# MILLINGTON AND SUTHERLAND WILLIAMS ON THE PROCEEDS OF CRIME

# MILLINGTON AND SUTHERLAND WILLIAMS ON

# THE PROCEEDS OF CRIME

## FOURTH EDITION

MARK SUTHERLAND WILLIAMS *LLB (Hons.) (Exon.)*
*Judge of the First-Tier Tribunal*
*Barrister of the Inner Temple*
*Barrister of the Eastern Caribbean Supreme Court*

MICHAEL HOPMEIER *MA (Oxon.) LLM (Lond.)*
*Circuit Judge*
*Barrister of the Middle Temple*

RUPERT JONES *MA (Oxon.)*
*Barrister of the Middle Temple*

OXFORD
UNIVERSITY PRESS

# OXFORD
UNIVERSITY PRESS

Great Clarendon Street, Oxford, OX2 6DP,
United Kingdom

Oxford University Press is a department of the University of Oxford.
It furthers the University's objective of excellence in research, scholarship,
and education by publishing worldwide. Oxford is a registered trade mark of
Oxford University Press in the UK and in certain other countries

© Mark Sutherland Williams 2013

The moral rights of the author have been asserted

First edition published in 2003
Fourth edition published in 2013

Impression: 1

Published in the United States of America by Oxford University Press
198 Madison Avenue, New York, NY 10016, United States of America

British Library Cataloguing in Publication Data

Data available

Library of Congress Control Number: 2013937231

ISBN 978-0-19-967291-2

Printed in Great Britain by
CPI Group (UK) Ltd, Croydon, CR0 4YY

*Trevor John Millington OBE, LLB (Hons.) (Wales)*

*1958–2012*

*Barrister of the Middle Temple*

*Liveryman of the Worshipful Company of Scriveners*

*Fellow of the Society for Advanced Legal Studies*

*Fellow of the Royal Society of Arts*

*Friend*

*General Editor*

MARK SUTHERLAND WILLIAMS
*Judge of the First-Tier Tribunal*
*Profumo Scholar of the Inner Temple*

*Editors and Contributors*

MICHAEL HOPMEIER

*Circuit Judge*

RUPERT JONES
*Barrister of the Middle Temple*

*Contributors*

SHEENA CASSIDY
*3 Paper Buildings*
*Barrister of the Inner Temple*

JAMES CHEGWIDDEN
*6KBW College Hill*
*Barrister of Lincoln's Inn*

JAMES DENNISON
*2 Dr Johnson's Buildings*
*Barrister of the Inner Temple*

MATHEW GULLICK
*3 Paper Buildings*
*Barrister of Gray's Inn*

WILLIAM HAYS
*6KBW College Hill*
*Barrister of the Middle Temple*

PAUL JARVIS
*6KBW College Hill*
*Barrister of Lincoln's Inn*

IAIN MACWHANNELL
*Thompson Cooper Law*
*Barrister of the Middle Temple*

PAUL O'DOHERTY
*3 Paper Buildings*
*Barrister of the Middle Temple*

OLIVER POWELL
*3 Paper Buildings*
*Barrister of Gray's Inn*
*Barrister of the Eastern Caribbean Supreme Court*

SARAH WHITEHOUSE
*6KBW College Hill*
*Barrister of Lincoln's Inn*

# FOREWORD

*David Green CB, QC*

Since it came into effect in 2003, the Proceeds of Crime Act 2002 (POCA) has had a fundamental impact on how law enforcement agencies tackle acquisitive crime. Although there are a few cases to which predecessor legislation (such as the Criminal Justice Act 1988) still applies, the vast majority of criminals coming before the courts are now dealt with under the provisions of POCA. It is a lengthy and complex statute, which has already spawned a plethora of case law.

The law enforcement landscape has also changed significantly over the same period. The emergence of a cadre of civilian accredited financial investigators has enhanced and sharpened the availability of financial investigation. Considerable sums have been removed from criminals and either returned to victims or to the Exchequer. The Asset Recovery Agency, the body originally established to lead this area of work, ceased to exist in 2008 when its functions were transferred to the Serious Organised Crime Agency, and some of its powers to the Director of Public Prosecutions and the Director of the Serious Fraud Office.

New legislation continues to develop. The Bribery Act 2010 was a significant improvement in the UK's anti-corruption laws and the government will introduce legislative underpinning for Deferred Prosecution Agreements, dealing with certain corporate criminality. The interplay with POCA in major cases brought under these statutes will be important.

POCA is a vital tool in the fight against economic crime as it strikes at the main motivation for such criminality and diminishes funds available for investment in future criminal conduct. However, POCA goes much further than confiscation. It sets out money-laundering offences that criminalise anyone dealing with criminal proceeds. The introduction of entirely new civil recovery and cash seizure/forfeiture powers has provided a means of pursuing traceable criminal property even in the absence of a conviction.

Despite the scope of the powers contained in it and its characterisation as 'draconian', the recovery of criminal property under POCA is still patchy. There are a number of challenges which staff in my own organisation and across law enforcement face on a regular basis. These include: extensive and complex third-party litigation; delaying tactics by defendants, including repeated changes in legal representation; the need for better international cooperation; and the risks involved in the vigorous pursuit of civil recovery cases in the High Court.

I have made the recovery of the proceeds of crime a top priority for the Serious Fraud Office, and I intend to enhance the existing team of specialist investigators and lawyers focusing on this activity. It is a routine feature of our cases, and is consistent with the Association of Chief Police Officers' objective of embedding financial investigation in the overall investigation process. The basic principle behind POCA—that crime should not pay—needs to be at the forefront of all investigations and prosecutions. That principle should apply whether the individual is a burglar, a drug dealer, a money launderer, or a sophisticated fraudster.

A decade after the enactment of POCA, this book offers a timely survey of its operation and the challenges faced by practitioners. It also highlights the strengths, weaknesses, and gaps in the regime.

All practitioners will be delighted that Mark Sutherland Williams persevered with the production of this fourth edition despite the untimely death of Trevor Millington OBE in February 2012. Personally, I recall Trevor's contribution to the (much-lamented) RCPO's reputation and expertise around the proceeds of crime with gratitude and respect. This fourth edition of what is now a flagship work will be greatly welcomed by all practitioners in this area of law.

David Green CB QC
Director
Serious Fraud Office
May 2013

# PREFACE TO THE FOURTH EDITION

It has been a turbulent time. In the short number of years since the publication of the third edition of this book, the UK, like much of the developed world, has faced both economic downturn and swathing cuts to funding in the public sector. This has led to a contraction in work for many in legal services, particularly those in the private sector, who have seen a noticeable decrease in the quantity of work and in many cases the quality of work, often engendered by uncertainty and restraint as a result of the difficult financial climate.

Whilst nations still proclaim the need to have proper and effective asset recovery powers and procedures in place, in reality the recovery of criminally obtained assets has itself dropped some way down the list of national priorities. For many reasons this is understandable. The need to address the pressing economic and other issues of the day has overtaken many areas of potential legislation and, it appears inevitably, the funding necessary to ensure effective asset recovery has been unavailable.

Nonetheless, the point may now be approaching where there should be a re-examination of the effectiveness of the UK's proceeds of crime legislation and a new and reinvigorated emphasis placed on the recovery of ill-gotten gains. A well-run, well-thought-out, asset recovery scheme should be self-funding. It should to a large degree be recession proof. The National Fraud Authority, Annual Fraud Indicator (AFI) Report 2012 suggests that fraud alone is costing the UK around £73 billion a year. This figure reflects other similar reports and surveys. Even if the actual figure were only half this amount, when one considers the additional acquisitive criminal offences that take place in the UK each year, one can begin to see what a large role proceeds of crime, money laundering, and related offences play in, and cost, the UK economy. Moreover, there appears to be a truism in the notion that City fraud and other types of criminal activity tend to increase in times of recession, as individuals become more desperate to maintain certain types of living, and are therefore more willing to take risks in order to fund their lifestyle choices. In many respects it is disappointing to note that since the introduction of the Proceeds of Crime Act in 2002 there does not appear to have been any marked improvement or breakthrough in terms of recovery, in fact, the opposite. In 2003 estimations suggested that the annual proceeds of crime figures circulating in the UK were likely to be between £19 billion and £48 billion. Today's statistics suggest, if anything, that the situation has got worse. Home Office figures drawn from UK-based asset recovery suggest that in England, Wales, and Northern Ireland, from cash forfeitures, criminal confiscation, civil recovery, and taxation, the following amounts were recovered:

| 2006–07 | 2007–08 | 2008–09 | 2009–10 | 2010–11 |
|---------|---------|---------|---------|---------|
| £125.26m | £135.7m | £148m | £153.71m | £161m |

Even by adding to this a further £10.5 million recovered in Scotland (Crown Office and Procurator Fiscal Service, news release, May 2012), the amounts, though superficially attractive, begin to wain by comparison to the true proceeds of crime figures being channelled through the UK economy.

There are no easy fixes to the problem. But a re-examination and discussion about what else could be done may now be overdue. In particular, there should be a re-examination of the part the private sector could play in confiscation and the UK recovery of criminal assets. On one view, there appears to have been a marked reluctance by those in authority to engage with stakeholders in the private sector and draw upon their expertise. To give but one example, there has been a noticeable withdrawal from the use of court appointed receivers in the recovery of the proceeds of crime, with many experienced insolvency practitioners reporting falls in their appointments. The justification appears to be one of cost. But in circumstances where prosecuting agencies lack both the resources and manpower to themselves effectively pursue assets and confiscation orders both nationally and abroad, a dialogue should be opened to see how receivers may be able to assist more and, if so, the terms of their engagement. The danger is that before long many receivers will have left this area of the law altogether, with the risk that years of experience will be lost for good.

Nor must one overlook the part that the defence Bar and legal profession can play in this. A properly funded defence practice, with access if need be to restrained funds on an appropriately capped basis, would ensure that not only Legal Aid Agency funding is protected, but also that legal arguments can be properly made and resourced, with the benefit to the Crown of avoiding often unnecessary and costly appeals. Properly funded representation may also result in agreement on issues being reached at an early stage with the consequent saving in costs.

There remain changes on the horizon. The new Crime and Courts Act 2013 will counter the effect of *Perry* in the Supreme Court and amend Part 5 of POCA on civil recovery to allow for property to be recoverable outside the jurisdiction if there is some connection between the case and the UK. Moreover, the courts continue to clarify the law in this area, making recovery and confiscation not only more certain, but more realistic in terms of the sums involved. These are all steps in the right direction.

As Baroness Scotland QC once suggested, there is a delicious irony in the recovery of the proceeds of crime. Not only does it accord with what most law-abiding individuals want to see, namely the stripping of ill-gotten gains from the criminal classes, but it also means that once recovered those funds can be utilised and invested back into law enforcement, schools, hospitals, and other worthy causes. The important role of the proceeds of crime practitioner is thus ensured, and no doubt will continue.

In this fourth edition, we have strived to keep to the original formula, namely that of a straightforward, easily digestible work on this, at times, complex area of the law. Whether we have succeeded we will leave for others to decide. The mistakes are our own, and any views expressed are not intended to be binding upon or representative of the various editors and contributors to this work.

Mark Sutherland Williams writes; it appears that Trevor Millington had been ill for a short while, although quite how ill no one, including himself, had fully appreciated. It came, as they say, like a bolt out of the blue. He was fifty-three years of age. The impact of his death reverberated around the whole of the proceeds of crime community. Trevor had played a pivotal role in the development of this area of the law in his twenty-five years working within it. The suddenness of the loss was felt not only by his friends, but by many who had encountered Trevor both professionally and socially over the years. He was a one-off. Committed to his work. A raconteur. A loyal friend. It is both with sadness, but with thanks to a remarkable life, that this edition is dedicated to his memory.

Trevor and I had been in the middle of planning this fourth edition when events took over. That he would have wanted the book to continue I have no doubt, but the enormity of the task appeared at the time to be a daunting prospect. I need not have been concerned. Mutual friends stepped forward, and as a result a book that could be regarded as a *liber amicorum* to Trevor Millington has been produced. I am immensely grateful to those who have contributed in this way. They represent many of the most high-profile and well-regarded asset forfeiture practitioners currently working in the UK. Especially, I must thank my co-editors, Michael Hopmeier and Rupert Jones. Both knew Trevor well. Both have extensive expertise in this area of the law. Michael is the judge that teaches judges about it; Rupert is one of the leading asset forfeiture practitioners at the Bar. I feel in very privileged company.

Lastly, I must thank my wife and family and Trevor's good friends, Margaret, Marion and John, and Warren for their abiding support.

Michael Hopmeier wishes to thank all those who have assisted in his research for up-to-date information and authorities; and to his family and friends for their support and patience whilst he has been engaged on this work.

Rupert Jones wishes to thank his wife, his children, and his parents for their support during the course of this project.

All of our thanks go to Roxanne Selby, Amy Jones, Emma Brady, Ellen Carey, and Eleanor Walter at our publishers, Oxford University Press, for their kind assistance and patience; and our particular thanks for the further contributions of David Perry QC (appeals); Master Evan Bell (Northern Ireland); Lisa Arbon-Donovan of Knapp Richardson (costs); Shahmeem Purdasy (civil recovery); and Fiona Alexander (appendices).

Lastly, we thank David Green CB, QC, for kindly agreeing to pen the Foreword to this fourth edition.

Mark Sutherland Williams
Michael Hopmeier
Rupert Jones
Temple, London
May 2013

# BIOGRAPHIES

*Judge Mark Sutherland Williams*

Whilst at the Bar, Mark Sutherland Williams appeared as counsel in a number of the most significant cases decided in the proceeds of crime field. He co-drafted the receivers' guidelines in *Capewell*; and was the first counsel to be instructed to obtain an interim receiving order under POCA and a property freezing order under SOCPA. He also drafted and obtained the first external restraint order under the new legislation. He was junior counsel in the House of Lords cases of *Capewell*, *Briggs-Price*, and *Islam*. His career at the Bar was also notable for his involvement in a number of the country's most high-profile drug importation cases, including Operations *Stealer* and *Extend*. In 1999 he was instructed to draft the witness statements of Baroness Thatcher and John Major for the BSE public inquiry. He was a co-founder of the Proceeds of Crime Lawyers Association and acted as its Treasurer from 2008 to 2011. He has spoken at both national and international conferences on asset forfeiture law. He was head of the 3 Paper Buildings Asset Forfeiture Group for over ten years. In 2011 he was appointed a full-time Judge of the First-Tier Tribunal.

*His Honour Judge Michael Hopmeier*

Michael Hopmeier was at the Bar for over thirty years before his appointment as a full-time circuit judge in 2009, sitting at Kingston-upon-Thames Crown Court. He had been sitting as a recorder since 1994, in crime, civil, and family law. He appeared in the first Asil Nadir case in 1993, leading for the defence of Mr Nadir's co-defendant and undertook, whilst at the Bar, many high-profile fraud cases, both prosecuting (for the SFO and CPS Special Casework Unit) and defending. His practice at the Bar also involved commercial work, including the drafting of commercial agreements for banks and other financial institutions. He specialises in economic crime and confiscation and lectures to judges at the Judicial College on the Proceeds of Crime Act. He is the author of *A Guide to Restraint and Confiscation* (latest edition January 2013), which is published by the Judicial College for the assistance of judges. He was a contributor to the (EU) Fenix Programme in Lisbon and has written a number of articles for practitioners on aspects of asset recovery. Since 2008 he has regularly lectured abroad on behalf of the EU, ERA (Academy of European Law), the Commonwealth Secretariat, the Proceeds of Crime Lawyers Association, and Philja (Philippine Judicial Academy) on areas of economic crime and asset recovery. He is a committee member of the European Criminal Law Association (ECLA (UK)) and the Wadham College Law Society.

*Rupert Jones*

Rupert Jones was called to the Bar as a member of Middle Temple in 2000 following a degree in experimental psychology. After initially practising in criminal law, he has specialised in the field of asset forfeiture and proceeds of crime for many years and has appeared as counsel in some of the most significant cases in the area such as: *CPS v Eastenders Group & Brandon Barnes; Gayle Horne, and others v Central Criminal Court; Minshall v UK; Larkfield Limited v RCPO; Stephen Lamb (Re Pigott) v RCPO; Marion Gibson v RCPO; Robert Minshall v Marylebone Magistrates' Court; Paul Hansford v Southampton Magistrates' Court; Telli v RCPO; and HMRC v Capewell.* He has lectured on asset forfeiture law at conferences and seminars for the Proceeds of Crime Lawyers Association and for the LLM course on international commercial fraud at SOAS. He has been recommended by Chambers and Partners as a leading practitioner in the field. He is appointed to the Attorney General's Panel of Counsel to undertake civil work and is therefore instructed on behalf of various government departments in tax recovery and national security cases involving civil anti-terrorist measures. He is a registered Pupil Supervisor.

# CONTRIBUTORS

**Sheena Cassidy** specialises in cases involving restraint and confiscation proceedings where conflict arises under the Matrimonial Causes Act 1973 or the Trusts of Land and Appointment of Trustees Act 1996 as well as in relation to third party interest generally. She has been ranked in Chambers UK and the Legal 500 as a leading junior in proceeds of crime and asset forfeiture. (Chapters 16 and 22)

**James Chegwidden** practises in civil and employment law as well as asset forfeiture. He has acted for the Crown and the defence in confiscation, cash forfeiture, and excise cases. He is a Grade 2 panellist for the CPS's specialist Proceeds of Crime Unit. (Chapter 9)

**James Dennison** was called to the Bar in 1986, initially dealing with criminal cases. He has specialised in confiscation law since 1999 and is regularly instructed by prosecuting authorities, both UK and worldwide, to advise and then to present their positions in court. (Chapters 2 and 6)

**Mathew Gullick's** asset forfeiture work has seen him appear in the Crown Court, the High Court, and both divisions of the Court of Appeal. He is appointed to the Attorney General's panel of junior counsel to the Crown in civil matters. He appeared for the Home Secretary (intervening) in *R v Lambert* 2012. (Chapter 8)

**William Hays** practises in asset forfeiture, criminal, and public law. He was appointed to the Attorney General's panel of civil counsel in 2012, is a member of the Serious Fraud Office's panel of counsel, and was junior counsel to the Crown in the Supreme Court cases of *Waya*, *Varma*, and *Re Peacock*. (Chapters 11 and 18)

**Paul Jarvis** is ranked in Chambers UK as a leading criminal practitioner. He prosecutes and defends in cases of serious fraud and has extensive experience of the confiscation legislation gathered both at first instance and before the appellate courts. (Chapter 9)

**Iain MacWhannell** is a commercial lawyer. His practice focuses on tax, commercial fraud, and financial services. Prior to coming to the Bar, Iain worked for two years in the VAT & Excise Litigation Department of HM Revenue & Customs. (Chapter 25)

**Paul O'Doherty** specializes in commercial law, fraud, and the proceeds of crime. (Chapters 13 and 14)

**Oliver Powell** is a commercial litigator with a practice that encompasses asset forfeiture; civil recovery; commercial fraud; and indirect tax. His expertise has been recognised by his appointment to both the CPS and the SFO Advocate Panels. (Chapters 15 and 23)

**Sarah Whitehouse** is junior Treasury Counsel and on the Attorney General's list of Special Advocates. (Chapters 7 and 11)

With thanks to the further contributions of

David Perry QC
*6KBW College Hill*

Master Evan Bell
*Master of the High Court (Northern Ireland)*

Lisa Arbon-Donovan
*Costs Lawyer and Costs Draftsman, Knapp Richardson*

Fiona Alexander
*Barrister*

Shahmeem Purdasy
*Barrister and New York Attorney*

# CONTENTS

# TABLE OF CASES

# TABLES OF LEGISLATION

# SECONDARY LEGISLATION

# TABLES OF EUROPEAN LEGISLATION

# TABLE OF INTERNATIONAL
# TREATIES AND CONVENTIONS

# ABBREVIATIONS

The following abbreviations are used throughout this work:

| | |
|---|---|
| A1P1 | Article 1 Protocol 1 to the European Convention on Human Rights |
| AFAR | Arab Forum on Asset Recovery |
| AFU | Asset Freezing Unit |
| AJA | Access to Justice Act 1999 |
| ARA | Assets Recovery Agency |
| ASBO | Anti-social Behaviour Order |
| CARIN | Camden Asset Recovery Inter Agency Network |
| CCRC | Criminal Cases Review Commission |
| CDD | Customer Due Diligence |
| CDS | Criminal Defence Service |
| CEMA | Customs and Excise Management Act 1979 |
| CICA | Crime (International Co-operation) Act 2003 |
| CJA 1987 | Criminal Justice Act 1987 |
| CJA 1988 | Criminal Justice Act 1988 |
| CLS | Community Legal Service |
| CPR | Civil Procedure Rules |
| CPS | Crown Prosecution Service |
| CrimPR | Criminal Procedure Rules (where amended, 2013) |
| DFID | Department for International Development |
| DPA | Deferred Prosecution Agreement |
| DPP | Director of Public Prosecutions |
| DTA | Drug Trafficking Act 1994 |
| DTOA | Drug Trafficking Offences Act 1986 |
| ECHR | European Convention on Human Rights |
| ECtHR | European Court of Human Rights |
| EESC | European Economic and Social Committee |
| FATF | Financial Action Taskforce |
| FCIB | First Curacao International Bank |
| FIU | Financial Intelligence Unit |
| FSA | Financial Services Authority |
| HMRC | HM Revenue and Customs |
| HRA | Human Rights Act 1998 |
| ICAR | International Centre for Asset Recovery |
| IRO | Interim Receiving Order |
| JARD | Joint Assets Recovery Database |
| LA | Limitation Act 1980 |
| LASPO | Legal Aid, Sentencing and Punishment of Offenders Act 2012 |
| LIVR | Limited Intelligence Value Report |
| LSC | Legal Services Commission |
| MCA | Magistrates' Courts Act 1980 |
| MCA 1973 | Matrimonial Causes Act 1973 |
| MLA | mutual legal assistance |
| MRO | Management Receivership Order |
| MTIC | missing trader intra-community |

| NCA | National Crime Agency |
|-----|------------------------|
| NCIS | National Criminal Intelligence Service |
| OSCE | Organization for Security and Co-operation in Europe |
| PACE 1984 | Police and Criminal Evidence Act 1984 |
| PCC(S)A | Powers of Criminal Courts (Sentencing) Act 2000 |
| PFO | Property Freezing Order |
| PII | public interest immunity |
| POCA | Proceeds of Crime Act 2002 |
| RCPO | Revenue and Customs Prosecution Office |
| RCU | Regional Confiscation Unit |
| SAR | Suspicious Activity Report |
| SCA | Serious Crime Act 2007 |
| SFO | Serious Fraud Office |
| SOCA | Serious Organised Crime Agency |
| SOCPA | Serious Organised Crime and Police Act 2005 |
| StAR | Stolen Assets Recovery Initiative |
| TA | Terrorism Act 2000 |
| TAFA | Terrorist Asset-Freezing etc. Act 2010 |
| TFEU | Treaty on the Functioning of the European Union |
| TLATA | Trusts of Land and Appointment of Trustees Act 1996 |
| UKBA | UK Border Agency |
| UNCAC | United Nations Convention against Corruption |
| UNODC | United Nations Office for Drugs and Crime |
| UNTOC | United Nations Convention against Transnational Organised Crime |
| VATA 1994 | Value Added Tax Act 1994 |

# 1

## SETTING THE SCENE

## A. Introduction

Every school child knows that you cannot have the penny and the sweet.

Toulson LJ, *R v Pattison* [2008]

The purpose of this introductory chapter is to consider why Parliament decided to enact **1.01** confiscation legislation and to give a brief overview of the mechanics of the Proceeds of Crime Act 2002 (POCA). Also provided are an outline of the functions of some of the key law enforcement agencies having conduct of restraint and confiscation cases under the legislation and a summary of some of the most significant developments in this fast-moving area of law since the publication of the third edition of this work. This work is intended to assist all those interested or concerned in this area of the law, including practitioners and those involved in the administration of justice, in both understanding the current legislation and procedures and applying them in practice to proceedings in court. As will be seen hereinafter, this work will concentrate on the provisions and implementation of the Proceeds of Crime Act 2002 and their practical application. For a detailed commentary of previous proceeds of crime legislation, the reader is directed to earlier editions of this work.

## B. Why Was Confiscation Law Enacted?

### The genesis of the confiscation regime

The first confiscation enactment to reach the statute book was the Drug Trafficking Offences **1.02** Act 1986 (DTOA) which came into force on 10 January 1987. It was introduced following

1

a recognition by Parliament that the profits made from drug trafficking were so great that the deterrent effect of even lengthy terms of imprisonment were insufficient: the convicted criminal could spend his sentence secure in the knowledge that his ill-gotten gains (often well invested in the meantime) would be available to him on his release. The legislation also reflected the recognition by Parliament that existing forfeiture provisions were inadequate for the purpose of depriving the offender of the fruits of his crime.

**1.03**  The enactment of the DTOA followed a report by a committee chaired by Mr Justice Hodgson in 1984, which recommended that the courts should be empowered to confiscate the proceeds of criminal offences of which defendants had been convicted. This led to the enactment of the DTOA, which imposed a mandatory obligation on the court to confiscate the proceeds of drug trafficking of those convicted of such offences. Some two years later, Parliament passed the Criminal Justice Act 1988 (CJA), which, in broad terms, extended the confiscation regime imposed by the 1986 Act to cover all indictable offences together with a small number of offences triable only summarily where the benefits accruing to the defendant were likely to be unusually high.

**1.04**  The DTOA confiscation regime was augmented by a number of provisions in the Criminal Justice (International Co-operation) Act 1990 which came into force on 1 July 1991. Section 15 of the Act provided for the payment of interest on unpaid confiscation orders and s 16 empowered the prosecutor to apply to the court for confiscation orders to be increased where further realisable property was identified. Part III of the Act introduced entirely new provisions empowering customs officers to apply to a magistrates' court for the detention and forfeiture of drug trafficking money being imported or exported in cash.

**1.05**  On 3 February 1995 the Drug Trafficking Act 1994 (DTA) came into force. It consolidated the provisions of the DTOA and the Criminal Justice (International Co-operation) Act 1990. It also strengthened the provisions of the DTOA by implementing many of the recommendations of the Home Office Working Group on Confiscation.

**1.06**  In October 1998 the Performance and Innovation Unit of the Cabinet Office examined once again the UK's asset recovery arrangements with a view to improving the efficiency of the recovery process and increasing the amount of illegally obtained assets recovered. It proposed the creation of a new agency with lead responsibility for asset recovery and the consolidation of existing laws on confiscation and money laundering into a single piece of legislation. It also proposed the introduction of new powers to recover criminal assets through civil proceedings without, controversially, the need for a criminal conviction. As a result the Proceeds of Crime Act 2002 (POCA) consolidated the law and created the Assets Recovery Agency (ARA). In 2008, following some criticism, deemed by many to have been unfair, the ARA was abolished and its civil recovery powers transferred to the Serious Organised Crime Agency (SOCA) and the Directors of the lead prosecuting agencies (Crown Prosecution Service (CPS) and Serious Fraud Office (SFO)). By contrast in the EU a number of specialised asset recovery agencies have been set up. Thus, for example, in the Netherlands the Bureau Ontnemingswetgeving OM (BOOM) has been operating for many years. In France an asset recovery agency was set up in July 2010, which commenced working in February 2011, namely AGRASC—the Agency for the Recovery and Management of Seized and Confiscated Assets.

## C. The Object of the Confiscation Regime

One of the most successful weapons which can be used to discourage offences that are committed in order to enrich the offenders is to ensure that if the offenders are brought to justice, any profit which they have made from their offending is confiscated.

*R v Sekhon*, 16 December 2002, The Lord Chief Justice

It is important to appreciate at the outset of any study of the law relating to restraint and confiscation orders that POCA (and previously the DTA and the CJA) is concerned with confiscating the *value* of the defendant's proceeds of the offences of which he has been convicted, and not the actual proceeds themselves. It follows from this that once the court has determined the amount by which the defendant has benefited from his criminal conduct, all assets in which he has an interest, whether legitimately acquired or not, are vulnerable to confiscation up to the amount of that benefit. The Crown Court (under POCA) is thus entitled, pre-conviction, to restrain the defendant from dissipating assets that have been acquired perfectly legitimately for the purpose of ensuring that they remain available to satisfy a confiscation order in the amount of his benefit. **1.07**

It is also important to appreciate that, contrary to the position in some countries (eg the USA and many EU countries), a confiscation order in criminal proceedings in the UK is not an *in rem* order against the defendant's realisable property, but an *in personam* order against the defendant himself. This has a number of important consequences. In particular, the mere making of a confiscation order does not divest the defendant of his legal title to whatever realisable property was taken into account by the court in making the order. Thus the making of a confiscation order does not, itself, entitle any person in possession of the defendant's property to pass the same over to the enforcing magistrates' court in satisfaction of the confiscation order. Unless the property is being handed over pursuant to a receivership order or the defendant has expressly consented to the property being forwarded to the court, any person who does so will be vulnerable to a civil action for conversion. **1.08**

## D. The Proceeds of Crime Act 2002: A Summary

The Proceeds of Crime Act 2002 received Royal Assent on 24 July 2002. It was intended to replace and improve the existing legislation, namely the DTA and the CJA. The main implementation date for Part 2 of the Act, the confiscation provisions, was 24 March 2003. The transitional provisions stipulate that the CJA and the DTA shall continue to apply to all offences committed before 24 March 2003 or which overlap that date. The three Acts have coexisted side by side for some time, however as time goes by the vast majority of confiscation cases are likely to be governed by the provisions of POCA (as amended). In practice, therefore, most new confiscation orders are now being made under POCA, although some orders under the old legislation are still being enforced in the High Court and elsewhere. The other implementation dates on which POCA came into force are considered, where relevant, in the relevant chapters herein. For a detailed analysis of the provisions of the CJA and the DTA, please see earlier editions of this work. **1.09**

POCA provides for confiscation orders in relation to persons who benefit from criminal conduct and for restraint orders to prohibit persons, including third parties, from dealing with **1.10** property. It also allows for the recovery of property that is or represents property obtained through unlawful conduct or is intended to be used in unlawful conduct; and it has made new provisions about money laundering and investigations relating to benefit from criminal conduct or to property that is or represents property obtained through unlawful conduct.

**1.11**  POCA together with its amendments and its related rules of procedure provides a comprehensive code governing confiscation law. Under it there is no distinction between drug trafficking offences and other offences (except in relation to the 'criminal lifestyle' provisions). Powers that were formerly exercised by the High Court in relation to restraint orders and the supervision and enforcement of confiscation orders are exercised by the Crown Court. The Act also made provision for 'civil recovery' where the defendant has not been convicted or even charged with an offence. Civil recovery orders are made in the High Court and take effect *in rem*.

### Northern Ireland

**1.12**  A summary of the proceeds of crime applicable to Northern Ireland may be found at Appendix 20.

## E.  Agencies Responsible for the Enforcement of the Legislation

### The Serious Organised Crime Agency

**1.13**  The effect of Sch 8 to the Serious Crime Act 2007 was to transfer the civil recovery and revenue functions of the ARA to SOCA. SOCA is itself a creature of statute established by s 1 of the Serious Organised Crime and Police Act 2005 (SOCPA). By s 2(1) of the Act:

> SOCA has the functions of—
>
> (a) preventing and detecting serious organised crime, and
> (b) contributing to the reduction of such crime in other ways and to the mitigation of its consequences.

**1.14**  By s 3(1) of SOCPA, SOCA has the following function as to information in relation to crime:

> ... gathering, storing, analysing and disseminating information relevant to—
>
> (a) the prevention, detection, investigation or prosecution of offences, or
> (b) the reduction of crime in other ways or the mitigation of its consequences.

**1.15**  By s 3(2) of SOCPA, SOCA is empowered to disseminate such information to police forces, special police forces, law enforcement agencies, or such other persons as it considers appropriate in connection with its functions under s 3(1). Section 3(4) defines 'law enforcement agencies' in very broad terms to include the Commissioners of HM Revenue and Customs or any other government department, the Scottish Administration, any other person charged with the duty of investigating offences or charging offenders, and any other person outside the UK carrying on activities similar to those carried on by SOCA or a police force.

**1.16**  The general powers of SOCA are set out in s 5(2) of the Act which provides as follows:

> SOCA may—
>
> (a) institute criminal proceedings in England and Wales or Northern Ireland;

(b) at the request of the chief officer of a police force or of a special police force, act in support of any activities of that force;

(c) at the request of any law enforcement agency, act in support of any activities of that agency;

(d) enter into other arrangements for co-operating with bodies or persons (in the United Kingdom or elsewhere) which it considers appropriate in connection with the exercise of SOCA's powers under section 2 or 3 or any activities within subsection (3).

By s 5(3) of SOCPA, SOCA may carry on activities in relation to other crime if they are car- **1.17** ried on for the purposes of any of the functions conferred on SOCA.

It should be noted that SOCA has no prosecutorial function and is not responsible for the **1.18** conduct of criminal proceedings in relation to the offences it investigates. By s 38 of the Act, prosecutions are conducted by the Director of Public Prosecutions.

The criteria that SOCA requires to be satisfied before it will embark on a civil recovery or **1.19** revenue investigation are set out on the Agency's website at <http://www.soca.gov.uk> and are as follows:

• Criminal investigation and prosecution must have been considered and either failed or been impossible, eg because of lack of resources within the law enforcement agency.

• For civil recovery, there must be evidence of criminal conduct that is supported to the civil standard of proof (ie on the balance of probabilities) and that has generated the funding or acquisition of the referred recoverable property. The Civil Evidence Rules will apply and evidence may include hearsay, statements by co-accused, or other material that could not be used in a criminal case. The professional opinion of an experienced police officer who knows the subject may also be used as evidence from an expert witness.

• For tax cases, there must be material to give rise to reasonable suspicion that there is criminality that has produced an untaxed income. The suspicion may rest in whole or in part on reliable intelligence.

• Recoverable property must have been identified to a value of at least £10,000 and acquired within the previous twelve years (or twenty years for Part 6 Tax).

• All relevant case papers both criminal and financial (where applicable) are to be made available for inspection and use by the Agency in assessing this referral for adoption. (If documents are not made available to the Serious Organised Crime Agency then this may affect whether the case is adopted.)

In their Annual Accounts and Report for 2011/12 SOCA refer expressly to the fact that their **1.20** '...Work utilising the asset recovery provisions of the Proceeds of Crime Act 2002 continued to be a critical component of SOCA's operational strategy...'.

The functions of SOCA will be incorporated into the new National Crime Agency formed **1.21** pursuant to s 1 of the Crime and Courts Act 2013, which received the Royal Assent on 25 April 2013.

### The National Crime Agency

In June 2011 the details relating to the proposed new agency were set out in a Home **1.22** Office document entitled *The National Crime Agency: A plan for the creation of a national crime-fighting capability.*

**1.23** The Crime and Courts Act 2013 covers a wide range of subjects. Part 1 provides the statutory basis for the new National Crime Agency (NCA), which the government hopes will be fully operational by the end of 2013. The NCA is to tackle serious organised crime, encompassing the work of a number of existing organisations, including SOCA. The NCA will have four 'Commands', three dealing with organised crime, border policing, and economic crime and the fourth comprising the Child Exploitation and Online Protection Centre.

**1.24** The Economic Crime Command will provide an improved capability to deal with fraud and economic crimes, including those carried out by organised criminals.

### The Crown Prosecution Service

**1.25** The CPS is responsible for the restraint and confiscation aspects of all prosecutions instituted by the police and HM Revenue and Customs. Following the merger of the CPS with the Revenue and Customs Prosecution Office (RCPO), the Central Confiscation Branch and the Asset Forfeiture Division have combined, and are now referred to as 'The Proceeds of Crime Unit'. Based in London, the Proceeds of Crime Unit deals with the confiscation aspects of CPS prosecutions. The Proceeds of Crime Unit's work is not limited to prosecution-related casework but extends to civil litigation too, though it has dealt with few civil cases. In 2010 it obtained its first civil recovery order. The Proceeds of Crime Unit Branch also has the conduct of the restraint and confiscation aspects of cases brought by SOCA in those cases where the CPS is the lead prosecuting authority. Other POCA cases are generally dealt with locally in CPS area offices.

### HM Revenue and Customs

**1.26** On 18 April 2005 the Inland Revenue and HM Customs and Excise merged to form one new Department known as HM Revenue and Customs (HMRC). HMRC is responsible for mounting criminal investigations into precisely the same offences for which its predecessors had responsibility, including money laundering and tax frauds. The one significant difference is that HMRC has no prosecutorial function: this is the responsibility of the Revenue and Customs Division of the merged CPS. HMRC does, however, retain responsibility for applications before the magistrates' court for the inland detention and forfeiture of cash under Pt 5 of POCA. The effect of ss 5, 6, and 50 of the Commissioners for Revenue and Customs Act 2005 is such that references in any enactment, statutory instrument, or other document to the 'Commissioners of Customs and Excise' is deemed to be a reference to the Commissioners of HMRC, and similarly references to 'Customs Officers' are deemed to be references to officers of HMRC.

### The UK Border Agency

**1.27** The UK Border Agency (UKBA) took over the role of Customs at airports and ports throughout the UK from 5 August 2009.

**1.28** Section 26 of the Borders, Citizenship and Immigration Act 2009 made various transfer provisions. The Scheme gives effect to the transfer of specified property, rights, and liabilities from the Commissioners for Revenue and Customs to the Secretary of State for the Home Department and the Director of Border Revenue in connection with the exercise of the

Commissioners' functions. The Secretary of State's functions are exercised by delegation to the Chief Executive of UKBA.

On 26 March 2013 the Home Secretary announced that the UKBA would be abolished and its work returned to the Home Office. **1.29**

### The Serious Fraud Office

The SFO was established under the Criminal Justice Act 1987 (CJA 1987) to investigate and prosecute cases of serious fraud. The CJA 1987 gives the SFO a number of investigatory powers not vested in other law enforcement agencies, including the power under s 2 to require any person whom the Director has reason to believe has relevant information, or a person under investigation, to attend for interview and provide information and documentation. **1.30**

The Act provides no definition of what constitutes a 'serious fraud' and the SFO does not take on every case referred to it. According to the SFO website (<http://www.sfo.gov.uk>): **1.31**

> The SFO investigates and, where appropriate, prosecutes cases of serious or complex fraud (including cases of domestic or overseas bribery and corruption) which, in the opinion of the Director of the SFO, call for the multi-disciplinary approach and legislative powers available to the SFO. In deciding what cases to adopt, the Director will consider all the circumstances of the case including:
> - the scale of loss (actual or potential);
> - the impact of the case on the UK economy;
> - the effect of the case on the UK's reputation as a safe place to do business;
> - the factual or legal complexity and the wider public interest.

The SFO has its own specialist confiscation unit, the Asset Recovery Unit, handling that aspect of their cases. **1.32**

### HMCS Regional Confiscation Units

There were originally sixty-three independent offices in forty-two areas that dealt with confiscation enforcement through magistrates' courts. There are now nine dedicated Regional Confiscation Units (RCUs) which are located in the South West, South East, London, North West (Bolton), North West (Merseyside and Cheshire), North East, Wales, Midlands East, and Midlands West. The benefits of those RCUs include: **1.33**

- delivery of 'total confiscation' by ensuring the end-to-end multi-agency confiscation process has been designed into the delivery mechanism;
- a central point of contact for internal colleagues and stakeholders from other agencies, eg police prosecutors;
- improved communication links with other asset recovery agencies/stakeholders;
- opportunities for joint training/awareness with other agencies raising the profile and ensuring all are working to the same goal;
- consolidating casework management processes;
- driving forward best practice;
- ensuring a singular and dedicated focus;
- performance improvement; and
- engagement with Local Criminal Justice Boards.

## F. The International Element

**1.34** Drug trafficking, in nearly every case, at some stage involves the smuggling of controlled drugs from one country to another. There is also an international element in many other organised criminal activities, including tax and other frauds, people smuggling, and money laundering. Practitioners will have noted the prevalence of particular countries or regions of the world connected with fraud and money laundering, offering apparent safe havens for the deposit of ill-gotten gains. The issue of such havens was raised as a matter of concern at the G8 Summit in Northern Ireland in June 2013. It is not surprising therefore that the various Acts make provision for assets held in the UK by defendants being prosecuted in other jurisdictions to be restrained and ultimately realised in satisfaction of a foreign confiscation order. Similarly UK confiscation legislation can apply to assets that a defendant owns overseas, and prosecuting authorities frequently seek the assistance of overseas jurisdictions, by means of letters of request, to restrain such assets and, after conviction, realise the same in satisfaction of a confiscation order. The High Court and Crown Court also have the power to make a 'repatriation order' directing a defendant to bring within the jurisdiction of the court assets he holds overseas. Countries throughout the world have recognised the importance of cooperation in relation to the identification, restraint, and seizure of the proceeds of crime, including, in particular, corruption, committed in their own countries but where the proceeds of crime have been sent to or deposited in other countries. It is significant that following the 'Arab Spring', new regimes are seeking the repatriation of assets alleged to have been wrongly removed from their respective countries. Thus the first Arab Forum on Asset Recovery was held in September 2012 in Doha, Qatar.

### The strength of UK powers

**1.35** On 12 March 2012 the European Commission proposed a new Directive of the European Parliament and Council on the freezing and confiscation of proceeds of crime in the European Union. The UK Minister of State for Crime Prevention announced in September 2012 that the UK government had decided not to opt in at this stage stating that:

> The Government welcomes the overall aims of the Directive and recognises the benefits of increased international cooperation to recover assets held overseas... The UK has strong powers which are successfully used to tackle criminal finances. Our powers are already compliant with or stronger than many of those contained in the Directive.

## G. Money Laundering

**1.36** Closely related to restraint and confiscation law is the law relating to money laundering. Those who participate in drug trafficking and other criminal offences that yield huge profits need to conceal their proceeds from law enforcement authorities to prevent confiscation and also to disguise the true source of their ill-gotten gains. Consequently, POCA has criminalised money laundering activities and, as the threat of money laundering has increased, so the provisions have become increasingly more draconian.

**1.37** The legislation now extends to financial institutions and others who hold money on behalf of clients. The Money Laundering Regulations 2003 and 2007 (as amended in 2011 and 2012) make it a criminal offence not to report suspicious transactions to law enforcement authorities, and impose a positive obligation to introduce systems and staff training with a view to detecting such transactions. On 5 February 2013 the EU Commission adopted two proposals to reinforce the EU's existing rules on anti-money laundering and fund transfers, namely:

- a (fourth) European Money Laundering Directive on the prevention of the use of the financial system for the purpose of money laundering and terrorist financing; and
- a regulation on information accompanying transfers of funds to secure 'due traceability' of these transfers.

The proposals are a response to changes made to the requirements issued by the Financial **1.38** Action Taskforce (FATF) in February 2012 and a review conducted by the Commission on the implementation of the Third Money Laundering Directive.

## H. Recent Developments in Confiscation Law

Since the third edition of this work was published in 2010 there have been many significant **1.39** developments in confiscation law, both in terms of statute and case law. Recent cases are considered in detail in the following chapters of this work under their respective subjects. At the time of writing, appeals on important points are pending in the Supreme Court in the cases of *R v Ahmad and Ahmed* [2012] EWCA Crim 391 and *R v Sumal* [2012] EWCA Crim 1840.

Of note, following the significant and much cited case of *R v May, Jennings and Green* [2008] **1.40** UKHL 28 (where the House of Lords laid down important principles as well as guidance as to how the courts should approach their consideration of confiscation applications in the Crown Court) the Supreme Court returned to this area of the law in its decision of *R v Waya* [2012] UKSC 51, focusing on the key issue

(1) of whether a confiscation order made under POCA 2002 could violate a defendant's right to the peaceful enjoyment of his possessions, guaranteed by article 1 of the First Protocol to the Convention for the Protection of Human Rights and Fundamental Freedoms 1950 (known as the 'A1P1' (Article 1, Protocol 1) issue).

The Supreme Court held that although POCA had removed all discretion from the Crown **1.41** Court, the European Convention on Human Rights (ECHR) 1950 Protocol 1 Article 1 required that the deprivation of property had to be proportionate to the legitimate aim of removing from criminals the pecuniary proceeds of their crime, but no more. A judge could therefore refuse to make a disproportionate confiscation order. Thus the judgment places a responsibility on Crown Court judges not to make confiscation orders which would otherwise involve a violation of A1P1. *Waya* has now been considered in a number of cases referred to in the chapters following. Pre-*Waya* cases have been considered in *R v Harvey* [2013] EWCA Crim 1104. See recently *R v Sale* [2013] EWCA Crim 1306.

## I. Deferred Prosecution Agreements

Finally, looking ahead, some mention should be made of Deferred Prosecution Agreements **1.42** (DPAs) set out in s 45 and Sch 17 of the Crime and Courts Act 2013, which are likely to be brought into effect in 2014. The Act received the Royal Assert on 25 April 2013.

DPAs would be a new weapon in the armoury of prosecutors in dealing with corporate finan- **1.43** cial and economic crime. A comprehensive discussion of the provisions can be found in the

House of Commons Research Paper 13/4, 9 January 2013. It appears that the agreements are based largely on similar remedies applied in the USA.

**1.44**   Under paragraph 5(3) of Sch 17 the person under investigation would have to comply with a non-exhaustive list of suggested requirements:

> (3) The requirements that a DPA may impose on P include, but are not limited to, the following requirements—
>   (a) to pay to the prosecutor a financial penalty;
>   (b) to compensate victims of the alleged offence;
>   (c) to donate money to a charity or other third party;
>   (d) to disgorge any profits made by P from the alleged offence; . . . . . . .

**1.45**   The requirement of 'disgorging profits' as set out in s (3)(d) above is a new concept; how this provision will be interpreted, as well as the extent to which particular asset-recovery cases will be dealt with under the proposed DPAs, will no doubt be of interest to many practitioners. Judges will be asked to declare that the entering into of a DPA with the party is likely to be in the interests of justice and they must approve such agreements as being 'fair, reasonable and proportionate' before they can come into force.

**1.46**   On 27 June 2013 the director of the SFO and the DPP published a draft Code of Practice for prosecutors. The consultation closes on 20 September 2013.

# 2

## RESTRAINT ORDERS

## A. Introduction

An application for a restraint order to prevent the dissipation of assets is frequently the first **2.01** step a prosecutor will take in the confiscation process. Restraint orders are most commonly sought shortly before, or just after, criminal proceedings have been commenced—although they can be sought at any stage prior to the conclusion of those proceedings. Indeed, it is by no means unusual for a restraint order to be made after a confiscation order has been made for the purpose of protecting assets against dissipation during the enforcement process. Further, under the Proceeds of Crime Act 2002 (POCA), a restraint order may be made as soon as a criminal investigation is started in England and Wales with regard to an offence. An example of a POCA restraint order is set out in Appendix 9.

### Purpose of restraint orders

The purpose of a restraint order is to preserve realisable property for the purposes of satisfying **2.02** any confiscation order which may be or has been made. Many months, or even years, may elapse between a criminal investigation getting underway and a defendant ultimately standing trial. The aims of the legislation would clearly be defeated if a defendant against whom a confiscation order may be made could deal freely with his assets while awaiting trial: he would be able to dispose of his property to ensure he was effectively 'judgment proof' by the time the confiscation hearing took place. POCA, in common with the legislation that preceded it, gives the court jurisdiction to make restraint orders to prevent a defendant dealing with his property pending the conclusion of the criminal proceedings brought against him and, thereafter, the satisfaction of any confiscation order that may be made. Restraint orders may also be made to prevent a defendant dealing with his property pending the determination of an application to increase a confiscation order that has already been both made and satisfied.

### Freezing orders distinguished

**2.03**  Although the Court of Appeal held in *Re Peters* [1988] QB 571 that the jurisdiction to make restraint orders is 'clearly analogous' to the jurisdiction to make freezing orders (formerly Mareva injunctions), there are a number of important distinctions between the two forms of relief. The jurisdiction to make freezing orders stemmed initially from the inherent jurisdiction of the High Court before being enshrined in s 37(3) of the Supreme Court (now Senior Courts) Act 1981, whereas the restraint order has always been a creature of statute. Further, the purpose of the freezing order is to preserve assets to meet any award of damages that might be made in favour of the claimant in a civil action. The restraint order, in contrast, is intended to preserve a defendant's assets with a view to making them available to satisfy any confiscation order that might be, or has been, made against him following his conviction for a criminal offence.

**2.04**  Of most practical importance, POCA makes specific provision as to the way in which the court must exercise its discretion when considering applications for restraint and receivership orders and applications by defendants and affected third parties to vary or discharge such orders. By s 69(2) of POCA:

> (2)  The powers—
> (a)  must be exercised with a view to the value for the time being of realisable property being made available (by the property's realisation) for satisfying any confiscation order that has been or may be made against the defendant;
> (b)  must be exercised, in a case where a confiscation order has not been made, with a view to securing that there is no diminution in the value of realisable property;
> (c)  must be exercised without taking account of any obligation of the defendant or a recipient of a tainted gift if the obligation conflicts with the object of satisfying any confiscation order that has been or may be made against the defendant;
> (d)  may be exercised in respect of a debt owed by the Crown.

This provision, often referred to as 'the legislative steer', led the Court of Appeal in *Serious Fraud Office v Lexi Holdings PLC (In Administration)* [2009] 2 WLR 905 to hold that the court has no jurisdiction to vary a restraint order to allow an unsecured bona fide creditor of the defendant to be paid from restrained funds. This is in marked contrast to the position in relation to freezing orders where the court will not allow a claimant who has not obtained judgment to gain priority over other creditors of the defendant.

**2.05**  A further distinction between restraint orders and freezing orders is that the court has no power, when making a restraint order, to require the prosecutor to give an undertaking to indemnify third parties in respect of any liability which may flow from compliance with the order: see *Re R (Restraint Order)* [1990] 2 All ER 569. A freezing order, in contrast, will not normally be granted unless such an undertaking is given by the claimant. Similarly, as an essential prerequisite to obtaining a freezing order, the claimant will be required to give an undertaking to pay damages to the defendant if it later transpires that the order should not have been granted. In relation to restraint orders, however, r 59.2(4) of the Criminal Procedure Rules (CrimPR) provides that a prosecutor applying for a restraint order shall not be required to give any such undertaking. Further, s 72 of POCA imposes strict limitations on the circumstances in which an acquitted defendant can seek compensation from the prosecutor for any loss he has suffered as a result of being subject to the restraint order. Finally, and perhaps most controversially of all, s 41(4) of POCA precludes the release of restrained funds to meet legal fees incurred by the defendant if they relate to the offence with which he is charged or in respect of which he is under investigation. This provision not only includes the criminal proceedings but extends to the restraint proceedings themselves: see *Customs and Excise Commissioners v S* [2005] 1 WLR 1338.

## B.  Restraint Orders

### When does POCA apply?

Under the Proceeds of Crime Act 2002 (Commencement No 5, Transitional Provisions, **2.06** Savings and Amendment) Order 2003, SI 2003/333, from 24 March 2003 all applications for restraint orders are made to the Crown Court under POCA where it is alleged that the offences to which the application relates were committed on or after that date. Proceedings that have been instituted in the High Court prior to that date under the Criminal Justice Act 1988 (CJA) and the Drug Trafficking Act 1994 (DTA) will continue to be heard in that court even after the commencement date. Applications for the variation or discharge of such orders, for the appointment of management and enforcement receivers, or for certificates of inadequacy therefore remain within the jurisdiction of the High Court. Similarly, rare applications for restraint orders in cases where the offences are alleged to have been committed before POCA came into force will continue to be made in the High Court under the CJA and DTA (for which, see earlier editions of this work).

### Procedure—without notice applications

The procedure for restraint proceedings under POCA is governed by Pt 59 CrimPR and **2.07** is dealt with in Chapter 7 on procedure. Applications for restraint orders are usually made without notice to the defendant (ex parte) for the reason that if he is put on notice there is a risk he may dissipate his assets including those which are sought to be restrained. The application must follow the format set out in r 59.1 CrimPR, which is set out in Chapter 3 para 3.07 and for further details on procedure see Chapter 7.

### Conditions for obtaining restraint orders under POCA

Section 40(1) of POCA provides that the Crown Court may make a restraint order if any one **2.08** or more of the following conditions are satisfied.

*The first condition: criminal investigations*

By s 40(2) of POCA the first condition is that:                                                                    **2.09**

    (a)   a criminal investigation has been started in England and Wales with regard to an offence; and

    (b)   there is reasonable cause to believe that the alleged offender has benefited from his criminal conduct.

This condition represents a significant departure from the position under the old legislation. Restraint orders can only be made under the CJA and DTA when the defendant has been charged with an offence to which the legislation applies or the prosecutor is in a position to say that he will be so charged at a future date.

**2.10** A 'criminal investigation' is defined in s 88(2) of POCA in the following terms:

> A criminal investigation is an investigation which police officers or other persons have a duty to conduct with a view to it being ascertained whether a person should be charged with an offence.

The term therefore extends to investigations conducted by all law enforcement authorities and not just the police. By s 40(9)(a) of POCA, references to 'the defendant' are to be construed as references to the alleged offender and, by s 40(9)(b), references to 'the prosecutor' are to the person the court believes will have the conduct of any proceedings for an offence.

*The second condition: criminal proceedings already started*

**2.11** By s 40(3) of POCA, the second condition is that:

(a) proceedings for an offence have been started in England and Wales and not concluded, and
(b) there is reasonable cause to believe that the defendant has benefited from his criminal conduct.

This condition is in similar terms to the previous legislation and is the provision under which most applications for restraint orders are made. By s 85(1) of POCA, proceedings for an offence are started:

(a) when a justice of the peace issues a summons or warrant under section 1 of the Magistrates' Courts Act 1980 in respect of an offence;
(b) when a person is charged with the offence after being taken into custody without a warrant;
(c) when a bill of indictment is preferred under section 2 of the Administration of Justice (Miscellaneous Provisions) Act 1933 in a case falling within subsection (2)(b) of that section (preferment by Court of Appeal or High Court judge).

Again, this definition will be familiar to practitioners as being in identical terms to the CJA and DTA. Section 85(3) to (6) of POCA provides a much more comprehensive definition of the phrase 'proceedings are concluded' than under the old legislation, and is in the following terms:

(3) If the defendant is acquitted on all counts in proceedings for an offence, the proceedings are concluded when he is acquitted.
(4) If the defendant is convicted in proceedings for an offence and the conviction is quashed or the defendant is pardoned before a confiscation order is made, the proceedings are concluded when the conviction is quashed or the defendant is pardoned.
(5) If a confiscation order is made against the defendant in proceedings for an offence (whether the order is made by the Crown Court or the Court of Appeal) the proceedings are concluded—
(a) when the order is satisfied or discharged, or
(b) when the order is quashed and there is no further possibility of an appeal against the decision to quash the order.

**2.12** It is a common misconception that proceedings conclude on the making of a confiscation order and that any restraint order is discharged at that point. Section 85(5)(a) makes it plain that proceedings only conclude when the confiscation order is satisfied (or discharged) and the restraint order may thus remain in force until full payment is made. As previously noted, it is by no means uncommon for restraint orders to be sought for the first time after the making of a confiscation order for the purpose of preventing any dissipation of assets pending the enforcement of the order or the determination of any appeal.

Section 85(6) to (8) sets out the rules for determining when proceedings conclude in cir- **2.13** cumstances where the prosecutor exercises his right of appeal under s 31(2) of the Act. The section, as amended by the Constitutional Reform Act 2005 with effect from the 1 October 2009, provides that:

(6) If the defendant is convicted in proceedings for an offence but the Crown Court decides not to make a confiscation order against him, the following rules apply—

(a) if an application for leave to appeal under section 31(2) is refused, the proceedings are concluded when the decision to refuse is made;

(b) if the time for applying for leave to appeal under section 31(2) expires without an application being made, the proceedings are concluded when the time expires;

(c) if on appeal under section 31(2) the Court of Appeal confirms the Crown Court's decision, and an application for leave to appeal under section 33 is refused, the proceedings are concluded when the decision to refuse is made;

(d) if on appeal under section 31(2) the Court of Appeal confirms the Crown Court's decision, and the time for applying for leave to appeal under section 33 expires without an application being made, the proceedings are concluded when the time expires;

(e) if on appeal under section 31(2) the Court of Appeal confirms the Crown Court's decision, and on appeal under section 33 the Supreme Court confirms the Court of Appeal's decision, the proceedings are concluded when the Supreme Court confirms the decision;

(f) if on appeal under section 31(2) the Court of Appeal directs the Crown Court to reconsider the case, and on reconsideration the Crown Court decides not to make a confiscation order against the defendant, the proceedings are concluded when the Crown Court makes that decision;

(g) if on appeal under section 33 the Supreme Court directs the Crown Court to reconsider the case, and on reconsideration the Crown Court decides not to make a confiscation order against the defendant, the proceedings are concluded when the Crown Court makes that decision.

(7) In applying subsection (6) any power to extend the time for making application for leave to appeal must be ignored.

(8) In applying subsection (6) the fact that a court may decide on a later occasion to make a confiscation order against the defendant must be ignored.

The effect of these provisions is to permit the restraint order to remain in force until appeal proceedings have been determined by the Court of Appeal or Supreme Court in accordance with ss 31 and 33 of the Act.

*The third condition: application for reconsideration to be made*

By s 40(4) of POCA (as amended by para 22(2) of Pt 1 to Sch 8 of the Serious Crime Act **2.14** 2007), the third condition is that:

(a) an application by the prosecutor has been made under sections 19, 20, 27 or 28 and not concluded, or the court believes that such an application is to be made, and

(b) there is reasonable cause to believe the defendant has benefited from his criminal conduct.

Sections 19 and 20 of POCA allow the prosecutor to apply to the Crown Court to recon- **2.15** sider a case in the light of fresh evidence where no confiscation order was made. Sections 27 and 28 of POCA permit the prosecutor to apply to the Crown Court for confiscation orders to be made against defendants who abscond. The effect of s 40(4) is to give the court jurisdiction to make restraint orders to prevent assets being dissipated while such applications are pending.

**2.16**   By s 86(1) of POCA, such applications are concluded:

(a) in a case where the court decides not to make a confiscation order against the defendant, when it makes the decision;

(b) in a case where a confiscation order is made against him as a result of the application, when the order is satisfied or discharged, or where the order is quashed and there is no further possibility of an appeal against the decision to quash the order;

(c) in a case where the application is withdrawn, when the person who made the application notifies the withdrawal to the court to which the application was made.

The effect of this section is very similar to s 85 in that it defines the word 'concluded' in such a way as to allow the restraint order to remain in force pending any appeal or until such time as any confiscation order has been satisfied.

*The fourth condition: reconsideration of benefit*

**2.17**   By s 40(5) of POCA (as amended by para 22(3) of Pt 1 to Sch 8 of the Serious Crime Act 2007), the fourth condition is that:

(a) an application by the prosecutor has been made under section 21 and not concluded, or the court believes that such an application is to be made, and

(b) there is reasonable cause to believe that the court will decide under that section that the amount found under the new calculation of the defendant's benefit exceeds the relevant amount (as defined in that section).

**2.18**   Section 21 of POCA permits the court, on an application by the prosecutor, to make a new calculation of benefit and increase the confiscation order accordingly in the light of evidence that was not available at the time the original order was made.

*The fifth condition: reconsideration of available amount*

**2.19**   By s 40(6) of POCA (as amended by para 22(4) of Pt 1 to Sch 8 of the Serious Crime Act 2007), the fifth condition is that:

(a) an application by the prosecutor has been made under section 22 and not concluded, or the court believes that such an application is to be made, and

(b) there is reasonable cause to believe that the court will decide under that section that the amount found under the new calculation of the available amount exceeds the relevant amount (as defined in that section).

**2.20**   Under s 22 of POCA the Crown Court may, on the application of the prosecutor or an enforcement receiver, increase a confiscation order when it appears that the value of the defendant's realisable property exceeds that found to be available at the time the confiscation order was made. In such circumstances, the court may increase the order to such an amount as it believes just, provided it does not exceed the amount found to be the defendant's benefit from the criminal conduct concerned.

**2.21**   By s 86(2) applications under ss 21 and 22 are concluded:

(a) in a case where the court decides not to vary the confiscation order concerned, when it makes that decision;

(b) in a case where the court varies the confiscation order as a result of the application, when the order is satisfied or discharged, or when the order is quashed and there is no further possibility of an appeal against the decision to quash the order;

(c) in a case where the application is withdrawn, when the person who made the application notifies the withdrawal to the court to which the application was made.

**Undue delay**

Section 40(7) of POCA provides that the second condition is not satisfied if the court **2.22** believes there has been undue delay in continuing proceedings or the prosecutor does not intend to proceed. Section 40(8) provides that the third, fourth, and fifth conditions are not satisfied if the court believes there has been undue delay in continuing the application or that the prosecutor does not intend to proceed. Delay and applications for the discharge of restraint orders are considered in Chapter 5.

**Conduct and benefit**

Each of the five conditions in s 40 of POCA requires the prosecutor to prove that there is rea- **2.23** sonable cause to believe the defendant has benefited from his criminal conduct. Section 76(1) of POCA defines 'criminal conduct' in these terms:

> (1) Criminal conduct is conduct which—
>     (a) constitutes an offence in England and Wales, or
>     (b) would constitute such an offence if it occurred in England and Wales.

In many cases it will be obvious from the circumstances of the alleged offence that there is **2.24** reasonable cause to believe that the defendant has benefited from such conduct: the bank robber who steals vast sums of money from a bank or the large-scale, long-term drug dealer have both clearly benefited. There are, however, many situations in which the position is less clear—what, for example, of the professional man who launders the proceeds of a client's crime through his client account and only retains control over it for a very short time? Or the tobacco smuggler who is arrested and has his bounty seized before he has the chance to sell it on?

The Act itself provides some assistance in defining benefit. Section 76(4) to (7) provides: **2.25**

> (4) A person benefits from conduct if he obtains property as a result of or in connection with the conduct.
> (5) If a person obtains a pecuniary advantage as a result of or in connection with conduct, he is to be taken to obtain as a result of or in connection with the conduct a sum of money equal to the value of the pecuniary advantage.
> (6) References to property or a pecuniary advantage obtained in connection with conduct include references to property or a pecuniary advantage obtained both in that connection and some other.
> (7) If a person benefits from conduct his benefit is the value of the property obtained.

The leading authorities on benefit are the decisions of the House of Lords in *R v May* [2008] **2.26** 2 WLR 1131 and the Supreme Court in *R v Waya* [2012] 3 WLR 1188. These decisions are considered in more detail in Chapters 8 and 9, but, in summary, in the former their Lordships decided that:

(1) Benefit is the total value of the property or advantage obtained, not the defendant's net profit after deductions of expenses and payments to co-conspirators.
(2) In determining whether the defendant has obtained property or a pecuniary advantage, the Court should apply ordinary common law principles governing entitlement and ownership.
(3) A defendant obtains property if in law he owns it, whether alone or jointly, which will ordinarily connote a power of disposition or control.

(4) A defendant ordinarily obtains a pecuniary advantage if (amongst other things) he evades a liability to which he is personally subject.

(5) Mere couriers or other minor contributors to an offence, rewarded by a specific fee and having no interest in the property or the proceeds of sale, are unlikely to be found to have obtained that property.

**2.27** In *Waya* the court affirmed the correctness of the decision in *May*. The majority further held, in an important judgment, that:

(1) the primary aim of the legislation was to remove from criminals the pecuniary proceeds of their crime, the deterrent effect being secondary;

(2) if a disproportionate order was sought, the judge has to refuse to make such an order since there would otherwise be a breach of Article 1 of the First Protocol of the European Convention on Human Rights 1950 (ECHR);

(3) an example of a disproportionate order would be where a defendant had restored the proceeds of crime since any order in those circumstances would be an additional financial penalty that would not satisfy the statutory process;

(4) the court invited to make a confiscation order should focus on that which had in fact and in law been obtained by a given defendant;

(5) even if the defendant did not retain criminally acquired property, it yet remained as a benefit and a confiscation order up to the value of the proceeds could follow against legitimately acquired assets.

**2.28** The question of pecuniary advantage was considered by the House of Lords in the earlier case of *R v Cadman-Smith* [2002] 1 WLR 54. The defendant had pleaded guilty to an offence of being knowingly concerned in the fraudulent evasion of excise duty. He had attempted to smuggle 1.25 million cigarettes into the country in a boat which he sailed up the Humber estuary past customs' posts at Immingham and Hull before he reached Goole, where the boat was stopped and searched and the contraband seized by customs' officers. At the confiscation hearing the court determined that he had benefited from the offence to the extent of £130,000, being the amount of the duty evaded, and a confiscation order for £46,250 was made. The Court of Appeal quashed the order on the basis that the defendant had not benefited because the cigarettes had been seized by customs officers before he had the opportunity of selling them. The prosecution appealed to the House of Lords and, in allowing the appeal, their Lordships ruled that the defendant had obtained a pecuniary advantage by evading duty on the cigarettes at the point of importation and it was immaterial that he had not been able to sell them on at the time of his arrest.

**2.29** There is a plethora of authority on the issue of benefit, and further rulings can be expected from the Court of Appeal as it applies the decisions in *May* and *Waya* to the facts of individual cases. It is submitted, however, that these cases are of limited relevance in the context of an application for a restraint order made at the early stages of an investigation or prosecution. As Laws LJ observed in the Court of Appeal's judgment in *Jennings v CPS* [2005] EWCA Civ 746; 4 All ER 391 (where a restraint order had been made under the CJA):

> When a restraint order is applied for, the court is not only ignorant of the defendant's future fate at the hands of the jury. There may be other defendants; the court is, of course, equally ignorant of the jury's future view of them. Indeed it may be unclear who, if anyone, will stand his trial beside the defendant whom the court is considering. There may be large unanswered questions as to the respective roles of different defendants, as to who did what with the crime's proceeds,

and the ultimate extent and destination of those proceeds. There may be other uncertainties. In all these circumstances, it may often be appropriate in a case where there are several prospective defendants to make restraint orders against each of them, so as to protect, as against each, the whole sum which represents the proceeds of the crime so far as the court can at that stage ascertain it. While of course the Crown must lead evidence as to the amount of the proceeds, and the defendant's acts in getting—'obtaining'—the proceeds, and also the defendant's assets so far as they are known, the exercise is quite unlike the later exhaustive investigation undertaken by the trial judge in deciding what, if any, confiscation order to make. At the restraint order stage the court makes no final decision as to the defendant's 'benefit' or 'realisable property'. It is concerned only, as I have said, to make a protective order so that in the particular case the satisfaction or fulfilment of any confiscation order made or to be made will be efficacious. Given the court's obligation under s 82(2) [the forerunner of s 69(2) of POCA], there will be cases where it will advisedly make orders to preserve the same sum of money in the hands of multiple defendants.

### Proving a risk of dissipation of assets

An applicant for a freezing order must satisfy the court that there is a real risk of assets being **2.30** dissipated in order to be entitled to relief. There is no express provision in POCA, or in the previous legislation, requiring the prosecutor to establish that such a risk exists as a condition precedent to obtaining a restraint order. As no such requirement appeared in the legislation, prosecutors initially contended that, on an application for a restraint order, it was unnecessary for them to establish a risk of dissipation. However, this argument was rejected by the Court of Appeal in *Re AJ and DJ* (Unreported, 9 December 1992).

In many cases, the risk of dissipation will speak for itself. As Glidewell LJ acknowledged in **2.31** *Re AJ and DJ*:

> I accept that in many and perhaps the substantial majority of cases where offences involving a gain exceeding £10,000 are concerned, the circumstances of the alleged offences themselves will lead to a reasonable apprehension that, without a restraint or charging order, realisable assets are likely to be dissipated. In drug trafficking offences, this is likely to be so in almost every case. Thus the onus on the prosecution will often not be difficult to satisfy.

Similarly, in relation to cases where there is an allegation of dishonesty, Longmore LJ observed **2.32** in *Jennings v CPS* [2005] 4 All ER 391:

> In a case where dishonesty is charged, there will usually be reason to fear that assets will be dissipated. I do not therefore consider it necessary for the prosecutor to state in terms that he fears assets will be dissipated merely because he thinks there is a good arguable case of dishonesty. As my Lord has said, the risk of dissipation will generally speak for itself. Nevertheless prosecutors must be alive to the possibility that there may be no risk in fact. If no asset dissipation has occurred over a long period, particularly after a defendant has been charged, the prosecutor should explain why asset dissipation is now feared at the time of application for the order when it was not feared before.

These cases, relating to orders made under the old legislation after defendants had been **2.33** charged, were decided by the Civil Division of the Court of Appeal. In *R v B* [2008] EWCA Crim 1374; [2009] 1 Cr App R 14, the Court of Appeal (Criminal Division) had to consider the issue of delay and the risk of dissipation in relation to a restraint order made under POCA at a time when the defendant was still under investigation. On 17 May 2007 the defendant was arrested by officers from SOCA investigating an alleged offence of concealing or disguising criminal property contrary to s 327 of POCA. Thereafter, he was admitted to bail and re-interviewed by SOCA officers on four occasions, during which time he made no attempt to dissipate assets. On 20 November 2007, on the application of the Revenue and Customs

Prosecutions Office 'RCPO', then the prosecuting authority for SOCA, a restraint order was made under POCA. The order included a provision requiring the defendant to disclose the full extent of his assets and, in compliance with this provision, he made a witness statement which disclosed the existence of a donor account with a credit balance in excess of US$1 million of which RCPO was wholly unaware. He made no attempt to dissipate the funds in that account. Further, on 26 November the restraint order was varied to release a company bank account that had been restrained without justification and thereafter the defendant did not take the opportunity to remove any of the funds held in that account.

**2.34** The defendant applied to discharge the restraint order on the grounds that there was no evidence to show that he would dissipate assets, but this was refused by the Crown Court judge. The defendant's appeal to the Court of Appeal was allowed and the restraint order discharged. Moses LJ stated:

> Furthermore, in the light of the facts that we have identified of this appellant not taking the opportunity with which he was presented to dissipate his assets, it was incumbent both on the prosecution and the judge by way of reasoning to explain how it could be said that there was a real risk that he would dissipate his assets in the future when he had had every opportunity to do so in the past. In our view no such explanation has ever been forthcoming, no reasoning has been advanced upon which such a conclusion could be based.

His Lordship added:

> Of course in many cases a Crown Court Judge will have a better opportunity than this court to evaluate evidence, but it should be noted that in a case such as this the only proper safeguard of the rights of one whose property is to be interfered with by a restraint order is careful scrutiny by the judge both on the ex parte hearing and on any application to vary or discharge not only of the issue as to whether there is reasonable cause to believe that the alleged offender has benefited from his criminal conduct, but whether there is a real risk that assets will be dissipated. It should be noted that in the case on which the prosecution founded its argument, *Jennings*, the application was made after the subject of the restraint order had been prosecuted and indeed during the trial. Here, where a citizen has not even been charged, and still has not been charged, it is particularly important to see that there is a proper basis for such a serious order.

**2.35** The longer the prosecutor delays in making his application for a restraint order, the more difficult it will be to establish there is a risk of assets being dissipated and the greater will be the duty on him to justify the necessity for a restraint order. Those acting for defendants and affected third parties should be vigilant in ensuring the prosecuting authority has established a risk of dissipation in relation to restraint orders obtained without notice, particularly where there has been a considerable delay between the start of the investigation and the application for a restraint order being made. It should always be borne in mind that one of the effects of a POCA restraint order, in contrast to those under the CJA and DTA, is currently to preclude a defendant from using his assets to fund his defence to the criminal charges that he faces. For further on the risk of dissipation in relation to the discharge of restraint orders, see Chapter 5.

### The scope and duration of restraint orders

*Parties restrained by the order*

**2.36** Section 41(1) of POCA provides that:

> If any condition set out in section 40 is satisfied the Crown Court may make an order (a restraint order) prohibiting any specified person from dealing with any realisable property held by him.

Section 41(1) gives the court very wide powers to restrain dealing in realisable property not only by the defendant, but by any other person or body holding assets in which the defendant has an interest or which represent gifts made by the defendant. Members of a defendant's family and business associates often find themselves affected by restraint orders. Wives frequently find themselves restrained from dealing with the matrimonial home and with funds held in joint bank accounts. Banks and other financial institutions holding accounts belonging to the defendant will also be bound by the terms of the restraint order. Business assets held by the defendant in conjunction with an innocent business partner are equally vulnerable to restraint.

*Property restrained by the order*

By s 41(2) of POCA:  **2.37**

> A restraint order may provide that it applies—
> (a) to all realisable property held by the specified person whether or not the property is described in the order;
> (b) to realisable property transferred to the specified person after the order is made.

By s 83 of POCA, 'realisable property' includes any free property held by the defendant and any free property held by the recipient of a tainted gift. Section 82 provides that property is free unless an order is in force in relation to it under a number of provisions including s 27 of the Misuse of Drugs Act 1971 (forfeiture order), s 143 of the Powers of Criminal Courts (Sentencing) Act 2000 (deprivation order), ss 23, 23A, or 111 of the Terrorism Act 2000 (forfeiture order), or ss 245A, 246, 255A, 256, 266 (being orders made under the civil recovery regime), 295(2), or 298(2) (being orders made in cash seizure proceedings) of POCA.

Section 84 of POCA contains a number of important provisions in relation to property. It  **2.38**
provides:

> (1) Property is all property wherever situated and includes—
> (a) money;
> (b) all forms of real or personal property;
> (c) things in action and other intangible or incorporeal property.
> (2) The following rules apply in relation to property—
> (a) property is held by a person if he holds an interest in it;
> (b) property is obtained by a person if he obtains an interest in it;
> (c) property is transferred by one person to another if the first one transfers or grants an interest in it to the second;
> (d) references to property held by a person include references to property vested in his trustee in bankruptcy, permanent or interim trustee (within the meaning of the Bankruptcy (Scotland) Act 1985) or liquidator;
> (e) references to an interest held by a person beneficially in property include references to an interest which would be held by him beneficially if the property were not so vested;
> (f) references to an interest, in relation to land in England and Wales or Northern Ireland, are to any legal estate or equitable interest or power;
> (g) references to an interest, in relation to land in Scotland, are to any estate, interest, servitude or other heritable right in or over land, including a heritable security;
> (h) references to an interest, in relation to property other than land, include references to a right (including a right to possession).

The standard for determining whether a defendant has an interest in property for the pur-  **2.39**
poses of making a restraint order pre-confiscation is that the court must be satisfied that there is a good arguable case for such (*per* paragraph 38 of the judgment of Simon Brown LJ in *CPS*

*v Compton and others* [2002] EWCA Civ 1720). The court will have regard to the practical realities of the situation. In *D (UK) Ltd v Revenue and Customs Prosecutions Office* [2005] EWCA Crim 2919, a restraint order was varied, on the prosecutor's application, to include some £366,000 held in the account of a company known as 'R' on the basis that it should be available for confiscation at the end of a trial involving an alleged fraudster, Mrs S. On appeal, it was argued that the order should not have been so varied as Mrs S had no interest in the money in the company bank account. This argument was rejected by the Court of Appeal and, in dismissing the appeal, Longmore LJ said:

> If, therefore, Revenue and Customs can show that there is a good arguable case that the money in R's account in R's bank was part of the benefit obtained by the alleged fraudster, Mrs S, that money will be liable to restraint until a confiscation order is made. In our judgment, Revenue and Customs do not have to show that there is any enforceable right to the money as between the fraudsters. If they can show an arguable case of fraud in which R (or any other party which may claim entitlement to the money) were participating, money retained in the execution of the fraud is, for the purposes of this legislation, the fraudster's money. No doubt the legal title to the chose in action constituted by R's account at the bank while it is in credit is in R, but the beneficial interest lies with any of the fraudster participants in the fraudulent scheme. It is thus an existing beneficial interest which can be subject to a restraint order, not, as Counsel sought to persuade the full court in his supplemental skeleton argument in order to obtain leave to appeal, 'an inchoate future benefit'.

**2.40**   In *R v Walbrook and Glasgow* [1994] Crim LR 613, the Court of Appeal held that a contingent interest under a will was capable of constituting 'property'.

*Capping the amount restrained*

**2.41**   Restraint orders are often obtained at an early stage of an investigation or prosecution before the full extent of the defendant's realisable property is known, but when restraint action is considered appropriate to prevent dissipation. Prosecutors frequently rely on the wide terms of s 41(2) of POCA to restrain all assets in which the defendant has an interest, whether in his possession at the time the order was made, or coming into his possession at some time thereafter. In cases to which the statutory assumptions do not apply because it cannot be shown that the defendant has a 'criminal lifestyle' and where the amount of the defendant's benefit can be readily ascertained, the prosecutor should not restrain assets significantly in excess of that benefit. By way of example, if it can only be asserted that a defendant has benefited from crime to the extent of £1 million, it would clearly be oppressive for the order to restrain assets worth over £5 million. However, in *Re K* [2005] EWCA Crim 619 it was contended that the maximum amount of benefit of which there was prima facie evidence was £477,000 and there was no justification for making a restraint order to cover a greater amount. The judge rejected this argument, ruling that he was entitled to have regard to the statutory assumptions which, if applied, may result in a confiscation order being made in a much larger amount. The Court of Appeal upheld the judge's ruling and rejected the contention that the restraint order should be restricted to assets to the value of £477,000. In delivering the judgment of the Court, Laws LJ said:

> In our view, the judge's reasoning demonstrates a common sense approach to the facts and we see no reason why this Court should interfere with it. It seems to us the judge was perfectly justified in looking to these assumptions as a feature of the case that might very well be in play at a later stage. The reality here is, in our judgment, that at the stage at which the judge was dealing with the matter in January 2005, and in the light of such information as he then had, he was entitled to make an order unlimited in amount. There was

strong evidence of control of the companies by S and M. The companies were significantly engaged, on the Commissioners' evidence, in the defendants' criminality. We have already referred to the judge's finding, unchallenged here, that there is a substantial case that the defendants have used the companies as a façade behind which they were hiding the proceeds of smuggling. In our judgment, it would have been artificial for the judge to conclude that the realisable assets were to be treated as strictly limited to the ill gotten gains that were expressly demonstrated.

Those acting for defendants subject to restraint orders should nevertheless be vigilant in **2.42** ensuring that the order does not restrain more assets than necessary to secure any confiscation order that may be made and, if it does, invite the prosecutor to consent to an appropriate variation, failing which an application to the court should be made. In the case of a restraint order made after a confiscation order has been made, where the benefit figure is already determined, the order should be similarly limited.

*Limited companies*

It is by no means uncommon for a defendant subject to a restraint order to have an interest in **2.43** a limited company incorporated under the Companies Acts. Any shares held in a company are likely to constitute realisable property of the defendant and thus be liable to restraint. However, as limited companies enjoy a legal personality of their own, company assets will not normally constitute 'realisable property' of the defendant within the meaning of POCA. There are, however, a number of exceptions to this general rule. Firstly, property that a defendant gives to a company is likely to be caught by s 77 of POCA as a tainted gift in the same way as tainted gifts to any other third party. The second and most important exception relates to companies under the control of the defendant that have been used to facilitate the commission of the criminal offences with which he has been charged or which are subject to investigation. This occurs most frequently in money laundering cases and in so called 'MTIC' (missing trader intra community) or VAT 'carousel' frauds where a series of buffer companies are created or used to facilitate the fraudulent activity. In these circumstances, the court may lift the corporate veil of the company and treat the assets of the company as being the assets of the defendant and therefore liable to restraint and confiscation under the Act.

An early authority in relation to restraint proceedings was *Re H (Restraint Order: Realisable* **2.44** *Property)* [1996] 2 All ER 391. The three defendants had been charged with excise duty evasion offences in relation to which it was alleged there was a loss to the Exchequer in excess of £100 million. They owned, together with a third party, 100 per cent of the issued share capital of two family companies through which it was alleged the frauds had been committed. On this basis, the High Court made restraint and management receivership orders that included the assets of the companies. The defendants sought variations to the orders removing all references to the companies, contending that the court had no jurisdiction to restrain them. The Court of Appeal rejected the defendants' contention ruling that, where a corporate structure had been used as a device or facade to conceal criminal activity, the court could lift the corporate veil and treat the assets of the company as the realisable property of the defendant for the purposes of the Act. Rose LJ (with whom Aldous LJ and Sir Iain Glidewell agreed) said:

> As to the law, the general principle remains that which was enunciated in *Salmon v Saloman* [1897] AC 22, [1895–9] namely that a company duly formed and registered is a separate legal entity and must be treated like any other independent person with its own rights and liabilities distinct from those of its shareholders.

But a succession of cases throughout the twentieth century show, as Danckwerts LJ said in *Merchandise Transport Ltd v British Transport Commission, Arnold Transport (Rochester) Ltd v British Transport Commission* [1961] 3 All ER 495 at 518, [1962] 2 QB 173 at 206–207:

> …where the character of a company, or the nature of the persons who control it is a relevant feature, the court will go behind the mere status of the company as a legal entity and will consider who are the persons as shareholders or even as agents who direct and control the activities of a company which is incapable of doing anything without human assistance.

**2.45**   In *Adams v Cape Industries plc* [1990] Ch 433; 2 WLR 657, Slade LJ, giving the judgment of the Court of Appeal, cited the same passage and added:

> The correctness of this statement has not been disputed. The court also assumed to be correct the proposition that the court will lift the corporate veil where the defendant by the device of a corporate structure attempts to evade (i) limitations imposed on his conduct by law…
>
> Clearly, as a matter of law, the corporate veil can be lifted in appropriate circumstances.

The Court in *Re H* then went on to review the facts and concluded:

> As to the evidence, it provides a prima facie case that the defendants control these companies, that the companies have been used for fraud, in particular the evasion of excise duty on a large scale; that the defendants regard the companies as carrying on a family business and that company cash has benefited the defendants in substantial amounts.

In these circumstances, the Court held it was appropriate to lift the corporate veil of the companies and treat them as the realisable property of the defendants.

**2.46**   The court is entitled to lift the corporate veil even if it is shown that the company in question is engaged in significant legitimate trading activity. In *Re K* [2005] EWCA Crim 619 the judge found there was a substantial arguable case that the defendants had used various companies as a facade behind which they were hiding the proceeds of their smuggling activities. He lifted the corporate veil on the companies notwithstanding that he accepted they were also engaged in legitimate trading activity. The companies appealed, contending that the judge had failed to ask himself the correct question, namely whether the companies were facades or shams set up by the defendants to conceal the true position. The Court refused the defendants permission to appeal on this point. Laws LJ in delivering the judgment of the Court observed:

> In our judgment the judge's ruling here did no more than reflect the reality of the situation. There was a pressing case on the evidence that albeit none of the defendants had formal control of the companies as office holders they used the companies without the least let or hindrance to facilitate and execute their fraudulent designs. The judge's decision was, in our judgment, plainly in line not only with the dictum from *Re H* but also other authority, not least *Merchandise Transport Limited v British Transport Commission* [1962] 2 QB 173, *Adams v Cape Industries plc* [1990] 1 Ch 433, *Yukong Line* [1998] 1 WLR 794 and *Compton* to which we have already referred and which in truth replicated the test in *H*.

The Court held that the phrase 'lifting the corporate veil' may be somewhat misleading and in reality the true question is whether assets of the company may be treated as realisable property of the defendant. This approach was followed by Ouseley J in *Re D* [2006] EWHC Admin 254.

**2.47**   In *R v Seager and Blatch* [2009] EWCA Crim 1303; [2010] 1 WLR 815, the Court of Appeal considered the issue of lifting the corporate veil in the context of cases where a defendant has been convicted of managing a company in breach of a director's disqualification order. On the facts of these cases, the Court of Appeal found that the corporate veil of the companies in question should not have been lifted. Aikens LJ, in delivering the judgment of the court said:

> A court can 'pierce' the carapace of the corporate entity and look at what lies behind it only in certain circumstances. It cannot do so simply because it considers it might be just to do so. Each of these circumstances involves impropriety and dishonesty. The court will then be entitled to look for the legal substance, not just the form. In the context of criminal cases the courts have identified at least three situations where the corporate veil can be pierced. First if an offender attempts to shelter behind a corporate façade, or veil to hide his crime and his benefits from it: see *Re H and others*, per Rose LJ at 402A; *Crown Prosecution Service v Compton and others* [2002] All ER (D) 395, paragraph 44–48, per Simon Brown LJ; *R v Grainger*, paragraph 15 per Toulson LJ. Secondly, where an offender does acts in the name of the company which (with the necessary *mens rea*) constitute a criminal offence which leads to the offender's conviction, then 'the veil of incorporation is not so much pierced as rudely torn away': per Lord Bingham in *Jennings v CPS*, paragraph 16. Thirdly, where the transaction or business structures constitute a 'device', 'cloak' or 'sham', ie an attempt to disguise the true nature of the transaction or structure so as to deceive third parties or the courts: *R v Dimsey* [2000] QB 744 and 772 (per Laws LJ), applying *Snook v London and West Riding Investment Ltd* [1967] 786 at 802 per Diplock LJ.

Applying these principles to the case of *Blatch*, Aikens LJ said:                      **2.48**

> Mr Blatch was not hiding behind the companies to conceal his offence of contravening the disqualification to act as a company director. He was doing the opposite. He was brazenly continuing to operate and control the companies despite his ban. That was the essence of his offence. There was no question of Mr Blatch using the companies for any illegal purpose, such as avoiding the payment of VAT or money laundering, or defrauding his creditors from which he benefited. There was no evidence before the judge that Mr Blatch used the companies as a shield to hide benefits that he had obtained from his offence of contravening the disqualification.
>
> We accept that Mr Blatch performed acts in the names of the companies whilst illegally acting as a 'director' of them. But the position is very different from that in *Jennings v CPS*. There the company was the vehicle used to perpetrate the 'advanced fee fraud' of the appellant (an employee) and his co-accused, who was the controlling shareholder and director of the company. The corporate structure was, effectively, a sham. Once the corporate veil was pierced, or torn aside, then the property in question was to be regarded as the joint property of those who controlled the company. That was why the restraining order against dissipation of the appellant's property was held to be effective, because the property restrained was to be regarded as the appellant's (jointly with his co-accused), rather than that of the company. In the present case the acts of Mr Blatch, when purporting to be a director, were done on behalf of the companies and they meant that he contravened the disqualification. But the existence of the companies themselves and the legitimacy of their business cannot be in doubt. No one has said that they are to be disregarded as legitimate legal entities.

The Court found that the facts were very different from those in *Re H*. Aikens LJ stated:     **2.49**

> The case of *Re H* was different on the facts. There, Rose LJ, who gave the leading judgment, held that the evidence showed that the defendants controlled the family companies, which had been used for fraud to evade excise duty on a large scale and that company cash had benefited the defendants in substantial amounts: see page 402A. In those circumstances it was obviously appropriate to lift or pierce the corporate veil.

The Court took a similar view of the facts in *Seager*. Aikens LJ stated:

> Mr Seager did not use (the company) as a façade to hide benefits from his crime of contraven-
> ing the undertaking. He did not use the company for other illegal activities. The business of
> the company was legitimate. Although Mr Seager purported to do acts in the name of the
> company (eg enter the lease and operate a bank account in its name), there was no evidence
> that this was a 'sham', with the consequence that he was, in practice, the lessee or the person
> beneficially entitled to any credit in the bank account. Even if Mr Seager did, as a 'shadow'
> director, dispose of property and money on behalf of the company, that would not, by itself,
> prove that he owned it.

**2.50**  The Court of Appeal's decision in *Seager and Blatch* serves as a reminder of the limits on the
powers of the court to lift the corporate veil of companies in which those subject to restraint
and confiscation orders have an interest. It appears that the decision of Ouseley J in *Re D*
[2006] EWHC Admin 254 was not cited in the Court of Appeal in *Blatch and Seager*.

**2.51**  The Court of Appeal returned to the position as regards lifting the corporate veil and restraining companies in *Windsor v CPS* [2011] EWCA Crim 143; [2011] 1 WLR 1519. There was
considerable criticism of the manner in which the order had been both sought and made.
The Court expressed concern at the fact that the judge hearing the application had had an
extremely limited time in which to review the papers and, further, stated that it would be
preferable to list complex cases either before a High Court judge sitting in the Crown Court
with experience of such frauds or a circuit judge with similar experience. Further criticism
was made of the approach of the judge who:

> did not seek to identify the nature and extent of those assets of the company in which the
> alleged offenders might have a beneficial interest, or which might represent their benefit from
> criminal conduct; he did not make any attempt to separate the proceeds of crime from the
> proceeds of legitimate trading; he did not advert to the consequences of the orders upon the
> companies or their minority shareholders, or indeed to the other creditors of the companies.

It is now clear, if it was not before, that if it is wished to lift the corporate veil and restrain
the assets of a company there must be an examination of the various factors set out above, as
well as clear and compelling reasons for taking such a potentially drastic step. The Supreme
Court has recently examined the general principles involved in lifting the corporate veil in
*Prest v Petrodel Resources Ltd* [2013] UKSC 34. In *R v Sale* [2013] EWCA Crim 1306 the
Court of Appeal at paragraphs 41–2 of its judgment stated that the principles in *Seager and
Blatch* should be applied in light of *Prest*.

**2.52**  Another avenue open to a prosecutor wishing to secure company assets would potentially be
to institute criminal proceedings against the company itself if the evidence justified such a
course. In this event the company would become a defendant in its own right and be liable
to restraint and confiscation action. This did not, however, find favour with the Court of
Appeal in *Re H*. Rose LJ said in this regard:

> In my judgment the Customs and Excise are not to be criticised for not charging the com-
> panies. The more complex commercial activities become, the more vital it is for prosecuting
> authorities to be selective in whom and what they charge, so that issues can be presented
> in as clear and short a form as possible. In the present case, it seems to me that no useful
> purpose would have been served by introducing into criminal proceedings the additional
> complexities as to the corporate mind and will, which charging the companies would have
> involved. Conversely, there could have been justified criticism had the companies been
> charged merely as a device for obtaining orders under the Act in relation to their assets.

*Legitimately acquired assets*

It is a common misconception that restraint orders may only be made in relation to assets **2.53** that represent, directly or indirectly, the proceeds of the defendant's criminal conduct. This view is erroneous because, as we have seen, s 83 of POCA defines realisable property as any free property held by the defendant or the recipient of a tainted gift, and s 84 defines property as being 'all property' wherever situated.

These definitions thus make no distinction between assets that have been acquired legiti- **2.54** mately and those which have not. All realisable property of the defendant is liable to restraint, and ultimately confiscation, up to the full amount of his benefit, even if it is acquired legiti- mately many years before the commission of the offences. This was confirmed in *R v Chrastny (No 2)* [1991] 1 WLR 1385 where, in delivering the judgment of the court in a case to which the Drug Trafficking Offences Act 1986 applied, Glidewell LJ said:

> In our view it is quite clear that that definition embraces legitimately acquired property. We cannot read into the Act of 1986 any inference that that definition is limited to illegitimately acquired property; that is to say the proceeds of drug trafficking. The statute is undoubtedly draconian and the decision on that point may seem harsh; the statute is harsh. The statute is in essence one that seeks to ensure that anybody who has benefited from drug trafficking shall, to the extent to which he or she can do so, be deprived of the whole of that benefit.

In *R v Peacock* [2012] UKSC 5; [2012] 1 WLR 550, the Supreme Court ruled that a confisca- **2.55** tion order made under the provisions of the DTA could subsequently be varied upwards, on the application of the prosecutor, to take account of the value of assets legitimately acquired after the original order had been made. It follows from that judgment that the Crown's appli- cation to the High Court for a restraint order to cover those assets, pending the application to revise the order, had been properly made and granted.

In the case of a third party donee of a 'tainted gift' from a defendant, it must be borne in mind **2.56** that it is the value of the gift, rather than the gift itself, that is an asset of the defendant. Thus in the case of *Dickens* [1990] 2 QB 102 the defendant had given his wife a Range Rover, pur- chased for £15,000, which she sold on to another. The court held that, despite the fact that she had sold the vehicle on, the value of the gift was properly included within the amount that made up the confiscation order. It follows, therefore, that any assets held by a third party, however and whenever acquired, may be restrained up to the value of any gift made to them.

*Duration of restraint orders*

By r 59.2(7) of the Criminal Procedure Rules (CrimPR): **2.57**

> (7) Unless the Crown Court otherwise directs, a restraint order made without notice has effect until the court makes an order varying or discharging it.

In practice, the Crown Court rarely 'otherwise directs' and the majority of restraint orders remain in force until a further order of the court is made. The court will invariably give all parties affected by the order permission to apply to vary or discharge it upon giving the court and prosecutor a number of clear days' notice in writing. In any event r 59.3 of the CrimPR allows any person affected by a restraint order to apply for it to be varied or discharged on giving (unless the Crown Court specifies a shorter period) at least two clear days' notice.

This procedure met with the approval of the Court of Appeal (Civil Division) in *Ahmad v* **2.58** *Ahmad* [1998] EWCA Civ 1246 when complaint was made by the appellant third party that a CJA restraint order did not have a return date on which she could attend and argue why the order should not continue in that form. In rejecting this criticism, Thorpe LJ said:

> In my opinion that would not be a sensible practice since in the majority of cases I suspect that the return date, inter partes, would achieve little useful purpose. I can see no objection to the practice whereby the order obtained ex parte contains an obligation to serve with liberty to apply on short notice. This is certainly the practice that obtains in ancillary relief litigation in the Family Division and it has proved to work effectively.

This is not to say that the prosecutor should automatically seek a restraint order of indefinite duration. Indeed, in the later case of *Customs and Excise Commissioners v S* [2005] 1 WLR 1338 the Criminal Division of the Court of Appeal expressed a somewhat different view. Scott Baker LJ said:

> It also seems to us, in the light of the statutory prohibition on the use of restrained funds for legal expenses, that these orders should ordinarily be made with a short return date rather than left open ended for the defendant to apply to vary or discharge. In that way the court can exercise close supervision over orders that are by their nature draconian.

**2.59** It is submitted that prosecutors should consider each case on its own particular facts. If the circumstances of a particular case are such that it is clear that there should be an early hearing at which the court can determine whether the order should remain in force and, if so, on what terms, the prosecutor should ask the court to fix a return date rather than inviting the court to leave the order open ended. If it is not so clear then it is suggested that the court should be invited to fix a return date for a number of weeks in the future, with the stipulation that the date may be administratively vacated should it not be required. If this course is taken then the court retains a degree of control and oversight over the conduct of the order. Whichever course is taken, the prosecutor should ensure that a witness statement is served on the court whenever fresh information is received that could have a bearing either on the original decision to grant the order or as to its ongoing existence or ambit.

### The legislative steer

**2.60** For commentary on what has become termed 'the legislative steer', and its application to restraint orders, see Chapter 5.

### Exceptions to an order

**2.61** By s 41(3) of POCA:

> (3) A restraint order may be made subject to exceptions, and an exception may in particular—
> (a) make provision for reasonable living expenses and reasonable legal expenses;
> (b) make provision for the purpose of enabling any person to carry on any trade, business, profession or occupation;
> (c) be made subject to conditions.

The section gives the court a discretion, which must be exercised in accordance with the legislative steer in s 69 of the Act, as to what exceptions and conditions should be made on making a restraint order. The exceptions made and conditions imposed will inevitably depend on the particular facts of individual cases, but the more frequent requirements are detailed below.

*Reasonable living expenses*

The court will normally require the order to make provision for the release of reasonable sums **2.62** (typically around £300 per week) for the payment of general living expenses. As restraint orders are normally made before the defendant has been convicted of any offence and he is therefore entitled to the benefit of the presumption of innocence, it is right and proper that he should be allowed to meet his general living expenses pending the determination of the criminal proceedings. As Lawton LJ observed in *CBS United Kingdom Limited v Lambert* [1982] 3 All ER 537:

> Even if a plaintiff has good reason for thinking that a defendant intends to dispose of assets so as to deprive him of his anticipated judgment, the court must always remember that rogues have to live and that all orders, particularly interlocutory ones, should as far as possible do justice to all parties.

Further, where a restraint order prevents a spouse or partner of the defendant from dealing with realisable property (eg money in a bank account) the order should also make provision for the release of funds to meet his or her reasonable living expenses unless there is evidence to show that he or she has access to adequate unrestrained funds. The order should also make provision for the defendant to deal freely in any payments he receives from the Department for Work and Pensions by way of state benefits.

In *R v AW* [2010] EWCA Crim 3123 there was a suggestion by the Crown, at one stage, that **2.63** s 69 of the Act should be viewed as:

> An overriding provision which meant the discretionary possibility of an exception being made in respect of reasonable living expenses could not properly be exercised without first treating the defendant in question as impoverished to the extent of being forced to claim on benefits. The question would then be what his position would be when he had achieved all the benefits that he could achieve on the basis that any assets he had to his name were entirely locked up in a restraint order.

Although the point was not in the event pursued, Rix LJ observed that:

> although it is in each case a matter of balance and ultimate discretion for the court, there is no need in principle for a defendant to show that he and his family, even his estranged family, even the children of a divorced wife, are reduced to poverty before a proper claim can be made in terms of the rubric of reasonable living expenses.

If the defendant or an affected third party considers the amounts payable under the restraint **2.64** order by way of general living expenses is insufficient for his legitimate needs, he should invite the prosecutor to agree to the order being varied by consent to allow a greater amount to be released for such purposes. If the prosecutor does not agree to the variation sought, it will be necessary for a formal variation application to be made to the court. This subject is considered in more detail in Chapter 5 where it will be seen that, in determining such applications, the court has to strike a difficult balance between ensuring the defendant has sufficient funds available to meet reasonable living expenses on the one hand and complying with the 'legislative steer' imposed by s 69 of POCA to ensure that the value of the defendant's realisable property is made available to satisfy a confiscation order on the other. If delay occurs in the application then it may be appropriate, and is permissible, for amounts payable by way of living expenses to be backdated; see *R v AW* [2010] EWCA Crim 3123. However, it is unlikely that capitalised lump sums in respect of future living expense liabilities will be released, see *Re Peters* [1988] 1 QB 871.

*Businesses*

**2.65** The court will not, at the pre-confiscation stage, allow a restraint order to operate in such a way as to prevent a business in which the defendant has an interest from trading profitably and legitimately, see s 41(3)(b) of POCA. As Stanley Burnton J said in *Re G* [2001] EWHC (Admin) 606:

> Particular caution is required if it appears that, in addition to engaging in fraudulent transactions, the company is carrying on a legitimate business that may be closed down by the order. It may not be appropriate to treat the assets of the company as those of the defendant in such circumstances. Freezing injunctions in civil proceedings normally contain an exception to the prohibition against dealing with property to enable the person restrained to deal with his assets in the ordinary course of business.

Accordingly, most restraint orders will make provision for the release of business bank accounts for the purpose of facilitating legitimate trading activity subject to profit and loss accounts, bank statements, and related documentation being produced to the prosecutor on a regular basis. The standard form of words used appears in paragraph 19(6) of the precedent restraint order in Appendix 9. In more complex cases, or where there is evidence to suggest the business may be being used to facilitate the commission of offences, the appointment of a management receiver to run the business may prove necessary. This is considered in Chapter 4.

*Legal expenses*

**2.66** Although s 41(3)(a) of POCA gives the court jurisdiction to make provision in a restraint order for the release of funds to pay reasonable legal expenses, s 41(4) POCA imposes strict limitations on the court's powers in this regard. It provides:

> (4) But an exception to a restraint order must not make provision for any legal expenses which—
> (a) relate to an offence which falls within subsection (5), and
> (b) are incurred by the defendant or by the recipient of a tainted gift.

**2.67** Section 41(5) provides that the offences caught by s 41(4)(a) are:

> (a) the offence mentioned in section 40(2) or (3) if the first or second condition (as the case may be) is satisfied;
> (b) the offence (or any of the offences) concerned, if the third, fourth or fifth condition is satisfied.

**2.68** In *Customs and Excise Commissioners v S* [2005] 1 WLR 1338 the Court of Appeal held that s 41(4) prohibited the release of restrained funds to meet legal expenses incurred in relation to the restraint proceedings as well as such expenditure incurred in defending the criminal proceedings. This is in contrast to the position for restraint orders under the CJA and DTA where the release of funds for such expenditure was permitted. The Court upheld the prosecutor's contention that the words 'relate to an offence' in s 41(4) are sufficiently wide to cover the restraint proceedings as no restraint order could be made unless an investigation was underway in relation to an offence or a person had been charged with an offence. In reaching this conclusion, the court found it significant that the prohibition in s 41(4) extended to legal expenses incurred by recipients of tainted gifts. As Scott Baker LJ observed:

> This makes clear that the legislation is not directed simply at excluding legal expenses in connection with the defendant's criminal proceedings—the underlying offence—but in the restraint proceedings themselves, otherwise the provision in relation to recipients of tainted gifts would be unnecessary.

The Court was influenced by the fact that Sch 11, para 36(4) to POCA expressly amended the Access to Justice Act 1999 to make public funding available in relation to restraint proceedings, and that s 252 of the Act imposed a similar prohibition on the release of funds to meet legal expenses incurred in relation to proceedings for an interim receiving order brought under the civil recovery provisions.

**2.69** The Court considered, but rejected, a submission by the defendant that s 41(4) amounted to a breach of his right to a fair trial under Art 6 of the ECHR. The Court observed that the defendant faced 'an overwhelming factual difficulty' because he was represented throughout and it was not suggested that he did not have a fair hearing. The Court noted that Art 6(3) applied only to criminal hearings where the defendant had been charged with an offence and found, following *R (McCann) v Crown Court at Manchester* [2003] 1 AC 787, that it was 'impossible to conceptualise the restraint proceedings as criminal'. Further, the Court noted that in *X v UK* (1984) 6 EHRR 366 the European Commission distinguished civil proceedings from criminal proceedings holding that:

> Only in exceptional circumstances, namely where the withholding of legal aid would make the assertion of a civil claim practically impossible, or where it would lead to an obvious unfairness of the proceedings, can such a right be invoked by virtue of Article 6(1).

**2.70** Finally, the Court considered whether s 41(4) amounted to a breach of the defendant's right to peaceful enjoyment of his possessions under Art 1 of the First Protocol to the Convention. Again, the Court answered in the negative, noting that *Raimondo v Italy* (1994) 18 EHRR 237 made it plain that there is a distinction to be drawn between depriving a person of his possessions and temporary measures to prevent him using them. As Scott Baker LJ said:

> A restraint order constitutes a control in the use of property which will be lawful if, as in the present case, it serves a legitimate aim, namely the preservation of property believed to be the proceeds of crime for confiscation so as to deprive offenders of their benefit from crime.

The Court was nonetheless troubled by the possible consequences of its ruling on those affected by restraint orders. In the concluding paragraph of the judgment, Scott Baker LJ stressed that 'This is not a conclusion we have reached with any enthusiasm'. Section 41(4) has attracted calls for its amendment to restore the position for POCA restraint orders to that which it was under the CJA and DTA, where restrained funds could be released for such legal expenses. However, s 46 of the Crime Courts Act 2013 (not yet in effect) does not go this far (see below).

**2.71** The Court of Appeal followed the decision of *Customs and Excise Commissioners v S* in *AP & U Limited v Crown Prosecution Service and Revenue & Customs Prosecutions Office* [2007] EWCA Crim 3128; [2008] 1 Cr App R 39. The defendant applied to the Crown Court for the release of restrained funds to secure legal representation at the confiscation hearing. The Crown Court judge refused the application, ruling that he was bound by the decision in *S*. The defendant appealed, arguing that his rights under the ECHR had been violated. The Court followed the decision in *S*, refused to make a declaration of incompatibility, and dismissed the appeal. In delivering the judgment of the Court, Latham LJ said:

> An important point, not dealt with, at least expressly, in any of the cases to which we have been referred, is that a restraint order relates to funds which the prosecution believe could well be the proceeds of crime. To permit, therefore, monies which could well be the proceeds of crime being used to pay lawyers for the benefit of the defendant who is either suspected of being, or has been found to be, a criminal raises a clear social issue. Parliament, it seems to us, is entitled to take the view that funds which may have criminal origins should not be so used.

Parliament had to take into account the consequences, namely that other means would have to be provided to enable defendants to have legal representation during restraint and confiscation proceedings. The course adopted was to provide state aid.

**2.72**  The case of *AP* had an interesting sequel in that the trial judge, His Honour Judge Mole QC, ultimately stayed the confiscation proceedings as an abuse of process because no counsel of sufficient experience could be found who was prepared to act for the defendant at the legal aid rate of £178.25 per day. The solicitors acting for the defendant had approached eighteen sets of chambers in London and in the provinces, but no one was prepared to act for those rates of payment. In staying the proceedings the trial judge said:

> I am driven to the conclusion, I have to say reluctantly, that in the exceptional, possibly unique position of P, he cannot have a fair trial of this confiscation issue without representation by the counsel he wishes to have and, in my view, needs. To use the language of *McLean and Buchanan*, I do think it is inevitable he will suffer real prejudice without the assistance of counsel.

> The principle underlying confiscation is a just one so long as the confiscation is carried out justly. The overriding principle is, in my judgment, that for these serious matters, the defendant must be able to have a fair trial and in this case I am confident that he cannot, unrepresented by counsel. I therefore stay these proceedings as an abuse of the process of the Court.

The Crown Prosecution Service did not appeal the judge's ruling. It is submitted that the outcome of this litigation is most unsatisfactory. In consequence, a convicted drugs dealer was allowed to retain his ill-gotten gains in a case where the Crown alleged his benefit from criminal conduct exceeded £4 million. Section 41(4) of POCA was introduced to overcome some of the abuses that occurred in cases to which the CJA and DTA applied where vast amounts of restrained funds were being dissipated in legal fees. Particular care had been taken by the draftsman to amend the Access to Justice Act 1999 to make it clear that public funding should be available for proceedings under POCA (see Sch 11, para 36(4) to POCA). This has to be balanced against the need to ensure that defence solicitors and counsel are adequately remunerated to ensure that those facing restraint and confiscation proceedings are properly represented to enable justice to be done between the parties.

**2.73**  Section 46 of the Crime and Courts Act 2013 many potentially add new subsections to s 41 of POCA namely, (2A), (2B), (5A), and (5B). However, this section and the amendments are not currently in force. If and when they do come into force, the effect will be to allow restrained assets to be used to pay towards legal aid contributions in circumstances which will be prescribed in further legislation. However, POCA will continue to prohibit the use of restrained assets to fund private defence costs, in order to prevent restrained assets from being unnecessarily dissipated. Defendants whose restrained income would otherwise put them over the threshold should continue to receive legal aid, subject to any prescribed contributions. Any unrestrained income would still be taken into account for the purpose of these potential amendments.

### Legal expenses for unrelated proceedings

**2.74**  Section 41(4) does not preclude the release of restrained funds to meet legal expenses incurred in connection with proceedings that are wholly unrelated to the offence. If, for example, the defendant wishes to pursue or defend civil proceedings or even criminal proceedings totally unrelated to the offences in relation to which the restraint order has been made (eg proceedings for a road traffic offence) the prohibition will not apply. The authorities suggest, however, that the court will take a broad view as to the nature of proceedings that relate to the offence. In *AP & U Limited v Crown Prosecution Service and Revenue and Customs Prosecutions Office* [2007] EWCA Crim 3128; [2008] 1 Cr App R 39, one of the issues the Court of Appeal had to consider was whether the prohibition extended to judicial review proceedings. U Limited, a company describing itself as a money transmitting business, transferred some 7 million euros on behalf of clients to the account of a company called Currency Solutions Ltd at the Laiki Bank in the UK. On 6 February 2007 Currency Solutions made a formal disclosure report under POCA to SOCA requesting consent to continue providing facilities to U Limited. After initially giving consent, SOCA refused permission to the bank to provide further facilities to U Limited, which thereupon commenced judicial review proceedings.

U Limited was under investigation for alleged money laundering offences and was subject **2.75** to a restraint order made under POCA. The company sought a variation to the restraint order for the purpose of meeting legal fees incurred in connection with the judicial review proceedings. The Crown Court judge agreed that funds should be released for this purpose and varied the restraint order accordingly, but the Crown exercised its right of appeal against that decision. The key issue for the Court of Appeal was whether the judicial review proceedings related to the offence within the meaning of s 41(4). The Court held that they did and allowed the Crown's appeal. Latham LJ said:

> The Crown's case is simply that the events in February 2007, that is the circumstances surrounding the disclosure reports, were all matters connected with the money laundering which, in general terms, was the offence into which the criminal investigation had been started, as disclosed in the witness statement relied upon by the Crown before the Judge applying for the restraint order. [Counsel for U Ltd] has valiantly attempted to persuade us that there is no proper connection between the events of February 2007 and the offence or offences into which the criminal investigation began. In particular he pointed to the fact that no money laundering offences were committed if consent was given for the transaction disclosed. But that fails to grapple with the Crown's argument. Consent may relieve the bank of any criminal responsibility for a transaction in question; but that does not mean that in relation to others involved in the transaction, it may not amount to or form part of a dishonest money laundering scheme. The Crown's case is that the disclosure reports were triggered by transactions which were suspected of being part of such a scheme. That being so, it seems to us that there is a sufficiently clear connection between the offence or offences into which there was the investigation to mean that the judicial review proceedings 'related to' that offence or offences.

Further, it is not possible to avoid the prohibition in s 41(4) of POCA by arguing that the **2.76** payment of legal fees constitutes a living expense allowable under s 41(3)(a). In *McInerney v Financial Services Authority* [2009] EWCA Crim 997; [2010] 1 WLR 650, the defendant was being prosecuted by the Financial Services Authority for alleged money laundering offences. A restraint order had been made which released £250 per week to him for ordinary living expenses. The defendant applied to the Legal Services Commission for public funding to seek a judicial review of the Financial Services Authority's power to prosecute offences contrary to POCA. The Legal Services Commission agreed to provide public funding, but subject to the defendant making a contribution of £117.66 per month. This contribution was assessed on the basis of the defendant's entitlement to £250 per week living expenses from restrained funds. The defendant thereupon sought confirmation from the Financial Services Authority that the monthly contributions could be paid from the allowance made for his ordinary living expenses. The authority refused to give the confirmation sought, contending that payment of the contribution would constitute a breach of s 41(4) as it was not possible to make an exception to the order for the payment of legal expenses. The defendant then sought a variation to the restraint order to make it clear that he was not prohibited from paying the contribution. The judge refused the application saying that to accede to it would be 'an attempt to do serious injury to the wording of the statute'.

**2.77** The defendant thereupon appealed to the Court of Appeal, contending that, on a proper reading of s 41 of the Act, it placed no limitations on what the defendant may do with any money allowed to him by way of general living expenses. He contended that he could spend the £250 per week allowed in any way he pleased without being in breach of the Act or in contempt of court. He could therefore choose to use the money to instruct a lawyer to defend him in the restraint proceedings or on the criminal charges. The Court of Appeal rejected this argument and dismissed the appeal. Hooper LJ said:

> We agree with the judge. Payments to the LSC are not ordinary living expenses and thus McInerney would be in contempt of court to pay money to the LSC and the LSC would be in breach of the restraint order to receive it. Furthermore section 41(3)(a) makes a distinction between living expenses and legal expenses and if a contribution to the LSC is a legal expense, a payment to the LSC would not be a payment towards ordinary living expenses.

He added:

> It follows that a judge who discovers that a contribution is being made to the LSC is likely to impose a condition that no such contribution should be made, indeed if not bound to do so in the light of sections 41(4) and 69.

**2.78** See above for the potential effect of s 46 of the Crime and Courts Act 2013 on s 41 POCA which may yet allow restrained funds to be paid towards legal aid contributions. The terms and conditions on which the court will release restrained funds to pay legal expenses in cases where the s 41(4) prohibition does not apply are considered in more detail in Chapter 5.

### Costs and expenses incurred in complying with the restraint order

**2.79** Third parties affected by restraint orders will from time to time incur costs in ensuring they are properly complied with. Banks and other financial institutions, for example, will incur costs in identifying accounts affected by the order and freezing them in compliance with it. By r 59.2(5) of the CrimPR:

> (5) The Crown Court may require the applicant for a restraint order to give an undertaking to pay the reasonable expenses of any person, other than the person who is prohibited from dealing with realisable property by the restraint order, which are incurred in complying with the restraint order.

As this requirement does not extend to persons who are prohibited from dealing with realisable property, the defendant, his spouse or partner, any company in relation to which the corporate veil has been lifted, and any recipient of a tainted gift will generally be excluded from the terms of any such undertaking given by the prosecutor.

### Undertakings in damages

**2.80** Rule 59.2(4) of the CrimPR provides that the Crown Court must not require the applicant for a restraint order to give any undertaking to pay damages sustained as a result of the order to any person who is prohibited from dealing with assets by it. This is in marked contrast to the position in relation to freezing orders where the applicant will normally be required to give an undertaking in damages as a condition precedent to the making of the order.

### Restrictions

Section 58 of POCA imposes a number of restrictions on third parties exercising various **2.81** rights they may otherwise have in relation to realisable property caught by a restraint order. By s 58(2), no distress may be levied against property subject to a restraint order except with the leave of the Crown Court and subject to any conditions it may impose.

Similarly, by s 58(3) and (4), where a restraint order applies to a tenancy of any premises, no **2.82** landlord or any person to whom rent is payable may exercise a right of forfeiture by way of peaceable re-entry without the leave of the Crown Court. This is in contrast to the position under the old legislation where it has been held that the exercise of a right to forfeiture does not constitute a breach of any restraint order affecting the property: see *Re R (Restraint Order)* [1990] 2 All ER 569.

By s 58(5) POCA, where any court in which proceedings are pending (for example civil pro- **2.83** ceedings in the County Court or High Court) in relation to any property is satisfied that a restraint order has been applied for or made in respect of that property, that court may either stay the proceedings or allow them to continue on such terms as it thinks fit. Although s 58 appears to give the appropriate court a very wide discretion as to how it may exercise its powers, it is clear from the terms of s 69(1)(a) of POCA that the relevant court's discretion under s 58 must still be exercised in accordance with the legislative steer under s 69(2) and (3) to preserve the value of realisable property in order to satisfy any confiscation order. Section 69 of POCA is considered in more detail in Chapter 5.

Further, s 58(6) of POCA provides that before the relevant court exercises its power under **2.84** s 58(5), it must give the applicant for the restraint order and any receiver appointed under the Act an opportunity to be heard. In *Serious Fraud Office v Lexi Holdings PLC (In Administration)* [2008] EWCA Crim 1443; [2009] 2 WLR 905, the Court of Appeal reminded practitioners of the importance of complying with s 58 where property in respect of which they are litigating is subject to a restraint order. In noting that the section had not been complied with, Keene LJ said:

> We entirely accept that the reason why section 58 was not drawn to the attention of those judges was because counsel then appearing for Lexi was himself unaware of it. It was an innocent oversight. Nonetheless, steps do need to be taken to ensure that the terms of section 58 are observed. Some thought might usefully be given to the possibility of creating a register of restraint orders and applications for such orders, though that would not have cured the problem in the present case, since all involved were aware of the existence of the restraint order. The SFO and other prosecuting authorities could usefully publicise more widely the general tenor of section 58 and no doubt the relevant Bar Associations could play a role. This is not just a matter for the criminal courts and criminal lawyers: the duty under section 58 applies to all courts in which proceedings about such property take place and very often those will be the civil courts.

### Variation and discharge of restraint orders

Section 42(3) to (7) of POCA deals with the variation and discharge of restraint orders. This **2.85** is dealt with in more detail in Chapter 5.

## C. Northern Ireland

**2.86** A summary of the relevant proceeds of crime provisions applicable to Northern Ireland may be found at Appendix 20.

## D. Protecting Real Property

**2.87** By r 93(1) of the Land Registration Rules 2003 (SI 2003/1417) a POCA restraint order may be registered as a restriction against the title to the property at the Land Registry. By r 92(1), the application must be made by the prosecutor on Form RX1. The restriction will be entered in the charges register in Form EE set out in Sch 4 to the Land Registration Rules 2003 and will preclude any dealing in the property without the consent of the prosecutor or further order of the court.

# 3

## ANCILLARY ORDERS: SEIZURE, DISCLOSURE, AND REPATRIATION OF ASSETS

## A. Introduction

Practitioners may be surprised, on seeing a restraint order for the first time, to note the **3.01** extent and breadth of its terms. In many instances, the order will go way beyond restraining the defendant from dealing in his assets but, in addition, will require him to make a witness statement disclosing the full extent and location of all his realisable property and even to repatriate assets held overseas. Section 41(7) of the Proceeds of Crime Act 2002 (POCA) empowers the Crown Court to make any such order as it believes appropriate for the purpose of ensuring the restraint order is effective. In this chapter, we examine the powers of the court to make ancillary orders and the conditions and limitations to which they are subject.

## B. Seizure of Assets

By s 45 of POCA: **3.02**

    (1) If a restraint order is in force, a constable or a customs officer may seize any realisable property to which it applies to prevent its removal from England and Wales.

    (2) Property seized under subsection (1) must be dealt with in accordance with the directions of the court which made the order.

The Act is silent as to the degree of proof the officer must have that the asset may be removed from England and Wales before he can seize it. It is submitted that the standard must be the same as that required to obtain a restraint order, namely that there is a good arguable case that the asset may be removed: see *Compton v CPS* [2002] EWCA Civ 1720. Substantial proof is not required and, it is submitted, there is no requirement that the evidence should be in a form admissible in a criminal trial.

**3.03** Once an asset has been seized, it must be dealt with in accordance with the court's directions under s 45(2). Although no procedures are laid down in POCA or in rules of court, it is submitted that the proper course is for the prosecutor to issue an application seeking the court's directions as to how the asset should be dealt with. The application notice should be served on all parties who, to the prosecutor's knowledge, claim to have an interest in the property. If the asset is of particularly high value, it may be appropriate for the prosecutor to apply for the appointment of a management receiver to take possession of it pending the conclusion of the proceedings.

**3.04** POCA appears to confer an unlimited discretion on the court to give such directions as it sees fit as to how the seized property should be dealt with. It is submitted that the court must exercise its discretion in accordance with the legislative steer in s 69 of the Act. The court should be particularly mindful of its power under s 69(4) to order that property must not be sold if it cannot be replaced.

## C. Disclosure Orders

**3.05** The prosecutor should have full information as to the nature, extent, and location of all the defendant's realisable property to police the restraint order effectively. When the prosecutor applies for a restraint order, he will have much information about the defendant's realisable property from a variety of sources. In the last analysis, however, the extent of a defendant's realisable property is a matter within his own knowledge. Thus, from the very early days of the legislation, prosecutors have asked courts making restraint orders to include a provision requiring the defendant to swear an affidavit disclosing the full extent of his realisable property. Although the early cases required disclosure on affidavit, since the advent of the Civil Procedure Rules the usual requirement is for the defendant to make the required disclosure in a witness statement verified by a statement of truth.

### Jurisdiction to make disclosure orders under POCA

**3.06** The power of the High Court to make disclosure orders ancillary to restraint orders under the predecessor regimes such as the Criminal Justice Act (CJA) and the Drug Trafficking Act 1994 (DTA) flowed from the inherent jurisdiction of the High Court: *Re O* [1991] 1 All ER 330. As the Crown Court is a creature of statute and has no such inherent jurisdiction, POCA makes express statutory provision empowering the court to make ancillary orders to restraint orders. Section 41(6) and (7) of POCA provides as follows:

> (6) Subsection (7) applies if—
>    (a) a court makes a restraint order, and
>    (b) the applicant for the order applies to the court to proceed under subsection (7) (whether as part of the application for the restraint order or at any time afterwards).
> (7) The court may make such order as it believes is appropriate for the purpose of ensuring the restraint order is effective.

This provision enables the Crown Court to continue making disclosure and repatriation orders in precisely the same way as the High Court together with any other form of order it considers necessary to ensure the restraint order is effective. An example of a POCA restraint order, including disclosure and repatriation provisions, is found at Appendix 9.

**Procedure for application**

The Procedure for making applications under section 41(7) POCA is provided in Part 59 of **3.07** the Criminal Procedure Rules (CrimPR) and covers ancillary orders in addition to restraint orders. For further details on procedure see Chapter 7. The requirements under Rule 59.1 are identical to those for restraint orders:

> 59.1—(1) This rule applies where the prosecutor, or an accredited financial investigator, makes an application under section 42 of the Proceeds of Crime Act 2002 for—
>
>     (a) a restraint order, under section 41(1) of the 2002 Act; or
>
>     (b) an ancillary order, under section 41(7) of that Act,
>
> for the purpose of ensuring that a restraint order is effective.
>
> (2) The application may be made without notice if the application is urgent or if there are reasonable grounds for believing that giving notice would cause the dissipation of realisable property which is the subject of the application.
>
> (3) An application for a restraint order must be in writing and supported by a witness statement which must—
>
>     (a) give the grounds for the application;
>
>     (b) to the best of the witness' ability, give full details of the realisable property in respect of which the applicant is seeking the order and specify the person holding that realisable property;
>
>     (c) include the proposed terms of the order.
>
> (4) An application for an ancillary order must be in writing and supported by a witness statement which must—
>
>     (a) give the grounds for, and full details of, the application;
>
>     (b) include, if appropriate—
>
>         (i) any request for an order for disclosure of documents to which rule 61.9 applies (rules applicable to restraint and receivership proceedings: disclosure and inspection of documents),
>
>         (ii) the identity of any person whom the applicant wants the court to examine about the extent or whereabouts of realisable property,
>
>         (iii) a list of the main questions that the applicant wants to ask any such person, and
>
>         (iv) a list of any documents to which the applicant wants to refer such a person; and
>
>     (c) include the proposed terms of the order.
>
> (4) An application for a restraint order and an application for an ancillary order may (but need not) be made at the same time and contained in the same documents.
>
> (5) An application by an accredited financial investigator must include a statement that, under section 68 of the 2002 Act, the applicant has authority to apply.

**The problem of self-incrimination**

There is a real risk that by requiring a defendant to disclose his assets he might incriminate **3.08** himself both in relation to the offence with which he has been charged and other offences as well. Full compliance with a disclosure order might, for example, result in the defendant admitting money laundering offences. The courts have from the outset been vigilant to protect the defendant's right against self-incrimination by insisting that the prosecutor must not make any use of the disclosure statement during any criminal trial. In *Re a Defendant*, The Independent, 2 April 1987, Webster J ruled that the disclosure order was only to take effect upon the prosecutor giving an undertaking

> not to use any of the information obtained as a result of compliance with the order for any purpose or in connection with any criminal proceedings taken or contemplated against the defendant or for any purpose other than a purpose arising under the Drug Trafficking Offences Act 1986.

**3.09** The Court of Appeal made it clear in *Re O* [1991] 1 All ER 330 that the CJA could not be construed in such a way as to abrogate the privilege against self-incrimination. The Court ruled, however, that the privilege was capable of protection by the imposition of conditions upon the use to which information provided in disclosure statements may be put. The Court considered the practice that had developed following *Re a Defendant* and Lord Donaldson MR said:

> We were told that in another case the CPS was required to give an undertaking limiting the class of person to whom the disclosed information could be given and the purposes for which it could be used. I would not wish to be taken to criticise such an approach, but consider it preferable to impose a condition in the order rather than seek an undertaking.

The Court suggested that the condition should be in the following terms:

> No disclosure made in compliance with this order shall be used as evidence in the prosecution of an offence alleged to have been committed by the person required to make that disclosure or by any spouse of that person.

**3.10** In *Re T (Restraint Order: Disclosure of Assets)* [1992] 1 WLR 949 the defendant contended that this condition was insufficient to protect his privilege against self-incrimination in a drug trafficking case. It was contended that, by complying with the disclosure order, the defendant would suffer an enhanced penalty by increasing the size of the confiscation order that would be made against him and, in consequence, render him liable to serve a longer term of imprisonment in default of payment than would otherwise be the case. The Court of Appeal rejected this argument, ruling that the purpose of the legislation was to compel the defendant to make reparation in respect of the unjust enrichment he had obtained from his criminal activities and, that by making such reparation, he did not incur punishment. There was thus no question of self-incrimination. As Leggatt LJ said:

> Compliance with the order to swear an affidavit does not expose the defendant to any such risk: the condition to which the order is subject precludes the risk of further prosecution on that account; a confiscation order is different in nature from forfeiture: and even if it were right to regard a confiscation order as penal in character, disclosure on affidavit does not render the defendant liable to the imposition of a form of order to which he would not otherwise be subject.
>
> Disclosure of assets in conjunction with the statutory assumptions merely facilitates assessment of the amount to be recovered in the defendant's case, once it has been determined that he has benefited from drug trafficking, and does not in my view amount to self incrimination. Confiscation applies to the value of the defendant's proceeds of drug trafficking, whereas forfeiture extends to things used for the commission of crime and is therefore punitive. It is true that disclosure of assets exposes the defendant to the risk of a confiscation order greater in amount than could be made in the absence of disclosure. But it is not self incriminating because a person does not by making reparation incur punishment.

**3.11** In *R v Martin and White* (1998) 2 Cr App R 385 the Court of Appeal had to consider a complaint by a defendant that the condition approved in *Re O* had been breached by the prosecutor during the course of his trial. Prosecuting counsel, who had been supplied with a copy of the disclosure affidavit by those instructing him, had cross-examined the defendant on inconsistencies between the evidence he gave on oath to the jury and the contents of the affidavit. The defendant contended that this represented a breach of the condition and, furthermore, that there should be a species of 'Chinese Wall' preventing the affidavit coming into the possession of those having conduct of the prosecution until such time as the defendant is convicted.

The Court of Appeal ruled that there had been no such breach by the prosecutor because **3.12** the affidavit had not been adduced as evidence in the prosecution of an offence but merely used in cross-examination as to credit. Rose LJ added that it would be 'an affront to common sense' if the defendant could make two wholly contradictory statements on oath and avoid being challenged in any way as to the inconsistency. Further, the Court rejected the suggestion that the disclosure affidavit should have been withheld from those having the conduct of the prosecution until after conviction. Rose LJ said:

> We cannot accede to the submission that such an affidavit should remain detached from those engaged in prosecution. To attempt to debar the prosecution from sight of such an affidavit would be both impracticable and wrong, not least because the conduct of the prosecutor is or should be under the immediate supervision of the court. We are not prepared to contemplate the prosecution being kept in ignorance of any such affidavit until a confiscation order is sought.

The Court was nonetheless troubled by the use to which the affidavit had been put and the **3.13** circumstances in which it had been used without prior reference to the trial judge. Rose LJ emphasised that:

> We cannot envisage circumstances in which any such affidavit could become admissible in evidence during a criminal trial at the behest of the Crown, either in the course of the prosecution or, as was thought to have happened here, by being purportedly proved by way of cross examination of the accused. We would hope and expect that, in future cases, the Crown and the court will be alert to the limitations subject to which an order for disclosure by affidavit is made.

The Court also held that prosecuting counsel should not rely on the disclosure statement **3.14** without first seeking the leave of the judge. Rose LJ said:

> Such use of the affidavit should be subject to safeguards aimed at reconciling the proviso with the immediate needs of the Crown. In our judgment, prosecuting counsel should seek prior directions from the judge as to the precise use which can be made of the affidavit. This will alert the judge and defence counsel as to the situation and enable the judge to maintain an oversight that reconciles use of the affidavit with the proviso.

The wording of the condition as approved in *Re O* has subsequently been reviewed by the **3.15** High Court in the light of the incorporation of the European Convention on Human Rights (ECHR) into English law. In *Re C (Restraint Order: Disclosure)* (4 September 2000) the prosecutor sought an order of committal against the defendant for failing to comply with the disclosure provisions in a DTA restraint order. In response, counsel for the defendant expressed concern that compliance with the disclosure order might put those investigating the criminal case on the track of some evidence they would otherwise have been unaware of, which could prove gravely prejudicial to the defendant. Collins J held that this submission had considerable force and that any such use of the disclosure statement would constitute a breach of the defendant's right to a fair trial under Art 6 of the Convention, given the ruling of the European Court of Human Rights in *Saunders v UK* (1996) 23 EHRR 313. The judge also expressed doubt as to whether the decision in *Martin and White*, which was made prior to the Convention being incorporated in English law, was consistent with Art 6. Collins J said:

> It does not matter in what form the information is used, whether as evidence, whether because it enables other evidence to be obtained which could not otherwise have been discovered or whether it is used merely as a weapon in cross examination of the defendant. Whatever use in the criminal trial is prima facie a breach, it seems to me, of Article 6.

**3.16** Collins J ruled that the wording of the condition should be tightened to make it plain that the information disclosed should not be used against the defendant in the course of the criminal trial. The revised wording of the condition is set out in paragraph 13 of the example restraint order in Appendix 9. Collins J recognised that there may be circumstances in which the interests of justice dictate that the contents of a disclosure statement should be disclosed to a co-accused. It may be, for example, that the contents of a disclosure statement made by defendant A may exonerate or at the very least assist the defence of defendant B. The judge emphasised that, whatever the circumstances, the court must retain ultimate control over the use to which the disclosed information is put and that in circumstances such as these an application for directions should be made to determine how, if at all, the disclosed information might be revealed to the co-accused.

**3.17** In the case of *R v JS* [2009] EWCA Crim 2972 the Court of Appeal followed the approach of Collins J in *Re C*. In *JS* the defendant and his co-defendant were awaiting trial and restraint orders had been made against both. Paragraph 9(2) of the defendant's restraint order specified that there should be no disclosure of any material disclosed in compliance with the order to any co-defendant in the criminal proceedings. The Crown wished to seek a management receivership order against the defendant. The co-defendant asked to see the material relied on in the receivership application including trading records supplied by the defendant, so that he could make representations in the receivership application under s 49(8) POCA. The Crown Court granted a variation of para 9(2) of the defendant's order so that the material could be disclosed to the co-defendant for that purpose. The Court of Appeal quashed that order on the basis that disclosure of the material was prima facie prohibited by para 9(2) of the order and the co-defendant had not put forward any specific reason why he should see the material. The Court held it to be essential that an analysis be conducted of how access to the materials might assist the co-defendant in relation to any relevant submissions. Lord Justice Hooper also stated:

> We do not need to decide whether an order of the kind made in this case could ever properly be made when material has been previously disclosed with the protection afforded by paragraph 9(2) or similar provision. But in our view there was no justification for making the order in this case and it is difficult to imagine a case when such an order would be justified upon an application to appoint a receiver.

**3.18** It should be noted that the condition as revised by the ruling of Collins J in *Re C* does not preclude the use of the disclosure statement in a confiscation hearing after the defendant has been convicted. In *Re E and Re H* (Unreported, 24 May 2001) an application by the defendants for an order preventing the prosecutor relying on the disclosure statement at the confiscation hearing was robustly rejected by the High Court. In delivering his judgment, Henriques J said:

> The absurd consequence of counsel's submission is that where a prosecuting authority are aware of assets disclosed and verified they would not be able to rely on that information in the confiscation proceedings. Nothing could be more absurd. If the defendant gave different information or no information when it was sought under section 73(A) known assets would have to be returned. Counsel suggests that is a necessary consequence of Parliament not clearly revoking the privilege against self incrimination. He suggests, in any event, that individuals might themselves obtain Mareva injunctions. Such a course is fanciful and it would dismember a now sophisticated and highly developed procedure for recovering assets from criminals and returning them to their rightful source. The absurdity of the consequence exposes the fallacy of the argument which unhappily falls at the first hurdle of binding precedent.

Dyson LJ took a similar line in refusing permission to appeal against the ruling of Henriques J **3.19** in *Customs and Excise Commissioners v El Heri* [2001] EWCA Civ 1782 where he said:

> Counsel submits that unless the prohibition on the use of disclosed material is extended to the confiscation proceedings, then there will be a significant erosion of the privilege against self incrimination, an erosion for which there is no sufficiently clear statutory authority. I am not persuaded that the confiscation proceedings attract the privilege against self incrimination. I accept that the outcome of confiscation proceedings may properly be described as a penalty and may also be described as part of the sentencing process, since they arise in criminal proceedings. But no authority has been cited to me which shows that the privilege against self incrimination extended to proceedings which take place following a conviction. Be that as it may, the authorities to which I have referred clearly point to the conclusion that the judge was right in this case. I do not accept that the law has been materially changed in this regard by Article 6 of the ECHR.

Disclosure orders are also subject to the usual rule of civil procedure that they may not be used for **3.20** any ancillary or collateral purpose. In *Re R* (Unreported, 21 October 1992) Macpherson J said:

> As a matter of general principle, it seems to me in the highest degree undesirable that these affidavits should go to anybody other than the court and the parties involved. The reasons for that are obvious. They may not be used in other criminal proceedings. There will be reticence, if not downright secretion of facts by individuals, if they feel that these affidavits may go elsewhere. In ordinary circumstances—this appears to be such a case—these affidavits should be kept locked in the Central Office and not disclosed to anyone.

### Disclosure and third parties

It has been seen that restraint orders can, and frequently do, bind third parties not charged **3.21** with any offence who may have control or possession of realisable property or claim an interest in it. In *Re D (Restraint Order: Non party)* The Times, 26 January 1995 the High Court held that the power to order disclosure extended to such third parties. The father of the defendant had been restrained from dealing with a number of bank accounts and was required to swear an affidavit disclosing details of transactions through accounts held in his name. Turner J dismissed the father's application to remove the disclosure requirement from the order in so far as it affected him. The judge held that the court did have jurisdiction to compel a third party to make such disclosure. He held that as the purpose of requiring disclosure was to police compliance with the restraint order and that third parties could be restrained from dealing with realisable property, it followed that the inherent jurisdiction of the court to order disclosure applied equally to third parties as it did to the defendant.

### Disclosure orders against solicitors

Solicitors from time to time may hold information that may assist the prosecutor in polic- **3.22** ing a restraint order and the question arises as to the extent to which they may be compelled to disclose such information. The information may take many forms and may include, for example, the name and address of persons known to be affected by the order and details of assets caught by the order such as a bank account used by the defendant or an affected third party to pay the solicitor's fees. The leading authority is *Re W* [2008] EWHC 2780 (Admin). The background to the case was the defendant's conviction for fraud, which resulted in a finding that he had benefited from criminal conduct to the extent of £33 million and the making of a confiscation order for £9.4 million. The defendant escaped from prison and was eventually arrested in Switzerland. An enforcement receiver was appointed, but he was only able to recover a small proportion of the amount outstanding under the order.

**3.23** One of the defendant's assets was a development plot in Spain, which the trial judge found had been purchased in the name of a Spanish company by the defendant's wife using money supplied by the defendant. The defendant contended that the property was not realisable because it had been stolen by a Spanish lawyer, but the judge rejected this contention. Two days before the hearing of the application to appoint a management receiver, London solicitors applied to intervene in the proceedings on behalf of an entity referred to as Estevez Consulting Group who claimed that the property was not owned by the defendant but by a Mr Estevez. Two days later, the solicitors advised the prosecutor that in fact a company called Achedina Veinte SL owned the property. It appeared to the prosecutor that this company was owned beneficially by the defendant.

**3.24** Thereafter the intervenor failed to comply with a court order to file evidence as a result of which the prosecutor applied to strike out the intervention. In response, it was contended that Mr Estevez, who was alleged to be the agent for Achedina, was dealing with the solicitors through an interpreter, and was eager to put in evidence, but had not yet had the opportunity to do so. On the evening prior to the strike-out hearing, the solicitors served a witness statement to the effect that they had discovered the interpreter was in fact the sole director of the company and the person who had been giving them instructions. The interpreter herself produced a witness statement referring to Mr Estevez as a friend and accountant. She said that the company was owned by a British Virgin Islands trust company known as Candis. The court thereupon ordered the production of the trust deed. Eleven days before the deadline for compliance, the solicitors sent a letter to the prosecutor advising that their client was unable to comply with the disclosure order, in consequence of which the prosecutor instituted another strike-out application. Shortly before the hearing, the solicitors advised that their clients would no longer be pursuing the intervention and the court struck it out, ordering the intervenor to pay the prosecutor's costs of £17,849.63. The costs were never paid.

**3.25** The prosecutor believed that the defendant and his wife were the beneficiaries of Candis and the owners of the land in Spain and that it was they who initiated and controlled the third-party intervention. The prosecutor thereupon sought disclosure from the solicitors for the dual purposes of enabling the receiver to take possession of the property and enforcing the costs order made in his favour. The information sought included details as to when the solicitors first received instructions to act, whether the instructions were oral or in writing, the identity of the person who instructed them, and that person's address and telephone number. The prosecutor also sought disclosure of the date on which funds were remitted to the solicitors to cover the costs of the proceedings, the identity of the person remitting the funds, and the sort code and account number of any cheque transfer. The solicitors provided the names and addresses sought, but not the date on which they were instructed or the financial information requested by the prosecutor.

**3.26** Ouseley J ordered the solicitors to disclose the information sought by the prosecutor. He found as a fact that where one saw the involvement of the defendant's wife as beneficiary of the trust owning the property, one also saw the hand of the defendant. The judge expressed himself as being satisfied that the disclosure sought would be of value to the enforcement receiver in preventing the defendant evading the confiscation order and of assistance in making sure that the defendant's assets were realised. As to the legal basis for making the disclosure order Ouseley J said:

> Counsel (for the prosecutor) puts the legal principles which he says should govern the exercise of the admitted jurisdiction as follows. He says that I should follow the principles in *Norwich Pharmacal v Customs & Excise Commissioners* [1973] AC 133. He adopts the succinct summary of those principles from Mr Justice Lightman in *Mitsui & Co Ltd v Nexen Petroleum (UK) Ltd*

[2005] EWHC 625 Ch in which, at paragraph 21, he said the principles required for *Norwich Pharmacal* relief were:

i) a wrong must have been carried out, or arguably carried out, by an ultimate wrongdoer;

ii) there must be the need for an order to enable an action to be brought against the ultimate wrongdoer;

iii) the person against whom the order is sought must: (a) be mixed up in so as to have facilitated the wrongdoing; and (b) be able or likely to be able to provide the information necessary to enable the ultimate wrongdoer to be sued.

He points out that in *Re D (Restraint Order: Non-Party)* TLR, 25 January 1995, Mr Justice Turner had held that disclosure could be ordered within the context of a restraint order under section 8 of the Drug Trafficking Offences Act 1986 against a person who was not a party in the criminal proceedings, and he applied the broad principles of *Norwich Pharmacal* although the precise test is not discussed.

Counsel for the solicitors, whilst accepting that an order for disclosure can be made, submits that because it is confidential information, whether applying *Norwich Pharmacal* or not, a stricter test or an additional point needs to be added. For these purposes he relies on *Finers and others v Miro* [1991] 1 WLR 35, 40D to 41C, where Lord Justice Dillon, with whose judgment the others concurred, made a number of comments about the circumstances in which disclosure could be ordered in respect of privileged information. The court said that privilege could not apply if the solicitors were consulted—even though he did not realise it or was himself acting innocently—to cover up or stifle a fraud:

On the material before us I conclude that it does seem probable that the defendant may have consulted Mr Stein for the purpose of being guided and helped, albeit unwittingly on the part of Mr Stein, in covering up or stifling a fraud on the insurance company of which there is a prima facie case resting on solid grounds.

Counsel submits that it is necessary for there to be a higher test to reflect the fact the information sought here is confidential, whereas in *Norwich Pharmacal* cases the information may well not be confidential but merely information which the third party simply does not wish to supply.

In support of his submission, Counsel referred to Article 8 of the European Convention on Human Rights and the tests there to be satisfied in Article 8(2) for an interference with Article 8 rights to be justified. It is not necessary separately to consider that issue. Counsel was minded to agree—and he would have been certainly wrong not to have done—that if the *Finers v Miro* test was satisfied then Article 8(2) would also have been satisfied. There is in my judgment nothing in Article 8 which imposes a higher test than that which emerges from *Finers v Miro*. Counsel for the prosecutor was not disposed to take issue, as I understand his submissions, with the sort of language put forward in *Finers v Miro* in relation to confidential information.

For my part, I consider that Counsel for the solicitors makes a sound point in relation to the approach which a court ought to adopt in relation to confidential information. However I accept Counsel for the prosecutor's submission that on the application of that test it is manifestly satisfied here for the reasons I have given. There is a substantial amount outstanding on a confiscation order made as a result of a conviction for a very serious fraud on the public purse.

The judge emphasised that he was making the order for the purpose of advancing the **3.27** enforcement of the confiscation order and hindering the 'manifest attempts' of the defendant at evading it. The order was not made, nor was it refused, for the other purpose sought by the prosecutor, namely the enforcement of the costs order made against the intervener. He said:

Quite what the test should be for that may be debatable, certainly very debatable in the absence of the background which I have described. If an abuse of process is required I am minded to consider that that is exactly what the intervention was. But in the light of the way in which the arguments have developed on what I see as the main basis for the making of this order, it is unnecessary for me to reach any firm conclusion. If there are any difficulties in relation to the use of the information I am ordering to be disclosed for the purpose of enforcement of costs it will be open to the prosecutor to revert to this court for the purpose of seeing whether it can indeed use the information to that end.

**3.28**   It should be noted that information sought by the prosecutor in *Re W* is not protected by legal professional privilege since it has nothing to do with the provision of legal advice by the solicitor to the client. The authority for this is *R (On the application of Miller Gardner Solicitors) v Minshull Street Crown Court* [2002] EWHC 3077 (Admin), where Fulford J, with whom Rose LJ agreed, said:

> In *R v Manchester Crown Court ex parte Rogers* [1999] 1 WLR 832 this court held that a record of an attendance at a solicitor's office by a client for an appointment, which I observe must involve giving the name of the client, was a communication between client and solicitor, but not one that attracted legal professional privilege. In his judgment at page 839, Lord Bingham CJ considered the function and nature of the document with which the court was concerned, and he concluded that:
>
>> It records nothing which passes between the solicitor and the client and it has nothing to do with obtaining legal advice. It is the same sort of record as might arise if a call were made to a dentist or a bank manager. A record of an appointment does involve a communication between the client and the solicitor's office but it is not in my judgment, without more, to be regarded as made in connection with legal advice. So to hold would extend the scope of legal privilege beyond its proper sphere . . .
>
> That decision provides strong support for the proposition that the provision of an individual's name, address and contact number cannot, without more, be regarded as being made in connection with legal advice. It records nothing which passes between the solicitor and client in relation to the obtaining of or giving of legal advice. Taking down the name and telephone number is a formality that occurs before the legal advice is sought or given. As My Lord observed during argument, providing these details does no more than create the channel through which advice may later flow: see in this regard the case of *Studdy v Sanders and others* [1823] 2 D and R 347.
>
> It follows, in my judgment, that the identity of the person contacting the solicitor is not information subject to legal professional privilege and the telephone numbers of the brothers, equally, are not covered by this protection; neither are the dates when one or other of those men phoned the office. Moreover, the record of appointments in the office diary and attendance notes, insofar as they merely record who was speaking to the solicitor and the number they were calling from, fall within the same category.

**3.29**   Further, information or documentation is not protected by legal professional privilege if it is held with the intention of furthering a criminal purpose: see *R v Central Criminal Court ex p Francis and Francis* [1988] 3 All ER 775 considered in more detail in Chapter 17.

**3.30**   The fact that the information has been provided to the solicitors is not necessarily a bar to disclosure. In *A v A; B v B* [2000] 1 FLR 701 Charles J reviewed the extent to which confidential information is protected from disclosure to persons having a legitimate interest in gaining access to it: the issue that fell to be determined was the extent of the court's power to disclose financial information revealed during the course of ancillary relief proceedings to the Inland Revenue. At p 713F Charles J summarised the position in these terms: 'Generally, in the absence of a statutory provision or rule that prohibits, or restricts, the proposed use, or disclosure of material there is no absolute duty of confidence and a court has a discretion to authorise, or order, disclosure of confidential information.'

The court will normally exercise its discretion in favour of disclosure where the proper **3.31** administration of justice would otherwise be defeated. In *Price Waterhouse v BCCI Holdings (Luxembourg) SA* [1992] BCLC 583 at 601f Millet J (as he then was) said: 'The duty of confidentiality . . . is subject to a limiting principle. It is subject to the right, not merely the duty, to disclose information where there is a higher public interest in disclosure than in maintaining confidentiality.'

In *A v A; B v B* Charles J went on to consider the types of case where the public interest in **3.32** disclosure should outweigh the duty of confidentiality. At p 722C he said: 'There is a well accepted and strong public interest in the proper and efficient investigation and prosecution of crime.' At p 722E–F he added:

> There is also a well accepted and strong public interest in the proper, fair and efficient admin-istration of justice. A part of the public interest in the administration of justice, and also a free standing public interest, is that solicitors, as officers of the court, and the persons employed by them should perform their duties honestly and efficiently and thus, for example, not mislead the court.

It is submitted that there is compelling public interest in divesting criminals of the proceeds **3.33** of their nefarious activities and, to that end, in ensuring the proper and effective enforce-ment of restraint, confiscation, and receivership orders. In most circumstances this should outweigh any duty of disclosure owed by solicitors to their clients.

### Form of disclosure orders

A typical disclosure order appears in paragraphs 12 and 14 of the draft restraint order at **3.34** Appendix 9. Many orders impose two distinct obligations on the defendant: firstly, to give initial disclosure in writing within seventy-two hours of the order being served and, sec-ondly, within fourteen days thereafter to serve a witness statement on the prosecutor, sup-ported by a statement of truth, verifying the information provided in the initial disclosure. In *Re E and Re H* (Unreported, 24 May 2001) the defendant disputed the necessity for his disclosure statement to be verified by a statement of truth. In rejecting this submission, Henriques J said:

> It is particularly appropriate in a case involving very large sums of money such as this that a disclosure of assets should be accompanied by a statement of truth. With prosecution for contempt as the only sanction and a two year maximum sentence discounted by way of good character, pleas and possible parole, many a fraudster would not be deterred from a partial or inaccurate disclosure of assets.

### Disclosure from the prosecutor

The defendant does not have the right to seek disclosure of information or documentation **3.35** held by the prosecutor for the purpose of assisting him to comply with his disclosure obliga-tions under a restraint order. In *Re S and W* (Unreported, 7 February 2000) the defendants, who were both in custody, sought orders requiring the prosecutor to disclose documents they claimed were in his possession and which they required to assist in complying with the disclosure provisions in DTA restraint orders made against them. Tucker J dismissed the application saying:

> The point taken on behalf of Her Majesty's Customs and Excise is that if these defendants were aware of the information which Customs and Excise had obtained, they might have been tempted to tailor their own information to that which they were aware that Customs and

Excise already had. I see the force in that submission. I rather doubt whether the court has the power, in any event, to order disclosure on the part of Her Majesty's Customs and Excise. Even if I had that power, I would not be minded in my discretion to exercise it.

These orders are, and are intended to be, Draconian in their provisions. They are aimed at restricting the use by the defendants of ill-gotten gains obtained by them by allegedly criminal activities. The terms of the order are clear. The accounts may be numerous and it may be expensive for the defendants to obtain the information from their banks but the obligation is, nevertheless, laid on the defendants to do so. I am not going to relieve that obligation by making any order against Her Majesty's Customs and Excise; therefore, I decline to do so. It is for the defendants to obtain the information.

The judge nonetheless indicated that he had some sympathy with the position in which the defendants found themselves and, without making any order, invited the prosecutor to assist in so far as he felt able to do so.

**3.36** It may be that on an occasion a third party seeks to obtain the material disclosed by a defendant in response to a restraint order for some other purpose such as parallel litigation. In *T v (1) B (2) Revenue & Customs Prosecutions Office* [2008] EWHC 3000 (Fam); [2009] 1 FLR 1231, a mother in child maintenance proceedings sought an order from the Family Division of the High Court to be joined to the restraint proceedings and have access to the disclosure statement of the father and documents arising from his restraint order proceedings in the Crown Court. Sir Mark Potter, President of the Family Division, held that the application was in effect to vary the restraint order and that while he enjoyed the jurisdiction of the Crown Court it would be inappropriate for him to exercise it. The President decided that the matter should be heard by the Crown Court which granted the restraint order with the prosecutor having the opportunity to present a reasoned response as to whether disclosure prejudiced the prosecutor and that the Court deciding the matter needed to have the disclosure statement and documents before it so as to rule upon them. The President also observed:

> as it seems to me, provided there is no reason to suppose or suspect collusion, tainted knowledge or improper motive on the part of an applicant in seeking leave to make use of a witness statement or statements made in the course of restraint proceedings for the purposes of pursuing a bone fide claim for maintenance, other ancillary relief or relief under Schedule 1, then the Judge should be prepared favourably to consider the making of such an order in the interests of justice.

**3.37** Prosecuting agencies usually employ separate legal teams or divisions dealing with restraint and confiscation in addition to those dealing with the prosecution itself. This is because of the need to ensure so-called 'Chinese walls' and that no improper use is made in the prosecution of material compulsorily disclosed by a defendant in restraint proceedings. A defendant's disclosure statement is not usually passed from the restraint and confiscation team to the prosecution team, except in the circumstances envisaged by the authorities above and below. This, however, may cause difficulties such as in relation to the prosecutor's disclosure obligations. In *R v S* [2009] EWCA Crim 2870 the prosecutor applied to the Court of Appeal to have sight of the Court's judgment dealing with variation of the defendant's restraint order. The Court had ordered that its judgment was not to be disclosed to others, and in particular that it was not to be disclosed to the prosecutor (being the prosecution team as distinct from the Restraint and Confiscation team in the Asset Forfeiture Division). The prosecution was, however, concerned that documents in the hands of its Asset Forfeiture Division might be documents that it ought to consider for the purpose of fulfilling its disclosure obligations, and wished to see what had been disclosed. The Court of Appeal held that if it was right that the documents were ones that the prosecution ought to consider for the purpose of fulfilling its disclosure obligations then the proper forum for an application was to the judge who was in charge of the restraint proceedings. Therefore the proper course was for the prosecutor to return to the judge and seek a variation of the restraint order so that all the relevant material was made available to it. The procedure set out for the obtaining of information from those subject to restraint orders had to be observed and the duty to ensure a fair trial fell upon the trial judge.

The position may sometimes be complicated by the fact that the prosecutor has obtained **3.38** information from a foreign jurisdiction pursuant to letter of request with the guarantee it only be used in criminal and confiscation proceedings. In *P v P* [2012] EWHC 1733 (Fam); [2013] 1 FLR 1003 Mr Justice Moylan determined an application by a former wife for disclosure from her husband of all the documents connected to his ongoing restraint and confiscation proceedings in support of her ancillary relief proceedings. The CPS intervened and opposed the application on the basis that the documents which the wife sought contained information consisting of or derived from material received from foreign governments or other authorities pursuant to requests for mutual legal assistance (MLA). The information had been provided only on the basis it be used in the criminal and confiscation proceedings and not for other purposes. In balancing the public interest in the MLA scheme against the wife's need to have access to the documents to pursue her ancillary relief claim fairly, Moylan J exercised his discretion and granted the disclosure order to the wife as sought and ordered that the documents should be disclosed by the husband or failing that, the CPS.

### Advising the defendant or third party required to disclose

The practitioner's task in advising a client, whether he be a defendant or an affected third **3.39** party, who is required to make disclosure under the terms of a restraint order is an important and complex one. Serious consequences for the client may flow from a failure to give full and complete disclosure of assets, whereas too much disclosure may cause unnecessary prejudice to the client at a later stage in the proceedings. Although each case must be considered on its own particular facts, we endeavour in this section to offer practical guidance to the practitioner faced with this important task.

The disclosure order usually requires compliance within a relatively short timescale: most **3.40** orders require initial disclosure within seventy-two hours and full disclosure in a witness statement verified by a statement of truth within fourteen or twenty-one days thereafter. The practitioner needs to consider at the outset whether it will be possible for the client to comply with these time frames. There may be many legitimate reasons why compliance will not be possible: for example, the client may be remanded in custody at a prison some distance from his solicitor's office and a legal visit may take some time to arrange; or it may be necessary to obtain or produce many documents in support of the statement. If it is not going to be possible to comply with the time limits imposed by the order, the prosecutor should be approached as a matter of urgency and asked to agree to the order being varied by consent to extend the time for compliance. It is unlikely that the prosecutor will refuse to agree a short extension provided a proper explanation is advanced as to why it is necessary. However, given that the prosecutor requires the disclosure information to police the restraint order effectively, a lengthy or open-ended extension is unlikely to be acceptable and any extension agreed will be expressed in terms of days rather than weeks or months. If the prosecution will not consent to the order being varied, an application should be made to the court for an extension of time. The matter should not be left in abeyance, because the prosecutor may well institute contempt proceedings in the absence of proper compliance with the order or an application to court for further time to comply.

**3.41** As far as initial disclosure is concerned, the client should be asked to list all the assets in which he has an interest in as much detail as possible. As initial disclosure may have to be given within seventy-two hours, the prosecutor will not expect it to be full and comprehensive provided the defendant has listed all the assets in which he has an interest to the best of his ability. If time permits, the list should be typed and the client invited to check it carefully and sign it before it is sent to the prosecutor. A handwritten list will suffice if there is insufficient time to provide the prosecutor with a typed copy before the deadline expires.

**3.42** Once the initial disclosure has been provided, work should begin on the preparation of the witness statement, which will need to be served usually no later than fourteen days thereafter. Great care should be taken in the preparation of the statement because the order requires it to be verified by a statement of truth, and potentially serious consequences will flow from any material inaccuracy or non-disclosure. The client should be advised very carefully of these possible consequences, which include proceedings for contempt of court and criminal prosecution together with the risk of serious damage to the client's credibility at any confiscation hearing if he has been shown to be untruthful in his disclosure statement. Further, the client should not assume that the full extent of the prosecutor's knowledge of the defendant's assets is set out in the officer's witness statement in support of the restraint application. The prosecutor's investigation will inevitably continue until the confiscation hearing takes place and, indeed, may even continue after a confiscation order has been made given the court's powers under POCA to increase orders in the light of fresh evidence. The client would therefore be well advised to disclose all his assets at the outset, whether the prosecutor appears to be aware of them or not, in order to avoid any risk of contempt proceedings or being embarrassed at the confiscation hearing.

**3.43** The client should be taken through every subparagraph of the disclosure order and asked to provide full details of the assets he holds that are caught by each provision. If he cannot remember the precise details, the relevant financial institutions should be approached for confirmation of the position: banks may be contacted, for example, to advise as to account numbers and the balances standing to the credit of all the client's accounts. The prosecutor may also be approached for assistance if he has taken up documentation relating to the client's assets during house searches at the time of the arrest. The prosecutor may, however, rely on *Re S and W* (Unreported, 7 February 2000) as authority for the proposition that he is not required to provide such documentation.

**3.44** Once the client has provided all the required information, work should commence on drafting the witness statement. It is submitted that the proper approach is to address each subparagraph of the disclosure order in turn, in the order in which they appear in the restraint order, and identify with full particularity each and every asset required to be disclosed. Once the draft has been completed and typed, the client should check it and the effect of his signing the statement of truth fully explained. If he is satisfied it sets out fully all the assets in which he has an interest, he should sign the statement of truth and it should be served on the prosecutor.

**3.45** After the disclosure statement has been served, the defendant's legal representatives should be vigilant to ensure it is not abused by the prosecutor or put to any improper use. The legal representative's suspicions should be aroused if, within a short time of a disclosure statement being served, the prosecutor serves further evidence in the criminal proceedings that appears to mirror facts disclosed by the defendant. In such circumstances, an enquiry of the prosecutor as to how the new evidence was obtained would be perfectly justified. If the evidence has been obtained legitimately and quite independently of the disclosure statement, the prosecutor should be able to demonstrate this through a proper audit trail. As Collins J said in *Re C (Restraint Order: Disclosure)* (Unreported, 4 September 2000):

> I am not prepared to assume that any prosecuting authority is going deliberately to fail to comply with the requirements and surreptitiously obtain evidence based on the material disclosed as a result of the order. I cannot approach my task, nor could any court, on that assumption. If there is a misuse, if there is an attempt to produce and rely on material obtained as a result of disclosure it would, I would have thought, normally be difficult to conceal that exercise because of the requirements of prior disclosure and because of the need for there to be a prima facie case before the High Court could be persuaded to make a restraint order.

> A restraint order is based upon an affidavit by the applicant which is itself based upon information given by the officer in the case. If further information suddenly came to light after disclosure it would indeed be suspicious. I do not doubt that the trial judge who could see among other things the affidavit of the officer which had obtained the restraint order would be able to ascertain whether there had been any bad faith, which is what it would amount to on the part of the prosecution. That, as I say, is not something I should take into account in my judgment in deciding whether the order in a particular form should or should not be made.

## D. Oral Examination

Criminal Procedure Rule 59.1(4)(b)(ii)–(iv) (as set out above at para 3.07 and in Chapter 7) also anticipates that ancillary orders made under s 41(7) POCA may include the court ordering the holding of a hearing with an oral examination of a defendant or third party. Such an enquiry could include questions to be asked of the defendant regarding realisable property or of parties who may be able to give relevant evidence concerning the extent or whereabouts of that property. The power to hold a hearing with oral questioning of defendants and third parties, as opposed merely to setting a written list of questions to be answered in a disclosure witness statement, has historically rarely been used. It is submitted it should only be employed where it is proportionate and 'is appropriate for the purpose of ensuring that the restraint order is effective' as required by s 41(7) POCA. **3.46**

## E. Repatriation of Assets

### Introduction

The legislation applies to all realisable property of the defendant wherever it is situated in the world: see s 84(1) POCA. As most serious organised crime involves an international element, it is by no means an infrequent occurrence that those involved in such offences have the ability to invest their ill-gotten gains in overseas jurisdictions. Indeed, as money laundering operations have become more sophisticated and funds can be transferred from country to country more or less instantaneously by means of electronic transfer, those involved in criminal activity can move the proceeds of their nefarious activities overseas with ease in an attempt to conceal them from the UK law enforcement agencies. **3.47**

**3.48**   As we shall see in Chapter 19, international cooperation between countries can often facilitate the restraint and confiscation of assets in foreign jurisdictions in support of criminal proceedings brought in the UK. The process can, however, be a long and drawn out one and not all countries are willing to cooperate, particularly in cases involving tax fraud. In such circumstances the prosecutor may seek a repatriation order requiring the defendant to bring the assets in question within the jurisdiction of the court pending the determination of the proceedings.

### Jurisdiction to make repatriation orders

**3.49**   As with disclosure orders, the Crown Court's jurisdiction to make repatriation orders is to be found in s 41(7) POCA.

**3.50**   In *DPP v Scarlett* [2000] 1 WLR 515 the jurisdiction to make repatriation orders was considered by the Court of Appeal. The Court had no hesitation in confirming that the jurisdiction to make repatriation orders in support of restraint proceedings did exist. Beldam LJ (with whom Roch and Judge LJJ agreed) said:

> If a power to order full disclosure of assets on affidavit is inherent in a restraint order, the order should also include power to order the return of those assets within the jurisdiction. Both powers are essential to the purpose of the restraint order and to the realisation of those assets which is the purpose of the express statutory power given by Parliament.

**3.51**   The power to order repatriation is a discretionary one and it does not follow that the court will order it in every case where assets are located overseas. The court may well require an explanation as to why the prosecutor has chosen to rely on the repatriation remedy rather than seeking mutual legal assistance to restrain the asset in the jurisdiction in which it is located. There may be many reasons why such action would prove impractical: the country in question may not be prepared to assist, a letter of request may have been sent and not been met with a timely response, or the necessity to prevent threatened dissipation of assets may require urgent action to be taken. Whatever the reason, the prosecutor must be prepared to justify the use of the repatriation remedy to the court's satisfaction.

### Form of repatriation orders

**3.52**   The draft restraint order at Appendix 9 incorporates repatriation provisions at paragraph 16. The usual form of order requires the asset to be brought within the jurisdiction within twenty-one days and for the prosecutor to be informed of its location within seven days thereafter. If the asset is in the form of money, the order will require it to be deposited in an interest-bearing account and for the prosecutor to be notified of its location within the same period. As with disclosure orders, if compliance within the periods specified in the order proves impossible for any reason, the prosecutor must be approached with a view to an extension of time being agreed by consent and, in default of agreement, an application to the court should be made.

## F. Writ of *Ne Exeat Regno*

**3.53**   An ancillary order in support of a restraint order can be creatively drafted so long as it satisfies the statutory requirement under s 41(7) POCA. It may range further than simply a disclosure or repatriation order or an order for an oral examination. For example, the High Court has long had a jurisdiction to issue a writ of *ne exeat regno* (literally 'do not leave the realm') in support of Mareva or freezing injunctions to compel defendants to surrender their passports and not to leave the jurisdiction. The High Court set down the applicable criteria in *Fenton v Callis* [1969] 1 QB 200, which require that: (a) the cause of action must be one in which the defendant would have been liable to arrest at law; (b) it constitutes a good cause of action—at least a good arguable case; (c) it provides probable cause for believing the defendant would otherwise quit England; and (d) the defendant's absence from England would materially prejudice the plaintiff in prosecuting the action. For examples of its use in case law see also *B v B (Injunction: Restraint On Leaving Jurisdiction: Passport Surrender)* [1998] 1 WLR 329; *Allied Arab Bank v Taj El Arefin Hajjar and others* [1988] QB 787; and *Al Nahkel for Contracting & Trading Ltd v Lowe* [1986] QB 235.

In the case of Raymond Woolley, Keith Lindblom QC (as he then was) sitting as a deputy **3.54** High Court judge ordered that the defendant surrender his passport and not leave the jurisdiction in support of a High Court restraint order extant under the CJA. Mr Woolley had returned to the jurisdiction having previously absconded from prison and fled to Switzerland with a confiscation order unpaid. There was therefore an obvious flight risk and his presence was required in order to satisfy the outstanding confiscation order which the restraint order remained in place to enforce.

The Crown Court has made similar types of orders under s 41(7) POCA, even in **3.55** pre-conviction cases, where there has been a flight risk and the orders have been necessary to ensure the restraint orders were effective. These orders may even be applied prior to defendants being charged with any criminal offence. However, such orders are likely to be used sparingly and only if truly necessary for the restraint order as opposed to the prosecution. Their use must also be proportionate, particularly if they might amount to bail-type conditions (such as residence or reporting to the police station etc). The Crown Court made such orders against the defendants in *R v AA & SA* [2011] Lloyd's Rep FC 71 to secure their attendance at the contempt of court proceedings for breaching their restraint orders in circumstances where they had previously fled the jurisdiction to avoid the service of restraint orders.

# 4

## MANAGEMENT RECEIVERS

## A. Introduction

A restraint order, coupled with disclosure and repatriation provisions, will in most cases **4.01** prove sufficient to preserve the value of realisable property pending the making and enforcement of a confiscation order. Banks will immediately freeze a defendant's accounts on being served with a copy of the order and the registration of a restriction at the Land Registry will effectively prevent any dealing in real property. As to the running of businesses caught by the order, conditions requiring the defendant to deliver accounts, bank statements, and associated documentation at regular intervals will normally be sufficient for the prosecutor to satisfy himself that the business is being properly run for legitimate trading activities. The defendant himself will also be aware that any dealing in realisable property in breach of the order will constitute a contempt of court for which he may be committed to prison.

In some cases, however, a restraint order alone will not be an effective means of preserving **4.02** the value of a defendant's assets pending the determination of the proceedings. The defendant may, for example, be in custody or have absconded leaving valuable assets unmanaged. In consequence, a house, often the most valuable asset in a defendant's estate available for confiscation, may be left unoccupied or fall into a state of disrepair and attract the attention of squatters, burglars, or vandals. It may be left uninsured and mortgage payments may fall into arrears. Similar considerations may apply to other valuable assets including cars, boats, and light aircraft. A business or company under the control of the defendant may need closer supervision than that afforded by requiring the defendant to submit business records on a regular basis. Further, the prosecutor has neither the qualifications nor experience necessary to make important decisions relating to the management of a restrained business. It would not, for example, be in a position to judge whether the release of a large sum of money from a restrained bank account to fund a particular business venture represents a good business risk or not.

**4.03** In circumstances such as these, further measures need to be taken to manage and preserve the realisable property of the defendant while the restraint order remains in force. The Proceeds of Crime Act 2002 (POCA) gives the court power, on the application of the prosecutor, to appoint a receiver to take possession of and manage the defendant's realisable property pending the conclusion of the proceedings. Receivers appointed for such purpose are referred to as 'management receivers' to distinguish them from 'enforcement receivers' who are appointed after a confiscation order has been made to realise the defendant's assets in satisfaction of the order. A draft management receivership order is found at Appendix 10.

**4.04** In *Capewell v Customs and Excise Commissioners* [2005] 1 All ER 900 the Court of Appeal emphasised how management receivership orders can seriously interfere with the business and personal life of the defendant, and that the costs of appointing a receiver should always be proportionate to the benefits to be derived from the appointment. Once the overall objective of the receivership has been achieved and there is no further benefit to be derived without disproportionate cost, the receiver should be discharged. The Court also approved a number of guidelines drawn up by counsel which should be followed by the court and the prosecutor on the hearing of applications for the appointment of management receivers and adhered to by all parties once the appointment has been made.

**4.05** It is of considerable importance to any study of the law and procedure relating to receivers under POCA and the previous legislation (the Criminal Justice Act (CJA) and the Drug Trafficking Act 1994 (DTA)) to note that the court has had power to appoint receivers for various purposes for many hundreds of years and that a considerable body of case law has developed in relation thereto. In *Capewell v HM Revenue and Customs* [2007] UKHL 2; [2007] 1 WLR 386 Lord Walker of Gestingthorpe summarised the position in these terms:

> The Court's power to appoint a receiver, as part of its auxiliary equitable jurisdiction is of very ancient origin. It was described in *Hopkins v Worcester and Birmingham Canal Proprietors* (1868) LR 6 Eq 437, 447 as one of the oldest remedies in the Court of Chancery. It was used in a wide variety of situations where there was a need for the interim protection of property (and the income of property), including disputes about partnerships, sales or mortgages of land, and administration of estates. Receivers could also be appointed by way of equitable execution. The receiver, being appointed by the Court, was an officer of the Court. His duty was to act impartially, and in accordance with the directions of the Court in administering the property to which the receivership extended.

> In short, the appointment of a receiver was in many cases the most effective way of 'holding the ring' between warring litigants until the disputed issues could be finally determined. Because it is a useful procedure, Parliament has from time to time extended the range of situations in which a receiver or manager could be appointed—for instance, in order to enforce the repairing obligations of the absentee landlord of a block of flats (see Landlord and Tenant Act 1987 section 21). The provisions of section 77(8) of CJA 1988, section 26(7) of DTA 1994 and section 48 of POCA 2002 are a further important extension of the situations in which the court has a statutory power to appoint a receiver. Sections 48, 50 and 52 of POCA 2002 provide for three types of receivers (management receivers, enforcement receivers and Director's receivers, the latter appointed by the Director of the Assets Recovery Agency) but it is unnecessary to go into those details on this appeal.

## B. Jurisdiction to Appoint Management Receivers

### Applications to appoint management receivers

Applications for the appointment of management receivers should follow the procedure laid **4.06** down in Part 60 of the Criminal Procedure Rules (CrimPR), which governs all receiverships under POCA. Rule 60.1(1)–(3) provides:

> 60.1—(1) This rule applies to an application for the appointment of a management receiver under section 48(1) of the Proceeds of Crime Act 2002 and an application for the appointment of an enforcement receiver under section 50(1) of the 2002 Act.
>
> (2) The application may be made without notice if—
>   (a) the application is joined with an application for a restraint order under rule 59.1;
>   (b) the application is urgent; or
>   (c) there are reasonable grounds for believing that giving notice would cause the dissipation of realisable property which is the subject of the application.
>
> (3) The application must be in writing and must be supported by a witness statement which must—
>   (a) give the grounds for the application;
>   (b) give full details of the proposed receiver;
>   (c) to the best of the witness' ability, give full details of the realisable property in respect of which the applicant is seeking the order and specify the person holding that realisable property;
>   (d) where the application is made by an accredited financial investigator, include a statement that, under section 68 of the 2002 Act, the applicant has authority to apply; and
>   (e) if the proposed receiver is not a person falling within section 55(8) of the 2002 Act and the applicant is asking the court to allow the receiver to act—
>     (i) without giving security, or
>     (ii) before he has given security or satisfied the court that he has security in place, explain the reasons why that is necessary.

For further details on procedure see Chapter 7. A draft management receivership order is found at Appendix 10.

### The power to appoint management receivers

Sections 48 and 49 of POCA give the Crown Court jurisdiction to appoint management **4.07** receivers for the purpose of managing and preserving the value of realisable property pending the conclusion of the criminal proceedings. By s 48 of POCA the appointment can only be made over realisable property to which a restraint order applies:

> (1) Subsection (2) applies if—
>   (a) the Crown Court makes a restraint order, and
>   (b) the applicant for the restraint order applies to the court to proceed under subsection (2) (whether as part of the application for the restraint order or at any time afterwards).
> (2) The Crown Court may by order appoint a receiver in respect of any realisable property to which the restraint order applies.

The standard of proof applicable in determining whether property is realisable for the pur- **4.08** pose of restraint and receivership orders prior to a confiscation order being made is that of a 'good arguable case' as laid down by the Court of Appeal in *CPS v Compton and others* [2002] EWCA Civ 1720, in which Simon Brown LJ stated at paragraph 38:

> All that I think it appropriate on this appeal to add by way of comment on the approach to adopt to the exercise of section 26 powers is that if, on the documents, a good arguable case

arises for treating particular assets as the realisable property of the defendant—here on the basis that the company's corporate veil should properly be pierced—then the relevant restraint (and possibly receivership) order(s) should ordinarily be made. That essentially is the test for the grant of Mareva relief. So too should it be the test for the exercise of the section 26 powers. It is, of course, open to third parties (or the defendant himself where the order is made without notice) to apply to set it aside.

**4.09**  A receiver would normally only be appointed over the assets of a limited company if the corporate veil is lifted and the assets of the company are treated as the assets of the defendant (see Chapters 2 and 5 on lifting the corporate veil and the applicable test). The exception is if a company is in receipt of an asset which represents a tainted gift from the defendant. Equally if a defendant holds shares in a company then these might be subject to a receivership order even if the corporate veil cannot be lifted and the assets of the company itself cannot be made the subject of the receivership.

**4.10**  A management receiver may be appointed over non-corporate assets held in the name of parties other than a defendant. The Court of Appeal in *In the matter of Stephen Michael Pigott sub nom Stephen Lamb v RCPO* [2010] EWCA Civ 285; [2010] STC 1190 dismissed an appeal against an order of the High Court appointing a management receiver over a property in the name of a third party. The prosecutor had sought a management receiver to be appointed over the property to stop its value depreciating pending determination of an appeal against the confiscation order and the possible appointment of an enforcement receiver. The High Court had relied on the finding of the Crown Court in confiscation proceedings under the CJA that a property registered in the legal title of a third party, Mr Lamb, was realisable property beneficially held by the defendant, Mr Pigott. It was therefore satisfied that there was a good arguable case that the Defendant owned the property as required by the test in *Compton*. The High Court therefore included it within a management receivership order, despite Mr Lamb opposing the appointment partly on the basis that he was the true owner of the property and that there had been no final determination of the issue. Rix LJ suggested that any final resolution as to the beneficial ownership of the property subject to the receivership claimed by the third party claim legal title holder, Mr Lamb, should preferably be made at the time of the enforcement receivership application rather than at the management receivership stage. It is to be noted that generally, once confiscation proceedings have been finally resolved, the prosecutor will be in a better position than the receiver to litigate ownership issues in later enforcement proceedings. The prosecutor should be in possession of all the relevant evidence and this will also save costs.

*Simultaneous restraint and receivership*

**4.11**  Section 48(1)(b) of POCA and Criminal Procedure Rule 60.1 give statutory effect to what had become the practice by prosecutors of applying for restraint and management receivers under the old legislation at the same time. In *Re P (Restraint Order: Sale of Assets)* [2000] 1 WLR 473 the Court of Appeal suggested that restraint and management receivership orders should only be sought simultaneously in cases of urgency. Simon Brown LJ (as he then was) said:

> But to justify the making of composite orders on an ex parte basis there must, in my judgment, be an urgency about the matter (or a need not to alert the defendant) such as to preclude putting the defendant on notice, and the order initially made should be in the narrowest terms necessary to meet the strict requirements of the situation.

These dicta are now codified within s 49(8), see below, which precludes the receiver being **4.12** granted the powers to manage, deal with, and realise property on a without-notice application. In addition Criminal Procedure Rule 60.2(2) limits without-notice applications to those seeking to grant the receiver power to take possession of property. If a prosecutor or receiver wishes to seek the power to manage, deal with, or realise property then a further application must be made on notice to the defendant and any party affected pursuant to r 60.2(6).

It is paramount that prosecutors think very carefully before applying without notice for the **4.13** appointment of a management receiver at any time and particularly prior to a defendant being charged with a criminal offence, ie while they are still subject to a criminal investigation. This is even more imperative if a restraint order and management receiver is sought over a company's assets. The prosecutor will have to satisfy the court of the following grounds: (a) that there is reasonable cause to believe the defendant has benefited from criminal conduct; (b) that there is a good arguable case that the property held by any company is realisable, ie that the corporate veil should be lifted; (c) that there is a real risk of dissipation so as to require a restraint order; (d) that a restraint order on its own will not suffice; (e) that the discretion should be exercised in favour of appointment in accordance with s 69 POCA and the *Capewell* Guidelines (set out below); and (f) that an application for a receivership order cannot be made on notice because it is urgent or there are reasonable grounds for believing that giving notice of the application would cause the dissipation of realisable property which is the subject of the application. Such applications and appointments are likely to be rare. An example of the Court of Appeal discharging such an appointment due to a failure to satisfy grounds (a) and (b) is to be found in *Windsor and others v Crown Prosecution Service* [2011] EWCA Crim 143; [2011] 1 WLR 1519.

It is important to note that under s 48(1)(b) of POCA only the applicant for the restraint **4.14** order may make an application for the appointment of a management receiver: neither the defendant nor an affected third party (such as a judgment creditor) may apply for the appointment of a receiver to manage restraint assets. In *Re M* [1992] QB 377; 1 All ER 537, a defendant did apply, under the old legislation, for the appointment of a management receiver. Otton J held that he had no *locus standi* to make the application, saying:

> ... in my judgment, it is unthinkable that an application for the appointment of a receiver by or on behalf of an accused to preserve assets intended for the satisfaction of a confiscation order could be entertained by the court. A restraint order may only be made upon the application of a prosecutor and, bearing in mind that the making of an order appointing a receiver can only be exercised upon the making of a restraint order, it would follow, in my judgment, that an application for the appointment of a receiver can similarly only be made by a prosecutor.

### Powers of management receivers

The powers the court may confer on management receivers are set out in POCA as supple- **4.15** mented by the general law of receivership as it has developed over the years. By s 49 POCA:

(1) If the court appoints a receiver under section 48 it may act under this section on the application of the person who applied for the restraint order.
(2) The court may by order confer on the receiver the following powers in relation to any realisable property to which the restraint order applies—
    (a) power to take possession of the property;
    (b) power to manage or otherwise deal with the property;
    (c) power to start, carry on or defend any legal proceedings in respect of the property;

    (d)  power to realise so much of the property as is necessary to meet the receiver's remuneration and expenses.

(3)  The court may by order confer on the receiver power to enter any premises in England and Wales and to do any of the following—

    (a)  search for or inspect anything authorised by the court;

    (b)  make or obtain a copy, photograph or other record of anything so authorised;

    (c)  remove anything which the receiver is required or authorised to take possession of in pursuance of an order of the court.

(4)  The court may by order authorise the receiver to do any of the following for the purpose of the exercise of his functions—

    (a)  hold property;

    (b)  enter into contracts;

    (c)  sue and be sued;

    (d)  employ agents;

    (e)  execute powers of attorney, deeds or other instruments;

    (f)  take any other steps the court thinks appropriate.

(5)  The court may order any person who has possession of realisable property to which the restraint order applies to give possession of it to the receiver.

(6)  The court—

    (a)  may order a person with an interest in realisable property to which the restraint order applies to make to the receiver such payment as the court specifies in respect of a beneficial interest held by the defendant or the recipient of a tainted gift.

    (b)  may (on payment being made) by order, transfer, grant or extinguish any interest in the property.

(7)  Subsections (2), (5) and (6) do not apply to property for the time being subject to a charge under any of these provisions—

    (a)  section 9 of the Drug Trafficking Offences Act 1986 (c32);

    (b)  section 78 of the Criminal Justice Act, 1988 (c33);

    (c)  Article 14 of the Criminal Justice (Confiscation) (Northern Ireland) Order 1990 (SI 1990/2588 (NI17));

    (d)  section 27 of the Drug Trafficking Act 1994 (c37);

    (e)  Article 32 of the Proceeds of Crime (Northern Ireland) Order 1996 (SI 1996/1299 (NI9)).

(8)  The court must not—

    (a)  confer the power mentioned in subsection (2)(b) or (d) in respect of property, or

    (b)  exercise the power conferred on it by subsection (6) in respect of property,

    unless it gives persons holding interests in the property a reasonable opportunity to make representations to it.

(8A)  *see below*

(9)  The court may order that a power conferred by an order under this section is subject to such conditions and exceptions as it specifies.

(10)  Managing or otherwise dealing with property includes—

    (a)  selling the property or any part of it or interest in it;

    (b)  carrying on or arranging for another person to carry on any trade or business the assets of which are or are part of the property;

    (c)  incurring capital expenditure in relation to the property.

**4.16**  Most of the powers the court may vest in the receiver under s 49 of POCA reflect powers the High Court has for many years conferred on receivers appointed under the CJA and DTA pursuant to its inherent jurisdiction. Section 49(8) of POCA imposes an important restriction on the court's power to confer powers on management receivers. The powers: to manage or otherwise deal with property (s 49(2)(b)); to realise assets to meet the costs and expenses of the receiver (s 49(2)(d)); and to require a person holding realisable property to make payments to the receiver after which property rights may be granted, transferred, or extinguished (s 49(6)), may not be exercised until persons having an interest in the property have been given a reasonable opportunity to make representations to the court. Thus, in cases where the receiver is appointed without notice to the defendant or interested third parties, a further application on notice will have to be made before any of the powers referred to in s 49(8) can be conferred on the receiver.

There is, however, an important exception to this rule in relation to property that is perish-   **4.17**
able or needs to be sold before its value diminishes. Section 82(1) of the Serious Crime Act 2007 added s 49(8A) to POCA which provides:

> (8A)  Subsection 8 so far as relating to the power mentioned in subsection (2)(b) does not apply to property which—
>   (a)  is perishable, or
>   (b)  ought to be disposed of before its value diminishes.

The effect of this subsection is that defendants and affected third parties need not be given an opportunity to make representations before the court empowers a receiver to manage or otherwise deal with property where that property is perishable or ought to be disposed of before its value diminishes. This is a useful power for receivers because the delay caused by giving an opportunity to make representations can often result in the property diminishing in value to the detriment of all concerned. It is submitted that the power should be exercised sparingly where there is a genuine risk of the property in question depreciating in value and the prosecutor or receiver should be in a position to justify the urgent necessity to deal with property without giving the defendant or affected third parties the opportunity to make representations. Particular care should be exercised in relation to property which is irreplaceable or may have considerable sentimental value to those claiming an interest in it.

### Intangible property

The powers of management receivers extend to intangible property. In *Manning and Sinclair*   **4.18**
*v Glatt* [2003] EWCA Civ 1977 the Court of Appeal, in refusing an application for permission to appeal, rejected the contention that a management receiver's powers under the CJA were confined to tangible property. Jacob LJ said:

> We explored with Counsel the various possibilities of different kinds of action that might involve receivers who have been appointed. Could they, if appointed as receivers over a lease, take proceedings for unpaid rent or for possession? Or could they defend proceedings if, for example, there was an application for a third party debt order? All those examples to my mind indicated very clearly that unless this Act was restricted to physical objects Counsel's arguments disintegrated. I can think of no reason whatever why the Act should have been limited, as Counsel submitted. The power is to take possession of any realisable property. One focuses on anything, therefore, which can be converted into money. Almost all forms of property can be so converted. The word 'possession' takes its flavour from the kind of property. The Act would serve no useful or meaningful purpose if confined to chattels . . . once one has arrived at the position that the receiver can take possession of all realisable property, it must follow that he has the power to look after that property by taking proceedings or defending them, as well as any other necessary action. Of course if the receiver acts in some improper way there may well be proceedings which can be taken, and if the receiver is ever in doubt as to what he should be doing he has, of course, express power to apply to the court. But that is much the same as the position of any other receiver appointed by the court, or indeed others concerned with insolvency, for example trustees in bankruptcy or liquidators of companies. The remedy lies not in challenging the receiver's powers, but in any misuse of them.

Sedley LJ added:

> ...Receivers must have an implied power to resort to the courts in order to preserve the defendant's property. Once this is accepted there can be no bright line which restricts either the kinds of proceedings which the receiver may bring or defend, or the kinds of realisable property to which the receivership may relate. The proper control of the receiver, precisely because he is an officer of the court, lies where necessary in the hands of the court. There is no reason why the defendant himself should not be able to alert the court to any possible irregularities of the kind with which Counsel is understandably concerned in the present case.

### Management receivers' power of sale

**4.19** Upon appointment the receiver must not only act only within the terms of his appointment under the order but also subject to the legislative steer under s 69 POCA, which applies as much to the exercise of a receiver's powers as it does to the exercise of the court's. If the receiver is in any doubt as to the extent and exercise of his powers then he should apply to court for directions under section 62 of POCA on notice to all parties. The power to realise or sell realisable property under s 49(2)(d) and (10)(a) of POCA causes particular problems in relation to management receiverships. The primary role of a management receiver is, of course, to manage and preserve the defendant's realisable property pending the making or enforcement of a confiscation order. This is in contrast to the position of an enforcement receiver who is appointed to sell off realisable property and pay the proceeds into court in satisfaction of a confiscation order that has already been made and that is no longer subject to an appeal. Nonetheless, a situation may arise in which a management receiver wishes to sell a particular asset because, for example, it is depreciating in value or in order to pay the receiver's fees under s 49(2)(d) of POCA. The course of action may be opposed by a defendant who claims that the asset in question is of sentimental value or irreplaceable and that sale would preclude the return of the asset to him in the event of an acquittal.

**4.20** In terms of the threat to sell, POCA does not, however, leave the defendant without a remedy. By s 69(3)(c) of POCA:

> in a case where a confiscation order has not been made against a defendant, property must not be sold if the court so orders under subsection (4).

Section 69(4) provides:

> If on an application by the defendant, or by the recipient of a tainted gift, the court decides that property cannot be replaced it may order that it must not be sold.

**4.21** By s 69(5) an order made under subs (4) may be revoked or varied. It should be noted that the court is not compelled to order that irreplaceable assets should not be sold: the Act provides that the court 'may' order that the asset is not to be sold, not that it must do so. Unless, however, there are very compelling reasons to the contrary, it is submitted that the proper course would be to order that irreplaceable assets should not be sold prior to the defendant's conviction. This is not to say that it will never be appropriate for a court to empower a management receiver to sell assets. If a defendant is deliberately exposing his assets to the risk of dissipation or depreciation, for example, by not paying the mortgage and insurance premiums on a property, or not effecting essential repairs, by abandoning an asset or causing wanton damage, an order for sale may well be entirely appropriate. The sale of an asset may also be appropriate to make funds available to meet receivership costs and expenses or the general living expenses of the defendant where no other funds are available within the receivership estate.

For further on the legislative steer, see Chapter 5 para 5.35. For the position under the CJA **4.22** and DTA, see *Re P (Restraint Order: Sale of Assets)* [2000] 1 WLR 473.

## C. Exercising the Discretion to Appoint Management Receivers: The *Capewell* Guidelines

The power to appoint a management receiver is a discretionary one, although the court must **4.23** have regard to the 'legislative steer' in s 69 of POCA in determining how that discretion should be exercised. While the need to preserve property to meet any confiscation order must carry great weight, it is not the only issue the court must take into account in the exercise of its discretion. As the Court of Appeal observed in *Re P (Restraint Order: Sale of Assets)* [2000] 1 WLR 473, a balance has to be struck between the preservation of property and allowing the defendant to continue with the ordinary course of his life at a time when he is presumed innocent. The court will need to be satisfied that a restraint order alone will be insufficient to prevent dissipation of the defendant's realisable property and the appointment of a receiver is an appropriate and proportionate measure in all the circumstances. The appointment of a receiver is inevitably an expensive exercise and the court will need to be satisfied that the costs involved do not outweigh the potential benefits to the defendant's estate. Further, in *Hughes v Customs and Excise Commissioners* [2000] 4 All ER 633 the Court of Appeal held that the court must always take account of the fact that, if acquitted, significantly depleted assets may be returned to the defendant given that the receiver is entitled to look to the receivership estate for the payment of his remuneration and expenses. Simon Brown LJ said:

> Given that restraint orders can, as perhaps these very cases show, bear heavily upon the individuals involved and may leave acquitted defendants with substantially depleted assets, the court should, in deciding whether initially to make and whether thereafter to vary or discharge such orders, weigh up the balance of the competing interests with the greatest care. The Court's concern to safeguard an accused's property against dissipation or removal abroad must always be weighed against the possibility that the price to be paid will fall upon an innocent man.

Since the Court of Appeal judgment in *Hughes*, courts have become increasingly concerned **4.24** about the costs of management receiverships and the risk that they could have to be borne by a defendant who is ultimately acquitted. In *Capewell v Customs and Excise Commissioners* [2005] 1 All ER 900, at the Court's invitation, counsel on both sides prepared a set of guidelines for the appointment of management receivers. Although the Court did not hear detailed argument on the guidelines, it commended them as a 'useful checklist' for those involved in future cases. The guidelines are in the following terms:

#### Application by the Prosecutor

1. Within the witness statement in support of the application to appoint a management receiver, the prosecutor should set out the reasons the prosecutor seeks the appointment of a receiver, and what purpose the prosecutor believes the receivership will serve.
2. The witness statement in support of the application should also give an indication of the type of work that it is envisaged the receiver may need to undertake, based on the facts known to the prosecutor at the time of the appointment.
3. The witness statement in support of the application should specifically draw to the Court's attention the proposition that the assets over which the receiver is appointed will be used to pay the costs, disbursements and other expenses of the receivership (even if the defendant is acquitted or the receivership is subsequently discharged).

4. The letter of acceptance of appointment from the receiver, which must be exhibited to the applicant's witness statement, should contain the time charging rates of the staff the receiver anticipates he may need to deploy.

5. In appropriate cases, where it is possible, and this will not be in every case, the receiver should give in his letter of acceptance an estimate as to how much the receivership is likely to cost.

6. The prosecutor's witness statement in support of the application should inform the Court of the nature of the assets and their approximate value (if known) and the income the assets might produce (if known).

7. If the prosecutor or receiver is unable to comply with any of the above requirements the prosecutor should explain the reasons for the failure in the prosecutor's application to the court and the matter will be left at the discretion of the court.

### Upon appointment

8. Upon the appointment of a receiver, the Judge should consider whether it is appropriate, in all the circumstances, to reserve any future applications to himself, with a view to minimising costs.

9. Upon the appointment of a receiver, the Judge should consider whether it is appropriate, in all the circumstances, to set a return date, balancing the need for such a hearing with the interests of the defendant, who ultimately will bear the costs of such a hearing.

10. The receiver should inform the parties by written report as soon as reasonably practicable, if it appears to him that any initial costs estimate will be exceeded, or receivership costs are increasing, or are likely to increase to a disproportionate level. Such a report should also be filed with the Court. In such circumstances the parties and the receiver shall be at liberty to seek directions from the Court.

### Reporting requirements

11. Unless the Court directs otherwise, the receiver should report 28 days after his appointment and quarterly thereafter.

12. Unless the Court directs otherwise, the report should be served on the prosecutor and the defendant and filed with the Court.

13. Every report should set out the costs incurred to date; the work done; the projected costs until the next report; a summary of how those costs attach to the matters that led to the appointment or to the matters that may have arisen; and, where appropriate, an estimated final outcome statement.

14. Every report should contain a statement that the receiver believes that his costs are reasonable and proportionate in all the circumstances.

15. If the receiver is unable to fulfil any of the above reporting requirements, he should give, as soon as reasonably practicable, an explanation, by way of written report to be filed at Court and served on the parties, of why this is the case, and those parties shall be at liberty to seek directions from the Court.

### Lawyers and other agents

16. The parties should always be told that lawyers or other agents have been instructed unless it is not practicable or in the interests of justice to do so (for example, to make an urgent without notice application to secure assets).

17. If lawyers or other agents are instructed the receiver should ask for monthly bills or fee notes. The receiver should endeavour to keep a close control on such fees and satisfy himself that the costs being incurred are reasonable and proportionate in all the circumstances.

18. The receiver should notify the parties as soon as reasonably practicable if it appears to him that any lawyers' or other agents' costs are rising to a disproportionate level, and those parties shall be at liberty to apply to the Court for directions.

**General**

19. Nothing in these guidelines should be read as supplanting the appropriate rules of court, particularly CPR 69, and the relevant statutory provisions.
20. Judges appointing receivers should always bear in mind that the costs of the receivership may fall on an innocent man. They should also bear in mind that the interests of justice dictate that receiverships are a necessary and essential tool of the criminal justice system for preserving and managing assets to satisfy confiscation orders if the defendant is convicted.
21. Management receivership orders should be endorsed with the appropriate penal notice. It will be a term of most orders that defendants should cooperate with and comply with, as soon as possible and forthwith, directions and requests of the receiver, so as to enable the receiver to efficiently and cost-effectively carry out the duties, functions and obligations of his office. It is therefore in the defendant's interest to avoid, as far as possible, the need for the receiver to return to Court for further orders or directions, the cost of which will ultimately fall on the defendant's estate.

The *Capewell* Guidelines seek to achieve a balance between the rights of all concerned: the **4.25** prosecutor, concerned to protect and preserve the value of realisable property pending the determination of the proceedings; the defendant, anxious to prevent his business and personal life being unduly interfered with and the costs of any receivership escalating out of control; and the receiver's desire to have sufficient powers to act effectively and be properly remunerated for his work. The Guidelines achieve this by making it clear that, although the power to appoint a management receiver is an essential tool in the criminal justice system to ensure assets are properly preserved, prosecutors must give proper thought to the objectives the receivership is intended to achieve and consider whether the cost will be proportionate having regard to the benefits likely to accrue to the defendant's estate. The receiver too is enjoined to have proper regard to the principle of proportionality, to report regularly to the parties and the court on the state of progress and the likely costs involved. He must also advise the parties promptly if costs are likely to increase to an amount beyond that estimated in his reports or to the extent that they cease to be proportionate. If a defendant fails to cooperate with the receiver in the proper discharge of his duties after being given due warning, the receiver should bring the matter promptly to the court's attention on an application for directions rather than allow the matter to drift with further unnecessary costs being incurred.

It should also be noted that the defendant has an important role to play in ensuring that **4.26** receivership costs do not escalate out of control. As Guideline 21 makes plain, it is incumbent on the defendant to cooperate with the receiver by complying promptly and fully with his requirements to enable him to discharge his duties, functions, and obligations as an officer of the court efficiently and cost-effectively. Indeed, it is in the defendant's interests to cooperate because the consequence of any failure to do so is likely to be an application by the receiver for further directions. In particularly serious cases, any such failure could result in the receiver or prosecutor instituting contempt proceedings. A draft management receivership order is found at Appendix 10.

## D. Status of the Receiver on Appointment

**4.27** On appointment, a management receiver becomes an officer of the court, accountable to the court for his actions. He is not the agent of either party in the proceedings: see *Re Andrews* [1999] 1 WLR 1236 at 1242 approving Cairns LJ's statement in *Gardner v London Chatham and Dover Railway Co (No 1)* (1867) LR 2 Ch App 201 at 211–12:

> When the court appoints a manager of a business or undertaking it in effect assumes the management into its own hands; for the manager is the servant or officer of the court, and upon any question arising as to the character or details of the management it is the court which must direct and decide.

**4.28** Although appointed on the application of the prosecutor, the receiver must act entirely independently and the prosecutor does not have the right to direct him to exercise his powers in a particular way. When the court appoints a management receiver, it effectively assumes the management of the defendant's estate and the receiver is entitled to refer to the court all issues that arise about that management and about the nature and extent of the estate for it to determine: see *Re G, Manning v G (No 4)* [2003] EWHC 1732 (Admin).

**4.29** It is inevitable that the receiver will work very closely with the prosecuting authority because they will have access to a great deal of information as to the location and status of assets subject to the receivership order. Further, where there is no conflict of interest between the receiver and the prosecuting authority, they may arrange, with a view to saving costs, to be represented by the same counsel on the hearing of any subsequent application in relation to the receivership.

**4.30** The court may from time to time ask the prosecutor to litigate a particular issue on behalf of the receiver, such as the ownership of a particular asset identified in the receivership order. The advantage of this course is that the prosecutor can often litigate such issues more economically than the receiver, to the mutual advantage of all concerned. Where the prosecutor litigates such issues pursuant to an order of the court, he is entitled to the same indemnity from the receivership estate as the receiver: see *Sinclair (Heath) (The former court appointed receiver) v Louis Glatt & others* [2008] EWHC 798 (Admin). Indeed, the expenses that can be recovered by the receiver from the receivership estate would include, in an appropriate case, litigation costs and even the costs of defending an action brought against the receiver by the defendant: see *Sinclair v Dhillon and others* [2012] EWHC 3517 (Admin) and *Glatt v Sinclair* [2010] EWHC 3069 (Admin); [2011] 6 Costs LR 943 (although note that the substantive decision which gave rise to the costs order in the latter case was overturned by the Court of Appeal: [2011] EWCA Civ 1317; [2012] 1 Costs LO 48; see para 4.33 below).

**4.31** It follows from the receiver's status as an officer of the court that any obstruction of the receiver in the performance of his duties under the court's order will constitute a contempt of court. It is for this reason that the standard practice is to endorse all receivership orders with a penal notice (see *Capewell* Guideline 21). A wide range of acts and omissions can constitute obstruction of the receiver including: putting assets beyond the receiver's reach; refusing to deliver up assets or documents of title relating to them; refusing to sign powers of attorney or other documents allowing the receiver to take control of assets; submitting false or forged documents to the receiver intending him to act on them as genuine; and threatening or assaulting the receiver, members of his staff, or agents.

## E. Duties and Liabilities of the Receiver

### Liability in negligence

Like all professionals, a receiver owes a duty of care to those affected by his actions during the **4.32** course of a receivership. This does not, however, mean that the receiver will be held liable in relation to every act or omission that results in loss to the state. If, for example, the receiver is managing a business, he is entitled to take decisions in relation to the running of the business that involve an element of risk, provided that the risk is not such that no reasonable and prudent person in the receiver's position would have taken it. In order to succeed in an action against a receiver, the defendant or aggrieved third party would have to establish negligence on the part of the receiver.

In *Louis Glatt v Heath Sinclair* [2011] EWCA Civ 1317 the Court of Appeal, overturning **4.33** the High Court, gave a former defendant (the claimant) permission to sue the receiver for breach of duty based on a substantial price difference between the sale price of a property obtained by the receiver and that of its immediate subsequent sale. At paragraphs 11–12 of the judgment Kitchin LJ stated:

> 11. There is no dispute between the parties as to the test for the grant of permission and I am satisfied that the judge properly directed himself in referring to the following guidance given by Jonathan Parker LJ in *McGowan v Chadwick* [2001] EWCA Civ 1758 at [78]:
>
>> As to the approach which the court should take on such an application, it is a matter for the court's discretion whether or not to give permission, and accordingly no hard and fast rules can be laid down as to the requirements which a prospective claimant must meet or as to the manner in which he brings forward his application. What can, in my judgment, safely be said is that permission will not be granted unless the applicant satisfies the court that his claim is a genuine one, in the sense that the allegations which he seeks to make are such as to call for an answer from the receiver. On the one hand, the receiver must not be subjected to vexatious or harassing claims; on the other hand, as Nevill J observed, the court must see that justice is done.
>
> 12. As for the duties of a receiver, this too is largely a matter of common ground, as it was before the judge. In circumstances such as those arising in these proceedings, a receiver is under a duty to those interested in the property over which he is appointed to act in good faith and to take reasonable steps to obtain a proper price: see for example, *Downsview Nominees Ltd v First City Corporation Ltd* [1993] AC 295 (PC) at page 315 C–D; *Medforth v Blake* [2000] Ch 86 (CA) at page 98 C–D. In this context 'proper price' means the best price reasonably obtainable at the time, as Pill LJ explained in *Mortgage Express v Trevor Mardner* [2004] EWCA Civ 1859 at paragraphs [5] to [9].

Further, POCA itself gives the receiver some protection against liability to the defendant and **4.34** third parties. By s 61:

> If a receiver appointed under section 48, 50 or 52—
> (a) takes action in relation to property which is not realisable property,
> (b) would be entitled to take the action if it were realisable property, and
> (c) believes on reasonable grounds that he is entitled to take the action,
>
> he is not liable to any person in respect of any loss or damage resulting from the action, except so far as the loss or damage is caused by his negligence.

Thus, even where the receiver acts in relation to property that turns out not to be realisable property under the legislation, he will enjoy protection from liability for his actions provided that he was not negligent and had reasonable grounds for believing he was entitled to act in relation to the property in question. The only other form of compensation a defendant might obtain in relation to the appointment of a receiver is in the limited circumstances where s 72 of POCA applies—see Chapter 22.

**4.35**    The receiver will be personally liable in relation to any contracts he enters into in his capacity as receiver. He will not, however, be liable in relation to any contracts already in force at the time of his appointment, save to the extent that he adopts them and allows them to continue.

### Employment of agents

**4.36**    In all but the most straightforward cases, the receiver will need to instruct agents to assist and advise him in the proper discharge of his duties and the receivership order will normally empower him to do so. The receiver will frequently need to instruct a solicitor to provide legal advice and litigation support, expert valuers to value assets subject to the receivership, and property management agents to manage real property. The receiver must ensure that the costs of any such agents are reasonable and proportionate having regard to the benefits that are likely to accrue to the receivership estate. It is the practice of some receivers to instruct City solicitors to advise them and, although it is normally possible to negotiate a discount on the firms' charge-out rates, the costs of these firms can rapidly escalate. Although it may be justifiable for the receiver to instruct a City firm in highly complex receivership cases, the use of such a firm to act on a straightforward conveyancing transaction in relation to a property located in the provinces would not. In such a case the receiver would be expected to instruct a high street solicitor in the area where the property is located. In *Re D* [2006] EWHC 254 (Admin), solicitors acting for a company affected by restraint and management receivership orders sought the release of some £110,000 by way of legal fees for advising and representing the company. This amount represented a third of the company's entire asset base. Ouseley J ruled that this was disproportionate and released only £50,000 to the solicitors. It is submitted that the same principle applies to receivers and their agents: the services of agents must be obtained at a cost that is proportionate in all the circumstances and not necessarily from the receiver's first choice of professional advisers.

**4.37**    When the receiver intends to instruct an agent, he should notify the parties as soon as possible except where this is not practicable or in the interests of justice to do so (see *Capewell* Guideline 16). The receiver should also ask for monthly bills or fee notes and satisfy himself that the amounts claimed are reasonable and proportionate (see *Capewell* Guideline 17). The duties of the receiver in this regard are considered in more detail at paragraph 4.55 below. Finally, the receiver must notify the parties immediately if it appears to him that the costs of his agents are rising to a disproportionate level (see *Capewell* Guideline 18).

**4.38**    Receivers must, therefore, take great care to ensure the reasonableness and proportionality of their actions in relation to the appointment of agents. If they are unable to satisfy the court that their agents' fees and disbursements are reasonable and proportionate having regard to all the circumstances of the case, they run the risk of the same being disallowed in whole or in part. The court will not expect receivers to get it right every time and, it may be that it is willing to give receivers appointed under POCA rather more latitude than those appointed in civil cases. This is because, as Lord Donaldson MR observed in *Re O* [1991] 1 All ER 330, the legislative contemplation is that some of those claiming an interest in realisable property may be of a 'dishonest disposition' who do their expert best to deal with it in such a way that it is outside the grasp of the court and the receivers whom it appoints.

### Receivers' accounts and reports

By r 60.7(1) of the CrimPR the Crown Court may order a management or enforcement **4.39** receiver to prepare and serve accounts. The letter of agreement between the receiver and the prosecuting authority on whose application he is appointed will invariably require the preparation and service of accounts on the court, prosecutor, and defendant at regular intervals, and the receivership order itself will provide that the receiver must act in accordance with that letter of agreement.

Rule 60.7 CrimPR gives all parties served with the receiver's accounts certain important **4.40** rights. Firstly, under CrimPR r 60.7(2) any party served with the accounts may apply for an order permitting him to inspect any document in the possession of the receiver relevant to those accounts. This does not entitle a defendant or affected third party to have full access to the receiver's file, but merely to documents that are of relevance to the accounts he has submitted. Secondly, by CrimPR r 60.7(3), any party may, within fourteen days of being served with the accounts, serve notice on the receiver:

 (a) specifying any items in the accounts to which he objects;
 (b) giving the reason for such objection; and
 (c) requiring the receiver within 14 days of receipt of the notice, either—
   (i) to notify all the parties who were served with the accounts that he accepts the objection, or
   (ii) if he does not accept the objection to apply for an examination of the accounts in relation to the contested item.

By CrimPR r 60.7(4), when the receiver applies for the examination of the accounts he must **4.41** file the accounts and a copy of the notice served on him under para (3). If the receiver fails either to accept the objection or apply for an examination of his accounts under CrimPR r 60.7(3)(c), any party to the receivership proceedings may apply to the Crown Court for an examination of the accounts in relation to the contested item: CrimPR r 60.1(5). At the conclusion of the examination of the accounts the court shall certify the result: CrimPR r 60.7(6).

The duty of the receiver to serve accounts on the defendant also extends to any reports he **4.42** may prepare as to the progress of the receivership. If the receiver considers that particularly sensitive issues alluded to in his report should be withheld from the defendant he should refer the matter to the court and be in a position to justify departing from the usual rule: see *Re G, Manning v G (No 4)* [2003] EWHC 1732 (Admin) and *Capewell* Guideline 12.

## F.  Remuneration of Receivers

Those appointed as management receivers under POCA are normally chartered account- **4.43** ants or licensed insolvency practitioners working for large accountancy firms. They accept appointments under the legislation because they are commercially viable enterprises that are entitled to charge fees in order to make a profit for themselves or their employers. The remuneration of receivers has been one of the most controversial aspects of management receiverships in recent years as there is a real danger that the costs can escalate out of control unless there is careful monitoring by the court, the prosecutor, and the defendant. This gives rise to two distinct but interrelated issues that have been the subject of much litigation, namely who is liable to pay the receiver's fees and how is control exercised over the amounts claimed?

### The historical background

**4.44** The position at common law has always been that the receiver looks to the estate under management for payment of his remuneration, costs, and expenses. This rule flows from the status of the receiver as an independent officer of the court rather than an agent of the prosecutor or other parties to the proceedings. In *Boehm v Goodall* [1911] 1 Ch 151 Warrington J summarised the position thus:

> I think it is of the utmost importance that receivers and managers in this position should know that they must look for their indemnity to the assets which are under the control of the court. The court cannot indemnify receivers but can, and will, do so out of the assets, so far as they extend, for expenses properly incurred, but it cannot go further.

**4.45** This principle was upheld by the Court of Appeal in the more recent case of *Evans v Clayhope Ltd* [1988] 1 WLR 358. In that case, the court had appointed a receiver and manager to manage property which was the subject of an action pending the trial. The court held that it had no power, before the issues in the action had been determined, to make an interim order requiring one of the parties to pay the remuneration or expenses of the receiver and that, accordingly, the receiver was entitled to recover his remuneration and expenses only from such funds as were under the control of the court pursuant to the receivership. Nourse LJ said:

> *Boehm v Goodall* was a decision based on statements of principles of high authority. In my judgment it was correctly decided and it applies in this case. Moreover the decision is one of jurisdiction, and unless any part of the receiver and manager's remuneration and expenditure can be treated as 'costs', no question of discretion arises.

**4.46** The position at common law is thus clear: the receiver is entitled to look only to the estate under management for the payment of his remuneration and expenses. In a number of cases, the Court of Appeal and House of Lords have had to consider the extent to which this rule applies to receivers appointed under confiscation legislation and, in particular, whether the position is different where the defendant is acquitted or the management receiver is discharged for any reason. In *Re Andrews* [1999] 1 WLR 1236 a management receiver appointed under the CJA was discharged following the defendant's acquittal. The defendant thereafter discovered that some £10,000 had been taken from his estate by way of receiver's fees and he sought an order that this sum be reimbursed by the prosecuting authority. The Court of Appeal upheld the judge's ruling that he had no power to do so and that, the acquittal notwithstanding, he the receiver was entitled to draw his remuneration and expenses from the estate under management. Aldous LJ said:

> Despite the persuasive submissions of Counsel who appeared for the appellant, in my judgment the remuneration of the receiver was not costs incidental to proceedings in the civil division of the High Court. By order of the Court the receiver assumed control of the company and of the £42,000. Most of the time of the receiver was spent supervising the running of the company. For example, she spent time supervising disposal and acquisition of lorries for the benefit of the company. As yet the receiver has not produced accounts but they will show expenditure and income. Part of the expenditure will consist of her charges which were paid for at least in part out of the money available from the £42,000 that came from the appellant. Such charges cannot in my view be recoverable in these proceedings. These charges are expenses of the receivership and are therefore not recoverable by a successful party in proceedings in which a receiver has been appointed. That conclusion can be demonstrated to be right

if it be assumed that the only property that was taken into receivership was the company. If so, the receiver's remuneration would be incurred as a charge for running the company which hopefully would have made a profit even after the remuneration of the receiver had been deducted. It would by no means have been certain that the same position would have been achieved without the accountancy advice of the receiver. In such a case would the receiver's remuneration be recoverable by the owners of the company, if they were successful in the proceedings in which the receiver was appointed? If so would the amount recoverable be the amount charged by the receiver or that sum less the income derived from work done by the receiver? I believe the first question should be answered in the negative. The remuneration of a receiver is an expense of the receivership not costs incidental to the proceedings in which he is appointed. To answer in the affirmative would lead to the difficulty posed by the second question.

The Court also agreed with the prosecutor's submission that the defendant's claim was in **4.47** reality a claim for compensation under s 89 of the CJA (the predecessor of s 72 of POCA) dressed up as a claim for costs because he could not bring himself within the strict requirements of the section. Aldous LJ said:

I would add that in my judgment counsel was right in his submission that this really was a claim for compensation dressed up as an application for an award of costs; and it is therefore most significant that by section 80 Parliament laid down a carefully regulated code for such a claim. Consequently, in my judgment section 89 is the proper avenue for a compensation claim of this kind, provided of course the claimant can bring himself within the rather strict requirements of the section.

The Court of Appeal in *Andrews* made it clear that it had not considered the provisions of the **4.48** European Convention on Human Rights (ECHR) in reaching its decision. The issue came before the Court of Appeal again in *Hughes v Customs and Excise Commissioners* [2002] 4 All ER 633, and on this occasion the court considered it afresh in the light of the Convention. In this case, the acquitted defendant claimed that it would represent a breach of his rights under Art 1 of the First Protocol to the ECHR for the costs of the management receivership to be met from the estate under management. It would, he contended, be disproportionate and arbitrary to deprive an unconvicted or acquitted defendant of his assets in the absence of provision for the payment of compensation. He was successful at first instance but, on the prosecutor's appeal, the Court of Appeal upheld its earlier decision in *Andrews*. The Court ruled that statutory receivers appointed under the DTA and CJA should be treated in precisely the same way as their common law counterparts except where the legislation provided to the contrary. Accordingly, the costs of the receiver were to be met from the fund under management rather than by the prosecutor, even when the defendant is acquitted or the receiver discharged.

The Court found nothing in its decision that conflicted with the ECHR. Simon Brown LJ **4.49** stated:

It is common ground that acquitted defendants are not, save in the most exceptional circumstances, entitled to compensation for being deprived of their liberty while on remand or indeed for any other heads of loss suffered through being prosecuted. In my view, it is no more unfair, disproportionate or arbitrary that they should be uncompensated too for any effects that restraint and receivership orders may have had upon their assets.

In *Capewell v HM Revenue and Customs* [2007] 1 WLR 386 the House of Lords held that the **4.50** Court of Appeal had been wrong to assume that r 69.7 of the Civil Procedure Rules (CPR) which applied to CJA and DTA receiverships, could have the effect of overruling the Court's previous ruling in *Hughes*. Lord Walker of Gestingthorpe said:

> In my opinion, CPR 69.7 has not had that far-reaching and surprising result. The function of CPR 69 is to set out a procedural code applicable to the generality of receiverships of all types. Its text gives no indication that its draftsman had particularly in mind the new species of receiverships in support of restraint orders and confiscation orders. No doubt its provisions do in general apply to such receiverships but they cannot override the scheme inherent in the detailed provisions of the CJA 1988. That scheme is for the receiver's remuneration and expenses to be paid out of the receivership assets, but in a way which counts towards satisfaction of any confiscation order, and subject to the statutory long-stop already mentioned. If an individual subject to a restraint order is not ultimately convicted and made subject to a confiscation order, section 89 of the CJA gives a statutory right to compensation in some circumstances. But Parliament has deliberately framed the right to compensation in narrow terms. That is an aggrieved individual's only right to compensation as such. He would not normally have the benefit of an undertaking in damages since (as Simon Brown LJ observed in *Hughes* at para 50) a prosecutor cannot be required to give an undertaking in damages as a condition of obtaining the appointment of a receiver. An aggrieved individual's only other recourse would be to challenge the amount of the receiver's remuneration as the respondent has done in this case. There is a similar scheme under POCA 2002 and the Crown Court (Confiscation, Restraint and Receivership) Rules 2003 (SI 2003/421) made under that Act, but in these new provisions it is made perfectly clear that receivership expenses and remuneration are to come out of the assets subject to the receivership.
>
> The Court of Appeal was in my opinion wrong to suppose that CPR 69.7 has made (or could have made) a fundamental change either in the general law of receivership, or in the position of receiverships under CJA 1988 and other comparable statutory powers. I would allow this appeal on that ground. There is also a further, narrower ground for concluding that the order of the Court of Appeal cannot be upheld. In the original order appointing Mr Sinclair as receiver, Jackson J directed that 'the costs of the receivership' (which in the context must mean expenses and remuneration) were to be paid in accordance with the agreement letter of 21 November 2002. That order was not appealed at the time (although it was contemplated that an early application would be made for discharge of the receiver) nor has there been any subsequent application for permission to appeal from it out of time. A receiver takes on heavy responsibilities when he accepts appointment, and he is entitled to the security of knowing that the terms of his appointment will not be changed retrospectively—even if an appellate court later decides that the receivership should have been terminated at an earlier date.

**4.51** The decision in *Hughes* therefore remains good law, CPR 69.7 notwithstanding and CrimPR r 60.6, the successor to the Crown Court Rules, appears to confirm this for POCA receiverships. The position was summarised by Lord Justice Longmore at para 1 of *Sinclair v Glatt* [2009] 1 WLR 1845:

> This appeal is about the entitlement of a receiver, appointed pursuant to section 77 of the Criminal Justice Act 1988 ('the Act') to get in the assets of a money launderer who has been convicted of various money-laundering offences, to recover his remuneration costs and expenses. It is now settled that such a receiver, like a receiver at common law, is entitled to recover his remuneration, costs and expenses from the assets which he has been appointed to receive ('the receivership assets'). That is so whether or not he ought to have been appointed in the first place or the order appointing him has been discharged, see *Mellor v Mellor* [1992] 1 WLR 517. Even if the defendant, whose assets have been caught by the order appointing the receiver, is subsequently acquitted or has his conviction quashed, the receivership assets must bear the costs of the receivership; this is also the position if, as in the present case, a confiscation

order is made but subsequently quashed, *Hughes v Customs and Excise Commissioners* [2003] 1 WLR 177. Even if the receiver carries on his receivership unnecessarily and should have agreed that his receivership should have been discharged at a time before a court application is made to terminate his receivership, the receivership assets bear those costs reasonably incurred up to the date he is actually discharged, *Capewell v Revenue and Customs Commissioners* [2007] 1 WLR 386.

The above decisions may not be as harsh as they first appear. The defendant will have ben- **4.52** efited from a professional manager administering his assets and business. In many cases, following his acquittal, the defendant will get back assets that are far better managed and maintained than at the time the receiver took office. Inevitably, managing those assets incurs much expenditure. Houses and other real property will need to be insured, kept in good repair, and mortgage repayments and council tax liabilities met. If there is a business to run, staff and trading expenses will need to be paid and proper accounts prepared and main- tained. All these items of expenditure are essential to the proper management of the defend- ant's estate and would have to be met regardless of whether a receiver is in office.

As Lord Walker pointed out in *Capewell*, the position under POCA is clearer than it was **4.53** under the predecessor regimes of the CJA and DTA. Section 49(2)(d) of POCA allows the Crown Court to give management receivers power to:

realise so much of the property as is necessary to meet the receiver's remuneration and expenses.

Similarly, CrimPR r 60.6(5) makes specific provision that the receiver is to receive his remu- neration by realising property in respect of which he is appointed, ie from the estate under his management. It is submitted that the combined effect of these provisions is to apply the common law rules in relation to the remuneration of receivers to management receivers appointed under POCA. Rule 60.6 CrimPR is considered below. However, the position is uncertain following the Court of Appeal's decision in *CPS v The Eastenders Group* [2012] EWCA Crim 2436; [2013] 2 All ER 437 which is the subject of an appeal to the Supreme Court—see para 4.67 below. The Court of Appeal has decided that a receiver may not be permitted to draw his remuneration from the receivership assets under management (the receivership estate) where this would constitute a breach of Article 1 of the First Protocol to the ECHR, nor be permitted to exercise a lien over the assets for that purpose. Whether a breach has occurred will depend on the precise facts involved.

In historical cases the prosecutor undertook, in the letter of agreement, to indemnify the **4.54** receiver as to his remuneration and expenses in the event that there were insufficient assets available within the estate under his management. Such indemnities were often made subject to conditions, such as a requirement that the receiver notify the prosecutor immediately if he considered there was a risk he may need to call on the indemnity, and/or a provision capping the amount the prosecutor was prepared to pay. This type of contractual indemnity offered by the prosecutor has become less common since the introduction of POCA. Moreover, POCA does not contain an equivalent statutory indemnity for the receiver as was provided under s 88(2) of the CJA. Many receivers are now prepared to act without an indemnity or subject to a conditional fee agreement.

### Controlling the receiver's remuneration and expenses

In the *Hughes* case, the Court of Appeal ruled that receivers' remuneration and expenses **4.55** must be approved by the court and the previous practice of such fees being vetted and approved by the prosecutor alone was wrong. Arden LJ drew attention to paragraph 22.6 of the Chancery Guide which provides that:

> The receiver's remuneration must be authorised by the Court. Unless the court directs it to be fixed by reference to some fixed scale, or percentage of sums collected, it is assessed by the court, but in the first instance the receiver should submit his remuneration claim to the parties for approval. If the claim is accepted by the parties, the court should not normally be concerned to intervene, but it must at least formally authorise the remuneration.

This, it is submitted, is a more equitable regime because it gives the defendant the right to make representations if he considers the receiver's claim is excessive. The previous system whereby fees were simply agreed between the prosecutor and the receiver left little avenue of redress open to a defendant who wished to challenge the receiver's claim.

**4.56** Indeed, it must not be thought that a receivership order gives the receiver a 'blank cheque' to charge whatever fees he thinks appropriate, pursue whatever enquiries he chooses, or pay the fees of agents he engages without holding up their invoices to critical scrutiny. In *Mirror Group Newspapers v Maxwell* [1998] BCC 324 Ferris J described as 'profoundly shocking' a receivership in which nothing at all had been realised for the benefit of creditors in an estate valued in excess of £1.5 million, and the majority of the funds had been applied in satisfaction of the costs of the receivers and their lawyers. He issued a timely reminder to receivers as to their duties as office holders and fiduciaries. He said that the test for determining whether a receiver had acted properly in undertaking particular tasks at a particular cost must be:

> whether a reasonable prudent man, faced with the same circumstances in relation to his own affairs, would lay out or hazard his own money in doing what the office holders have done. It is not sufficient, in my view, for office holders to say that what they have done is within the scope of the duties or powers conferred on them. They are expected to deploy commercial judgment, not to act regardless of expense. This is not to say that a transaction carried out at a high cost in relation to the benefit received, or even an expensive failure, will automatically result in the disallowance of expenses or remuneration. But it is to be expected that transactions having these characteristics will be subject to close scrutiny.

**4.57** The learned judge took a similarly robust line in relation to the fees of lawyers and other professionals engaged to advise receivers. He said:

> At the very least they must subject the bills to critical scrutiny. If they simply pay them without scrutiny they will obviously be vulnerable. They may be able to negotiate certain reductions, thus facilitating an argument that the negotiated reductions are preferable to the possibility of obtaining greater reductions at greater costs. In an appropriate case (but not I would expect one where the issues are as complex and the amounts as large as in this case) they may be able to obtain a certificate from the Law Society as to the proper amount of their solicitors bill. Finally they can require the bills to be taxed pursuant to Section 70 of the Solicitors Act 1975.

**4.58** The concerns expressed by Ferris J led to new rules being introduced in the High Court in relation to remuneration of receivers with effect from 2 December 2002. In so far as CJA and DTA cases are concerned the new rules are to be found in CPR 69.7. In relation to POCA cases, the rules, which are in almost identical terms, are to be found in CrimPR r 60.6. Rule 60.6 provides:

> (1) This rule applies where the Crown Court appoints a receiver under section 48 or 50 of the Proceeds of Crime Act 2002 and the receiver is not a member of staff of the Crown

Prosecution Service (and it is immaterial whether the receiver is a permanent or temporary member or he is on secondment from elsewhere).

(2) The receiver may only charge for his services if the Crown Court—
   (a) so directs; and
   (b) specifies the basis on which the receiver is to be remunerated.

(3) Unless the Crown Court orders otherwise, in determining the remuneration of the
receiver, the Crown Court shall award such sum as is reasonable and proportionate in all
the circumstances and which takes into account—
   (a) the time properly given by him and his staff to the receivership;
   (b) the complexity of the receivership;
   (c) any responsibility of an exceptional kind or degree which falls on the receiver in con-
       sequence of the receivership;
   (d) the effectiveness with which the receiver appears to be carrying out, or to have carried
       out, his duties; and
   (e) the value and nature of the subject matter of the receivership.

(4) The Crown Court may refer the determination of a receiver's remuneration to be ascertained by the taxing authority of the Crown Court and rules 78.4 and 78.7 shall have
effect as if the taxing authority was ascertaining costs.

(5) A receiver appointed under section 48 of the 2002 Act is to receive his remuneration by
realising property in respect of which he is appointed in accordance with section 49(2)(d)
of the 2002 Act.

(6) A receiver appointed under section 50 of the 2002 Act is to receive his remuneration
by applying to the magistrates' court office for payment under section 55(4)(b) of the
2002 Act.

**4.59** All parties to the proceedings should examine receivers' claims for remuneration with care
and challenge any discrepancies or concerns. In particular, the hourly rates claimed should
be checked to ensure they are in accordance with the letter of agreement between the prosecutor and the receiver which will always be annexed to the witness statement in support
of the receivership application. The number of hours spent on each task should also be
examined to ensure reasonableness and proportionality, having regard to the particular circumstances of the case. The grade of fee earner performing particular tasks is also open to
challenge: it does not, for example, require the receiver himself to write letters about routine
issues; this can properly be delegated to more junior staff on lower charge-out rates. Care
should also be taken to check that receivers are not claiming for overheads such as handover
meetings when a fee earner is leaving the firm, drawing cheques, bank reconciliations, and
the like. All these overheads are included in the hourly rate and should not attract separate
entries on the invoices. Similar checks should be undertaken in relation to invoices rendered
by agents engaged by the receiver such as solicitors, surveyors, estate agents etc. In many cases
it will be possible to resolve any disputes by negotiation with the receiver but, if this proves
impossible, the Crown Court should be asked to refer the matter to the taxing authority in
accordance with CrimPR r 60.6(4).

### The mechanics of drawing remuneration

**4.60** A receiver must draw his remuneration in accordance with the order of the court appointing
him, which will normally incorporate the letter of agreement with the prosecutor on the
mechanics of drawing his fees. Prior to any confiscation order being made against a defendant, subject to the terms of his appointment, s 49(2)(d) of POCA and CrimPR 60.6(5) allow
the receiver to realise realisable property to meet his fees.

**4.61**    Often a management receiver remains in office after a confiscation order has been made, eg because the confiscation order is subject to appeal so s 50(1)(c) of POCA bars their appointment as an enforcement receiver. In those circumstances it is prudent for any sums held by the receiver first to be paid into the Magistrates' Court towards satisfaction of the defendant's confiscation order so that he receives the appropriate credit and avoids the possibility of interest accruing for late payment of those sums. Thereafter the receiver might draw back his remuneration and expenses from the Magistrates' Court. In the case of *Paul Hansford (Claimant) v Southampton Magistrates' Court (Respondent) & Revenue and Customs (Interested Party)* [2008] EWHC 67 (Admin); [2008] 4 All ER 432, the Divisional Court held that a management receiver acting post confiscation was not entitled under s 81(1) CJA to retain sums in respect of his fees and disbursements out of the proceeds of realisation from the sale of property of a defendant against whom a confiscation order had been made. The Court held the receiver was required to apply those sums towards the satisfaction of the confiscation order as soon as they were received and draw back his remuneration from the Magistrates' Court under s 81(5) of the CJA. It is to be noted, however, that s 81 CJA, in applying to both management and enforcement receivers, is worded significantly differently from the terms of the corresponding s 54 of POCA, which is limited to the application of sums in the hands of enforcement receivers alone. In accordance with s 55(4) of POCA the designated officer will repay from the sums paid into the magistrates' court by an enforcement receiver the remuneration and expenses of any management receiver, to the extent that they have not already been met by virtue of the exercise of his power of sale under s 49(2)(d), in priority to repaying the remuneration and expenses of any enforcement receiver.

### The receiver's lien

**4.62**    The receiver has a lien over the assets forming part of the receivership estate for payment of his remuneration and expenses. In *Mellor v Mellor & others* [1992] 1 WLR 517 it was held by the High Court that the receiver's lien over the assets gave him a continuing right to possession even after the discharge of the receivership order. In *Sinclair v Glatt and others* [2009] EWCA Civ 176; [2009] 1 WLR 1845 the Court of Appeal held that the receiver's lien extended to assets over which the defendant had no beneficial entitlement but only held a bare legal interest because they remained realisable property for the purposes of the CJA. The defendant had been subject to restraint and management receivership orders which were ultimately discharged when his confiscation order was quashed by the Court of Appeal. During the course of the management receivership, Munby J made a ruling to the effect that the executors of the defendant's late mother's estate were beneficially entitled to various assets subject to the order and that the defendant held no beneficial interest therein but merely held bare legal title. The receiver thereafter asserted a lien for his remuneration and expenses against those assets and, in a further ruling, Munby J upheld the receiver's claim notwithstanding that the estate of the defendant's late mother was beneficially entitled to them. The Court of Appeal upheld the judge's ruling that the receiver was entitled to exercise his lien over the assets as they remained realisable property for the purposes of the Act. Longmore LJ, with whom Stanley Burnton and Elias LJJ agreed, held that there was an element of 'artificiality' in the submission that the lien could not attach to property over which the defendant only had a bare legal interest. He said:

> A further reason why Counsel cannot be right to say that 'realisable property' cannot include a defendant's bare legal interest is its artificiality. Counsel has to accept that if a defendant has

a 10% (or even 1%) beneficial interest in the property, it would then be realisable property and that the receiver's lien would then attach. Such a construction would create anomaly and defy practical sense.

The Court also rejected a submission from the defendant's wife that the receivership assets **4.63** should not be made available to meet the receiver's lien until her own ancillary relief application in divorce proceedings had been determined. Longmore LJ said:

> Mrs Glatt has not yet obtained any property adjustment or other order in her matrimonial proceedings; she is, therefore, in no position to make any claim to the receivership assets in her own name. There is no suggestion by her or by Mr Glatt that any assets are not properly the subject-matter of the receivership order. The fact that if the confiscation order had not been quashed, Mrs Glatt would have been afforded an opportunity before any asset was realised to show that she had an interest of her own in such assets (see *Re Norris*) is nothing to the point since she does not currently assert that she has any such interest. The most she has is the hope that, in due course, a court might make a property transfer order in her favour. If she does obtain such an order, and the receivership order had been outstanding, she might have been able to extract what by then would have become her assets but there is no reason why the receiver could not exercise his lien for his charge up to the time of any such transfer. It follows that there is no point in preventing the receiver from now exercising his lien and Counsel's first argument that the entire proceedings should be deferred until after the resolution of Mrs Glatt's proceedings for ancillary relief must fail.

The Court was similarly unimpressed with an argument advanced on behalf of the wife to the **4.64** effect that the court had a discretion to balance the competing claims of the wife and receiver and conclude that the receiver should look to his indemnity from the prosecutor for payment of his remuneration and expenses. Longmore LJ said:

> That would be contrary to the decisions of this court in *Mellor* and *Hughes* in which it was determined that a receiver appointed under the Act had the same powers as his common law counterpart and that he must be entitled to assess the value of the receivership assets included in the receivership order when determining whether or not to take on the receivership.

Finally, the court considered whether the decision represented a breach of property rights **4.65** under Art 1 to the First Protocol of the ECHR and concluded that it did not. The Court held that the statutory measures in relation to the receiver's costs were in the public interest, appropriate for and achieving their aim, proportionate in striking a fair balance between the demands of the general interests of the community and the requirements of the protection of individual rights. Longmore LJ noted that counsel for the receiver and prosecutor had conceded that in an extreme case, where a party wholly unconnected with the defendant stood to lose an entire asset because it was eaten up by receiver's costs, Art 1 might have a part to play in determining how much the receiver was entitled to claim and from which asset it would be payable. He emphasised that, in the instant case, none of the parties could claim to have no connection with the defendant. The court observed that the wife's claim under Art 1 to the First Protocol was 'even more hopeless' since she had no property interest of which she would be deprived if the receiver exercised his lien.

However, in *Brandon Barnes v Eastenders Cash & Carry Plc & CPS* [2012] EW Misc 6 **4.66** (CCrimC) (04 April 2012) Case No: U20110135/1/2011, Underhill J, as he then was, sitting in the Central Criminal Court, considered the European Convention argument on a different factual basis. The receiver applied for his remuneration and expenses to be drawn from the exercise of his lien over the estate under management, namely the assets of the Eastenders companies. He had previously been discharged from office by the Court of Appeal on the basis that two conditions for his appointment were not satisfied: (a) there was no reasonable cause to believe the defendants had benefited from criminal conduct and (b) the corporate veil should not have been lifted and the assets of the companies were not therefore assets of the defendants and therefore not realisable property—see *Windsor and others v CPS* [2011] 1 WLR 1519. In addition to opposing the receiver's application, the Eastenders companies applied for compensation from the CPS under s 72 POCA in the event their assets were drawn upon to pay the receiver's remuneration. Underhill J made no order on either application because he ruled that it would breach the companies' right under Art 1 of the First Protocol were their assets to be drawn upon for the receiver's remuneration when the Court of Appeal had subsequently decided that the receiver should never have been appointed. Following a further application by the receiver on 8 May 2012, the learned judge ruled that the CPS should pay the receiver's remuneration and expenses. That decision was appealed to the Court of Appeal Criminal Division.

**4.67** The Court of Appeal unanimously allowed the appeal in part and ruled that there was no power, whether under POCA or otherwise, to order the CPS to pay the receiver's remuneration and expenses—see paras 69–71 of the judgment of Laws LJ in *Crown Prosecution Service v The Eastenders Group & Anor* [2012] EWCA Crim 2436; [2013] 2 All ER 437. However, by a majority, with Laws LJ dissenting, the Court ruled that allowing the receiver to exercise a lien over the assets of the companies would breach their right to peaceful enjoyment of their property under Article 1 of Protocol 1 to the Convention. This was because such a deprivation of possession of property would not be subject to conditions provided for by law so as to comply with Art 1 as neither of the two conditions set out above for the appointment of the receiver were satisfied—see paras 77–81 of the judgment. Therefore the receiver was likely to be left without payment of his remuneration or expenses unless he could sue the prosecutor for them, a potential action contemplated at para 84 of the judgment. The Court of Appeal had certified a point of law of general public importance raised in the case at the time of their decision but refused permission to appeal and the appeal is due to be heard in 2014. However, in May 2013 the Supreme Court granted the receiver permission to appeal. Further to the Court of Appeal's decision, in a judgment dated 26 April 2013, [2013] EWHC 1057, Underhill J ordered the receiver to repay the companies for the expenses which had already been paid out from their assets during the currency of the receivership.

## G. Discharge of the Receiver

**4.68** Receivers and the prosecuting authorities that apply for their appointment should be vigilant in reviewing both the economic viability of the receivership and the continued necessity for having a receiver in office. At any point during the receivership, the receiver, prosecutor, defendant or any other affected party may apply under section 62 of POCA to the Crown Court for directions as to the exercise of the receiver's powers. The Court may make such order as it believes appropriate under section 62(4) of POCA. If the point comes when it is apparent that the receivership would no longer serve any useful purpose or that it is no longer economically viable, an application should be made to the Crown Court for the receiver's discharge under section 63 of POCA.

Equally if the statutory or discretionary criteria for the appointment of the receiver are not met **4.69** then the receivership should be discharged—see above and in particular the case of *Windsor and others v Crown Prosecution Service* [2011] 1 WLR 1519, also dealt with in Chapter 5.

A defendant who considers that a management receivership order should be discharged for **4.70** these reasons should initially invite the receiver and the prosecutor to justify why it is necessary for the receiver to stay in office. If he considers the response unsatisfactory, the defendant should himself apply to discharge the receivership. He should serve a witness statement in support of his application setting out his grounds for seeking the discharge of the receiver together with his own proposals for the effective management of his assets pending the conclusion of the proceedings.

Section 63 of POCA (as amended by para 30 of Sch 8 to the Serious Crime Act 2007) makes **4.71** provision for the discharge and variation of receivership orders. It provides:

(1) The following persons may apply to the Crown Court to vary or discharge an order made under any of sections 48 to 51—
  (a) the receiver;
  (b) the person who applied for the order;
  (c) any person affected by the order.
(2) On an application under this section the court—
  (a) may discharge the order;
  (b) may vary the order.
(3) But in the case of an order under section 48 or 49—
  (a) if the condition in section 40 which was satisfied was that proceedings were started or an application was made, the court must discharge the order on the conclusion of the proceedings or of the application (as the case may be);
  (b) if the condition which was satisfied was that an investigation was started or an application was to be made, the court must discharge the order if within a reasonable time proceedings for the offences are not started or the application is not made (as the case may be).

It is thus a matter for the court's discretion as to whether the receivership order should be **4.72** discharged or not, save where s 63(3) applies when the court must discharge the order. When exercising its discretion under s 63(2), the court must have regard to the legislative steer in s 69. In *Capewell v Customs and Excise Commissioners (No 2)* [2005] EWCA Civ 964 the Court of Appeal gave guidance as to the issues the court should take into account in determining whether a management receivership order should be discharged. Carnwath LJ said:

On the question of discharge, cost is of course a factor, but it is not the primary issue. The overriding consideration is whether the receivership is still serving a valid purpose, within the overall objective set by section 82. The relevant questions for the court are likely to be—

(i) For what purposes, within the overall objective, was the receivership authorised?
(ii) To what extent have those purposes been achieved or overtaken?
(iii) To the extent that they have not yet been achieved or overtaken, is the continuation of the receivership (as opposed to a restraint order or some other order) necessary to achieve them?
(iv) In any event, having regard both to the overall objective and to fairness to the defendant, is the additional cost of continuing the receivership proportionate to the likely financial gain?

We would add that fairness to the defendant cannot be measured purely in financial terms. Even without accepting all of Mr Capewell's evidence, it requires little imagination to understand how a receivership of this kind can seriously interfere with the ordinary business and personal life of those affected and their families. The premise of the 1988 Act is that such a burden may have to be accepted in the public interest. But it is for the court to decide in individual cases where the balance lies, weighing all the benefits and burdens, both public and private.

**4.73** Any application for a receiver's discharge should be made in accordance with the procedure laid down in CrimPR r 60.3 requiring a formal written application and seven days' notice to all parties. Even if there are insufficient grounds to justify the discharge of the receiver, the defendant or an affected third party is always entitled to seek the court's directions (see section 62 of POCA) if he considers the receiver is abusing his power or is otherwise acting improperly: see *Manning & Sinclair v Glatt* [2003] EWCA Civ 1977. Following discharge of the receivership, receivers appointed under the legislation still remain officers of the court. Therefore in *Glatt and others v Sinclair* [2013] EWCA Civ 241, The Times, 8 May 2013, the Court of Appeal held that the discharge did not extinguish the receiver's common law entitlement to be indemnified from the receivership estate for his remuneration and expenses incurred both before and after discharge.

**4.74** Section 64 of POCA (as amended by para 31 of Sch 8 to the Serious Crime Act 2007) makes provision for the discharge of management receivers on the appointment of an enforcement receiver. It provides:

(1) This section applies if—
    (a) a receiver stands appointed under section 48 in respect of realisable property (the management receiver), and
    (b) the court appoints a receiver under section 50.
(2) The court must order the management receiver to transfer to the other receiver all property held by the management receiver by virtue of the powers conferred on him by section 49.
(3) *repealed by para 31(3) of Schedule 8 to the Serious Crime Act 2007.*
(4) Subsection (2) does not apply to property which the management receiver holds by virtue of the exercise by him of his power under section 49(2)(d).
(5) If the management receiver complies with an order under subsection (2) he is discharged—
    (a) from his appointment under section 48;
    (b) from any obligation under this Act arising from his appointment.
(6) If this section applies the court may make such a consequential or incidental order as it believes is appropriate.

**4.75** The management receiver cannot be compelled to deliver up to the enforcement receiver assets he holds for the purpose of meeting his remuneration and expenses: see s 64(4). Once he complies with an order under s 64(2), the management receiver is discharged from office and from any obligation consequent upon it: see s 64(5).

## H. Taxation and Receivers

**4.76** Management and enforcement receivers appointed under POCA are not liable to pay tax pursuant to the Taxes Management Act 1970 in respect of their dealings in and realisations of realisable property pursuant to their orders of appointment: see s 448 and Pt 1 of Sch 10 to POCA. The same principle applies to receivers appointed under the CJA and DTA: see *IRC v Dayman and Piacentini*, The Times, 10 February 2003.

# 5

# APPLICATIONS TO VARY AND DISCHARGE RESTRAINT ORDERS

## A. Introduction

Restraint orders are typically granted following applications made without notice to the **5.01** defendant if they are urgent or if there are reasonable grounds for believing that giving notice would cause the dissipation of realisable property which is the subject of the application pursuant to the Criminal Procedure Rules (CrimPR) r 59.1(2). In addition applications are often granted on the papers without even a hearing pursuant to CrimPR r 61.3—for further on procedure see Chapter 7. Rule 61.3 provides:

> **Applications to be dealt with in writing**
>
> **61.3.** Applications in restraint proceedings and receivership proceedings are to be dealt with without a hearing, unless the Crown Court orders otherwise.

The Court of Appeal, in various authorities cited below (*SFO v Lexi Holdings, Windsor v CPS* and *Stanford International Bank v SFO*), has emphasised that a hearing of the application should take place whenever there are issues of any complexity which require determination by a Judge. Whatever the form of the application, a defendant is likely to have little opportunity to contest the making of the order. The defendant or other affected party may, however, apply to vary or discharge the order under s 42(3) of the Proceeds of Crime Act 2002 (POCA):

> An application to discharge or vary a restraint order or an order under section 41(7) may be made to the Crown Court by—
> (a) the person who applied for the order;
> (b) any person affected by the order.

The procedure to be followed in an application to discharge or vary the order is set out in the CrimPR at Pt 59, r 59.3 for those affected by the order and rr 59.4 and 59.5 for the person who applied for the order—see Chapter 7 for further details. Rule 59.3 provides:

> 59.3.—(1) This rule applies where a person affected by a restraint order makes an application to the Crown Court under section 42(3) of the Proceeds of Crime Act 2002 to discharge or vary the restraint order or any ancillary order made under section 41(7) of the Act.
> (2) The application must be in writing and may be supported by a witness statement.
> (3) The application and any witness statement must be lodged with the Crown Court.
> (4) The application and any witness statement must be served on the person who applied for the restraint order and any person who is prohibited from dealing with realisable property by the restraint order (if he is not the person making the application) at least two days before the date fixed by the court for hearing the application, unless the Crown Court specifies a shorter period.

**5.02** Further, the restraint order itself will invariably give all parties affected by it permission to apply for its discharge or variation on giving two clear days' notice in writing to the court and the prosecutor. A party aggrieved by a restraint order should always apply for the order to be varied or discharged before embarking on an appeal. Indeed, an appeal to the Court of Appeal by a person affected by a restraint order only lies against a decision of the Crown Court on an application made under s 42(3) of the Act. There is no immediate right of appeal against the making of a restraint order without first seeking its variation or discharge: see s 43 of the Act. In this chapter we consider the grounds on which applications for the variation and discharge of POCA restraint orders might be made by prosecutors, defendants, and third parties.

## B. Applications to Discharge Restraint Orders

### On the conclusion of proceedings

**5.03** By s 42(6) of POCA:

> If the condition in section 40 which was satisfied was that proceedings were started or an application was made, the court must discharge the order on the conclusion of the proceedings or of the application (as the case may be).

Once proceedings conclude, the restraint order must be discharged—s 42(6) gives the court no discretion in the matter. It should, however, be noted that the definition of the expression 'conclusion of proceedings' in s 85 of POCA is such that proceedings do not conclude when the defendant is convicted and sentenced, but only upon the satisfaction of any confiscation order. In practice, the prosecutor should apply promptly for the restraint order to be discharged in the event of the defendant being acquitted or on the satisfaction of a confiscation order. If he does not, in the absence of a satisfactory explanation, the defendant should make his own application for the order to be discharged.

### Delay by the prosecutor

**5.04** A restraint order can, and often does, have a significant impact on a defendant and others affected by it. The order imposes draconian restrictions on the extent to which he is entitled to deal with his assets at a time when he may not have been convicted of any offence and is entitled to be presumed innocent. Accordingly, the prosecutor is expected to proceed expeditiously once a restraint order has been obtained and to prosecute any associated criminal proceedings without undue delay. This principle has been applied for many years by the civil courts in cases where freezing orders (formerly Mareva injunctions) have been granted: see, for example, *Lloyds Bowmaker Ltd v Britannia Arrow Holdings Ltd* [1988] 1 WLR 1337.

Section 42(7) of POCA puts this principle on a statutory footing in cases where the restraint **5.05** order has been made pre-charge when a person is subject to a criminal investigation. It provides:

> If the condition in section 40 which was satisfied was that an investigation was started or an application was to be made, the court must discharge the order if within a reasonable time proceedings for the offence are not started or the application is not made (as the case may be).

What constitutes a 'reasonable time' is an issue of fact to be determined on the facts of indi- **5.06** vidual cases. The application of some specific facts were considered at paragraphs 89–90 of the Court of Appeal's judgment in *SFO v Lexi Holdings* [2009] 2 WLR 905. The equivalent provision in art 9 of the POCA (External Requests & Orders) Order 2005 was also considered by Gross J in *SFO v Al Zayat* [2008] Lloyd's Rep FC 390 at para 58 of his judgment. If the investigation being conducted relates to a complex fraud with a vast quantity of documentation to examine and overseas enquiries to pursue, it is likely to be reasonable for the investigation to take longer to complete than a more straightforward investigation where all the evidence is to be found in the UK. In determining what constitutes a 'reasonable time' the court is entitled to take into account the progress of the investigation from the time it started and not just from the date on which the restraint order was made. Where an investigation is taking longer to complete than was expected at the time a restraint order was made, in compliance with his ongoing duty to give full and frank disclosure of all material facts, the prosecutor should inform the court of the position so it may determine whether it is appropriate for the restraint order to remain in force and, if so, on what terms.

### Procedural irregularities by the prosecutor or absence of risk of dissipation

A procedural irregularity by the prosecutor in obtaining the restraint order may be a suf- **5.07** ficient basis to seek its discharge although, as indicated above, this could prove a short-lived victory for the defendant because it is always open to the prosecutor to remedy the defect and apply for a new order. If the irregularity is of a minor or technical nature that can easily be remedied, the defendant and any affected third party would be well advised not to pursue an application for the discharge of the order as litigating the matter could prove costly and may even serve no useful purpose.

If the irregularity is a serious one, an application to discharge the order may well be appropri- **5.08** ate, particularly if it is not easily capable of remedy.

Laws LJ expanded upon this principle at paras 50–57 of his judgment in the Court of Appeal **5.09** in *Jennings v CPS* [2005] 4 All ER 391 and Longmore LJ laid down guidelines on dissipation and delay at paras 61–66—see also Chapter 2. In particular, at paras 61 and 65 of his judgment Longmore LJ stated:

> 61. (1) Duty to set out reasons for fearing asset dissipation.
>
> Fear of dissipation of assets is the reason for seeking a restraint order. Such fear must, in fact, exist before an order should be applied for. But in a case where dishonesty is charged, there will usually be reason to fear that assets will be dissipated. I do not therefore consider it necessary for the prosecutor to state in terms that he fears assets will be dissipated merely because he or she thinks there is a good arguable case of dishonesty. As my Lord has said, the risk of

dissipation will generally speak for itself. Nevertheless prosecutors must be alive to the possibility that there may be no risk in fact. If no asset dissipation has occurred over a long period, particularly after a defendant has been charged, the prosecutor should explain why asset dissipation is now feared at the date of application for the order when it was not feared before.

. . .

65. (5) Delay.

As my Lord has said, delay will not usually be a significant fact on its own. But, as stated in (1) above, it may be relevant if there has been delay between the defendant being charged and the date of the application, if there has been no dissipation of the assets meanwhile. It is then incumbent on the Crown to explain why dissipation was not initially seen as a major risk but now is.

**5.10** For an example of a restraint order being discharged where the prosecution failed to establish the requisite risk of dissipation see *R v B* [2008] EWCA Crim 1374; [2009] 1 Cr App R 14 where a suspect had made no attempt to dissipate his assets despite having a clear opportunity to do so over a significant period of time. For further details, see Chapter 2.

*Further grounds for discharge—failure to meet statutory criteria*

**5.11** A discharge application may also be appropriate where the statutory criteria which are required to exist before a restraint order can be made have not been established. Applications for the discharge of the order on this basis should be confined to cases where there is no evidence to show that one or more of the statutory criteria exist. The Crown Court judge will not attempt to usurp the function of the jury by assessing the strengths and weaknesses of the criminal case—if the statutory criteria have been made out, it is unlikely the court will consider discharging an order in the absence of some serious procedural irregularity by the prosecutor. Laws LJ in *Jennings* stated at paragraph 44:

> When a restraint order is applied for, the court is not only ignorant of the defendant's future fate at the hands of the jury. There may be other defendants; the court is, of course, equally ignorant of the jury's future view of them. Indeed it may be unclear who, if anyone, will stand his trial beside the defendant whom the court is considering. There may be large unanswered questions as to the respective roles of different defendants, as to who did what with the crime's proceeds, and the ultimate extent and destination of those proceeds. There may be other uncertainties. In all these circumstances, it may often be appropriate in a case where there are several prospective defendants to make restraint orders against each of them, so as to protect, as against each, the whole sum which represents the proceeds of the crime so far as the court can at that stage ascertain it. While of course the Crown must lead evidence as to the amount of the proceeds, and the defendant's acts in getting—'obtaining'—the proceeds, and also the defendant's assets so far as they are known, the exercise is quite unlike the later exhaustive investigation undertaken by the trial judge in deciding what, if any, confiscation order to make. At the restraint order stage the court makes no final decision as to the defendant's 'benefit' or 'realisable property'. It is concerned only, as I have said, to make a protective order so that in the particular case the satisfaction or fulfilment of any confiscation order made or to be made will be efficacious.

**5.12** An example of the statutory criteria not being met for the making of restraint orders is the case of *Alexander Windsor and others v Crown Prosecution Service* [2011] EWCA Crim 143; [2011] 1 WLR 1519. The Court of Appeal allowed appeals against the Crown Court's making of without-notice restraint and receivership orders against suspects (the defendants) who had not been charged with any criminal offence. The Crown Court judge had previously refused to discharge the orders following a contested hearing. The Court of Appeal held that the prosecutor had failed to establish on the evidence before the Crown Court judge that there was reasonable cause to believe that the alleged offenders had benefited from criminal conduct for the purposes of s 40(2)(b) POCA. Hooper LJ stated at paras 53–60 of his judgment:

> 53. Before charge—and all the more so before arrest—there will be many uncertainties. The law does not require certainty at this stage but uncertainty is not in itself a reason for making a restraint order as some of the respondent's submissions might suggest. The court must sharply focus on the statutory test: is the judge satisfied that there is a reasonable cause to believe that the alleged offender has benefited from his criminal conduct? It is that test which the court must apply and it requires a detailed examination of the material put before it. The presence of uncertainties does not prevent there being reasonable cause to believe, but the judge must still be satisfied that there is reasonable cause to believe.
> ...
> 57. An application of this complexity should be listed before a judge with sufficient time to read and absorb the papers and with sufficient time to conduct a proper hearing. It would, in our view, be preferable to list applications of this complexity before a High Court Judge sitting in the Crown Court with experience of complex frauds or a Circuit Judge with similar experience.
> ...
> 59. Given that applications of this kind are made ex parte and given the draconian consequences of restraint orders and receivership orders, it is vitally important, in the interests of the absent alleged offenders, that the hearing is as fair as is possible in the circumstances. Giving those affected an early opportunity to apply to set aside or vary the restraint orders and receivership orders (whilst important) is not a substitute for a fair ex parte hearing.
> 60. We add this. It has often been said when interpreting the confiscation legislation in a manner adverse to those affected by Part 2 orders that it is 'draconian'. Judges asked to exercise their discretion to make restraint (and receivership) orders of the kind with which this appeal is concerned should bear in mind the draconian consequences of such orders, albeit of course applying the legislation and, in particular, section 69.

**5.13** The Court of Appeal therefore emphasised the high level of scrutiny required before a judge should make restraint and receivership orders under POCA. The Court proceeded to remit the case back to the Crown Court for a fresh application for restraint orders to be heard on notice to the defendants with consideration of further evidence. However at that subsequent hearing Mackay J dismissed the application for fresh restraint orders.

**5.14** As is dealt with in Chapter 2, the court must be satisfied that there is a 'good arguable case' that property is realisable property in order for it to be subject to restraint or receivership orders prior to a confiscation order being made—see *CPS v Compton and others* [2002] EWCA Civ 1720. Therefore, an application to discharge a restraint order might be made on the basis that there is no good arguable case that the property subject to the order is realisable property for the purposes of ss 41 and 83 of POCA because the defendant or suspect holds no interest in it. The Court of Appeal in *Windsor* quashed the receivership orders on the additional basis that the companies' property was not realisable property for the purposes of s 48(2) POCA, see paras 16, 18, 94, and 109 of the judgement. The reasoning was that the corporate veil should not have been lifted and the assets of the companies should not have been treated as the assets of the defendants. The same applied for the purposes of the restraint orders over the companies' assets. In the case of *Bond v Crown Prosecution Service sub nom In The Matter Of Simon Price* [2011] EWHC 2330 (Admin) the applicants, the daughter and stepson of the defendant, sought to discharge restraint and receivership orders in respect of land in France on the basis that the defendant had no interest in the land. Their application was dismissed on its facts.

**Failure to give full and frank disclosure**

**5.15** Applications for restraint orders made without notice to the defendant are subject to the duty that the applicant for such relief must give full and frank disclosure of all material facts. The defendant has neither the right nor the opportunity to be present or represented when the application is made. The procedure therefore constitutes an exception to the principle of natural justice that both sides should be heard before the court makes an order. In consequence, the prosecutor is required to give full and frank disclosure of all material facts in his witness statement in support of the application. This obligation requires him to disclose any weaknesses in his case of which he is aware, any information that might be favourable to the defendant, and any innocent explanation that he may have advanced when being interviewed. The prosecutor's duty of full and frank disclosure is considered in more detail in Chapter 7 para 7.07, and it will be seen that a serious failure to comply with this duty may result in the order being discharged. Some caution does need to be exercised in considering whether an application to discharge the order should be made on this basis, because it is always open to the prosecutor to apply for a further order on the basis of an amended witness statement that remedies any previous deficiencies in his case.

**5.16** Further, in *Jennings v Crown Prosecution Service* [2005] 4 All ER 391 the Court of Appeal held that the public interest in the restraint and confiscation of the proceeds of crime dictated that the court should not be too ready to discharge a restraint order where there has been a failure to give full and frank disclosure. At paras 62 and 63 of his judgment Longmore LJ stated:

> 62. (2) Failure to discharge the duty.
>
> If there is a duty on the prosecutor to inform the court why, on the facts of a particular case, there is fear of dissipation and the prosecutor fails to discharge that duty, it would be a strong thing to discharge the order altogether. If an application is made by a defendant to discharge or vary the order on the grounds that it is unreasonable to fear that his assets will be dissipated, the court will decide that question on the evidence. If the court considers that the prosecutor failed to consider whether there was a risk of dissipation when he should have done or failed to put relevant documentary material before the court but that the public interest still requires an order, the judge can deprive the prosecution of their costs as Leveson J indeed did in this case. If the public interest requires that an order should be made, an order should still be made.
>
> 63. (3) Duty to make full and frank disclosure.
>
> This duty applies to applicants for restraint orders as much as to applicants for freezing orders.
>
> 64. (4) Failure to discharge the duty.
>
> See the answer to (2) above. The fact that the Crown acts in the public interest does, in my view, militate against the sanction of discharging an order if, after consideration of all the evidence, the court thinks that an order is appropriate. That is not to say that there could never be a case where the Crown's failure might be so appalling that the ultimate sanction of discharge would be justified.

**5.17** Just such a case was considered by the Court of Appeal in the case of *Stanford International Bank v Serious Fraud Office and others* [2010] EWCA Civ 137; [2010] 3 WLR 941, where the Court set aside an external restraint order made under art 8 of the Proceeds of Crime Act 2002 (External Requests and Orders) Order 2005. Nevertheless, the Court, after considering whether to exercise its discretion to grant the restraint order afresh, did so. It is to be noted that the bank sought permission to appeal this decision to the Supreme Court who held that the Appellant did not require permission in order to proceed with its appeal—see *S.I.B. v SFO*

[2012] UKSC 3. The Court of Appeal in its judgment laid down useful guidelines on restraint order applications. At paras 190-1–190-91 of his judgment Hughes LJ stated:

> 190. I conclude that there were serious and material failures of the duty of candour in this case. It matters not where the responsibility for it lies as between the US prosecutors and the SFO as the DoJ's English agents and (presumably) advisors. The applicants failed to disclose: i) the existence of the Antiguan proceedings, the prior appointment of receivers over SIB and the pending application to wind it up; ii) the correspondence between the Antiguan receivers and the banks; and they misstated or at least failed to explain: iii) the risk of Jack J's order being discharged; and iv) the consequential need for urgency.

> 191. Whilst I respectfully agree with the view expressed by Slade LJ in *Brinks Mat v Ellcombe* [1988] 1 WLR 1350 that it can be all too easy for an objector to a freezing order to fall into the belief that almost any failure of disclosure is a passport to setting aside, it is essential that the duty of candour laid upon any applicant for an order without notice is fully understood and complied with. It is not limited to an obligation not to misrepresent. It consists in a duty to consider what any other interested person would, if present, wish to adduce by way of fact, or to say in answer to the application, and to place that material before the judge. That duty applies to an applicant for a restraint order under POCA in exactly the same way as to any other applicant for an order without notice. Even in relatively small value cases, the potential of a restraint order to disrupt other commercial or personal dealings is considerable. The prosecutor may believe that the defendant is a criminal, and he may turn out to be right, but that has yet to be proved. An application for a restraint order is emphatically not a routine matter of form, with the expectation that it will routinely be granted. The fact that the initial application is likely to be forced into a busy list, with very limited time for the judge to deal with it, is a yet further reason for the obligation of disclosure to be taken very seriously. In effect a prosecutor seeking an ex parte order must put on his defence hat and ask himself what, if he were representing the defendant or a third party with a relevant interest, he would be saying to the judge, and, having answered that question, that is what he must tell the judge. This application is a clear example of the duty either being ignored, or at least simply not being understood. This application came close to being treated as routine and to taking the court for granted. It may well not be the only example.

Hughes LJ at paras 204-2–204-13 of his judgment went on to give some practical guidance **5.18** on matching suitable judicial expertise to the case and on managing restraint order applications and associated litigation, so far as can be accomplished, in a coordinated manner. He concluded thus:

> The need for this procedure to work properly in the few cases where it will be called for underlines still further the essential requirement that applicants for restraint orders make full disclosure to the initial judge of potential complications. The present case is a vivid illustration. The failure of the prosecution to discover and reveal the pending and all too patent Antiguan winding up proceedings, and to tell the judge what was happening in the equally patent civil freezing order proceedings, was inexcusable, wherever the responsibility for it lay. It was equally inexcusable that notice of the lengthy proceedings before Lewison J was never given to the prosecutors, nor was that judge's attention drawn to Article 17(5) of the ERO.

## C. Applications to Vary the Restraint Order

In the majority of cases, the most appropriate means of seeking to mitigate the harsher effects **5.19** of a restraint order is to apply for it to be varied in some respect. Applications to vary restraint orders are most commonly made to release funds to pay legal fees and to increase the amount payable to the defendant and his dependants by way of general living expenses.

**Legal fees**

**5.20**   We have seen in Chapter 2 that s 41(4) of POCA imposes strict limitations on the release of restrained funds to pay legal fees in contrast to the position under the old legislation—the Criminal Justice Act 1988 (CJA) and the Drug Trafficking Act 1994 (DTA). Funds may not be released to the defendant or the recipient of a tainted gift in connection with the offence or offences with which the defendant has been charged or is under investigation. This prohibition includes the restraint proceedings (see *Commissioners and Customs and Excise v S* [2005] 1 WLR 1338) and any related judicial review proceedings (see *AP & U Limited v Crown Prosecution Service and Revenue and Customs Prosecutions Office* [2007] EWCA Crim 3128; [2008] 1 Cr App R 39).

**5.21**   Furthermore the prohibition in s 41(4) POCA currently prevents a restrained defendant from making contributions towards the Legal Aid Agency from his living expenses allowance in order to bring a publicly funded action for judicial review of the decision to prosecute him—see *Crown Prosecution Service v Susan Jane Campbell: Michael Joseph Mcinerney v Financial Services Authority: Medicines & Healthcare Products Regulatory Agency v Graeme Trevor Carlton Sub Nom Re M (Restraint Order: Reasonable Living Expenses)* [2009] EWCA Crim 997. The above cases are dealt with in Chapters 2 and 22. As noted in Chapter 2, the amendments to s 41 of POCA made under the Crime and Courts Act 2013 may come into effect in due course and allow the release of restrained property for legal aid contributions to fund legal expenses for a defendant's criminal and restraint proceedings.

**5.22**   Funds paid to a solicitor by a defendant prior to restraint and held by the solicitor thereafter will not be subject to restraint if the solicitor holds the beneficial interest in them thereafter and not the defendant. In the case of *Irwin Mitchell (Appellants) v Revenue & Customs Prosecutions Office (Respondent) & Abdullah Allad (Interested Party)* [2008] EWCA Crim 1741; [2009] 1 WLR 1079 the Court of Appeal held that a POCA restraint order did not apply to an amount of £5,000 paid by the defendant into a solicitor's client account before the order was made, where the firm had already incurred fees up to that amount because the defendant ceased to have a beneficial interest in them. At para 40 of the judgment Toulson LJ stated:

> It was submitted on behalf of RCPO that if Irwin Mitchell's argument is correct, there would be nothing to stop a solicitor from taking a very large payment on account before a restraint order is made and using the money to pay for services provided after notice of the restraint order. That is not so. On Irwin Mitchell's argument if at the time when the firm received notice of the restraint order it had taken £100,000 on account of fees and done £5000 worth of work, the client would have a substantial beneficial interest in the money paid to the solicitors, which at that moment would be potentially available to satisfy a future confiscation order. It would be a breach of the order for the client to incur further expenditure which would enable the solicitors to extinguish his beneficial interest in that money. The solicitors would aid and abet him in that breach if they agreed to continue to run up legal costs and to recoup themselves by recourse to the remaining £95,000 of the money in the account.

**5.23**   The effect of the prohibition currently imposed by s 41(4) is that restrained funds may now only be released to meet legal fees incurred by the defendant in proceedings wholly unrelated to the criminal prosecution. They may also be available potentially to meet legal fees incurred by third parties who can prove that they hold an interest in the restrained funds and that they do not have access to other unrestrained assets for this purpose. In such circumstances the court may be prepared to accede to the release of restrained funds to permit the legal expenses to be paid so long as they are bona fide and justified and this is in accordance with the legislative steer under s 69 of POCA. The court will not, however, sign a 'blank cheque' allowing the defendant or third party to expend whatever sums he wishes on legal expenses. The order will limit such expenditure to expenses actually, reasonably, and properly incurred in the proceedings. As a condition precedent to the release of funds for such purposes the variation order will provide that the following details must be provided to the prosecutor:

(a) the source of the fund to be used to meet the costs;
(b) the general nature of the costs incurred;
(c) the time spent and the grade of fee earners involved; and
(d) the hourly rate charged by each grade of fee earner.

**5.24** The variation order will also make provision for the resolution of any dispute between the parties as to the amount payable by providing that, in the event of the prosecutor considering that the amount claimed has not been actually, reasonably, and properly incurred, the claim shall be subject to detailed assessment by a costs judge with 65 per cent of the amount claimed being paid in the interim. The assessment will be on the indemnity basis in accordance with r 48.8 of the CPR but without the provisions of r 48.8(2) applying.

**5.25** There are now many ways in which civil litigation can be funded including through insurance policies, membership of trade unions and professional associations, conditional fee agreements, and 'no win, no fee' arrangements. It is submitted that a defendant or third party subject to a POCA restraint order who wishes to have funds released to pursue or defend unrelated civil litigation must also establish that funding through these means is not available to him. Ultimately, however, it is a matter for the discretion of the court to decide whether funds caught by a POCA restraint order should be released to meet legal fees incurred in connection with proceedings unrelated to the criminal offence with which the defendant is charged or for which he is under investigation.

**5.26** As above, any applicant seeking to release funds pre-confiscation is required to prove (a) that there is a good arguable case they hold an interest in the restrained property which they seek to be released; and (b) that they hold no other alternative unrestrained funds or have no access to any other funds, including public funding, upon which they can draw. These latter principles are derived from the judgments of the Court of Appeal in *SFO v X* [2005] EWCA Civ 1564, dealt with at para 5.34 below, and Ouseley J in the case of *Serious Organised Crime Agency v Azam and another* [2011] EWHC 1551 (Admin). In *Azam*, Ouseley J examined the release of legal fees to a third party from a property freezing order in civil recovery proceedings under Part 5 POCA. Although the statutory provisions under s 245C differ from restraint proceedings under Part 2 POCA, it is submitted that his reasoning in deciding the application may be similarly applicable. However, it is important to note the stage which proceedings have reached and whether a confiscation order has been made and appeals dismissed. Collins J in *Re D* [2006] EWHC 1519 (Admin) refused the release of funds under the previous legislation to a third party for legal expenses post confiscation and where public funding might be available—see para 5.65 below.

### General living expenses

**5.27** Most restraint orders will make provision for the release of funds (usually around £300 per week) to a defendant not in custody for the purpose of meeting his general living expenses—see Chapter 2. At the time the prosecutor applies for a restraint order, the information he has as to the personal circumstances of the defendant may well be very limited. He may not, for example, know the defendant's marital status, or whether he has any dependant children to care for. It is also unlikely that the prosecutor will know the extent of the defendant's legitimate financial commitments such as mortgage repayments, public utility bills, and the like. If the defendant considers the amount allowed by way of general living expenses is insufficient, he may ask the prosecutor to consent to the order being varied to permit an upward variation and, in default of agreement, can apply to the court for the restraint order to be so varied. The leading authority on the variation of restraint orders to meet general living expenses under the previous legislation, the CJA, is *Re Peters* [1988] 3 WLR 182. In *Re Peters*, the Court of Appeal allowed an application by the defendant for the release of restrained funds to meet school fees for his children, albeit only until the outcome of his criminal trial and not in relation to expenses that might be anticipated to accrue thereafter. It is to be noted that the 'legislative steer' under s 82 CJA is more flexibly worded than that under s 69 of POCA. In delivering his judgment, Lord Donaldson MR observed: 'Mr. Peters as an unconvicted accused person who might be acquitted, was entitled to ask that his son's education should not be interrupted, that he himself should be adequately clothed and that he should be able to pay the costs of his defence.' Similarly, Mann LJ said: 'In my experience a restraint order does not, and properly does not, prevent the meeting of ordinary and reasonable expenditure. That which is or is not ordinary expenditure may vary from time to time.'

**5.28** What constitutes 'ordinary and reasonable expenditure' is an issue to be determined having regard to the circumstances of each individual case. The principles on which the court acts in varying POCA restraint orders are considered under the legislative steer under s 69 of POCA and the case law below. This includes the dicta to the effect that the defendant is not entitled to a 'Rolls Royce lifestyle' (see *Re D and D*, unreported 1992 at para 5.49 below). In *R v AW* [2010] EWCA Crim 3123 the Court of Appeal allowed an appeal against a judge's refusal to make an exception for reasonable living expenses from a POCA restraint order. The appeal was compromised for the most part with the prosecution agreeing that an order could properly be made to take allowance of the needs of a defendant's dependants. The Court made obiter observations at paras 13–16 of the judgment including that the introduction in POCA of the legislative steer in s 69(2)(b) that the restraint powers be exercised '*With a view to securing that there is no diminution in the value of realisable property*' did not overrule the prior case law decided under the previous regimes of the CJA and DTA. The Court concluded at para 16:

> Nevertheless, merely by way of observation and not by way of decision by any means, we would simply observe that our present understanding of cases in the bundle before us, which the parties have not joined issue in argument before us on, cases such as Re: Peters [1988] 3 WLR 182 and Re: P Restraint Order Sale of Assets [2000] 1 WLR 473, is that, although it is in each case a matter of balance and ultimate discretion for the court, there is no need in principle for a defendant to show that he and his family, even his estranged family, even the children of a divorced wife, are reduced to poverty before a proper claim can be made in terms of the rubric of reasonable living expenses. I refer in particular to what Lord Donaldson of Lymington MR said in Re: Peters at 188 to 189 and to what Simon Brown LJ said in Re: P at pages 480 to 481.

**5.29** It is unlikely that the court will sanction any increase in living expenses until the defendant has fully complied with his disclosure obligations under the order because, until such time as the required information has been supplied, it is unlikely that sufficient information will be available on which to reach a decision. A detailed breakdown of the expenditure the proposed variation is intended to fund will also be required so the court might be satisfied that it is genuinely necessary for the purpose of meeting ordinary and reasonable expenditure. A defendant who wishes to have funds released to meet such expenses as mortgage repayments and valuable investments including pensions and life insurance policies etc may not encounter any resistance from the court or prosecutor. Indeed, in most cases, it will be in the prosecutor's interests to ensure that mortgages do not fall into arrears as the properties to which they relate will then become liable to repossession by the lender and therefore valuable equity therein may be reduced or no longer available to meet a confiscation order. This would therefore diminish the value of realisable property available to meet a confiscation order when the purpose of a restraint order is to preserve that value. A defendant who seeks to have funds released to fund an extravagant lifestyle is likely to incur more resistance from the prosecutor and find the court reluctant to accede to his requests. The court will only sanction the release of such funds as are necessary to enable the defendant to meet ordinary and reasonable expenditure but not automatically at a level which enables the same lifestyle he enjoyed prior to the making of the order.

### Companies and other business entities

It is by no means unusual, especially in tax fraud cases, that the defendant has an interest in **5.30** a company or other business entity engaged in legitimate trading. In the absence of special provision, the business bank accounts may be frozen and it would not be able to deal with its assets. This would have the effect of preventing the business trading and cause it to close down. The court will not, however, allow a restraint order to prevent a defendant or his business trading legitimately prior to him being convicted: see s 41(3)(b) POCA and *Re G* [2001] EWHC 606 (Admin). If a restraint order does not provide for such a business to trade legitimately, the defendant would be entitled to apply to the court for the order to be varied appropriately. The court will require safeguards to be incorporated to prevent any such variation being abused. In particular, the court is likely to insist on accounts and other business records being produced to the prosecutor at regular intervals. The usual provisions of the release of business accounts and assets appear in para 19(6) of the draft restraint order at Appendix 9. Where the affairs of a restrained business are unusually complex, or it has a very high turnover, or there is a suggestion that it has been used to facilitate the commission of criminal offences, the appointment of a management receiver may well be appropriate. For further details see Chapter 2 on lifting the corporate veil over companies' assets and Chapter 4 on receivership.

### Unsecured third-party creditors

The Crown Court has no jurisdiction to vary a POCA restraint order to release funds to **5.31** enable an unsecured third-party creditor of the defendant to be paid. This is in marked contrast to the position under a freezing order made in support of a civil claim, where a third-party creditor may intervene and apply for the order to be varied so as to enable, but not compel, the defendant to make payment of the amount owed. The reason for this is that a claimant who obtains a freezing order does not acquire an interest in the frozen assets, nor does he acquire precedence over other creditors of the defendant: see *Iraqi Ministry of Defence v Arcepey Shipping Co SA (The Angel Bell)* [1981] QB 65.

The position is very different where a defendant's assets are frozen pursuant to a restraint **5.32** order. Since its inception, confiscation legislation has made specific provision as to the way in which the court must exercise its discretion to make, vary, and discharge restraint orders— see *Re Peters* [1988] 3 WLR where the court described s 82 of the CJA as a 'legislative steer' as to the manner in which the discretion should be exercised.

The legislative steer in s 69 of POCA is worded very differently to the previous legisla- **5.33** tion and, in *Serious Fraud Office v Lexi Holdings PLC (In Administration)* [2008] EWCA

Crim 1443; [2009] 2 WLR 905, the Court of Appeal held it precluded the release of funds restrained by POCA restraint orders for the purpose of paying third-party creditors of the defendant. The effect of the decision is that unless the creditor can assert a proprietary claim over restrained assets, he will be unable to secure their release for the purpose of satisfying his claim. The *Lexi Holdings* decision is considered in more detail at para 5.36 below.

### Burden of proof

**5.34**   It is for the applicant for a variation to a restraint order to satisfy the court that he should be entitled to the variation he seeks. In *Serious Fraud Office v X* [2005] EWCA Civ 1564, a case concerning the release of restrained funds to meet legal fees under the CJA, Sir Anthony Clarke MR (with whom Brooke and Buxton LJJ agreed) said:

> If a defendant against whom a restraint order has been made wishes to vary the order in order to enable him to use the funds or assets which are the subject of the order, which I will call 'the restrained assets', in order to pay for his defence, it is for him to persuade the court that it would be just for the court to make the variation sought. I would call that the burden of persuasion.

As X had failed to show that he did not have assets overseas which could be used to meet his legal expenses, the Court held that the order should not be varied for this purpose.

## D.  The Principles on which the Court Acts: the 'Legislative Steer'

**5.35**   In determining applications for the release of restrained funds for whatever purpose the court has to achieve a difficult balance between ensuring assets are available to satisfy a confiscation order on the one hand and ensuring that the defendant has sufficient funds available to meet legitimate expenditure on the other. Section 69 of POCA contains mandatory provisions with which the court is required to comply when exercising its powers under the Act, and these are particularly relevant in the context of variation applications. It is therefore convenient to consider them here. Section 69 (as amended by para 34 of Sch 8 to the Serious Crime Act 2007) provides:

> (1) This section applies to—
>> (a) the powers conferred on a court by sections 41 to 59 and sections 62 to 67;
>> (b) the powers of a receiver appointed under section 48 or 50.
> (2) The powers—
>> (a) must be exercised with a view to the value for the time being of realisable property being made available (by the property's realisation) for satisfying any confiscation order that has been or may be made against the defendant.
>> (b) must be exercised, in a case where a confiscation order has not been made, with a view to securing that there is no diminution in the value of realisable property;
>> (c) must be exercised without taking account of any obligation of the defendant or a recipient of a tainted gift if the obligation conflicts with the object of satisfying any confiscation order that has been or may be made against the defendant;
>> (d) may be exercised in respect of a debt owed by the Crown.
> (3) Subsection (2) has effect subject to the following rules—
>> (a) the powers must be exercised with a view to allowing a person other than the defendant or a recipient of a tainted gift to retain or recover the value of any interest held by him;
>> (b) in the case of realisable property held by a recipient of a tainted gift, the powers must be exercised with a view to realising no more than the value for the time being of the gift;

> (c) in a case where a confiscation order has not been made against the defendant, property must not be sold if the court so orders under subsection (4).
>
> (4) If on an application by the defendant, or by the recipient of a tainted gift, the court decides that property cannot be replaced it may order that it must not be sold.
>
> (5) An order under subsection (4) may be revoked or varied.

Similar, but by no means identical, provisions appear in s 82 of the CJA and s 31 of the DTA. **5.36** These provisions under the old legislation were described in *Re Peters* [1988] 3 WLR 182 as amounting to a 'legislative steer' as to the manner in which the court's discretion should be exercised. The legislative steer in s 69 is drafted more restrictively than under the previous legislation and its construction fell to be determined by the Court of Appeal in *Serious Fraud Office v Lexi Holdings PLC (In Administration)* [2008] EWCA Crim 1443; [2009] 2 WLR 905.

A restraint order had been obtained by the SFO against an individual known as 'M' on the **5.37** basis that he was subject to a criminal investigation into an alleged offence of conspiring to defraud the Cheshire Building Society and associated money laundering offences. The administrators of Lexi alleged it had been the victim of substantial frauds committed by M and others and judgment in default was eventually entered in its favour by the Chancery Division of the High Court for some £625,250 plus interest. Lexi thereafter applied to the Central Criminal Court for the restraint order to be varied to permit M to satisfy the judgment. Lexi sought the variation both on the basis that it had a proprietary claim and as a bona fide judgment creditor. The application was opposed by the SFO, but the judge made the variation sought so as to allow payment to be made to Lexi from M's restrained assets. The judge held that the court had a 'reasonably wide discretion' under POCA so as to do justice. He held that there was no significant change in statutory policy or underlying principle from the pre-2002 Act regime and agreed with the reasoning of Davis J in *Re X* [2004] 3 WLR 906. The SFO appealed, with permission, to the Criminal Division of the Court of Appeal.

The Court of Appeal (which included Davis J, as he then was, in its composition) allowed the **5.38** SFO's appeal. The Court noted that there were significant differences between the wording of the legislative steer in s 69 of POCA and under the previous legislation. Keene LJ said:

> It is true that some of the provisions in that section contain the phrase 'with a view to' which as has been said in several of the authorities indicates a degree of flexibility in the court's approach and simply gives a 'legislative steer'. Section 69(2)(c), however, is different. It does not contain that phrase and does appear to be in mandatory terms: the powers 'must be exercised without taking account of any obligation…'. Moreover, the feature of its equivalent provision in the earlier legislation which so influenced Davis J. in *Re X* has changed: it is now clear that this provision does apply in the situation where there is a restraint order but no confiscation order in existence, because the words 'or may be made' have been added. This must be taken to represent a deliberate tightening up of the legislation by Parliament.

He went on:

> On the face of it, section 69(2)(c) does require the courts to ignore any debt owed by the restrained person to an unsecured third party creditor, so that the existence of such a debt would not empower the court to vary a restraint order unless there was no conflict 'with the object of satisfying any confiscation order'. On that last aspect we are wholly unpersuaded by Counsel for Lexi's argument about the meaning to be attached to those words. His contention that the 'object' is that of depriving the offender of the proceeds of crime is unsustainable. That is the object of the confiscation order itself, whereas this provision is referring to the object of 'satisfying' any confiscation order, i.e. providing a sufficient quantum of assets to meet the sum

identified, already or in due course, in a confiscation order. Counsel's interpretation would render the presence of that word 'satisfying' unnecessary and would, in our judgment, distort the natural meaning of section 69(2)(c). If he were right, the provision would enable any third party creditor to obtain a variation of the restraint order and so to be paid and indeed Counsel submits that this is what should happen. The provision would in fact have virtually no effect in practice. In our view, the latter part of paragraph (c) is, as Counsel for the SFO argues, indicating merely that if the court can see that a confiscation order, existing or prospective relates to an amount which the defendant has ample assets to meet, then it may be that a debt to a third party creditor can properly be allowed to be paid from the restrained assets.

**5.39** The Court also noted that Lexi's argument appeared inconsistent with the procedures to be followed at the confiscation stage. Keene LJ said:

> ... of the greatest significance, the payment of third party creditors at the restraint order stage seems to us to be inconsistent with the position which obtains at the confiscation order stage. Section 9 of the 2002 Act provides that the available amount of the defendant's assets when one comes to quantify the amount to be specified in the confiscation order is to be ascertained in the following way:
>
> (1) For the purpose of deciding the recoverable amount, the available amount is the aggregate of—
>   (a) the total of the values (at the time the confiscation order is made) of all the free property then held by the defendant minus the total amount payable in pursuance of obligations which have priority, and
>   (b) the total of the values (at that time) of all tainted gifts.
> (2) An obligation has priority if it is an obligation of the defendant—
>   (a) to pay an amount due in respect of a fine or other order of a court which was imposed or made on conviction of an offence and at any time before the time the confiscation order is made, or
>   (b) to pay a sum which would be included among the preferential debts if the defendant's bankruptcy had commenced on the date of the confiscation order or his winding up had been ordered on that date.
> (3) 'Preferential debts' has the meaning given by section 386 of the Insolvency Act 1986 (c45).
>
> It will be seen that, when the court decided on the amount to be specified in the confiscation order, it has to use the total of the values of the property the defendant holds, less only 'priority' obligations such as fines and preferential debts. The existence of obligations owed to ordinary third party creditors is to be disregarded when a confiscation order is made. It seems to this court that it would have been wholly illogical for the legislature to have decided to allow third party debts to be paid during the period when assets are supposedly being preserved by a restraint order when such debts are to be left out of account at the stage when the confiscation order is made. We can see no reason why Parliament should have decided to allow unsecured creditors to reduce the assets during the restraint phase when such creditors could not reduce the assets at the confiscation stage. If that were the position, it would put a premium on well advised creditors getting in quickly during the restraint phase before their opportunity is lost, and we do not accept that that situation is one which was ever intended.

**5.40** Although the effect of s 69 may appear to be harsh so far as innocent third parties are concerned, the Court emphasised that they were not necessarily left without a remedy. The Court noted that a restraint order is essentially a temporary measure preserving assets pending the making and enforcement of a confiscation order. As Keene LJ said:

> A restraint order is therefore performing a holding operation. Of course, it has to be acknowledged that that operation may, and has been known to, last a considerable time. Nonetheless, the limited duration of restraint orders is a relevant factor when considering its adverse effects

on third party creditors and when seeking to ascertain the intention of Parliament. The restraint order will eventually be discharged and either replaced by some other order such as a confiscation order or not replaced at all.

The Court also noted that the potential harshness of s 69(2)(c) was mitigated to some extent **5.41** by other powers available to the Crown Court once an offender is convicted. As Keene LJ observed:

> ...the court has the power under section 130 of the Sentencing Act to make a compensation order in favour of a person who has suffered loss resulting from the offence or any other offence which is taken into consideration. As Counsel for the SFO points out, such a compensation order takes priority over a confiscation order: see section 13(5) and (6) of the 2002 Act. Not every creditor will be helped by this provision, since he may not qualify under section 130, but some will be assisted. Indeed, if a victim of the defendant's criminal conduct has started or intends to start civil proceedings against him 'in respect of loss, injury or damage sustained in connection with the conduct', then the court, by virtue of section 6(6) need not make a confiscation order at all. The duty to make one where it is determined that the defendant has benefited from his criminal conduct becomes simply a power in those circumstances described in section 6(6). When one bears in mind that the criminal conduct leading to 'loss, injury or damage' may be *general* criminal conduct if the defendant has a criminal lifestyle and not merely the *particular* criminal conduct covered by the offences in question (plus those taken into consideration), it can be appreciated that a considerable number of persons may qualify as 'victims' for this purpose. This too must tend to reduce the number of third parties ultimately affected adversely by the 2002 Act.

Finally, the court noted that the victims themselves may benefit from the defendant's assets **5.42** being held under restraint pending the determination of the criminal proceedings. They too could lose out if the total value of the defendant's assets was reduced by claims brought by other third-party creditors being entertained by the court at the restraint stage.

This important decision makes it clear that the effect of s 69(2)(c) is such that POCA restraint **5.43** orders may not be varied to allow unsecured third-party creditors of the defendant to be paid from restrained funds.

It is submitted that the Court's approach in the *Lexi Holdings* case should be welcomed, **5.44** bringing some much needed certainty into the law relating to the release of assets to pay unsecured third-party creditors of a defendant. Prosecutors can now take a consistent approach to all applications to vary POCA restraint orders for such purposes, and defendants, victims, and creditors alike know where they stand in relation to such matters. This consistency of approach will ensure that no unsecured creditor can 'jump the gun' and gain an advantage over others, including a victim, by reducing the amount of assets available to meet compensation and confiscation orders.

This approach will also overcome the risk of abuse by associates of a defendant making bogus **5.45** third-party claims at his behest with a view to reducing the fund available for confiscation. Although defendants are of course entitled to a presumption of innocence at the pre-conviction stage, one must remain mindful of the fact that, as Lord Donaldson MR observed in *Re O* [1991] 1 All ER 330: 'Whatever may be the position in an individual case, the legislative contemplation is that restraint orders will be made in circumstances in which it is thought that some of those having interests in the property may well be of a dishonest disposition.'

Of course, not all payments to third parties will fall foul of s 69(2)(c). There is, for example, **5.46** no difficulty with a management receiver paying off trade debts with a view to retaining and preserving the value of the business of a company, since the payment of such a debt would preserve an asset greater in value. Similarly, there can be no objection to allowing rent or mortgage payments to be made either on the basis that they constitute a living expense or because they preserve and maintain the defendant's interest in property. In both cases the value of the realisable property is not diminished but preserved because such payments allow a company to continue trading or making profits, or prevent the mortgagee foreclosing, potentially reducing the value of the equity in the property.

**5.47** Section 69 also provides for a stricter legislative steer compared to that contained in the previous legislation in other respects, in particular in relation to the sale of assets that are likely to depreciate in value. There is now specific provision under s 69(2)(b) that the powers of the courts and receivers must be exercised, in a case where a confiscation order has not been made, with a view to securing that there is no diminution in the value of realisable property.

**5.48** Section 69(4) POCA protects the position of unconvicted defendants in possession of property that 'cannot be replaced' in that it gives the court a power to order that it must not be sold in cases where a confiscation order has not yet been made. The reason for this provision is set out in the Guidance Notes to the Act in these terms:

> The provision has regard to the fact that the defendant has not been convicted at this stage and should not, therefore, be obliged to lose irreplaceable assets.

It should be noted that the court is not compelled to order that irreplaceable assets should not be sold: s 69(4) provides that the court 'may' order that the asset is not to be sold, not that it must do so. Unless there are very compelling reasons to the contrary, such as a deliberate intention on the part of the defendant to dispose of property or it is depreciating significantly in value, it is submitted that the proper course would be to order that irreplaceable assets should not be sold prior to the defendant's conviction. It is likely therefore that the racehorses in *Re P (Restraint Order: Sale of Assets)* [2000] 1 WLR 473 described by the defendant as 'well-loved family pets', would not have been sold even if POCA had been in force at the time the decision was made.

**5.49** Another consequence of the legislative steer is that the court will not give effect to a proposed variation which allows a defendant to pursue a luxurious lifestyle or live beyond his legitimate means: see *Re D and D* (Unreported, 28 October 1992). In that case Hutchison J commented: 'As I suggested, perhaps a court which is making a variation will think that he may have to content himself in the exigencies in which he finds himself with something less than a Rolls Royce lifestyle until his guilt or innocence is established.' The defendant may well find that he has to tighten his belt and economise on his normal expenditure while the restraint order remains in force.

**5.50** Further, and quite independently of the legislative steer, the Court of Appeal held in *Serious Fraud Office v X* [2005] EWCA 1564 that the authorities in relation to the variation of freezing orders (formerly Mareva injunctions) are also relevant to applications to vary restraint orders. The Court drew particular attention to the judgment of Robert Goff J in *A v C (No 2)* [1981] QB 962 at p 963:

> In the present case, I have had to consider the position where the defendant has, or may have, other assets from which the relevant payment may be made. I have still to apply the basic principle, i.e. that I can only permit a qualification to the injunction if the defendant satisfies the court that the money is required for a purpose which does not conflict with the policy

underlining the Mareva jurisdiction. I do not consider that in normal circumstances a defendant can discharge that burden of proof simply by saying 'I owe someone some money'. I put to the defendants' counsel, in the course of argument, the example of an English based defendant with two bank accounts, one containing a very substantial sum which was not subject to the Mareva injunction, and the other containing a smaller sum which was. I asked counsel whether it would be sufficient for the defendant simply to say, 'I owe somebody some money, please qualify the injunction to permit payment from the smaller account without giving any consideration to the possibility of payment from the larger account.' Counsel was constrained to accept that that would not be sufficient because it would not satisfy the court that the payment out of the smaller account would not conflict with the principle underlying the Mareva jurisdiction. The whole purpose of selecting the smaller account might be to prevent the money in that account from being available to satisfy a judgment in the pending proceedings. In my judgment, a defendant has to go further than that; precisely what he has to prove will depend, no doubt, upon the circumstances of the particular case. At all events, in the present case, if the defendants making the application have other assets freely available—and I do not know, on the evidence, whether they have or not—it would be open to counsel for the plaintiffs to submit, on the evidence, that it would be wrong for the court to vary the Mareva injunction. All I can say at present is that, on the evidence before the court, the defendants have not discharged the burden of proof which rests upon them.

## E. The Source for Payment of Legal Fees and General Living Expenses

The order will require the defendant to nominate a source for the payment of any sums **5.51** released by way of legal fees and general living expenses. As a general rule, he has an unfettered right to nominate any restrained source he chooses for this purpose. He must, however, bear in mind that if he fails to disclose the nominated asset in his disclosure statement or claims it does not belong to him, the court and prosecutor may have some difficulty in acceding to its release for such purposes.

### Assets not legitimately acquired

It would seem that a defendant is entitled to use assets the Crown alleges have not been **5.52** legitimately acquired as the source for payment of any sums released to him. In *Re D and D* (Unreported, 28 June 1992) large sums of money were found in the homes of the defendants when they were arrested. They were later charged with alleged drug trafficking offences and restraint orders were obtained that specifically identified the seized money as one of the restrained assets. The order further provided that the money was to be paid into an interest-bearing account if it was not required as an exhibit in the criminal proceedings. The prosecutor decided the money was not so required and duly paid it into an interest-bearing account in accordance with the terms of the order. The defendants then applied for the money to be released to pay their legal fees and general living expenses. The prosecutor objected, contending that the money had not been legitimately acquired and should not therefore be released for these purposes.

Hutchison J overruled the prosecutor's objections and granted the defendants' application **5.53** for the release of the seized funds. The learned judge ruled that it would breach the presumption of innocence for a finding to be made prior to the defendants' trial that the funds had not been legitimately acquired. In any event, given that both legitimately and illegitimately acquired assets could be used to satisfy any confiscation order, it was inappropriate, the learned judge ruled, to restrict a defendant to using only assets the prosecutor was satisfied were legitimately acquired to pay his legal fees and general living expenses prior to conviction.

**Assets that are prosecution exhibits**

**5.54**  It happens from time to time that restrained assets (particularly cash taken up at the time of a defendant's arrest) become an exhibit in the criminal proceedings. In *Re C* (Unreported, 1993) the court considered the extent to which exhibited assets could be released to fund general living expenses. The defendant was found in possession of substantial sums of money when he was arrested and which were duly included in a DTA restraint order. In due course the money became an exhibit in the criminal case and, at committal proceedings, the prosecutor gave an undertaking to the examining magistrates to produce the money along with all the other exhibits at trial. Laws J ruled that the court did have a discretion to order the release of the money notwithstanding that it was an exhibit in the criminal case and notwithstanding the prosecutor's undertaking. The judge said:

> In my judgment, the court is not deprived of the jurisdiction to release money for living expenses simply on the Crown's assertion that it intends to put the relevant cash before the jury. Nor do I accept that where money in cash form, or for that matter any other property, has been accorded the formal status of an exhibit, this court lacks all power to release it in whole or in part to permit living expenses within the general context of a restraint order. Any undertaking by the Crown given to the magistrates' court to produce exhibits at trial will surely be released pro tanto by the High Court's superior order. The question, therefore, is one of discretion.

**5.55**  The judge then went on to consider the manner in which the court should exercise its discretion. The crucial test seems to be whether it is essential that the original exhibit must be produced to the criminal court if the prosecutor is to do justice to his case. Laws J said:

> The court will certainly give great weight to what after proper consideration are said to be the evidential needs of the prosecution. There will be situations in which that weight is obviously conclusive. Not only that: in my judgment there can be no question of making allowances for living or other expenses within a restraint order if to do so would curtail or circumscribe the Crown's function of properly presenting, by evidence, the case to the jury.

**5.56**  The judge found in the instant case that there was no reason why the prosecution could not produce photographs of the money and describe in the fullest detail the circumstances in which it was found and still do justice to its case. He therefore ordered the release of some of the money to meet the general living expenses of the defendant's family.

## F. Release of Funds after a Confiscation Order has been Made

**5.57**  The right of defendants and affected third parties to draw on restrained funds for whatever purpose does not continue indefinitely. It is submitted that this right comes to an end on the making of a confiscation order or, if there is an appeal against conviction and/or the confiscation order, when all domestic avenues of appeal have been exhausted. Many of the authorities make reference to the defendant being entitled to have funds released to fund general living expenses because, at the time the restraint order is made, he has not been convicted of any offence and is therefore entitled to a presumption of innocence. In *Re Peters* [1988] 3 WLR 182, by way of example, Lord Donaldson MR justified the release of funds to meet general living expenses on the basis that Mr Peters was an unconvicted accused person who might be acquitted and therefore entitled to ask that his son's education should not be interrupted and that he himself should be adequately clothed. Clearly, this consideration does not apply after the defendant has been convicted and all domestic avenues of appeal have been exhausted.

In *Re P* [1998] EWHC 1049 (Admin) the defendant had been convicted of drug trafficking offences and a confiscation order made. An appeal to the Court of Appeal (Criminal Division) had been dismissed but the defendant sought the release of funds for various purposes in connection with pursuing the matter with the European Court of Human Rights and the Criminal Cases Review Commission, including studying for a law degree to assist him in conducting his legal affairs. Laws J rejected the application saying: 'I am afraid that it is clear beyond any doubt that none of these matters could justify a variation of the restraint order. The fact is that, so far as the domestic criminal litigation is concerned in this case, Mr. P is well past the end of the road.' The Court of Appeal upheld Laws J's order in an unreported judgment of 25 January 2000. **5.58**

In *Re C* [2008] EWHC 3377 (Admin) Sullivan J, sitting in the High Court, took the view that the fact of the defendant's conviction entitled the court to draw in the purse strings somewhat so far as the release of funds to meet general living expenses is concerned. The defendant had been convicted of conspiracy to defraud, the amount involved being in the region of £1.8 million. She was subject to a CJA restraint order which had been varied to allow the release of £420 per week by way of general living expenses and £750 per month to pay rent. Further one-off payments had been authorised in relation to a Spanish property she owned. The defendant made a further application for the restraint order to be varied to allow the release of a lump sum payment of £1,000 to buy Christmas presents for her children before the likely imposition of a custodial sentence on 12 December. Sullivan J refused the application saying: **5.59**

> Whilst I of course have sympathy with the position in which the applicant finds herself, it has to be said it is one of her own making, and if she does not have funds, one is not in the position to buy presents for other people. That sadly will be the position of many people this Christmas. The applicant has funds only as a result of the fraud, so in effect she would be buying Christmas presents for her children out of money which is not by rights hers to give away as presents.
>
> The other factor is this: I have indicated the amount of her weekly allowance and her monthly rental allowance. By my calculation that amounts to a net payment equivalent of more than £30,000 a year. It does seem to me that since that comfortably exceeds the gross national average wage and those on average wages are able by careful saving to give presents to their children, there is no good reason why this particular applicant should not be in a similar position. The presents might not be as generous as she might wish, but there certainly is no reason why someone who is on 'net earnings' in excess of £30,000 a year should not be able to buy presents out of those monies.

In *Stodgell v Stodgell* [2009] EWCA Civ 243; [2009] 2 FLR 244, a case dealing with the competing ancillary relief and restraint proceedings under the Matrimonial Causes Act 1973 and CJA, the Court of Appeal refused permission to appeal to a wife against a decision of Holman J to the effect that all payments by way of general living expenses from the restrained fund should come to an end. The defendant husband had been convicted of tax fraud offences and a CJA confiscation order was made against him for £903,453. The order remained unpaid in its entirety whilst substantial payments were being made from the restrained fund to pay general living expenses for the wife together with legal fees incurred in ancillary relief payments. Holman J in his first instance judgment [2008] EWHC 1925 (Admin); [2009] 2 FLR 218 noted that everyone except the Crown, who were the victims of the offence, appeared to be drawing on the restrained funds and ruled the payments had to stop. The Judge stated at para 81 of his judgment: **5.60**

I have already expressed my great sympathy for the wife and indeed for (the child), but I echo also a comment from Lord Justice Mann in *Re Peters* [1988] 1 QB 871 at 881 that 'There is, in light of section 13(2) [viz the identical legislative steer in an earlier Act] no room for the intrusion of sympathy.' Unless and until the confiscation order has been satisfied in full, both the wife and (the child) will have to live at the standard and by the means provided by the state out of welfare and other benefits and entitlements.

He added:

The result has been that the funds needed to satisfy the confiscation order have been even further reduced by a combination of maintenance payments for the wife and, separately, (the children), and by the provision of her and her husband's legal costs. In my view this has simply got to stop. All members of this family have got to face and bear the reality of what has happened and of the criminal confiscation order and that the available funds cannot continue simply to be drawn as if from a piggy-bank.

5.61   The Court of Appeal refused the wife permission to appeal against Holman J's decision and also the earlier decision in the same case of Charles J, [2008] EWHC 2214 (Admin) to allow the release of some funds. Hughes LJ (with whom Lloyd and Thorpe LJJ agreed) said:

...I am for my part entirely sure that the judge was right. Indeed, as it seems to me he would have been wrong to make any other order. He was right for the reasons which he gave and which I have only imperfectly summarised. They also included the very rapid haemorrhaging of the pot by the incurring of very substantial costs.

The judge also noted that s 69 of POCA represented a 'significant tightening of the rules' in cases to which it applies. At para 14 Hughes LJ stated:

I should just briefly draw attention to the significant tightening of the statutory rules made in the subsequent statute, the Proceeds of Crime Act 2002—see section 69(2)(c) and the recent decision of this court and the Criminal Division in *SFO v Lexi Holdings* [2008] EWCA Crim 1443. But the impact of that on ancillary relief, particularly interim periodical payments, must, as it seems to me, await full argument and will undoubtedly be fact-sensitive.

5.62   It is submitted that the right to draw on the restrained fund, for whatever purpose, comes to an end once domestic avenues of appeal against a confiscation order and the underlying conviction have been exhausted. This is particularly so where, as in *Stodgell v Stodgell*, the lifestyle enjoyed by the defendant and his family has been funded by offences of dishonesty and no recompense has been made to the victim of those offences.

5.63   In consequence, restraint orders made for the first time after all domestic appeals against a confiscation order have been exhausted need not contain a provision for the automatic payment of general living expenses. Further, all parties who are dependent on restrained funds to meet general living expenses would be well advised to make contingency plans as to how such expenses will be met in the event of the defendant being convicted. If they do not, they may well find that in this eventuality restrained funds are no longer available to meet these expenses or, at the very least, the court significantly reduces the amount payable.

5.64   The point has arisen in two other cases. In *Re L* [2008] EWHC 3321 (Admin) the High Court ruled that payments of restrained funds for legal and living expenses should come to an end where confiscation orders remain unsatisfied long after all domestic avenues of appeal have been exhausted. Furthermore in *Re S* [2010] EWHC 917 (Admin) Sir Michael Harrison dismissed an application by the former wife of the defendant under s 77(7) of the CJA to vary a restraint order to provide funds to apply to discharge the restraint order because the case had reached the post-confiscation stage, there was no appeal outstanding, and there was a settled confiscation order. In those circumstances, unless there were very strong reasons permitting the release of funds to a third party, it was obligatory to follow the legislative steer in s 82(2) and s 82(6) of the CJA. The learned judge also distinguished the factual and legal position from that concerned in *RCPO v Briggs Price and O'Reilly* [2007] EWCA Civ 568. It is submitted that the same reasoning would apply with even more force under s 69 of POCA to any third party seeking such a variation of a restraint order made under s 41.

The legislative steer also precludes the release of funds to an affected third party to resist an **5.65** application for the appointment of an enforcement receiver to realise assets in satisfaction of the confiscation order, see *Re D* [2006] EWHC 1519 (Admin). Once the position is reached where the prosecutor is applying for the appointment of an enforcement receiver, the defendant not only stands convicted but all appeals against the order and the underlying conviction will have been dismissed. At this stage, it would seem entirely consistent with the legislative steer and the policy underlying the legislation for affected third parties to rely on public funding or, if they are available, unrestrained assets for the purpose of securing advice and representation in relation to the receivership application or any associated litigation. Similarly, where this point has been reached, neither the defendant nor any affected third party is entitled to continue drawing on the restrained funds for the payment of general living expenses.

# 6

# ENFORCEMENT OF RESTRAINT AND RECEIVERSHIP ORDERS: CONTEMPT OF COURT

## A. Introduction

Restraint and receivership orders can only in most cases serve their intended purpose to the **6.01** extent that there are effective sanctions available to the court to deal with any breach of the order committed by a defendant or third party affected by it. In some cases it may be possible to register the restraint order against title to property at HM Land Registry. In this chapter we examine the powers of the court to deal with breaches of restraint and receivership orders, the procedures that must be followed to bring a person before the court in relation to any such breach, and offer guidance to practitioners who are instructed in such proceedings.

### Ways in which breaches may be committed

Breaches of restraint and receivership orders may be committed in a variety of ways. The **6.02** most common types of breach brought before the court are:

(a) a defendant or affected third party dealing or attempting to deal with restrained assets;
(b) a defendant failing to comply with the terms of a disclosure order either by not disclosing at all or by failing to disclose his interest in a particular asset;
(c) a defendant failing to comply with the terms of a repatriation order;

(d) a defendant or affected third party failing to comply with the terms of a receivership order, for example by refusing to deliver up assets to the receiver or refusing to sign a power of attorney in favour of the receiver; and

(e) obstructing the receiver in the performance of his duties, for example by assaulting, threatening, or abusing him, producing forged documentation intending the receiver to act on it as being genuine, or making untruthful statements to the receiver as to the extent of his realisable property.

### Sanctions available for breaches of restraint and receivership orders

**6.03** POCA and indeed the old legislation do not give the prosecutor or receiver any specific remedy in relation to breaches of restraint and receivership orders. Any breach of the order is to be dealt with as a contempt of court in the same way as a breach of another form of court order. As with other instances of disobedience to an order of the court, the ultimate sanction available to the court is an order committing the contemnor to prison or, if the contemnor is a body corporate, an order sequestrating the company's assets.

### Jurisdiction

**6.04** When POCA transferred the power to make restraint and receivership orders from the High Court to the Crown Court no provisions were made, either in the Act itself or in rules of court, as to how breaches of such orders should be dealt with. This led to some uncertainty as to the correct venue for contempt proceedings and, in particular, to doubts as to whether the Crown Court had any jurisdiction at all to entertain applications by a prosecutor or receiver for the committal of a defendant alleged to be in breach of such orders. These doubts were laid to rest by the Court of Appeal in *R v M* [2008] EWCA Crim 1901. A restraint order had been made against M under POCA and the prosecutor alleged that thereafter he had made a number of transactions in breach of the order. The prosecutor contended that these breaches amounted to a contempt of court and applied to the Crown Court for an order for committal. The Crown Court held that it had jurisdiction to entertain the prosecutor's application and M appealed against that ruling to the Court of Appeal.

**6.05** The Court of Appeal held that s 45(4) of the Supreme Court Act 1981 clearly gave the Crown Court jurisdiction to determine contempt proceedings brought in relation to breaches of POCA restraint and receivership orders. The section provides:

> The Crown Court shall in relation to ... Any contempt of court, the enforcement of its order and all other matters incidental to its jurisdiction have the like powers, rights, privileges and authority as the High Court.

It should be noted that the Supreme Court Act 1981 was renamed as the Senior Courts Act 1981 as from October 2009 by the Constitutional Reform Act 2005; the wording of s 45(4) is, however, unchanged.

**6.06** The defendant contended that the word 'contempt' in s 45(4) could only be construed as meaning criminal contempt because, when the Supreme Court Act was enacted, there were no restraint orders nor any other order which could be made by the Crown Court which carried the contempt sanction in the event of a breach. The Court rejected this argument, Bean J saying:

> We do not accept that the meaning of the statute is that only such types of contempt as might have arisen in the Crown Court in 1981 are covered, nor that only such orders as the Crown Court would have been enforcing as the law stood in 1981 are covered.

The defendant also sought to rely on *DPP v Channel 4 Television Company Limited* [1993] **6.07**
2 All ER 517. In that case a Crown Court judge had made production orders against Channel
4 under terrorism legislation. Channel 4 refused to comply, relying on the journalist's duty
of protecting the confidentiality of his source. The DPP brought proceedings for contempt
in the Divisional Court. In the course of his judgment Woolf LJ said that in 'this type of case'
the contempt proceedings should invariably be heard by a Divisional Court. The Court of
Appeal held that the reference to 'this type of case' by Woolf LJ meant an application against
the media which raised substantial issues of principle. He was not, the Court held, referring
to all contempt applications, nor even all civil contempt applications emanating from the
work of the Crown Court. In a clear statement of principle, Bean J said: 'We can see no reason why the contempt proceedings should not be tried by a single judge in the court whose
restraint order the defendant has said to have breached, just as would occur in the case of a
freezing injunction.'

It is submitted that this statement of principle must be correct as the clear intention of **6.08**
Parliament in enacting POCA was to make the Crown Court a 'one stop shop' dealing with
all matters relating to restraint, receivership, and confiscation orders and their enforcement.
This dispensed with the rather cumbersome procedure under the old legislation whereby
cases passed to and fro between the High Court and the Crown Court, with the former
responsible for making restraint, management, and enforcement receivership orders and
determining applications for certificates of inadequacy, and the latter being responsible for
making the confiscation order and reducing the same when a certificate of inadequacy had
been granted. The Criminal Procedure Rules (CrimPR) have now been amended to incorporate Crown Court contempt hearings.

## B. Procedure in Crown Court Applications

### Contempt of the Crown Court

The procedure that should be followed in Crown Court contempt cases was first codified **6.09**
in 2009; the present rules are set out in the CrimPR. It should be noted that, despite the
Crown Court application being governed by the CrimPR, the contempt constituted by
breach of a restraint order under POCA is a civil, not a criminal, contempt: in *OB v Director
of the Serious Fraud Office* [2012] EWCA Crim 67 the appellant had been made subject to
a restraint order which he breached. He thereafter left the UK. He was subsequently extra-
dited from the United States to face charges relating to his fraudulent behaviour but not in
relation to the contempt. The SFO then successfully applied for his committal to prison for
breaching the order. On appeal it was submitted on his behalf that, since the breach was a
criminal contempt, the appellant enjoyed the protection of the specialty principle and the
court therefore had no jurisdiction, or was wrong, to commit him to prison. The Court of
Appeal dismissed his appeal. Gross LJ held, following a wide-ranging review of the authorities, that the breach was civil, not criminal, and thus the appellant had been correctly dealt
with. Whilst the argument that since proceedings are taken in the Crown Court they are
criminal in nature may appear superficially attractive, the Court ruled that the physical
venue in which the proceedings take place cannot determine whether the contempt is civil
or criminal. Additionally the Court noted that the fact of a custodial punishment is neutral;
what matters is the nature of the contempt (breach of an existing order of the court) and

the purpose of the punishment (coercive as well as punitive); added to the fact that nothing in the predecessor regimes to POCA supported the contention that contempt constituted by a breach of a restraint order was a criminal rather than a civil contempt, the Court had no hesitation in affirming that a breach is civil, not criminal, in nature. It is suggested that this approach is clearly right and, moreover, in line with the general approach of the courts towards the confiscatory regime.

**6.10** In a subsequent ruling in the same case, at [2012] EWCA Crim 901, the court rectified an apparent statutory drafting mistake and affirmed that there was a right of appeal to the Supreme Court from a decision of the Court of Appeal Criminal Division ('CACD') in cases of contempt of court.

### Criminal Procedure Rules

**6.11** Part 62 of the CrimPR deals with applications for the punishment for contempt of court of those who disobey court orders, who indulge in any conduct which the court may deal with as a civil contempt, or who disclose prosecution material without authority.

**6.12** It appears that the rules were first introduced to provide much needed clarity about the procedure to be followed when dealing with the disobedience of a respondent to a restraint order made under POCA.

**6.13** Rule 62.1 confirms that the rules in Part 62 of the CrimPR apply where it is alleged that there has been a failure to comply with a restraint (or other ancillary) order made under r 59 (see r 62.9(1)); such an allegation may be made by any party or other person directly affected, as well as by the court of its own initiative. Rule 62.2 states that the court must not exercise its power to punish for contempt of court in the respondent's absence, unless his behaviour makes it impracticable to proceed otherwise, or he has had at least fourteen days in which to make representations and introduce evidence, or he was present when the hearing was arranged.

**6.14** In terms of procedure, r 62.9 deals with applications to punish for contempt of court. The rules set out what a person who wants the court to exercise its power to punish the respondent must do to initiate the proceedings. The application must be made in writing and served on both the court and the respondent. It must identify the respondent, explain that it is an application for him to be dealt with for contempt of court and give sufficient details about the conduct in question that is alleged to amount to contempt of court. The application must also include a warning notice to the respondent that the court can impose imprisonment or a fine, or both, for contempt of court and that the court may deal with the application even if the respondent does not turn up at the hearing. Applications of this type must be personally served on the person accused of the contempt.

**6.15** If, as invariably will be the case, the applicant wishes to rely on any written evidence (or other hearsay) then r 62.11 mandates that this must be served on the court and the respondent at the same time as the application. Thereafter the respondent has only seven days to file any written evidence in response. Any witness statement served must contain a declaration of truth (r 62.12) and any notice of hearsay must set out the evidence (or attach the document that contains it) and identify the person who made the statement that is hearsay (r 62.13). If there is a desire by either party to cross-examine the maker of any such evidence then an application must be made under r 62.14, in writing, giving the reasons for seeking permission. A person accused of disobeying an order, 'the respondent', must apply within seven days of service of the hearsay to cross-examine the person. When an applicant wants to cross-examine a person, they must apply to do so not more than three days after service of the hearsay by the respondent. The court may decide an application of either type without a hearing, but must not dismiss an application unless the person making it has had an opportunity to make representations at a hearing.

Rule 62.15 sets out the procedure to be followed if any party wants to challenge the credibility or consistency of a person who made a statement which another party wants to introduce as hearsay. Written notice must be served on the court and the party seeking to introduce the material. Again, in the case of the respondent this has to be done within seven days of receiving the material from the applicant; the applicant must comply within three. If such an application is received by either party then they may call the person to give oral evidence instead. No permission is required from the court but a notice of intention must be served on the court and the other party as soon as practicable after the challenge has been made. If the party who receives the challenge is unable, or decides not, to call the person involved then the procedure to be followed is set out in s 5(2) of the Civil Evidence Act 1995:  **6.16**

> (2) Where in civil proceedings hearsay evidence is adduced and the maker of the original statement, or of any statement relied upon to prove another statement, is not called as a witness—
>> (a) evidence which if he had been so called would be admissible for the purpose of attacking or supporting his credibility as a witness is admissible for that purpose in the proceedings; and
>> (b) evidence tending to prove that, whether before or after he made the statement, he made any other statement inconsistent with it is admissible for the purpose of showing that he had contradicted himself.
>
> Provided that evidence may not be given of any matter of which, if he had been called as a witness and had denied that matter in cross-examination, evidence could not have been adduced by the cross-examining party.

Rule 62.17 sets out the court's power to vary any of the time limits under rr 62.11, 62.14, and 62.15, set out above. The court can extend or shorten such a time limit, even after it has expired but, if a party wants an extension of time, they must apply when serving the statement, notice, or application for which the extension of time is needed and they must explain the delay.  **6.17**

The procedure at the hearing itself is governed by r 62.10. The Crown Court has jurisdiction to hold such a hearing in private but must announce, in general terms, the result of such a hearing in public; see r 62.2(3). Rule 62.10 is in the following terms:  **6.18**

> (1) At the hearing of an allegation under rule 62.9, the court must—
>> (a) ensure that the respondent understands (with help, if necessary) what is alleged;
>> (b) explain what the procedure at the hearing will be; and
>> (c) ask whether the respondent admits the conduct in question.
> (2) If the respondent admits the conduct, the court need not receive evidence.
> (3) If the respondent does not admit the conduct, the court will receive—
>> (a) the application or written statement served under rule 62.9;
>> (b) any other evidence of the conduct;
>> (c) any evidence introduced by the respondent; and
>> (d) any representations by the respondent about the conduct.
> (4) If the respondent admits the conduct, or the court finds it proved, the court must—
>> (a) before imposing any punishment for contempt of court, give the respondent an opportunity to make representations relevant to punishment;

  (b) explain, in terms the respondent can understand (with help, if necessary)
   (i) the reasons for its decision, including its findings of fact, and
   (ii) the punishment it imposes, and its effect; and
  (c) in a magistrates' court, arrange for the preparation of a written record of those findings.

**6.19** If the conduct is either admitted or proved, the court will proceed to sentence once the contemnor has been given an opportunity to make representations relevant to his punishment. By reason of s 45 of the Senior Courts Act 1981, the Crown Court has an inherent power to imprison (for a maximum of two years), or fine (to an unlimited amount), or both, a respondent for such behaviour. This power is constrained for those under the age of twenty-one, and in all cases subject to the early release provisions, as discussed below. If the court suspends the sentence, and the respondent is not at that stage present, then he must be served with a notice to that effect by the applicant (see r 62.3).

**6.20** Rule 62.4 sets out the procedure to be followed when the respondent wants to apply to discharge the order for imprisonment for contempt of court. A written application must be made, explaining why it would be appropriate for the order to be discharged and the result of any appeal that there may have been. The respondent must serve the application on the court and on the applicant who applied for the respondent's punishment. If the respondent wants one, they can ask for a hearing.

### Sentence

**6.21** If the defendant admits the contempt, or the court finds the case proved, the court must then proceed to sentence. The contemnor will of course have the right to address the court in mitigation before sentence is imposed. Any such mitigation should include an unequivocal apology, an undertaking not to commit any further breaches of the order and, if possible, proposals for remedying the contempt. The maximum sentence that may be imposed for contempt of court is two years' imprisonment: see s 14(1) of the Contempt of Court Act 1981. Consecutive sentences may be imposed for separate breaches, so long as the total sentence imposed on any one occasion does not exceed the maximum. Under s 89 of the Powers of Criminal Courts (Sentencing) Act 2000, no respondent who is under twenty-one may be imprisoned for contempt of court. Under s 108 of that Act, a respondent who is at least eighteen but under twenty-one may be detained if the court is of the opinion that no other method of dealing with him or her is appropriate. Under s 14(2A) of the Contempt of Court Act 1981, a respondent who is under seventeen may not be ordered to attend an attendance centre. Sentences of imprisonment for contempt of court are subject to the early release provisions set out in s 258 of the Criminal Justice Act 2003; a respondent who is imprisoned for contempt of court must be released unconditionally after serving half the term.

**6.22** The court will invariably treat breaches of restraint and receivership orders very seriously, especially where the dissipation of assets is involved. In *R v Kenny* 2013 EWCA Crim 1 the Court of Appeal also held that a breach of a restraint order could of itself constitute the offence of perverting the course of justice. Unless the contemnor has taken prompt steps to recover assets so dissipated, the almost inevitable consequence will be an immediate sentence of imprisonment. Indeed, in relation to freezing orders, there is clear authority to the effect that any dissipation of assets should be visited by immediate imprisonment. In *Popishal v Phillips*, The Times, 20 January 1988, the Court of Appeal said that it was 'of the highest importance to the public as well as to the parties that Mareva injunctions issued to prevent the dissipation of assets should be obeyed and not disregarded and certainly not flouted'. The Court held that where property had been sold in breach of such an order, an immediate custodial sentence was appropriate, irrespective of whether it was necessary to ensure compliance with the injunction.

A similar approach was adopted by Stanley Burnton J, as he then was, in *R v Selby* (Unreported, **6.23** QBD (Admin) 16 June 2006) where a six-month sentence of imprisonment was imposed for dissipating assets in breach of a CJA restraint order. In passing sentence the learned judge said:

> Any order of this court is regarded by the court as a matter of the greatest importance. It is necessary that they be complied with and, if not complied with, that punishment follows, otherwise the orders become pointless; compliance with the law would fall into disrepute. The courts necessarily regard a breach of any court order, particularly an order of the kind involved in this case, as a serious matter.

Keith J adopted the same approach in *CPS v Ellis* [2009] EWHC 876 (Admin) where the **6.24** defendant had failed to disclose the existence of bank accounts and used funds in those accounts in breach of the restraint order. He imposed a sentence of nine months' imprisonment, saying to the defendant: 'These were serious contempts of court. You deliberately set out to do what you could to conceal your assets in order to avoid having to comply with the confiscation order and you disposed of at least some of your assets.' He added: 'I have to say that your breaches are too serious for a sentence of imprisonment of immediate effect to be avoided.'

If the contemnor is already serving a sentence of imprisonment at the time of being sen- **6.25** tenced for contempt of court, the contempt sentence will be consecutive to the earlier sentence unless the court otherwise directs. In practice it is highly unlikely that the court would so direct.

As noted above, the contemnor has the right under s 258 of the Criminal Justice Act **6.26** 2003 to be released from custody after serving one half of the term for which he was committed.

### Suspended committals

The court has power to direct that the execution of an order for committal be suspended **6.27** for such period or on such terms or conditions as it may specify. In the context of restraint orders, this provision gives the court jurisdiction to suspend the committal provided the defendant remedies his breach by, for example, serving his disclosure statement or repatriating assets within a specified period of time. The court may also suspend the committal on terms that the defendant henceforth comply with the terms of the order, notwithstanding that the effect of this is to suspend the committal indefinitely: see *Griffin v Griffin* The Times, 28 April 2000. If the committal is suspended and the contemnor thereafter commits another breach of the restraint order, the court can activate the suspended committal and impose another sentence for the new contempt to be served consecutively, provided the overall limit of two years imposed by s 14 of the Contempt of Court Act 1981 is not exceeded: see *Villiers v Villiers* [1994] 2 All ER 149.

In *Re M* [2009] EWHC 2163 (Admin) Ockelton DHCJ found that the application revealed **6.28**

> an attitude to the order which is entirely unsatisfactory, and is indeed contemptuous. It beggars belief that a person under a restraint order, as Mr M was, was prepared to act as a sort of

informal banker to his family and friends, essentially lending them money, normally a credit card company's money, to be repaid in due course...it is difficult to see that Mr M has, in respect of [dealing with bank accounts], or perhaps in general, done anything at all differently as the result of the restraint order. He appears to have completely ignored it so far as his financial dealings were concerned.

He nevertheless suspended the term of six months' imprisonment on the basis, amongst other mitigation, that the breaches had been admitted. The terms of that suspension included a requirement that M had to provide financial disclosure to the applicant on an ongoing basis.

### Effect of being in contempt

**6.29** The potential consequences of being in contempt extend well beyond being sentenced to a term of imprisonment. The court has a discretion to refuse to hear a person who is in contempt until such time as the contempt has been purged: see *Hadkinson v Hadkinson* [1952] 2 All ER 567 and *X Ltd v Morgan Grampian* [1990] 2 All ER 1. The discretion may only be exercised on an application made by the contemnor and may not be used to prevent him defending an application brought by the prosecutor in the proceedings. This can be a powerful weapon against a defendant who flagrantly disobeys a restraint or receivership order as it can preclude him seeking a variation while he remains in contempt.

### Sentencing authorities

**6.30** In *R v Roddy* [2010] EWCA Crim 671 the Court of Appeal considered the relationship between matters for which a defendant was sentenced following a criminal trial and those which arose in the course of the trial. The defendant was the subject of a restraint order which specifically referred to a property in Manchester. Six days after being served with the order he sold the property, cashed at a pawn brokers the sale cheque he was given, and then took the money with him to the Republic of Ireland. Some months later he returned to the UK, under a false name, but was arrested and stood trial for various drugs offences. During the course of his evidence he admitted the sale, in breach of the order, but claimed that he had done so in order to pay off debts owed by his girlfriend to drug dealers. That account was rejected by the jury. The Recorder sentenced him to seven years' imprisonment on the criminal matters with a further twenty months for his admitted contempt by selling the property. The Court of Appeal (Nicol J) ruled that

> ...this was a flagrant contempt of court...a deterrent sentence was needed to mark the fact that the court will not tolerate a frustration of the administration of justice...[but it] was quite separate from the drugs charges. The Recorder was perfectly entitled to impose this sentence consecutively to the imprisonment for those offences...we do not think that a consecutive sentence offends the principle of totality.

However, the Court also noted that it would, were the allegations in a criminal trial to be the same as those underpinning an allegation of contempt, 'be wrong in principle to hold the same matters against [him] when it came to sentencing him for the contempt of court'.

**6.31** Having referred to *R v Adewunmi* [2008] EWCA Crim 71 the Court noted additionally that 'even when a breach of a restraining order has been deliberate, cunning, sophisticated and sustained, twenty months was too great a punishment on an admission of guilt' and reduced the sentence to one of fifteen months.

Nicol J was a member of the Court that considered the sentence of *R v Baird* [2011] EWCA **6.32**
Crim 459. Mr Baird was subject to a restraint order which, as is usual, required him to
provide to the prosecutor various financial details including the names and addresses of all
the persons holding such assets, including financial institutions or banks, and all accounts
held by him, or in which he had an interest. It was accepted that he did not comply with
those provisions and he was sentenced to a total of eighteen months for that breach. In
his appeal he relied on dicta in *Adewunmi* and *Roddy* in support of his argument that the
sentence was excessive. The Court declined to alter the sentence, finding that the cases
were of no assistance since those sentences were punitive and deterrent, rather than coercive. That passed on Baird fell into the latter category and, as such, the defendant could
purge his contempt at any stage simply by cooperating with the prosecutor and making
full disclosure.

*R v Samra* [2011] EWCA Crim 2799 involved twenty-six separate breaches of a restraint **6.33**
order involving the use of bank accounts and the failure to disclose substantial overseas
assets; one related to a (false) witness statement disclosing assets of £5 in India when the real
figure was in excess of £700,000. The Court declined to grant leave to appeal against the
sentence of twelve months with the following observations:

> We take the view that once a suspect is served with an order restraining him from dealing
> with his assets, if he quite deliberately seeks to avoid the consequences of that order then
> a sentence of imprisonment—and immediate imprisonment—must follow. We have con-
> sidered whether the sentence of 12 months was too long. Having considered all the circum-
> stances here, and including the number of breaches that there were and the amounts of money
> involved, we are satisfied that 12 months was the appropriate figure. As a matter of principle,
> any sentence for contempt in these circumstances must be made consecutive to the sentence
> for the indictable offences.

In *R v Shepard (Terence)* [2012] EWCA Crim 1716 the appellant had utilised two bank **6.34**
accounts in breach of a restraint order. The prosecution accepted that his use of the two
accounts reflected, at least in part, the profits of (legitimate) ticket sales but the Court of
Appeal held, when dismissing his appeal against a sentence of twelve months' imprisonment, that 'these were serious contempts of their kind, involving as they did the use of two
different bank accounts at different times after Shepherd had been arrested for the offences
of fraudulent trading. His use of the two accounts demonstrated a complete disregard for
orders of the court.'

The appellant in *R v Hussain (Abbas)* [2012] EWCA Crim 1714 took the somewhat unusual **6.35**
course of trying to persuade the Crown Court, and the Court of Appeal, that his action
of cashing a cheque should be treated as a contempt of court in that it was done in breach
of a restraint order—rather than being placed on an indictment as an allegation of an act
tending and intended to pervert the course of justice. In that course he was unsuccessful.
The reasoning was that, that if he should be treated as a civil contemnor, then any attempt
to criminally prosecute him would inevitably founder on an abuse of process application.
The trial judge took the view that there were aggravating features in that whilst the cheque
was cashed in breach of the restraint order, it was in itself obtained by fraud. Following that
ruling the defendant pleaded guilty. It does not appear that the case of *Re S* [1999] EWHC
466 (Admin) was cited to the Court; had it been then, it is suggested, the Court would have
referred to it with approval.

# C. The Hearing

### Preliminary matters

**6.36**  In Crown Court cases, the hearing will take place before a Crown Court judge sitting in open court. Advocates should therefore be robed.

**6.37**  If the prosecutor brings a contempt application during the course of the criminal trial or shortly before it is due to commence, the defendant may be able to argue with some force that it would be oppressive to require him to respond to it at that time when all his resources need to be directed towards defending the criminal proceedings. This is particularly so if it can be shown that the prosecutor has been aware of the facts giving rise to the committal application, but has been guilty of an unreasonable delay in bringing the proceedings. In such circumstances, the court would be entitled to strike out the committal application as an abuse of process or adjourn it pending the determination of the criminal proceedings. The court is, however, unlikely to strike out or adjourn a committal application where the alleged breach occurs shortly before or during the criminal trial.

### The burden and standard of proof

**6.38**  The burden is on the person bringing the contempt proceedings (in this context, the prosecutor or receiver) to prove his case. The respondent to the application cannot be compelled to adduce evidence in his defence, although in most cases he would be well advised to file an affidavit or a statement verified by a statement of truth responding to the allegations of contempt made against him. The standard of proof required is proof beyond reasonable doubt. This is an exception to the usual rule that the standard of proof in civil proceedings is proof on a balance of probabilities and is justified on the basis that in contempt proceedings the liberty of the subject is at stake. High Court PD 81.9 specifically states as follows:

> In all cases the Convention rights of those involved should particularly be borne in mind. It should be noted that the standard of proof, having regard to the possibility that a person may be sent to prison, is that the allegation be proved beyond reasonable doubt.

**6.39**  In *R (on the application of Minshall) v City of Westminster Magistrates' Court & HM Revenue and Customs* [2007] EWHC 214 (Admin) the High Court had to consider whether a defendant would be guilty of contempt of court if he genuinely believed the restraint order had been discharged. In the event, the court did not need to make a definitive ruling because it rejected the evidence of the defendant in this regard but, in a helpful review of the cases, Langstaff J said:

> As to this, I was invited to give consideration to the case of *Intelli v Squatriti and others* [1993] 1 QB 83, a decision of the Court of Appeal. In that case Farquharson LJ said:
>
> 'The question for us is whether the evidence now available establishes beyond a reasonable doubt that they did intend to act in contempt of the court's authority.'
>
> He referred to finding it impossible on the evidence to say that he was convinced that the appellants had the necessary intention. Taylor LJ applied the same test, that the judge could not have been sure that the appellant had knowingly breached the court order. The Vice-Chancellor, Sir Donald Nicols, said in the last sentence of the report, 'that the conclusion had to be that a knowing breach of the order by the appellants had not been proved'. All three members of the court, therefore, approached the question whether contempt was made out by asking whether or not the respondent, the appellants in that case, had known that what they did was in breach of the order.

However, shortly after that decision, the House of Lords had cause to consider the question of knowledge in the case of *Director General of Fair Trading v Pioneer Concrete (UK) Ltd and Another* [1995] 1 AC 456. There, following extensive citation of authority, their Lordships adopted the earlier view, which had been expressed by Warrington J in the case of *Stancomb v Trowbridge Urban District Council* [1910] 2 Ch 190 at 194. Lord Nolan said that in his judgment the decision in the *Stancomb* case was good law.

It is plain that their Lordships considered that it was not necessary for an alleged contemnor to know that what he did was in breach of the relevant order. The decision in *Irtelli* was one in which it appears from the note of argument that no argument was addressed to the requisite mental intention of the respondent. No case was cited which related to it. Although *Irtelli* was itself not cited to their Lordships in *Pioneer Concrete*, other relevant authority was. It is plain that what was in issue in *Pioneer* was the mental element. I have no hesitation in concluding that I am bound by the view expressed in the House of Lords, which I consider to be ratio.

I am fortified in this conclusion by considering the cases of *Bird and Hadkinson* 4 March 1999 a decision of Neuberger J, as he then was, and *Adam Phones Limited v Goldsmidt and others* [1999] 4 All ER 486, a decision of Jacob J, as he then was, in each of which the court followed the *Pioneer Concrete* approach and not that indicated by *Irtelli*.

Langstaff J then addressed directly the issue of whether a defendant who believed the restraint **6.40** order had been discharged would be in breach. He said:

It seems to me that this is an interesting question of law which, as will be plain from my conclusions of fact, I do not need to decide in the present case. I do not, therefore, do so. However, should it be relevant I consider that in any case in which a defendant knows of the existence of an order, but subsequently forms a view that it may very well have been discharged, without making any adequate inquiry (as it were, a wilful shutting of eyes) he will be bound by the order. This seems to me to represent the policy and principle underlying the cases of *Pioneer Concrete* and those others, to which I have referred.

I leave for further consideration the question whether if he knew of the existence of the order, but then believed genuinely that the order had been discharged, he should be treated as guilty of contempt rather than the matter simply going to a question of penalty. There is much force in the observations which Jacob J made in saying that had it been a matter open to him in that particular case, that of *Adam v Goldsmidt*, he might have inclined to finding that there had been no contempt.

It is submitted that this approach is correct. If the defendant genuinely believes on reason- **6.41** able grounds (for example, because his solicitor told him so) that the restraint order had been discharged, it would be wrong to find him guilty of contempt. If, however, he fails to make due enquiry, or wilfully shuts his eyes to the question of whether the order has been discharged or not, he can properly be found guilty of contempt and his belief as to the position of the restraint order would only amount, if at all, to mitigation.

In *Togher v Customs and Excise Commissioners* [2001] EWCA Civ 474 the Court of Appeal **6.42** emphasised the importance of those facing contempt proceedings being legally represented whenever imprisonment was contemplated as the appropriate sanction for the breach. Robert Walker LJ said at para 37:

I consider next the criticisms which Mr. Togher makes of the procedure followed at the committal hearing, including the absence of any legal representation for Mr. Togher in a matter in which his personal liberty was at stake. Counsel for the Commissioners has pointed out, correctly, that the restraint order gave Mr. Togher the opportunity of applying for a variation of the restraints on his bank account so as to enable him to pay for legal representation but that he did not make such an application, nor did he ask for an order for cross-examination of the Customs and Excise witnesses on their affidavits.

These observations are no doubt correct but they seem to me rather to miss the point. Legal representation is important for defendants because lawyers understand the need for applications of that sort and defendants who are not lawyers may not do so, even assuming them to be hardened criminals. It is easy for anyone who is not a lawyer, especially if he is under stress, to overlook the need to interrupt Counsel (which is what Mr. Togher would have had to do) in order to raise this sort of preliminary point. This court has said that in matters of civil contempt, as soon as it appears that there is an appreciable risk of imprisonment, an unrepresented defendant should be asked by the judge whether he or she wishes to be represented: see *Newman v Modern Bookbinders* [2000] 2 All ER 814, 822. It does not appear that Mr. Togher was asked that question at the hearing on 15th November 1995.

## D. Procedure on High Court Applications

### Contempt of the High Court

**6.43**  The parties follow the provisions of the CPR in relation to contempt proceedings in the High Court. The rules in relation to High Court proceedings are to be found in Part 81 of the CPR (at <http://www.justice.gov.uk/courts/procedure-rules/civil/rules/part-81-applications-and-proceedings-in-relation-to-contempt-of-court>) and in the Practice Direction accompanying the rules (at <http://www.justice.gov.uk/courts/procedure-rules/civil/rules/practice-direction-81-applications-and-proceedings-in-relation-to-contempt-of-court>).

**6.44**  The High Court's power to punish breaches of its orders by committal and sequestration of assets is comprehensively set out in CPR 81. Rules 81.4 and 81.20 provide as follows:

81.4
(1) If a person—
    (a) required by a judgment or order to do an act does not do it within the time fixed by the judgment or order; or
    (b) disobeys a judgment or order not to do an act,
    then, subject to the Debtors Acts 1869 and 1878 and to the provisions of these Rules, the judgment or order may be enforced by an order for committal.
(2) If the time fixed by the judgment or order for doing an act has been varied by a subsequent order or agreement of the parties under rule 2.11, then references in paragraph (1)(a) to the time fixed are references to the time fixed by that subsequent order or agreement.
(3) If the person referred to in paragraph (1) is a company or other corporation, the committal order may be made against any director or other officer of that company or corporation.
(4) So far as applicable, and with the necessary modifications, this Section applies to undertakings given by a party as it applies to judgments or orders.

81.20
(1) If—
    (a) a person required by a judgment or order to do an act does not do it within the time fixed by the judgment or order; or
    (b) a person disobeys a judgment or order not to do an act,
    then, subject to the provisions of these Rules and if the court permits, the judgment or order may be enforced by a writ of sequestration against the property of that person.
(2) If the time fixed by the judgment or order for doing an act has been varied by a subsequent order or agreement of the parties under rule 2.11, references in paragraph (1)(a) to the time fixed are references to the time fixed by that subsequent order or agreement.

(3) If the person referred to in paragraph (1) is a company or other corporation, the writ of sequestration may in addition be issued against the property of any director or other officer of that company or corporation.

(4) So far as applicable, and with the necessary modifications, this Section applies to undertakings given by a party as it applies to judgments or orders.

### Strict compliance required

At the outset, it must be emphasised that the court has held on many occasions that, as the liberty of the subject is at stake, strict compliance with all the required procedures is essential: see, for example, *Gagnon v McDonald*, The Times, 14 November 1984. Any failure by the prosecutor to comply with these procedures may result in the application being dismissed, although a court may waive any procedural defect in the commencement or conduct of a committal application if it is satisfied the defendant has suffered no injustice as a result: see PD 81.16.2.   **6.45**

### Contents of the application notice

The High Court application notice must state that the application is made in the proceedings in question and set out its title and reference number, which must correspond with the title and reference number of those proceedings (PD 81.13.1). In accordance with CPR 81.10(3)(a) the application notice must:   **6.46**

> set out in full the grounds on which the committal application is made and must identify, separately and numerically, each alleged act of contempt including, if known, the date of each of the alleged acts.

Once the application notice has been issued, it may only be amended with the court's permission: see PD 81.13.2(2). The test as to whether an application notice provides sufficient detail as to the alleged acts of contempt complained of is set out in the judgment of Nicholls LJ in *Harmsworth v Harmsworth* [1988] 1 FLR 349:   **6.47**

> The test is, does the notice give the person alleged to be in contempt enough information to enable him to meet the charge? In satisfying this test it is clear that in a suitable case if lengthy particulars are needed, they may be included in a schedule or other addendum either at the foot of the notice so as to form part of the notice rather than being set out in the body of the notice itself. The rules require that the notice itself must contain certain information. The information is required to be available to the respondent to the application from within the four corners of the notice itself. From the notice itself the person alleged to be in contempt should know with sufficient particularity what are the breaches alleged.

The application notice or letter must also contain a prominent notice setting out the possible consequences of the court making a committal order and the respondent not attending the hearing: see PD 81.13.2(4). Annex 3 to the Practice Direction incorporates a form of notice that might be used. It reads as follows:   **6.48**

IMPORTANT NOTICE

The Court has power to send you to prison, to fine you or seize your assets if it finds that any of the allegations made against you are true and amount to a contempt of court. You must attend court on the date shown on the front of this form. It is in your own interest to do so. You should bring with you any witnesses and documents which you think will help you put your side of the case. If you consider the allegations are not true you must tell the court why. If it is established that they are true, you must tell the court of any good reason why they do not amount to a contempt of court, or, if they do, why you should not be punished. If you need advice, you should show this document at once to your solicitor or go to a Citizens' Advice Bureau or similar organisation.

It is submitted that this form of words should be used in every case so the respondent is left under no illusions as to the gravity of the proceedings and what he should do in response to them.

### The evidence in support of the application

**6.49** The High Court application notice must be accompanied by an affidavit setting out the evidence relied on in support of each and every allegation of contempt made against the defendant: see CPR 81.10(3)(a). The affidavit should exhibit all documentation on which the applicant wishes to rely. This is the only instance in restraint and confiscation proceedings where a witness statement verified by a statement of truth will not suffice: the evidence must be in affidavit form.

### Proving service of the order

**6.50** The first issue the affidavit must address is the service of the restraint or receivership order on the person who is alleged to be in breach of it. In all but the most exceptional circumstances, the prosecutor must be in a position to prove that the order was personally served on the person who is said to have disobeyed it. It is obviously only right and proper that a person should not face the loss of his liberty for disobeying an order unless it can be proved that he had knowledge of the terms of that order at the time he disobeyed it.

**6.51** Further, the prosecutor must prove that the order was endorsed with a penal notice in accordance with CPR 81.9 which provides that:

(1) Subject to paragraph (2), a judgment or order to do or not do an act may not be enforced under rule 81.4 unless there is prominently displayed, on the front of the copy of the judgment or order served in accordance with this Section, a warning to the person required to do or not do the act in question that disobedience to the order would be a contempt of court punishable by imprisonment, a fine or sequestration of assets.

Paragraph 2 of the Rule refers to 'undertakings' to do, or not to do, such an act and is thus unlikely ever to be relevant in the context of breaches of a restraint order.

**6.52** The penal notice appears at the top of the draft restraint and receivership orders at Appendices 9 and 10 respectively. In rare circumstances, the court may dispense with proof of personal service of the order. The court is given this discretion under CPR 81.8(1), which provides that in respect of an order requiring the defendant to abstain from doing any act, the order may be enforced by committal notwithstanding that service has not been effected in the prescribed manner where the party sought to be committed has notice of the order either by:

(a) being present when the order was made; or
(b) being notified of its terms, whether by telephone, email, or otherwise.

**6.53** It should be noted that this provision can only be used where the contemnor is alleged to be in breach of the prohibitory terms of a restraint order, ie the provisions restraining him from dealing with assets. It used to be thought that where it was sought to commit the defendant for breach of a requirement in the order to perform a positive act (eg to make a disclosure statement or repatriate assets) only personal service would suffice. CPR 81.8(2), however, permits the court to dispense with personal service even in those circumstances if it is thought 'just to do so' or, in the alternative, that an order was made permitting service by an alternative method. The affidavit should provide full details of the circumstances in which the order was served on the alleged contemnor and, it is submitted, should exhibit a copy of the order to enable the court to be satisfied it contains all the required information.

### Proving the breach

The prosecutor's affidavit should set out clearly and fully the facts relied on to prove each **6.54** breach alleged against the defendant. The affidavit should also exhibit all documentation relied on by the prosecutor to establish the breach. As the liberty of the subject is in issue, the court will require the best evidence possible to establish the breach and, it is submitted, hearsay evidence should be avoided, particularly when direct evidence is readily available.

### Serving the application

Once the proper officer of the court has issued the application and given it a return date it **6.55** must, together with the supporting evidence, be served personally on the alleged contemnor unless the court otherwise directs. If it proves impossible to effect personal service because, for example, the defendant is deliberately evading service, then an application should be made to the court for an order allowing service by an alternative method; see CPR 81.10(5). Once service has been effected, the prosecutor should cause an affidavit of service to be sworn to enable the court to proceed in the alleged contemnor's absence should he fail to attend. If the application relates to a writ of sequestration to enforce an order it must not, somewhat quixotically, be executed on a Sunday, Good Friday, or Christmas Day. This indulgence does not extend to other applications.

### The defendant's response

Any written evidence by the defendant in response to the contempt application must also be **6.56** given on affidavit: see PD 81.14.1. Even if the defendant has not filed any such evidence, he may still give oral evidence at the hearing if he chooses, but if he does so he will be liable to cross-examination: see CPR 81.28(2). Further, he may with the permission of the court, call witnesses to give oral evidence regardless of whether they have sworn an affidavit. The court does, however, have power to direct the alleged contemnor to swear an affidavit or produce statements from witnesses of fact upon whom he wishes to rely and serve them in sufficient time to enable the prosecutor to consider them and file any necessary evidence in reply. The alleged contemnor retains the right not to have such evidence adduced at the hearing, although the wise course is normally to file evidence setting out his case in detail and, if appropriate to make a full and frank admission of the contempt: see *Re B (A Minor) (Contempt Evidence)*, The Times, 11 November 1995. Further, the judge is entitled to make appropriate inferences from the alleged contemnor's failure to offer any explanation to the court as to his conduct.

## E. The Hearing

### Preliminary matters

In High Court cases, the hearing will also be heard in public but the court is specifically **6.57** given jurisdiction under CPR 39 to hear the application in private if any of the following circumstances pertain:

(a) publicity would defeat the object of the hearing;
(b) it involves matters relating to national security;

(c) it involves confidential information (including information relating to personal financial matters) and publicity would damage that confidentiality;

(d) a private hearing is necessary to protect the interests of any child or protected party;

(e) it is a hearing of an application made without notice and it would be unjust to any respondent for there to be a public hearing;

(f) it involves uncontentious matters arising in the administration of trusts or in the administration of a deceased person's estate; or

(g) the court considers this to be necessary, in the interests of justice.

**6.58** The court may also order that the identity of any party or witness must not be disclosed if it considers non-disclosure necessary in order to protect the interests of that party or witness. It is submitted that the Crown Court has similar jurisdiction regarding both the hearing and the ability to prevent identification. A defendant in, for example, a high-profile case that has attracted a lot of publicity may wish to ask the court to hear the application in private if there is a risk that hearing it in public could prejudice his defence in the criminal proceedings. If the court does decide to hear the application in private and decides to make a committal order it must, under CPR 81.28(5), state in public:

(a) the name of the respondent;

(b) in general terms the nature of the contempt of court in respect of which the committal order is being made; and

(c) the length of the period of the committal order.

**6.59** By PD 15.4, the court may, on the hearing date:

(1) give case management directions with a view to a hearing of the committal application on a future date; or

(2) if the committal application is ready to be heard, proceed to hear it.

**6.60** The court must always have regard to the need for the alleged contemnor to have details of the alleged acts of contempt and the opportunity to respond to the application: see PD 15.5. Further, by PD 15.6, the court must also have regard to the need for the respondent to be:

(1) allowed a reasonable time for responding to the committal application including, if necessary, preparing a defence;

(2) made aware of the availability of assistance from the Community Legal Service and how to contact the Service;

(3) given the opportunity, if unrepresented, to obtain legal advice; and

(4) if unable to understand English, allowed to make arrangements, seeking the assistance of the court if necessary, for an interpreter to attend the hearing.

**6.61** Once a committal application has been issued, it may only be discontinued with the permission of the court (PD 81.16.3). Thus the prosecutor is not entitled to withdraw a committal application, even if the defendant has remedied the breach complained of by, for example, filing a disclosure statement or repatriating assets. The proper course is for the prosecutor to write to the court, enclosing a letter of agreement from the defendant, seeking permission to discontinue the application. If the court agrees, the application can be discontinued without the necessity for the parties to attend court and the hearing date can be vacated.

### Procedure at the hearing

**6.62** The court clerk or associate will open proceedings by identifying the defendant, reciting each of the allegations of contempt contained in the application to him, and asking whether he admits or denies them. The prosecutor, upon whom the burden of proving the contempt rests, will then open his case, read his affidavits, and call any witnesses required to attend for cross-examination. The defendant will then have the opportunity of addressing the court, reading his affidavits, and calling evidence. By CPR 81.28(2), if the person sought to be committed expresses a wish to give oral evidence on his own behalf, he shall be entitled to do so. The parties will then have the right to make closing addresses before the judge considers his decision. If the court concludes that the prosecutor has not proved his case beyond reasonable doubt, the committal application will be dismissed. If, however, the court finds the case has been proved to the criminal standard, it will proceed to consider the appropriate sentence.

### Purging contempt

A defendant imprisoned for contempt of court has the right under CPR 81.31 to go back to court at any time and seek his discharge on the ground that he has purged, or wishes to purge, his contempt. In order to convince a judge that it is appropriate to release him, the defendant will have to show that he is now suitably contrite and henceforth will comply with the terms of the order. The chances of a defendant being discharged will be enhanced if he is able to advance proposals as to how the harm caused by his breach of the order might be remedied.   **6.63**

The application for the contemnor's discharge should be made in writing and attested by the governor (or other senior officer) of the prison to which the contemnor has been committed. It must show that he has purged, or wishes to purge, the contempt and be served on the person (if any) at whose instance the warrant of committal was issued at least one day before the application is made (CPR 81.31). Whilst not a requirement, it is clearly preferable that, if he is available, the application should be made to the judge who heard the original application. The judge has a wide discretion as to what cause of action to take: he may refuse the application, which will mean the original sentence remains unchanged; he may accede to it, in which case the contemnor will be released immediately; he may direct the contemnor's release at a future date prior to the end of the original sentence; or alternatively he may suspend it on terms.   **6.64**

### Sentence

Relevant sentencing authorities are set out in the Crown Court contempt section of this chapter at para 6.09.   **6.65**

### Appeals

The contemnor has the right of appeal to the Court of Appeal (Criminal Division) against the Crown Court's finding of contempt or the sentence it imposes. Permission to appeal against a contempt sentence is not normally required and the court has jurisdiction to grant bail pending the determination of the appeal.   **6.66**

# 7

# PRACTICE AND PROCEDURE IN CROWN COURT RESTRAINT AND MANAGEMENT RECEIVERSHIP CASES UNDER POCA

## A. Introduction

One of the most striking features of confiscation legislation is the extent to which it makes **7.01** use of remedies normally employed in the civil courts for the purpose of protecting assets against dissipation and realising assets in satisfaction of a confiscation order after conviction. The use of restraint and receivership orders in proceeds of crime cases can create a dilemma for experienced criminal practitioners who rarely have cause to venture into the civil courts where these remedies are more commonly employed. Court procedures and terminology are different. In this chapter, we examine the rules and procedures in so far as they affect restraint and management receivership applications in the Crown Court to assist the practitioner in pursuing the right course from the outset so as to protect the client's interests and avoid incurring judicial displeasure and adverse costs orders.

# B. The Overriding Objective

**7.02**  It is important to note at the outset that the overriding objective in r 1 of the CrimPR applies with equal force to restraint and receivership applications as it does to criminal proceedings in general, including of course the confiscation proceedings themselves. Rule 1 provides as follows:

> 1.1  The overriding objective
>> (1)  The overriding objective of this new code is that criminal cases be dealt with justly.
>> (2)  Dealing with a criminal case justly includes—
>>> (a)  acquitting the innocent and convicting the guilty;
>>> (b)  dealing with the prosecution and the defence fairly;
>>> (c)  recognising the rights of a defendant, particularly those under Article 6 of the European Convention on Human Rights;
>>> (d)  respecting the interests of witnesses, victims and jurors and keeping them informed of the progress of the case;
>>> (e)  dealing with the case efficiently and expeditiously;
>>> (f)  ensuring that appropriate information is available to the court when bail and sentence are considered; and
>>> (g)  dealing with the case in ways that take into account—
>>>> (i)  the gravity of the offence alleged,
>>>> (ii)  the complexity of what is in issue,
>>>> (iii)  the severity of the consequences for the defendant and others affected, and
>>>> (iv)  the needs of other cases.
>
> 1.2.  The duty of the participants in a criminal case
>> (1)  Each participant, in the conduct of each case, must—
>>> (a)  prepare and conduct the case in accordance with the overriding objective;
>>> (b)  comply with these Rules, practice directions and directions made by the court; and
>>> (c)  at once inform the court and all parties of any significant failure (whether or not that participant is responsible for that failure) to take any procedural step required by these Rules, any practice direction or any direction of the court. A failure is significant if it might hinder the court in furthering the overriding objective.
>> (2)  Anyone involved in any way with a criminal case is a participant in its conduct for the purposes of this rule.
>
> 1.3.  The application by the court of the overriding objective
>
> The court must further the overriding objective in particular when—
>> (a)  exercising any power given to it by legislation (including these Rules);
>> (b)  applying any practice direction; or
>> (c)  interpreting any rule or practice direction.

**7.03**  By r 3.1 of the CrimPR, the court must further the overriding objective by actively managing the case. By r 3.2, 'active case management' includes:

(a)  the early identification of the real issues;
(b)  the early identification of the needs of witnesses;

(c) achieving certainty as to what must be done, by whom, and when, in particular by the early setting of a timetable for the progress of the case;

(d) monitoring the progress of the case and compliance with directions;

(e) ensuring that evidence, whether disputed or not, is presented in the shortest and clearest way;

(f) discouraging delay, dealing with as many aspects of the case as possible on the same occasion and avoiding unnecessary hearings;

(g) encouraging the participants to co-operate in the progression of the case; and

(h) making use of technology.

By r 3.3 the parties are under a duty to assist the court in fulfilling its duties under r 3.2 and **7.04** to apply to the court for directions if they are needed to further the overriding objective. The expression 'overriding objective' was first used in the CPR, which brought into effect the recommendations of Lord Woolf's report on the civil justice system. The aim of the overriding objective, in the context of civil proceedings, is to encourage the parties to resolve their differences without recourse to litigation and, in those cases where litigation is unavoidable, to narrow down the issues in dispute as much as possible. In the context of restraint and receivership proceedings, the parties will be expected to serve their evidence on each other and on the court well in advance of any hearing, together with skeleton arguments summarising the case they propose to advance. They will also be expected to agree bundles of documents and serve them on the court so that the judge has the opportunity of considering them in advance of the hearing. In the more complex cases, the judge will give directions as to the various steps the parties must take and the timescale within which they must be completed. Any party to the proceedings who does not comply with such directions risks sanctions being imposed in costs. The duty of active case management imposed on the court by the rules means that the court takes a much more 'hands on' approach to case management than has hitherto been the case. In the past, particularly in civil cases, case management was largely in the hands of the parties who were able to agree amongst themselves how the case would progress, often granting one another significant extensions of time in which to carry out various steps in the litigation prescribed by the rules or by order of the court. This is no longer the case under the overriding objective, and the parties will be expected to comply with their obligations within the period specified by the rules or in the court's directions. If they are unable to do so, they will be expected to advance very compelling reasons to the court as to why not.

## C. Procedure on Applications for Restraint Orders

### Applications for restraint orders or ancillary orders

By r 59.1 of the CrimPR:  **7.05**

(1) This rule applies where the prosecutor, or an accredited financial investigator, makes an application under section 42 of the Proceeds of Crime Act 2002 for—

(a) a restraint order, under section 41(1) of the 2002 Act; or

(b) an ancillary order, under section 41(7) of that act,

for the purpose of ensuring that a restraint order is effective.

(2) The application may be made without notice if the application is urgent or if there are reasonable grounds for believing that giving notice would cause the dissipation of realisable property which is the subject of the application.

(3) An application for a restraint order must be in writing and supported by a witness statement which must—
  (a) give the grounds for the application;
  (b) to the best of the witness's ability, give full details of the realisable property in respect of which the applicant is seeking the order and specify the person holding that realisable property;
  (c) include the proposed terms of the order.

(4) An application for an ancillary order must be in writing and supported by a witness statement which must—
  (a) give the grounds for, and full details of, the application;
  (b) include, if appropriate—
    (i) any request for an order for disclosure of documents to which rule 61.9 applies (rules applicable to restraint and receivership proceedings: disclosure and inspection of documents),
    (ii) the identity of any person whom the applicant wants the court to examine about the extent or whereabouts of realisable property,
    (iii) a list of the main questions that the applicant wants to ask any such person, and
    (iv) a list of any documents to which the applicant wants to refer such a person; and
  (c) include the proposed terms of the order.

(5) An application for a restraint order and an application for an ancillary order may (but need not) be made at the same time and contained in the same documents.

(6) An application by an accredited financial investigator must include a statement that, under section 68 of the 2002 Act, the applicant has authority to apply.

**7.06** Rule 59(1) expressly provides that the application may be made without notice to the defendant and persons holding realisable property but only if the application is urgent or if there are reasonable grounds to believe that the giving of notice would cause the dissipation of assets.

### The duty of full and frank disclosure

**7.07** Rule 59.1(3) sets out the issues the prosecutor's witness statement in support of the restraint application must address. It should not, however, be thought that the prosecutor need do no more than provide in his witness statement the information required by r 59.1(3). Applications for restraint orders are subject to the usual rule of civil procedure that a litigant who asks the court to make an order without giving notice to the other parties to the action must give full and frank disclosure of all material facts whether they support his case or not. The requirement to give full and frank disclosure is imposed because the defendant has no opportunity to attend and address the court as to why the order should not be made. If granted, a restraint order can have a drastic effect on the defendant, his family and business, and, in contrast to the position in relation to freezing orders, he will only have very limited rights to compensation in the event of his acquittal. In *Director of the Serious Fraud Office v A* [2007] EWCA Crim 1927, [2008] Lloyds Rep FC 30, Hughes LJ explained the duty of full and frank disclosure in the context of applications for restraint orders as follows:

> A restraint order is a far-reaching order. Although it takes away no property or assets from the person under investigation, and is by definition temporary in application, it prevents him from using the frozen property in any way until the criminal investigation and any ensuing prosecution is over. That may restrict him considerably in what he can do by way of business or private activity. If it turns out that the person is not shown to be guilty of crime, he may in the meantime have lost a good deal because of the restrictions put upon him by the order. His ability to recover any losses from those who asked for the order is in a domestic case strictly limited by section 72 to cases in which there has been serious default by an investigator of a kind which caused the investigation to continue when otherwise it would not have done. The

restriction of a restraint order may sometimes last for a long time, though it can be reviewed if it is persisting unfairly. The order has been called draconian, and so it may (deliberately) be.

Because the initial application is commonly made without notice, the court will not at that stage hear evidence on both sides. For this reason, as with other without notice applications, the court insists on full and complete disclosure by the applicant of everything which might affect the decision whether or not to grant the order. There is a high obligation on the applicant to put everything relevant before the Judge, whether it may help or hinder his cause.

In short, full and frank disclosure is essential to enable the court to determine the application for a restraint order fairly.

### What additional matters should be disclosed?

There can be no exhaustive list of the matters which should be disclosed as each case is dif-  **7.08**
ferent and must be judged on its own particular facts. It is submitted that the following matters should be disclosed by the prosecutor if he is to comply with his duty of full and frank disclosure:

(a) particulars of any defence put forward by the defendant in interview or which would appear to be available to him from the facts known to the prosecutor;

(b) details of any innocent explanation advanced by the defendant as to his possession of substantial assets that appear to be inconsistent with his known legitimate sources of income;

(c) details of any legitimate business operated by the defendant, so the court can be satisfied any restraint order makes proper provision to enable the company to continue in bona fide trading pending the conclusion of the proceedings;

(d) details, in so far as they are known, of the defendant's domestic circumstances and financial commitments, including his marital status, details of any children or other dependent relatives he may have, and the extent of any mortgage obligations. If the defendant has at any time been made bankrupt, this too should be disclosed;

(e) particulars of any interest held by a third party in realisable property in respect of which the order is being sought;

(f) where it is alleged that a company controlled by the defendant has facilitated the criminal conduct complained of, all the facts relied on in support of this contention should be disclosed together with full details of the corporate structure, including the date on which the company was incorporated, the share capital, the names of the company's officers and shareholders, and, when known, the approximate annual turnover of the company;

(g) details of any civil proceedings brought against the defendant by any victim of the offence and any efforts the defendant may have made to compensate the victim voluntarily; and

(h) full details of all facts relied on in support of the contention that the defendant will dissipate assets if a restraint order is not made.

The duty to give full and frank disclosure is a continuing one that does not come to an end  **7.09**
once a restraint order has been made. The duty extends to disclosing subsequently discovered facts. If further information comes to light after the order has been made that could be relevant to the exercise of the court's discretion whether or not to make a restraint order and, if so, on what terms, the prosecutor must make full and prompt disclosure. The proper course in such circumstances is for the prosecutor to make a further witness statement deposing as to the new matters and then refer the matter back to the court, on notice to the defendant

and affected third parties, to enable the court to determine what action should be taken having regard to those matters.

### The consequences of non-disclosure

**7.10**   The usual consequence of material non-disclosure is that the court will discharge the order. The court will also be at pains to ensure that a prosecutor who obtains a restraint order without full disclosure will be deprived of any advantage he may have derived from the failure to disclose. As the Court of Appeal made clear in *Brinks Mat Ltd v Elcombe* [1988] 1 WLR 1350, the court does nonetheless have some discretion in the matter and, if it considers any non-disclosure to be of a minor nature, it may either direct the order to continue or discharge it and make a new order on the same or different terms.

**7.11**   In *Jennings v CPS* [2005] 4 All ER 391 the Court of Appeal was at pains to stress the public interest in ensuring that assets were available to meet any confiscation order that might be made in the defendant's cases. Longmore LJ said:

> The fact that the Crown acts in the public interest does, in my view, militate against the sanction of discharging an order if, after consideration of all the evidence, the court thinks that an order is appropriate. That is not to say that there could never be a case where the Crown's failure might be so appalling that the ultimate sanction of discharge would be justified.

**7.12**   As Laws LJ observed in *Jennings v CPS* this has to be balanced against the importance of requiring the Crown to comply strictly with the rules. He said:

> It seems to me that there are two factors which might point towards a different approach being taken to without notice applications for restraint orders in comparison to applications in ordinary litigation for freezing orders; but they pull in different directions. First, the application is necessarily brought (assuming of course that it is brought in good faith) in the public interest. The public interest in question is the efficacy of s 71 of the Act of 1988. Here is the first factor: the court should be more concerned to fulfil this public interest if that is what on the facts the restraint order would do, than to discipline the applicant—the Crown—for delay or failure of disclosure. But secondly, precisely because the applicant is the Crown, the court must be alert to see that its jurisdiction is not being conscripted to the service of any arbitrary or unfair action by the State, and so should particularly insist on strict compliance with its rules and standards, not least the duty of disclosure.

**7.13**   Further, a failure to give full and frank disclosure will only attract the sanction of the restraint order being discharged if the facts that have not been disclosed are material to the exercise of the court's discretion whether or not to grant the order and, if so, on what terms. Minor failings to disclose peripheral issues will not normally result in the order being discharged. In the *Jennings* case the defendant's solicitors had written to the Greater Manchester CPS advising of his intention to remortgage his home in order to pay off some outstanding liabilities. As a result of an oversight this letter was not passed on to the Central Confiscation Branch of the CPS in London and complaint was made that it was not disclosed in the witness statement made in support of the restraint application. In rejecting the contention that the restraint order should have been discharged on this basis, the Court of Appeal pointed out that the letter did not necessarily assist the defendant because it showed that he was living beyond his means. As Laws LJ said:

> Plainly the letter displayed a willingness on the applicant's part to disclose to the CPS transactions which he intended to carry out relating to his property. But it cuts both ways. The letter tends also to show that the appellant was living beyond his means. He was having to borrow

to pay tax: and he was proposing to turn unsecured debt into a secured loan, thus giving the lender a statutory priority over the Crown. At the very least Leveson J was not plainly wrong to hold that the impact of disclosure of the letter would only have been 'to increase the concern of dissipation of assets, rather than reduce it'. And the failure to disclose it was inadvertent. In the circumstances I am quite unable to hold that the failure was such as to require the court to discharge the restraint order, and then consider as a separate exercise whether to impose a fresh order.

The Court of Appeal took a similar approach in *Director of the Serious Fraud Office v A* [2007] **7.14** EWCA Crim 1927. In that case the Director appealed against the decision of a Crown Court judge to discharge a restraint order it had obtained following a request from the government of Iran pursuant to the Proceeds of Crime Act 2002 (External Requests and Orders) Order 2005. The Iranian judge who made the original request for the order did not disclose that the request came from the military branch of the Iranian judicial organisation. The failure to make that disclosure led the judge to discharge the order. The Court of Appeal held that this was not sufficiently material to justify the discharge of the order and allowed the Director's appeal. Hughes LJ said:

> . . . the difficulty lies in ascertaining why he found that the fact that the investigation judge was in this instance operating within the framework of the military courts made a crucial difference to whether a restraint order should be made. If the investigating judge's explanation of his own position and of the nature of the investigation is correct, it is not easy to see why it should. If he is right, it is not easy to see why it makes a significant difference that, as a career lawyer, he is in this instance investigating a case proceeding within the military court structure when he operates in a similar way in what he says is a parallel system of civil courts governed essentially by the same rules. If he is right, it is not easy to see why even if the investigator were a military officer that makes a significant difference where the trial will be before a properly constituted civil court. It might or might not be different if (the defendant) were being investigated by a biased or politically motivated officer with a view to a show trial with a pre-ordained end. But there is no finding that that is the case, or even that the contrary has not been sufficiently shown.

He added:

> To say, as the Judge did, that the fact that the external request emanated from the military branch of the judicial organisation of Iran would have been a factor relevant to his decision is to beg the question of what its effect would have been upon that decision and why. To answer that unanswered question involves answering the antecedent questions likewise unresolved, (i) how much if any of the investigating judge's explanation of the non-disclosure can be accepted, and (ii) what is the import of the undisclosed origin of the request. Without the answer to any of those questions, it is impossible to know whether the non-disclosure was sufficiently significant to justify the immediate discharge of the order. In any event, the Judge has not considered whether the order should, on its merits, stand or fall. If the conclusion drawn by the Crown Court had been one of deliberate deception, then providing there was sufficient reason for reaching it that might well provide a basis for discharging the restraint order, but in the absence of such a conclusion and, if it be reached, consideration whether or not the order should stand on its merits, we are unable to say that the Judge directed himself correctly.

Prosecutors must nonetheless remain vigilant to ensure that witness statements in support **7.15** of applications for restraint orders made without notice to the defendant give full and frank disclosure of all material facts. If a prosecutor has any doubt as to whether a particular fact should be disclosed, he should err on the side of disclosure. This is not to say that it is incumbent on him to disclose every minute detail of the case and the court must, it is submitted, give the prosecutor some latitude to reflect the fact that in many cases restraint orders have to be obtained as a matter of great urgency to prevent assets of substantial value being dissipated. Indeed, in *Brinks Mat Ltd v Elcombe* [1988] 1 WLR 1350 Slade LJ deprecated the practice of applying for orders to be discharged alleging non-disclosure on very slender grounds. When material non-disclosure does occur in restraint cases, it is rarely attributable to bad faith on the part of the prosecutor. In most instances, it arises from a breakdown in communication between those responsible for the financial investigation and those dealing with the prosecution side of a case at a time when there is an understandable concern to have a restraint order in place at the earliest opportunity to prevent any dissipation of assets. In such circumstances, it is perhaps not surprising that, from time to time, misunderstandings arise in the passing of information between those having the conduct of different aspects of the case. The failure to pass on the letter in the case of *Jennings v CPS* [2005] 4 All ER 391 is a classic example of this and was, rightly it is submitted, described by Laws LJ as 'unimpressive but, plainly, not malicious'. Minor failings of this nature are, in the absence of bad faith on the part of the prosecutor, unlikely to result in the restraint order being discharged.

*Cross-disclosure*

**7.16** In *R v Randhawa* [2012] EWCA Crim 3 the court determined that in a case where there are two defendants, the question whether D2 can require disclosure of evidence provided by D1 in restraint proceedings depends upon the application of the correct disclosure case and the facts of the particular case.

**The order**

**7.17** By r 59.2 of the CrimPR:

(1) The Crown Court may make a restraint order subject to exceptions, including but not limited to, exceptions for reasonable living expenses and reasonable legal expenses, and for the purpose of enabling any person to carry on any trade, business or occupation.

(2) But the Crown Court must not make an exception for legal expenses where this is prohibited by section 41(4) of the Proceeds of Crime Act 2002.

(3) An exception to a restraint order may be made subject to conditions.

(4) The Crown Court must not require the applicant for a restraint order to give any undertaking relating to damages sustained as a result of the restraint order by a person who is prohibited from dealing with realisable property by the restraint order.

(5) The Crown Court may require the applicant for a restraint order to give an undertaking to pay the reasonable expenses of any person, other than a person who is prohibited from dealing with realisable property by the restraint order, which are incurred in complying with the restraint order.

(6) An order must include a statement that disobedience of the order, either by a person to whom the order is addressed, or by another person, may be contempt of court and the order must include details of the possible consequences of being held in contempt of court.

(7) Unless the Crown Court otherwise directs, an order made without notice has effect until the court makes an order varying or discharging it.

(8) The applicant for a restraint order must—
  (a) serve copies of the order and of the witness statement made in support of the application on the defendant and any person who is prohibited by the order from dealing with realisable property; and
  (b) notify any person whom the applicant knows to be affected by the order of its terms.

Rule 59.2(1) makes it clear that the restraint order may be made subject to an exception **7.18** permitting a person to carry on any trade, business, or occupation. In *Re AW* [2010] EWCA (Crim) 3123 an exception to the restraint order can include a reasonable allowance for needs of a defendant's dependants.

Rule 59.2(2) limits the court's power to make an exception for the payment of legal expenses **7.19** where this is prohibited by s 41(4) of POCA. Section 41 of POCA will need to be considered in the light of the provisions of Sections 46 and 47 of the Crime and Courts Act 2013. Rule 59.2(7) provides that a POCA restraint order has effect until the court makes an order varying or discharging it unless the court directs otherwise. In fact, this provision merely gives effect to what had been the practice of the High Court for many years and which was expressly approved by the Court of Appeal in *Ahmad v Ahmad* [1998] EWCA Civ 1246.

The court suggested in *Customs and Excise Commissioners v S* [2005] 1 WLR 1338 that **7.20** POCA restraint orders should contain a provision advising as to the availability of public funding. Scott Baker LJ said:

> We think these orders should state clearly on their face that public funding is available. It is plainly desirable that defendants to restraint orders should in the ordinary course of events have legal representation. It would also be helpful if such orders direct defendants to the central unit at which their public funding application will be processed. Time will often be of the essence; it is crucial that public funding applications in these matters should be dealt with, with the greatest expedition.

By CrimPR r 61.10(1) the order must state the name and judicial title of the person making **7.21** it, bear the date on which it was made, and be sealed by the Crown Court. The seal may be placed on the order by hand or by printing a facsimile of the seal on the order whether electronically or otherwise: see r 61.10(2). The standard practice is for the prosecutor to submit a draft of the order he seeks with the application and to be responsible for drawing up the final version of the order as approved by the court. This is in accordance with r 61.15(1), which provides that orders shall be drawn up by the court unless it directs a party to draw it up or a party, with the permission of the court, agrees to draw it up or the order is made by consent under r 61.10. A draft POCA restraint order appears at Appendix 9.

### Hearings

Where the prosecutor applies for the restraint order without notice, there is rarely a formal **7.22** hearing of the application and the judge considers the matter in his private room without any attendance by the parties. This is in accordance with r 61.3 of the CrimPR, which provides that applications in restraint and receivership proceedings are to be dealt with without a hearing unless the Crown Court orders otherwise. This rule gives effect to the procedure that applies in the High Court in relation to applications under the old legislation where the judge considers the application without a hearing and only requires the prosecutor to attend if there are aspects of the application that concern him. Of course it is always open to the prosecutor to request a hearing and, it is submitted, he should always do so where there are unusual features to the application that call for an explanation.

In *R v B* [2008] EWCA Crim 1374 the Court of Appeal held that the Crown Court judge **7.23** should normally give reasons for making a restraint order. Moses LJ said:

> ...those facts do serve to demonstrate how serious it is to make an order such as this and therefore the obligation upon any judge either considering it *ex parte* or on an application

to vary or discharge to see that those bases are not only established but that there are good reasons for making and reaching the conclusion that they have been established. After all, the giving of reasons for making such a decision not only tells the subject of such an order why they have been made, but afford a powerful discipline to the judge who is obliged to consider whether the grounds have been established. We note that pursuant to the Criminal Procedure Rules 61.3 such applications are to be dealt with without a hearing unless the Crown Court orders otherwise. But we wish to stress that the fact that they are to be dealt with without a hearing does not in any way obviate the need for careful scrutiny by the court on an *ex parte* application, lest rights enshrined in the European Convention on Human Rights should be infringed. In the instant case it is by no means clear why it was that the judge on the *ex parte* application made this order notwithstanding the fact that there had been an opportunity to dissipate the assets which had not been taken.

**7.24** Where a hearing does take place, in accordance with the procedure established in relation to freezing injunctions in *Interroute Telecommunications (UK) Ltd v Fashion Group Ltd* [1999] TLR 762, the prosecutor should take a full note of the hearing and serve the same on the defendant along with a copy of the restraint order and supporting evidence. In *Director of the Assets Recovery Agency v Singh* [2004] EWHC Admin 2335 McCombe J held that the *Interroute* principle in relation to freezing orders applied equally to applications for interim receiving orders under Pt V of POCA. He said:

> I can see no reason why the common practice in relation to without notice applications in the High Court should not be followed in cases of this type, unless the judge hearing the application expressly decides that, for good reason, a note should not be served on the affected parties and provided that that decision is recorded on the face of the order, so that all affected parties may know that that decision also is susceptible to the customary provision to apply to vary or discharge the order.

**7.25** It is submitted that this principle should also apply to applications for restraint orders made without notice and that the best practice is for the prosecutor to prepare and serve a note of the hearing on the defendant.

### Service of the order

**7.26** Once the restraint order has been made the prosecutor must serve it together with the witness statement in support and, if applicable, his note of the hearing, on the defendant and any person holding realisable property and must notify any person affected by the order of its terms: see CrimPR r 59.2(8). The rules as to service, service by an alternative method, and service outside the jurisdiction are found in r 57 and are considered at para 7.62 below.

**7.27** The court will normally expect the prosecutor to give an undertaking to serve the order as soon as reasonably practicable. In *PS Refson & Co Ltd v Saggars* [1982] 3 All ER 111 the High Court held that 'as soon as reasonably practicable' meant 'forthwith'. Nourse J, with the concurrence of the Vice-Chancellor, gave a warning to the profession that any failure to comply with undertakings as to service constitute a contempt of court and that solicitors acting on behalf of a party can also be held in contempt for failing to implement any such undertakings given on behalf of a client.

## D. Procedure on Applications to Vary or Discharge the Order

**7.28** In Chapter 5 we considered the grounds on which a defendant or affected third party might apply to the court for a restraint order to be varied or discharged. In this section we examine the procedures that should be followed on the making of such an application. Applications to discharge the order should normally be confined to those instances where the prosecutor's evidence appears to be insufficient to justify the making of the order or where there has been a serious breach of the duty to give full and frank disclosure of all material facts. In most cases, it will be more appropriate to make an application to vary the order to mitigate its harsher effects. In practice, the most commonly made applications for variations include:

(a) requests for more time to comply with disclosure and repatriation requirements;
(b) requests for an increase in the amount payable by way of general living expenses; and
(c) applications to release a particular asset either to effect a sale or on the ground that it is not realisable property of the defendant.

### Variation by consent: consulting the prosecutor

Any person seeking a variation to a restraint order should always approach the prosecutor **7.29** before making an application to the court to discover whether the proposed variation, or a mutually acceptable compromise, can be agreed on a 'by consent' basis. A person who applies directly to the court for the order to be varied without first consulting the prosecutor risks being penalised in costs and, if the application is made on the advice of his legal representatives, the court might be minded to make a wasted costs order against those responsible.

In approaching the prosecutor, the applicant should provide precisely the same information **7.30** that he would incorporate in his evidence in support were the matter to be determined by the court. Further, if the variation requested is an increase in the amount payable by way of general living expenses, the applicant should ensure that he has first complied with his disclosure obligations under the order. It is unlikely that the prosecutor would be in a position to accede to a request for an increase before those obligations have been met because he will not have sufficient information on which to base a decision in the absence of full details of the defendant's assets. In *Re O* [1991] 1 All ER 330 the Court of Appeal upheld the decision of Macpherson J not to entertain a variation application until the defendants had given full disclosure of their assets.

Any consent order agreed must be drawn up by the parties in terms that comply with **7.31** CrimPR r 61.11. It must be expressed as being 'by consent' and must be signed by the legal representative acting for each of the parties to whom the order relates or by the party if he is a litigant in person: see r 61.11(4). The application may be dealt with without a hearing in accordance with r 61.11(3).

Defendants, affected third parties, and their legal advisors should take care in agreeing the **7.32** terms of 'by consent' variations and only agree to the same if they are content to be legally bound by them. A consent order is treated as a binding contract between the parties and, as the Court of Appeal held in *Weston v Dayman* [2006] EWCA Civ 1165, the Court will only entertain an application to vary an order made by consent in exceptional circumstances. Arden LJ said:

> I would accept that the court should accede to an application for variation where it is just to do so but in my judgment one of the aspects of justice is that a bargain freely made should be upheld. Mr. Weston clearly obtained benefits under the order. It may well be that those benefits are not as great as he thought, but that is not a matter for the court. In those circumstances I do not consider it would be right for this court to exercise its discretion to vary the order as sought

**Applying to the court**

**7.33** Where an approach to the prosecutor does not result in agreement as to the terms of any variation, the only way forward is for an application to be made to the court for the order to be varied. The procedure is set out in r 59.3 of the CrimPR which provides:

(1) This rule applies where a person affected by a restraint order makes an application to the Crown Court under section 42(3) of the Proceeds of Crime Act 2002 to discharge or vary the restraint order or any ancillary order made under section 41(7) of the Act.

(2) The application must be in writing and may be supported by a witness statement.

(3) The application and any witness statement must be lodged with the Crown Court.

(4) The application and any witness statement must be served on the person who applied for the restraint order and any person who is prohibited from dealing with realisable property by the restraint order (if he is not the person making the application) at least two days before the date fixed by the court for hearing the application, unless the Crown Court specifies a shorter period.

**7.34** This rule is in very similar terms to sc 115 r 5 in relation to applications in the High Court to vary restraint orders made under the old legislation. The interpretation provisions in rr 57.1, 57.2, and 57.3 provide assistance in computing time. By r 57.2(2):

A period of time expressed as a number of days shall be computed as clear days.

**7.35** 'Clear days' is defined in r 57.2(3) in these terms:

(3) In this rule 'clear days' means that in computing the number of days—

(a) the day on which the period begins; and

(b) if the end of the period is defined by reference to an event, the day on which that event occurs, are not included.

**7.36** Further, under r 57.2(4), when the period is five days or less and includes a day that is not a business day, that day does not count for the purpose of computing time. 'Business day' is defined in r 57.1 as being any day other than:

(i) a Saturday, Sunday, Christmas Day or Good Friday; or

(ii) a bank holiday under the Banking and Financial Dealings Act 1971 in England and Wales.

**7.37** The effect of these provisions is to provide very similar rules as to service as applied under sc 115 in relation to applications under the old legislation. The position remains that two clear days' notice must be given by the defendant or affected third party of any application to vary or discharge a restraint order. Thus, if an application to vary or discharge a restraint order is served on the prosecutor on a Monday, the first day on which the same may be heard at the Crown Court would be the following Thursday.

**Variation applications by the person who applied for the order**

**7.38** Thus far, we have considered only the procedures to be followed when an application to vary a restraint order is made by the defendant or an affected third party. There may, however, be circumstances in which the prosecutor wishes to apply for the order to be varied, for example by including new assets discovered since the restraint order was made or, indeed, by deleting assets from the order if further enquiries reveal that he has restrained more assets than are necessary to satisfy a confiscation order in the amount of the defendant's benefit.

**7.39** The procedure to be adopted on such applications is set out in r 59.4 of the CrimPR which provides:

(1) This rule applies where the applicant for a restraint order makes an application under section 42(3) of the Proceeds of Crime Act to the Crown Court to vary the restraint order or any ancillary order made under section 41(7) of the 2002 Act (including where the court has already made a restraint order and the applicant is seeking to vary the order in order to restrain further realisable property).

(2) The application may be made without notice if the application is urgent or there are reasonable grounds for believing that giving notice would cause the dissipation of realisable property which is the subject of the application.

(3) The application must be in writing and must be supported by a witness statement which must—

(a) give the grounds for the application; and

(b) where the application is for the inclusion of further realisable property in a restraint order give full details, to the best of the witness's ability, of the realisable property in respect of which the applicant is seeking the order and specify the person holding that realisable property;

(c) where the application is to vary an ancillary order include, if appropriate—

(i) any request for an order for disclosure of documents to which rule 61.9 applies (rules applicable to restraint and receivership proceedings: disclosure and inspection of documents),

(ii) the identity of any person whom the applicant wants the court to examine about the extent or whereabouts of realisable property,

(iii) a list of the main questions that the applicant wants to ask any such person; and

(iv) a list of any documents to which the applicant wants to refer such a person; and

(d) include the proposed terms of the variation.

(4) An application made by an accredited financial investigator must include a statement that, under section 68 of the 2002 Act, the applicant has authority to apply.

(5) The application and witness statement must be lodged with the Crown Court.

(6) Except where, under paragraph (2), notice of the application is not required to be served, the application and witness statement must be served on any person who is prohibited from dealing with realisable property by the restraint order at least 2 days before the date fixed by the court for hearing the application, unless the Crown Court specifies a shorter period.

(7) If the court makes an order for the variation of a restraint order, the applicant must serve copies of the order and of the witness statement made in support of the application on—

(a) the defendant;

(b) any person who holds realisable property to which the restraint order applies (whether before or after the variation); and

(c) any other person whom the applicant knows to be affected by the order.

Rule 59.4 is in very similar terms to sc 115 r 6 in relation to such applications made to the **7.40** High Court under the old legislation, and introduced no procedural changes to the way in which applications for variations by the prosecutor should be made.

### Hearing the variation application: the *Lexi Holdings* decision

Where an application for the variation of a restraint order is contested a hearing will almost **7.41** certainly be necessary. Any such hearing may be held in chambers: see CrimPR r 61.4. In many cases the issues the court is required to determine will be relatively straightforward and will not occupy a great deal of court time: for example, whether the defendant should be entitled to an increase in the amount payable by way of general living expenses. Some applications, however, will be more complicated and may even occupy a number of days of court time. In such circumstances the court should consider listing the matter for directions initially so that it can make orders as to the timescale for the service of evidence and skeleton arguments and the agreement of bundles by the parties.

**7.42** A small number of variation applications can prove highly complex and may well involve issues of law far removed from those normally determined by the Crown Court. Just such a situation arose in *Serious Fraud Office v Lexi Holdings PLC (In Administration)* [2008] EWCA Crim 1443 where the Court had to determine whether a third-party creditor had a proprietary claim to restrained assets and, if not, whether a restraint order could properly be varied to allow a third-party judgment creditor of the defendant to be paid. The Court, having determined the point of law at issue, gave some important guidance as to how complex cases of this nature should be dealt with in the future. Keene LJ said:

> We cannot leave this appeal without commenting on some procedural matters which have come to light during the hearing. First, there can be little doubt that the issues which arose in this case concerning beneficial interests, equitable charges and tracing were far from straight-forward. They are not part of the daily work of most Crown Court judges, and indeed this constitution of the Court of Appeal was deliberately arranged to ensure that appropriate expertise in matters normally falling within the jurisdiction of the Chancery Division was available. Sometimes issues may arise in restraint order proceedings about equitable interests which are not unduly complicated and can readily be dealt with in the Crown Court. In other cases the sums involved may not warrant any unusual steps. But there may be other times when the complexities are such that it may not be wise for the Crown Court judge to embark on seeking to decide those issues. In such a case where a relaxation of the restraint order is sought, consideration should be given to adjourning those variation proceedings to enable the issues to be determined in proceedings before a specialist Chancery Circuit Judge or High Court Judge of the Chancery Division. Alternatively, those arranging the listing of such cases in the Crown Court should seek to ensure that they are heard before a judge with the relevant experience and expertise.

**7.43** Where such issues are involved, the parties should inform the court as soon as possible so arrangements can be made for the case to be listed before a judge with the appropriate expertise.

## E. Receivership Proceedings

**7.44** The CrimPR makes extensive provision in relation to applications for the appointment of management and enforcement receivers. These are necessary because the Crown Court, being a creature of statute, does not have the same inherent jurisdiction as the High Court. In consequence most of the provisions are not replicated in sc 115 dealing with the High Court's jurisdiction under the old legislation.

### The application for appointment

**7.45** Rule 60.1 provides:

> (1) This rule applies to an application for the appointment of a management receiver under section 48(1) of the Proceeds of Crime Act 2002 and an application for the appointment of an enforcement receiver under section 50(1) of the 2002 Act.
> (2) The application may be made without notice if—
>   (a) the application is joined with an application for a restraint order under rule 59.1;
>   (b) the application is urgent; or
>   (c) there are reasonable grounds for believing that giving notice would cause the dissipation of realisable property which is the subject of the application.

(3) The application must be in writing and must be supported by a witness statement which must—
   (a) give the grounds for the application;
   (b) give full details of the proposed receiver;
   (c) to the best of the witness's ability, give full details of the realisable property in respect of which the applicant is seeking the order and specify the person holding that realisable property;
   (d) where the application is made by an accredited financial investigator, include a statement that, under section 68 of the 2002 Act, the applicant has authority to apply; and
   (e) if the proposed receiver is not a person falling within section 55(8) of the 2002 Act and the applicant is asking the court to allow the receiver to act—
      (i) without giving security, or
      (ii) before he has given security or satisfied the court that he has security in place, explain the reasons why that is necessary.
(4) Where the application is for the appointment of an enforcement receiver, the applicant must provide the Crown Court with a copy of the confiscation order made against the defendant.
(5) The application and witness statement must be lodged with the Crown Court.
(6) Except where, under paragraph (2), notice of the application is not required to be served, the application and witness statement must be lodged with the Crown Court and served on—
   (a) the defendant,
   (b) any person who holds realisable property to which the application relates, and
   (c) any person whom the applicant knows is affected by the application, at least 7 days before the date fixed by the court for hearing the application, unless the Crown Court specifies a shorter period.
(7) If the court makes an order for the appointment of a receiver, the applicant must serve copies of the order and of the witness statement made in support of the application on—
   (a) the defendant;
   (b) any person who holds realisable property to which the order applies; and
   (c) any other person whom the applicant knows to be affected by the order.

**7.46** Most law enforcement authorities who apply for the appointment of receivers select the person they apply to the court to appoint from an approved panel that have agreed to adhere to prescribed standards in the conduct of the receivership. The members of the panel are typically insolvency practitioners who are partners in firms of chartered accountants or solicitors. The prosecutor will select a member of the panel either on a rota basis or because of his known expertise in a particular type of case and invite him to accept the appointment by sending him a 'letter of agreement' setting out the terms of the proposed appointment and inviting him to confirm his acceptance of them. The letter of agreement should always be exhibited to the prosecutor's witness statement in support of the application and the receivership order will usually provide that the receiver must act in accordance with the letter of agreement.

**7.47** Rule 60.1(2) permits applications for the appointment of management receivers to made without notice if the application is joined with an application for a restraint order under rule 59.1, or in urgent cases or where there are reasonable grounds to believe assets would be dissipated were notice to be given. Prosecutors must, however, have due regard to the decision of the Court of Appeal in *Re P (Restraint Order: Sale of Assets)* [2000] 1 WLR 473 where the Court emphasised that such applications should only be made in cases of genuine urgency and that the receiver's powers should be confined to those strictly necessary to meet the justice of the situation. A draft management receivership order appears at Appendix 10 and an enforcement receivership order at Appendix 11.

### Applications for the conferment of powers on receivers

**7.48** Rule 60.2 of the CrimPR deals with applications for the conferment of powers on receivers made pursuant to s 49 of POCA. As r 60.2 is in almost identical terms to r 60.1, it is not reproduced here.

### Applications to vary or discharge receivership orders

**7.49** Rule 60.3 makes provision for applications (by persons including those referred to in r 60.1(7)(b) and (c) above) to vary or discharge receivership orders. These, too, must be made in writing and served on all affected parties at least seven days before the hearing unless the court specifies a shorter period. If the court decides to make an order varying or discharging the order, the applicant must serve copies of the order on any persons whom he knows to be affected by it. For the relevant questions a court needs to address when considering discharge of a receivership order, see *Capewell v Customs and Excise Commissioners* [2005] 1 All ER 900; [2004] EWCA Civ 1628 at para 50, (summarised at para 18.33 below).

### Security

**7.50** Rule 60.5 deals with the provision of security by receivers who are not members of staff of the CPS or the Revenue and Customs Prosecutions Office. By r 60.5(2):

> (2) The Crown Court may direct that before the receiver begins to act, or within a specified time, he must either—
> (a) give such security as the Crown Court may determine; or
> (b) file with the Crown Court and serve on all parties to any receivership proceedings evidence that he is already has in force such security,
> to cover his liability for his acts and omissions as a receiver.

The Crown Court may terminate the receiver's appointment if he fails to give security or satisfy the court as to the security he has in place by the date specified: see r 60.5(3).

**7.51** The Crown Court has a discretion whether or not to require the receiver to give security and does not have to require it in every case. It is submitted that the Crown Court could properly dispense with the provision of security where the person the prosecutor seeks to appoint comes from an experienced receiver in the employ of a reputable firm of chartered accountants which has a proven track record for conducting receiverships in a proper manner. The purpose of the security is to ensure the defendant's estate is properly protected in the event that the receiver acts improperly. If, in reality, there is no real risk that the receiver will abuse his position, it is submitted that security could properly be dispensed with. It is worthy of note that the High Court, where it appoints a receiver under the DTA and CJA, is not bound to require security in cases where the proposed receiver has already acted in previous cases under the legislation. The Crown Court, it is submitted, could properly apply the same rule in deciding whether or not to exercise its discretion in favour of requiring security.

### Receivers' remuneration and accounts

**7.52** Rule 60.6 and Rule 60.7 respectively deal with receivers' remuneration and accounts. As these provisions are dealt with in detail in Chapter 3, they are not reproduced again here.

### Non-compliance by a receiver

**7.53** Rule 60.8 makes provision for dealing with a receiver who fails to comply with any rule, practice direction, or direction of the Crown Court. By r 60.8(1) the Crown Court may order him to attend a hearing to explain his non-compliance. At the hearing the court may make any order it considers appropriate, including an order terminating the receiver's appointment, reducing or disallowing his remuneration, or requiring him to pay the costs of any party.

## F. Provisions as to Evidence and the Service of Documents

### Evidence

Rule 61.5 of the CrimPR gives the Crown Court power to control the evidence in restraint **7.54** and receivership proceedings by giving directions as to:

(a) the issues on which it requires evidence;
(b) the nature of the evidence which it requires to decide those issues; and
(c) the way in which the evidence is to be placed before the court.

The court may use its powers under r 61.5(1) to exclude evidence that would otherwise be admissible (see r 61.5(2)), and may limit the scope of cross-examination (see r 61.5(3)).

### Evidence should be in writing

Rule 61.6 of the CrimPR imposes a general rule that unless the court otherwise orders, evi- **7.55** dence in restraint and receivership proceedings should be in writing. The parties may apply under r 61.6(2) for permission to cross-examine a person who has tendered written evidence. If a person is required to attend for cross-examination and fails so to attend, his evidence may not be used unless the court gives permission: see r 61.5(3). This accords with the procedures of the High Court in restraint and receivership applications under the old legislation where evidence is normally given in affidavit or witness statement form. It is submitted that cross-examination should be ordered only in cases where there is a complete conflict of evidence between the parties. Rule 61.7 empowers the court, on the application of any party to the proceedings, to issue a witness summons requiring a witness to attend court to give evidence or produce documents to the court.

Witness statements required to be served under the rules must be verified by a statement **7.56** of truth contained in the statement itself: see r 57.7(1). By r 57.7(2) a statement of truth is defined as:

> ... a declaration by the person making the witness statement to the effect that the witness state-ment is true to the best of his knowledge and belief and that he made the statement knowing that, if it were tendered in evidence, he would be liable to prosecution if he wilfully stated in it anything which he knew to be false or did not believe to be true.

The effect of this provision appears to be that statements of truth should be in the same form as that in witness statements tendered under s 9 of the Criminal Justice Act 1967 rather than the form required under the CPR. If a person making a witness statement fails to verify the witness statement by a statement of truth, the court may direct that it shall not be admissible in evidence: see r 57.7(4).

### Hearsay evidence

Rule 61.8 of the CrimPR makes provision as to the admission of hearsay evidence in restraint **7.57** and receivership proceedings. It provides that the duty imposed by s 2(1) of the Civil Evidence Act 1995 to give notice of an intention to rely on hearsay evidence does not apply to evidence in restraint and receivership proceedings. See also s 46 POCA.

**Expert evidence**

**7.58** By r 57.9(1) of the CrimPR, a party to restraint or receivership proceedings who wishes to adduce expert evidence (whether of fact or opinion) must, as soon as practicable:

(a) serve on the other parties a statement in writing of any findings or opinion which he proposes to adduce by way of such evidence; and

(b) serve on any party who requests it in writing, a copy of (or if it appears to the party proposing to adduce the evidence to be more practicable, a reasonable opportunity to examine)—

(i) the record of any observation, test, calculation or other procedure on which the finding or opinion is based; and

(ii) any document or other thing or substance in respect of which the observation, test, calculation or other procedure mentioned in sub-paragraph (1)(b)(i) has been carried out.

**7.59** A party may waive his right to be served with the documents etc. referred to in r 57.9(1) but, if he does not waive that right, expert evidence that has not been served in accordance with this rule may not be admitted without the leave of the court (see r 57.9(3)) except where r 57.10 applies. Rule 57.10 makes special rules to deal with cases where a party fears that compliance with r 57.9 might lead to intimidation or attempted intimidation of the witness or that the course of justice may otherwise be interfered with. In such circumstances, he shall not be obliged to comply with r 57.9 but must serve a notice on the other party stating that the evidence is being withheld and the reasons for withholding it.

**Disclosure and inspection of documents**

**7.60** Where any issue arises in restraint or receivership proceedings as to whether property is realisable property the Crown Court may make an order under r 61.9 of the CrimPR for disclosure and inspection of documents. In such circumstances Pt 31 of the CPR has effect as if the proceedings were proceedings in the High Court: see r 61.9(3). Part 31 of the CPR makes provisions for the disclosure and inspection of documents and for the service of lists of documents by the parties.

**Court documents**

**7.61** Rule 61.10 of the CrimPR makes various miscellaneous requirements as to court documents. These are primarily administrative provisions that give effect to the practices and procedures that apply in High Court proceedings under the old legislation. Rule 61.10(1) provides that Crown Court orders must state the name and judicial title of the judge that made them and the date on which they are made, and must be sealed by the court. By r 61.10(2), the Crown Court may place the seal on the order by hand or by printing a facsimile of it on the order, whether electronically or otherwise. A document purporting to bear the court's seal is admissible in evidence without further proof (see r 61.10(3)).

**Service of documents**

**7.62** Service of documents in restraint and receivership proceedings is, in common with all other cases to which the CrimPR apply, governed by the rules in Part 4 of the CrimPR. These rules provide for service by various different methods but where a document may be served by electronic means the general rule is that it will be served using that method (rule 4.2 (2)). Rule 4.3(1) provides that a document may be served by means of handing it to the appropriate person. The document can be served on:

(a) an individual by handing it to him or her;

(b) a corporation by handing it to a person holding a senior position in that corporation;
(c) an individual or corporation who is legally represented in the case by handing it to that representative;
(d) the prosecution by handing it to the prosecutor or to the prosecution representative;
(e) the court officer by handing it to a court officer with authority to accept it at the relevant court office;
(f) the Registrar of Criminal Appeals by handing it to a court officer with authority to accept it at the Criminal Appeal Office.

**7.63** Rule 4.4 contains provisions for serving documents by leaving them at an appropriate address or by posting them. Rules 4.5 and 4.6 permit service via document exchange and by electronic means respectively provided that the recipient has not refused to accept service by these methods. By r 4.10 documents served by post or left at a document exchange are, unless the contrary can be shown, deemed to have been served on the second day after posting or being deposited at the document exchange. Where documents are served by electronic means they are deemed to be served on the next business day after they are transmitted.

**7.64** Rule 57.11(2) allows an order made in restraint and receivership proceedings to be enforced against a defendant or party affected by it notwithstanding that it has not been served in accordance with the rules, provided the court is satisfied that he had notice of it by being present when it was made.

### Service by an alternative method

**7.65** Rule 4.9 of the CrimPR makes provision for service by an alternative method. The court's order authorising service by an alternative method must specify the method of service allowed and the date when the document will be deemed to have been served (see r 4.9(2)).

### Service outside the jurisdiction

**7.66** Rule 57.12 of the CrimPR allows documents to be served outside England and Wales with the permission of the court. The document may be served by any method permitted by the law of the country in which it is to be served (see r 57.12(2)). However, nothing in the rule or in any court order authorises or requires any person to do anything in the country where the document is to be served which is against the law of that country (see r 57.12(3)). Where a document is required to be served a certain time before the date of a hearing and the recipient does not appear at the hearing, that hearing must not take place unless the Crown Court is satisfied the document has been duly served (see r 57.12(4)).

### Proof of service

**7.67** By r 57.13 of the CrimPR, where the rules require an applicant for an order to serve a document on another person, he must lodge a certificate of service with the Crown Court within seven days of the service of the document stating the method and date of service and, where the document is served in accordance with an order for service by an alternative method, such other information as the court may require (see r 57.13(2)). Where a document in restraint and receivership proceedings is to be served by the court, and the court is unable to serve it for any reason, it must send a notice of non-service stating the method attempted to the party who requested service (see r 57.13(3)).

### Consent orders

**7.68** Rule 61.11 of the CrimPR makes provision in relation to consent orders. By r 61.11(2) any party to the proceedings may apply for a judgment or order in agreed terms and such an application may be dealt with without a hearing. By r 61.11(4) such a judgment or order must be drawn up in the terms agreed, must be expressed as being 'by consent', and must be signed by the legal representative acting for each of the parties or by the party himself if he is a litigant in person.

### Slips and omissions

**7.69** Rule 61.12 of the CrimPR introduces a 'slip rule' whereby the Crown Court may at any time correct an accidental slip or omission made in an order in restraint and receivership proceedings. A party may apply for a correction without notice (see r 61.12(2)).

### Supply of documents from court records

**7.70** By r 61.13(1) of the CrimPR, no document relating to restraint or receivership proceedings may be supplied to any person to inspect or copy unless the Crown Court gives permission. Given the sensitivity of restraint proceedings, the court should normally be very reluctant to give such permission, especially at the pre-conviction stage. This is particularly so in relation to the defendant's disclosure statement or any document he produces to the court under compulsion. The court should, it is submitted, follow the ruling given by Macpherson J in *Re R* (Unreported, 21 October 1992) to the effect that such statements should be held in the court office 'under lock and key' and disclosed to no one (see Chapter 3 para 3.20). An application for permission under r 61.13(1) must be made on notice to the parties to the proceedings (see r 61.13(2)).

**7.71** Rule 61.14(2) provides that the judge presiding at proceedings for the offence may be supplied with documents relating to restraint and receivership proceedings but otherwise such documents must not be disclosed in proceedings for an offence (see r 61.14(2) and (3)).

### Preparation of documents

**7.72** Rule 61.15 of the CrimPR makes provision for the preparation of documents by the court and the parties. By r 61.15(1), orders in restraint and receivership proceedings should be drawn up by the Crown Court unless:

(a) the Crown Court orders a party to draw it up;
(b) a party, with the permission of the Crown Court agrees to draw it up; or
(c) the order is made by consent under r 61.10.

**7.73** By r 61.15(2) the Crown Court may direct that orders drawn up by a party must be checked by the court prior to sealing, or that before an order is drawn up by the court the parties must lodge an agreed statement of its terms. It is submitted that the better course in most cases would be for the parties to draw up the order for the court's approval given the length and complexity of most restraint and receivership orders. Where an order is to be drawn up by a party to the proceedings, he must do so within seven days after the date on which he was ordered or permitted to draw it up and, if he fails to lodge it within that period, any other party may draw it up and lodge it at the court for sealing (see r 61.15(3)).

**Change of solicitor**

Rule 61.16 of the CrimPR requires a party who changes his solicitor to notify the court and all the other parties to the proceedings. By r 61.17, a solicitor may apply to the court for an order that he has ceased to act for a party to restraint and receivership proceedings. If the solicitor has died, been made bankrupt, ceased to practise, or cannot be found, any other party to the proceedings may apply to the court for an order that he has ceased to act (see r 61.18). **7.74**

**Costs**

Rules 61.19 to 61.21 make provision for the payment of costs in restraint and receivership proceedings. The rules as to costs are considered in detail in Chapter 22 below and are therefore not reproduced here. **7.75**

# 8

# PREPARING FOR CONFISCATION HEARINGS

# A. Introduction

### The evolution of confiscation

**8.01** In *R v Sekhon* [2002] EWCA Crim 2954; [2003] 1 WLR 1655, the then Lord Chief Justice considered the evolving history of confiscation law, starting out by noting (para 1) that one of the most successful weapons that could be used to discourage offences that are committed in order to enrich offenders is to ensure that if the offenders are brought to justice any profit which they have made from their offending is confiscated.

**8.02** The Hodgson Committee report, 'The Profits of Crime and their Recovery' (Howard League for Penal Reform, 1984), made a number of recommendations which form the background of the modern confiscation provisions. The report recommended the repeal of the Criminal Bankruptcy Order and its replacement with confiscation and sentences in default, designed to catch the profits of major crime. Following these recommendations, a confiscation regime was introduced in relation to drug trafficking under the guise of the DTOA. As well as including the powers of restraint and confiscation, that Act also contained a statutory assumption to the effect that a drug trafficker's assets were the proceeds of crime and therefore liable to confiscation. The CJA introduced a new power to make a confiscation order in the case of certain crimes other than drug trafficking offences.

**8.03** Section 1 of the DTOA imposed a mandatory obligation on the court to hold a financial enquiry whenever a defendant was convicted of a drug trafficking offence. This resulted in a considerable waste of court time, both in cases where it was patently obvious that there had been no benefit (or any benefit was of a purely nominal amount) and also in cases where the defendant was accepted to have no realisable property.

**8.04** In cases that commenced after the DTA came into force (on 1 February 1995), the mandatory obligation on the court to hold a financial enquiry in every case was relaxed. Under s 2(1) of the DTA, the court was only obliged to hold a mandatory enquiry when either the prosecutor asked it to proceed under s 2 or if the court considered it appropriate to proceed under s 2, even though the prosecutor had not asked it to do so.

**8.05** Under s 71(1) of the CJA, a confiscation hearing could be held by the Crown Court whenever a defendant had been convicted of an indictable offence (other than a drug trafficking offence), but it was contingent upon the prosecutor giving written notice and/or the court considering it appropriate to proceed.

**8.06** Under section 6 of POCA the Crown Court must hold a confiscation hearing if a defendant has either been convicted of an offence in the Crown Court, or has been committed to the Crown Court for sentencing (or committed with a view to a confiscation order being considered) and the court has been asked to proceed by the prosecutor or the court believes it is appropriate to do so. Relevant parts of the amended Act are set out in Appendix 1.

### The transitional arrangements

**8.07** The transitional arrangements introduced following the commencement of POCA provided that offences committed before the effective date of the legislation, namely 24 March 2003, should remain under the DTA or the CJA (SI 2003/333).

For the purposes of this fourth edition, we have focused substantially on POCA as opposed **8.08** to the two preceding Acts. During the lifetime of this edition more than a decade will have elapsed since the passing of POCA. The effects of the transitional provisions, therefore, are now considerably diluted, with the vast majority of cases now falling squarely within the scope of POCA. For cases where the DTA or CJA do still apply, the second edition of this work gives a detailed commentary on the practice and procedure to be followed.

### The wake-up call

The purpose of this first of two chapters on confiscation hearings is to focus on the steps usu- **8.09** ally required prior to the hearing. The concerns of the Court of Appeal in relation to preparation for confiscation hearings were summarised concisely in the Court of Appeal case of *R v Baden Lowe* [2009] EWCA Crim 194; [2009] 2 Cr App R (S) 81, where the Court made the following two important observations (para 21):

(i) It is essential that the court (hearing the proceedings) finds and sets out all the relevant facts in its ruling (or judgment), including the facts that are agreed before it. It is evident that many confiscation hearings are not prepared in advance as they should be. There are many complaints that Defence Statements are inadequate. Timetables set out in the Criminal Procedure Rules or the court's directions frequently slip. Sometimes it is only at the last minute, either immediately before the court sits or even in the course of a hearing, that some matters are agreed and the real issues emerge, considerably burdening the task of the judge hearing the proceedings. If identifying the issues is left to the last minute, then insufficient attention is paid to ensuring that any procedural steps needed for the evidence to be admissible are taken. In an occasional case, where difficult issues arise, it may be the case that counsel with more experience of such issues is needed. Difficulties are from time to time compounded by the lack of a properly paginated bundle. It is, in the experience of many in this court, that, for reasons such as those we have outlined, it is not always clear from the ruling (or judgment) below what the facts were on which the issues which arose were determined. As the task of the court hearing the confiscation proceedings is to apply the statutory provisions to the facts (as agreed or found), it is essential that the ruling (or judgment) sets out all the relevant facts, as agreed and as found.

(ii) Too many authorities are cited to courts. Advocates should bear the observations in *May* at paragraph 48(4) clearly in mind before any authority is cited to the judge hearing the proceedings or in this court. We were provided with a large bundle of authorities which were unnecessary.

### When do POCA confiscation hearings have to be held?

Under s 6(1) of POCA the Crown Court must proceed with a confiscation hearing if the **8.10** following two conditions are satisfied:

(2) The first condition is that a defendant falls within any of the following paragraphs—
    (a) he is convicted of an offence or offences in proceedings before the Crown Court;
    (b) he is committed to the Crown Court for sentence in respect of an offence or offences under Section 3, 4 or 6 of the Sentencing Act;
    (c) he is committed to the Crown Court in respect of an offence or offences under Section 70 of the Proceeds of Crime Act 2002 (committal with a view to a confiscation order being considered).

(3) The second condition is that—
    (a) the prosecutor asks the Court to proceed under [Section 6 of POCA]; or
    (b) the court believes it is appropriate to do so.

Section 6(1) therefore imposes a mandatory obligation on the court to hold a financial enquiry whenever subss (2) and (3) are satisfied. The Sentencing Act referred to is the Powers of Criminal Courts (Sentencing) Act 2000 (see s 88(5) of POCA).

**8.11** This duty on the court to proceed in respect of confiscation if the conditions set out in s 6 of POCA are satisfied has been held by the UK Supreme Court to apply even where an absolute discharge or a conditional discharge has been imposed for the offence(s) in question—see *R v Varma* [2012] UKSC 42; [2012] 3 WLR 776 (para 58).

**8.12** In *R v Moulden* [2008] EWCA Crim 2561; [2009] 1 WLR 1173 the Court of Appeal held (para 20) that the words 'proceedings before the Crown Court' in s 6(2)(a) meant proceedings under a single indictment. The Court found that where there were two indictments and therefore two sets of proceedings, one of which fell under POCA and one under the CJA, the two statutory frameworks should be independently applied.

### The steps to confiscation—in a nutshell

**8.13** In summary, the route to the confiscation hearing is likely to include:

(1) *Conviction of the defendant for an acquisitive crime.* While the confiscation process may commence prior to conviction, ordinarily the court and prosecutor are only likely to focus on the timetable for confiscation once a conviction has been secured, not least because of resource issues and the potential that the defendant may be acquitted. Lack of such focus early on in the proceedings may, however, hamper the efforts of the prosecutor and make the court's task more difficult in the confiscation hearing later on (a point reflected in the Court of Appeal's judgment in *R v Baden Lowe* (above)).

(2) *The prosecutor will ask the court to proceed under s 6 of POCA.* The application is often made orally after the jury has returned its verdict. The court may at this stage order the defendant to provide information pursuant to s 18 of POCA to assist in the enquiry. In the alternative, although rarely applied in practice, the court may proceed to hold a confiscation hearing of its own motion.

(3) *The prosecutor will provide or the court will order a statement of information from the prosecutor, pursuant to s 16 of POCA.* This is essentially the prosecuting authority's opportunity to state its case. It will often be the product of an ongoing financial investigation and will make reference to restraint proceedings where assets have been frozen. The prosecutor will put figures on what is believed to be the defendant's benefit, the burden of which rests with the prosecutor on the balance of probabilities. The prosecutor may also make reference to available assets and whether it contends there are hidden assets, although the burden of proof in respect of the extent of his realisable assets rests with the defendant.

(4) *Within the statement of information the Crown will identify whether the case is a particular or general criminal conduct matter.* If it is a general criminal conduct matter or a lifestyle offence, the statutory assumptions under s 10 of POCA will apply. If it is a particular criminal conduct matter they will not.

(5) *The defendant will be required to respond to the statement of information within a set time frame, pursuant to s 17 of POCA.* A failure to address the issues may lead to the court treating the defendant as accepting the allegations in the prosecutor's statement.

(6) *The prosecutor may serve a further statement of information (at any time), pursuant to s 16(6).*

(7) *The court may at any time order the defendant to provide further specified information, pursuant to s 18 of POCA.*

(8) *The court may postpone confiscation proceedings and sentence the defendant, pursuant to s 14 of POCA.* However, if it decides to do this it cannot exercise its powers to order s 16 and s 17 statements when it is not proceeding under s 6. It may postpone for beyond two years if exceptional circumstances apply.

(9) *The court may sentence the defendant, if it is proceeding under s 6, prior to making the confiscation order (R v Gilleeney [2009] EWCA Crim 193; [2009] 2 Cr App R (S) 80).* There is no requirement to complete the proceedings under s 6 within a particular period, or before sentence.

The confiscation hearing itself is considered in more detail in the next chapter of this book. **8.14** A draft directions order may be found at the end of this chapter, and the relevant sections of the Act are reproduced at Appendix 1. Whilst deceptively simple, the path to confiscation can be full of pitfalls, and the practice and procedure is considered in more detail below.

### The discretion to ask the court to proceed

*Oppression*

In *R v Paulet* [2009] EWCA Crim 288 the Court of Appeal held that there might be limited **8.15** and exceptional cases where it would be considered oppressive for the Crown to seek a confiscation order. This reflected the view of previous constitutions of the Court of Appeal that where the making of a confiscation order would be oppressive, then the appropriate course of action would be to stay the confiscation proceedings (see eg *R v Shabir* [2008] EWCA Crim 1809; [2009] 1 Cr App R (S) 84). The Court of Appeal invited the Director of Public Prosecutions (DPP) to give guidance to prosecutors about the policy to be followed and to identify proceedings in which the commencement of confiscation proceedings would be appropriate, in order to establish a consistency of approach. In May 2009 that policy was issued by the CPS in a document entitled: 'Guidance for Prosecutors on the Discretion to Instigate Confiscation Proceedings'. That guidance was later approved by the Court of Appeal in *R v Nelson & Others* [2009] EWCA Crim 1573; [2010] 1 QB 678.

*Proportionality*

In *R v Waya* [2012] UKSC 51; [2012] 3 WLR 1188, the view taken by the UK Supreme **8.16** Court was that the concept of abuse of process does not need to be resorted to in such situations. The correct question is whether or not the confiscation order would amount to a disproportionate interference with the defendant's rights under Art 1 Protocol 1 of the ECHR and so would be unlawful by reason of the Human Rights Act 1998. Article 1 of Protocol 1 provides that:

> Every natural or legal person is entitled to the peaceful enjoyment of his possessions. No one shall be deprived of his possessions except in the public interest and subject to the conditions provided for by law and by the general principles of international law. The preceding provisions shall not, however, in any way impair the right of a State to enforce such laws as it deems necessary to control the use of property in accordance with the general interest or to secure the payment of taxes or other contributions or penalties.

If a disproportionate interference with the defendant's property rights is established, it was held in *Waya* that the court must act in a manner which is compliant with the defendant's rights and make a proportionate order. The Supreme Court decided to 'read in' the necessary words into s 6 of POCA to require the court not to make a confiscation order which would be disproportionate under Art 1 Protocol 1 of the ECHR.

**8.17**  Although *Waya* marks a significant change in the legal route by which confiscation proceedings that would otherwise result in an order being made may be halted, despite the apparently mandatory wording of section 6 of POCA, it does not appear that the Supreme Court intended that the classes of cases in which no confiscation order would be made (either because the prosecuting authority decided not to proceed, or because the court determined that the making of an order would be wrong), or in which the effects of applying the provisions of POCA would be mitigated, would be widened significantly by this change of legal emphasis. It is also of note that Lord Judge CJ, who gave the judgments of the Court of Appeal in both *Paulet* and *Nelson & Others*, sat as an additional Justice of the Supreme Court in *Waya* and agreed with the majority judgment. That judgment was co-authored by Sir Anthony Hughes, also sitting as an additional Justice, who had given the judgment of the Court of Appeal in *Shabir* in which it was expressly stated (para 25) that the power to stay for oppression provided the remedy in the case of any disproportionality.

**8.18**  It had previously emphasised that the cases in which a confiscation order would be classed as a disproportionate interference with a defendant's rights under Art 1 Protocol 1 of the ECHR are very limited; as the House of Lords had said in *Green* (para 16), it cannot be disproportionate to deprive a defendant of a criminal benefit which he has in fact and in law obtained. Thus the argument that it was disproportionate and so a criminal breach of their rights under Art 1 Protocol 1 to make confiscation orders against two defendants, each in the total amount of their joint benefit, was rejected by the Court of Appeal in *R v Lambert* [2012] EWCA Crim 421; [2012] 2 Cr App R (S) 90. So too, in *Waya*, the Supreme Court emphasised that its choice of compliance with Art 1 Protocol 1 as the route by which the lawfulness of a confiscation order was to be judged does not involve the reintroduction of a general judicial discretion (para 24) and, applying the observations of Lord Bingham in *May*, that a confiscation order may legitimately require a defendant to pay far more than his net profit from the crime and may require multiple defendants to pay a sum obtained successively by each of them (para 26).

**8.19**  That said, however, the Supreme Court in *Waya*, despite disapproving of the use of abuse of process doctrine as a mechanism to determine whether confiscation proceedings are appropriate, gave no clear answer to the question of what circumstances might give rise to a disproportionate confiscation order, instead stating that these would need to be resolved 'case by case as the need arises' (para 34). It cited as an example of disproportionality the situation of stolen goods or money which had been entirely restored to the loser, but gave no clear indication of the other situations which might lead to a mitigation of the confiscation order on the basis of disproportionality. It remains to be seen (at the time of writing) to what extent, if any, the Court of Appeal will seek to widen the scope of the concept of disproportionality in this context, although the opportunity for so doing would appear to be limited in the light of the endorsement of the principles already set out by the House of Lords in *May*.

**8.20**  However, one consequence of *Waya* may well be that confiscation orders will in future be made in cases where previously the power to stay for abuse of process would have been exercised and so no confiscation order would have been made at all. Rather than simply stay the proceedings, the Supreme Court has indicated that the court should instead make a confiscation order which is proportionate (para 16). The judgment in *Waya* and its consequences are considered in more detail in Chapter 9. *Waya* has been applied in *R v Axworthy* [2012] EWCA Crim 2889, *R v Hursthouse* [2013] EWCA Crim 517, and *R v Jawad* [2013] EWCA Crim 644. See also *R v Warwick* [2013] NICA 13 and *R v Harvey* [2013] EWCA Crim 1104 for discussion of pre-*Waya* cases.

In *R v Lambert* [2012] EWCA Crim 421; [2012] 2 Cr App R (S) 90, the two defendants had **8.21** engaged in a conspiracy to grow cannabis on a commercial scale. The 'criminal lifestyle' provisions were not, however, applied on the facts of the case by the Crown Court, which made orders against each of the defendants in the total amount of their joint benefit from the particular offending, as each had assets in excess of the joint benefit. The argument that this produced a disproportionate result was rejected by the Court of Appeal. The defendants had argued that this was a breach of their rights under Art 1 Protocol 1 of the ECHR and that it would be proportionate to 'apportion' the benefit from their offending between the two of them. The Court of Appeal held that this was not permissible, relying on the statement made by Lord Bingham in *May* that apportionment between offenders jointly liable was contrary to both principle and statute and that in *Green* that it would not be disproportionate to deprive an offender of what he had in fact and in law obtained. *Lambert* was decided prior to the hearing in *Waya* but was not cited in argument to the Supreme Court, and the Supreme Court did not discuss the concept of apportionment in its judgment, nor the impact of its finding that the Court could in circumstances of disproportionality make an order lower than what would otherwise be required by the statutory scheme on the historic rejection of apportionment as a methodology.

### The standard and burden of proof

The court must decide any question arising under s 6(4) and (5) of POCA on the 'balance of **8.22** probabilities' (pursuant to s 6(7), see Appendix 1).

In *R v Barwick* [2001] 1 Cr App R (S) 129 the Court of Appeal held that in confiscation **8.23** proceedings under the CJA it was for the prosecution to establish that the defendant had benefited from an offence and the value of that benefit. Once that had been established, it was for the offender to prove, on a balance of probabilities, that the amount that might be realised was less than the value of his calculated benefit (see also *R v Layode* (CA, 12 March 1993), *R v Carroll* [1991] Crim LR 720, and *R v Ilsemann* (1990) 12 Cr App R (S) 398).

In *R v Barnham* [2005] EWCA Crim 1049; [2006] 1 Cr App R (S) 83 the Court confirmed: **8.24**

> 40 . . . Once the prosecution has established the benefit there is no requirement on it to provide a *prima facie* case. At the second stage the burden of proof shifts to a defendant to establish, if he can, his realisable assets to the satisfaction of the court. By the second stage a defendant will know exactly how the court has determined the benefit attributable to him and must prove by evidence what his realisable assets are. It is for him to show why the confiscation order should not be 'the value of (*his*) proceeds of drug trafficking'. If he proves that he has no, or appreciably less, realisable assets than the amount of the benefit determined by the court the order will be made in the lesser sum. Provided the judge keeps well in mind the principle that the risk of serious injustice to the defendant must be avoided and does not just pay lip service to that principle, the order will be in the amount assessed as either the amount of benefit or such other sum as the defendant shows represents his realisable assets.
>
> 41. To hold that the prosecution must, in some way, show a prima facie case that the defendant has hidden assets in our judgment would defeat the object of the legislation. It is designed to enable the court to confiscate a criminal's ill-gotten gains. The expression 'hidden assets'

is indicative of the fact that the prosecution can have no means of knowing how and where a defendant may have dealt with or disposed of the proceeds of his criminal activities.

8.25 Similarly, the Court of Appeal in *R v Granger* [2007] EWCA Crim 139 held that:

> 13. Moreover, it is not enough for a defendant to accept that he has had money and say in general terms that it has disappeared. A defendant seeking to avert or minimise a proposed confiscation order needs to be specific about where his money has come from and gone to, if the judge is to be invited to hold a defendant has no realisable assets.

### Victims and restitution

8.26 As with most acquisitive crime, frequently an innocent third party will have suffered a loss, eg householders and insurance companies in burglary cases, building societies in mortgage fraud cases, HM Revenue and Customs in VAT and income tax frauds etc. Section 6(6) of POCA permits the court to treat its duty to decide the recoverable amount and make a confiscation order as a discretionary power if it believes that a victim of the criminal conduct has at any time started or intends to start proceedings against the defendant in respect of loss, injury, or damage sustained in connection with the conduct.

8.27 If, for example, it transpires that a building society that has suffered loss as a result of a mortgage fraud has instituted civil proceedings against the defendant in which it is seeking the recovery of a sum equating to the benefit the defendant has derived from the offence, the court may form the view that it would not be proper to make a confiscation order against the defendant because of the element of double recovery involved. Section 7(3) specifies how the court should approach the recoverable amount in such circumstances; see Appendix 1.

8.28 However, the potential for such a claim is not something upon which the court should speculate. In *R v Hockey* [2007] EWCA Crim 1577; [2008] 1 Cr App R (S) 50, the Court of Appeal found that the judge at first instance had erred by expressing the view that a confiscation order would be inappropriate in circumstances where financial institutions may have a legitimate interest. This was a mortgage fraud case, and the lenders concerned had not at any time indicated that they had started or intended to start proceedings, instead being content to continue to accept the mortgage payments despite the mortgages having been fraudulently obtained (see paras 27–30). In such circumstances a confiscation order ought to have been made.

8.29 The case of *Hockey* is a salutary reminder to financial institutions (and those who represent them) that if they wish to make a claim against a defendant then they must notify the prosecutor or court expeditiously, or risk losing the opportunity to mount effective action.

8.30 The Court of Appeal considered *Hockey*, amongst other cases, in *R v Morgan and Bygrave* [2008] EWCA Crim 1323. In that case the court, striking a cautionary note, found:

> 30 ... it may amount to an abuse of process for the Crown to seek a confiscation order which would result in an oppressive order to pay up to double the full restitution which the defendant has made or is willing immediately to make, and which would thus deter him from making it ... Whilst confiscation may well be draconian or penal in effect, it does not, as the House of Lords observed in R v May [2008] UKHL 28, at paragraph 48(1), operate as a fine.

8.31 This approach was adopted with even more firmness by the UK Supreme Court in *Waya* (above), where it was held that where the defendant has restored the entirety of the proceeds of his offending to the victim, then the making of a confiscation order would inevitably be disproportionate (paras 27–30):

27. Similarly, it can be accepted that the scheme of the Act, and of previous confiscation legislation, is to focus on the value of the defendant's obtained proceeds of crime, whether retained or not. It is an important part of the scheme that even if the proceeds have been spent, a confiscation order up to the value of the proceeds will follow against legitimately acquired assets to the extent that they are available for realisation.

28. The case of a defendant such as was considered in *Morgan and Bygrave* is, however, a different one. To make a confiscation order in his case, when he has restored to the loser any proceeds of crime which he had ever had, is disproportionate. It would not achieve the statutory objective of removing his proceeds of crime but would simply be an additional financial penalty. That it is consistent with the statutory purpose so to hold is moreover demonstrated by the presence of section 6(6). This subsection removes the duty to make a confiscation order, and converts it into a discretionary power, wherever the loser whose property represents the defendant's proceeds of crime either has brought, or proposes to bring, civil proceedings to recover his loss. It may be that the presence of section 6(6) is capable of explanation simply as a means of avoiding any obstacle to a civil action brought by the loser, which risk would not arise if repayment has already been made. But it would be unfair and capricious, and thus disproportionate, to distinguish between a defendant whose victim was about to sue him and a defendant who had already repaid. If anything, an order that the same sum be paid again by way of confiscation is more disproportionate in the second case than in the first. Unlike the first defendant, the second has not forced his victim to resort to litigation.

29. The principle considered above ought to apply equally to other cases where the benefit obtained by the defendant has been wholly restored to the loser. In such a case a confiscation order which requires him to pay the same sum again does not achieve the object of the legislation of removing from the defendant his proceeds of crime, but amounts simply to a further pecuniary penalty—in any ordinary language a fine. It is for that reason disproportionate. If he obtained other benefit, then an order confiscating that is a different matter.

# B. Confiscation in the Magistrates' Court

### Introduction

Section 97 of SOCPA permits the Secretary of State to make an order enabling magistrates' **8.32** courts to make confiscation orders under Pt 2 of POCA in a sum less than £10,000. Whilst s 97 of SOCPA came into force as long ago as 1 July 2005, no enabling order has yet been made by the Secretary of State at the time of writing.

When (or rather, if, given the passage of eight years since the passing of SOCPA) such an order **8.33** is eventually made, magistrates will have the power to fix confiscation hearings pursuant to the POCA scheme following a trial or a guilty plea, where the sum to be confiscated is less than £10,000.

To some extent these provisions, once introduced, will ease the burden on prosecutors **8.34** in determining whether or not to ask the magistrates to refer a case to the Crown Court. However, the issue of whether to commit will still arise in a number of cases.

### Section 70: committal by a magistrates' court

Section 70 of POCA states: **8.35**

(1) This section applies if—
    (a) a defendant is convicted of an offence by a magistrates' court, and

     (b) the prosecutor asks the Court to commit the defendant to the Crown Court with a view to a confiscation order being considered under Section 6.

  (2) In such a case the magistrates' court must—

     (a) commit the defendant to the Crown Court in respect of the offence and

     (b) may commit him to the Crown Court in respect of any other offence within sub-section (3).

  (3) An offence falls within this sub-section if—

     (a) the defendant has been convicted of it by the magistrates' court or any other Court, and

     (b) the magistrates' court has power to deal with him in respect of it.

The effect of s 70 is that a defendant may be committed to the Crown Court for confiscation proceedings following a conviction of any offence (triable either way or summarily) in the magistrates' court. The requirement to commit a defendant to the Crown Court is mandatory once the prosecutor has asked the magistrates' court to do so (see s 70(2)).

**8.36**  Where the defendant is convicted of an either way offence, s 70(5) requires the magistrates' court to state whether it would have committed the defendant to the Crown Court for sentencing in any event. It appears this subsection is required because, under s 71(3)(b), the Crown Court's sentencing powers following a committal for confiscation are otherwise limited to the sentencing powers of the magistrates' court, illustrated by the reduction in sentence from twelve to six months' imprisonment in *R v Smith* [2012] EWCA Crim 1954 where 'the only reason for the committal was to enable the court to make a confiscation order' (para 1) and the magistrates were not of the view that their sentencing powers were insufficient—the Crown Court did not therefore have power to impose any sentence greater than six months.

**8.37**  The application to commit to the Crown Court should be made at an early stage; a prosecutor who delayed making the application in an either way case until the magistrates, having retired to consider sentence, had returned to court and were about to pronounce sentence (in the erroneous belief that this course of action would have been to the defendant's advantage because the Crown Court would not on committal have imposed a higher sentence than that pronounced by the magistrates) was said to have acted 'misguidedly' and been guilty of 'bad practice' by the Divisional Court in *R (on the application of Baguley) v Blackpool Magistrates' Court* [2009] EWHC 3652 (Admin) (paras 8 and 10).

**The circumstances where a magistrates' court may commit**

**8.38**  When considering s 6(2)(b) of POCA, the Powers of Criminal Courts (Sentencing) Act 2000 (PCC(S)A) specifies the powers under which a magistrates' court may commit to the Crown Court. Section 3 of the PCC(S)A provides a general power to commit adult offenders summarily convicted of an offence triable either way; s 4 confers a power to commit adult offenders convicted of a triable either way offence as a result of a guilty plea indicated before the mode of trial procedures have been embarked upon; and s 6 gives a general power to commit for sentence, which may be used to supplement a committal under the various provisions of the PCC(S)A.

**8.39**  It follows that defendants appearing before the Crown Court on appeal from decisions of the magistrates' court do not fall under s 6(2)(b) of POCA, nor do those defendants who are committed outside ss 3, 4, and 6 of the PCC(S)A, eg committal for breach of a community order or return to custody under s 116 of the PCC(S)A.

### The discretion to commit

The 2009 guidance for prosecutors referred to at para 8.15 above is also likely to have a direct **8.40** bearing on whether prosecutors should seek the committal of defendants in confiscation matters before magistrates' courts.

As well as abuse of process arguments (which, even after *Waya*, would appear to still be **8.41** relevant, at least to the question of whether or not there should be a committal for confiscation), public policy considerations may also arise because s 70(1)(a) confers on the prosecutor a discretion as to whether he should ask the magistrates' court to commit following a defendant's conviction. How and when that discretion is exercised will ultimately depend on the circumstances of the individual case. The Code for Crown Prosecutors emphasises that deciding on what is in the public interest is not simply a matter of adding up factors on each side. It will be for the lawyer who has control of the case to determine how important each factor is in the circumstances of the individual case and go on to make an overall assessment. This approach was confirmed by the Court of Appeal in *R v Benjafield* [2003] 1 AC 1099, a DTA case, where the Court held that the discretion 'will have to be exercised taking into account all relevant considerations, so as to avoid the risk of injustice'.

It has long been the view that it is not in the public interest to automatically make referrals; **8.42** not least because such a course would entail no exercise of any discretion and would leave prosecutors exposed to potential judicial review actions (see para 5.6 et seq of the Code for Crown Prosecutors).

However, there are a number of factors that are common to all confiscation matters, which **8.43** may assist the prosecutor on the decision he is being asked to make in relation to s 70(1)(b):

(1) It is an established principle that prosecutors should seek to carry out a financial enquiry in every case where such an enquiry would be both relevant and appropriate. There is therefore a presumption that a case lawyer should consider whether the confiscation scheme is likely to be applicable.
(2) The fact that Parliament has legislated for the prosecutor to seek confiscation orders in summary matters is a clear indication that this power is to be considered and *used* by prosecutors.
(3) It would not be in the public interest to allow a repeat offender to see the consequences of his criminality go unchecked.

Whether it is appropriate to ask the magistrates' court to refer a case to the Crown Court for **8.44** the purpose of making a confiscation order will depend very much on the facts of the individual case, including the seriousness of the matter, whether the individual is a repeat offender, and the sums/loss involved. The fact that the chances of recovering realisable assets ('the available amount') are very low is also a consideration, but may not be determinative. This may also be the case where the alleged benefit is insignificant, but to set a financial cut-off point below which referrals should not be made would amount to a fettering of the prosecutor's discretion. Inevitably, internal resources may also in practice be a factor in influencing matters.

The approach taken to arguments concerning Art 1, Protocol 1 of the ECHR, proportionality, **8.45** and the protection of an individual's property by the Supreme Court in *Waya* was not made in the context of a decision to commit, and we suggest that it is more appropriate for any disproportionality arguments to be considered at the confiscation hearing in the Crown Court, particularly given their fact-sensitive nature. In any event, whilst the decision to seek a committal and indeed the decision by the magistrates to commit would both potentially be judicially reviewable on public law grounds (eg if it were alleged that the decision to request committal had been made in bad faith), the question of any disproportionate interference with a defendant's rights under Art 1 Protocol 1 of the ECHR would only, we suggest, arise as and when the court is deciding whether to make a confiscation order or not. Committing a defendant to the Crown Court for a confiscation hearing does not, of itself, involve any interference with his property rights.

### Committal: practice and procedure

**8.46** In relation to confiscation proceedings themselves, the timetable in the magistrates' court is likely to be as follows:

(1) The defendant is convicted.
(2) The prosecutor asks the magistrates' court to commit.
(3) The matter is listed at the Crown Court for directions.
(4) The directions hearing deals with the serving of the prosecutor's statement, the defence reply, the time estimate for the confiscation hearing etc.
(5) The defendant is sentenced. (A timetable should ideally be set and the matter postponed in relation to the confiscation hearing before sentence is passed.)
(6) A confiscation hearing may be postponed for up to two years from the date of conviction to allow for the financial reports etc to be prepared (s 14(5)).

**8.47** Once committed, the Crown Court will follow the confiscation procedure set out in s 6 et seq of POCA (see s 70(4)(a)).

## C. The Basics of Confiscation under POCA

### If section 6(1)–(3) is satisfied, how must the court proceed?

**8.48** Section 6(4) states:

The court must proceed as follows:
(a) it must decide whether the defendant has a criminal lifestyle;
(b) if it decides that he has a criminal lifestyle it must decide whether he has benefited from his general criminal conduct;
(c) if it decides that he does not have a criminal lifestyle it must decide whether he has benefited from his particular criminal conduct.

**8.49** Under s 6(4) the court must, when considering a confiscation hearing, decide whether the defendant has a 'criminal lifestyle'. If it decides he has a criminal lifestyle the court must then decide whether he has benefited from his 'general criminal conduct'. If the court decides that the offender does not have a criminal lifestyle, it must decide whether he has benefited from his 'particular criminal conduct'.

### How is 'criminal lifestyle' defined?

**8.50** Section 75 of POCA provides:

(1) A defendant has a criminal lifestyle if (and only if) the following condition is satisfied.
(2) The condition is that the offence (or any of the offences) concerned satisfies any of these tests—
(a) it is specified in Schedule 2;

(b) it constitutes conduct forming part of a course of criminal activity;

(c) it is an offence committed over a period of at least six months and the defendant has benefited from the conduct which constitutes the offence.

In respect of s 75(2)(a), the offences specified in Sch 2 are termed 'lifestyle' offences.

### What are 'lifestyle offences'?

Lifestyle offences are defined under Sch 2 to POCA, and include (at para 1) drug trafficking **8.51** offences, namely:

(1) An offence under any of the following provisions of the Misuse of Drugs Act 1971—
  (a) Section 4(2) or (3) (unlawful production or supply of controlled drugs);
  (b) Section 5(3) (possession of controlled drugs with intent to supply);
  (c) Section 8 (permitting certain activities relating to controlled drugs);
  (d) Section 20 (assisting in or inducing the commission outside the UK of an offence punishable under a corresponding law).
(2) An offence under any of the following provisions of the Customs & Excise Management Act 1979 if it is committed in connection with a prohibition or restriction on importation or exportation which has effect by virtue of Section 3 of the Misuse of Drugs Act 1971—
  (a) Section 50(2) or (3) (improper importation of goods);
  (b) Section 68(2) (exploration of prohibited or restricted goods);
  (c) Section 170 (fraudulent evasion).
(3) An offence under either of the following provisions of the Criminal Justice (International Co-operation) Act 1990—
  (a) Section 12 (manufacture or supply of a substance for the time being specified in Schedule 2 to that Act); or
  (b) Section 19 (using a ship for illicit trafficking of controlled drugs).

Other offences specified in Sch 2 include money laundering, namely s 327 of POCA (con- **8.52** cealing, etc criminal property) and s 328 of POCA (assisting another to retain criminal property) (but not s 329, acquisition, use, and possession of criminal property). Lifestyle offences also include: directing terrorism under s 56 of the Terrorism Act 2000; people trafficking under ss 25, 25A, or 25B of the Immigration Act 1971; arms trafficking under s 68(2) of the Customs & Excise Management Act 1979 (exportation of prohibited goods), and s 170 of the same Act (fraudulent evasion); or an offence under s 31 of the Firearms Act 1968 (dealing in firearms or ammunition by way of trade or business).

Also included under Sch 2 are: trafficking people for sexual exploitation; trafficking people **8.53** for exploitation; counterfeiting; intellectual property offences under the Copyright, Designs and Patents Act 1988 and the Trade Marks Act 1994 (unauthorised use of trade marks); certain prostitution and child sex offences under the Sexual Offences Acts of 1956 and 2003; blackmail under s 21 of the Theft Act 1968; and acting as a gangmaster.

Paragraph 10 of Sch 2 incorporates inchoate offences, namely: attempting; conspiring; incit- **8.54** ing; aiding or abetting; or counselling or procuring, the commission of any offence specified in Sch 2.

### 'Criminal lifestyle' and relevant benefit of not less than £5,000

Under s 75(4) an offence does not satisfy the test in s 75(2)(b) or (c) unless the defendant **8.55** obtains a relevant benefit of not less than £5,000. The term 'relevant benefit' is given two definitions under s 75, dependant upon whether or not the court is proceeding under s 75(2)(b) or s 75(2)(c).

### How is 'relevant benefit' defined?

**8.56** Under s 75(5), 'relevant benefit' for the purposes of s 75(2)(b) (where the offence constitutes conduct forming part of a course of criminal activity), is defined as:

(a) benefit from conduct which constitutes the offence;
(b) benefit from any other conduct which forms part of the course of criminal activity and which constitutes an offence of which the defendant has been convicted;
(c) benefit from conduct which constitutes an offence which has been or will be taken into consideration by the Court in sentencing the defendant for an offence mentioned in paragraph (a) or (b).

**8.57** Under s 75(6), 'relevant benefit' for the purposes of subs (2)(c) (where the offence has been committed over a period of at least six months and the defendant has benefited from the conduct which constitutes the offence), is defined as:

(a) benefit from conduct which constitutes the offence;
(b) benefit from conduct which constitutes an offence which has been or will be taken into consideration by the court in sentencing the defendant for the offence mentioned in paragraph (a).

### Criminal conduct and benefit

**8.58** Section 6(4)(b) and (c) refers to 'criminal conduct'. Criminal conduct is defined at s 76(1) as being:

(1) conduct which
    (a) constitutes an offence in England and Wales; or
    (b) would constitute such an offence if it occurred in England and Wales.

Section 76 adds:

(4) A person benefits from conduct if he obtains property as a result of or in connection with the conduct.
(5) If a person obtains a pecuniary advantage as a result of or in connection with conduct, he is to be taken to obtain as a result of or in connection with the conduct a sum of money equal to the value of the pecuniary advantage.
(6) References to property or a pecuniary advantage obtained in connection with conduct include references to property or a pecuniary advantage obtained in both that connection and some other.
(7) If the person benefits from conduct his benefit is the value of the property obtained.

### General criminal conduct

**8.59** Section 76(2) states:

General criminal conduct of the defendant is all his criminal conduct, and it is immaterial—

(a) whether conduct occurred before or after the passing of this Act;
(b) whether property constituting a benefit from conduct was obtained before or after the passing of this Act.

The phrase 'general criminal conduct' therefore encompasses all of the defendant's criminal conduct, both conduct for the offence(s) in question and criminal conduct other than the offence in question, on the basis that the defendant has a criminal lifestyle.

### Particular criminal conduct

Section 76(3) defines the 'particular criminal conduct' of the defendant as being:  **8.60**

(3) ...all his criminal conduct which falls within the following paragraphs—

   (a) conduct which constitutes the offence or offences concerned;

   (b) conduct which constitutes offences of which he was convicted in the same proceedings as those in which he was convicted of the offence or offences concerned;

   (c) conduct which constitutes offences which the court will be taking into consideration in deciding his sentence for the offence or offences concerned.

### The relationship between general and particular conduct

By virtue of its definition, 'general criminal conduct' is inclusive of 'particular criminal con-  **8.61**
duct'. Under the POCA regime courts must therefore consider the defendant's benefit from his general criminal conduct, where the court has found, upon conviction, that the defendant has a criminal lifestyle. If the court concludes that the defendant does not or has not had a criminal lifestyle, confiscation is by reference to his benefit from the particular criminal conduct on which he has been convicted (this is similar, although not identical, to the former provisions of the CJA that dictated simple and extended benefit).

### When does a defendant's conduct form part of his criminal activity?

Under s 75(3):  **8.62**

Conduct forms part of a course of criminal activity if the defendant has benefited from the conduct and—

(a) in the proceedings in which he was convicted he was convicted of three or more other offences, each of three or more of them constituting conduct from which he has benefited, or

(b) in the period of six years ending with the day when those proceedings were started (or if there is more than one such day, the earliest day) he was convicted on at least two separate occasions of an offence constituting conduct from which he has benefited.

### When does a person benefit from criminal conduct?

Under s 76(4) a person benefits from criminal conduct if he obtains property as a result  **8.63**
of or in connection with that conduct. If a person benefits from criminal conduct, his benefit is the value of the property obtained (s 76(7)). The meaning of these apparently simple provisions has been the subject of much case law, which is considered in detail in Chapter 9.

Under s 6(5) of POCA, if the court decides under s 6(4)(b) or (c) that the defendant has ben-  **8.64**
efited from criminal conduct, it must next decide the recoverable amount (see s 7 of POCA) and then make a confiscation order requiring him to pay that amount in full.

### Transitional provisions

Conduct shall not form part of a course of criminal activity under s 75(3)(a) of the Act where  **8.65**
any of the three or more offences mentioned in s 75(3)(a) (see para 8.62 above) was committed before 24 March 2003 (SI 2003/531). (See *R v Moulden* [2008] EWCA Crim 2648; [2009] 1 WLR 1173.)

**8.66** The transitional provisions set out in SI 2003/531 state that where the court is applying the rule in s 75(5) of the Act in relation to the calculation of relevant benefit for the purposes of determining whether or not the test in s 75(2)(b) is satisfied by virtue of conduct forming part of a course of criminal activity under s 75(3)(a), the court must not take into account benefit from conduct constituting an offence mentioned in s 75(5)(c) of the Act which was committed before 24 March 2003.

**8.67** However, conduct shall form part of a course of criminal activity under s 75(3)(b) of the Act if the offences that the defendant was convicted of on at least two separate occasions in the period mentioned in s 75(3)(b) were committed before 24 March 2003.

**8.68** Similarly, where the court is applying the rule in s 75(5) in relation to the calculation of relevant benefit for the purposes of determining whether or not the test in s 75(2)(b) of the Act is satisfied by virtue of conduct forming part of a course of criminal activity under s 75(3)(b), the court may take into account benefit from conduct constituting an offence committed before 24 March 2003.

**8.69** Under SI 2003/531, where the court is applying the rule in s 75(6) in relation to the calculation of relevant benefit for the purpose of determining whether or not the test in s 75(2)(c) of the Act is satisfied, the court must not take into account benefit from conduct constituting an offence mentioned in s 75(6)(b) of the Act which was committed before 24 March 2003.

## D. Postponement of POCA Confiscation Hearings

### The statutory scheme

**8.70** Under s 14(1) of POCA the court may:

    (a) … proceed under Section 6 before it sentences the defendant for the offence (or any of the offences) concerned, or
    (b) postpone proceedings under Section 6 for a specified period.

The court may order more than one postponement and the period of postponement may be extended (as per s 14(2)). However, a period of postponement must not end after the 'permitted period' has finished (s 14(3)).

**8.71** Pursuant to r 58.2 of the CrimPR, the Crown Court may grant a postponement without holding a hearing.

### What is the 'permitted period'?

**8.72** 'Permitted period' is defined at s 14(5) as being a period of two years starting with the date of conviction. This section therefore extends the period of postponement previously permitted under the DTA and CJA from six months to two years. This means that the court no longer has to find 'exceptional circumstances' to postpone beyond six months. Further, it appears the court may now postpone a confiscation hearing under POCA for any reason, eg because no court is available (as happened in *R v Neish* [2010] EWCA Crim 1011; [2010] 1 WLR 2395). Previously it had to be on the grounds that 'further information' was required. Where the court is satisfied exceptional circumstances exist, the period may be extended beyond two years, adopting similar considerations to those that have developed under the DTA and CJA (see s 14(4) and para 8.75 below).

### Date of conviction

The defendant's date of conviction is defined in s 14(9) as being the date on which the **8.73** defendant was convicted of the offence concerned, or where there are two or more offences and the convictions were on different dates, the date of the latest.

### Further postponements

Section 14(8) provides that where proceedings have been postponed already for a period and **8.74** an application to extend the period further is made before the previous period of postponement ends, the application may be granted, even though the previous period (by the time the application is heard) may have ended. In effect this means that provided the application is submitted to the court before the postponed period comes to an end, the application may be granted. It should be noted that in *R v Iqbal* [2010] EWCA Crim 376; [2010] 1 WLR 1985, the Court of Appeal held that an application to extend a period of postponement must be made before the previously permitted period has expired.

### Postponement beyond two years

There is no limit to the period of postponement where the court finds that there are 'excep- **8.75** tional circumstances' (s 14(4)). The Act does not define when circumstances are exceptional, although some guidance may be found from previous case law in relation to the DTA or CJA. In practice, only in exceptional circumstances should the need for postponement take the final date of making any confiscation order beyond the two-year period and the timetabling should reflect this.

### What amounts to exceptional circumstances?

In *R v Jagdev* [2002] EWCA Crim 1326; [2002] 1 WLR 3017 the Court of Appeal held that **8.76** the purpose of the power to postpone confiscation proceedings was to enable the judge to reach a fair conclusion on the confiscation issue; and that where there was a real prospect that the hearing might have been wasted and an unjust order made if the judge had proceeded to hear the case (in *Jagdev* because of an awaited decision of the Court of Appeal), then the judge was entitled to hold that there were exceptional circumstances.

In *R v Cole* (The Independent, 30 April 1998 (CA)), the trial judge had become ill after a dif- **8.77** ficult and complex trial. The issue was whether this constituted exceptional circumstances. Judge LJ stated:

> The judgment whether circumstances are exceptional or not must be made by the Court considering whether to make a confiscation order. Here the Judge was in hospital on the date when he had indicated that he would determine the confiscation issue... Having studied the statutory code we do not consider that it was intended or drafted so as to preclude the Listing Officer making sensible arrangements for the conduct of the Crown Court business, normally after discussion with the Trial Judge or the Resident Judge...

The Court of Appeal has shown a marked reluctance to interfere with the exercise of the **8.78** discretion of the sentencing judge to find exceptional circumstances. It is not a question of whether or not the Court of Appeal would find the circumstances in question to be exceptional, but whether the judge was entitled to conclude that they were (see *R v Gadsby* [2001] EWCA Crim 1824; [2002] 1 Cr App R (S) 97). Nor is it necessary for the sentencing judge to use the expression 'exceptional circumstances' to describe the reason for the postponement (although it is submitted it is better that he does) (see *R v Chuni* [2002] EWCA Crim 453; [2002] 2 Cr App R (S) 82 (para 32)), or, it appears, even for the postponing judge to consider whether such circumstances exist, provided that they do in fact exist (see *R v T* [2010] EWCA Crim 2703). A broad approach on the issue of exceptional 'circumstances' was adopted by the Court of Appeal in *R v Johal* [2013] EWCA Crim 647.

**8.79** In *Steele and Shevki* [2001] 2 Cr App R (S) 40; [2001] Crim LR 153, Judge LJ returned to this subject and stated:

> These decisions involve the Court's discretion, judicially exercised when the statutory conditions are present, taking full account of the preferred statutory sequence... For example, to take account of illness on one side or the other, or the unavailability of the Judge, without depriving a subsequent order for confiscation of its validity.

**8.80** In *Sekhon* [2003] 1 WLR 1655 the Court of Appeal held that the decision as to whether to postpone and as to whether exceptional circumstances existed involved the consideration of the same types of issues that courts were regularly required to determine when engaged in case management and that the strict compliance with procedural requirements relating to issues of that nature would not normally be expected to go to jurisdiction.

**8.81** This rationale is reflected in s 14(11) of POCA which provides:

> (11) A confiscation order must not be quashed only on the ground that there was a defect or omission in the procedure connected with the application for or the granting of a postponement.

However, s 14(12) should also be noted, which provides:

> (12) But subsection (11) does not apply if before it made the confiscation order the court—
> (a) imposed a fine on the defendant;
> (b) made an order falling within section 13(3);
> (c) made an order under section 130 of the Sentencing Act (compensation orders).

**8.82** In *R v T* [2010] EWCA Crim 2703, exceptional circumstances were found to exist where the defendant had absconded whilst on bail, was convicted in his absence, was recaptured shortly before the end of the two-year period and subsequently contrived to avoid attending court for a confiscation hearing fixed within the two-year period by telling the Prison Service that he was not required at court. The judge who postponed that hearing to a date outside the two-year period had not considered the issue of exceptional circumstances (although the Court of Appeal decided that they had in fact existed), and the Court of Appeal noted 'the importance that this court attaches to the need for judges in the Crown Court to be very alive to the provisions of section 14 of the Proceeds of Crime Act, and to ensure that their judgments are expressly loyal to those provisions' (para 13).

### Postponement for a specified period

**8.83** Under s 14(1)(b) of POCA, the period of the postponement must be for a specified period. However, that does not mean that a judge must specify the very date the substantive hearing is to begin. In *R v Knights* [2005] UKHL 50; [2006] 1 AC 368, a CJA 1988 case, the judge purported to postpone the confiscation proceedings under s 72(A)(1) of the CJA by arranging for the case to be mentioned with a view to fixing a hearing. The appeal was heard by the House of Lords immediately following the case of *Soneji and Bullen*. Both cases raised broadly similar questions as to whether non-compliance with the strict requirements of the

1988 Act (which correspond with the DTA and, save for the extension to two years, POCA) disabled the court from making confiscation orders.

The argument advanced suggested that the court was only allowed to postpone for a precise **8.84** period of time and had to stipulate a date when the actual determination was to take place. It was argued that a date for mention was insufficient because it did not deal with the substantive hearing. Because it was anticipated that there would have to be a further postponement, it was argued that the initial postponement should not have been made without the court expressing itself satisfied that there were exceptional circumstances to justify such a course.

Lord Brown stated that when postponing the determination in confiscation proceedings, **8.85** the judge was required to specify the particular period of the postponement: he could not simply adjourn the proceedings generally. However, the judge was not bound to specify the very date when the substantive hearing was to begin; it was sufficient when postponing the proceedings to give directions for the service of statements and to specify a date when the proceedings were next to be listed, whether for disposal or for such further directions as might be needed (or to fix a final hearing date).

In *Knights* the House of Lords held that it was only if the timetable initially set made it **8.86** likely that the limit would ultimately be exceeded that the court had on the occasion of the first postponement to address the question of whether exceptional circumstances existed to justify the directions proposed. Although the House of Lords held that the judge *should* have addressed the question of exceptional circumstances, it found that that did not deprive the court of jurisdiction to make the confiscation order. Even if a judge were to postpone confiscation proceedings in a particular case without specifying any return date at all, the court would not, applying the approach now laid down in *Soneji*, be precluded from restoring the proceedings to the list for hearing and thereafter making an appropriate order (in *R v Soneji and Bullen* [2005] UKHL 49; [2006] 1 AC 340, the House of Lords held that a failure to comply with the procedural requirements of s 72(A) of the CJA 1988 did not result in the invalidity of the proceedings, where a judge had made the order more than six months after conviction, owing to listing difficulties, without having made a finding of exceptional circumstances).

### No requirement to find further exceptional circumstances

In *R v Steel and Shevki* [2001] 2 Cr App R (S) 40; [2001] Crim LR 153, it was held that **8.87** once the court had postponed a determination on the grounds that there are exceptional circumstances it is not then necessary for the court to find further exceptional circumstances for subsequent postponements (see also *R v Zelzele* [2001] EWCA Crim 1763; [2002] 1 Cr App R (S) 62).

### Who may apply for a postponement?

A postponement or extension may be made upon application by either the defendant, or by **8.88** the prosecutor, or alternatively by the court of its own motion (see s 14(7)).

### The effect of the court failing to follow the postponement provisions

Section 14(11) states that a confiscation order *must not* be quashed on the sole ground that **8.89** there was a defect or omission in the procedure connected with the application for the granting of a postponement.

**8.90**  In effect this prevents confiscation orders being quashed because of some procedural irregularity in the postponement procedures. There is an exception to this rule if, before the court made the confiscation order, it imposed a fine on the defendant, or made an order falling within s 13(3) of POCA (ie a compensation order, a forfeiture order, or a deprivation order), or made an order under s 130 of the PCC(S)A (compensation orders), then, under s 14(12), a procedural irregularity of that type is likely to lead to the confiscation order being quashed.

**8.91**  However, in *R v Donohoe* [2006] EWCA Crim 2200; [2007] 1 Cr App R (S) 88, the Court of Appeal held that the making of a technically erroneous order for the forfeiture of illegal drugs did not have the effect of depriving the court of the jurisdiction to make a confiscation order. The Court held that it would frustrate the object of POCA to hold that the erroneous imposition of a trivial fine rendered the court powerless to proceed with the substantive confiscation proceedings.

### Postponement pending appeal

**8.92**  Under s 14(6) of POCA, if:

(a)  the defendant appeals against his conviction for the offence (or any of the offences) concerned, and

(b)  the period of three months (starting with the day when the appeal is determined or otherwise disposed of) ends after the period found under sub-section (5), the permitted period is that period of three months.

Section 14(6) provides in circumstances where a defendant has appealed that the postponement shall not, save where the court is satisfied that there are exceptional circumstances, exceed three months after the date on which the appeal is determined or otherwise disposed of.

### Sentencing

**8.93**  In *R v Gilleeney* [2009] EWCA Crim 193; [2009] 2 Cr App R (S) 80, the Court of Appeal considered the disjunctive nature of s 14(1) and emphasised the importance of judges stating plainly whether they were acting under s 14(1)(a) and going ahead with confiscation proceedings under s 6 or whether they were postponing the whole issue of confiscation, pursuant to s 14(1)(b).

**8.94**  In *Gilleeney*, the court concluded that the judge at first instance had been proceeding under s 14(1)(a) (and thereby s 6) when he had ordered the Crown to supply a s 16 statement of information within six months. Importantly, the Court found that the fact that the judge was proceeding under part 6, and had not postponed the proceedings, did not prevent the court from then sentencing the defendant (para 14): 'A power to sentence in advance of the completion of the s 6 proceedings can be read into s 14(1), a view reinforced by *Soneji*.' The Court added, at para 15:

> Section 14(1)(a) plainly contemplates that proceedings under section 6 may commence before sentences are imposed. The present tense is used in the paragraph and proceedings under section 6 commenced with the requirement that the prosecution give the court statements of information within 6 months, under section 16(1). There is no requirement to complete the proceedings under section 6 within a particular period, or before sentence, or that a direction under section 14(1)(a) requires directions beyond that to provide statements of information.

**8.95**  This was an important development, as courts and commentators had previously proceeded on the basis that the court could only move to sentence in cases where the court had postponed the confiscation proceedings. Nevertheless, the Court of Appeal's ruling does appear to be consistent with the more relaxed approach to the statutory scheme to ensure that technical arguments on the legislation do not overcome the overriding object, an example of which is reflected in *R v Soneji and Bullen* [2005] UKHL 49; [2006] 1 AC 340 in which the House of Lords held that a confiscation order *must not* be quashed on the sole ground that there was a defect or omission in the procedure.

Similarly, if the court postpones proceedings under s 6 it may proceed to sentence the **8.96** defendant for the offence (or any of the offences) concerned, by virtue of s 15(1). Section 15(2) provides:

> In sentencing the defendant for the offence (or any of the offences concerned) in the postponement period the Court must not (a) impose a fine on him, (b) make an order falling within section 13(3) [ie a compensation order, a forfeiture order, or a deprivation order], or (c) make an order for the payment of compensation under Section 130 of the Sentencing Act.

The purpose of this section is to prevent sentencing being delayed while confiscation is being considered.

It is suggested that in certain cases the defendant may benefit if the judge decides not to **8.97** sentence until the confiscation hearing is over. For example, where new information surfaces concerning the defendant's criminal lifestyle, or lack of it, during the confiscation hearing, or where an assumption may have been made in respect of the defendant, which is also relevant to sentencing, and the defence are able to show at the confiscation hearing that it has no application. In those circumstances it may be to the defendant's benefit if the judge does not sentence until the confiscation hearing is over, and all of the facts have been considered.

### Power to vary sentence

Under s 15(3), if the court decides to sentence the defendant for the offence concerned in **8.98** a postponement period, once that period has ended the court may vary the sentence by imposing a fine on him, or making an order falling within s 13(3) (compensation, forfeiture, or deprivation orders), or making an order for the payment of compensation under s 130 of the PCC(S)A. However, the court may only proceed under s 13(3) within a period of twenty-eight days starting from the last day of the postponement period (s 15(4)). In practice this means that a court may vary the sentence within twenty-eight days of the end of the postponement period by making one or more of the orders referred to in s 13(3), ie a fine or ancillary order. This is intended to enable the court to order, for example, the forfeiture and destruction of drugs, if the court had not done so already.

The postponement provisions set out in s 15 only apply to circumstances where the court **8.99** has passed sentence following a postponement under s 14(1)(b) of the Act. The court should take care therefore to specify whether it is proceeding under s 14(1)(a), namely going ahead with confiscation proceedings, or whether it is postponing the same under s 14(1)(b).

## E. Preparatory Steps for a POCA Hearing

### Section 16 statements of information

Under s 16(1) of POCA if the court is proceeding under s 6(3)(a) (where the prosecutor has **8.100** asked the court to proceed under the confiscation provisions), the prosecutor must provide the court with a statement of information, within 'any period' that the court orders. Section 16 is set out in Appendix 1.

**8.101** Alternatively, if the court is proceeding under s 6(3)(b) (where the court believed it was appropriate to proceed to a confiscation hearing without an invitation from the prosecutor), it may order the prosecutor to give it a statement of information, and the prosecutor must present such a statement within the time frame the court orders (see s 16(2)).

**8.102** It is important to note that s 16 statements may only be ordered if the court is proceeding under s 6, and not if the court has decided to postpone the confiscation proceedings under s 14(1)(b).

### The purpose of section 16 statements

**8.103** Section 16(3) provides that if the prosecutor believes the defendant has a criminal lifestyle, the statement of information should include matters the prosecutor believes are relevant in connection with deciding the following issues:

   (a)  whether the defendant has a criminal lifestyle;
   (b)  whether he has benefited from his general criminal conduct;
   (c)  his benefit from the conduct.

**8.104** The prosecutor's statement serves a number of purposes. Firstly, it enables the defence and the court to be put on notice of the Crown's case and prevent the defence from being taken by surprise. Secondly, it identifies the real issues in terms of the Crown's case, thereby saving court time in relation to matters that are not really disputed. In *R v Comiskey* (1991) 93 Cr App R 227, Turner J, in delivering the judgment of the Court, said (at p 231): 'it is very desirable that those responsible for the prosecution of offences should make full use of this (section)' (when dealing with the use of the corresponding s 11 statements under the DTA).

**8.105** The Court of Appeal considered the purpose of the prosecutor's statement in *R v Benjafield* (2001) 2 Cr App R (S) 221, at para 107. In finding that such statements did not contravene Art 6 of the ECHR the Court held that:

> A statement serves the useful purpose of forewarning the defendant of the case of the prosecution which he will have to meet as to his assets. It should assist the defendant by making clear the matters with which he has to be prepared to deal. It is right that, as the rules require, the prosecution should identify any information which would assist the defendant.

### The content of section 16 statements

**8.106** Under s 16 of POCA, the prosecutor should give to the court a statement with as much relevant detail as possible relating to the defendant's benefit from criminal conduct. It should achieve what it says on the can, namely it should be a 'statement of information'.

**8.107** The actual content of the statement will partly depend on whether the prosecutor alleges the defendant has had a criminal lifestyle. Under s 16(4), the statement should include information relevant to the making of the assumptions if the prosecutor believes that the defendant has had a criminal lifestyle.

If the prosecutor does not believe the defendant has had a criminal lifestyle, the statement of **8.108** information becomes a statement of matters the prosecutor believes are relevant in deciding whether or not the defendant has benefited from his *particular* criminal conduct and, if so, his benefit from that conduct (see s 16(5)).

Under r 58.1 of the CrimPR, when the prosecutor is required under s 16 of the Act to give a **8.109** statement to the Crown Court, the prosecutor must also, as soon as practicable, serve a copy of the statement on the defendant. Any statement given to the Crown Court by the prosecutor under s 16 of the Act must, in addition to the information required by the Act, include the following information, pursuant to r 58.1(2) of the CrimPR:

(1) the name of the defendant;
(2) the name of the person by whom the statement is made and the date on which it is made; and
(3) where the statement is not given to the Crown Court immediately after the defendant has been convicted, the date on which, and the place where the relevant conviction occurred.

It will be noted, pursuant to r 57.7 of the CrimPR, that witness statements should be verified **8.110** with a statement of truth in confiscation proceedings.

In practice, the statement of information will ordinarily include: **8.111**

(1) an outline of the nature of the offence(s) that the defendant has been convicted of, together with references to the indictment, the factual background, the date of conviction, any sentence that has been passed, and the timetable for confiscation;
(2) relevant details of the defendant himself, including age, address, marital status, and dependants. This will also include reference to previous occupations, income derived from the same, and any previous relevant convictions;
(3) the history of any restraint order proceedings, including whether a receiver has been appointed;
(4) the extent of the benefit alleged, and whether the case is one of general or particular criminal conduct—this will often include reference to admissions made at trial or the evidence given, and may also extend to relevant sentencing remarks and the basis of plea;
(5) if a general criminal conduct matter, or a lifestyle offence, reference to the assumptions that the court is being invited to draw;
(6) the nature of the assets the Crown maintains are realisable (whilst there is no duty upon the Crown to prove the available amount—formerly the 'realisable assets'—it is clearly helpful if it refers to what is known in terms of the defendant's property and wealth);
(7) the extent of any allegation of hidden assets and the basis for such a belief;
(8) the amount of the confiscation order the Crown is seeking;
(9) occasionally, reference to decided case law or the statute itself.

### A duty of full and frank disclosure?

If the prosecutor believes that the defendant has a criminal lifestyle, the statement must **8.112** include information relevant to the making of the assumptions (s 16(4)). To avoid criticism of the Crown, it is suggested that the statement should also include information about matters known to the prosecutor that might contribute to the court concluding that making an assumption would amount to a serious risk of injustice.

### The financial investigation

**8.113**  The financial investigator has a number of tools upon which he can call when conducting his enquiry (see Chapter 17). These include:

- Production Orders—s 345 of POCA, requiring disclosure of information;
- Account Monitoring Orders—s 370 of POCA, placing an ongoing duty on financial institutions to provide information for a period of up to 90 days from the day on which such an order is made;
- Customer Information Orders—s 364 of POCA, requiring a financial institution to provide any customer information in relation to a specified individual;
- Search and Seizure Warrants—s 352 of POCA, giving power to the court to make warrants authorising officers to enter premises and seize material likely to be of substantial value to the investigation, where a production order has been made and not complied with.

### When should the section 16 statement be served?

**8.114**  Under s 16(1) and (2) the prosecutor must give the statement of information to the court 'within the period the Court orders'. It is suggested, however, that in matters flowing from criminal trials the best practice is to serve the s 16 statement prior to said trial whenever possible and, except in the most complex cases, not later than the return of the jury. This will enable the trial judge to be in the best possible position to give directions as to how the POCA proceedings should proceed after conviction or a timely guilty plea.

### Upon whom should the prosecutor's statement be served?

**8.115**  Section 16(1) of POCA states that the statement of information must be given to the court. Rule 58.1 of the CrimPR requires a copy to be served on the defendant as soon as is practicable.

**8.116**  There is no requirement in the CrimPR that a statement should be served on solicitors acting on behalf of the co-accused. This is possibly because statements frequently disclose personal matters relating to the defendant's financial affairs and exhibit his disclosure statements sworn in compliance with a restraint order. Because it is in the public interest that the defendant should be encouraged to make full and frank disclosure of all his realisable property in such statements, it is suggested that he is not likely to do so if the statement was to come into the hands of third parties.

### The defendant's statement

**8.117**  Section 17 of POCA reads as follows:

> (1) If the Prosecutor gives the Court a Statement of Information and a copy is served on the defendant, the Court may order the defendant—
>    (a) to indicate (within the period it orders) the extent to which he accepts each allegation in the statement, and
>    (b) so far as he does not accept such an allegation to give particulars of any matters he proposes to rely on.

The purpose of s 17 is to identify areas of dispute for the confiscation hearing, so that evidence may be adduced only in relation to the disputed points, thus narrowing the issues and saving court time. Under r 58.1 of the CrimPR where, under s 17 of the Act, the Crown Court orders the defendant to indicate the extent to which he accepts each allegation in a statement given by the prosecutor, the defendant must state in writing his position and provide a copy to the Crown Court. One of the other purposes of s 17 is to avoid the defendant ambushing the Crown by not disclosing in advance what his case is. In addition, s 17(1) anticipates giving the prosecution the opportunity of making enquiries into the correctness of the defendant's assertions.

Once again it is important to note that a defence statement under s 17 may only be triggered **8.118** if the prosecutor gives the court a statement of information and the court is therefore proceeding under s 6, and not if the court has decided to postpone the confiscation proceedings under s 14(1)(b).

When considering s 17(1)(a), the defence should consider the prosecutor's statement para- **8.119** graph by paragraph and state whether each allegation is admitted or denied. (This is analogous to a defence in civil proceedings and a similar approach should be adopted when drafting the defendant's statement.) Where an allegation is denied, any facts relied upon to support that denial should be fully set out, with exhibits/evidence if necessary. The statement should also be verified by a statement of truth (CrimPR r 57.7).

The importance of obtaining independent corroboration of the defendant's assertions can- **8.120** not be overemphasised. In *R v Walbrook and Glasgow* [1994] Crim LR 613, the Court of Appeal held that where a defendant wanted to show that the amount of his realisable assets available for confiscation was less than the amount of his benefit as certified by the court, he had to produce clear and cogent evidence; 'vague and generalised assertions unsupported by evidence would rarely if ever be sufficient'.

It must also be remembered that at this stage the defendant is likely to stand convicted of an **8.121** offence, whether by guilty plea or by the verdict of a jury, and may therefore have something of a credibility problem.

### Defendant's acceptance conclusive

Under s 17(2) of POCA, if the defendant accepts to any extent an allegation in the statement **8.122** of information, the court may treat his acceptance as conclusive of the matters to which it relates for the purpose of deciding the issues referred to in s 16(3) (general criminal conduct) or s 16(5) (particular criminal conduct), as the case may be. Great care therefore should be taken only to admit assertions made in the prosecutor's statement that are genuinely accepted.

It should be noted, however, that the defendant's acceptance will not necessarily be binding **8.123** on appeal. In the case of *R v Emmett* [1998] AC 773, a DTOA case, the defendant pleaded guilty at the Crown Court stage. It was agreed between counsel that the benefit figure amounted to £100,000 and various sums were agreed in respect of his realisable assets. The judge made an agreed confiscation order. In the Court of Appeal the Crown submitted that the general right to appeal against a confiscation order was excluded by virtue of the DTOA's corresponding provision to s 17(2) of POCA, following the defendant's acceptance of any allegation in a statement tendered by the prosecutor which had been acted upon by the court. However, the Court of Appeal ruled that there was a strong presumption that, except by specific provision, the legislature will not exclude a right of appeal as of right, or with leave, where such a right is ordinarily available (as per *R v Cain* [1985] AC 46, 55g–56d). On appeal to the House of Lords, Lord Steyn held that unless the Act expressly or by necessary implication excluded a right of appeal, there is, as a matter of jurisdiction, a right of appeal against a confiscation order in all cases. However, he went on to state, at p 782, that:

> it is of course true that if there is an appeal, the Court of Appeal may have to take account of the fact that a Judge has decided to treat an acceptance of an allegation in a prosecution statement as conclusive, and the Court of Appeal may have to give proper and due weight to that consideration.

### Failure to respond by the defendant

**8.124**  If the defendant fails in any respect to comply with an order under s 17(1) he may be treated, under s 17(3), as having accepted every allegation in the statement of information, apart from:

    (a)  any allegation in respect of which he has complied with the requirement;
    (b)  any allegation that he has benefited from his general or particular criminal conduct.

Thus, if the defendant fails to respond to a statement of fact in relation to his assets or the available amount, that fact may be deemed by the court to be true.

**8.125**  However, there should not be any automatic assumption that the defendant has accepted an allegation that he has benefited from general or particular criminal conduct. This is because, at the time this legislation was introduced, and as part of the explanatory notes that accompanied POCA, it was considered inappropriate that the defendant's silence should be conclusive of the two principal issues before the court.

### Consequences of the defendant failing to respond to the prosecutor's statement

**8.126**  The defendant who fails to respond to orders of the court made under s 17 of POCA runs the risk of having a confiscation order made in the full amount of the benefit figure as alleged by the prosecution.

**8.127**  In *R v Comiskey* (1991) 93 Cr App R 227, the Court of Appeal held that once the prosecution have proved benefit, the burden then passes to the defendant to show, on a balance of probabilities, the value of his realisable property was less than this sum. If he fails to discharge that burden, the court must make a confiscation order in the full amount by which it has certified he has benefited from his crime.

**8.128**  As a result, the Court of Appeal has shown a reluctance to interfere with confiscation orders made in circumstances where the defendant has failed to respond to the prosecutor's statement and has failed to give evidence at the confiscation hearing.

**8.129**  In *R v Layode* (Unreported, CA, 12 March 1993) the defendant failed to respond to the prosecutor's financial statement or give evidence at the confiscation hearing. The Court of Appeal dismissed the defendant's appeal against the confiscation order. McPhearson J, in delivering the judgment of the court, observed that: 'if the Judge was wrong about the realisable assets and the bank accounts, the Appellant had nobody but himself to blame in this regard'. He added that the case underlined the importance of a defendant submitting evidence.

### Disclosure evidence inadmissible: section 17(6)

**8.130**  A potential danger arises if information is passed to the criminal case team before or during the trial that reveals matters contained within the defendant's disclosure statement, following disclosure ordered pursuant to a restraint order. The prosecutor must be alert to the fact that such disclosure is protected from cross-examination by the Crown, pursuant to the restraint order itself and *Re O (Restraint Order)* [1991] 2 QB 520, 530 (CA); *Re C (Restraint Order: Identification)* The Times, 24 April 1995; *Re C (Restraint Order: Disclosure)* (4 September 2000) (DTA 7/2000) at paras 42 and 43; and *Re D* [2001] EWHC Admin 668.

A similar danger may arise if the prosecutor was allowed to utilise disclosures made in a **8.131** defendant's reply to a s 16 statement, particularly if the trial were ongoing or further trials were anticipated. As a result some protection is included within POCA. Under s 17(6):

> No acceptance under section 17 (the defendant's response to the prosecutor's statement) that the defendant has benefited from criminal conduct is admissible in evidence in proceedings for an offence.

This protection is also given to witness statements generally in POCA matters by r 57.8 of **8.132** the CrimPR, although r 57.8 does not apply where:

(a) the witness gives consent in writing to some other use of it;
(b) the Crown Court gives permission for some other use; or
(c) the witness statement has been put in evidence at a hearing held in public.

### The problem of self-incrimination

One of the purposes of s 17(6) is to prevent the defendant invoking his privilege against **8.133** self-incrimination as a justification for failing to respond to a prosecutor's statement. This provision is analogous to the conditions under which disclosure orders are made in restraint order cases and which are designed to protect the defendant's privilege against self-incrimination.

The purpose of a s 17 defendant's statement in response is not to assist the prosecution **8.134** to advance their case. However, the reality, it is suggested, is that there will often be an overlap between the criminal investigation and preparation for the confiscation hearing, particularly in criminal cases involving financial investigations, and often to the detriment of the defendant (see *Re J* [2001] EWHC Admin 713 at para 20 challenging *R v Martin and White* (1998) 2 Cr App R 385, and *Re C (Restraint Order: Disclosure)*, (4 September 2000) (DTA/7/2000); and on self-incrimination: *Re E and Re H* [2001] EWHC Admin 472; *Istel v Tully* [1993] AC 45 at pp 55–7; and *Re: T (Restraint Order: Disclosure of Assets)* (1993) 96 Cr App R 194).

Section 17(6) is intended to encourage the defendant to be more forthcoming in his **8.135** disclosure, whereas if the protection afforded by s 17(6) did not exist, the defendant may be reluctant to admit benefit from criminal conduct that had not been the subject of a prosecution.

### Further provision of information by the defendant

Section 18 applies either where the court is proceeding under s 6 of POCA in a matter where **8.136** s 6(3)(a) applies (namely where the prosecutor has asked the court to proceed) or where s 6(3)(b) applies (where the court believes it is appropriate to do so).

Section 18(2) enables the court to order the defendant to provide information 'at any time' **8.137** for the purpose of assisting the court to carry out its confiscatory function.

**8.138**  Under r 58.1(4) of the CrimPR, where the Crown Court orders the defendant to give to it any information under s 18 of the Act, the defendant must provide the information in writing and must, as soon as practicable, serve a copy of it on the prosecutor.

**8.139**  The primary purpose of s 18 is to allow the court to make an order where the defendant is relying, or has relied, on certain matters, and the court considers it requires more information to assist it in determining the point in question.

**8.140**  It would appear that because s 18 is triggered when the court is proceeding under s 6 it may not exercise its s 18 powers in circumstances where it has postponed the confiscation proceedings, unless it can be argued that it requires the information to determine whether it should now entertain proceedings itself under s 6.

**8.141**  If the defendant fails to comply with the court's order, without reasonable excuse, s 18(4) allows the court to draw any inference it believes appropriate. Section 18(5) states that:

> Subsection 4 does not affect any power of the Court to deal with the defendant in respect of a failure to comply with an order under this section.

For example, the court's power to punish the defendant for contempt of court in refusing to comply with the order would exist in addition to the court's power to draw an inference or rely on an assumption as a result of the defendant's failure to comply.

**8.142**  It will be noted that pursuant to r 57.7 of the CrimPR, such statements provided should bear a statement of truth.

**8.143**  In terms of the type of information the court may require to assist it with its functions, there can be no exhaustive list, but examples would include:

(1)  particulars of any sources of income, including bequests;
(2)  identification of all bank and building society accounts anywhere in the world, whether jointly or solely held;
(3)  particulars of any real property anywhere in the world in which the defendant holds an interest;
(4)  details of any unit trusts, pension policies, bonds, shares, or debentures in which the defendant holds an interest;
(5)  details of any cash held and from where it was sourced;
(6)  particulars of any motor vehicles, boats, works of art, livestock, or jewellery owned;
(7)  details of any safe deposit boxes held;
(8)  details of all charge and credit cards held;
(9)  details of any other transfers made to or from the defendant in the previous six years.

### Further protection against self-incrimination

**8.144**  Section 18(9) contains a similar provision to that in s 17(6), in that it protects the defendant from incriminating himself and others in the making of any admission or reply to s 18. However, if the information disclosed leads the prosecuting authority to other new information or evidence, s 18 does not appear to prevent the authorities from using that other evidence.

**Prosecutor's acceptance conclusive**

Under s 18(6) of POCA, any acceptance by the prosecutor of any assertion contained in a **8.145** defendant's statement may be treated by the court as being conclusive for the purposes of the POCA enquiry.

**Failure to provide the information ordered**

The position of a defendant who fails to provide information under s 18(2) of POCA is dealt **8.146** with in s 18(4) which provides as follows:

> If the Defendant fails without reasonable excuse to comply with an order under this section the Court may draw such inference as it believes is appropriate.

**Further statements by the prosecutor**

Section 16(6) provides: **8.147**

> (6) If the Prosecutor gives the Court a statement of information—
>   (a)  he may at any time give the Court a further statement of information;
>   (b)  he must give the Court a further statement of information if it orders him to do so and he must give it within the period the Court orders.

A practice developed under the DTA and the CJA of the prosecutor submitting a further statement if there were matters in the defendant's statement with which he disagreed or which called for further comment. Section 16(6) of POCA endorses this practice and provides for a further statement to be tendered by the prosecutor either acting on his own volition or in compliance with an order of the court.

**Securing the attendance of witnesses**

Once s 16 and s 17 statements have been served, the parties should advise each other of **8.148** which witnesses they require at the hearing. It should be borne in mind that certain civilian witnesses, especially those employed by financial institutions, may not be prepared to attend the court voluntarily. In such cases witness summonses should be sought from the appropriate officer of the Crown Court.

**Expert evidence**

The procedure to be followed for adducing expert evidence in confiscation hearings and the **8.149** exceptions to same are set out in rr 57.9 and 57.10 of the CrimPR.

**Service of documents**

The procedure relating to the service of documents in relation to Pt 2 of POCA is set out in **8.150** r 57.11 of the CrimPR. The procedure for alternative service and service outside the jurisdiction is contained in CrimPR rr 57.12 and 57.13 respectively.

**Northern Ireland**

The proceeds of crime provisions relevant to Northern Ireland are summarised in **8.151** Appendix 20.

**An example timetable for confiscation**

**8.152** While each case will always have its own peculiar attributes so that any order will need to be drafted to cover the particular facts and issues in the case (and many cases may begin with a s 18 order against the defendant), a draft directions order is set out below:

*IN THE.............. CROWN COURT..............*                     *T.....................*

R

V

.........

Draft/ORDER

Upon hearing Counsel/Solicitor for the Prosecution and Counsel/Solicitor(s) for the Defendant (s) and upon the Defendant(s) appearing in Court
And upon the request of the Prosecution that confiscation proceedings be instituted and the Court proceeding pursuant to Section 6 of the Proceeds of Crime Act 2002

It is Ordered and Directed that:–

1. Pursuant to Section 18 of the Proceeds of Crime Act 2002 (hereinafter referred to as 'POCA') the Defendant(s) do provide replies in writing to a request for information served on the Defendant (s) on..........., by 4.00pm on.................. 2014;
**The Defendant(s) is/are expressly warned that if he/she/they fail without reasonable excuse to comply with Paragraph 1 above, then pursuant to Section 18(4) POCA the court may draw such inference as it believes is appropriate.**
2. The Prosecution do serve upon the Court and the Defendant(s) by 4.00pm on the................ 2014 a written Statement pursuant to Section 16 POCA;
3. The Defendant do serve upon the Court and the Prosecution a written Response pursuant to Section 17 POCA by 4.00pm on................ 2014 (together with any witness statements and documents, including experts' reports, relied upon);
4. The Prosecution do serve upon the Defence and the Court a written Response to the Defendant's Response (if so advised) by 4.00pm on........... 2014;
5. (The Prosecution and the Defence to agree an up-to-date valuation for the Property at ........................................... ('the Property') by 4.00pm on.......... In default of agreement as to valuation, the Prosecution and the Defence to each obtain 1 valuation report on the Property on which they propose to rely, to be served on the Court no later than........... 2014;)
6. The Prosecution to provide the Court and the Defence with written details of (a) the costs of the trial proceedings and (b) the confiscation proceedings to date (to include an estimate of the costs of the mention hearing on...............2014), by 4.00pm on.................. 2014;
7. The Defence, in relation to the Defendant(s) (in so far as all or any of the costs were incurred under a Representation Order) to provide the Court with written details of (a) the costs of the trial proceedings and (b) the costs of the confiscation proceedings to date (to include an estimate of the costs of the mention hearing on ................ 2014), by 4.00pm on the.................... 2014;
8. The Prosecution to prepare and serve upon the Court and the Defence an indexed and paginated bundle of relevant Confiscation documents, including any relevant trial documents and a chronology, for the final confiscation hearing together with a document setting out the outstanding issues in the Confiscation Proceedings by no later than 4.00pm on................ 2014;

9. Skeleton submissions in respect of any contested issues of law to be raised by any party at the final confiscation hearing to be served on the other parties and the Court on or before...................... 2014;

10. This matter to be listed for a readiness and directions hearing on............................... 2014 at 2.00pm, time estimate....... hour(s). Confiscation trial advocates to attend (if available). Matter reserved to HHJ................. (if available). The Defendant(s) to attend Court by 10.00am on the........ 2014 to meet with his/her/their advisers;

11. The final Confiscation Hearing date (in default of disposal on..............) to be fixed at the readiness and directions hearing;

(Matter to be listed for final Confiscation hearing at 10.00am on................2014. Time estimate....days. The Defendant(s) to attend. Matter reserved to HHJ..............;)

12. Any application by any party for any extension of time in respect of the periods set out above must be made before the time expires and upon not less than 48 hrs written notice to the other side and the Court. Any party seeking an extension of time must as soon as possible obtain the other side's written response to such application and serve such response on the Court;

13. In accordance with Cr.PR rule 3.5(2)(1) the parties are on notice that a failure to comply with these directions may result in an adverse order as to costs being made against a defaulting party;

14. Prosecution application for trial costs (and the consideration and/or determination of any financial orders) to be adjourned/postponed to be determined at the confiscation hearing or further order. The Defendant's(s') liability, if any, for a Recovery of Defence Costs Order or to make a contribution to his/her publicly funded costs to be determined at the Confiscation hearing or further order;

15. Documents required to be served by the parties under this Order shall be served where possible on the Court and parties by email or other electronic format. Documents to be served on the Court may be sent to the following email address...................…......... (Judge's clerk). The email address of the Prosecution is............................. The email address(es) of the Defendant's(s') solicitors is/are...........................................;

16. Costs, including the costs of today, are reserved.

HHJ................

.......................... 2014

173

# 9

# THE CONFISCATION HEARING

## A. Introduction

In the preceding chapter of this book the steps towards the final confiscation hearing were **9.01** set out. In this chapter consideration will be given to what happens at the final hearing itself and in particular how the Crown Court arrives at a final sum of money that the defendant will be obliged to pay pursuant to any confiscation order.

**9.02**   Before addressing the statutory provisions in detail it is as well to look at how the courts have approached that exercise in recent years. The provisions of POCA (and its statutory predecessors) that allow a court to impose a confiscation order on a convicted defendant may, on first impressions, appear straightforward, but in fact they betray a complexity that has challenged the House of Lords and the UK Supreme Court on numerous occasions.

### *May, Jennings,* and *Green*—the watershed

**9.03**   The House of Lords in *R v May* [2008] UKHL 28; [2008] 1 AC 1028, *Jennings v Crown Prosecution Service* [2008] UKHL 29; [2008] 1 AC 1046, and *R v Green* [2008] UKHL 30; [2008] 1 AC 1053, reviewed the earlier authorities and offered some guidance to Crown Court judges on the way to approach the statutory confiscation regimes. In *R v Clark & Severn* [2011] EWCA Crim 15; [2011] 2 Cr App R (S) 55, the Court of Appeal went so far as to describe the decision of the House of Lords in *May* as a 'watershed authority' (para 13).

**9.04**   How then did the confiscation landscape look in the aftermath of the *May, Jennings* and *Green* decisions? A number of observations can be made.

**9.05**   Firstly, the lower courts were required to focus on answering the three questions posed by Lord Bingham in *May* after having made appropriate findings of fact, namely: Has the defendant benefited from the relevant criminal conduct? If the answer to that question is negative, the inquiry ends. If the answer is positive, the second question is: What is the value of the benefit the defendant has so obtained? The third question is: What sum is recoverable from the defendant?

**9.06**   In answering those questions, the courts were invited to look to the language of the relevant Act and the facts of the particular case, rather than the extensive case law in this area.

**9.07**   Secondly, in answering the first of those questions ('Has the defendant (D) benefited from relevant criminal conduct?') the courts were permitted to reflect on whether the nature of the defendant's criminality meant that he had not obtained property at all, or at least not the property that was the subject matter of his crime. Thus, couriers or custodians or other very minor contributors to an offence might not have benefited in the same amount as others involved in the commission of the offence, especially where they participated in the crime for a fee and had no 'interest' in the property that passed through their hands. The consequence of this approach was that more and more defendants have sought to argue that they were merely couriers or custodians of stolen or contraband goods in order to avoid a finding that they had obtained the goods themselves.

**9.08**   Thirdly, the notion that where a number of defendants jointly obtained property as a result of or in connection with their crime there should be some apportionment between them was laid to rest except where it might be disproportionate or in breach of Art 1 Protocol 1 (A1P1) to make a confiscation order for the full amount against all of them. It is fair to note that Lord Bingham in *May* devoted little time to considering when an argument under A1P1 might arise and how it could be resolved. Uncertainty therefore lingered around when A1P1 might be invoked and so whenever a defendant felt there was a yawning gap between his benefit as calculated by operation of the provisions of the relevant Act and the proceeds of his criminal conduct that actually came to him he would typically seek to stay the confiscation proceedings as an abuse of process rather than rely on any disproportionality argument under A1P1. This is precisely what occurred in two unrelated cases: *R v Morgan* [2008] 4 All ER 890 and *R v Shabir* [2009] 1 Cr App R (S) 497. In *Shabir*, the prosecution sought a confiscation order in the sum of £400,000 in circumstances where it was agreed that the defendant had only received £464 that could be directly attributed to his criminality. In the event an order was made in the amount of £212,464. The Court of Appeal quashed the order and held that the confiscation proceedings ought to have been stayed as an abuse of process given the enormous disparity involved. The Court was keen to emphasise, though, that the power of the Crown Court to stay confiscation proceedings should be exercised 'with considerable caution' (para 24) and it should not be used as a substitute for the general discretion that Parliament had seen fit to deny judges in such cases.

### Guidance

The Court of Appeal in *R v Sivaraman* [2008] EWCA Crim 1736; [2009] 1 Cr App R (S) 80;  **9.09**
[2008] Crim LR 989, a case decided after *May, Jennings*, and *Green*, offered this summary of the guidance issued by Lord Bingham in those cases, at para 12:

> In the trio of cases recently decided by the House of Lords a number of matters were made plain:
> (1)  The legislation is intended to deprive the defendants of the benefit they have gained from the relevant conduct within the limits of their available means. It does not operate by way of fine: *May*, paragraph 48(1); *Jennings*, paragraph 13.
> (2)  The benefit gained is the total value of the property or pecuniary advantage gained, not the particular defendant's net profit: *May*, paragraph 48(1).
> (3)  In considering what is the value of the benefit which the defendant has obtained, the court should focus on the language of the statute and apply its ordinary meaning (subject to any statutory definition) to the facts of the case: *May*, paragraph 48(3) and (4); Jennings paragraph 13.
> (4)  'Obtained' means obtained by the relevant defendant: *Jennings*, paragraph 14.
> (5)  A defendant's acts may contribute significantly to property or to a pecuniary advantage being obtained without that defendant obtaining it: *Jennings*, paragraph 14.
> (6)  Where two or more defendants obtain property jointly, each is to be regarded as obtaining the whole of it. Where property is received by one conspirator, what matters is the capacity in which he receives it, that is, whether for his own personal benefit, or on behalf of others, or jointly on behalf of himself and others. This has to be decided on the evidence: *Green*, paragraph 15. By parity of reasoning, two or more defendants may or may not obtain a joint pecuniary advantage; it depends on the facts.

### Stays

The Court of Appeal in *CPS v N* [2009] EWCA Crim 1573 shared these sentiments and  **9.10**
bemoaned the fact that applications by defendants to stay confiscation proceedings were on the increase. In that Court's view, in the vast majority of cases the application of the statutory language would lead to a just result and so any attempt by the defence to halt the process by claiming that it was being abused should be given short shrift. Nevertheless, the Court did recognise situations where confiscation proceedings could be stayed and these included where those proceedings were not fair (see *AP and U v CPS* [2007] EWCA Crim 3128). Similarly, where the defendant had voluntarily restored the proceeds of his crime to the loser, or was ready and willing to do so, it *might* be an abuse of process for the prosecution to press ahead with confiscation proceedings because that 'would result in an oppressive order to pay up to double the full restitution which the defendant has made or is willing immediately to make and which would thus deter him from making it'.

In *R v Bhanji* [2011] EWCA Crim 1198 the Court of Appeal held that a confiscation hear-  **9.11**
ing may proceed despite the defendant's absence because of chronic illness. The court must weigh up the impact of the absence on the fairness of the hearing. The interests of justice require a determination. The availability of other relevant evidence and the fact that this is treated as part of post-conviction sentencing rather than trial are both relevant factors.

**The shifting landscape—*Waya***

**9.12** The decisions of the House of Lords in *May, Jennings,* and *Green* therefore had major ramifications for the way in which the courts conducted confiscation proceedings and the arguments taken by parties to those proceedings. In only a few short years, however, that landscape had shifted yet again, this time by the decision of the UK Supreme Court in *R v Waya* [2012] UKSC 51; [2012] 3 WLR 1188. See also *R v Harvey* [2013] EWCA Crim 1104.

**9.13** The issues in the appeal related to the first and second questions posed by Lord Bingham in *May*: what was the appellant's benefit from his crime and what was the value of that benefit?

**9.14** In answering those questions the Supreme Court did not speak with one voice. The majority opinion was written by Lord Walker and Sir Anthony Hughes, with whom Lord Judge LCJ, Baroness Hale, Lord Kerr, Lord Clarke and Lord Wilson agreed, whereas the minority opinion was written by Lord Phillips and Lord Reed. The first thirty-five paragraphs of the majority judgment contain an overview of the statutory provisions of POCA and give consideration to the effects of the Human Rights Act 1998 (HRA) on the confiscation regime. The minority (at para 83) expressed its admiration for and endorsement of the majority's reasoning and conclusions in those paragraphs. It follows that paragraphs 1–35 of the majority's judgment represent the shared views of each member of the Supreme Court in *Waya*. The views expressed in those paragraphs, whilst strictly *obiter*, should be followed in all future confiscation proceedings: see *R v Hursthouse* [2013] EWCA Crim 517 and *R v Jawad* [2013] EWCA Crim 644, at para 8.

**9.15** In those paragraphs the Court commented on the strict nature of the confiscation regime in POCA and on the difficulties often faced by judges in the lower courts when applying that regime on account of 'the extremely involved statutory language' (para 4). As to that language, the Court noted that Parliament 'has framed the statute in broad terms with a certain amount of what Lord Wilberforce (in a tax case) called "overkill" ' (para 8). In the same paragraph, the Court went on to say this:

> Although the statute has often been described as 'draconian' that cannot be a warrant for abandoning the traditional rule that a penal statute should be construed with some strictness. But subject to this and to HRA, the task of the Crown Court judge is to give effect to Parliament's intention as expressed in the language of the statute. The statutory language must be given a fair and purposive construction in order to give effect to its legislative policy.

**9.16** The Court endorsed the guidance of Lord Bingham in *May* as to the three questions that the Crown Court judge should answer (para 7) and went on to do what the House of Lords had declined to do in *May* and consider the full impact of the HRA on the confiscation regime.

*Human rights*

**9.17** At para 12, the Court in *Waya* said that it is 'clear law' that A1P1

> imports, via the rule of fair balance, the requirement that there must be a reasonable relationship of proportionality between the means employed by the state in, inter alia, the deprivation of property as a form of penalty, and the legitimate aim which is sought to be realised by the deprivation.

**9.18** In addition, as A1P1 is one of the Convention rights to which the HRA applies, so s 3(1) of that Act requires that so far as it is possible to do so legislation must be 'read and given effect in a way which is compatible' with it (para 13).

**9.19** It followed, in the Court's view, that where s 6(5) of POCA requires the Crown Court judge, having made a determination as to the defendant's benefit, to decide the recoverable amount and to make a confiscation order requiring the defendant to pay that amount, it is necessary to read in a further requirement that the court should only make a confiscation order requiring the defendant to pay the recoverable amount where such an order would *not* be disproportionate and thus a breach of A1P1 (para 16). This necessity arises 'in order to ensure that the statute remains Convention-compliant' with the result that a Crown Court judge should 'if confronted by an application for an order which would be disproportionate, refuse to make it but accede only to an application for such sum as would be proportionate'. The minority described the use of A1P1 in this context as 'novel and imaginative' (para 83).

*The position going forward*

Undoubtedly the Court in *Waya* modified the approach advocated by the House of Lords in **9.20** *May*. Now the lower courts must not only answer the three questions posed in *May* but must also consider whether a confiscation order in the sum of the recoverable amount arrived at once those questions have been answered would be disproportionate within the context of A1P1.

It is important to realise that the Crown Court will not have to consider whether the defend- **9.21** ant's benefit as determined by operation of the statute is disproportionate until it has decided on the recoverable amount because A1P1 will only be engaged once the court has decided on what form the confiscation order should take, as it is only then that the risk of interference with the defendant's peaceful enjoyment of his possessions is threatened.

Drawing on the reasoning of the minority in paragraph 84 of *Waya*, the questions any Crown **9.22** Court judge should answer are now these:

(a) What is the defendant's benefit under the statute?
(b) What is the value of the defendant's benefit?
(c) What is the recoverable amount?
(d) Would a confiscation order in the sum of the recoverable amount be disproportionate to the purpose of the statute? If so what would be a proportionate order?

Aside from an addition to the number of questions that any Crown Court judge will need **9.23** to answer, the Supreme Court in *Waya* left untouched the view of the House of Lords in *May* that the lower courts should apply the language of the statute and avoid, if possible, extensive reference to the established case law. In *R v Beazley* [2013] EWCA Crim 567 the Court held it was not unfair or disproportionate to apply the confiscation regime and the criminal lifestyle provisions to defendants convicted of unauthorised trademark offences. Whether there will be any practical difference in future between adopting a purposive interpretation of the legislation as favoured by the majority in *Waya* (para 8) or the natural construction that was found to be attractive to the minority (para 103) remains, however, to be seen.

## B. Statutory Benefit

Once the Crown Court has decided to proceed to a confiscation hearing, section 6(4) of **9.24** POCA is engaged. It reads thus:

> The court must proceed as follows—
> (a) it must decide whether the defendant has a criminal lifestyle;
> (b) it if it decides that he has a criminal lifestyle it must decide whether he has benefited from his general criminal conduct;

(c) if it decides that he does not have a criminal lifestyle it must decide whether he has benefited from his particular criminal conduct.

**9.25** The statute therefore draws a clear distinction between cases where the defendant has a criminal lifestyle and cases where he does not. Where he does, the court must determine whether he has benefited from his general criminal conduct (ie from his criminal lifestyle). Where the defendant does not have a criminal lifestyle, the focus of the court's attention will be on what he obtained as a result of or in connection with the particular crime or crimes he committed and no more.

### General criminal conduct

*What amounts to a 'criminal lifestyle'?*

**9.26** Section 75(1) of POCA provides that a 'defendant has a criminal lifestyle if (and only if)' s 75(2) is satisfied:

(2) The condition is that the offence (or any of the offences) concerned satisfies any of these tests:
(a) it is specified in Schedule 2;
(b) it constitutes conduct forming part of a course of criminal activity;
(c) it is an offence committed over a period of at least six months and the defendant has benefited from the conduct which constitutes the offence.

**9.27** The reference here to 'the offence (or any of the offences)' refers to the crime or crimes committed by the defendant and which led to the commencement of confiscation proceedings against him, as set out in s 6(2). This definition does not extend to include an offence or offences that have been formally taken into consideration by the court at the sentencing stage.

**9.28** Where the defendant has been convicted of a number of offences he will have a criminal lifestyle provided that at least one of those offences satisfies any of the three tests in s 75(2). The Judge has a duty to determine whether the defendant has a 'criminal lifestyle'—*R v Molloy* [2013] EWCA Crim 682.

**9.29** **The first test** If any of the offences concerned are found in Sch 2 then the defendant will have a criminal lifestyle whether he has benefited from those offences or not. The offences contained in Sch 2 are as follows

- Asylum and Immigration (Treatment of Claimants, etc.) Act 2004, section 4 (exploitation).
- Copyright, Designs and Patents Act 1988, section 107(1) (making or dealing in an article that infringes copyright), section 107(2) (making or possessing an article designed or adapted for making a copy of a copyright work), section 198(1) (making or dealing in an illicit recording), and section 297A (making or dealing in unauthorised decoders).
- Criminal Justice (International Co-operation) Act 1990, section 12 (manufacture or supply of a substance or the time being specified in Schedule 2 to that Act) and section 19 (using a ship for illicit traffic in controlled drugs).
- Customs and Excise Management Act 1979,
  (i) section 50(2) or (3) (improper importation of goods), section 68(2) (exploration of prohibited or restricted goods), and section 170 (fraudulent evasion), if any of these offences are committed in connection with a prohibition or restriction on importation or exportation which has effect by virtue of section 3 of the Misuse of Drugs Act 1971.

(ii) section 68(2) (exportation of prohibited goods), and section 170 (fraudulent evasion), if any of these offences are committed in connection with a firearm or ammunition.

- Firearms Act 1968, section 3(1) (dealing in firearms or ammunition by way of trade or business). Those terms have the same meaning as they do in section 57 of that Act.
- Forgery and Counterfeiting Act 1981, section 14 (making counterfeit notes or coins), section 15 (passing etc counterfeit notes or coins), section 16 (having counterfeit notes or coins), and section 17 (making or possessing materials or equipment for counterfeiting).
- Gangmasters (Licensing) Act 2004 (acting as a gangmaster other than under the authority of a licence, possession of false documents etc.).
- Immigration Act 1971, sections 25, 25A and 25B (assisting unlawful immigration etc).
- Inchoate offences, including (i) an offence of attempting, conspiring or inciting the commission of an offence specified in this Schedule, (ii) an offence under section 44 of the Serious Crime Act 2007 of doing an act capable of encouraging or assisting the commission of an offence specified in this Schedule, and (iii) an offence of aiding, abetting, counseling or procuring the commission of such an offence.
- Misuse of Drugs Act 1971, section 4(2) or (3) (unlawful production or supply of controlled drugs), section 5(3) (possession of controlled drug with intent to supply), section 8 (permitting certain activities relating to controlled drugs), and section 20 (assisting in or inducing the commission outside the UK of an offence punishable under a corresponding law).
- Proceeds of Crime Act 2002, section 327 (concealing etc criminal property) and section 328 (assisting another to retain criminal property) (but not section 329 acquisition use and possession of criminal property).
- Sexual Offences Act 1956, sections 33 or 34 (keeping or letting premises for use as a brothel).
- Sexual Offences Act 2003, section 14 (arranging or facilitating commission of a child sex offence), section 48 (causing or inciting child prostitution or pornography), section 49 (controlling a child prostitute or a child involved in pornography), section 50 (arranging or facilitating child prostitution or pornography), section 52 (causing or inciting prostitution for gain), section 53 (controlling prostitution for gain), and sections 57 to 59 (trafficking for sexual exploitation).
- Terrorism Act 2000, section 56 (directing the activities of a terrorist organisation).
- Theft Act 1968, section 21 (blackmail).
- Trade Marks Act 1994, section 92(1), (2) or (3) (unauthorised use etc of trade mark).

**The second test**    Under the second test in section 75(2), the defendant will have a crimi- **9.30** nal lifestyle where the offence or offences of which he stands convicted 'constitute conduct forming part of a course of criminal activity'. This test caters for the situation where no single offence of which the defendant has been convicted demonstrates that he enjoys a criminal lifestyle but when taken together with the defendant's other convictions (whether acquired at the same time or on some earlier occasion) reveal that to be the case.

Section 75(3) and (4) seeks to clarify when this second test will be satisfied:    **9.31**

(3)  Conduct forms part of a course of criminal activity if the defendant has benefited from conduct and—
(a)  in the proceedings in which he was convicted he was convicted of three or more other offences, each of three or more of them constituting conduct from which he has benefited or

> (b) in the period of six years ending with the day when those proceedings were started (or,
> if there is more than one such day, the earliest day) he was convicted on at least two
> separate occasions of an offence constituting conduct from which he has benefited.
> (4) But an offence does not satisfy the test in subsection (2)(b) or (c) unless the defendant
> obtained relevant benefit of not less than £5,000.

**9.32** This subsection draws a distinction between a situation where the defendant has a criminal lifestyle on account of the number and types of offences he was convicted of in the substantive criminal proceedings that led to the commencement of confiscation proceedings and a situation where that is not the case but nevertheless the number and type of the defendant's *previous* criminal convictions demonstrates that the test is met.

**9.33** The reference to 'benefit' in s 75(3) and 'relevant benefit' in s 75(4) is explained in s 75(5), which provides as follows:

> (5) Relevant benefit for the purposes of subsection 2(b) is—
> (a) benefit from conduct which constitutes the offences;
> (b) benefit from any other conduct which forms part of the course of criminal activity
> and which constitutes an offence of which the defendant has been convicted;
> (c) benefit from conduct which constitutes an offence which has been or will be taken
> into consideration by the court in sentencing the defendant for an offence mentioned
> in paragraph (a) or (b).

**9.44** Furthermore, s 76(4) states that a defendant 'benefits from conduct if he obtained property as a result of or in connection with the conduct'. The meaning and significance of this section is considered later in this chapter.

**9.45** Drawing s 75(2), (3), (4), and (5) together, the offence or offences of which the defendant has been convicted will constitute conduct forming part of a course of criminal activity in two situations.

**9.46** The first situation is where the defendant has been convicted in criminal proceedings of an offence from which he has benefited and in the proceedings in which he was convicted he was also convicted of at least three other offences from which he also benefited and the total benefit from those four offences and any other offences taken into consideration at the time is not less than £5,000. Some examples will illustrate how this will work in practice.

*Example 1*: The defendant appears in the Crown Court on an indictment containing four counts of burglary. His benefit from each burglary was £1,500. There are no offences to be taken into consideration. As the defendant benefited from each of these burglaries and his total benefit exceeds £5,000 then these convictions will represent a course of criminal activity sufficient to affix the defendant with a criminal lifestyle.

*Example 2*: The defendant appears in the Crown Court on an indictment containing four counts of burglary and two further burglaries to be taken into consideration. His benefit from each burglary was £1,000. As the defendant's total benefit from all of the burglaries, including those to be taken into consideration, is £6,000 his convictions will represent a course of criminal activity like that in example 1.

*Example 3*: The defendant appears in the Crown Court on an indictment containing three counts of burglary with two further burglaries to be taken into consideration. His benefit from each of these five burglaries was £1,500. There would be no course of criminal activity because the defendant would not have been convicted of four offences in the same set of proceedings.

*Example 4*: The defendant appears in the Crown Court on an indictment containing three counts of burglary and one count of attempted burglary with two further burglaries to be taken into consideration. His benefit from each of these five burglaries was £1,500 but he did not benefit from the attempted burglary because he was disturbed in the act and fled empty-handed. There would be no course of criminal conduct because although the defendant was convicted of four offences in the same set of proceedings, he did not benefit from all four offences.

The second situation is where the defendant has been convicted in criminal proceedings of **9.47** an offence from which he has benefited and in the six-year period before he was charged with that offence he was convicted on two separate occasions of an offence constituting conduct from which he has benefited. Again, some examples will illustrate how this will work in practice.

*Example 1*: The defendant is convicted in the Crown Court on 1 January 2013 of burglary from which his benefit was £2,000. On the 1 January 2012 he had been convicted of another burglary from which he had benefited to the same amount. On the 1 January 2011 he had been convicted of yet another burglary from which he had benefited to the same amount as well. This would constitute a course of criminal activity because the defendant was convicted of three offences on three different occasions and he benefited from each one where the total benefit was not less than £5,000.

*Example 2*: As in example 1, only this time the benefit from each of the three burglaries was only £1,000 but as to the 1 January 2011 conviction, two further burglary offences had been taken into consideration where the benefit from each was also £1,000. This would constitute a course of criminal activity because the defendant was convicted of three offences on three different occasions and he benefited from each one where the total benefit from those offences and the two taken into consideration was not less than £5,000.

**The third test**    This arises where the offence or any of the offences that the defendant stands **9.48** convicted of was committed over a period of at least six months and the defendant has benefited from conduct that constitutes the offence (see *R v Bajwa* [2011] EWCA Crim 1093 and *R v Molloy* [2013] EWCA Crim 682). Section 75(6) provides as follows:

(6) Relevant benefit for the purposes of subsection 2(c) is—
    (a) benefit from conduct which constitutes the offence;
    (b) benefit from conduct which constitutes an offence which has been or will be taken into consideration by the court in sentencing the defendant for the offence mentioned in paragraph (a).

If any of the offences of which the defendant stands convicted were committed over a period **9.49** of at least six months, the defendant must nevertheless have benefited from the offences in order to have a criminal lifestyle. Thus, if the defendant is convicted of a conspiracy to defraud that lasted longer than six months but from which he did not benefit and a separate count of theft from which he benefited in the sum of £5,000, the third test will not be met because his benefit from the offence that was committed over a period of at least six months did not come to at least £5,000.

The effect of s 75(6)(b) then is that where a defendant is being sentenced in respect of two **9.50** offences (one of which was committed over a period of at least six months and the other that was not) the court cannot amalgamate the benefit he received from each to see if it comes to not less than £5,000. Where, however, there is an offence to be taken into consideration where the defendant benefited to a sum not less than £5,000, then that can be amalgamated with the benefit he obtained in respect of the offence committed over a period of at least six months and so the third test would be met on the latter scenario but not the former.

### When does the defendant benefit from his general criminal conduct?

*General rules*

**9.51** If the defendant has a criminal lifestyle then under s 6(4)(b) the court must decide whether he has benefited from his general criminal conduct. Section 76(2) provides that the general criminal conduct of the defendant 'is all his criminal conduct', irrespective of when that conduct occurred. Moreover, by s 76(1), criminal conduct is conduct that constitutes an offence in England and Wales or that would constitute an offence if it occurred in England and Wales. It follows that the definition of criminal conduct is not just limited to offences committed by the defendant in England and Wales but encompasses any conduct on his part committed anywhere in the world if it would amount to an offence had he committed it within this jurisdiction.

**9.52** The defendant's general criminal conduct will therefore include (i) the offence or offences of which he stands convicted, (ii) any previous offences of which he was convicted in England and Wales, (iii) any conduct occurring in England and Wales that amounts to the commission of a criminal offence but in respect of which the defendant has not been convicted, and (iv) any conduct occurring outside this jurisdiction that would qualify under (iii) if it had occurred in this jurisdiction. But general criminal conduct does not include any criminal offences committed overseas (except where the conduct would qualify under (iv)) or any other conduct occurring overseas where on the same facts no offence would have been committed in England and Wales.

**9.53** As to (i) and (ii), it will in all likelihood be obvious from the defendant's antecedents what those offences were and the circumstances of them should be readily ascertainable too. Thus, it should be a straightforward matter for the prosecution to establish the defendant's benefit from his commission of those offences pursuant to s 76(4).

**9.54** As to (iii) and (iv), where the defendant does not have a domestic criminal conviction to his name, that task will be harder because the prosecution will have to prove the defendant's guilt before it can go on to establish his benefit from that proven conduct. It should be borne in mind that where a defendant has been acquitted of a criminal offence, it would be wrong for the prosecution to seek to reopen that acquittal in confiscation proceedings by proving the defendant's guilt afresh so that his benefit from that offence can form part of his benefit from his general criminal conduct: see *R v Briggs-Price* [2009] UKHL 19. See also *R v Sakhizada* [2012] EWCA Crim 1036.

### Statutory assumptions

**9.55** Not only can the prosecution seek to rely on conduct falling within (i), (ii), (iii), and (iv) above to show the defendant's benefit from his general criminal conduct but by virtue of s 10, the court is obliged to make four assumptions against the defendant for the purpose of deciding whether he has benefited from his general criminal conduct and deciding his benefit from that conduct. These assumptions are as follows:

(2) The first assumption is that any property transferred to the defendant at any time after the relevant day was obtained by him—
   (a) as a result of his general criminal conduct, and
   (b) at the earliest time he appears to have held it.

(3) The second assumption is that any property held by the defendant at any time after the date of conviction was obtained by him—
   (a) as a result of his general criminal conduct, and
   (b) at the earliest time he appears to have held it.

(4) The third assumption is that any expenditure incurred by the defendant at any time after the relevant day was met from property obtained by him as a result of his general criminal conduct.

(5) The fourth assumption is that, for the purpose of valuing any property obtained (or assumed to have been obtained) by the defendant, he obtained it free of any other interests in it.

Under s 10(8), the relevant day is the first day of the period of six years ending with either **9.56** the day when proceedings for the offence concerned were started against the defendant, or if there are two or more offences and proceedings for them were started on different days, the earliest of those days. Proceedings will start against the defendant when he is charged with the offence of which he stands convicted and in respect of which the confiscation proceedings were commenced.

The assumptions will only come into play where the prosecution can prove to the civil stand- **9.57** ard that property was transferred to the defendant (the first assumption) or that property was held by the defendant (the second assumption) or that expenditure was incurred by the defendant (the third assumption). It follows that the court must not assume, for example, that the defendant incurred expenditure and then make the further assumption that that expenditure was met from property obtained by the defendant as a result of his general criminal conduct.

### The first assumption

As to the first assumption, the relevant day will be calculated by determining when the **9.58** defendant was first charged with the offence or offences of which he stands convicted and then settling on the date six years beforehand. Any property transferred to the defendant from that date onwards, up to and including the final confiscation hearing itself, will be subject to this assumption. Section 84(2)(c) provides that 'property is transferred by one person to another if the first one transfers or grants an interest in it to the second' and by virtue of s 84(2)(f) and (h), references to an interest in land 'are to any legal estate or equitable interest or power' and references to an interest in relation to property other than land 'include references to a right (including a right to possession)'. These definitions will be considered in more detail later in this chapter but it is clear from the language of the subsections themselves that property need not be handed over in its entirety to the defendant for it to have been transferred to him. It will be enough in most cases that some interest in the property has been ceded to him and if that can be proven then the first assumption will bite.

### The second assumption

As to the second assumption, this relates to property held by the defendant at any time **9.59** after the date of his conviction for the offences in respect of which confiscation proceedings were initiated. Section 84(2)(a) states that 'property is held by a person if he holds an interest in it' and 'interest' is further defined in s 84(2)(f) and (h) as set out above. Where the defendant has divested himself of any such interest in property held by him before the date of his conviction then in the ensuing confiscation proceedings this assumption will not apply.

### The third assumption

**9.60** As to the third assumption, that relates to expenditure incurred by the defendant during the period set down under the discussion of the first assumption. If the prosecution can show that expenditure was incurred then the assumption applies.

### The fourth assumption

**9.61** As to the fourth assumption, this applies whenever the defendant has obtained property, whether as a result of the successful application of the first and second assumptions or because the prosecution has been able to show that the defendant has benefited from his general criminal conduct in some other way. The assumption is that he obtained that property free from the interests that anyone else has in it. This assumption avoids the difficulties inherent in s 79(3) so far as valuing separate interests in property is concerned. The scope of s 79(3) is therefore confined to cases where either the defendant does not have a criminal lifestyle or he does and the fourth assumption has been rebutted. Section 79(3) will be considered later in this chapter.

### Rebutting the assumptions

**9.62** Although the court is required by s 10 to make these assumptions where the defendant has a criminal lifestyle, the section does set out two ways in which the assumptions can be rebutted. They are contained in s 10(6):

> (6) But the court must not make a required assumption in relation to particular property or expenditure if—
>    (a) the assumption is shown to be incorrect, or
>    (b) there would be a serious risk of injustice if the assumption were made.

**9.63** The first way in which the assumptions can be rebutted is for the defendant to show that the assumptions are incorrect. In other words, if the defendant can establish that the property transferred to him came from a legitimate source and was transferred to him for a perfectly lawful reason then the court should not make the assumption that he obtained that property as a result of his general criminal conduct. It may not be necessary for the defendant to adduce any cogent evidence to establish the legitimacy of that property provided there is some evidence from which the court could reach that conclusion.

**9.64** The second way in which the assumptions can be rebutted is where there would be a serious risk of injustice if the assumptions were made. The focus of the court here is not on whether the assumptions themselves are flawed but on whether the effect of making the assumptions would be to create a real risk of the defendant suffering an injustice. This may be so where, for example, the defendant's criminal lifestyle consists of buying and selling stolen goods. If he buys one stolen object, then sells it and buys another one with the proceeds and so on the application of the assumptions would hold that the value of the stolen objects, the money the defendant used to buy them, and the money the defendant received from their sale should all count as his benefit even though what the minority in *Waya* would describe as his 'real' benefit would be limited to the profit he made from each sale. In these circumstances, the defendant may well have a strong argument that injustice will flow if the assumptions applied in full on these facts.

A serious risk of injustice does not arise just because the defendant will suffer real hardship if **9.65** a confiscation order is made in the full amount of the benefit as derived by operation of the assumptions (see *R v Jones*, The Times, 8 August 2006) but where there is a risk that a confiscation order in that amount would be disproportionate to the purpose of the legislation, as explained in *Waya*, a serious risk of injustice would follow.

There is one other way in which the defendant may be able to defeat the assumptions without **9.66** recourse to s 10(6). If a confiscation order was made against the defendant in some earlier proceedings that took place since the relevant day (ie on a date after the day six years before the defendant was charged with the offences of which he stands convicted and in respect of which the current confiscation proceedings have been commenced) and his benefit in those proceedings was determined by reference to his general criminal conduct then, by virtue of s 10(9), the relevant day for the purposes of the current proceedings is the day on which the defendant's benefit was calculated in those earlier proceedings and the second assumption would not apply to any property which was held by the defendant on or before the relevant day.

### Particular criminal conduct

*General rules*

If the defendant does not have a criminal lifestyle then the court must decide whether he **9.67** has benefited from his particular criminal conduct. In order to make that determination the court must have regard to ss 76 and 84 of POCA, which are set out in full below.

76. Conduct and benefit
(1) Criminal conduct is conduct which –
 (a) constitutes an offence in England and Wales, or
 (b) would constitute such an offence if it occurred in England and Wales.
(2) General criminal conduct of the defendant is all his criminal conduct, and it is immaterial –
 (a) whether conduct occurred before or after the passing of this Act;
 (b) whether property constituting a benefit from conduct was obtained before or after the passing of this Act.
(3) Particular criminal conduct of the defendant is all his criminal conduct which falls within the following paragraphs—
 (a) conduct which constitutes the offence or offences concerned;
 (b) conduct which constitutes offences of which he was convicted in the same proceedings as those in which he was convicted of the offence or offences concerned;
 (c) conduct which constitutes offences which the court will be taking into consideration in deciding his sentence for the offence or offences concerned.
(4) A person benefits from conduct if he obtains property as a result of or in connection with the conduct.
(5) If the person obtains a pecuniary advantage as a result of or in connection with conduct, he is to be taken to obtain as a result of or in connection with the conduct a sum of money equal to the value of the pecuniary advantage.
(6) References to property or a pecuniary advantage obtained in connection with conduct include references to property or a pecuniary advantage obtained both in that connection and some other.
(7) If a person benefits from conduct his benefit is the value of the property obtained.
 ...

84. Property: general provisions

    (1) Property is all property whenever situated and includes—

        (a) money;

        (b) all forms of real and personal property;

        (c) things in action and other intangible or incorporeal property.

    (2) The following rules apply in relation to property—

        (a) property is held by a person if he holds an interest in it;

        (b) property is obtained by a person if he obtains an interest in it;

        (c) property is transferred by one person to another if the first one transfers or grants an interest in it to the second;

        (d) references to property held by a person include references to property vested in his trustee in bankruptcy, permanent or interim trustee (within the meaning of the Bankruptcy (Scotland) Act 1985 (c.66)) or liquidator;

        (e) references to an interest held by a person beneficially in property include references to an interest which would be held by him beneficially if the property were not so vested;

        (f) references to an interest, in relation to land in England and Wales or Northern Ireland, are to any legal estate or equitable interest or power;

        (g) references to an interest in relation to land in Scotland, are to any estate, interest, servitude or other heritable right in or over land, including a heritable security;

        (h) references to an interest, in relation to property other than land, include references to a right (including a right to possession).

**9.68** When determining whether the defendant has benefited from his particular criminal conduct, the focus of the court will be on s 76(4)—a person benefits from conduct if he obtains property as a result of or in connection with the conduct. That section has consistently been interpreted to mean that the *only* way a defendant can benefit from his particular criminal conduct is where he obtains property as a result of or in connection with that conduct. A number of words and expressions in that section betray a complexity that may not be obvious from a first reading. In particular, the meaning of 'obtains' has bedevilled the criminal courts for some time now and a satisfactory all-embracing definition is still some way off, if, indeed, it is achievable at all.

**9.69** Breaking s 76(4) down into its component parts creates the following series of questions that a court will need to answer:

    (1) What 'conduct' counts?

    (2) What does 'property' mean?

    (3) How does the defendant 'obtain' property?

    (4) When will the defendant obtain property 'as a result of' his conduct?

    (5) When will the defendant obtain property 'in connection with' his conduct?

**9.70** It is worth bearing in mind here the view of the House of Lords in *May* and the UK Supreme Court in *Waya* that the Crown Court should follow the language of the Act and avoid, where possible, reference to the case law unless those authorities clarify an ambiguity in the statutory text.

*What 'conduct' counts?*

**9.71** Section 76(3) makes it clear that the 'conduct' here will be a combination of the conduct that constitutes the offence or offences in respect of which confiscation proceedings were initiated, conduct that constitutes another offence or offences of which the defendant was convicted in the same proceedings, and conduct which constitutes offences 'which the court will be taking into consideration in deciding his sentence' for the offences of which he was convicted.

In practice this means that where a defendant is convicted in the same proceedings in the **9.72** Crown Court of, say, burglary, and there is a schedule of several additional offences of burglary that the defendant wishes the judge to take into consideration when sentencing him (commonly referred to as a 'TIC Schedule'), the 'conduct' for the purposes of s 76(3) will be the burglary count on the indictment and all of the burglary offences listed in the schedule.

What of the situation where in the example above there was no schedule but the judge was **9.73** nevertheless satisfied to the criminal standard, having heard the evidence given at trial, that the defendant had committed more burglaries than just the one charged in the indictment? It may even be that the defendant confessed in his evidence to having committed other burglaries but either way does this mean that the judge would be entitled to include those other offences in the list of 'conduct' under s 76(3)? The language of the statute would appear to preclude this although there would be no bar to the Crown Court judge using these findings when making an assessment of the defendant's benefit from his general criminal conduct should he have a criminal lifestyle.

*What is 'property'?*

By virtue of s 84(1), property includes (but is not therefore limited to) 'money', 'all forms **9.74** of real and personal property', and 'things in action and other intangible or incorporeal property'.

**'Money'**  This means physical currency of the sort that a bank robber might take. Where **9.75** it is alleged that the defendant obtained a pecuniary advantage, s 76(5) provides that 'he is taken to obtain as a result of or in connection with the conduct a sum of money equal to the value of the pecuniary advantage'. Thus, if the defendant smuggles contraband cigarettes into the UK, thereby avoiding having to pay the excise duty chargeable on them, the pecuniary advantage he secured for himself will become, by operation of s 76(5), an equivalent sum of money in his hands that will be 'property' (see *R v David Cadman-Smith* [2002] 1 WLR 54).

The essence of a pecuniary advantage here is that the defendant has, by his criminal conduct, **9.76** avoided a financial obligation that he was bound to satisfy. Hence in the case of a defendant convicted of evading some form of lawful taxation the issue will be whether that defendant was bound to pay that tax. In the case of the smuggler of contraband cigarettes, the Court of Appeal in *R v James* [2011] EWCA Crim 2991; [2012] 1 WLR 2641; [2012] 2 Cr App R (S) 44; [2012] Lloyd's Rep FC 168; [2012] Crim LR 307; The Times, 20 January 2012, held that a party to such an operation would only have been liable to pay the excise duty where he was either holding the tobacco products at the time they reached the excise duty point (ie the driver) or he caused the products to reach that point and retained a connection with them at that time (ie the haulier). If he was simply a warehouseman who loaded the contraband onto the lorry then his involvement in the enterprise was *de minimis* and he would not attract personal liability to pay the duty in which case his benefit from criminal conduct could not be the duty thereby evaded (see also *R v Chambers* [2008] EWCA Crim 2467, *R v Mitchell* [2009] EWCA Crim 214).

**9.77** **'All forms of real and personal property'** This means, again, something tangible that can be held or felt or seen. Real property would obviously include land and fixtures, such as buildings, on the land. Personal property would include objects irrespective of their size or weight or worth.

**9.78** **'Things in action and other intangible or incorporeal property'** This means something that cannot be held or felt or seen but nevertheless something that the law recognises as being of some value. In *Waya*, for example, the majority held that the 'property' was the bundle of rights that the appellant obtained before the purchase of his flat was completed. It would be fruitless to attempt to define these terms with any more precision here. If doubt arises in any given case, reference can be made to the established works in other areas of the law to decide whether the thing in question is a chose in action or some other form of intangible or incorporeal property (like a trademark).

*How does the defendant 'obtain' property?*

**9.79** This is clearly a vexing issue arising out of the confiscation regime created by POCA. On one view of the wealth of authorities on the meaning of 'obtains' it would be easier to define it by reference to what it is not, rather than what it is. It does not mean 'retains', because it is not necessary for the defendant to have 'had' the property for any length of time in order to have obtained it. It does not mean 'holds' because the property need not be tangible and, in any event, it is possible for the defendant to obtain tangible property even though he never saw it or held it. It does not mean 'possesses' because it is not necessary for the defendant to have ever had the property under his personal custody or control. What then does 'obtains' mean?

*What does 'obtains' mean?*

**9.80** The starting point is s 84(2)(b)—'property is obtained by a person if he obtains an interest in it'. The heading to s 84(2) identifies the words in quotations as a rule to be applied 'in relation to property'.

*What does 'interest' mean?*

**9.81** Where the 'property' is land, s 84(2)(f) states that 'references to an interest ... are to any legal estate or equitable interest or power'. The obvious point to make is that where the defendant has a legal estate or equitable interest or power he will already have property because those things will satisfy the definition of 'property' in s 84(1)(b) and/or (c). But if the prosecution wishes to assert that the defendant in fact obtained the land itself rather than just a limited interest in it, s 84(2)(b) would come into play to justify the conclusion that because the defendant has an interest in the land so he obtained the land. Supposing then that the defendant fraudulently obtained the leasehold interest in a building. That leasehold interest would be 'property' but so would the building itself because the leasehold would be an 'interest' in the building. It would be open to the prosecution in this example to say that the 'property' was either the leasehold or the building itself.

**9.82** Where the 'property' is said to be something other than land, s 84(2)(h) provides that 'references to an interest ... include references to a right (including a right to possession)'. There is a clear contrast then between the position where the property is land and where it is not. In the former case POCA provides a definition of what an 'interest' in land is but in the latter it simply indicates what an 'interest' includes without saying more. This strongly implies that in relation to property other than land interests other than legal or equitable ones will suffice. Such interests will include a right (itself undefined), including a right to possession. Thus a defendant who steals the contents of a person's pocket and thereby acquires a right of possession over those contents will have obtained them because he will have an interest in them.

In *May*, Lord Bingham's guidance included a passage where he suggested that a defendant **9.83** ordinarily obtains property if in law he owns it, whether alone or jointly, which will ordinarily connote a power of disposition or control. This guidance needs to be approached with caution. Lord Bingham was not saying that a defendant *only* obtains property where he owns it because that would exclude thieves and like offenders. Instead, His Lordship appears to be saying, first, that where the defendant has ownership of the property then ordinarily he will have obtained it and secondly that where he has the power to control or dispose of the property then that may also indicate that he has obtained it whether he owns it or not.

### Couriers and custodians

The 'exceptions' to this are where the defendant is a courier or custodian of the property **9.84** and he received a set fee for the limited role he played in the overall enterprise. So, on Lord Bingham's analysis, the drugs mule would not ordinarily obtain the drugs that he was paid a set fee to carry from one location to another. In *R v Allpress* [2009] 2 Cr App R (S) 58, the Court of Appeal followed this analysis and held that it also applied to the courier or custodian of cash (paras 82 and 84). The situation was different, however, where the 'custodian' was a money launderer who was in sole operational control of an account into which the proceeds of crime had been transferred because as soon as the transfer was complete he acquired the funds represented by the debit his bank owed to him. While those funds were in his account he was the only person who could control or dispose of them and so, following the guidance of Lord Bingham in *May*, he obtained them. Moreover, this accords with Lord Bingham's observation in the same case that custodians who are money launderers may well obtain the property they have custodianship over: see the decision of the Northern Ireland Court of Appeal in *R v Warwick* [2013] NICA 13.

The couriers or custodians of property who perform their functions for a fee and who there- **9.85** fore do not stand ready to draw value from the property itself are not concerned in that property and so have no 'interest' in it; hence they do not obtain it.

It may be, following *Waya*, that the courts take a step back from the aspect of the guidance **9.86** in *May* relating to couriers and custodians and simply look to the language of the Act, interpreted in accordance with its ordinary meaning, to make a determination as to whether a particular defendant has obtained property or not, in which case those who hold property for even a short time and who expect to be rewarded for their efforts from a source other than that property could find themselves obtaining that property after all.

### Joint benefit

*Obtaining 'with' others*

In a straightforward case where a defendant commits an acquisitive crime by himself there **9.87** may be little difficulty in determining what property he thereby obtained but where there is more than one defendant that determination becomes more difficult. Where a number of defendants acting in concert set out to obtain property from the commission of crime determining the benefit of each defendant may not be as straightforward.

Where a group of defendants come together to commit crime, the first question will often **9.88** be whether any property was generated by their enterprise. In a case where a number of defendants plot to rob a bank, if the defendants are arrested during the planning stage and then charged and convicted of a conspiracy to rob, it follows that their crime will not have advanced sufficiently for *any* of them to have obtained anything from it. In these circumstances, it may not be necessary for the court to go any further.

**9.89** If, however, the group had put its plan into action and the robbery had been successful with one of the robbers (D1) making off with a substantial amount of money, the next question will be to ask whether D1 took that money for himself or 'or behalf of the conspirators as a whole', an expression used by David Clarke J in the Court of Appeal in *R v Green* [2007] 3 All ER 751 at para 45 and endorsed by Lord Bingham in the House of Lords. If the former, then the court will need to see what property the other defendants obtained as a result of their involvement in the crime. If the latter, then the court would be entitled to conclude that each robber obtained *all* of the stolen money.

**9.90** An example of how the court should draw this distinction can be seen in the case of *R v Sivaraman* [2008] EWCA Crim 1736; [2009] 1 Cr App R (S) 80; [2008] Crim LR 989, referred to earlier in this chapter. The defendant was the manager of a service station from which his employer was selling agricultural 'red diesel' without paying the excise duty chargeable on that fuel. The defendant pleaded guilty on the basis that he had taken delivery of a volume of the converted diesel in respect of which the duty evaded came to £128,000. He maintained that he had been paid £15,000 for his role in the criminal enterprise. The Crown Court judge found his benefit to be £128,000 but the Court of Appeal disagreed. Referring to the judgment of Lord Bingham in *May*, the Court said this at para 13:

> ...participants in a joint criminal offence (including conspiracy) may benefit jointly to the same extent by each obtaining the same property or pecuniary advantage; or the value of the benefit received by them may differ as between one and another. To circuit judges and recorders who do not come from a civil law background, it may seem rather daunting; but, as Lord Bingham said, it is essentially a matter of applying concepts which are themselves in most cases relatively straightforward (that is, obtaining property or obtaining a pecuniary advantage) to the facts as established and trying to avoid becoming enmeshed in case law in the process: *May* at [46(3)] and [46(4)]. The thrust of Lord Bingham's advice was clear: the court needs to find the facts and to apply the words of the statute to them in as commonsensical a way as possible.

**9.91** The Court went on at para 19 to add this:

> 19. The greater the involvement of a defendant in a conspiracy, the greater will be the appropriate level of punishment. But it does not follow that the greater the involvement the greater the resulting benefit to that defendant. Within the statutory definitions contained in the Act, what benefit a defendant gained is a question of fact. As we have said, the critical question in relation to the conduct of the appellant in supervising the bunkering operations carried out under his control was the capacity in which he was acting. Was he, in point of fact, a joint purchaser of the fuel for resale as DERV who, by his conduct, jointly gained the pecuniary advantage of being able to resell it as DERV without having incurred the duty which would have had to be paid on purchasing DERV; or was he acting just as an employee? The judge did not find the former. Indeed, it is plain that he believed the position to be the latter. Otherwise he would have had no misgiving in finding that the appellant obtained benefit of the amount which he felt obliged to find. It would be wrong for this Court to make a different finding.

**9.92** As the employee had not been acting in the capacity of a joint purchaser of the 'red diesel' so his benefit could not be the duty evaded but rather the specific reward that he obtained from his employer for the performance of his role, namely £15,000.

In *Allpress*, the Court of Appeal cited *Sivaraman* and said this at para 30:  **9.93**

> In *Sivaraman* the court also addressed two misconceptions which subsequent cases suggest
> may still be common. One was that in assessing benefit in a conspiracy case each conspirator
> is to be taken as having jointly obtained the whole benefit obtained by 'the conspiracy'. A con-
> spiracy is not a legal entity but an agreement or arrangement which people may join or leave
> at different times. In confiscation proceedings the court is concerned not with the aggregate
> benefit obtained by all parties to the conspiracy but with the benefit obtained, whether singly
> or jointly, by the individual conspirator before the court. The second misconception is a vari-
> ant of the first. It is that anybody who has taken part in a conspiracy in more than a minor
> way is to be taken as having a joint share in all benefits obtained from the conspiracy. This is
> to confuse criminal liability and resulting benefit. The more heavily involved a defendant is in
> a conspiracy, the more severe the penalty which may be merited, but in confiscation proceed-
> ings the focus of the inquiry is on the benefit gained by the relevant defendant. In the nature
> of things there may well be a lack of reliable evidence about the exact benefit obtained by any
> particular conspirator, and in drawing common sense inferences the role of a particular con-
> spirator may be relevant as a matter of fact, but that is a purely evidential matter.

*Conspiracies*

Problems commonly arise where the defendant is a party to a conspiracy, where the imple-  **9.94**
mentation of the criminal agreement results in a loss to the victim but there is little or no
evidence as to where the money taken from the victim went. If it can be shown that it went to
one conspirator then the question posed in *Green* (see para 9.89 above) needs to be answered,
but if nothing is known of its destination then the Crown Court may have to grope towards
the determination of each conspirator's benefit almost in the dark.

Of course, the court is entitled to draw robust inferences from the facts as the court finds  **9.95**
them to be; so if in the sort of case envisaged in the preceding paragraph the court was not
assisted by any evidence from the defendants, those defendants should not be surprised if
the court concluded that the monies generated by their crime was obtained by each jointly.

It may be that the defendants do assist the court and either seek to explain that they obtained  **9.96**
nothing or a set fee for their involvement, as was the case in *Sivaraman*. If the court believes
their evidence that they received a fee then in all likelihood their benefit will be limited to
that fee because the court will have accepted that they did not share in the proceeds generated
by the conspiracy. If, on the other hand, the court does not believe their evidence, is it bound
to conclude that they all obtained those proceeds jointly?

In *R v McIntosh* [2011] EWCA Crim 1501, the Court of Appeal heard a case where the issue  **9.97**
was the determination of the realisible amount and not the determination of the appellant's
benefit but the observations of the Court may be pertinent to the exercise of both functions.
At para 15, the Court said:

> ... there is no principle that a court is bound to reject a defendant's case that his current realis-
> able assets are less than the full amount of the benefit, merely because it concludes that the
> defendant has not revealed their true extent or value, or has not participated in any revelation
> at all. The court must answer the statutory question ... in a just and proportionate way. The
> court may conclude that a defendant's realisable assets are less then the full value of the benefit
> on the basis of the facts as a whole. A defendant who is found not to have told the truth or who
> has declined to give truthful disclosure will inevitably find it difficult to discharge the burden
> imposed upon him. But it may not be impossible for him to do so. Other sources of evidence,
> apart from the defendant himself, and a view of the case as a whole, may persuade a court that
> the assets available to the defendant are less then the full value of the benefit.

**9.98**    At the stage of determining a defendant's benefit this may mean that even if the court rejects the defendant's evidence it may still find against the assertion (doubtless made by the prosecution) that each defendant obtained the entire sum generated by the conspiracy, if 'the facts as a whole' point towards a different conclusion. There is thus no default position of joint benefit in the absence of credible evidence from the defendants to the contrary. See *R v Mahmood* [2013] EWCA Crim 525 and *R v Saben* [2013] EWCA Crim 575 for further consideration of *McIntosh*.

**9.99**    The Crown Court judge in *R v Clark & Severn* (above) erred in assuming that such a default position existed—see paras 28–32 of the judgement. *Clark & Severn* illustrates the dangers that lie in wait for the Crown Court judge who extrapolates from the absence of evidence to the conclusion that there must have been joint benefit as between the conspirators. Although the Court of Appeal in *Clark & Severn* expressed a view as to the options available to the judge (that either the appellant Clark was an 'equity partner' in the conspiracy or a 'mere' bailee for reward) it gave little guidance on how the judge could draw that distinction on the evidence.

**9.100**    It follows from cases such as *McIntosh* and *Clark & Severn* that the Crown Court must consider all of the evidence and make a determination of a given defendant's benefit based on that evidence. The court cannot simply default to a conclusion of joint benefit because it has received no assistance from the defendant. While it is not an enviable task to sift through the evidence to find pointers one way or another, it is a necessary one.

*Obtaining 'through' others*

**9.101**    It may happen that a defendant uses an agent to commit a crime on his behalf. If that agent has a guilty mind then in all likelihood he will become a co-defendant and so the position will be analogous to that considered under the 'Obtaining "with" others' heading. If, on the other hand, the agent is innocent different considerations apply.

**9.102**    Where the innocent agent is a natural person and he obtains property, does it follow that the defendant will have obtained that property too? Suppose the defendant (D) persuades another person (P) that he, the defendant, is owed money by someone else (V) when in fact there is no such debt. D tells P that V has left that money in his wallet in his coat pocket and that the coat is hanging in the cloakroom unattended. On D's instruction P goes to V's coat, takes the money from the wallet and then goes to find D. On the way he is intercepted by V, who recovers the money and alerts the police. On those facts D was clearly concerned to ensure that the money P took found its way to him. He planned to take that money for himself and used an innocent agent to do it so it should make no difference to the determination of his benefit that he did not have the chance to lay his own hands on it. On the ordinary meaning of 'obtains' there can be little doubt that D obtained the money that P took at his request.

**9.103**    That seems relatively straightforward but it becomes more complicated where the agent is a legal person, such as a company. A company has a separate legal identity from those who own it and those who run it. Where the company is a limited company, any 'acts done in the name of and on behalf of… [the] company are treated in law as the acts of the company, not of the individuals who do them. That is the veil which incorporation confers' (*Jennings*, para 16).

**9.104**    Where, therefore, the company is used by those in control of it as a vehicle for fraud, their acts are treated as the company's acts and so it would seem that where the company obtains the property generated by those acts those in control of the company do not unless the veil of incorporation can be moved aside thereby enabling the courts to see just where that property ends up (see *R v Seagar and Blatch* [2009] EWCA Crim 1703, at para 76, where the Court of Appeal commented on the circumstances in which the corporate veil can be displaced so that the controllers of a company can be held to have obtained property transferred to the company).

### Casual Connection

It is not enough that the defendant both engaged in criminal conduct and obtained prop- **9.105** erty: in order for that property to constitute his benefit there must be a causal connection between the crime and the obtaining. It is important to remember that POCA offers two tests of causation. The first is the 'as a result of' test. The second is the 'in connection with' test. The first test suggests that the court's mind should be directed towards property coming to the defendant after his criminal conduct occurred. The money taken by the bank robber is an obvious example of property that he obtains as a result of his crime. The second test is different. It suggests that property obtained even before the crime was committed could also form part of the defendant's benefit. Where, for example, the getaway driver buys a second-hand car so he can carry out his role in the robbery planned for later that day, could that car have been obtained by him in connection with his crime? In *Sumal* [2012] EWCA Crim 1840 it was held that rental income from a property that was unlicensed contrary to s 95(1) of the Housing Act 2004 did not amount to a person's benefit under s 76(4) POCA. At the time of writing, it should be noted that there is an appeal pending in *Sumal* to the Supreme Court.

In a case where the defendant had been convicted of excise duty evasion by bringing contra- **9.106** band cigarettes across to the UK without declaring them, the Court of Appeal in *R v Waller* [2009] 1 Cr App R (S) 449 held that not only did the excise duty evaded constitute the appellant's benefit but so did the cigarettes themselves and they were to be valued by reference to what the defendant paid for them overseas. The Court arrived at this conclusion for a number of reasons but principally because the defendant had obtained the cigarettes in connection with the commission of his crime. *Waller* remained good law for only three years before the Court of Appeal overruled it in *R v Ahmad and Ahmed* [2012] EWCA Crim 391; [2012] 1 WLR 2335; [2012] 2 All ER 1137; [2012] STC 1239; [2012] 2 Cr App R (S) 85; [2012] Lloyd's Rep FC 413; [2012] Crim LR 468; [2012] STI 546; The Times, 29 May 2012. In that case, the Court of Appeal reasoned that whilst the costs incurred by the defendant in committing his crime cannot be deducted from his benefit it does not follow that they should be added to his benefit. The Court said this at para 35: 'To make a confiscation order which includes within the benefit the costs of committing a crime seems to be contrary to the object of the legislation and that part of the confiscation order would, it seems to us, to operate by way of a fine.'

At the time of writing an appeal in *Ahmad* is pending to the Supreme Court—for the certified point, see para 74 of the judgment.

For this reason it was inappropriate to include within the defendant's benefit a sum of money **9.107** reflecting the costs incurred by the defendant in committing the crime itself. At para 53 of its judgment the Court of Appeal took this conclusion and turned to the question of the bank robber. In its opinion: 'The robber's benefit is what he steals, the robber cannot deduct the costs of undertaking the robbery but surely those costs should not be added on to the benefit?'

**Evidence at the hearing**

**9.108**  Normally the court will hear from witnesses (on behalf of the prosecution and the defendant) giving live evidence. However hearsay may be admitted. The ordinary rules of criminal evidence do not strictly apply in confiscation hearings. The proceedings are quasi-civil in nature. Confiscation proceedings are an extension of the sentencing hearing. The Civil Evidence Act 1995 does not apply to confiscation hearings. The Criminal Justice Act 2003 is also not strictly applicable. However, when admissibility and weight of hearsay are in issue it is the most appropriate framework within which to make a decision. The statutory criteria should not be applied rigidly, bearing in mind fairness to all parties, the legislative steer in s 69 of POCA, and that the ultimate decision will be made by a judge sitting in a post-conviction context. The procedure has to be flexible and fair. See *R v Clipston* [2011] EWCA Crim 446. It is important that the Judge receives and identifies evidence on which findings are made. Thus in *R v Jaffery* [2013] EWCA Crim 360, whilst a prosecutor was entitled to submit that a money launderer in that case must have received a reward for his services being 'not less than x per cent'of the sums laundered, any findings by the Judge as to a 'not less than' figure, needed to be supported by evidence.

## C. Valuing Benefit

**9.109**  If a person benefits from (general or particular) criminal conduct his benefit is the value of the property obtained (s 76(7)). In *R v Sivaraman*, the Court of Appeal held, at para 12, that in determining the value of the defendant's benefit the focus should be on the language of the statute and the courts should give that language its ordinary meaning. The relevant sections of POCA are ss 79 and 80, which read as follows:

> 79. Value: the basic rule
> (1) This section applies for the purpose of deciding the value at any time of property then held by a person.
> (2) Its value is the market value of the property at that time.
> (3) But if at that time another person holds an interest in the property its value, in relation to the person mentioned in subsection (1), is the market value of his interest at that time, ignoring any charging order under a provision listed in subsection (4).
> (4) The provisions are—
>     (a) section 9 of the Drug Trafficking Offences Act 1986 (c.32);
>     (b) section 78 of the Criminal Justice Act 1988 (c.33);
>     (c) Article 14 of the Criminal Justice (Confiscation) (Northern Ireland) Order 1990 (S.I. 1990/2588 (N.I. 17));
>     (d) Section 27 of the Drug Trafficking Act 1994 (c.37);
>     (e) Article 32 of the Proceeds of Crime (Northern Ireland) Order 1996 (S.I. 1996/1299 (N.I. 9)).
> (5) The section has effect subject to sections 80 and 81.
>
> 80. Value of property obtained from conduct
> (1) This section applies for the purpose of deciding the value of property obtained by a person as a result of or in connection with his criminal conduct; and the material time is the time the court makes its decision.
> (2) The value of the property at the material time is the greater of the following—
>     (a) the value of the property (at the time the person obtained it) adjusted to take account of later changes in the value of money;
>     (b) the value (at the material time) of the property found under subsection (3).

(3) The property found under this subsection is as follows:
    (a) if the person holds the property obtained, the property found under this subsection
       is that property;
    (b) if he holds no part of the property obtained, the property found under this subsection
       is any property which directly or indirectly represents it in his hands;
    (c) if he hold part of the property obtained, the property found under this subsection is
       that part and any property which directly or indirectly represents the other part in
       his hands.
(4) The references in subsection (2)(a) and (b) to the value are to the value found in accordance with section 79.

It is now clearly established that by virtue of s 79(1), the provisions of s 79 apply *both* to the **9.110** valuation of the defendant's benefit from his criminal conduct and to the valuation of his assets at the stage when the court is considering whether the defendant can afford to satisfy a confiscation order in the full amount of his benefit. This was the conclusion reached by the Court of Appeal in *R v Rose* [2008] 1 WLR 2113 and endorsed by the majority of the Supreme Court in *Waya* at para 65. Thus, s 79 falls to be considered by the Crown Court when answering questions (b) and (c) of the checklist in *May* as revised by a consideration of *Waya*.

By virtue of s 79(2) the value of property is its market value. The House of Lords considered **9.111** this question in *R v Islam* [2009] UKHL 30. The majority (Lord Hope, Baroness Hale, and Lord Mance) held, at para 16, that 'the essence of market value is simply . . . the price that would be paid for the goods as between a willing buyer and a willing seller'. It followed that for the purposes of calculating the defendant's benefit the property obtained by him, which could not be lawfully traded, nevertheless had value and that value would be calculated by reference to the amount that he could sell it for on the black market.

Section 79(3) contains a general provision for valuation. It provides that when the court **9.112** comes to value property it must first decide whether any person other than the defendant holds an interest in the property and, if they do, the court will have to value the defendant's limited interest ignoring any charging order under any of the enactments mentioned in subsection (4). In *Waya*, the majority favoured this interpretation of s 79(3):

> What that section means is that lawfully co-existing interests in property are to be valued individually. It does not mean that the loser's right to recover the property from the thief, which is a claim to totally defeat anything the thief has obtained, is to be treated as a co-existing partial interest for the very purpose of valuing what he has obtained.

Unlike s 79, s 80 applies *only* to the valuation of property obtained by the defendant as a **9.113** result of or in connection with his criminal conduct and so it cannot be employed at the stage of assessing the value of the defendant's existing assets.

Moreover, s 80 applies at 'the material time', which is the time the Crown Court makes its **9.114** decision about the value of the defendant's benefit. By virtue of s 80(2) that value will either be the value of the property at the time the defendant obtained it (adjusted to take account of later changes in the value of money) or its value at the time the court makes its decision, whichever is the greater. In *R v Oyebola* [2013] EWCA Crim 1052, rental income from a property that had been purchased through mortgage fraud was found to constitute a benefit. See further *R v Morgan* [2013] EWCA Crim 1307.

Where the defendant still 'holds' the property at the time the court makes its decision then **9.115** it should be a relatively straightforward task for the court to work out what that property was worth at the time the defendant obtained it and what it is worth at the time of the final hearing and ascribe the higher of those two values to it.

**9.116** Where, however, the defendant does not 'hold' the property at the time the court makes its decision because, for example, he has sold it, then s 80(3)(b) and (c) comes into play. It requires the court to consider whether any property 'held' by the defendant at the time the court makes it decision represents, in whole or in part, the property obtained by the defendant as a result of or in connection with his crime. The former will be referred to as the 'representing property' and the latter the 'original property'.

**9.117** Section 80(3) allows the Crown Court to trace the value of the original property as it moves from one form to another and finally into the representing property 'held' by the defendant at the time the court makes it decision. What section 80(3) does not do is 'give any guidance as ... to how the test of direct or indirect representation is to be applied': *Waya* (para 56). The majority of the Supreme Court felt that this omission might signal that Parliament intended ss 80(3)(b) and 80(3)(c) 'to apply only when the facts are relatively straightforward'. Where the evidential trail leading from the original property runs cold it may be impossible for the Crown Court to conclude that any property held by the defendant at the time of its decision represents the original property, in which case the value of the original property can only be assessed by reference to its market value at the time the defendant obtained it.

## D. Recoverable Amount

### What sum is recoverable from the defendant?

**9.118** Section 7 of POCA provides that:

> (1) The recoverable amount for the purposes of section 6 is an amount equal to the defendant's benefit from the conduct concerned.
> (2) But if the defendant shows that the available amount is less than that benefit the recoverable amount is—
>     (a) the available amount, or
>     (b) a nominal amount, if the available amount is nil.

Under s 7 the method of calculation in terms of assessing the recoverable amount is the same as in the DTA and the CJA. The recoverable amount is the amount of the defendant's benefit from either his general criminal conduct or his particular criminal conduct (as the case may be). However, if the amount available for confiscation is, after consideration by the court, found to be less than the benefit in question, the confiscation order must be made in the lesser amount. The word 'nominal' is defined in the Oxford English Dictionary as meaning 'virtually nothing'.

**9.119** The House of Lords in *R v May* [2008] UKHL 28 noted that:

> The answering of this third question is a very important stage in the procedure for making confiscation orders since, however great the payments a defendant may have received or the property he may have obtained, he cannot be ordered to pay a sum which it is beyond his means to pay.

**9.120** The House continued (para 41):

In many cases the assessment of the realisable amount poses complex and difficult problems for the trial judge, often exacerbated by lack of information... But the statutory provisions governing the assessment are detailed, and the problems which arise are not, in the main, questions of principle. It is not in doubt that assets legitimately acquired may be included within the realisable amount, provided of course that the defendant's total benefit from the relevant criminal conduct is not exceeded.

### The 'available amount'

Section 9(1) and (2) of POCA provides:                                                          **9.121**

(1) For the purposes of deciding the recoverable amount, the available amount is the aggregate of—
  (a) the total of the values (at the time the confiscation order is made) of all the free property then held by the defendant minus the total amount payable in pursuance of obligations which then have priority, and
  (b) the total of the values (at that time) of all tainted gifts.
(2) An obligation has priority if it is an obligation of the defendant—
  (a) to pay an amount due in respect of a fine or other order of a Court which was imposed or made on conviction of an offence and at any time before the time the confiscation order is made, or
  (b) to pay a sum which would be included amongst preferential debts if the defendant's bankruptcy had commenced on the date of the confiscation order or his winding up had been ordered on that date.

Under s 9(1), the 'available amount' is the value of all the defendant's property, minus **9.122** certain prior obligations of the defendant, such as earlier fines, plus the value of all tainted gifts made by the defendant. It is, in effect, equivalent to the term 'the amount that might be realised' in the earlier confiscation legislation, and is calculated in the same way. Such an amount is to be considered as at the time of the making of the order itself: subsequent increases in the available amount can be dealt with via an application under s 22 (see Chapter 10).

Section 82(3) defines free property as follows:                                                **9.123**

Property is free unless an order is enforced in respect of it under any of these provisions—
(a) forfeiture orders under Section 27 of the Misuse of Drugs Act 1971;
(b) ...
(c) ...
(d) deprivation orders under Section 143 of the Sentencing Act;
(e) Section 23 or 111 of the Terrorism Act 2000 (forfeiture orders);
(f) Section 246, 266, 295(2) or 298(2) of this Act (certain civil recovery orders under Pt 5).

### Burden of proof

Thus far, the burden of proof, at each stage, has been on the Crown. Once the Crown has **9.124** discharged the burden of satisfying the court of the fact of benefit and the amount of the defendant's proceeds, the burden shifts onto the defendant to show that the value of his realisable assets is less than the amount of his benefit (see *R v Comiskey* [1991] 93 Cr App R 227). The reason for this is that the defendant is the person who is in the best position to know the extent and value of his own assets. As Tucker J said in delivering the judgment of the Court of Appeal in *Comiskey* (at p 231):

The Act was intended to avoid a situation where a drug dealer serves his sentence with equanimity, knowing that on his release substantial funds will be available to enable him to live in

199

comfort. With this in mind, a successful drugs dealer will take care to ensure, so far as he can, that the proceeds of his trade will be hidden away so as to be untraceable. The Act is designed to oblige him to disclose his assets, or to face the risk that if he does not do so, the court will make certain assumptions against him, and that he may have to serve an additional sentence of imprisonment if he does not comply with an order.

**9.125** The standard of proof is on a balance of probabilities (s 6(7)). If the defendant fails to participate in the hearing or fails to discharge this burden, a confiscation order will be made in the full amount of his benefit.

**9.126** In *R v Benjafield* (2002) 2 Cr App R (S) 70, Lord Steyn confirmed (at para 12): 'The fact that the appellant did not testify is a powerful point against him.'

**9.127** In *R v Afraz Siddique* [2005] EWCA Crim 1812, the Court held that in circumstances where a defendant had failed to provide evidence about his realisable assets for the purposes of the confiscation order, the judge was entitled to conclude that the appellant had not satisfied him that his realisable assets were less than the benefit of the drug trafficking. The Court held (at para 27) that:

> The appellant had the opportunity of seeking to persuade the court about his realisable assets. He declined to take it, for no doubt the very good reason that either there was no, or no credible, evidence he could give and/or he would be exposed to penetrating cross-examination which could only make his position worse. The fact that his credibility may already have been badly damaged is not a shield behind which he can hide. If it were, defendants in the position of the appellant would refuse to give evidence and yet successfully maintain that their realisable assets were less than the benefit. Such a position would be nonsensical, given the structure of the DTA and its compliance with Article 6, and would place judges hearing confiscation proceedings in an impossible position.

**9.128** That said, where a court *does* conclude that the defendant has not revealed the true extent or value or his realisable assets, or has not participated in any revelation at all, or has lied about the extent of his assets, it is nevertheless not *bound* to reject a defendant's case that his current realisable assets are less than the full amount of the benefit. In *R v McIntosh and Marsden* [2012] 1 Cr App R (S) 60, Moses LJ held that rather, the court's task is to answer the statutory question about the recoverable amount in s 7 in a just and proportionate way. The court may conclude that a defendant's realisable assets are less than the full value of the benefit on the basis of the facts as a whole, irrespective of whether the defendant is wholly believed. The judge, after considering previous dicta in *Glaves v Crown Prosecution Service* [2011] EWCA Civ 69, said as follows (at 348—9):

> A defendant who is found not to have told the truth or who has declined to give truthful disclosure will inevitably find it difficult to discharge the burden imposed upon him—but it may not be impossible for him to do so. Other sources of evidence, apart from the defendant himself, and a view of the case as a whole, may persuade a court that the assets available to the defendant are less than the full value of the benefit.

### Difficulty of realisation

**9.129** Whether or not a defendant may have difficulty in realising his assets to produce a liquidated amount of money is not a relevant consideration when deciding what amount is available to him: *R v Modjiri* [2010] 1 WLR 2096, applying the principle enunciated earlier by the Divisional Court in *R v Liverpool Magistrates' Court, Ex p Ansen* [1998] 1 All ER 692. It may often arise, particularly as concerns tainted gifts, that the gifts of the defendant are, in practical terms, extremely difficult to recover, but they are nonetheless intended under s 9(1)(b) to be included as 'available' to the defendant. Hickinbottom J notes in *Re L* [2010] EWHC 1531 (Admin) that a justification for such a draconian policy is that while a defendant personally may have great difficulty realising a certain asset, the Crown has a number of enforcement options available to it which may enable realisation on the defendant's behalf.

### Hidden assets

In *R v Ilsemann* [1991] Crim LR 141 the Court of Appeal considered the issue of 'hidden assets' and held: **9.130**

> it was a misconception to say that the amount of the confiscation order should be limited to the amount which the prosecution could prove to be the value of the defendant's assets known to them. If the defendant wished to say that that was all that was realisable, it was for him to satisfy the court to this effect.

(See also *R v Cokovic* [1996] 1 Cr App R (S) 131.)

In *R v Wright* [2006] EWCA Crim 1257, the Court of Appeal returned to the subject of hidden assets. In *Wright* the judge at first instance had made a confiscation order in the sum of £100,000 but had not given specific reasons as to how he had come to that conclusion. A benefit figure of £4,630,823 had been identified and the appellant's realisable assets were put at a sum of just over £50,000. It was apparent and assumed therefore that the judge had concluded that the appellant must have hidden assets in the sum of the balance. The appellant appealed on the basis that there was no evidence that he had such hidden assets. The principles in *R v Barwick* [2001] 1 Cr App R (S) 129 were accepted by the Court of Appeal. They make clear that the burden of establishing that the realisable assets are in a lesser sum than the benefit is with the defendant. The question for the Court in *Wright* was whether the judge was entitled to add £50,000 by way of realisable assets upon the evidence before him. The Court of Appeal (Pill LJ) stated: **9.131**

> Of course there are many ways in which assets can be hidden, including assets being held temporarily by some other person on the defendant's behalf. The burden was on the appellant, an appellant who hitherto had had a lavish lifestyle. It was for the judge to form a judgement on realisable assets in those circumstances. As he correctly pointed out, he had had no assistance from the appellant himself by way of oral evidence, or even by way of signed statements. (See para 20).

The Court of Appeal concluded in *Wright* that the judge was entitled to reach the conclusion he did. There was, the Court said, no rule of law that a judge was not entitled to find on appropriate facts that there are hidden assets. The Court concluded that the judge had been modest in his assessment of the situation. **9.132**

In *R v Barnham* [2005] EWCA Crim 1049, the Court of Appeal ruled that the Crown was not under an obligation to make out a prima facie case that a defendant had hidden assets before a defendant could be expected to deal with such an allegation. The correct approach was that once the prosecution had established the existence of benefit, there was no requirement on it to provide a prima facie case in relation to realisable or hidden assets. Once benefit was established, the burden of proof shifted to the defendant to prove, if he could, his realisable assets to the satisfaction of the court. By that stage the defendant would know exactly how the court had determined benefit attributable to him and he had to prove by evidence what his realisable assets were. It was for him to show why the confiscation order should not **9.133** be the value of the proceeds of drug trafficking. This was only fair, it said, given that 'hidden assets' by definition were indicative of the fact that the prosecution could not know how and where a defendant might have disposed of or dealt with the proceeds in question; see further *R v Valentine* [2006] EWCA Crim 2717. The European Court of Human Rights, to which Mr Barnham appealed, dismissed the appeal ((2009) 48 EHRR 30; Crim LR 200), holding that no violation of the defendant's Art 6 rights had occurred. Rather, it concluded that it was not unfair of a court to require a defendant such as Mr Barnham to explain satisfactorily what had happened to the property he had obtained as a result of his activities and which had generated the benefit figure. If such explanation were to be entirely unsatisfactory, a court's finding of hidden assets would not be inconsistent with Art 6.

**9.134**   The above rationale was echoed in the DTA case of *R v Peacock* [2009] EWCA Crim 654 where the Court of Appeal held (at para 24):

> Realisable property . . . is not confined to that which is specifically identified. Money received is a realisable asset even though its source is described generically and its exact provenance is not established. Further, a court is entitled to draw reasonable inferences as to the existence of realisable assets from evidence satisfying it to the requisite standard of proof.

**9.135**   In *Telli* [2008] 2 Cr App R (S) 48, the Court accepted the inclusion of a sum to account for hidden assets as part of the available amount where a defendant had not disclosed the nature and extent of his realisable assets. As the defendant had not established that his assets were less than the benefit figure, he had not satisfied the court that the total value of all his realisable property was less than the value of the proceeds of his crimes, and thus any shortfall was accounted for by hidden assets. However, in *Glaves* [2011] EWCA Civ 69, the Court of Appeal qualified this by holding that a defendant's failure to account for all his assets does not *require* a court to find that he therefore has hidden assets up to the full benefit sum. The defendant's failure to account satisfactorily for his assets was one element of the evidence, but not necessarily the determinative one. It would be possible for a court, despite a defendant's lack of complete candour, to settle on an available amount lower than the benefit figure and not to make a finding of hidden assets, if it felt that such a course was appropriate. See also *Re Pearson* [2012] EWHC 1704 (Admin) and *Shakil* [2012] EWCA Crim 1966. See also *R v Druce* [2013] EWCA Crim 40.

### Assets not restricted to those derived from criminal activity

**9.136**   As with DTA and CJA cases, any asset of the defendant, whether legitimately acquired or not, is vulnerable to confiscation in order to satisfy a confiscation order made under POCA (see *R v Currey* (1995) 16 Cr App R (S) 421 and *R v Chrastny (No 2)* [1991] 1 WLR 1385).

### Market value

**9.137**   Section 79 states that in deciding the value at any time of property held by a person, its value is the market value of the property at that time (s 79(2)). But if at that time another person has an interest in the property, its value, in relation to the person who holds the property, is the market value at the time of the person who holds the property's interest, ignoring any charging order (see s 79(3) and s 79(4) for the provisions relating to charging orders). (See also para 9.111).

### Costs of sale

**9.138**   In *R v Davies* [2004] EWCA Crim 3380, the Court of Appeal held that it was 'quite right' to deduct the costs of any sale (eg estate agent's costs) from the value of the house that was to be sold in order to satisfy the confiscation order (see para 15, reflecting *R v Cramer* (1992) 13 Cr App R (S) 390 and the terms of the order in *R v Lemmon* (1991) 13 Crim App R (S) 66).

### Contract services

In *Re Adams* (2005) LS Gaz 13 January 28, QBD (Lightman J), the Court held that a **9.139** consultancy contract entered into by the defendant under which he would be entitled to £52,000 pa for his services, was not 'realisable property' within s 74(1) and s 102(1) of the CJA, because the contract was for the provision of services where the identity of the provider was of the essence and any entitlement to payment under the contract for services would only arise if the services were provided by the defendant. The Court found that such conditional and future entitlement 'was not property' but a chose in action personal to the party. In *R v Najafpour* [2009] EWCA Crim 2723, the Court of Appeal stated that commission, owed as a debt, could not be treated as a realisable asset under the confiscation scheme.

### Assets jointly held

Where assets are jointly held between co-defendants, the Court must determine what por- **9.140** tion of the asset is held by each defendant when considering each defendant's available amount for the purposes of s 7: *R v Gangar (Shinder Singh)* [2012] Crim LR 808 (CA). In that case, the Court of Appeal reiterated that a partial interest in an asset cannot, at the available amount stage, be treated as a 100 per cent interest. This was further confirmed by the Supreme Court in *Waya* [2012] 3 WLR 1188 at 1212.

Similarly, where the defendant owns an asset jointly with an innocent third party (eg a **9.141** matrimonial home held jointly with his wife) it constitutes a realisable asset of the defendant to the extent of his interest in it. Thus, if the defendant has a 50 per cent interest in an asset with another party, 50 per cent of its value can be taken into account in assessing the amount to be realised. The means by which such assets are realised, the procedure, and the rights of third parties in relation thereto are considered fully in Chapter 16. It should be emphasised at this stage that any third party claiming to have an interest in realisable property does not have the right to be heard or be legally represented at the confiscation hearing except in his capacity as a witness on behalf of the defendant, if he chooses to call him. The third party's right to be heard arises at the enforcement stage. It is, however, still the task of the court to assess the defendant's actual realisable property, whether third parties give evidence or not, and so it is entirely appropriate for the defendant to bring evidence as to other persons' interest in a disputed asset to enable the court to make its findings on as complete a picture of the evidence as possible: *R v Harriott (Paula)* [2012] EWCA Crim 2294.

### Pension funds

For the proposition that private pension funds can form part of confiscation orders, see *R v* **9.142** *Ford* [2008] EWCA Crim 966. In *R v Chen* [2009] EWCA Crim 2669, the Court confirmed that whilst a pension policy did on its face constitute free property, the judge at first instance had been wrong in his assessment of its value, as the policy could not be realised. Once assets have been identified as realisable property they may be recovered from any trust or company; see *In the matter of May* [2009] EWHC 1826 (QB).

### Detained cash

**9.143** Cash that has been detained but not yet forfeited under the cash forfeiture provisions of POCA is to be taken to be part of the free property of the defendant and thus is part of the available amount: *R v Weller* [2009] EWCA Crim 810. If such cash ultimately is forfeited in the cash forfeiture hearing which eventually follows, it will then be appropriate for the defendant to apply to the Crown Court to vary the confiscation order downwards in the same amount under s 23, so as to avoid the possibility of the defendant paying the same amount of money to the Crown twice.

### Matrimonial homes and other property

**9.144** The determination and application of interests in matrimonial homes and beneficial interests in property in confiscation proceedings, together with case law relating thereto, is considered fully in Chapter 16. Trial judges may often be called upon to determine beneficial interests within confiscation proceedings. The court considered whether the registration of an interest was a sham in *Liscott v CPS* [2013] EWHC 501.

### Recoverable amount: victims

**9.145** By ss 6(6) and 7(3), where the victim of the criminal conduct has started or intends to start proceedings against the defendant in respect of loss, injury, or damage sustained in connection with the conduct, the recoverable amount will be an amount which:

(1) the court believes is just, but
(2) does not exceed the amount found under s 7(1) or (2) as the case may be.

### Court must give reasons

**9.146** Under s 7(5) if the court decides the available amount, it must include in the confiscation order a statement of its findings as to the matters relevant for deciding that amount. In *Birmingham City Council v Ram* [2007] EWCA Crim 3084 Toulson J commented (at para 28): 'the judge was not required as a matter of law to deal with each point on which there was a conflict of evidence. He had to deal with the essential issues in dispute and state his reasons for his conclusions.'

## E. Tainted Gifts

**9.147** The legislature is alive to the possibility that defendants and those involved in nefarious activities may seek to divest themselves of valuable assets in order to circumvent the confiscation regime. In order to ensure such 'gifts' are caught as realisable assets, the Act makes specific provision for them to be taken into account as part of the 'available amount' under s 9(1)(6) of POCA.

**9.148** Under s 77(1) of POCA, the issue of whether a gift of assets or property is tainted will be considered if:

(a) no court has made a decision as to whether the defendant has a criminal lifestyle, or
(b) the court has decided that the defendant has a criminal lifestyle.

### When is a gift tainted?

**9.149** Under s 77 of POCA, a gift becomes tainted if:

(2) ... it was made by the defendant at any time after the relevant day.

(3) A gift is also tainted if it was made by the defendant at any time and was of property—

    (a) which was obtained by the defendant as a result of or in connection with his general criminal conduct, or

    (b) which (in whole or in part and whether directly or indirectly) represented in the defendant's hands property obtained by him as a result of or in connection with his general criminal conduct.

Under s 77(9), the 'relevant day' referred to in s 77(2) is the first day of the period of six years **9.150** ending with:

    (a) the day when proceedings for the offence concerned were started against the defendant, or

    (b) if there are two or more offences and proceedings for them were started on different days, the earliest of those days.

Under POCA, therefore, a gift is tainted: **9.151**

(1) if it is made by the defendant to any person in the period beginning six years before the commencement of proceedings, (under s 77(2)),

(2) if it was made by the defendant at any time and the gift was from the proceeds of crime (under s 77(3)).

Section 77(5) adds a further situation where a gift will be tainted, but, by virtue of s 77(4), **9.152** it only applies if the court has decided that the defendant does not have a criminal lifestyle:

(5) A gift is tainted if it was made by the defendant at any time after—

    (a) the date on which the offence concerned was committed, or

    (b) if his particular criminal conduct consists of two or more offences and they were committed on different dates, the date of the earliest.

For the purposes of s 77(5), an offence which is a continuing offence is committed on the **9.153** first occasion when it is committed (as per s 77(6)), and the defendant's particular criminal conduct for the purposes of s 77(5) includes any conduct which constitutes offences which the court has taken into consideration in deciding his sentence for the offence or offences concerned (s 77(7)).

It should be noted that the gift might be a tainted gift whether it was made before or after **9.154** the passing of POCA (as per s 77(8)). Further, like the earlier legislation, gifts made by the defendant to other persons may be placed under restraint prior to the criminal trial or confiscation hearing.

### Gifts and their recipients

Section 78(1) provides: **9.155**

If the defendant transfers property to another person for a consideration whose value is significantly less than the value of the property at the time of the transfer, he is to be treated as making a gift.

This section is designed to prevent defendants from benefiting under the legislation if they sell property for an under value. Under POCA a 'gift' includes a transaction for a consideration which is significantly less than the value of the gift at the time of the transfer, eg if a defendant sells a painting worth £100,000 for £5,000.

**9.156**  This is a departure from the earlier legislation, where an undervalued transaction was defined as the difference between the value of the property when the defendant received it and its value at the time of the transfer.

**9.157**  References to a recipient of a tainted gift are to a person to whom the defendant has made the gift (s 78(3)).

**9.158**  The provision is only triggered when property is 'transferred'. It is important to establish what property right has in fact transferred in a given transaction before assessing whether there has been a sale at undervalue. This is a matter determined by the law of property in the ordinary way. In *Richards* [2008] EWCA Crim 1841, Toulson LJ considered that a transfer from one criminal to another of legal title to a set of five properties was, on the evidence in that case, not in fact a transfer of the whole beneficial interest but only of the bare legal interest, beneficial interest remaining in the donor. As such, given that only a right of nominal worth was transferred, it would not be possible to consider the value of the properties a 'tainted gift', which requires transfer at a value 'significantly less' than the value of the property. (However, by virtue of the same conclusion the value of the houses always remained the property of the transferring defendant in the normal way, and thus could be included in the available amount, albeit not as a tainted gift.)

**9.159**  Whether consideration for a transfer is 'significantly less than the value of the property at the time of the transfer' is a matter for the court deciding on confiscation in each particular case, based on the evidence.

**9.160**  Courts must, however, when considering undervalue, take into account the various potential financial motives of a defendant by entering into a given transaction, and not adopt a narrow approach. In *RCPO v Johnson* [2012] EWCA Civ 1000, a defendant's disposal to another of his share in an aircraft under a hire-purchase agreement was deemed initially by the sentencing judge to make no commercial sense, and it was therefore treated as a tainted gift. The Court of Appeal disagreed, considering that the transfer was commercially well balanced: it relieved the defendant of 'substantial existing and future liabilities with respect to the aircraft' and thus was no gift.

**9.161**  An interest-free loan given to a third party without consideration of equal value is capable of being construed as a tainted gift, because it amounts to a transfer of property at an undervalue within the meaning of s 78(1). In *R v Craft* [2012] EWCA Crim 1356, the Court considered that where a defendant's girlfriend received an interest-free loan of £140,000 to purchase a property in her name, the only consideration being a mere charge over the property given to the defendant, but without any right to enforce sale, the transfer of the £140,000 was a tainted gift and thus the defendant's available amount would be increased by that amount. For further information see *Heron v SOCA* [2013] CA (Civ Div) unreported.

### Value of tainted gifts

**9.162**  Under s 81 of POCA:

(1) The value at any time (the material time) of a tainted gift is the greater of the following—
    (a) the value at the time of the gift of the property given, adjusted to take account of later changes in the value of money;
    (b) the value (at the material time) of the property found under subsection (2).
(2) The property found under this subsection is as follows—

(a) if the recipient holds the property given, the property found under this subsection is that property;

(b) if the recipient holds no part of the property given, the property found under this subsection is any property which directly or indirectly represents it in his hands;

(c) if the recipient holds part of the property given, the property found under this subsection is that part and any property which directly or indirectly represents the other part in his hands.

Section 81 sets out how the court is to work out the value of property held by a person. These **9.163** principles broadly reproduce the previous legislation. The references under s 81 to value are to the value found in accordance with s 79 (as per s 81(3)).

### Defendant does not have to be able to realise gift

In *R v Tighe* [1996] Crim LR 69 the Court of Appeal held that Parliament had contemplated **9.164** that money might continue to be realisable even though it had been the subject of a gift or gifts by the defendant. The fact that a gift had been made would not save the offender from a confiscation order. The recovery of the money was only one factor of which the court must take account in exercising its discretion. In *Tighe* the appellant had deliberately put out of his control monies already outside of the jurisdiction. On that basis the judge had been correct in refusing to take account of the fact that the appellant might not be able to recover the money. See also *R v Smith (Wallace Duncan)* [1996] 2 Cr App R 1.

## F. Proportionality

Once the Crown Court judge has established that the defendant has benefited from his **9.165** criminal conduct (whether general or particular) and he or she has valued that benefit and determined what the defendant's assets are then it should be possible to arrive at the recoverable amount. By virtue of s 6(5)(b), the judge is then required to make a confiscation order obliging the defendant to pay a sum of money equal to the recoverable amount unless, according to the Supreme Court in *Waya*, such a confiscation order would be disproportionate. If it would be, then the judge must decide what a proportionate confiscation order would be and make a confiscation order in that amount only.

That principle is simple to state but as the Supreme Court acknowledged at para 20 in *Waya*, **9.166** '[t]he difficult question is when a confiscation order sought may be disproportionate'. As an aid to answering that question, the minority created the concept of 'real' benefit (para 84). In their opinion, where the defendant's benefit, as determined by operation of the statute, exceeds the defendant's 'real' benefit then the Crown Court judge 'must decide whether it is proportionate to base the confiscation order on the POCA benefit'. However, in seeking to answer the 'difficult question' of when a confiscation order will be disproportionate, Crown Court judges should have regard to a number of observations spread throughout the judgment of the majority in *Waya*.

The first is that A1P1 does not vest in the Crown Court judge a wide-ranging discretion to **9.167** do what he or she wants. At para 24 the majority said this:

> . . . it must be clearly understood that the judge's responsibility to refuse to make a confiscation order which, because disproportionate, would result in an infringement of the Convention right under A1P1 is not the same as the recreation by another route of the general discretion

once available to judges but deliberately removed. An order which the judge would not have made as a matter of discretion does not thereby ipso facto become disproportionate. So to treat the jurisdiction would be to ignore the rule that the Parliamentary objective must, so long as proportionately applied, be respected.

**9.168** The second is that, following the decision of the House of Lords in *May*:

> a legitimate, and proportionate, confiscation order may have one or more of three effects: (a) it may require the defendant to pay the whole of a sum which he has obtained jointly with others; (b) similarly it may require several defendants each to pay a sum which has been obtained, successively, by each of them, as where one defendant pays another for criminal property; (c) it may require a defendant to pay the whole of a sum which he has obtained by crime without enabling him to see off expenses of the crime...Although these propositions involve the possibility of removing from the defendant by way of confiscation order a sum larger than may in fact represent his net proceeds of crime, they are consistent with the statute's objective and represent proportionate means of achieving it [para 26].

**9.169** The third is that:

> To make a confiscation order...when [the defendant] has restored to the loser any proceeds of crime which he ever had, is disproportionate. It would not achieve the statutory objective of removing his proceeds of crime but would simply be an additional financial penalty [para 28].
>
> The principle considered above ought to apply equally to other cases where the benefit obtained by the defendant has been wholly restored to the loser. In such a case a confiscation order which required him to pay the same sum again does not achieve the object of the legislation of removing from the defendant the proceeds of his crime, but amounts simply to a further pecuniary penalty—in any ordinary language a fine. It is for that reason disproportionate. If he obtained other benefit then an order confiscating that is a different matter [para 29].

**9.170** The Court of Appeal in *R v Axworthy* [2012] EWCA Crim 2889, referred to para 29 of *Waya* when deciding to quash a confiscation order in circumstances where the criminal property had been recovered by the loser. In that case, the appellant's mother had leased a motor vehicle. The appellant subsequently informed the lessor that the vehicle had been stolen. That was a lie. The appellant had in fact moved the vehicle to his flat in Ibiza. The lessor tracked the vehicle down and brought it back to the UK. Following conviction for offences of theft and attempting to pervert the course of justice, the Crown Court made a confiscation order against him to the full value of the vehicle, £22,010. This decision serves to emphasis the observations in paras 28 and 29 of *Waya* that *any* recovery in full of the criminal property by the loser will suffice and not just recovery initiated by the defendant. It follows that even where the defendant is reluctant to return that which he took, or positively resists the loser's efforts to get it back from him, it will be disproportionate to make a confiscation order against him: see *R v Hursthouse* [2013] EWCA Crim 517. It is worth emphasising here that the Supreme Court in *Waya* was only addressing the situation where the defendant has in fact made restoration in full. Where a compensation order has been made against a defendant that requires him to repay his victim in full the mere fact the property taken by the defendant may be restored is not sufficient to render disproportionate a confiscation order that includes the value of such property: see *R v Jawad* [2013] EWCA Crim 644, at para 21.

**9.171** The fourth is that:

> There may be other cases of disproportion analogous to that of goods or money entirely restored to the loser. That will have to be resolved case by case as the need arises. Such a case

might include, for example, the defendant who, by deception, induces someone else to trade with in a manner [CAF1] otherwise lawful, and who gives full value for goods or services obtained. He ought no doubt to be punished and, depending on the harm and the culpability demonstrated, maybe severely, but whether a confiscation order is proportionate for any sum beyond profit may need careful consideration' [para. 34].

Clearly, the Supreme Court wants to reign in at the outset the enthusiasm that Crown Court **9.172** judges may have for using A1P1 as a revived form of discretion to alter confiscation orders in the interest of justice or by some other similar standard. A1P1 should only be invoked to ensure that confiscation orders are proportionate and for no other reason. That is an exercise in judgment, not discretion. See *R v Harvey* [2013] EWCA Crim 1104 for discussion of pre-*Waya* cases. See also *R v Sale* [2013] EWCA Crim 1306.

## G. Time for Payment

Section 11 indicates the period the court should allow the defendant to pay the amount due **9.173** under the confiscation order. Section 11(1) states that the amount ordered to be paid must be paid on the making of the order (ie immediately), but this is subject to certain provisions:

  (2) If the defendant shows that he needs time to pay the amount ordered to be paid, the court making the confiscation order may make an order allowing payment to be made in a specified period.
  (3) The specified period—
      (a) must start with the day on which the confiscation order is made, and
      (b) must not exceed six months.

It is for the defendant to show that he needs more time to pay (eg because he envisages the **9.174** sale of his home). If within the specified period the defendant applies to the Crown Court for the period to be extended and the court believes there are exceptional circumstances, it may make an order extending the period (see s 11(4)). However, the court must not make an order under either s 11(2) or (4) unless it gives the prosecutor a right to be heard and make representations at any such application.

Section 11(5) states the extended period: **9.175**

  (a) must start with the day on which the confiscation order is made, and
  (b) must not exceed 12 months.

Similarly, an order under s 11(4) may be made after the end of the specified period, but must not be made after the end of the period of twelve months starting on the day on which the confiscation order is made (see s 11(6)). Therefore, no more than twelve months may be granted from the day on which the confiscation order is made.

The court may direct payment of any amount ordered to be paid under a confiscation order **9.176** by instalment (see s 139(1)(b) PCC(S)A). Payment should be made to the magistrates' court, pursuant to CrimPR r 52.2. Occasionally, the court will split the time-to-pay period, eg £10,000 within one month of the making of the order, the balance within six months.

### Appeal does not stop clock

In circumstances where an appeal had been lodged, the Court of Appeal took a robust **9.177** approach to the period set for payment in the case of *R v May, Lawrence and others* [2005] EWCA Crim 367, where Keene LJ held at para 5 that:

No authority has been cited for the proposition that the time to pay a confiscation order runs from the date of the determination of an appeal against it, and in our judgment the proposition is unsound in law. In principle the fact that an appeal is pending does not operate so as to suspend the operation of any sentence or order.

**9.178**   He added at para 7 that:

There is no reason why steps preparatory to the raising of the money specified in the confiscation order should not have been taken while May's appeal was pending. The appellant was not entitled to assume that his appeal would be successful and, as indicated above, as a matter of law time was running during that period. Moreover, it would be wrong as a matter of principle for appellants to be encouraged to believe that bringing an appeal would be likely to lengthen the time given for payment, even if the appeal was unsuccessful.

### Imprisonment in default

**9.179**   Under s 38(2) and (5) of POCA, the provisions of the PCC(S)A apply to the enforcement of a confiscation order in the same way as they apply to the imposition of a fine by the Crown Court. The effect of this provision is that the court must impose a prison sentence to be served in default of payment. It will be noted that, as with the previous legislation, the serving of the sentence in default does not extinguish the debt.

**9.180**   The penalties available for default in payment are set out in s 139(4) of the PCC(S)A and are as follows:

| | |
|---|---|
| An amount not exceeding £200 | 7 days |
| An amount exceeding £200 but not exceeding £500 | 14 days |
| An amount exceeding £500 but not exceeding £1,000 | 8 days |
| An amount exceeding £1,000 but not exceeding £2,500 | 45 days |
| An amount exceeding £2,500 but not exceeding £5,000 | 3 months |
| An amount exceeding £5,000 but not exceeding £10,000 | 6 months |
| An amount exceeding £10,000 but not exceeding £20,000 | 12 months |
| An amount exceeding £20,000 but not exceeding £50,000 | 18 months |
| An amount exceeding £50,000 but not exceeding £100,000 | 2 years |
| An amount exceeding £100,000 but not exceeding £250,000 | 3 years |
| An amount exceeding £250,000 but not exceeding £1,000,000 | 5 years |
| An amount exceeding £1,000,000 | 10 years |

**9.181**   The imposition of a default sentence was held to be mandatory in *R v Popple* [1992] Crim LR 675 and s 38(2) of POCA provides that the default sentence must be served consecutively to any sentence of imprisonment imposed for the substantive offence. It should be noted, however, that the above sentences are the maximum that may be imposed and it does not follow that the maximum sentence available for a particular amount should automatically be imposed in every case.

**9.182**   In *R v Szrajber* (1994) 15 Cr App R (S) 821, Crim LR 543 a CJA confiscation order was made against the defendant in the sum of £407,188 and a five-year sentence of imprisonment imposed for default in making payment, being the maximum period that could be ordered in respect of a sum between £250,000 and £1 million. The trial judge imposed the maximum sentence assuming it was a fixed period that she was required to impose. The Court of Appeal ruled, however, that the periods set out in the table were maximum periods and the court had discretion to impose a period below the maximum. The normal procedure would be for the court to impose a default sentence that fell between the maximum and minimum of the band being considered. So, for a confiscation order in the sum imposed against the defendant, a default sentence between three and five years should normally be imposed. In determining the proper sentence the court had to have regard to the circumstances of the case, to the overall seriousness of the matter, and in particular to the purpose for which the default sentence was imposed, namely to secure payment of the sum ordered to be confiscated. It was not necessary to approach the matter on a strict arithmetical basis. In the circumstances, the court varied the default sentence to four years. *Szrajber* was followed in the case of *R v Cox* [2008] EWCA Crim 3007, where the five-year maximum was reduced to four years, and where the Court commented that the judge should have been given more assistance on the issue than she was. As to the length of the default sentence see also *R v Castillo* [2011] EWCA Crim 3173 and *R v Patel* [2012] EWCA Crim 2736.

In *R v French* (1995) 16 Cr App R (S) 841, the court held that the period of imprisonment **9.183** in default should be such, within the maximum permitted, as to make it completely clear to the defendant that he had nothing to gain by failing to comply with the order. In *R v Simon Price* [2010] 2 Cr App R (S) 44, the Court adopted the reasoning in *R v Pigott* [2009] EWCA Crim 2292 in determining that the purpose of the default sentence was to ensure that the defendant complied with the order, and that it was wrong in principle to take into account the sentence for the substantive offence, ie the principle of totality in sentence did not have application. See also *Aspinwell* [2011] 1 Cr App R (S) 54.

### The form of order

The judge must give adequate reason for the order made: see *R v Waithe* [2012] EWCA Crim **9.184** 1168; *R v McCreesh* [2011] EWCA Crim 641. The court should give full reasons for its decision as to the facts it finds proven and the calculation of relevant figures. It should set out which assets it ascribes to the defendant and, if necessary, why. Reasons should be given even where the figures are 'agreed'.

It is permissible and not unusual for parties to reach agreement as to the figures which are to **9.185** form the basis of a confiscation order. Such agreement is likely to be binding on the defendant unless the Court of Appeal finds that there are 'exceptional circumstances'—eg where erroneous advice was given: *R v Hirani* [2008] EWCA Crim 1463; *R v Ayankoya* [2011] EWCA Crim 1488.

The confiscation order itself is then drawn up and inputted on two forms which are now **9.186** held on the computer systems in court operated by Crown Court clerks, namely, forms 5050 and 5050A. Care should be taken to ensure that the forms are completed correctly. Form 5050 will also include any details as to compensation payable out of the confiscation order as well as the default sentence. Form 5050A contains details of the schedule of available or realisable assets. This is clearly an important document and may be referred to in further applications (eg to vary). Where the defendant 'agrees' the value of assets it is suggested that the schedule should reflect this fact. Similarly where the prosecution has asserted that the defendant has hidden assets and the defendant effectively accepts he has hidden assets (eg because he agrees with the prosecution to pay an amount by way of an order which is in excess of the particular assets identified by the prosecution) it is suggested that the schedule should have an entry for 'Hidden Assets, location unknown .... value not less than £x.' as agreed by the defendant.

### Costs

**9.187**  In *R v Macatonia* [2009] EWCA Crim 2516 the Court confirmed that a costs order could be made, notwithstanding the existence of an outstanding confiscation order, because a costs order is designed to compensate the prosecutor for such expense. The costs order is not an additional punishment, but should not be 'grossly disproportionate' to the confiscation order imposed (see also *R v Dove* [2000] 1 Cr App R (S) 136 and *R v Constantine* [2010] EWCA Crim 2406, where the Court found that an order for costs in respect of both the trial and confiscation proceedings can be made more than twenty-eight days after the end of any postponement period under s 15(4) POCA where an issue in the original sentence had been adjourned).

**9.188**  However, in *R v Malakasuka* [2011] EWCA Crim 2477 the Court determined that where the benefit figure substantially exceeds the realisable assets, a confiscation order is likely to take everything the defendant has; and in those circumstances there should not normally be a costs order.

### Serving the default sentence does not extinguish the debt

**9.189**  Under s 38(5) where the defendant serves the term of imprisonment or detention in default of paying any amount due under a confiscation order, his serving that term does not prevent the confiscation order from continuing to have effect, so far as any other method of enforcement is concerned.

### Early release

**9.190**  The liability to serve the full default sentence is reduced by half following the introduction of s 258 of the Criminal Justice Act 2003. It applies to those defendants committed to prison after 4 April 2005 as a result of a default in the payment of a sum adjudged to be paid on conviction:

> (2)  As soon as a person to whom this section applies has served one-half of the term for which he was committed, it is the duty of the Secretary of State to release him unconditionally.
> (3)  Where a person to whom this section applies is also serving one or more sentences of imprisonment, nothing in this section requires the Secretary of State to release him until he is also required to release him in respect of that sentence or each of those sentences.

### Interest on unpaid sums

**9.191**  If the amount to be paid by a person under a confiscation order is not paid by the time it was required to be paid, the defendant must pay interest on that amount for any period after which it remains unpaid (see s 12(1)). Under s 12(2), the rate of interest is the same as that for interest on civil judgment debts (see s 17 of the Judgments Act 1838, currently 8 per cent). The payment of interest is mandatory in all cases, the interest being treated as part of the amount to be paid under the confiscation order (s 12(4)).

### Term in default: a penalty

**9.192**  In *Togher (Appellant) v Revenue & Customs Prosecutions Office (Respondent) & Doran (Intervenor)* [2007] EWCA Civ 686 Collins J had held at first instance that the term of imprisonment in default was not a penalty, but a means of enforcement. The Court of

Appeal, however, rejected this, Thomas LJ delivering the judgment of the court, finding (at para 470):

> The confiscation order and the default sentence were imposed following a conviction for a criminal offence. The nature and purpose of the confiscation and the term in default is to punish the offender. In *R v Clark & Bentham* [1997] 2 Cr App (S) 99, Lord Bingham CJ giving the judgment of the Court of Appeal Criminal Division made it clear that a judge should approach the period of imprisonment to be served in default by asking the question—what period of imprisonment not exceeding the statutory maximum is necessary to coerce the defendant into realising and paying the sum due under the confiscation order? The procedures for the making of the confiscation order and the imposition of the term in default were those of a criminal court. Both the confiscation order and the term in default were severe in their consequences. In my view it is artificial to seek to categorise separately the confiscation order and the term in default; to categorise the term in default as the means by which the penalty is to be enforced is to disregard the overall scheme and to put form before substance. In my view each is a penalty within the meaning of Article 7(1), but both should be considered together. If they are, they plainly are a penalty within the meaning of Article 7(1).

**Unreasonable delay**

In *Bullen and Soneji v UK* [2009] Lloyd's Rep FC 210, the ECtHR held that there had been **9.193** a violation of Art 6(1) following a delay of approximately five years and six months (including appeals to the Court of Appeal (Criminal Division) and the House of Lords) in the final determination of the confiscation proceedings. The Strasbourg Court reiterated that the reasonableness of the length of the proceedings must be assessed in the light of the circumstances of the case with reference to: the complexity of the case; the conduct of the applicants and the relevant authorities; and what was at stake for the applicants (para 58, applying *Pelissier and Sassi v France* no 25444/94 and *Caplik v Turkey* no 57019/00).

In *Lloyd v Bow Street Magistrates' Court* [2003] EWHC 2294 (Admin) the court ruled **9.194** that an unreasonable delay on the part of the prosecutor in taking enforcement action would amount to a breach of the defendant's rights under Art 6 of the ECHR if an attempt was made to implement the default sentence. The Court made it plain, however, that its decision applied only where enforcement action took the form of implementing the default sentence and had no application in respect of the use of civil remedies, such as the appointment of an enforcement receiver. This position has, however, been slightly modified by *R (on the application of Deamer) v Southampton Crown Court* [2006] EWHC 2221 (Admin) where the Divisional Court held that where there had been no unexplained or unjustifiable delay on the part of the prosecutor a committal in default was not unreasonable even though six years had elapsed. The issue of delay is returned to in the enforcement chapter of this book. On this issue see also *R v Leicester Magistrates' Court* [2013] EWHC 919.

## H. The Effect of a Confiscation Order on Sentence and the Court's Other Powers

Once the court has made a confiscation order it must then proceed in respect of the offence **9.195** or offences concerned in the terms set out in s 13(2) and (4) of POCA:

(2) The court must take account of the confiscation order before—
  (a) it imposes a fine on the defendant, or
  (b) it makes an order falling within subsection (3).
(3) …
(4) Subject to subsection (2) the court must leave the confiscation order out of account in deciding the appropriate sentence for the defendant.

**9.196**  Orders falling within subs (3) include compensation orders under s 130 of the Sentencing Act; forfeiture orders under s 27 of the Misuse of Drugs Act 1971; deprivation orders under s 143 of the Sentencing Act 2000; and forfeiture orders under s 23 of the Terrorism Act 2000.

**9.197**  Section 13 therefore requires the court to have regard to the confiscation order before imposing a fine or other order involving payment by the defendant, except for a compensation order, but otherwise it directs the court to ignore the confiscation order when sentencing the defendant.

### The relationship between the confiscation order and compensation

**9.198**  Under s 13(5):

(5) Subsection (6) applies if—
  (a) the Crown Court makes both a confiscation order and an order for the payment of compensation under section 130 of the Sentencing Act against the same person in the same proceedings, and
  (b) the court believes he will not have sufficient means to satisfy both the orders in full.
(6) In such a case the court must direct that so much of the compensation as it specifies is to be paid out of any sums recovered under the confiscation order; and the amount it specifies must be the amount it believes will not be recoverable because of the insufficiency of the person's means.

### Orders for the payment of prosecution costs

**9.199**  Orders for the payment of costs should only be made where the defendant has the ability to pay them. If a confiscation order is made in what the court finds to be the full value of a defendant's realisable property, no order for costs should be made. In *R v Szrajber* [1994] Crim LR 543 the defendant's benefit from the offences was found to be £524,000, but his realisable property was valued at £407,188 and a confiscation order accordingly made in this lesser sum. In addition, an order for the payment of costs was made in the sum of £65,428. The Court of Appeal quashed the order for costs on the basis that a confiscation order had been made in the full amount of the defendant's benefit from the offence and accordingly he had no further assets at his disposal from which the order for costs could be paid.

**9.200**  In *R v Ghadami* [1997] Crim LR 606 the Court of Appeal held that when it came to considering the question of an order to pay the costs of the prosecution, other debts should be taken into account (eg a confiscation order). It could then be seen that the appellant was a man without assets. In *Ghadami* the order to pay the costs of the prosecution was quashed (see also *R v Ruddick* The Times, 6 May 2003 (CA)).

## I. Appeals

The defendant's right of appeal in relation to POCA confiscation matters is considered fully in Chapter 18. **9.201**

Under s 31(1) and (2), subject to 31(3), and s 89 of POCA, the prosecutor's right of appeal is without restriction, subject to leave. Section 32(1) confirms that on an appeal the Court of Appeal may confirm, quash, or vary the confiscation order. **9.202**

## J. Defendants who Die or Abscond

### Introduction

Sections 27 and 28 of POCA give the court jurisdiction, in certain circumstances, to make confiscation orders in relation to s 6 of POCA for defendants who abscond. It will be noted that previously these powers were vested in the High Court and that in effect the power to deal with absconded defendants now rests with the Crown Court. **9.203**

### The defendant who dies

There is no provision in POCA for the court to proceed with confiscation in circumstances where the defendant dies following his conviction, but before a confiscation order is made. The previous provision under s 19 of the DTA for the High Court to make a confiscation order against a drug trafficker who died after conviction, but before the Crown Court could make a confiscation order was not re-enacted under POCA (it was considered, according to the explanatory notes that accompany POCA, that the recovery of benefit where the perpetrator is dead was better dealt with under the Civil Recovery Procedures in Pt 5 of POCA). **9.204**

### The defendant who absconds post-conviction

Section 27(2) and (3) of POCA gives the Crown Court the power to make confiscation orders post-conviction and provides as follows: **9.205**

(1) The section applies if the following two conditions are satisfied.
(2) The first condition is that a defendant absconds after—
    (a) he is convicted of an offence or offences in proceedings before the Crown Court,
    (b) he is committed to the Crown Court for sentencing in respect of an offence or offences under section 3, 4 or 6 of the Sentencing Act, or
    (c) he is committed to the Crown Court in respect of an offence or offences under section 70 (committal with a view to a confiscation order being considered).
(3) The second condition is that—
    (a) the prosecutor or the director applies to the Crown Court to proceed under this section, and
    (b) the court believes it is appropriate to do so.

*Procedure*

If this section applies the court must then proceed under s 6 in the same way as it would proceed if the two conditions mentioned in s 6 were otherwise satisfied; but in the case of the absconded defendant this is subject to s 27(5): **9.206**

(5) If the court proceeds under section 6 as applied by this section, this Part has effect with these modifications—

(a) any person the court believes is likely to be affected by an order under section 6 is entitled to appear before the court and make representations;

(b) the court must not make an order under section 6 unless the prosecutor has taken reasonable steps to contact the defendant;

(c) Section 6(9) applies if the reference to subsection (2) were to subsection (2) of this section;

(d) sections 10, 16(4), 17 and 18 must be ignored;

(e) sections 19, 20 and 21 must be ignored while the defendant is still an absconder.

Subsection (5)(c) imports that the defendant must fall within the paragraphs set out in 6(2).

**9.207**  For the purposes of s 27 the following sections of POCA must be ignored: s 10 (assumptions to be made in cases of a criminal lifestyle); s 16(4) (the requirement that a statement of information by the prosecutor under s 16(3) must include information the prosecutor believes is relevant in connection to the making of the required assumptions or for the purpose of enabling the court to decide if the circumstances are such that it must not make an assumption); s 17 (the defendant's response to the statement of information); and s 18 (provision of information by the defendant). It is suggested that the requirement that the defendant need not respond to the prosecutor's statement is perhaps not surprising in the circumstances.

**9.208**  Furthermore, ss 19 (no order made: reconsideration of case), 20 (no order made: reconsideration of benefit), and 21 (order made: reconsideration of benefit) must be ignored while the defendant is still an absconder (see s 27(5)(e)).

**9.209**  However, once the defendant ceases to be an absconder s 19 has effect as if subs (1)(a) read:

(a) at a time when the first condition in Section 27 was satisfied the court did not proceed under Section 6.

**9.210**  Similarly if the court does not believe it is appropriate for it to proceed under s 27, once the defendant ceases to be an absconder, s 19 has effect as if subs (1)(b) read:

(b) there is evidence which was not available to the prosecutor on the relevant date.

**9.211**  The special considerations which apply to proceedings held in the absence of an absconded defendant were set out by the Court of Appeal and House of Lords in *R v Hayward* [2003] AC 1 and in *R v Gavin & Tasie* [2010] EWCA Crim 2727 the Court held that where a defendant voluntarily absents himself from the jurisdiction the court has discretion as to whether to proceed or not, applying Convention principles. Where a defendant is involuntarily absent through the actions of the state then the court may find that it would be an abuse to proceed to confiscation in his absence.

### The defendant who absconds pre-conviction

**9.212**  Section 28 deals with the position where proceedings have been instituted against the defendant, but at the relevant time there has been no conviction recorded against him. Section 28 provides as follows:

(1) This section applies if the following two conditions are satisfied.

(2) The first condition is that—

(a) proceedings for an offence or offences are started against a defendant but are not concluded,

(b)  he absconds, and

(c)  the period of two years (starting with the date the court believes he absconded) has ended.

(3)  The second condition is that—

(a)  the prosecutor applies to the Crown Court to proceed under this section, and

(b)  the Court believes it is appropriate for it to do so.

### Two-year rule

In the circumstances set out in s 28, it will be noted that a confiscation order may only be **9.213** made against an absconder if two years have elapsed from the time he absconds (s 28(2)(b)).

### *Procedure*

If s 28 applies, the court must proceed under s 6 in the same way as it would proceed if the **9.214** two conditions mentioned in s 6 are satisfied (s 28(4)). Any person the court believes is likely to be affected by an order under s 6 is entitled to appear before the court and make representations (s 28(5)(a)).

The court is not entitled to make an order under s 6 unless the prosecutor has taken reason- **9.215** able steps to contact the defendant (s 28(5)(b)).

Under s 28(5)(b)–(e), the following sections of the confiscation provisions of POCA must **9.216** be ignored when proceeding under s 28: s 10 of POCA (assumptions to be made in cases of a criminal lifestyle); s 16(4) (the requirement that a statement of information by the prosecutor under s 16(3) must include information the prosecutor believes is relevant in connection to the making of the required assumptions or for the purpose of enabling the court to decide if the circumstances are such that it must not make an assumption); ss 17–20 (the defendant's response to a statement of information; provision of information by the defendant; and where no confiscation order is made: reconsideration of case and benefit); as must be s 21, while the defendant is still an absconder (confiscation order made: reconsideration of benefit). However, once the defendant has ceased to be an absconder s 21 does have effect.

### What happens if the defendant later returns?

If the court makes an order under s 6 as applied by s 28, and the defendant is later convicted **9.217** in proceedings before the Crown Court of the offence or any of the offences concerned, s 6 does not apply so far as that conviction is concerned (s 28(7)). In other words, when a court has made a confiscation order under s 28 it cannot go on to make another confiscation order if the defendant returns and is convicted.

### Variation and discharge of absconder's confiscation order

Section 29 deals with varying orders made under s 28 and s 30 deals with the discharging of **9.218** orders made under s 28. Both are considered in more detail in Chapter 10.

# 10

# RECONSIDERATION OF CONFISCATION ORDERS

## A. Introduction

**10.01**   When it makes a confiscation order the Crown Court will usually attempt to determine accurately the value of the defendant's realisable property. Nonetheless, the valuation process is something of an inexact science and it frequently happens that the sum realised on sale of a particular asset is either less or more than that anticipated at the time a confiscation order is made. For example, fluctuations in the property market may mean that when a house is sold it may be worth significantly more or less than was originally anticipated. Further, as the objective of many criminals is to conceal the extent of their benefit from criminal conduct and the extent and location of their assets, it may well be that at the time of a confiscation hearing the prosecutor is unable to put before the court evidence which gives a full picture of a defendant's wealth.

**10.02**   The Proceeds of Crime Act gives the prosecutor the right to apply to the court for the various determinations made during the course of a confiscation hearing to be revised in the light of new evidence. Similarly, POCA gives the defendant the right to seek a reduction in the amount of a confiscation order where the value of his realisable assets proves inadequate to satisfy the order in full.

**10.03**   This chapter primarily considers the variation and discharge of orders made under POCA. The numbers of DTA and CJA cases are inevitably decreasing and the effects of the transitional provisions are therefore now considerably diluted; as a result, the reader is referred to earlier editions of this work for a detailed examination of the previous legislation.

**10.04**   Although the case of *R v Waya* [2012] UKSC 51 considered in chapters 8 and 9 has not yet been considered in cases involving the reconsideration of orders, it seems likely that the principle of 'proportionality' will fall to be considered by judges in such cases.

## B. Variation and Discharge under the Proceeds of Crime Act 2002

### The slip rule

**10.05**   Section 155(1) of PCC(S)A (as amended) provides that confiscation orders can be varied within fifty-six days.

**10.06**   The application of this section to confiscation cases was confirmed in the case of *R v Bukhari* [2008] EWCA Crim 2915, that case dealing with the then strict twenty-eight-day limit; thereafter the correct route was by way of appeal. Appeals against confiscation orders are considered separately in Chapter 18.

# C. Reconsideration of Case where no Confiscation Order was Originally Made

Section 19 of POCA applies where no confiscation hearing was held after the original conviction.

**10.07**

Section 19(1) states:

**10.08**

This section applies if—
(a) the first condition in section 6 is satisfied, and no court has proceeded under that section;
(b) there is evidence which was not available to the prosecutor on the relevant date;
(c) before the end of the period of six years starting with the date of conviction the prosecutor applies to the Crown Court to consider the evidence; and
(d) after considering the evidence the Court believes it is appropriate for it to proceed under section 6.

The first condition of s 6 of POCA (s 6(2)) is that a defendant must fall within one of the following categories:

**10.09**

(a) he is convicted of an offence or offences in proceedings before the Crown Court;
(b) he is committed to the Crown Court for sentencing in respect of an offence or offences under ss 3, 4 or 6 of the Powers of Criminal Courts (Sentencing) Act 2000 (PCCSA); or
(c) he is committed to the Crown Court in respect of an offence or offences under s 70 of POCA (committal with a view to a confiscation order being considered).

Once the court has established that s 19(1) is satisfied the court must proceed under s 6 (s 19(2)) and in doing so must apply s 19(3) to (8). The court must consider the benefit obtained at the time of the original decision not to proceed and can only take into account benefit after that date which was a result of or in connection with conduct occurring before that date.

## Time limit

Importantly, it will be noted that in all cases, an application must be made to the Crown Court within six years of the original conviction (see s 19(1)(c)).

**10.10**

## How are the 'relevant date' and the 'date of conviction' defined?

The 'relevant date' referred to in s 19(1)(b) is defined in s 19(9) as either:

**10.11**

(a) if the court made a decision not to proceed under section 6, the date of that decision; or
(b) if the court did not make such a decision, the date of conviction.

Under s 19(10) the date of conviction is either:

(a) the date on which the defendant was convicted of the offence concerned, or
(b) if there were two or more offences and the convictions were on different dates, the date of the latest.

It should be noted that the purpose of s 19 is to allow the prosecutor to return to court when new evidence which could support an application for confiscation is discovered. It is therefore inappropriate for a prosecutor who had possession of evidence relating to the defendant's assets and conduct etc at the time of his trial and conviction, but chose not to apply for a confiscation order then, to apply for reconsideration under s 19 at a later date in circumstances where no new evidence has arisen.

**10.12**

**The status of previous orders of the court and compensation**

**10.13** Section 19(8) states that where a compensation order under s 130 of the PCC(S)A was made following the trial, the court cannot order payment of that compensation out of a confiscation order made at a reconsideration hearing under s 19. It follows that the payment of any compensation should only be ordered out of confiscated monies under s 13(6) of POCA where a confiscation order was also made in the original proceedings.

**10.14** Under s 19(7), POCA requires the court to take into account certain orders already made against the defendant in the original proceedings, namely fines, forfeiture, and compensation orders.

**Procedure: applications under section 19 of POCA**

**10.15** See para 10.40 below.

**Statements of information**

**10.16** Under s 26 of POCA, if the court proceeds under s 6 (the making of a confiscation order) in pursuance of s 19, the prosecutor must give the court a statement of information within the period the court orders (see para 10.41 below).

# D. Reconsideration of Benefit: Hearing Held but No Confiscation Order Originally Made

**10.17** Section 20 of POCA applies when a confiscation hearing was originally held and the court decided on that occasion that the defendant had a criminal lifestyle, but had not benefited from his general criminal conduct; or did not have a criminal lifestyle and did not benefit from his particular criminal conduct. Section 20 of POCA only applies if two specified conditions are satisfied.

**The first condition**

**10.18** Section 20(2) states:

> The first condition is that in proceeding under section 6 the court has decided that—
> (a) the defendant has a criminal lifestyle but has not benefited from his general criminal conduct, or
> (b) the defendant does not have a criminal lifestyle and has not benefited from his particular criminal conduct.

**The second condition**

**10.19** The second condition under s 20(4) is that:

> (a) there is evidence that was not available to the prosecutor when the court decided that the defendant had not benefited from his general or particular criminal conduct,
> (b) before the end of the period of six years starting with the date on which the prosecutor applies to the Crown Court to consider the evidence, and
> (c) after considering the evidence the court concludes that it would have decided that the defendant would have benefited from his general or particular criminal conduct (as the case may be) if the evidence had been available to it.

The 'date of conviction' is defined at s 19(10) as the date on which the defendant was convicted of the offence concerned or, if there are two or more offences and the convictions were on different dates, the date of the latest (see s 20(13)). If the court considers that the two conditions are satisfied, it must make a fresh decision as to benefit and make a new confiscation order.

### The status of previous orders of the court

Under s 20(11)(c) and (d), POCA requires the court to take into account certain orders **10.20** already made against the defendant in the original proceedings, namely fines, forfeiture, and compensation orders.

### Compensation

Section 20(12) states that where a compensation order under s 130 of the PCC(S)A was **10.21** made following the trial, the court cannot order payment of that compensation out of a confiscation order made at a reconsideration hearing under s 20. It follows that the payment of any compensation should only be ordered out of confiscated monies under s 13(6) of POCA where a confiscation order was also made in the original proceedings.

### Procedure: applications under section 20 of POCA

See para 10.40 below.                                                                           **10.22**

### Statements of information

Under s 26 of POCA, if the court proceeds under s 6 (the making of a confiscation order) in **10.23** pursuance of s 20, the prosecutor must give the court a statement of information within the period the court orders (see para 10.41 below).

## E. Where a Confiscation Order has been Made: Reconsideration of Benefit

Section 21 of POCA applies if:                                                                  **10.24**

   (1) ...
- (a) the court has made a confiscation order,
- (b) there is evidence which was not available to the prosecutor at the relevant time,
- (c) the prosecutor [...] believes that if the court were to find the amount of the defendant's benefit in pursuance of this section, it would exceed the relevant amount,
- (d) before the end of the period of six years starting from the date of conviction the prosecutor [...] applies to the Crown Court to consider the evidence, and
- (e) after considering the evidence the court believes it is appropriate for it to proceed under this section.

When reconsidering the defendant's benefit, the court must make a new calculation of the **10.25** defendant's benefit from the conduct concerned (s 21(2)). In effect this enables a confiscation order already made to be increased.

Under s 21 there is no restriction as to the number of times that the prosecutor may return **10.26** to the Crown Court to seek an increase in the defendant's benefit figure, although it will have been noted that s 21(1)(d) imports a limitation date of six years starting from the date of conviction.

**10.27**   If a court has already sentenced the defendant for the offence (or any of the offences) concerned, s 6 of POCA has effect as if the defendant's particular criminal conduct included conduct which constitutes offences which the court has taken into consideration in deciding his sentence for the offence or offences concerned (as per s 21(3)).

**10.28**   When the court is reconsidering the defendant's benefit under s 21, s 8(2) of POCA does not apply. Instead the court must:

> (4) ...
>> (a)  take account of conduct occurring up to the time it decided the defendant's benefit for the purposes of the confiscation order;
>> (b)  take account of the property obtained up to that time;
>> (c)  take account of property obtained after that time if it was obtained as a result of or in connection with conduct occurring before that time.

**10.29**   In terms of general criminal conduct and the deducting of aggregate amounts, when applying s 8(5) of POCA in relation to reconsidering a defendant's benefit, the confiscation order previously made against the defendant must be ignored (s 21(5)).

### When is the relevant time?

**10.30**   By s 21(12), the relevant time is:

> (a)  when the court calculated the defendant's benefit for the purposes of the confiscation order, if this section [21] has not applied previously;
> (b)  when the court last calculated the defendant's benefit in pursuance of this section, if this section has applied previously.

### What is the relevant amount?

**10.31**   Under s 21(13) the relevant amount is:

> (a)  the amount found as the defendant's benefit for the purposes of the confiscation order, if this section [21] has not applied previously;
> (b)  the amount last found as the defendant's benefit in pursuance of this section, if this section has applied previously.

### When is the date of conviction?

**10.32**   The date of conviction is:

> (a)  the date on which the defendant was convicted of the offence concerned; or
> (b)  if there are two or more offences and the convictions are on different dates, the date of the latest (see s 21(14) applying s 19(10)).

### The assumptions

**10.33**   When considering s 10 of POCA (assumptions to be made in cases of criminal lifestyle) in s 21 cases:

> (a)  the first and second assumptions do not apply with regard to property first held by the defendant after the time the court decided his benefit for the purposes of the confiscation order;

(b) the third assumption does not apply with regard to expenditure incurred by him after that time;

(c) the fourth assumption does not apply with regard to property obtained (or assumed to have been obtained) by him after that time (see s 21(6)).

### Revised benefit and relationship with the recoverable amount

**10.34** If the amount found under the new calculation of the defendant's benefit under s 21 exceeds the relevant amount, the court must make a new calculation of the recoverable amount for the purposes of s 6, and, if it exceeds the amount required to be paid under the confiscation order previously ordered, the court may vary the order by substituting for the amount required to be paid such amount as it believes is just (s 21(7)).

**10.35** When making the new calculation for the recoverable amount for the purposes of s 6, the court must take the new calculation of the defendant's benefit and apply s 9 of POCA (the available amount) as if references to the time the confiscation order was made were to the time of the new calculation of the recoverable amount, and as if references to the date of the confiscation order were to the date of that new calculation (s 21(8)).

**10.36** Under s 21(9), in applying s 21(7)(b) (where the court is considering varying an order to substitute it for an amount it believes 'just') the court must have regard to:

(a) any fine imposed on the defendant for the offence (or any of the offences) concerned;

(b) any order which falls within section 13(3) of POCA [compensation orders, forfeiture orders or deprivation orders] which have been made against the defendant in respect of the offence (or any of the offences) concerned and have not already been taken into account by the court in deciding what is the free property held by him for the purposes of section 9;

(c) any order which has been made against the defendant in respect of the offence (or any of the offences) concerned under section 130 of the Sentencing Act (compensation orders).

The purpose of s 21(9)(b) and (c) is to avoid double recovery and equally to prevent a defendant from being allowed a reduction twice in respect of the same property.

### The status of previous orders of the court

**10.37** Under s 21(9)(b) and (c), POCA requires the court to take into account certain orders already made against the defendant in the original proceedings, namely fines, forfeiture, and compensation orders.

### Exception to rule

**10.38** By s 21(10), the court cannot take a compensation order into account in one specified circumstance when reconsidering the defendant's benefit. If the court has made a direction under s 13(6) (compensation to be paid out of any sums recovered under the confiscation order), in applying s 21(7)(b) (where the defendant's benefit exceeds the amount required to be paid under the confiscation order) the court must not have regard to an order falling within s 21(9)(c) (compensation orders).

### Changes in the value of money

**10.39** When deciding under s 21 whether one amount exceeds another, the court must take account of any change in the value of money (s 21(11)).

## F. Procedure: Applications under Sections 19, 20, or 21 of POCA

**10.40**   Where the prosecutor makes an application under s 19, 20, or 21 of POCA (application for reconsideration of a decision to make a confiscation order or benefit assessed for purposes of a confiscation order) the application must be in writing and give details of:

(a) the name of the defendant;

(b) the date on which and the place where any relevant conviction occurred;

(c) the date on which and the place where any relevant confiscation order was made or varied;

(d) the grounds for the application;

(e) an indication of the evidence available to support the application (see CrimPR r 58.3). Under r 58.3(3) any application for reconsideration of a decision to make a confiscation order or reconsideration of benefit assessed for the purposes of a confiscation order, must be lodged with the Crown Court, and the application must be served on the defendant at least seven days before the date fixed by the court for hearing the application, unless the Crown Court specifies a shorter period (see r 58.3(4)).

### Statements of information

**10.41**   Under s 26 of POCA if the court proceeds under s 6 (the making of a confiscation order) in pursuance of either s 19 (no order made: reconsideration of case) or s 20 (no confiscation order made: reconsideration of benefit) or the prosecutor applies under s 21 of POCA (where a confiscation order has been made and the court has to reconsider the benefit figure), the prosecutor must give the court a statement of information within the period the court orders (see s 26(1) and (2)(a)).

**10.42**   Section 16 of POCA (the provision of a statement of information) applies accordingly (with appropriate modification where the prosecutor applies under s 21); as does s 17 (the defendant's response to the statement of information), and s 18 (the provision of information by the defendant) where s 6(3)(a) or s 6(3)(b) applies (ie the prosecutor has asked the court to proceed under s 6 or the court believes it is appropriate for it to do so), or the court is considering whether or not to proceed under s 6 (s 26(2)(b)).

## G. Increase in Available Amount

### Where a confiscation order has been made: reconsideration of the available amount

**10.43**   The purpose of s 22 of POCA is to allow the court to recalculate the available amount in circumstances where a confiscation order has previously been made in an amount lower than the defendant's assessed benefit, because at that time there was insufficient realisable property to satisfy an order in the full amount. Under the previous legislation this was sometimes referred to as a 'Certificate of Increase'.

**10.44**   Section 22 of POCA applies if:

(1)   ...

(a) a court has made a confiscation order,

(b) the amount required to be paid was the amount found under section 7(2) [where the defendant was able to show that the available amount was less than the benefit figure], and

(c) an applicant falling within section 22(2) [ie the prosecutor or a receiver appointed under section 50 of POCA (an enforcement receiver)] applies to the Crown Court to make a new calculation of the available amount.

Where the above circumstances apply the court must make the new calculation, and in doing **10.45** so it must apply s 9 of POCA (calculation of the available amount) as if references to the time the confiscation order is made were to the time of the new calculation, and as if reference to the date of the confiscation order were to the date of the new calculation (s 22(3)). Evidence that pre-dates the confiscation order can be taken into consideration by the court as long as that evidence was not before the court at the time of the original hearing. This section operates in a similar way as the 'Certificate of Increase' provisions operated under the DTA. The purpose of these provisions was identified by Rose LJ in *R v Tivnan* [1999] 1 Cr App R (S) 92 who held:

> ...we see no ambiguity. The plain words of the statute, in our judgment, provide for the making of an application for a further certificate and for an increase in the amount recovered under the confiscation order at any time after the original confiscation order was made. By this means drug dealers can be deprived of their assets until they have disgorged an amount equivalent to all the benefit which had accrued to them from drug dealing.

It will be noted that, unlike ss 19, 20, and 21, there is no limitation to the time when an application may be made and the prosecutor or a receiver may apply on more than one occasion.

Under s 22(4), if the amount found under the new calculation exceeds the relevant amount **10.46** the court may vary the order by substituting for the amount required to be paid such amount as:

(a) it believes is just, but
(b) does not exceed the amount found as the defendant's benefit from the conduct concerned.

In deciding what is 'just' the court must have regard in particular to: **10.47**

(5) ...
   (a) any fine imposed on the defendant for the offence (or any of the offences) concerned;
   (b) any order which falls within section 13(3) (compensation orders, forfeiture orders or deprivation orders) and has been made against him in respect of the offence (or any of the offences) concerned and has not already been taken into account by the court in deciding what is the free property held by him for the purposes of section 9 of POCA [the available amount];
   (c) any order which has been made against the defendant in respect of the offence (or any of the offences) concerned under Section 130 of the Sentencing Act (compensation orders).

### Hidden assets

In deciding what is 'just' the court must have regard to an order falling within subs (5)(c) **10.48** (orders made under s 130 of the Sentencing Act (compensation orders)), if a court has made a direction under s 13(6) of POCA, to avoid the defendant being able to offset the impact of the compensation order on both occasions (subs (6)). For the amount to be recovered from unidentified assets (not confined to that which is specifically identified) and for reasonable inferences as to the existence of realisable assets, see *Re Peacock* [2012] UKSC 5 and *R v Lee* [2012] EWCA Crim 954.

### What is the 'relevant amount' under section 22?

**10.49** Under s 22(8) the relevant amount is:

(a) the amount found as the available amount for the purposes of the confiscation order, if section 22 had not applied previously;

(b) the amount last found as the available amount in pursuance of section 22, if section 22 has applied previously.

**10.50** The amount found as the defendant's benefit from the conduct concerned is:

(9) ...

(a) the amount so found when the confiscation order was made, or

(b) if one or more new calculations of the defendant's benefit have been made under section 21 of POCA, the amount found on the occasion of the last such calculation.

### Changes in the value of money

**10.51** When deciding under s 22 whether one amount exceeds another, the court must take account of any change in the value of money (see s 22(7)).

### Procedure: applications under section 22 of POCA

**10.52** Under r 58.4 CrimPR, where the prosecutor or a receiver makes an application under s 22 of POCA for a new calculation of the available amount, in circumstances where a confiscation order has already been made, the application must be in writing and must be supported by a witness statement. That application and any witness statement must be lodged with the Crown Court and served upon:

(a) the defendant;

(b) the receiver, if the prosecutor is making the application and a receiver has been appointed under s 50 of POCA (an enforcement receiver); and

(c) the prosecutor if the receiver is making the application,

at least seven days before the date fixed by the court hearing the application, unless the Crown Court specifies a shorter period (see r 58.4(1) to (4)).

### Increase in the available amount: ECHR

**10.53** In *Saggar* [2005] EWCA Civ 174, the Court of Appeal held that where the state had granted to itself the right to reopen the issue of confiscation under s 16 of the DTA (for a certificate of increase), the reasonable time requirement under Art 6(1) of the ECHR was triggered and extended throughout the period starting from the original proceedings, and not just from the institution of the s 16 application.

## H. Inadequacy of Available Amount

### Introduction

**10.54** Section 23 of POCA replaces the previous procedure where defendants or the receiver had to apply to the High Court for a certificate of inadequacy.

**10.55** Applications by defendants attaching to the inadequacy of their realisable assets, and thereby their inability to meet their confiscation orders, are commonplace. Pending applications are regularly raised as a reason for the default sentence not to be implemented at enforcement hearings.

Prior to s 23, the legislative provisions for subsequent applications by defendants in respect **10.56** of confiscation orders were contained in s 17 of the DTA and s 83 of the CJA, each as amended by POCA and by the PCC(S)A. They were in the same terms, save for provisions in the latter referring to magistrates' courts. The sections provided for an application to the High Court for a certificate of the inadequacy of the defendant's realisable property to pay the amount previously ordered. Where a certificate was issued by the High Court the defendant could apply to the Crown Court to have substituted for the amount originally ordered such lesser amount as the Crown Court thought just in all the circumstances.

The earlier sections thus provided a wholly different procedure to enable a defendant to **10.57** come back to the Crown Court to ask for a reduction in the amount originally ordered. It was formerly the High Court which had to consider the adequacy of realisable property: it is now the Crown Court which has to consider whether the available amount is inadequate for the payment of the outstanding balance. In terms of procedure, if a defence solicitor wishes to seek public funding for a s 23 application, he should apply to the Crown Court, not to the enforcement magistrates' court (which has no power to grant a representation order for s 23 proceedings).

### Section 23

Section 23(1) applies to POCA cases if: **10.58**

(a) a court has made a confiscation order, and
(b) the defendant, or a receiver appointed under s 50 of POCA (an enforcement receiver) applies to the Crown Court to vary the order under section 23.

When an application is being considered under s 23, the Crown Court must calculate the available amount, and in doing so it must apply s 9 of POCA (calculation of the available amount) as if references to the time the confiscation order was made were to the time of the current calculation and as if references to the date of the confiscation order were to the date of the current calculation (see s 23(2)). As a result, under s 23 the available amount is to be assessed as under s 9, but at the time of the calculation under s 23.

The court may disregard any inadequacy which it believes is attributable (wholly or partly) **10.59** to anything done by the defendant for the purpose of preserving property in circumstances where it is held by the recipient of a tainted gift (s 23(5)).

Under s 23(3), if the court finds that the available amount (as so calculated) is inadequate for **10.60** the payment of any amount remaining to be paid under the confiscation order, it may vary the order by substituting it for a smaller amount as the court believes is just. It should also alter the default sentence accordingly, by s 39(2) of POCA. The terms of s 23(3) are discretionary. What is 'just' will depend on all the circumstances and is not merely an arithmetical exercise based upon the extent of the inadequacy found but will include the reasons for the shortfall which may include the defendant's actions—see *Briggs* [2003] EWCA Crim 3298, a case under the DTA. For example, it may be 'just' only to reduce the confiscation order by a nominal sum if the inadequacy is attributable to wilful dissipation of assets by the defendant in preference to satisfying his confiscation order. It will have been clearly noted that a confiscation order is made *in personam* (against the defendant) rather than *in rem* (against the defendant's assets). The court can therefore take into account any assets held by the defendant at the time of the reconsideration.

**10.61**  There is no limit to how often the defendant can return to court for reconsideration. A defendant who does not acquire any new assets may well have an interest in returning to court in order to obtain an order which reduces his liability and default sentence pro rata. However, this does not mean that the defendant must return to court each time an asset is sold at an undervalue to have his order reduced. Because the order is made against him, his total assets may well still be sufficient to satisfy the order. The court, in exercising its discretion to vary the order, will scrutinise the reasons why the asset has not been realised for the sum set at confiscation or is otherwise unavailable. The court will no doubt look carefully at the original order and schedule of assets set out at the time of the court order in forms 5050 and 5050A.

**10.62**  If the defendant or others are going to rely upon this provision they must demonstrate to the court firm and clear evidence of their reduced circumstances—per *Gokal v SFO* [2001] EWCA Civ 368 where Keene LJ stated:

> As has been said many times in the authorities, it is not enough for the defendant to come to court and say that his assets are inadequate to meet the confiscation order, unless at the same time he condescends to demonstrate what has happened since the making of the order to the realisable property found by the trial judge to have existed at the time when the order was made.

**10.63**  *Gokal* was applied in *R v Younis* [2008] EWCA Crim 2950 where the Court held, applying the 'hard edged rule' in *Re McKinsley* [2006] 1 WLR 3420, that s 23 should not be seen as an opportunity to re-litigate matters already determined against the defendant in the Crown Court (para 11). The hearing is not an appeal. However, the court may examine whether there would be a real risk of injustice if the order were to continue in its present terms.

**10.64**  In *R v Glaves* [2011] EWCA Civ 69, the court held that there was no rule of law, on an application for a certificate of inadequacy, that the application was bound to fail unless the applicant gave full disclosure of what had happened to his assets (including 'hidden assets'). In *Alves* [2011] EWCA Crim 1375, the confiscation order was reduced because the realisable amount was found to include a half share of the equity in a house and the value of a VW Beetle car when the car and the entire equity in the house were, and remained, the property of the appellant's former wife. The Crown accepted that at the time of the confiscation order, the applicant, on a proper analysis, had no interest in these items and had none at the time of the appeal.

**10.65**  The Court of Appeal in *R v Barry Ward* [2010] EWCA Crim 1932 held that it had no jurisdiction to hear an appeal from the Crown Court against a decision not to vary a confiscation order under s 23 POCA. It held that an order made under s 23 was excluded from the definition of 'sentence' by virtue of the Criminal Appeal Act 1968.

**Procedure: variation of confiscation order due to inadequacy of available amount**

**10.66**  Rule 58.5 CrimPR applies where the defendant or a receiver makes an application under s 23 of POCA for the variation of a confiscation order to a lower amount. Under r 58.5 the application must be in writing and may be supported by a witness statement, and any application and accompanying witness statement must be lodged with the Crown Court. That application and any witness statement must be served on:

(a) the prosecutor;
(b) the defendant, if the receiver is making the application; and
(c) the receiver, if the defendant is making the application and a receiver has been appointed under s 50 (an enforcement receiver)

at least seven days before the date fixed by the court for hearing the application, unless the Crown Court specifies a shorter period. Where appropriate, the application should also include any accrued interest.

It will also be noted that in *Re T* [2005] EWHC 3359 (Admin) Collins J held (in a DTA case)  **10.67** that the court did have jurisdiction to grant bail in an appropriate case where the outcome of a certificate of inadequacy application was awaited.

### Practice

In *Re B* [2008] EWHC 3217 (Admin), DHCJ Holgate QC gave a helpful distillation of the  **10.68** principles that have been established with regard to the consideration of inadequacy applications in a CJA matter (para 74):

(1) The burden lies on the applicant to prove, on the balance of probabilities, that his realisable property is inadequate for the payment of the confiscation order (see *Re O'Donoghue* (2004) EWCA Civ 1800, per Laws LJ at para 3).
(2) The reference to realisable property must be to 'whatever are his realisable assets as a whole at the time he applies for the certificate of inadequacy. If they include assets he did not have when the confiscation order was made, that is by no means a reason for leaving such fresh assets out of consideration.' (ibid and see also *Re Phillips* [2006] EWHC 623 (Admin)).
(3) A section 83 application cannot be used to go behind a finding made at the confiscation hearing or embodied in the confiscation order as to the amount of the defendant's realisable assets. Such a finding can only be challenged by way of an appeal against the confiscation order. (See *Gokal v Serious Fraud Office* (2001) EWCA Civ 368, Per Keene LJ at paras 17 and 24).
(4) It is insufficient for a defendant to say under section 83 'that his assets are inadequate to meet the confiscation order, unless at the same time he condescends to demonstrate what has happened since the making of the order to the realisable property found by the trial Judge to have existed when the order was made' (see *Gokal* at para 24 and *Re O'Donoghue* at para 3).
(5) The confiscation hearing provided an opportunity for the Defendant to show that his realisable property was worth less than the Prosecution alleged. It also enabled the Defendant to identify any specific assets which he contended should be treated as the only realisable property. The section 83 procedure, however, is intended to be used only where there has been a genuine change in the Defendant's financial circumstances. It is a safety net intended to provide for post-confiscation order events. (See *McKinsley v Crown Prosecution Service* (2006) EWCA Civ 1092 per Scott Baker LJ at paras 9, 21–24, 31 and 35).
(6) A section 83 application is not to be used as a 'second bite of the cherry'. It is not an opportunity to adduce evidence or to present arguments which could have been put before the Crown Court Judge at the confiscation hearing (para 38 of *Gokal* and paras 23, 24 and 37 of *McKinsley*).
(7) The clarification of a third party's interest in property may be a post confiscation order event. The extent of any such interest may have to be decided by a civil court. (*Re Norris* (2001) UKHL 34 and *McKinsley* at para 39).

(8) In a section 83 application the definition of realisable property includes a chose in action or a right to a sum of money which the applicant is entitled to recover, irrespective of any difficulty in its actual recovery, unless the applicant proves on the balance of probabilities that it is impossible to recover that sum (*R v Liverpool Magistrates' Court ex parte Ansen* [1998] 1 All ER 692 at page 701d–e and *Re Houssan Ali* [2002] EWCA Civ 1450 at para 1.11).

### Not a route to appeal

**10.69** An inadequacy application should only be sought in cases where, since the making of the confiscation order, the value of the defendant's realisable property has decreased for some reason. It is not an appropriate remedy for a defendant who is aggrieved by the Crown Court's findings when it made the confiscation order: in such circumstances the defendant's remedy is an appeal to the Court of Appeal (Criminal Division).

**10.70** In *Re N* [2005] EWHC QBD 3211 (Admin), Toulson J endorsed a 'hard-edged rule' in respect of certificate of inadequacy applications. He expressed concern that the provisions set out in s 17 of the DTA and the corresponding provisions of POCA were being used by defendants as an appeal route, whereas the proper course would have been to pursue the matter in the Court of Appeal.

**10.71** This was further confirmed in *P v Customs and Excise Commissioners* [2005] EWHC 877 (Admin), where Beatson J stated (at para 18) that it was '...well established that the procedure under [s 17]...is not to be used as a device to appeal against the original finding that an item of property is realisable property within the legislation'. He added at para 20: 'In applying for a certificate of inadequacy, an applicant must show what has happened to the realisable property or to part of it since the making of the confiscation order.'

### Evidence

**10.72** In *Gokal v Serious Fraud Office* [2001] EWCA Civ 368, at paras 16 and 17, Keene J considered a similar problem:

> The evidence in support of the recent application for a certificate took the form of a witness statement...In the witness statement it is said that the appellant 'seeks to prove that he has no realisable property to be applied in satisfaction of the confiscation order'. Apparently an attempt was going to be made to produce evidence at this stage to show that the money which went into the appellant's personal bank account has been dissipated. This would take the form of schedules produced by accountants which were available at the time of the appeal to the Court of Appeal but not produced to that court. This is not a proper basis on which to seek a certificate. It amounts to an attempt to go behind the original confiscation order finding as to the amount of the defendant's realisable assets. Such a finding can only be challenged by way of an appeal against the confiscation order...An application for a certificate does not provide an opportunity to try to make good deficiencies in the case presented at the time of the confiscation order or at the appeal against it.

**10.73** In *R v T* (QBD (Admin), 1 February 1996) McCullough J said:

> It is not sufficient for a defendant simply to assert at the time of his application for a certificate of inadequacy that he has no realisable property. He must explain what has become of the realisable property whose existence formed the basis of the confiscation order. If a defendant is at liberty simply to rely upon the assertion of the present lack of realisable property to justify the issue of a certificate of inadequacy, then it is open to him...to subvert the decision which formed the basis of the confiscation order. That is plainly wrong in principle.

**Hidden assets**

A particular difficulty arises for a defendant where there has been a finding of hidden assets **10.74** by the Crown Court. The finding implies that he has been less than frank about the extent of his assets. In such cases it would appear to be extremely difficult to obtain a certificate of inadequacy, particularly in cases where the defendant is still maintaining that he has no assets. In *Telli v RCPO* [2007] EWHC 2233 the court held that:

> … absent identification of all the realisable property held by him, a defendant normally will be unable to satisfy the court that the amount that might be realised at the time the confiscation order is made is less than the amount assessed to be the proceeds of his drug trafficking. Assets which he hides from the gaze of Customs and Excise may, for all anyone knows, be equal to or in excess of the value of his proceeds of drug trafficking. For that reason, no court should be satisfied that they are to be quantified at a lesser amount.

> 37. Secondly, it is incumbent upon a court to assess the *current* value of the realisable property in order to determine whether it is inadequate to meet the outstanding sum. Once it is appreciated that the property held by the defendant includes unidentified assets forming part of the total value of the realisable property at the time of the order, it is impossible for Telli to establish that the realisable property is inadequate now to meet payment of the outstanding amount. The order was made in 1996. If a defendant fails to identify all the assets he holds, no-one will know their true value and by the time of the application, the value of the assets he failed to identify may have increased, particularly after 10 years. Absent consideration of current value, no court could be satisfied that the realisable property was inadequate. If the assets remain unidentified no conclusion can be reached as to their current value.

However in *Glaves v CPS* [2011] EWCA Civ 69 the Court of Appeal held that even if the **10.75** defendant held assets that were unidentified at the time of making the confiscation order and at the time of the application for a certificate, it was still open to the defendant to attempt to obtain a certificate on the grounds that his identified assets had diminished in value such that he could not now pay the full amount outstanding under the confiscation order. *Glaves* was considered in *Pearson, Re* [2012] EWHC 1704 (Admin) in which Collins J held that the existence of hidden assets did not of itself preclude the making of a certificate of inadequacy. However, it was incumbent on the court, in such an application, to have evidence of, or to be able to assess, the current value of any assets, including, generally, hidden assets. On the facts of that case, the burden of proof was on the defendant to show that the amount of hidden assets, having regard to their present value, of which the court had no evidence, was insufficient, so as to justify the grant of a certificate of inadequacy.

**Burden and standard of proof**

In *Re O'Donoghue* [2004] 176 EWHC (Admin), Lightman J reaffirmed that the burden of **10.76** proof was on the defendant to establish that the value of his assets was inadequate to satisfy the whole value of the confiscation order. He added that it was not sufficient for him to merely state that his assets were inadequate, without demonstrating what had happened since the making of the confiscation order that had made them so.

**Assets difficult to realise**

The fact that particular assets prove difficult for a defendant to realise does not necessarily **10.77** mean they cease to be realisable property (see *Re R*, The Independent, 4 November 2002). In *R v Liverpool Justices ex p Ansen* [1998] 1 All ER 692 the assets taken into account in making a confiscation order included a deposit he had put down on a summer house in Turkey and that was held by German agents; a deposit he had put down and was entitled to reclaim in relation to some Waterford Wedgwood articles; and a loan he had apparently made to his junior counsel at trial. He had been unable to realise any of these amounts in satisfaction of a confiscation order and accordingly applied for a certificate of inadequacy. In refusing the defendant's application, May J said:

> [Counsel for the Prosecutor] submits that the fact that an asset may be difficult to realise is simply not relevant. The provisions of the Act, he submits, define 'realisable property' in terms of section 5 and do not address any question of whether in practical terms it is difficult to recover the money. I agree with that submission for two reasons. Firstly, the definition of 'realisable property' includes property held by the defendant and by definition 'property' is held by any person if he holds an interest in it and the 'interest' in property includes a right. Accordingly, if as Mr. Ansen's affidavit indicates, the sum of approximately £8,500 held by agents in Germany is an amount which he is entitled to recover, then it is realisable property by definition irrespective of any difficulty in its actual recovery.
>
> Secondly, s 5(1)(b) of the DTA, referring, as it does, to 'realisable property' including 'gifts caught by the Act', necessarily means that circumstances may arise where gifts which an applicant has made may be practically, even legally, irrecoverable, but they are nevertheless still regarded as realisable property under this draconian Act. The purpose of these draconian procedures is obvious: they are intended, as has often been said, to make it as difficult as possible for those who traffic in drugs to get away with the proceeds of that traffic.

### Inadequacy and gifts

**10.78**  Where the defendant has made a gift caught by the relevant Act, the defendant cannot obtain a certificate of inadequacy purely on the grounds that he cannot compel realisation of the property from the donee: *Re L* [2010] EWHC 1531 (Admin). The effect of ss 83 and 74 of the CJA is that it is necessary for the court to find as a fact that the donee has insufficient property to satisfy the value of the gift. See also *R v Kim Smith* [2013] EWCA Crim 502.

**10.79**  Under s 23(5) POCA, the court may disregard any inadequacy which it believes is attributable (wholly or partly) to anything done by the defendant for the purpose of preserving property held by the recipient of a tainted gift from any risk of realisation under this Part.

### Inadequacy of available amount in bankruptcy cases

**10.80**  Section 23(4) POCA states that if a person has been adjudged bankrupt or his estate has been sequestrated (or if an order for the winding up of a company has been made), the court must take into account the extent to which realisable property held by that person or that company may be distributed among creditors ('company' for these purposes means any company that may be wound up under the Insolvency Act 1986 (see s 23(6)). In *Re R* [2009] EWHC 1700 (Admin), the defendant was adjudged bankrupt after the confiscation order. The application for a Certificate of Inadequacy was refused. The applicant failed to discharge the onus on him to show what his realisable assets were. In *R v Shahid (Abdul)* [2009] EWCA Crim 831, a bankruptcy order was made prior to the confiscation order. It was held on appeal that the fact that assets were in the hands of a trustee in bankruptcy did not affect the judge's power to make a confiscation order, although it might affect enforcement by s 102(8) POCA.

### Court must give its reasons

In *Re Forwell* [2003] EWCA Civ 1608, the Court of Appeal held that where a court, when **10.81**
dealing with an inadequacy application, decided to disregard any inadequacy, it was expressly
required to set out its reasons for so doing.

### Inadequacy of available amount: discharge of confiscation order

Section 24 is a provision that previously did not exist under either the DTA or the CJA. **10.82**
Section 24 of POCA applies if:

(a)  a court has made a confiscation order,
(b)  the designated officer for a magistrates' court applies to the Crown Court for the dis-
     charge of the order; and
(c)  the amount remaining to be paid under the order is less than £1,000 (s 24(1)).

In such a case the court must calculate the available amount and in so doing it must apply s 9
(calculation of available amount) as if references to the time the confiscation order is made were
to the time of the original calculation and as if references to the date of the confiscation order
were to the date of the original calculation (see s 24(2)).

Under s 24(3) if the court: **10.83**

(a)  finds that the available amount (as so calculated) is inadequate to meet the amount
     remaining to be paid, and
(b)  is satisfied that the inadequacy is due wholly to a specified reason or a combination of
     specified reasons,

it may discharge the confiscation order.

### Under section 24 what are 'specified reasons'?

The specified reasons are: **10.84**

(4)  ...
    (a)  in a case where any of the realisable property consists of money in a currency other
         than sterling, the fluctuations in currency exchange rates occurred;
    (b)  any reason specified by the Secretary of State by Order.

For the procedure to be followed by magistrates' courts for applications under s 24, see
para 10.87.

### Small amount outstanding: discharge of confiscation order

Under s 25 of POCA, if: **10.85**

(a)  a court has made a confiscation order,
(b)  a justices' chief executive applies to the Crown Court for the discharge of the order, and
(c)  the amount remaining to be paid under the order is £50 or less,

the court may discharge the order (see s 25(1) and (2)).

This section only applies where the magistrates' court is enforcing a confiscation order. The **10.86**
intention is that certain confiscation orders should be discharged where their final recovery
becomes uneconomic.

**Procedure: application by magistrates' court to discharge a confiscation order**

**10.87** Under r 58.6 of the CrimPR, where a magistrates' court makes an application under s 24 or s 25 of POCA for the discharge of a confiscation order, the application must be in writing and supported by a witness statement which must give details of:

(a) the confiscation order;
(b) the amount outstanding under the order; and
(c) the grounds for the application (see r 58.6(2)).

**10.88** That application and witness statement must be served on:

(a) the defendant;
(b) the prosecutor; and
(c) any receiver appointed under s 50 (enforcement receiver) of the Act, under r 58.6(3).

**10.89** Once such an application has been made the Crown Court may determine the application without a hearing, unless any of the persons listed in r 58.6(3) indicates, within the period of seven days beginning on the day after the day on which the application was served on him, that he would like to make representations (see r 58.6(4)).

**Procedure where the Crown Court discharges a confiscation order**

**10.90** Under r 58.6(5) CrimPR, if the Crown Court makes an order discharging the confiscation order, the appropriate court officer must at once send a copy of the order to:

(a) the designated officer of the magistrates' court who applied for the order;
(b) the defendant;
(c) the prosecutor; and
(d) any receiver appointed under s 50 of the Act (an enforcement receiver).

# I. Variations and Discharge for Defendants who Abscond

**Introduction**

**10.91** Sections 27 and 28 of POCA give the court jurisdiction, in certain circumstances, to make confiscation orders in relation to s 6 of POCA for defendants who abscond. These powers are considered in some depth in Chapter 9. Here consideration is given to applications to vary and discharge such orders.

**Variation and discharge of orders under section 28**

**10.92** Section 29 deals with varying orders made under s 28, and s 30 deals with the discharging of orders made under s 28. If the court discharges a confiscation order under s 30 it may make such consequential or incidental orders as it believes are appropriate (see s 30(5)).

**Variation of order**

**10.93** POCA identifies certain circumstances where, if the court makes a confiscation order in circumstances where the defendant has absconded, such an order may later be varied. The variation provisions have effect only where the defendant applies to the court on the grounds the original order, made in his absence, is too large.

The circumstances are set out in s 29(1) which apply if: **10.94**

(a) the court makes a confiscation order under s 6 as applied by s 28 (where the defendant is neither convicted nor acquitted);
(b) the defendant ceases to be an absconder;
(c) he is convicted of an offence (or any of the offences) mentioned in s 28(2)(a) (ie he is now convicted of an offence where previously proceedings had been started against him, but had not been concluded);
(d) the defendant believes that the amount required to be paid was too large (taking the circumstances prevailing when the amount was found for the purposes of the order), and
(e) before the end of the relevant period the defendant applies to the Crown Court to consider the evidence on which his belief is based.

### What is the relevant period?

Under s 29(3) the relevant period referred to in subs (1)(e) is the period of twenty-eight days **10.95** starting with:

(a) the date on which the defendant was convicted of an offence mentioned in s 28(2)(a), or
(b) if there are two or more offences and the convictions were on different dates, the date of the latest.

It should be noted that the defendant only has twenty-eight days from his conviction to apply for a variation of an order made in his absence under s 29.

### Procedure on applications for a variation made by a former absconder

Under r 58.7 CrimPR, where the defendant makes an application under s 29 of POCA for a **10.96** variation of a confiscation order, that application must be made in writing and supported by a witness statement which must give details of:

(a) the confiscation order made against an absconder under s 6 of the Act as applied by s 28 of the Act;
(b) the circumstances in which the defendant ceased to be an absconder;
(c) the defendant's conviction of the offences concerned; and
(d) the reason why he believes the amount required to be paid under the confiscation order was too large (r 58.7(2)).

That application and witness statement must be lodged with the Crown Court and must be **10.97** served on the prosecutor at least seven days before the date fixed by the court for hearing the application, unless the Crown Court specifies a shorter period (r 58.7(3) and (4)).

### Powers of the court

If (after considering the evidence) the court concludes that the defendant's representations **10.98** are well founded:

> 29(2) ...
> (a) it must find the amount which should have been the amount required to be paid (taking the circumstances prevailing when the amount was found for the purposes of the order), and
> (b) it may vary the order by substituting for the amount required to be paid such amount it believes is just.

However, in a case where s 28(2)(a) applies to more than one offence the court must not make an order under s 29 unless it is satisfied that there is no possibility of any further proceedings being taken or continued in relation to any such offence in respect of which the defendant has not been convicted (s 29(4)).

### Discharge of confiscation order where the defendant has absconded

**10.99** Under s 30 of POCA, if the court makes a confiscation order under s 6, as applied by s 28 (defendant neither convicted nor acquitted) and the defendant is later tried for the offence (or offences) concerned and acquitted on all counts, and the defendant then applies to the Crown Court to discharge the confiscation order made in his absence, the court must discharge that confiscation order (see s 30(1) and (2)).

### Discharge of order: undue delay or proceedings not continuing

**10.100** Under s 30(3) if the court makes a confiscation order under subs 6, as applied by s 28 (a confiscation order in circumstances where the defendant is neither convicted nor acquitted, ie pre-conviction), and the defendant ceases to be an absconder, and the defendant was never tried for the offence(s) concerned, the defendant may apply to the Crown Court to discharge the order.

**10.101** The court may discharge the order if it finds that there has been undue delay in continuing the proceedings mentioned in s 28(2) (ie the proceedings for the offence(s) have been started against the defendant, but have not been concluded), or the prosecutor does not intend to proceed with the prosecution.

**10.102** Unlike s 30(2), s 30(4) is discretionary. If the court discharges a confiscation order under s 30 it may make such other consequential or incidental orders as it believes are appropriate (s 30(5)).

### Procedure: application for discharge made by a former absconder

**10.103** Under r 58.8 CrimPR, if a defendant makes an application under s 30 of POCA for discharge of a confiscation order, that application must be in writing and supported by a witness statement which must give details of:

(a) the confiscation order made under s 28 of the Act;
(b) the date on which the defendant ceased to be an absconder;
(c) the acquittal of the defendant if he had been acquitted of the offences concerned; and
(d) if the defendant has not been acquitted of the offence concerned—
   (i) the date on which the defendant ceased to be an absconder;
   (ii) the date on which the proceedings taken against the defendant were instituted; and a summary of steps taken in the proceedings since then; and
   (iii) any application given by the prosecutor that he does not intend to proceed against the defendant.

**10.104** Under r 58.8(3) CrimPR once that application and witness statement have been made they must be lodged with the Crown Court. Further, under r 58.7(4) they must be served on the prosecutor at least seven days before the date fixed by the court for hearing the application, unless the Crown Court specifies a shorter period.

If the Crown Court orders the discharge of the confiscation order, the court must serve **10.105** notice on the magistrates' court responsible for enforcing the order (see r 58.8(5)).

### Compensation: confiscation order made against absconder

Rule 58.11(1) CrimPR applies to an application for compensation under s 73 of POCA **10.106** (where a confiscation order has been varied or discharged under either s 29 or s 30 of POCA and an application has been made to the Crown Court by a person who held realisable property and who has suffered a loss as a result of the making of that order). Under r 58.11(2) the application must be in writing and supported by a witness statement which must give details of:

(a) the confiscation order made under s 28 of POCA;
(b) the variation or discharge of the confiscation order under ss 29 or 30 of POCA;
(c) the realisable property to which the application relates; and
(d) the loss suffered by the applicant as a result of the confiscation order.

Once the application and witness statement are made they must be lodged with the Crown **10.107** Court (r 58.11(3)) and served on the prosecutor at least seven days before the date fixed by the court for hearing the application, unless the Crown Court specifies a shorter period.

The rules applying to general compensation under s 72 of POCA are set out in r 58.10 **10.108** CrimPR.

### Reconsideration of term of imprisonment in default

Section 39 of POCA provides for the reconsideration and variation of prison terms in certain **10.109** circumstances including provision for reduction and increase in default terms. Thus under s 39(5) of POCA there is provision for the prosecutor to make an application to increase the term of imprisonment in default of payment of a confiscation order. The CrimPR in relation to same are found at r 58.9, which provides:

(2) The application must be made in writing and give details of—
    (a) the name and address of the defendant;
    (b) the confiscation order;
    (c) the grounds for the application; and
    (d) the enforcement measures taken, if any.
(3) On receipt of the application, the court must—
    (a) at once send to the defendant and the magistrates' court responsible for enforcing the order, a copy of the application; and
    (b) fix a time, date and place for the hearing and notify the applicant and the defendant of that time, date and place.
(4) If the Crown Court makes an order increasing the term of imprisonment in default, the court must, at once, send a copy of the order to—
    (a) the applicant;
    (b) the defendant;
    (c) where the defendant is in custody at the time of the making of the order, the person having custody of the defendant; and
    (d) the magistrates' court responsible for enforcing the order.

# 11

# ENFORCEMENT OF CONFISCATION ORDERS

## A. Introduction

A confiscation order under POCA is an *in personam* order against the defendant requiring **11.01** him to pay a sum of money. It is not an *in rem* order against the property taken into account by the court in making the order. A confiscation order does not therefore divest the defendant or any interested third party of title to property in contrast to a Civil Recovery Order under Pt 5 of POCA, which does. Any person who attempts to sell the defendant's property for the purpose of satisfying a confiscation order will be vulnerable to civil proceedings for conversion if he does so without consent or an appropriate order of the court. This principle should be borne in mind by all those in possession of a defendant's realisable property, particularly officers of prosecuting authorities who may, for example, be in possession of money taken from the defendant on his arrest.

**11.02**   The defendant may decide to satisfy the order voluntarily. Where he does not, a further order of the court will be necessary to enforce the confiscation order. In some cases, particularly those involving assets subject to third-party claims (especially ancillary relief applications in relation to the matrimonial home) or assets located overseas, enforcement proceedings can become lengthy and protracted. In other cases, such as those involving so-called 'hidden assets', the respective law enforcement agencies may struggle to locate, let alone realise, the property in the absence of cooperation from the defendant. In practice, there will be little the court can do other than consider activation of the default sentence for non-payment. In this chapter, we examine the powers available to the court to enforce confiscation orders under the Proceeds of Crime Act 2002 (POCA).

**11.03**   In 2003 the Home Office published its 'National Best Practice Guide to Confiscation Order Enforcement'. It was revised in 2005 and again in 2010. Its purpose is to improve performance and promote consistency of approach in the enforcement of confiscation orders. Information about obtaining the Guide is available on the internet at <http://www.gov.uk/government/publications/confiscation-order-enforcement-national-best-practice-guide>.

**11.04**   It should be emphasised the Guide is precisely that and does not purport to prescribe the legal procedures that must be followed in individual cases. In the words of the Introduction: 'The guide aims to set the minimum acceptable standards for the confiscation order process. It is not intended to be prescriptive, so where local processes already deliver the same standard or better there may be no need for change.'

**11.05**   The Guide does not have the force of law and the mere fact that a particular law enforcement agency has failed to follow the procedures it recommends does not, without more, give a defendant a right of redress.

## B.  Roles of Law Enforcement Agencies in the Satisfaction of Confiscation Orders

**11.06**   The legislation gives different agencies a variety of roles in the enforcement process which can appear at first sight to be confusing. The position is set out below.

### The enforcing magistrates' court

**11.07**   Primary responsibility for the enforcement of confiscation orders rests with the magistrates' court. All moneys realised in satisfaction of the order are paid to the designated officer at the court (CrimPR r 52). As confiscation orders may be enforced as if they were fines (s 35 of POCA), the magistrates' court has power to issue distress warrants. The magistrates' court may in certain cases also make orders under s 67 of POCA directing banks, other financial institutions, and law enforcement agencies to pay over funds they are holding and which belong to the defendant in satisfaction of the confiscation order. The enforcing magistrates' court normally takes the lead in enforcing confiscation orders where the amounts involved are relatively small and there are no third-party claims to the assets involved. Nevertheless, the court should liaise closely with the prosecutor, who has the right to attend and make representations at any hearing when the activation of the default sentence is being considered. Section 109 of the Coroners and Justice Act 2009 permits a live video link to be used in magistrates' court enforcement proceedings. The court will wish to know why the order has not been paid and will wish to hear detailed proposals for prompt payment if it is not to consider committing the defaulter to prison. For more on the role of the magistrates' court, see para 11.72 below.

### The prosecutor

The prosecutor too has an important role to play in the enforcement of confiscation orders. **11.08** It is the prosecutor, and only the prosecutor, who may apply to the Crown Court for the appointment of an enforcement receiver under s 50 of POCA. In respect of confiscation orders under the previous legislation, applications are to the High Court under s 80 of the Criminal Justice Act (CJA) and s 29 of the Drug Trafficking Act 1994 (DTA), for further on which, see earlier editions of this work. The enforcing magistrates' court and, indeed, the defendant himself, have no standing under these sections to apply for an enforcement receiver to be appointed. As the National Best Practice Guide makes clear, the prosecutor is under a continuing duty to assist the enforcing magistrates' court in the efficient and expeditious enforcement of confiscation orders. It states: 'The financial investigator and prosecuting authority have a continuing responsibility to support the enforcement authority wherever their assistance could improve enforcement outcomes.'

In practical terms, the prosecutor's role involves close liaison with the enforcing magistrates' **11.09** court, by keeping the court informed of any action the prosecutor himself is taking to realise assets (for example, by the appointment of a receiver); advising the court of the location of assets; and, in appropriate cases, appearing at enforcement hearings before the justices to assist them in discharging their responsibilities under the legislation.

### The Crown Court

Once a confiscation order has been made, the Crown Court has a reduced role to play in its **11.10** enforcement other than to determine applications by the prosecutor for the appointment of enforcement receivers in POCA cases. In POCA cases it is the Crown Court (and not the magistrates' court) that is permitted to extend time for payment of the confiscation order (for more on this topic, see para 11.100 below).

### The National Crime Agency

Since the demise of the Assets Recovery Agency, the Serious Organised Crime Agency **11.11** (SOCA) has been responsible for maintaining the Joint Assets Recovery Database (JARD), which plays a key role in the enforcement of confiscation orders and is described in more detail below. SOCA will be abolished and its functions will become part of a new 'National Crime Agency' in the near future following the implementation of ss 1 and 15 of the Crime and Courts Act 2013.

## C. The Joint Asset Recovery Database

JARD holds records of all restraint, confiscation, cash seizure, and civil recovery orders **11.12** made throughout the UK (except Scotland). Also recorded are brief details of the assets taken into account in the making of such orders. Importantly, it shows the balance outstanding on confiscation orders at any time, and the daily rate of interest being charged, where applicable.

**11.13** The following agencies have access to and maintain data on JARD: all Police Services; Regional Asset Recovery Teams; HM Revenue and Customs; SOCA; the Department for Work and Pensions; the Department for Business, Innovation and Skills; the Crown Prosecution Service; the Northern Ireland Director of Public Prosecutions; magistrates' courts in England and Wales. It is estimated that the system is used by over 5,000 officers and staff across the asset recovery community.

**11.14** JARD is described in these terms in the National Best Practice Guide:

> JARD was a brainchild of the Concerted Inter Agency Criminal Finance Action group (CICFA) in 2003. Its purpose is to improve the overall performance of the criminal justice system (CJS) in removing the proceeds of crime through better day to day management of asset recovery at case and order level.
>
> It is the master repository for data concerning asset recovery activity in the UK and is used to produce national statistics for the agencies involved, the Asset Recovery Working Group (ARWG—the successor to CICFA), and other government departments including the Home Office. Data is drawn from JARD for the operation of agency incentivisation schemes funded from the Asset Recovery Incentive Scheme (ARIS), which is another reason for agencies to ensure that their data is accurate and up to date. In addition, statistics from JARD enable ARWG and others concerned with CJS performance regarding asset recovery to identify where systemic problems exist and can identify projects, or policy or legislative changes needed to address them.

## D. Voluntary Satisfaction by the Defendant

**11.15** In most circumstances, the prosecutor should give the defendant an opportunity to satisfy the confiscation order voluntarily before taking enforcement action in the courts. It is very much to the defendant's advantage to cooperate with the court and prosecutor in the voluntary satisfaction of the confiscation order for the following reasons:

(1) He will be liable to pay interest, at the same rate applicable to civil judgments, currently 8 per cent, on any amount outstanding when the time allowed for payment expires: see s 12 of POCA, s 10 of the DTA, and s 75A of the CJA. The amount of interest must be treated as part of the amount to be paid under the confiscation order under s 12(4) of POCA. Section 39(5) of POCA, like the DTA and CJA provisions, also gives the court power, on the application of the prosecutor, to increase the default term if the effect of adding interest to the capital sum due is to increase the maximum period of imprisonment for which he would be liable. Interest is added to the amount outstanding by operation of law and the court does not have a discretion not to add interest to the amount due, see *Hansford v Southampton Magistrates Court* [2008] 4 All ER 432; [2008] EWHC 67 (Admin).

(2) It will reduce the risk of the prosecutor applying for the appointment of an enforcement receiver to realise the defendant's assets in satisfaction of the order.

(3) If the order is satisfied prior to time to pay expiring, the defendant will avoid any risk of having to serve the default term of imprisonment for non-payment.

(4) Any restraint order made in the defendant's case does not necessarily come to an end once a confiscation order is made. It is most likely to remain in force until the confiscation order is satisfied. The sooner the defendant satisfies the confiscation order, the sooner he will be free of the restrictions imposed by the order and be able to resume a normal lifestyle.

(5) Voluntary satisfaction of an order may avoid assets being sold by bailiffs at a public auction where they may not realise the values attributed to them in the Crown Court proceedings.

Once a confiscation order has been made, the prosecutor will invariably write to the defend- **11.16** ant or his solicitors inviting proposals for payment. For the reasons outlined above, it is very much in the defendant's interests to reply constructively. If the defendant fails to respond in constructive terms, he may well find that the court is unsympathetic if the prosecutor invites the court to appoint an enforcement receiver or consideration is being given to the implementation of the default sentence. Conversely, if the defendant demonstrates from the outset an intention to satisfy a confiscation order voluntarily, the court may be reluctant to accede to a prosecutor's application for a receiver to be appointed until the defendant has been afforded a reasonable opportunity to act on that intention.

There will, of course, be some circumstances where voluntary satisfaction is inappropri- **11.17** ate: for example, where a defendant has shown, by his previous conduct, that he cannot be trusted to realise assets himself or where the assets in question are subject to third-party claims that need to be determined. In many cases, the defendant will be in some difficulty in satisfying the confiscation order voluntarily because he will be serving a lengthy sentence of imprisonment. This need not, however, prevent him signing letters of authority permitting the prosecutor to pay over to the court money seized at the time of his arrest or permitting banks to pay over money held in his bank accounts. Similarly, so far as real property is concerned, there is no reason why the defendant cannot give his solicitor instructions to effect a sale notwithstanding the fact that he is in prison.

If a restraint order is in force, it will usually be necessary to seek a variation before dealing with **11.18** the defendant's property. It is important that those holding assets on behalf of a defendant or who are instructed to act for him on the sale of property should check the terms of the restraint order very carefully before taking any action. It will not normally be necessary for the restraint order to be varied to enable money held by the defendant or a third party to be paid into court in satisfaction of the confiscation order. This is because most restraint orders contain a provision to the effect that nothing in the order shall prevent the payment of money into court in satisfaction of a confiscation order: see para 19(7) of the draft restraint order at Appendix 9.

Solicitors should be vigilant to ensure that such a variation is obtained prior to taking steps to **11.19** realise restrained property on behalf of a client. In the absence of such a variation, a solicitor or any other professional person instructed to effect a sale of realisable property on behalf of a client could be vulnerable to proceedings for contempt of court if he assists in any way in the sale of an asset subject to a restraint order. In most instances, the prosecutor will be prepared to agree that the restraint order should be varied by consent to allow a sale to take place, but they will want to be assured that the property is not sold at an undervalue, possibly to an associate of the defendant, and that, once the sale is completed, the net proceeds are paid directly into court and not given to the defendant or placed under his control. These concerns can normally be met by the inclusion of a number of conditions in the variation order. These usually include the following:

(1) a term that the property shall be valued by at least two independent valuers who are members of a recognised trade association and be sold in an arm's length transaction to a bona fide purchaser for value, for not less than the average of the two valuations.

(2) an undertaking by the defendant to instruct a named solicitor to act for him in relation to the transaction and that he will not terminate that solicitor's retainer without the agreement of the prosecutor or, in default of agreement, the permission of the court.

(3) an undertaking by the solicitor to pay the net proceeds of sale into court in satisfaction of the order forthwith on completion of the transaction.

(4) a term that all fees payable to solicitors, valuers, estate agents, and other professionals in relation to the transaction shall be agreed with the prosecutor in advance of being incurred.

**11.20** Where real property is involved, it is usual for the prosecutor to give an undertaking to apply for the discharge of any restriction registered at the Land Registry on being notified that the proceeds of sale have been paid into court. The above conditions and undertakings are by no means exhaustive and others may be required having regard to the particular circumstances of individual cases.

**11.21** Restraint orders usually contain a provision which permits variation where consent is reached in writing between the parties. Defendants and affected third parties should take great care, when agreeing consent orders with the prosecutor, to check the terms proposed and ensure they are content to be bound by them. Once a consent order has been agreed, it has the status of a contract between the parties and will be interpreted as such. In *Weston v Dayman* [2008] 1 BCLC 250; [2006] EWCA Civ 1165, the claimant, who had been subject to CJA restraint and management receivership orders, agreed a consent order for the discharge of the receiver on his acquittal. One of the terms of the consent order was that the receiver would not be liable for any failure by her to manage properly the claimant's estate. Notwithstanding this provision, the claimant instituted proceedings against the receiver claiming damages, alleging she had acted in breach of duty by failing to take proper care of a motor yacht. The Court of Appeal upheld the judge's ruling that summary judgment should be entered in favour of the defendant receiver, holding that the claimant was bound by the terms of the consent order he had freely entered into whereby the receiver was released from any such liability. Although it would be open to a defendant to apply for a consent order to which he is party to be varied or set aside, it is submitted this would only be appropriate in exceptional circumstances. As Arden LJ observed in *Weston v Dayman*:

> I would accept that the court should accede to an application for variation where it is just to do so but in my judgment one of the aspects of justice is that a bargain freely made should be upheld. Mr. Weston clearly obtained benefits under the order. It may well be that those benefits are not as great as he thought, but that is not a matter for this court. In those circumstances I do not consider it would be right for this court to exercise its discretion to vary the order as sought.

**11.22** A variation to a restraint order will not be sanctioned by the court if it does not result in the realisation of the full value of the defendant's interest in the property to which the variation relates, at least in cases where the proposed variation will not secure the full satisfaction of the confiscation order. In *Re Barnes and Barnes* [2004] EWHC 2620 (Admin), CJA confiscation orders were made against the defendants (who were husband and wife) in the sums of £42,845.73 and £63,320.73 respectively. The realisable assets of the defendants included their half shares in the matrimonial home which amounted to some £21,316.50. They sought a variation to the restraint order to permit them to take out a second mortgage on the property which would enable them to pay £38,715 into court in part satisfaction of the confiscation orders. They proposed to pay off the balance in monthly instalments of

£60. The prosecutor refused to agree a variation to the restraint order in these terms and the defendants made an application to court for the order to be so varied. Lightman J refused the defendants' application, ruling that the variation sought was incompatible with the legislative steer in s 82(2) of the CJA. He said:

> In my judgment, the language of section 82(2) of the Criminal Justice Act 1988 is mandatory and requires the power to be exercised with a view to securing the full realisation of the realisable property, so far as necessary to secure the full satisfaction of the confiscation order. An exercise of power for the purpose of anything less than full realisation of value can only be sanctioned if it is clear that that exercise, or that exercise jointly with something else (for example, a further payment to the Crown) will fully discharge the debt due to the Crown.
>
> In this case, assuming—and this is a considerable assumption—that the building society, after being correctly informed as to the full and true facts, is prepared to agree to the proposed remortgage, there will be a shortfall due to the Crown of some £8,000 to £10,000, and this shortfall will arise because the defendants propose a remortgage and not a sale. I do not think that the court has jurisdiction to vary the restraint order with a view to authorising a transaction which does not realise the full value of the property, or at least sufficient to enable the confiscation order to be satisfied. The adverse consequences for the defendant (which are the plight of their own criminal conduct) and the adverse consequences to the community in the costs of providing housing are nothing to the point.

**11.23** If a defendant refuses to cooperate in the voluntary satisfaction of a confiscation order, or, for whatever reason, it is inappropriate to allow him to do so, it will be necessary to invoke the powers of the court to ensure the order is paid. These powers are examined below.

## E. General Living Expenses and Legal Fees

**11.24** We saw in Chapter 5 that the right to draw on restrained funds for the payment of general living expenses and, in restricted circumstances, for the payment of legal fees, does not continue indefinitely but comes to an end on the making of a confiscation order or, if an appeal is lodged, when all domestic avenues of appeal have been exhausted. Many restraint orders now make provision for such payments to come to an end on the making of a confiscation order but, if they do not, it is likely that the prosecutor will invite the defendant to consent to a variation precluding the release of further funds for such purposes and, if consent is not forthcoming, make an appropriate application to the court.

**11.25** This principle, sometimes described as 'turning off the tap', applies both to cases where the restrained funds are tainted and where they are not. An example of the latter scenario is a case where assets are accumulated as a result of the defendant's dishonest failure to pay tax. This was the position in *Stodgell v Stodgell* [2009] 2 FLR 244; [2009] EWCA Civ 243, a CJA case in which considerable sums had been released to pay general living expenses of the defendant's family and to meet legal expenses incurred by the defendant's wife in ancillary relief proceedings. Following the making of the confiscation order, Holman J directed the payments to cease. This decision was upheld by the Court of Appeal. Hughes LJ said:

> The spouses both lived well on a domestic economy which included the non-payment of tax and penalties. For the same reason, counsel's careful submissions about 'taint' do not, as it seems to me, provide the wife with any arguable ground of appeal. 'Taint' is not a statutory expression. Of course it is relevant where assets can be traced to acquisition from the proceeds of crime, but that is not the only case in which justice requires that the confiscation order

should be met before there can be any question of allocating the assets between husband and wife. Another such case, of which this is one, is where the domestic economy and the assets accumulated are only of the size they are because the husband failed to pay the tax due. If this husband had paid his tax and penalties, his assets would be nil rather than either £880,000 or £750,000. For that reason, it is not critical that the Devon house and the London flat were not acquired from crime. What is critical, as it seems to me, is that they could not have been and cannot be preserved without non payment of the tax and the penalties.

**11.26**   The court indicated that in its view the judge would have been wrong to make any other order. Although this case was decided under the CJA, the Court noted that the legislative steer in POCA represented a 'significant tightening of the statutory rules'. It is therefore likely that, at the enforcement stage, the court will not allow the dissipation of further funds by way of general living expenses and legal fees, and defendants and affected third parties should prepare for this contingency by arranging other sources of funding or, if appropriate, apply for state benefits.

## F. Enforcement Receivers under POCA

### The power to appoint enforcement receivers

**11.27**   Section 50 of POCA empowers the Crown Court to appoint receivers for the purpose of enforcing confiscation orders. In contrast to the position in relation to management receivers, the primary purpose of an enforcement receiver is to realise assets in satisfaction of the confiscation order, although enforcement receivers will inevitably have to manage the assets prior to realisation. For the general principles of receivership law see Chapter 4 on Management Receivers, a significant part of which applies equally to enforcement receivers.

**11.28**   Section 50 of POCA provides:

> (1) This section applies if—
>   (a) a confiscation is made,
>   (b) it is not satisfied, and
>   (c) it is not subject to appeal.
> (2) On the application of the prosecutor the Crown Court may by order appoint a receiver in respect of realisable property.

**11.29**   The remedy is a discretionary one: the court is not bound to appoint a receiver even where the conditions in s 50(1) have been met. The court may, for example, consider whether the defendant could reasonably satisfy the order voluntarily and, if so, whether he has been given a sufficient opportunity to do so. The court may also consider whether other less expensive methods of enforcement might be equally effective, including (in a case where assets are located abroad) a request for legal assistance via a letter of request. The court must, however, exercise its discretion judicially and in accordance with the legislative steer in s 69 of POCA. It is submitted that the correct approach is that outlined by Munby J in *Re HN* [2005] EWHC 2982 (Admin), a case heard in the High Court under the CJA. He said:

> On the face of it, once a confiscation order has been made, the Crown is entitled to demand the appointment of an enforcement receiver in order to realise the funds with which to discharge the confiscation order. That, after all is no more than the 'legislative steer' in section 82(2) would normally demand. On the other hand, since the effect of my ruling is potentially

to throw onto the defendant's assets the burden of meeting the receiver's costs, disbursements and fees, it may be proper, in an appropriate case to defer the appointment of a receiver for a short period to give the defendant the opportunity himself (subject of course to suitable safeguards) to realise the assets—something he may perhaps be able to do more advantageously and at lesser expense than a receiver.

The court will not, on an application for the appointment of an enforcement receiver, enter- **11.30** tain any challenge *by the defendant* to the validity of the confiscation order to which it relates. In *Customs and Excise Commissioners v Togher* [2005] EWCA Civ 274 the defendant contended that a confiscation order made against him under the DTA was invalid because it should have been made under the Drug Trafficking Offences Act 1986. Sedley LJ, in refusing the defendant leave to appeal, said:

> This submission is, in my judgment, entirely misconceived. The confiscation order exists. It has the authority of the Criminal Division of the Court of Appeal and of the Crown Court. Customs and Excise are not only entitled but are required, as a matter of public duty, to enforce it if they can. The time for challenging its validity is past. The place for challenging its validity in any event is not the receivership proceedings consequent upon it.
>
> I am tempted to go into the reasons why it seems to me that the underlying argument is a bad one. But to do so would be to accept the very thing that I do not accept, which is that it is open to the Administrative Court, or therefore to this court, in receivership proceedings, to embark upon the question whether the order upon which Customs and Excise rely is a properly made order. The time and place for such a challenge are not here and are not now.

Section 50 does not require that any time allowed for payment by the Crown Court **11.31** should have elapsed before an enforcement receiver can be appointed. The fact that time to pay has not expired will be a matter the court will wish to take into account in deciding whether or not to make the order but there is nothing wrong in principle, it is submitted, in making an enforcement receivership order before the expiration of the period. The prompt appointment of an enforcement receiver after the making of a confiscation order will assist in ensuring that the order is satisfied within the time allowed for payment and so is entirely consistent with the legislative steer. This is particularly so in cases where assets are going to take a considerable time to realise, where there are third-party claims to resolve, or where the defendant fails to advance his own proposals for the voluntary satisfaction of the order.

### Orders subject to appeal

Section 50(1)(c) precludes the appointment of an enforcement receiver while the confisca- **11.32** tion order is subject to appeal. By s 87(2) of POCA:

> A confiscation order is subject to appeal until there is no further possibility of an appeal on which the order could be varied or quashed; and for this purpose any power to grant leave to appeal out of time must be ignored.

A confiscation order is therefore only subject to appeal if an appeal has been lodged within the time limits prescribed by rules of court or if permission to appeal has been granted out of time. If an application for permission to appeal out of time has been lodged but not determined, or if the defendant merely indicates an intention to appeal out of time, the order will not be 'subject to appeal' within the meaning of s 87(2). Although a confiscation order will not technically be 'subject to appeal' if an application for permission to appeal out of time has been made, the fact that such an application has been lodged may be a matter the court will wish to consider in deciding whether or not to appoint an enforcement receiver.

**11.33** If a confiscation order is subject to appeal the prosecutor may, of course, still apply for the appointment of a management receiver to manage and preserve realisable property pending the determination of the appeal, but, unlike an enforcement receiver, he would not have power to realise assets in satisfaction of the confiscation order.

**11.34** In *Re P* [1998] EWHC 1049 (Admin) (a decision upheld on appeal, see also Chapter 5), it was held that a confiscation order is not 'subject to appeal' if there is a pending application to the Criminal Cases Review Commission or to the European Court of Human Rights in relation to it. Laws J said:

> The fact is that, so far as the domestic criminal litigation is concerned in this case Mr. P is well past the end of the road. The Commission may, of course, investigate a matter after all other criminal legal processes have been exhausted. Indeed, that is their very role. However, it is quite clear to me that while they are doing so, and the fact that they are doing so, are no basis for altering, suspending or varying the effect of a restraint order and therefore, the execution of a confiscation order once that has been made. The same applies in relation to his application to the European Court of Human Rights.

**11.35** *Re P* was followed in *R v Bullen and Soneji* [2006] EWCA Crim 1125 where the Court of Appeal expressed itself as being '...wholly unimpressed by the suggestion that the period allowed for payment should be extended uncertainly into the future so that the defendants can pursue their petition before the European Court of Human Rights'. Further, it is important to appreciate that, in the absence of a specific order of the court, a pending appeal does not suspend the obligation to pay the confiscation order and time continues to run. In *R v May (Confiscation Order: Time to Pay)* [2005] EWCA Crim 367 the Crown Court made a confiscation order for £3,264,277 and ordered the defendant to pay within three years. He appealed against the order to the Court of Appeal, but his appeal was dismissed. He then contended that the three-year period for payment should run from the date on which his appeal was dismissed and not from the date on which the confiscation order was made. Keene LJ described this proposition as 'unsound in law' and said:

> We do not find this argument persuasive. There is no reason why steps preparatory to the raising of the money specified in the confiscation order should not have been taken while May's appeal was pending. The appellant was not entitled to assume that his appeal would be successful and, as indicated above, as a matter of law time was running during that period. Moreover, it would be wrong as a matter of principle for appellants to be encouraged to believe that the bringing of an appeal would be likely to lengthen the time given for payment, even if the appeal was unsuccessful.

**11.36** The decision in *May* was followed by the Court of Appeal in *R v Bullen and Soneji* [2006] EWCA Crim 1125. In that case, confiscation orders were made against the defendants for £375,000 and £30,284 respectively. The trial judge, being aware of the defendants' intention to appeal against the orders, allowed eighteen months to pay from the date on which the Court of Appeal determined the appeals. In due course, the Court of Appeal allowed the appeals and quashed the confiscation orders.

**11.37** The Crown thereafter successfully appealed to the House of Lords and the confiscation orders were reinstated. The defendants contended that the eighteen-month period should run from the date on which the House of Lords allowed the Crown's appeal. The Court of

Appeal rejected this argument and ordered the defendants to pay in full within twenty-eight days. In delivering the judgment of the Court, Fulford J said:

> ...in our view they have had ample time to raise, speedily, adequate funds. Given the time that has elapsed, it is our view that a sufficient—indeed generous—opportunity has been afforded to the defendants to put their affairs in order so they can pay these sums. As the decision of this Court in *R v May* [2005] EWCA Crim 367 makes clear, the obligation to pay a confiscation order within a specified period remains in force from the date it was imposed. The clock does not stop running whilst an appeal is pending, save by judicial authorisation, in other words, time continues to run unless there is a court order to the contrary.

**11.38**  Defendants subject to confiscation orders who appeal against the order, or against the conviction that resulted in the order being made, would be well advised to make contingency plans for the prompt satisfaction of the order in the event that the appeal is unsuccessful. If they do not do so, they may find enforcement action being taken shortly after the appeal is dismissed.

### Powers of enforcement receivers

**11.39**  The powers the Crown Court may give an enforcement receiver are set out in some detail in s 51 of POCA which provides:

(1) If the court appoints a receiver under section 50 it may act under this section on the application of the prosecutor.

(2) The court may by order confer on the receiver the following powers in relation to the realisable property—
   (a) power to take possession of the property;
   (b) power to manage or otherwise deal with the property;
   (c) power to realise the property, in such manner as the court may specify;
   (d) power to start, carry on or defend any legal proceedings in respect of the property.

(3) The court may by order confer on the receiver power to enter any premises in England and Wales and to do any of the following—
   (a) search for or inspect anything authorised by the court;
   (b) make or obtain a copy, photograph or other record of anything so authorised;
   (c) remove anything which the receiver is required or authorised to take possession of in pursuance of an order of the court.

(4) The court may by order authorise the receiver to do any of the following for the purpose of the exercise of his functions—
   (a) hold property;
   (b) enter into contracts;
   (c) sue and be sued;
   (d) execute powers of attorney, deeds or other instruments;
   (e) take any other steps the court thinks appropriate.

(5) The court may order any person who has possession of realisable property to give possession of it to the receiver.

(6) The court—
   (a) may order a person holding an interest in realisable property to make to the receiver such payment as the court specifies in respect of a beneficial interest held by the defendant or the recipient of a tainted gift;
   (b) may (on the payment being made) by order transfer, grant or extinguish any interest in the property.

(7) Subsections (2), (5) and (6) do not apply to property for the time being subject to a charge under any of these provisions—
   (a) section 9 of the Drug Trafficking Offences Act 1986 (c32);
   (b) section 78 of the Criminal Justice Act 1988 (c33);

(c) Article 14 of the Criminal Justice (Confiscation) (Northern Ireland) Order 1990 (SI 1990/2588 (NI 17));

(d) section 27 of the Drug Trafficking Act 1994 (c37);

(e) Article 32 of the Proceeds of Crime (Northern Ireland) Order 1996 (SI 1996/1299 (NI 9)).

(8) The court must not—

    (a) confer the power mentioned in subsection (2)(b) or (c) in respect of property, or

    (b) exercise the power conferred on it by subsection (6) in respect of property,

    unless it gives persons holding interests in the property a reasonable opportunity to make representations to it.

(8A) Subsection (8), so far as relating to the power mentioned in subsection (2)(b), does not apply to property which–

    (a) is perishable; or

    (b) ought to be disposed of before its value diminishes.

(9) The court may order that a power conferred by an order under this section is subject to such conditions and exceptions as it specifies.

(10) Managing or otherwise dealing with property includes—

    (a) selling the property or any part of it or interest in it;

    (b) carrying on or arranging for another person to carry on any trade or business the assets of which are or are part of the property;

    (c) incurring capital expenditure in respect of the property.

**11.40** The powers under s 51(2) are in very similar terms to those given to management receivers under s 49(2) of POCA and which are considered in Chapter 4 above. There is, however, one significant difference in that s 51(2)(c) of POCA allows the court to empower the receiver to realise the property in such manner as it may direct. The equivalent power in relation to management receivers in s 49(2)(d) is confined to the realisation of assets to pay the receiver's remuneration and expenses. This difference reflects the different purposes for which management and enforcement receivers are appointed: the primary role of the management receiver being to manage and preserve property, and the primary role of the enforcement receiver being to realise assets in satisfaction of the confiscation order. In addition s 51(2)(b) of POCA, like s 49(2)(b), provides for the court to make orders empowering the receiver to manage or deal with the property generally which includes selling it under s 51(10). Section 51(8) of the Act protects the interests of third parties to the extent that the powers set out in s 51(2)(b) and (c) and (6) cannot be conferred on the receiver unless and until they have been given a reasonable opportunity to make representations. Section 51(8) is now subject to the qualification contained in s 51(8A), an amendment inserted by reason of s 82 of the Serious Crime Act 2007. The effect of the amendment is that, where the enforcement receiver is concerned with perishable property, or property which ought to be disposed of before its value diminishes, he may manage or otherwise deal with that property, even though he has not given persons holding an interest in the property a reasonable opportunity to make representations. The purpose of the amendment is to ensure that the receiver need not delay where to do so would lead to the perishing of property or the diminution of the value of property.

### Application of the proceeds of realisation

**11.41** Sections 54 and 55 of POCA deal with the way in which the proceeds of realisation must be dealt with both by the enforcement receiver and the enforcing magistrates' court. Section 54(1) and (2) provides as follows:

(1) This section applies to sums which are in the hands of a receiver appointed under section 50 if they are—

    (a) the proceeds of the realisation of property under section 51;

(b) sums (other than those mentioned in paragraph (a)) in which the defendant holds an interest.

(2) The sums must be applied as follows—

(a) first, they must be applied in payment of such expenses incurred by a person acting as an insolvency practitioner as are payable under this subsection by virtue of section 432;

(b) second, they must be applied in making any payments directed by the Crown Court;

(c) third, they must be applied on the defendant's behalf towards satisfaction of the confiscation order.

By s 54(6), the receiver applies the sums in satisfaction of the confiscation order under **11.42** s 54(2)(c) by paying them to the designated officer of the magistrates' court responsible for enforcing the order. It is important to note that an enforcement receiver appointed under POCA is not entitled to deduct his own remuneration and expenses before paying the proceeds of realisation into court unless the court specifically directs otherwise. The only payments he is permitted to make under s 54 prior to remitting funds to the enforcing magistrates' court are the expenses of an insolvency practitioner pursuant to s 432 of POCA (s 54(2)(a)) and any payments the Crown Court directs should be made (s 54(2)(b)). Under s 54(2)(b) of POCA the Crown Court may have directed within the receivership order that prior payments be made before payments towards satisfying the confiscation order such as compensation to a victim of the offence or, for example, even the costs of realising assets. However, these types of orders are unlikely to be made unless there is good reason such as that the defendant holds sufficient assets to satisfy these prior payments in addition to satisfying his confiscation order. Therefore, if the receivership order includes such a provision, the net proceeds of realisation of assets may be paid to the magistrates' court towards satisfaction of the confiscation order rather than the gross proceeds. The Court of Appeal (Mummery and Laws LJJ) when refusing permission to appeal to the applicant in *In the Matter of Brian Roger Allen and In the Matter of the CJA 1988* [2003] EWCA Civ 1168 held that s 81(1) of the CJA (the predecessor to s 54(2) of POCA) allowed the High Court to include such a provision within the terms of an enforcement receivership order. The High Court had directed that the receiver had the power to discharge from the proceeds of sale of the defendant's assets the costs of and incidental to the sale before applying them towards the confiscation order. Once the receiver has paid the sums he holds to the enforcing magistrates' court, he must apply to the designated officer to be reimbursed in respect of his fees: s 55(4). The purpose of this provision is to ensure that in most circumstances the gross amount realised by the receiver is credited against the amount outstanding under the confiscation order.

Section 54(3) to (5) deals with the position where the receiver remains in possession of funds **11.43** after the confiscation order has been paid in full. By s 54(3) he must distribute such funds among such persons who held (or hold) interests in the property concerned as the Crown Court directs and in such proportions as it directs. The Crown Court must give persons who held (or hold) an interest in the property concerned a reasonable opportunity to make representations before making a direction under s 54(3): see s 54(4).

Section 55 sets out how funds must be dealt with when received by the designated officer in **11.44** the magistrates' court. The section applies to all funds received on account of the amount payable under a confiscation order, whether received from an enforcement receiver or otherwise. Section 55(2) provides that the receipt of those sums by the court reduces the amount payable under the order, but the designated officer is required to apply the sums received as follows:

> (3) First, he must apply them in payment of such expenses incurred by a person acting as an insolvency practitioner as—
>   (a) are payable under this subsection by virtue of section 432, but
>   (b) are not already paid under section 54(2)(a).
> (4) If the designated officer received the sums under section 54 he must next apply them—
>   (a) first, in payment of the remuneration and expenses of a receiver appointed under section 48 to the extent that they have not been met by the exercise by that receiver of a power conferred under section 49(2)(d);
>   (b) second, in payment of the remuneration and expenses of the receiver appointed under section 50.
> (5) If a direction was made under section 13(6) for an amount of compensation to be paid out of sums recovered under the confiscation order, the designated officer must next apply the sums in payment of that amount.

**11.45**  The effect of these provisions is that the court must first pay the costs of an insolvency practitioner in accordance with s 432 if the receiver himself has not already paid those costs. Next he must pay any remuneration and expenses still owed to a management receiver and then, but only then, may he pay the remuneration and expenses of the enforcement receiver. Finally, the court may pay any compensation ordered by the Crown Court to be paid under s 13(6). This is the provision which applies in cases where the court believes that the defendant's means are insufficient to meet both the compensation order and the confiscation order.

**11.46**  The question arises as to whether the receiver is entitled to realise sufficient assets to pay both the confiscation order and his own remuneration and expenses. It is submitted that he can, for two reasons. Firstly, it is settled law that the remuneration and expenses of a receiver appointed under the legislation fall to be paid from the receivership estate: see in particular the decision of the House of Lords in *Capewell v HM Revenue and Customs* [2007] 1 WLR 386; [2007] UKHL 2. Indeed, the expenses that can be recovered by the receiver from the receivership estate would include, in an appropriate case, litigation costs and even the costs of defending an action brought against the receiver by the defendant: see *Sinclair v Dhillon and others* [2012] EWHC 3517 (Admin) and *Glatt v Sinclair* [2010] EWHC 3069 (Admin); [2011] 6 Costs LR 943; (although note that the substantive decision which gave rise to the costs order in the latter case was overturned by the Court of Appeal: [2011] EWCA Civ 1317; [2012] 1 Costs LO 48).

**11.47**  Secondly, at least in cases where the appointment of the enforcement receiver was necessitated by the defendant's failure to discharge the confiscation order voluntarily, the interests of justice dictate that he, and not the Crown, should meet these costs so long as he has the means to meet both them and the confiscation order. As Munby J said in *Re HN & others* [2005] EWHC 2982 (Admin):

> If it becomes necessary to have a receiver, why should the Crown be left paying his costs, disbursements and fees? On the contrary, in most such cases, at least where there is a sufficiency of assets, the only proper order is that the burden of meeting those costs, disbursements and fees should be thrown on the defendant rather than on the Crown. Why, after all, should the public purse be expected to pay for something necessitated by a solvent criminal's failure to discharge a confiscation order? I can think of no good reason.

## G. Procedure on Applications for the Appointment of Enforcement Receivers under POCA

### Initiating the application

The procedures to be followed on applications for the appointment of enforcement receivers **11.48** under s 50 POCA are set out in parts 60 and 61 of the Criminal Procedure Rules (CrimPR). By r 60.1(3) the application must be in writing and supported by a witness statement which must:

(a) give the grounds for the application;

(b) give full details of the proposed receiver;

(c) to the best of the witness' ability, give full details of the realisable property in respect of which the applicant is seeking the order and specify the person holding that realisable property;

(d) where the application is made by an accredited financial investigator, include a statement that, under section 68 of the 2002 Act, the applicant has authority to apply; and

(e) if the proposed receiver is not a person falling within section 55(8) of the 2002 Act and the applicant is asking the court to allow the receiver to act—

(i) without giving security, or

(ii) before he has given security or satisfied the court that he has security in place, explain the reasons why that is necessary.

The applicant must provide the Crown Court with a copy of the confiscation order it is **11.49** sought to enforce against the defendant (see r 60.1(4)). It is submitted that the best practice is to exhibit a copy of the order in the witness statement lodged in support of the application. Although not specifically required by the rules, it is submitted that the letter of agreement between the prosecutor and the receiver should also be exhibited to the witness statement. The letter of agreement is, in essence, a contractual document between the receiver and the applicant prosecutor dealing with such matters as reporting arrangements, the maintenance and inspection of records, the instruction of agents, drawing remuneration, and maintaining confidentiality. The receiver's response, which will normally include an estimate of the likely costs involved and a table setting out the rates to be claimed by each grade of fee earner likely to be involved, should also be exhibited.

Letters of agreement for many years included a contractual indemnity under which the pros- **11.50** ecutor agreed to indemnify the receiver in relation to his remuneration and expenses in the event that the value of any assets realised proved insufficient to meet the same. Increasingly, however, receivers are prepared to reach agreement without any indemnity being provided or to proceed on the basis of a conditional fee agreement. There is no statutory indemnity under POCA for the prosecutor to pay the receiver as was previously provided under s 88(2) of the CJA. In this way the receiver takes a degree of risk and is incentivised to locate and realise the defendant's property.

Finally, the prosecutor should also exhibit or lodge with the Crown Court a draft of the **11.51** receivership order he seeks.

### Service of the application

**11.52**  Although r 60.1(2) of the CrimPR allows applications for the appointment of enforcement receivers to be made without notice in limited circumstances, it is submitted that it would rarely, if ever, be appropriate for such applications to be made other than on notice to the defendant and affected third parties. Where the application is to be made on notice, the application and witness statement in support must be lodged with the Crown Court and served on: the defendant; any person who holds realisable property to which the application relates, and any other person whom the applicant knows to be affected by the application such as third parties holding a potential interest in realisable property. Service should be effected at least seven days before the date of the hearing (see r 60.1(6)).

### The defendant's response to the application

**11.53**  It is important that the defendant should determine well in advance of the hearing date what his response should be. Where a defendant has been sentenced to a long term of imprisonment and has a substantial confiscation order to meet he will, in most instances, have no grounds for resisting the application. In such circumstances, he should write promptly to the court and prosecutor consenting to the appointment of the receiver so that the matter may proceed on a 'by consent' basis, thereby saving the time and expense of a contested hearing in the Crown Court. If the defendant is in a position to satisfy the order voluntarily, he should make a witness statement setting out realistic proposals as to how this might be achieved. The court will need to be satisfied that any such proposal is genuine and the court will almost certainly insist on a consent order setting out a clear timescale within which assets must be realised together with conditions and undertakings to ensure assets are sold to bona fide purchasers at the proper market value and the proceeds of sale are paid promptly into court. If the defendant failed to keep to the terms of such a consent order it would be open to the prosecutor to ask the court to reconsider the question of appointing an enforcement receiver. A consent order might even include the appointment of a receiver but suspended so that it only comes into force should the defendant fail to realise property or satisfy his confiscation order by a certain date.

**11.54**  One argument that will find little favour with the court is that the defendant would prefer to serve the default term of imprisonment for non-payment rather than satisfy the confiscation order. This is for the simple reason that serving the default term does not expunge the debt: see s 38(5) of POCA.

**11.55**  If the defendant contends that an asset the prosecutor wishes to be included in the enforcement receivership order does not constitute realisable property, this should be dealt with in his witness statement and documentary evidence exhibited in support of his claim. The defendant is estopped from arguing that property in which he was found to hold an interest during the confiscation proceedings is not realisable property for the purposes of the enforcement receivership proceedings. However, he may wish to argue that other property included within the proposed receivership which was not considered at the time of the confiscation hearing is not realisable property. Ideally, evidence should also be obtained from the person the defendant alleges to be the true owner of the property. Indeed, wherever possible, independent evidence should be obtained to corroborate the defendant's testimony. It must be remembered that at the enforcement stage the defendant stands convicted and, particularly if he pleaded not guilty at trial, may face something of a credibility problem having been disbelieved by the jury.

## Third parties

Section 51(8) of POCA precludes the court (subject to section 51(8A)) from empower- **11.56** ing receivers to realise property in which a third party has an interest until such time as the person in question has been given a reasonable opportunity to make representations to the court. This does not always mean that the third party is entitled to legal representation at any hearing at which they make representations—see *R v Mohammed Arif Gaffar* [2012] EWCA Crim 2350. It is an important protection for third parties because, even if called by the defendant as a witness, they have no right to appear as a separate party or be represented at the confiscation hearing when the court is determining the extent and value of the defendant's realisable property. Indeed, the only opportunities the law allows for a third party to prevent property in which he claims an interest being realised in satisfaction of a confiscation order is in the restraint or receivership proceedings. This was confirmed by the House of Lords in *Re Norris* [2001] 1 WLR 1388; [2001] UKHL 34, a case under the Drug Trafficking Offences Act 1986. In considering the different purposes of the confiscation and receivership proceedings, Lord Hope of Craighead said:

> The scheme of the Act, so far as third party interests are concerned, is for their claims to be resolved in the High Court. The question for the High Court, when proceedings reach this stage, relates not to the amount of money which the defendant must pay—that has already been fixed by the order made in the Crown Court—but to the powers which the receiver is to be authorised to exercise. It is at this stage that third parties are entitled to have their claims heard and determined. This is when, as a matter of both substance and procedure, representations may be made as to their interests, if any, in the property which the receiver wishes to realise.

> Provisions designed to protect the interests of third parties are conspicuously absent from the rules of procedure that apply at the stage of the hearing in the Crown Court. Third parties are not entitled to participate in the criminal proceedings in that court. But the issue for the Crown Court is not whether any property in which a third party might have an interest is to be confiscated. The order which it makes is an order which is directed against the defendant only, and it is simply an order for the payment of a sum of money. The question of realisation, if the exercise of powers by a receiver is needed in order to make good the order which the defendant is required to satisfy, is reserved for the High Court.

> I do not therefore, with respect, agree with the observation by Tuckey LJ, that the situation which has arisen in this case is exactly that which the doctrine of abuse of process is designed to prevent. The scheme of the Act itself shows that this proposition must be unsound. It cannot be an abuse of process for a third party holding an interest in property, to which a right is given by section 11(8) of the Act to make representations to the High Court, to seek to exercise that right just because he or she gave evidence in the Crown Court in support of the defendant's case that the property was not to be valued and taken into account as realisable property.

Although POCA has transferred the power to make enforcement receivership orders from **11.57** the High Court to the Crown Court, the principle remains the same. As Lord Hobhouse of Woodborough observed in *Re Norris*, the interests of the defendant and a third party are not necessarily identical. He said:

> It was wrong to say that her interests were identical with those of her husband. Indeed their proprietary interests were in principle opposed to each other. There were competing rights of property giving rights to one spouse against the other. It was in the interests of the defendant to put forward to the Crown Court the interest of his wife because he could use it to get a reduction in the confiscation order which was going to be made against him. But the wife's interests were not and are not the same as those of her husband. She wishes to preserve for herself and

her children the right to live at [the matrimonial home] against her husband if necessary and against anyone claiming through him. The defendant also has an interest in mitigating the sentence of imprisonment he was going to receive. The proceedings in the Crown Court were for the benefit of the defendant and the Customs and Excise and not Mrs Norris.

**11.58** The legislative steer in s 69 of POCA provides further protection for third parties and the recipients of tainted gifts. Section 69(3) lays down a number of rules with which the court and enforcement receiver must comply in exercising powers under the Act. Section 69(3) provides:

> Subsection (2) has effect subject to the following rules—
> (a) the powers must be exercised with a view to allowing a person other than the defendant or recipient of a tainted gift to retain or recover the value of any interest held by him;
> (b) in the case of realisable property held by a recipient of a tainted gift, the powers must be exercised with a view to realising no more than the value for the time being of the gift;
> (c) in a case where a confiscation order has not been made against the defendant, property must not be sold if the court so orders under subsection (4) [irreplaceable property].

**11.59** The protection afforded to third parties by s 69 at the enforcement stage is not absolute. First of all, s 69(3)(c) does not apply to enforcement receivers as, at the stage they are appointed, a confiscation order will have been made. Moreover, s 69(3)(a) and (b) are concerned with preserving not the property or gift itself but the 'value' of the third party's interest or of the gift. The court may therefore empower the receiver to sell assets in which the defendant and a third party have a joint interest while preserving the value of the third party's interest. If, for example, a defendant and a third party each have a half share in a property the court may order the sale of the property but direct that an amount of money proportionate to the third party's interest should be paid to him from the proceeds of sale, with the balance being paid into court in satisfaction of the confiscation order. An alternative way of proceeding is to give the third party the option of buying out the defendant's interest in the property. In this event, the court will order the third party to pay to the receiver a sum of money equivalent to the value of the defendant's interest in the property and, on payment being made, direct that the defendant's interest in the property be transferred to the third party.

### Advising third parties served with an application to appoint an enforcement receiver

**11.60** As soon as a solicitor is instructed by a third party affected by an application to appoint an enforcement receiver, he should notify the court, the prosecuting authority, and any solicitor acting on behalf of the defendant of his interest in the matter. If the client is unable to fund the case privately and meets the eligibility criteria, an emergency application for public funding should be made. As third parties, like defendants, are only entitled to seven days' notice of the hearing of an application to appoint an enforcement receiver, the solicitor may find it necessary to seek an adjournment. Although the court will view such a request sympathetically, given that the public interest dictates that the confiscation order should be satisfied promptly, it may well not be prepared to adjourn the entire receivership application. The court will frequently order that the enforcement receiver be appointed with powers to realise assets that are free from third-party claims, but impose a stay on the receiver's powers of realisation over those assets which are subject to third-party claims pending their determination. At the same time, the court may exercise its case-management functions to impose directions as to how the third-party claim should proceed, imposing requirements, for example, as to the timescale within which the third party's evidence must be served, along with any response by the prosecutor and the defendant.

Once any necessary adjournment has been obtained and funding secured, the third party's **11.61** witness statement in support of his claim should be prepared. Where documentary evidence exists to support the claim, it should be exhibited to the witness statement. If there are other persons who are in a position to confirm the veracity of the third party's claim, witness statements should also be taken from them. Such independent evidence is particularly important in cases where no documentary evidence exists to support the third-party claim.

Once the third party's evidence has been served, it may be prudent to enter into without **11.62** prejudice negotiations with the prosecutor and the defendant. In many cases, the fact of the third party having an interest in the asset in question will be beyond dispute. The real issue is more commonly the extent of that interest. As all the parties will be anxious to resolve the matter expeditiously with the minimum of costs, and the court will encourage the parties to reach agreement wherever possible, it may well be that all concerned would be willing to take a commercial view and not press for the highest amount for which they could contend.

Although the prosecutor acts in the public interest in taking proceedings to enforce a con- **11.63** fiscation order, this does not mean that he should not negotiate with the defendant and interested third parties to reach a mutually acceptable compromise where this is justified by the evidence. In *Grimes v CPS* [2004] 1 FLR 910; [2003] EWCA Civ 1814 the Court of Appeal accepted that the prosecutor had public duties to perform in relation to the confiscation order but, in the words of Brooke LJ:

> That does not in my judgment mean that the CPS were entitled to behave, as litigants far too often behaved before the CPR came in, by simply standing back and saying 'We will make no offer at all for the court to consider when it decides what order as to costs is a reasonable one to make. We will simply see you in court.'
>
> The CPS has a duty under CPR 1.3 to help the court to further the overriding objective, and it would be the reverse of justice if the court were to be perceived to be upholding a policy which led the CPS to think that it did not have to make any offer at all and could come to court for an expensive contested hearing, simply leaving the successful party to lose much of its success by an order for costs which it could not recover.

He added:

> To some extent both parties were at fault for not doing all they could to resolve this dispute without the uneconomic costs of a hearing before a High Court judge, and it may well be that mediation is a more appropriate way of resolving many of these disputes now that experience of mediation, and of successful mediation, has grown so much.

All parties to receivership proceedings should, it is submitted, bear these remarks in mind **11.64** and should be willing to make what Brooke LJ described as a 'well pitched offer' to compromise the proceedings. A party to the proceedings who refuses to accept such an offer is at risk of having costs awarded against him.

### Determination of the interests of third parties in property the subject of the application

The Crown Court may exercise its discretion to appoint a receiver over realisable prop- **11.65** erty in which the defendant holds the sole beneficial interest. However, if jointly held property is proposed to be included it may adjourn or suspend the appointment over that property pending a trial of the issue of whether and to what extent third parties hold beneficial interests in the property. The principles which the court will use to determine any beneficial interests of the defendant and third parties in property sought to be included in the enforcement receivership application are given detailed consideration in Chapter 16. For a recent example of the principles applied in the appointment an enforcement receiver under s 29 DTA, see *CPS v Liscott; Laurence Lawrence* [2013] EWHC 501 (Admin). The procedure for the determination of third-party disputes is contained within Pts 60 and 61 of the CrimPR. The practice is dealt with in some detail again in Chapter 16. The Crown Court, acting under CrimPR r 61.5, is likely to set directions of the type suggested in Chapter 16 for the trial of any issue. Interestingly, the Crown Court has not been given explicit power under POCA nor under the CrimPR to make declarations in respect of the property interests to which the application relates. This is in contrast to RSC Order 115.7(4)(c) which gives the High Court that power, if it did not already hold it under its inherent jurisdiction, in respect of applications for enforcement receivers under s 29 DTA or s 80 CJA. However, the Crown Court clearly has the duty and power to recognise the interests of third parties in property for the purposes of determining receivership applications—see s 51(6), (8), and (9) together with s 69(3)(a) POCA.

### The matrimonial home: rights of spouses etc

**11.66**  It should also be noted that different considerations may apply in relation to the proposed realisation of the matrimonial home. In certain circumstances, the spouse of a defendant may be allowed to remain in the property notwithstanding that he or she has less than a 100 per cent interest in it—see Chapter 16.

### The court's order

**11.67**  If the parties cannot reach agreement, the application for the appointment of an enforcement receiver will proceed to a full contested hearing before a Crown Court judge following the procedure set down in Parts 60 and 61 of the CrimPR. In most cases, where there is a substantial confiscation order that remains unsatisfied and the defendant has made little effort to satisfy the order voluntarily, or it is impracticable to allow him to do so, the court will exercise its discretion in favour of appointing a receiver, reflecting the legislative steer under s 69 of POCA. The terms of the appointment will depend on the findings the court makes in determining any third-party claims as to the ownership of certain assets. If a third party is successful in his claim that the defendant holds no interest in a particular asset, it will of course form no part of the receivership order. If, however, the court finds that the asset is subject to shared ownership by the defendant and the third party, it will be included in the order. If the court determines the asset is owned by the defendant and a third party, it may proceed in one of two ways:

(1)  the court may order the defendant and third party to give possession of the asset to the receiver to realise and that the receiver should pay to the third party a sum of money from the proceeds of sale proportionate to his interest in it; or

(2)  the court may order the third party to pay to the receiver a sum of money equivalent to the defendant's interest in the property. On payment of this sum, the court will direct that the defendant's interest in the property should be extinguished and transferred to the third party. The court will need to be satisfied that the third party has sufficient funds before making an order in these terms, but will usually be prepared to give

the third party a reasonable time in which to raise any necessary finance (see s 51(6) of POCA).

The court may also need to conduct a cost–benefit analysis of the proposed terms of the order **11.68** for receivership, particularly where assets are difficult to locate or realise. A good example of this arose in *Re Johnson* [2011] EWHC 593. In that case the defendant owned certain assets located in the United Arab Emirates and Tanzania. The question for the court was whether the most effective method of realising these out-of-jurisdiction assets was by way of a letter of request 'LOR' (as the prosecution contended) or by way of the enforcement receiver 'ER' (as the defendant contended). The prosecution, which was concerned to achieve cost-effectiveness for the tax payer, considered that the costs of the receiver were likely to exceed the value of the property he would be able to realise. Rafferty J ultimately found in favour of the defendant, albeit in doing so she approved the prosecutor's approach. She said:

> I shall permit the ERO to pursue the out-of-jurisdiction assets... Though one understands and applauds the Crown's vigilance and its recognition of its status as guardian of the public purse, nevertheless it is now March 2011 and not a great deal has been achieved. LOR may be effective, but the likelihood is that the man of business who maintains an office in Dubai enjoys an advantage in finding and, it should be remembered, selling, assets if discoverable... I am impressed by the restraint with which the ER has expressed himself in correspondence and by his willingness to operate on a conditional fee basis, thus exposing his firm to commercial risk. Though the arguments for the Crown have merit, it is plain to me that the better risk is in the use of the ER's skills.

### Status of the enforcement receiver on appointment

As with a management receiver, on appointment an enforcement receiver becomes an **11.69** officer of the court accountable to the court for his actions—see Chapter 4 for the general principles of receivership law. Although appointed on the application of the prosecutor, an enforcement receiver is entirely independent of the prosecutor who has no power to require him to exercise his powers in a particular way. This is not to say that the prosecutor and receiver should not work closely together during the course of the receivership. Indeed, the receiver is still bound by the legislative steer under s 69 of POCA and in practice, the prosecuting authority's financial investigation officers will work very closely with the receiver and his staff as they are in the best possible position to advise as to the realisable property owned by the defendant and its current location. Similarly where, during the course of a receivership, the defendant or a third party makes an application to the court, the prosecutor frequently liaises closely with the receiver because he may have access to information and documentation relevant to the court's consideration of the claim. Where no conflict of interest arises, the prosecutor and receiver frequently instruct the same counsel with a view to saving costs. It is submitted that these practices are perfectly proper provided the receiver does nothing to compromise his independence as an officer of the court.

The prosecutor is also responsible for monitoring the receiver's fees and, prior to applying **11.70** to the enforcing magistrates' court to draw his remuneration and expenses, must seek the prosecutor's approval. The defendant should also be given the opportunity to make representations if he has any interest in the amount being claimed. In many cases he will have no such interest since the full amount realised by the receiver will be paid in gross and credited towards the confiscation order. Most letters of agreement will also require the receiver to seek approval from the prosecutor to the appointment of agents such as solicitors, property managers, and valuers.

### Directions or variation and discharge of the receivership

**11.71**  A receiver may apply to the court to seek directions as to the exercise of his powers under s 62 of POCA. Alternatively he may seek to vary the terms of his appointment or to discharge his office (typically once his duties are completed) under s 63 of POCA. These applications are governed by CrimPR r 60.3 but the procedural rules cannot limit the grounds on which a receiver's discharge might be sought—see *McCracken v CPS* [2011] EWCA Civ 1620; [2012] Lloyd's Rep FC 148. In addition s 63 of POCA allows a prosecutor, defendant, or third party to seek the receiver's discharge at an earlier date if, for example, the receiver is not acting in accordance with the legislative steer under s 69 of POCA as required or if it can be demonstrated that the receiver has acted in an unreasonable or dilatory fashion. For an example of such an attempt see *Re Dahner* [2010] EWHC 3397 (Admin). Equally an application might be made to discharge or vary an enforcement receivership where the property the subject of the order is not realisable property in which the defendant holds an interest—see Chapter 16 on third-party interests.

## H. The Powers of the Magistrates' Court

**11.72**  The appointment of an enforcement receiver, although often an effective remedy to secure payment of the amount due under a confiscation order, is also an expensive one. Its use should normally be confined to larger and more complex confiscation orders and those where there are houses or other substantial assets to be sold, overseas properties to be dealt with, third-party claims to be determined, or other compelling reasons why the magistrates' court's powers are inadequate. In cases where there are no third-party claims and the assets are easy to realise, such as money held in bank accounts or by the prosecutor, jewellery, or motor vehicles of relatively low value, recourse should always be had to the sanctions available to the magistrates' court responsible for enforcing the order.

**11.73**  Magistrates' courts are involved in the enforcement process because s 35(2) of POCA provides that ss 139(2) to (4) and 140(1) to (4) of the Powers of Criminal Courts (Sentencing) Act 2000 (PCC(S)A) shall apply in relation to the enforcement of confiscation orders in the same way as they apply to the enforcement of fines. Sections 9(1) of the DTA and s 75(1) of the CJA made similar provision in relation to confiscation orders made under the old legislation. In consequence, all the powers of the magistrates' court that are available for the enforcement of fines are also available for the purpose of enforcing confiscation orders.

### Distress warrants

**11.74**  Section 76(1) of the Magistrates' Courts Act 1980 (MCA) empowers the magistrates' court to issue a distress warrant. Such a warrant empowers bailiffs to take possession of and sell property belonging to the defendant to satisfy the confiscation order. It is particularly useful in relation to motor vehicles, jewellery, and other goods belonging to the defendant since it provides a quick and inexpensive means of realisation. Distress warrants may also assist in cases where the prosecutor is in possession of property taken from the defendant at the time of his arrest and which the defendant will not authorise the prosecutor to hand over to the court. In such circumstances, the issue of a distress warrant protects the prosecutor from any civil action for conversion if he hands the property to the bailiff. A distress warrant may not be issued until time to pay has expired.

### Third-party debt orders and charging orders

By s 87 of the MCA, the Magistrates' Court may enforce the order in the High Court or in a **11.75** County Court otherwise than by the issue of a writ of *fieri facias*, imprisonment, or attachment of earnings. This includes the designated officer applying for a third-party debt order (formerly known as a 'garnishee order') under Pt 72 of the Civil Procedure Rules. The application is in two stages: the County Court will first make an interim order freezing the funds in question pending a hearing at which the third party must attend and provide information regarding any funds he holds belonging to the defendant. At the second stage, a hearing will take place at which the County Court will decide whether to make a final third-party debt order instructing the third party to pay the sum in question to the enforcing Magistrates' Court. Further enforcement measures include an application for deduction from state benefits. Such orders are likely to be sought less frequently now the enforcing Magistrates' Court has its own powers in relation to seized funds under s 67 of POCA which are considered below.

The combined effect of s 35 of POCA and s 87 of the MCA is that one enforcement **11.76** route available to the Magistrates' Court is to treat the confiscation order as a quasi civil judgment debt potentially allowing the designated officer to obtain charging orders on a defendant's property from either the High Court or County Court—see *Designated Officer For Sunderland Magistrates' Court v (1) George Knowles Krager (2) Lorraine Amanda Mason* [2011] EWHC 3283 (Ch).

### Seized money

Section 67 of POCA gives the enforcing Magistrates' Court power to direct banks and build- **11.77** ing societies holding money belonging to a defendant to pay it to the court in satisfaction of the confiscation order. The section also applies to money held by police and customs officers. Section 67(1) to (3) specifies the money to which the section applies and provides:

(1) This section applies to money which—
    (a) is held by a person, and
    (b) is held in an account maintained by him with a bank or building society.
(2) This section also applies to money which is held by a person and which—
    (a) has been seized by a constable under section 19 of the Police and Criminal Evidence Act 1984 (c60) (general power of seizure, etc.), and
    (b) is held in an account maintained by a police force with a bank or building society.
(3) This section also applies to money which is held by a person and which—
    (a) has been seized by a customs officer under section 19 of the 1984 Act as applied by an order made under section 114(2) of that Act, and
    (b) is held in an account maintained by the Commissioners of Customs and Excise with a bank or building society.

If the seized cash falls into any one of these categories, the justices may make an order requir- **11.78** ing the bank or building society to pay the money to the court, provided the conditions set out in s 67(4) of POCA (as amended by para 33 of Pt 1 of Sch 8 to the Serious Crime Act 2007) have been satisfied. These are:

(a) a restraint order has effect in relation to the money;
(b) a confiscation order is made against the person by whom the money is held;

(c) a receiver has not been appointed under s 50 in relation to the money;

(d) any period allowed under s 11 for payment of the amounts ordered to be paid under the confiscation order has ended.

**11.79** It is important to note that the section only applies when a restraint order is in force and any time allowed for payment by the Crown Court has ended. If no restraint order is in force, a third-party debt order will have to be sought. If the bank or building society fails to comply with an order under s 67 it may be fined up to £5,000 (see s 67(6)). For the purposes of the section, a bank is a deposit-taking institution within the meaning of the Banking Act 1987 and 'building society' has the same meaning as in the Building Societies Act 1986 (see s 67(8)).

**11.80** Rule 58.12(1) of the CrimPR sets out the information that an order under s 67 must contain. It provides:

> An order under section 67 of the Proceeds of Crime Act 2002 requiring a bank or building society to pay money to a magistrates' court officer ('a payment order') shall—
>
> (a) be directed to the bank or building society in respect of which the payment order is made;
>
> (b) name the person against whom the confiscation order has been made;
>
> (c) state the amount which remains to be paid under the confiscation order;
>
> (d) state the name and address of the branch at which the account in which the money ordered to be paid is held and the sort code of that branch, if the sort code is known;
>
> (e) state the name in which the account in which the money ordered to be paid is held and the account number of that account, if the account number is known;
>
> (f) state the amount which the bank or building society is required to pay to the court officer under the payment order;
>
> (g) give the name and address of the court officer to whom payment is to be made; and
>
> (h) require the bank or building society to make payment within a period of seven days beginning on the day on which the payment order is made, unless it appears to the court that a longer or shorter period would be appropriate in the particular circumstances.

**11.81** Service of the order should be effected in accordance with r 4.3 of the CrimPR. In summary, the order may be served by handing it to a person holding a senior position in the bank or building society, or by leaving it at, or sending it by first class post (or the equivalent to first class post) to, the principal office of the bank or building society in question. The order may also, subject to the exceptions contained in the CrimPR, be served by DX or by electronic means.

### Activation of the default term

*Introduction: the enforcement hearing*

**11.82** Section 76(2) of the MCA gives the Magistrates' Court power to issue a warrant of commitment to activate the default term of imprisonment imposed by the Crown Court in the event of non-payment of a confiscation order. The only exception to the Magistrates' Courts' jurisdiction is where the Crown Court orders immediate payment of the confiscation order under s 11(1) of POCA together with a default term of imprisonment for non-payment. In those circumstances the Crown Court may itself immediately impose the default term if any of the conditions under s 139(3) of the PCC(S)A are satisfied as applied by s 35(2) of POCA. These conditions include, by virtue of s 139(3)(a) PCC(S)A, if the defendant 'appears to the court to have sufficient means to pay the sum forthwith' or, under s 139(3)(b), 'it appears to the court that he is unlikely to remain long enough at a place of abode in the United Kingdom to enable payment of the sum to be enforced by other methods'. Otherwise, in order to give consideration to the activation of the default term, it will be necessary to convene an enforcement hearing at the Magistrates' Court at which the defendant will be required to attend. If the defendant fails to attend, a warrant may be issued for his arrest under s 83 of the MCA. This is because s 35(2) POCA and s 140(1) of the PCC(S)A have the effect of treating the confiscation order as if it were a fine imposed upon conviction by the Magistrates' Court and hence Pt 3 of the MCA (ss 75–96) apply, subject to the exceptions set out in s 35(3) of POCA and modifications as described in the case law below. Therefore the default term may not be activated in a defendant's absence (he must be present due to s 82(5) MCA) except in the very limited circumstances set out in s 82(5A)–(5F) of the MCA. The power to issue a warrant for the defendant's arrest under s 83 MCA only applies in cases where the justices are considering activation of the default term and does not extend to cases where only civil remedies are being considered. In *R (on the application of Rustim Necip) v City of London Magistrates' Court* [2010] 1 WLR 1827; [2009] EWHC 755 (Admin), the defendant had already served his default term, but the Magistrates' Court convened a further enforcement hearing to consider whether any other means of enforcement might be appropriate. The defendant did not appear and a warrant was issued for his arrest. The Divisional Court quashed the warrant holding that the power to issue a warrant under s 83 was ancillary to the power under s 82 to activate the default term of imprisonment. As it was no longer open to the court to impose the default term, there was no power to issue a warrant under s 83. Richards LJ said:

> An arrest warrant can be issued under section 83 only for the purpose of enabling inquiry to be made under section 82 or for securing attendance at a hearing required under section 82(5). But the provisions of section 82 are all concerned with the issue of a warrant of commitment. They impose a raft of restrictions on the exercise of the power to issue such a warrant, so as to ensure in effect that a warrant of commitment is a remedy of last resort. They are not dealing with the situation where a period of imprisonment in default of payment has already been served and where there can therefore be no possible question of the issue of a warrant of commitment.

He added:

> Thus there is nothing in section 82, as it seems to me, to cover a case where there is no question of a warrant of commitment being issued and the court is concerned only with whether some other method of enforcement of the confiscation order should be adopted.
>
> As I read section 83, it is purely ancillary to section 82. It can be used to secure attendance for section 82 purposes but it cannot be used so as to secure attendance for some other purpose.

**11.83** The decision in *Necip* has unfortunate consequences for enforcing Magistrates' Courts wishing to consider civil methods of enforcement when, for whatever reason, activation of the default term is no longer an available remedy. If defendants realise that the court has no means of compelling their attendance for such purposes they will simply refuse to attend court, with the consequence that the justices are effectively powerless to enforce the order.

**11.84** The only duty of the justices is to enquire into the defendant's proposals for payment and to determine whether any other method of enforcement might be effective. If the defendant advances no such proposals, or no other methods of enforcement appear to the court to be appropriate, it is entitled to issue the warrant of commitment.

**11.85** It is important that the justices should resist the temptation to act as a court of appeal against the making of the confiscation order. The court is only concerned with the enforcement of the order and, if the defendant is aggrieved by it, he has the right to appeal to the Court of Appeal. Similarly, if he claims that his assets are insufficient to meet the confiscation order, he may apply for a certificate of inadequacy. In *R v Harrow Justices, ex parte DPP* [1991] 1 WLR 395 Stuart-Smith LJ observed:

> The mere fact that a confiscation order has been made is evidence that, at the date of its imposition, there were realisable assets available to meet the requirements of the order. Even if at the date when the Justices have to consider the question of enforcement, the value of realisable assets are less than they were at the date of the confiscation order, it is open to the defendant to apply for a certificate of inadequacy ... which will lead to a reduction in the amount of the original order.

*The prosecutor has the right to attend and make representations*

**11.86** When the justices are determining whether or not to issue the warrant of commitment, they are entitled to hear representations from the prosecuting authority as to the position in relation to the confiscation order. In *R v Hastings and Rother Justices ex p Anscombe* (1998) 162 JP 340: [1998] Crim LR 812 Schiemann LJ observed:

> The applicant also seeks to quash the decision of the justices to hear the representative of the Customs and Excise who informed them as to the current situation as best it was known to him and who informed them amongst other things of the undisputed fact that, in breach of bail, the applicant had previously left the jurisdiction. I see nothing wrong either in the fact that the representative was heard or that he saw it appropriate to put this fact before the magistrates who were being asked to adjourn the proceedings. Had they adjourned Mr Anscombe would have been released from prison and might have chosen this opportunity to go abroad again.

**11.87** Similar sentiments were expressed by the Divisional Court in *R v Harrow Justices ex p DPP* (above). In that case Stuart-Smith LJ said:

> Given the *inter partes* nature of the procedure leading to the making of a confiscation order, it will be in the nature of things that the prosecution will in all probability have information available which would be relevant to the justices' consideration. More compellingly, the prosecution has a legitimate interest in being heard before the justices come to any decision.

**11.88** In *Garrote v City of London Magistrates' Court* [2002] EWHC 2909 the Divisional Court quashed a committal warrant where the enforcing magistrates' court failed to adjourn the case to give the prosecutor the opportunity to attend and make representations. A confiscation order had been made against the defendant in the sum of £1,373,405.47 under the CJA in its unamended form and a receiver had been appointed to realise assets in satisfaction of the order. After realising assets located within the jurisdiction to the extent of £114,725.72, the receiver was discharged. The prosecutor and the receiver were satisfied that all the assets within the jurisdiction had, so far as possible, been realised, and there was no suggestion that the defendant had failed to cooperate or had misled the authorities. The prosecutor sought the realisation of overseas assets by means of letters of request to the countries in which they were located.

**11.89** The enforcing magistrates' court nonetheless had the defendant produced from prison for an enforcement hearing. The prosecutor did not attend and was not represented. The defendant's counsel sought an adjournment to allow enquiries to be made as to whether the prosecutor was aware of the hearing and wished to attend to make representations and to establish the position in relation to letters of request forwarded to overseas countries in which assets were located. The court refused the application and issued the committal warrant to activate the default sentence. The defendant sought judicial review of the justices' decision. The High Court found that the justices had acted unreasonably in not adjourning to seek the prosecutor's representations and quashed the committal warrant. Gibbs J said:

> My conclusions about this regrettable chain of events already summarised, and about this application, are as follows. The justices apparently failed to consider all methods of enforcement short of issuing the committal warrant. Despite receiving the letter dated 18th January 2002 from the Crown Prosecution Service saying that assets were still being pursued, the magistrates failed to offer the prosecution the opportunity to be heard in relation to the legitimate public interest that their position should be known. There is no sign that the magistrates conducted, or even considered conducting, the balancing exercise which Silber J rightly referred to as being necessary in a situation such as this. Alternatively, if the justices did attempt to conduct such a balancing exercise, they did so without the benefit of any, or any adequate, information.
>
> In the result, it follows that the magistrates' decision was neither a rational one, nor was it conducted with regard to the appropriate legal considerations. The only way in which the magistrates could have dealt with the matter properly was to adjourn for the purposes of obtaining information about the progress of the prosecution regarding assets pursued both in this country and abroad, but in particular abroad.

It is therefore essential that the enforcing magistrates' court should consult the prosecutor **11.90** before listing an enforcement hearing and give him the opportunity to attend and make representations. If the court neglects to do this and issues the committal warrant, the decision will be vulnerable to challenge by way of judicial review at the instance both of the prosecutor and the defendant.

### Legal representation of the defendant

The defendant is, of course, entitled to be legally represented at the enforcement hearing and, **11.91** in appropriate circumstances, public funding is available for representation by a solicitor. The right to funding does not, however, extend to representation by counsel or an advocate at public expense. In *Taylor v City of Westminster Magistrates' Court* [2009] EWHC 1498 (Admin) the defendant was facing an enforcement hearing in relation to a confiscation order for £633,530.45 made in 1996 of which £258,530.47 remained outstanding. He sought public funding for representation by counsel. The basis of the application was that it would be necessary to argue complex delay points relating to the European Convention on Human Rights (ECHR) as to whether the default sentence should be served concurrently or consecutively with a sentence imposed for an unrelated offence and that it would be necessary to consider copious amounts of correspondence reflecting the conduct of the parties. The defendant's application was refused by the district judge on the basis that the conditions set out in Regulation 12(1) of the Criminal Defence Service (General) (No 2) Regulations 2001 (SI 1437/2001) had not been met. Regulation 12 provided:

> (1) A representation order for the purpose of proceedings before a magistrates' court may only include representation by an advocate in the case of:
> (a) any indictable offence, including an offence which is triable either way; or
> (b) extradition hearings under the Extradition Act 2003
> where the court is of the opinion that because of circumstances which make the proceedings unusually grave or difficult, representation by both a litigator and an advocate would be desirable.

267

**11.92**   The District Judge found that the enforcement hearing did not amount to 'proceedings before a magistrates' court in the case of an indictable offence' but was merely incidental to such proceedings. As to the second limb regarding the proceedings being unusually grave or difficult, the District Judge found that the defendant's case was 'far too vague and rather woolly', and the delay point under the ECHR was not particularly complex. The defendant applied for judicial review of the District Judge's decision, but his application was dismissed by the High Court. The court found that the District Judge had been correct to hold that the enforcement hearing did not amount to proceedings before a magistrates' court in the case of an indictable offence within the meaning of Regulation 12(1). Cranston J (with whom Pill LJ agreed) said:

> In my view, regulation 12 does not extend to confiscation enforcement proceedings in the magistrates' court, however serious the underlying events. The District Judge was correct to conclude that he had no jurisdiction to make a representation order in this case. The basic principle of interpretation is that a regulation such as this must be construed in context. That means that consideration must be given to this regulation in the context of the 2001 regulations themselves but also against the background legislative scheme, its scope and purpose. Confiscation enforcement proceedings are criminal proceedings for the purposes of the 1999 Act and the 2001 Regulations and fall within the scope of section 12(2)(b) of the 1999 Act. However, the confiscation legislation makes clear that enforcement of a confiscation order is deemed to be equivalent to the enforcement of a fine through the magistrates' court. That is far from being proceedings in the case of an indictable offence.

He added:

> Regulation 12 has no application as a matter of statutory interpretation because such proceedings are not 'in the case of . . . an indictable offence'. Rather they are, in their statutory context, quite separate proceedings: the enforcement of a confiscation order is to be treated as the enforcement of a fine. In my view, the meaning of regulation 12 within its statutory context is that a representation order in the magistrates' court may only be extended to cover the instruction of a court advocate where the case before the court involves proceedings in the case of an indictable offence in the strict sense or extradition proceedings.

*Applications to adjourn the enforcement hearing*

**11.93**   The court has a discretion to adjourn the enforcement hearing if it considers it appropriate to do so. It not infrequently happens that the listing of an enforcement hearing focuses the defendant's attention on applying for a certificate of inadequacy. The mere fact that the defendant asserts he is taking such steps does not necessarily mean that the justices must adjourn the enforcement hearing pending the outcome of the application for a certificate of inadequacy. The justices must, of course, exercise their discretion judicially but, if there has been a long delay by the defendant in lodging his application for a certificate of inadequacy, the court would be entitled to refuse an application for an adjournment. If, on the other hand, the defendant has acted with all due expedition and a hearing is pending, the better course may be to adjourn the enforcement proceedings to await the outcome of the application. In *R v Liverpool Magistrates' Court ex p Ansen* [1998] 1 All ER 692 there had been a delay of two years between the confiscation order being made and the justices issuing the warrant of commitment during which time no application had been made by the defendant for a certificate of inadequacy. He brought judicial review proceedings against the justices for, inter alia, refusing his application for the hearing to be adjourned to allow an application for a certificate of inadequacy to be made. In rejecting this argument, May J said:

> The next matter relied upon is that the magistrate did not adjourn the matter before him so that the applicant could be given time to make an application to the High Court for a certificate of inadequacy. The evidence of the magistrate here is that he did not do so because he reckoned that the applicant had had quite adequate time to do this and that an adjournment for that purpose should be refused. In my judgment, that was a perfectly proper decision for the magistrate to make.

The court took a similar view in *R v Hastings and Rother Justices ex p Anscombe* (above) where **11.94** it found that an application for a certificate of inadequacy—which would involve an attempt by the defendant to challenge the factual findings made in the Crown Court—would have had no prospect of success. Schiemann LJ said:

> The justices could have adjourned the proceedings in front of them in order to see whether or not the High Court would issue a certificate of inadequacy and, if so, whether an application would be made by the defendant to the Crown Court to reduce the amount of the order and of the period to be served in default. An application for an adjournment was made to them. The only grounds put forward appear to have been the promised application to the High Court for the certificate of inadequacy which in turns seems to have been based on the contention that the sums which the Crown Court had held had been salted away had never been salted away. That assertion was not open to the appellant as I have indicated earlier in this judgment. I see no error of law in the failure by the justices to exercise in Mr Anscombe's favour their discretion to adjourn.

The refusal of an enforcing magistrates' court to adjourn an enforcement hearing was again **11.95** challenged in *McLeod v City of Westminster Magistrates' Court* [2009] EWHC 807 (Admin). A CJA confiscation order for £170,962 was made against the defendant on 18 October 2007 to be paid in full by 18 July 2008. On 30 January 2008 the RCPO wrote to the defendant advising that they were the enforcing authority and inviting his proposals for payment. The letter contained a warning that, in the absence of satisfactory proposals, the appointment of an enforcement receiver would be considered. No response was received to this letter, but on 8 July 2008 the defendant's solicitors asked the prosecutor to agree a three-month extension of time in which to pay. The prosecutor responded advising that there was no power under the CJA to extend time to pay. An enforcement hearing was then listed before the magistrates' court on 23 September 2008 on which occasion the defendant appeared unrepresented. The hearing was adjourned until 4 November 2008 to allow the defendant the opportunity to secure legal representation and on this date he appeared represented by counsel. Counsel sought a further adjournment to enable both parties to consider the possibility of a receiver being appointed and to allow the defendant to realise his share of the matrimonial home which was held in his wife's name. Counsel explained that the defendant was going through divorce proceedings and the property had been on the market since the confiscation order was made. The prosecutor pointed out that the defendant had provided no evidence he was going through a divorce or that the property was on the market. The defendant had only raised the possibility of a receiver being appointed on the day of the hearing. In the light of these submissions, the district judge refused the application for an adjournment and activated the default term of imprisonment. The district judge found that the defendant had been given every opportunity to produce evidence and said he was not prepared to act on his unsupported assertions. He found that the adjournment application amounted to a 'delaying tactic' by the defendant.

**11.96** The defendant sought judicial review of the district judge's decision. Whilst the application was pending the RCPO wrote to the defendant's solicitors asking for confirmation of the position in relation to the divorce proceedings as it was necessary to consider whether to intervene in any related ancillary relief application. Again, no response was forthcoming. The Divisional Court dismissed the application and was critical of the defendant's contention that the district judge had failed to exercise his discretion judicially. May LJ said: 'To my mind this is an unfortunate submission, taken alone, when the district judge plainly addressed all the submissions that were made to him and made a reasoned judicial decision on them.' He added:

> In my judgment the case that the District Judge failed to properly exercise his judicial discretion, and/or that he came to a wrong decision on 4 November, is simply not made out. The date for payment of the amount ordered by agreement in the confiscation proceedings was well past, and the applicant had had more than a year to arrange to sell the house to raise the amount required. In practice, he had had an additional period after the expiry of the nine month period that he had been given at the confiscation proceedings as time to pay.

**11.97** The Divisional Court was also critical of the defendant's failure to produce evidence and respond to correspondence from the prosecutor. May LJ said:

> There was no evidence before the court and in my judgment it was well within the District Judge's judicial discretionary competence to decline to accept assertions by counsel, unsupported by evidence from one who had been convicted of conspiracy to cheat. The applicant had been warned on 23 September 2008 when the matter was first adjourned that he risked a committal order, and he had had six weeks or so in which to produce evidence. He had had legal aid since the beginning of October 2008.

Referring to the prosecutor's correspondence, he added:

> The submission in that respect is simply not helped by the fact that we are told that no response was received to that letter nor to the one that had been written to the applicant's wife. In those circumstances, this court is in no better position from the point of view of evidence than was the District Judge.

**11.98** The conclusion of the Divisional Court in *McLeod* may be contrasted with the conclusion reached in *Barnett v Director of Public Prosecutions* [2009] EWHC 2004 (Admin). In that case the Divisional Court decided that the magistrates' court should have adjourned on the basis that there remained alternative methods of enforcement and the defendant was in no way responsible for the collapse of the sale of a property, and he and his solicitors had cooperated with the court and prosecutor in attempting to realise his assets. In *R (On The Application Of Agogo) v North Somerset Magistrates' Court* [2011] EWHC 518 (Admin) the Divisional Court also quashed a committal warrant where the Magistrates' Court had failed to adjourn to allow a defendant legal representation where he faced lengthy imprisonment.

**11.99** A number of principles can be established from these cases. The Magistrates' Court has a discretion whether or not to accede to applications for the adjournment of enforcement hearings. The discretion must be exercised judicially and, if it is found to have been exercised in a manner which is *Wednesbury* unreasonable, it will be vulnerable to challenge. A defendant who asks the court to exercise the discretion to adjourn in his favour must be able to show the court that he has cooperated with the enforcement authorities in responding to correspondence, realising assets voluntarily where possible, and by acting promptly upon any stated intention to seek a certificate of inadequacy. Further, he must provide evidence to support his assertions: in the absence of evidence to corroborate a defendant's assertions, the court is entitled to reject his claims, particularly in cases where he has been convicted of offences of dishonesty.

*Applications to extend the time allowed for payment*

In POCA cases, the Crown Court, but not the Magistrates' Court, has power to extend the **11.100** time to pay provided the total period allowed for payment does not exceed twelve months and that any application for an extension is made prior to the expiration of the initial period allowed for payment: see s 11 of POCA. In cases to which the old legislation applies, there is no statutory provision similar to s 11 of POCA and it has been held that the court has no inherent jurisdiction to extend the deadline for payment. In *Revenue and Customs Prosecutions Office v Kearney* [2007] EWHC 640 (Admin) a CJA confiscation order was made against the defendant for £143,000 and he was given twelve months in which to pay. After the expiration of the twelve-month period, the defendant applied to the Crown Court for the time to pay to be extended. The prosecutor opposed the application, contending the court had no jurisdiction to extend time to pay, but the judge held that the Crown Court had an inherent jurisdiction to grant an extension and noted that s 11 of POCA gave the court such a power in cases to which that Act applied. He extended time to pay by a further four months. The prosecutor appealed to the Divisional Court by way of case stated.

The Divisional Court allowed the prosecutor's appeal, holding there was no inherent juris- **11.101** diction to extend time to pay CJA and DTA confiscation orders. Gross J (with whom Smith LJ agreed) said:

> The reality of the confiscation order is that it is to pay a given amount within a given period or face a sentence of imprisonment in default. The given period of time to pay is an integral part of the order. For my part, I am satisfied that the introduction of any power such as that purportedly exercised by the judge here into the pre-POCA regime would, as submitted by the prosecutor, give rise to some difficulty. But that is in a sense by the by. There is no such power which is capable of being inferred from the provisions of POCA, a different regime which in any event would not have assisted the respondent as he was out of time. The right answer was for the respondent to seek to persuade the Magistrates in the exercise of their discretion, not then to activate the default sentence so that any injustice, if such there was, could have been addressed. Here that course was not followed. The learned judge had, with respect, no jurisdiction to make the order which he did.

A similar approach was adopted by the Divisional Court in the later case of *Crown* **11.102** *Prosecution Service v Greenacre* [2008] 1 WLR 438; [2007] EWHC 1193 (Admin) in which it was held that the enforcing Magistrates' Court had no power to extend time to pay. A confiscation order for £818,953.45 was made against the defendant under the CJA and he was given six months to pay. When the six-month period expired, the defendant applied to the Crown Court for an extension of the time to pay. The Crown Court judge correctly found that he had no power to grant the extension, but concluded that the magistrates' court did have such power. He therefore proceeded to sit as a district judge in accordance with s 66 of the Courts Act 2003 and granted an extension of time. A number of further extensions were granted by the Magistrates' Court until, nearly a year later, the prosecutor wrote to the court contending that it had no power to grant an extension of time. The District Judge concluded that he did have such power under s 75(2) of the MCA and granted a further extension of time. The prosecutor appealed to the Divisional Court by way of case stated.

**11.103**  The Divisional Court allowed the prosecutor's appeal, holding that the enforcing Magistrates' Court too had no jurisdiction to extend the time to pay. Laws LJ, with whom Tomlinson J agreed, said:

> First, it is to be noted that the effect of section 75(5)(a) of the Criminal Justice Act 1988 is that the magistrates' court has no power to remit the whole or any part of a confiscation order. One then notes that section 75A(1)(b) of the same Act provides that the amount of interest required to be paid when a confiscation order is not paid on time 'shall, for the purposes of enforcement, be treated as part of the amount to be recovered under the confiscation order'. If the magistrates' court can, under section 75(2) of the 1980 Act, allow further time to pay in the case of a Crown Court confiscation order, that would vary the date from which interest began to accrue and thereby, as it seems to me, would be tantamount to a partial remittal of the confiscation order; but that the magistrates' court cannot do. This is in my judgment a powerful consideration militating against any legislative intent that section 75(2) of the Magistrates' Courts Act might be deployed to allow the magistrates' court to extend time for payment of a Crown Court confiscation order.

**11.104**  In the light of these judgments, a defendant who needs further time to realise assets in satisfaction of a POCA confiscation order should, first of all, seek an extension from the Crown Court. Where this fails (or where the confiscation order was imposed under the old law under which there was no power to extend) the defendant would be better advised to seek an adjournment of the enforcement hearing rather than to seek an extension of time to pay. The court will want to be satisfied that an adjournment will serve a useful purpose and is not merely delaying the inevitable, and it will no doubt require clear and cogent evidence from the defendant that there is a very real likelihood of further assets being realised if the proceedings are so adjourned.

*The court has no discretion to waive interest payments*

**11.105**  The enforcing Magistrates' Court has no power to waive interest payments due on an unpaid confiscation order. In *Hansford v Southampton Magistrates' Court* [2008] 4 All ER 432; [2008] EWHC 67 (Admin), the defendant sought to argue that the enforcing magistrates' court had a discretion, in appropriate circumstances, not to make a defaulter liable to pay the full amount of interest due from the date on which he becomes liable to pay until the date of the enforcement hearing. The defendant contended that the words 'shall be liable to pay interest' in s 75A(1)(a) of the CJA were ambiguous (the wording of s 12 POCA is that the defendant 'must pay interest'). The words could be given an 'absolute construction' meaning bound to pay or a 'discretion construction' meaning at risk of paying. Bearing in mind the punitive consequences for the defendant the statutory ambiguity should be resolved in his favour. The court held that there was no such ambiguity and that the court had no discretion to waive any interest that had accrued on an unpaid confiscation order. Dyson LJ said:

> Section 75A(1) and (2) are provisions which prescribe the consequences of court orders. There is no role for the court here. They follow automatically if the necessary conditions are satisfied. One of the conditions is that a court has made a confiscation order. If a confiscation order has been made and the sum required to be paid under it has not been paid when it is required to be paid, the consequence follows that the defendant pays interest at the rate defined in subsection (3). The provision accords no role to the court here. The lack of role for the court is not only to be contrasted with those other provisions where a court function is specified; it is to be contrasted with subsection (2) where the court is given the power (but not the duty) to increase the default term of imprisonment or detention if the effect of subsection (1) is to increase the maximum period applicable.

The contrast between subsection (2) on the one hand and subsections (1) and (3) on the other is striking and fatal to counsel's argument. Where Parliament intends to give the court a discretion, it does so expressly and uses the word 'may' which is well understood to connote a discretion.

Section 79(2) of the MCA operates so that the default term a defendant is liable to serve **11.106** will be reduced pro rata in accordance with the proportion of the confiscation order that has been satisfied. However, if the interest that has accrued on the order outweighs the payments made towards it then the defendant will receive no benefit. In the case of *R (on the application of the CPS) v City of London Magistrates' Court; Keith Hartley* [2007] EWHC 1924 (Admin) Sedley LJ described the relationship as follows at para 7 of his judgment:

> What the enforcing justices have to work with, therefore, is something like a measuring jug. It has a fixed capacity which cannot be exceeded, but within it the amount of the debt may both fall as the capital sum is paid off and rise as interest accrues on the balance. When they come to activate a default term, the justices must activate the same proportion of it as the amount in the jug—that is principal and interest together—bears to its capacity.

*Issuing the warrant of commitment*

The enforcing Magistrates' Court should only issue the warrant of commitment after consid- **11.107** ering all the other available enforcement options and concluding that they are unlikely to be effective: see *R v Harrow Justices ex p DPP* [1991] 1 WLR 395 and *Garotte v City of London Magistrates' Court* [2002] EWHC 2909. Where the Magistrates' Court has decided to issue a warrant of commitment the defendant is not permitted to rely on the 'slip rule' (s 142(1) of the MCA) to reopen the decision, save where it is necessary to correct a mistake: *Roman Zykin v CPS* (2009) 173 JP 361; [2009] EWHC 1469 (Admin).

The decision in *Garrote* was followed in *Barnett v Director of Public Prosecutions* [2009] **11.108** EWHC 2004 (Admin), a case where the Divisional Court was required to consider whether a decision to commit the defendant to prison for non-payment of a confiscation order was lawful. In that case a POCA confiscation order had been made against the defendant for £86,605.74 to be paid within six months and with a default sentence of two years' imprisonment. The main assets available to satisfy the order were funds in a bank account and the defendant's equity in a property valued at £59,000. The property proved difficult to market and in November 2007 the Crown Court extended time to pay until April 2008. Enforcement proceedings were taken in the magistrates' court but adjourned on a number of occasions as it appeared that a sale of the property was imminent. One week before the adjourned hearing was to take place in January 2009 the sale fell through because the proposed purchaser failed to put his solicitor in funds. In the light of this, the defendant's solicitors wrote to the court and the prosecutor asking for a further adjournment. The prosecutor consented, but, in view of the imminence of the hearing, the court took the view that the case should remain in the list. The application for an adjournment was ultimately refused and the district judge concluded that the only way of enforcing the order was to commit the defendant for the default sentence which he duly did. The defendant appealed by way of case stated to the Divisional Court.

The court held that the District Judge had been wrong to refuse the adjournment and activate **11.109** the default sentence as alternative methods of enforcement were available. Maddison J said:

> There is no statutory requirement that a court should be satisfied that no alternative means of enforcement are available for it to commit a defendant to prison in circumstances such as

these. But there is clear case law authority to that effect in cases such as *R v Harrow Justices ex parte DPP* [1991] 1 WLR 935 and *R v City of London Justices ex parte Garrote* [2003] EWHC 2909.

In my judgment the district judge was wrong in both his conclusions. He should have granted the application for a further adjournment. The fact that the application was made with the agreement of the Crown Prosecution Service, as the enforcement authority, was not determinative of the issue but it was certainly an important matter to be taken into account. Despite the disappointing and very recent collapse of the intended sale of the property for £130,000, there was no reason to believe at the time that the property could not be sold for some such amount. There was never a suggestion that the property was inherently unsaleable. It could have been sold at auction if all else failed or by the mortgagees following repossession or indeed still on the open market. There was no suggestion that the appellant would block or refuse to co-operate with any such sale. The district judge had previously adjourned the enforcement hearings because efforts were being made to sell the property. The memorandum of 19 January 2009 which was before the district judge spoke of the appellant's wish that the sale proceed without delay. Depending on the price achieved, it might well then be necessary to apply to the court for a variation of the confiscation order under Section 23 of the 2002 Act by reducing the amount specified in the order to be paid. But there remained the prospect that the sum still due under the confiscation order would, at least in part, be satisfied.

It follows, in my view, that the district judge was demonstrably wrong to refuse the application to adjourn the proceedings and to conclude that no other method of enforcement remained other than to commit the appellant to prison. In my view, his decisions can properly be described as *Wednesbury* unreasonable.

**11.110** This case is clear authority for the proposition that, although it is not necessary to prove wilful refusal or culpable neglect to pay as a condition precedent to activating the default term (as otherwise required by s 82(4) of the MCA), the court must be satisfied that no other alternative methods of enforcement are appropriate. Each case will, of course, turn on its own facts—for example *Barnett* was distinguished in *Jestin v Dover Magistrates' Court* [2013] EWHC 1040 (Admin). The principle that a warrant of committal is an enforcement method of last resort has been repeated on numerous occasions (eg see para 11.107 above and para 19 of the judgment in *Lloyd v Bow Street Magistrates' Court* [2004] 1 Cr App R 11; [2003] EWHC 2294 (Admin)). In contrast in *Munir v Bolton Magistrates' Court* [2010] EWHC 3974 Charles J appeared to depart from it. He suggested (at para 10) that, before the court may commit the defendant to prison, it must be satisfied that there has been wilful refusal to pay the confiscation order. It is submitted that *Munir* should not be followed. The view expressed by Charles J, which is contained in a judgment delivered *ex tempore*, appears to have been based on s 82(4) of the MCA, which applies where the court is required to inquire into the defendant's means. This, however, overlooks the fact that, as explained in *R v Hastings and Rother Justices ex p Anscombe* (above), where the court is considering an application for committal in respect of non-payment of a confiscation order (as distinct from a fine) there is no requirement to inquire into the defendant's means. Furthermore in *R (on the application of Craig Matthew Johnson) (Claimant) v Birmingham Magistrates' Court (Defendant) & Crown Prosecution Service (Interested party)* [2012] EWHC 596 (Admin), the Divisional Court held that the test in s 82(4) was that the court had to have regard to other methods of enforcement, it did not have to have tried them all. In that case, the fact that a receiver was in office and assets were located outside the jurisdiction did not abrogate the defendant of his duty to satisfy his confiscation order.

### Default term: practical matters

The default term of imprisonment for non-payment of a confiscation order unarguably forms **11.111** part of the sentence imposed for the offences of which a defendant is convicted. Therefore the imposition of the default term of imprisonment does not constitute a new or separate charge. It is within the scope of the original substantive sentence of which the confiscation order is part—see paras 22–24 of the Divisional Court's judgment in *R (on the application of the Director Of Revenue & Customs Prosecutions) (Claimant) v Birmingham Magistrates' Court (Defendant) & Raymond Woolley* [2010] EWHC 12 (Admin): [2010] Lloyd's Rep FC 286. Where the committal warrant is issued by the justices, the term is to be served consecutively to the term of imprisonment imposed for the substantive offence: see s 38 of POCA, s 9(2) of the DTA, and s 75(3) of the CJA. Section 38 of POCA provides as follows:

(1) Subsection (2) applies if—
   (a) a warrant committing the defendant to prison or detention is issued for a default in payment of an amount ordered to be paid under a confiscation order in respect of an offence or offences, and
   (b) at the time the warrant is issued the defendant is liable to serve a term of custody in respect of the offence (or any of the offences).
(2) In such a case the term of imprisonment or detention under section 108 of the Sentencing Act (detention of persons aged between 18 to 20 for default) to be served in default of payment of the amount does not begin to run until after the term mentioned in subsection (1)(b) above.
(3) The reference in subsection (1)(b) above to the term of custody the defendant is liable to serve in respect of the offence (or any of the offences) is a reference to the term of imprisonment or detention in a young offender institution, which he is liable to serve in respect of the offence (or any of the offences).
(4) For the purposes of subsection (3) consecutive terms and terms which are wholly or partly concurrent must be treated as a single terms and the following must be ignored—
   (a) any sentence suspended under section 118(1) of the Sentencing Act which has not taken effect at the time the warrant is issued;
   (b) in the case of a sentence of imprisonment passed with an order under section 47(1) of the Criminal Law Act 1977 (c45) (sentences of imprisonment partly served and partly suspended) any part of the sentence which the defendant has not at that time been required to serve in prison;
   (c) any term of imprisonment or detention fixed under section 139(2) of the Sentencing Act (term to be served in default of payment of fine etc) for which a warrant committing the defendant to prison or detention has not been issued at that time.
(5) If the defendant serves a term of imprisonment or detention in default of paying any amount due under a confiscation order, his serving that term does not prevent the confiscation order from continuing to have effect so far as any other method of enforcement is concerned.

Where the defendant commits further offences other than those which led to the confiscation **11.112** order, it is now clear that the issuing of the committal warrant may be postponed pending the expiry of the additional sentence: *RCPO v Taylor (George)* [2010] EWHC 715 (Admin). In that case, the defendant was made the subject of a confiscation order and sentenced to a term of imprisonment. Upon his release he committed a further offence for which he was imprisoned for twenty years. He had not yet satisfied the confiscation order. The prosecutor had two options. The first was to delay the instigation of enforcement proceeding to await the defendant's release date, which might lead to an argument that the prosecutor had brought about unreasonable delay that was incompatible with the defendant's article 6.1 rights (on which, see below). The alternative was to instigate the enforcement process but invite the court to postpone the issuing of the warrant committing the defendant to prison until the expiry of the defendant's further sentence. The defendant argued that the court had no power to postpone. This argument was accepted by the district judge, who stated a case for the opinion of the High Court. That Court decided that s 77(2) of the MCA gave the magistrates' court power to postpone the issuing of the warrant where it was in the interests of justice to do so. In appropriate cases the interests of justice would be met by postponing the issue of the warrant of commitment until the defendant has completed any sentence he is currently serving. It is submitted that this decision is plainly right, if only for the reason that it avoids a situation whereby, where the defendant is sentenced for further offences, the default term is rendered entirely futile.

**11.113** Offenders committed to prison to serve the default term for non-payment of a confiscation order have the right to be released from custody unconditionally under s 258 of the Criminal Justice Act 2003 after serving half of the default term. It is submitted the provision contained in s 264 of the Criminal Justice Act 2003 whereby consecutive sentences are 'aggregated' does not apply to default terms.

## I. Delay in Taking Enforcement Action

### Introduction

**11.114** Delays in the enforcement of confiscation orders can occur for a variety of reasons: the defendant may abscond or be obstructive or there may be administrative failings or a breakdown in communication by the law enforcement agencies responsible for enforcing confiscation orders. Lengthy appeal processes can also cause delay since prosecutors cannot seek to appoint enforcement receivers and may not normally seek the imposition of the default term to enforce confiscation orders whilst they remain subject to appeal. In *R v Chichester Magistrates' Court ex p Crowther* [1998] EWHC Admin 960 the High Court held that even a culpable delay by the prosecutor does not constitute a bar to the enforcement of the order. This changed, however, with the decision of the Divisional Court in *Lloyd v Bow Street Magistrates' Court* [2004] 1 Cr App R 11; [2003] EWHC Admin 2294 where the decision of a magistrates' court to activate the default term was quashed by reason of a lengthy delay by the prosecutor in taking action to enforce a confiscation order. As a result of the decision in *Lloyd*, a substantial body of case law has built up dealing with the circumstances in which a delay will result in enforcement proceedings being stayed.

### Activation of the default term

*Delay by the prosecutor*

**11.115** An unreasonable delay in taking enforcement proceedings will act as a bar to the activation of the default term of imprisonment. Whether the delay is unreasonable is a matter of fact to be determined having regard to the circumstances of individual cases. In *Lloyd* a CJA confiscation order had been made against the defendant on 21 June 1996 for £33,236 with an eighteen-month sentence of imprisonment to be served in default of payment. On 10 July 1997, when £26,897.37 was still outstanding, the CPS wrote to the defendant advising him of their intention to apply for the appointment of an enforcement receiver unless the amount owing was paid within fourteen days. No further payments were made, but it was not until 30 November 1998 that the CPS issued an application for the appointment of a receiver. The receiver was duly appointed by an order of the court dated 15 January 1999. Thereafter, it appears there was a breakdown of communication between the CPS and the receiver, the latter claiming never to have received a copy of the order appointing him. The CPS did not write to the receiver to establish what progress had been made in realising the defendant's assets but, on 6 December 1999, wrote to the enforcing magistrates' court saying that no assets had been realised and inviting the court to issue the warrant of commitment. In January 2001 the court issued a summons requiring the defendant to attend for consideration to be given to the warrant being issued, but the hearing did not take place until 9 October 2002 when the defendant was committed to prison.

**11.116** The High Court quashed the warrant of commitment, holding that the delay constituted a breach of the defendant's right under Art 6.1 of the ECHR to a fair trial within a reasonable time. At first sight this might seem surprising, because the primary obligation to satisfy a confiscation order is on the defendant and not on the prosecuting authority or enforcing magistrates' court. If there is a delay it is normally the result of the defendant failing to comply with the terms of the order. This contention was firmly rejected by Dyson LJ in *Lloyd*. He said:

> We do not see how the fact that the defendant is in breach of his continuing duty to satisfy the confiscation order can be relevant. In our view, the conduct of the defendant can have no bearing on the question whether he has a right to have proceedings against him in respect of that conduct instituted and determined within a reasonable time. It is common ground that a defendant is entitled to have a substantive criminal charge against him determined within a reasonable time. That right is predicated on the basis that the defendant is alleged to have broken the law by committing a crime. The fact that a defendant is alleged to have committed a crime is plainly not a reason for denying him the right to have the criminal charged determined within a reasonable time. Indeed, the existence of the criminal charge is the very reason why he has that right. Similarly, in our view, the fact that a defendant is alleged to be in breach of a confiscation order is no reason to deny him the right to have proceedings brought to enforce the order by commitment to prison determined within a reasonable time.

He added:

> Convicted criminals who are the subject of confiscation orders do not attract sympathy and are not entitled to favoured treatment. But there is nothing surprising about a requirement that, if the prosecuting authorities/magistrates' court seek to enforce a confiscation order, they should do so within a reasonable time. It is potentially very unfair on a defendant that he should be liable to be committed to prison for non-payment of sums due under a confiscation order many years after the time for payment has expired, and long after he has been released from custody and resumed work and family life.

**11.117** In a clear warning to the enforcement authorities, Dyson LJ concluded:

> If the authorities whose task it is to enforce confiscation order are so slow in communicating with one another, or in activating enforcement mechanisms that they become in breach of Article 6.1, then the appropriate remedy my well be (as in this case) that the weapon of imprisonment in default is lost. The sooner this is appreciated by all agencies of the criminal justice system, the better.

**11.118** If, of course, the defendant himself is responsible for the delay or, due to the complexity of his financial affairs, his assets take an unusually long time to realise, Art 6.1 will not assist him. As Dyson LJ said:

> It follows that, in deciding what is a reasonable time, regard should be had to the efforts made to extract the money by other methods, for example (as in the present case) by the appointment

of a receiver. If a receiver has been appointed within a reasonable time and has proceeded with reasonable expedition, then the fact that all of this may have taken some time will not prevent the court from concluding that there has been no violation of the defendant's Article 6.1 rights if the unsuccessful attempts to recover the money have led to delay in the institution of proceedings to commit. Likewise, if the defendant has been evasive and has avoided diligent attempts to extract the money from him, he will be unable to rely on the resultant delay in support of an argument that his right to a determination within a reasonable time has been violated.

**11.119** In *R (on the application of Deamer) v Southampton Magistrates' Court* [2006] EWHC 2221 (Admin), the High Court reiterated that a stay on enforcement would only be granted where the delay by the enforcing authority was unreasonable and unjustified.

**11.120** The defendant had applied for judicial review of the District Judge's decision. The Court dismissed the application, Aikens J observing:

> In my view, the District Judge cannot be criticised for her conclusion that the period up to the end of the appointment of the receiver is unexceptional. As to the period when Mr Deamer's solicitors were apparently seeking evidence for the application of a certificate of inadequacy, it seems to me that they were trying to get information to back such an application. At the same time the RCPO were hoping that the information would provide material to show that Mr Deamer indeed had assets to pay the confiscation order. I agree with the District Judge's view that the RCPO might have been naïve in this regard. But I have reached the firm conclusion that it cannot be said that the District Judge's finding on the facts was in any way unreasonable. The solicitors for Mr Deamer did indicate that investigations were going on in the USA, even if they had produced no results.
>
> In my view it cannot be said that the District Judge's conclusion on the reasonableness of RCPO's activity and their stance in relation to these investigations is either irrational or perverse or unreasonable.

**11.121** The decision in *Deamer* makes it clear that mere delay by itself will not be sufficient to justify a stay of the enforcement proceedings. The delay must be one for which the enforcement agency is responsible and which is unreasonable and unjustifiable on the facts. If the defendant causes or contributes to any such delay, it will not normally be appropriate to order a stay of proceedings. This is particularly so where, as in *Deamer*, the enforcement agency had throughout made its intention of enforcing the order abundantly clear.

**11.122** Plainly, whether delay in a particular case is of a nature and duration such as to justify a stay of proceedings is a question of fact and judgment in light of all the circumstances. Illustrative decisions include *Stone v Plymouth Magistrates' Court* [2007] EWHC 2519 (Admin), a case where the Divisional Court quashed a committal warrant that had been issued some thirteen years after a confiscation order had been made in relation to drug trafficking offences. The court said it 'had no doubt' that the delay had been such as to breach the defendant's Art 6.1 rights. A similar approach was taken in *R (on the application of Flaherty) (Claimant) v City of Westminster Magistrates Court (Defendant) & Crown Prosecution Service (Interested Party)* [2008] EWHC 2589 (Admin). A more recent example of the High Court finding unreasonable delay by the prosecutor and the receiver is *Altaf Syed; Trevor Hamilton-Farrell v City of Westminster Magistrates' Court* [2010] EWHC 1617 (Admin).

*Delays caused by the appeal process*

**11.123** In all the cases examined thus far, the allegation was that the prosecutor was responsible for the delays that occurred. In *Minshall v Marylebone Magistrates' Court* [2010] 1 WLR 590;

[2008] EWHC 2800 (Admin), the High Court had to consider the position when all parties accepted that the prosecutor was not at fault, but that the delay had occurred during a lengthy appeal process triggered by the defendant exercising his right of appeal against conviction and the resulting confiscation order. The High Court ruled that as the state is responsible for the appeal mechanism, a delay in the appeal process could amount to an unreasonable delay within the meaning of Art 6.1, but held that on the facts of the defendant's case the delay was reasonable.

However, in *Minshall v The United Kingdom*, (2012) 55 EHRR 36; [2011] ECHR 2243, the **11.124** Strasbourg Court found that, contrary to the view taken by the Divisional Court, there had been a breach of Article 6.1. This was on the basis of the period of unreasonable delay attributable to the state, namely the period while Minshall's case was stayed pending the outcome of the decision of the House of Lords in *Soneji*. In order to understand this reasoning, it is necessary to examine the facts of *Bullen and Soneji v The United Kingdom* [2009] ECHR 28.

On the facts of *Bullen and Soneji* there had been a lengthy delay as a result of appeal proceedings **11.125** taken in respect of the confiscation orders. The applicants had pursued an appeal to the Court of Appeal and the Crown had appealed to the House of Lords. On the basis of this delay the applicants complained that their Art 6.1 rights had been violated. The Court found that the relevant period of delay had been five years and six months, beginning on the date of the applicants' conviction, on which day they became liable to a confiscation order, and ending with the date of the decision of the House of Lords to allow the Crown's appeal and reinstate the confiscation orders. The government contended that the prosecutor had acted with reasonable expedition at all times and that any delays were not attributable to the state. If the applicants had not raised objections to the Crown Court's jurisdiction to make the confiscation orders, the proceedings would have been concluded much earlier.

The European Court of Human Rights held unanimously that the applicants' Art 6.1 **11.126** rights had been violated. The Court reiterated that Art 6.1 rights applied throughout proceedings for the determination of a criminal charge and extended to the confiscation proceedings. The Court in accordance with the criteria it had previously set out in many judgments such as *Crowther v The United Kingdom* 53741/00 [2005] ECHR 45, held that the reasonableness of the length of the proceedings must be assessed 'in the light of the circumstances of the case and with reference to the following criteria: the complexity of the case, the conduct of the applicants and the relevant authorities and what was at stake for the applicants'.

The Court found that the applicants could not be criticised for exercising their legal entitle- **11.127** ment to have the question of the Crown Court's jurisdiction to make the confiscation orders challenged on appeal and the delay that arose in consequence could not be attributed to their conduct. The Court went on to consider what was at stake for the applicants and noted that they faced confiscation orders in which they were required to pay substantial sums of money—£30,284 and £75,350 with default sentences of twelve and twenty-one months respectively. The Court concluded that:

> In the light of the importance of what was at stake for the applicants in this case and without discounting the complexity of the legal issue in question, the Court finds the period of delay attributable to the State, when taken cumulatively, to be unreasonably long and in breach of the reasonable time requirement as provided in Article 6 of the Convention.

**11.128**   As the applicants did not make a claim for just satisfaction, the Court made no order other than declaring that there had been a violation of the applicants' Art 6.1 rights in relation to the delay.

**11.129**   In summary, therefore, delays in the appeal process may give rise to a breach of Art 6.1, the remedy for which may be to refuse to commit the defendant to prison for non-payment. As to whether there has been a breach of Art 6.1 will depend on all the circumstances. The conduct of the parties will clearly be a highly relevant feature. In *Minshall*, the Court was plainly correct to take into account the defendant's non-cooperative stance, even if, on the facts, its ultimate decision was disapproved of by the ECtHR. The court will, however, also need to consider what is at stake for the defendant and, where a substantial confiscation order and lengthy default sentence is involved, the court is likely to look at delay, including delay occasioned by any appeal proceedings, with particular care. The case should act as a reminder to prosecutors to pursue confiscation investigations with all due expedition.

### Other methods of enforcement

**11.130**   In *Lloyd v Bow Street Magistrates' Court* [2004] 1 Cr App R 11; [2003] EWHC 2294 (Admin), the Divisional Court emphasised that its decision applied only to the enforcement of confiscation orders by means of committal to prison and did not extend to civil methods of enforcement. In *Joyce v Dover Magistrates' Court* [2008] EWHC 1448 (Admin), the High Court had to consider the effect of a delay when an attempt was being made to enforce a confiscation order by the employment of civil remedies. A confiscation order had been made against the defendant as long ago as 1993. It was accepted that the delay was such that it was no longer appropriate to enforce the confiscation order by activation of the default term of imprisonment, but the Court proceeded to hold an enforcement hearing to determine whether any of the civil means of enforcing the order would be appropriate. The defendant asked the district judge to stay the enforcement hearing as an abuse of process, but he declined to do so giving the following reasons:

> (1) Mr Joyce has made no payments whatsoever in the 14 years since this order was made; (2) that there has never been any offer of any sort of satisfaction in any form from Mr Joyce relating to this order; (3) not only has there never been any attempt by Mr Joyce to reach a resolution of the order, he himself delayed enforcement proceedings for some significant period by indicating periodically that he would be seeking a certificate of inadequacy, which in the event he never pursued; (4) Mr Joyce has throughout been aware of his continuing liability to satisfy this order; (5) for the 3 year period from March 2004 to April 2007 Mr Joyce was unlawfully at large, fully aware of his duty to surrender to the court, but failed to do so. I cannot see how, taking these factors into account, that it can be maintained that it would be an abuse of the process of this court to enforce any of the methods of enforcement available, other than committal to prison. Given Mr Joyce's own responsibility for some significant periods of delay, his complaint that the enforcement authorities should be prevented by this court from seeking satisfaction of this long outstanding debt is in my view wholly unsustainable.

**11.131**   The defendant sought judicial review of the district judge's decision. There was an issue between the parties as to whether Art 6.1 rights extended to the enforcement of confiscation orders by the employment of civil remedies, but the Court declined to rule on this point because it was accepted that the law of abuse of process applied to such proceedings and that these gave the defendant as much protection as the ECHR. Maurice Kay LJ said:

> There is a debate in the skeleton arguments about the position under Article 6 of the ECHR, and the right to a fair hearing within a reasonable time. The submission on behalf of the respondent

is that Article 6 does not apply to this stage of the enforcement of a confiscation order by means other than a warrant of commitment, because it does not involve a determination of civil rights and obligations, nor is it now the determination of a criminal charge. However, this is something of a sterile debate, because it is common ground that the common law of abuse of process is applicable to these proceedings and that this is no less protective than Article 6 would be. In the circumstances, I propose to deal with the case on a common law basis.

The Court concluded that there was no abuse of process in the defendant's case and dismissed his claim for judicial review. Maurice Kay LJ said: **11.132**

For my part I do not doubt that enforcement proceedings such as these do not fall outside the ambit of abuse of process. For example, if the enforcement authority were to manipulate the procedure, a finding of abuse could follow. But in the present case, no manipulation or bad faith is suggested. It is put as a case of culpable delay, pure and simple. Moreover, it is not suggested that the passage of time would prevent a fair assessment of the claimant's means and ability to discharge the order. Such matters are within the knowledge of the claimant.

The Court also stressed that an application for judicial review could only succeed if it could **11.133** be shown that the decision of the enforcing magistrates' court was *Wednesbury* unreasonable. Maurice Kay LJ concluded:

In this application for judicial review the question becomes whether that conclusion and the reasoning which led to it are vitiated on *Wednesbury* grounds. This is common ground. In my judgment, they are not so vitiated. I accept that there may be cases in which delay is so extensive and so culpable, or unexplained, that a stay will be appropriate. However, the District Judge's reasons for refusing a stay in the present cased are, in my judgment, unassailable.

It is clear therefore that the employment of civil methods of enforcement is vulnerable to **11.134** challenge where the delay is such as to amount to an abuse of process. In the case of *Joyce* a significant factor in the failure of the application was the defendant's own conduct which had played a major part in the delay. If he had cooperated with the enforcement authorities, not absconded, and pursued his stated intention of applying for a certificate of inadequacy the outcome may well have been different.

The principle in *Joyce* was followed in *CPS v Derby and South Derbyshire Magistrates' Court* **11.135** [2010] EWHC 370 (Admin), a case which illustrated the fact that the victims of crime may have an interest in the ongoing availability of civil means of enforcement. In that case the defendant, a convicted thief, had been made the subject of both a confiscation order and a compensation order. Following protracted attempts to enforce the order, the case came before a deputy district judge to consider an application for a warrant of commitment. The judge found there had been an unreasonable delay by the CPS in bringing the application. On this basis, not only did he decide to stay the committal proceedings as an abuse of process, but he also stayed any available civil means of enforcing the confiscation order and the compensation order. The effect of this ruling was that the magistrates' court could play no further part in securing any payments. On appeal, the Divisional Court concluded that the deputy district judge had been entitled to stay the committal proceedings, but his decision to stay the other available means of enforcing the order had been unreasonable. In overturning the decision, the Court noted that the effect of the lower court's decision had been to deprive the victims of any further possibility of compensation.

# 12

# THE INSOLVENT DEFENDANT

## A. Introduction

It is not unusual for a defendant to become insolvent either before or during the course **12.01** of restraint and confiscation proceedings. There are a number of possible reasons for this. A defendant who has a business experiencing cash flow difficulties may be tempted to commit criminal offences as a means of alleviating his problems. He may, for example, commit income, corporation, or value added tax offences, or even become involved in other criminal offences such as drug trafficking in the hope of raising funds to overcome his financial difficulties. Once a defendant has been arrested and charged he may be unable to continue to work and meet his debts, especially if he has been remanded in custody, and third-party creditors may institute civil proceedings to recover debts owing to them. It is also not uncommon for a defendant to try and make himself bankrupt with a view to rendering any restraint or confiscation proceedings ineffective. Finally, in cases where the Crown has suffered a significant loss, for example in a VAT carousel or 'MTIC' fraud, law enforcement agencies may institute civil proceedings to recover their loss and seek the appointment of a provisional liquidator over the companies involved. In this chapter we examine the provisions of The Proceeds of Crime Act 2002 (POCA) in relation to the insolvent defendant.

## B. The Position under POCA

Part 9 of POCA deals with insolvency and maintains the 'first come, first served' rule in the **12.02** previous legislation. That is to say that, in most circumstances, a restraint order will take priority provided it was first in time and, similarly, insolvency proceedings will take precedence if they were brought before a restraint order is made.

### Bankruptcy

Bankruptcy is dealt with by ss 417 to 419 of POCA. Section 417 deals with the position **12.03** where the bankruptcy post-dates the restraint order and provides that in such circumstances the restrained assets shall be excluded from the defendant's estate for the purposes of the bankruptcy. By s 417(1) and (2) of POCA (as amended by para 69 of Pt 1 to Sch 8 of the Serious Crime Act 2007):

(1) This section applies if a person is adjudged bankrupt in England and Wales.

(2) The following property is excluded from his estate for the purposes of Part 9 of the 1986 Act—

    (a) property for the time being subject to a restraint order which was made under section 41, 120 or 190 before the order adjudging him bankrupt;

    (b) any property in respect of which an order under section 50 is in force;

    (c) any property in respect of which an order section 128(3) is in force;

    (d) any property in respect of which an order under section 198 is in force.

**12.04** References to 'the 1986 Act' are to the Insolvency Act 1986: see s 434(1)(d) of POCA. It is important to note that the key date for determining priority is the date on which a restraint or enforcement receivership order is made. The date on which a confiscation order is made is immaterial for this purpose. Thus, if a confiscation order has been made in a case where there is no restraint or enforcement receivership order in force, the bankruptcy order will take precedence even if it post-dates the confiscation order. If a prosecutor wishes to protect assets to satisfy a confiscation order, he should always seek a restraint order in any cases where there is a real risk of a bankruptcy order being made. The date on which the bankruptcy order is made determines which order has priority and not the date on which the petition is lodged: see s 417(1).

**12.05** Section 418 of POCA (as amended by para 70 of Pt 1 of Sch 8 to the Serious Crime Act 2007) deals with the position where the bankruptcy order is first in time and provides:

(1) If a person is adjudged bankrupt in England and Wales the powers referred to in subsection (2) must not be exercised in relation to the property referred to in subsection (3).

(2) These are the powers—

    (a) the powers conferred on a court by sections 41 to 67 and the powers of a referred appointed under section 48 or 50;

    (b) the powers conferred on a court by sections 120 to 136 and Schedule 3 and the powers of an administrator appointed under section 125 or 128(3).

    (c) the powers conferred on a court by sections 190 to 215 and the powers of a receiver appointed under section 196 or 198.

(3) This is the property—

    (a) property which is for the time being comprised in the bankrupt's estate for the purposes of Part 9 of the 1986 Act;

    (b) property in respect of which his trustee in bankruptcy may (without leave of the court) serve a notice under section 307, 308 or 308A of the 1986 Act (after acquired property, tools, tenancies etc);

    (c) property which is to be applied for the benefit of creditors of the bankrupt by virtue of a condition imposed under section 280(2)(c) of the 1986 Act;

    (d) in a case where a confiscation order has been made under section 6 or 156 of this Act, any sums in the hands of a receiver appointed under section 50 or 198 of this Act after the amount required to be paid under the confiscation order has been fully paid;

    (e) in a case where a confiscation order has been made under section 92 of this Act, any sums remaining in the hands of an administrator appointed under section 128 of this Act after the amount required to be paid under the confiscation order has been fully paid.

**12.06** This section again gives effect to the 'first come, first served' rule by providing that if the order adjudging the defendant bankrupt comes first in time, the court may not make restraint or receivership orders over any property referred to in s 418(3).

Section 419 makes provision in relation to tainted gifts and provides that no order under **12.07**
the Insolvency Act 1986 may be made in relation to property that amounts to a tainted gift
provided it is subject to a restraint or enforcement receivership order.

### Winding up of companies

Section 426 of POCA makes similar provision in relation to the winding up of companies. **12.08**
By s 426(2)(a), where a court has made a winding-up order or the company passes a resolution for its voluntary winding up, the functions of the liquidator (or any provisional liquidator) may not be exercised in relation to property subject to a restraint order made before the
relevant time. Section 426(9) defines the relevant time as:

(a) if no order for the winding up of the company has been made, the time of the passing of
the resolution for voluntary winding up;
(b) if such an order has been made, but before the presentation of the petition for the winding
up of the company by the court such a resolution has been passed by the company, the
time of the passing of the resolution;
(c) if such an order has been made, but paragraph (b) does not apply, the time of the making
of the order.

Section 426(4) and (5) deals with the situation where the order or resolution for winding **12.09**
up pre-dates a restraint order and provides that the powers of the court to make restraint
and receivership orders must not be exercised in a way mentioned in s 426(6) in relation to
property held by the company and in relation to which the functions of the liquidator are
exercisable. Section 426(6) provides:

(6) the powers must not be exercised—
(a) so as to inhibit the liquidator from exercising his functions for the purpose of distributing property to the company's creditors;
(b) so as to prevent the payment out of any property of expenses (including the remuneration of the liquidator or any provisional liquidator) properly incurred in respect
of the property.

### Floating charges

Creditors, particularly financial institutions, frequently hold a floating charge over a compa- **12.10**
ny's assets as security for a loan. The terms of the charge will normally empower the creditor
to appoint an administrative receiver, without the necessity to make an application to court,
for the purpose of taking control of the assets subject to the charge. The relationship between
such charges and restraint orders and court-appointed receivers is provided for in s 430 of
POCA. Again, the rule is generally one of 'first come, first served'. By s 430(2) the functions
of a receiver appointed pursuant to a floating charge are not exercisable in relation to property subject to a restraint order made prior to the appointment of the receiver. Similarly, if the
receiver is appointed prior to the application for the restraint order, s 430(4) provides that
the administrative receivership shall take precedence, and the powers of the court to make
restraint orders and to appoint management and enforcement receivers shall not be used in
a way mentioned in s 430(6). By s 430(6):

The powers shall not be exercised—
(a) so as to inhibit the receiver from exercising his functions for the purpose of distributing
property to the company's creditors;
(b) so as to prevent the payment out of any property of expenses (including the remuneration
of the receiver) properly incurred in the exercise of his functions in respect of the property.

### Limited liability partnerships

**12.11**  By s 431 of POCA, the provisions as to the winding up of companies and floating charges apply equally to limited liability partnerships that are capable of being wound up under the Insolvency Act 1986.

### Protection of insolvency practitioners

**12.12**  Section 432(1) and (2) of POCA gives protection to insolvency practitioners who mistakenly deal in realisable property providing that they will only be liable to pay damages for their actions if they are negligent. The section also empowers them to recover their remuneration and expenses, and gives them a lien over the property and the proceeds of sale for payment.

### Relationship between insolvency and external restraint orders

**12.13**  The principles above do not apply to the relationship between insolvency and restraint orders emanating from external requests from foreign jurisdictions; for those principles see the Court of Appeal's judgment in *Stanford International Bank Ltd (acting by its joint liquidators) v SFO* [2010] 3 WLR 941 (at the time of writing the subject of an appeal to the Supreme Court). At para 74 of his judgment the Chancellor noted that Part 9 of POCA has not been replicated in the Proceeds of Crime Act 2002 (External Requests and Orders) Order 2005.

## C. Insolvency and Confiscation Orders

**12.14**  In the case of *R v Shahid* [2009] EWCA Crim 831; [2009] 2 Cr App R (S) 105, the Court of Appeal held that the mere fact that a bankruptcy order has been made does not necessarily preclude the making of a confiscation order under the CJA even though difficulties might arise at the enforcement stage. On 30 September 2005 a confiscation order was made against the defendant for £135,524.60 notwithstanding that on 1 September 2005 a bankruptcy order had been made in respect of the defendant on his own petition for bankruptcy. The appellant argued that the bankruptcy order deprived the judge of jurisdiction to make the confiscation order some four weeks later. The Court of Appeal disagreed and dismissed the appeal. Keith J said:

> As a matter of principle, we do not think that a bankrupt's assets being in the hands of the trustee in bankruptcy affects the position at all. The bankruptcy may be highly relevant to the enforcement of a confiscation order, but not to the making of such an order in the first place. That, we think, is the explicit effect of section 102(8) of the 1988 Act, which defines what is meant by the phrase 'property held by a person' which relates back, inter alia, to the definition of 'realisable property' in section 74(1) of the 1988 Act, which refers to 'any property held by the defendant'. Section 102(8) reads:
>
>> 'References to property held by a person include a reference to property vested in the trustee in bankruptcy, permanent or interim trustee within the meaning of the Bankruptcy (Scotland) Act 1985 or liquidator.'
>
> So if the property held by the defendant for the purposes of making a confiscation order includes property vested in his trustee in bankruptcy, it is impossible to say that a confiscation order cannot be made against a bankrupt.

**12.15**  The wording of s 102(8) of the CJA is replicated in s 84(2)(d) of POCA meaning that property vested in his trustee in bankruptcy or liquidator is still property held by the defendant for the purposes of making a confiscation order. Keith J added in *Shahid*:

In our view, the difficulties which are said to arise as a result of the tension between these two legal processes are significantly reduced when one focuses, once again, on the making of the confiscation order as opposed to its enforcement. The prosecution accepts that its powers may well be severely restricted when it comes to the enforcement of a confiscation order, which is where the tension really lies. We have not been persuaded that the making of a confiscation order, which will focus on what the offender's realisable assets are rather than how their realisation can be enforced, brings the tension between confiscation and bankruptcy into play. Indeed, as Hallett LJ pointed out in the course of argument, if the public interest is a relevant factor at all, the public interest would not be served if a defendant was able to avoid a confiscation order by the simple expedient of applying for his own bankruptcy before the hearing of the application for a confiscation order takes place. It is no argument to say that the prosecution could protect itself by making an application for a restraint order, because the circumstances entitling the prosecution to apply for a restraint order may either not be known to the prosecution or may not even exist.

The same position applies under POCA. Under s 9(1)(a) of POCA, when determining the **12.16** value of the available amount of a defendant in order to make a confiscation order against him, only sums required to meet priority obligations are to be deducted from the free property held by a defendant. Section 9(2)(b) of POCA provides that priority obligations include obligations to pay a sum which would be included among preferential debts under s 386 of the Insolvency Act 1986 if the defendant's bankruptcy had commenced on the date of the confiscation order or his winding up had been ordered on that date. Preferential debts are limited to those defined under Sch 6 to the Insolvency Act 1986. No other unsecured debts owed by the defendant, apart from criminal fines under s 9(2)(a) of POCA, are priority obligations so that their value cannot be deducted from the available amount when calculating a confiscation order so that a confiscation order is capable of being made despite the existence of a bankruptcy order.

However, as Keith J foresaw, the problem is likely to come at the enforcement stage where, **12.17** absent a restraint order coming first in time, the bankruptcy order will take precedence over any confiscation order and, unless the value of the defendant's estate is greater than that necessary to pay off his creditors, the confiscation order will stand little chance of being satisfied. If the prosecutor has obtained a restraint order prior to any bankruptcy order being made, this problem will not arise as satisfaction of the confiscation order will take priority over the bankruptcy. This problem was confronted head on in the enforcement of Mr Shahid's confiscation order, as anticipated, because no restraint order had been in place prior to his bankruptcy. In *R (on the application of Shahid) v Birmingham Magistrates' Court (Defendant) & Department for Work & Pensions (Interested Party)* [2010] EWHC 2969 (Admin), the Divisional Court (Richards LJ, Cranston J) quashed the order of the magistrates' court committing Mr Shahid to prison to serve his default term for non-payment of his confiscation order. The Court relied on the fact that Mr Shahid had been granted a certificate of inadequacy by the High Court under s 83(1) of the CJA because his assets were vested in the trustee in bankruptcy who indicated no funds would be returned to him. However, Mr Shahid's confiscation order had not yet been varied by the Crown Court pursuant to s 83(4) of the CJA so that the original confiscation order remained in place. Enforcement proceedings were therefore remitted back to the magistrates' court by the Divisional Court on the basis that they may or may not be pursued depending on the terms of the variation of the confiscation order yet to be made by the Crown Court. Assuming the bankruptcy was still in effect, Mr Shahid's assets remained vested in the trustee, and there were no newly acquired assets, the likely outcome was that the Crown Court would reduce Mr Shahid's confiscation order to a nil sum and that the magistrates' court enforcement proceedings would therefore be withdrawn.

**12.18** Therefore prosecutors and financial investigators should always be alive to the risk of a defendant petitioning for his own bankruptcy as a means of evading a confiscation order, and also of the risk that third-party creditors may seek to protect their position by means of bankruptcy proceedings and, wherever the circumstances justify it, seek a restraint order to protect assets for the purpose of satisfying the confiscation order.

## D. Interaction between Restraint and Insolvency Proceedings

**12.19** It is by no means uncommon for restraint and insolvency actions to proceed concurrently in respect of companies holding realisable property. This is particularly common in VAT 'carousel' or 'MTIC' fraud cases where there has been a significant loss—often many millions of pounds—to the Exchequer. It is understandable that, in such circumstances, the government department suffering the loss, usually HMRC, wishes to pursue every remedy at its disposal to recoup the loss that has been sustained. In circumstances where the restraint and insolvency proceedings are serving separate and distinct purposes it is submitted this course of action is entirely unobjectionable.

**12.20** Problems can arise, however, when restraint and insolvency proceedings are pursued in relation to the same assets. This is particularly so where a management receiver has been appointed and both he and a liquidator or provisional liquidator are pursuing the same assets. They will both be seeking to claim their remuneration and expenses from the assets under their control and may well each have solicitors and other agents acting for them at considerable expense. In such circumstances, there is a real risk of a duplication of effort and the receiver and liquidator competing for the same assets which, one way or another, will all go to the benefit of the Crown if the proceedings are successful, whether in the liquidation proceedings or by way of the satisfaction of a confiscation order.

**12.21** It is submitted that it cannot be sensible for this to be allowed to occur and that all law enforcement agencies should have regard to the following principles:

(1) A restraint order is not a remedy in itself but is an interim order intended to preserve assets to make them available to satisfy a confiscation order. It follows from this that once a restraint order is in place, law enforcement agencies should not, without good and sufficient reason, change tactics and institute proceedings in the civil courts in relation to the same assets.

(2) If civil proceedings are instituted, the duty under s 6 of POCA to make a confiscation order becomes a mere power: see s 6(6). The institution of civil proceedings in these circumstances would represent a significant change in circumstances and, in compliance with his ongoing duty to give full and frank disclosure, the prosecutor should notify the court forthwith.

(3) Guidance issued by the Home Secretary and Attorney General indicates that benefit derived from criminal activities should normally be recovered through prosecution and the making of confiscation orders.

This does not necessarily mean that civil proceedings should never be brought in cases where **12.22** restraint and confiscation orders are actively being pursued. Indeed, there may be compelling reasons why, on the facts of individual cases, civil proceedings should be brought. If, for example, civil proceedings will allow assets to be recovered that would otherwise be unavailable then such a course would be entirely justified. Law enforcement agencies should, however, proceed with caution and only resort to civil proceedings where there is some appreciable benefit to be gained from doing so. There should also be close liaison with prosecutors to ensure that there is no duplication of effort and that they comply with the ongoing duties to provide full and frank disclosure.

# 13

## CIVIL RECOVERY: PROPERTY FREEZING ORDERS; RECEIVERS; AND LEGAL EXPENSES

## A. Introduction

**13.01**  Civil recovery of the proceeds of crime includes both recovery in the High Court (under Chapter 2 of Pt 5 of POCA) and the recovery of cash in summary proceedings (under Chapter 3 of Pt 5 of POCA). As a result, Pt 5 of the Act has two purposes: firstly, to enable the relevant agency to recover in civil proceedings before the High Court property that is, or represents, property obtained through unlawful conduct; and secondly, to enable cash which is, or represents, property obtained through unlawful conduct, or which is intended to be used in unlawful conduct, to be forfeited in civil proceedings before a magistrates' court.

**13.02**  The second of these objectives is considered fully in Chapter 15.

**13.03**  The first objective, to enable the relevant agency ('the enforcement authority') to recover property in civil proceedings before the High Court, is considered in this and the next chapter.

**13.04**  For ease of reference we have divided civil recovery into two parts. First, in this chapter, we give an overview of the legislation in relation to civil recovery and then look at the interim measures anticipated by the Act, namely Property Freezing Orders (PFOs), Management Receiving Orders (MROs), and Interim Receiving Orders (IROs), before considering insolvency, compensation, and how to obtain the release of funds to cover legal expenses in civil recovery cases.

**13.05**  In the next chapter we consider recovery orders themselves; decisions concerning the ECHR; the pension provisions; and the Pt 6 taxation powers.

## B. Overview in Relation to Civil Recovery

### The rise and fall of the Assets Recovery Agency

**13.06**  The civil recovery provisions came into force on 24 February 2003, SI 2003/120. The Act, in its original form, created a new government agency, known as the Assets Recovery Agency

(ARA). ARA's task was to implement the new legislation and spearhead the new powers in relation to civil recovery.

Whilst ARA enjoyed a measurable success before the courts (particularly with challenges to **13.07** the legislation), it nevertheless failed to come close to collecting its target figures. One of the problems cited was delays with legal aid, which created a considerable backlog in claims. The cost of ARA, which employed 162 staff, to June 2005, was £29 million. This led the press and other commentators to question whether it represented value for money, which in turn applied pressure on ministers to consider yet more reform.

As a result, s 74 of the Serious Crime Act 2007 (SCA) abolished ARA with effect from 1 April **13.08** 2008. Schedule 8 of the SCA transferred the civil recovery powers of ARA to SOCA and extended those powers to the DPP, the Director of the RCPO (now merged with the CPS), and the Director of the SFO.

In SOCA's first year it collected £16.7 million in relation to civil and tax recovery, exceeding **13.09** the government's rather modest target of £16 million, with the other agencies contributing a further £2 million plus. This compared with £7.7 million in ARA's last year of operation (SOCA annual report 2009). Progress has been steady; in the 2011/12 financial year, SOCA froze £5.6 million pursuant to civil and tax powers, with a further £14.1 million recovered pursuant to civil recovery orders and civil recovery consent orders. The Crime and Courts Act 2013 includes the abolition of the Serious Organised Crime Agency, and the creation of the National Crime Agency (NCA) (see ss 1–16). Subject to Parliamentary processes the ambition is that it will be fully operational by December 2013. Section 1 of the Crime and Courts Act 2013 provides:

(1) A National Crime Agency, consisting of the NCA officers, is to be formed.
(2) The NCA is to be under the direction and control of one of the NCA officers, who is to be known as the Director General of the National Crime Agency.
(3) The NCA is to have—
   (a) the functions conferred by this section;
   (b) the functions conferred by the Proceeds of Crime Act 2002; and
   (c) the other functions conferred by this Act and by other enactments.
(4) The NCA is to have the function (the 'crime-reduction function') of securing that efficient and effective activities to combat organised crime and serious crime are carried out (whether by the NCA, other law enforcement agencies, or other persons).
(5) The NCA is to have the function (the 'criminal intelligence function') of gathering, storing, processing, analysing, and disseminating information that is relevant to any of the following—
   (a) activities to combat organised crime or serious crime;
   (b) activities to combat any other kind of crime;
   (c) exploitation proceeds investigations (within the meaning of section 341(5) of the Proceeds of Crime Act 2002), exploitation proceeds orders (within the meaning of Part 7 of the Coroners and Justice Act 2009), and applications for such orders.
(6) The NCA must discharge the crime-reduction function in the following ways (in particular).
(7) The first way is by the NCA itself—
   (a) preventing and detecting organised crime and serious crime,
   (b) investigating offences relating to organised crime or serious crime, and

(c) otherwise carrying out activities to combat organised crime and serious crime, including by instituting criminal proceedings in England and Wales and Northern Ireland.

(8) The second way is by the NCA securing that activities to combat organised crime or serious crime are carried out by persons other than the NCA.

(9) The third way is by the NCA securing improvements—

(a) in co-operation between persons who carry out activities to combat organised crime or serious crime, and

(b) in co-ordination of activities to combat organised crime or serious crime.

(10) The crime-reduction function does not include—

(a) the function of the NCA itself prosecuting offences; or

(b) the function of the NCA itself instituting criminal proceedings in Scotland.

(11) In this Part, a reference to activities to combat crime (or a particular kind of crime, such as organised crime or serious crime) is a reference to—

(a) the prevention and detection of crime (or that kind of crime),

(b) the investigation and prosecution of offences (or offences relating to that kind of crime),

(c) the reduction of crime (or that kind of crime) in other ways, and

(d) the mitigation of the consequences of crime (or that kind of crime);

and references to the carrying out of activities to combat crime (or a particular kind of crime) are to be construed accordingly.

**13.10**  As a result, the civil recovery function of SOCA will be transferred to the new NCA. The other amendments and the broadening of the scope of the NCA's role may be seen as consistent with one of the main purposes of the Proceeds of Crime Act, namely the reduction of crime.

**13.11**  Under s 2A of the amended POCA, the various directors are required to exercise their functions under POCA 'in the way best calculated to contribute to the reduction of crime'.

**13.12**  In doing so the directors must have regard to guidance issued by the Secretary of State and the Attorney General. Importantly, pursuant to s 2A(4), that guidance must indicate that 'the reduction of crime is in general best secured by means of criminal investigations and criminal proceedings'.

**13.13**  Section 2A(4) appears to give a steer in that it signals that criminal investigations and criminal proceedings should be seen as the preferential route for the reduction of crime. As a secondary route, POCA anticipates that where criminal investigations or proceedings cannot be taken forward, other methods, such as civil recovery, may be deployed.

### The enforcement authority

**13.14**  The power to recover in civil proceedings before the High Court is reserved to the 'enforcement authority'. The definition of enforcement authority is set out at s 316(1) of the Act and includes SOCA (soon to be the NCA), the DPP (the CPS), and the Director of the SFO.

### Proceedings even on acquittal

**13.15**  Under s 240(2) it is possible to invoke civil recovery and cash forfeiture proceedings even though proceedings have not been brought for a criminal offence in connection with the property, eg where there may be insufficient grounds for a prosecution, or the suspect is outside of the jurisdiction, or has died:

The powers conferred by this Part are exercisable in relation to any property (including cash) whether or not any proceedings have been brought for an offence in connection with that property.

It should be noted that cases where criminal proceedings have been brought include cases **13.16** where a defendant has been acquitted, as they too fall within the scheme of Pt 5. In *Director of the Assets Recovery Agency v Taher and others* [2006] EWHC 3402 (Admin), Collins J confirmed the effect of the legislation:

> The legislation provides that if the Director is able to establish on the balance of probabilities that assets are the proceeds of crime, they are recoverable even if there has been a prosecution which has not succeeded and even if there has been no prosecution, because, for example, the view has been taken that evidence would not be sufficient to establish criminality beyond reasonable doubt.

This reasoning has been extended to circumstances where the respondent's conviction had been quashed because his arrest had been unlawful (*Serious Organised Crime Agency v Olden* [2009] EWHC 610). For acquitals by foreign courts, see *SOCA v Namli, and others* [2013] EWHC 1200 QB.

### Standard and burden of proof

Section 241(3) states: **13.17**

> The court . . . must decide on *a balance of probabilities* whether it is proved:
> (a) that any matters alleged to constitute unlawful conduct have occurred, or
> (b) that any person intended to use any cash in unlawful conduct.

The standard of proof applicable is that which normally applies to civil matters, ie the balance of probabilities, and not the criminal standard of beyond reasonable doubt. It will be noted that the Act is specific in that it states that the burden is on 'the balance of probabilities' and not 'to the civil standard'. POCA is thus proactively encouraging the courts to apply a 51/49 per cent 'more likely than not' balance of probabilities test.

Griffith Williams J considered the issue of standard and burden of proof in *SOCA v Gale and* **13.18** *others* [2009] EWHC 1015. He observed as follows (at 9):

> The burden of proof is on the claimant and the standard of proof they must satisfy is the balance of probabilities. While the claimant alleged serious criminal conduct, the criminal standard of proof does not apply, although 'cogent evidence is generally required to satisfy a civil tribunal that a person has been fraudulent or behaved in some other reprehensible manner. But the question is always whether the tribunal thinks it more probable than not'—see *Secretary of State for the Home Department v Rehman* [2003] 1 AC 153 at paragraph 55 *per* Lord Hoffmann.

The standard of proof appropriate in deciding whether matters alleged to constitute unlaw- **13.19** ful conduct have occurred was considered by Collins J in *R (on the application of the Director of the Assets Recovery Agency) v (1) Jia Jin He and (2) Dan Dan Chen* [2004] EWHC 3021 (Admin), in which he found that 'cogent' evidence, although no gloss, was required. He stated:

> As a general rule, no doubt, criminal conduct may be regarded as less probable than non-criminal conduct. But where there is evidence from which a court can be satisfied that it is more probable than not that criminal conduct has been involved, it does not seem to me that that is something that is so improbable as to require a gloss on the standard of proof. However, I recognise, and it is no doubt right, that since it is necessary to establish that there

has been criminal conduct in the obtaining of the property, the court should look for cogent evidence before deciding that the balance of probabilities has been met. But I have no doubt that Parliament deliberately referred to the balance of probabilities, and that the court should not place a gloss upon it, so as to require that the standard approach is that appropriate in a criminal case. Apart from anything else, if that were necessary, then the effectiveness of, in particular, Part 5 of the Act would be to a considerable extent removed... It is plain that Parliament deliberately imposed a lower standard of proof as the standard appropriate for these proceedings.

**13.20**  In the case of *Gale and others v SOCA [2011] UKSC* 49 the issue was considered by the Supreme Court, which was unanimous in rejecting the proposition that the criminal standard of proof should be applied in civil recovery proceedings.

**13.21**  In *Director of the Assets Recovery Agency v Jeffrey David Green* [2005] EWHC 3168 (Admin), The Times, 27 February 2006, Sullivan J stated (at para 19) that when read in the context of s 240 and the remainder of s 241, it was plain that Parliament envisaged that in civil recovery proceedings the Director would identify the matters alleged to constitute unlawful conduct in sufficient detail to enable the court 'not to decide whether a particular crime had been committed by a particular individual, but to decide whether the conduct so described was unlawful under the criminal law of the UK' (or the criminal law of the United Kingdom and the foreign country in question). He stated that any litigant in civil proceedings seeking to recover property upon the basis that it had been obtained by unlawful conduct would be expected to identify (a) the property, and (b) the conduct that was said to be unlawful (para 23). For a recent example of *Green* being followed see *SOCA v Hymans and others* [2011] EWHC 3332 (QB).

### Civil proceedings

**13.22**  In *Jia Jin He* Collins J stated that there was 'no doubt' that in domestic law proceedings under Pt 5 are classified as civil proceedings (para 47). In so finding, he adopted the decision of Coghlin J in the *Director of the Assets Recovery Agency v Walsh* [2004] NIQB 21 where his Lordship considered the three principal criteria identified in *Engel v The Netherlands (No 1)* (1976) 1 EHRR 647 (para 13) for civil proceedings namely:

(i)  the manner in which the domestic state classifies the proceedings [although this normally carries comparatively little weight and is regarded as a starting point rather than determinative—see *Ozturk v Germany* (1984) 6 EHRR 409 at 421 and 422];

(ii)  the nature of the conduct in question classified objectively bearing in mind the object and purpose of the Convention;

(iii)  the severity of any possible penalty—severe penalties, including those with imprisonment in default and penalties intended to deter, are pointers towards a criminal classification of proceedings—see *Schmautzer v Austria* (1995) 21 EHRR 511.

**13.23**  Having applied the approach in *Engel* (confirmed as appropriate by the House of Lords in *R v H* [2003] 1 All ER 497) Coghlin J found the civil recovery scheme to be civil in nature, a view Collins J in *Jia Jin He* concurred with.

### The distinction between recovery proceedings and confiscation proceedings

**13.24**  There are a number of fundamental differences between the two schemes, including the distinct procedural requirements that govern the appropriate proceedings.

In *Director of the Assets Recovery Agency v Ashton* [2006] EWHC 1064 Newman J **13.25**
endorsed (at para 50) the following distinctions between civil recovery and confiscation
proceedings:

- No conviction is necessary in recovery order proceedings (indeed civil recovery proceedings may be brought where no offence has been charged or where a defendant has
  been tried and acquitted), whereas a confiscation order can only be made if there has
  been a conviction.
- No one stands in jeopardy.
- Enforcement is through a trustee, as opposed to an enforcement magistrates' court.
- Confiscation proceedings are dealt with by criminal courts (albeit operating on the civil
  standard—see the CrimPR), and often by the judge who oversaw the criminal trial.
- Confiscation proceedings are initiated by the prosecutor, or the judge of his own motion.
- A confiscation order is not directed towards particular assets *per se*. A defendant may use
  any resource to satisfy the order made against him, whereas in civil recovery the property
  itself is the target of the claim.

See further para 13.67.

### Civil recovery in the High Court: proceedings for recovery orders

Proceedings for a recovery order may be taken by the appropriate Director in the High Court **13.26**
against any person whom the enforcement authority thinks holds recoverable property (see
s 243(1)).

### Definitions within POCA

Chapter 4 of Pt 5 of POCA sets out various definitions which apply to both the civil recovery **13.27**
scheme and the cash forfeiture provisions. It deals particularly with recoverable property, namely:

| | |
|---|---|
| Property obtained through unlawful conduct | s 304 |
| Tracing property | s 305 |
| Mixing property | s 306 |
| Recoverable property accruing profits | s 307 |
| General and other exceptions and exemptions | ss 308 and 309 |
| Granting interests | s 310 |
| Obtaining and disposing of property | s 314 |
| Property | s 316(4) |

These sections are considered more closely below.

### Definition of 'property'

Under s 316(4) property is all property wherever situated and includes: **13.28**

(a) money,
(b) all forms of property, real or personal, heritable or moveable,
(c) things in action and other intangible or incorporeal property.

It should be noted that under s 308(9), property is not recoverable if it has already been taken
into account when calculating the amount to be paid under a confiscation order.

Under s 316 'recoverable property' (defined in s 304 as 'property obtained through unlawful **13.29**
conduct') is to be read in accordance with ss 304 to 310, which deal with property obtained

through 'unlawful conduct'; tracing property; mixing property; recoverable property and accruing profits; and general exceptions and exemptions including the granting of interests. In short, recoverable property is property that has been obtained through unlawful conduct or property that represents such property (see *Singh v Director of the Assets Recovery Agency* [2005] EWCA Civ 580, [2005] 1 WLR 3747).

**13.30**  Under s 316(5) any reference to a person's property (whether expressed as a reference to the property he holds or otherwise) is to be read as follows:

(1)  In relation to land, it is a reference to any interest which he holds in the land.
(2)  In relation to property other than land it is a reference to the property (if it belongs to him), or to any other interest which he holds in the property (s 316(5) to (7)).

### Property obtained through unlawful conduct

**13.31**  Under s 242(1) a person obtains property through unlawful conduct (whether his own conduct or another's) if he obtains property by or in return for that conduct.

**13.32**  In deciding whether any property was obtained through unlawful conduct, it is immaterial 'whether or not any money, goods or services were provided in order to put the person in question in the position to carry out the conduct in question' (s 242(2)(a)). Nor is it necessary to show that the conduct was of a particular kind, if it can be shown that the property was obtained through conduct of one of a number of kinds, each of which would have fallen within the definition of 'unlawful conduct' (see s 242(2)).

**13.33**  It follows that a person will obtain property through unlawful conduct if he obtains it by his conduct, eg by stealing, or if he obtains it in return for unlawful conduct, eg by taking a bribe to award a contract. In *SOCA v Turrall and others* [2013] EWHC 2256 (Admin) the Court drew inferences to conclude multiple items of property were derived from unlawful conduct.

### Unlawful conduct

**13.34**  Conduct occurring in any part of the UK is unlawful conduct if it is unlawful under the criminal law of that part of the UK (s 241(1)).

**13.35**  Furthermore, under s 241(2) conduct which:

(a)  occurs in a country outside the United Kingdom and is unlawful under the criminal law of that country, and
(b)  if it occurred in a part of the United Kingdom, would be unlawful under the criminal law of that part,

is also unlawful conduct.

The effect of s 241(2) is to enable property obtained through unlawful conduct abroad to be recovered. For further information on territorial limits, see para 13.61.

### How is 'recoverable property' defined?

**13.36**  'Recoverable property' is defined as property obtained though unlawful conduct (s 304). The definitions of 'property' and 'unlawful conduct' are set out above.

### How is 'associated property' defined?

**13.37**  Associated property is defined by s 245(1):

(1) 'Associated property' means property of any of the following descriptions (including property held by the Respondent which is not itself the recoverable property)—

    (a) any interest in the recoverable property,

    (b) any other interest in the property in which the recoverable property subsists,

    (c) if the recoverable property is a tenancy in common, the tenancy of the other tenant,

    (d) if (in Scotland) the recoverable property is owned in common, the interest of the other owner,

    (e) if the recoverable property is part of a larger property, but not a separate part, the remainder of that property.

This broad definition is intended to deal with circumstances in which only part of the prop-  **13.38**
erty is recoverable, or where there is more than one interest in the property and some of it is not recoverable. In those circumstances the non-recoverable part is described as 'associated property'.

The guidance notes that accompanied POCA give the following examples in terms of (a) to  **13.39**
(e) above:

> In paragraph (a) the associated property might be a tenancy in a recoverable freehold. In paragraph (b), where a lease in a freehold block of flats has been purchased with recoverable property, another lease in the same block bought with legitimate money would be associated property. In paragraphs (c) and (d) where two people buy a car together, one with recoverable cash and one with legitimate cash, the share of the person who bought with legitimate cash is the associated property. In paragraph (e), where a painting is recoverable property but it had been framed using legitimate money, the frame would be associated property.

Section 245(2) adds that references to property 'being associated with recoverable property'  **13.40**
are to be read accordingly, and that no property is to be treated as associated with the recoverable property where the recoverable property consists of rights under a pension scheme (within the meaning of ss 273 to 275 of POCA) (see s 245(3)).

### The tracing of property

The Act envisages the tracing of property (s 305), which may include an audit trail exercise.  **13.41**
Where property was originally obtained through unlawful conduct (or would have been recoverable property), property that represents the original property is also recoverable. For example, a person steals a valuable painting (the original property), it is sold and the cash received from the sale is later used to purchase a Mercedes motor car. The Mercedes becomes recoverable property, being representative of the proceeds of a crime.

### Mixed property

The Act also stipulates that where a person's 'recoverable property' is mixed with other prop-  **13.42**
erty, the portion of the mixed property that is said to relate to unlawful conduct becomes 'recoverable property' (see s 306—mixing property). For example, where there are two joint company directors, and one uses the company account for legitimate monies, and the other to launder the proceeds of crime. The 'honest' director withdraws a large sum of cash and as part of an investigation that cash is seized. The portion of the cash that he has on him that relates to legitimate money from the business does not fall within the recovery scheme. However, the portion that he holds that represents the proceeds of a crime does stand to be forfeited, whether that particular director knew about it or not.

### Accruing profits

**13.43** As one might expect, where a person who has 'recoverable property' obtains further property because of profits that have accrued on that recoverable property, those profits also become recoverable and are to be treated as 'property obtained through unlawful conduct' (eg increase in the value of an investment or in the value of a house) (see s 307—accruing profits).

### Disposal of recoverable property

**13.44** Section 308 provides that:

(1) If—
   (a) a person disposes of recoverable property, and
   (b) the person who obtains it on the disposal does so in good faith, for value and without notice that it was recoverable property,
   the property may not be followed into that person's hands and, accordingly, it ceases to be recoverable.

Whether a person who obtains the recoverable property on the disposal falls within the section 308 exception to recoverability depends very much on the circumstances of the individual case—see eg *SOCA v Lundon and others* [2010] EWHC 353 (QB) and *SOCA v Coghlan and Burgoyne [2012]* EWHC 429 (QB).

### Granting interests

**13.45** Section 310 provides:

(1) If a person grants an interest in his recoverable property, the question of whether the interest is also recoverable is determined in the same manner as it is in any other disposal of recoverable property.
(2) Accordingly, on his granting an interest in the property in question,
   (a) where the property in question is property obtained through unlawful conduct, the interest is also to be treated as obtained through that conduct;
   (b) where the property in question represents property, in his hands, obtained through unlawful conduct, the interest is also to be treated as representing, in his hands, the property so obtained.

In other words, gifting a property or granting an interest in any other way is unlikely to save the property from civil recovery.

## C. Property Freezing Orders

### Introduction

**13.46** Section 98 of SOCPA inserted s 245A into POCA. Section 245A(1) states:

Where the enforcement authority may take proceedings for a recovery order in the High Court, the authority may apply to the court for a property freezing order (whether before or after starting the proceedings).

**13.47** Section 245A reflects s 246(1) of POCA, in that it anticipates that the Director will be at liberty to apply for a PFO before he has started his CPR Pt 8 claim for civil recovery (s 316(1), as amended, defines 'enforcement authority').

## Draft PFO

A draft PFO is found at Appendix 17.                                                **13.48**

## Definition

Section 245A(2) defines a PFO as an order that:                                    **13.49**

(a) specifies or describes the property to which it applies, and

(b) subject to any exclusions (see section 245C(1)(b) and (2)), prohibits any person to whose property the order applies from in any way dealing with the property.

## PFO without notice

By s 245A(3), the relevant Director may apply for a PFO without giving notice, if the cir-   **13.50**
cumstances are such that notice of the application would prejudice any right of the enforcement authority to obtain a recovery order in respect of any property. This provision, like
IROs and restraint orders under POCA, is to safeguard against the possibility that a respondent may attempt to either secrete his assets or transfer them out of the jurisdiction once put
on notice that the relevant Director intends to seek a PFO. Clearly, whilst that risk is always
a possibility, when making an *ex parte* application it is still incumbent upon the enforcement
authority to at least state what its belief is in relation to the risk of dissipation and the facts
upon which it bases that belief.

## Factors giving rise to the risk of dissipation

One of the purposes of seeking a PFO is the risk that assets may be lost which might other-   **13.51**
wise be the subject of a civil recovery order. In *Director of the Assets Recovery Agency v Keenan*
[2005] NIQB 67, Coughlin J stated that assets obtained through the proceeds of crime were
'... by their very nature assets likely to be at particular risk of dissipation'.

In many cases, the risk of dissipation will speak for itself. But of relevance will be the nature   **13.52**
of the allegations against the respondent; whether or not those allegations have been proven
(and therefore impact upon his credibility and integrity as a result); the ease with which the
assets can be transferred, including whether or not the respondent has any bank accounts
or connections overseas; and whether or not he has attempted to deal with his assets in the
past. His cooperation with the authorities may also be relevant, particularly if he has a history of either evading court orders or failing to cooperate. The respondent's geographical
location may also be a factor: a defendant who is either out of the country or being detained
in prison is still able to deal with his assets fairly easily through the cooperation of others,
particularly (it might be said) bearing in mind the technological age in which we live.

## Duty of full and frank disclosure

It is important to remember that a person applying for an injunction without notice is under   **13.53**
a duty of full and frank disclosure of all the material facts. The grant of either a PFO (or an
IRO) is a discretionary remedy, and the enforcement authority is not therefore entitled to
either order as of right. Accordingly, it is very important that the evidence put before the court
should be as complete as possible and should demonstrate compelling reasons why such relief
is necessary.

In *R v Kensington Income Tax Commissioners ex p de Polignac* [1917] 1 KB 486, the court held   **13.54**
that there was a duty on all applicants to make full and fair disclosure of all material facts.

In *Siporex Trade SA v Condel Commodities Ltd* [1986] 2 Lloyd's Rep 428, Bingham J (as he then was) said:

> The scope of the duty of disclosure of a party applying *ex parte* for injunctive relief is, in broad terms, agreed between the parties. Such an applicant must show the utmost good faith and disclose his case fully and fairly. He must, for the protection and information of the defendant, summarise his case and the evidence in support of it... must identify the crucial points for and against the application, and not rely on general statements and the mere exhibiting of numerous documents.

**13.55** In *Brinks Mat Ltd v Elcombe* [1988] 1 WLR 1350, Ralph Gibson LJ said that the duty to make full and frank disclosure encapsulated the following duties and principles:

(1) the duty of the applicant to make a full and fair disclosure of all material facts;
(2) the material facts are those which it is material for the judge to know in dealing with the application as made, materiality is to be decided by the court and not by the assessment of the applicant or his legal advisers;
(3) the applicant must make proper inquiries before making the application;
(4) the extent of the inquiries which will be proper and therefore necessary, must depend on all the circumstances of the case;
(5) if material non-disclosure is established the court will be astute to ensure that a plaintiff who obtains an *ex parte* injunction without full disclosure is deprived of any advantage he may have derived by that breach of duty;
(6) whether the fact not disclosed is of sufficient materiality to justify or require immediate discharge of the order without examination of the merits depends on the importance of the fact to the issues which were to be decided by the judge on the application;
(7) It is not for every omission that the injunction will be automatically discharged. The court has a discretion, notwithstanding proof of material non-disclosure which justifies or requires the immediate discharge of the *ex parte* order, nevertheless to continue the order or to make new terms.

**13.56** In *Director of the Assets Recovery Agency v Satnam Singh* [2004] EWHC Admin 2335 McCombe J considered the above authorities (at para 42 of the judgment) and the duty upon the Director to make full and frank disclosure at the time of a without-notice hearing (in *Singh* the court was considering an application for an IRO). Having considered the authorities, his Lordship found that there had been a failure to disclose certain things to the court, but that this did not afford grounds to discharge the order. He stated he considered it a situation to which the remarks of Slade LJ in *Brinks Mat* were particularly applicable. The non-disclosure was attributable to an innocent lack of knowledge on the part of the Director and her advisers and the order should therefore be maintained. He did, however, adopt the procedure established in *Interoute Telecommunications (UK) Ltd v Fashion Gossip Ltd*, The Times, 10 November 1999, which establishes that the applicant should provide to the respondent a note of what has taken place during the *ex parte* hearing. McCombe J stated (para 47):

> For the future, I can see no reason why the common practice in relation to without notice applications in the High Court should not be followed in cases of this type, unless the judge hearing the application expressly decides that, for good reason, a note should not be served on affected parties and provided that that decision is recorded on the face of the order, so that all

affected parties may know that the decision also is susceptible to the customary permission to apply to vary or discharge the order.

It follows that if the enforcement authority is going without notice for an application, it is **13.57** important that notes are made during the hearing and that those notes are provided to any party affected by the injunction. In *Interoute* Lightman J said that this was essential so that each party might know exactly what had occurred, and the basis for granting the injunction, in order to be able to make an informed application for discharge. It should also be noted that the duty to provide full notes applies regardless of whether the respondent asks for them (see *Thane Investments Ltd v Tomlinson*, The Times, 10 December 2002 (ChD)). (While these cases relate to freezing orders one can see that there must be an overlap between the jurisdictions and it is submitted that they represent good practice in relation to applications for both PFOs and IROs.) The reasoning of McCombe J in *Singh* was adopted by Coghlin J in *Director of the Assets Recovery Agency v Gerard Malachy Keenan* (NIHC, 23 September 2005) (para 23).

The scope of proper disclosure cannot be underestimated. As authorities have found in the **13.58** restraint order regime, an order can properly be challenged where there has been material non-disclosure, see eg *Re: Stanford International Bank (In Receivership)* [2010] EWCA Civ 137 where a restraint order was set aside for misrepresentation and material non-disclosure (though the Court reimposed the order after hearing full argument) and *R v Windsor & Hare & others (Eastenders PLC)* [2011] EWCA Crim 143.

### Criteria for granting a PFO

The court may make a PFO if it is satisfied that the conditions in s 245A(5), and where **13.59** applicable s 245A(6) are met. Section 245A(5) states:

The first condition is that there is a good arguable case
(a) that the property to which the application for the order relates is or includes recoverable property, and
(b) that if any of it is not recoverable property, it is associated property.

Section 245A(6) reads:

The second condition is that, if
(a) the property to which the application for the order relates includes property alleged to be associated property, and
(b) the enforcement authority has not established the identity of the person who holds it,
the authority has taken all reasonable steps to do so.

Once again, these conditions mirror those that relate to an application for an IRO under s 246 of the Act.

Whilst the expression 'good arguable case' is not defined in the Act, it is a familiar expression **13.60** to practitioners seeking injunctions under the freezing order scheme. In *The Niedersachsen* [1983] 2 Lloyd's Rep 600, 605A it was held a good arguable case related to the merits of the substantive claim and the evidence as a whole. See the case of *Serious Organised Crime Agency v Khan [2012] EWHC 3235 (Admin)* for a recent example of the test being satisfied, and a PFO being granted, even though there were extensive factual disputes and further investigations required. A 'good arguable case' is considered further below.

**Territorial limits**

**13.61** A recent decision limited the territorial scope of PFOs. Overturning the Court of Appeal's decision, the Supreme Court in *Perry & others v SOCA and Perry & others v SOCA (No 2) [2012] UKSC 35* held that POCA Pt 5 did not give the High Court of England and Wales power to impose PFOs (and therefore orders in civil recovery proceedings) in respect of property situated outside the jurisdiction of the court. Further, a disclosure order under POCA Pt 8 did not authorise the sending of information notices to persons outside the jurisdiction of the court. This important decision warrants careful consideration.

**13.62** The appellants were Mr Perry, who had been convicted of fraud in Israel, and members of his family, who lived outside the UK. The appeals concerned SOCA's efforts to deprive the appellants of the fruits of the fraud by way of a future civil recovery order. SOCA had obtained a worldwide PFO under s 245A and a disclosure order under s 357.

**13.63** The appellants appealed on the basis that the High Court of England and Wales did not have jurisdiction to impose PFOs and authorise disclosure notices in respect of property and persons situated outside the jurisdiction ([2011] EWCA Civ 578, [2011] 1 WLR 2817, and [2010] EWCA Civ 907; [2011] 1 WLR 542).

**13.64** In relation to PFOs, the Court of Appeal had held that an order could be made in respect of any form of property, wherever it was situated; the natural meaning of the words 'wherever situated' in s 316(4) being applied without restriction. In relation to the disclosure order appeal, the Court of Appeal upheld the validity of the disclosure notices.

**13.65** The issues before the Supreme Court were whether the court's power to impose PFOs under s 245A applied exclusively to property within the UK; and whether a disclosure order under s 357 authorised the sending of notices to persons outside the UK.

**13.66** By a majority decision, with Lord Judge and Lord Clarke dissenting on the PFO appeal, the Supreme Court held that the High Court of England and Wales had no jurisdiction to make a PFO in relation to property outside England and Wales. The Court found that many of the POCA provisions applied only to property within the UK, as summarised by Lord Phillips in the leading judgment:

> 14. The words 'wherever situated' do not describe the type of property to which Part 5 applies. Rather they indicate the location of the property to which the provisions of Part 5 can apply. The definition is repeated no less than eight times in POCA—sections 84(1), 150(1), 232(1), 316(4), 326(9), 340(9), 414(1) and 447(4). POCA is peppered with references to 'property'. All fall within the definition. But the definition cannot be applied so as to add to the words 'property', wherever it appears, the words 'wherever situated'. As I shall demonstrate, most of the provisions of POCA apply only to property within England and Wales, Scotland or Northern Ireland. By way simply of example, I can refer to section 45(1) which confers on a constable the power to seize property 'to prevent its removal from England and Wales'. Some provisions refer, however, to property worldwide. Whether or not the location of 'property' to which a provision of POCA refers is subject to a territorial restriction depends upon the context. I so held, when giving the only reasoned speech in *King v Director of the Serious Fraud Office* [2008] UKHL 17; [2009] 1 WLR 718, para 37. For these reasons I do not attach to the words in the definition 'wherever situated' the weight that they have carried with the courts below. In order to decide on the scope of the application of Part 5 of POCA it is necessary to consider both the structure and the language of the Act having regard to relevant principles of international law.

The effect was to draw a further distinction between civil recovery and confiscation. Whilst **13.67** there was a presumption against a statute having extraterritorial effect, this had been departed from with respect to confiscation:

> 18. Confiscation of the proceeds of crime is, however, an activity in respect of which States have departed from these principles. Of particular relevance is the Strasbourg Convention, to which the United Kingdom is a party. The question of whether the exorbitant effect of Part 5 of POCA for which SOCA contends would involve a breach of international law must be considered in the light of the Strasbourg Convention...

The Strasbourg Convention on Laundering, Search, Seizure and Confiscation of the **13.68** Proceeds of Crime envisages the courts in one state making an order confiscating property situated in another state. However, that scheme was founded on the premise of the conviction of the owner of the property by the court in the state making the order, as opposed to the wider jurisdiction that is conferred by Pt 5 of POCA, which allows for recovery without conviction.

Lord Phillips noted the *in personam* nature of confiscation under POCA, having regard to **13.69** property worldwide, and that no power was granted to the UK authorities to secure or realise property that was situated outside the jurisdiction (and where the UK authorities have to rely on the 'Enforcement Abroad' provisions of s 74 and request assistance from the authorities of the other country).

In relation to civil recovery, it is clear that the focus of Pt 5 is on the property (*in rem*) rather **13.70** than the particular defendant. Lord Phillips noted that ss 245A–255 make separate provision for PFOs in England and Wales, in Scotland and in Northern Ireland, which he found indicated that the provisions were designed to apply separately within the jurisdictions of the UK. Further, Pt 5 itself contained no enforcement provisions to compare with s 74; Lord Phillips observed that if Parliament had intended that it should extend to property outside the UK, provisions parallel to s 74 would have been included, and the fact that they did not indicated that Pt 5 was not intended to have extraterritorial effect.

A difficulty faced by the majority of their Lordships in reaching this conclusion is the enigma **13.71** of s 286, which on its face confers on the Court of Session in Scotland the jurisdiction to make an order with extraterritorial effect. The issue appears, however, to have been neatly sidestepped, with Lord Phillips simply stating that it did not lead him to change his conclusion, at least in so far as England and Wales and Northern Ireland were concerned. The court held therefore:

> 78. The High Court of England and Wales has no jurisdiction under Part 5 to make a recovery order in relation to property outside England and Wales. It follows that the court had no jurisdiction to make the worldwide property freezing order that was made in this case. The PFO appeal should be allowed and the property freezing order redrawn so that it applies only to property within the jurisdiction of the Court.

In their dissenting judgment, Lords Judge and Clarke refer to the poor drafting of POCA. **13.72** They present a cogent argument for extraterritorial effect based on the purpose of POCA (to deprive those engaged in criminal conduct of the property representing the proceeds of crime) and that the expression in question—'all property wherever situated'—had to have the same meaning, wherever it appeared in the Act. It is submitted that there is considerable force in their position. In *SOCA v Hymans* [2011] EWHC 3332 QB, *Perry* was followed and put into effect: a PFO made in April 2011 which included properties in France and Spain had to be varied to remove them as there was no jurisdiction under s 245A to make a worldwide freezing order. Of import, in *Serious Organised Crime Agency v (1) James Thomas O'Docherty (Aka Mark Eric Gibbons) (2) Manncherty Sl* [2013] EWCA Civ 518 the Court of Appeal held that *Perry* would not have retrospective effect. In other words, the Supreme Court's decision in *Perry* did not enable an individual who had had overseas property made the subject of a civil recovery order prior to the *Perry* decision to challenge the earlier order on the basis of the *Perry* decision. (For further information see paras 17.66 et seq and 19.21 et seq.)

### Amendments to POCA by the Crime and Courts Act 2013

**13.73** The Crime and Courts Act 2013 reversed, so far as possible, the effect of *Perry* by making a number of changes to POCA. The amendments to Chapter 2 of Pt 5 of POCA ensure the High Court in England and Wales and the Court of Session in Scotland can make an order against property situated outside the jurisdiction of the court where there is or has been a connection between the case and the relevant part of the UK (s 282A of POCA). A non-exhaustive list of connecting factors is set out in a new Sch 7A. New ss 282B–282F of POCA facilitate the enforcement outside the UK of orders made under Chapter 2 of Pt 5 of POCA and the transmission of requests for evidence held outside the UK. These provisions have retrospective effect and came into force on Royal Assent (s 282A of POCA and s 61(11) (c) and (d) of the Crime and Courts Act 2013).

**13.74** New s 282B of POCA makes provision for an enforcement authority in England and Wales or Scotland to ask the Secretary of State to transmit a request to freeze property situated abroad to the government of the country concerned before an order under Chapter 2 of Pt 5 of POCA is made. The Crime and Courts Act 2013 also inserts s 282C into POCA. This facilitates the transmission by a receiver of a request abroad to freeze property before a civil recovery order is made. Similar provision is made for Scotland. In addition, new s 282D of POCA facilitates the transmission abroad of a request by an interim receiver or an interim administrator where it is thought there may be relevant evidence held outside the UK. Inserted s 282E of POCA ensures that evidence obtained under s 282D cannot be used for any purpose other than for carrying out the functions of the interim receiver or interim administrator, or for the purposes of certain proceedings, unless appropriate consent has been obtained. New s 282F of POCA makes provision about how a civil recovery order made in England and Wales or Scotland may be enforced abroad by an enforcement authority or the trustee for civil recovery. POCA Pt 8 has also been amended (this will come into force by order). The main changes are to the definition of civil recovery to clarify that the focus of an investigation can be a person or property and also to clarify that there can be an investigation into property that has not yet been clearly identified. Further there is a new s 375A of POCA which makes provision for evidence to be obtained from overseas if a person or property is subject to a civil recovery investigation, a detained cash investigation, or an exploitation proceeds investigation. Similar provision is made for Scotland. For further see para 17.67.

### Variation and setting aside of the PFO

**13.75** Pursuant to s 245B of the amended Act, the court may at any time vary or set aside a PFO (s 245B(1)).

**13.76** Section 245B(2) requires the court to set aside a PFO if it subsequently makes an IRO that applies to all of the same property which a PFO covers. Where the court makes an IRO that applies to some *but not all* of the property to which the PFO applies, it must vary the PFO so as to exclude any property to which the IRO applies (s 245B(3)). It therefore becomes apparent that as a result of s 245B(3), the legislation anticipates that IROs and PFOs will not be mutually exclusive and may operate in tandem with each other.

If the court decides that any property to which the PFO applies is neither recoverable prop- **13.77** erty nor associated property it must vary the order so as to exclude the property (s 245B(4)). This subsection is directory and clearly affords the court little discretion once property has been identified as no longer being recoverable. However, before exercising any power to vary or set aside a PFO, the court must (as well as giving the parties to the proceedings an opportunity to be heard) give such an opportunity to any person who may be affected by the court's decision (see s 245B(5))—although this subsection does not apply where the court is acting as required by s 245B(2) or (3) (see subs (6)). For practice and procedure in applying for variations, see below.

### Exclusions and variations

The power to vary a PFO includes (in particular) power to make certain exclusions. These **13.78** include:

(a)  power to exclude property from the order; and
(b)  power, otherwise than by excluding property from the order, to make exclusions from the prohibition on dealing with the property to which the order applies (see s 245C(1)).

Exclusions from the prohibition on dealing with the property to which the order applies may **13.79** also be made when the order is made. Such exclusions may make provision for the purpose of enabling any person to:

(a)  meet his reasonable living expenses; or
(b)  carry on any trade, business, profession, or occupation.

However, such an exclusion may be made subject to conditions (see s 245C(2)–(4)). Section 245C(5) states that where the court exercises the power to make an exclusion for the purpose of enabling a person to meet legal expenses that he has incurred, or may incur, in proceedings under this part of the Act (note, not legal expenses in relation to other proceedings), it must ensure that the exclusion:

(a)  is limited to the reasonable legal expenses that the person has reasonably incurred or that he reasonably incurs,
(b)  specifies the total amount that may be released for legal expenses in pursuance of the exclusion, and
(c)  is made subject to the required conditions (see s 286A (below)) in addition to any conditions imposed under subs (4).

The court has a discretion in deciding whether to make an exclusion for the purpose of ena- **13.80** bling a person to meet legal expenses, and in exercising that discretion it:

(a)  must have regard (in particular) to the desirability of the person being represented in any proceedings under Pt 5 of the Act in which he is a participant, and
(b)  must, where the person is the respondent, disregard the possibility that legal represen- tation of the person in any such proceedings might, were an exclusion not made, be funded by the Legal Aid Agency.

**13.81**  The test the court is likely to apply was set out by Stanley Burnton J in *Director of the Assets Recovery Agency v Creaven* [2005] EWHC 2726 (Admin). For practice and procedure in applying for such an exclusion, see below.

**13.82**  The issue of obtaining funding from frozen assets to meet legal expenses is considered at the end of this chapter. See in particular, *SOCA v Amis Azam and others* [2013] EWHC 1480 (QB).

### The legislative steer

**13.83**  What can be described as a 'legislative steer' is found at s 245C(8), where the amended Act states that the power to make an exclusion must, subject to s 245C(6), be exercised with a view to ensuring, so far as practicable, that the satisfaction of any right of the enforcement authority to recover the property obtained through unlawful conduct is not unduly prejudiced. Section 245C(8) does not apply where the court is acting as required by s 245B(3) or (4), see s 245C(9).

**13.84**  It is perhaps worthy of note that whilst comparison is sometimes useful when looking at freezing orders/Mareva injunctions precedents, and considering them against PFOs, it must be borne in mind that, unlike the freezing order jurisdiction, POCA contains a legislative steer that courts are required to consider. Courts are also likely to have regard to the overall purpose of the Act: namely to recover the proceeds of crime. So, for example, whilst in *PCW (Underwriting Agencies) Ltd v Dixon* [1983] 2 All ER 158 (QBD) Lloyd J stated 'justice and convenience require that [the frozen respondent] should be able to pay his ordinary bills and continue to live as he has been accustomed to live before' the same considerations will not necessarily apply in a POCA matter.

### Restriction and staying of other proceedings

**13.85**  Under s 245D, while a PFO has effect, the court must stay any action, execution, or other legal process in respect of the property to which the order applies and no distress may be levied against the property to which the order applies except with the leave of the court and subject to any terms the court may impose.

**13.86**  Similarly, under s 245D(2), if a court (whether the High Court or any other court) in which proceedings are pending in respect of any property is satisfied that a PFO has been applied for or made in respect of the property, it may either stay the proceedings or allow them to continue on any terms it thinks fit.

**13.87**  If a PFO applies to the tenancy of any premises, no landlord or other persons to whom rent is payable may exercise the right of forfeiture by peaceable re-entry in relation to the premises in respect of any failure by the tenant to comply with any terms or conditions of the tenancy, except with the permission of the court and subject to any terms the court may impose (see s 245D(3)).

**13.88**  Before exercising any power conferred by s 245D of POCA, the court must (as well as giving the parties to any of the proceedings concerned an opportunity to be heard) give such an opportunity to any person who may be affected by the court's decision.

### Ancillary orders and disclosure

**13.89**  In *AJ Bekhor & Co Ltd v Bilton* [1981] QB 923 (CA) the Court held that it had an inherent power to make such ancillary orders (including disclosure) as appeared to be just and

convenient in order to ensure that a freezing order was effective. See also *SOCA v Perry*
[2009] EWHC 1960 (Admin).

However the reach of the existing disclosure order power was somewhat constrained by Lord **13.90**
Phillips in *Perry & others v SOCA and Perry & others v SOCA (No 2)* [2012] UKSC 35, where
the Supreme Court found at para 94:

> 94. The point is a very short one. No authority is required under English law for a person to
> request information from another person anywhere in the world. But section 357 authorises
> orders for requests for information with which the recipient is obliged to comply, subject to
> penal sanction. Subject to limited exceptions, it is contrary to international law for country
> A to purport to make criminal conduct in country B committed by persons who are not
> citizens of country A. Section 357, read with section 359, does not simply make proscribed
> conduct a criminal offence. It confers on a United Kingdom public authority the power to
> impose on persons positive obligations to provide information subject to criminal sanction
> in the event of non-compliance. To confer such authority in respect of persons outside the
> jurisdiction would be a particularly startling breach of international law. For this reason alone
> I consider it implicit that the authority given under section 357 can only be exercised in respect
> of persons who are within the jurisdiction.

This reasoning was quite independent of the Supreme Court's basis for holding that a recovery order can only be made against property within the jurisdiction. In order to address the
effect of the judgment in *Perry*, amendments to Pt 5 of POCA were included in ss 48, 49 and
schs 18 and 19 of the Crime and Courts Act 2013 (CCA) which was passed in April 2013 (see
para 13.74 above). New s 375A of POCA will make provision for evidence to be obtained
from a court, tribunal, government, or authority outside the United Kingdom ('receiving
country') if a person or property is subject to a civil recovery investigation, a detained cash
investigation, or an exploitation proceeds investigation (as defined in s 341). It will enable
a judge to make a request for assistance upon an application by an appropriate officer or a
person subject to the investigation, providing that the judge thinks there is relevant evidence
in a country or territory outside the United Kingdom. However a senior appropriate officer
or the relevant Director may make a direct request for assistance if it is thought that there is
relevant evidence in a country or territory outside of the United Kingdom. The meanings
of 'appropriate officer', 'senior appropriate officer' and 'relevant Director' are found in ss
352(5A) and 378 of POCA as above. In the case of urgency, a request may be sent via the
International Criminal Police Organization (Interpol or Europol) or any person competent
to receive it under any provisions adopted under the EU Treaties, for onward forwarding to
the receiving country.

New s 375A(10) of POCA will provide a power to make rules of court as to the practice and **13.91**
procedure to be followed in connection with proceedings relating to requests for assistance
made by a judge. New s 375B of POCA will provide that evidence obtained by a request for
assistance under new s 375A must not be used for any purpose other than for the purpose
of the investigation for which it was obtained or for the purposes of certain proceedings.
However, the court, tribunal, government, or authority that received the request and provided the evidence can consent to the use of the evidence for other purposes.

### PFOs: practice and procedure

The Civil Recovery Proceedings Practice Direction sets out the procedure to be followed in **13.92**
relation to proceedings in the High Court under POCA. Paragraph 2.1 stipulates that the

venue for issuing applications should be the Administrative Court. Paragraph 5.1 states that an application for a PFO must be made to a High Court judge in accordance with Pt 23 of the CPR. Under CPR r 23.3 the general rule is that an applicant must file an Application Notice which must then be served on each respondent (see r 23.4).

**13.93** Paragraph 5.3 of the Practice Direction allows for applications to be made without notice pursuant to s 245A(3) of the Act, and Art 147(3) of the Order in Council (meaning the Proceeds of Crime Act 2002 (External Requests and Orders) Order 2005).

**13.94** Paragraph 5.4 provides that an application for a PFO must be supported by written evidence which must:

(1) set out the grounds on which the order is sought; and
(2) give details of each item or description of property in respect of which the order is sought, including:
   (a) an estimate of the value of the property; and
   (b) the additional information referred to in para 5.5.

**13.95** The additional information referred to in para 5.5 requires that the written evidence must state in relation to each item or description of property in respect of which the PFO is sought:

   (a) whether the property is alleged to be
      (i) recoverable property or
      (ii) associated property,
      and the facts relied upon in support of that allegation; and
   (b) in the case of any associated property
      (i) who was believed to hold the property; or
      (ii) if the enforcement authority is unable to establish who holds the property, the steps that have been taken to establish their identity; and
   (c) identify a nominee.

**13.96** Paragraph 5.6 of the Practice Direction stipulates that a draft of the order that is sought must be filed with the Application Notice. This should, if possible, also be supplied to the court in an electronic form compatible with the word processing software used by the court.

**13.97** Rule 23.8 CPR deals with situations where applications may be dealt with without a hearing. While some judges will be prepared to deal with PFO applications on the papers alone, many still require the attendance of counsel on behalf of the relevant Director to explain the history and necessity of the order being applied for.

**13.98** Rule 23.9 CPR deals with the service of the application and r 23.11 sets out the powers of the court to proceed in the absence of a party. Rule 23.10 does not apply to PFOs (see para 5.2).

**13.99** Paragraph 5A of the Practice Direction states that where a PFO is made before a claim for a recovery order has been commenced it must:

(1) specify a period within which the enforcement authority must either start the claim or apply for the continuation of the order while it carries out its investigation; and
(2) provide that the order shall be set aside if the enforcement authority does not start the claim or apply for its continuation before the end of that period.

### Exclusions when making a PFO: legal costs

Paragraph 5B.1 of the Civil Recovery Practice Direction sets out the court's power to make **13.100** exclusions for the purpose of enabling a respondent to meet his reasonable legal costs so that he may:

(1) take advice in relation to the order;
(2) prepare a statement of assets in accordance with para 7A.3; and
(3) if so advised, apply for the order to be varied or set aside.

The total amount specified in the initial exclusion will not, according to the Practice Direction, normally exceed £3,000. This exclusion is dealt with at the end of this chapter.

### Applications to vary or set aside a PFO

Pursuant to para 7.1 of the Practice Direction an application to vary or set aside a PFO can **13.101** be made at any time by (1) the enforcement authority, or (2) any person affected by the order.

Unless the court otherwise directs or exceptional circumstances apply, a copy of the applica- **13.102** tion notice must be served on every party to the proceedings and any other person who may be affected by the court's decision.

This is an important proviso as it appears that the Practice Direction accompanying the leg- **13.103** islation does not make any provision for return dates where applications for discharge and variation might otherwise be argued.

### Compensation

The compensation provisions within Pt 5 are considered under 'Compensation in IRO and **13.104** PFO cases' below.

## D. Management Receiving Orders

### Introduction

Section 83 of the SCA was introduced on 6 April 2008 (SI 2008/755) and amends POCA **13.105** to provide for a new type of receiver in civil recovery proceedings whose only function is to manage property subject to a PFO.

The role of the management receiver is distinct from the role of the interim receiver as the lat- **13.106** ter has the additional responsibility of investigating the property that he manages and then reporting his findings to the enforcement authority and the court. The new management receiver will have no investigation function and so theoretically will have less of an influence on the progress and final outcome of the case. Accordingly, the role does not have the same level of independence and therefore can be performed by a member of staff of the enforcement authority that is pursuing the civil recovery case.

### The legislative scheme

Section 83(1) of the SCA inserts after s 245D of POCA the following provision: **13.107**

> 245E *Receivers in connection with property freezing orders*
> (1) Subsection (2) applies if—
>   (a) the High Court makes a property freezing order on an application by an enforcement authority, and

>    (b) the authority applies to the court to proceed under subsection (2) (whether as part of the application for the property freezing order or at any time afterwards).
>    (2) The High Court may by order appoint a receiver in respect of any property to which the property freezing order applies.

**13.108** Section 245E(4) and (5) provides that the enforcement authority must nominate a suitably qualified person for appointment as a receiver and that such a person may be a member of staff of the enforcement authority.

**13.109** The term 'suitably qualified person' is not defined in the amended legislation, although in the past management receivers have been insolvency practitioners who hold accountancy qualifications.

### Independence

**13.110** There appears to be little requirement for the receiver to be seen as independent in this role, as it is apparent that the legislation anticipates that the appointment can be made 'in house'. This might give rise to challenge, not least because a respondent may have justifiable reservations about cooperating with a receiver who is employed by the claimant pursuing his property.

**13.111** Theoretically, a receiver appointed by the High Court is an officer of the court, and has historically been seen as an individual who could 'hold the ring' between the parties (albeit defendants and respondents might greet such an assertion with some scepticism, as receivers in a management or enforcement role have generally been viewed as an extension of the state in that they were often perceived as doing the bidding of those who sought their appointment and upon whom, to a degree, they depend for future work).

**13.112** It is perhaps a reflection of this concern that s 245G(1) specifies that in terms of the supervision of the receiver, any of the following persons may at any time apply to the High Court for directions as to the exercise of the functions of a receiver appointed under s 245E:

>    (a) the receiver,
>    (b) any party to the proceedings for the appointment of the receiver or the property freezing order concerned,
>    (c) any person affected by any action taken by the receiver,
>    (d) any person who may be affected by any action proposed to be taken by the receiver.

**13.113** The court may make such directions it considers appropriate, provided that the court has given the opportunity for the receiver, the parties to the proceedings for the appointment of the receiver and for the property freezing order concerned, and any other person who may be interested, to be heard (s 245G(2)).

**13.114** The amended Act does not limit the role of management receiver exclusively to those employed by the agency seeking the appointment, and it is apparent that an outside receiver may be appointed, or even an individual who is seconded to the authority concerned (s 245E(6) and (7)).

**13.115** The purported independence of court-appointed receivers is considered further under 'The status and independence of the interim receiver' at para 13.132.

### Power to apply without notice

Pursuant to s 245E(3) an application for an MRO may be made without notice if the circumstances are such that notice of the application would prejudice any right of the enforcement authority to obtain a recovery order in respect of any property:  **13.116**

    (6)   The enforcement authority may apply a sum received by it under section 280(2) in making payment of the remuneration and expenses of a receiver appointed under this section.

    (7)   Subsection (6) does not apply in relation to the remuneration of the receiver if he is a member of the staff of the enforcement authority (but it does apply in relation to such remuneration if the receiver is a person providing services under arrangements made by the enforcement authority).

### Remuneration of the management receiver

Section 245E(6) allows for the remuneration and expenses of the receiver to be met from the realised proceeds of a recovery order, *unless* he is an employed member of staff (s 245E(7)).  **13.117**

### The receiver's powers

The management powers of the receiver are set out in para 5 of Sch 6 (set out in Appendix 8 of this book), and pursuant to s 245F(2), the High Court may authorise or require the receiver to exercise any of the powers mentioned therein (which include the power of sale over property which is diminishing in value or is perishable; and the power to carry on any trade or business within the receivership estate).  **13.118**

In addition, the High Court has a broad discretion to order any other steps be taken in connection with the management of the property (including securing the detention, custody, or preservation of the property concerned, s 245F(2)(b)).  **13.119**

Furthermore, the court may order any person in respect of whose property the receiver is appointed to transfer or repatriate his assets pursuant to the receiver's direction or to do anything else he is 'reasonably required to do by the receiver' (s 245F(3)). What amounts to 'reasonable' in this context is not defined, although it is apparent that for the receivership to function the receiver must have some form of control over those holding the assets or property over which he is appointed, and the receiver and court will want to ensure that those assets are preserved and maintained without the repeated need to return to the court for further directions, directions that may be costly both in terms of legal fees, but also in terms of risk in that the assets might be dissipated in the intervening period.  **13.120**

In a similar vein, the court may order that any person in respect of whose property the receiver is appointed should bring any documents relating to the property which are in his possession or control to a place specified by the receiver or to place them in the custody of the receiver (s 245F(4)). Subsection (5) provides that 'document' means anything in which information of any description is recorded, and could therefore encompass computer records.  **13.121**

Whilst an individual could suggest that he was prohibited from following the receiver's request by virtue of the extant PFO, which prevents any dealing with the property, the legislation anticipates this by incorporating within s 245F(6) a clause which permits a person to comply with the requirements imposed.  **13.122**

### Protection for the receiver

**13.123** By s 245F(7), if the receiver deals with property which is not property in respect of which he is appointed (ie property outside the receivership estate), but at the time of dealing with it he believes on reasonable grounds that he is entitled to do so, the management receiver will not be liable to any person in respect of any loss or damage resulting from his dealing with the property concerned, except so far as any loss or damage is caused by his negligence.

**13.124** This proviso gives the receiver a large degree of protection and reassurance in terms of the powers he has to operate, save for any steps he takes in relation to property outside the receivership which could be categorised as negligent (eg failing to make proper enquiries in terms of ownership, or overlooking information that he had previously been provided with, which has led to a loss to the true owner).

### Variations to management receiving orders

**13.125** The court may at any time vary or set aside the powers of the management receiver or any of the directions it has set, or equally set aside the appointment of the receiver as a whole (s 245G(3)).

**13.126** Before exercising this power the court must ensure that the relevant parties have been given an opportunity to be heard, including the receiver, the parties to the proceedings, and any other person affected by the court's decision (s 245G(4)).

### Practice and procedure

**13.127** The Civil Recovery Proceedings Practice Direction sets out the procedural steps that relate to applications for MROs. Pursuant to para 5.1, the applications must be made to a High Court judge in accordance with CPR Pt 23.

**13.128** The right to apply without notice set out by s 245E(3) is confirmed by para 5.3, and para 5.6 requires the applicant to file a draft of the order sought at the time the application is made.

**13.129** Applications for directions are provided for by paras 6.1 and 6.2 of the Practice Direction, and equally the procedure to be followed for applications to vary or set aside the order are set out in paras 7.1 and 7.2. Unless exceptional circumstances apply, in both cases the application must be served on all parties to the proceedings, including the receiver, the enforcement authority, and any other person who may be affected by the court's decision.

## E. Interim Receiving Orders

### The role of the interim receiver

**13.130** The role of the interim receiver is two-fold. Firstly, there is a management role which is to secure the detention, custody, or preservation of property to which the order applies (s 247(1)) (similar to that of a management receiver appointed while a restraint order is extant). Secondly, there is an investigative role whereby the interim receiver should investigate on behalf of the court (a) whether the property to which the order applies is recoverable property; and (b) whether there is any other recoverable property (related to the same unlawful conduct) and, if there is, who holds it (see s 247(2)).

In *Director of the Assets Recovery Agency v Wilson and Wilson* [2007] NIQB 49 Higgins J **13.131**
observed (at 10):

> The role of the interim receiver is that of a court-appointed expert to investigate the origin
> and ownership of assets and to report to the court on those assets. In the absence of evidence
> to the contrary, such a report will be compelling evidence in any application based upon it. Its
> detailed contents relating to accountancy matters are accepted as fact unless shown otherwise.

### The status and independence of the interim receiver

Interim receivers should be considered independent officers of the court. It is the court that **13.132**
appoints them. Their independence is underlined in that the Act stipulates that they must
not be a member of the enforcement authority's staff. The interim receiver is under a duty
to report *to the court* any material change in circumstances (s 255(1)). It is the court that
determines the receiver's powers on a case-by-case basis within the framework prescribed by
s 247 and Sch 6 to POCA (Appendix 8). At any time, the interim receiver can apply to the
court for directions as to the exercise of his powers (s 251(1)). Only the court is able to direct
an interim receiver, and it follows that he or she should be beyond the direction of the parties. In addition, the court may vary or set aside an IRO at any time (s 251(2)). It will also be
noted that there is no requirement for an independent person to supervise when the interim
receiver is exercising the powers conferred by Sch 6.

Once an IRO is made, the relevant director is deemed no longer to be carrying on a civil **13.133**
recovery investigation (s 341(3)(b)). While the director may still receive information by
virtue of the gateway provisions in Pt 10 of POCA, in practice it is generally the position
that the investigation will cease on the granting of an IRO. The imposition of the investigative function upon the interim receiver confers a unique role amongst receivers in UK
jurisprudence. A vital aspect of the scheme is that the interim receiver is not a witness for the
enforcement authority and is not supervised by the enforcement authority. He is the court's
investigator and it can be expected that the report will be used to determine which issues can
be agreed and which remain in dispute.

In *Director of the Assets Recovery Agency v Jackson* [2007] EWCA (QB) 2553 King J said: **13.134**

> 29. It is obviously clear from this legislative framework and these statutory provisions govern-
> ing the appointment of the Receiver and her investigative and reporting functions under the
> supervision of the court rather than the Director, that the Receiver is not the agent of any of
> the parties. In my judgment, she is akin to an officer of the court and is reporting and giving
> evidence to the court in that capacity independent of the parties. It is further obviously right
> that the Receiver's report should be used in advance of the final hearing as a means by which
> to establish such facts as can be agreed between the parties and to identify the matters in dis-
> pute in need of resolution by the court. Further, in principle, I am prepared to accept that the
> Receiver's findings as to recoverable property should be given considerable persuasive weight
> by the court and to that extent her report enjoys special status.
>
> 30. However, this said, I also agree with the respondent's submissions that the Receiver's
> findings of recoverable property are not binding on the court, that it is the primary evidential
> material underlying her findings and said by her to justify them, which is of crucial impor-
> tance together with any additional evidence called before the court and that it is the duty of
> the court, in determining any area of dispute between the parties carefully to scrutinise and
> weigh that evidence in order to determine whether the claim to recoverable property is made
> out... The statutory provisions referred to do not alter either the burden or standard of proof
> which is upon the claimant to establish the existence of recoverable property on the balance of

probabilities by cogent evidence. The findings of the receiver do not in themselves reverse the burden of proof so as to put any onus on the respondent to disprove her findings...

### Challenging the findings of the interim receiver

**13.135** If a party wishes to dispute the correctness of the findings of an interim receiver, they should in the first instance notify the receiver in writing of the matter that they take issue with for the receiver to consider. Similar considerations apply where a party believes that a receiver has taken account of evidence which is either not relevant or is incorrect. Thereafter the interim receiver should either reply in writing or prepare a further report for the court. Whether it is desirable for interim receivers to meet with the parties in the absence of the other parties is a moot point. Clearly there will be occasions where it is appropriate to give the other party notice that a meeting is going to take place and to invite their observations and/or attendance. On the other hand, to require a third party to attend on every occasion will not only lead to additional costs for that party, as well as potential inconvenience, but may well inhibit the subject matters that need to be discussed. The interim receiver is not acting as mediator, but is trying to establish the facts in order to report them to the court. The minutes of any such meeting, if a party has not attended, can thereafter be circulated, subject to the agreement of the party attending.

**13.136** Occasionally, respondents may wish to appoint their own forensic accountant or expert witness to deal with issues that arise. For funding in relation to the same, see para 13.252.

### Applications for an IRO

**13.137** Where the enforcement authority is considering taking proceedings for a recovery order in the High Court, the relevant director may apply to the court for an IRO (whether before or after starting proceedings) (see s 246(1)). An example of such an order is found at Appendix 16.

**13.138** An application for an IRO may be made without notice if the circumstances are such that notice of the application would prejudice any right of the enforcement authority to obtain a recovery order in respect of any property (see s 246(3)), for example, because of the risk of dissipation.

**13.139** It is a requirement of s 247(2) that an IRO must require the interim receiver to take any steps which the court thinks necessary to establish:

    (a) whether or not the property to which an order applies is recoverable property or associated property;

    (b) whether or not any other property is recoverable property (in relation to the same unlawful conduct) and if it is, who holds it (s 247(1)).

### Loss of power to investigate

**13.140** It should be noted that up to the issuing of the claim form or until an IRO is made the enforcement authority has access to the civil investigation powers set out in Pt 8 of POCA. Once an IRO is made or a claim form for civil recovery is issued the enforcement authority ceases to have the powers set out in Pt 8 (s 341(3)) and the duty of taking further steps to establish facts about the property is placed with the interim receiver acting under the court's direction.

**13.141** The relevant authority also loses the power to obtain a disclosure order under s 357. This is because s 391(3) provides that an application for a disclosure order must state that certain property specified in the application is subject to a civil recovery investigation. Section 341(3) provides that an investigation is not a civil recovery investigation if an IRO applies in relation to the property. Therefore the only person who can use compulsory questioning powers is the interim receiver. The enforcement authority would thus be prohibited from doing so.

**Previous interim receiver investigations**

In *Director of The Assets Recovery Agency v Szepietowski and others* [2006] EWHC 2406 **13.142** (Admin), The Times, 25 October 2006, the Court considered whether, on an application for the appointment of an interim receiver over certain property, an enforcement agency would be entitled to rely on information about property which had only come to light as a result of investigations conducted pursuant to a previous IRO which related to *different* wrongdoing by the proposed defendant. Silber J found it would be permissible, on the basis that:

(1) if the applicant could not use information obtained by the interim receiver relating to *different* unlawful conduct, it would undermine the 'general purposes' of the civil recovery provisions;

(2) there would be a serious loophole in the Act that would confer a form of immunity from the provisions of the Act on a wrongdoer who had property, which had been obtained through 'unlawful conduct';

(3) there was no basis at common law for restricting the use of that information in the absence of a provision in the first IRO preventing the use of the information obtained.

**Purpose and conditions**

Under s 246(2) an IRO is an order for:                                                      **13.143**

(a) the detention, custody, or preservation of property; and

(b) the appointment of an interim receiver.

A court may make an IRO on the application of the relevant director if it is satisfied that **13.144** either of the following two conditions is met:

(1) that there is a good arguable case that the property to which the application for the order relates is or includes 'recoverable property', and that, if any of it is not recoverable property, it is 'associated property' (see s 246(5));

(2) that if the property to which the application for the order relates includes property alleged to be associated property, and the enforcement authority has not established the identity of the person who holds it, the authority has taken all reasonable steps to do so (see s 246(6)).

If either of these conditions is met, an application can be made to the High Court to make an IRO and this may be done before the director issues a claim form for a recovery order. The application may also be without notice if the enforcement authority believes that giving notice would prejudice its right to recover the property (s 246(3)).

Often it may be necessary to apply *ex parte* in circumstances where alerting the potential **13.145** parties may cause the property to be either hidden or dissipated.

**'Good arguable case'**

The expression 'good arguable case' is not defined in the Act although it is already used in **13.146** applications for injunctions to freeze disputed property in civil courts under the freezing injunction regime formerly known as Mareva injunctions. In *The Niedersachsen* [1983] 2 Lloyd's Rep 600, 605A it was held a 'good arguable case' related to the merits of the substantive claim and was described as 'one which is more than barely capable of serious argument, but not necessarily one which the judge considers would have a better than 50 per cent chance of success'. The courts have also observed that 'it is not enough to show an arguable case, namely one which a competent advocate can get on its feet. Something markedly better than that is required, even if it cannot be said with confidence that the Plaintiff is more likely to be right than wrong' (*Orri v Moundreas* [1981] Com LR 168, Mustill J QBD).

**13.147**  In *Director of The Assets Recovery Agency and Szepietowski and others* [2007] EWCA 766, The Times, 21 August 2007, Waller LJ stated:

> the ARA must first establish a good arguable case that a certain kind of unlawful conduct occurred and then a good arguable case that property was obtained though that kind of unlawful conduct. What the ARA is not required to do is to establish a good arguable case that any property was obtained through a specific criminal offence, even of the general kind alleged [para 26].

He added at para 28:

> ...in considering whether a good arguable case has been established, it will be necessary to examine first whether it is arguable on the evidence that unlawful conduct of the kind asserted by the ARA has taken place i.e. mortgage fraud. Next needs to be considered whether it is arguable that the property sought to be frozen represents property originally obtained through such unlawful conduct, but not necessarily through specific examples of that conduct; and finally, if there is some evidence that property was obtained though unlawful conduct, consideration needs to be given to any untruthful explanation or a lack of explanation where opportunity has been given to provide it. An untruthful explanation or a failure to offer an explanation may add strength to the arguability of the case.

### Application for an IRO: practice and procedure

**13.148**  Under para 5.1 of the Civil Recovery Proceedings Practice Direction, an application for an IRO must be made:

(1)  to a High Court judge; and
(2)  in accordance with CPR Pt 23.

Rule 23 CPR requires both written evidence in support and a draft order.

**13.149**  The application may be made without notice in the circumstances set out in s 246(3) of the Act (para 5.3(2)).

**13.150**  Under para 5.5, CPR Pt 69 (the court's power to appoint a receiver) and its Practice Direction apply to an application for an IRO with the following modifications:

(1)  paragraph 2.1 of the PD supplementing Part 69 does not apply;
(2)  the enforcement authority's written evidence must, in addition to the matters required by paragraph 4.1 of that PD, also state in relation to each item or description of property in respect of which the order is sought—
   (a)  whether the property is alleged to be—
      (i)   recoverable property;
      (ii)  associated property, and the facts relied upon in support of that allegation; and

(b) in the case of any associated property—
    (i) who is believed to hold the property;
    (ii) if the enforcement authority is unable to establish who holds the property, the steps that have been taken to establish their identity; and
(3) the enforcement authority's written evidence must always identify a nominee and include the information in paragraph 4.2 of the PD [claim form for a recovery order].

**13.151** There must, under para 5.6, be filed with the application notice a draft of the order sought. This should if possible also be supplied to the court in electronic form. An example draft order is found at Appendix 16.

**13.152** In *R (on the application of the Director of the Assets Recovery Agency) v H*, The Independent, 8 November 2004, McCombe J held that it is important that the jurisdiction within s 246 of POCA should be exercised carefully, so that people are not wrongfully injuncted, or injuncted for a period longer than is required. Equally, a court should not permit an individual to attack the basis upon which the order is made simply by choosing a snapshot in time where the evidence remains incomplete and thereby 'crawl away' from the consequences of various suspicions until the investigation is complete and matters are capable of clear resolution.

### IRO made before commencement of claim for civil recovery

**13.153** Pursuant to para 5A of the Civil Recovery Proceedings Practice Direction, an IRO which is made before a claim for a recovery order has been commenced must:

(1) specify a period in which the enforcement authority must either start the claim or apply for the continuation of the order while it carries out its investigations; and
(2) provide that the order shall be set aside if the enforcement authority does not start the claim or apply for its continuation before the end of that period.

### Duty of full and frank disclosure

**13.154** This is considered at para 13.53 above.

### The need for expedition

**13.155** In *Director of the Assets Recovery Agency v (1) Jia Jin He (2) Dan Dan Chen* [2004] EWHC 3021 (Admin) Collins J commented at para 81:

> . . . It is plain that there is a need for expedition. The receiver has an obligation to report as soon as practicable and there is a serious interference with Mr. He's property and his ability to carry on business if the reality is that he is not in any way involved in criminal conduct and it is not to be regarded as recoverable property. The matters which the receiver has to investigate are of some complexity, and it is not surprising that she has taken some time to resolve them. But the time is nigh when enquiries must be brought to a conclusion.

### Other powers of the High Court

**13.156** The High Court has an inherent discretion in civil proceedings to make such and any orders in law that it considers appropriate when making interlocutory injunctions (see *AJ Bekhor & Co Ltd v Bilton* [1981] QB 923 (CA)). This discretion is reflected in s 246(8) which states that the power to make an IRO is not limited by ss 247 to 255 of POCA.

### Functions of an interim receiver

**13.157**   The enforcement authority must nominate a suitably qualified person for appointment as an interim receiver. This will usually be an independent licensed insolvency practitioner. It may not be a member of the staff of the agency in question (s 246(7)).

**13.158**   The IRO made by the High Court may authorise or require the interim receiver to:

(a)  exercise any of the powers mentioned in Sch 6 to POCA;

(b)  take any other steps the court thinks appropriate,

for securing the detention, custody, or preservation of the property to which the order applies or of taking any steps under subs (2) (s 247(1)).

### Contents of the order

**13.159**   Schedule 6 of POCA is reproduced at Appendix 8. The powers it invests in an interim receiver include the following:

(1)  The power to seize property to which the order applies.

(2)  The power to obtain information or require a person to answer any questions.

(3)  The power to enter any premises in the UK to which the interim order applies and take the following steps:

    (a)  carry out a search or inspection of anything described in the order;

    (b)  make or obtain a copy, photograph, or other record of anything so described, and

    (c)  remove anything which the receiver is required to take possession of in pursuance of the order.

(4)  The power to manage any property to which the order applies, including selling or otherwise disposing of assets comprised in the property which are perishable or which ought to be disposed of before their value diminishes, or where the property comprises assets of a trade or business, or incurring capital expenditure in respect of the property.

**13.160**   The power to sell depreciating assets remains the most controversial of these, and can include cars and other high-value items. In such circumstances it is submitted that the receiver should give the respondent/owner sufficient notice of the sale to allow them the opportunity to make representations, either by correspondence or by way of an application to the High Court, if the costs of such a course are not prohibitive.

**13.161**   Schedule 6 also anticipates that the IRO may give the interim receiver access to any premises that he may need to enter in pursuance of Sch 6 para 3. The order may also require any person to give the interim receiver any assistance he may need for taking the steps mentioned above.

**13.162**   An IRO may also require any person to whose property the order applies to bring or repatriate the property to a place in England and Wales specified by the interim receiver, or place it into the custody of the interim receiver (if, in either case the person to whose property the order applies is able to do so), and/or to do anything he is reasonably required to do by the interim receiver for the preservation of the property (see s 250(1)).

**13.163**   The IRO may also require any person to whose property the order applies to bring any documents relating to the property which are in his possession or control to a place (in England and Wales) specified by the interim receiver or to place them in the custody of the interim receiver. For these purposes 'document' means anything in which information of any description is recorded (s 250(2)). This presumably would extend to computer files.

A person who ignores or contravenes such an order would potentially be liable to committal **13.164** proceedings in the High Court for contempt (see *SOCA v McKinney* [2008] NIQB 111).

### Restrictions on dealing with property

Under s 252(1) of POCA: **13.165**

> An interim receiving order must, subject to any exclusion made in accordance with this section, prohibit any person to whose property the order applies from dealing with the property.

Exclusions may be made when the IRO is made or on an application to vary the order (see s 252(2)). Under s 252(3) an exclusion may, in particular, make provision for the purpose of enabling any person:

(a) to meet his reasonable living expenses or
(b) to carry on any trade, business, profession or occupation, and may be made subject to conditions.

The purpose of this section is to ensure that IROs prevent any dealing with the property that **13.166** they cover. It also anticipates that from time to time there will be exclusions to that rule. 'Dealing' with property includes disposing of it, taking possession of it, or removing it from the UK (see s 316(1)).

Any excluded property must either be specified or described in general terms in the order **13.167** (s 252(5)).

### Contents of the order in terms of reporting by the receiver

Section 255(2) states that an IRO must require the interim receiver to report his findings to **13.168** the court and serve copies of his reports on the enforcement authority, and on any person who holds any property to which the order applies or who may otherwise be affected by the report. This requirement is considered in more detail under 'Reporting to the enforcement authority and the court', below.

### Protection against self-incrimination

Under Sch 6 para 2(3) to POCA, any answer given by a person in pursuance of the require- **13.169** ments set out in para 2 may not be used in evidence against him in criminal proceedings (see also para 2(4)(b)). However, it should be noted that contempt proceedings for any failure to cooperate or fully disclose may arise.

### Protection for the receiver

Section 246(3) provides legal protection for the receiver if he mistakenly, but honestly, deals **13.170** with property that is not the property specified in the order, providing that those dealings are not caused by his or her own negligence.

### Applications to clarify the receiver's powers

The interim receiver, any party to the proceedings, and any person affected by any action **13.171** taken by the interim receiver, or who may be affected by any action proposed to be taken by him, may at any time apply to the court for directions in relation to the interim receiver's functions. Once such an application has been made and the matter is before the court, before giving any directions the court must (as well as giving the parties to the proceedings an opportunity to be heard) give such an opportunity to the interim receiver and to any person who may be interested in the application (see s 251(1) and (2)). Such directions may be used to clarify the powers of the receiver in relation to certain property.

### Applications for directions

**13.172**  Under para 6.1 of the Practice Direction, an application for directions in relation to the interim receiver's functions may, under s 251 of the Act, be made at any time by:

(1)  the interim receiver;
(2)  any party to the proceedings; and
(3)  any person affected by any action taken by the interim receiver, or who may be affected by any action proposed to be taken by him.

**13.173**  The application must always be made by application notice, which must be served on:

(1)  the interim receiver (unless he is the applicant);
(2)  every party to the proceedings; and
(3)  any other person who may be interested in the application.

### Power to vary or set aside

**13.174**  The court may at any time vary or set aside an IRO (see s 251(3)). However, before exercising that power the court must give such opportunity to the interim receiver, and to any person who may be affected by the court's decision, an opportunity to be heard, including the parties to the proceedings themselves (s 251(4)).

**13.175**  Section 252(6) of POCA provides that the power to make exclusions to an IRO has to be exercised with a view to ensuring that the satisfaction of any right of the enforcement authority to recover property obtained through unlawful conduct is not unduly prejudiced. The power to make exclusions to a freezing order made in support of a claim under Pt 5 should be exercised on that basis. In general a court is unlikely to permit a respondent who has property available that is not recoverable property to use property that is claimed to be recoverable property to meet his expenditure pending the hearing.

### Application to vary or discharge an IRO: practice and procedure

**13.176**  Under the Civil Recovery Practice Direction (para 7.1), an application to vary or discharge an IRO may be made at any time by:

(1)  the enforcement authority; or
(2)  any person affected by the order.

**13.177**  Paragraph 7.2 of the Practice Direction states that a copy of the application notice must be served on:

(1)  every party to the proceedings;
(2)  the interim receiver; and
(3)  any other person who may be affected by the court's decision.

**13.178**  The difficulty in making an application for discharge prematurely was illustrated in *Director of the Assets Recovery Agency v Molloy* [2006] NIQB 49, where Coghlin J dealt with an application to discharge in circumstances where it was suggested ARA had not identified any relevant unlawful conduct on the part of the respondent, nor identified any property alleged to have been obtained as a result of such unlawful conduct. Coghlin J held that while no property had been specifically identified as representing the product of unlawful conduct, such identification may have been unlikely at the stage of the application he was dealing with because of extensive and complex property arrangements. He added:

> it is the specific task of the interim receiver to investigate that property for the purposes of establishing whether or not it is recoverable property...a good deal of progress has already been made and it has become necessary to amend Sch 2 of the original receiving order so as to exclude a substantial amount of property which is no longer regarded as recoverable. However, at this stage, I remain of the view that there is a good arguable case that the property to which this interim receiving order relates is or includes recoverable property...and, accordingly, I dismiss this application.

### Non-specified recoverable property

As soon as an interim receiver believes that property not specifically referred to in the order is recoverable then he should take steps to seize and take possession of that property. It is only by doing this that the risk of dissipation is minimised pending an application to the court to seek directions in respect of the non-specified property. Such an application therefore should be made forthwith in order to protect the interests of all the parties affected, as well as to inform the court as to what has happened. It may also be that the interim receiver will be required to give evidence and be cross-examined in relation to the property itself. **13.179**

The court may then either order that the property be returned or extend the order itself to specifically include it and in so doing clarify that the newly discovered asset is potentially recoverable property. Such a conclusion is essential to the effective working of Pt 5 of POCA and its purpose of recovering the proceeds of crime. **13.180**

### Exclusion of property which is not recoverable

If the court decides that any property to which an IRO applies is neither recoverable property nor associated property, it must vary the order so as to exclude it (s 254(1)). **13.181**

Under s 254(2) the court may (importing discretion) also exclude property providing the enforcement authority's rights to recover the remaining property is not prejudiced: **13.182**

> The court may vary an interim receiving order so as to exclude from the property to which the order applies any property which is alleged to be associated property if the court thinks the satisfaction of any right of the enforcement authority to recover the property obtained through unlawful conduct will not be prejudiced.

Under s 245(3) the court may exclude any property within this section on any terms or conditions that the court thinks 'necessary or expedient'. **13.183**

### Exclusion of property to cover legal expenses

The issue of release of restrained funds to cover a respondent's legal costs is set out at the end of this chapter. **13.184**

**Interim receiver's expenses**

**13.185**   Section 99 of SOCPA amended s 280 of POCA (Applying realised proceeds) to insert after subs (2):

(3)   the enforcement authority may apply a sum received by it under sub-section (2) in making payment of the remuneration and expenses of
   (a)   the trustee or
   (b)   any interim receiver appointed in, or in anticipation of, the proceedings for the recovery order.

(4)   Sub-section (3)(a) does not apply in relation to the remuneration of the trustee if the trustee is a member of the staff of the enforcement authority concerned.

This effectively allows for the enforcement authority to recompense the interim receiver (and the trustee for civil recovery) from sums which represent the realised proceeds of property following a successful civil recovery order claim, after payments referred to in s 280(2) of POCA have been made. This directly mirrors the manner in which receivers are paid pursuant to Pts 2 and 4 of the Act.

**Interim receiverships over land**

**13.186**   The purpose of s 248 of POCA is to ensure that where an IRO is made over land, its effect may be reinforced by taking action at the Land Registry to prevent the disposal or dissipation of the land in question. The 'Registration Acts' (namely the Land Registration Act 1925, the Land Charges Act 1972, and the Land Registration Act 2002) apply in relation to IROs as they would apply in relation to orders which affect any other land where an order is made by the court for the purpose of enforcing judgments or other pending land actions (see s 248(1) and (2)).

**13.187**   Section 248(3) prohibits the registering of title under the Land Registration Act 2002 in respect of property covered by an IRO.

**13.188**   It should be noted that a person applying for an IRO should be treated for the purposes of s 57 of the Land Registration Act 1925 (inhibitions) as an interested person in relation to any registered land to which the application relates (see s 248(4)).

**Restriction on existing proceedings and rights**

**13.189**   Whilst an IRO has effect, the court may stay any action, execution, or other legal process in respect of the property to which the order applies. No distress may be levied against the property to which the order applies except with the leave of the court and subject to any terms the court may impose (see s 253(1)).

**13.190**   Section 253(2) allows the court in which proceedings are pending in respect of the property to stay them or impose terms on their continuation.

**13.191**   Section 253(3) deals with the situation where IROs apply to tenancies on premises. A landlord may not exercise a right of forfeiture by peaceful re-entry on a property affected by an order.

**13.192**   When exercising the powers conferred by s 253 the court must give the opportunity to the interim receiver (if appointed) and any other person who may be affected by the court's decision, including the parties, to be heard (s 253(4)).

## Reporting to the enforcement authority and the court

Section 255(1) reads:  **13.193**

(1) An interim receiving order must require the interim receiver to inform the enforcement authority and the court as soon as reasonably practicable if he thinks that—
  (a) any property to which the order applies by virtue of a claim that it is recoverable property is not recoverable property,
  (b) any property to which the order applies by virtue of a claim that it is associated property is not associated property,
  (c) any property to which the order does not apply is recoverable property (in relation to the same unlawful conduct) or associated property, or
  (d) any property to which the order applies is held by a person who is different from the person it is claimed holds it, or if he thinks that there has been any other material change of circumstances.

The Act therefore lays a proactive duty upon the receiver to inform both the enforcement authority and the court of circumstances where, eg, he believes that property covered by an IRO claimed to be recoverable property, is in fact not recoverable. By virtue of this section, it is submitted, there must also be an ongoing duty within the receivership to keep matters under review to ensure that s 255 is complied with.

This duty is a corollary to s 247(2) which requires the interim receiver to take any steps which  **13.194** the court thinks are necessary to establish whether or not the property to which the order applies is recoverable property or associated property.

Under s 255(2), an IRO must require the interim receiver:  **13.195**

(a) to report his findings to the court,
(b) to serve copies of his reports to the enforcement authority and on any person who holds any property to which the order applies or who may otherwise be affected by the report.

This formalises the receiver's duty to produce a formal report of his findings and ensure that he serves copies of that report on all those who may be affected by it. These reports may then be used as a basis to establish agreed facts in relation to disputed matters.

## F. The Legislative Steer and Third-Party Creditors

Section 252(6) of POCA states:  **13.196**

The power [of the Court] to make exclusions [regarding the general prohibition against dealing with receivership property] must be exercised with a view to ensuring, so far as is practicable, that the satisfaction of any right of the enforcement authority to recover the property . . . is not unduly prejudiced.

There is a distinct contrast between s 69(2)(c) of POCA (which deals with the legislative steer under Pt 2 of the Act (restraint and confiscation)) and s 252(6) under Pt 5. This may well be deliberate and designed to reflect that one section is concerned with confiscation of a criminal's benefit, whereas the other concerns the civil recovery of property. As a result it may be inappropriate to draw too much upon the case law that has arisen in relation to, for example, the payment of third-party debts/creditors, under the earlier legislation. Nevertheless, in *Serious Fraud Office v Lexi Holdings PLC (In Administration)* [2008] EWCA

Crim 1443 the Court of Appeal held that restraint orders made under POCA may not be varied to permit defendants to pay off unsecured third-party creditors, and it is submitted that their Lordships' reasoning therein may have persuasive application to any variations sought (outwith legal expenses) under the civil recovery scheme.

**13.197** Should s 252(6) of POCA be interpreted by reference to case law in the civil law jurisdiction of freezing/Mareva injunctions? It is submitted that the answer is no, and that s 252(6) is *sui generis*. Under freezing order/Mareva injunctions a bona fide creditor can recover their debts. This was confirmed by Lord Donaldson in *Re Peters* at p 879, who stated:

> The interest of the potential judgement creditor has to be balanced against those of actual creditors, whether secured or unsecured, and of the defendant himself who may succeed in the action and should be fettered in his dealing with his own property to the least possible extent necessary to ensure the interests of justice are not frustrated.

**13.198** In IRO and PFO matters it is appropriate for the court or the receiver to consider all approaches for the settlement of secured or unsecured debts (which are bona fide) on their merits. It would not, however, be appropriate, it is suggested, to release property from civil restraint when that property was the probable proceeds of unlawful conduct, because to do so would be to frustrate the purpose of the Act.

**13.199** An interim receiver will often be able to assist the court with this question, and where a court is faced with a dispute between the receiver and a respondent (or third party) as to the proposed course of a receivership, the court is likely to give greater weight to the disinterested views of the receiver, particularly if supported by professional advice and expertise (see *Re Piper* [2000] 1 WLR 473).

**13.200** Although s 252(6) may not be particularly robust, it must still be considered by the court, and the approach of the court therefore cannot be as liberal as that which a court might adopt when considering freezing order injunctions. A distinction may also be drawn in cases where the nexus to unlawful conduct has not yet been established in relation to any given asset and where the possibility at least must exist that that property will not be subject to civil recovery.

## G. The Insolvent Respondent

### Introduction

**13.201** Receiverships where an individual has been adjudged bankrupt have always been subject to different rules in proceeds of crime legislation—see eg s 15(2) of the DTOA and its corresponding provisions, together with s 32 of the DTA and s 84 of the CJA. In such cases the powers of a receiver have never been exercisable in relation to property within the bankrupt's estate or to property that is to be applied for the benefit of creditors.

**13.202** Voluntary arrangements were not similarly protected (see *Re M* [1992] QB 377 at p 381). So a receiver could have utilised his full powers before a defendant was adjudged bankrupt under the CJA or DTA. In *Re M*, Otton J concluded that the restraint order prohibits 'any person' from dealing with any realisable property, 'This prevents the debtor from petitioning for his own bankruptcy' (p 382).

Section 311 of POCA deals with insolvency in civil recovery proceedings under Pt 5. **13.203**
Proceedings for a recovery order may not be taken or continued in respect of property:

(1) that is an asset of a company which is being wound up;
(2) where the company or an individual has entered into a voluntary arrangement;
(3) where an interim trustee has already been appointed over it, pursuant to the Insolvency Acts; or
(4) where it is an asset comprised in the estate of an individual who has been adjudged bankrupt (see s 311(3) of POCA).

A potential flaw exists in that, knowing this, an individual may prefer to rack up debts/force **13.204**
his petition for bankruptcy rather than be subjected to civil recovery proceedings.

Unlike the situation in *Re M*, s 311 does not merely provide for a respondent who has actually **13.205**
been adjudged bankrupt, but also for individuals and companies who have entered into a voluntary arrangement under Pt 1 or Pt 8 of the Insolvency Act 1986. As a result, the diluted legislative steer in s 252 and the broadening of the categories to include voluntary arrangements has potentially made it easier for respondents to avoid civil recovery. Whether in practice individuals would pursue such a line is a moot point. Any suggestion of contrivance would be likely to be viewed dimly by the court, and might lead to the court interpreting s 252(6) in a more robust fashion.

### Insolvency and IROs

In *Q3 Media Ltd* [2006] EWHC 1553 (Ch D) Rimer J considered the issue of insolvency where **13.206**
an interim receiver had been appointed. The effect of a company being subject to an IRO and the supremacy of such an order was underlined. In relation to an application by a company's prospective creditor for an administration order over the company, although the court was satisfied that the company was unable to pay its debts, it was not satisfied that an order was likely to achieve the purpose of administration, as the company was subject to an IRO under s 246 of POCA. It was likely that all the company's assets were recoverable property and not available to creditors. Rimer J held that the basis of W's claim was that X were creditors and their claim was a claim in restitution, not a claim for a debt. Therefore it might be that W's claim was on behalf of prospective creditors, not creditors, and Q was waiting to see how X would make good their claim. However, in the circumstances, the court was satisfied that Q was unable to pay its debts as even if the applicants were regarded as prospective creditors, the unexplained failure to pay justified the inference that it was unable to pay. There was a good arguable case that all of Q's assets were recoverable property, given the IRO, and that Q was unable to pay its debts, so that the Insolvency Act 1986, Sch B1, para 11(A) had been satisfied. However, the court could not be satisfied under para 11(B), Sch 1 to the 1986 Act that the making of the administration order would be reasonably likely to achieve the purpose of administration, because if Q's assets were recoverable property they would be available to meet the creditors' demands. An administration order therefore was not granted at that stage.

## H. Compensation in IRO and PFO Cases

### Ability to claim

Where an IRO or a PFO is made by the court, and the court later decides that the prop- **13.207**
erty is neither recoverable property nor associated property, the person whose property

it is may make an application to the High Court for compensation (see s 283(1) and s 316(1)).

**13.208** The ability to claim compensation does not extend to property in respect of which a declaration has been made under s 281 (victims of theft), or in circumstances where an order under s 276 has been made (a consent order) (see s 283(2)).

**13.209** Under s 272(5):

> (5) If—
>> (a) a property freezing order, an interim receiving order [...] applied at any time to the associated property or joint tenancy, and
>> (b) the court is satisfied that the person who holds the associated property or who is an excepted joint owner has suffered loss as a result of the [...] order [...],
>> a recovery order making any provision by virtue of subsection (2) or (3) [of section 272] may require the enforcement authority to pay compensation to that person.

The criterion which the court is to apply is set out in s 272(6) and it is an amount the court thinks reasonable, having regard to the person's loss and any other relevant circumstance.

### Time limit for compensation application

**13.210** Where the court has decided that no recovery order should be made in respect of property the application for compensation must be made within a period of three months beginning:

> ...in relation to a decision of the High Court, with the date of the decision, or if any application is made for leave to appeal, with the date on which the application is withdrawn or refused or (if the application is granted) on which any proceedings on appeal are finally concluded (s 283(3)(a)).

**13.211** If the proceedings in respect of the property have been discontinued, the application for compensation must be made within the period of three months beginning with the discontinuance (see s 283(4)).

**13.212** If, but for s 269(2) (circumstances where a right of pre-emption, right of irritancy, right of return, or other similar right does not operate as a result of the vesting of any property under a recovery order), any right would have operated in favour of, or become exercisable by any person, that person may make an application to the court for compensation. Such an application must be made within three months (s 269(6)) beginning with the vesting referred to in s 269(2).

### The test the court should apply

**13.213** If the court is satisfied that the applicant has suffered loss as a result of the PFO or IRO, it may require the relevant enforcement authority to pay compensation to him under s 283(5). Similarly, if the court is satisfied that in consequence of the operation of s 269, the right of the applicant can no longer be operated or exercised by him, it may require the relevant agency to pay compensation to him. (It will be noted that these are discretionary awards and will clearly depend on the facts and evidence in the case.)

**13.214** The amount of compensation to be paid under s 283 is the amount that the court 'thinks reasonable' having regard to the loss suffered and any other relevant circumstances (see s 283(9)).

## I. Legal Expenses in Civil Recovery Proceedings

### Introduction

Section 98 and Sch 6 of SOCPA amends POCA to allow respondents who are subject to **13.215** civil proceedings to have access to their frozen assets in order to fund the costs of their legal representation. Such access was originally prohibited by s 252(4) of POCA.

The amended legislation is aimed at resolving funding difficulties and allowing matters to **13.216** proceed at a faster pace. It has the advantage of avoiding frustrating delays whilst Legal Aid Agency funding is explored. Equally, it has the disadvantage that defence firms must now go to the enforcement authority and in effect make their case for funding arrangements in which the relevant authority is not only a party, but the claimant of the property concerned. The concept of what are 'reasonable' legal expenses is left somewhat open by the amended legislation. It is intended that the courts will resolve any disagreement between the parties, although one can see that this has the potential to give rise to delay, with potential arguments being made in relation to both the HRA and judicial review, particularly bearing in mind that the legislation appears to afford employees of the relevant authority a discretion.

It is important to note that the regulations are designed to ensure that the assets can only be **13.217** used to fund what is described as 'a reasonable defence', and presumably therefore not to fund proceedings that extend or frustrate the legal process by unjustifiably diminishing the assets on legal fees. At the time of their introduction the Legal Aid Minister, Bridget Prentice, said:

> These measures will achieve a balance that will ensure that the tax payer does not foot the bill for defendants who can afford to pay their own legal costs, while also ensuring that frozen assets are not misused to fund a 'champagne defence'. They will ensure that funds are only released for legal costs where reasonable and proportionate.

In a press release issued at the time it was anticipated that the new measures would save around £3 million a year from the Legal Aid budget.

Whilst the intention of the legislation may be sound, it is suggested that Sch 6 to SOCPA **13.218** which seeks to amend s 286A of POCA and the amended Practice Direction in civil recovery proceedings together with the Proceeds of Crime Act 2002 (Legal Expenses in Civil Recovery Proceedings) Regulations 2005 have made this process unnecessarily complicated. As will be seen, defence firms are expected to carry out the work and only then submit their invoices to the enforcement authority for consideration of payment. Although the regulations anticipate a controlled and staged cost plan, clearly some work undertaken will lead to other enquiries which may not be anticipated at the beginning of an application. Furthermore, a respondent's solicitors may not wish to disclose every aspect of the work that they anticipate they will carry out to the person bringing the claim against them.

### Background to the provisions

Paragraph 15 of Sch 6 to SOCPA inserts into s 266 (Recovery Orders) subss 8(A) and 8(B), **13.219** which state:

> 8(A) A recovery order made by a court in England and Wales or Northern Ireland may provide for payment under section 280 of reasonable legal expenses that a person has reasonably incurred, or may reasonably incur, in respect of—

    (a)  the proceedings under this Part in which the order is made, or

    (b)  any related proceedings under this Part.

  8(B) If regulations under section 286B apply to an item of expenditure, a sum in respect of the item is not payable under section 280 in pursuance of provision under section 8(A) unless—

    (a)  the enforcement authority agrees to its payment, or

    (b)  the court has assessed the amount allowed by the regulations in respect of the item and the sum is paid in respect of the assessed amount.

**13.220**    Section 280(2) (application of the realised proceeds of a recovery order) is amended by para 18 of Sch 6 to SOCPA to insert after para (a):

  (aa) Next, any payment of the legal expenses which, after giving effect to section 266(8B), are payable under this sub-section in pursuance of a provision under section 266(8A) contained in the recovery order.

**13.221**    Paragraph 20 of Sch 6 inserts a new para 286B into POCA which sets out the Lord Chancellor's powers in terms of making provision for the purposes of remuneration allowable to representatives for work undertaken in civil recovery cases (which he has done, see below).

### The legal expenses regulations

**13.222**    Provision for legal expenses were introduced by the Proceeds of Crime Act 2002 (Legal Expenses in Civil Recovery Proceedings) Regulations 2005, SI 2005/3382 (as amended by SI 2008/523), which came into force on 1 January 2006 (see regulation 1).

### Legal expenses at the conclusion of proceedings

**13.223**    Part 4 of the Regulations deals with the agreement or assessment of expenses at the conclusion of civil recovery proceedings. It sets out the procedure for determining the amount payable in respect of legal expenses once the High Court has made a recovery order which vests property in the trustee for civil recovery and provides for the payment of those expenses out of that property. If the expenses are not agreed with the enforcement authority, proceedings must be commenced for them to be assessed by the court. Part 4 applies regardless of whether interim payments have been made under Pt 3, and the amount which must be paid is reduced by the amount of any interim payments.

**13.224**    Regulation 12 applies where a person seeks the enforcement authority's agreement to the payment of a sum in respect of his legal expenses pursuant to s 266(8B)(a) of the 2002 Act or Art 177(11)(a) of the Proceeds of Crime Act 2002 (External Requests and Orders) Order 2005.

**13.225**    In determining the amount which may be paid in respect of legal expenses with its agreement, the enforcement authority must have regard to the provisions of Pt 5 of the Regulations which apply on the assessment of those expenses by the court (reg 12(2)). Regulation 12(3) states:

  Where the enforcement authority agrees to the payment of the sum which a person seeks in respect of his legal expenses—

    (a)  it shall give that person and the trustee for civil recovery notice of the agreed sum; and

    (b)  the sum payable in respect of those expenses shall be the agreed sum.

**Expenses to be assessed if not agreed**

Unless the enforcement authority agrees to the payment of the sum which a person seeks **13.226** in respect of his legal expenses pursuant to a provision made in a recovery order, that person must commence proceedings for the assessment of those expenses in accordance with reg 13(2).

**Two-month time limit**

Regulation 13(2) states: **13.227**

(a) In relation to civil recovery proceedings in England and Wales, [a person] must commence proceedings for the detailed assessment of those expenses in accordance with CPR Part 47, subject to the modifications that—
  (i) r 47.7 shall have effect as if it provided that he must commence those proceedings not later than two months after the date of the recovery order; and
  (ii) r 47.14(2) shall have effect as if it is provided that he must file a request for a detailed assessment hearing not later than two months after the expiry of the period for commencing the detailed assessment proceedings.

**Practice and procedure**

The Proceeds of Crime Act 2002 (Legal Expenses in Civil Recovery Proceedings) Regulations **13.228** 2005 came into force on 1 January 2006 (SI 2005/3382, as amended by SI 2008/523). Part 2 of those Regulations set out the general conditions required before money can be released to pay legal fees. Pursuant to regulation 4 an exclusion must specify:

(a) the stage or stages in civil recovery proceedings to which it relates; and
(b) the maximum amount which may be released in respect of legal expenses for each stage to which it relates.

If the solicitor acting for the person to whose legal expenses the exclusion relates, becomes **13.229** aware that:

(a) that person's legal expenses in respect of any stage in civil recovery proceedings have exceeded or will exceed the maximum amount specified in the exclusion for that stage; or
(b) that person's total legal expenses in respect of all the stages to which the exclusion relates have exceeded or will exceed the total amount that may be released pursuant to the exclusion,

the solicitor must give notice to the enforcement authority and the court as soon as reasonably practicable. This obviously places a proactive duty upon the solicitor and the respondent's legal advisers (see reg 5 and PD7A.8).

Where a person has incurred legal expenses in relation to a stage in civil recovery proceedings **13.230** specified in an exclusion:

(a) during any period when a property freezing order or IRO has effect, a sum may only be released in respect of those expenses in accordance with Pt 3 of the Regulations;
(b) where the court makes a recovery order which provides for the payment of that person's reasonable legal expenses in respect of civil recovery proceedings, the sum payable in respect of his legal expenses shall be determined in accordance with Pt 4 of the

Regulations, regardless of whether a sum has been released in respect of any of these expenses under Pt 3.

### Legal expenses at the commencement of proceedings

**13.231**  Paragraph 5B.1 of the Civil Recovery Proceedings Practice Direction (not to be confused with the Legal Expenses in Civil Recovery Proceedings Regulations) sets out the court's power to make exclusions for the purpose of enabling a respondent to meet his reasonable legal costs so that he may:

(1)  take advice in relation to the order;
(2)  prepare a statement of assets in accordance with para 7A.3; and
(3)  if so advised, apply for the order to be varied or set aside.

As a result, when a court makes a PFO or an IRO it may also make an exclusion to enable the respondent to meet his reasonable legal costs so that (for example) when the claim is commenced: (1) he may file an Acknowledgment of Service and any written evidence on which he intends to rely; or (2) he may apply for a further exclusion for the purpose of enabling him to meet his reasonable costs of the proceedings (see PD 5B.2).

**13.232**  The total amount specified in the initial exclusion will not, according to the Practice Direction, normally exceed £3,000. This clearly affords both the enforcement authority and the court some latitude in relation to the amount and there may be instances where initial exclusions will exceed that figure (particularly, for example, if the respondent has to make inquiries overseas or if a preliminary hearing or conference is envisaged which require further work, or if the respondent is separated from the individual who now holds the appropriate records).

**13.233**  The Practice Direction also provides that when an exclusion is made for the purpose of enabling a person to meet his reasonable legal costs, it should specify:

(1)  the stage or stages in civil recovery proceedings to which it relates;
(2)  the maximum amount which may be released in respect of legal costs for each specified stage; and
(3)  the total amount which may be released in respect of legal costs pursuant to the exclusion (para 7A.7).

### Considerations for the court

**13.234**  The court, in deciding whether to make an exclusion for the purpose of enabling a person to meet legal expenses in respect of proceedings must:

(a)  have regard (in particular) to the desirability of the person being represented in any proceedings under this Part in which he is a participant; and
(b)  where the person is the respondent, disregard the possibility that legal representation of the person in any such proceedings might, were an exclusion not made, be funded by [legal aid].

**13.235**  The steer set out at s 252(6) of POCA, namely that the court's power 'be exercised with a view to ensuring that the satisfaction of any right of the enforcement authority to recover the property obtained through unlawful conduct is not unduly prejudiced', is now subject to s 252(4A).

Section 252(6) requires the court to have regard to equality of arms arguments and the desir-  **13.236**
ability of persons being legally represented. It tells the court to disregard the possibility that
legal representation might be funded by the legal aid scheme.

The amended subs (4) states:  **13.237**

> Where the court exercises the power to make an exclusion for the purpose of enabling a person
> to meet legal expenses that he incurred, or may incur, in respect of proceedings under this Part,
> it must ensure that the exclusion (a) is limited to reasonable legal expenses that the person has
> reasonably incurred or that he reasonably incurs, (b) specifies the total amount that may be
> released for legal expenses in pursuance of the exclusion, and (c) is made subject to the required
> conditions (see section 286A) in addition to any conditions imposed under sub-section (3).

The issue of legal funding was considered by Morgan J in *Director of the Asset Recovery Agency*  **13.238**
*v Patrick Fleming and others* [2007] NIQB 16. His Lordship indicated that for an exclusion
to be made in respect of legal expenses:

1. The defendants must file an affidavit containing a statement of assets.
2. The court must be satisfied that the defendants had no other assets, beyond those subject
   to the IRO, available to them to discharge their legal expenses.
3. The court must have regard in particular to the desirability of the person being represented in proceedings under Pt 5 of the Act.
4. Subject to section 252(4A) the power to make exclusions must be exercised with a view
   to ensuring, so far as practicable, that the satisfaction of any right of the enforcement
   authority to recover the properly obtained through unlawful conduct is not unduly
   prejudiced.
5. The exclusion must be limited to the legal expenses that are reasonable.
6. The exclusion must be limited to reasonable legal expenses that must, have been, or will
   be reasonably incurred.
7. The exclusion must specify the stage or stages in civil recovery proceedings to which it
   relates.
8. The exclusion must specify the maximum amount which may be released in respect of
   legal expenses for each stage to which the exclusion relates and the total for the entire
   exclusion if it covers more than one stage.
9. Any question over the amount of an exclusion for a reasonable legal expenses should
   normally be referred to the Taxing Master.
10. The defendant shall then comply with the procedure set out in the 2005 regulations (as
    amended) for payment and notification.

### Practice and procedure: Part 3 of the Regulations

Part 3 sets out the procedure for the release of frozen property to make interim payments  **13.239**
of legal expenses during civil recovery proceedings. Once expenses have been incurred,
the person may seek the enforcement authority's agreement to the release of an interim
payment in respect of those expenses. The amount which may be released is the amount
which the relevant agency agrees or 65 per cent of the amount claimed, whichever is the
greater.

A request for the enforcement authority's agreement to the release of a sum in respect of legal  **13.240**
expenses must be made in writing to the relevant agency by the person to whose expenses the
exclusion relates (see reg 8).

**13.241** The request must describe the stage or stages in the civil recovery proceedings in relation to which the legal expenses were incurred; summarise the work done in connection with each stage; be accompanied by any invoices, receipts, or other documents which are necessary to show that the expenses have been incurred; and identify any item or description of property from which the person making the request wishes the sum to be released.

**13.242** A person may not make a request under this regulation in respect of legal expenses which he has not yet incurred; or more than once in any two-month period.

### The enforcement authority's response

**13.243** Pursuant to reg 9, the enforcement authority is required to respond to a request to release legal fees not later than twenty-one days after it receives the request and such a response must set out:

    (a) whether it agrees to the release of the requested sum; and

    (b) if it does not agree to the release of the requested sum:

        (i) the amount (if any) which it agrees may be released; and

        (ii) the reasons for its decision.

**13.244** Where an IRO applies to the property from which it is proposed that the requested sum should be released, the enforcement authority must at the same time send copies of the request and the notice referred to in reg 9(1) to the interim receiver.

**13.245** In determining the amount which may be released in respect of legal expenses with its agreement, the enforcement authority must have regard to the provisions of Pt 5 of the Regulations, which set out the basis for assessment of legal expenses and which apply on the assessment of those expenses by the court (reg 9(3)).

### Release of an interim payment

**13.246** Pursuant to the Legal Expenses Regulations (reg 10), the sum which may be released is the greater of:

    (a) the amount which the enforcement authority agrees may be released; and

    (b) 65 per cent of the requested sum.

The sum may only be released to (i) the solicitor who is instructed to act in the civil recovery proceedings for the person to whose legal expenses the exclusion relates; or (ii) where appropriate, to the solicitor who was so instructed when the legal expenses to which the sum relates were incurred.

**13.247** There is no provision for the sum that is to be released to go to the respondents themselves. If the enforcement authority does not agree the amount to be released, only 65 per cent of the requested sum may be released at this stage.

### Evidence for the purpose of meeting legal costs

**13.248** Pursuant to para 7.3 of the Practice Direction, the evidence in support of an application for the purpose of enabling a person to meet his reasonable legal costs must:

    (1) contain full details of the stage or stages in civil recovery proceedings in respect of which the costs in question have been or will be incurred;

(2) include an estimate of the costs which the person has incurred and will incur in relation to each stage to which the application relates (see precedent H of the Costs Precedent annexed to the Practice Direction);

(3) include a statement of assets containing the information set out in para 7A.3 (unless the person has previously filed such a statement in the same civil recovery proceedings and there has been no material change in the facts set out in the statement);

(4) where the court has previously made an exclusion in respect of any stage to which the application relates, explain why the person's costs will exceed the amount specified in the exclusion for that stage; and

(5) state whether the terms of the exclusion have been agreed with the enforcement authority.

### Ongoing opportunity

The Practice Direction goes on to state that when the court makes an order or gives direc-  **13.249**
tions in civil recovery proceedings, it will at the same time consider whether it is appropriate to make or vary an exclusion for the purpose of enabling any person affected by the order or directions to meet his reasonable legal costs (see para 7A.1).

### Statement of assets

The court will not make an exclusion for the purpose of enabling a person to meet his reason-  **13.250**
able legal costs (other than as provided for by para 5B.1) unless that person has made and filed a statement of assets. Paragraph 7A.3 defines a statement of assets as being a witness statement which sets out all the property which the maker of the statement owns, holds, or controls, or in which he has an interest, giving the value, location, and details of all such property. To that extent it is similar to a disclosure statement provided in restraint proceedings, albeit without the requirement to give details dating back six years. Such a statement must bear a statement of truth.

Paragraph 7A.3 also provides that the information given in a statement of assets under the  **13.251**
Practice Direction will be used only for the purpose of the civil recovery proceedings. What it does not do is provide that the maker of the statement will be afforded some form of guarantee that the information that he or she supplies will not then be utilised by the enforcement authority in terms of pursuing further assets.

### Legal costs and forensic accountants

In *Director of the Asset Recovery Agency v Patrick Fleming and others* [2007] NIQB 16, Morgan  **13.252**
J was asked by the respondent to consider making an exclusion for legal expenses in order for a forensic accountant to be employed. He indicated that the following matters should be taken into account in such applications (para 20):

(a) If a party considers that the interim receiver has not considered relevant evidence, he should first request of the receiver in writing that the matter be investigated. If this request is not met sufficiently or is not accepted then the defendant can apply to the court for a direction that the receiver so investigate.

(b) If a party considers that the interim receiver has considered evidence which is not relevant, or is incorrect, it should notify the interim receiver in writing of this view. If this request is not met sufficiently or is not accepted then the defendant can apply to the court for a direction in respect of same.

(c) If a party has taken action as above, the interim receiver should make a further report to the court stating her conclusions as to the matters raised.

(d) If a party wishes to explore the methodology or findings of a report, that party may request a meeting with the interim receiver. If such a meeting occurs, all parties should be invited and the meeting should be properly minuted for the court.

(e) If a party then wishes to challenge the methodology or findings in an interim receiver's report, that party should apply to the court for a legal expenses exclusion for the retention of a forensic accountant with an affidavit setting out in a focused way which aspects of the report it takes issue with.

(f) If a sufficiently detailed affidavit is sworn and served, the court should allow time for both the interim receiver and the other parties to make any replying affidavits they wish.

(g) Upon receipt and consideration of any replying affidavits, the court should reach a determination as to whether there are any issues on which it may be reasonable to incur expenditure for expert witnesses through a legal expenses exclusion.

(h) In reaching a decision the court may wish to hear from its interim receiver in a preliminary hearing in order to be satisfied as to whether there is any substance to the defendant's claims and also to ensure that the court's interim receiver is carrying out her functions properly.

(i) The court should set out the specific areas on which the defendant will be entitled to have his own expert witness and the exclusion orders shall specify those areas.

**13.253** He added that where the court decides to make a legal expenses exclusion in respect of a forensic accountant the respondent should normally file an affidavit setting out the hourly rate of the forensic accountant who is going to do the work, the basis for that rate, the work involved in dealing with the issues, the time required to be spent on a specific issue including the time for any meetings, and the length of time envisaged in respect of evidence. Where there is a dispute in relation to these matters the court will normally rely upon the Taxing Master (para 21).

### Legal expenses following the making of a recovery order

**13.254** Pursuant to para 7B.1 of the Civil Recovery Proceedings Practice Direction, where the court:

(1) makes a recovery order in respect of property which was the subject of a property freezing order or interim receiving order; and

(2) had made an exclusion from the property freezing order or interim receiving order for the purpose of enabling a person to meet his reasonable legal costs,

the recovery order will make provision under section 266(8A) of POCA or Art 177(10) of the External Requests Order.

Effectively where the court makes a recovery order which provides for the payment of a person's reasonable legal costs in respect of civil recovery proceedings, it will at the same time make an order for the detailed assessments of those costs, if they are not agreed. Parts 4 and 5 of the Regulations, Pt 47 of the CPR, and r 49A of the Practice Direction on Costs apply to a detailed assessment pursuant to such an order (see para 7B.2).

### Part 4 of the Regulations

**13.255** Part 4 sets out the procedure for determining the amount payable in respect of legal expenses once the High Court has made a recovery order which vests property in the trustee for civil recovery and provides for the payment of those expenses out of that property. If the expenses are not agreed with the enforcement authority, proceedings must be commenced for them to be assessed by the court. Part 4 applies regardless of whether any interim payments have been made under Pt 3, and the amount which must be paid is reduced by the amount of any interim payments.

### Setting aside the exclusion

The court may set aside any exclusion which it has made for legal expenses or reduce any amount specified in such an exclusion, if it is satisfied that the person has property which the PFO or IRO does not apply to and from which he may meet his legal costs (Practice Direction 7A.4). **13.256**

The court's approach to this issue was considered in *SOCA v Szepietowski* [2009] EWHC 344 (Ch); [2010] 1 WLR 1316 (Henderson J), a case which involved a trustee defending recovery order proceedings against trust assets. The case concerned S who was a solicitor who had received money from a client which SOCA alleged had been obtained by unlawful conduct. That money was held in an offshore trust; S was the sole trustee and the client was sole beneficiary. SOCA applied for a civil recovery order and an interim receiving order was made over assets of S. (As part of the background there had been a claim against S in a personal capacity in the same proceedings, with criminal allegations against him including mortgage fraud, which was settled.) **13.257**

It was found that S had substantial available assets. S argued that, because he was defending the claim in his capacity as a trustee, he was entitled to be indemnified out of the relevant trust fund in respect of his costs. It was argued that this general rule of trust law should be applied so far as possible to be consistent with the provisions of the exclusion order regime, contending that Parliament's intention was not that a trustee who was defending civil recovery proceedings would have to either fund the defence from assets available to him in his personal capacity or choose not to defend the proceedings at all. That argument was rejected. The exclusion order regime is silent about persons being sued as a trustee or when holding another fiduciary capacity; Henderson J held that that omission was not accidental. He considered that Parliament's intention must have been for the regime to apply to all persons in whom recoverable property was allegedly vested. There was no discretion to disregard the available personal assets. **13.258**

Whilst Henderson J acknowledged there would clearly be difficulties for a trustee defendant with available personal assets, his analysis was that the trustee defendant with available personal assets was not compelled to defend the proceedings at his own expense. In the majority of cases defending the proceedings would mean a temporary funding only of the defence by the trustee because on a successful defence the trustee could recover his costs from SOCA and by way of indemnity out of the relevant trust fund. Conversely, if the defence failed the court still has discretion to provide for his costs out of the fund under s 266(8A): a recovery order may provide for payment of 'reasonable legal expenses that a person has reasonably incurred, or may reasonably incur' in respect of recovery proceedings. It was noted by the court that only if the trustee had acted unreasonably in defending the proceedings would the court be likely to refuse to make a costs order in his favour. **13.259**

A trustee who acts reasonably, and has available personal assets, will not be able to obtain an exclusion order while the litigation is in progress, but should still be able to recover **13.260** all or most of his costs at the conclusion of the case; on the other hand, a trustee defendant without personal assets could obtain an exclusion in the same way as a non-trustee defendant. This may seem unduly unfair to the trustee with ample available assets but, as Henderson J put it, the regime 'cannot be stigmatised as unreasonable or unduly onerous for trustee defendants, bearing in mind the very strong public interest that property representing the proceeds of crime should be recovered with as few deductions made from it as possible'.

**13.261** The matter was considered further in another application in the same proceedings, *SOCA v Szepietowski* [2009] EWHC 1560 (Ch). The court rejected an argument by S that Practice Direction 7A.4 should be disregarded because it was in conflict with the Act and the Proceeds of Crime Act 2002 (Legal Expenses in Civil Recovery Proceedings) Regulations 2005. A non-statutory Practice Direction could not override legislation and if there was a conflict, logically the legislation would prevail. However, as a matter of fact there was no conflict here. The court had the power to set aside or vary an interim order under POCA and that included the varying or setting aside of exclusions in respect of property subject to the order. It was also noted that the compulsory obligation to apply Practice Directions could be overridden by the exercise of CPR case management powers in certain circumstances.

**13.262** The making of a legal costs exclusion order was put into its proper context by Henderson J in this second judgment: the making of an exclusion order did not automatically mean that an order under s 266(8A) would be made in the event of the court deciding to make a recovery order. An order under s 266(8A) was discretionary and it was that order which allowed for actual payment of costs as opposed to the exclusion order which simply identified the assets from which costs could be paid in due course if appropriate. For an example of a costs exclusion order being granted post-*Szepietowski*, see *SOCA v (1) Amir Azam (2) A* [2011] EWHC 1551 (Admin).

### Costs judge assessment

**13.263** Where there is dispute, the court will normally refer to a costs judge any question relating to the amount which an exclusion should allow for reasonable legal costs in respect of proceedings or a stage of the proceedings (Practice Direction 7A.5).

### Basis for assessment of legal expenses

**13.264** Part 5 of the Legal Expenses Regulations provides that the court is to assess legal expenses on the standard basis. It also specifies the hourly rates of remuneration which may be allowed in respect of work done by legal representatives. Higher rates may be allowed for cases involving substantial novel or complex issues of law or fact, and the rates are increased for legal representatives whose offices are situated in certain London postal code areas and districts.

**13.265** Pursuant to reg 16, the court must give effect to (a) any provision made in the recovery order for the purpose of enabling a person to meet his reasonable legal expenses in civil recovery proceedings; and (b) subject to subpara (a), the terms of any exclusion made for the purpose of enabling that person to meet those legal expenses (including the required conditions).

**13.266** The standard basis of assessing a person's legal expenses is set out in CPR r 44.4.

Remuneration for work done by a legal representative may only be allowed at the appropriate  **13.267**
hourly rate shown Table 13.1.

**Table 13.1  Rates of remuneration for legal representatives**

| Solicitors and their employees | | |
| --- | --- | --- |
| Senior solicitor (of at least 8 years' standing) | £187.50 | £225.00 |
| Solicitor (of at least 4 years' and less than 8 years' standing) | £150.00 | £187.50 |
| Junior solicitor (of less than 4 years' standing) | £107.50 | £131.25 |
| Trainee solicitor, paralegal, or other fee earner | £75.00 | £93.75 |
| Counsel | | |
| Queen's Counsel | – | £275.00 |
| Senior junior counsel (of at least 10 years' standing) | £150.00 | £225.00 |
| Junior counsel (of less than 10 years' standing) | £100.00 | £150.00 |

Several points arise from this table. Firstly, in relation to England and Wales, a reference  **13.268**
to number of years' standing as a solicitor or counsel is to be interpreted as referring to the
number of years of general qualification within the meaning of the Courts and Legal Services
Act 1990.

Secondly, the higher hourly rates as specified in the third column may only be allowed where  **13.269**
the case involves substantial novel or complex issues of law or fact. These are not defined
further in the Regulations; however, most courts will be adept at recognising same.

Thirdly, the rates specified in the table can be increased by 20 per cent for legal representa-  **13.270**
tives whose offices are situated in central London, namely EC1–4, SW1, W1, and WC1–2,
and increased by 10 per cent for legal representatives whose offices are situated in outer
London (meaning all other postcode districts and postcode areas including BR, CR, DA, E,
N, NW, SE, SW, UB, and W).

Fourthly, it is perhaps indicative of the current climate that there has been no movement in  **13.271**
the fees since the rates were introduced.

### Civil legal aid

It is important to note that civil legal aid remains available for cases where access to assets is  **13.272**
not possible.

# 14

# CIVIL RECOVERY: RECOVERY ORDERS; THE ECHR; AND TAXATION

# A. Introduction

**14.01** For ease of reference we have divided civil recovery into two parts. In this chapter we consider recovery orders themselves; the ECHR; the pension provisions; and the Pt 6 taxation powers.

**14.02** In the previous chapter we gave an overview of the legislation in relation to civil recovery and considered the interim measures anticipated by the amended Act, namely PFOs, MROs, and IROs, together with the provisions for the release of funds to cover legal expenses in civil recovery cases.

### The purpose of civil recovery

**14.03** The purpose of the legislation was considered in *R (on the application of the Director of the Assets Recovery Agency) v Ashton (Paul)* [2006] EWHC 1064 (Admin), where Newman J stated (at para 41):

> What, in my judgment, Parliament is here doing is seeking to enforce some measure of recovery for the benefit of the State. It is seeking to make a recovery for the State which is in the public interest of the State, so that the proceeds of crime should not be at large in society for the benefit of those who happen to be in possession of it at the time.

> Crime, when it is committed, is not simply a crime against the individual victim of the crime. Crime, when it occurs, is an offence against the good order of the State and, apart from the victim, it puts the State to enormous expense to resolve questions in connection with [it].

**14.04** In *Director of the Assets Recovery Agency v Creaven* [2005] EWHC 2726 Admin; [2006] 1 WLR 622, Stanley Burnton J held that it was the clear policy of the Act to deprive respondents of property obtained through unlawful conduct (unless they could establish a statutory defence), and for that property to be transferred for the benefit of the community.

### The reduction of crime

**14.05** Section 2A of POCA (as amended by the SCA, ss 74(2) and Sch 8 (para 124) and brought into force by SI 2008/755 on 1 April 2008) provides that:

> (1) A relevant authority must exercise its functions under this Act in the way which it considers is best calculated to contribute to the reduction of crime.
> (2) In this section 'a relevant authority' means—
>> (a) SOCA,
>> (b) the Director of Public Prosecutions,
>> (c) the Director of Public Prosecutions for Northern Ireland,
>> (d) .....
>> (e) the Director of the Serious Fraud Office.

**14.06** The various directors must have regard to guidance issued by the Secretary of State and the Attorney General. Importantly, pursuant to s 2A(4), that guidance must indicate that 'the reduction of crime is in general best secured by means of criminal investigations and criminal proceedings'. Section 2A(4) appears to give a steer in that it signals that criminal investigations and criminal proceedings should be seen as the preferential route for the reduction of crime. As a secondary route, POCA anticipates that where criminal investigations or proceedings cannot be taken forward, other methods, such as civil recovery, may be deployed. The Crime and Courts Act 2013 includes the abolition of the Serious Organised Crime Agency, and the creation of the National Crime Agency (NCA) (see ss 1–16, and Chapter 13 at para 13.09). Subject to Parliamentary processes the ambition is that it will be fully operational by December 2013.

# B. Recovery Orders

## Introduction

Proceedings for a recovery order may be taken by the relevant enforcement authority in the **14.07** High Court against any person who the enforcement authority thinks holds recoverable property (see s 243(1) of POCA).

Section 266(1) of POCA enables the court, if satisfied that any property is recoverable, to **14.08** make a 'recovery order'. Once made, the recovery order must vest the recoverable property in the 'trustee for civil recovery' (see s 266(2)). In practice this will either be the interim receiver (an insolvency practitioner) or an employee of SOCA (soon to be the NCA) or the agency concerned.

## Financial threshold

Section 287 of the Act anticipates the setting of a figure below which the relevant enforce- **14.09** ment authority will not be able to seek a recovery order. That figure has been set at £10,000 (see SI 2003/175).

## Claims for a recovery order: practice and procedure

Under the Practice Direction for Civil Recovery Proceedings a claim by the enforcement **14.10** authority for a recovery order must be made using the CPR Pt 8 procedure (see para 4.1). The claim form must:

(1) identify the property in relation to which a recovery order is sought;
(2) state, in relation to each item or description of property—
    (a) whether the property is alleged to be recoverable property or associated property; and
    (b) either—
        (i) who is alleged to hold the property; or
        (ii) where the enforcement authority is unable to identify who holds the property, the steps that have been taken to try to establish their identity;
(3) set out the matters relied upon in support of the claim;
(4) give details of the person nominated by the enforcement authority to act as trustee for civil recovery in accordance with section 267 of the Act [or article 178 of the Order in Council in external request matters].

The evidence in support of the claim must include the signed, written consent of the per- **14.11** son nominated by the relevant enforcement authority to act as trustee for civil recovery if appointed by the court (PD 4.4).

References to the claim form also include the Particulars of Claim when they are served **14.12** subsequently (s 243(4)).

## A stand-alone claim

In *Director of the Assets Recovery Agency v Creaven* [2005] EWHC 2726 Admin; [2006] 1 **14.13** WLR 622, Stanley Burnton J held that a claim under Pt 5 of the Act differed from both the conventional personal and conventional proprietary claim. It differed from a conventional personal claim in that it was confined to identified property, although not all of the property needed to be identified when the initial claim was brought. It differed from a conventional proprietary claim in that a respondent held no personal liability.

**14.14** After an order was made the property was transferred to a trustee for civil recovery. Accordingly, a claim under Pt 5 was to be regarded as *sui generis*, a statutory creation of a special kind.

### Procedure the enforcement authority must follow

**14.15** Under s 243(2) the enforcement authority must serve a claim form:

(a) on the respondent, and
(b) unless the court dispenses with service, on any other person who the authority thinks holds any associated property which the authority wishes to be subject to a recovery order, wherever domiciled, resident or present.

### Settlement agreements

**14.16** The enforcement authority will usually be prepared to settle matters, providing that they are suitable for settlement, and the settlement does not abuse the agency's strategic aims. As a result SOCA has been amenable to seeing civil recovery claims settled by mediation and agreement. A draft Civil Recovery agreement may be found at Appendix 18.

### Consent orders

**14.17** The court may make an order staying any proceedings for a recovery order on terms agreed by the parties for the disposal of proceedings if each person to whose property the proceedings, or the agreement, relates, is a party both to the proceedings and the agreement (s 276(1)). A consent order, as well as staying the proceedings, may make provision under s 276(2) for:

(a) ... any property which may be recoverable property to cease to be recoverable, [and]
(b) make any further provision which the court thinks appropriate.

**14.18** Section 280 applies to property vested in the trustee for civil recovery, or money paid to him, in pursuance of an agreement. Under s 280(2) the trustee must pay out of the sums that he receives:

(a) first, any payment required to be made by him by virtue of section 272,
(b) second, any payment or expenses incurred by a person acting as an insolvency practitioner which are payable ... by virtue of section 432(10), and any sum which remains to be paid to the enforcement authority.

(Section 432(10) states that whether or not an insolvency practitioner has ceased to act or has disposed of any property, he or she is entitled to payment of their expenses under s 280.)

**14.19** This section should also be read in the light of amendments made to s 280(2) by SOCPA, which inserted subpara (aa) and allows for payment of a respondent's agreed legal expenses (see Chapter 13).

**14.20** For consent orders involving pensions, see below.

**14.21** A draft civil recovery order may be found at Appendix 18.

### Summary judgment

The enforcement authority is entitled to apply for summary judgment, pursuant to Pt 24 of the **14.22**
CPR in cases where the evidence lodged reveals that a respondent has no real prospect of succeeding on the claim or issue, and where there is no other compelling reason for the case not to
be disposed of before a hearing (see CPR r 24.2) or where the respondent has failed to engage in
the Court's process (see *SOCA v (1) Li (2) Fan and 2 others* [2013] QBD, Admin (unreported)).

In *Director of the Assets Recovery Agency v Brian Colin Charrington* [2005] EWCA Civ 334, **14.23**
the Court of Appeal considered the position of summary judgments following a decision of
Collins J where an order for summary judgment under Pt 24 of the CPR had been made. The
genesis of the Director's claim was a seizure by Customs in June 1992 of some £2.25 million
in cash at the respondent's home, after the respondent had been arrested in connection with
the importation of very substantial quantities of cocaine into the UK. Factually, the respondent had been an informant and had told officers at the time he was interviewed that he had
been acting as an informant and that he had been asked to launder money from the sale of
drugs. A note had been found at his premises which appeared to corroborate this. Partly as a
result of this a decision was taken that the respondent should not be prosecuted (see para 4 of
their Lordships' judgment). The burden therefore fell on the Director to prove that the cash
in question was the proceeds of crime.

The defence put forward by the respondent was that the cash represented a commission paid **14.24**
to him for his part in a legitimate transaction concerning diamonds and had nothing whatsoever to do with the importation of drugs or laundering the proceeds of criminal drug sales.
Two statements were deployed in support of this case. Collins J held at first instance that:

> It is a strong thing to give summary judgment without the matter being tested by the giving
> of evidence and cross-examination of relevant witnesses. But it is necessary for me to form a
> view if this application is brought before me. It seems to me that the story that is now given is
> truly incredible. Everything that was said at the material time and the note that was discovered
> (and I of course recognise that he now says it was a fabrication) all point in the direction that
> Charrington was indeed involved and heavily involved in these importations of cocaine and
> was laundering the money on behalf of those who were behind the importation. That is what
> he admitted, that is what he told a number of officers, that was the information that he himself
> gave in order to enable himself not to be prosecuted. At no time was the diamond suggestion
> raised until the question arose of seeking this confiscation, for want of a better word, on behalf
> of the Director of the Assets Recovery Agency.

Collins J stated that in the circumstances he had no hesitation in rejecting the evidence that **14.25**
was now sought to be relied upon. He said 'I cannot imagine that any judge would believe
it, were it to be put forward.'

In the Court of Appeal, Laws LJ held that in his judgment, on the material before him, **14.26**
Collins J was not only right but 'obviously right' to dismiss the respondent's explanation out
of hand for the reasons which he had given.

In *Woodstock v Director of the Assets Recovery Agency* [2006] EWCA Civ 741, however, the **14.27**
Court of Appeal held that where at a summary judgment stage it was not possible to say that
a respondent was bound to be disbelieved on his contention that the source of his money
was loaned from friends as opposed to being from unlawful conduct, there was a triable issue
that needed to be determined and in such circumstances summary judgment was not an
appropriate remedy.

**14.28** There is nothing to prevent respondents also seeking summary judgment in a civil recovery claim (or its striking out) if the particulars of claim are not sufficiently clear or pertinent, or contain insufficient material to support the claim. However, where inferences may be drawn from the particulars, or where the pleadings were sufficiently clear, such an application would be unlikely to succeed (see *Director of the Assets Recovery Agency v Olupitan and Makinde* [2006] EWHC 1906 (Admin)).

### What the enforcement authority needs to prove

**14.29** The purpose and object of the Act is to ensure that individuals who are enjoying the benefit of crime are deprived of its proceeds. It should be remembered that the burden of proof that the property is recoverable is with the enforcement authority, albeit on a civil standard.

**14.30** In *Director of the Assets Recovery Agency v He and Chen* [2004] EWHC 3021 (Admin), Collins J held (at para 66) that the standard of proof required under s 241(3) is the balance of probabilities, a standard to which the court 'should not place a gloss upon, so as to require that the standard approaches that appropriate in a criminal case' (confirmed in *Director of the Assets Recovery Agency v Taher* [2006] EWHC 3406 (Admin)). In other words, his Lordship was suggesting that courts should not place a gloss on the civil standard—and certainly not raise the bar to that approaching the standard in criminal matters.

**14.31** Section 242(2)(b) provides that it is not necessary to show that the conduct was a particular kind, if it is shown that the property was obtained through conduct of one of a number of kinds, each of which would have been unlawful conduct.

### Does the enforcement authority need to establish a specific criminal offence?

**14.32** The short answer is no. In *Director of the Assets Recovery Agency v Green* [2005] EWHC 3168 (Admin), The Times, 27 February 2006, Sullivan J held that the director need neither allege nor prove the commission of any specific criminal offence. However, nor should he merely set out the matters that are alleged to constitute the particular kind or kinds of unlawful conduct (para 47). He must prove that, on the balance of probabilities, the property was obtained by or in return for a particular kind or one of a number of kinds of unlawful conduct (para 50).

**14.33** He also held that a claim for civil recovery could not be sustained solely upon the basis that a defendant had no identifiable lawful income to warrant his lifestyle:

> The purpose of the Act was to strike a fair balance between the interests of the State and society in general and the civil rights of the individual. If Parliament had wished the Agency to be able to recover property simply by alleging and thereafter persuading the court on the balance of probabilities that it had been obtained by or in return for some unspecified unlawful conduct, it could have said so, but it had not.

**14.34** Sullivan J's view was approved by the Court of Appeal in *The Director of Assets Recovery Agency v Szepietowski and others* [2006] EWHC 3228 (Admin), with the possible qualification in the judgment of Moore-Bick LJ, who said at para 107:

> ... It is sufficient in my view for the director to prove that a criminal offence was committed, even if it is impossible to identify precisely when or by whom or in what circumstances and that the property was obtained by or in return for it. In my view Sullivan J was right therefore to hold that in order to succeed the Director need not prove the commission of any specific criminal offence in the sense of proving that a particular person committed a particular offence

on a particular occasion. Nonetheless, I think it is necessary for her to prove that specific property was obtained by or in return for a criminal offence of an identifiable kind (robbery, theft, fraud or whatever) or, if she relies on section 242(2), by or in return for one or other of a number of offences of an identifiable kind. If, as I think, that is what the judge meant in paragraph 50 of his judgment, I respectfully agree with him.

Griffith Williams J considered the same issue in *SOCA v Gale and others* [2009] EWHC **14.35** 1015 and held:

> With respect to Sullivan J, I consider his second answer is too restrictive. While a claim for civil recovery may not be sustained solely upon the basis that a respondent has no identifiable lawful income to warrant his lifestyle, the absence of any evidence to explain that lifestyle may provide the answer because the inference may be drawn from the failure to provide an explanation or from an explanation which was untruthful (and deliberately so) that the source was unlawful.

Griffith Williams J concluded this aspect of his ruling by citing *Director of the Assets Recovery* **14.36** *Agency v Olupitan* [2007] EWHC (QB) 162 (at 22); *Director of the Assets Recovery Agency v Jackson* [2007] EWHC (QB) 255 (at 115); and *R v Anwoir & others* [2008] 2 Cr App R 36 at para 21, finding:

> ... that there are two ways in which the Crown can prove in money laundering offences that property was derived from crime—either by proving it derived from unlawful conduct of a specific kind or kinds or by evidence of the circumstances in which the property was handled, such as to give rise to the irresistible inference that it could only have been derived from crime.

### What is a 'trustee for civil recovery'?

A trustee for civil recovery is a person appointed by the court to give effect to a recovery order **14.37** (s 267(1)). Whenever a court makes a recovery order or a consent order under s 276, the court must also appoint a trustee for civil recovery. It is the duty of the enforcement agency to nominate a suitably qualified person for the appointment (see s 267(2)).

The person nominated is likely to be the interim receiver in situ, or an insolvency prac- **14.38** titioner (the agencies concerned retain an 'approved' list of suitably qualified individuals and firms), or an employee of the enforcement authority. Much will depend upon the complexity and issues involved in realising the assets in question. If, for example, assets are held outside the jurisdiction, a trustee in the form of an insolvency practitioner is likely to be appointed, because of the jurisdictional issues involved. If, on the other hand, the realisation is a straightforward matter over a modest number of assets, the relevant author- ity is likely to nominate a member of its own staff, not least because it is more cost effective to do so.

### What are the functions of the trustee?

Pursuant to s 267(3) the functions of the trustee are: **14.39**

   (a) to secure the detention, custody or preservation of any property vested in him by the recovery order,

   (b) in the case of property other than money, to realise the value of the property to the benefit of the enforcement authority, and

   (c) to perform any other functions conferred on him by virtue of [Chapter 5].

Under s 267(4) of the Act, in performing his functions the trustee acts on behalf of the enforcement authority and must comply with any directions given by that authority.

**14.40**   The trustee's duty is to realise the value of the property vested in him by the recovery order, so far as practicable, in the manner best calculated to maximise the amount payable to the enforcement authority (s 267(5)).

### Powers of the trustee for civil recovery

**14.41**   Schedule 7 to POCA sets out the powers of the trustee for civil recovery, as follows:

(1) Power to sell the property or any part of it or interest in it.
(2) Power to incur expenditure for the purpose of—
    (a) acquiring any part of the property, or any interest in it, which is not vested in him,
    (b) discharging any liabilities, or extinguishing any rights, to which the property is subject.
(3)
    (1) The power to manage property;
    (2) Managing property involves doing anything mentioned in paragraph 5(2) of Schedule 6. [See Appendix 8]
(4) Power to start, carry on or defend any legal proceedings in respect of the property.
(5) Power to make any compromise or other arrangements in connection with any claim relating to the property.
(6)
    (1) For the purposes of or in connection with, the exercise of any of his powers—
        (a) power by his official name to do any of the things mentioned in subparagraph (2),
        (b) power to do any other act which is necessary or expedient.
    (2) Those things are—
        (a) holding property,
        (b) entering into contracts,
        (c) suing and being sued,
        (d) employing agents,
        (e) executing a power of attorney, deed or other instrument.

**14.42**   It has already been observed that references to a recovery order include an order under s 276 (consent orders) and references to 'property vested in a trustee by a recovery order' include property vested in him in pursuance of an order under s 276 (see s 267(7)).

### The twelve-year limitation

**14.43**   Section 288 of POCA adds s 27A to the Limitation Act 1980 (LA). It deals with actions for recovery of property obtained through unlawful conduct and states that none of the time limits given in the LA apply to any proceedings under Chapter 2 of Pt 5 of POCA (civil recovery of the proceeds of unlawful conduct). Under s 27A(2):

> Proceedings under that chapter [Chapter 2 of Pt 5 of POCA] for a recovery order in respect of any recoverable property shall not be brought after the expiration of the period of 12 years from the date on which the Director's cause of action accrued.

Proceedings are brought when (a) a claim form is issued, or (b) an application is made for an interim receiving order, whichever is the earlier.

**14.44**   The application of the twelve-year rule was considered in *Director of The Assets Recovery Agency v Szepietowski and others* [2007] EWCA 766 The Times, 21 August 2007 (para 18). Importantly, the Court held that the burden was on the respondent to persuade the court that a limitation defence had such good prospects of success that it fatally undermined the Director's case. In *Szepietowski*, by failing to provide an explanation for the source of the funds used, the respondent had provided no relevant dates by reference to which the limitation point could at an interim stage be decided (para 42). The Court of Appeal held that s 32(1)(b) of the LA applied and that concealment from the ARA during the course of an investigation would lead to the limitation period recommencing on discovery of the concealment (or when the matter concealed could have been discovered with reasonable diligence) (para 58). (The application of s 32 LA was further endorsed in *SOCA v Gale and others* [2009] EWHC 1015 at para 145.)

### Can civil recovery powers be used retrospectively?

The answer appears to be yes. Retrospectivity is made express by s 316(3) of POCA. This **14.45** subsection was considered in the judgment of Waller LJ in the case of *Director of The Assets Recovery Agency v Szepietowski and others* [2007] EWCA 766, The Times, 21 August 2007 (para 18).

Further, the powers can be used prior to the creation of the enforcement authority, subject to the **14.46** limitation issue outlined above. Provided the property is recoverable the identity of the enforcement authority is irrelevant. The allocation of the claimant does not qualify the cause of action.

### Rights of pre-emption

Under s 269 of POCA, recovery orders take precedence and have effect in relation to any **14.47** property, even in circumstances where provision (of whatever nature) would otherwise prevent, penalise, or restrict the vesting of the property.

The right of pre-emption, the right of irritancy, the right of return, or other similar rights **14.48** do not operate or become exercisable once property has been vested under a recovery order. (Section 269(2) defines a right of return as any right under a provision for the return or aversion of property in specified circumstances.)

It follows that a person who has the first right to buy a property when it changes hands will **14.49** not be able to exercise his right to prevent the vesting of recoverable property in the trustee. He should, however, have first right to buy the property when the trustee comes to sell it (s 269(3)).

Under s 283(6), if a person holding any such right suffers a loss as a result of the property **14.50** vesting in the trustee, he is entitled to apply to the court for compensation and the court may order compensation to be paid (s 283(8)).

### The vesting of recoverable property

By s 266(8) a recovery order may impose conditions about the manner in which the trustee **14.51** for civil recovery deals with the property vested for the purpose of realising it, and under s 266(7) a recovery order may sever any property. It should be noted that s 266 is subject to both s 270, which deals with associated and joint property (below) and sections 271 to 278, which deal with associated and joint property, payments in respect of pension schemes, consent orders, and limits on recovery.

### Associated and joint property

Section 271 of POCA (agreements about associated and joint property) and s 272 (associ- **14.52** ated and joint property: default of agreement) apply if the court makes a recovery order in respect of any recoverable property which falls into the following four categories (see s 270(1) to (3)):

(a) the property to which the proceedings relate includes property which is associated with the recoverable property and is specified or described in the claim form, and

(b) if the associated property is not the respondent's property the claim form or application form has been served on the person whose property it is or the court has dispensed with service,

(c) the recoverable property belongs to joint tenants, and

(d) one of the tenants is an excepted joint owner.

**14.53** Sections 270 to 272 have been created because joint tenants are, as a matter of law, treated as though they are the single owner of the property in issue. That would also include joint bank accounts or real property held jointly.

### 'Excepted joint owner'

**14.54** Under s 270(4) which came into force on 30 December 2002 (SI 2002/3015):

> An excepted joint owner is a person who obtained the property in circumstances in which it would not be recoverable as against him; and references to the excepted joint owner's share of the recoverable property are to so much of the recoverable property as would have been his if the joint tenancy had been severed.

For the definition of associated property, see s 245 and Chapter 13.

### Associated and joint property: agreements

**14.55** Section 271 is intended to deal with situations where an agreement can be reached with the enforcement authority to permit a person to make a payment to the trustee rather than vesting property in the trustee.

**14.56** Where s 271 of POCA applies, and the enforcement authority and the person who holds the associated property who is the excepted joint owner agree, the recovery order may, instead of vesting the recoverable property in the trustee for civil recovery, require the person who holds the associated property or who is the excepted joint owner to make a payment to the trustee (s 271(1)).

**14.57** A recovery order which includes such a requirement may, so far as is required for giving effect to the agreement, include provision for vesting, creating, or extinguishing any interest in property. In effect, the joint owner is buying out the interest the enforcement authority has in the property.

### Associated and joint property: calculating the amount

**14.58** The amount to be paid is the amount which the enforcement authority and the person who holds the associated property (or who is the excepted joint owner) agree represents:

(a) in a case within s 270(2), the value of the recoverable property;

(b) in a case within s 270(3), the value of the recoverable property less the value of the excepted joint owner's share.

**14.59** However, if an IRO applied at any time to the associated property or joint tenancy, and the enforcement authority agrees that the person has suffered a loss as a result of the IRO, the amount of the payment may be reduced by any amount the enforcement authority and that person agree is reasonable, having regard to that loss and to any other relevant circumstances (see s 271(4)).

If there is more than one such item of associated property or excepted joint owner, the total **14.60** amount to be paid to the trustee and the part of that amount which is to be provided by each person who holds any such associated property or who is an excepted joint owner, is to be agreed between both (or all of them) and the enforcement authority.

Upon agreement, the recovery order must provide that the property concerned ceases to be **14.61** recoverable (see s 271(6)).

### Associated and joint property: default of agreement

Section 272 applies where no agreement can be reached in relation to either associated or **14.62** joint property, but the court thinks it would be just and equitable to make provision concerning that property (see s 272(1)). Under s 272(2) the recovery order may provide:

(a) for the associated property to vest in the trustee for civil recovery or (as the case may be) for the excepted joint owners interest to be extinguished or,

(b) in the case of an excepted joint owner, for the severance of his interest.

In relation to s 272(2)(a) above, a recovery order may also provide: **14.63**

(a) for the trustee to pay an amount to the person who holds the associated property or who is an excepted joint owner, or

(b) for the creation of interests in favour of that person, or the imposition of liabilities or conditions, in relation to the property vested in the trustee, or for both (s 272(3)).

Pursuant to s 272(4), when making provision in a recovery order under subss (2) or (3) the **14.64** court must have regard to the following:

(a) the rights of any person who holds the associated property or who is an excepted joint owner and the value to him of that property or, as the case may be, of his share (including any value which cannot be assessed in terms of money),

(b) the enforcement authority's interest in receiving the realised proceeds of the recoverable property.

Section 272(4)(a) particularly acknowledges the rights of third parties and directs the court **14.65** to take into account those rights.

### Interests

An interest in relation to land held in England and Wales means any legal estate and any **14.66** equitable interest or power. In relation to property other than land, 'interest' includes any right 'including a right of possession of the property' (see s 316(1)).

### Public interest immunity

The issue of public interest immunity in civil recovery proceedings arose in the case of **14.67** *Director of the Assets Recovery Agency v Personal Representative of Paul Patrick Daly (Dec'd)* [2006] NIQB 36, where Coghlin J was shown some eighty-seven intelligence documents referred to in an affidavit. It was thereafter submitted that having carried out an ex parte exercise he should recuse himself from sitting as a judge for the purpose of determining the substantive recovery order proceedings. Coghlin J accepted that the concept of fairness enshrined in Art 6 of the ECHR should be considered in this context. He balanced the interests of the parties with the efficient operation of the justice system, including additional delays, expense, and frustration on the part of other litigants which were likely to result from a decision to split the function of determining disclosure from that of determining the substantive issues (paras 8 and 9). Taking those matters into account, he stated that the basic test remained that set out by Lord Steyn in *Lawal v Northern Spirit Ltd* [2004] 1 All ER 197 at para 22, namely the 'indispensable requirements of public confidence in the administration of justice'.

**14.68** He observed that in *R v May* [2005] 3 All ER 523, the judge had dealt with several public interest immunity (PII) applications and then went on to deal with confiscation proceedings brought under the CJA. In that case the appellant had relied upon the decision of the Strasbourg Court in *Edwards v UK* [2004] ECHR 39647/98. In the Court of Appeal, Keene LJ attributed considerable importance to the judge's statement in *May* that he had ignored anything revealed to him which attracted PII, and felt able to distinguish the case of *May* from *Edwards v UK*.

**14.69** In *Edwards* the Court was not pronouncing upon a situation in which the judge had expressly stated that he had ignored the undisclosed material for the purpose of a subsequent ruling, but had been concerned with a situation in which the judge made a determinative ruling on an issue of fact which he had decided by reference to undisclosed material. And there it seems the distinction lies. As a result, in *Daly* Coghlin J was quite satisfied that he could exclude from his consideration the reports/observations that he had been shown in ex parte hearings, and thus was able to go on and consider the recovery order claim.

**14.70** The Court of Appeal has recently taken a flexible approach to PII where the material which SOCA seeks to withhold from disclosing to a respondent are intelligence reports which *adversely* affected that respondent's case (as opposed to adversely affecting SOCA's case or adversely affecting a co-respondent's case) but which SOCA did not wish to rely upon. In *SOCA v (1) Hakan Yaman Namli and (2) Topinvest Holdings International Ltd* [2011] EWCA Civ 1411 the respondent's case was not adversely affected by the withholding of the intelligence materials and the Court of Appeal was prepared to endorse the judge's approach of limiting disclosure rather than requiring SOCA to make an application to withhold from disclosure under CPR r 31.19. For a contrast in approach, see *SOCA v Pelekanos* [2009] EWHC 2307 (QB) where SOCA attempted to rely on intelligence. Hamblen J said that the evidence amounted to un-attributable multiple hearsay which could not be investigated and was effectively unchallengeable. As a result, the Court found it could attach no real weight to the evidence.

## C. Safeguards and Exemptions in Civil Recovery

### Overview

**14.71** Civil recovery is subject to a number of safeguards and restrictions to ensure fairness and compatibility with relevant civil law principles. These include the following:

- Parties will have the same rights of appeal as in other High Court actions.
- There is protection for third parties who have an interest in the property in the provisions about associated and joint property (ss 270 to 272).
- Where the true owner of the property concerned comes forward during civil recovery proceedings, the property will be returned to the true owner and will not be recovered by the enforcement authority (s 281).

- Property will not be recoverable from people who obtain recoverable property where they have purchased it for full value, in good faith and without notice of its unlawful origins (s 308).
- The court may refuse or limit a recovery order if a person satisfies it that he obtained the property in good faith; that as a result of receiving the property (or in anticipation of receiving it) he took steps which he would not otherwise have taken; that when he took the steps he had no notice that the property was recoverable; and that recovery would cause him to suffer detriment as a result of those steps (s 266(3) and (4)).
- There are limits on recovery in order to prevent double recovery (ss 278 and 279).
- The court cannot include in a recovery order measures that are incompatible with rights under the ECHR (s 266(3)(b)).
- If the enforcement authority loses the case, the court will be able to award compensation for any financial loss suffered by the respondent as a result of an interim receiving order applying to his property (s 283).
- There is to be a financial threshold below which civil recovery proceedings may not be pursued (s 287), namely £10,000.
- There is a twelve-year limitation period on when civil recovery proceedings can be brought, starting at the time the original property was generated by unlawful conduct (s 288).
- There are certain exemptions which provide that proceedings for civil recovery may not be taken in respect of certain people in prescribed circumstances (s 282, which provides an order-making power to add further exemptions). Further exemptions in relation to property are set out in s 308 and may be made by order under s 309. An order has been made under s 309 (SI 2003/336).

### Exclusions, exemptions, and exceptions

Exclusions to recovery orders are provided for under s 266(3) and the court may not make **14.72** in a recovery order:

(a) any provision in respect of any recoverable property if each of the conditions in subs (4) is met and it would not be just and equitable to do so, or

(b) any provision which is incompatible with any of the Convention rights (within the meaning of the HRA).

Under s 266(4) the conditions referred to in subs (3)(a) are that: **14.73**

(a) the respondent obtained the recoverable property in good faith,

(b) he took steps after obtaining the property which he would not have taken if he had not obtained it or he took steps before obtaining the property which he would not have taken if he had not believed he was going to obtain it,

(c) when he took the steps, he had no notice that the property was recoverable,

(d) if a recovery order were made in respect of the property, it would, by reason of the steps, be detrimental to him.

In deciding whether it would be 'just and equitable' to make a provision in the recovery order **14.74** where the conditions set out in s 266(4) are met, the court must have regard to:

(6) ...

(a) the degree of detriment that would be suffered by the respondent if the provision were made,

(b) the enforcement authority's interest in receiving the realised proceeds of the recoverable property.

(See also s 308(1).) It should be further noted that the exemptions set out at s 281 (victims of theft) and s 282 (other exemptions) apply to this section of the Act.

### Where the court must not make a recovery order

**14.75**  Under s 278(3), the court is not to make a recovery order if it thinks that the enforcement authority's right to recover the original property has been satisfied by a previous recovery order or a consent order under s 276. If an order is made under s 298 for the forfeiture of cash, and the enforcement authority subsequently seeks a recovery order in respect of related property, the order under s 298 is to be treated, for the purposes of s 278, as if it were a recovery order obtained by the relevant authority in respect of the forfeited property. This avoids double counting and/or the proceeds of the same criminal conduct being recovered twice (see also s 282(1)).

**14.76**  However, by s 278(6) where the court has made the recovery order in respect of any property, s 278 does not prevent the recovery of any profits which have accrued in respect of that property.

**14.77**  In *Satnam Singh v Director of the Assets Recovery Agency* [2005] EWCA Civ 580; [2005] 1 WLR 3747, it was held that if an order were quashed on appeal (in *Singh* a confiscation order), eg on a technicality, the fact the order was made over the property in question once before did not prohibit the agency from making a further claim.

**14.78**  The Proceeds of Crime Act 2002 (Exemptions from Civil Recovery) Order 2003, SI 2003/336 provides that certain property is not recoverable property for the purposes of Pt 5 of POCA, eg s 27 of the Misuse of Drugs Act 1971, s 6 of the Knives Act 1997, s 43 of the DTA, s 3 of the Obscene Publications Act 1959, and s 23 of the Terrorism Act 2000, and less-used statutes such as the Salmon and Freshwater Fisheries (Protection) (Scotland) Act 1951 and other enactments. This is because these sections make particular provision for forfeiture themselves.

### Victims of criminal conduct

**14.79**  Section 278(8) is designed to ensure that where a victim of unlawful conduct has recovered, through civil litigation, property which was obtained through unlawful conduct, the enforcement authority cannot secure an order under the civil recovery scheme for that property (see also s 281).

### Recovery orders and confiscation orders

**14.80**  Section 278(9) and (10) envisages circumstances where property has been taken into account in deciding the amount of the person's benefit from criminal conduct for the making of a confiscation order and the enforcement authority subsequently seeks a recovery order in respect of the same property. For the purposes of s 278(9), the confiscation order is to be treated as if it were a recovery order. This again avoids double counting and/or the proceeds of the same criminal conduct being recovered twice.

**14.81**  As stated above in *Satnam Singh v Director of the Assets Recovery Agency* [2005] EWCA Civ 580; [2005] 1 WLR 3747, it was held that if a confiscation order was quashed on appeal the ARA would not be prevented from making a civil recovery claim (see below).

## Supplementary provisions to recovery

Section 279 gives examples of the enforcement authority's right to recover original property **14.82** (meaning property obtained through unlawful conduct, s 278(2)). Section 279(2) states:

(2) If—
    (a) there is a disposal, other than a part of disposal, of the original property, and
    (b) other property (the representative property) is obtained in its place,
the enforcement authority's right to recover the original property is satisfied by the making of a recovery order in respect of either the original property or the representative property.

(3) If—
    (a) there is a part disposal of the original property and
    (b) other part property (the representative property) is obtained in place of the property disposed of,
the enforcement authority's right to recover the original property is satisfied by the making of a recovery order in respect of the remainder of the original property together with either the representative property or the property disposed of.

## Exemptions to the recovery scheme

Sections 281 and 283 set out exemptions to the recovery order scheme. Under s 281(1), **14.83** where a person affected by a recovery order claims that any property alleged to be recoverable property, or any part of the property, belongs to him, he may apply for a declaration under s 281. The court may make a declaration to the effect sought by the person claiming the property providing the following conditions are met:

(3) …
    (a) the person was deprived of the property he claims, or of property which it represents, by unlawful conduct,
    (b) the property he was deprived of was not recoverable property immediately before he was deprived of it, and
    (c) the property he claims belongs to him.

The person who makes the claim must have true title to the property concerned (s 281(3) (c) and s 278(8)).

If the innocent individual is successful in his application and the court makes a declaration, **14.84** the property is no longer recoverable (subs (4)). Section 281 therefore gives a true owner precedence over the enforcement authority for property which, for example, has been stolen in the past. 'The court' means the High Court (see s 316(1)).

## Other exemptions

Section 282 lists the circumstances in which proceedings for a recovery order may not be **14.85** taken. They include:

(1) Proceedings in respect of cash alone (unless the proceedings are also taken in respect of other property). This means that the enforcement authority may not take civil recovery proceedings in respect of cash unless they are simultaneously taking proceedings against other property held by the same person. (Cash seizures fall within the domain of either the police or HMRC.)

(2) Proceedings against the Financial Services Authority in respect of any recoverable property held by the Authority.

(3) Proceedings which relate to a collateral security charge; a market charge; a money market charge; or a system charge (s 282(4)).

(4) Proceedings against any person in respect of any recoverable property which he holds by reason of his acting, or having acted, as an insolvency practitioner ('acting as an insolvency practitioner' is defined by s 433).

**14.86** Further the Secretary of State may add to this list of exemptions in a prescribed order (see s 282(1)). Any such order must be approved by both Houses of Parliament (see s 459(6)(a)).

### Exemptions or exceptions to property being 'recoverable'

**14.87** Under ss 308 to 310 there are certain general exceptions and exemptions to the civil recovery rules, some of which appear to be repetitive of the above.

**14.88** General exceptions include a situation where a person disposes of recoverable property and the person who obtains it on the disposal does so in good faith, for value, and without notice that it was recoverable property. In such circumstances the property may not be followed into the person's hands and, accordingly, it ceases to be recoverable (s 308(1) and s 266(4)).

**14.89** Similarly, if in pursuance of a judgment in civil proceedings the defendant makes a payment to the claimant or the claimant otherwise obtains property from the defendant (which may otherwise have been recoverable property), that payment (property) ceases to be recoverable (see s 308(3)). Alternatively, if a payment is made to a person in pursuance of a compensation order under s 130 of the PCC(S)A 2000, the payment (property) ceases to be recoverable (s 308(4)).

**14.90** If a payment is made to a person in pursuance of a restitution order under s 148(2) of the PCC(S)A 2000 or a person otherwise obtains any property or money in pursuance of such an order, the property ceases to be recoverable. A similar provision applies in respect of restitution orders under s 308(6) and (7).

**14.91** Under s 308(8), the property is not recoverable while a restraint order applies under ss 41, 120, or 190 of POCA. Nor is it recoverable if it has already been taken into account in deciding the amount a person has benefited from for the purpose of making a confiscation order (see s 308(9) and s 278(9) and (10)).

**14.92** In *Satnam Singh v Director of the Assets Recovery Agency* [2005] EWCA Civ 580; [2005] 1 WLR 3747, the Court of Appeal held (at para 18) that where a previous court had quashed a confiscation order it must inevitably follow that no order was made 'under the corresponding provision' of a relevant enactment for the purposes of s 308(9) of POCA. This, in the view of Latham LJ, was 'precisely what Parliament intended'. The purpose of s 308(9) was to prevent double recovery. He stated at para 19:

> Its effect is to ensure that the only mechanism for recovery in relation to property taken into account if a confiscation order has been made is that provided for under the confiscation order. But if criminal proceedings are brought, but no confiscation order is made or the property in question has not been taken into account in determining benefit for the purpose of any confiscation order that has been made, I can see no justification under the 2002 Act for precluding the respondent from seeking to obtain a recovery order in relation to the proceeds of crime.

**14.93** He went on to hold that the clear intention of Parliament was to ensure that, so far as possible, criminals should be deprived of the possibility of benefiting from their own crimes: 'To permit the technicality which resulted in the confiscation order being quashed to preclude recovery by the civil recovery route would be to perpetrate a mischief which the 2002 Act was clearly designed to prevent.'

Other exemptions within the Act include where an order provides that property is not recov- **14.94** erable if it is prescribed property or if it is disposed of in pursuance of a prescribed enact- ment (see s 309(1) and (2)). 'Prescribed property' means prescribed by an order made by the Secretary of State (see s 309(4)). (Any order made by the Secretary of State is subject to the affirmative resolution procedure provided under s 459(6)(a) of POCA.)

### Insolvency and recovery orders

Proceedings for a recovery order may not be taken or continued in respect of property **14.95** which falls under the following categories, unless the appropriate court gives permission and the proceedings are taken or (as the case may be) continued in accordance with the terms imposed by that court (see s 311(1) and (3)):

(a) an asset of a company being wound up;
(b) an asset of a company and a voluntary arrangement under Pt 1 of the Insolvency Act 1986;
(c) an order under s 286 of the Insolvency Act 1986;
(d) an asset comprised of an estate of an individual who has been adjudged bankrupt;
(e) an asset of an individual and a voluntary arrangement under Pt 8 of the Insolvency Act 1986.

An application under s 311, or under any provision of the Insolvency Act 1986, for permis- **14.96** sion to take proceedings for a recovery order may be made without notice to the person. That, however, does not affect any requirement for notice of an application to be given to any person acting as an insolvency practitioner or to the official receiver (see s 311(4) and (5)).

Insolvency and civil recovery are also considered at para 13.201 of Chapter 13. **14.97**

### Publicity and civil recovery

It was previously commonplace for the ARA to post on its website recent successes and **14.98** issue corresponding press releases, and SOCA (soon to be the NCA) have tended to adopt a similar policy. The High Court in Northern Ireland considered the use of website publicity in *In the matter of Colin Armstrong* [2007] NIQB 20. Gillen J concluded that the use of the website in this manner was both proportionate and furthered the legitimate aim of ensuring that crime was reduced (para 15). In so finding, he dismissed arguments based upon Art 2 and Art 8 of the ECHR.

### Territorial limits

A recent decision limited the territorial scope of PFOs. Overturning the Court of Appeal's **14.99** decision, the Supreme Court in *Perry & others v SOCA and Perry & others v SOCA (No 2)* [2012] UKSC 35, held that POCA Pt 5 did not give the High Court of England and Wales power to impose PFOs (and therefore orders in civil recovery proceedings) in respect of property situated outside the jurisdiction of the court. Further, a disclosure order under POCA Pt 8 did not authorise the sending of information notices to persons outside the jurisdiction of the court.

The Crime and Courts Act 2013 reversed, so far as possible, the effect of *Perry* by making **14.100** a number of changes to POCA and the Civil Jurisdiction and Judgments Act 1982. The amendments to Chapter 2 of Pt 5 of POCA ensure the High Court in England and Wales (and the Court of Session in Scotland) can make an order against property situated outside the jurisdiction of the court where there is or has been a connection between the case and the relevant part of the UK (s 282A of POCA). A non-exhaustive list of connecting factors is set out in a new Schedule 7A. The case of *Perry* is considered in detail in Chapter 13, at para 13.61.

## D. The Impact of the European Convention on Human Rights on Civil Recovery

**14.101** The ECHR has featured in a number of civil recovery cases, as perhaps it inevitably would bearing in mind the controversial nature of the legislation.

### Article 1—interference with property

**14.102** In *Director of the Assets Recovery Agency v (1) Jia Jin He (2) Dan Dan Chen* [2004] EWHC 3021 (Admin) Collins J considered Art 1 of the First Protocol which prohibits interference with property. He referred to the Italian cases of *Arcuri v Italy* (App No 52024–99) and *M v Italy* (App No 12386–86), where the European Court had held that recovery provisions did not fall foul of Art 1, provided that the measure in question was regarded as proportionate. At para 74 Collins J stated, in upholding the principle:

> Whilst the situation in this country is not, I hope, as dire as that represented by the activities of the Mafia in Italy, nonetheless Parliament has quite clearly decided that these measures are necessary in order to fight crime, and in particular to ensure, as far as possible, that those involved in crime should be unable to enjoy the fruits of their criminal activities.

### Article 6(1)

**14.103** In *Director of the Assets Recovery Agency v Satnam Singh* [2004] EWHC 2335 (Admin); [2005] ACD 36, McCombe J rejected an argument advanced in relation to Art 6(1) of the ECHR that sought to join the overall length of the criminal proceedings with those of the recovery proceedings (a total of nine years from arrest for the substantive matter). While Art 6(1) provides that in the determination of the civil rights and obligations of an individual (or in criminal proceedings), everyone is entitled to a fair and public hearing 'within a reasonable time', McCombe J was inclined to the view that the recovery proceedings represented separate civil proceedings in which no question of relevant delay arose (para 40).

### Article 6(2)

**14.104** In *Director of the Assets Recovery Agency v Walsh* [2004] NIQB 21, Coghlin J held that proceedings under the 2002 Act were civil proceedings to which Art 6(2) did not apply. Coghlin J held: 'It seems to me that, in substance, proceedings by way of a civil recovery action under the provisions of Part 5 of POCA differ significantly from the situation of a person charged with a criminal offence within the meaning of Article 6.'

**14.105** In *R (on the application of the Director of the Assets Recovery Agency) (Paul) v Ashton* [2006] EWHC 1064 (Admin), Newman J held that the imposition of a civil recovery order under s 243 of POCA was not punitive and could not therefore violate Art 6 of the ECHR (no punishment without law). He held that civil recovery orders had a compensatory aspect in that they are a manifestation of Parliament's intention to recover expenses incurred in investigating crime, and the fact that deprivation of property is involved does not constitute a penalty because the holder of the property to which the order relates had no right to hold it in the first place. (See also *Director of the Assets Recovery Agency v Charrington* [2005] EWCA Civ 334.)

In the case of *Gale and others v SOCA* [2011] UKSC 49 the issue has now been considered **14.106** by the Supreme Court, which was unanimous in rejecting the proposition that the criminal standard of proof should be applied in civil recovery proceedings.

In civil recovery proceedings, for the purposes of s 241(3) of POCA, the court could apply **14.107** the civil standard of proof in determining whether property recovered was the product of criminal conduct on the part of the defendants without breaching Art 6 of the ECHR. It was also decided that an order for costs made in favour of SOCA against a person against whom a recovery order had been made could include the investigation costs which were incurred by an interim receiver.

The appellants, Mr Gale and his former wife, appealed against a Court of Appeal decision **14.108** ([2010] EWCA Civ 759; [2010] 1 WLR 2881) which upheld a civil recovery order made against them, and ordered that the costs of SOCA included the investigation costs incurred by an interim receiver.

The civil recovery order was based on a finding, on the balance of probabilities under s **14.109** 241(3), that property held by the appellants was derived from criminal activity on the part of one or both of them, namely drug trafficking, money laundering, and tax evasion in the UK and other jurisdictions. The judge's finding was made even though Mr Gale had not been convicted of drug trafficking; he had, however, been prosecuted and acquitted in Portugal. An interim receiver had also been appointed and his investigation had incurred substantial costs. The agency paid those costs and the Court of Appeal ordered recovery of these costs from the appellants.

The appeal was based on the argument that a finding that the property was the product of **14.110** crime required proof that the appellants had been guilty of criminal conduct, meaning that they were entitled to the presumption of innocence under Art 6(2) of the ECHR and the rebuttal of that presumption required proof of guilt to the criminal standard. There was a further strand to the argument that no adverse finding could be made against Mr Gale in respect of conduct of which he had been acquitted in Portugal.

Lord Phillips (with whom Lord Mance, Lord Judge, and Lord Reed agreed) analysed the **14.111** Strasbourg case law in this area, concluding that a number of the leading cases dealing with the application of Art 6(2) after acquittal were mutually inconsistent and that in others it was not easy to identify the principle underlying them. He concluded that the case law was sufficiently confusing that it would benefit from being considered by the Grand Chamber.

The Court found that Mr Gale's acquittal did not prevent the English court in proceedings **14.112** under POCA from considering the evidence which had formed the basis of the charges in Portugal. On the issue of whether the criminal standard had to be applied to the proof of criminal conduct in POCA proceedings, the ECHR had found in the cases of *Phillips v United Kingdom* (41087/98) 11 BHRC 280 and *Van Offeren v the Netherlands* (19581/04) that:

> In each case the court held that confiscation proceedings in relation to the benefits of drug trafficking did not involve charging the defendant with a criminal offence so as to bring them within the scope of article 6(2). In each case the applicant had been convicted of drug offences and in the confiscation proceedings related to property held by him the issue was whether article 6(2) was infringed by a presumption that this property was derived from similar offences. In holding that it was not, the court treated the confiscation procedure as analogous to the sentencing process. It does not seem to me that the analogy is very precise. The important

point is, however, that the ECHR approved of the confiscation of property on the basis that it was derived from drug trafficking without treating the proof that it was so derived as involving criminal charges and thus involving the application of article 6(2).

**14.113** Whilst a later decision of *Geerings v Netherlands* (30810/03) seemed to indicate the contrary, the Supreme Court was influenced by the fact that the ECtHR had not sought to depart from the position in *Phillips* and *Van Offeren*. Lord Phillips stated that the views on the standard of proof expressed in *R v Briggs-Price (Robert William)* [2009] UKHL 19; [2009] 1 AC 1026, which were acknowledged as obiter, nonetheless supported the conclusion that criminal conduct in this context had to be established on the civil and not the criminal standard. He concluded the judge had been right to apply the civil standard and dismissed the appeal on this ground.

**14.114** Turning then to the investigation costs, pursuant to s 51 of the Senior Courts Act 1981, which governs the court's jurisdiction in civil proceedings, costs were in principle recoverable provided they were costs of and incidental to the proceedings. It first had to be determined whether the receiver's expenses in the investigation fell into this definition and, if so, whether there was any rule or authority which prevented the court from having jurisdiction to order the appellants to bear the costs of the investigation. The Supreme Court in *Gale* held that the investigation was an essential part of the civil recovery proceedings and there was no reason why these could not be costs of the proceedings. For a recent example of *Gale* being followed see *SOCA v Hymans and others* [2011] EWHC 3332 (QB).

### Article 7—civil proceedings

**14.115** Article 7 was specifically referred to in the case of *Director of the Assets Recovery Agency v (1) Jia Jin He (2) Dan Dan Chen* [2004] EWHC 3021 (Admin). In that matter Collins J held that there was 'no doubt' recovery proceedings were civil, and that Art 7 did not apply as no penalty was involved (para 69).

**14.116** In a considered judgment, his Lordship reviewed the structure and basis of the Act (para 1 et seq), together with the tests in *Engel v Netherlands (No 1)* (1976) 1 EHRR 647 (at 678–9) which dictate whether proceedings should be classified as civil or criminal (para 49). Furthermore he considered two European authorities, namely *Arcuri v Italy* and *M v Italy* (17 DR 59), where the European Court settled that preventative confiscation measures that did not involve a finding of guilt do not constitute a penalty (and therefore were not in contravention of Art 7) (see para 56 of the judgment).

**14.117** His Lordship went on to consider the standard of proof required in such claims, and concluded that Parliament had intentionally imposed a lower standard in civil recovery proceedings, namely that of the balance of probabilities (para 66).

**14.118** In *R (on the Application of the Director of the Assets Recovery Agency) v Paul Ashton* [2006] EWHC 1064 (Admin), Newman J adopted the decision of Collins J in *Jia Jin He* and noted that his Lordship had rejected the suggestion that a heightened civil standard of proof applied where criminal conduct was said to be involved. At para 39 Newman J stated that he regarded the judgments which had preceded this matter to be 'an impeccable catalogue of features which are relevant when considering the issue of Article 7'.

### Article 7—a criminal penalty?

**14.119** It is now established that confiscation proceedings, following on and attaching to a criminal conviction, represent a 'penalty', not least because a prison sentence in default flows from non-payment, and the confiscation order is treated as a fine, pursuant to (eg) s 9 of the DTA. (See *R v Benjafield* [2002] UKHL 2 (para 82), *Rezvi* [2002] UKHL 1, and *Phillips v UK* (2001) EHRR No 41087/98.) Part of the reasoning in *Rezvi* was that the purpose of confiscation proceedings was to '...punish convicted offenders'.

The impact of Art 7 and the issue of 'penalty' in civil recovery proceedings was considered by the Court of Appeal in *Director of Assets Recovery Agency v Charrington* [2005] EWCA Civ 334, where Laws LJ embraced the argument that it was untenable to suggest that recovery orders should be treated as criminal (para 17). He described as 'entirely right' both Collins J's ruling (which was not appealed), and that of Coghlin J in the case of *Director of Assets Recovery Agency v Walsh* (QBD NI, 1 April 2004) where Coghlin J said: '...what seems to me of greater importance is the fact that there is no arrest nor is there any formal charge, conviction, penalty or criminal record...' (para 18). **14.120**

Laws LJ roundly dismissed the argument that the case of *Charrington* should be classified as criminal proceedings for the purposes of Art 6 and Art 7 of the ECHR (para 14). His Lordship adopted the submissions of the Director, who maintained that the argument that proceedings for recovery orders should be treated as criminal for Convention purposes was untenable. He cited the fact that the ECtHR has twice considered and rejected that argument in cash forfeiture proceedings under the DTA (see *Butler v UK* (2002) App No 41661-98 and *Webb v UK* (2004) App No 56054-00). It was submitted that it was inconceivable that the reasoning of the ECtHR would not apply equally to the cash forfeiture provisions in Pt 5 of POCA (s 298) which replaced the DTA provisions. It followed that the argument being advanced on behalf of *Charrington* involved inviting the Court of Appeal to decide that the High Court civil recovery procedures under Pt 5 were 'criminal' in nature, whereas the magistrates' court procedures under Pt 5 were to be regarded as 'civil'. The Director submitted that there was no prospect of the court so holding and Laws LJ concurred with that view and adopted it in his judgment. **14.121**

The case of *Walsh* went to appeal in Northern Ireland (Kerr LCJ, Nicholson LJ, and Campbell LJ, *Walsh v Director of the Assets Recovery Agency* [2005] NICA 6), and the Court found, applying the three tests set out in *Engel v Netherlands* that: **14.122**

(1) all the available indicators point strongly to recovery cases being classified as a form of civil proceedings.

   'the Appellant is not charged with a crime...He is not liable to imprisonment or fine if the recovery action succeeds. There is no indictment and no verdict. The primary purpose of the legislation is restitutionary rather than penal.' [para 27].

(2) In terms of the nature of the proceedings the allegation made does not impute guilt and there is no prosecutorial function [para 29].

(3) The primary purpose of the legislation is to recover the proceeds of crime; it is not to punish the appellant in the sense normally entailed in a criminal sanction [para 39].

The Court in *Walsh* (which was primarily considering Art 6(1)) refrained from expressing any final view as to whether recovery of assets was penal within the autonomous meaning of the term (see para 39). **14.123**

Subsequently, the matter was further considered in *Scottish Ministers v McGuffie* [2006] SC(D) 26/2, in which the Court was invited to find that the petitioners were seeking to impose a criminal penalty retrospectively by asking for the appointment of an interim administrator pursuant to s 256 of the Act. It was accepted by the respondent that if there **14.124** was no criminal penalty then his challenge to the petition would fail. Lord Kinclaven, having considered *Walsh* above, stated (see para 127):

The proceedings are directed against property (*in rem*) rather than against Mr. McGuffie's person. The recovery procedures are under the control of the civil court. Mr. McGuffie's guilt is not in issue. He is not facing a criminal charge. He is not an accused person. He cannot be arrested or remanded or compelled to attend. There has been no formal accusation by the prosecuting authorities. He will not be subject to a criminal conviction or finding of guilt. He will not be imprisoned. He will not receive a sentence. A civil recovery order will not form any part of his criminal record.

**14.125** Lord Kinclaven went on to list further features which distinguished civil recovery proceedings:

- The orders sought by the petitioners did not amount to a retrospective criminal penalty within the meaning of Art 7 of the Convention.
- The orders sought by the petitioners were part of a regime for the civil recovery of property that was, or represented, property obtained through unlawful conduct rather than a regime of punishment.
- They were not at the instance of the Lord Advocate or a prosecuting authority.
- They had been initiated by civil petition.
- They were being heard in a civil court.
- The procedures involved for making and implementing the order were clearly civil rather than criminal.
- The proceedings were directed against property rather than against the respondent's person.
- The respondent would not be subject to a criminal conviction or a finding of guilt.
- A civil recovery order would not form any part of his criminal record.

For features that distinguish confiscation and civil recovery proceedings, see Chapter 13.

### Article 7—retrospectivity

**14.126** In *Jia Jin He* Collins J held (at para 69):

The authorities to which I have already referred make it plain that there is no question of any penalty involved in these proceedings. Furthermore, there has been no conviction of a criminal offence leading to a penalty. Of course, property cannot be recoverable unless, at the time it was acquired, it was obtained through unlawful conduct. That conduct must have been criminal at that time. To that extent, the prohibition against retrospectivity will apply, but only because the Act says that the property must be property which was obtained by criminal conduct. In those circumstances, it is quite clear that Article 7 has no application.

**14.127** In *R (on the Application of the Director of the Assets Recovery Agency) v Paul Ashton* [2006] EWHC 1064 (Admin) Newman J also considered whether the civil recovery procedure offended Art 7 of the ECHR governing retrospectivity, and found that it did not. (Leave to appeal his judgment was subsequently refused.)

**14.128** Similarly in *McGuffie* Lord Kinclaven stated (at para 127): 'In my opinion, on a fair valuation of all the circumstances, the orders sought by the Scottish Ministers in the present case do not amount to a retrospective criminal "penalty" within the meaning of Article 7.'

### Article 8

**14.129** In relation to Art 8, the right to family and personal life, Collins J in *Jia Jin He* held it added nothing to what he had said about proportionality in relation to Art 1.

## Proportionality generally

In *Director of Assets Recovery Agency v John and Lord* [2007] EWHC 360 (QB) Tugendhat J **14.130** found it doubtful that monies received from unlicensed street trading would amount to property obtained through unlawful conduct. He stated:

> 76. The provisions of s. 266 are to be contrasted with the way that the criminal law is framed. The penalty for unlicensed trading is set by Parliament. But it is not a mandatory penalty. Criminal statutes set a maximum penalty, and the courts impose a sentence within that maximum in accordance with the law on sentencing. Sentences must be proportionate to the offender's culpability and to the harm which the offence caused, was intended to cause or might foreseeably have caused, and fines must be proportionate to the offender's means: Criminal Justice Act 2003 ss. 143(1), 164(2) and (3). It cannot have been the intention of Parliament that a breach of a regulatory statute for which, on conviction, a fine of £50 pound is appropriate (that is the fine imposed on Mr John for each of his offences of unlicensed trading), should automatically also result in a civil recovery order in respect of all the money he received in making lawful sales while committing that offence.

For a broader discussion on proportionality in the civil recovery and confiscation con- **14.131** text, see *Gilligan v The Criminal Assets Bureau* [1998] 3 IR 185 (in the context of the Irish Constitution); *Raimondo v Italy* (1994) 18 EHRR 371; and *McIntosh v Lord Advocate* [2001] 2 All ER 638.

# E. Pension Schemes

## Introduction

Pension policies can be of great value, but their actual value is often, pursuant to the terms **14.132** of the pension policy, unrealisable until a certain age, or until the policy itself dictates or matures. Money paid into a policy tends to become locked in, with even the policy holder powerless to realise it, or in the alternative, an ability to realise it, but at a considerable undervalue due to the excessive penalties involved and incurred. Parliament appears to have acknowledged this practical problem and legislated for it accordingly within POCA. Not only is the realisation of pension schemes and policies important to the success of the Act and the recovery of the proceeds of crime, but it would also represent a considerable loophole in the legislation if those involved in criminal activity were aware that they could pay tens of thousands of pounds into pension schemes in the safe knowledge that it would place those funds beyond the reach of civil recovery and that in years to come those individuals could look forward to living off a nest egg representing the proceeds of ill-gotten gains.

Section 273(1) and (2) of POCA applies to recoverable property consisting of rights under **14.133** a pension scheme. A recovery order in respect of the property must, instead of vesting the property in the trustees for civil recovery, require the trustees or managers of the pension scheme to pay to the trustee within a prescribed period the amount determined by the trustees or managers of the pension scheme to be equal to the value of the right, and to give effect to any other provision made within ss 273, 274, and 275. This is subject to what is said later in Pt 5 of the Act concerning consent orders (s 276), consent orders and pensions (s 277), and the limit on recovery (s 278).

The requirement of the trustee or managers of the pension scheme to pay to the trustee for **14.134** civil recovery an amount equal to the value of the rights of the pension scheme overrides the provisions of the pension scheme itself, to the extent that if they conflict with the provisions of the order, the order must take priority (see s 273(3)).

**14.135** Subsection (5) of s 273 provides that any statutory provisions, eg s 159 of the Pension Schemes Act 1993, will not frustrate the enforcement authority's or the interim receiver's ability to pursue the recovery of the value of pension rights.

### What does a pension scheme mean within this part of the Act?

**14.136** A pension scheme means an occupational pension scheme or a personal pension scheme. Under s 275(4), these expressions have the same meaning as in the Pension Schemes Act 1993.

**14.137** References to a pension scheme also include retirement annuity contracts; and annuity or insurance policies purchased or transferred for the purposes of giving effect to rights under an occupational pension scheme or a personal pension scheme and/or an annuity purchase, for the purpose of discharging any liability in respect of a pension credit under s 29(1)(b) of the Welfare Reform and Pensions Act 1999.

### Trustees or managers

**14.138** In relation to an occupational pension scheme or a personal pension scheme, the 'trustees or managers' mean either:

(a) in the case of the scheme established under a trust, the trustees
(b) in any other case, the managers (s 275(5)).

**14.139** In relation to a retirement annuity contract or other annuity, references to the trustees or managers are to the provider of the annuity, and in relation to an insurance policy references to the trustees or managers are to the insurer (see s 275(7)).

### The Proceeds of Crime Act 2002 (Recovery from Pension Schemes) Regulations 2003

**14.140** The Proceeds of Crime Act 2002 (Recovery from Pension Schemes) Regulations 2003 were introduced by SI 2003/291 and came into force on 17 March 2003. These Regulations make provision as to the exercise by trustees or managers of pension schemes of their powers when a civil recovery order is made under s 273(2) of POCA and requires them to make a payment to the trustee for civil recovery in respect of the rights of a member of that scheme.

### Calculation and verification of the value of rights under pension schemes

**14.141** Regulation 2(1) applies where the High Court makes a pension recovery order (other than in respect of rights derived from a pension sharing transaction under a destination arrangement) in a pension scheme.

**14.142** It provides for the calculation and verification of the cash equivalent of the value of pension rights which are recoverable property under the Act. This is by reference to the method applying for the purposes of the provision of information in respect of pensions on divorce, separation, and nullity under the Pensions on Divorce etc (Provision of Information) Regulations 2000, SI 2000/1048 and the equivalent regulations applying in Scotland and Northern Ireland.

**14.143** A 'destination arrangement' means a pension arrangement under which some or all of the rights are derived, directly or indirectly, from a pension sharing transaction. A 'pension sharing transaction' means an order or provision falling within s 28(1) of the Welfare Reform and Pensions Act 1999 (activation of pension sharing).

The trustees or managers of the pension scheme in respect of which the pension recovery **14.144** order has been made must calculate and verify the cash equivalent of the value (at the valuation date of the rights which are the subject of the pension recovery order) and must pay to the trustee for civil recovery a sum equal to that cash equivalent (reg 3).

In relation to the calculation and verification by the trustees or managers of the cash equiva- **14.145** lent referred to above:

(a) in the case of a pension scheme wholly or mainly administered in England and Wales, reg 3 of the Pensions on Divorce etc. (Provision of Information) Regulations 2000 (information about pensions and divorce: valuation of pension benefits), except para (2) thereof, shall have effect as it has effect for the valuation of benefits in connection with the supply of information and in connection with domestic and overseas divorce etc in England and Wales, with the modification that, for 'the date on which the request for the valuation was received' in each case where it appears in that regulation, there shall be substituted 'the valuation date for the purposes of the Proceeds of Crime Act 2002 (Recovery from Pension Schemes) Regulations 2003';

(b) in the case of a pension scheme wholly or mainly administered in Scotland, reg 3 of the Divorce etc. (Pensions) (Scotland) Regulations 2000 (valuation), except para (11) thereof, shall have effect as it has effect for the valuation of benefits in connection with the supply of information in connection with divorce in Scotland, with the modification that, for 'the relevant date' in each case where it appears in that regulation, there shall be substituted 'the valuation date for the purposes of the Proceeds of Crime Act 2002 (Recovery from Pension Schemes) Regulations 2003'; and

(c) in the case of a pension scheme wholly or mainly administered in Northern Ireland, reg 3 of the Pensions on Divorce etc. (Provision of Information) Regulations (Northern Ireland) 2000 (information about pensions on divorce: valuation of pension benefits), except para (2) thereof, shall have effect as it has effect for the valuation of benefits in connection with the supply of information in connection with domestic and overseas divorce etc in Northern Ireland, with the modification that, for 'the date on which the request for the valuation was received' in each case where it appears in that regulation, there shall be substituted 'the valuation date for the purposes of the Proceeds of Crime Act 2002 (Recovery from Pension Schemes) Regulations 2003'.

### Calculation and verification of the value of rights under destination arrangements

As stated above, 'destination arrangement' means a pension arrangement under which **14.146** some or all of the rights are derived, directly or indirectly, from a pension sharing transaction. Regulation 3(1) of the Proceeds of Crime Act 2002 (Recovery from Pension Schemes) Regulations 2003 applies where the High Court makes a pension recovery order in respect of rights derived from a pension sharing transaction under a destination arrangement in a pension scheme. The trustees or managers of the pension scheme in respect of which the pension recovery order has been made must calculate and verify the cash equivalent of the value at the valuation date of the rights which are the subject of the pension recovery order and must pay to the trustee for civil recovery a sum equal to that cash equivalent. Regulation 3 provides:

> (3) In relation to the calculation and verification by the trustees or managers of the cash equivalent referred to in paragraph (2)—
> 
> > (a) in the case of a pension arrangement in a scheme that is wholly or mainly administered in either England and Wales or Scotland, regulation 24 of the Pension Sharing

> (Pension Credit Benefit) Regulations 2000 (manner of calculation and verification of cash equivalents) shall have effect as it has effect for the calculation and verification of pension credit for the purposes of those regulations; and
>
> (b) in the case of a pension arrangement in a scheme that is wholly or mainly administered in Northern Ireland, regulation 24 of the Pension Sharing (Pension Credit Benefit) Regulations (Northern Ireland) 2000 (manner of calculation and verification of cash equivalents) shall have effect as it has effect for the calculation and verification of pension credit for the purposes of those regulations.

### Approval of manner of calculation and verification of the value of rights

**14.147**   Regulation 4 makes provision for circumstances where the person with the pension rights which are recoverable property is a trustee or manager of the scheme in question. In such circumstances, an actuary must approve the method of calculation and verification of the cash equivalent value.

**14.148**   The manner in which the trustees or managers have calculated and verified the value of the rights must be approved by:

(a) a Fellow of the Institute of Actuaries; or
(b) a Fellow of the Faculty of Actuaries.

**14.149**   Regulation 4 goes on to provide:

> (3) Where the person referred to in paragraph (2) is not able to approve the manner in which the trustees or managers have calculated and verified the value of the rights which are the subject of a pension recovery order, he must give notice in writing of that fact to the trustee for civil recovery and the trustees or managers of the scheme.
>
> (4) Where the trustees or managers of the scheme have been given notice under paragraph (3), they must re-calculate and re-verify the value of the rights which are the subject of a pension recovery order for the purposes of regulation 2 or 3.

### Time for compliance with a pension recovery order

**14.150**   Regulation 5 prescribes the period for paying the amount of those pension rights to the trustee for civil recovery:

> 5 (1) In this regulation, 'the prescribed period' means the period prescribed for the purposes of section 273(2)(a) of the Act.
>
> (2) Subject to paragraphs (3) and (4), the prescribed period is the period of 60 days beginning on the day on which the pension recovery order is made.

**14.151**   Under reg 5(3), where an application for permission to appeal the pension recovery order is made within the period referred to in para (2), the prescribed period is the period of sixty days beginning on:

(a) the day on which permission to appeal is finally refused;
(b) the day on which the appeal is withdrawn; or
(c) the day on which the appeal is dismissed, as the case may be.

**14.152**   Where the person referred to in reg 4(2) gives notice, in accordance with reg 4(3) and within the period referred to in para (2), to the trustee for civil recovery and trustees or managers of the scheme that he is unable to approve the manner in which the trustees or managers have calculated the value of the rights which are the subject of the pension recovery order, the prescribed period is the period of sixty days beginning on the day on which such notice is given (reg 5(4)).

'Valuation date' means a date within the period prescribed by reg 5 in respect of which the trustees or managers of the pension scheme decide to value the relevant person's pension rights in accordance with regs 2 or 3. **14.153**

### Costs of the trustees or managers of the pension scheme

The trustees or managers of the pension scheme may recover costs incurred by them in: **14.154**

(a) complying with the recovery order, or
(b) providing information, before the recovery order was made, to the enforcement authority or the interim receiver (see s 273(4)).

### Consequential adjustment of liabilities under pension schemes

A recovery order made by virtue of s 273(2) must require the trustees or managers of the pension scheme to make such reduction in the liabilities of the scheme as they think necessary in consequence of a payment made in pursuance of s 273(2). **14.155**

Accordingly, by s 274(2), the order must require the trustees or managers to provide for the liabilities of the pension scheme to cease in respect of the respondent's recoverable property to which s 273 applies. For provision as to the exercise by trustees or managers of pension schemes of their powers see the Proceeds of Crime (Recovery from Pension Schemes) Regulations 2003, SI 2003/291. **14.156**

Section 274(1) envisages that the recovery order itself will include a condition that stipulates that the trustees or managers of the pension scheme will reduce their liabilities to the extent they think necessary following the payment made under the order. Section 274(3) states that the trustees' or managers' powers include the power to reduce the amount of any benefit or future benefit to which the respondent is or may be entitled under the scheme, and any future benefit to which any other person may be entitled under the scheme in respect of that property. **14.157**

### Consent order: pensions

Section 277 of POCA envisages orders by consent being made where recoverable property includes rights under a pension scheme. Section 277(2) states that: **14.158**

> A consent order made under section 276 [which deals with consent orders generally in civil recovery, see para 14.17 above]—
> (a) may not stay the proceedings on terms that the rights are vested in any other person, but
> (b) may include provision imposing the following requirement, if the trustees or managers of the scheme are parties to the agreement by virtue of which the order is made.

The requirement is that the trustees or managers of the pension scheme make a payment in accordance with the agreement and give effect to any other provision made by virtue of s 277 in respect of the scheme (s 277(3)). Section 277(4) states: **14.159**

> The trustees or managers of the pension scheme have power to enter into an agreement in respect of the proceedings on any terms on which [a consent] order made under section 276 may stay the proceedings.

Section 277(6) makes it clear that a consent order made under s 276 overrides the provisions of the pension scheme to the extent that they conflict with the requirements of the order. **14.160**

**14.161**   The consent order may provide for the recovery by the trustees or managers of the scheme (whether by deduction from any amount which they are required to pay in pursuance of the agreement or otherwise) of costs incurred by them in complying with the order, or providing information before the order was made to the enforcement authority or interim receiver (s 277(7)).

## F. Civil Recovery and Taxation

### Summary of taxation provisions

**14.162**   Part 6 of POCA sets out the revenue functions and tax powers of the civil recovery scheme. Pursuant to the SCA, these powers were extensively transferred to SOCA following the abolition of the ARA on 1 April 2008 (s 74(2) and Sch 8, para 93 SCA; and SI 2008/755). This includes the ARA's power to issue tax assessments where the income can be linked to criminality. In turn, the Crime and Courts Act 2013 includes the abolition of the Serious Organised Crime Agency, and the creation of the National Crime Agency (NCA) (see ss 1–16). Subject to Parliamentary processes the ambition is that it will be fully operational by December 2013, after which point the NCA will inherit SOCA's role.

**14.163**   Section 317(1) of POCA sets out the qualifying condition which must be satisfied before the Director of SOCA can take over general Revenue functions (defined at s 323(1)). The condition is that the Director must have reasonable grounds to suspect that income, profits, or gains arising or accruing to a person (including a company) in respect of a chargeable period are chargeable to tax and arise or accrue as a result of that person's, or another's, criminal conduct. Criminal conduct is defined in s 326. If this condition is satisfied, then subs (2) allows the Director to serve a notice on HMRC that has the effect of vesting certain functions of the Revenue in the Director. The notice served will specify a number of things. These will include adequate details to identify the relevant person or company, the chargeable periods in question, and also the particular functions that the Director wishes to assume responsibility for. These may be some or all of the functions listed in s 323(1). The notice will also specify the particular tax periods during which the income, profits, or gains are suspected of arising as a result of criminal conduct.

**14.164**   By s 317(7), the tax function may be vested in both the Director and HMRC officers concurrently. This allows, among other things, routine work to be carried out by HMRC notwithstanding that the functions are also vested in the Director.

**14.165**   Section 320 provides a right of appeal and all appeals against actions arising from the exercise by the Director of his Revenue functions will be to the Tax Tribunal. The right of appeal is equivalent to that available to taxpayers subjected to decisions made by HMRC.

**14.166**   Section 326 of POCA provides definitions and meanings for some of the terminology used in Pt 6 and in particular the terms 'criminal conduct' and 'criminal property'. For the purposes of Pt 6, 'criminal conduct' does not include an offence relating to a matter under the care and management of HMRC, for example tax fraud.

# 15

# THE SEIZURE AND RECOVERY OF CASH

# A. Introduction

**15.01**  The UK's first cash seizure provisions came into force on 1 July 1991 when Pt III of the Criminal Justice (International Co-operation) Act 1990 was enacted. That legislation proved to be necessary because the DTOA, together with similar provisions in other countries, had become a victim of their own success. Drug traffickers and money launderers could no longer risk transferring money from country to country by means of the electronic bank transfer system for fear of being detected, or the location of their money being discovered if they were arrested.

**15.02**  The money launderer became even more vulnerable following implementation of the First EC Money Laundering Directive, which required Member States to introduce legislation requiring financial institutions to keep proper records of transactions and report on money laundering. In consequence, Customs officers at ports and airports noticed that it was becoming increasingly common for large sums of money derived from drug trafficking to be imported into and exported from the UK in cash. They were powerless to intervene and detain such monies unless there was a prosecution for a drug trafficking offence ongoing, in which case the money could be the subject of restraint and confiscation orders. As a result, new legislation was required to combat the couriering of cash into and out of the UK.

## The DTA

**15.03**  Part II of the DTA gave the police and Customs officers the power to seize and detain for up to forty-eight hours drug trafficking money being imported or exported in cash. Magistrates' courts were given the power to order its further detention for periods of up to two years and, ultimately, to order its forfeiture.

**15.04**  The provisions of s 42 et seq of the DTA, although considered extensively in the first edition of this work, were repealed by POCA and are now consigned to history. In Chapter 24 we consider the cash seizure provisions of the Anti–Terrorism, Crime and Security Act 2001.

## The POCA regime

While undoubtedly the DTA scheme for the seizure and forfeiture of cash met with some **15.05** success in terms of both the amounts seized and the message it sent out to would-be drug smugglers and their money couriers (not least because of its draconian nature), it was nevertheless restricted to money that represented or was intended for drug trafficking. In this regard the scheme was viewed by many as flawed, because it made no provision for the forfeiture of cash being imported or exported in relation to other forms of criminal conduct.

As a result, a new scheme under POCA was enacted which expanded the DTA regime to **15.06** include cash related to *all* unlawful conduct. It also went further, by expanding the meaning of 'cash', allowing cash found anywhere in the UK to be seized (not just that which was being imported or exported) and in addition, added new search provisions.

In this chapter we will consider the revised regime governing the law relating to the seizure, **15.07** detention, and forfeiture of cash under ss 289–303 of POCA (see Appendix 5 of this book). These sections came into force on 30 December 2002 (SI 2002/3015) and replace the earlier provisions found in ss 42–48 of the DTA. They affect all cash seizures made on or after that date.

Sections 289–292 of POCA deal with the power to search premises and persons for cash (set **15.08** out in the second part of this chapter), and ss 294–300 deal with the seizure, detention, and forfeiture of cash generally.

The relevant court forms in relation to cash seizures under POCA are found in the Magistrates' **15.09** Court (Detention and Forfeiture of Cash) Rules 2002, SI 2002/2998, as amended by rr 91–96 of the Magistrates' Courts (Miscellaneous Amendments) Rules 2003, SI 2003/1236.

## Civil proceedings

Although some debate ensued under the previous statutory provisions as to whether forfeiture **15.10** provisions were civil or criminal, POCA draws a line under such discussion. The Introduction to Pt 5 of POCA (Civil Recovery of the Proceeds Etc of Unlawful Conduct) states in terms that forfeiture proceedings will be civil proceedings before the magistrates' court:

240(1) This Part has effect for the purposes of—
(a) ...
(b) enabling cash which is, or represents, property obtained through unlawful conduct, or which is intended to be used in unlawful conduct, to be forfeited in civil proceedings before a magistrates' court or (in Scotland) the sheriff.

This accords with the findings of courts under the DTA that the cash seizure provisions were **15.11** civil in nature (see *R v Dover and East Kent Magistrates' Court ex p Steven Gore* (23 May 1996, QBD); *R v Crawley Justices ex p Ohakwe* (1994) 158 JP Reports 78; and *Butler v UK* (App No 41661/98) (27 June 2002) 156 JP 357). Whilst the position as to forum appeared clear, Lewison J confirmed that it was Parliament's intention for cash forfeiture proceedings to be resolved in the magistrates' court in the matter of *Capper v Commissioner of Police of the Metropolis* [2010] EWHC 1704 (Ch). He concluded that to bring a claim in the High Court would be an abuse of process.

## UK Border Agency

The UKBA took over the role of Customs at airports and ports throughout the UK from **15.12** 5 August 2009. While the force and application of the cash forfeiture provisions remain unchanged, the switch has involved the handing over of responsibility from HMRC to the UKBA for cash seizures and investigations at borders in relation to travellers found in possession of cash in excess of the minimum amount. HMRC have retained responsibility in respect of inland cash seizures and investigations (see s 26 of the Borders, Citizenship and Immigration Act 2009). On 26 March 2013 the Home Secretary announced that the UKBA was to be abolished with its work returning to the Home Office. The Home Secretary told MPs that 'its performance was not good enough'. At the time of going to press further details were unclear. For the purposes of this chapter we have continued with the reference to the UKBA, but with the above caveat.

### Investigating the cash

**15.13** The SCA introduces the concept of a formal detained cash investigation (ss 75–77). Schedule 10 to the SCA amends the relevant parts of POCA from 6 April 2008 to allow for the same.

**15.14** Section 75 of the SCA alters s 341(3) of POCA to allow the production order provisions under Pt 8 of POCA to be used for investigating the provenance or intended destination of cash seized. Section 76 amends s 352(2) of POCA to allow for the search and seizure provisions under Pt 8 of POCA to be used for investigating the provenance or intended destination of cash seized. Section 77 gives effect to Sch 10 which makes further provision about the use of production orders and search and seizure warrants for detained cash investigations.

**15.15** The detained cash investigation is intended to be an addition to the existing types of investigation, namely a confiscation investigation, civil recovery investigation, and money laundering investigation.

**15.16** Pursuant to s 79, Sch 11 gives accredited financial investigators powers to recover cash (as described by s 453). The term 'accredited financial investigator' is further defined by the Proceeds of Crime Act 2002 (References to Financial Investigators) (Amendment) Order 2009 (SI 2009/2707).

## B. The Seizure and Forfeiture of Cash

### Preliminary matters

**15.17** The provisions under ss 294–303 of POCA (set out in Appendix 5) establish a civil procedure by which money suspected of being either recoverable property or intended by any person to be used in unlawful conduct may be seized, detained, and forfeited (see s 294). The proceedings for forfeiture are civil (see s 240(1)(b)), the burden being on the applicant (UKBA, HMRC, or the police) to demonstrate that the property is recoverable or the conduct is unlawful, on the balance of probabilities (s 241(3)).

### The circumstances in which cash may be seized

**15.18** Section 294(1) states:

> (1) A Customs Officer, a constable or an accredited financial investigator may seize any cash if he has reasonable grounds for suspecting it is—
> (a) recoverable property, or
> (b) intended by any person for use in unlawful conduct.

An officer may also seize an entire consignment of cash where he has reasonable grounds for suspecting part of it to be:

(a) recoverable property, or

(b) intended by any person for use in unlawful conduct, in circumstances where it is not reasonably practicable to seize only the 'suspicious' part (s 294(2)).

### The minimum amount that may be seized: £1,000

Section 294 does not authorise the seizure of cash if it is for less than the 'minimum amount' (see s 294(3)). The minimum amount was originally set at £10,000, but was subsequently reduced on 16 March 2004 to £5,000 (SI 2004/420), and on 31 July 2006 to £1,000 following the introduction of the Proceeds of Crime Act 2002 (Recovery of Cash in Summary Proceedings: Minimum Amount) Order 2006 (SI 2006/1699).  **15.19**

### Does the minimum amount need to be in the possession of a single person?

It is possible to foresee, particularly in relation to inland seizures, the practical difficulties of linking cash seized from separate individuals and treating it as one amount. However, some judicial guidance may be derived from the decision of *Customs and Excise Commissioners v Duffy* [2002] EWHC 425 (Admin) (decided under the DTA) where the defendants, who had all been travelling to Malaga, were stopped by a Customs officer at Gatwick Airport. They were found with £20,000 collectively in cash. Of the three defendants stopped, it was found they were carrying £7,000, £7,000, and £6,000 respectively (the minimum amount under the DTA being £10,000). The Divisional Court held that a court should approach the Act having in mind that the cash might be with one individual, more than one individual, or in fact no individuals at all. Kennedy LJ said that the sums should not be aggregated if the individuals are otherwise apparently unconnected, but if it can be shown that the money comes from a common source or has a common destination, that may lead the court to conclude that in reality it is a single amount of cash.  **15.20**

It is submitted that the alternative would give rise to a situation developing whereby an individual involved in transferring large sums of cash could ask eg three individuals to carry £950 each (£2,850 in total), in the knowledge that they would be able to avoid the bite of the legislation. Clearly it is important that the UKBA, HMRC, or the police are able to show that there is a nexus between the individuals or the cash concerned. Examples may include: the money having traces/being contaminated with residue of the same drug consignment; the travellers' tickets being booked at the same time or by the same individual; the individuals being known to each other or having a common tie. Any combination of these may suggest that the individuals were operating together and that the source of the money was therefore linked.  **15.21**

### The meaning of 'cash'

The meaning of cash has been expanded under s 289(6) to include:  **15.22**

(a) notes and coins in any currency,

(b) postal orders,

(c) cheques of any kind, including traveller's cheques,

(d) banker's drafts,

(e) bearer bonds and bearer shares.

Unlike the previous DTA regime, this entitles officers to seize cheques where the cheque is under suspicion. Where only part of the value of the cheque in question is under suspicion, s 296(2) allows an officer to pay that cheque into an interest-bearing account, and release the portion of the value of the cheque to which the suspicion does not relate (s 296(2)).

**15.23**  Cash also includes 'any kind of monetary instrument' (s 289(7)). It is submitted a 'monetary instrument' must be in such a form that it can be paid into an interest-bearing account, so as to comply with the requirements of s 296(2). It follows that if it cannot be, then it is likely to fall outside the seizure powers under POCA.

### How is 'unlawful conduct' defined?

**15.24**  Under s 241 of POCA 'unlawful conduct' is defined as either:

> (1)  Conduct occurring in any part of the United Kingdom which is unlawful under the criminal law of that part of the UK (s 241(1)); or
>
> (2)  Conduct which—
>  (a)  occurs in a country outside the United Kingdom and is unlawful under the criminal law of that country, and
>  (b)  if it occurred in a part of the United Kingdom, would be unlawful under the criminal law of that part [of the UK] (s 241(2)).

### Does the 'unlawful conduct' have to be specified?

**15.25**  There is a requirement for the police or the UKBA to satisfy the court that the cash relates to unlawful conduct, although that need not be limited to identifying one particular kind. Section 242(2)(b) reads:

> (2)  In deciding whether any property was obtained through unlawful conduct—
>  (a)  ...
>  (b)  it is not necessary to show that the conduct was of a particular kind if it is shown that the property was obtained through conduct of one of a number of kinds, each of which would have been unlawful conduct.

**15.26**  Provided the court is satisfied, on the balance of probabilities, that the cash seized was obtained through (or intended to be used for) unlawful conduct of one kind or another, it is not necessary to narrow the test to a single particular type nor is there a limit to the number of kinds of unlawful conduct that an officer can rely upon. However it is not sufficient for an officer to rely on unlawful conduct of an unspecified type. Whilst the Act does not provide a definition or definitive list of the kinds of unlawful conduct, in practice most cases are likely to involve an allegation of a particular kind of unlawful conduct, not least because the facts will dictate same. Examples invariably include income from a shop where no tax has been declared, or cash with an unusually high contamination of drugs. The explanatory note to POCA provides that the kinds of unlawful conduct will include 'drug dealing, money laundering, brothel-keeping or other unlawful activities'.

**15.27**  It is also submitted that such a course is also preferable if the defendant is to know, notwithstanding these being civil proceedings, the case he has to answer. This approach also appears to be in line with *R (Director of Assets Recovery Agency) v Green* [2005] EWHC 3168 (Admin) where Sullivan J held that in civil proceedings under Pt 5 of POCA, the applicant did not need to allege the commission of any specific criminal offence, but did have to set out the matters alleged to constitute the particular kind of unlawful conduct by which the property was obtained. He stated that if Parliament had wished the applicant to be able to recover property by simply alleging, and thereafter persuading the court that on the balance of probabilities, it had been obtained by some unspecified unlawful conduct, it could have said so, but did not. It follows therefore that to merely allege that the defendant has no identifiable lawful income, and therefore the cash 'must be' the proceeds of unlawful conduct is not enough; some evidence is required.

*Green* was followed in *Director of the ARA v Szeptietowski* [2007] EWCA Civ 766 and *R v*   **15.28**
*NW SW RC and CC* [2008] EWCA Crim 2, where Laws LJ held:

> 37. ... it would be anomalous, not to say bizarre, if the Crown were not required to identify the class of crime in question in a criminal prosecution while the Director is so required in a civil enforcement suit. Sullivan J's description of the legislative purpose of POCA, adopted by Moore-Bick LJ, is surely no less apt as a guide for the application of Part 7 as it is for that of Part 5.

> 38. In short, we do not consider that Parliament can have intended a state of affairs in which, in any given instance, no particulars whatever need be given or proved of a cardinal element in the case, namely the criminal conduct relied on. It is a requirement, to use Sullivan J's expression, of elementary fairness.

Whilst it is correct to observe that the Court in *NW* was considering civil recovery under Pt   **15.29**
5 of the Act in the context of s 340, it would be difficult to construe the cash forfeiture provisions, which also appear under Pt 5, in a different way. This approach was also confirmed by the High Court in the matter of *Carol Angus v United Kingdom Border Agency* [2011] EWHC 461 (Admin). In applying the provisions of s 242(2)(b) Davies J confirmed that in cash forfeiture proceedings an officer did have to show that the money seized had been obtained through conduct of one or more kind(s), each of which would have been unlawful conduct:

> 27. Part 5 of the Act is concerned with civil recovery. It provides two statutory regimes for recovery, it does not distinguish between the two regimes in the statutory provisions which identify what has to be proved in order to succeed in the relevant proceedings. The effect of the respondent's submission would be to create two different ways of interpreting section 242(2)(b) depending upon whether the litigation is High Court civil recovery proceedings or magistrates/Crown Court cash forfeiture. The section makes no such distinction, the wording is clear, the Explanatory Note underlines the unified approach. Had it been the intention of Parliament to create two separate tests for one section, it would have been made clear in the wording of the statute. To read into section 242 two separate tests, is to place upon it a meaning which is not simply strained and unreasonable, it is wrong in law ...

> 29. Applying the provisions of section 242(2)(b) of the Act, our answer to the question is as follows: in a case of cash forfeiture, a customs officer does have to show that the property seized was obtained through conduct of one of a number of kinds each of which would have been unlawful conduct.

### How is 'recoverable property' defined?

'Recoverable property' is defined as property obtained though unlawful conduct (s 304) (ie   **15.30**
property obtained through conduct which is unlawful under UK criminal law and/or the criminal law of a country outside the UK). To fully understand this definition in the context of cash seizures, 'property' should be read as meaning 'cash' (and its various meanings under s 289(6)) (see s 232(1) and s 414: 'Property is all property wherever situated and includes— (a) money...').

**15.31**   Chapter 4 of Pt 5 of POCA sets out various definitions that apply to both the civil recovery scheme and the cash forfeiture provisions. It deals particularly with recoverable property, namely:

| | |
|---|---|
| Property obtained through unlawful conduct | s 304 |
| Tracing property | s 305 |
| Mixing property | s 306 |
| Recoverable property accruing profits | s 307 |
| General exceptions and other exemptions | ss 308 and 309 |
| Granting interests | s 310 |
| Obtaining and disposing of property | s 314 |

**15.32**   Under s 311, if the cash concerned is 'an asset of a company being wound up' or if there is, prima facie, an arguable case that it is (or one of the other terms imposed by s 311), then an application for further detention may not be made unless the court that is dealing with the winding-up petition/bankruptcy gives leave.

### The tracing of property

**15.33**   The Act envisages, under s 305, the tracing of property. Where the original property was obtained through unlawful conduct, any property subsequently obtained with it also has the potential to become 'recoverable property'. For example, a person steals a valuable painting (the original property). The painting is then sold and the cash received from the sale is later seized at an airport under POCA. Following an investigation the cash can be traced back to the stolen painting. The cash therefore becomes recoverable property, it being the proceeds of a crime.

### Mixed property

**15.34**   The Act also stipulates that where a person's 'recoverable property' is mixed with other property, the portion of the mixed property that is said to relate to unlawful conduct becomes 'recoverable property' (see s 306). In terms of s 294, the recoverable property is likely to be mixed cash. For example, where there are two joint company directors, one uses the company account for legitimate monies, the other to launder the proceeds of crime. The 'honest' director withdraws a large sum and he is stopped going through the airport and the cash is seized. The portion of the cash which he has on him that relates to legitimate money from the business does not fall within the scheme; however, the portion which was paid in as part of the laundered proceeds of a crime does stand to be forfeited, whether that particular director knew about it or not.

### Property that is not 'recoverable'

**15.35**   POCA also affords certain 'defences' under which property should not be considered recoverable (see ss 304–310, SI 2003/336 and Chapter 13). General exceptions include a situation where a person disposes of recoverable property and the person who obtains it does so in good faith, for value, and without notice that it was recoverable property. In such circumstances the property may not be followed into that person's hands and, accordingly, it ceases to be recoverable (s 308(1)).

**15.36**   Similarly, if in pursuance of a judgment in civil proceedings the defendant makes a payment to the claimant or the claimant otherwise obtains property from the defendant, that property ceases to be recoverable (see s 308(3)); or if a payment is made to a person in pursuance of a compensation order under s 130 of the PCC(S)A, the property ceases to be recoverable (s 308(4)).

In cash seizure cases these are all matters that in practice will need to be raised by the defend- **15.37** ant/traveller. It may be that as part of their enquiries the police/UKBA/HMRC (or the court) will enquire of the defendant/traveller as to whether or not any of the exemptions or exceptions apply to the cash seized. Unless the court/police/UKBA/HMRC are positively advised otherwise, they are likely to assume that they do not.

### The re-seizure of cash

In *Chief Constable of Merseyside Police v Hickman* [2006] EWHC 451 (Admin); Mitting J **15.38** held that money that had been seized pursuant to a criminal enquiry and s 19 of the Police and Criminal Evidence Act 1984 (PACE 1984), could be re-seized at any time under s 294 of POCA. There were no time limits on the exercise of the power to seize money under the cash forfeiture provisions of POCA, and there was no reason why the police should be prevented from 'seizing' cash already in their possession, the position being analogous to that of property found on an individual after arrest. The approach was followed in *Cook v Serious Organised Crime Agency* [2010] EWHC 2119 (Admin). In *Iqbal v Luton & South Bedfordshire Magistrates' Court* [2011] EWHC 705 (Admin) Pill LJ held that where property had been retained on suspicion of money laundering under s 22 PACE 1984, the police were entitled to a 'short period of grace' between the expiry of that power and the exercise of their s 294 power to re-seize under POCA. Section 22(1) PACE 1984 permits the police to retain any property for a short period while considering the position (see *Gough v Chief Constable of the West Midlands Police* [2004] EWCA Civ 2006). The court also confirmed that: (i) on the premise that an original seizure is lawful; and (ii) that the decision to re-seize under s 294 POCA is made 'within a reasonable time', there is no requirement to return the cash before it is re-seized.

### Ongoing criminal proceedings

In *R v Payton* (2006) 150 SJ 741, the Court of Appeal considered the difficult situation of **15.39** where cash seizure proceedings may be ongoing and taking place either in advance of or in parallel with a defendant's criminal trial. The concern was that such proceedings would lead to a potential unfairness to the defendant if he was required to give or call evidence. To ensure that a defendant's entitlement to a fair trial was not compromised, the Court of Appeal stated that it was essential that there should be proper communication between the cash-seizing authority and the prosecuting authority. In practice cash seizure cases are usually adjourned pending the outcome of any criminal proceedings.

## C. Practice and Procedure

### The initial enquiry

The money may only be seized if the officer has 'reasonable grounds', upon enquiry, for sus- **15.40** pecting the money is recoverable property or is intended by any person for use in unlawful conduct (s 294(1)). If the officer, or his senior officer, as the case may be, believes 'reasonable grounds' for such a suspicion do not exist, or conversely the explanation is credible, the cash should not be detained. It must be borne in mind that 'cash' also means traveller's cheques, cheques, and any other kind of monetary instrument.

**15.41** In order to ascertain whether the cash is recoverable or is intended by any person for use in unlawful conduct a short interview is often held. While the provisions of PACE 1984 do not apply in civil proceedings (see *Revenue & Customs v Pisciotto* [2009] EWHC 1991 (Admin)), officers should nevertheless consider what is best practice, particularly bearing in mind that at this stage it remains a possibility that, subject to further investigation, a criminal charge (eg money laundering) may arise. A signed endorsement in the officer's notebook, confirming that the contents of the interview have been read back to the interviewee and that the contents are a 'true and accurate record' therefore remains important for all parties. It is particularly pertinent for officers given that interviewees may subsequently change their account as to the provenance of the money. The caution is not appropriate when acting solely under s 294.

**15.42** At this preliminary stage there is no compulsion for an individual to stay and answer questions. If the individual elects to continue their journey or does not wish to answer any questions, that is their prerogative.

**15.43** Once the decision to seize has been made, the individual should be informed that the matter will be listed before a magistrates' court within forty-eight hours.

### Procedure prior to the first hearing and venue

**15.44** The first application under s 295(4) for the extension of the period for which the cash (or any part of it) may be detained beyond the initial forty-eight hours may be made on Form A, and sent to the magistrates' court where the applicant wishes to make the application. Unlike the DTA, there is no restriction on which magistrates' court the applicant may use.

**15.45** This is also reflected in SI 2003/638, which amends the magistrates' jurisdiction so that for the purposes of s 52 of the MCA, any magistrates' court has jurisdiction to hear such an application, whether or not it relates to a matter arising within the commission area for which the court is appointed.

**15.46** Where the reasonable grounds (under s 295(4)) for the suspicion leading to the seizure in question are connected to a previous order made under s 295(2) of the Act, then the application may be sent to the magistrates' court that made the previous order (r 4(2) of the Magistrates' Court (Detention and Forfeiture of Cash) Rules 2002, SI 2002/2998).

**15.47** Under r 4(3) of the same rules, a copy of the written application and notification of the hearing of the application should be given by the applicant to the person from whom the cash was seized (except where cash is seized as a result of an unattended despatch, eg an unattended letter or parcel, or where unattended cash is seized).

### The first detention hearing for the seized cash

**15.48** Under s 295(1) of POCA, while the police or a Customs/UKBA officer continue to have reasonable grounds for suspicion that the cash seized falls under s 294, it may be detained, initially for a period of forty-eight hours (to allow further enquiries to be made).

**15.49** At the first detention hearing the period for detention of the cash (or any part of it) may be extended by the magistrates' court, but not for a period of beyond six months beginning with the date of the order (s 295(2)(a)). Thereafter, the period of detention may be extended on a six-monthly basis, but not beyond the end of a period of two years beginning from the date of the first order. In other words, the maximum order for continued detention, before having to return to the magistrates' court for a further order, is six months. The maximum period for the investigation is two years.

It should be noted that at this stage there is no obligation to notify any third party who may **15.50** be affected by the first application (see r 4(3) Magistrates' Court (Detention and Forfeiture of Cash) Rules 2002, SI 2002/2998). However, the rules envisage the magistrates' court giving notice of any order made by the court not only to the person from whom the cash was seized, but also to any other person known to be affected by the order (Form C—see r 4(9) as above).

Under the Act a single justice of the peace may exercise the powers of the magistrates' court **15.51** to make the first order extending the period (s 295(3)).

### Unattended despatches

Where seized cash is found in a means of unattended despatch (eg an unattended letter or **15.52** parcel), copies of the written application and notification of the hearing of the application must be sent by the police/UKBA/HMRC to the sender and intended recipient of the unattended item (r 4(4)).

Where the seized cash is contained in an unattended despatch, and the sender or intended **15.53** recipient is not known, the applicant (understandably) is not required to send out copies of the written application and notification (see r 4(5)).

Under the Magistrates' Courts Rules it is not in the court's power to decline to hear an **15.54** application solely on the ground that it has not been proved that the sender and intended recipient have been given a copy of the written application and notification of the hearing in unattended despatch cases (see r 4(6)).

Where unattended cash is seized (other than where the cash is found in an unattended des- **15.55** patch), the applicant need not give a copy of the written application and notification of the hearing to any person (see r 4(7)).

### The forty-eight-hour rule

The forty-eight-hour rule should be complied with in all cases. SOCPA, however, has **15.56** amended the rule to allow for greater latitude in relation to the meaning of '48 hours'. Section 100 of SOCPA inserts into s 295 of POCA the following provision:

> (1B) In calculating a period of 48 hours in accordance with this subsection, no account shall be taken of—
> (a) any Saturday or Sunday,
> (b) Christmas Day,
> (c) Good Friday,
> (d) any day that is a bank holiday..., or
> (e) any day prescribed...as a court holiday... [in Scotland].

This section avoids the pitfall that formerly arose in terms of getting the matter before **15.57** magistrates within forty-eight hours when the seizure took place at weekends (see *R v Uxbridge Magistrates' Court ex p Henry* [1994] Crim LR 581 and *Walsh v Customs and Excise*

*Commissioners* [2001] EWHC 426 (Admin), both cases in which the Court found that the forty-eight-hour time limit must be strictly complied with).

**15.58**   It is perhaps worthwhile remembering that the overriding purpose of POCA is to recover the proceeds of crime. To return, for example, £100,000 of cash that can be linked to unlawful conduct, on the basis that an officer was ten minutes late in lodging an application, or on some other technicality, may, it is suggested, offend against the overall intention of Parliament. One remedy, presumably (and subject to abuse arguments), would be to return the money, and then re-seize it. (See also *Chief Constable of Merseyside Police v Reynolds* [2004] EWHC 2862 (Admin).)

### The test the court will apply at further detention hearings

**15.59**   Under s 295(4), once an application has been made it is for the court to decide whether or not to make an order, if satisfied, in relation to any cash to be further detained, that either of the following conditions are met:
Condition 1:

> 295(5)... that there are reasonable grounds for suspecting that cash is *recoverable property* and that either—
> (a) its continued detention is justified while its *derivation* is further investigated, or consideration is given to bringing (in the UK or elsewhere) proceedings against any person for an offence with which the cash is connected, or
> (b) proceedings against any person for an offence with which the cash is connected have been started and have not been concluded [emphasis added].

If there are such reasonable grounds, that test/condition is met and the court may order a period of further detention.
Condition 2:

> 295(6)... that there are reasonable grounds for suspecting that the cash is intended to be used in *unlawful conduct* and that either—
> (a) its continued detention is justified while *its intended use is further investigated* or consideration is given to bringing (in the United Kingdom or elsewhere) proceedings against any person for an offence with which the cash is connected, or
> (b) proceedings against any person for an offence with which the cash is connected have been started and have not been concluded [emphasis added].

Under s 295(4) either of the above conditions must be met. It is not necessary for both conditions to be met.

**15.60**   It is important to reiterate, therefore, that the officer must not only show that he has reasonable grounds for suspecting that either the cash is recoverable property or the cash is intended to be used in unlawful conduct, but also that its continued detention is justified pending further investigation into its derivation or intended use; or consideration is being given to bringing proceedings against any person for an offence with which the cash is connected (or that proceedings against any person for an offence with which the cash is connected have been started and have not been concluded).

### Interest

**15.61**   Under s 296, if cash is detained for more than forty-eight hours, it must at the first opportunity be paid into an interest-bearing account and held there; and the interest accruing on it must be added to it on its forfeiture or release.

It is suggested that this requirement could present some difficulty to law enforcement offic-  **15.62**
ers. The banking of cash is not likely to be a problem; the banking of bearer bonds, banker's
drafts, cheques, and the like, is. In practical terms cheques can be 'stopped'. They are likely to
be made payable to third parties. The above requirement therefore requires special arrangements to be put in place with the banks to ensure acceptance of any monetary instrument,
without, presumably, adopting usual banking protocols.

### Interest—what does 'at the first opportunity' mean?

Section 296(3) states that payment of money into an interest-bearing account at the earliest  **15.63**
opportunity does not apply if the cash or, as the case may be, the part to which the suspicion
relates, is required as evidence of an offence or evidence in proceedings under Chapter 3 of the Act.

One assumes that would cover a situation where the evidence was still being gathered, eg  **15.64**
forensic testing of the money. It follows that, if the police or the relevant agency want to
submit the money for forensic testing for traces of drugs, they would not be obliged to
pay it into an interest-bearing account until the results are back and the defence has been
given the opportunity to test the money themselves (affording the defence the opportunity
of testing the money themselves was always considered best practice in DTA cases, and
avoids any argument that the defence were not given such an opportunity).

In cases where no forensic testing is required, and the cash is not required as a physical  **15.65**
exhibit, a strict interpretation of POCA appears to dictate that 'at the first opportunity'
is after forty-eight hours have passed, in other words as soon as the banks open, the cash
should be banked. It is submitted that an element of reasonableness should be implied, ie
as soon as reasonably practicable. While that more lenient interpretation may afford the
police, UKBA, or HMRC officers further time, the failure to pay the money in at the first
opportunity could later lead to criticism and potential compensation as s 302(2) provides:

> (2) If for any period beginning with the first opportunity to place the cash in an interest bear-
> ing account after the initial detention of the cash for 48 hours, the cash was not held in an
> interest bearing account while detained, the court may order an amount of compensation
> to be paid to the applicant.
> (3) The amount of compensation to be paid under subsection (2) is the amount the court
> thinks would have been earned in interest in the period in question if the cash had been
> held in an interest bearing account.

While in many cases the loss of interest will only be for a nominal amount, in cases where the  **15.66**
cash seized is a more significant sum the potentially accruing interest is likely to be of more
importance.

### Release of money to which no suspicion attaches

Under s 296(2) the police or Customs officer must, on paying the seized cash into a bank  **15.67**
account, release any part of that cash to which the suspicion does not relate.

## D. Continued Detention Hearings: Practice

### Form A

Applications for the continued detention of seized cash under s 295(4) may be made on  **15.68**
Form A (see r 5(1) of the Magistrates' Court (Detention and Forfeiture of Cash) Rules 2002,

SI 2002/2998, as amended by r 93 of the Magistrates' Courts (Miscellaneous Amendments) Rules 2003, SI 2003/1236).

**15.69** On receipt of Form A the justices' clerk/legal advisor should fix a date for the hearing of the application. The court must then notify that date to the relevant agency and every person to whom notice of the previous orders has been given (r 5(3)). It should be noted that the justices' clerk is required to give seven days' notice for a continued detention hearing. Accordingly best practice dictates that Form A should be submitted to the clerk in good time prior to the existing order running out (eg at least eight or nine days prior). This will allow the clerk time to issue the hearing notice and comply with the seven-day requirement.

**15.70** Once this has been done it is then the duty of the applicant to send a copy of the application to every person to whom notice of previous related orders made under s 295(2) of the Act has been given (see r 5(2)).

### Two-year investigation

**15.71** The Act, like the DTA before it, envisages a period of up to two years for the investigation to take place. The magistrates may allow a period up to a maximum of three months from the date of the order, but not beyond the end of a period of two years from the date of the first order (s 295(4)). It should be noted that, as in the initial detention application, the magistrates are entitled to conclude that only part of the cash seized should continue to be detained.

**15.72** If the court refuses to grant a further detention, it will not necessarily lead to the release of the cash. The applicant is still at liberty to bring an application for forfeiture within forty-eight hours and/or an appeal, the effect of the magistrates' decision being to refuse a further extension, as opposed to ordering its release (see *Chief Constable of Lancashire Constabulary v Burnley Magistrates' Court* [2003] EWHC 3308 (Admin)).

### Form C

**15.73** Form C relates to rr 4(9) and 5(6). It is a notice to persons affected by an order for continued detention of seized cash. It reflects the Act, in that the person from whom the cash was seized may apply for the release of the detained cash or any part of it under s 297 of the Act. Under the Magistrates' Courts (Miscellaneous Amendments) Rules 2003, SI 2003/1236, Form C is omitted from the Schedule and is no longer a mandatory requirement of the rules (r 9(6)).

### Service of documents

**15.74** Under r 9 any notification or document required to be given or sent to any person under the Magistrates' Court (Detention and Forfeiture of Cash) Rules 2002, SI 2002/2998 may be given by post or by fax to his last known address, or to any other address given by that person for the purpose of service of documents under the rules (presumably including solicitors).

### Procedure at the continued detention hearing

**15.75** Although the Magistrates' Courts Rules are themselves silent, Form A envisages that the police, UKBA, or HMRC officer applying for the order will state on oath that at least one of the two grounds in s 295(4) is satisfied.

**What if the correct forms have not been served or the proper procedure not followed?**

Caution should be taken to ensure that the proper procedures set out in the Magistrates' **15.76** Court (Detention and Forfeiture of Cash) Rules 2002 are met. However, since the introduction of the Magistrates' Courts (Miscellaneous Amendments) Rules 2003, SI 2003/1236 the requirement to use any of the forms is considerably diluted and, in cases other than Form A and G, omitted This reflects the case law that had developed in relation to cash seizure cases, which dictated that use of the forms was directory rather than mandatory.

In *R v Luton Justices ex p Abecasis*, The Times, 30 March 2000, the Court of Appeal held that **15.77** Form C under the DTA was no more than a request to continue the existing order and that it did not have to be served on the person whose cash has been seized. All that was required, the Court held, is that the clerk to the justices should fix a date for the hearing and notify the person whose cash had been seized that the hearing was so listed. Where that was done, the substance of the rule was complied with. (See also *R (On the application of Gorvievski) v HM Customs & Excise* [2003] EWHC 2773 (Admin) where the court confirmed a technical failure to fully comply with the rules did not invalidate the order subsequently made). (See also *Halford v Colchester Magistrates' Court* [2000] All ER (D) 1527.)

A similar problem arose in the POCA case of *Chief Constable of Merseyside Police v Reynolds* **15.78** [2004] EWHC 2862 (Admin). In *Reynolds* an order for continued detention was made at 10 am on 11 February 2004 for a further period of ninety days. It was argued, by way of case stated, that the order must have expired at midnight on 10 May 2004. The next hearing for further detention had taken place on the morning of 11 May 2004. Furthermore, the request for an extension of time had not been served seven days prior to the hearing, as is required by r 5 of the Magistrates' Courts (Detention and Forfeiture of Cash) Rules 2002, SI 2002/2998.

In relation to the latter point the Court (Rose LJ and Leveson J) held that the requirement **15.79** in r 5 was merely directory and not mandatory (following *Halford* and *Abecasis*) and as such, had no merit.

In terms of the expiry period, the Court held 11 February should be excluded when calcu- **15.80** lating the ninety-day period (by reference to *Marren v Dawson Bentley & Co* [1961] 3 All ER 270 and *Radcliffe and Bartholomew* [1892] 1 QB 161, which establish that the day a cause of action arises or an offence is committed is to be excluded in computing a limitation period and that the principle applied whether the statute in question was dealing with civil or criminal cases). For a similar decision on the application of the *Abecasis* principle, and the refusal of further detention on the merits, see *Chief Constable of Lancashire Constabulary v Burnley Magistrates' Court* [2003] EWHC 3308 (Admin) and *Gorgievski v Customs and Excise Commissioners* [2003] EWHC 2773 (Admin).

These cases should not of course be regarded as an invitation to the police or other officers **15.81** not to comply with the Rules. Leveson J commented in *Reynolds* that such arguments 'are entirely avoidable if the application is not made at the last moment'.

**Insolvency and further detention hearings**

An application for an order for the further detention of any cash for which s 311(3) applies **15.82** (assets subject to insolvency proceedings) may not be made under s 295 unless the appropriate court gives permission (s 311(2)).

**Early release of the cash—to the person from whom the cash was seized**

**15.83** Section 297(2) of POCA authorises the court to release the cash prior to the expiration of a detention order. A magistrates' court may only direct the release of the cash under s 297 (either in whole or in part) if the following condition is met: the court must be satisfied, on an application from the person *from whom the cash was seized*, that the conditions in s 295(5) and (6) for the detention of the cash that is to be released are no longer met (s 297(2) and (3)). The burden at this interim stage is on the person from whom the cash was seized, to the civil standard (*R (on the application of the Chief Constable of Greater Manchester) v City of Salford Magistrates' Court and Sarwar and Sons (Knitwear Ltd)* [2008] EWHC 1651 (Admin)).

**15.84** An application under s 297(3) of the Act for the release of detained cash must be made in writing and sent to the magistrates' court (see r 6(1)). If the applicant (the person from whom the cash was seized) has been given notice of an order under s 295(2) (continued detention) in respect of the detained cash, then the application should be sent to the magistrates' court who sent him that notice. Once an application has been received, the court must send a copy of the application to the police/UKBA/HMRC (r 6(3)(a)), and every person to whom notice of the order made under s 295(2) of the Act has been given (r 6(3)(c)). The justices' clerk must then fix a hearing date (see r 6(4)).

**15.85** Only a person from whom the cash was seized is entitled to make such an application under s 297(3). A third party affected by the order therefore will have no right to do so (but does under s 301).

**Form D**

**15.86** The requirement for the magistrates' court to make a direction for the release of the detained cash on Form D if it is satisfied that the condition set out in s 297(3) has been met is omitted by the Magistrates' Courts (Miscellaneous Amendments) Rules 2003, SI 2003/1236 and is no longer a requirement, although anecdotally in practice courts are still using the forms for administrative convenience.

**15.87** Form D appears to envisage that the court will hear oral evidence and representations.

**15.88** The court may either order the immediate release of the money or the release of the money on a date not more than seven days from the date of the direction, unless a later date is agreed by the applicant.

**15.89** Cash cannot be released where s 298(4) of POCA applies (ie while forfeiture proceedings are ongoing).

**Applications for early release by victims or other owners**

**15.90** Section 301 is part of the supplementary provisions to the cash forfeiture regime, and allows a person who claims that any cash detained under Chapter 3 of POCA belongs to him to apply to a magistrates' court for the release of the cash (or a part of it) (s 301(1)).

**15.91** The application may be made in the course of proceedings under s 295 (detention of seized cash) or s 298 (forfeiture) or 'at any other time' (s 301(2)).

**15.92** An application under s 301(1) of the Act for the release of detained cash must be made in writing and sent to the magistrates' court concerned (see r 6(1)).

Section 301 is divided into two parts:  **15.93**

(a)  for victims of unlawful conduct (s 301(3)); and
(b)  for other owners of the cash where s 295(5) and (6) is no longer met (s 301(4)).

### Section 301(3): victims of unlawful conduct

Section 301(3) states:  **15.94**

> (3)  If it appears to the court...concerned that—
> (a)  the applicant was deprived of the cash to which the application relates, or of property which it represents, by unlawful conduct,
> (b)  the property he was deprived of was not, immediately before he was deprived of it, recoverable property, and
> (c)  that cash belongs to him,
> the Court may order the cash to which the application relates to be released to the applicant.

All three requirements must be met. An example of where s 301(3) may apply would be if a third party was to come forward who claimed that the money had been stolen from him at an earlier time, ie he was the victim of an unlawful event.

### Section 301(4): third-party applications/other owners

Section 301(4) states:  **15.95**

> (4)  If—
> (a)  the applicant is not the person from whom the cash to which the application relates was seized,
> (b)  it appears to the court...that that cash belongs to the applicant,
> (c)  the court...is satisfied that the conditions in section 295 for the detention of the cash are no longer met or, if an application has been made under section 298 [forfeiture], the court decides not to make an order under that section in relation to that cash, and
> (d)  no objection to the making of an order under this subsection has been made by the person from whom the cash was seized,
> the court...may order the cash to which the application relates to be released to the applicant or to the person from whom it was seized.

All four criteria must be met before release can be sanctioned. Section 301(4)(c) implies that there must no longer be any reasonable grounds for suspecting the cash is recoverable property and no longer any reasonable grounds for suspecting that the cash is intended for use in unlawful conduct.

### Objection to release under section 301(4) from the person from whom the cash was seized

Section 301(4)(d) is important because if the person from whom the cash was seized objects  **15.96**
to the third party's claim to being the true owner of the money, whatever the merits of the third party's claim, the court will not be able to release it. It is in effect a veto, held by the person from whom the cash was seized. Section 301(4)(d), according to the explanatory notes that accompany POCA, is intended to prevent the court from becoming embroiled in a complicated ownership dispute between the party from whom the cash was seized and the rightful owner of the cash prior to the forfeiture hearing.

### Form F: Order for release under section 301(4)

**15.97** Although the importance of Form F has diminished since its omission from the Magistrates' Courts (Miscellaneous Amendments) Rules 2003, SI 2003/1236, anecdotally some courts are still using the form or similar for the purposes of administrative convenience where it appears to the court that:

(a) the sum was not seized from the applicant;
(b) the sum (whether in full or in part) belongs to the applicant;
(c) the conditions in s 295 of POCA for detaining the sum are no longer met;
(d) the court has decided not to order forfeiture of the sum under s 298(2) of POCA; and
(e) no objection to the making of the order was made by the person from whom the sum was seized or alternatively the cash was unattended.

**15.98** Form F anticipates that any release of the sum under s 301(4) will include any interest accruing thereon, as per s 296(1). Under Rule 6(7):

> A Direction under section 297(2) of the Act and an Order under section 301(3) or (4) of the Act shall provide for the release of the cash within seven days of the date of the making of the Order or Direction, or such longer period as, with the agreement of the Applicant, may be specified, except that cash shall not be released while section 298(4) [where a forfeiture application has been made and proceedings have not been concluded] applies.

### Joinder

**15.99** Under r 6(5), at the hearing of an application under s 301(1) the court may, if it thinks fit, order that the applicant be joined as a party to the proceedings in relation to the detained cash.

### Applications for the return of the cash: standard of proof

**15.100** In *Customs and Excise Commissioners v Mukesh Shah* (1999) 163 JP 759 (a DTA case) the court accepted that it was for the applicant to satisfy the magistrates on the balance of probabilities to release the cash if they were satisfied that there were no, or no longer any, grounds for its detention or, on an application made by any other person, the detention of the cash was not for that or any other reason justified.

### Can officers agree to the release of cash?

**15.101** Yes. Under s 297(4) of POCA, a police, UKBA, or HMRC officer may (after notifying the magistrates' court under whose order the cash is being detained) release the cash in whole or in part, if he is satisfied the detention of the cash is no longer justified. It is always advisable therefore for a defendant to first write to either the police or the relevant agency and set out the defendant's case for the return of the cash prior to contemplating court action.

### Transfer of proceedings

**15.102** Under r 10 of the Magistrates' Court (Detention and Forfeiture of Cash) Rules 2002, SI 2002/2998, any person who is a party to, or affected by, proceedings under Chapter 3 of Pt 5 of POCA may, at any time, make application to the court dealing with the matter for the proceedings to be transferred to a different petty sessions area (r 10(1)). Applications should be made in writing (r 10(2)) and should specify the grounds on which they are made. The magistrates' court must send a copy of the application to the parties to the proceedings and any other people affected by the proceedings and fix a date for the hearing of the application under r 10(3) and (4).

### Transfer: what test is to be applied?

Under r 10(5) the court may grant the application for transfer if it is satisfied that it would **15.103** be more convenient or fairer for proceedings to be transferred to a different petty sessions area. Rule 10(6) sets out the steps that the magistrates' court should follow if the application is granted.

## E. Applications for Forfeiture of Detained Cash

### Forfeiture proceedings

When the police, UKBA, or HMRC have completed their enquiries into the provenance of **15.104** the detained monies and consider they have sufficient evidence, on the balance of probabilities, to establish the cash or any part of it is:

(a) recoverable property or
(b) intended by any person for use in unlawful conduct,

an application for forfeiture on Form G should be made (see s 298 of POCA).

By s 298(2): **15.105**

> (2) The court may order the forfeiture of the cash or any part of it if it is satisfied that the cash or part—
> (a) is recoverable property, or
> (b) is intended by any person for use in unlawful conduct.

As distinct from powers to detain under s 295(5) and (6), there is no express requirement contained within s 298(2) that the court must be satisfied, either at the time the cash was seized or beforehand, that the relevant public authority had 'reasonable grounds' for suspecting that it had been obtained through or intended for use in unlawful conduct. The proper test for the court and the only question that need concern it is whether it can be satisfied (to the requisite standard) that the cash had been obtained or was intended for use in unlawful conduct (*Secretary of State for the Home Department v Tuncel* [2012] EWHC 402 (Admin)).

### Form G

An application under s 298(1) for forfeiture of the detained cash is made on Form G (r 7(1), as **15.106** amended by the Magistrates' Courts (Miscellaneous Amendments) Rules 2003, SI 2003/1236) and sent to the Justices' Chief Executive to whom applications for the continued detention of the cash under s 295(4) of the Act have been sent (if no applications in respect of the cash have been made under s 295(4) then the application must be sent to the Justices' Chief Executive of the court before which the police or Customs wish to make the application).

Where the 'reasonable grounds for suspicion' that led to the initial seizure of the cash are **15.107** connected to the 'reasonable grounds for suspicion' which led to the seizure of cash under another order (made under s 295(2)), the application should be sent to the Justices' Chief Executive for the magistrates' court that made the first order.

Form G should then be sent to every person to whom notice of any order made under **15.108** s 295(2) (continued detention) has been given, and to any other person identified by the court as being affected by the application.

**15.109**   Form G requires the police, UKBA, or HMRC officer to state the grounds for his belief that the cash is recoverable property or is intended by any person for use in unlawful conduct.

**15.110**   It is the applicant's responsibility and not the court's to send a copy of the application to the various parties. This may well therefore require an enquiry by the applicant to the court or in circumstances where parallel criminal proceedings are ongoing, to the solicitors instructed in the criminal matter (*Harrison v Birmingham Magistrates' Court* [2011] EWCA Civ 332). In *Harrison* the Court of Appeal expressed concern that the Rules contained no explicit provision allowing a defendant to demonstrate that service of notice of the proceedings had been ineffective, and so to ask for a forfeiture order to be set aside. The court described it as being in accordance with 'the most elementary principle of natural justice' that in such circumstances a defendant should be able to retrieve the opportunity to participate in the proceedings. To meet that concern, a presumption of effective service (unless the contrary is shown) has been introduced. Rule 9 (as amended by the Magistrates' Courts (Detention and Forfeiture of Cash) (Amendment) Rules 2012 (SI 2012/1275)) provides:

> Any notification or document required to be given or sent to any person under these Rules may be given by post or by facsimile to his last known address, or to any other address given by that person for the purpose of service of documents under these Rules, and, if so given or sent, shall be deemed to have been received by that person unless the contrary is shown.

**15.111**   If the recipient of that notification is not the person from whom the cash was seized, but someone who claims that the cash belongs to him, and the court decides not to make a forfeiture order, the recipient 'third party' of Form G may then apply to the court under s 301(4) for the release of the cash to them (as per Form G).

### Effect of lodging an application

**15.112**   Once an application for forfeiture (Form G) has been made the cash may not be released until any proceedings in pursuance of that application (including any proceedings on appeal) are concluded.

### Power for prosecutors to appear in cash recovery proceedings

**15.113**   Section 84 of the SCA permits the CPS to take forward cash recovery proceedings on behalf of a constable or HMRC if asked to do so and it is considered appropriate. It inserts s 302A into POCA, which also allows designated staff who are not prosecutors, together with outside contractors, to appear in cash seizure proceedings. The amendments made by this section are further amended by para 12 of Sch 11 to the Act to include accredited financial investigators. Previously these matters were exclusively dealt with by either the relevant police force's solicitors' office, or HMRC's solicitor's office.

## F. The Hearing

### Hearing for directions

**15.114**   Once Form G has been issued the justices' clerk/legal advisor must set a date for a directions hearing (see r 7(4)). At the directions hearing, the court may give directions relating to the management of the proceedings, including the date of the hearing.

Importantly, under r 7(6) if neither the person from whom the cash was seized, nor any **15.115** other person who was affected by the detention of the cash, seeks to contest the application, the court may decide the application at the directions hearing. It is therefore imperative that parties attend directions hearings, or at least make it clear on the record that they intend to contest the hearing. Failure to do so may lead to the court making an order in the defendant's absence. This rule was tested in *Leigh v Uxbridge Magistrates' Court* [2005] EWHC 1828 (QBD) where Goldring J, while expressing no principle, quashed an order for forfeiture made by the magistrates' court and remitted the matter back to the justices in circumstances where it was apparent that the defendant had made it clear through his solicitors and counsel on previous occasions that he would be contesting the hearing, but nevertheless failed to attend the directions hearing.

For the non-appearance of the defendant, complainant, or both at the hearing of the com- **15.116** plaint, see ss 55–57 of the MCA.

### What type of directions may be ordered?

Rule 7(5) appears to give the court a wide discretion: **15.117**

> The Court may give Directions relating to the management of the proceedings, including Directions as to the date of the hearing of the application.

The court will be concerned to ensure that any witnesses who may be required are available and therefore parties should be prepared to notify the court of what witnesses they are likely to be calling and the length of their evidence. Enquiries should be made about whether any evidence can be agreed or reduced to admissions, eg the date of the seizure and the amount of the cash. Enquiry should also be made about the service of witness statements by way of mutual disclosure.

Enquiries should be made as to whether or not any expert witnesses will be called (eg forensic **15.118** scientists), and whether or not any interpreters are required. Whilst courts are often happy to assist in the arrangement of interpreters, it should be remembered that these are civil proceedings and such costs will need to be met (in advance of the hearing) by the party requiring the interpreter.

### The forfeiture hearing

The purpose of the hearing is to determine whether, in accordance with s 298(2), the detained **15.119** cash is recoverable property or is intended by any person for use in unlawful conduct. If the court is so satisfied, it may order its forfeiture under s 298.

### Procedure at hearings made on complaint

Rule 11(1) states: **15.120**

> At the hearing of an application under Chapter 3 of Part 5 of the Act (either searches for cash or seizure of cash), any person to whom notice of the application has been given may attend and be heard on the question of whether the application should be granted. The fact that any such person does not attend should not prevent the Court from hearing the application.

Rule 11(2) states: **15.121**

> ... proceedings on such an application shall be regulated in the same manner as proceedings on a Complaint, and accordingly for the purposes of these rules the application shall be

deemed to be a Complaint, the Applicant a Complainant, the Respondents to be Defendants, and any notice given by the Justices' Chief Executive under Rules 5(3), 6(4), 7(4), 8(4) or 10(4) to be a Summons: but nothing in this rule should be construed as enabling a Warrant of Arrest to be issued for failure to appear to any such Notice.

**15.122**   The rules in relation to the hearing of a complaint, procedure, and the jurisdiction of the magistrates' court are set out at s 51 et seq of the M CA.

**15.123**   Section 52 confirms jurisdiction; s 53 deals with procedure and states that at the hearing of a complaint, the court shall, if the defendant appears, state to him the substance of the complaint. Section 54 sets out the adjournment provisions, which may take place 'at any time'; and s 55 confirms that if a defendant does not appear the court may proceed in his absence. Similarly, under s 56, where at the time and place appointed for the hearing or adjourned hearing of a complaint the defendant appears but the complainant does not, the court may dismiss the complaint or, if evidence has been received on a previous occasion, proceed in the absence of the complainant. By s 57, where neither party attends, the court may dismiss the complaint; and s 58 deals with the transfer of proceedings.

### Order of evidence and speeches

**15.124**   Rule 14 of the Magistrates' Courts Rules 1981 sets out the order of evidence and speeches in civil cases made on complaint:

 (1)  On the hearing of a complaint the complainant shall call the evidence and before doing so may address the court.

 (2)  At the conclusion of the evidence for the complainant, the defendant may address the court, whether or not he afterwards calls evidence.

 (3)  At the conclusion of the evidence, if any, for the defence, the complainant may call evidence to rebut that evidence.

 (4)  At the conclusion of the evidence for the defence and the evidence, if any, in rebuttal, the defendant may address the court if he has not already done so.

 (5)  Either party may, with the leave of the court, address the court for a second time, but where the court grants leave to one party it shall not refuse leave to the other.

 (6)  Where the defendant obtains leave to address the court for a second time, his second address shall be made before the second address, if any, of the complainant.

**15.125**   It is important to note that the applicant's only opportunity to fully address the court without leave comes when he opens his case. From the applicant's point of view, therefore, it is important that he gives as full an opening as he can, although depending on the facts of the case, he may apply for leave to address the court again for a second time.

**15.126**   Similarly, if the defendant chooses to address the court in opening and before he calls evidence he loses his opportunity to make a closing speech without further leave. The usual rules apply, in that either party may address the court on a point of law at any time.

**15.127**   Although the defendant is at liberty to make a submission of no case to answer after the applicant's case, some caution should be exercised, because if it fails and the defendant has been asked to choose between calling evidence and making a submission, he will not be entitled to call evidence thereafter. See *Boyce v Wyatt Engineering* [2001] EWCA Civ 692.

**Matters to be sworn under oath**

By r 11(3):  **15.128**

> At the hearing of an application under Chapter 3 of Part 5 of the Act, the Court shall require the matters contained in the application to be sworn by the Applicant under oath, may require the Applicant to answer any questions under oath and may require any response from the Respondent to the application to be made under oath.

# G. Rules of Evidence

## Burden and standard of proof

The burden is on the applicant to prove the criteria set out in s 298(2) (*Muneka v Customs and*  **15.129** *Excise Commissioners* [2005] EWHC 495 (Admin)). The standard of proof, however, is that applicable in civil proceedings (ie proof on the balance of probabilities—see s 240(1)(b)). Once the applicant has satisfied the court to the required standard, it is for the defendant to show, also on the balance of probabilities, that the suggestion advanced by the applicant is incorrect.

In *Butt v Customs and Excise Commissioners* (2002) 166 JP 173 money in the possession of  **15.130** the appellant's nephew was seized by Customs officers. The appellant's nephew had been travelling to Amsterdam on a single ticket with a large sum of cash in brown paper packages in a locked case. The defence argued that the justices had not borne in mind the remarks made by Lord Bingham in *B v Chief Constable of Avon and Somerset* [2001] 1 WLR 340 to the effect that in serious cases the difference between civil and criminal standards is 'in truth largely illusory'. In dismissing the appeal the Court held that Parliament had explicitly provided that the civil standard of proof should apply in proceedings under s 43 of the DTA, namely 'more probable than not'. A forfeiture order made under the 1994 Act, they stated, involved no aspersions on the character of the applicant. Indeed, in this case the justices made no finding that the monies actually belonged to the appellant. The proceeding was effectively an action *in rem*, the Court's findings only applying to the cash.

## Are previous convictions admissible?

In contrast to the position in criminal proceedings, any previous conviction of a person  **15.131** claiming an interest in the money is admissible and adverse inferences may be made against him in relation to same.

The effect of previous convictions was illustrated in the DTA case of *Ali v Best* (1997) 161 JP  **15.132** 393. In March 1992 the appellant had been convicted of an offence of possessing one ounce of heroin with intent to supply. In August 1994 Customs officers at Dover stopped him as he was about to leave the country and a holdall in the boot of his car was found to contain £48,830 in cash. No drugs were found in the vehicle and no traces of drugs were found on the bank notes. The justices ordered the money to be forfeited, and the appellant appealed by way of case stated. The High Court dismissed the appeal, McCowan J commenting in delivering the judgment of the court:

> In my judgment, evidence of that previous conviction and the facts of it were clearly admissible. The question that remains is, how cogent was it? In my judgment, it did have some cogency. It certainly called for an answer. The answer that he gave, apparently in interview, was

that the money had come from trading in Cypriot antiques and, as he told the Customs officer when stopped, he was intending to use it to buy a Mercedes or two. He did not, however, go into the witness box. In my judgment [counsel for the respondent] is entitled to rely on that fact that he did not choose to give any explanation on oath. This is not a criminal case, this is a civil case and in my judgment in those circumstances, this is a matter which can properly be relied upon by the respondent.

15.133   In *R v Isleworth Crown Court ex p Kevin Marland* (1998) 162 JPR 251 the Court held that in civil cases the rules concerning the admission of previous convictions were less circumscribed because the underlying intention is not to protect one side, but to be fair to both sides. If the facts of the previous conduct are sufficiently similar to the facts sought to be proved in the instant case as to be logically probative, then evidence of previous conduct is admissible and that would include spent convictions, subject only to the judge's discretion to exclude them on such grounds as oppression, unfairness, or surprise. Mrs Justice Smith held:

> ... it matters not whether the evidence is of a conviction or whether it is of past conduct which has not resulted in the conviction ... When exercising its discretion to admit spent convictions the Court must be satisfied that justice cannot otherwise be done. Justice means justice to both parties. These convictions were plainly of some relevance to the issues in the case ... because of the lapse of time, they may be said to have less probative value than if they were more recent. Some tribunals might well have considered the prejudicial effect out-weighed the probative value. However that is not to say that I think the decision to admit them was obviously wrong—I do not.

### Is there a need for direct evidence of the unlawful conduct?

15.134   No. In *Butt v Customs and Excise* [2001] EWHC 1066 (Admin), the court held that in applications under s 43 of the DTA there was no need for direct evidence of connection to drugs for the purpose of discharging the burden of proof.

### The drawing of inferences and illustrative cases

15.135   The drawing of inferences was a common thread through a number of cases under the DTA. In *Bassick and Osborne v Customs and Excise Commissioners* (1997) 161 JP 377, the magistrates came to the conclusion, having paid particular regard to the circumstances surrounding Bassick's possession of the cash seized, that it was more likely than not that the money directly or indirectly represented a person's proceeds of, or was intended by any person for use in, drug trafficking. Bassick was unemployed at the time he was stopped and on his way to Amsterdam with £21,520 in cash in various denominations, with a single flight ticket that had been bought shortly before the departure time of the aircraft. He possessed a note giving him instructions on how to reach an address in Amsterdam, and he had made no arrangements for his return journey or for his accommodation abroad. The magistrates had also noted his evasive demeanour and that of his witnesses when they testified. Accordingly the magistrates ordered forfeiture. There was nothing to suggest that either of the two defendants had been convicted of criminal offences involving drugs. There was nothing to suggest that they had been associated with people who were known to be connected with drug trafficking, nor was there anything to suggest that they were known to a person or persons in Amsterdam who were known to be so involved. On appeal Watkins LJ said:

> I can see no flaw in the way in which they (the Justices) approached it, and none in the decision which they reached upon it. It seems to me that there was ample material to allow them

to come to the conclusion which they did . . . the overbearing fact is that these Justices simply did not believe Osborne and Bassick.

A similar decision was reached in *R v Dover and East Kent Magistrates' Court ex p Steven Gore* **15.136** (QBD, 23 May 1996) where Auld LJ held:

> . . . the Magistrates were entitled and indeed bound, to take into account all the circumstances (of the case): the circumstances in which the money was seized; the amount of the money; the fact that it was contaminated albeit slightly with traces of cannabis or cannabis resin; the refusal of the applicant before caution to give an explanation as to who had given him the money, at a time when it might be expected that he would or could have given an explanation. The Magistrates were entitled to take into account the answers he gave in interview that I have summarised, an account which, putting aside any refusals to answer, raised more questions than it answered. I have no doubt that the Magistrates were entitled to apply the civil burden of proof to conclude as they did and to order the forfeiture of the money accordingly.

In *Muneka v Customs and Excise Commissioners* [2005] EWHC 495 (Admin), a case that was **15.137** dealt with under s 298 of POCA and concerned an appellant who was stopped at Heathrow with £22,760 in cash in his possession while on his way to Albania via Hungary, Moses J held:

> In my judgement, in this context the fact that there was no explanation for the source of that money, no reasonable explanation as to why he was taking that cash to Albania, the fact that there were discrepancies in his explanations as to the source of the money and as to its final destination, taken together, did establish, both source and intention . . . on the balance of probabilities.

### Hearsay in civil cases

The Magistrates' Courts (Hearsay Evidence in Civil Proceedings) Rules 1999, SI 1999/681, **15.138** set out the rules applying to hearsay in magistrates' courts.

These Rules make provision for the requirements of the Civil Evidence Act 1995 in relation **15.139** to hearsay evidence in civil proceedings in magistrates' courts and:

- the procedure to call a witness for cross-examination on hearsay evidence (r 4);
- a notice requirement where a party tenders hearsay evidence (but does not call the person who made the statement to give oral evidence) and another party wishes to attack the credibility of the person who made the statement or allege that he has made another statement inconsistent with it (r 5); and
- the service of documents required by the Rules (r 6).

However, a failure to comply with the duty to give notice should not affect the admissibility **15.140** of hearsay evidence (see s 1(1) of the Civil Evidence Act 1995 and s 1(2) which is specifically adopted by r 2(2)). It then becomes a question of weight for the justices to determine. In assessing the weight, all the relevant circumstances should be considered including the fact that the individual who makes the statement has not been tendered in cross-examination and therefore the evidence has not been tested. The desirability of serving a hearsay notice is obvious, as a party may find itself liable for costs if a witness statement tendered at the hearing reveals new evidence that the other side has not had the opportunity of exploring, or evidence that amounts to an ambush.

**15.141**   Section 4(2) of the Civil Evidence Act 1995 provides some guidance that may assist the court when assessing what weight should be given to hearsay. That guidance includes:

> (i)   whether it would have been reasonable and practicable to have produced the person who made the statements rather than relying on a hearsay report of them;
>
> (ii)  whether the person who originally made the statements made them contemporaneously with the matters stated;
>
> (iii) whether the evidence is multiple hearsay, in other words whether the hearsay witness is in fact repeating something which itself is hearsay;
>
> (iv)  whether anyone involved has a motive to conceal or misrepresent matters;
>
> (v)   whether the original statement was made for some purpose or produced in collaboration with others;
>
> (vi)  whether the attempt to rely on hearsay rather than calling the person who made the original statement is designed to prevent a proper evaluation of its weight by the court.

**15.142**   In the Crown Court the position is slightly different, although the same principle appears to apply. In *R v Wadmore and Foreman* [2006] EWCA Crim 686, a case that concerned an application for an Anti-social Behaviour Order (ASBO), the Court of Appeal held that ASBOs amounted to civil proceedings in a criminal court. The CrimPR do not apply to civil cases. The CPR do not apply in criminal courts. The Magistrates' Courts (Hearsay Evidence in Civil Proceedings) Rules do not apply to the Crown Court. The Court of Appeal therefore assumed, without deciding, that as the case was civil in nature, hearsay evidence was admissible under s 1 of the Civil Evidence Act 1995. There were no applicable procedural rules and the Court thought that the Magistrates' Court Rules should be applied by analogy.

**Lies told by the defendant**

**15.143**   In *Nevin v Customs and Excise Commissioners* (QBD, 3 November 1995), Smedley J stated:

> While the prescribed Civil Standard of proof would not, of course, allow the Justices to act without satisfactory evidence on the intended use of the money, they are not required to direct themselves, for example, in relation to lies told by a defendant, as the Judge would direct a jury in a criminal trial. That is not to say that they should overlook the possibility that lies may have the purpose of concealing something other than the misconduct presently alleged. But a suspect who gives an account of his reasons for carrying the money which the Justices reject as untruthful cannot complain if the Justices go on to infer from other relevant evidence, that by itself might not have been enough to satisfy them, that the true reason was for the use of [drug trafficking].

**15.144**   This passage was specifically referred to and approved by Moses J in *Muneka v Customs and Excise Commissioners* [2005] EWHC 495 (Admin), in which he stated:

> Those comments apply with added force in the context of this case where it is not necessary to identify any criminal activity such as drug trafficking; all that has to be identified is that the source was criminal activity or the intended destination was use for criminal activity. A lie in that context may well entitle the fact-finding body to infer what the source or intention for which the cash was to be used was in reality on the balance of probabilities.

**15.145**   In Moses J's judgment the fact that the appellant had lied was evidence upon which the district judge was entitled to conclude that the suggestions in relation to unlawful conduct being put to him were in fact true on the balance of probabilities:

> The District Judge was entitled to ask herself: why should this appellant have lied about the source and destination of that cash? He must have appreciated that such lies could have had

no reasonable explanation, other than that the suggestions made to him as to their source and as to destination were in fact true.

Moses J went on to cite *Bassick and Osborne* (1993) 161 JP 377 as authority for the proposition that lies in a particular context may establish a positive case as to the source of the money.   **15.146**

### Record of proceedings and reasons

Under r 11(4) there is a duty for the legal advisor and/or the court to keep a record of any   **15.147** statements made under oath that are not already recorded in the written application. In other words, the court must keep a record of proceedings, which may later be referred to in any appeal. Such a record should include the magistrates' reasons for concluding that the cash was obtained through or was intended for use in unlawful conduct (ie the premise for which they say it was liable to forfeiture). A failure to give adequate reasons may result in a forfeiture order being appealed by way of case stated (*Wiese v UKBA* [2012] EWHC 2019 (Admin)).

### Sensitive material

Although PII applications do not feature in magistrates' courts, exclusion of evidence on the   **15.148** grounds of public policy applies equally to civil proceedings as it does in criminal. The test is whether the production of a document or other piece of evidence would be 'injurious to the public interest'; ie whether the withholding of a document/information is necessary for the proper functioning of a government department. For example, the disclosure of the document may jeopardise an ongoing operation, or the methods deployed or the cooperation received from others in the investigation of an offence.

It is important to remember that the issue the court is having to decide is that set out in s   **15.149** 298(2), namely whether the seized cash is recoverable property or is intended by any person for use in unlawful conduct. Considerations such as why the individual was stopped in the first place, or what information the police held on that individual, are largely irrelevant to the test the court is having to apply, which focuses on the provenance of the cash and its intended/previous purpose. (By analogy see *Hoverspeed v Customs and Excise Commissioners* [2002] EWCA Civ 1804 at paras 44–9.)

### Joint owners

Under s 298(3), where the recoverable property belongs to joint owners, the order for forfei-   **15.150** ture of the cash may not apply to any amount the court thinks is attributable to an innocent joint owner's share. Section 270(4) states:

> An excepted joint owner is a person who obtained the property in circumstances in which it would not be recoverable as against him; and references to the 'excepted joint owner's share' of the recoverable property are to so much of the recoverable property as would have been his if the joint tenancy had been severed.

In other words, the court must not forfeit the cash that is attributable to the innocent part-   **15.151** ner's share (eg if two business partners held a joint bank account, and one of those partners had been trading legitimately and paying legitimate money into it whereas the other one (unbeknown to the other) had been paying in drug trafficking proceeds, if the illegitimate partner were to withdraw all of the cash in the account and it was subsequently seized, the court would have to distinguish between the clean and the 'dirty' money. The court would be entitled to return to the innocent partner his share of the money.)

# H. Costs and Compensation

**15.152**  The successful party may apply for his costs against the unsuccessful party. However, as in all costs matters, the court does have an element of discretion and would, for example, be entitled to refuse costs against a successful party whose behaviour had led the applicant to believe his case was stronger than it really was or where the case has been dismissed on a technicality rather than on the merits.

### Costs payable at each application and not carried forward

**15.153**  In *R v Dover Magistrates' Court ex parte Customs and Excise Commissioners*, The Times, 12 December 1995, a series of orders were made by the magistrates' court for continued detention of the money. During that period notice was given that an application for forfeiture had been lodged by Customs. Having put in that notice of application for forfeiture, Customs then gave notice that they did not intend to proceed with their application. The defendant's representatives applied for an order from the magistrates that Customs should pay the defendant's costs. The magistrates made the order, and directed that if costs could not be agreed then they would assess the costs themselves. Subsequently, the magistrates further ordered that the costs should be paid in accordance with the bill submitted by the defendant's solicitors. On appeal, the issue for the Divisional Court was whether it was right for the defendant's schedule of costs to include costs not only in relation to the proposed forfeiture hearing, but also in relation to the earlier continued detention hearings. Section 52(3) of the Courts Act 1971 provides that where:

> (b) a complaint is made to a Justice of the Peace acting for any area but the complaint is not proceeded with, a Magistrates' Court for that area may make such order as to costs to be paid by the Complainant to the Defendant as it thinks just and reasonable.

**15.154**  In the *Dover* case there was a complaint made to the justices asking for forfeiture. Under s 64(1) of the MCA:

> (1)  On the hearing of a complaint a Magistrates' Court shall have power in its discretion to make such order as to costs that—
>> (a)  on making the order for which the complaint is made, to be paid by the Defendant to the Complainant;
>> (b)  on dismissing the complaint, to be paid by the Complainant to the Defendant,
> as it thinks just and reasonable...

The distinction between the two is that s 64 of the MCA deals with cases where the complaint has been heard and determined, whereas s 52 of the Courts Act deals with cases where the complaint is 'not proceeded with'.

**15.155**  The Divisional Court had to determine whether or not there was one complaint initiated by the first detention proceedings which continued up to and including the forfeiture proceedings; or whether there were separate complaints in respect of continued detention and forfeiture. Staughton LJ in the judgment of the court held that it was clear that there was more than one complaint: 'There was a complaint for forfeiture and at least one complaint if not more for detention.' He explained:

> First, in the circumstances of this case, the costs of detention proceedings fall to be dealt with under section 64. That says that where a complaint has succeeded the Court may award the costs to the Complainant, and where it has failed it may award the costs to the Defendant.

That seems to me inconsistent with the court, in this case, awarding the costs of the detention proceedings, which have succeeded, to the Defendant. The second reason is this: it seems to me implicit in section 52 that what the Court may award is the cost of the proceedings in question. I cannot accept that section 52 gives the Magistrates carte blanche to award any other costs on any other matter whatsoever if they think it just and reasonable to do so. In my opinion the power relates to the cost of the proceedings in question.

It is therefore incumbent on the parties to ensure that costs are dealt with at the end of each **15.156** individual application for continued detention. Costs may not be 'reserved' to later hearings, although it should be noted that once a forfeiture application has been lodged any hearing that takes place following the lodging of the application, eg a pretrial review, forms part of the same application and therefore costs need not be dealt with until the hearing itself.

### Costs under section 64 of the Magistrates' Courts Act 1980

The court has a discretion to make an award of costs in favour of the successful party. The **15.157** successful party must specify the sum and such order must be such costs as the court thinks 'just and reasonable' (see *Orton v (1) Truro Crown Court and (2) West Cornwall Magistrates' Court* [2009] EWHC 168 (Admin)). The magistrates' court does not enforce these costs. There is no imprisonment in default. It is not treated as a fine. They merely create a civil debt between the applicant and the defendant. Enforcement is a matter for the county court, if the successful party thinks it is worth enforcing. When considering a costs order against a defendant, his means may be a relevant factor, because the court has to consider what sum is just and reasonable in the circumstances of the case. At this stage of the proceedings the court may be minded to infer that the defendant is of sufficient means if they have sat through a hearing where details of large sums of cash have been given. Conversely, if the applicant has just been awarded, by virtue of the court's finding, a large amount of money, then the court may not be minded to grant costs at all.

Pursuant to s 64(2) the amount ordered to be paid shall be specified in the order and s 64(3) **15.158** confirms that the costs ordered shall be enforceable as a civil debt. For further information on costs, see para 22.05.

### Can successful defendants obtain their costs?

In *Perinpanathan v City of Westminster Magistrates' Court and 2 others* [2009] EWHC 762 **15.159** (Admin) the test for the award of costs to a successful defendant was considered and set out. The Divisional Court adopted the words of Lord Bingham in *Bradford Metropolitan District Council v Booth* (2000) 164 JP 485, a case where the local council had refused to renew Mr Booth's private hire operator's licence on the grounds Mr Booth had broken a condition, but in which Mr Booth had appealed to the magistrates' court and had been successful. He sought his costs on the basis that they should follow the event (CPR 44.3). Lord Bingham stated:

23. I would accordingly hold that the proper approach to questions of this kind can for convenience be summarised in three propositions:

24. (1) Section 64(1) confers a discretion upon a Magistrates' Court to make such order as to costs as it thinks just and reasonable. That provision applies both to the quantum of the costs (if any) to be paid, but also as to the party (if any) which should pay them.

25. (2) What the court will think just and reasonable will depend on all the relevant facts and circumstances of the case before the court. The court may think it just and reasonable that costs should follow the event, but need not think so in all cases covered by the subsection.

26. (3) Where a complainant has successfully challenged before justices an administrative decision made by a police or regulatory authority acting honestly, reasonably, properly and on grounds that reasonably appeared to be sound, in exercise of its public duty, the court should consider, in addition to any other relevant fact or circumstances, both (i) the financial prejudice to the particular complainant in the particular circumstances if an order for costs is not made in his favour; and (ii) the need to encourage public authorities to make and stand by honest, reasonable and apparently sound administrative decisions made in the public interest without fear of exposure to undue financial prejudice if the decision is successfully challenged.

**15.160**  The magistrates' court in *Parinpanathan* had refused to award costs, on the basis that the cash seizure had been properly brought by the police. The Divisional Court concluded that they had acted properly, Goldring LJ commenting (at para 29):

> ...I accept that there is a difference between administrative decisions such as those referred to in *Bradford* and the present case. The distinction is limited, however. In one case a police officer (at possible risk to someone's livelihood) is saying that the person will not have an on-licence, for example. In the other, he is saying the person will not have his (or in this case her) money returned. In taking both decisions, it is crucial that the police act honestly, reasonably, properly, and on grounds that reasonably appear to be sound. In both cases there is a need to make and stand by honest, reasonable and apparently sound decisions in the public interest without fear of exposure to undue financial prejudice, in one case if the decision is successfully challenged, in the other if the application fails. There is a real public interest that the police seek an order for forfeiture if they consider that on the evidence it is more probable than not that the money was intended for an unlawful purpose. It would be quite contrary to the public interest if, due to fear of financial consequences, it was decided not to seek its forfeiture, but simply return the money. The public duty requires the police to make an application in such circumstances.

**15.161**  The appellant challenged the Divisional Court's decision (*Perinpanathan v City of Westminster Magistrates' Court* [2010] EWCA Civ 40). In their judgment, the Court of Appeal applied *Bradford* on the premise that the CPR did not apply to cash forfeiture proceedings. On the basis that *Bradford* did apply, and that the actions of the public body were properly carried out, the starting point and the default position in relation to costs was that no order should be made. In the present case, the Court of Appeal held that the police did act responsibly and given that the defendant had challenged the seizure, the only avenue available to the police was to make the forfeiture application. A public authority should not be deterred from making such an application because of concerns about its liability for the defendant's costs. However, notwithstanding the Court's refusal to pay costs to the successful party in this instance, the police/UKBA/HMRC should not assume that they may proceed with impunity. The position was distilled by the Master of the Rolls (at para 77):

> The effect of our decision is that a person in the position of the appellant, who has done nothing wrong, may normally not be able to recover the costs of vindicating her rights against the police in proceedings under section 298 of POCA, where the police have behaved reasonably. In my view, this means that Magistrates should exercise particular care when considering whether the police have acted reasonably in a case where there is an application for costs against them under section 64. It would be wrong to invoke the wisdom of hindsight or to set too exacting a standard, but, particularly given the understandable resentment felt by a person in the position of the appellant if no order for costs is made, and the general standards of behaviour that can properly be expected from the police, it must be right to scrutinise their behaviour in relation to the seizure, the detention, and the confiscation proceedings, with some care when deciding whether they acted reasonably and properly.

### Legal Aid Agency funding

Pursuant to Sch 11 para 36 to POCA, the Access to Justice Act 1999 (AJA) was amended **15.162**
by POCA to insert at Sch 2 para 2(3) of the AJA a provision that allowed for Legal Services
Commission (LSC) funding to be obtained for an order or direction under ss 295, 297,
298, 301, or 302 of POCA (the cash forfeiture and supplementary matters provisions). In
particular, this allowed for advocacy to be met by LSC funding.

In practice, solicitors should complete a Legal Aid Merits form and also the appropriate **15.163**
Means form. This may then be submitted to the relevant Legal Aid office who will then
decide whether or not it should be granted. Whether it is granted depends on the amount of
money involved. Anything less than £10,000 is likely to be refused.

Practical difficulties might arise, including the fact that the claimant has just had a large amount **15.164**
of cash seized from him. This obviously gives rise to a question in relation to their means and
will often lead to delay while the Legal Aid Agency investigate matters. Often as a result defendants in cash seizure cases are left either defending themselves or with their advisers sometimes
acting on a conditional fee arrangement. The Jackson reforms are likely to lead to further cuts
to this type of funding. Anecdotally the sums available for advocacy have been very limited.

Quite why the cash seizure provisions are dealt with differently to those for civil recovery else- **15.165**
where under Pt 5 of the Act is not immediately clear. In civil recovery matters heard before the
High Court, judges were fairly robust in resisting applications from the (former) ARA whilst
LSC funding was being determined. It was in part the robust attitude of the judiciary that led
to the amendments to the SOCPA that now allow for restrained funds to be utilised to fund
representation being introduced (based on arguments such as equality of arms etc). It could
equally be argued that it is unfair for a defendant to have to respond to a complaint made by
either the police or another agency until his legal aid funding has been determined.

### May funds be released from the detained cash to fund continued detention and forfeiture applications?

The short answer appears to be no. In a decision made under the old legislation, *Customs and* **15.166**
*Excise Commissioners v Harris* (1999) 163 JPR 408, Forbes J held:

> I am satisfied that there is no proper basis for extending to the Magistrates a power to make
> any order for the release of lawfully detained cash which has been seized pursuant to the provi-
> sion of Section 42 of the 1994 Act, because of the absence of any specific Statutory power to
> make such an order and it is plain that the 1994 Act contains no provision empowering the
> Magistrates to make any such order.

Similarly, POCA does not provide any mechanism for monies to be released to fund defendants' litigation expenses.

### Wasted costs

The power of the magistrates' court to make a wasted costs order is governed by s 145A of the **15.167**
MCA and SI 1991/2096. Costs are further considered in Chapter 22.

### Compensation

Under s 302(1) of POCA compensation may be paid to either the person from whom the **15.168**
cash was seized or the person to whom the cash belongs.

**15.169**   Section 302(1) states:

> If no forfeiture order is made in respect of any cash claimed under this Chapter, the person to whom the cash belongs or from whom it was seized might make an application to the Magistrates' Court for compensation.

**15.170**   Under s 302(4) if the court is satisfied, presumably on the balance of probabilities, that, taking account of any interest to be paid under s 296 the applicant has suffered a loss as a result of the detention of the cash, and that the circumstances are 'exceptional', the court may order compensation, or additional compensation, to be paid to him.

**15.171**   The amount of compensation to be paid under subs 4 is the amount the court thinks reasonable, having regard to the loss suffered and any other relevant circumstances (see s 302(5)).

**15.172**   This section applies to compensation for loss incurred as a result of the detention of the cash. Therefore, if an individual has suffered loss for any other reason, there is no recourse under this section.

**15.173**   Section 302 does not define what 'exceptional circumstances' are, nor does it give any indication as to the type of losses that would be considered appropriate. For example, ordinarily in a civil case the successful party would be entitled to claim their legal costs. That clearly does not come under the heading of compensation. Loss of earnings, however, in having to attend court in order to defend the forfeiture application, may be included. The question is whether or not loss of earnings would constitute 'exceptional circumstances'. 'Exceptional' has a dictionary meaning of 'not ordinary; uncommon; rare; hence, better than the average; superior; unusual; beyond the norm'.

**15.174**   The court will also need to satisfy itself, again on the balance of probabilities, that the loss was 'as a result of the detention of the cash'.

### Application for compensation

**15.175**   Under r 8(1) an application for compensation under s 302(1) must be made in writing and sent to the Justices' Chief Executive before which the applicant wishes to make the application. However, under r 8(2), if the applicant has been given notice of an order under s 295(2) of the Act in respect of the cash which is the subject of the application, then the application must be sent to the Justices' Chief Executive who sent him that notice. The Justices' Chief Executive will send a copy of the application to either the police or the relevant Agency and then fix a date for the hearing of the application (see r 8(3)). It is apparent therefore that the Rules anticipate a separate and distinct hearing—the prerequisite being an application in writing. Applications for compensation under s 302(1) of POCA must be made within the six-month time limit as provided for by s 127 of the MCA. The time limit is stringent and there is no provision contained within the Act or elsewhere for it to be extended (*Atkinson v DPP* [2004] EWHC 1457 (Admin)). The six-month time limit will start to run from the date on which cash forfeiture proceedings were discontinued (*Davis v Chief Constable of Leicestershire* (Admin) (18 July 2012)).

## I. Appeals

### Appeals against forfeiture

**15.176**   Section 299 of POCA was amended by s 101 of SOCPA because of an ambiguity as to its meaning. While the original s 299(1) appeared to allow 'any party to the proceedings' the ability to appeal against an order made under s 298, this was qualified by the words 'for the forfeiture of cash'. This meant that while any party may appeal an order for forfeiture there was no provision for the complainant (the police/UKBA/HMRC) to appeal a refusal to grant forfeiture, although somewhat ironically a complainant could appeal an order for forfeiture.

The substituted s 299 now states:                                                                                          **15.177**

(1)  Any person to proceedings for an order for the forfeiture of cash under section 298 who is aggrieved by an order under that section or by the decision of the court to make such an order may appeal.

In other words, both the complainant and the defendant now have a right of appeal from the magistrates' court hearing to the Crown Court. Such a hearing will normally be *de novo* (s 9(3) of the Supreme Court Act 1981), with the facts being re-examined in the court above, and with the opportunity for both parties to serve further evidence before the hearing takes place (while the original s 299(3) expressly stated that the appeal was by way of rehearing, the substituted legislation does not).

The appeal is to the Crown Court and notice must be lodged before the expiration of thirty  **15.178**
days from when the order or decision was made (substituted s 299(2)).

This section also has the effect of allowing the Crown Court to hear the appeal in the most  **15.179**
appropriate way, for example on a point of law only.

### Can the thirty-day period for the date of the appeal be extended?

It appears not. In *R v West London Magistrates' Court ex p Rowland Omo Lamai* (QBD, 6 July  **15.180**
2000), a DTA case, the High Court held that the thirty-day period could not be extended by either a Crown Court or a magistrates' court; and that the thirty day statutory deadline was a deadline without flexibility.

### Funding the appeal

The provision under s 44(4) of the DTA for the release of cash in order to fund an appeal in  **15.181**
DTA cases no longer exists under the corresponding provisions of s 299 (although it should be noted that substituted s 299(3) states that the court hearing the appeal may make 'any order it thinks appropriate'. It is anticipated that there is likely to be argument as to whether this can be extended to ordering release of part of the cash in order to fund the appeal, particularly where the appellant's arguments have merit, he can demonstrate that he has no other available funds, and that he requires representation, ie 'equality of arms' at the Crown Court. By implication ECHR arguments would arise if such a request were refused without proper consideration.)

### Costs in appeal proceedings

The Crown Court's powers to award costs are set out in ss 48(2)(c) and 52 of the Senior  **15.182**
Courts Act 1981. Although not directly applicable, helpful guidance as to the Crown Court's jurisdiction to award costs on appeal and costs incurred in the magistrates' court proceedings is also given in rr 76.2, 76.6, and 76.11 of the CrimPR.

### Judicial review

While there remains obvious scope for judicial review proceedings in cash seizure cases,  **15.183**
in *M v Bow Street Magistrates' Court*, The Times, 27 July 2005, the court held that in

proceedings under the Anti-Terrorism, Crime and Security Act 2001 it was premature to seek permission to challenge by way of judicial review a district judge's decision on a preliminary ruling when the judge had not yet determined any of the factual issues or received evidence in relation to the substantive matter. The Divisional Court held that it would be impossible to know precisely how the legal issues would arise until the evidence was heard and the facts were found. Appeals in cash seizure cases are further considered in Chapter 18 at, 18.101.

## J. Searches and Seizure of Cash

**15.184** The second part of the regime under POCA deals with the power to search and seize cash found on either premises or on an individual. These provisions also came into force on 30 December 2002 (SI 2002/3015). Many of the procedural rules that apply to cash seizures under the seizure and detention provisions of s 294 apply equally to cash searches.

### Cash on premises

**15.185** Section 289 states:

> (1) If a Customs Officer, a constable or an accredited financial investigator who is lawfully on any premises has reasonable grounds for suspecting that there is on the premises cash—
>  (a) which is recoverable property or is intended by any person for use in unlawful conduct, and
>  (b) the amount of which is not less than the minimum amount,
> he may search for the cash there.

### The minimum amount: £1,000

**15.186** Under s 303, the 'minimum amount' is defined as the amount in sterling specified in an order made by the Secretary of State (£1,000—SI 2006/1699) and for that purpose the amount of any cash held in a currency other than sterling must be taken to be the sterling equivalent.

**15.187** These search powers can only be exercisable, therefore, if the suspected cash is thought to exceed the threshold of £1,000.

### The definition of 'cash'

**15.188** Under s 289(6) cash means:

> (a) notes and coins in any currency,
> (b) postal orders,
> (c) cheques of any kind (including travellers cheques),
> (d) bankers drafts,
> (e) bearer bonds and bearer shares
> found at any place in the UK.

**15.189** Section 289(1) is only exercisable on private premises where the police or HMRC have lawful authority to be present (see Code B PACE 1984 and s 164 Customs and Excise Management Act 1979 (CEMA)). An officer could also be lawfully present on private premises if he is there at the invitation of the owner.

**Cash on the suspect**

Under s 289(2):                                                                                                      **15.190**

> (2) If a Customs Officer, a constable or an accredited financial investigator has reasonable
> grounds for suspecting that a person (the suspect) is carrying cash—
>> (a) which is recoverable property or is intended by any person to be used in unlawful
>> conduct, and
>> (b) the amount of which is not less than the minimum amount [£1,000],
> he may exercise the following powers.
> (3) The officer, constable or accredited financial investigator may, so far as he thinks it neces-
> sary or expedient, require the suspect—
>> (a) to permit a search of any article he has with him;
>> (b) to permit a search of his person.

This section does not require the person to submit to an intimate search or a strip search
(within the meaning of s 164 CEMA 1979) (see s 289(8)). However, under s 289(4) an
officer exercising his powers under s 289(3)(b) may detain the suspect for 'so long as is necessary for the exercise'.

Under s 289(5) the powers conferred by s 289(1) and (2) are exercisable only so far as is   **15.191**
reasonably required for the purpose of finding cash and are exercisable by a Revenue and
Customs officer only if he has reasonable grounds for suspecting the unlawful conduct in
question relates to an assigned matter within the meaning of CEMA. Areas within the meaning of CEMA include drug trafficking, money laundering, and excise evasion. (See also the
Proceeds of Crime 2002 (Cash Searches: Code of Practice) Order 2008 (SI 2008/947).)

**Unlawful conduct**

See s 241, para 15.24 above.                                                                                  **15.192**

**Safeguards for the new search powers**

The powers conferred by s 289 may only be exercised when the appropriate approval has   **15.193**
been given unless it is not practicable to obtain that approval before exercising the power
(s 290(1)).

The appropriate approval means the approval of a 'judicial officer' or, if that is not practica-   **15.194**
ble, the approval of a senior officer (s 290(2)). Under s 290(3)(a) a 'judicial officer' means a
justice of the peace (JP/magistrate).

A senior officer means, in relation to the exercise of the power by a Revenue and Customs   **15.195**
officer, a Revenue and Customs officer of a rank designated by HMRC as equivalent to that
of a senior police officer and in relation to the exercise of the power by a constable, a senior
police officer (an inspector or above) (see s 290(4)). The grading and seniority of accredited
financial investigators are framed by s 453.

If judicial approval is not obtained prior to a search, and cash is either not seized or is released   **15.196**
before the matter comes before a court (ie within forty-eight hours) the officer concerned
must prepare a written statement giving the particulars of the circumstances which led him
to believe that the powers were exercisable and why it was not practicable to obtain the
approval of a judicial officer (ie a magistrate). Once that is prepared they must submit it to
'the person appointed by the Secretary of State' (see s 290(6) to (8)).

**15.197**  There is therefore in effect a three-stage process in exercising these searches in terms of prior approval:

(1) the officer concerned must seek the approval of a judicial officer (magistrate) before exercising the power;

(2) if it is not practicable to obtain a magistrate's approval, the officer concerned should seek the approval of a senior officer; and

(3) the power to search may still be exercised if, in the circumstances, it is not practical to obtain the approval of either of the above before exercising the power (s 290(1)).

### Report on exercise of powers

**15.198**  The report submitted to the 'appointed person', where judicial approval has not been sought, forms the basis of an annual report (s 291). The appointed person may draw general conclusions and make appropriate recommendations as to the circumstances and manner in which the powers conferred by s 289 are being exercised (see s 291(2)).

### The Code of Practice

**15.199**  A Code of Practice exists for officers in connection with the exercise of the search powers conferred by s 289 of POCA (The Proceeds of Crime Act 2002 (Cash Searches: Code of Practice) Order 2008, SI 2008/947).

**15.200**  Under s 292(6) a failure by an officer to comply with a provision of the Code does not of itself make him liable to criminal or civil proceedings.

**15.201**  Under 292(7) the Code is admissible in evidence in criminal or civil proceedings and is to be taken into account by a court or tribunal in any case in which it appears to the court or tribunal to be relevant.

**15.202**  The Code of Practice was introduced by The Proceeds of Crime Act 2002 (Cash Searches: Code of Practice) Order 2002, SI 2002/3115 and came into force on 30 December 2002.

### Procedure at hearings

**15.203**  Rule 11(1) states:

> At the hearing of an application under Chapter 3 of Part 5 of the Act (either searches for cash or seizure of cash), any person to whom notice of the application has been given may attend and be heard on the question of whether the application should be granted. The fact that any such person does not attend should not prevent the Court from hearing the application.

For further on procedure following the discovery and seizure of cash under the search powers, see para 15.44 et seq above.

## K. Compatibility of the Forfeiture Provisions with the ECHR

**15.204**  In *Butler v UK* (App no 41661/98) (27 June 2002) the ECtHR took the view that a forfeiture order was a preventative measure and could not be compared to a criminal sanction. The Court further held that the court proceedings '... afforded the applicant ample opportunity to contest the evidence against him and to dispute the making of a forfeiture order and that the complaint before them was "manifestly ill-founded"'. In short, therefore, for the time being this area of the law appears to be ECHR friendly.

## L. The Control of Cash (Penalties) Regulations

The Control of Cash (Penalties) Regulations 2007 (SI 2007/1509) came into force on 15 **15.205**
June 2007, and were made under s 2(2) of the European Communities Act 1972 (c 68) to
give effect to Community Regulation 1889/2005 which, under Art 3, requires any person
entering or leaving the EU and carrying cash amounting to €10,000 or more to declare that
amount.

The intention is to introduce a harmonised control and information procedure for large-scale **15.206**
movements of cash in or out of the EU.

The Regulations provide for penalties for failing to declare movements of cash and an appeal **15.207**
mechanism to the Tax Tribunal (reg 5).

Cash is defined in SI 1889/2005 as including not only currency (banknotes and coins that **15.208**
are in circulation as a medium of exchange), but also

> bearer negotiable instruments including monetary instruments in bearer form such as trav-
> ellers cheques, negotiable instruments (including cheques, promissory notes, and money
> orders) that are either in bearer form, endorsed without restriction, made out to a fictitious
> payee, or otherwise in such form that title thereto passes upon delivery, and incomplete instru-
> ments (including cheques, promissory notes, and money orders) signed, but with the payee's
> name omitted.

Regulation 3 gives effect to the obligation to create a system of penalties. Regulation 4 **15.209**
enables a person subject to a penalty to require a review of the decision to impose that
penalty. Regulations 5, 6, and 7 create a right of appeal from the review decision to the
Tax Tribunal, the powers of the tribunal in respect of the appeal, and a requirement that,
save in the case of hardship, the penalty be paid as a condition of appealing. Article 4 of the
Community Regulation creates a power to detain cash where there has been a breach of
Art 3, and reg 8 enables the Commissioners to retain the amount of a proposed penalty from
any money detained until determination of an appeal.

In terms of the likely penalty and the discretion to impose same, the explanatory notes **15.210**
accompanying the Regulations state as follows:

> ...the Commissioners for HMRC are being given the option of imposing a penalty not
> exceeding £5000 for non-compliance with the obligation to declare. This gives them the
> opportunity to exercise discretion to impose a lesser amount or to limit action to issuing a
> warning letter. Factors which would influence the action taken may include the amount of the
> undeclared cash in any particular case and the number of previous occasions that the person
> concerned has been identified as failing to comply with the obligation to declare.

# 16

# THIRD PARTIES

## A. Introduction

The draconian nature of confiscation law is such that restraint and confiscation orders will **16.01** inevitably have an effect on parties, other than the defendant, who are in possession of, or hold an interest in, his realisable property. The purpose of this chapter is to consider the rights and obligations of third parties who find themselves holding realisable property subject to restraint and confiscation proceedings. In *R v Judge and Woodbridge* (1992) 13 Cr App R (S) 685, the court rejected the defendant's contention that it was 'unfair and oppressive' to make a confiscation order in an amount which would necessitate the sale of the matrimonial home. Similarly, in *R v Crutchley and Tonks* (1994) 15 Cr App R (S) 627 the Court of Appeal ruled that the value of the offender's interest in his home may be incorporated in a confiscation order to the extent that it forms part of his realisable property.

## B. Restraint Orders

### Jurisdiction to bind third parties

**16.02** The power to restrain parties other than the defendant from dealing in his realisable property is found in s 41 of POCA (formerly s 26(1) Drug Trafficking Act 1994 (DTA) and s 77(1) Criminal Justice Act 1988 (CJA)), for which see earlier editions of this work).

**16.03** Section 41(1) of POCA reads:

> If any condition set out in section 40 is satisfied the Crown Court may make an order (a Restraint Order) prohibiting any specified person from dealing with any realisable property held by him.

The purpose of the legislation is that a restraint order may be made against any specified person. This includes both the defendant (or the person under investigation), and any other person holding realisable property.

**16.04** Section 41(1) and (2) therefore empowers the court to prohibit third parties from dealing with realisable property. The provisions are wide enough to restrain third parties from dealing with assets in which the defendant holds an interest.

**16.05** It is, of course, an essential prerequisite to restraining a third party that the defendant has some interest in the property: the prosecutor may not restrain assets in which the defendant has no interest whatever, except where the asset in question is a gift caught by the Act (see ss 77–78 of POCA).

### Obligations of third parties

**16.06** Once a third party is given notice or is served with a copy of a restraint order, he must not allow the defendant to deal with any realisable property caught by the order in a manner inconsistent with its terms. Any failure to do so will render the third party vulnerable to proceedings for contempt of court. In practice, third parties are often named on the restraint order, particularly where an asset is held in the joint names of the defendant and the third party, or where it is alleged that an asset held by the third party is in fact held by that party on trust for the defendant. In such circumstances, the third party is also directly restrained from himself dealing with that asset, including dealing with his own share in it.

**16.07** If the order contains any exceptions, the third party should only allow the defendant to avail himself of that exception once he has satisfied himself that the conditions precedent have been satisfied. For example, the release of monies to pay a defendant's general living expenses is frequently conditional upon him giving notice to the prosecutor of the source of any monies he intends to use for this purpose. A financial institution may wish to check with the prosecuting authority that conditions of this nature have been fulfilled before releasing money for such purposes. However, many restraint orders are now worded in such a way as to provide protection to banks in this way, by providing that 'No bank need enquire as to the application or proposed application of any money withdrawn by the Defendant if the withdrawal appears to be permitted by this order.'

The third party should also check whether he holds other assets belonging to the defend- **16.08** ant which, although not specifically named in the order, are caught by the general restraint provisions. These assets too should not be released to the defendant, because most restraint orders are 'global'—they apply to all realisable property whether or not described in the order (s 41(2)(a) of POCA). The exception is that the restraint order is worded in such a way as to be limited to specific assets, such as where the value of the defendant's benefit from criminal conduct is known to be less than the realisable property available. A restraint order may specifically restrain the defendant from dealing with monies held in a current account at a particular bank. However, it may transpire that the defendant also holds a deposit account at the same bank, of which the prosecutor was unaware when he obtained the restraint order. In most circumstances therefore, the bank should also take steps to freeze that account.

A third party served with a restraint order would be well advised to seek legal advice on its **16.09** terms at an early stage. The third party has to steer a difficult course between preventing any dealing with assets properly caught by the order, and allowing defendants access to assets that are not strictly within its terms. Any failure to do the former may result in contempt proceedings being brought by the prosecutor, and any failure to do the latter may result in an action being brought against the third party by the defendant for breach of contract or other relief. In order to prevent being caught in this position, the third party should, when in doubt, apply to the Crown Court to vary the order under r 59.3 of the Criminal Procedure Rules (CrimPR) and s 42(3) POCA restraint orders—see Chapter 5 on the variation of restraint orders.

## Rights of third parties

Restraint and confiscation law has to strike a balance between ensuring that realisable prop- **16.10** erty in the hands of third parties is properly restrained on the one hand and ensuring that the third party does not suffer loss on the other. Inevitably this is a difficult balance to achieve, the two aims being to some extent in conflict. Third parties should, however, be aware of the rights they have in order to keep to a minimum any potential loss suffered as a result of complying with any order.

## Reasonable costs and expenses

Most third parties will inevitably incur costs in complying with the terms of the order. In **16.11** most cases, it will be necessary to take legal advice on the terms of the order, and in the case of orders affecting commercial organisations, the time of fee-earning staff will be occupied in setting up systems to ensure the order is complied with. Banks, for example, will have to put a 'freeze' on the defendant's bank accounts to prevent money being withdrawn from its branches by cheque or cash card. By r 59.2(5) of the CrimPR the court '... may require the applicant for a restraint order to give an undertaking to pay the reasonable expenses of any person, other than a person who is prohibited from dealing with realisable property by the restraint order, which are incurred in complying with the restraint order'.

It is usual for the prosecutor to give an undertaking to pay the reasonable costs and expenses **16.12** of third parties (except the recipients of gifts caught by the Act), which are incurred:

(a) in ascertaining whether any assets caught by the order are within his possession or control; or
(b) in securing compliance with the terms of the order.

**16.13** Typically such an undertaking is in the following terms:

> [The Prosecutor] will pay the reasonable costs of anyone other than the Defendant (and his wife) which have been incurred as a result of compliance with this Order including the costs of ascertaining whether that person holds any of the Defendant's assets SAVE THAT [the Prosecutor] will not pay any legal or accountancy costs so incurred without first giving their consent in writing.

This undertaking only extends to costs incurred for the purposes set out and for no other reason and only 'reasonable' costs and expenses are caught.

**16.14** In the majority of cases, such issues can be resolved by agreement between the prosecutor and the third party concerned. Where the parties are unable to resolve any dispute as to liability or quantum, the third party should make an application to the court.

### Restraint orders and joint owners of property

**16.15** In *Re G (Restraint Order)* (QBD, 19 July 2001) Stanley Burnton J laid down guidelines for what should and should not be included in restraint orders. An order made against the defendant had also included his wife. Stanley Burnton J considered that s 77 of the CJA (which corresponds with s 26 of the DTA and s 41 of POCA) empowered the High Court (and now under POCA the Crown Court) to make a restraint order prohibiting any person from dealing with any realisable property. He stated such a person might be someone other than the defendant, provided he or she holds realisable property. He added:

> There are therefore two possible bases under the 1988 Act for making a restraint order prohibiting the wife of a defendant from dealing with a bank account in their joint names: (a) that the credit balance in the bank account constitutes realisable property; and (b) that the wife's interest in the joint bank account may be the result of a gift or gifts caught by Part VI of the 1988 Act. On the same basis the real property in joint names may also be made the subject of a Restraint Order prohibiting both husband and wife from dealing with the property. Of course, in many cases basis (b) will be inapplicable, either because no gift has been made (as where the wife's interest results from her own earnings) or because of the requirement of section 74(10) that the gift must have been made after the earliest of the offences in question. In addition if a joint bank account is used for domestic expenses and has a modest credit balance, it is debatable whether the payments into the account made by the defendant are a 'gift' ... if, as in the present case, a wife is to be prohibited from dealing with any property, the order should make clear on its face that she is the subject of the order. In the case of civil proceedings, this may be done by making her a Respondent to the application, and a defendant in the proceedings. RSC Order 115 Rule 2A would seem to prevent making the wife, against whom no criminal proceedings have been instituted and, as far as I am aware, is not to be charged, a defendant to proceedings such as the present. However, the 'Notice to the Defendant' at the beginning of the Restraint Order should be supplemented so as to become 'Notice to the Defendant and to (the wife)', giving the full name of the wife. It is not sufficient for the application of the Order for the wife to be found only in the operative paragraphs of the Order.

**16.16** Stanley Burnton J went on to add that unless there is evidence that the wife has adequate separate means, it is essential that the order permits her to spend an adequate weekly sum on ordinary living expenses, and to pay for her separate legal advice and representation. It is not appropriate, he held, to rely on her right to apply to vary the order for this purpose. Lastly, he stated the order should include an undertaking by the prosecutor to serve the order and the witness statement in support on the wife as soon as practicable. CrimPR r 59.2(8) now makes such service mandatory (sc115.4(3) applies to High Court DTA/CJA cases).

He added that the above considerations are equally applicable to anyone who is a cohab- **16.17**
itee of the defendant. They should be borne in mind whenever a third party is named in
the restraint order. In certain circumstances, eg where a company said to be owned by the
defendant is included in the order, thought will need to be given as to whether specific
provision should be made ensuring that the company is permitted to utilise such assets as
will enable it to carry out its ordinary course of business. CrimPR r 59.1 (in similar terms to
s 41(3) of POCA) specifically provides that:

> The Crown Court may make a restraint order subject to exceptions, including, but not limited
> to, exceptions for reasonable living expenses and reasonable legal expenses, and for the pur-
> pose of enabling any person to carry on any trade, business or occupation.

### Use of assets

The restraint order only prevents dealing with the property. Hence, a third party may continue **16.18**
to use an asset in such a way that does not constitute dealing with it. A third party may therefore continue to reside in a restrained property pending the making and enforcement of a
confiscation order, and may continue to drive round in a restrained motor vehicle. What they
may not do is attempt to sell the asset without first obtaining a variation order from the court.

### What remedies are available to a person who denies the defendant has an interest in a restrained asset?

It may happen that a third party denies that the defendant has an interest in a restrained asset. **16.19**
If this is correct, and the asset does not constitute a gift caught by the Acts, then the asset will
not constitute 'realisable property'. A third party who so contends would be entitled to apply
to the High Court under the pre-POCA regime, and now the Crown Court under s 42(3)
of POCA, for a variation releasing the asset in question from the terms of the order—see
Chapter 5. For restraint orders in force prior to a confiscation order being made the standard
on which the court will normally decide the issue is whether there is a good arguable case that
it is realisable property. It should be borne in mind that the function of the restraint order
is to preserve the status quo pending the making and enforcement of a confiscation order. It
does not take away title to property, but merely restrains any dealing in it. Accordingly,
previously the High Court, and now for POCA cases the Crown Court, will not normally
be willing to become embroiled in an argument as to ownership of property at the restraint
stage, but will often prefer issues as to the ownership of property to be resolved at the confiscation and enforcement stage (see *Re Norris* as cited below and *Lamb v RCPO sub nom Re
Pigott* [2010] EWCA Civ 285; [2010] Lloyd's Rep FC 405).

Applications for the release of property will usually be confined at the restraint stage to those **16.20**
cases where the prosecution's evidence fails to establish any interest in the asset or where the
applicant has clear and incontrovertible evidence that the defendant has no interest whatever
in the asset. In *SCF Finance Co Ltd v Masri* [1985] 1 WLR 876 the Court of Appeal emphasised, in relation to freezing injunctions, that a mere assertion that a third party owns an asset
need not be accepted without proper enquiry, and the court had jurisdiction in appropriate
circumstances to order the trial of an issue in relation to any such dispute. If, however, the
third party argues that the continued inclusion of his asset within the restraint order is likely
to have a detrimental effect on, eg, his business dealings, the case for an immediate hearing as
to the beneficial interests in that property will be much stronger. The third party will need to
consider his position carefully—if the defendant is ultimately acquitted, he will potentially

waste costs in litigating his interest at the restraint stage. It would, however, always be advisable to make the prosecution aware of the third party's alleged interest at an early stage, in order to ensure that it is not later claimed that the application is being brought only as a result of a confiscation order having been made.

### Living expenses

**16.21** A dependant with no other reasonable source of income is likely to be entitled to a sum from restrained funds in order to meet their weekly and monthly outgoings. If the defendant is in prison a figure will be fixed with them in mind. If the defendant is at liberty, a figure will be fixed for both him and his dependants. In *R v AW* [2010] EWCA Crim 3123 the Court considered that an exception to a restraint order for living expenses could include the needs of the defendant's wife and children, even where the defendant's wife had separated from him. The Court further considered that expenditure on reasonable living expenses could not properly be considered 'dissipation' of assets. Lord Justice Rix noted that '[T]here is no need in principle for a defendant to show that he and his family, even his estranged family, even the children of a divorced wife, are reduced to poverty before a proper claim can be made in terms of the rubric of reasonable living expenses.'

**16.22** 'Reasonable costs and expenses' will be met. School fees may be payable. But such items would cease to be allowable once the defendant was convicted, as per *Re Peters* [1988] 3 All ER 46. The Court of Appeal held that under a Drug Trafficking Offences Act 1986 restraint order, payment of school fees for the defendant's son for a period after the result of his trial was known could not be allowed. As Mann LJ said at p 52: 'I fully understand that [the court below] may have been influenced by the disruption of the son's education should a confiscation order be made, but in my judgment there is, in the light of section 31(2) no room for the intrusion of sympathy.'

**16.23** In the majority of cases, such issues can be resolved by agreement between the prosecutor and the third party concerned. Where the parties are unable to resolve any dispute as to liability or quantum, the third party should make an application to the court—see Chapters 2 and 5.

### Legal expenses

**16.24** In *Re D* [2006] EWHC 1519 (Admin), the question arose as to whether third parties who assert an interest in property that is the subject of a restraint order and which was due to be considered as part of a confiscation order have a right to receive legal funding from that property. There were a number of properties that were in the name of members of the defendant's family. It was part of the case against the defendant that that had been done deliberately in order to conceal the true situation (namely that they were actually his benefit from his unlawful conduct). Counsel suggested that by virtue of s 82(4) of the CJA everyone who has an alleged interest in property should have the opportunity to establish the existence of that interest, and be provided with monies from the proceeds of the property, to pay for legal representation. Collins J described this as a 'quite hopeless submission'. He stated:

> The powers must be exercised to ensure that the third parties have a proper opportunity of pursuing their claim. That they will do in the way that any litigation is to be pursued. If they have the means, they will have to pay for it: if they do not have sufficient means, then they may apply for public funding. But what they cannot do is to obtain funding from the property which they are asserting they have an interest in when their interest is being disputed.

The position under the previous legislation was again considered in *Re S* [2010] EWHC **16.25** 917. The wife of the defendant had applied to release funds under restraint to pay her legal expenses of making an application to discharge the restraint order. The Court considered both *Re D* and *Revenue and Customs Prosecutions Office v Briggs-Price and O'Reilly* [2007] EWCA Civ 568 and found the application by the defendant's wife to be very different from the position in *Briggs-Price*, principally as there was now a 'settled' confiscation order in place, in which case there had to be very strong reasons to permit release of funds to a third party in a post-confiscation situation. The court did not, however, state that a restraint order should never be varied to permit payment towards a third party's legal expenses. For further on this topic generally see Chapters 2 and 5.

### Restraint orders and limited companies

In *Re G (Restraint Order)* (2001) (above) Stanley Burnton J (as he then was) held, leaving **16.26** gifts aside, that there were two bases upon which a prosecutor may apply for a restraint order prohibiting dealings in the assets of a company controlled by a defendant, but against which no criminal charge is to be made, namely:

(1) that the company holds realisable property within the meaning of (the applicable Act); and
(2) that the company has no genuine separate existence from the defendant, and is used by him as a device for fraud.

### The corporate veil

In the case of (2) above, the court treats the assets of the company as if they were in the name **16.27** of the defendant. The court is said to pierce or 'lift the corporate veil'. This topic is covered in depth in Chapters 2 and 5. The application to lift the corporate veil will often come in the witness statement that supports the application for the restraint order. The wording will be in similar terms to the following: 'I invite the Honourable Court to lift the corporate veil in respect of Tosca Limited as I believe the sole purpose of the company and its bank accounts was and continues to be to perpetrate a fraud and provide a conduit for its proceeds.'

In *Re G* Stanley Burnton J held that while the phrase 'lifting the corporate veil' was helpful **16.28** shorthand, it had no place in an injunction (in the restraint order itself), because the object of that was to set out clear and specific prohibitions affecting the defendant and the other persons affected by the order and to impose equally clear obligations on the applicant. He stated as follows: 'If the evidence before the court raises a *prima facie* case justifying a lifting of the corporate veil, and to treat the property of the company as the property of the Defendant, the order should prohibit the company, in addition to the Defendant, from dealing with its property.'

Notwithstanding Stanley Burnton J's above observation, it is commonplace to find within a **16.29** restraint order the following additional injunction:

AND IT IS ORDERED THAT: The assets of Tosca Limited be treated as the personal assets of the Defendant

thus reflecting the fact that the court has in fact lifted the corporate veil over that company.

The principles relating to the lifting of the corporate veil in this context are no different **16.30** from those applicable in other areas of the law: see *Re H (Restraint Order: Realisable Property)* [1996] 2 All ER 391 and *Trustor AB v Smallbone* [2001] 1 WLR 1177 (especially at para 23). They were more recently encapsulated in the judgment of the Court of Appeal in *R v Seager* *and Blatch* [2010] 1 WLR 815, which dealt with an appeal against confiscation orders. Aikens LJ said at [76]:

> A court can 'pierce' the carapace of the corporate entity and look at what lies behind it only in certain circumstances. It cannot do so simply because it considers it might be just to do so. Each of these circumstances involves impropriety and dishonesty. The court will then be entitled to look for the legal substance not just the form. In the context of criminal cases the courts have identified at least three situations when the corporate veil can be pierced. First if an offender attempts to shelter behind a corporate façade or veil to hide his crime and his benefits from it: see In re H, at p 402, per Rose LJ; Director of Public Prosecutions v Compton [2002] EWCA Civ 1720, paras 44–48, per Simon Brown LJ and R v Grainger [2008] EWCA Crim 2506 at [15], per Toulson LJ. Secondly, where an offender does acts in the name of a company which (with the necessary mens rea) constitute a criminal offence which leads to the offender's conviction, then 'the veil of incorporation has been not so much pierced as rudely torn away': per Lord Bingham in Jennings v Crown Prosecution Service [2008] AC 1046, para 16. Thirdly, where the transaction or business structures constitute a 'device', 'cloak' or 'sham', ie, an attempt to disguise the true nature of the transaction or structure so as to deceive third parties or the courts: R v Dimsey [2000] QB 744, 772, per Laws LJ, applying Snook v London and West Riding Investment Ltd [1967] 2 QB 786, 802, per Diplock LJ.

**16.31** In many cases, in addition, it will be appropriate to appoint a receiver under the power conferred by the relevant statute to take possession of the property of the company and to manage it (see *Re H* and *CPS v Compton* [2002] EWCA Civ 1720 above). In *R v Sale* [2013] EWCA Crim 1306 the Court of Appeal at paragraphs 41–42 of its judgment stated that the principles in *Seager and Blatch* should be applied in light of the Supreme Court's judgment in *Prest v Petrodel Resources Ltd* [2013] UKSC 34.

**16.32** It should also be noted that at the stage of the application for a restraint order without notice prior to a confiscation order being made, the court will have no more than a prima facie case before it. The court must be satisfied that there is a good arguable case that the property is realisable, ie that the defendant holds an interest in it. The same would apply to lifting the corporate veil—see Simon Brown LJ at para [38] of *Compton*:

> ...if, on the documents, a good arguable case arises for treating particular assets as the realisable property of the defendant—here on the basis that the company's corporate veil should properly be pierced—then the relevant restraint (and possibly receivership) order(s) should ordinarily be made. That essentially is the test for the grant of *Mareva* relief. So too should it be the test for the exercise of the section 26 powers. It is, of course, open to third parties (or the defendant himself where the order is made without notice) to apply to set it aside.

**16.33** The company in question may subsequently be able to establish that it has a legitimate existence as a legal person carrying on a lawful business. The order must therefore also be addressed to the company and the applicant's witness statement served on it, as required by CrimPR r 59.2(8) (or sc 115.4(3) for CJA/DTA cases). The order should provide that the company should be entitled to spend up to a maximum sum (which is liable to be increased) on its separate legal advice and representation (as per Stanley Burnton J in *Re G*) albeit under POCA this could only be for legal proceedings unrelated to the defendant's restraint or prosecution.

**16.34** Stanley Burnton J also held that particular caution was required if it appeared that, in addition to engaging in fraudulent transactions, the company was carrying on a legitimate business that may be closed down by the order. In those circumstances it may not be appropriate to treat the assets of the company as those of the defendant. This has been illustrated by the cases of *Windsor and others v CPS* [2011] 1 WLR 1519 (dealt with in Chapters 2 and 5) and *Crown Prosecution Service v G* [2010] EWHC 1117, in which the court considered that it was not enough to show that criminal funds had been injected into a business for the corporate veil to be lifted and a restraint order made against the company in terms that its assets were to be treated as those of the criminal. G had invested £200,000 of monies which appeared to have been stolen from a German bank into the relevant company. In discharging a restraint order made against the company, Treacy J considered:

> The available evidence does not appear to me to show a substantial arguable case of use of a corporate structure as a device or façade to conceal criminal activity in circumstances where substantial trading activity took place to continue an already existing genuine business, and where the loan was openly recorded. Whilst what occurred no doubt enabled G to invest what appear to be part of his ill-gotten gains, I am not persuaded that on the evidence an arguable case is demonstrated to show that G was attempting to hide behind the corporate veil so as to conceal his crime and his benefits from it.

**16.35**  Freezing injunctions in civil proceedings normally contain an exception to the prohibition against dealing with property to enable the person restrained to deal with his assets in the ordinary course of business. A restraint order may be made subject to such a specified exception where appropriate.

**16.36**  Where the company is not a company limited by guarantee, but is merely a company which is a trading name for the defendant, eg Alfredo Germont trading as Alfredo Germont Fuels, it has no separate legal identity because it is not a registered company. It is therefore incorrect and unnecessary for it to be separately restrained. The restraint order itself would prevent the defendant from dealing with the assets of Alfredo Germont Fuels because he is prohibited from dealing with any assets that he holds.

### Prosecutor does not have to give an undertaking in damages

**16.37**  In contrast to the position in relation to freezing injunctions, the prosecutor cannot be required to give an undertaking in damages. This provision is to be found in the CrimPR r 59.2(4) (POCA cases) or sc115.4(1) (CJA/DTA cases) and which states as follows:

> (4) The Crown Court must not require the applicant for a restraint order to give any undertaking relating to damages sustained as a result of the restraint order by a person who is prohibited from dealing with realisable property by the restraint order.

### Unsecured creditors and POCA

**16.38**  The legislative steer under POCA is worded differently to the CJA/DTA. It is to be found in s 69(2) of the Act and provides:

> (2) The powers—
>   (a) must be exercised with a view to the value for the time being of realisable property being made available (by the property's realisation) for satisfying any confiscation order that has been or may be made against the defendant;
>   (b) must be exercised, in a case where a confiscation order has not been made, with a view to securing that there is no diminution in the value of realisable property;
>   (c) must be exercised without taking account of any obligation of the defendant or a recipient of a tainted gift if the obligation conflicts with the object of satisfying any confiscation order that has been or may be made against the defendant;
>   (d) may be exercised in respect of a debt owed by the Crown.

The legislative steer in s 69 is therefore drafted more restrictively than under the previous legislation, and it was the construction of this section that fell to be determined in the case of *Lexi Holdings* (also dealt with in Chapter 5).

**16.39**   In *Serious Fraud Office v Lexi Holdings PLC (In Administration)* [2008] EWCA Crim 1443; [2009] 2 WLR 905 the Court held that restraint orders made under POCA may not be varied to permit defendants to pay unsecured third-party creditors. The Court also took the opportunity to give important guidance to practitioners on how applications to vary restraint orders, often involving complex points of law far removed from the usual work of the Crown Court, should be dealt with.

**16.40**   In *Lexi Holdings* a restraint order had been obtained by the SFO against an individual known as 'M' on the basis that he was subject to a criminal investigation into an offence of conspiracy to defraud the Cheshire Building Society and associated money laundering offences. The administrators of Lexi alleged it had been the victim of substantial frauds committed by M and others and judgment in default was eventually entered in its favour for some £625,250 plus interest. Lexi thereafter applied to the Central Criminal Court for the restraint order to be varied to permit M to satisfy the judgment. Lexi sought the variation both on the basis that it had a proprietary claim and as a bona fide judgment creditor. The application was opposed by the SFO, but the judge at first instance made the variation sought so as to allow payment to be made to Lexi from M's restrained assets. The judge held that the court had a 'reasonably wide discretion' under POCA 'to do justice'. He found that there was no significant change in statutory policy or underlying principle from the pre-2002 Act regime and agreed with the reasoning of Davis J in *Re X* [2004] EWHC 861 (Admin); [2005] 1 QB 133. The SFO appealed, with permission, to the Criminal Division of the Court of Appeal.

**16.41**   The Court (Keene LJ, Davis J, and the Recorder of Swansea) allowed the SFO's appeal. The court noted there were significant differences between the wording of the legislative steer in s 69 of POCA and under the previous legislation. Keene LJ said:

> It is true that some of the provisions in that section contain the phrase 'with a view to' which as has been said in several of the authorities indicates a degree of flexibility in the court's approach and simply gives a 'legislative steer'. Section 69(2)(c), however, is different. It does not contain that phrase and does appear to be in mandatory terms: the powers 'must be exercised without taking account of any obligation…'. Moreover, the feature of its equivalent provision in the earlier legislation which so influenced Davis J. in *Re X* has changed: it is now clear that this provision does apply in the situation where there is a restraint order but no confiscation order in existence, because the words 'or may be made' have been added. This must be taken to represent a deliberate tightening up of the legislation by Parliament.

**16.42**   Keene LJ went on:

> On the face of it, section 69(2)(c) does require the courts to ignore any debt owed by the restrained person to an unsecured third party creditor, so that the existence of such a debt would not empower the court to vary a restraint order unless there was no conflict 'with the object of satisfying any confiscation order'. On that last aspect, we are wholly unpersuaded by [Counsel for Lexi's] argument about the meaning to be attached to those words. His contention that the 'object' is that of depriving the offender of the proceeds of crime is unsustainable. That is the object of the confiscation order itself, whereas this provision is referring to the object of 'satisfying' any confiscation order, i.e. providing a sufficient quantum of assets to meet the sum identified, already or in due course, in a confiscation order. Counsel's interpretation would render the presence of that word 'satisfying' unnecessary and would, in our judgment, distort the natural

meaning of section 69(2)(c). If he were right, the provision would enable any third party creditor to obtain a variation of the restraint order and so to be paid and indeed Counsel submits that this is what should happen. The provision would in fact have virtually no effect in practice. In our view, the latter part of paragraph (c) is, as [Counsel for the SFO] argues, indicating merely that if the court can see that a confiscation order, existing or prospective, relates to an amount which the defendant has ample assets to meet, then it may be that a debt to a third party creditor can properly be allowed to be paid from the restrained assets.

The Court also noted that Lexi's argument appeared to be inconsistent with the procedures to be followed at the confiscation stage. Keene LJ said:  **16.43**

> ... of the greatest significance, the payment of third party creditors at the restraint order stage seems to us to be inconsistent with the position which obtains at the confiscation order stage. Section 9 of the 2002 Act provides that the available amount of the defendant's assets when one comes to quantify the amount to be specified in the confiscation order is to be ascertained in the following way:
>
> (1) For the purpose of deciding the recoverable amount, the available amount is the aggregate of—
>   (a) the total of the values (at the time the confiscation order is made) of all the free property then held by the defendant minus the total amount payable in pursuance of obligations which have priority, and
>   (b) the total of the values (at that time) of all tainted gifts
> (2) An obligation has priority if it is an obligation of the defendant—
>   (a) to pay an amount due in respect of a fine or other order of a court which was imposed or made on conviction of an offence and at any time before the time the confiscation order is made, or
>   (b) to pay a sum which would be included among the preferential debts if the defendant's bankruptcy had commenced on the date of the confiscation order or his winding up had been ordered on that date.
> (3) 'Preferential debts' has the meaning given by section 386 of the Insolvency Act 1986 (c45).
>
> It will be seen that, when the court decides on the amount to be specified in the confiscation order, it has to use the total of the values of the property the defendant holds, less only 'priority' obligations such as fines and preferential debts. The existence of obligations owed to ordinary third party creditors is to be disregarded when a confiscation order is made. It seems to this court that it would have been wholly illogical for the legislature to have decided to allow third party debts to be paid during the period when assets are supposedly being preserved by a restraint order when such debts are to be left out of account at the stage when the confiscation order is made. We can see no reason why Parliament should have decided to allow unsecured creditors to reduce the assets during the restraint phase when such creditors could not reduce the assets at the confiscation stage. If that were the position, it would put a premium on well advised creditors getting in quickly during the restraint phase before their opportunity is lost, and we do not accept that that situation is one which was ever intended.

The Court emphasised that unsecured third parties were not necessarily left without a remedy. It noted that a restraint order is essentially a temporary measure preserving assets pending the making and enforcement of a confiscation order. Keene LJ said:  **16.44**

> A restraint order is therefore performing a holding operation. Of course, it has to be acknowledged that that operation may, and has been known to, last a considerable time. Nonetheless, the limited duration of restraint orders is a relevant factor when considering its adverse effects on third party creditors and when seeking to ascertain the intention of Parliament. The restraint order will eventually be discharged and either replaced by some other order such as a confiscation order or not replaced at all.

**16.45** The Court also noted that the potential harshness of s 69(2)(c) was mitigated to some extent by other powers available to the Crown Court once an offender is convicted. As Keene LJ observed:

> ... the court has the power under section 130 of the Sentencing Act to make a compensation order in favour of a person who has suffered loss resulting from the offence or any other offence which is taken into consideration. As [Counsel for the SFO] points out, such a compensation order takes priority over a confiscation order: see section 13(5) and (6) of the 2002 Act. Not every creditor will be helped by this provision, since he may not qualify under section 130, but some will be assisted. Indeed, if a victim of the defendant's criminal conduct has started or intends to start civil proceedings against him 'in respect of loss, injury or damage sustained in connection with the conduct', then the court, by virtue of section 6(6) need not make a confiscation order at all. The duty to make one where it is determined that the defendant has benefited from his criminal conduct becomes simply a power in those circumstances described in section 6(6). When one bears in mind that the criminal conduct leading to 'loss, injury or damage' may be *general* criminal conduct if the defendant has a criminal lifestyle and not merely the *particular* criminal conduct covered by the offences in question (plus those taken into consideration), it can be appreciated that a considerable number of persons may qualify as 'victims' for this purpose. This too must tend to reduce the number of third parties ultimately affected adversely by the 2002 Act.

**16.46** Finally, the Court noted that the victims themselves may benefit from the defendant's assets being held under restraint pending the determination of the criminal proceedings. They too could lose out if the total value of the defendant's assets was reduced by claims by other third-party creditors being entertained by the court at the restraint stage.

**16.47** It is submitted that the Court's ruling in *Lexi* brings some certainty into the law relating to the release of restrained assets to pay unsecured third-party creditors of a defendant. Advisers can now maintain a consistent approach to all applications to vary POCA restraint orders for such purposes, and defendants, victims, and creditors alike know where they stand in relation to such matters. This consistency of approach will ensure that no unsecured creditor can 'jump the gun' and gain an advantage over others, including a victim, by reducing the amount of assets available to meet compensation and confiscation orders.

**16.48** This approach will also help to overcome the risk of abuse by associates of a defendant making bogus third-party claims at his behest with a view to reducing the fund available for confiscation. Although defendants are of course entitled to a presumption of innocence at the pre-conviction stage, one must remain mindful of the fact that, as Lord Donaldson MR observed in *Re O* [1991] 1 All ER 330: 'whatever may be the position in an individual case, the legislative contemplation is that restraint orders will be made in circumstances in which it is thought that some of those having interests in the property may well be of a dishonest disposition'.

**16.49** Of course, not all payments to third parties will fall foul of s 69(2)(c). There is, for example, no difficulty with a management receiver paying off trade debts with a view to retaining and preserving the value of the business of a company, since the payment of such a debt would preserve an asset greater in value. Similarly, there can be no objection to allowing rent or mortgage payments to be made either on the basis that they constitute a living expense or because they preserve and maintain the defendant's interest in property. In both cases the value of the realisable property is not diminished but preserved because such payments allow a company to continue trading or making profits, or prevents the mortgagee foreclosing, potentially reducing the value of the equity in the property.

### Third-party claims and practice

In a postscript to the *Lexi Holdings* judgment, the Court gave some important guidance to **16.50** practitioners as to how similar problems in relation to POCA restraint orders should be dealt with in the future. First, the Court recognised that the issues arising in the *Lexi Holdings* case were not part of the daily work of most Crown Court judges. Where the points at issue are not unduly complicated, they could readily be dealt with in the Crown Court, but there would be other occasions in which the complexities of the case were such that it would be unwise for a Crown Court judge to attempt to determine the issues. In such circumstances Keene LJ suggested that:

> . . . where a relaxation of a restraint order is sought, consideration should be given to adjourning those variation proceedings to enable the issues to be determined in proceedings before a specialist Chancery Circuit Judge or High Court Judge of the Chancery Division. Alternatively, those arranging the listing of such cases in the Crown Court should seek to ensure that they are heard by a judge with the relevant experience and expertise.

It should be borne in mind that POCA does not appear to give judges of the Crown Court **16.51** the ability to make declarations as to beneficial interests in property in contrast to the High Court's power for CJA and DTA cases as provided by its inherent jurisdiction and in RSC Order 115.7(4)(c), see Chapter 11 on enforcement receivers. Whilst the Crown Court can, for example, vary a restraint or receivership order to take into account a third party's interest and must exercise its powers with a view to allowing the third party to retain or recover its value under s 69(3)(a) of POCA, it appears likely that for declarations as to beneficial interests, third parties may still need to have their application heard in the civil courts. Secondly, the Court in *Lexi Holdings* reminded practitioners of their obligations under s 58(5) and (6) of POCA in cases where restraint orders had been made in relation to assets in respect of which they are litigating on behalf of third parties. These provisions require that the prosecutor and any receiver appointed under the Act are to be given the opportunity of making representations before the relevant court decides whether to stay third party litigation in relation to restrained assets or to allow that litigation to continue. The Court of Appeal noted that this section had not been complied with in the instant case. In conclusion Keene LJ said:

> We entirely accept that the reason why section 58 was not drawn to the attention of those judges was because counsel appearing then for Lexi was himself unaware of it. It was an innocent oversight. Nonetheless, steps do need to be taken to ensure that the terms of section 58 are observed. Some thought might usefully be given to the possibility of creating a register of restraint orders and applications for such orders, though that would not have cured the problem in the present case, since all involved were aware of the existence of the restraint order. The SFO and other prosecuting authorities could usefully publicise more widely the general tenor of section 58, to increase the awareness of it in the legal profession, and no doubt the relevant Bar Associations could play a role. This is not just a matter for the criminal courts and criminal lawyers: the duty under section 58 applies to all courts in which proceedings about such property take place and every so often those will be the civil courts. We shall direct that a copy of this judgment, together with a note drawing attention to this postscript, be sent to the Chairman of the Judicial Studies Board and to the Family and Civil Procedure Rules Committees.

An application by a third party for recognition of their interest in restrained assets under **16.52** POCA/CJA/DTA will be determined, whether by the Crown Court or High Court, using civil law and on the ordinary principles of contract, property, or trust law save in so far as the statutory provisions provide otherwise eg gifts for the purposes of the Acts. For examples, see *Larkfield v RCPO* [2010] 3 All ER 1173; [2010] EWCA Civ 521 and *Revenue & Customs*

*Prosecutions Office v Johnson and Backhouse* [2011] EWHC 1950). Practitioners should familiarise themselves with the relevant provisions of Pts 59–61 of the CrimPR, Pt 23 of the CPR and RSC Order 115 in terms of admissibility of evidence and the procedure to be followed. In *Backhouse v Revenue & Customs Prosecution Office* [2012] EWCA Civ 1000, Lord Justice Aikens stated:

> I agree that this appeal should be allowed for the reasons that Pill LJ has given. I also particularly wish to associate myself with his remarks at [8] above about the lack of a clear definition of the issues in this case. When civil claims are made under the Proceeds of Crime Act 2002 and their statutory predecessors, it seems to me that it is vitally important that the issues between the parties must be clearly identified. In simple cases that can be done very shortly. In more complicated cases, such as this one was by the time it reached the judge for trial, it will be better for the RCPO to set out its case in points of claim and for the defendant to respond to that in points of defence. In these more complicated cases it may then be appropriate for a List of Issues to be drawn up in the way that it is done in cases in the Commercial Court.

16.53  The advantage of this approach will not only be to make presentation of the case easier from the court's point of view, but also to establish at an early stage what the key issues in the case are likely to be.

## C. Confiscation Orders and their Enforcement

16.54  A confiscation order is an *in personam* order against the convicted defendant and not an *in rem* order against specific items of property. The consequence of this is that third parties who hold an interest in realisable property do not have a right to be heard at the confiscation hearing in the Crown Court or to have counsel make representations to the court on their behalf. If the defendant wishes the third party to be called as a witness on his behalf for the purpose of establishing the extent of his interest in realisable property, he may of course do so (see *Re Norris* below).

16.55  This may at first sight seem to be a denial of justice to the third party. However, this is not necessarily the case, because the mere making of a confiscation order does not take away the owner's title to the property. It may be that the defendant will be able to satisfy the confiscation order by realising assets other than those in which a third party claims to have an interest. In this event the third party concerned will not be troubled further. It is only if the defendant fails to satisfy the order voluntarily and the Crown seeks the appointment of a receiver that a third party holding an interest in realisable property need become involved as a party to the proceedings.

### No right to be heard at confiscation stage

16.56  So far as representation of a third party in confiscation proceedings in the Crown Court is concerned, there is no provision contained in POCA for representation or argument to be presented by the third party at the stage when the confiscation order is made. This is so even in cases where the Crown Court is likely to consider that the assets in which the third party claims an interest are the realisable property of the defendant.

16.57  In this respect the position is the same as that which existed under the CJA and DTA. The third party is not, however, left without protection. In *Re Norris* [2001] 1 WLR 1388 the House of Lords held that having convicted a person of a drug trafficking offence the Crown Court had to assess the value of his proceeds of drug trafficking and the amount of his realisable property for the purpose of making the necessary confiscation order. At that hearing the defendant's wife, who was not a party to the proceedings, had given detailed evidence on the defendant's behalf that the matrimonial home belonged either wholly or substantially to her. The judge disbelieved her evidence and made a confiscation order against the defendant on the basis that the full value of the house formed part of his realisable property. Mrs Norris then sought to assert her beneficial interest in the property before the High Court at the enforcement stage. The prosecution asserted that, the Crown Court having made a determination that the entirety of the home was realisable property of the defendant, it was an abuse of process for Mrs Norris now to assert the contrary. The House of Lords held that the assertion of an interest in the property by a third party should be resolved at the enforcement stage. Their Lordships confirmed that a third party was not precluded from asserting his or her interest by reason of having previously made assertions as to the ownership of the property when called as a witness for the defence in the confiscation proceedings even had their assertions not been accepted. Mrs Norris had not been represented at the confiscation hearing and had not been party to those proceedings. It would be a denial of justice to prevent her from asserting her rights at the enforcement stage.

A third party should, however, be careful to ensure that they do not make contrary assertions **16.58** at the enforcement stage to those they may have made at the confiscation hearing. In *Re Y* [2011] EWHC 2427, the prosecutor applied for summary judgment against the respondents who were the defendant's wife and children who had each been convicted of money laundering and were all the subject of joint confiscation proceedings. The Crown had alleged that three assets were tainted gifts from the defendant to the family. The family did not dispute this, presumably on the basis that any confiscation orders to be made against themselves were thereby minimised. At the point at which the receiver was appointed, however, they asserted that the three assets belonged to them. The court held that it was an abuse of process for the family as interested parties in receivership proceedings to claim entitlement to assets included in a confiscation order made against the defendant when they had been party to the same confiscation proceedings and had not then disputed the defendant's entitlement to those assets. The distinction with *Norris* is clear—the family was party to and represented at the confiscation hearing and chose not to dispute the assertion that the assets belonged to the defendant.

When making a confiscation order the Crown Court will disregard what a former wife may **16.59** obtain in other proceedings over and above any interest which she holds at the time the confiscation order is made. The mere right of the wife to apply for relief under the Matrimonial Causes Act 1973 (MCA 1973) does not amount to 'an interest' falling within the terms of s 69(3)(a) of POCA: see s 84(2)(f) of POCA. At that stage, the Crown Court has no regard to, and makes no allowance for, any possible adverse consequences for a former spouse and her child when deciding the amount to be confiscated. The court's function is simply to conduct an arithmetical exercise to determine the assets available for confiscation: see *R v Ahmed and Qureshi* [2004] EWCA Crim 2599.

In that case Latham LJ stated: **16.60**

> 11. ... The court is merely concerned with the arithmetic exercise of computing what is, in effect, a statutory debt. That process does not involve any assessment, in our judgment, of the way in which that debt may ultimately be paid, any more than the assessment of any other debt. No questions therefore arise under Article 8 at this stage in the process.

12. Different considerations, will, however arise if the debt is not met and the prosecution determine to take enforcement action, for example by obtaining an order for a Receiver. As the House of Lords explained in *Re Norris* [2001] 1 WLR 1388, this is the stage of the procedure in which a third party's rights can not only be taken into account but resolved... It would be at that stage that the court would have to consider whether or not it would be proportionate to make an order selling the home in the circumstances of the particular case... The court would undoubtedly be concerned to ensure that proper weight is given to the public policy objective behind the making of confiscation orders, which is to ensure that criminals do not profit from their crime. And the court will have a range of enforcement options available with which to take account of the rights of third parties such as other members of the Ahmed family.

16.61   As is apparent from the case of *R v Modjiri* [2010] 1 WLR 2096, at the confiscation stage the defendant's beneficial interest in property should be taken into account notwithstanding that there may be difficulties in realising it at the enforcement stage. In *R v Harriott* [2012] EWCA Crim 2294, the Court of Appeal considered that, although third party interests were to be advanced at the enforcement stage, the Crown Court nonetheless had to determine the extent of the defendant's realisable property. The judge had been incorrect to consider that the alleged equitable interest must be asserted in separate proceedings before he could take account of it at the confiscation stage.

By way of contrast with the position at the stage the confiscation order is made, POCA gives a right to an affected third party to make representations in relation to the making and variation etc of restraint orders and the enforcement of confiscation orders: see ss 42(3), 49(8), 51(8), and 63(1). These provisions give effect to the requirement in s 69(3)(a) of POCA to allow persons other than the defendant and the recipient of the tainted gift to retain or recover the value of his or her interests. POCA treats the function of the Crown Court at the confiscation stage as a limited one which does not involve the consideration of the practical effects of an order properly made on third-party interests. However, if an order is made in separate proceedings determining a third party to be the beneficial owner of assets otherwise contended to be realisable assets of the defendant, the Crown Court must have regard to it in determining the 'available amount'. In confiscation proceedings, the Crown Court is not absolved of determining the extent of the realisable assets of the defendant even if these are jointly held with third parties. The court must still determine the extent of the interest the defendant holds—see *R v Harriott* (above).

16.62   Similarly, if an order determining that a third party holds an interest in realisable property is made in separate proceedings after the confiscation order but before enforcement, the Crown Court must, on the application of the prosecutor or the defendant, have regard to it in any application to adjust 'the available amount' under s 23 of POCA. This is the case so long as the prosecutor or receiver has been given notice of the civil proceedings in which that order was made, per s 58(5) and (6) of POCA. If the prosecutor or receiver was not given such notice, it may argue that any such order should be set aside until it has been heard on the question of the beneficial interests held in the property.

### Enforcement proceedings

16.63   Enforcement Receivership is dealt with in some detail in Chapter 11. When this stage of the proceedings is reached, third parties claiming to hold an interest in realisable property have a right to be heard because a receivership order effectively extinguishes the property rights of those holding realisable property. However, the rights of third parties are protected in a number of ways.

Where the Crown applies for an enforcement receiver (under s 50 of POCA, s 29 DTA, or **16.64** s 80 CJA), the court has the power to allow a third party claiming an interest in the property to reopen the question of ownership previously determined in the confiscation proceedings in the Crown Court, but should not permit the re-litigation of issues by the defendant which had been decided in the Crown Court on the same, or substantially the same, evidence and submissions (see *Re Norris* [2001] 1 WLR 1388).

### The right to be given notice of the proceedings

CrimPR r 60.1(6)(b) (sc1 15.7(2)(b) in CJA/DTA cases) provides that the application seeking **16.65** the appointment of an enforcement receiver under s 50 of POCA must be served, inter alia, upon:

> Any person holding any interest in the realisable property to which the application relates.

The application, together with the evidence in support, must be served not less than seven **16.66** days prior to the hearing date.

### The right to make representations

Section 51(8) of POCA states: **16.67**

> The court must not—
> (a) confer the power mentioned in subsection (2)(b) or (c) in respect of property, or
> (b) exercise the power conferred on it by subsection (6) in respect of property,
>
> unless it gives persons holding interest in the property a reasonable opportunity to make representations to it.

A right merely to be given notice of the proceedings will, by itself, not be sufficient to protect the third party's interest in the property. Accordingly, s 51(8) of POCA provides that the Crown Court shall not exercise the powers given to it unless a reasonable opportunity has been given to persons holding an interest in the property to make representations to the court (the same applies in the High Court under s 29(8) of the DTA and s 80(8) of the CJA).

It should be noted that the only persons who have a right to be given notice of and make **16.68** representations in receivership proceedings are those who have an interest in the defendant's realisable property. Thus, a bank holding a deposit account in the name of the defendant would have no right to make representations, whereas the defendant's spouse in whose name the matrimonial home was jointly held with the defendant clearly would. It is also worth noting that in *R v Gaffar* [2012] EWCA Crim 2350, the Court considered that there was no breach of the ECHR where an interested party was unrepresented at a hearing to determine whether an enforcement receiver should be appointed to realise property. The interested party could make representations on his own behalf, had previously been represented, was willing to give evidence and the issues in question had been straightforward. Accordingly, his right to effective access to the courts had not been breached and the judge's refusal to grant an adjournment had not been unreasonable.

### What steps should be taken on behalf of the third party on receipt of an application to appoint an enforcement receiver?

The third party's solicitor should firstly go on the record by notifying the court, the prosecut- **16.69** ing authority that issued the application, and the solicitors for the defendant, of his interest in the case. If the client is unable to fund the case privately and meets the eligibility criteria, an emergency application for public funding should be made. Once funding has been resolved, work should commence on preparing a witness statement setting out in detail the precise nature of the third-party interest in the property. Where documentary evidence supporting the third party's claim exists (eg in relation to an interest in a jointly owned property) this should be produced and exhibited to the witness statement. If there are other persons who are in a position to confirm the extent of the third party's claim, witness statements should also be taken from them. Such independent corroboration is particularly important in cases where no documentary evidence exists confirming the third party's claim.

**Seeking an adjournment and setting directions**

**16.70**    As third parties are only entitled to seven days' notice of the hearing, there may be insufficient time to obtain public funding, conduct all the necessary enquiries, draft and serve witness statements, and brief counsel before the return date on the application. In such circumstances an adjournment should be sought. As the public interest requires that confiscation orders should be satisfied promptly, it may well be that the court would not be prepared to adjourn the entire receivership application. It has become increasingly common for the court to appoint a receiver to enable him to begin realising assets that are free of third-party claims. In order to protect the position of the third party, the court will order a stay on the receiver's powers of realisation in respect of those assets in which the third party claims an interest pending the determination of the claim. The Court of Appeal in *Lamb v Revenue and Customs Prosecutions Office* [2010] EWCA Civ 285 held that the fact that there was a dispute as to whether an asset was in fact realisable property of the defendant or belonged to a third party did not preclude the court from including that asset in a management receivership order pending the resolution of that dispute at the enforcement stage.

**16.71**    In order to ensure that the third party claim is determined expeditiously, the court may make directions as to how the case should proceed under CrimPR r 61.5. The court may direct that the third party should serve his Points of Dispute and evidence in support within a specific time frame and that the prosecutor and defendant be at liberty to serve any list of issues and evidence in rebuttal within a specified period thereafter. Parties may then notify each other whether they require witnesses to attend for cross examination for the purposes of CrimPR r 61.6. See the case of *Backhouse*, above, on the importance of parties specifying the issues in dispute.

**16.72**    Before the hearing, it may be prudent for the third party to enter into negotiations with the prosecutor and defendant. As all parties will be anxious to resolve the matter expeditiously and at minimum cost, it may well be that the prosecutor and defendant would be prepared to take a commercial view and not press for the highest amount for which they could argue.

**Powers of the court and receiver in relation to third parties**

**16.73**    Under s 69(3)(a) of POCA, the powers of the court and the receiver must be exercised with a view to allowing a person, other than the defendant or a recipient of a tainted gift, to retain or recover the value of any interest held by him. It follows that the confiscation and enforcement powers conferred on the court and the receiver by the Act must be exercised with a view to allowing an innocent third party to retain or recover the value of any interest in realisable property held by him. Just as the High Court had the duty under s 82 CJA and s 31 DTA, it is the duty of the Crown Court under s 69(3)(a) of POCA to ensure that the value of the third party's interests in realisable property is preserved, and that duty is in priority to the duty of the court to preserve assets for payment of a confiscation order.

It is important to remember that while there is no right to be heard at the confiscation hear-  **16.74**
ing, a third party may be heard at the restraint or receivership stage of proceedings including at the enforcement stage (see *Re Nomis* cited above).

It should be noted that under s 84 of POCA, references to an interest in relation to land in  **16.75**
England and Wales are to a legal estate, or equitable interest or power (see s 84(2)(f)). This means that mere rights such as a right of occupation are not protected under s 69(3)(a).

### The role of the defendant

As already observed, the third party should serve his application and evidence on the defend-  **16.76**
ant as well as the prosecutor and should also involve him in any negotiations. The reason for this is that the defendant has a clear interest in the outcome of the proceedings. The greater the interest the court rules the third party has in the asset, the less the defendant will have from the proceeds of sale to satisfy the confiscation order. Accordingly, he may well wish either to dispute the third party's claim in its entirety or at least argue that the extent of the third party's interest is not as great as that claimed. As there is such a potential conflict of interest between the defendant and third party, the practice of their being represented by the same solicitors should generally be discouraged, even when there remains a close relationship between the defendant and the third party.

### The hearing

If the parties are unable to agree, the matter will usually be listed for hearing before a judge  **16.77**
in the Crown or High Courts. Applications for the resolution of third-party interests for the purpose of appointing management or enforcement receivers under ss 48 and 50 of POCA or varying their appointments under s 63 of POCA will proceed under Parts 60 and 61 of the CrimPR in the Crown Court. Those for the purposes of ss 26 and 29 of the DTA or ss 77 and 80 of the CJA will proceed under RSC Order 115.7 in the High Court with any applications being made in accordance with CPR Pt 23. The proceedings will determine:

(a) whether the third party has any interest in the asset at all; and
(b) if so, the extent of that interest.

The third party will normally be the applicant for relief so will open the proceedings and call  **16.78**
his or her evidence, followed by any of the defendant, prosecution, and/or receiver. Often a management receiver will be in place or the enforcement receiver will have been appointed but the trial of issue adjourned. In those circumstances the receiver will be able to become a party and conduct the proceedings by seeking directions or by seeking to vary his order under ss 62 or 63 of POCA. However it will usually be more time and cost efficient for the prosecution to litigate the issue of beneficial interests and it may have access to evidence and investigative techniques which the receiver does not.

Witness statement evidence will be admissible under the Criminal or Civil Procedure Rules  **16.79**
and will ordinarily stand as the witness's evidence in chief. Under CrimPR r 61.6 any party may apply to cross-examine a witness upon the statement and should the witness fail to attend their evidence will not be used without the court's permission. Hearsay evidence is

admissible under CrimPR r 61.8. Once all the evidence has been heard, the parties will have the right to make a closing address to the court in the usual way.

### The court's order

**16.80**  The order the court makes will depend on its findings of law and fact. If the court finds that the third party is the sole owner of the property in dispute, then clearly it cannot be incorporated in the receivership order because it is not realisable property of the defendant. Equally, if the court rules that the defendant is the sole owner of the asset, the entire net proceeds of sale will be applied to the satisfaction of the confiscation order and the third party will get nothing. Such situations are deceptively simple, as the matter becomes increasingly more complex when the court rules that the third party does have some interest in the asset.

**16.81**  In such circumstances, the court has a number of options under s 51(6) of POCA (or s 29 of the DTA and s 80 of the CJA). Firstly, it could order the receiver to sell the asset and pay to the third party from the net proceeds of sale an amount proportionate to his interest in the property. If, for example, the net proceeds of sale of the property in question were £50,000 and the third party's interest in the property was found to be 50 per cent, £25,000 would go to the third party and £25,000 towards the satisfaction of the confiscation order.

**16.82**  Alternatively, where the third party has the means to 'buy out' the defendant's interest in the property, the court may, under s 51(6)(a) of POCA (or s 29(6)(a) of the DTA and s 80(6) of the CJA), order the third party to pay to the receiver an amount equivalent to the value of the beneficial interest of the defendant in that property or, as the case may be, of the recipient of a gift caught by the Act. The court may order under s 51(6)(b) of POCA (or s 29(6)(b) of the DTA and s 80(6) of the CJA) that once such payment has been made, the defendant's interest in the property should be transferred to the third party and/or that the defendant's interest in the property be extinguished.

**16.83**  Section 51(6) of POCA states:

> The court—
> (a) may order a person holding an interest in realisable property to make to the receiver such payment as the Court specifies in respect of a beneficial interest held by the Defendant or the recipient of a tainted gift;
> (b) may (on the payment being made) by order transfer, grant or extinguish any interest in the property.

### Application of sums and third parties

**16.84**  Under s 54 of POCA, sums held by the receiver appointed by the Crown Court under s 50 of POCA that are the proceeds of the realisation of property under s 51, or sums in which the defendant holds an interest, must be applied as follows:

(a) they must be applied in payment for such expenses incurred by a person acting as an insolvency practitioner as are payable under this subsection by virtue of s 432;
(b) they must be applied in making any payments directed by the Crown Court; and
(c) they must be applied on the defendant's behalf towards satisfaction of the confiscation order. (See s 54(2).)

It follows, therefore, that where a third party had been successful in establishing their interest, under 54(2)(b) that interest should be satisfied in terms of the repayment of any money owing in priority to satisfaction of the confiscation order.

# D. Specific Third-Party Claims

### Beneficial interests in property

Often, third parties, be they the spouse or civil partner of the defendant, a cohabitee, family **16.85** member, or business partner, will assert that property held by the defendant in fact belongs beneficially to them. On occasion, the prosecution will seek to include an asset in a third party's name within the defendant's realisable property for the purposes of making the confiscation order on the basis that the 'reality' is that the asset belongs to the defendant. By virtue of s 84(2)(a) of POCA a person holds property if he holds any interest in it, whether it be legal or beneficial.

In determining what is realisable property for the purposes of ss 83–84 of POCA, the extent **16.86** of the defendant's interest therein, who is the beneficial owner of property, and in what share, the court is to have regard to ordinary principles of civil law. These are typically principles of contract, property, trust and company law and may also include concepts such as 'lifting the corporate veil'. The court must in addition apply the provisions of POCA, for example s 69 on the legislative steer and ss 77–78 on tainted gifts, which may modify the outcome that would otherwise be arrived at.

When considering joint interests in real property the court should begin by determining the case as if it were an application under the Trusts of Land and Appointment of Trustees Act 1996 ('TLATA'). In *Serious Fraud Office v Lexi Holdings PLC (In Administration)* [2008] EWCA Crim 1443; [2009] 2 WLR 905 the Court of Appeal noted that it may be appropriate for such questions to be determined by a judge of the Chancery Division of the High Court sitting as a Crown Court judge. Whether a decision to transfer a case to a specialist judge is taken may well depend on the complexity of the issues.

The starting point for the court will be the legal title—the burden is upon the party seeking to **16.87** establish that the beneficial interests in the property are held otherwise than as per the legal title. Following the speech of Baroness Hale, with whom the majority of the House of Lords agreed, at para 56 of *Stack v Dowden* [2007] UKHL 17; [2007] 2 AC 432 there is a presumption that property held in joint names is beneficially owned by the legal owners in equal shares and that property held in sole legal ownership is held in sole beneficial ownership. It is for the party asserting that the beneficial interests in property are not held as per the legal title to demonstrate that position.

### *Sole name cases*

In 'sole name' cases, where a property is held in the name of one party ('A') and another party **16.88** ('B') seeks to establish a beneficial interest in the same, B must firstly surmount the hurdle of showing that he or she has *any* interest in it ('the first question') before the court considers the extent of that interest ('the second question'). To obtain a positive answer to the first question, B must ordinarily show *either* a common intention, agreement, or understanding between the parties which he or she then relied upon to his or her detriment, *or* that he or she has made a financial contribution to its purchase: *Lloyds Bank plc v Rosset* [1991] 1 AC 107 (although in *Stack v Dowden*, it was considered that the test set out in *Lloyds v Rosset* may have set the bar too high).

**16.89** The Court of Appeal's judgment in *Oxley v Hiscock* [2004] 3 WLR 715 provides a useful starting point on this area of the law. At paras 68 and 69 of his judgment Lord Justice Chadwick, having reviewed the authorities, provided a summary:

> 68. . . . cases in which the common features are: (i) the property is bought as a home for a couple who, although not married, intend to live together as man and wife; (ii) each of them makes some financial contribution to the purchase; (iii) the property is purchased in the sole name of one of them; and (iv) there is no express declaration of trust. In those circumstances the first question is whether there is evidence from which to infer a common intention, communicated by each to the other, that each shall have a beneficial share in the property. In many such cases—of which the present is an example—there will have been some discussion between the parties at the time of the purchase which provides the answer to that question. Those are cases within the first of Lord Bridge's categories in *Lloyds Bank Plc v Rosset*. In other cases—where the evidence is that the matter was not discussed at all—an affirmative answer will readily be inferred from the fact that each has made a financial contribution. Those are cases within Lord Bridge's second category. And, if the answer to the first question is that there was a common intention, communicated to each other, that each should have a beneficial share in the property, then the party who does not become the legal owner will be held to have acted to his or her detriment in making a financial contribution to the purchase in reliance on the common intention.
>
> 69. In those circumstances, the second question to be answered in cases of this nature is 'what is the extent of the parties' respective beneficial interests in the property?' Again, in many such cases, the answer will be provided by evidence of what they said and did at the time of the acquisition. But, in a case where there is no evidence of any discussion between them as to the amount of the share which each was to have—and even in a case where the evidence is that there was no discussion on that point—the question still requires an answer. It must now be accepted that (at least in this Court and below) the answer is that each is entitled to that share which the court considers fair having regard to the whole course of dealing between them in relation to the property. And, in that context, 'the whole course of dealing between them in relation to the property' includes the arrangements which they make from time to time in order to meet the outgoings (for example, mortgage contributions, council tax and utilities, repairs, insurance, and housekeeping) which have to be met if they are to live in the property as their home.

**16.90** In *Grant v Edwards* [1986] Ch 638, it was held by the Court of Appeal that where an excuse was provided for not putting a party's name on a property, that of itself could be considered enough to demonstrate the common intention of the parties. At p 649 of the judgment, Nourse LJ stated that:

> these facts appear to me to raise a clear inference that there was an understanding between the plaintiff and the defendant, or a common intention, that the plaintiff was to have some sort of proprietary interest in the house; otherwise no excuse for not putting her name onto the title would have been needed.

**16.91** As regards the 'detriment' that must be shown, in the same case, Sir Nicholas Browne-Wilkinson VC considered that:

> As at present advised, once it has been shown that there was a common intention that the claimant should have an interest in the house, any act done by her to her detriment relating to the joint lives of the parties is, in my judgment, sufficient detriment to qualify. The acts do not have to be inherently referable to the house.

*Joint names cases*

**16.92** In 'joint names' cases, the first question is presumed to already have been answered in the affirmative—the fact that a property is held in joint names is strong evidence that the parties gave thought to ownership, and decided that it should be joint. A party wishing to demonstrate that the property is to be held other than in equal shares must show an agreement or understanding to that effect. The mere fact of contribution to the purchase price in different shares will not be sufficient to displace that presumption (per *Stack v Dowden*).

In determining the extent of each party's share in the property (ie the 'second question'), the court will initially consider whether there was an agreement as to what those shares would be. In *Stack v Dowden*, Baroness Hale confirmed that: 'The search is to ascertain the parties' shared intentions, actual, inferred or imputed, with respect to the property in light of their whole course of conduct in relation to it' (para 60). **16.93**

That agreement can either be express, or inferred from the objective facts of the case. In the event that the court cannot find that there was an express or inferred agreement as to the extent of the shares, it may impute an agreement, that the shares would be whatever the court considers fair, having regard to the whole course of dealing between the parties (*Jones v Kernott* [2011] UKSC 53). The 'whole course of dealing' is not limited to financial contributions and will include eg contributions by way of bringing up a family. As regards the extent of that interest, Baroness Hale, at para 61 of *Stack v Dowden*, cited with approval the view of the Law Commission that there was much to be said for the adoption of: 'a "holistic approach" to quantification, undertaking a survey of the whole course of dealing between the parties and taking account of all conduct which throws light on the question what shares were intended'. At para 69, she continued: **16.94**

> In law, 'context is everything' and the domestic context is very different from the commercial world. Each case will turn on its own facts. Many more factors than financial contributions may be relevant to divining the parties' true intentions. These include: any advice or discussions at the time of the transfer which cast light upon their intentions then; the reasons why the home was acquired in their joint names... the purpose for which the home was acquired; the nature of the parties' relationship; whether they had children for whom they both had a responsibility to provide a home; how the purchase was financed, both initially and subsequently; how the parties arranged their finances, whether separately or together or a bit of both; how they discharged the outgoings on the property and their other household expenses...

### If criminal funds are used to fund the property, is the position affected?

In *Gibson v Revenue and Customs Prosecutions Office* [2008] EWCA Civ 645; [2009] 2 WLR 471, the Court of Appeal considered the beneficial interests in a property with legal title held in the joint names of a husband and wife. It held that, despite the proceeds of the husband's criminal offending having been used to fund payments under the mortgage on a jointly-held property, this could not operate to reduce Mrs Gibson's 50 per cent share in the property. In his confiscation proceedings at the Crown Court the husband was found to hold the sole beneficial interest in the property. At the enforcement stage of proceedings in the High Court, in line with the guidance in *Norris* [2001] 1 WLR 1388, Mrs Gibson sought to assert her interest in the matrimonial home, which was held in joint names with Mr Gibson. The High Court had found that, although that property had been purchased before the commencement of Mr Gibson's criminality, a large number of mortgage payments had been made from funds which were the direct proceeds of Mr Gibson's crime. It also made findings that Mrs Gibson had had knowledge of this. It then applied the principles as he considered them to be as set out in *Customs and Excise Commissioners v A; A v A* [2003] 2 WLR 210 and *CPS v Richards* [2006] 2 FLR 1220, **16.95** and in light of Mrs Gibson's guilty knowledge he determined her share of the property to be 12.5 per cent.

16.96 The Court of Appeal allowed the appeal, and applying the House of Lords decision in *Stack v Dowden* [2007] UKHL 17, declared her share of the property to be 50 per cent. Accordingly, only 50 per cent would remain available for satisfaction of the confiscation order. Lord Justice May considered at para 18 that:

> [I]t seems to me quite impossible for the law, in the guise of public policy, to attribute to Mr and Mrs Gibson an intention which they plainly did not have and would never have assented to. The prosecution cannot, in my view, by the language of imputation achieve a confiscation of Mrs Gibson's assets which the law does not otherwise enable, by imposing on her a notional and fictitious intention. Indeed Mr Bartlett accepted in oral submission that Mr and Mrs Gibson did not change their intention, but that they changed the means of preserving the property.

16.97 There is logic in this approach. The two cases which the High Court had relied upon were cases relating to applications under the MCA 1973—ie cases in which the court was being invited to make orders using its discretion under that Act to redistribute assets upon divorce. Mrs Gibson had not sought an exercise of the court's powers under the MCA 1973, but had merely sought to assert her rights under trust principles. The property being in joint names and having been purchased from originally legitimate funds, there was therefore a presumption that she owned 50 per cent of it.

16.98 However, Arden LJ left open the question of how a property knowingly purchased with the proceeds of crime from the outset would be dealt with:

> 24. If the Gibsons had at the outset entered into an agreement to acquire the property jointly and to use the proceeds of crime to pay off the mortgage in whole or as to at least a substantial part, the agreement would be likely to have been wholly unenforceable.

In such circumstances a court may have determined Mrs Gibson not to have held any beneficial interest in the property. In addition, in such circumstances, the wife may also have been guilty of money laundering with any interest she held in the property being liable to be recovered under confiscation proceedings against her following conviction or in civil recovery proceedings under Part 5 of POCA.

16.99 *Gibson* was decided before *Jones v Kernott* (16.94 above) —where an actual agreement (be it express or inferred) about ownership is not shown, the court would be in a position to 'impute' an intention to the parties to own the property in such shares as the court considered 'fair', it is arguable that this would not include a share of criminal funds.

16.100 Furthermore, *Gibson* was a case decided on specific facts where the property was held in joint names, the couple was not divorcing, there was no contribution to the property's initial purchase from tainted funds, and there was no suggestion that the wife's interest in the property had been a gift for the purposes of the DTA. Had the wife's interest in the property been determined to be a gift from her husband then it would have been recoverable as realisable property. The Court of Appeal in *Gibson* found support for its position in *R v Buckman* [1997] 1 Cr App R (S) 325, where Brooke LJ said (p 329) that the correct approach, where property is held in joint names, is for the court to start with the prima facie position as to where the beneficial interests lay and then go on to find whether there are gifts caught by the Act which ought then to increase the realisable value of the property within the meaning of s

6 of the DTA. On this basis, if Mrs Gibson's beneficial interest was not wholly or partly a gift caught by the Act, and if it was not otherwise within the confiscatory ambit of the legislation, it did not fall to be confiscated.

In *In the Matter of Stephen Edwards v CPS* [2011] EWHC 1688, it was held that a presumption of the beneficial interest in a property being held as per the legal interest could be displaced where the source of the funds used for purchase emanated from criminal monies. At para 39, Cranston J stated: **16.101**

> The flow of unlawful monies from 1996 has a bearing on the issues before me, since how a purchase is financed is one of the factors identified by Baroness Hale in Stack v Dowden [2007] UKHL 17, [2007] 2 AC 432, [2007] 2 All ER 929 as relevant to the common intention of the parties as to beneficial ownership of the property purchased.

Therefore Mrs Edwards was held not to be entitled to 50 per cent of the beneficial interest in a property which had been substantially purchased from the proceeds of crime.

### Significant capital payments

*Gibson* concerned a case where the tainted funds paid towards the property were the ongoing monthly mortgage repayments. In ordinary TLATA cases, where one party has made a significant improvement to a property (eg by way of an extension) from funds which were exclusively theirs, it is still arguable after *Stack v Dowden* that this is evidence that the parties intended that contribution to be taken into account in determining their beneficial interests. The principles of equitable accounting also remain relevant (see eg *Re Pavlou (a bankrupt)* [1993] 1 WLR 1046). In circumstances where one joint owner of a property has made a significant contribution to the same, the other party would be expected to account to them for that contribution. In *W v W* [2012] EWHC 2469 (Fam), the wife of the defendant asserted a 50 per cent interest in the matrimonial home and a 50 per cent interest in a holiday chalet, each of which were held in joint names with the defendant. The Crown argued that payments made by the defendant should be treated as gifts. Ryder J considered that: **16.102**

> In so far as regular payments, such as ordinary amounts of mortgage and payments of regular outgoings are concerned, there is a well established answer to this submission, namely that the wife provides consideration by bringing up the children and looking after the home i.e. the payments are not gifts at all (see for example, para [10] of Gibson). The Crown is on stronger ground, however, in relation to irregular or extraordinary payments.

In the circumstances, he considered that, in relation to sums of €500,000 and £56,000 paid by the defendant towards renovating the holiday chalet from tainted funds, the wife should provide an equitable account for those sums.

In cases where property is stolen, or obtained through fraud, it is arguable that the thief, or person committing the fraud, holds the proceeds of the same on a constructive trust for the victim. See eg the comments of the Court in *Westdeutsche Landesbank Girozentrale v Islington LBC* [1996] AC 669. At p 715, Lord Browne Wilkinson noted: **16.103**

> The argument for a resulting trust was said to be supported by the case of a thief who steals a bag of coins. At law those coins remain traceable only so long as they are kept separate: as soon as they are mixed with other coins or paid into a mixed bank account they cease to be traceable at law. Can it really be the case, it is asked, that in such circumstances the thief cannot be required to disgorge the property which, in equity, represents the stolen coins? Moneys can only be traced in equity if there has been at some stage a breach of fiduciary duty, ie if either before

the theft there was an equitable proprietary interest (eg the coins were stolen trust moneys) or such interest arises under a resulting trust at the time of the theft or the mixing of the moneys. Therefore, it is said, a resulting trust must arise either at the time of the theft or when the moneys are subsequently mixed. Unless this is the law, there will be no right to recover the assets representing the stolen moneys once the moneys have become mixed. I agree that the stolen moneys are traceable in equity. But the proprietary interest which equity is enforcing in such circumstances arises under a constructive, not a resulting, trust. Although it is difficult to find clear authority for the proposition, when property is obtained by fraud equity imposes a constructive trust on the fraudulent recipient: the property is recoverable and traceable in equity.

**16.104** It may therefore be said that where the offence in question is one of theft or fraud, the prosecution will be in a position to argue that the defendant was not in a position to transfer ownership of those tainted funds to the other joint owner, as they were subject to a constructive trust in favour of the victim of the offence. However, in *Halifax Building Society v Tomas* [1996] Ch 217 it was considered that there is no universal principle that wherever there is a personal fraud the fraudster will become a trustee for the party injured by the fraud.

**16.105** Similar arguments were considered in the case of *Independent Trustee Services Ltd v (1) GP Noble Trustees Ltd (2) Susan Morris* [2012] 3 All ER 210—in that case, a sum of £1.48 million had been paid to Mrs Morris by her husband pursuant to a financial order made between them on their divorce. That sum represented trust monies misappropriated by Mr Morris from pension funds. The Court of Appeal considered that Mrs Morris had a defence to a claim by the beneficiaries for repayment of the sum—she had not known about the offending and the giving up of her claims on divorce upon payment of the sum amounted to consideration—she was, in reality, a bona fide purchaser for value without notice and so could defeat the beneficiaries' claim. However, upon that financial remedy order being set aside (as it had been on her application), the beneficiaries of the trust monies were able to reassert their interest in the funds.

### Recipients of gifts for the purposes of the Acts

**16.106** Gifts which meet the statutory definitions in POCA (ss 77–78), as set out in Chapter 9, will constitute realisable property and hence become recoverable at the enforcement stage under the Acts. In this situation conventional property law will not necessarily apply to the recoverability of property representing gifts and the legislative steer in POCA does not protect the recipient (see s 69(2)(c) and (3)(a) and (b)). A third party who is a recipient of a gift from the defendant as determined in confiscation proceedings under POCA, CJA, or DTA will not receive the same protection under law as they might in normal circumstances even though they may hold the full beneficial interest in the gift. The third party may have the opportunity to challenge whether the property was in fact a gift for the purposes of the Act at the enforcement stage under the principles set out above in *Re Norris* (because they were not party to or represented at the confiscation hearing even if they were a witness). However, if the third party does not challenge the finding that their property was a gift or that challenge fails and the property is deemed to remain a gift as part of any restraint or receivership proceedings then under s 69(3)(b) of POCA the powers of the court or receiver will be exercised to realise the value of that gift. This may be effected either by the third party making a realistic alternative offer such as a payment to the magistrates' court or to the receiver to the value of the gift. Alternatively, if the recipient cannot do so, the court may use its discretion to appoint the receiver to sell the recipient's property which represents the value of the gift. In *Re B (Confiscation Order)* [2008] EWHC 690 (Admin); [2008] 2 FLR 1 the High Court appointed an enforcement receiver (under s 80 of the CJA) over the 50 per cent interest in a property which it found had been a gift to the wife by her husband for the purposes of the Act. The wife also held her undisputed share, the remaining 50 per cent interest in the property, which was not realisable property. Even though the gift was not made by the husband to the wife in order to evade confiscation proceedings and the wife was innocent of any wrongdoing, the Court reluctantly gave the receiver the power of sale over the property in order to realise the 50 per cent interest in the property representing the gift. However the power was suspended for six months in order to enable her to attempt other payment methods. A receiver was appointed with immediate effect over a property which wholly represented a gift from mother to son in *Re Ford-Sagers sub nom Brenda Ford-Sagers v Theodore Ford-Sagers* [2011] EWHC 2217 (Admin).

### Position of wives

Wives enjoy little more protection under the Acts than other third parties. The law of **16.107** England and Wales does not recognise any general concept of 'family property'. This was noted in *Stack v Dowden* where, in discussion of previous decisions of the House of Lords (as was), Lord Walker of Gestingthorpe noted at para 16 that: '[The Court] was almost unanimous in rejecting any general doctrine of "family assets" and in the view that (at least as between husband and wife) the presumption of advancement was no longer appropriate for determining property disputes.' Accordingly, the starting point for wives, as with any other third party, is whether they can demonstrate a beneficial interest in property held by the defendant. Practitioners are perhaps more likely to find themselves advising wives on their position under confiscation legislation than any other third party. The first occasion on which a solicitor is likely to be approached is immediately after a restraint order has been served. At this stage, the wife may well be in a state of some distress; not only may her husband be in custody facing serious criminal charges, but she may find herself served with a restraint order freezing all of her husband's realisable property, including items in which she may hold a joint interest. It is possible to give her some reassurance at this stage.

Firstly, although the matrimonial home may be subject to restraint or charging orders, she **16.108** is entitled to remain in residence pending the conclusion of the proceedings. The restraint order merely prevents her from disposing of realisable property and does not prevent its use pending the determination of the proceedings against her husband. The same principle would apply to motor vehicles, namely that they may continue to be used by the wife, but not sold. The wife should be advised that if at any time she wishes to sell an asset, she must not do so, but should return to the solicitor forthwith. It may well be that if she wishes to move to a smaller house or buy a smaller motor vehicle, the prosecution and defendant would readily consent to a variation of the restraint order to enable her to do so, subject to the new asset being immediately made subject to restraint and any surplus funds being paid into an interest-bearing account pending the conclusion of the proceedings. As well as being warned of the potential consequences of an unlawful sale, a wife should also be advised that, in so far as she is able, she should ensure that the asset is properly maintained in the interim. If she were to allow a property to deteriorate, or fail to keep up mortgage payments, this could provide a basis for the prosecution applying to appoint a pre-conviction management receiver.

Joint bank accounts can create particular problems when they are restrained. It may well **16.109** be that the wife's salary is paid into such an account, or that they contain other monies belonging solely to her. First, she should be advised to open a bank account in her sole name and arrange for all future salary payments, together with any other payments to which she alone is entitled, to be paid into that account. The prosecution should be notified that she intends to do this. Secondly, as to any monies belonging solely to her that are already in the account at the time the restraint order is served, she should be asked to provide documentary evidence (eg salary advice, letter from her employer, etc) to prove her entitlement. This should then be forwarded to the prosecution who will normally consent to the order being varied to release from the account monies belonging solely to her that do not constitute realisable property of the defendant. If the prosecution will not agree, an application to court should be considered.

**16.110**  The wife is also entitled, pending the conclusion of the criminal proceedings against her husband, to expect her reasonable needs to be provided for. She would, therefore, be entitled to ask the court to vary the restraint order to allow reasonable sums to be released from the restraint order to pay the reasonable living expenses of herself and her family if she has no independent and sufficient assets or income of her own. This is the case even where she has separated from the defendant—see eg *R v AW* [2010] EWCA Crim 3123.

**16.111**  Restraint orders typically contain a proviso that spending limits for living expenses may be increased on the following terms:

> The Defendant and Mrs X may agree with the (Prosecutor) that the above spending limits for living expenses should be increased, and the Defendant (and the Prosecutor) may agree this order may be varied in any respect but any such agreement must be in writing.

Where agreement cannot be reached in relation to living expenses the matter should be listed before the court for determination.

**16.112**  In so far as a wife is able to show that she is beneficially entitled to property, she will be able to retain the same. When advising a wife, serious consideration should therefore be given to bringing a claim under TLATA, as set out in the paragraphs above. This will be relevant whether or not she intends to divorce the defendant. If she does intend to proceed with a divorce (or judicial separation), she may make an application under the MCA 1973 for financial relief. However, the powers of the court when faced with an application under the MCA 1973 are discretionary—accordingly, if she can prove a pre-existing beneficial interest, she will not need to rely upon the provisions of the Act.

**16.113**  The court may give the wife the option of buying out her husband's interest in the property. She may be able to persuade the court to exercise its discretion under s 51(9) of POCA (or s 29(5) of the DTA or s 80(5) of the CJA) to direct that the house should not be realised for a specific period to give her a reasonable opportunity either of finding alternative accommodation or raising the finance to buy out her husband's interest in the property. She may well also find the receiver, anxious to avoid a forced sale, will have some sympathy for her position and will be prepared to negotiate.

### Matrimonial proceedings and the position under POCA

**16.114**  Where parties to a marriage end that marriage through divorce or judicial separation, either party to the marriage may apply for financial orders under Part II of MCA 1973. The court may make a variety of orders in favour of the applicant, including orders for periodical payments (maintenance), lump sum payment orders, transfer of property orders, or pension sharing orders, and order certain variations of nuptial trusts. On the whole, when considering an application for financial remedy, the court does not take particular account of beneficial interests held by the spouses. The orders made are pursuant to the court's discretion, rather than being related to the parties' proprietary interests in assets. In ordinary financial remedy proceedings, there is therefore limited value in either party asserting an interest in particular assets (although this can become more relevant where the marriage is a short one, and where the court is less concerned with 'sharing' the assets).

Section 25 of MCA 1973 sets out a list of considerations for the court when determining an application for financial remedy—these have been expanded upon by authority. In brief, the statutory considerations are: **16.115**

- 'first consideration' must be given to the welfare while a minor of any child of the family who has not attained the age of eighteen,
- the income, earning capacity, property, and other financial resources which each of the parties to the marriage has or is likely to have in the foreseeable future, including, in the case of earning capacity, any increase in that capacity which it would in the opinion of the court be reasonable to expect a party to the marriage to take steps to acquire;
- the financial needs, obligations, and responsibilities which each of the parties to the marriage has or is likely to have in the foreseeable future;
- the standard of living enjoyed by the family before the breakdown of the marriage;
- the age of each party to the marriage and the duration of the marriage;
- any physical or mental disability of either of the parties to the marriage;
- the contributions which each of the parties has made or is likely in the foreseeable future to make to the welfare of the family, including any contribution by looking after the home or caring for the family;
- the conduct of each of the parties, if that conduct is such that it would in the opinion of the court be inequitable to disregard it;
- the value to each of the parties to the marriage of any benefit which, by reason of the dissolution or annulment of the marriage, that party will lose the chance of acquiring.

Where a confiscation order has been made, the court is not precluded from exercising its discretion in the wife's favour under MCA 1973. She may still seek an order under the Act, notwithstanding the restraint and/or confiscation order. Whilst the court must have regard to the 'legislative steer' of the Act, this does not 'oust' the court's statutory discretion to make an order under s 23 or s 24 of MCA 1973. The leading authority remains *Customs and Excise Commissioners v A and another; A v A* [2002] EWCA Civ 1039; [2003] 2 WLR 210, in relation to the DTA, in which Schiemann LJ stated (At p 222): **16.116**

> In my judgment, there is nothing in the provisions of either the 1973 Act or the 1994 Act which requires the court to hold that either statute takes priority over the other when the provisions of each are invoked in relation to the same property. Both statutes confer discretion on the court, which the court may or may not choose to exercise, to make orders. The terms of those orders will depend on the facts of the individual case.

However, the court also considered that: 'There can be no question of the 1973 Act being used as a means to circumvent the provisions of the 1994 Act, and I am confident that the judges will be acutely alert to ensure that this is not the case' (per Judge LJ). **16.117**

**16.118**  It is unlikely to be enough for a wife to simply assert eg that the marriage has been a long one, and therefore she should retain half of the assets. Factors which were relevant in *A v A* included:

(a)  the wife already beneficially held more than 50 per cent in the property she was seeking to have transferred to her;

(b)  the husband's criminal conduct had begun after the parties had separated—the wife had had no involvement or knowledge whatsoever of that conduct;

(c)  a significant proportion of the confiscation order had already been paid—some £29,000 remained outstanding.

**16.119**  It is also likely that the more the wife can couch her arguments in terms of needs (in particular, the needs of any minor children), the more likely she will be to obtain a favourable order. If she greatly overstates her claim, relief granted may nevertheless be limited to those needs (see eg *MN v SN* [2005] EWHC 2623).

**16.120**  Section 41 of POCA confers on the Crown Court the power to make a restraint order prohibiting any specified person from dealing with any realisable property held by him and the subsequent ss 41 to 60 deal with the Crown Court's powers in relation to restraint, receivers, and enforcement of confiscation orders.

**16.121**  Section 42(3) of POCA permits an application to discharge or vary a restraint order to be made to the Crown Court by the person who applied for the restraint order or any person affected by that order (such as a wife).

**16.122**  Section 69 of POCA provides the following legislative steer to courts exercising powers under ss 42 to 60:

(2)  The powers—
   (a)  must be exercised with the view for the value for the time being of realisable property being made available (by the property's realisation) for satisfying any confiscation order that has been made or may be made against the defendant;
   (b)  must be exercised, in a case where a confiscation order has not yet been made with a view to securing that there is no diminution in the value of the realisable property . . .
(3)  Sub-section (2) has effect subject to the following rule—
   (a)  the powers must be exercised with a view to allowing a person other than the defendant or recipient of the tainted gift to retain or recover the value of any interest held by him . . .

**16.123**  By use of the phrase 'with a view to' in the preceding subsections, the language of s 69 of POCA retains the same terminology as that which appeared in s 31 of the DTA and s 82 of the CJA. There is nothing in the wording of POCA to suggest that the meaning of those words is different, or should be applied any differently, from the interpretation of the Administrative Court in *Customs & Excise v A*.

**16.124**  In *Stodgell v Stodgell* [2009] EWCA 243; [2009] 2 FLR 244 Lord Justice Hughes stated: 'I should just briefly draw attention to the significant tightening of the statutory rules made in the subsequent statute, the Proceeds of Crime Act 2002—see section 69(2)(c) and the recent decision of this court and the Criminal Division in *SFO v Lexi Holdings* [2008] EWCA Crim 1443.' However, no guidance was given as to what impact that might have on an application under the MCA 1973, and to date, no authority appears to specifically deal with the point.

Although, like s 69(2)(c), the wording of s 69(2)(b) of POCA did not appear in the previous legislation and appears to tighten the legislative steer pre-confiscation it still employs the phrase 'with a view to'. Therefore the subsections are likely to retain such 'elasticity' as to permit a diminution in the available amount. It is submitted they will continue to contemplate striking an appropriate balance between the same competing public policy considerations of confiscating the proceeds of crime and making proper financial provision for a wife, per para 42, *Webber v Webber and CPS* [2006] EWHC 2893 (Fam); [2007] 1 WLR 1052; [2007] 2 FLR 116, where the President of the Family Division held:

> 42. .... For the reasons given in *Customs & Excise v A*, injustice may be caused by too rigid an application of the confiscation principle where the interests of an 'innocent' or former spouse are concerned. Removal of the discretion of the High Court to make financial provision in such circumstances would be a substantial change in the law and the jurisdiction of the High Court and it is clear to me that the effect of MCA 1973 remains unaltered in that respect.
>
> 43. Thus, at the time that the matter came before me, it was clear that the High Court had the power to make a property adjustment order in favour of the wife to an extent which went beyond the half share conceded by the CPS not to be tainted as the proceeds of crime.

**16.125** In *Webber v Webber* it was considered more appropriate for the financial remedy proceedings to be disposed of first. However, whether the financial remedy or confiscation proceedings should be determined first is likely to depend on a number of factors—eg if there may be a surplus of assets depending on the confiscation figure, it is likely to be preferable for the size of the confiscation order to be determined first so that the wife and prosecution can know whether there is genuinely likely to be a dispute between them. In *Webber* the President indicated:

> 52. .... it was plainly preferable that the ancillary relief application should be disposed of first. By that means, on restoration of the adjourned hearing of the confiscation proceedings in the Crown Court [the judge] would be in a position to judge whether the amount available was 50% of the proceeds of sale, as conceded by the CPS, or required adjustment in the light of the findings of the High Court judge hearing the ancillary relief application.

**16.126** It appears, therefore, that where an innocent wife has asked for her financial remedy application to be dealt with at the same time as confiscation, the appropriate course may be for the financial remedy matter to be disposed of first by the High Court (or other family court), thus enabling the Crown Court judge to make the appropriate determination in relation to what assets remain. The prosecutor would still retain a right to intervene in such proceedings under s 58(5) and (6) of POCA if there is a restraint order in place. The alternative would be to attempt to transfer both matters to a judge entitled to sit in both the Family Division of the High Court and the Crown Court to determine both sets of proceedings at the same hearing. For further discussion on the order of proceedings see para 16.133. Directions may be set in accordance with the guidelines laid down by Munby J in *W v H, and Her Majesty's Customs & Excise* [2004] EWHC 526 and the Family Procedure Rules 2010.

**16.127** Under s 58(5) of POCA, if a court in which proceedings are pending in respect of any property is satisfied that a restraint order has been applied for or made in respect of the property, the court may either stay the proceedings or allow them to continue on any terms it thinks fit. Thus, if a restraint or receivership order is in place over the assets, the legislative steer set out in s 69 of POCA, as dealt with above, will apply to the family court proceedings where the court is considering a lump sum or a property adjustment order under s 24 or s 25 of the MCA 1973.

### Exercise of the court's discretion—'taint'

**16.128**  The case of *Crown Prosecution Service v Richards & Richards* [2006] EWCA Civ 849; [2006] 2 FLR 1220 was one in which the court found that the majority of the assets had been 'tainted' by the husband's criminal activities—the proceeds of his crimes could be traced into the matrimonial assets over which the wife sought an order, and the great majority of the assets had been acquired from those proceeds. Further, it was found that the wife had in fact been aware of her husband's criminal activities, and of the fact that the proceeds of his crimes had been used towards the matrimonial assets.

**16.129**  The Court of Appeal considered that in such a case, the court should not exercise its discretion in the wife's favour. At para 26 of the judgment Lord Justice Thorpe noted:

> Where assets are tainted and subject to confiscation they should ordinarily, as a matter of justice and public policy, not be distributed. This is not to say that the court is deprived of jurisdiction under the 1973 Act nor to say that no circumstances could exist in which an order would be justified; an example of a seriously disabled child living in specially adapted accommodation was mooted in argument. It is to say that, in most cases, and certainly in this one, the fact that the assets are tainted is the decisive factor in any balance. The error of the judge lay in thinking that the requirement to conduct a balancing exercise meant that in every case all factors are relevant. In cases such as this the knowledge of the wife, throughout her married life, that the lifestyle and the assets she enjoyed were derived from drug trafficking is dispositive.

**16.130**  It further considered whether, in such a case, it would be possible to make an order for the benefit of the parties' son who was innocent of any wrongdoing. However, it concluded: 'This is, of course, another sad example, all too familiar to family judges, of the fact that the court cannot protect children from every consequence of their parents' behaviour.'

**16.131**  It accordingly becomes important for both the prosecutor and the applicant to establish the extent of the wife's knowledge of and involvement in the criminality. It will also be important for the prosecutor to consider whether it is possible to trace the proceeds of the defendant's crimes into the available assets—a process which is not usually required under the criminal legislation.

### Exercise of the court's discretion—'debt'

**16.132**  *Stodgell v Stodgell* [2009] EWCA 243; [2009] 2 FLR 244 was a case in which the husband had evaded paying the full amount of his income tax due over a lengthy period. The amount of the confiscation order made against him (some £900,000) was comprised of the amount of tax owing, coupled with interest and penalties. The assets available were, by the time the court considered the wife's financial remedy application, less than this. It was agreed that the wife had no beneficial interest in the assets, and was seeking an order purely pursuant to the court's discretion. Holman J had considered that no order should be made in her favour. The Court of Appeal agreed. Whilst the wife herself had been ignorant of the wrongdoing, this in itself was not enough for an order to be made in her favour. In particular, where HMRC could have simply elected to bring civil proceedings for the amount of the debt due, thus bankrupting the defendant, the reality was that there were no assets left from which to make an order in the wife's favour. *Stodgell* was a tax case and has not yet been applied in subsequent authorities. However, it is arguable that similar considerations will arise where there can be said to be an 'equal and equivalent' civil debt to the amount of the confiscation order.

**MCA 1973 order made first**

In *Customs & Excise v A*, the prosecution had been willing to concede that, had an order **16.133** under MCA 1973 been made prior to the restraint order, it would have taken priority. The Court did not agree with that position. Judge LJ (as he then was) stated at para 92 that:

> Looking at the matter generally, the outcome should not depend on whether an order made under the 1973 Act had been concluded in the wife's favour before the confiscation was made against her husband. Carried to its logical conclusion that would offer a material advantage to a spouse who rushed into divorce and ancillary relief proceedings as soon as she discovered the slightest grounds for suspicion that her husband was involved in drug dealing and a corresponding disadvantage if she delayed...A further consequence would be an unseemly competition between the prosecution and the Crown Court, where the wife would not be heard, and the solicitors acting for the wife in ancillary proceedings, from which the prosecution would be absent. First come, first served, would be unlikely to produce a just result. These are persuasive arguments for the view that, notwithstanding any perceived 'priority', the decision of the courts should not be confined to enforcement of a confiscation order first and exclusively, but even where a confiscation order has been made, provided the circumstances justify (for example, as here, where a wholly innocent spouse and property untarnished by drug dealing or its profits are involved), the enforcement process should at least acknowledge the existence of the 1973 Act and the power of the court to exercise its discretion by taking account of the interests of the innocent spouse as well as the criminal defendant.

For further on timing of the orders see paras 16.125–16.126 above. The importance of the **16.134** timing of an order was, however, illustrated in *Independent Trustee Services Ltd v (1) GP Nobel Trustees Ltd (2) Susan Morris* [2012] 3 All ER 210. Mr Morris had paid Mrs the sum of £1.48 million pursuant to a financial remedy order. Unbeknown to her, this money originated directly from pension funds from which Mr Morris had misappropriated significant sums. Mrs Morris later discovered that her husband had not provided full disclosure of his assets to her (a requirement in financial remedy proceedings) and had the order set aside on the basis of non-disclosure. In the meantime, the beneficiaries of the pension schemes were successful in the Chancery Division in obtaining an order that they were the beneficial owner of the misappropriated trust monies, including the £1.48 million.

The Court of Appeal considered that, until the financial remedy order had been set aside, **16.135** Mrs Morris had a defence to any claim by the beneficiaries—she was a bona fide purchaser without notice. She had not known of her husband's offending and the giving up of her financial remedy claims had amounted to good consideration for the transfer of the funds. However, once that order was set aside, she was no longer able to defeat the claims of the beneficiaries.

**Costs**

In *Crown Prosecution Service v Piper* [2011] EWHC 3570 the Court held that the applicant **16.136** wife held a 50 per cent beneficial interest in the matrimonial home (by reason of trust principles). The Court made an order for costs against the CPS, who had contested the claim in its entirety and had not made any admissible offers to settle. Holman J stated:

> My overall view is that although I am very sympathetic to the CPS, I cannot justifiably in this case depart from the general rule. Janet Piper is not tainted by the criminal offending. From the first in this intervention she has put forward a properly judged and not exaggerated claim. She has been wholly successful, and it would be unjust to her now to deny her her costs

**16.137**  In family proceedings the 'normal rule' is that the court makes no order as to costs—ie each party will pay their own costs (see eg r 28.3 of the Family Procedure Rules 2010). However, where a third party is involved (ie the prosecutor), the court will revert to principles more akin to those in ordinary civil procedure, and may make costs orders against unsuccessful parties. It is therefore wise for all parties to consider negotiation if they wish to avoid adverse costs awards.

### Trusts

**16.138**  For confiscation orders and family trusts, see *R v Stannard* [2005] EWCA Crim 2717. In *R v Sharma* [2006] EWCA Crim 16; [2006] 2 Cr App R (S) 63, the Court of Appeal held that there was no room for the application of trust principles and the application of the normal legal consequences that might flow from the receipt of money for others when determining whether a person had benefited from criminal conduct. The definition of how benefit arises under s 76(4) POCA is to be followed. However, the principles do apply when it comes to determining beneficial interests in realisable property under ss 83 and 84 of POCA for the purpose of enforcing confiscation orders. In *Larkfield Ltd v RCPO and others* [2010] EWCA Civ 521; [2010] 3 All ER 1173 the Court of Appeal held that the usual principles of company and trust law applied in determining third-party interests in confiscation enforcement. Those principles are always subject to other doctrines such as lifting the corporate veil or property representing gifts for the purposes of the Act, however they did not apply on the facts of the case.

### Tenants

**16.139**  By virtue of s 84 of POCA, references to an interest in relation to land in England and Wales are to a legal estate, or equitable interest or power (see s 84(2)(f) of POCA), rather than rights such as a right of occupation. Accordingly, such rights are not protected under s 69(3)(a). However, in *LMB (in her capacity as enforcement receiver of EN) v EN, MA & JS* [2009] EWHC 2884 the Court took the view that the power under s 80(4) of the CJA to 'order any person having possession of realisable property to give possession of it' to a receiver could not be extended to cover tenants protected by contract and/or statute. The Court considered that clearer language would be required to expropriate a property right without compensation to the tenants. It noted that the general scheme of the confiscation legislation is to realise the criminal's assets, but not to infringe the property rights, procedural and/or substantive, of other parties who may themselves be innocent.

### Banks

**16.140**  Banks and other financial institutions frequently find themselves affected by the terms of restraint orders, as they remain a popular repository for the proceeds of crime. The bank should, on receiving a restraint order, ensure that any accounts specified in the order which they hold are frozen forthwith. Further, if the restraint order is in purely general terms, any further accounts in which the defendant holds an interest of which they are aware should be similarly restrained. The bank is not, however, under an obligation to search through its records in an attempt to trace any other accounts the defendant may hold, unless the prosecuting authority is prepared to pay for the reasonable costs of such an exercise.

**16.141**  The bank is also entitled to look to the prosecutor for reimbursement of its reasonable costs and expenses in complying with the order. Inevitably, however, there will from time to time be cases that are of greater than average complexity and involve the bank in more work. In such cases the bank would be justified in seeking a higher payment.

The restraint order does not prevent the bank from exercising any existing rights it may **16.142** have in relation to set-off or to combine accounts. This principle is well illustrated by *Re K (Restraint Order)* [1990] 2 All ER 562. A restraint order was served on the Bank of India in respect of bank accounts that contained a total of £639,541.87. A separate account, however, had an overdraft of £337,585.59 and the bank applied to the Court for a variation to the restraint order to enable it to combine the deposit and overdraft accounts so that the overdraft would be paid off leaving some £320,000 in the deposit accounts. Otton J allowed the application, ruling that a bank had an inherent right to combine the accounts and that by doing so it was merely carrying out an accounting exercise to determine the customer's indebtedness to the bank. The Court also ruled that, on the facts of the case, the bank had a right of set-off and that the exercise of that right did not constitute disposing of or diminishing or in any way dealing with the money and that by so doing the bank was not in contravention of the restraint order.

A more difficult problem arises in relation to a bank that has an office within the jurisdiction **16.143** of the court, but the account of the defendant is held at a branch overseas. If there is an agreement in force with the country in question, the account can be restrained by an order made in the courts of that jurisdiction, but considerable problems arise in relation to the defendant whose account is in a country where no such agreement exists.

### Banks: no duty of care

In *Customs and Excise Commissioners v Barclays Bank plc* [2006] UKHL 28, Barclays Bank **16.144** appealed against the decision that it owed a duty of care to Customs (a third party) to take reasonable care to ensure that no payments were made out of customer accounts that were subject to freezing injunctions. Customs had frozen two accounts while they sought payment of outstanding VAT, and the restraints specifically prohibited disposal of or dealing with any of the debtor companies' assets. The bank had been notified of the injunctions by fax. Only a matter of hours after receiving the freezing injunctions, Barclays had authorised transfers of substantial sums from the accounts. As a result Customs attempted to claim damages against Barclays for the sums paid out in breach of the freezing order.

The bank submitted that it did not owe a duty of care to avoid causing financial harm to **16.145** another unless it had voluntarily undertaken responsibility towards that other person.

The House of Lords held that the presence or absence of a voluntary assumption of respon- **16.146** sibility did not necessarily provide the answer in all cases. When the Court granted Customs their application, the purpose was to protect Customs by preventing the companies from parting with their assets. The freezing injunctions were directed at the companies as opposed to the bank. Barclays, itself a third party, would be in contempt of court only if it knowingly failed to freeze customer accounts subject to the freezing injunctions and authorised transfers of sums from the accounts after being notified of the court orders (see *Z Ltd v A-Z and others, sub nom Mareva Injunction* [1982] QB 558; [1982] 2 WLR 288, *A-G v Times Newspapers* [1991] 2 WLR 994 and *A-G v Punch Ltd* [2002] UKHL 50).

The Court held the failure to operate a system for freezing accounts did not mean that **16.147** Barclays was liable to Customs who had obtained the orders. Notification of the order placed a duty on Barclays to respect the order of the court, but it did not of itself generate a duty of care to Customs. Having obtained a freezing order and notified the bank, Customs could expect that any responsible bank would respect the order, but it could not rely on the bank doing so.

**16.148** Ultimately, Customs had to rely on the court to ensure that Barclays did not flout the orders and to punish Barclays if it did so. There was nothing that could be regarded as a voluntary assumption of responsibility by the bank for the way in which it would go about freezing the companies' accounts and there was nothing that involved Barclays in entering into any kind of relationship with Customs that required it to exercise such care as the circumstances required. The Court held that Barclays and Customs were about as far from being in a relationship 'equivalent to contract' as they could be, and therefore the Court held that in the circumstances it would not be fair to hold that Barclays owed a duty of care to Customs.

### The insolvent defendant: the position of the trustee in bankruptcy

**16.149** It happens from time to time that defendants involved in offences to which POCA, the DTA, and the CJA apply are made bankrupt. There are a variety of reasons for this. If the defendant is in custody, he will not be earning any income and will be unable to run any business he might own. Further, he may well already be in financial difficulty at the time of committing the alleged offences and, indeed, his impecunious state may well provide an explanation for his offending in the first place.

**16.150** In *R v Shahid (Abdul)* [2009] EWCA Crim 831 the Court of Appeal held that where a bankruptcy order had been made against an offender and all his assets were in the hands of his trustee in bankruptcy, it did not affect a judge's power to make a confiscation order—see Chapter 12 for further details. The Court found that whilst it might affect the enforcement of the confiscation order, it would not affect the making of it. For circumstances in which a court may interfere with a settlement following bankruptcy, see *Avis v (1) Turner (2) Avis* [2007] EWCA Civ 748.

## E. Conclusion

**16.151** Anecdotally, prosecuting authorities are very conscious of the difficulties that restraint orders can cause to innocent third parties and, in so far as the legislation allows, endeavour to deal with them fairly and in a way which takes account of their property rights. In the first instance, third parties and their solicitors who have any doubts as to their position, or who wish to deal with a particular asset, would be well advised to contact the prosecuting authority which obtained the restraint order to see if a mutually acceptable agreement can be reached.

# 17

# INVESTIGATIONS

## A. Introduction

If investigations by law enforcement agencies to trace the proceeds of criminal conduct are to **17.01** be truly effective, it is essential that they should have powers to compel third parties such as financial institutions, solicitors, accountants, etc to disclose information and produce documentation that may be relevant to their enquiries. Indeed, following the trail of the money often leads investigators to evidence of substantive offences such as frauds, drug trafficking, and the like.

In this chapter, we examine the powers of the court under the Proceeds of Crime Act 2002 **17.02** (POCA) to make production orders, account monitoring orders, customer information orders, and search and seizure warrants compelling third parties to hand over material they hold to law enforcement authorities to assist their investigations into criminal conduct. We also examine the powers given to the Crown Court and a magistrates' court under the Serious Organised Crime and Police Act 2005 (SOCPA) to make financial reporting orders against persons convicted of certain criminal offences.

**17.03**   The relevant provisions are now to be found in Pt 8 of POCA which came into force on 24 February 2003: see the Proceeds of Crime Act 2002 (Commencement No 4 Transitional Provisions and Savings) Order 2003, SI 2003/120. They apply to all investigations occurring after that date, irrespective of whether the investigation is in support of ongoing restraint and confiscation proceedings under the Drug Trafficking Act 1994 (DTA) or Criminal Justice Act 1988 (CJA).

# B. Defining Investigations

**17.04**   In addition to giving the Crown Court power to make production orders (s 345) and grant search and seizure warrants (s 352), Pt 8 of POCA also added a number of additional powers to the investigator's armoury, such as the ability to apply for disclosure orders (s 357), customer information orders (s 363), and account monitoring orders (s 370). The latter three powers were not, for example, contained within the CJA, which only provided for production orders (s 93H) and search and seizure warrants (s 93I).

**17.05**   Part 8 prescribes five types of investigation in relation to which these orders may be obtained: a confiscation investigation; a civil recovery investigation; a detained cash investigation; a money laundering investigation; and an exploitation proceeds investigation. These are defined in s 341(1)–(5) of POCA. This chapter will concentrate on confiscation, civil recovery, detained cash, and money laundering investigations which are defined in the following terms:

> **341 Investigations**
>
> (1)  For the purposes of this Part a confiscation investigation is an investigation into—
>> (a)  whether a person has benefited from his criminal conduct, or
>> (b)  the extent or whereabouts of his benefit from criminal conduct.
>
> (2)  For the purposes of this Part a civil recovery investigation is an investigation into—
>> (a)  whether property is recoverable property or associated property,
>> (b)  who holds the property, or
>> (c)  its extent or whereabouts.
>
> (3)  But an investigation is not a civil recovery investigation if—
>> (a)  proceedings for a recovery order have been started in respect of the property in question,
>> (b)  an interim receiving order applies to the property in question,
>> (c)  an interim administration order applies to the property in question, or
>> (d)  the property in question is detained under section 295.
>
> (3A)  For the purposes of this Part a detained cash investigation is—
>> (a)  an investigation for the purposes of Chapter 3 of Part 5 into the derivation of cash detained under section 295 or a part of such cash, or
>> (b)  an investigation for the purposes of Chapter 3 of Part 5 into whether cash detained under section 295, or a part of such cash, is intended by any person to be used in unlawful conduct.
>
> (4)  For the purposes of this Part a money laundering investigation is an investigation into whether a person has committed a money laundering offence.

**17.06**   The definition of 'confiscation investigation' in s 341(1) allows for such an investigation to continue even after a confiscation order has been made so long as the statutory criteria under s 341(1)(a) or (b) are met. The Divisional Court in *Horne and others v Central Criminal Court (1) CPS (2) HMRC* [2012] 1 WLR 3152 considered the situation where a prosecutor sought to obtain a disclosure order under s 357 of POCA and search and seizure warrants under s 352 of POCA. These orders were sought against the relatives of Raymond May who were deemed to hold relevant information regarding his assets following the making of a CJA confiscation order against him many years before. The confiscation proceedings had determined the extent of Mr May's benefit from criminal conduct, being the value of property obtained as a result of or in connection with unlawful conduct under s 71(4) of CJA. Unusually, however, the proceedings had not determined the whereabouts of that benefit. Therefore the investigation could continue post confiscation into the whereabouts of his benefit from criminal conduct for the purposes of s 341(1)(b) of POCA. That investigation necessitated searching his partner's property and car and asking questions of her, his wife, and his son. In identifying the whereabouts of his benefit, the prosecutor hoped to take enforcement action against the property representing the benefit to the extent that it also represented realisable property which might be used to satisfy the outstanding confiscation order.

The Divisional Court upheld this approach ruling that it was a lawful confiscation investigation and the dominant purpose of the investigation was not to identify legitimately acquired realisable property, for which there is no jurisdiction under s 341, but to identify benefit from criminal conduct. This benefit itself might also constitute or represent illegitimately acquired realisable property which might in turn be realised to satisfy a confiscation order. Therefore a confiscation investigation may proceed into realisable property to the extent it also represents benefit from criminal conduct so long as the statutory criteria are satisfied and this is the dominant purpose (see *ex parte Bowles*, cited below). However, law enforcement agencies remain prevented from seeking Pt 8 orders purely to obtain information for the purpose of identifying legitimately acquired realisable property. Where a confiscation order has already determined whether a defendant has benefited from criminal conduct and the extent and whereabouts of his benefit from such conduct there will be no jurisdiction to make any of the Pt 8 orders.

The definition of a civil recovery investigation under s 341(2)–(3) of POCA is to be amended by s 49 and Sch 19 to the Crime and Courts Act 2013 which was passed in April 2013. Schedule 19 has not yet come into force as of the time of writing. When it does, it will make the following substitution and addition to s 341:

(2)  For the purposes of this Part a civil recovery investigation is an investigation for the purpose of identifying recoverable property or associated property and includes investigation into—
   (a)  whether property is or has been recoverable property or associated property,
   (b)  who holds or has held property,
   (c)  what property a person holds or has held, or
   (d)  the nature, extent or whereabouts of property.
(3)  But an investigation is not a civil recovery investigation to the extent that it relates to—
   (a)  property in respect of which proceedings for a recovery order have been started,
   (b)  property to which an interim receiving order applies,
   (c)  property to which an interim administration order applies, or
   (d)  property detained under section 295.

After s 341 it will also insert a new subsection—

**341A Orders and warrants sought for civil recovery investigations**
Where an application under this Part for an order or warrant specifies property that is subject to a civil recovery investigation, references in this Part to the investigation for the purposes of which the order or warrant is sought include investigation into—

    (a) whether a person who appears to hold or to have held the specified property holds or has
        held other property,

    (b) whether the other property is or has been recoverable property or associated property, and

    (c) the nature, extent or whereabouts of the other property.

# C. Courts and Judges having Jurisdiction to Make Orders

## Judges

**17.07** In relation to confiscation or money laundering investigations in England and Wales, a judge entitled to exercise the jurisdiction of the Crown Court is empowered to make orders under Pt 8: see s 343(2)(a) of POCA.

**17.08** In relation to civil recovery or detained cash investigations, only a judge of the High Court has jurisdiction to make orders under Pt 8: see s 343(3) of POCA.

## Courts

**17.09** Similarly, s 344 of POCA provides that the court having jurisdiction in relation to confiscation or money laundering investigations is the Crown Court and, in relation to civil recovery or detained cash investigations, the High Court.

# D. Production Orders

## Jurisdiction to make the order

**17.10** Section 345(1) of POCA gives a judge power to make a production order if he is satisfied that all the requirements for making an order have been fulfilled. By s 345(2) applications for production orders must state that:

    (a) a person specified in the application is subject to a confiscation investigation or a money laundering investigation, or

    (b) property specified in the application is subject to a civil recovery investigation.

**17.11** In accordance with s 345(3) the application must also state that:

    (a) the material is sought for the purpose of the investigation;

    (b) the order is sought in relation to material, or material of a description, specified in the application;

    (c) a person specified in the application appears to be in possession or control of the material.

## Requirements for making the order

**17.12** These are set out in s 346 of POCA which provides as follows:

    (1) These are the requirements for the making of a production order.

    (2) There must be reasonable grounds for suspecting that—

        (a) in the case of a confiscation investigation, the person the application for the order specifies as being subject to the investigation has benefited from his criminal conduct;

        (b) in the case of a civil recovery investigation, the property the application of the order specifies as being subject to the investigation is recoverable property or associated property;

        (ba) in the case of a detained cash investigation into the derivation of cash, the property the application for the order specifies as being subject to the investigation, or a part of it, is recoverable property;

    (bb) in the case of a detained cash investigation into the intended use of cash, the prop-
        erty the application for the order specifies as being subject to the investigation, or a
        part of it, is intended by any person to be used in unlawful conduct;
    (c) in the case of a money laundering investigation, the person the application of the order
        specifies as being subject to the investigation has committed a money laundering offence.
    (d) …
(3) There must be reasonable grounds for believing that the person the application specifies
    as appearing to be in possession or control of the material so specified is in possession or
    control of it.
(4) There must be reasonable grounds for believing that the material is likely to be of sub-
    stantial value (whether or not by itself) to the investigation for the purposes of which the
    order is sought.
(5) There must be reasonable grounds for believing that it is in the public interest for the
    material to be produced or for access to it to be given having regard to—
    (a) the benefit likely to accrue to the investigation if the material is obtained;
    (b) the circumstances under which the person the application specifies as appearing to be
        in possession or control of the material holds it.

**17.13** Most of these requirements are similar to those for obtaining production orders under the old legislation. In particular, there is no requirement that a person has been charged with a criminal offence—it is sufficient that there is a confiscation, civil recovery, detained cash, or money laundering investigation taking place.

**17.14** By s 345(4) the production order, once made, is an order either:

    (a) requiring the person the application for the order specifies as appearing to be in possession
        or control of material to produce it to an appropriate office for him to take away, or
    (b) requiring that person to give an appropriate officer access to the material,
    within the period stated in the order.

**17.15** The period specified for compliance is seven days unless the judge considers, on the facts of a particular case, that a longer or shorter period would be appropriate: see s 345(5). Section 349 requires information held on a computer to be produced in a visible and legible form.

**17.16** Section 347 empowers the judge to make an order to grant entry to allow an appropriate officer to enter premises to obtain the material required to be produced under the order. By s 348(5) the appropriate officer may take copies of any material produced, or to which access is given, in compliance with a production order. Section 348(6) provides that material produced in compliance with a production order can be retained for as long as necessary in connection with the investigation for the purposes of which the order was made. If the appropriate officer has reasonable grounds for believing that the material may be required for the purpose of any legal proceedings and it might otherwise be unavailable for those purposes, he may retain it until the proceedings are concluded.

### Legal professional privilege

**17.17** Section 348(1) provides that a production order does not require a person to produce or give access to privileged material. By s 348(2) 'privileged material' is defined as:

    any material which the person would be entitled to refuse to produce on grounds of legal
    professional privilege in proceedings in the High Court.

**17.18** Legal privilege is defined in s 10 of the Police and Criminal Evidence Act 1984 (PACE). The mere fact that a lawyer is holding material on behalf of a client does not automatically mean that it is subject to legal professional privilege. In *R v Central Criminal Court ex p Francis and Francis* [1988] 3 All ER 775 the House of Lords held that documents were not subject to legal professional privilege if they were held with the intention of furthering a criminal purpose. This applies regardless of whether the intention was that of the person holding the documents or of any other person. Thus, a solicitor's file in relation to a conveyancing transaction on a property would not be subject to legal privilege in circumstances where the property was being purchased for a criminal purpose, for example, to launder the proceeds of drug trafficking.

**17.19**  In *R (on the application of Miller Gardner Solicitors) v Minshull Street Crown Court* [2002] EWHC 3077 (Admin) the Divisional Court held that personal details held by a firm of solicitors, such as a client's name and address, telephone number, and date of birth, were not subject to legal professional privilege.

### Excluded material

**17.20**  Section 348(2) of POCA provides that a production order does not require a person to produce or give access to excluded material within the meaning of s 11 of PACE.

### Government departments

**17.21**  A production order may be made in relation to material held by a government department as defined in the Crown Proceedings Act 1947 (see s 350(1) of POCA). The order may require any officer of the department (whether named in the order or not) who may for the time being be in possession or control of the material to which it relates to comply with it (see s 350(2)).

### Who may apply for a production order?

**17.22**  An application for a production order must be made by 'an appropriate officer'. This phrase is defined in s 378 of POCA (as amended by para 116 of Pt IV of Sch 8 to the Serious Crime Act 2007) and varies in accordance with the nature of the investigation in relation to which the application is made. By s 378(1), as so amended, in relation to confiscation investigations, the following are appropriate officers:

    (a)  a member of SOCA's staff;
    (b)  an accredited financial investigator;
    (c)  a constable; and
    (d)  a Customs officer.

**17.23**  As to civil recovery investigations, members of SOCA's staff, along with the relevant directors, are appropriate officers (see s 378(3) as so amended). The expression 'relevant director' means the Director of Public Prosecutions, the Director of Revenue and Customs Prosecutions, and the Director of the Serious Fraud Office (see s 352(5A)). In relation to detained cash and money laundering investigations, s 378(3A) and (4) provides that accredited financial investigators, constables, and officers of Revenue and Customs are appropriate officers.

### Procedure on applications: Crown Court

**17.24**  Applications for production orders may be made ex parte to a judge in chambers (see s 351(1) of POCA). The application should follow the procedure laid down in the Criminal Procedure Rules (CrimPR) rr 6.14 and 6.15, which require the application to be in writing and to address each of the relevant statutory criteria. This procedure appears to be based on the judicial guidelines in *R v Middlesex Guildhall Crown Court ex p Salinger*, The Independent,

26 March 1992, a case involving similarly worded provisions in terrorism legislation. The Court gave the following guidance:

(a) The application should be accompanied by a written statement upon which the officer wishes to rely to persuade the judge that the statutory conditions have been fulfilled. The statement need not disclose the nature or source of sensitive information. The officer should appear before the judge and be prepared to supplement the statement by oral evidence. The judge should not normally enquire into the nature and identity of the source of information, but it may be necessary for the officer to amplify the nature of the information itself, particularly if it has not been fully disclosed in the written statement.

(b) If the judge decides to make the order, he should give directions as to what, if any, information should be served with the order. This should normally be in writing and take the form of the written statement from the officer in support of the application. The information the judge requires the officer to give should be as full as possible without compromising security.

(c) If the judge decides it is inappropriate for any such information to accompany the order, he should consider whether it ought to be made available in the event of an application being made to vary or discharge the order.

The Court emphasised in its concluding words that the aim should be to provide as much information as possible, provided this is consistent with the security of the operation.

Any person affected by a production order may apply to have it varied or set aside under **17.25** s 351(3) of POCA. By r 6.20 of the CrimPR a person who proposes to apply for the variation or discharge of a production order must do so in writing as soon as practicable after becoming aware of the grounds for doing so.

In *ex p Salinger* (above), the Divisional Court ruled that applications to vary or set aside **17.26** production orders should, if possible, be made before the same judge who made the ex parte order, and it was desirable that the same officer that gave evidence at the ex parte hearing should attend. The Court said that questions as to the nature or identity of the source of information should not be permitted and, if the nature of the information is sensitive in the sense that it may compromise the security of the investigation, the judge should not allow the questions. He should tell the respondent in such circumstances that he has been given information which satisfies him that the conditions are met, but that such information cannot be disclosed.

### Procedure on applications: High Court

Applications for production orders and other Pt 8 POCA orders or warrants in support of **17.27** civil recovery or detained cash investigations are made to the High Court and are governed by the Civil Recovery Proceedings Practice Direction accompanying the CPR.

The application must be made to a High Court judge by filing an application notice: see **17.28** para 8.1 of the Practice Direction at Appendix 14. By para 8.2, the application may be made without notice to the respondent. Paragraph 10 requires that the application must be supported by written evidence which must be filed with the application notice. Paragraph 10.2 provides that the evidence must set out all the matters on which the applicant relies in support of the application including the matters required to be stated in the Act and all material facts of which the court should be aware. By para 10.3 the applicant must also file with the application notice a draft of the order sought. If possible, this should be supplied to the court on disk in a form compatible with any word processing software used by the court.

**17.29** The application will be heard and determined in private unless the judge directs otherwise (see para 11.1 of the Practice Direction at Appendix 14).

**17.30** An application for the variation or discharge of a Pt 8 order or warrant made pursuant to a civil recovery or detained cash investigation may be made by any person affected by it (see para 12.1 of the Practice Direction at Appendix 14). Any person making such an application must first notify the applicant under para 12.3. Paragraph 12.4 provides that any application for the variation of a Pt 8 order or warrant should be made to the judge who made the order or, if he is unavailable, to another High Court judge (Appendix 14). Further specific paragraphs of the Civil Recovery Proceedings Practice Direction apply to the different types of Pt 8 order and warrant. These are set out at Appendix 15 (para 13 on production orders, para 14 on search and seizure warrants, para 15 on disclosure orders, para 16 on customer information orders, and para 17 on account monitoring orders).

### Complying with the order

**17.31** Once the order has been sealed by the court, the officer should serve it promptly on the person or company to whom it is addressed. The recipient of a production order will normally have seven days in which to comply with the order unless the judge has exercised his discretion under s 345(5) of POCA to order a longer or shorter period. On no account should a person served with a production order divulge to a third party, particularly a client in relation to whom he is required to produce information, the fact that the order has been made. Any such disclosure could constitute an offence of prejudicing an investigation contrary to s 342 of POCA.

**17.32** It sometimes happens that information required to be disclosed under a production order is held on a computer. This is dealt with in s 349 of POCA which provides:

    (1) This section applies if any of the material specified in an application for a production order consists of information contained in a computer.

    (2) If the order is an order requiring a person to produce the material to an appropriate officer for him to take away, it has effect as an order to produce the material in a form in which it can be taken away by him and in which it is visible and legible.

    (3) If the order is an order requiring a person to give an appropriate officer access to the material, it has effect as an order to give him access to the material in a form in which it is visible and legible.

A person served with a production order may therefore have to print out the information covered by the order which he holds on computer or transfer it onto a disk or memory stick to allow the officer to take it away with him or have access to it.

**17.33** In contrast to the position with restraint orders, there is no requirement for the prosecutor to give an undertaking to pay the costs of innocent third parties, such as financial institutions or professional advisers, incurred in complying with a production order. Any such costs will therefore have to be borne by those named in the order and may not be reclaimed from the applicant.

**17.34** Once the appropriate officer has obtained material pursuant to a production order, it may be retained by him for so long as it is necessary to retain it (as opposed to copies of it) in connection with the investigation for the purposes of which the order was made (see s 348(6)). However, by s 347(7) of POCA:

(7) But if an appropriate officer has reasonable grounds for believing that—
    (a) the material may need to be produced for the purposes of any legal proceedings, and;
    (b) it might otherwise be unavailable for those purposes,
    it may be retained until the proceedings are concluded.

In *R (on the application of Cummins) v Manchester Crown Court* [2010] EWHC 2111 (Admin) **17.35** the Divisional Court held that SOCA could not be prevented from applying for a production order under s 345 of POCA against material they had originally seized under a search warrant but had returned to the applicant because they accepted the warrant was unlawful.

### Failure to comply with production orders

By s 351(7) of POCA: **17.36**

Production orders and orders to grant entry have effect as if they were orders of the court.

The effect of this provision is that any breach of a production order may be dealt with by the Crown Court as a contempt of court and may lead to imprisonment, the imposition of a fine, or the sequestration of assets. The jurisdiction of the Crown Court to deal with breaches of its order as a contempt of court is considered in Chapter 6.

Where the production order is made by the High Court pursuant to a civil recovery investigation, any failure to comply with the order will, of course, fall to be dealt with by the High Court rather than the Crown Court. **17.37**

## E. Search and Seizure Warrants

Section 352 of POCA gives the court power to issue search and seizure warrants empowering **17.38** appropriate officers to enter premises and seize material likely to be of substantial value to the investigation for the purpose of which the order is made. The requirements that must be fulfilled before a warrant may be issued are that a production order has already been made and has not been complied with and there are reasonable grounds for believing that the required material is on the premises, or that the requirements of s 353 have been met (see s 352(6)). Section 353 allows the court to issue search and seizure warrants in circumstances where it is not possible to make a production order. These instances include cases in which it is not practicable to communicate with a person in relation to whom a production order could be made, where consent would not be given without a warrant, or where the investigation might be seriously prejudiced if immediate entry to the premises could not be effected.

Appropriate officers should take great care to satisfy themselves that the statutory require- **17.39** ments have been satisfied before applying for a search warrant and give full and frank disclosure in the written statement in support. In *Power-Hynes v Norwich Magistrates Court* [2009] EWHC 1512 (Admin), a case concerning search warrants under PACE, Stanley Burnton LJ said:

...They must make full and frank disclosure to the justice of the peace, or district or circuit judge of the facts justifying the application, which will include the justification for applying for a search warrant rather than another remedy, in the present case a production order under section 9 and Schedule 1 to PACE.

**17.40**  At para 19 of the judgment his Lordship stated: 'I have no doubt that the description in the warrant of the articles to be sought was too vague and did not identify so far as practical the articles to be sought, as required by section 15(6)(b) of PACE.'

**17.41**  For additional requirements in relation to search warrants in support of civil recovery or detained cash investigations, see s 356 of POCA and the Civil Recovery Practice Direction: paras 8 and 14, reproduced at Appendices 14 and 15.

**17.42**  Further, appropriate officers should take great care to ensure that the written statement and warrant set out clearly which conditions in ss 352 and 353 were relied on in obtaining the warrant and that it properly identifies the properties to be searched and the nature of the material for which the officer is entitled to search. If proforma statements and warrants are used, care should be taken both by the applicant and court officials to ensure that any provisions that are inapplicable are properly crossed out. In *Redknapp v Commissioner of City of London Police* [2008] EWHC 1177 (Admin) where the Divisional Court quashed a search warrant made under s 9 of PACE 1984, Latham LJ said:

> ...the first thing that has to be said is that the failures that I have already referred to are wholly unacceptable. This court has complained in the past about slipshod completion of application forms such as this, the last occasion being the judgment of Underhill J in *R (on the application of 'C') v The Chief Constable of 'A' Police and another* [2006] EWHC 2352 (Admin). The obtaining of a search warrant is never to be treated as a formality. It authorises the invasion of a person's home. All the material necessary to justify the grant of a warrant should be contained in the information provided on the form. If the magistrate or judge in the case of an application under section 9, does require any further information in order to satisfy himself that the warrant is justified, a note should be made of the additional information so that there is a proper record of the full basis upon which the warrant has been granted.

**17.43**  It is submitted that the same principles should apply to search warrants made under POCA which can be equally intrusive. In the case of *Energy Financing Team Ltd and others v Director Of The Serious Fraud Office* [2006] 1 WLR 1316 Lord Justice Kennedy, sitting in the Divisional Court, at para 24 of his judgment set out guidance generally applicable to search and seizure warrants under various Acts. At subpara 5 of his guidance he stated that the 'warrant needs to be drafted with sufficient precision to enable those executing it and those whose property was affected by it to know whether any individual document or class of documents fall within it'. At para 37 of his judgment Crane J stated '...a warrant should be capable of being understood by those carrying out the search and by those whose premises are being searched, without reference to any other document'. These dicta were distinguished in the case of *Horne and others v Central Criminal Court* (see above) at para 32 where HMRC relied upon the terms of s 353(6) of POCA, which allows for a warrant not to specify the material sought

> if it cannot be identified at the time of the application but it a) relates to the person specified in the application, the question whether he has benefited from his criminal conduct or any question as to the extent or whereabouts of his benefit from his criminal conduct, and b) is likely to be of substantial value (whether or not by itself) to the investigation for the purposes of which the warrant is sought.

**17.44**  Other applicable statutory criteria must still be made out. The Court of Appeal in *Windsor and others v CPS* [2011] 1 WLR 1519 quashed restraint orders against defendants and connected companies on the basis there was no reasonable cause to believe they had benefited from criminal conduct. The Divisional Court went on to quash PACE 1984 warrants on the same basis because it was 'in substance the same issue as whether there were reasonable grounds for believing that an indictable offence had been committed'—see *The Queen on the application of Sanjay Panesar t/a Anami Law v Bristol Crown Court* [2011] Lloyd's Rep FC 337.

## F. Judicial Discretion

Even where the conditions set out in ss 345 or 352 of POCA have been met, the court **17.45** retains a discretion as to whether or not a production order or search warrant should be granted: note the use of the phrase 'a judge may' in ss 345(1) and 352(1). This was confirmed by the Divisional Court in *R v Crown Court at Southwark ex p Customs and Excise Commissioners* [1989] 3 All ER 673, where similar provisions in s 27 of the DTOA were considered. Watkins LJ said:

> ... We see nothing in the words of section 27(2) of the 1986 Act to suggest that Parliament did not intend the circuit judge to have a discretion either to grant or to refuse an order although he be persuaded that the conditions contained in subsection (4) are satisfied. While we acknowledge that it is not easy to identify circumstances in which a judge might properly refuse to make an order when those conditions have been satisfied, we are not persuaded that this is a subsection in which 'may' can be construed as meaning 'must' or 'shall'.

The judge had imposed a condition that the material obtained under the production order **17.46** should not be removed from the jurisdiction without the leave of the court. The judge imposed the condition on the basis of evidence from an official of a bank affected by the order to the effect that there was a risk of reprisals against members of the bank's staff in Panama, their families, and properties. The Court indicated that this evidence was 'unimpressive' and should not influence the court to exercise its discretion in favour of those who would use it to avoid compliance with an embarrassing order. Watkins LJ said: 'The courts of this country are not to be deflected from making orders in aid of the international battle against drug trafficking for fear of reprisals no matter from where the threat of them emanates.'

In *R v Southwark Crown Court ex p Bowles* [1998] AC 641 the House of Lords considered **17.47** the powers under s 93H of the CJA, the equivalent of s 345 POCA, to make production orders. They emphasised the intrusive nature of such orders and the need for judges to scrutinise applications carefully before exercising the discretion to make an order. Lord Hutton cited the judgment of Bingham LJ (as he then was) in *R v Crown Court at Lewes ex p Hill* [1991] 93 Cr App R 60 where, in relation to similar powers under PACE 1984, the Court referred to the importance of achieving a balance between competing public interests. Bingham LJ said:

> The Police and Criminal Evidence Act governs a field in which there are two very obvious public interests. There is, first of all, a public interest in the effective investigation and prosecution of crime. Secondly, there is a public interest in protecting the personal and property rights of citizens against infringement and invasion. There is an obvious tension between these two public interests because crime could be most effectively investigated and prosecuted if the personal and property rights could be freely overridden and total protection of the personal and property rights of citizens would make investigation and prosecution of many crimes impossible or virtually so.

As Lord Hutton pointed out, Bingham LJ emphasised that circuit judges must exercise their **17.48** powers with great care and caution to ensure the proper balance between these two competing public interests is maintained. The Divisional Court again referred to this balance in

*Power-Hynes v Chief Constable of Norfolk* [2009] EWHC 1512 (Admin). Stanley Burnton
LJ said:

> In a case such as the present, the Court is faced with two competing interests. The first is the
> public interest in prosecuting and preventing crime. That interest requires the Court to be
> sympathetic to the position of police officers applying for a search warrant, particularly in a
> case involving financial fraud, and to be realistic in its assessment of the compliance of the
> police with the obligations imposed by Parliament and set out in the provisions of PACE to
> which I have referred. The Court should not impose unrealistic or impracticable obligations
> on police officers seeking a search warrant or on the justice of the peace or district or circuit
> judge to whom application is made for the warrant.
>
> The second interest is that of the person or persons whose home or office or other business
> premises may be the subject of a search. A police search for materials is a very real and serious
> intrusion into the private life of those whose premises are searched and may be very distressing
> for them, and if it is to be justified the officers seeking the warrant must take diligent steps to
> ensure that the statutory requirements are satisfied.

**17.49** The court must also take great care to ensure that the production order is not abused by
its use in cases where an application under s 9 of PACE is more appropriate. The statutory
requirements for obtaining a POCA production order are less stringent than those for an
order under PACE and there may be a temptation on the part of some investigators to rely
on the POCA production order wherever possible. In particular:

(a) applications for production orders can be made without notice, whereas Sch 1 para 7 to
PACE requires that applications under s 9 must be made on notice;

(b) section 9 applications must relate to a 'serious arrestable offence', whereas there is no
such requirement in relation to applications for production orders;

(c) a s 9 order can only be made where there are reasonable grounds for believing that an
offence has been committed; whereas a production order involves a lower threshold test,
namely that there are reasonable grounds to suspect that a person has benefited from
criminal conduct;

(d) applications under s 9 are further limited by a requirement that other methods of obtaining the material have failed or have not been tried because they were bound to fail; there
is no similar requirement in relation to an application for a production order.

**17.50** The House of Lords held in *R v Southwark Crown Court ex p Bowles* [1998] AC 641 that a
'dominant purpose' test should be applied in determining whether a s 93H CJA production order application or an application under s 9 PACE is the most appropriate means of
obtaining the required material. If the dominant purpose of the application is to obtain
information in furtherance of a criminal investigation, s 9 should be used. If, however, the
dominant purpose of the application is to obtain evidence in relation to an investigation into
the proceeds of criminal conduct, a production order application may properly be made.
Further, the House of Lords ruled that provided a production order had been obtained
because the dominant purpose of the application was to progress an investigation into the
proceeds of criminal conduct, it mattered not that evidence was found that assisted the
criminal investigation: this could still be relied upon in a criminal trial. Lord Hutton said:

> I consider that if the true and dominant purpose of an application under section 93H is to
> enable an investigation to be made into the proceeds of criminal conduct, the application
> should be granted even if an incidental consequence may be that the police will obtain evi-
> dence relating to the commission of an offence. But if the true and dominant purpose of the

application is to carry out an investigation whether a criminal offence has been committed and to obtain evidence to bring a prosecution, the application should be refused.

I further consider that if the police discover evidence of the commission of an offence in the course of an investigation consequent upon an order properly made under section 93H, the fact that the evidence was discovered in this way would not be a reason for the exclusion of the evidence under section 78 of PACE on the ground of unfairness at a trial where the prosecution sought to adduce such evidence.

# G. Customer Information Orders

Customer information orders were introduced by s 363 of POCA and put further powers at **17.51** the disposal of investigators. Production orders on bank accounts can only be effective if the investigator has at least some information as to the identity of the account and the financial institution at which it is maintained. A customer information order requires a financial institution covered by the order to provide to an appropriate officer any customer information it has in relation to the person specified in the order (see s 363(5)). In relation to an individual, s 364(2) defines 'customer information' as information as to whether the person holds or has held an account with the institution named in the order and, if so, information as to:

(a) the account or account numbers;
(b) the person's full name;
(c) his date of birth;
(d) his most recent address and any previous addresses;
(e) the date or dates on which he began to hold the account or accounts and, if he has ceased to hold the account or any of the accounts, the date or dates on which he did so;
(f) such evidence of his identity as was obtained by the financial institution under or for the purposes of any legislation relating to money laundering;
(g) the full name, date of birth, and the most recent address and any previous addresses of any person who holds or has held an account at the financial institution jointly with him;
(h) the account number or numbers of any other account or accounts held at the financial institution to which he is a signatory and details of the person holding the other account or accounts.

Section 364(4) defines customer information in similar terms in relation to companies or limited **17.52** liability partnerships or similar bodies incorporated or otherwise established outside the UK.

## Requirements for making orders

The requirements are set out in s 365 of POCA. In all cases there must be reasonable grounds **17.53** for believing that the information will be of substantial value to the investigation (s 365(5)) and that it is in the public interest for the information to be provided having regard to the benefit likely to accrue to the investigation if the information is obtained (s 365(6)). The other requirements vary according to the nature of the investigation in relation to which the information is being required:

(a) in a confiscation investigation, there must be reasonable grounds for suspecting that the person named in the application has benefited from criminal conduct (s 365(2));
(b) in a civil recovery investigation, there must be reasonable grounds for suspecting that the property specified in the application is recoverable or associated property and that the person holds some or all of the property (s 365(3));

(c) in a money laundering investigation, there must be reasonable grounds for suspecting that the person specified in the application has committed a money laundering offence.

**17.54** Applications for customer information orders may be made ex parte to a Crown Court judge and any person affected by an order once it is made may apply for it to be varied or set aside (see s 369(1) and (3) respectively and CrimPR rr 6.18 and 6.20). Section 369(7) (as amended by para 111 of Pt 4 of Sch 8 to the SCA) provides that an accredited financial investigator, member of SOCA's staff, a constable, or Customs officer may apply for a customer information order but only if he is a 'senior appropriate officer' or has been authorised to make the application by such an officer. Section 378(2) (as amended by para 116 of Pt 4 of Sch 8 to the SCA) defines a 'senior appropriate officer' as being a senior member of SOCA's staff, a police officer not below the rank of superintendent, a Customs officer designated by the Commissioners of Revenue and Customs as being of equivalent rank to superintendent, and an accredited financial investigator designated in an order made by the Secretary of State under s 453. Section 378(8) (as added by para 116 of Pt 4 of Sch 8 to the SCA) provides that a senior member of SOCA's staff is the Director General of SOCA or any member of SOCA's staff designated by the Director (whether generally or specifically) for this purpose.

### Discharge and variation

**17.55** By s 369(3) of POCA an application to vary or discharge a customer information order may be made by the person who applied for the order or by any person affected by it. The procedures to be followed on such applications are the same for all Pt 8 orders and are set out in r 6.20(2) of the CrimPR. By r 6.20.(2),

> (2) That applicant, respondent or person affected must—
>   (a) apply in writing as soon as practicable after becoming aware of the grounds for doing so;
>   (b) serve the application on—
>     (i) the court officer, and
>     (ii) the respondent, applicant, or any person known to be affected, as applicable;
>   (c) explain why it is appropriate for the order to be varied or discharged;
>   (d) propose the terms of any variation; and
>   (e) ask for a hearing, if one is wanted, and explain why it is needed.

### Offences

**17.56** It is an offence under s 366 for a financial institution to fail to comply with a customer information order without reasonable excuse (s 366(1)) or to knowingly or recklessly make a false statement when complying with such an order (s 366(3)). An offence contrary to s 366 is punishable by a fine not exceeding level 5 on the standard scale (see s 366(2)), and an offence contrary to s 366(3) is punishable on indictment with an unlimited fine (see s 366(4)).

## H. Account Monitoring Orders

**17.57** The court is empowered under s 370 of POCA to make account monitoring orders on the application of an appropriate person. The particular value of these orders to investigators is that they impose an ongoing duty on the financial institution named in the order to provide information for a period of up to ninety days from the date on which the order is made. In contrast, production orders merely require the disclosure of information in the possession of the financial investigator when the order is served. If the officer requires further information after a production order has been complied with, he will have to apply to the court for another order.

An account monitoring order is defined in s 370(6) as: **17.58**

> an order that the financial institution specified in the application for the order must, for the period stated in the order, provide account information of the description specified in the order to an appropriate officer in the manner, and at or by the time or times stated in the order.

The period stated in the order must not exceed ninety days (see s 370(7)).

The requirements that must be fulfilled before an account monitoring order can be made are **17.59** set out in s 371 and are identical to those for making customer information orders. Again the application may be made ex parte to a judge in chambers (s 373), and affected parties have the right to apply to set aside or vary the order (see s 375 respectively). Rules 6.19 and 6.20 of the CrimPR set out the procedures that must be followed for applications and for affected parties who intend to apply for the order to be varied or discharged. As with customer information orders, the applicant must apply in writing to the Court and serve a copy of the application on the person who applied for the order (see r 6.20).

## I. Disclosure Orders

By s 357(1) of POCA (as amended by para 108 of Sch 8 to the SCA) a judge may, **17.60** on an application by a relevant authority, make a disclosure order which is defined in s 357(4) as:

> an order authorising the relevant authority to give any person the relevant authority considers has relevant information notice in writing requiring him to do, with respect to any matter relevant to the investigation for the purposes of which the order is sought, any or all of the following—
> (a) answer questions, either at a time specified in the notice or at once, at a place so specified;
> (b) provide information specified in the notice, by a time and in a manner so specified;
> (c) produce documents, or documents of a description specified in the notice, either at or by a time so specified or at once, and in a manner so specified.

Disclosure orders under s 357 of POCA can be contrasted with those obtainable under **17.61** s 41(7) of POCA both in terms of the statutory criteria applicable for their use and for the breadth of their purpose and power if granted.

It is also important to note that the disclosure order itself gives the prosecuting or civil **17.62** recovery agency the wide-ranging authority to issue disclosure notices against specific individuals. Any person affected by the order (ie the respondent to the order or recipient of any disclosure notice) and the person who applied for the order (the prosecuting or civil recovery enforcement agency) may apply to discharge or vary the order under s 362(3) of POCA and CrimPR r 6.20.

A 'relevant authority' is defined in s 357(7) as being, in relation to a confiscation investiga- **17.63** tion, a prosecutor and, in relation to civil recovery and exploitation proceeds investigations, a member of SOCA's staff or the relevant director. The term 'prosecutor' includes the Director of Public Prosecutions and the Director of the Serious Fraud Office: see s 357(8).

**17.64**   Applications for disclosure orders may not be made in relation to detained cash nor money laundering investigations (see s 357(2)) but they can be used in confiscation investigations, civil recovery investigations, or exploitation proceeds investigations (see s 357(3)). Applications should follow CrimPR rr 6.14 and 6.17.

**17.65**   The requirements that must be fulfilled before an order can be made are set out in s 358 of POCA and are identical to those in relation to customer information orders and account monitoring orders, save that, as indicated above, they may not be made in relation to money laundering investigations. A person commits an offence under s 359 of POCA if he fails to comply with a disclosure order or knowingly or recklessly makes a false or misleading statement in response to such an order.

### Civil recovery investigations into property outside the jurisdiction

**17.66**   In *Perry v Serious Organised Crime Agency* [2012] UKSC 35; [2013] 1 AC 182; [2012] 3 WLR 379, the Supreme Court considered two joined appeals as to whether disclosure orders under s 357 of POCA and property freezing orders (PFOs) under s 245A of POCA could be made in pursuance of a Pt 5 Civil Recovery investigation into property held outside the jurisdiction of England and Wales. The Supreme Court held that a Pt 5 Civil Recovery Order could not be made against property in a foreign jurisdiction notwithstanding the terms of s 316(4) of POCA (see Chapters 13 and 14 on civil recovery for further details). Therefore the Supreme Court allowed the appeal holding that a PFO could not be obtained over property outside the jurisdiction. The Court also went on to consider whether disclosure notices issued under a disclosure order could be made to request information from a person outside the jurisdiction. At para 94 of his judgment, with which the majority agreed, Lord Phillips stated:

> The point is a very short one. No authority is required under English law for a person to request information from another person anywhere in the world. But section 357 authorises orders for requests for information with which the recipient is obliged to comply, subject to penal sanction. Subject to limited exceptions, it is contrary to international law for country A to purport to make criminal conduct in country B committed by persons who are not citizens of country A. Section 357, read with section 359, does not simply make proscribed conduct a criminal offence. It confers on a United Kingdom public authority the power to impose on persons positive obligations to provide information subject to criminal sanction in the event of non-compliance. To confer such authority in respect of persons outside the jurisdiction would be a particularly startling breach of international law. For this reason alone I consider it implicit that the authority given under section 357 can only be exercised in respect of persons who are within the jurisdiction.

> This reasoning was quite independent of the Supreme Court's basis for holding that a Civil Recovery Order can only be made against property within the jurisdiction.

**17.67**   Subsequent to the handing down of the decision in *Perry*, in *SOCA v Azam and others* [2013] EWHC 627 (QB) Sir Raymond Jack held that SOCA was not required to return to Mr Azam money which had been repatriated into the jurisdiction from Luxembourg pursuant to a PFO. Equally, SOCA was entitled to rely in civil recovery proceedings on evidence regarding a prosecution outside the jurisdiction in UAE obtained pursuant to a disclosure order. Both orders had been made and carried out prior to the decision in *Perry* on the basis of the law as it was understood at that time and, despite the subsequent change of law, their effect should not be reversed. For further on the retrospective effect of *Perry* on civil recovery orders previously made see *SOCA v O'Docherty and another* [2013] EWCA Civ 518.

In order to address the effect of the judgment in *Perry*, amendments to Pt 5 of POCA were **17.68** included in ss 48 and 49 and Schs 18 and 19 to the Crime and Courts Act 2013 (CCA) which was passed in April 2013. Section 48 of the CCA is in force and introduces a new s 282A and Sch 7A to POCA to extend the jurisdiction of civil recovery orders so that they can now be made in respect of property outside the jurisdiction of the UK if there is or has been a connection between the case and the relevant part of the UK. Likewise Sch 18 to the CCA 2013 is in force and introduces ss 282B–282F to POCA. These sections will facilitate the enforcement outside the UK of orders made under Chapter 2 of Pt 5 of POCA and the transmission of requests for evidence held outside the UK. However, at the time of writing, s 49 and Sch 19 to the CCA are not yet in effect. When in force, Pt 1 of Sch 19 will amend s 341 of POCA as set out above and Pt 2 of the Schedule will introduce ss 375A and 375B to POCA.

New section 375A of POCA will make provision for evidence to be obtained from a court, **17.69** tribunal, government, or authority outside the UK ('receiving country') if a person or property is subject to a civil recovery investigation, a detained cash investigation, or an exploitation proceeds investigation (as defined in s 341). It will enable a judge to make a request for assistance upon an application by an appropriate officer or a person subject to the investigation, providing that the judge thinks there is relevant evidence in a country or territory outside the UK. However, a senior appropriate officer or the relevant Director may make a direct request for assistance if it is thought that there is relevant evidence in a country or territory outside the UK. The meanings of 'appropriate officer', 'senior appropriate officer', and 'relevant Director' are found in ss 352(5A) and 378 of POCA as above. In the case of urgency, a request may be sent via the International Criminal Police Organization (Interpol or Europol) or any person competent to receive it under any provisions adopted under the EU Treaties, for onward forwarding to the receiving country.

New s 375A(10) of POCA will provide a power to make rules of court as to the practice and **17.70** procedure to be followed in connection with proceedings relating to requests for assistance made by a judge.

New s 375B of POCA will provide that evidence obtained by a request for assistance under **17.71** new s 375A must not be used for any purpose other than for the purpose of the investigation for which it was obtained or for the purposes of certain proceedings. However, the court, tribunal, government, or authority that received the request and provided the evidence can consent to the use of the evidence for other purposes. (For further information on territorial limits see para 13.61 et seq).

### Confiscation investigations outside the jurisdiction

International cooperation under POCA is dealt with in detail in Chapter 19. The position **17.72** appears to be as follows for confiscation investigations under Pt 2 of POCA following the Supreme Court's judgment in *Perry*: (a) the courts can continue to make confiscation orders over the value of realisable property held outside the jurisdiction and enforce any order against foreign property by letter of request to that jurisdiction under s 74 of POCA (see paras 34–38 of Lord Phillips' judgment); (b) a prosecuting agency will continue to be able to issue a disclosure notice pursuant to s 357 of POCA against a person within the jurisdiction and this may enquire in relation to property which may represent the benefit from criminal conduct whether held in the jurisdiction or outside; (c) however, it is unlikely that the prosecuting agency can issue a disclosure notice directly against a person outside the jurisdiction in respect of property which may represent benefit from criminal conduct whether this is held in the jurisdiction or outside (para 94 of Lord Phillips's judgment). Instead in order to obtain the information sought under a disclosure notice from an overseas recipient a prosecuting authority will need to send a letter of request to the foreign authorities in the hope they will pursue the investigation.

**17.73** The judgment in *Perry* leaves unresolved how any person is determined to be outside the jurisdiction and whether this is based on residence or where they happen to be at the time the notice is served. The Court of Appeal at paragraphs 50 and 66 of their judgment on the disclosure order appeal, [2010] EWCA Civ 907, had attempted to grapple with the issues of a person's links or connection to the jurisdiction of England and Wales.

### Hearings

**17.74** It is also worth noting that in the first-instance proceedings in *Perry* in the High Court, Foskett J expressed some concern about the practice of applications under s 357 being determined on the papers and, given the intrusive nature of disclosure orders, suggested that where complex points of law arise, the applicant should consider asking for an oral hearing (even on an ex parte basis which is permitted under s 362(1) of POCA).

## J. Statements Made in Response to Orders

**17.75** POCA restricts the use to which statements made pursuant to disclosure orders, customer information and orders and account monitoring orders may be put. By s 360, a statement made by a person in response to a requirement imposed on him under a disclosure order may not be used against him in criminal proceedings. Similar protection is afforded to financial institutions to comply with customer information orders (s 367) and account monitoring orders (s 372). These immunities do not, however, extend to confiscation proceedings, proceedings for contempt of court or perjury, or for an offence where, in giving evidence, a person makes a statement which is inconsistent with a statement made in complying with the order.

## K. Financial Reporting Orders under the Serious Organised Crime and Police Act 2005

**17.76** Section 76 of SOCPA gives the Crown and Magistrates' Courts jurisdiction to make financial reporting orders. Unlike production orders, account monitoring orders, and customer information orders, a financial reporting order may only be made after a defendant has been convicted of certain specified criminal offences. The explanatory note accompanying the Act describes the purpose of financial reporting orders in these terms: 'Such orders may be imposed as ancillary orders for certain trigger offences and would enable the financial affairs of serious acquisitive criminals to be monitored from the point of sentence.'

### Jurisdiction to make the order

**17.77** By s 76(1) a court sentencing or otherwise dealing with a person convicted of an offence specified in s 76(3) may also make a financial reporting order. Section 76(2) restricts the court's jurisdiction to make the order to cases where it is:

> satisfied that the risk of the person's committing another offence mentioned in subsection (3) is sufficiently high to justify the making of a financial reporting order.

In order to assess the risk of reoffending, it is submitted that the proper course is for the court **17.78** to look at the circumstances of the offence of which the defendant has been convicted, his role in its commission, and the nature of any previous convictions he may have.

### Offences to which section 76 applies

By s 76(3) the offences are: **17.79**

- an offence under any of the following provisions of the Theft Act 1968—
  - Section 15 (obtaining property by deception),
  - Section 15A (obtaining a money transfer by deception),
  - Section 16 (obtaining a pecuniary advantage by deception),
  - Section 20 (2) (procuring execution of a valuable security, etc.),
- an offence under either of the following provisions of the Theft Act 1978—
  - Section 1 (obtaining services by deception),
  - Section 2 (evasion of liability by deception),
- any offence specified in Schedule 2 to the Proceeds of Crime Act 2002 ('lifestyle offences').

The 'lifestyle offences' referred to in s 76(3)(c) are set out in detail in Chapter 8 and include **17.80** most drug trafficking and money laundering offences. The Secretary of State may by order add to or delete offences from this list (see s 76(4)).

A financial reporting order is not a penalty but a preventative measure intended to enable the **17.81** court to keep control over offenders who are likely to indulge in further criminal activity. It follows from this that Art 7 of the European Convention on Human Rights (ECHR) is not engaged and financial reporting orders can be made notwithstanding the fact that s 76 was not in force at the time of the commission of the relevant offences by the defendant: see *R v Adams* [2008] EWCA Crim 914 and *R v Wright* [2008] EWCA Crim 3207.

In the case of *Wright*, the appellant also contended that the judge adopted the wrong **17.82** approach in treating the order as an aid to enforcement of the confiscation order, that he was plainly wrong to conclude that there was a high risk of the defendant committing another specified offence, and that in reality such an order would have no utility. Before considering each of these points individually, the court noted the extent of the appellant's involvement in serious organised crime. Thomas LJ said:

> This appellant is a career criminal on an enormous scale. He was convicted of offences of importing and supplying cocaine over a period of three years or thereabouts in the late 1990s. The judge who made this order had presided over a trial which took something like three months and of which the appellant's evidence was a significant feature. He had heard the appellant give evidence that he had lived in effect throughout his adult life 'outside the system'—that is to say in such manner that there was no or virtually no recorded trace of his existence. He owned no property, he paid no tax, he had no social security or National Insurance or even perhaps national health identity, his passport was an Irish passport, he had no bank accounts, no car was registered in his name and so on. The judge also heard the appellant give evidence that whilst it was accepted he was a gambler on an enormous scale, he had lived almost entirely by cash and he was able, on the evidence, to put his hands on six figure sums of cash with the assistance of custodians, friends or associates, as and when he needed to.

The judge summed up the man he was dealing with in this way: 'You lived anonymously, you were a master criminal, manipulative, influential and powerful. At various times you were the controlling mind and financial backbone behind an international drug smuggling ring which extended from South America in particular Colombia through the Caribbean and to these shores.' Thomas LJ added:

> It was apparent that the appellant had lived for many years a lavish lifestyle in the United Kingdom and Spain and elsewhere, surrounded by a clique of loyal acolytes. In due course his benefit from drug trafficking was assessed in the confiscation proceedings at no less than £45 million. He was, in other words, one of the relatively rare major and criminal entrepreneurs to be caught and convicted. Catching him had not been straightforward. The investigation had been long and painstaking. When it got near to his associates this appellant decamped by private jet to North Cyprus where there is of course no extradition regime. He remained there for some years and it was only when he made the error (from his point of view) of returning not to this country but to Spain that he was traced and apprehended.

**17.83** The Court also noted that at the confiscation hearing, the defendant adopted a policy of 'blanket non-compliance'. He did not file a response to the prosecutor's statement and refused to give evidence.

**17.84** Against this background, it is perhaps not surprising that the Court of Appeal dismissed the appeal against the financial reporting order. As to the first point taken by the appellant, the Court agreed that a financial reporting order should not be seen as ancillary to the enforcement of a confiscation order, although it noted that:

> ...an indirect effect of information given under the financial reporting order might turn out to be of some assistance to those who are seeking to enforce a confiscation order. The obvious case in which that might happen is if a prosecution for a money laundering offence followed and revealed into the public domain the existence of assets against which the order could be enforced. There may be other situations in which such indirect effect might occur.

**17.85** The Court expressed itself as being satisfied the judge had applied the statutory criteria correctly and rejected this ground of appeal. As to the suggestion that the appellant was incapable of committing further offences given that he was sixty-one years of age and serving a sentence of imprisonment of thirty years as a category A prisoner, the Court again found against the appellant. Thomas LJ said:

> The judge gave proper consideration to the undoubted fact that at present at least the appellant is a category A prisoner and subject to the special restrictions which are imposed on such prisoners. He was satisfied that that would not necessarily prevent the appellant, no doubt with other people, from achieving what he wanted to achieve and we for our part entirely agree.

**17.86** The Court was, however, at pains to emphasise that financial reporting orders should not be made without careful consideration being given to what they are likely to achieve. Thomas LJ said:

> We should say that whilst this form of order is newly created it ought not to be thought that it is routinely to be made without proper thought. We do not seek to set out any general rules for when it will be appropriate or not. This is not the right place in which to do that. No doubt the paradigm case for such an order is the defendant with a history of unsatisfactory business or financial dealing who at some stage at least is likely to be at large and engaged in business, commercial or financial activity which would otherwise be unsupervised or unmonitored. But it is perfectly clear that the section embraces also the defendant who is going to be a prisoner and, at least in the case of the very exceptional facts of this prisoner, we have no doubt that an order can be appropriate.

**17.87** Finally, the Court accepted that the order would have some utility in the case of the appellant, Thomas LJ adding:

> We are quite sure that judges who are asked to make financial reporting orders should give careful consideration to whether it would actually achieve anything. They should certainly look at

alternative powers which are available to financial investigators if they would have much the same effect. We have applied our minds to precisely that question in this case. It is the fact that if the appellant were to maintain a stance of total non co-operation with the financial reporting order and of disobedience to it, it no doubt would achieve nothing. We do not, however, think that there is any basis on which we should properly assume that that will be his stance, even if his stance in the confiscation proceedings was of that kind. This order is expressed to last ten years. It would be quite wrong to make the assumption that he will simply ignore it for all that time and court the risk of the penalties which would follow. Nor should we make any assumption as to the period which he will actually serve in prison. We simply do not know.

One of the alternative remedies the court considered was the ability of the prosecutor to **17.88** apply for variations to the restraint order requiring the defendant to make further disclosure statements. The court rejected this as an appropriate alternative saying:

> We certainly accept that to make repeated applications for variations of a restraint order with a view to obtaining a direction for disclosure by the defendant is not a realistic substitute for the financial reporting order. On the assumption that it is at least possible that the defendant will make some kind of compliance with the order, it seems to us that it may have, albeit limited, some utility. He will be on the spot and required to set out his financial position at regular intervals. There is a not fanciful possibility that something may emerge from what he says, if he says anything, which may be of value to those who are monitoring his finances and may enable either the commission of further offences to be avoided or deterred or, failing that, the commission of further offences to be detected.

Although the Court in *Wright* avoided giving guidance to judges as to the circumstances in **17.89** which it would be appropriate to make financial reporting orders, it is clear that such orders are not necessarily inappropriate in cases where the defendant is serving a long sentence of imprisonment. This said, the court must always take care to satisfy itself that a financial reporting order would serve a useful purpose and not make them as a matter of routine in every case where the statutory criteria are satisfied.

In *R v Adams* [2008] EWCA Crim 914 a financial reporting order was challenged on the **17.90** additional ground that it was made not when the defendant was sentenced but at a subsequent hearing at which he was brought back before the court for a hearing in relation to the recovery of defence costs by the Legal Services Commission. The defendant contended that, when this hearing took place, the Court was *functus officio* so far as sentencing matters were concerned. The Court rejected this argument and dismissed the appeal, Latham LJ saying:

> We take the view that the judge was entitled to make the order. When the matter came back before him, it matters not in what guise, he was dealing with the offender within the meaning of section 76. That gave him the jurisdiction and the power to make the order.

More recent cases in which the Court of Appeal have upheld financial reporting orders **17.91** include *R v (1) Kenneth Mullen (2) R v Adrian Davison: R v Andrew Bingham* [2012] EWCA Crim 606 and *R v Kevin John Bell: R v Carl Richard Ian Burgess* [2011] EWCA Crim 2728. In both cases the Court came to the conclusion that the risks the appellants raised were sufficiently high notwithstanding pre-sentence reports or other risk assessments because the Court had regard to the totality of their history of offending.

### Duration of orders

By s 76(5) the order comes into force when it is made and has effect for the period specified **17.92** in it, beginning on the date on which it is made. If the order is made by a Magistrates' Court, the duration of the order must not exceed five years (see s 76(6)). If the order is made by the Crown Court, its duration must not exceed fifteen years, or twenty years if the defendant is sentenced to imprisonment for life (see s 76(7)). The duration of the order must be proportionate to the risk of reoffending and a lengthy order will rarely be justified against a defendant with few previous convictions who has not been convicted of a particularly serious offence.

### Effect of a financial reporting order

**17.93** By s 79(1) a person against whom a financial reporting order has been made must do the following:

> (2) He must make a report in respect of—
>   (a) the period of a specified length beginning with the date on which the order comes into force; and
>   (b) subsequent periods of specified lengths, each period beginning immediately after the end of the previous one.
> (3) He must set out in each report, in the specified manner, such particulars of his financial affairs relating to the period as may be specified.
> (4) He must include any specified documents with each report.
> (5) He must make each report within the specified number of days after the end of the period in question.
> (6) He must make each report to the specified person.

**17.94** By s 81(1) 'the specified person' means the person to whom reports under the order are to be made. Section 82(2) empowers the specified person, for the purpose of doing either of the things mentioned in s 82(4), to disclose a report to any person who he reasonably believes may be able to contribute to doing either of those things. Similarly, by s 82(3), any other person may disclose information to the specified person or to a person to whom the specified person has disclosed a report, for the purpose of contributing to doing either of the things mentioned in s 82(4). Section 82(4) provides:

> The things mentioned in subsections (2) and (3) are—
>
> (a) checking the accuracy of the report or of any other report made pursuant to the same order,
> (b) discovering the true position.

**17.95** By s 82(5) the specified person may also disclose a report for the purpose of the prevention, detection, or investigation of criminal offences in the UK and elsewhere. Section 82(6) provides that any disclosure made under the section does not breach:

> (a) any obligation of confidence owed by the person making the disclosure, or
> (b) any other restriction on the disclosure of information (however imposed).

This is subject to an important provision in s 82(7) to the effect that the section does not authorise any disclosure in contravention of the Data Protection Act 1998 of personal data which is not exempt from its provisions.

### Variation and revocation of financial reporting orders

**17.96** By s 80(1), an application for the variation or revocation of a financial report order may be made by the person in respect of whom it was made or by the person to whom reports are to be made under it. The application must be made to the court which made the order (s 80(2)) or, if the order was made on appeal, to the court which originally sentenced the person in respect of whom it was made.

### Failure to comply with financial reporting orders

It is an offence under s 79(10) to include false or misleading information in a report or **17.97** otherwise to fail to comply with the order without reasonable excuse. The offence is punishable by imprisonment for a maximum of fifty-one weeks, a fine not exceeding level 5 on the standard scale, or both.

# 18

# APPEALS

# A. Introduction

**18.01**  The purpose of this chapter is to consider in more detail the practice and procedure of making an appeal against the various orders available to the court, including restraint, confiscation, and receivership orders.

### Transfer of powers from the High Court to the Crown Court

**18.02**  Under s 91 of POCA, the CrimPR now govern restraint, receivership, and confiscation applications made in the Crown Court under the provisions of POCA.

**18.03**  The CrimPR make provision for three types of appeal under POCA. The first is an appeal under s 31 of POCA to the Court of Appeal (and from there to the Supreme Court under s 33 of POCA) by the prosecutor against a confiscation order or a failure of the Crown Court to make a confiscation order. The second is an appeal under s 43 of POCA to the Court of Appeal (and from there to the Supreme Court under s 44 of POCA) in respect of decisions of the Crown Court about restraint orders. The third is an appeal under s 65 of POCA to the Court of Appeal (and from there to the Supreme Court under s 66 of POCA) in respect of decisions of the Crown Court about receivers. The rules relating to these appeals are considered at the relevant stages of the appeal process set out below, and a thumbnail guide is included at the conclusion of this chapter.

**18.04**  Restraint and receivership applications under the DTA and the CJA are currently dealt with by the High Court and fall within its civil law jurisdiction. The appropriate rules of court relating to appeals under this earlier legislation are the CPR. Due to the passage of time since the introduction of POCA, the number of DTA and CJA cases has declined considerably. As a result this chapter focuses exclusively on POCA. Earlier editions of this work deal with the procedure for the DTA and CJA.

### Appeals distinguished from applications

**18.05**  It is important to understand the difference between an appeal and an application to vary. An appeal is appropriate where there is a legal challenge to the order made in the Crown Court, either in whole or in part. An application to vary is appropriate where there has been a change in the factual position following the Crown Court's order. For example, an application to vary a confiscation order would be appropriate where assets are sold but realise a lesser amount than that which was anticipated when the confiscation order was made.

**18.06**  The distinction is important because the Court of Appeal is not likely to view sympathetically an appeal against a confiscation order made on the basis that assets to the value of the order are no longer available, when the same could be dealt with more expeditiously and economically by a judge on an application for a certificate of inadequacy (the process of varying a confiscation order is usually referred to as an application for either a certificate of inadequacy or a certificate of increase). Equally, a Crown Court judge will not take kindly to being invited to consider matters of law on the validity of the confiscation order that should more appropriately be determined by the Court of Appeal.

### The Crown Court 'slip rule'

**18.07**  In other cases, an application under the 'slip rule' would be appropriate, in preference to either an appeal or an application to vary. Under s 155(1) of the PCC(S)A both the defendant and the Crown may apply to the Crown Court to vary or remedy an order. Such an application would be appropriate where, for example, the Crown Court proceeded on a false factual footing, or overlooked a statutory provision. Section 155(1) states:

> Subject to the provisions of this section, a sentence imposed, or other order made by the Crown Court when dealing with an offender may be varied or remedied by the Crown Court within the period of 56 days beginning with the day on which the sentence or other order was imposed or made.

The application of this section to confiscation orders was confirmed in the case of *R v Bukhari* **18.08** [2009] 2 Cr App R (S) 18; [2008] EWCA Crim 2915. The application must be brought within the strict fifty-six-day limit. Thereafter, the appropriate challenge is by way of appeal.

### Appeals by financial investigators under POCA

As noted earlier in this book, s 68(1) extends to 'accredited financial investigators' the power **18.09** to apply for a restraint order under ss 41 or 42 or to apply for an order appointing or empowering a management receiver under ss 48 or 49 of POCA or to apply for variation or discharge of a management receivership order under s 63 of POCA.

Section 68 of POCA also enables 'accredited financial investigators' to pursue appeals in **18.10** respect of restraint orders (under ss 43 and 44) and receivership orders (under ss 65 and 66). 'Accredited financial investigators' are defined as being:

(a) a police officer who is not below the rank of superintendent;
(b) a Revenue and Customs officer who is not below such grade as is designated by the Commissioners of Revenue and Customs as equivalent to that rank; or
(c) a person who falls within a description in an order made under s 453 of POCA, namely the Proceeds of Crime Act 2002 (References to Financial Investigators) Order 2009/975 SI 2009/975 (as amended), eg certain employees of the Department for Business, Innovation and Skills; the Financial Services Authority; the Department for Work and Pensions etc.

An application or appeal commenced by an accredited financial investigator may continue **18.11** even where there is a change in the identity of the person bringing the application or appeal. This is because s 68(4) of POCA states that where an application or appeal is made, any subsequent step in the application or appeal or any further application or appeal relating to the same matter may be taken, made, or brought by a different 'accredited financial investigator' (as defined). The purpose of this subsection is to ensure that an application or appeal is not thwarted by, for example, the subsequent ill health of an investigator who makes an application or appeal concerning an order for restraint or receivership.

## B. Restraint Order Appeals: Practice and Procedure

### Restraint orders: appeal by the prosecutor or other applicant

If, on an application for a restraint order under POCA, the Crown Court decides (for what- **18.12** ever reason) not to make an order, the person who applied for the order may appeal to the Court of Appeal against the decision (s 43(1)). Where the person who applied for the order is an 'accredited financial investigator' that person (or another person falling into that category) may also pursue an appeal.

**18.13**  On an appeal under s 43, the Court of Appeal may either confirm the decision or make such order as it believes is appropriate (see s 43(3)).

### Restraint orders: general right of appeal

**18.14**  Section 43(1) gives the prosecution a right of appeal where the Crown Court decides not to make a restraint order. There is no right of appeal, therefore, against the Crown Court's decision to make a restraint order. A person who wishes to challenge the imposition of a restraint order or its terms may only appeal against the Crown Court's decision not to vary or discharge the restraint order. In effect, therefore, there is a two-tier process: first, an application must be made to the Crown Court for the variation or discharge of the restraint order. The application may be made by the person who applied for the order, the defendant, or any person affected by the order. Once the Crown Court has decided the application the second stage is to appeal under s 43(2) to the Court of Appeal. Such an appeal may be pursued by the person who applied for the order, or any person affected by it (including the defendant).

**18.15**  The position is similar in respect of orders made under s 41(7) (an order for the purpose of ensuring that the restraint order is effective, such as an order for disclosure of the defendant's assets). There is no power to appeal such an order. A person dissatisfied by the order must first apply for its variation or discharge. The application may be made by the person who applied for the order, the defendant, or any person affected by the order. Once the Crown Court has decided the application the second stage is to appeal under s 43(2) to the Court of Appeal. Such an appeal may be pursued by the person who applied for the order, or any person affected by it (including the defendant).

**18.16**  It is important to realise that the application to vary or discharge a restraint order is often the first time the Crown Court judge will have the opportunity of listening to and understanding the defendant's objections. This is because restraint orders are usually applied for on an ex parte (without notice) basis, so as to maintain the element of surprise and avoid any dissipation of assets prior to the matter being listed. Occasionally it is necessary to set a 'return date' for the parties to attend *inter partes* (on notice).

### Procedure

**18.17**  By s 89(1) of POCA, an appeal to the Court of Appeal under Pt 2 of POCA lies only with the leave of that court. Under r 73.1 of the CrimPR, leave to appeal to the Court of Appeal under s 43 of POCA will only be given where:

(a)  the Court of Appeal considers that the appeal would have a real prospect of success; or
(b)  there is some other compelling reason why the appeal should be heard.
(2) An order giving leave may limit the issues to be heard and be made subject to conditions.

**18.18**  Rule 73.2 of the CrimPR sets out the procedure for giving notice of appeal. The notice of appeal must be served in the form set out in the Practice Direction on the Crown Court officer and must be accompanied by the documents listed at r 73.2(3). Unless otherwise directed, the appellant must serve the notice of appeal accompanied by a respondent's notice in the appropriate form on: on each respondent, any person who holds realisable property to which the appeal relates, and any other person affected by the appeal 'as soon as practicable' and in any event not later than seven days after the notice of appeal is served on the Crown Court officer. The appellant must provide the Crown Court officer with a certificate of service or, if service was not possible, the reasons why.

Rule 73.3 sets out the procedure for the service of a respondent's notice. A respondent 'may' **18.19** serve a respondent's notice on the registrar, unless he himself is seeking leave to appeal, or wishes to ask the Court of Appeal to uphold the Crown Court's decision for reasons different from (or additional to) those given by the Crown Court, in which case he 'must' serve such a notice. Any respondent's notice should be in the approved form and must be served on the registrar no later than fourteen days after the date the respondent is served with notification that the Court of Appeal has granted leave to appeal. Thereafter the respondent's notice must be served on the appellant and any other respondent as soon as practicable and, in any event, not more than seven days after it was served on the registrar.

Rules 73.4 to 73.6 of the CrimPR explain the procedure for amending, abandoning, staying, **18.20** and striking out appeals.

The Secretary of State has made certain provisions corresponding to the Criminal Appeal **18.21** Act 1968 to allow for the adoption of general procedures such as obtaining leave to appeal and transcripts (s 89(3) of POCA). The Proceeds of Crime Act 2002 (Appeals under Part 2) Order 2003, SI 2003/82 came into force on 24 March 2003, and has subsequently been amended by the Proceeds of Crime Act 2002 (Appeals under Part 2) Amendment Order 2013 (SI 2013/24). For a more detailed consideration of this order, see para 18.82 below.

### Hearing the appeal

Subject to the rules made under s 53(1) of the Senior Courts Act 1981 (distribution of busi- **18.22** ness between civil and criminal divisions), the criminal division of the Court of Appeal is the division to which appeals should be made (s 53(2)(a)).

Under r 73.7 of the CrimPR, appeals brought under s 43 of POCA will be limited to a review **18.23** of the decision of the Crown Court, unless the Court of Appeal considers that in the circumstances of an individual appeal it would be in the interests of justice to hold a rehearing. The Court of Appeal will allow an appeal where the decision of the Crown Court was:

(a) wrong; or
(b) unjust because of a serious procedural or other irregularity in the proceedings in the Crown Court.

The Court of Appeal may draw any inference of fact which it considers justified on the evidence **18.24** (CrimPR r 73.7(4)). At the hearing of the appeal a party may not rely on a matter not contained in his notice of appeal unless the Court of Appeal gives permission (CrimPR r 73.7(5)).

### Appeal to the Supreme Court

Following an appeal to the Court of Appeal under s 43, a further appeal lies to the Supreme **18.25** Court under s 44 of POCA. The appeal may be made by any person who is a party to the proceedings before the Court of Appeal (including the prosecution). The powers of the Court of Appeal are set out in s 44(3) and are either to:

(a) confirm the decision of the Court of Appeal, or
(b) make such order as it believes is appropriate.

An appeal to the Supreme Court lies only from a decision of the Court of Appeal, and only **18.26** the parties to the Court of Appeal proceedings may appeal. Section 33(3) of the Criminal Appeal Act 1968 (limitation on appeal from the Criminal Division of the Court of Appeal) does not prevent an appeal to the Supreme Court under Pt 2 of POCA (see s 90(1) of POCA). For the procedure to be followed for appeals to the Supreme Court, see r 71.10 of the CrimPR and the Practice Directions available on the Supreme Court's website.

## C. Receivership Order Appeals: Practice and Procedure

### Appeal by the prosecutor or applicant

**18.27**  Under POCA if, on an application for a receivership order made under ss 48 to 51 of POCA, the court decides *not* to make such an order, the person who applied for the order may appeal to the Court of Appeal against the decision (s 65(1) of POCA).

**18.28**  Applications under ss 48 to 51 are for: the appointment of a management receiver by the Crown Court; the powers to be given to the management receiver by the Crown Court; the appointment of an enforcement receiver by the Crown Court; and the powers to be given to an enforcement receiver by the Crown Court.

### General right of appeal against receivership orders

**18.29**  If, on the other hand, the court *makes* an order under any of the above sections, the person who applied for the order or any person affected by the order may appeal to the Court of Appeal in respect of the court's decision (s 65(2) of POCA).

### Appeal: receivership directions, variation, or discharge

**18.30**  On an application for an order under s 62 of POCA (namely, an application made by the receiver under s 62(2) for an order giving directions as to the exercise of the receiver's powers; or an application, pursuant to s 62(3), by any person affected by action taken by the receiver, or by any person who may be affected by the action the receiver proposes to take) if the court decides *not* to make the order applied for, the person who applied for the order may appeal to the Court of Appeal, under s 65(3) of POCA against that decision.

**18.31**  If, on the other hand, the court *does* make an order under s 62, then the person who applied for the order or any person affected by the order, including the receiver, may appeal to the Court of Appeal in respect of the court's decision (s 65(4) of POCA).

**18.32**  Where an application is made to discharge or vary an order made under s 62 of POCA (ie the receivership order itself or orders giving the receiver his powers), an appeal may be pursued under s 63 to the Court of Appeal against the decision of the Crown Court. Such an appeal may be pursued by the person who applied for the order, or any person affected by the court's decision, or the receiver.

**18.33**  In *Capewell v Customs and Excise Commissioners* [2005] 1 All ER 900; [2004] EWCA Civ 1628, the Court of Appeal considered the issues which were likely to be relevant to the question of whether or not to discharge a receiver. Giving the judgment of the Court, Carnwath LJ said (at para 50):

> On the question of discharge, cost is of course a factor, but it is not the primary issue. The overriding consideration is whether the receivership is still serving a valid purpose...The relevant questions for the court are likely to be:
> i)  For what purposes, within the overall objective, was the receivership authorised?
> ii)  To what extent have those purposes been achieved or overtaken?

iii) To the extent that they have not yet been achieved or overtaken, is the continuation of the receivership (as opposed to a restraint order or some other order) necessary to achieve them?

iv) In any event, having regard both to the overall objective and to fairness to the defendant, is the additional cost of continuing the receivership proportionate to the likely financial gain?

52. We would add that fairness to the defendant cannot be measured purely in financial terms.

## Procedure

As in restraint cases, by reason of s 89(1) of POCA an appeal to the Court of Appeal under **18.34** Pt 2 of POCA lies only with the leave of that court.

Under r 73.1 of the CrimPR leave to appeal to the Court of Appeal under s 65 of POCA will **18.35** only be given where:

    (a) the Court of Appeal considers that the appeal would have a real prospect of success; or
    (b) there is some other compelling reason why the appeal should be heard.

  (2) An order giving leave may limit the issues to be heard and be made subject to conditions.

Rule 73.2 of the CrimPR sets out the procedure for giving notice of appeal. The notice of **18.36** appeal must be served in the form set out in the Practice Direction on the Crown Court officer and must be accompanied by the documents listed at r 73.2(3). Unless otherwise directed, the appellant must serve the notice of appeal accompanied by a respondent's notice in the appropriate form on each respondent, any person who holds realisable property to which the appeal relates, and any other person affected by the appeal 'as soon as practicable' and in any event not later than seven days after the notice of appeal is served on the Crown Court officer. The appellant must provide the Crown Court officer with a certificate of service or, if service was not possible, the reasons why.

Rule 73.3 sets out the procedure for the service of a respondent's notice. A respondent 'may' **18.37** serve a respondent's notice on the registrar, unless he himself is seeking leave to appeal, or wishes to ask the Court of Appeal to uphold the Crown Court's decision for reasons different from (or additional to) those given by the Crown Court, in which case he 'must' serve such a notice. Any respondent's notice should be in the approved form and must be served on the registrar no later than fourteen days after the date the respondent is served with notification that the Court of Appeal has granted leave to appeal. Thereafter the respondent's notice must be served on the appellant and any other respondent as soon as practicable and, in any event, not more than seven days after it was served on the registrar.

Rules 73.4 to 73.6 of the CrimPR explain the procedure for amending, abandoning, staying, **18.38** and striking out appeals.

The Secretary of State has made certain provisions corresponding to the Criminal Appeal Act **18.39** 1968 to allow for the adoption of general procedures such as obtaining leave to appeal and transcripts (s 89(3)). The Proceeds of Crime Act 2002 (Appeals under Part 2) Order 2003, SI 2003/82 came into force on 24 March 2003 and has subsequently been amended by the Proceeds of Crime Act 2002 (Appeals under Part 2) Amendment Order 2013 (SI 2013/24, see para 18.82 below).

## Hearing the appeal

Subject to the rules made under s 53(1) of the Senior Courts Act 1981 (distribution of busi- **18.40** ness between civil and criminal divisions) the criminal division of the Court of Appeal is the division to which appeals should be made (see s 53(2)(a)).

**18.41**  Under r 73.7 of the CrimPR appeals brought under s 65 will be limited to a review of the decision of the Crown Court unless the Court of Appeal considers that in the circumstances of an individual appeal it would be in the interests of justice to hold a rehearing. The Court of Appeal will allow an appeal where the decision of the Crown Court was:

(a) wrong; or

(b) unjust because of a serious procedural or other irregularity in the proceedings in the Crown Court.

**18.42**  The Court of Appeal may draw any inference of fact that it considers justified on the evidence. At the hearing of the appeal a party may not rely on a matter not contained in his notice of appeal unless the Court of Appeal gives permission (r 73.7(5) of the CrimPR).

### The powers of the Court of Appeal on an appeal against a receivership order

**18.43**  On an appeal under any of the heads of s 65, the Court of Appeal may either confirm the decision or may make such order as it believes is appropriate (s 65(6)).

### Appeal to Supreme Court

**18.44**  An appeal lies to the Supreme Court from a decision of the Court of Appeal on an appeal under s 65. An appeal may be pursued by any person who was a party to the proceedings before the Court of Appeal. The Supreme Court may confirm the decision of the Court of Appeal or make such order as it believes is appropriate. For the procedure to be adopted for appeals to the Supreme Court, see r 71.10 of the CrimPR and the Practice Directions available on the Supreme Court website.

**18.45**  It has already been noted that s 33(3) of the Criminal Appeal Act 1968 (limitation on appeal from the Criminal Division of the Court of Appeal) does not prevent an appeal to the Supreme Court under Pt 2 of POCA (s 90(1)).

## D.  Confiscation Order Appeals: Practice and Procedure

### Appeals in confiscation order cases

**18.46**  Appeals against confiscation orders lie to the Court of Appeal (Criminal Division) (unless it is a rare High Court confiscation case, where the appeal will be to the Civil Division).

### Appeals involving the judge's discretion

**18.47**  Although the Court of Appeal does have the power to consider and interfere in matters involving the discretion of the trial judge, it will only do so in the following circumstances:

(1) where there has been a failure to exercise a discretion; or

(2) where the judge has failed to take into account a material consideration; or

(3) where the judge in the court below has taken into account an immaterial consideration.

In practice, the Court of Appeal has shown a marked reluctance to interfere in appeals that depend on the exercise of judicial discretion. Similarly, the Court of Appeal has been reluctant to interfere with factual determinations of the Crown Court. This reluctance was exemplified in *R v Olubitan* [2004] 2 Cr App R (S) 14, where it was said that the Crown Court was entitled to draw 'robust inferences' where appropriate. On the other hand, the Court of

Appeal may be more inclined to interfere with the Crown Court's decision where that court did not make clear factual findings, or where the inferences drawn were not properly supported by the evidence. This was the position in *R v McCreesh* [2011] EWCA Crim 641. In that case, Lord Judge CJ said (at para 31):

> We accept that very often in situations such as the present the courts may be justified in drawing robust inferences. But as the facts stood in this case we do not think that the judge was justified in reaching the conclusion that he did. Nor did he make the findings that were open to him to justify the conclusion that he asserted.

### Defendant's appeal

An appeal against a confiscation order lies as part of the sentencing process. Section 50(1) of the Criminal Appeal Act 1968 defines sentence as including confiscation orders imposed under POCA, as well as variations to confiscation orders made under ss 21, 22, and 29 (but no others). The definition of 'sentence' also includes confiscation orders made under the DTA and the CJA, and orders varying such confiscation orders.  **18.48**

The grounds of appeal must be drafted in terms of either mistake of law or mistake of fact. It should be underlined that an appeal to the Court of Appeal must not be used as a means to seek a rehearing where a confiscation ruling has been adverse to the client. Time limits for lodging appeals are likely to be closely scrutinised, see *R v Bestel* [2013] EWCA Crim 1305.  **18.49**

### *A right of appeal against the confiscation order in all cases*

The defendant's right of appeal exists as a right against all matters determined by the Crown Court during the confiscation proceedings (*R v Emmett* [1998] AC 773). In that case the defendant sought to appeal against a confiscation order made by agreement between the parties under the Drug Trafficking Offences Act 1986. Subsequently, the defendant sought to argue that his acceptance of certain allegations contained in the prosecutor's statement, and ultimately his agreement to the terms of the confiscation order, had been based upon a mistake of fact. The question for the House of Lords was whether the fact that the defendant had accepted the prosecutor's allegations debarred him from appealing to the Court of Appeal. Lord Steyn stated, following *R v Cain* [1985] 1 AC 46 (per Lord Scarman, at 55G–56D), that unless the relevant legislation expressly or by necessary implication excluded a right of appeal against sentence, there was as a matter of jurisdiction a right of appeal in all cases. Since the Drug Trafficking Offences Act 1986 contained no provision ousting the right of appeal it followed that the fact that the defendant had agreed the terms of the order did not prevent him from appealing.  **18.50**

The principle found in *R v Emmett* may be relied upon in cases where the appellant asserts that he accepted an allegation made in the prosecutor's statement, or agreed to one or more terms of a confiscation order, only on the basis of a mistake of fact or mistake of law (see, eg, *R v Bell* [2011] EWCA Crim 6). Where the defendant makes such an assertion, the burden rests upon the appellant to persuade the Court of Appeal that his assertion is correct. This burden may not be easy to overcome. In *R v Emmett*, Lord Steyn said (at p 783):  **18.51**

> Lest it be thought, however, that my observations are some kind of open sesame to such appeals I would mention four matters. First, the question in such cases will not be what mistake Counsel made but what mistake the defendant made. Secondly, and particularly in regard to matters peculiarly within the knowledge of the defendant, the burden on the defendant of proving a mistake may not easily be discharged. Thirdly, the focus in such cases will be on

a material and causatively relevant mistake viz. a material mistake which in fact induced the defendant to accept the correctness of a [prosecutor's] statement. Fourthly, even if the defendant can persuade the Court of Appeal on these three points, the Court of Appeal may still have to consider whether, absent a material mistake, the particular confiscation order would nevertheless have been inevitable. If that is the case, the appeal may have to be dismissed on the grounds that on a global view of the case no injustice can be shown.

### Fresh evidence

**18.52**  In *R v Stroud* [2004] EWCA Crim 1048, the Court of Appeal held that where a defendant sought to adduce fresh expert evidence on appeal against a confiscation order, the considerations as to admissibility were the same as those applicable in appeals against conviction.

### Substitution of new order or a direction to proceed afresh

**18.53**  In *R v Hirani* [2008] EWCA Crim 1463, the Court of Appeal confirmed that it did have jurisdiction in an appeal against a confiscation order to substitute a new order in place of the original. Where the Court of Appeal has quashed a confiscation order, but is not in a position to substitute a new order (perhaps because factual issues remain which are better resolved in the Crown Court) the Court of Appeal may, by reason of s 11(3A) of the Criminal Appeal Act 1968, direct the Crown Court to proceed afresh. Where this course is taken, the Court of Appeal has power to give directions so as to ensure that any confiscation order made in respect of the appellant by the Crown Court does not deal more severely with him than the order just quashed: s 13(3C). The Crown Court must comply with any such directions.

**18.54**  The s 11(3A) procedure was introduced as a result of amendments contained in the Coroners and Justice Act 2009. It was designed to avoid the situation whereby a confiscation order is quashed by the Court of Appeal but that court is not in a position to carry out an effective confiscation enquiry. It is submitted, however, that the procedure may give rise to difficulties. The terms of s 6 of POCA are mandatory. It is unclear what the Crown Court should do if, having proceeded afresh, the statute compels a confiscation order which is greater than the order previously quashed by the Court of Appeal. Other difficult questions may also arise as to whether any given order is more 'severe' than another, particularly as, following the making of a confiscation order, it is open to the prosecution to apply to increase it at a later stage if further assets come to light.

### The effect of the appeal process on the process of enforcement

**18.55**  Lodging an appeal in a confiscation order case does not stop the 'time to pay' period set by the Crown Court from running. The Court of Appeal took a robust approach to the period set for payment in the case of *R v May (Confiscation Order: Time to Pay)* [2005] EWCA Crim 367, where Keene LJ held at para 5 that:

> the proposition that the time to pay a confiscation order runs from the date of the determination of an appeal against it . . . is unsound in law. In principle the fact that an appeal is pending does not operate so as to suspend the operation of any sentence or order.

He added (at para 7):

> There is no reason why steps preparatory to the raising of the money specified in the confiscation order should not have been taken while [the defendant May's] appeal was pending. The appellant was not entitled to assume that his appeal would be successful and, as indicated above, as a matter of law time was running during that period. Moreover, it would be wrong as a matter of principle for appellants to be encouraged to believe that bringing an appeal would be likely to lengthen the time given for payment, even if the appeal was unsuccessful.

The position is similar in respect of applications to the Criminal Cases Review Commission **18.56** ('CCRC'). The CCRC is not a court of appeal. It is therefore unlikely that an application to it would either slow or in any way inhibit the due processes of the confiscation scheme. This is reflected in the case law. In *Re P* (QBD, 6 November 1998) the defendant had been convicted in February 1995 of a conspiracy offence relating to drugs. On 17 July 1995 the court empowered the receiver to sell properties owned by the defendant. Following that, on 6 October 1995, the Crown Court made a confiscation order against the defendant in the sum of £557,000 with an order that he serve four years' imprisonment in default of payment. In June 1997 the Court of Appeal dismissed the defendant's appeal against his conviction. On that occasion his counsel did not pursue any complaint against the confiscation order.

In 1998 the defendant applied to the CCRC, arguing that he had been wrongly convicted. **18.57** He also lodged an application to the European Court of Human Rights. The defendant made an application to the Court to have funds released from the bite of the restraint order to enable him to meet the expenses associated with those two applications. Laws J held:

> The fact is that, so far as the domestic criminal litigation is concerned in this case, Mr P is well past the end of the road. The Commission may, of course, investigate a matter after all other legal processes have been exhausted. Indeed that is their very role. However, it is quite clear to me that whilst they are doing so, and the fact that they are doing so, are no basis for altering, suspending or varying the affect of the restraint order and therefore, in effect, the execution of a confiscation order once that has been made. The same applies in relation to his application to the European Court of Human Rights.

### Procedure

As noted above, a defendant's appeal against a confiscation order is to be treated as an appeal **18.58** against sentence. The applicable procedural rules may be found in r 68 of the CrimPR.

### Prosecutor's appeal

If the Crown Court makes a confiscation order the prosecutor may appeal to the Court of **18.59** Appeal against that order (s 31(1)). Conversely, if the Crown Court decides not to make a con- fiscation order the prosecutor may appeal to the Court of Appeal against that decision (s 31(2)). An appeal may be taken on any ground, of either a point of law or fact, and could, for example, allege that the court failed to take account of an item of property when calculating the available amount. The right of the prosecutor to appeal extends to a case where the Crown Court: refuses to proceed to confiscation (*R v Brack and Brack* [2007] EWCA Crim 1205); adjourns confis- cation proceedings *sine die* (*R v Hockey* [2008] 1 Cr App R (S) 50); or stays the confiscation proceedings as an abuse of process (*R v Nelson; R v Pathak; R v Paulet* [2010] QB 678).

There is, by reason of s 31(3) of POCA, no prosecutor's right of appeal against an order or **18.60** decision made in proceedings brought under: s 19 (no confiscation order made: reconsidera- tion of case); s 20 (no confiscation order made: reconsideration of benefit); s 27 (where the defendant has absconded after he has been convicted in the Crown Court or committed by the magistrates' court for sentence or with a view to a confiscation order being considered); or s 28 (where the defendant absconds before criminal proceedings have been concluded).

### Procedure

As with restraint and receivership appeals, under s 89(1) of POCA an appeal to the Court of **18.61** Appeal under Pt 2 of POCA lies only with the leave of that court.

**18.62**  Provisions for giving notice of appeal by the prosecutor are set out in r 72.1 of the CrimPR. Where a defendant is served with a notice of appeal under r 72.1 and wishes to oppose the granting of leave he must, not later than fourteen days after the date on which he received the notice of appeal, serve on the registrar and on the appellant a notice in the form set out in the Practice Direction (see r 72.2). Rule 72.3 of the CrimPR outlines the procedure to be followed when an appeal is to be either amended or abandoned.

**18.63**  Subject to the rules made under s 53(1) of the Senior Courts Act 1981 (distribution of business between Civil and Criminal Divisions) the Criminal Division of the Court of Appeal is the division to which appeals should be made (see s 53(2)(a)).

**18.64**  The Secretary of State has made certain corresponding provisions to the Criminal Appeal Act 1968 to allow for the adoption of general procedures such as obtaining leave to appeal and transcripts (s 89(3)). The Proceeds of Crime Act 2002 (Appeals under Part 2) Order 2003, SI 2003/82 came into force on 24 March 2003 and has subsequently been amended by the Proceeds of Crime Act 2002 (Appeals under Part 2) Amendment Order 2013 (SI 2013/24), see para 18.82 below).

*Appeal by the prosecutor: the Court of Appeal's powers*

**18.65**  Under s 32 of POCA, upon an appeal brought under s 32(1) by the prosecutor against the imposition of a confiscation order the Court of Appeal may confirm, quash, or vary the confiscation order.

**18.66**  If the appeal is against a decision not to make a confiscation order, the Court of Appeal may confirm the decision or, if it believes the decision is wrong, it may itself proceed under s 6 of POCA to make a confiscation order, or it may direct the Crown Court to proceed afresh under s 6.

**18.67**  If the Crown Court is directed to proceed afresh, it must comply with any other directions the Court of Appeal may make in relation to the hearing (s 32(3)).

**18.68**  The procedure for the provision of information, contained in ss 16 (prosecutor's statements), 17 (defendant's response), and 18 (provision of information by the defendant) apply to cases where the Court of Appeal is proceeding under s 6 or the Crown Court is proceeding afresh: s 32(10).

*Statutory modifications when making or varying a confiscation order or proceeding afresh*

**18.69**  By reason of s 32(4), if the Court of Appeal exercises its power under s 32 to make or vary a confiscation order, or the Crown Court proceeds afresh in pursuance of a direction made by the Court of Appeal under s 32(3), the court seized of the confiscation proceedings must have regard to any fine or other financial order falling within s 13(3) of POCA (compensation orders, deprivations orders, etc). The court need not have regard to any order falling within s 13(3) if a court has already taken it into account in deciding what free property is held by the defendant for the purpose of s 9 of POCA (the available amount). The purpose of s 32(4) is to ensure that any confiscation order that is made or varied as a result of the appeal proceedings takes into account any fine or financial order previously made against the defendant. It avoids a situation whereby the defendant is unable to meet both the confiscation order and any financial orders previously made against him in the proceedings.

*Further modifications when making a confiscation order or proceeding afresh*

Where, on an appeal against a decision not to make a confiscation order, the Court of Appeal **18.70**
proceeds under s 6 or the Crown Court proceeds afresh pursuant to a direction by the
Court of Appeal, s 32(6) to (10) applies. These provisions, together with s 32(4) (above),
are designed to modify the s 6 procedure having regard to the fact that a period of time has
elapsed since the earlier decision of the Crown Court not to make a confiscation order.
Section 32(6) and (7) provides:

> (6) If a court has already sentenced the defendant for the offence (or any of the offences) con-
> cerned, section 6 has effect as if his particular criminal conduct included conduct which
> constitutes offences which the court has taken into consideration in deciding his sentence
> for the offence or offences concerned.
> (7) If an order has been made against the defendant in respect of the offence (or any of the
> offences) concerned under section 130 of the Sentencing Act (Compensation Orders)—
>    (a) the Court must have regard to it, and
>    (b) Section 13(5) and (6) ... do not apply.

Thus, s 32(6) of POCA modifies the s 6 procedure where (as will usually be the case) the **18.71**
defendant has already been sentenced at the time the Court of Appeal is proceeding under
s 6 or the Crown Court is proceeding afresh. Moreover, s 32(7) modifies the way in which
compensation orders are treated in confiscation proceedings. First, if a compensation order
was previously made, the court proceeding afresh must have regard to it. This ensures that the
defendant (who may still own the property from which the compensation will be paid) is not
made the subject of orders which he is unable to meet. Secondly, s 13(5) and (6) is disapplied.
Section 13(5) and (6) is the provision which enables the court to order that compensation
be paid out of the sum collected under the confiscation order, where the defendant's means
are insufficient to meet both orders. The effect of section 32(7) is that this 'carving out' procedure is not available where the court is proceeding afresh in cases where the defendant was
previously made the subject of a compensation order.

Section 32(8) is a further modification to be observed where the Court of Appeal proceeds **18.72**
under s 6 or the Crown Court proceeds afresh. It provides:

> Section 8(2) does not apply, and the rules applying instead are that the court must—
> (a) take account of conduct occurring before the relevant date;
> (b) take account of property obtained before that date;
> (c) take account of property obtained on or after that date if it was obtained as a result of or
>    in connection with conduct occurring before that date.

Section 8(2) of POCA is the provision which requires the Crown Court to take into account conduct occurring up to the time that it makes its decision and to take account of property obtained
up to that time. Section 32(8) makes clear that those restrictions do not apply where a court is
proceeding afresh under s 6. The 'relevant date' is the date on which the Crown Court decided
not to make a confiscation order. Thus, the effect of s 32(8) is to require the court proceeding
afresh to consider the position, so far as conduct and property is concerned, which faced the court
in the original confiscation proceedings. The exception to this is that the court may take into
account property obtained *after* the date of the previous confiscation hearing, but only if such
property was obtained as a result of or in connection with conduct occurring *before* that date.

Section 32(9) also applies where the Court of Appeal proceeds under s 6 or the Crown Court **18.73**
proceeds afresh pursuant to a direction by the Court of Appeal. It is designed to protect the

defendant from the full application of the assumptions (found in s 10 of POCA) to events which take place after the date of the original confiscation hearing. It provides:

> (9) In section 10—
>> (a) the first and second assumptions do not apply with regard to property first held by the defendant on or after the relevant date; or
>> (b) the third assumption does not apply with regard to expenditure incurred by him on or after the date;
>> (c) the fourth assumption does not apply with regard to property obtained or assumed to have been obtained by him on or after that date.

**18.74** The effect of this provision, in general terms, is to limit the application of the assumptions to events occurring up to the date of the original confiscation hearing. However, by reason of s 32(8), it will still be open to the prosecution to allege that property obtained after confiscation hearing should count as benefit, but only if it can be shown that property was obtained as a result of or in connection with conduct occurring before the relevant date.

**Appeal to the Supreme Court following a prosecutor's appeal to the Court of Appeal**

**18.75** Under s 33(1), an appeal lies to the Supreme Court from a decision of the Court of Appeal on an appeal under s 31 of POCA.

**18.76** An appeal under this section lies at the instance of either the defendant or the prosecutor. On an appeal from a decision of the Court of Appeal to confirm, vary, or make a confiscation order the Supreme Court may confirm, quash, or vary the order (s 33(3)). On an appeal from the decision of the Court of Appeal to confirm the decision of the Crown Court not to make a confiscation order or from the decision of the Court of Appeal to quash a confiscation order the Supreme Court may:

(a) confirm the decision, or
(b) direct the Crown Court to proceed afresh under s 6, if it believes the decision was wrong (s 33(4)).

**18.77** It will have been noted already that s 33(3) of the Criminal Appeal Act 1968 (limitation on appeal from the Criminal Division of the Court of Appeal) does not prevent an appeal to the Supreme Court under Pt 2 of POCA (s 90(1)). For the procedure to be adopted when applying to appeal to the Supreme Court, see r 71.10 of the CrimPR and the Practice Directions available from the Supreme Court website.

*Supreme Court: no power to proceed under section 6*

**18.79** It will be noted that, unlike the Court of Appeal, the Supreme Court has no power itself to proceed under s 6. On an appeal from a decision of the Court of Appeal to confirm the decision of the Crown Court not to make a confiscation order or from a decision of the Court of Appeal to quash a confiscation order, the Supreme Court may only remit the case to the Crown Court with directions to proceed afresh under s 6. If proceeding afresh, the Crown Court must comply with any directions the Supreme Court has made (s 33(5)).

*Statutory modifications when the Supreme Court varies a confiscation order or the Crown Court proceeds afresh*

**18.80** Provision is made for certain matters to be taken into account where the Supreme Court varies a confiscation order or directs the Crown Court to proceed afresh. These are similar to the adjustments described above where the Court of Appeal varies a confiscation order, or proceeds under s 6 or the Crown Court proceeds afresh under s 6. Thus, where the Supreme Court varies a confiscation order, or the Crown Court proceeds afresh pursuant to a direction by the Supreme Court, that court must, by reason of s 33(6), have regard to any fine or other financial order falling within s 13(3) of POCA (compensation orders, deprivations orders, etc). The court need not have regard to any order falling with s 13(3) if a court has already taken it into account in deciding what free property is held by the defendant for the purpose of s 9 of POCA. The purpose of s 33(6) is to ensure that any confiscation order that is made or varied as a result of the appeal proceedings takes into account any fine or financial order previously made against the defendant. It avoids a situation whereby the defendant is unable to meet both the confiscation order and any financial orders previously made against him in the proceedings.

*Additional modifications where the Supreme Court directs the Crown Court to proceed afresh*

**18.81** Section 33(8)–(12) is in similar terms to the statutory modifications applicable to an appeal in the Court of Appeal, found in s 32(6)–(10) and discussed above. Section 33(8)–(12) applies where the Crown Court is proceeding afresh under s 6 in pursuance of a direction by the Supreme Court. As noted above, the purpose of these provisions is to modify the s 6 procedure having regard to the fact that a period of time has elapsed between the original Crown Court proceedings for confiscation and the date on which the Crown Court proceeds afresh. There are four key modifications. Firstly, the procedure is modified to take into account the fact that the defendant may have been sentenced since the original confiscation hearing. Secondly, the way compensation orders made in the proceedings interact with the s 6 procedure is modified. Thirdly, the effect of s 33(10) is to require the Crown Court to consider the position as regards 'conduct' and 'property' which faced the court on the date of the original confiscation proceedings. The exception to this is that the court proceeding afresh may take into account property obtained after the date of the previous confiscation hearing, but only if it is satisfied that it was obtained as a result of or in connection with conduct occurring before that date. Fourthly, the provisions also modify the application of the assumptions so that they do not apply to events occurring after the original confiscation proceedings.

# E. The Proceeds of Crime Act 2002 (Appeals under Part 2) Order 2003

## Practice and procedure: appeals to the Court of Appeal

**18.82** As foreshadowed in this chapter, the Secretary of State has made certain procedural rules corresponding to those contained in the Criminal Appeal Act 1968 which apply to the statutory appeals contained in Pt 2 of POCA. The Proceeds of Crime Act 2002 (Appeals under Part 2) Order 2003 (SI 2003/82) came into force on 24 March 2003. It has subsequently been amended by the Proceeds of Crime Act 2002 (Appeals under Part 2) Amendment Order 2013 (SI 2013/24.) These orders contain provisions that correspond with those contained in the Criminal Appeal Act 1968 for the purposes of the three new appeal routes introduced by POCA, namely:

(1) an appeal under s 31 of POCA to the Court of Appeal (and from there to the Supreme Court under s 33) by the prosecutor against a confiscation order or a failure of the Crown Court to make a confiscation order;

(2) an appeal under s 43 of POCA to the Court of Appeal (and from there to the Supreme Court under s 44 of POCA) in respect of decisions of the Crown Court about restraint orders; and

(3) an appeal under s 65 of POCA to the Court of Appeal (and from there to the Supreme Court under s 66 of POCA) in respect of decisions of the Crown Court about receivers.

The explanatory notes accompanying the amending Order confirm:

> This Order amends the Proceeds of Crime Act 2002 (Appeals under Part 2) Order 2003. It contains provisions which correspond to those under the Proceeds of Crime Act 2002 (External Requests and Orders) (Order 2005) (England and Wales) (Appeals under Part 2) Order 2012 (SI 2012 No 138). SI 2012 No 138 makes provision corresponding to provisions in the Criminal Appeal Act 1968 ('the 1968 Act') with modifications for the purposes of an appeal to the Court of Appeal (and from there to the Supreme Court) introduced by Articles 47(3) and 48(2) of the Proceeds of Crime Act 2002 (External Requests and Orders) Order 2005 ('the external requests order') that was made under sections 444 and 459(2) of the Proceeds of Crime Act 2002. The purpose of the amendments in this Order is to ensure consistency between appeals (to the Court of Appeal and then on to the Supreme Court) under part 2 of the Proceeds of Crime Act 2002 and those which relate to external requests and orders. It applies to appeals that are both ongoing at the time this Order comes into force and those commenced after.

### Initiating procedure

**18.83** Under Art 3(1) of the Proceeds of Crime Act 2002 (Appeals under Part 2) Order (as amended), a person who wishes to obtain the leave of the Court of Appeal to appeal to the Court of Appeal under Pt 2 of POCA, ie confiscation, restraint, and appointment of receivers, shall give notice of their application for leave to appeal in the manner directed by rules of court. Such a notice of application for leave to appeal shall be given within twenty-eight days from the date of the decision appealed against.

**18.84** Under Art 3(3) the time for giving notice may be extended (whether before or after it expires) by the Court of Appeal. Article 3 corresponds with the similar provisions contained in s 18 of the Criminal Appeal Act 1968.

### Disposal of groundless applications for leave to appeal

**18.85** Under Art 4 of the Proceeds of Crime Act 2002 (Appeals under Part 2) Order, if it appears to the registrar that a notice of application for leave to appeal to the Court of Appeal does not show any substantial ground of appeal, he may refer the application for leave to the Court of Appeal for summary determination.

**18.86** Where the case is so referred to the Court of Appeal, it may, if it considers that the application for leave is frivolous or vexatious and can be determined without adjourning it for a full hearing, dismiss the application for leave summarily, without calling on anyone to attend the hearing. This provision corresponds with s 20 of the Criminal Appeal Act 1968.

### Preparation of case for hearing

**18.87** Once an application has been received, and subject to Art 4, Art 5 states as follows:

(1) The registrar shall—
  (a) take all necessary steps for obtaining a hearing of any application for leave to appeal to the Court of Appeal under Part 2 of the Act of which Notice is given to him and which is not referred and dismissed summarily under Article 4;

(b) where an application for leave to appeal to the Court of Appeal under Part 2 of the Act is granted, take all necessary steps for obtaining a hearing of an appeal; and

(c) obtain and lay before the Court of Appeal in proper form all documents, exhibits and other things which appear necessary for the proper determination of the application for leave to appeal under Part 2 of the Act or the appeal under Part 2 of the Act.

**18.88**  Article 5 corresponds with s 21 of the Criminal Appeal Act 1968 and provides that the registrar must organise hearings for applications for leave to appeal and the appeals themselves. In the case of appeals in relation to confiscation orders, the registrar must also organise documents and exhibits for the appeal and provide them, in accordance with the rules of court, to the parties. Under Art 5(2), a party to an appeal may obtain from the registrar any document or thing, including copies or reproductions of documents, required for his appeal, in accordance with the rules of court. The registrar may make charges in accordance with such rules for those documents (see Art 5(3)).

### Right of defendant to be present

**18.89**  Under Art 6(1) of the Proceeds of Crime Act 2002 (Appeals under Part 2) Order (as amended), the defendant is entitled to be present, if he wishes, at the hearing of any appeal to the Court of Appeal to which he is a party, even though he may be in custody. However, if the defendant is in custody, he will not be entitled to be present:

(a) where the appeal is on some ground involving a question of law alone; or

(b) on an application for leave to appeal; or

(c) on any proceedings preliminary or incidental to an appeal, unless the Court of Appeal gives him leave to be present.

(See Art 6(2)). This article corresponds to s 22 of the Criminal Appeal Act 1968. The amended 2013 Order also provides, under Art 6(3), for the use of livelink facilities in appropriate cases.

### Rules of evidence in the Court of Appeal

**18.90**  For the purposes of an appeal under Pt 2 of POCA, the Court of Appeal may, if it thinks it necessary or expedient in the interests of justice:

(a) order the production of any document, exhibit or other thing connected with the proceedings, the production of which appears to them necessary for the determination of the case;

(b) order any witness to attend for examination and be examined before the Court of Appeal (whether or not the witness was called in the proceedings from which the appeal lies); and

(c) receive any evidence which was not adduced in the proceedings from which the appeal lies.

(2) The power conferred by paragraph (1)(a) may be exercised so as to require the production of any document, exhibit or other thing mentioned in that paragraph to—

(a) the Court;

(b) the appellant;

(c) the respondent;

(d) a party to the appeal.

(3) The Court of Appeal shall, in considering whether to receive any evidence, have regard in particular to—

(a) whether the evidence appears to the Court to be capable of belief;

    (b) whether it appears to the Court that the evidence may afford any ground for allowing the appeal;

    (c) whether the evidence would have been admissible in the proceedings from which the appeal lies on an issue which is the subject of the appeal; and

    (d) whether there is a reasonable explanation of the failure to adduce the evidence in those proceedings.

(See Art 7(1) of the Proceeds of Crime Act 2002 (Appeals under Part 2) Order, as amended by the 2013 Order.)

**18.91** Paragraph (1)(c) applies to any evidence of a witness (including the appellant) who is competent but not compellable. In paragraph (2)(c) 'respondent' includes a person who will be a respondent if leave to appeal is granted.

**18.92** For the purposes of an appeal or application for leave to appeal under Pt 2 of the Act, the Court of Appeal may, if they think it necessary or expedient in the interests of justice, order the examination of any witness whose attendance might be required under para (1)(b) to be conducted, in a manner provided by rules of court, before any judge or officer of the court or other person appointed by the court for the purpose, and allow the admission of any depositions so taken as evidence before the court (Art 7(5)(as amended).

### General provisions

**18.93** The CrimPR set out certain other general provisions to be adopted where the circumstances dictate; the relevant rules are listed below:

| | |
|---|---|
| Extension of time | r 71.1 |
| Applications for leave to be present, reception of evidence | r 71.2 |
| Examination of witnesses in court | r 71.3 |
| Supply of documentary and other exhibits | r 71.4 |
| Registrar's power to require information from court of trial | r 71.5 |
| Hearing by single judge | r 71.6 |
| Determination by full court | r 71.7 |
| Notice of determination | r 71.8 |
| Record of proceedings and transcript | r 71.9 |
| Appeal to the Supreme Court | r 71.10 |
| Service of Documents | r 4 |

### References to the European Court of Justice

**18.94** The Court of Appeal has power to refer a case to the European Court of Justice at any time before the determination of an appeal (see the Criminal Appeal (References to the European Court) Rules 1972, SI 1972/1786).

## F. Appeals in Connection with External Requests and Orders and Associated Receivership Orders

**18.95** In Chapter 19 we consider applications under the Proceeds of Crime Act 2002 (External Requests and Orders) Order 2005 (the 2005 Order) for restraint orders and confiscation orders following receipt of external requests and external orders, and for receivership orders. The 2005 Order makes provision for appeals in connection with these matters.

### Appeal to the Court of Appeal about restraint orders

Article 10(1) of the 2005 Order permits the relevant Director to appeal against a decision **18.96** of the Crown Court not to make a restraint order. On an application to vary or discharge a restraint order the decision of the Crown Court on the application may be appealed either by the relevant Director or by any person affected by the order (Art 10(2)). On appeal, the Court of Appeal may confirm the decision or make such order as it believes is appropriate (Art 10(3)). Thereafter, an appeal lies to the Supreme Court at the instance of any person who was a party to the proceedings in the Court of Appeal: Art 11(2). The Supreme Court may confirm the decision or make such order as it believes is appropriate (Art 11(3)).

### Appeal to the Court of Appeal about external orders

Article 23 concerns appeals to the Court of Appeal about external orders. By Art 23(1) if the **18.97** Crown Court decides not to give effect to the external order by registering it, the relevant Director may appeal to the Court of Appeal. If the Crown Court cancels the registration of the external order, or varies the property to which the external order applies, the relevant Director or any person affected by the registration may appeal to the Court of Appeal (Art 23(2)). On an appeal brought under either Art 23(1) or Art 23(2) the Court of Appeal may confirm or set aside the decision to register, or may direct the Crown Court to register the external order (Art 23(3)). Thereafter, an appeal lies to the Supreme Court at the instance of any person who was a party to the proceedings in the Court of Appeal: Art 24(2). The Supreme Court may confirm or set aside the decision of the Court of Appeal or direct the Crown Court to register the external order (Art 24(3)).

### Appeal to the Court of Appeal about receivers

Article 44 concerns appeals to the Court of Appeal about receivers. If the Crown Court **18.98** refuses an application for the appointment of an enforcement receiver or management receiver or, having granted such an application, decides not to give the receiver one or more of the powers applied for, the person who made the application may appeal to the Court of Appeal (Art 44(1)). On the other hand, if the Crown Court grants such an application, a similar right of appeal is available to the person who applied for the order and any person affected by it (Art 44(2)). On an application to discharge or vary a receivership order the decision of the Crown Court may be appealed by the person who made the application or any person affected by the court's decision, including the receiver (Art 44(5)). Where a receiver applies under Art 41 for directions as to the exercise of his powers, or an affected person applies to the Crown Court in that connection, the decision of the Crown Court may be appealed by the person who made the application, and any person affected by the order, including the receiver. On an appeal brought under Art 44 the Court of Appeal may confirm the decision or make such order as it believes is appropriate. Thereafter, an appeal lies to the Supreme Court at the instance of any person who was a party to the proceedings in the Court of Appeal: Art 45(2). The Supreme Court may confirm the decision or make such order as it believes is appropriate (Art 45(3)).

### Procedure for appeals under the 2005 Order

Appeals lie to the Court of Appeal (Criminal Division), subject to the rules of court made **18.99** under s 53(1) of the Senior Courts Act 1981.

**18.100**   The procedure for appealing to the Court of Appeal and to the Supreme Court are to be found in the Proceeds of Crime Act 2002 (External Requests and Orders) Order 2005 (England and Wales) (Appeals under Part 2) Order 2012/138.

## G.   Appeals against Orders for Cash Forfeiture or Condemnation

### Forfeiture appeals under POCA from the magistrates' court

**18.101**   Section 299 of POCA governs appeals against decisions made in proceedings for 'cash forfeiture' made under Pt 5 of POCA. The section was amended by s 101 of SOCPA because of an ambiguity as to its meaning. While the original s 299(1) appeared to allow 'any party to the proceedings' to appeal against an order made under s 298, this was qualified by the words 'for the forfeiture of cash'. This meant that while any party could appeal an order for forfeiture of cash, there was no provision for the complainant to appeal a *refusal* to grant forfeiture, although somewhat ironically a complainant could appeal an order *for* forfeiture.

**18.102**   The substituted s 299 now states:

> (1)   Any party to proceedings for an order for the forfeiture of cash under section 298 who is aggrieved by an order under that section or by the decision of the court not to make such an order may appeal...

**18.103**   In other words, both the complainant and the defendant now have a right of appeal from the magistrates' court hearing to the Crown Court. Such a hearing should be *de novo* (s 79(3) Senior Courts Act 1981), with the facts being re-examined in the court above, and with the opportunity for both parties to serve further evidence before the hearing takes place (whilst the original s 299(3) expressly stated that the appeal was by way of rehearing, the substituted legislation does not).

**18.104**   It will have been seen from Chapter 15 (seizure of cash under POCA) that once an application for forfeiture has been made, the seized cash may not be released until any proceedings in pursuance of that application (including any proceedings on appeal) are concluded. Under the previous legislation (s 42(7)) the money was not to be released until the application or criminal proceedings were concluded. (See further at para 15.176).

### Procedure on forfeiture appeals under POCA

**18.105**   The appeal is to the Crown Court; and notice must be lodged before the expiration of thirty days from when the order was made. It is a *de novo* hearing.

**18.106**   By reason of s 299(3) the Crown Court hearing the appeal may make any order it thinks appropriate.

**18.107**   Appeals in relation to the cash seizure provisions, including whether the thirty-day period can be extended and funding of the appeal and applications for judicial review, are further considered at para 15.176 et seq of Chapter 15.

**18.108**   The judge sits usually with two lay magistrates. The judge must give reasons for the court's decision. The reasoning required will depend on the circumstances of the case but must be enough to show that the court has identified the main issues and how it has resolved them (see *R v Harrow Crown Court ex p Dave* [1994] 1 WLR 98). The rules for the hearing of a 'complaint' should be adopted as the procedure of the court for such a hearing.

### Appeals in condemnation cases from the magistrates' court

Both HMRC and the defendant may appeal to the Crown Court against a decision of the magistrates' court to condemn property, or in the alternative invite the court to state a case for the High Court on a matter of law (see para 11 of Sch 3 to CEMA). The Crown Court's jurisdiction and powers of disposal are set out in ss 45 to 48 of the Senior Courts Act 1981. **18.109**

On appeal to the Crown Court the hearing is *de novo* (s 79(3) Senior Courts Act 1981) and involves a complete rehearing of the original case, including oral evidence. The CrimPR appear to have been adopted, albeit the appeal is civil in nature. Rule 63.2 of the CrimPR sets out the time limit (not more than twenty-one days from the date of the order) and the procedure (written notice to the magistrates' court). **18.110**

The procedure adopted at the hearing is the same as set out in the Magistrates' Courts Rules, discussed in Chapter 15 at para 15.122 et seq. Pending the rehearing, there is no restriction on either the complainant or the defence obtaining more evidence and adducing new evidence at the appeal. Appeals in condemnation cases, including procedure, are further considered at para 23.115 et seq of Chapter 23. **18.111**

### Appeal from the magistrates' court to the High Court by way of case stated

Under the Magistrates' Court Act 1980, s 111(1): **18.112**

> Any person who was a party to any proceedings before a Magistrates' Court or is aggrieved by the conviction, order, determination or other proceeding of the Court may question the proceeding on the ground that it is wrong in law or in excess of jurisdiction by applying to the justices composing the court to state a case for the opinion of the High Court on a question of law or jurisdiction involved...

The following points should be noted: **18.113**

(1) The application must be made in writing within twenty-one days of the decision and must state the point of law upon which the opinion of the High Court is sought.
(2) There is no power to state a case until the magistrates have reached a final decision in the matter.
(3) The right to appeal to the Crown Court is lost once an application to state a case to the High Court is made (see MCA, s 111(4)).
(4) The magistrates are entitled to refuse a request to state a case, but that decision is itself reviewable by the High Court on an application for judicial review (see *R v Huntington Magistrates' Court ex p Percy* (1994) COD 323, The Times, 4 March 1994).

The relevant parts of the CrimPR are set out at Pt 64, and deal with, inter alia, the making of the application; extension of the time limit; service of documents and content. **18.114**

## H. Appeals under Part 6 of POCA:
## Revenue Functions

**18.115**     An appeal in respect of the exercise by SOCA of general revenue functions is now to the Tax Chamber of the First-tier Tribunal (by reason of s 31 of the Taxes Management Act and Art 7 of the First-tier Tribunal and Upper Tribunal (Chambers) Order SI 2010/2655).

**18.116**     The applicable procedural rules are to be found in the Tribunal Procedure (First-tier Tribunal) (Tax Chamber) Rules, SI 2009/273 (as amended).

## I. The Criminal Cases Review Commission

**18.117**     The CCRC may refer to the Court of Appeal any conviction or sentence or other applicable finding. Thus it is within the competence of the CCRC to refer a confiscation order to the Court of Appeal provided the criteria for referral contained in s 13 of the Criminal Appeal Act 1995 are met. A reference shall not be made unless the CCRC is satisfied of three matters: firstly, that there is a real possibility that the confiscation order would not be upheld if the reference is made; secondly that this real possibility arises because of an argument on a point of law, or information, not raised in the proceedings; thirdly that an appeal against the confiscation order must have been determined or leave to appeal must have been refused. Where one or more of these three conditions is not met, the CCRC may, nevertheless, refer a case to the Court of Appeal if it appears that there are exceptional circumstances that justify a reference.

**18.118**     If the CCRC forms a negative view about an application it will invite further representations or comments, usually within twenty working days. This period is non-statutory and may be extended upon application to the Commission. However, if further representations are not received within twenty working days (in addition to any extension), or the representations raise no new issues, the case will be closed.

## J. Appeals against Findings of Contempt of Court

### Appeals in cases of findings of contempt of court by the High Court

**18.119**     An appeal lies against punishment imposed by a court for contempt of court: s 13 of the Administration of Justice Act 1960. Permission is not required to appeal a committal for contempt of court. By reason of s 13(1) of the Administration of Justice Act 1960 the defendant has the right of appeal to the Court of Appeal (Civil Division) from any order or decision. This means the defendant may appeal either against the sentence imposed for contempt or the finding of contempt itself or both. The powers of the Court of Appeal are found in s 13(3) of the Administration of Justice Act 1960, which reads:

> The court to which an appeal is brought under this section may reverse or vary the order or decision of the court below, and make such other order as may be just; and without prejudice to the inherent powers of any report referred to in subsection (2) of this section, provision may be made by rules of court authorising the release on bail of an appellant under this section.

**18.120**     The procedural rules, which are found in CPR Practice Direction 52 state that the appellant must serve the appellant's notice on the court from whose order or decision the appeal is brought (para 21.4 of the Practice Direction). In the case of appeals from the Queen's Bench Division the notice must be served on the Senior Master of the Queen's Bench Division, and service may be effected by leaving a copy of the notice of appeal with the clerk of the lists.

The High Court has the power to grant bail pending the outcome of any appeal: s 4 of the **18.121** Administration of Justice Act 1960.

There is a further provision for an appeal to the Supreme Court under s 13(4) subject to the **18.122** obtaining of permission.

### Appeals in cases of findings of contempt of court by the Crown Court

Section 18A of the Criminal Appeal Act 1968 states that a person who wishes to appeal **18.123** under s 13 of the Administration of Justice Act 1960 from any order or decision of the Crown Court in the exercise of its jurisdiction to punish for contempt of court shall give notice of appeal in such manner as may be directed by the rules of court. The usual procedural rules for appealing against sentence apply. They are found in Part 68 of the CrimPR. Notice of appeal is to be given within twenty-eight days from the date of the order or decision appealed against. The time for giving notice may be extended, either before or after expiry, by the Court of Appeal (s 18A(3) of the Criminal Appeal Act 1968).

The Court of Appeal may, if it thinks fit, grant an appellant bail pending the determination **18.124** of his appeal (s 19 of the Criminal Appeal Act 1968). It may also revoke it (s 19(1)(b) of the Criminal Appeal Act 1968).

## K. Thumbnail Guide to the Appeal Provisions within the Criminal Procedure Rules

Part 63—Appeals from the Magistrates' Court to the Crown Court against conviction or **18.125** sentence:

| | |
|---|---|
| Service of appeal notice | r 63.2 |
| Form of appeal notice | r 63.3 |
| Hearings and decisions | r 63.7 |
| Abandonment of appeal—notice and bail | r 63.8 |
| Variation of requirements | r 63.9 |
| Constitution of the Crown Court | r 63.10 |

Part 64—Appeal to the High Court by Way of Case Stated: **18.126**

| | |
|---|---|
| Application to Crown Court or magistrates' court to state case | r 64.2 |
| Preparation and submission of final case for magistrates' court | r 64.3 |
| Extension of time limit | r 64.5 |
| Content of case stated by magistrates' court | r 64.5 |

Part 66—Appeal to the Court of Appeal against ruling in Preparatory Hearing **18.127**

Part 67—Appeal to the Court of Appeal against ruling adverse to prosecution
Part 69—Appeal to the Court of Appeal regarding reporting or public access restriction
Part 68—Appeal to the Court of Appeal against conviction or sentence

**18.128** Part 71—Appeal to the Court of Appeal under the POCA 2002: General rules:

**18.129** Part 72—Appeal to the Court of Appeal under POCA 2002—Prosecutor's Appeal regarding Confiscation:

**18.130** Part 73—Appeal to the Court of Appeal under POCA 2002: Restraint or Receivership Orders:

**18.131** Part 74—Appeal to the Supreme Court:

**18.132** Part 75—Reference to the European Court:

### Confiscation: Attorney General's appeal

**18.133** In *A-G References Nos 114, 115, 116, 144 and 145 of 2002* [2003] EWCA 3374 the Court of Appeal held that it had jurisdiction to hear applications by the Attorney General to refer a sentence under s 36 of the CJA, on the basis that a judge had wrongly refused to make a confiscation order under the 1988 Act, and the Court could consider evidence as required. Attorney General's references may also be made where the terms of the confiscation order are considered to be unduly lenient.

# 19

# THE INTERNATIONAL ELEMENT

## A. Introduction

Organised crime transcends national frontiers. Organised criminals engage in a multitude **19.01** of cross-border criminal activities—such as drug trafficking, trafficking in human beings, illicit arms trafficking, fraud, money laundering, and corruption—generating huge profits. As Ognall J observed in *Re M* (Unreported, 9 July 1993): 'We live in an age when funds may be transferred from jurisdiction to jurisdiction as rapidly as it takes me to speak this sentence and when banks are increasingly multi-national operations.'

It is increasingly common, therefore, to find a person prosecuted for criminal offences in one **19.02** country owning or moving assets in or to another. Asset freezing and confiscation of proceeds of crime are essential tools in the fight against organised crime including also economic crime and corruption.

## B. Cooperation under POCA

### Preliminary matters

Sections 443 and 444 of POCA permit Orders in Council to be made permitting the **19.03** enforcement in the UK of orders made in England, Wales, Scotland, and Northern Ireland, as well as those made in other jurisdictions. Section 443 of POCA permit Orders in Council to be made permitting the enforcement of orders including confiscation and restraint orders made in one part of the UK in another part of it. Section 443 has been amended by paras 137(2) and 137(3) of Sch 8(6) to the SCA. Section 444 of POCA permits Orders in Council to be made permitting the enforcement of orders made by countries outside the UK in the UK. Section 444 has been amended by by s 108(2) of SOCPA and para 138 of Sch 8(6) to the SCA.

**19.04**  Nothing in s 444 requires overseas countries to be designated before orders made in their courts may be enforced in the UK. The removal of the requirement for designation is intended to expedite the process of obtaining restraint orders on behalf of overseas countries, enabling any country that identifies assets in the UK to forward a letter of request seeking a restraint order and, ultimately, confiscation of the property concerned.

**19.05**  Section 447 of POCA defines a number of the key expressions used in s 444. By s 447(1):

An external request is a request by an overseas authority to prohibit dealing with relevant property which is identified in the request.

**19.06**  By s 447(2):

An external order is an order which—
(a) is made by an overseas court where property is found or believed to have been obtained as a result of or in connection with criminal conduct, and
(b) is for the recovery of specified property or a specified sum of money.

**19.07**  By s 447(8) criminal conduct is defined as conduct which:

(a) constitutes an offence in any part of the United Kingdom, or
(b) would constitute an offence in any part of the United Kingdom if it occurred there.

### External requests and orders

**19.08**  By an Order in Council made under s 444 POCA, on 1 January 2006 the Proceeds of Crime Act 2002 (External Requests and Orders) Order 2005, SI 2005/3181 ('the External Requests 2005 Order') came into force. Parts 2, 3, 4, and 5 of the External Requests 2005 Order make provision in respect of 'external requests' as defined by POCA s 447(1) and 'external orders' as defined by POCA s 447(2).

**19.09**  The External Requests 2005 Order enables the powers conferred by Pts 2, 3, 4, and 5 of POCA to be exercised for the purpose of giving effect to external requests and external orders, so that the provisions of the External Requests 2005 Order mirror the provisions of POCA.

**19.10**  The External Requests 2005 Order has been amended by the Proceeds of Crime Act 2002 (External Requests and Orders) (Amendment) Order 2008, SI 2008/302.

### Action to be taken on receipt of an external request

**19.11**  Under Art 6(2) of the External Requests Order 2005, when an external request appears to the Secretary of State to be made in connection with criminal investigations or proceedings which relate to an offence involving serious or complex fraud and concerns relevant property in England or Wales he may refer it to the Director of the SFO to be processed.

**19.12**  Any other external request received by the Secretary of State in connection with criminal investigations or proceedings in the country from which the request was made and concerning relevant property in England and Wales may, under Art 6(1) of the External Requests Order 2005, be referred to the DPP or the Director of Revenue and Customs Prosecutions to be processed.

The Director to whom the request is referred is described in the External Requests Order **19.13** 2005 as 'the relevant Director': see Art 6(4).

### Powers of the Crown Court to make restraint orders

The External Requests Order 2005 follows the scheme of POCA by transferring the jurisdic-   **19.14** tion to make restraint orders and enforce external confiscation orders from the High Court to the Crown Court. By Art 7(1) the Crown Court may exercise the powers conferred by Art 8 to make restraint orders if either of the following conditions is satisfied:

7(2)  The first condition is that—
>  (a)  relevant property in England and Wales is identified in the external request,
>  (b)  a criminal investigation has been started in the country from which the external request was made with regards to an offence, and
>  (c)  there is reasonable cause to believe that the alleged offender named in the request has benefited from his criminal conduct.

7(3)  The second condition is that—
>  (a)  relevant property in England and Wales is identified in the external request,
>  (b)  proceedings for an offence have been started in the country from which the external request was made and not concluded, and
>  (c)  there is reasonable cause to believe that the defendant named in the request has benefited from his criminal conduct.

If either of these conditions is satisfied, the Crown Court may make a restraint order under   **19.15** Art 8(1) 'prohibiting any specified person from dealing with relevant property which is iden- tified in the external request and specified in the order'. By Art 8(2) the order may be made subject to exceptions and such exceptions may in particular:

(a)  make provision for reasonable living expenses and reasonable legal expenses in connec- tion with the proceedings seeking a restraint order or the registration of an external order;
(b)  make provision for the purpose of enabling any person to carry on any trade, business, profession, or occupation;
(c)  be made subject to conditions.

The terms of Art 8(2)(a) of the External Requests Order 2005 represent a significant depar-   **19.16** ture from the position under POCA because s 41(4) of POCA precludes the release of funds to meet legal expenses incurred in relation to the proceedings.

The departure from s 41 of POCA in Art 8(2) of the External Requests Order 2005 applies   **19.17** to restraint orders sought pursuant to external requests, but only in relation to the restraint proceedings or the registration of an external order. The defendant would not, under Art 8(2), be able to apply for the release of restrained funds to defend the criminal proceedings in the overseas jurisdiction making the request.

Article 8(2)(c) of the External Requests Order 2005 empowers the court to impose condi-   **19.18** tions subject to which funds are released under Arts 8(2)(a) and 8(2)(b).

The External Requests Order 2005 does not empower the Crown Court to make restraint   **19.19** orders prohibiting any dealing in assets located outside England and Wales. The House of

Lords so held in dismissing an appeal by the SFO in *King v Director of the Serious Fraud Office* [2009] UKHL 17.

**19.20** It followed from this case that in cases where the Crown Court is asked to make an order in response to an external request, the Crown Court has not only no power to restrain assets held outside the jurisdiction but also no power requiring the defendant to disclose the existence of assets held outside England and Wales.

### Power of the High Court to make property freezing or disclosure orders in civil proceedings

**19.21** In *Serious Organised Crime Agency v Perry* [2012] UKSC 35, the Court considered whether the High Court had power to make a worldwide PFO or an order requiring a defendant to disclose all his assets worldwide. SOCA sought a worldwide PFO and disclosure orders (within ss 357 and 359 POCA) against Mr Perry, following his conviction for serious offences outside the UK. Lord Phillips gave the lead judgement (supported by the majority). The Court recognized that POCA must be read in light of the 1990 Strasbourg Convention on Laundering, Search, Seizure and Confiscation of the Proceeds from Crime ('the Strasbourg Convention'). The Supreme Court held by a majority that Pt 5 of POCA did not give the High Court of England and Wales jurisdiction to impose PFOs or civil recovery orders in respect of property situated outside the UK.

**19.22** Similarly, the court had no power under Pt 8 of POCA to make disclosure orders relating to persons known to be outside the jurisdiction of the UK. Because ss 357 and 359 confer on a UK public authority the power to impose on persons positive obligations to provide information subject to criminal sanction in the event of non-compliance, it was considered that such authority could only be exercised over persons within its jurisdiction.

**19.23** Lord Judge and Lord Clarke provided a joint judgment in dissent in relation to whether there was jurisdiction to grant a worldwide PFO. At para 164, they state: 'In our judgment the expression "all property wherever situated" must have the same meaning in each of the sections in which it appears, including section 316(4).'

**19.24** In order to address the effect of the judgment in *Perry*, amendments to Pt 5 of POCA were included in ss 48, 49 and Schs 18 and 19 to the Crime and Courts Act 2013 (CCA) which was passed in April 2013. Section 48 of the CCA is in force and introduces a new s 282A and Sch 7A to POCA to extend the jurisdiction of civil recovery orders so that they can now be made in respect of property outside the jurisdiction of the UK if there is or has been a connection between the case and the relevant part of the UK. Likewise Sch 18 to the CCA 2013 is in force and introduces ss 282B–282F to POCA. These sections will facilitate the enforcement outside the UK of orders made under Chapter 2 of Pt 5 of POCA and the transmission of requests for evidence held outside the UK. However, at the time of writing s 49 and Sch 19 to the CCA are not yet in effect. When in force, Pt 1 of the Schedule will amend s 341 of POCA as set out above and Pt 2 of the Schedule will introduce ss 375A and 375B to POCA. New s 375A of POCA will make provision for evidence to be obtained from a court, tribunal, government, or authority outside the UK ('receiving country') if a person or property is subject to a civil recovery investigation, a detained cash investigation, or an exploitation proceeds investigation (as defined in s 341). It will enable a judge to make a request for assistance upon an application by an appropriate officer or a person subject to the investigation, providing that the judge thinks there is relevant evidence in a country or territory outside the UK. However a senior appropriate officer or the relevant Director may make a direct request for assistance if it is thought that there is relevant evidence in a country or territory outside the UK. In the case of urgency, a request may be sent via the International Criminal Police Organization (Interpol or Europol) or any person competent to receive it under any provisions adopted under the EU Treaties, for onward forwarding to the receiving country. New s 375B of POCA will provide that evidence obtained by a request for assistance under new s 375A must not be used for any purpose other than for the purpose of the investigation for which it was obtained or for the purposes of certain proceedings. However, the court, tribunal, government, or authority that received the request and provided the evidence can consent to the use of the evidence for other purposes. See also Chapter 17 on civil recovery investigations (para 17.66) and para 13.61 on territorial limits.

### Ancillary orders

Article 8(4) of the External Requests Order 2005 empowers the court to make such order as it **19.25** believes is appropriate for the purpose of ensuring the restraint order is effective. The orders most commonly sought under s 41(7) of POCA or Art 8(4) of the External Requests Order 2005 are disclosure orders. A disclosure order may be made against a third party holding the defendant's realisable property: see *Re D (Restraint Order: Non Party)* (1995), The Times, 26 January 1995.

### Applications for and the discharge and variation of restraint orders

By Art 9(1)(a) of the External Requests Order 2005 applications for restraint orders under **19.26** the order can only be made by the relevant Director (under Art 6(4) the DPP, the Director of Revenue and Customs Prosecutions, or the Director of the SFO). The application may be made ex parte to a judge in chambers (see Art 9(1)(b) of the External Requests Order 2005).

The relevant Director and any person affected by the order may apply for the restraint order **19.27** to be varied or discharged (Art 9(2)). The order must be discharged if no external confiscation order is made (Art 9(5)), if no external confiscation order is registered within a reasonable time (Art 9(6)), or if proceedings for an offence are not started within a reasonable time when the order has been obtained on the basis that the defendant is subject to a criminal investigation (Art 9(7)).

### Appeals

Article 10 of the External Requests Order 2005 makes provision for the relevant Director **19.28** and parties affected by restraint orders to appeal against decisions of the Crown Court to the Court of Appeal and Art 11 (as amended by Art 8(2) of the Constitutional Reform Act 2005 (Consequential Amendments) Order 2011/1242) provides for a further appeal to the Supreme Court.

### Hearsay evidence

Article 13 (3) of the External Requests Order 2005 makes provision for the admissibility **19.29** of hearsay evidence (as defined in Art 13(4)) in restraint proceedings subject to the terms of ss 2 to 4 of the Civil Evidence Act 1995.

### Management receivers

Articles 15 and 16 of the External Requests Order 2005 empower a Crown Court which **19.30** makes a restraint order to appoint management receivers on the same basis as under ss 48 and

49 of POCA. The application may be made at the same time as the application for a restraint order or any time thereafter (see Art 15(1)(b)).

### Procedural matters

**19.31** Rule 57.14 of the CrimPR provides that Pts 59 to 61 and 71 to 73 shall apply with the necessary modifications to applications under the External Requests Order 2005 in the same way as they apply to the corresponding provisions under Pt 2 of POCA.

**19.32** It is important to note that the duty of full and frank disclosure applies equally to applications for restraints under the External Requests Order 2005 as it does to applications in domestic cases under POCA. The relevant Director should therefore be vigilant to ensure that the overseas authority on whose behalf he is making the application has provided all the information the court will require to discharge this duty. The court will not, however, discharge a restraint order on this basis unless the failure to give full and frank disclosure goes to a matter central to the proceedings: see Buxton LJ in *Government of India v Ottavio Quattrocchi* [2004] EWCA Civ 40, a case decided under s76(1) CJA.

**19.33** The Criminal Division of the Court of Appeal adopted a similar approach in *Director of the Serious Fraud Office v A* [2007] EWCA Crim 1927, a case where the SFO obtained a restraint order against the defendant under the External Requests Order 2005, following receipt of a letter of request from Iran alleging that the defendant was guilty of a large-scale fraud on an Iranian government agency. In that case, the Court of Appeal allowed an appeal by the SFO against the judge's decision to discharge the order, holding that the non-disclosure complained of by the defendant on the facts of that case was not material. Hughes LJ concluded (at para 23):

> If the conclusion drawn in the Crown Court had been one of deliberate deception, then providing there was sufficient reason for reaching it that might well provide a basis for discharging the restraint order, but in the absence of such a conclusion and, if it be reached, consideration whether or [not] the order should stand on its merits, we are unable to say that the Judge directed himself correctly. The proper course is for the Judge's decision to discharge the restraint order to be quashed and the application for discharge to be remitted to the Crown Court for re-determination in the light of this judgment.

**19.34** The court will not, in deciding whether to make a restraint order, allow itself to become embroiled in detailed argument as to the merits of the proceedings brought in the requesting country, see *Government of India v Ottavio Quattrocchi*.

### Applications to give effect to external orders

**19.35** Articles 20 to 22 of the External Requests Order 2005 make provision for the Crown Court to give effect to external orders. By Art 2 of the External Requests Order 2005, 'external order' has the meaning given to it in s 447(2) of POCA.

**19.36** By Art 20(1) of the External Requests Order 2005, the relevant Director may make an application to the Crown Court to give effect to an external order. The application shall include a request to appoint the relevant Director as the enforcement authority for the order and the application may be made ex parte to a judge in chambers (see Art 20(3)). By Art 20(2), no application to give effect to an external order may be made otherwise than in accordance with Art 20(1). This provision effectively precludes overseas law enforcement agencies from making their own direct applications to the Crown Court to give effect to their orders; such applications may only be made by the relevant Director.

Article 21 of the External Requests Order 2005 sets out the conditions that must be satisfied **19.37** for the Crown Court to give effect to external orders. It provides:

(1) The Crown Court must decide to give effect to an external order by registering it where all of the following conditions are satisfied.

(2) The first condition is that the external order was made consequent upon the conviction of the person named in the order and no appeal is outstanding in respect of that conviction.

(3) The second condition is that the external order is in force and no appeal is outstanding in respect of it.

(4) The third condition is that giving effect to the external order would not be incompatible with any of the Convention rights (within the meaning of the Human Rights Act 1998) of any person affected by it.

(5) The fourth condition applies only in respect of an external order which authorises the confiscation of property other than money that is specified in the order.

(6) That condition is that the specified property must not be subject to a charge under any of the following provisions—
  (a) section 9 of the Drug Trafficking Offences Act 1986;
  (b) section 78 of the Criminal Justice Act 1988;
  (c) Article 14 of the Criminal Justice (Confiscation) (Northern Ireland) Order 1990;
  (d) section 27 of the Drug Trafficking Act 1994;
  (e) Article 32 of the Proceeds of Crime (Northern Ireland) Order 1996.

(7) In determining whether the order is an external order within the meaning of the Act, the Court must have regard to the definitions in subsections (2), (4), (5), (6), (8) and (10) of section 447 of the Act.

(8) In paragraph (3) 'appeal' includes—
  (a) any proceedings by way of discharging or setting aside the order, and
  (b) an application for a new trial or stay of execution.

The first condition, set out in Art 21(2) of the External Requests Order 2005, represents a **19.38** major change from the position that applied under the DTA and CJA to the extent that it requires that in order to give effect to the external order it must have been made on the conviction of the person named in it. This is in contrast to the position under the Designated Countries and Territories Orders where external orders could be registered even if they were made in civil proceedings. Part V of the External Requests Order 2005 creates a separate regime for the enforcement of external orders made in civil recovery proceedings. Applications in relation to the enforcement of such orders may only be made to the High Court.

The third condition specifically requires the court to satisfy itself that giving effect to the **19.39** order would not be incompatible with the Convention rights of anyone affected by it. This was considered by the House of Lords in *Barnette v Government of the United States of America* [2004] UKHL 37, a case involving s 97 CJA.

### Registration of the order

Where the Crown Court decides to give effect to an external order, Art 22(1) of the External **19.40** Requests Order 2005 provides that the court must:

(a) register the order in that court;
(b) provide for notice of the registration to be given to any person affected by it; and
(c) appoint the relevant Director as the enforcement authority.

If the order being registered is for a sum of money expressed in a currency other than sterling, **19.41** the amount to be recovered is taken to be the sterling equivalent calculated in accordance with the rate of exchange prevailing at the end of the working day immediately preceding the day when the Crown Court registered the order: see Art 25(2) of the External Requests Order 2005. The sterling equivalent is to be calculated by the relevant director: see Art 25(3). The notice of registration required to be served under Art 22(1)(b) must specify the sterling amount that is required to be paid: see Art 25(4). By Art 22(3), the Crown Court may cancel the registration of the order or vary the property to which it applies on the application of the relevant Director or any person affected by it and, under Art 22(4) of the External Requests Order 2005, must cancel the registration if it appears that the order has been satisfied.

### Appeals

**19.42** Article 23 of the External Requests Order 2005 makes provision for the relevant Director and any person affected by a registration to appeal to the Court of Appeal and Art 24 of the External Requests Order 2005 (as amended by article 8(2) of the Constitutional Reform Act 2005 (Consequential Amendments) Order 2011/1242) provides for a further appeal to the Supreme Court.

### Enforcement of the order

**19.43** Where the external order is for recovery of a specific sum of money, then by Art 26(2) of the External Requests Order 2005, payment of the external order is due on the day notice of registration is served. If the registration of the order is subject to an appeal to the Court of Appeal or Supreme Court, the duty to pay is delayed until the day on which the appeal is determined or withdrawn (Art 26(3)).

**19.44** Further, by Art 26(4) of the External Requests Order 2005 a person affected by an external order can, once it has been registered, apply to the court for time to pay. If the person affected shows that he needs time to pay, the Crown Court may allow payment to be made in a specified period which must not exceed six months (see Art 26(5)(b)). If, within that period, the person can show 'exceptional circumstances' the court may approve a further extension provided the total period allowed for payment does not exceed twelve months: see Art 26(7).

**19.45** Once an external order has been registered and any time to pay allowed by the Crown Court has expired, it may be enforced in similar ways to domestic confiscation orders: in particular Art 27 of the External Requests Order 2005 gives the court power to appoint enforcement receivers. These provisions are in identical terms to those in relation to the appointment of enforcement receivers in domestic cases.

### Outgoing requests: enforcement abroad

**19.46** Consideration has been given above only to the position where an overseas jurisdiction seeks assistance in the restraint and realisation of assets located in England and Wales. POCA also makes provision for letters of request for assistance to be sent to overseas countries seeking similar assistance in cases where defendants being prosecuted in England and Wales hold assets overseas against which restraint and enforcement action is sought. This is dealt with in s 74 of POCA, which makes provision in respect of the position both before and after a confiscation order is made. Section 74 (as amended by para 35 of Sch 8 and para 1 of Sch 14 to the SCA) provides:

> (1) This section applies if—
>> (a) any of the conditions in section 40 is satisfied,
>> (b) the prosecutor believes that realisable property is situated in a country or territory outside the United Kingdom (the receiving country), and

(c) the prosecutor sends a request for assistance to the Secretary of State with a view to it being forwarded under this section.

(2) In a case where no confiscation order has been made, a request for assistance is a request to the government of the receiving country to secure that any person is prohibited from dealing with realisable property.

(3) In a case where a confiscation order has been made and has not been satisfied, discharged or quashed, a request for assistance is a request to the government of the receiving country to secure that—

(a) any person is prohibited from dealing with realisable property;

(b) realisable property is realised and the proceeds are applied in accordance with the law of the receiving country.

(4) No request for assistance may be made for the purposes of this section in a case where a confiscation order has been made and has been satisfied, discharged or quashed.

(5) If the Secretary of State believes it is appropriate to do so he may forward the request for assistance to the government of the receiving country.

(6) If property is realised in pursuance of a request under subsection (3) the amount ordered to be paid under the confiscation order must be taken to be reduced by an amount equal to the proceeds of realisation.

(7) A certificate purporting to be issued by or on behalf of the requested government is admissible as evidence of the facts it states if it states—

(a) that property has been realised in pursuance of a request under subsection (3),

(b) the date of realisation, and

(c) the proceeds of realisation.

(8) If the proceeds of realisation made in pursuance of a request under subsection (3) are expressed in a currency other than sterling, they must be taken to be the sterling equivalent calculated in accordance with the rate of exchange prevailing at the end of the day of realisation.

**19.47** Section 74 provides for a similar scheme to that applicable under the CJA and DTA in relation to outgoing letters of request. Prior to the making of a confiscation order, a letter of request for assistance may only seek the restraint of assets held overseas by the defendant: see s 74(2). Once a confiscation order is made, however, the letter of request for assistance may seek both the restraint of assets and their realisation in satisfaction of the confiscation order. Once assets have been realised overseas in satisfaction of a confiscation order, the amount realised must be deducted from the amount due under the order: see s 74(6).

**19.48** Section 74 is, of course, without prejudice to the right of the prosecutor to enforce the order by the employment of domestic remedies. He may, for example, require the defendant to bring back assets to the jurisdiction pursuant to a repatriation order. But see *DPP v Scarlett* [2000] 1 WLR 515.

**19.49** The prosecutor may also appoint an enforcement receiver (Art 27 of the External Requests Order 2005), who may, pursuant to his order of appointment, require the defendant to sign such documents as are necessary to enable him to realise overseas assets and pay the proceeds into court in England and Wales. The remedy adopted by the receiver will inevitably depend on the facts of individual cases and the extent and speed of cooperation particular countries are able to offer. The letter of request route inevitably takes time and, if there is an immediate risk of dissipation, the prosecutor or receiver may well seek to use the repatriation route in relation to a defendant who is within the jurisdiction and can be brought before the court swiftly for contempt of court should he refuse to comply. If, on the other hand, there is no risk of dissipation and an asset is located in a country that is able to respond effectively and expeditiously to a letter of request, the prosecutor should normally pursue the letter of request route specifically provided for under s 74.

## C. Enforcement of POCA Confiscation Orders in Different Parts of the UK

**19.50**  Under s 443 of POCA, Orders in Council have been made in relation to s 443 Proceeds of Crime Act 2002 (Enforcement in different parts of the United Kingdom) Order 2002, SI 2002/3133 and to ss 443(1)(d), 443(1)(e), 443(3), and 443(4) Proceeds of Crime Act 2002 (Investigations in different parts of the United Kingdom) Order 2003/425 and Proceeds of Crime Act 2002 (Investigations in different parts of the United Kingdom) (Amendment) Order 2008/298.

**19.51**  By Arts 3, 4, 8, 9, 13, and 14 of the Proceeds of Crime Act 2002 (Enforcement in different parts of the United Kingdom) Order 2002, SI 2002/3133 restraint, receivership, and administration orders made in England, Wales, Scotland, and Northern Ireland automatically have effect throughout the UK. However enforcement proceedings

(a)  in the Crown Court in England and Wales (Art 5);
(b)  the Court of Session for Scotland (Art 10);
(c)  the High Court in Northern Ireland (Art 15)

can only be brought if the orders are registered in accordance with Arts 6, 11, or 16 of SI 2002/3133.

**19.52**  Once registration is effective, the court has the same powers of enforcement it would have if the order had been made in that jurisdiction.

## D. Assistance under the Crime (International Co-operation) Act 2003 (CICA)

**19.53**  In addition to POCA, under s 7(5) of CICA, the UK can authorise a designated prosecuting authority to issue a letter of request for mutual assistance (evidence) from another state and under ss 13 to 19 deal with incoming requests for evidence.

**19.54**  The 10th edition of the 'Mutual Legal Assistance Guidelines for the United Kingdom' was published in September 2012 and offers guidance to ensure that requests for assistance from the UK can be dealt with quickly by countries outside the UK. The guidance deals with both formal and informal requests for assistance.

## E. International Cooperation

### Introduction

**19.55**  As set out above by s 74 of POCA and/or s 7(5) of CICA, the UK can make a request for mutual legal assistance (MLA) to another country in order to recover criminal assets abroad. Whether and how those requests are dealt with will be determined by the legal framework of the requested country.

Sometimes informal, faster, and flexible channels among law enforcement authorities, supported by Interpol, Europol, or regional law enforcement authorities, may be used where coercive action is not required. However, information on overseas countries' implementation and adherence to Conventions, Directives, and legislation will be a crucial tool in preparing for international cooperation in asset recovery. **19.56**

Set out below, in summary form, are some of the international Conventions, organisations, and networks to promote best practice and to facilitate international cooperation and MLA. As will be seen, the need for cooperation both regionally and internationally has been recognised by countries throughout the world as necessary in the areas of asset recovery in the fight against crime and in particular corruption. **19.57**

### UK organisations

SOCA assumed its full function on 1 April 2006, its main functions being set up under SOCPA. In its Annual Plan 2012–13, SOCA notes that work to establish the NCA, which is expected to be fully operational in 2013, were ongoing. SOCA provides and manages, on behalf of the UK, the Suspicious Activity Reports Regime, the UK Financial Intelligence Unit (FIU), the Interpol and the Europol Bureau functions, one of the two UK Central Authorities for the European Arrest Warrant Regime, the National Compromise Database, and other similar functions. Pursuant to s 15 of the Crime and Courts Act 2013, as discussed elsewhere, SOCA is being abolished and its functions taken over by the new National Crime Agency. **19.58**

Since 2006, the Department for International Development (DFID) has provided support to UK law enforcement agencies to tackle money laundering from developing countries. In August 2012 it published figures on assets restrained, recovered, and returned between 2006 and 2012. Items identified for restraint orders amounted to £6,750,000 including forfeited funds of £1,115,000 (returned to Nigeria) and funds under confiscation orders (returned to Nigeria, Costa Rica, Uganda). Items restrained under a POCA restraint order amounted to £147,763,000. Items confiscated or forfeited amounted to £22,758,000. Items returned to developing countries or recovered or confiscated following a trial and a confiscation order amounted to £13,794,000. DFID is currently engaged in a Caribbean Criminal Assets Recovery Programme. **19.59**

### International organisations

The Basel Institute on Governance established the International Centre for Asset Recovery (ICAR) with the support of the governments of Switzerland, the UK, and the Principality of Liechtenstein in 2007. In its 'Business plan 2011–2013' adopted on 22 July 2010, it states that despite the positive international efforts and developments in the area of asset recovery 'in fact only very few cases in recent years have been successful in recovering stolen assets'. ICAR provides training programmes for financial investigations, MLA, and asset recovery, practitioners to support developing countries in pursuing investigations, a free online knowledge centre for asset recovery (<www.assetrecovery.org>), the informal social networking platform Asset Recovery Experts Network (AREN), the development of the Asset Recovery Intelligence System (ARIS) to assist in the identification of corruption-related transactions, and practical books and working papers. The plan for 2011 to 2013 includes for training to be provided 'to countries that have and demonstrate the necessary political will to recover stolen assets and where there is a potential for ongoing work on specific cases'. **19.60**

**19.61**   In 2007 the United Nations Office for Drugs and Crime (UNODC) and the World Bank jointly launched the Stolen Assets Recovery Initiative (StAR). The StAR/Interpol Asset Recovery Focal Point Database was established by Interpol in partnership with the StAR initiative on 19 January 2009. It is a secure contacts database of law enforcement officials who are available twenty-four hours a day, seven days a week, to respond to emergency requests for assistance when lack of immediate action may cause law enforcement to lose a money trail. In February 2013 seventy-four jurisdictions were part of the focal point database.

**19.62**   Interpol's anti-corruption and asset recovery initiatives are grouped under UMBRA. UMBRA deploys technical assistance to Interpol member countries to assist with operational support and capacity building. Interpol and StAR support the Global Focal Point Platform, a secure contacts database of law enforcement officials available twenty-four hours daily to respond to emergency requests for assistance. The Global Focal Point Platform is only available to authorised users and allows transmission of sensitive information between Focal Points. Interpol have worked with StAR to develop the communication tool. StAR-Interpol Asset Recovery Focal Points Meetings were held in December 2010 and July 2011 to discuss means of strengthening cooperation. The 4th StAR-Interpol asset recovery focal points meeting was held in Bangkok in July 2013 with some 65 countries participating.

**19.63**   The Camden Asset Recovery Inter Agency Network (CARIN) is an informal network of contacts and cooperative groups in the area of criminal asset identification established in 2004, following a recommendation at a Dublin conference co-hosted by the Criminal Assets Bureau of Ireland and Europol. The network of practitioners and experts aims to improve mutual knowledge and methodology for the cross-border identification, freezing, seizure, and confiscation of the proceeds of crime.

**19.64**   Financial Action Task Force (FATF) based at the OECD headquarters in Paris is an intergovernmental body with thirty-six members, and the participation of over 180 countries through a global network of regional bodies, established in 1989. The European Commission and fifteen EU Member States, including the UK, are FATF members. It has developed a comprehensive set of recommendations on how countries should fight money laundering. On 16 February 2012 Commissioner Michel Barnier announced FATF had adopted new standards aimed at strengthening global safeguards against money laundering and terrorist financing (MEMO/12/113). In October 2012 FATF published a paper on Best Practices on Confiscation (Recommendations 4 and 38) and a framework for ongoing work on asset recovery.

**19.65**   The OSCE (Organization for Security and Co-operation in Europe) is an organisation made up of fifty states from Europe, central Asia, and North America. It also maintains special relations with eleven countries in the Mediterranean region, Asia, and Australia. One of its tasks includes promoting good governance. It held a seminar in Vienna in September 2012 on Identifying Restraining and Recovering Stolen Assets in the OSCE Region which included consideration of asset recovery. This was followed by a declaration in Dublin of the OSCE Ministerial Council on Strengthening Good Governance and Combating Corruption, Money-laundering and the Financing of Terrorism. The importance of effective asset recovery and international cooperation was highlighted in the declaration.

**European Conventions and Directives**

Article 8 of the European Convention on the Suppression of Terrorism No. 17828 **19.66** (Strasbourg Convention, 1979) provides for mutual assistance in criminal matters in connection with the Convention.

The aim of the 2000 European Convention on Mutual Assistance in Criminal Matters is to **19.67** encourage and facilitate mutual assistance between judicial, police, and customs authorities on criminal matters. In particular, it supplements the 1959 Council of Europe Convention on Mutual Assistance in Criminal Matters, and its 1978 Protocol. According to the UK Explanatory Memorandum for the Convention on Mutual Assistance in Criminal Matters between the Member States of the European Union:

> The Convention is a significant development on the existing 1959 Council of Europe Convention on Mutual Assistance in Criminal Matters, to which all European Union Member States are Parties. One of the key new provisions is that, in general, assistance should be provided in accordance with the procedural requirements of the requesting Member State, whereas the presumption in the 1959 Convention is that the law of the requested Member State shall prevail.

Article 26 of the Council of Europe Criminal Law Convention on Corruption (1998) also **19.68** deals with the principle of mutual assistance.

The Council of Europe Convention on Laundering, Search, Seizure and Confiscation of **19.69** the Proceeds from Crime and on the Financing of Terrorism (Warsaw Convention, 16 May 2005) provides as follows:

> Article 15—General principles and measures for international co-operation
> 1 The Parties shall mutually cooperate with each other to the widest extent possible for the purposes of investigations and proceedings aiming at the confiscation of instrumentalities and proceeds.
> 2 Each Party shall adopt such legislative or other measures as may be necessary to enable it to comply, under the conditions provided for in this chapter, with requests:
>   a for confiscation of specific items of property representing proceeds or instrumentalities, as well as for confiscation of proceeds consisting in a requirement to pay a sum of money corresponding to the value of proceeds;
>   b for investigative assistance and provisional measures with a view to either form of confiscation referred to under a above.
>
> Article 21—Obligation to take provisional measures
> 1 At the request of another Party which has instituted criminal proceedings or proceedings for the purpose of confiscation, a Party shall take the necessary provisional measures, such as freezing or seizing, to prevent any dealing in, transfer or disposal of property which, at a later stage, may be the subject of a request for confiscation or which might be such as to satisfy the request.
> 2 A Party which has received a request for confiscation pursuant to Article 23 shall, if so requested, take the measures mentioned in paragraph 1 of this article in respect of any property which is the subject of the request or which might be such as to satisfy the request.

The European Union has provided several Framework Decisions and Council Decisions **19.70** to regulate freezing and confiscation of criminal assets. European Council Framework Decision 2001/500/JHA (OJ L182 of 05.07.2001) obliges Member States to enable confiscation, to allow value confiscation (confiscation of an amount of money equivalent to the value of the proceeds of a crime) where the direct proceeds of crime cannot be seized, and to ensure that requests from other Member States are treated with the same priority as domestic proceedings. European Council Framework Decision 2003/577/JHA (OJ L196/45 of 2.8.2003) provides for mutual recognition of freezing orders. European Council Framework Decision 2005/212/JHA (OJ L68/49 of 15.3.2005) harmonises confiscation laws. European Council Framework Decision 2006/783/JHA (OJ L328/59 of 24.11.2006) provides for mutual recognition of confiscation orders. Council Decision 2007/845/JHA (OJ L332/103 of 18.12.2007) on the exchange of information and cooperation between Asset Recovery Offices obliges Member States to set up or designate national Asset Recovery Offices as national central contacts which facilitate through enhanced cooperation the fastest possible EU-wide tracing of assets derived from crime.

**19.71**  The Council Directives needed to be reviewed in order to reflect the new FATF standards adopted on 16 February 2012. On 12 March 2012 the European Commission issued a proposal based on Arts 82(2) and 83(1) of the Treaty on the Functioning of the European Union (TFEU) for a Directive of the European Parliament and of the Council on the freezing and confiscation of proceeds of crime in the European Union (see COM (2012) 85 Final). The proposal will cover specific criminal activities listed in Art 83(1) and other criminal activities committed by criminal organisations falling within the definition of 'organised crime' in Framework Decision 2008/841/JHA (OJ L300/42 of 11.11.2008). The proposed Directive replaces Framework Decisions 2001/500/JHA and 2005/212/JHA in part, maintaining in force Arts 2, 4, and 5 of Framework Decision 2005/212/JHA to cover criminal activities which fall outside the scope of Art 83(1). The Commission's proposal is to simplify the rules concerning extended confiscation, third-party confiscation (concerning property transferred by the defendant to a third party who should have realised this was illegal or being transferred to avoid confiscation), limited non-conviction-based confiscations (confiscation where the defendant is deceased, permanently ill, or has fled so that a criminal conviction is not possible), precautionary freezing (freezing assets that risk disappearing as a precaution), effective execution (continued investigation of financial investigations to ensure effective enforcement), asset management (managing frozen or confiscated assets so that they do not lose economic value), and statistics (regularly collecting data on confiscation and asset recovery).

**19.72**  On 11 July 2012 the European Economic and Social Committee ('EESC') adopted an opinion on the proposal for a Directive on the freezing and confiscation of the proceeds of crime in the EU by a large majority. The EESC considered that the powers of the Asset Recovery Offices and Eurojust needed to be strengthened under the Directive and that it should promote better cooperation between the authorities responsible for dealing with trafficking, a common culture amongst relevant professionals, and that centralisation at European level in these areas will need to be considered.

### United Nations Conventions

**19.73**  In the United Nations Convention against Illicit Traffic in Narcotic Drugs and Psychotropic Substances of 1988, Arts 7(1) to 7(3) deal with the principle of MLA. Article 7(12) provides that a request for MLA should be executed in accordance with the domestic law of the requested State Party.

**19.74**  The United Nations Convention against Transnational Organised Crime (UNTOC/the Palermo Convention) was adopted on 15 November 2000 and is supplemented by three protocols. Article 12 of UNTOC explicitly obliges States Parties to adopt measures to enable confiscation of the proceeds of crime. Article 13 UNTOC deals with international cooperation for the purpose of confiscation. Article 18(17) provides that 'A request shall be executed in accordance with the domestic law of the requested States Parties and, to the extent not contrary to the domestic law of the requested States Parties and where possible, in accordance with the procedures specified in the request.'

The UNODC also operates the International Money Laundering Information Network, an **19.75** internet-based network assisting governments, organisations, and individuals to fight money laundering and the financing of terrorists. UNODC published its manual on MLA and extradition in September 2012 (at <http://www.unodc.org/documents/organized-crime/ Publications/Mutual_Legal_Assistance_Ebook_E.pdf>). The Manual on International Cooperation for the Purposes of Confiscation of Proceeds of Crime was published in September 2012 (at <http://www.unodc.org/documents/organized-crime/Publications/ Confiscation_Manual_Ebook_E.pdf>).

The United Nations Convention against Corruption (UNCAC) came into force on **19.76** 14 December 2005. As at 24 December 2012, it had been signed by 140 countries as parties to the Convention. It was the first international instrument which aimed to function as a multilateral MLA treaty and the first Convention to refer to the recovery of assets as a priority in the fight against corruption. The UK is a party to the Convention. The Convention established that MLA can be used for tracing proceeds of crime and the recovery of assets (see Art 46(3)(j) and (k)). Chapter V deals with asset recovery. Article 55 requires the establishment of international cooperation regimes for the purposes of confiscation. Article 58 encourages States Parties to establish FIUs to receive, analyse, and disseminate to the competent authorities reports of suspicious financial transactions. Such units have been in existence since the 1990s.

### Regional cooperation

On 21 May 2012, the G8 (France, Germany, Italy, Japan, the UK, the US, Canada, and Russia) **19.77** adopted its Action Plan on Asset Recovery within the framework of the Deauville partnership with Arab Countries in Transition. The G8 countries committed to a comprehensive list of actions aimed at promoting cooperation and case assistance, capacity-building efforts, and technical assistance in support of Arab countries in transition in recovering assets diverted by past regimes. The G8 countries also agreed on the launch of the Arab Forum on Asset Recovery (AFAR).

AFAR held its inaugural meeting in September 2012, co-organised by Qatar and the US **19.78** presidency of the G8. The Forum is an initiative to bring together the G8, Deauville Partners (Canada, Egypt, the EU, France, Germany, Italy, Japan, Jordan, Libya, Kuwait, Morocco, Qatar, Russia, Saudi Arabia, Tunisia, Turkey, the United Arab Emirates, the UK, and the US), and regional countries to raise awareness of effective measures for asset recovery, provide regional training, and discuss best practice.

On 17 December 2012 the UK Minister of State for Crime Prevention made a Written **19.79** Ministerial Statement that a task force has begun work to return stolen assets to the Egyptian, Libyan, and Tunisian peoples. To this end, a CPS prosecutor and Metropolitan Police financial investigator have been posted in Egypt and a regional asset recovery adviser would be posted to assist the authorities in Egypt, Libya, and Tunisia. Jeremy Brown wrote that on 27 November 2012, EU sanction regulations were amended to allow better information sharing between EU Member States and Arab Spring countries.

**Africa**

**19.80** Article 8 of the Southern African Development Community (SADC) Protocol against Corruption (2001) mandates each State Party to adopt measures necessary to identify, trace, seize, and confiscate proceeds of corruption.

**19.81** The 2003 African Union Convention on Preventing and Combating Corruption (AU Convention) includes provisions relating to the seizure, confiscation, and repatriation of the proceeds of corruption, as well as cooperation and mutual assistance between States Parties, and international cooperation to facilitate the repatriation of stolen or illegally acquired assets. The legal framework provided covers criminal offences including bribery, diversion of property by public officials, trading in influence, illicit enrichment, and money laundering.

**19.82** The Asset Recovery Inter-Agency Network of Southern Africa (ARINSA), inaugurated in 2010, brings together prosecutors and investigators to improve the tracing and confiscation of the proceeds of crime, particularly those associated with corruption. It has nine member countries from the Southern Africa region and is supported by UNODC and StAR. Through its network of contact points it aims to put prosecutors and investigators in contact with colleagues in thirty-five countries which are part of CARIN. Its secretariat is housed within South Africa's National Asset Forfeiture Unit.

**19.83** In the Africa Partnership Forum paper prepared for the December 2012 meeting of senior officials from Africa and its main development partners, it was noted that approximately $1.3 billion in stolen assets had been returned to African countries according to the StAR Asset Recovery Watch cases database as at November 2012. Of the $277 million returned to a foreign jurisdiction between 2006 and 2009, $20 million went to a developing country, of which $11 million went to Africa. There was a recognition that policy and legislative frameworks needed to be brought into line with UNCAC in many countries to facilitate the tracing and return of stolen assets, that institutional frameworks needed to be strengthened to enable them to identify and trace assets domestically and internationally, and that international cooperation was unduly slow, formalistic, and cumbersome.

**United States**

**19.84** Article XIV of the Inter-American Convention against Corruption (adopted 1996) provides for assistance and cooperation from the States Parties to each other.

**19.85** In 2010 the Department of Justice launched the Kleptocracy Asset Recovery Initiative led by its Asset Forfeiture and Money Laundering Section (AFMLS). This aims to provide support in cooperation in the recovery of stolen assets. The Initiative consists of a team of attorneys, investigators, and financial analysts responsible for investigating and prosecuting asset recovery cases. The US is a partner/State Party of StAR, CARIN, the Asset Recovery Focal Point Initiative, UNCAC, UNTOC, and the 1988 Vienna Convention.

**19.86** Whilst the US does not have a specific agency that deals with asset recovery, in 2012 the US Departments of State and Justice produced a handbook entitled 'US Asset Recovery Tools and Procedures, a Practical Guide for International Cooperation'.

# 20

## MONEY LAUNDERING

## A. Introduction

In this chapter we consider the money laundering provisions within POCA and outline the **20.01** European Directives relating to same. In the next chapter we look at the tipping-off provisions and the disclosure of suspicious transactions by the professions and the regulated sector.

The money laundering sections of Pt 7 of POCA came into force on 24 February 2003 **20.02** (SI 2003/120). These principal money laundering offences do not have effect where the conduct constituting the offence began before 24 February 2003. In those cases the previous legislation, namely the DTA, the Criminal Justice Act 1993, and the Criminal Justice (International Co-operation) Act 1990, continue to have effect (although these are far fewer due to the passage of time).

### The EU Money Laundering Directives

The above Acts were in part introduced to meet the UK's obligation under Art 9 of the 1991 **20.03** European Community Directive on the Prevention of the Use of the Financial System for the purpose of Money Laundering (Council Directive (EC) (1991/308)), which required contracting states to establish drug money laundering offences. This Directive, together with the Money Laundering Regulations 1993, was supplemented by the Council Directive

(EC) 2001/97 (the second EC Directive) and the Money Laundering Regulations 2001, SI 2001/3641. (The international and domestic history of offences relating to laundering drugs money is considered in some detail by the House of Lords in *R v Montila* [2004] UKHL 50.)

**20.04** Article 1 of the 1991 Directive, as amended by the 2001 Directive, defines money laundering as meaning the following conduct when committed intentionally:

(a) the conversion or transfer of property, knowing that such property is derived from criminal activity or from an act of participation in such activity, for the purpose of concealing or disguising the illicit origin of the property or of assisting any person who is involved in the commission of such activity to evade the legal consequences of his actions;

(b) the concealment or disguise of the true nature, source, location, disposition, movement, rights with respect to, or ownership of property, knowing that such property is derived from criminal activity or from an act of participation in such activity;

(c) the acquisition, possession, or use of property, knowing, at the time of receipt that such property was derived from criminal activity or from an act of participation in such activity;

(d) participation in, association to commit, attempts to commit, and aiding, abetting, facilitating, and counselling the commission of any of the actions mentioned in the foregoing indents;

Knowledge, intent, or purpose required as an element of the above-mentioned activities may be inferred from objective factual circumstances.

**20.05** Brooke LJ in *Bowman v Fels* [2005] EWCA Civ 226 emphasised that the 1991 and 2001 Council Directives were important to POCA's proper understanding. The Court interpreted 'so far as possible, the Act in the light of the wording and the purpose of the Directives in order to achieve the result pursued by the latter'.

**20.06** In his Lordship's judgment it was open to the UK Parliament to go further than the Directives and in some respects, in the Court's opinion, they did (see para 44). In particular, the UK legislation defined money laundering to include property known 'or suspected' to constitute or represent a benefit from criminal activity and applied it to the benefits of any type of criminal conduct (see s 330(3) of the 2002 Act). The extended definition of money laundering in the UK legislation (to embrace circumstances of suspicion) consolidates the distinction drawn in the Directives between money laundering and the requirement that the institutions and persons subject to the Directives should 'refrain from carrying out transactions which they know or suspect to be related to money laundering' (see also Case C-106/89 *Marleasing SA v LA Comercial Internacional de Alinentacion SA* [1990] ECR I-4135, para 8).

**20.07** The Third European Money Laundering Directive (Directive 2005/60/EC) came into effect on 15 December 2005 (see the OJ L309 25 November 2005 at pp 15–36). The Directive required EU members to bring into force the laws, regulations, and administrative provisions necessary to comply with the new Directive by 15 December 2007.

**20.08** As a result, the Money Laundering Regulations 2007 (SI 2007/2157) came into force on 15 December 2007 as part of the UK's response. They replace the 2003 Regulations. These Regulations provide for various steps to be taken by the financial services sector and other persons to detect and prevent money laundering and terrorist financing, and implement in part Directive 2005/60/EC (OJ L309, 25.11.2005, p 15) of the European Parliament and of the Council on the prevention of the use of the financial system for the purpose of money laundering and terrorist financing.

The revised Regulations include requirements that there be due diligence procedures in **20.09** place in relation to existing clients and customers and compel the financial, accountancy, legal, and other sectors to take steps to prevent their services being used for money laundering or terrorist financing. The Regulations also require firms to apply enhanced customer identification and monitoring measures, and require them to have appropriate anti-money laundering systems in place.

The Money Laundering (Amendment) Regulations 2011(SI 2011/1781) and 2012 (SI 2012/ **20.10** 2299) in turn amend the Money Laundering Regulations 2007.

These new Regulations represent something of a broadening of the existing scheme. For **20.11** example, under reg 3 of the 2012 Regulations the definition of 'estate agent' is amended, to include estate agents selling property outside the UK. Regulation 5 of the 2012 Regulations adds 'consumer credit financial institutions' to the list of persons who may be relied upon for the purposes of carrying out customer due diligence. Further, reg 8 of the 2012 Regulations adds a 'recognised investment exchange' to the list of relevant persons supervised by the Financial Services Authority for the purposes of the 2007 Regulations; and the 2011 Regulations amend reg 13 of the 2007 Regulations to include a 'junior ISA' within the scheme.

The remaining amendments provide for better cooperation between supervisory authorities **20.12** (see reg 9 of the 2012 Regulations, the sharing of information) and they vest certain miscellaneous powers into those authorities (regs 10–13 of the 2012 Regulations), including a power for enforcement authorities to impose a fine on persons who fail to comply with the requirements of a notice requiring the provision of information (reg 14).

Regulation 15 of the 2012 Regulations provides a right of appeal for a person who is **20.13** deemed by HMRC not to be 'fit and proper' for the purposes of registration under the 2007 Regulations.

## SOCPA

The money laundering provisions of POCA were further significantly amended by SOCPA. **20.14** From 1 April 2006 the National Criminal Intelligence Service (NCIS) ceased to exist and its functions and staff were absorbed into SOCA. One of the difficulties with the previous reporting regime was that NCIS had been inundated with insignificant and unnecessary 'suspicious activity reports' (SARs) in relation to suspected money laundering or terrorist property offences.

Sections 364 and 415 of POCA are amended by s 107 of SOCPA so that the meaning of **20.15** money laundering offences includes the principal money laundering offences that were in force before the 2002 Act. The purpose of this is to enable the investigation powers in Pt 8 of the Act to be used to investigate old money laundering offences.

### What is money laundering?

Money laundering is the process by which monies derived from criminal activities are converted **20.16** into funds or assets which appear to have an apparently legitimate source (see Appendix 21).

**20.17**  Money laundering was first made a criminal offence in relation to monies derived from drug trafficking by the DTOA. Subsequent legislation, notably the CJA and the DTA extended the number and ambit of these offences. POCA was intended to simplify and consolidate the existing statutory scheme.

### Why criminalise money laundering?

**20.18**  It has often been said that there would be fewer burglary offences committed if there were not those willing and able to receive and dispose of stolen property. Similarly, there would be less financially motivated crime committed if the criminal did not have at his disposal the means of concealing the origin of the proceeds of such offences by money laundering. The absence of legislation to prevent money laundering can result in a loss of confidence in a country's financial institutions, particularly if criminals can invest and transfer the proceeds of crime through banks with impunity. Furthermore, legitimate banks do not wish to have accounts they maintain tainted with the proceeds of crime, and many have withdrawn from countries where money laundering has not been pursued and where they are powerless to report suspicious transactions to law enforcement agencies without fear of an action for breach of confidence by the client. The absence of money laundering legislation can also serve to destabilise the political system of a country. The success of any terrorist organisation, for example, depends on its ability to raise and launder monies to fund their activities.

### How is money laundered?

**20.19**  Money laundering techniques vary in their degree of sophistication from the most simplistic to the highly complex. In its simplest form, money laundering occurs where a relative of a criminal, motivated by a misplaced sense of loyalty, agrees to pass the proceeds of a criminal enterprise through a bank account. The most sophisticated laundering operations involve the creation of front companies, trusts, etc, and the creation of bogus transactions to give the impression that monies come from a legitimate source. Most money laundering schemes can, however, be divided into three stages, regardless of the degree of complexity: placement, layering, and integration. A summary of each is set out below, and at Appendix 21.

#### Placement

**20.20**  At the placement stage, the launderer disposes of the so-called 'dirty money'. Cash is the most common medium of exchange used for many types of criminal transactions, particularly those related to drugs. As bank transfers and other non-cash means (credit cards, cheques) are usually used to finance the majority of legitimate transactions, the money launderer who carries out large financial transactions in cash risks drawing undesired attention to his illegally acquired money. He thus attempts through placement to put his funds into the financial system unnoticed, for example by engaging a number of people to make a series of small deposits on his behalf (a process known as 'smurfing') or by physically transporting the cash out of the country. It is at the placement stage that illegally acquired funds are often most vulnerable to detection.

#### Layering

**20.21**  After the funds have entered the financial system, the launderer further separates the illicit proceeds from their illegal source through layering. Layering occurs by conducting a series of financial transactions that, by reason of their frequency, volume, or complexities resemble legitimate financial transactions. The ultimate aim at this stage of the laundering process is to make tracing the funds back to their 'dirty' source as difficult as possible.

*Integration*

At the final integration stage, the launderer integrates the illicit funds into the economy. **20.22** He does this in such a way that the funds at this juncture appear to have originated from an entirely legal source, such as legitimate business earnings. At this stage the launderer will provide a legitimate explanation for the criminally derived funds. As a result, distinguishing between legitimate and illicit funds becomes extremely difficult, if not impossible to achieve. The profits may then be invested into other criminal enterprises, assets, and property, or used to support an extravagant lifestyle.

## B. Money Laundering under the Proceeds of Crime Act 2002

### Introduction

Part 7 of POCA introduces three principal money laundering offences: **20.23**

(a) s 327, concealing, disguising, converting, transferring, or removing from England and Wales criminal property;
(b) s 328, becoming concerned in an arrangement which a person knows or suspects facilitates the acquisition, retention, use, or control of criminal property by or on behalf of another person; and
(c) s 329, acquiring, using, or having possession of criminal property.

All of these money laundering offences apply to the laundering of an offender's own proceeds of crime, as well as those of someone else. The maximum sentence for these money laundering offences is fourteen years' imprisonment (see s 334). Sections 327–329 are found at Appendix 6.

Part 7 of POCA came into force on 24 February 2003 (SI 2003/120). The DTA and CJA **20.24** money laundering offences continue to be the principal Acts for all offences committed before that date (or which cross over that date), although these are becoming rare due to the passage of time since the introduction of POCA.

### The ingredients of the offence

Sections 327 to 329 require proof that the conduct concerned involves 'criminal property'. **20.25** Property is criminal property if it constitutes a person's benefit from criminal conduct, or it represents such a benefit (whether directly or indirectly), and the alleged offender knows or suspects that it constitutes such a benefit (s 340(3)).

In *R v Da Silva* [2006] EWCA Crim 1654, 2 Cr App R 35, the Court of Appeal held that **20.26** for a defendant to be convicted of an offence under s 93A(1)(a) of the CJA, he or she must think that there is a 'possibility, which is more than fanciful, that the relevant facts exist. A vague feeling of unease would not suffice.' This is subject, the Court held, to the further requirement that the suspicion so formed should be of 'a settled nature'. The court added, in the absence of a statutory definition, the dictionary definition would be likely to be an appropriate starting place.

**20.27**   The word 'suspect' is given various meanings in the Oxford English Dictionary. These include:

    (1)  an impression of the existence or presence of;

    (2)  believe tentatively without clear ground;

    (3)  be inclined to think;

    (4)  be inclined to mentally accuse; doubt the innocence of;

    (5)  doubt the genuineness or truth of a suspected person.

**20.28**   In *K Ltd v National Westminster Bank* [2006] EWCA Civ 1039 the Court noted that there was no legal definition within the Act of what 'suspicion' or 'suspect' should be held to mean, but confirmed that if the definition in *Da Silva* was sufficient for criminal cases, it was also sufficient for civil cases (para 16).

### Inchoate offences

**20.29**   Under s 340(11) of POCA, money laundering is an act which is not only defined by the three substantive offences, but is extended to all inchoate offences relating to them:

    (11) Money laundering is an act which—

        (a)  constitutes an offence under sections 327, 328 or 329,

        (b)  constitutes an attempt, conspiracy or incitement to commit an offence specified in paragraph (a),

        (c)  constitutes aiding, abetting, counselling or procuring the commission of an offence specified in paragraph (a), or

        (d)  would constitute an offence specified in paragraph (a), (b) or (c) if done in the United Kingdom.

Section 340 of POCA is found at Appendix 7. In *R v William and others* [2013] EWCA Crim 1262, the court confirmed that in a pecuniary advantage tax case, the 'criminal property' under s 340 was the entirety of the undeclared turnover, not just the tax due.

### Proof

**20.30**   In *R v Saik* [2006] 2 WLR 993 it was confirmed that the *mens rea* required for an offence of conspiracy to launder money was knowledge of its illicit origins. The House of Lords held that a mere suspicion that property might be the proceeds of crime was insufficient to establish guilt of conspiracy to engage in money laundering. To establish guilt, the Court held the accused had to be aware that the property involved was in fact the proceeds of crime or, in the case of unidentifiable property, intend that it should be. Lord Nicholls held that Parliament could not have intended that a person would be liable for conspiracy where he lacked the knowledge required to commit the substantive offence. When knowledge of a material fact was an ingredient of a substantive offence, it was also an ingredient of the crime of conspiracy to commit that offence. He went on to state that the ingredient of the substantive offence in s 93C(2) of the CJA was that the property in question had to emanate from a crime (*R v Montila* [2004] 1 WLR 3141). The prosecution had to prove that the conspirator had intended or known that that fact would exist when the conspiracy was carried out. Hence, where the property had not been identified when the conspiracy agreement had been reached, the prosecution had to prove that the conspirator had intended that it would become the proceeds of criminal conduct.

**20.31**   It is for the Crown to prove that the property is the proceeds of crime (see *R v El Kurd* [2001] Crim LR 234). In *R v Anwoir* [2008] 2 Cr App R 36 the Court of Appeal held (giving effect to *Director of the Assets Recovery Agency v Green* [2005] EWHC Admin 3168, The Times,

27 February 2006 and *R v Craig* [2007] EWCA Crim 2913), that the Crown may prove the property was 'criminal property' by showing either that it derived from conduct of a specific kind (or kinds) and that conduct of that kind was unlawful, or by evidence that the circumstances in which the property was handled were such as to give rise to an irresistible inference that it could only be derived from crime (para 21). *Anwoir* was subsequently followed in *R v F* [2009] Crim LR 45 and *R v Gillies* [2011] EWCA Crim 2140. For an arguably contra position to *Anwoir*, see *R v NW, SW, RC and CC* [2008] EWCA Crim 2, Laws LJ at paras 16 and 17.

### Conspiracy

In *R v Ali Hussain* [2005] EWCA Crim 87, the Court of Appeal held that offences under s 49(2) DTA and s 93C(2) CJA required proof that a defendant was in fact dealing with the proceeds of drug trafficking or other criminal conduct. A jury could only convict of conspiracy if the defendant *knew* he was dealing with the proceeds of drug trafficking or other criminal conduct and mere grounds to suspect were not enough. The Court stated (at para 151) that the consequence of their decision was that the prosecution has a heavier burden to discharge than it would have in order to prove the substantive offence. **20.32**

In *R v Montila* [2004] UKHL 50; [2004] 1 WLR 3141 the House of Lords decided that for offences under s 49(2) of the DTA and s 93C(2) of the CJA, it must be proved that the property was in fact the proceeds of drug trafficking or of other criminal conduct (reversing the Court of Appeal's decision). It was not enough that the defendant has reasonable grounds to suspect that the property was the proceeds of drug trafficking or of other criminal conduct, when in fact it is not (or could not be proved to be so). Lord Hope, giving the considered opinion of the committee said at para 27: **20.33**

> Sub-section (2) states that a person is guilty of an offence 'if knowing or having reasonable grounds to suspect that any property is…another person's proceeds of drug trafficking (s 49(2) of the 1994 Act) or of criminal conduct (s 93C(2) of the 1988 Act)' he does one or other of the things described to 'that property' for the purpose which the sub-section identifies. A person may have reasonable grounds to suspect the property is one thing (A) when in fact it is something different (B). But that is not so when the question is what a person knows. A person cannot know that something is A when in fact it is B. The proposition that a person knows that something is A is based on the premise that it is true that it is A. The fact that the property is A provides the starting point. Then there is the question whether the person knows that the property is A.

The Court said subsequent events may show that the property that he was dealing with had nothing whatever to do with any criminal activity at all, but resulted from the product of a windfall, eg a win on the National Lottery. See also *R v Harmer* [2005] EWCA Crim 1. **20.34**

In *R v Hussain* the Court of Appeal concluded that *R v Singh* [2003] EWCA Crim 3712 did not survive *Montila*. An intention to launder illicitly obtained money is not enough. The money must be proved to have been the proceeds of drug trafficking or other criminal conduct. **20.35**

In *R v Saik* [2006] 2 WLR 993 the House of Lords found that a conspiracy to commit an offence involved an agreement to convert another person's proceeds of criminal conduct. The agreement must be an agreement to do one or more of such acts for one or more of the stated purposes. Further, the intention must be that the property to be laundered is or would be criminal property (as defined—see s 340(3)), even if the property had not yet been specifically identified at the time of the conspiracy. **20.36**

**20.37** A central ingredient therefore of the substantive offence is that the property in question must emanate from a crime: *R v Montila* (above). Lord Nicholls held that the criminal provenance of the property is in fact necessary for the commission of the offence. Hence, where the property has not been identified when the conspiracy agreement is reached, the prosecution must prove the conspirator intended that the property would be the proceeds of criminal conduct (para 23).

**20.38** The phrase 'intend or know' in s 1(2) is a provision of general application to all conspiracies: in this context the word 'know' should be interpreted strictly and not watered down.

**20.39** In *R v Suchedina* [2006] EWCA Crim 2543, the Court of Appeal held that where a conviction for conspiracy to commit money laundering offences had been obtained in circumstances where the jury had been directed that the offence was made out in terms of *mens rea*, by proof either of knowledge or of reasonable grounds for suspicion as to the illicit origins of the money, such a conviction could no longer be regarded as safe, in the light of the ruling in *R v Saik*. See also *R v R* [2006] EWCA Crim 1974.

### The first money laundering offence: concealing etc

**20.40** The intention of s 327 was to simplify and replace s 49 of the DTA and s 93C of the CJA. In so doing, POCA no longer distinguishes between the proceeds of drug trafficking in relation to money laundering and the proceeds of other crimes.

**20.41** Under s 327(1) of POCA a person commits a money laundering offence if he:

(a) conceals criminal property;
(b) disguises criminal property;
(c) converts criminal property;
(d) transfers criminal property;
(e) removes criminal property from England or Wales or from Scotland or Northern Ireland.

In relation to s 327(1)(a) and (b) 'concealing' or 'disguising' criminal property includes concealing or disguising its nature, source, location, disposition, movement, or ownership of any rights with respect to it (s 327(3)). Sections 327–329 are found at Appendix 6.

### 'Criminal property'

**20.42** Criminal property is defined under s 340(3) as follows:

> (3) Property is criminal property if—
>> (a) it constitutes a person's benefit from criminal conduct or it represents such a benefit (in whole or part and whether directly or indirectly), and
>> (b) if the alleged offender knows or suspects that it constitutes or represents such a benefit.

**20.43** In *R v Gabriel* [2007] 1 WLR 2272 the Court of Appeal held that where a person in receipt of state benefits failed to declare income from a legitimate trade in goods to the Inland Revenue and the Department of Work and Pensions, his profits from the trade itself could not be said to constitute 'criminal property' within the meaning of s 340 of POCA. The failure to declare profits for the purposes of income tax may give rise to an offence, but that did not make the legitimate trading in goods an offence itself. The Court also held that where the prosecution allege that property is criminal property, it was sensible, by giving particulars either in advance or in opening, to set out the facts upon which the Crown relies and the inferences that the jury will be invited to draw. *Gabriel* however was distinguished in *R v IK* [2007] EWCA Crim 491, where the Court found that a person who cheated the Revenue obtained a pecuniary advantage as a result of criminal conduct within the meaning of s 340(6) of POCA and the proceeds of cheating the Revenue could amount to 'criminal property' within the meaning of s 340(5). The difference between *Gabriel* and *IK*, the Court held, was that in *IK* the prosecution had established a prima facie case for cheating, and therefore the judge had been wrong to withdraw that count from the jury.

In *R v Loizou* [2005] EWHC Crim 1579; The Times, 23 June 2005 the Court of Appeal **20.44** held, obiter, that the natural meaning of s 327(1) of POCA is that the property in question had to be criminal property at the time of the transaction. It was not sufficient that the property became criminal property within the meaning of the Act as a result of the transaction (see *Montila* above). In *R v Akhtar* [2011] EWCA Crim 146 the Court found that an appellant, who had knowingly submitted false mortgage applications, was not guilty of the offence, because when he entered into the relevant arrangements with the mortgage brokers the property in question could not be regarded as criminal property. For comparisons to the civil act of conversion, see *R v Fazal* [2010] 1 Cr App R 6, CA.

### 'Criminal conduct'

Criminal conduct is conduct which either constitutes an offence in any part of the UK, or **20.45** would constitute an offence in any part of the UK if it occurred there (s 340(2)).

It is immaterial who carried out the conduct, who benefited from it, or whether the conduct **20.46** occurred before or after the passing of POCA (see s 340(4)).

### 'Defences' to section 327(1)

Under s 327(2) a person does not commit such an offence if: **20.47**

(a) he makes an authorised disclosure under s 338 of POCA and (if the disclosure is made before he does the act mentioned in s 327(1)) he has the appropriate consent;
(b) he intended to make such a disclosure but has a reasonable excuse for not doing so;
(c) the act he does is done in carrying out a function he has relating to the enforcement of POCA or of any other enactment relating to criminal conduct or benefit from criminal conduct.

Occasionally, either the police or other enforcement authorities will themselves take possession of criminal property in the course of their duties and either convert or transfer it pending or as part of a further investigation. Section 327(2)(c) gives such authorities an appropriate exemption from the s 327(1) offence.

Section 102 of SOCPA amends Pt 7 of POCA to introduce a new 'defence' where conduct **20.48** is legal under local overseas law. The amendment came into force on 1 July 2005. Section 327(2) has inserted into it the following defence:

(2A) Nor does a person commit an offence under sub-section (1) if—
    (a) he knows, or believes on reasonable grounds, that the relevant criminal conduct occurred in a particular country or territory outside the United Kingdom, and
    (b) the relevant criminal conduct—
        (i) was not, at the time it occurred, unlawful under the criminal law then applying in that country or territory, and

(ii) is not of a description prescribed by an order made by the Secretary of State.

(2B) In sub-section (2A) 'the relevant criminal conduct' is the criminal conduct by reference to which the property concerned is criminal property.

**20.49** Section 328 (arrangements) and s 329 (acquisition, use, and possession) are amended in identical terms.

**20.50** The language used in POCA is different to that used in the CJA, in particular the draftsmen of POCA do not use the word 'defence' in the relevant parts of the statute. Nevertheless, it is clear that an individual will not have committed the offence in question if one of the 'exemptions' set out in the Act apply. Arguably it will be for the Crown to show that they do not apply, and therefore the burden will be on the prosecution. Having said that, there is something of an inevitability that the best case for applying the 'exemptions' will come from the defendant.

**20.51** The use of a third party to lodge, receive, retain, or withdraw money from an account does not amount to a defence, where the defendant had given his full cooperation throughout the period of conversion: *R v Fazal* [2010] 1 WLR 694; The Times, 26 June 2009.

### Threshold amounts

**20.52** Section 103 of SOCPA amends the threshold amounts in relation to money laundering. Section 327 (concealing etc) inserts subs (2C), which reads as follows:

(2C) A deposit-taking body that does an act mentioned in para (C) or (D) of sub-section (1) does not commit an offence under that sub-section if—

(a) it does the act in operating an account maintained with it, and

(b) the value of the criminal property concerned is less than the threshold amount determined under s 339A for the act.

**20.53** Under s 327(1)(D) of POCA, a bank or other deposit-taking body would need to make a disclosure to obtain consent before proceeding with any transaction that was suspected of involving criminal property. The SOCPA amendments will, in certain circumstances, allow deposit-taking bodies to continue to operate accounts without the need to seek consent in each case.

**20.54** The amendments do not apply to the duty to make a disclosure in respect of the initial opening of an account or, as the case may be, the time when the deposit-taking body first suspects that the property is criminal property (see s 338(2A) of POCA, s 106(5) of SOCPA).

**20.55** A bank or other deposit-taking body would not commit an offence in operating an account of a person suspected of money laundering when the amount of money concerned in the transaction is below £250 or such higher threshold amount as may be specified by a constable or Customs officer (or by a person authorised by the Director General of SOCA).

**20.56** Where a deposit-taking body requests a threshold amount higher than the £250 default threshold, one may be specified. This threshold amount of £250 may be varied by the Secretary of State.

**20.57** Where a threshold amount (above the £250 default level) has been specified for an account, the specified amount may be varied by any of the officers who could have specified it. Different thresholds may be specified in relation to the operation of the same account (for example, a threshold could be specified for deposits that are higher than the threshold specified for withdrawals).

### The second money laundering offence: arrangements

Under s 328 of POCA a person commits an offence:                               **20.58**

> (1) ...if he enters into or becomes concerned in an arrangement which he knows or suspects facilitates (by whatever means) the acquisition, retention, use or control of criminal property by or on behalf of another person.

This section replaces s 50 of the DTA and s 93A of the CJA. Sections 327–329 are found at Appendix 6.

It is for the prosecution to show not only that the person entered into an arrangement **20.59** which he knew or suspected would facilitate another person to acquire, retain, use, or control criminal property, but also that that person also knew or suspected that the property constituted or represented a benefit from criminal conduct. Importantly, the arrangement must be one which relates to property which was criminal property at the time when the arrangement began to operate: *R v Geary* [2011] 1 Cr App R 8, para 19, considering *Kensington International Ltd v Republic of Congo (and others)* [2008] 1 WLR 1144 CA.

In *Stephen Dare v CPS* [2012] EWHC 2074 the Court confirmed that for a defendant to be **20.60** found guilty of an offence under s 328(1), the 'another person' must be identified (or at least identifiable) at the time of the arrangement. In *Dare* the acts in questions were found to be too preparatory for that to have occurred, which led to the conviction being quashed (see paras 7–11 of the judgment.)

### 'Defences' to section 328(1)

As noted elsewhere in this chapter, the language used in POCA is different from that used in **20.61** the CJA; in particular the draftsmen of POCA do not use the word 'defence' in the relevant parts of the statute. Nevertheless, it is clear that an individual will not have committed the offence in question if one of the 'exemptions' set out in the Act applies.

Under s 328(2) certain 'safety-nets' therefore are afforded to a person who it is alleged com- **20.62** mitted such an offence as follows:

(a) he makes an authorised disclosure under s 338 and (if the disclosure is made before he does the act mentioned in subsection (1)) he has the appropriate consent;
(b) he intended to make such a disclosure but has a reasonable excuse for not doing so;
(c) the act he does is done in carrying out a function he had relating to the enforcement of any provision of POCA or of any other enactment relating to criminal conduct or benefit from criminal conduct.

These exemptions and the requirement for authorised disclosure under s 338 mirror those found under s 327.

For consideration of the duties of disclosure in relation to s 328 following the Court of **20.63** Appeal decision in *Bowman and Fels* [2005] 2 Cr App R 19 (which held that s 328 was not intended to cover legal professionals conducting ordinary litigation), see Chapter 21.

**20.64**   Section 328 has after subsection (4) had inserted a new 'safety-net', pursuant to SOCPA, which reads as follows:

> (5) A deposit-taking body that does an act mentioned in sub-section (1) does not commit an offence under that sub-section if—
>     (a) it does the act in operating an account maintained with it, and
>     (b) the arrangement facilitates the acquisition, retention, use or control of criminal property of a value that is less than the threshold amount determined under s 339A for the act.

**20.65**   In *Squirrel Ltd v National Westminster Bank plc (Customs & Excise Commissioners intervening)* [2005] 2 All ER 784, Laddie J held that once a bank suspected that a customer's account contained the proceeds of crime, it was obliged to report the matter to the relevant authority and not to carry out any transaction in relation to that account. Failing to do so would amount to an offence under s 328(1). That obligation remains the position unless and until consent for the transaction is given under s 335 of POCA, or if it were not, the relevant time limit had expired. Equally, if the bank told the customer why it was blocking the transaction or account, it would breach the tipping-off provisions set out at ss 333 and 338 of POCA. Laddie J noted that although the statutory provisions might cause hardship to companies, to force the bank to unblock the account would be tantamount to compelling it to commit a criminal offence and therefore sympathy for the company/customer's position could not override that consideration.

**20.66**   Questions of construction in relation to the money laundering provisions were further considered in *K Ltd v National Westminster Bank plc* [2006] EWCA Civ 1039, in particular s 328. The bank found itself in a predicament when its customer asked it to make a payment which the bank suspected would facilitate the use of criminal property and leave it open to the allegation of becoming 'concerned in an arrangement'. The customer, following the bank's refusal, made a claim for an interim injunction requiring the bank to comply with its instructions. It was argued on behalf of the customer that the bank, by refusing to honour its customer's instructions, was acting in breach of the contract whereby the bank had agreed to follow its customer's instructions. The Court found that there could be no doubt that if a banker knows or suspects that money in a customer's account is criminal property and, without making disclosure or without authorised consent (if disclosure is made), he processes a customer's cheque in such a way as to transfer the money in question into the account of another person, then he was facilitating the use or control of that criminal property, and thus committing an offence under s 328 of the 2002 Act. The Court held it would be no defence to a charge under that section that the bank was contractually obliged to obey its customer's instructions (para 9): 'If the law of the land makes it a criminal offence to honour the customer's mandate in these circumstances there can be no breach of contract for the bank to refuse to honour its mandate...'. In *Shah v HSBC Private Bank (UK) Ltd* [2010] 3 All ER 477, the Court distinguished the effect of *K Ltd*, in circumstances where the moratorium period had expired (or after consent had been given) and the bank still failed to execute the customer's instructions.

**20.67**   In *AP, U Limited v CPS, RCPO* [2007] EWCA Crim 3128, a case which essentially concerned the release of assets from restrained funds, the court confirmed that: 'Consent may relieve the bank of any criminal responsibility for a transaction in question; but that does not mean that in relation to others involved in the transaction, it may not amount to or form part of a dishonest money laundering scheme' (para 32).

#### The third money laundering offence: acquisition, use, and possession

Section 329(1) states that a person commits an offence if he:                    **20.68**

(a)  acquires criminal property;
(b)  uses criminal property;
(c)  has possession of criminal property.

Section 329 replaces s 51 of the DTA and s 93B of the CJA. In *Wilkinson, R (on the appli-* **20.69**
*cation of ) v DPP* [2006] EWHC 3012 (Admin) an issue arose over the CPS's seemingly
increasing practice of charging offences under s 329, as opposed to the offence of handling
stolen goods. Arguably it is easier to prove a s 329 offence, because the *mens rea* is 'knowing
or suspecting' as opposed to 'knowing or believing' (s 22 Theft Act 1968). The Court held
that if an offence was inappropriately charged the court should express a view and encourage
(but no more) the CPS to charge a lesser offence. However, it was ultimately a matter for
them and their own internal guidance.

In *CPS Nottinghamshire v Rose* [2008] EWCA Crim 239, the issue of whether s 329 charges **20.70**
were being brought in preference to handling stolen goods was returned to. The statistics did
not bear out such an assertion, and the Court found nothing wrong in the Crown proceeding with s 329 where it had the effect of simplifying the issues at the trial.

#### 'Defences' to section 329(1)

The offence under s 329 is only committed if the person concerned knows or suspects the **20.71**
property which has been acquired or used or which he has in his possession, constitutes or
represents his own or another's benefit from criminal conduct.

Under s 329(2) there are four specified exemptions available, as follows:                **20.72**

(a)  [the person] makes an authorised disclosure under s 338 and (if the disclosure is made
     before he does the act mentioned in s 338(1)) he has the appropriate consent;
(b)  he intends to make such a disclosure but has a reasonable excuse for not doing so;
(c)  he acquired or used or had possession of the property for adequate consideration;
(d)  the act he does is done in carrying out a function he has relating to the enforcement of
     any provision of this Act or of any other enactment relating to criminal conduct or benefit
     from criminal conduct.

In relation to s 329(2)(c) a person 'acquires property for inadequate consideration' if the **20.73**
value of the consideration is significantly less than the value of the property (see s 329(3)(a)).
A person also uses or has possession of property for inadequate consideration if the value of
the consideration is significantly less than the value of the use or possession (see s 329(3)(b)).

Further, it should be noted that the provision by a person of goods or services which he **20.74**
knows or suspects may help another to carry out criminal conduct is not 'consideration'
under s 329(3)(c).

Section 329 is also amended by SOCPA from 1 July 2005 to include a new 'defence' (2C), **20.75**
as follows:

(2C)  A deposit-taking body that does an act mentioned in sub-section (1) does not commit
      an offence under that sub-section if—
      (a)  it does the act in operating an account maintained with it, and
      (b)  the value of the criminal property concerned is less than the threshold amount
           determined under s 339A for the act.

**Burden of proof**

**20.76**   Under the CJA, the burden of proving the defence was with the defendant but, as in all cases where a burden rests on the defence, the standard of proof was to the civil standard. The burden was on the prosecution to prove the *mens rea* of the offence, but if the defendant wished to raise a defence to the effect that he did not know or suspect the nature of the transaction, the burden of proof was upon him to do so on a balance of probabilities (see *R v Colle* (1992) 95 Cr App R 67). The decision in *Colle* was approved by the Judicial Committee of the Privy Council in *A-G of Hong Kong v Lee Kwong-Kut* [1993] AC 951. The language used in POCA is different to that used in the CJA; in particular the draftsmen of POCA do not use the word 'defence' in the relevant parts of the statute. Nevertheless, it is clear that an individual will not have committed the offence in question if one of the 'exemptions' set out in, eg, s 327(2) apply. Arguably it is for the Crown to show that they do not apply, and therefore the burden will be on the prosecution. Having said that, there is something of an inevitability that the best case for applying the exemptions will come from the defendant.

**Maximum penalty**

**20.77**   Section 334 states:

(1) A person guilty of an offence under section 327, 328 or 329 is liable—
   (a) on summary conviction, to imprisonment for a term not exceeding six months or to a fine not exceeding the statutory maximum or to both, or
   (b) on conviction on indictment, to imprisonment for a term not exceeding 14 years or to a fine or to both.
(2) A person guilty of an offence under section 330, 331, 332 or 333 is liable—
   (a) on summary conviction, to imprisonment for a term not exceeding six months or to a fine not exceeding the statutory maximum or to both, or
   (b) on conviction on indictment, to imprisonment for a term not exceeding five years or to a fine or to both.

**Authorised disclosures**

**20.78**   All three of the money laundering offences afford a 'defence' or exemption to an individual if disclosure is authorised under s 338 of POCA. Section 338(1) states that disclosure will be authorised if:

(1) ...
   (a) it is a disclosure to a constable, a customs officer or nominated officer by the alleged offender that property is criminal property,
   (b) ... [repealed SOCPA s 105, Sch 17]
   (c) the first [second or third] condition set out below is satisfied.
(2) The first condition is that the disclosure is made before the alleged offender does the prohibited act.
(2A) The second condition is that: [inserted by SOCPA s 106]
   (a) the disclosure is made while the alleged offender is doing the prohibited act,
   (b) he began to do the act at a time when, because he did not then know or suspect that the property constituted or represented a person's benefit from criminal conduct, the act was not a prohibited act, and
   (c) the disclosure is made on his own initiative and as soon as it is practicable after he first knows or suspects that the property constitutes or represents a person's benefit from criminal conduct.
(3) The third condition is that—
   (a) the disclosure is made after the alleged offender does the prohibited act,

(b) he has a reasonable excuse for his failure to make the disclosure before he did the act, and

(c) the disclosure is made on his own initiative and as soon as it is practicable for him to make it.

[As amended by the Terrorism Act 2000 and Proceeds of Crime 2002 (Amendment) Regulations 2007, SI 2007/3398, Reg 3, Sch 2, para 6 from 26 December 2007.]

By s 338(6) references to 'the prohibited act' are to: **20.79**

(a) an act mentioned in s 327(1) (ie the concealing, disguising, converting, transferring, or removing of criminal property), or

(b) an act mentioned in s 328(1) (where a person knows or suspects that an arrangement he has entered into will facilitate the acquisition, retention, or use or control of criminal property), or

(c) an act mentioned in s 329(1) (where a person acquires criminal property, uses criminal property or has it in his possession).

For the 'defence' under s 338(1)(a) to be successful, the disclosure must be made in the **20.80** course of the defendant's employment (see s 338(5)).

It should be noted that an authorised disclosure is not to be taken to breach any restriction **20.81** on the disclosure of information (however imposed) (see s 338(4)).

By s 339(1) the Secretary of State may prescribe the form and manner in which a dis- **20.82** closure under s 338 must be made. That order may include a request to the discloser to provide additional information specified in the form. This is considered more fully in Chapter 21.

### Disclosure to a nominated officer

A nominated officer is a person nominated to receive disclosures under s 338 (see s 336(11)), **20.83** ie a person nominated to receive authorised disclosures relating to the money laundering offences under ss 327(1), 328(1), or 329(1), as the case may be.

The nominated officer will often be the person nominated by the alleged offender's employer **20.84** to receive authorised disclosures (see s 338(5)(a)).

### Appropriate consent

The three principal money laundering offences envisage that a person will have a defence if **20.85** the disclosure is authorised under s 338 and the person involved has 'appropriate consent'.

Under s 335(1) the appropriate consent is defined as: **20.86**

(a) the consent of a nominated officer to do a prohibited act if an authorised disclosure is made to the nominated officer;

(b) the consent of a constable to do a prohibited act if an authorised disclosure is made to a constable;

(c) the consent of a Customs officer to do a prohibited act if an authorised disclosure is made to a Customs officer.

References to a 'prohibited act' are references to the offences mentioned in ss 327(1), 328(1), or 329(1), as the case may be (see s 335(8)).

**20.87** Under s 335(1)(b), a constable includes a person authorised for the purposes of Pt 7 of POCA by the Director General of SOCA (see s 340(13)).

**20.88** By s 335(2), (3), and (4), a person must be treated as having the appropriate consent if he makes an authorised disclosure to a constable or a Customs officer and he does not receive, before the end of the 'notice period', a notice from a constable or Customs officer that consent to the doing of the act is refused; or alternatively, before the end of the notice period, he does receive notice from a constable or Customs that consent to the doing of the act is refused, but the 'moratorium period' has expired. POCA therefore envisages time limits under which Customs or the police must respond to requests for consent.

**20.89** For the right to ask for consent to be reviewed in the moratorium period and SOCA's obligation to do so, see *R (UMBS Online) v Serious Organised Crime Agency* [2008] 1 All ER 465.

### Notice period

**20.90** Section 335(5) states:

> The notice period is the period of seven working days starting with the first working day after the person makes the disclosure.

Section 335 puts a proactive duty on the nominated officer or law enforcement agency concerned to respond within the time limit of seven days. Failure to do so will mean the person who has disclosed the information can go ahead with what may otherwise be a prohibited act and without an offence being committed.

### Moratorium period

**20.91** Under s 335(6) the moratorium period is the period of thirty-one days starting with the day on which the person receives notice that consent to the doing of the act is refused.

**20.92** The effect of the moratorium period is that if a constable or Customs officer withholds consent within the seven-working-day period under s 335(5), then they are entitled to a further thirty-one calendar days in which to take further action in relation to the disclosures, for example seeking a court order to restrain the assets in question. However, if the discloser hears nothing more after the thirty-one-day period has expired, then they should be able to proceed with the transaction without the risk of committing any offence (a working day is defined as any day other than Saturday, Sunday, Christmas Day, Good Friday, or a Bank Holiday—see s 335(7)).

### Consent from a nominated officer

**20.93** Nominated officers must not give the appropriate consent to the doing of a prohibited act unless certain conditions set out in s 336(2)–(4) are satisfied (see s 336(1)). Those conditions are as follows:

(1) the discloser makes a disclosure that property is criminal property to a person authorised for the purposes of Pt 7 by the Director General of SOCA, and such a person gives consent to the doing of the act (s 336(2));

(2) the discloser makes a disclosure that property is criminal property to a person authorised for the purposes of Pt 7 by the Director General of SOCA, and before the end of the notice period he does not receive notice from such person that consent to the doing of the act is refused (s 336(3));

(3) the discloser makes a disclosure that property is criminal property to a person authorised for the purposes of Pt 7 by the Director General of SOCA, and before the end of the notice period he receives notice from such a person that consent to the doing of the act is refused, and the moratorium period has expired (s 336(4)).

The nominated officer must adhere very carefully to the above conditions. Failure to do so **20.94** may itself result in the committing of an offence by the nominated officer, for example, if he gives consent to a prohibited act in circumstances where none of the conditions are satisfied and the nominated officer knows or suspects that the act is prohibited under the money laundering regime (s 336(5)).

A nominated officer found to be guilty of such an offence stands liable, on summary con- **20.95** viction, to imprisonment for a term not exceeding six months, or to a fine not exceeding the statutory maximum, or to both; or on conviction on indictment, to imprisonment for a term not exceeding five years, or to a fine, or to both (see s 336(6)). The notice period and the moratorium period are identical to that set out under s 335(5) and (6), namely seven working days and thirty-one calendar days respectively (see s 336(7), (8), and (9)).

### The prohibited act

The prohibited act referred to in s 336(1) is an act which falls under either s 327(1) (conceal- **20.96** ing etc), s 328(1) (arrangements for money laundering), or s 329(1) (acquisition, use, and possession of criminal property for money laundering) as the case may be (s 336(10)).

### Protected disclosures

Disclosures under Pt 7 of POCA fall into two specified categories, either protected dis- **20.97** closures (under s 337) or authorised disclosures (under s 338). Authorised disclosures are considered above.

Section 337 sets out three conditions under which disclosure will not be taken to breach any **20.98** restriction on the disclosure of information (however imposed). The three conditions, all of which must be satisfied, are as follows:

(1) that the information or other matter disclosed came to the person making the disclosure (the discloser) in the course of his trade, profession, business, or employment (s 337(2));
(2) that the information or other matter:
    (a) causes the discloser to know or suspect, or
    (b) gives him reasonable grounds for knowing or suspecting, that another person is engaged in money laundering (s 337(3));
(3) that the disclosure is made to a constable, a Customs officer, or a nominated officer as soon as is practicable after the information or other matter comes to the discloser (s 337(4)).

The first condition, s 337(2), exempts a person who receives information in the course of **20.99** his trade or profession from any legal or other obligations that would otherwise prevent him from making disclosure to the authorities. This protection extends beyond the regulated sector to include, eg, accountants or solicitors giving free advice.

**20.100**   In terms of the suggestion that disclosing information may breach confidentiality undertakings, s 104 of SOCPA adds the following:

> 4A. Where a disclosure consists of a disclosure protected under subsection (1) and a disclosure of either or both of—
> (a)  the identity of the other person mentioned in subsection (3), and
> (b)  the whereabouts of property forming the subject-matter of the money laundering that the discloser knows or suspects, or has reasonable grounds for knowing or suspecting, that other person to be engaged in,
> the disclosure of the thing mentioned in paragraph (a) or (b) (as well as the disclosure protected under subsection (1)) is not to be taken to breach any restriction on the disclosure of information (however imposed).

### Form and manner of disclosures

**20.101**   Under s 339 of the Act, the Secretary of State is permitted to prescribe the form and manner in which a disclosure under ss 330, 331, 332, or 338 must be made. An order under this section may also provide that the form may include a request for the discloser to provide additional information specified in the form. (See also Chapter 21.)

**20.102**   While s 339(3) anticipates that the Secretary of State may ask for the discloser to provide additional information, it does not create any criminal offence if the discloser refuses to supply that additional information. Any additional information supplied appears, under s 339(4), to have been given immunity from any restriction on the disclosure of information, such as confidentiality clauses in contracts.

### Mode of trial

**20.103**   As these offences are triable either way, justices will be called upon to make decisions as to mode of trial. DTA and CJA case law suggests that rarely, if ever, will summary trial be appropriate. Further, the complexity of the case should also be taken into consideration. Money laundering cases frequently involve a detailed analysis of complex financial documentation which, together with the volume of evidence necessary to prove the case, means that any trial may be lengthy.

### Sentencing

**20.104**   The maximum sentence for these money laundering offences is fourteen years' imprisonment (see s 334).

**20.105**   In *R v Greaves and others* [2010] EWCA Crim 709, the Court of Appeal held (para 24):

> (a)  Offences contrary to sections 327 to 329 of the Proceeds of Crime Act, are separate free-standing offences to the offence or offences which give rise to the criminal property with which the Proceeds of Crime Act is concerned.
> (b)  Where the offender responsible for the primary crime is not the offender guilty of the Proceeds of Crime Act offence, the position is more straightforward than when they are the same. . . .
> (c)  Where the offenders are one and the same, if the conduct involved in the Proceeds of Crime Act offence in reality adds nothing to the culpability of the conduct involved in the primary offence, there should be no additional penalty. A person should not be punished twice for the same conduct. That can be achieved either by imposing 'no separate penalty'

on the Proceeds of Crime Act offence or by a concurrent sentence where the primary sentence is imprisonment.

(d) Where conduct involved in a Proceeds of Crime Act offence does add to the culpability of the conduct involved in the primary offence an additional penalty is appropriate: see *R v Brown* [2006] EWCA Crim 1996, [2007] 1 Cr App R (S) 77 and *R v Linegar* [[2009] EWCA Crim 648].

(e) Where the primary offence has a maximum sentence, that is the maximum which Parliament has thought appropriate for conduct constituting the offence. In a case where the Proceeds of Crime Act offence does not add to the culpability of the conduct involved in the primary offence, there should not be a consecutive sentence on the latter on the ground that the maximum permitted on the primary offence is too low. Any difficulty posed by a low maximum for the primary offence may possibly be avoided if it is foreseen by the prosecution. Thus in the present case there might have been a number of specimen substantive counts rather than one count of conspiracy.

(f) Where the conduct involved in the Proceeds of Crime Act offence does add to the culpability of the conduct involved in the primary offence, the maximum sentence permitted on the primary offence may be relevant to the sentence on the Proceeds of Crime Act offence because the seriousness of the primary offence reflects on the seriousness of the laundering: see, for instance, *R v Greenwood* [1995] 16 Cr App R (S) 614 and *R v Basra* [[2002] EWCA Crim 541]. But it does not as a matter of principle provide a limit: see *Linegar* [above]. If the Proceeds of Crime Act offence merits it, the sentence for it may add to that for the primary offence bringing it above the maximum for the latter, and it may if appropriate itself exceed the maximum on the latter: see *Linegar* [above].

In *R v Alexander and others* [2011] 2 Cr App R (S) 297 the Court gave further guidance, **20.106** concluding that when defendants are sentenced for a conspiracy to supply drugs and a conspiracy to conceal the proceeds of that conspiracy, such double or consecutive sentencing would be wrong, unless the second conspiracy added to the culpability of the first.

### Terrorism matters

Regulations in relation to terrorists acts and money laundering are considered in Chapter 24. **20.107**

# 21

# DISCLOSURE OF SUSPICIOUS TRANSACTIONS

## A. Introduction

Money laundering and confiscation law can only be truly effective if banks, financial institu- **21.01** tions, and professionals who handle money on behalf of clients, are compelled to disclose suspicious transactions to law enforcement authorities. The provisions of POCA and the related legislation encourage such disclosure by providing certain exemptions from criminal liability for money laundering and civil liability at the suit of the customer for any breach of confidentiality.

In this chapter we consider the main provisions of POCA in relation to disclosure of **21.02** suspicious transactions by the professions. The POCA provisions came into force on 24 February 2003.

POCA has been substantially amended in relation to money laundering and the disclosure **21.03** of suspicious transactions by virtue of SOCPA. According to the explanatory notes that accompanied SOCPA, these amendments were designed to improve the effectiveness of the civil recovery scheme and ease the money laundering reporting requirements on the regulated sector.

**21.04** As discussed in Chapter 20 of this book, many individuals launder money to conceal illegal activity, such as drug trafficking, tax evasion, and terrorism. It fuels criminal conduct, allowing drug dealers, smugglers, terrorists, arms dealers, and tax evaders to maintain control over their proceeds and ultimately to provide a legitimate cover for their sources of income. Law enforcement officials estimate that such individuals yearly launder $1 to $2 trillion worldwide through different types of financial institutions and businesses (see Appendix 21).

## B. Disclosure of Suspicious Transactions under POCA

### Businesses in the regulated sector

**21.05** The legislation distinguishes between businesses within and those outside the 'regulated sector'. The duty to report suspicious transactions under s 330 of POCA (below) is restricted to those businesses in the 'regulated sector'.

**21.06** The original definition of the regulated sector found in Appendix 9 of the 2002 Act was replaced by the Proceeds of Crime Act 2002 (Business in the Regulated Sector and Supervisory Authorities) Order 2003, SI 2003/3074. This has subsequently been further substituted by the Proceeds of Crime Act 2002 (Business in the Regulated Sector and Supervisory Authorities) Order 2007, SI 2007/3287, which came into force on 15 December 2007. The activities defined as constituting 'business' in the regulated sector include carrying out activities in the financial and property sectors; provision by way of business or services by a body corporate or unincorporated; or, in the case of a sole practitioner, by an individual, where trading involves participation in a financial or real property transaction.

**21.07** Businesses are included in the regulated sector if they engage in any of the following activities in the UK:

    (a) the acceptance by a credit institution of deposits or other repayable funds from the public, or the granting by a credit institution of credits for its own account;

    (b) the carrying on of one or more of the activities listed in points 2 to 12 and 14 of Annex 1 to the Banking Consolidation Directive by an undertaking other than—

        (i) a credit institution; or

        (ii) an undertaking whose only listed activity is trading on its own account in one or more of the products listed in point 7 of Annex 1 to the Banking Consolidation Directive and which does not act on behalf of a customer (that is, a third party which is not a member of the same group as the undertaking);

    (c) the carrying on of activities covered by the Life Assurance Consolidation Directive by an insurance company authorised in accordance with that Directive;

    (d) the provision of investment services or the performance of investment activities by a person (other than a person falling within Art 2 of the Markets in Financial Instruments Directive) whose regular occupation or business is the provision to other persons of an investment service or the performance of an investment activity on a professional basis;

    (e) the marketing or other offering of units or shares by a collective investment undertaking;

    (f) the activities of an insurance intermediary as defined in Art 2(5) of the Insurance Mediation Directive, other than a tied insurance intermediary as mentioned in Art 2(7) of that Directive, in respect of contracts of long-term insurance within the meaning given by Art 3(1) of, and Pt II of Schedule 1 to, the Financial Services and Markets Act 2000 (Regulated Activities) Order 2001;

(g) the carrying on of any of the activities mentioned in paragraphs (b) to (f) by a branch located in an EEA state of a person referred to in those paragraphs (or of an equivalent person in any other state), wherever its head office is located;

(h) the activities of the National Savings Bank;

(i) any activity carried on for the purpose of raising money authorised to be raised under the National Loans Act 1968 under the auspices of the Director of Savings;

(j) the carrying on of statutory audit work within the meaning of s 1210 of the Companies Act 2006 (meaning of 'statutory auditor' etc) by any firm or individual who is a statutory auditor within the meaning of Pt 42 of that Act (statutory auditors);

(k) the activities of a person appointed to act as an insolvency practitioner within the meaning of s 388 of the Insolvency Act 1986 or Art 3 of the Insolvency (Northern Ireland) Order 1989;

(l) the provision to other persons of accountancy services by a firm or sole practitioner who by way of business provides such services to other persons;

(m) the provision of advice about the tax affairs of other persons by a firm or sole practitioner who by way of business provides advice about the tax affairs of other persons;

(n) the participation in financial or real property transactions concerning—

    (i) the buying and selling of real property (or, in Scotland, heritable property) or business entities;

    (ii) the managing of client money, securities, or other assets;

    (iii) the opening or management of bank, savings, or securities accounts;

    (iv) the organisation of contributions necessary for the creation, operation, or management of companies; or

    (v) the creation, operation or management of trusts, companies, or similar structures, by a firm or sole practitioner who by way of business provides legal or notarial services to other persons;

(o) the provision to other persons by way of business by a firm or sole practitioner of any of the services mentioned in sub-para (4);

(p) the carrying on of estate agency work (within the meaning given by s 1 of the Estate Agents Act 1979 (estate agency work)) by a firm or a sole practitioner who carries on, or whose employees carry on, such work;

(q) the trading in goods (including dealing as an auctioneer) whenever a transaction involves the receipt of a payment or payments in cash of at least 15,000 euros in total, whether the transaction is executed in a single operation or in several operations which appear to be linked, by a firm or sole trader who by way of business trades in goods;

(r) operating a casino under a casino operating licence (within the meaning given by s 65(2) of the Gambling Act 2005 (nature of licence)).

The Terrorism Act 2000 and Proceeds of Crime Act 2002 (Business in the Regulated Sector) (No 2) Order 2012 (SI 2012/2299) extends the ambit to include estate agents selling property outside the UK within the scope of the definition.

The services referred to in subpara (1)(o) are:                                                    **21.08**

(a) forming companies or other legal persons;

(b) acting, or arranging for another person to act—

    (i) as a director or secretary of a company;

    (ii) as a partner of a partnership; or

    (iii) in a similar position in relation to other legal persons;

(c) providing a registered office, business address, correspondence or administrative address, or other related services for a company, partnership, or any other legal person or arrangement;

(d) acting, or arranging for another person to act, as—

(i) a trustee of an express trust or similar legal arrangement; or

(ii) a nominee shareholder for a person other than a company whose securities are listed on a regulated market.

**21.09** The amendments to the meaning of a 'business in the regulated sector' provided by Pt 1 of Sch 9 reflect changes to the scope of the regulated sector made by the EC's third money laundering Directive. The two major changes are the expanded definition of a trust or company service provider and the exemption for financial activity on an occasional or very limited basis.

**21.10** POCA intends, therefore, that the businesses listed above will employ a higher level of diligence in handling transactions than other businesses.

### Excluded businesses

**21.11** A business is not in the regulated sector if it consists of:

(a) the issuing of withdrawable share capital within the limit set by s 6 of the Industrial and Provident Societies Act 1965 (maximum shareholding in society), or the acceptance of deposits from the public within the limit set by s 7(3) of that Act (carrying on of banking by societies), by a society registered under that Act;

(b) the issuing of withdrawable share capital within the limit set by s 6 of the Industrial and Provident Societies Act (Northern Ireland) 1969 (maximum shareholding in society), or the acceptance of deposits from the public within the limit set by s 7(3) of that Act (carrying on of banking by societies), by a society registered under that Act;

(c) the carrying on of any activity in respect of which a person who is (or falls within a class of persons) specified in any of paras 2 to 23, 25 to 38, or 40 to 49 of the Schedule to the Financial Services and Markets Act 2000 (Exemption) Order 2001 is exempt;

(d) the exercise of the functions specified in s 45 of the Financial Services Act 1986 (miscellaneous exemptions) by a person who was an exempted person for the purposes of that section immediately before its repeal;

(e) the engaging in financial activity which fulfils all of the conditions set out in paras (a) to (g) of sub-para (3) of this paragraph by a person whose main activity is that of a high value dealer; or

(f) the preparation of a home information pack (within the meaning of Pt 5 of the Housing Act 2004 (home information packs)) or a document or information for inclusion in a home information pack.

**21.12** A business is also not in the regulated sector if it consists of financial activity where:

(a) the person's total annual turnover in respect of the financial activity does not exceed £64,000;

(b) the financial activity is limited in relation to any customer to no more than one transaction exceeding 1,000 euros, whether the transaction is carried out in a single operation, or a series of operations which appear to be linked;

(c) the financial activity does not exceed 5 per cent of the person's total annual turnover;

(d) the financial activity is ancillary to the person's main activity and directly related to that activity;

(e) the financial activity is not the transmission or remittance of money (or any representation of monetary value) by any means;

(f) the main activity of the person carrying on the financial activity is not an activity mentioned in para 1(1)(a) to (p) or (r); and

(g) the financial activity is provided only to customers of the person's main activity and is not offered to the public.

### Failure to disclose: regulated sector

Under s 330 of POCA (as amended by s 104 of SOCPA) a person commits an offence if each **21.13** of the following conditions is satisfied:

(2) The first condition is that he—
   (a) knows or suspects, or
   (b) has reasonable grounds for knowing or suspecting,
   that another person is engaged in money laundering.

(3) The second condition is that the information or other matter—
   (a) on which his knowledge or suspicion is based, or
   (b) which gives reasonable grounds for such knowledge or suspicion,
   came to him in the course of a business in the regulated sector.

(3A) The third condition is—
   (a) that he can identify the other person mentioned in section 330(2) or the whereabouts of any of the laundered property, or
   (b) that he believes, or it is reasonable to expect him to believe, that the information or other matter mentioned in section 330(3) will or may assist in identifying that other person or the whereabouts of any of the laundered property.

(4) The fourth condition is that he does not make the required disclosure to—
   (a) a nominated officer, or
   (b) a person authorised for the purposes of this Part by the Director General of the Serious Organised Crime Agency,
   as soon as is practicable after the information or other matter mentioned in sub-section (3) comes to him.

(5) The required disclosure is a disclosure of—
   (a) the identity of the other person mentioned in sub-section (2), if he knows it,
   (b) the whereabouts of the laundered property, so far as he knows it, and
   (c) the information or other matter mentioned in section 330(3).

The laundered property is the property forming the subject matter of the money laundering **21.14** that the individual knows or suspects (or has reasonable grounds for knowing or suspecting) that another person is engaged in (s 330(5A)). The 'reasonable grounds' element to the criteria introduces a negligence test within the legislation, which is also reflected in s 331.

Section 330 replaces s 52 of the DTA and is intended to create an obligation to report a **21.15** suspicion of money laundering to the authorities. In so doing, it widens the scope of the offences that it replaces under s 52 beyond reporting drug money laundering to reporting the laundering of the proceeds of *any* criminal conduct.

The obligation to disclose suspicions of money laundering will apply if the person required **21.16** to make a disclosure knows the identity of the person engaged in the money laundering offence, or the whereabouts of any of the laundered property, or information which may assist in uncovering the identity of the person engaged in the offence, or the whereabouts of any of the laundered property.

### What test should the court apply?

**21.17**  Section 330(8) reads:

> (8) In deciding whether a person committed an offence under this section the court must consider whether he followed any relevant guidance which was at the time concerned—
> (a) issued by a supervisory authority or any other appropriate body,
> (b) approved by the Treasury, and
> (c) published in a manner it approved as appropriate in its opinion to bring the guidance to the attention of persons likely to be affected by it.

Under s 330(8) an appropriate body is any body that regulates or is representative of any trade, profession, business, or employment carried on by the alleged offender (see s 330(13)).

**21.18**  The British Bankers Association has set up a Joint Money Laundering Steering Group, which has produced guidance notes on money laundering since 1990. It should be noted that guidance notes are just that, and cannot supplant the letter of the law, which the courts are bound to follow. Nevertheless s 330(8) provides that the court must at least take account of guidance notes issued by any supervisory authority providing that they have been approved by the Treasury.

### 'Defences' to failing to disclose in the regulated sector

**21.19**  A person does not commit an offence under s 330 if:

> (6) ...
> (a) he has a reasonable excuse for not making the required disclosure;
> (b) he is a professional legal advisor or relevant professional adviser and—
> > (i) if he knows either of the things mentioned in subsection (5)(a) and (b), he knows the thing because of information or other matter that came to him in privileged circumstances;
> > (ii) the information or other matter mentioned in subsection (3) came to him in privileged circumstances, or
> (c) subsection 7 or 7B applies to him.
> (7) This subsection applies to a person if—
> > (a) he does not know or suspect that another person is engaged in money laundering, and
> > (b) he has not been provided by his employer with such training as is specified by the Secretary of State by order for the purposes of this Section.

**21.20**  Section 102 of SOCPA amends s 330 of POCA to insert a further defence:

> (7A) Nor does a person commit an offence under this section if—
> > (a) he knows, or believes on reasonable grounds, that the money laundering is occurring in a particular country or territory outside the United Kingdom, and
> > (b) the money laundering—
> > > (i) is not unlawful under the criminal law applying in the country or territory, and
> > > (ii) is not of a description prescribed in an order made by the Secretary of State.

**21.21**  The Proceeds of Crime Act 2002 and Money Laundering Regulations 2003 (Amendment) Order 2006 (SI 2006/308) further inserts:

> (7B) This subsection applies to a person if—
> > (a) he is employed by, or is in partnership with, a professional legal adviser or a relevant professional adviser to provide the adviser with assistance or support,

> (b) the information or other matter mentioned in subsection (3) comes to the person
>     in connection with the provision of such assistance or support, and
> (c) the information or other matter came to the adviser in privileged circumstances.

Subsection (7) confirms that an individual does not commit an offence if the individual does **21.22**
not know or suspect that the person is engaged in money laundering and he has not been provided by his employer with such training as is specified by the Act. It is therefore a reasonable
excuse for an employee to raise that his employer has not given him adequate training, although
the employers themselves may then find themselves in jeopardy of the money laundering regulations. SI 2003/171 specifies training for the purposes of POCA.

Subsection 7A provides that an offence is not committed where the money laundering has **21.23**
occurred or is occurring outside the UK and money laundering is not unlawful in that particular country.

The language used in POCA is different from that used in the CJA—in particular the drafts- **21.24**
men of POCA do not use the word 'defence' in the relevant parts of the statute. Nevertheless,
it is clear that an individual will not have committed the offence in question if one of the
'exemptions' set out in the Act applies. Arguably it will be for the Crown to show that these
safety nets do not apply, and therefore the burden will be on the prosecution. Having said
that, there is something of an inevitability that the best case for applying the 'exemptions'
will come from the defendant.

### Legal and professional privilege

Legal professional privilege survives POCA. An individual does not commit an offence **21.25**
under this section if he has a reasonable excuse for not making the required disclosure; or he
is a professional legal adviser and the information came to him in privileged circumstances
(s 330(6), (7), or (7B)).

Section 330(6)(b) (as substituted by s 104(3) of SOCPA) provides a safety net where the **21.26**
person is a professional legal adviser or relevant professional adviser and the information or
other matter came to him in the circumstances set out in s 330(10).

'Relevant professional adviser' is defined by s 330(14), which is inserted by the Proceeds **21.27**
of Crime Act 2002 and Money Laundering Regulations 2003 (Amendment) Order 2006
(SI 2006/308) and includes accountants, auditors, and tax advisers who are members of a
professional body.

The effect of these amendments is to extend the defence available to professional legal advis- **21.28**
ers and to provide an exemption for a person employed by, or in partnership with, a professional legal adviser or a relevant professional adviser. The amendments came into force on
21 February 2006.

Section 330(10) states: **21.29**

> Information or other matter comes to a professional legal adviser or relevant professional
> adviser in privileged circumstances if it is communicated or given to him—
>
> (a) by (or by a representative of) a client of his in connection with the giving by the adviser
>     of legal advice to the client,
> (b) by (or by a representative of) a person seeking legal advice from the adviser, or
> (c) by a person in connection with legal proceedings or contemplated legal proceedings.

However, s 330(10) does not apply to information or other matter that is communicated or given to the legal adviser with the intention of furthering a criminal purpose (see s 330(11) and *Francis and Francis v Central Criminal Court* [1988] 3 All ER 775 (HL)).

**21.30**  The important decision of *Bowman v Fels* [2005] EWCA Civ 226 in relation to professional legal advisers is considered below.

### Failure to disclose: nominated officers in the regulated sector

**21.31**  Section 331 of POCA criminalises conduct where a nominated officer (otherwise the money laundering reporting officer—MRLO) receives a report under s 330 which causes him to know or suspect, or gives reasonable grounds for knowledge or suspicion, that money laundering is taking place, and where that nominated officer does not disclose that information 'as soon as practicable' after it comes to him.

**21.32**  A nominated officer is a person nominated to receive disclosures under s 338 (see s 336(11)), ie a person nominated to receive authorised disclosures relating to the money laundering offences under ss 327(1), 328(1), or 329(1), as the case may be.

**21.33**  The nominated officer will often be the person nominated by the alleged offender's employer to receive authorised disclosures (see s 338(5)(a)).

**21.34**  Section 331 states:

>  (1)  A person nominated to receive disclosures under section 330 commits an offence if the conditions in subsections (2) to (4) are satisfied.
>  (2)  The first condition is that he—
>      (a)  knows or suspects, or
>      (b)  has reasonable grounds for knowing or suspecting,
>  that another person is engaged in money laundering.
>  (3)  The second condition is that the information or other matter—
>      (a)  on which his knowledge or suspicion is based, or
>      (b)  which gives reasonable grounds for such knowledge or suspicion,
>  came to him in consequence of a disclosure made under section 330.
>  (3A)  The third condition is—
>      (a)  that [the individual] knows the identity of the other person mentioned in subsection (2), or the whereabouts of any of the laundered property, in consequence of a disclosure made under s 330,
>      (b)  that that other person, or the whereabouts of any of the laundered property, can be identified from the information or other matter mentioned in subsection (3), or
>      (c)  that [the individual] believes, or it is reasonable to expect him to believe, that the information or other matter will or may assist in identifying that other person or the whereabouts of any of the laundered property.
>  (4)  The fourth condition is that he does not make the required disclosure to a person authorised for the purposes of Part 7 [of POCA]...as soon as is practicable, after the information or other matter...comes to him. [as amended by s 104(4) of SOCPA].

**21.35**  The required disclosure must be made to either a person authorised by SOCA or in the form and manner prescribed under s 339 (see s 331(5)). The 'reasonable grounds' element of the criteria introduces a negligence test to the legislation.

**21.36**  The 'required disclosure' is a disclosure of: (a) the identity of the other person mentioned in s 3A(2), if disclosed to him under the applicable section, (b) the whereabouts of the laundered property, so far as disclosable to him under the applicable section, and (c) the information or other matter mentioned in s 3A(3).

By s 3A(5A), the 'laundered property' is the property forming the subject matter of the **21.37** money laundering that the individual knows or suspects that other person to be engaged in.

### 'Defence' available

A person does not commit an offence under s 331 if he has a 'reasonable excuse' for not dis- **21.38** closing the information or other matter (see s 331(6)). Similarly, a new subs (6A) has been inserted after subs (6) which is in identical terms to the inserted defences available under s 330 (set out above).

As stated previously, the language used in POCA is different from that used in the CJA; in **21.39** particular the draftsmen of POCA do not use the word 'defence' in the relevant parts of the statute. Nevertheless, it is clear that an individual will not have committed the offence in question if one of the 'exemptions' set out in the Act apply. The term 'reasonable excuse' is undesirably vague: what one person may consider reasonable, another may not.

### Considerations for the court

In deciding whether a nominated officer has committed an offence under s 331, the court **21.40** must consider whether he followed any relevant guidance which was at the time concerned issued by a supervisory authority or any other appropriate body and approved by the Treasury (see s 331(7)). An 'appropriate body' is a body which regulates or is representative of a trade, profession, business, or employment (see s 331(9)).

### Failure to disclose: other nominated officers

Under s 332, it is an offence where a nominated officer (otherwise the money laundering **21.41** reporting officer—MRLO) receives a report under either s 337 or s 338 (protected disclosures or authorised disclosures) which causes him to know or suspect that money laundering is taking place, and notwithstanding that, he does not disclose the report as soon as the information comes to him. The offence is committed if the following four conditions under s 332(1) to (4) are satisfied:

(1) that the person nominated knows or suspects that another person is engaged in money laundering;
(2) that the information or other matter on which his knowledge or suspicion is based came to him as a consequence of disclosure made under the applicable section;
(3) that—
    (a) he knows the identity of the other person mentioned in subs (2), or the whereabouts of any of the laundered property, in consequence of a disclosure made under the applicable section,
    (b) that other person, or the whereabouts of any of the laundered property, can be identified from the information or other matter mentioned in subsection (3) [(2) above], or
    (c) he believes, or it is reasonable for him to expect to believe, that the information or other matter will or may assist in identifying that other person or the whereabouts of any of the laundered property.
(4) that he does not make the required disclosures 'as soon as in practicable' after the information or other matter comes to him.

**21.42** Under s 332(5) a nominated officer is required to disclose to SOCA in the form prescribed by s 339.

**21.43** By subs 5B the 'applicable section' is s 337 (protected disclosures), or s 338 (authorised disclosures).

**21.44** The laundered property is the property forming the subject matter of the money laundering that the individual knows or suspects the other person to be engaged in (subs 5A).

### No breach of confidentiality

**21.45** Pursuant to s 104(7) of SOCPA, s 337 of POCA (protected disclosures) has inserted after subs (4) the following:

> (4A) Where a disclosure consists of a disclosure protected under sub-section (1) and a disclosure of either or both of—
> (a) the identity of the other person mentioned in sub-section (3), and
> (b) the whereabouts of property forming the subject matter of the money laundering that the discloser knows or suspects, or has reasonable grounds for knowing or suspecting, that other person to be engaged in,
> the disclosure of the thing mentioned in paragraphs (a) or in (b) (as well as the disclosure protected under sub-section (1)) is not to be taken to breach any restriction on the disclosure of information (however imposed).

**21.46** Authorised disclosures have a similar proviso under s 338(4).

### 'Defence' available

**21.47** It will be noted that under s 332(6) an individual does not commit an offence if he has a reasonable excuse for not making the required disclosure. SOCPA inserts a new defence in the guise of s 332(7), which is in identical terms to that set out in s 330 above. See para 21.13 above.

## C. Professional Legal Advisers

### Introduction

**21.48** Professional legal advisers continue to be exempt from the reporting obligations if the information or other matter comes to them in legally privileged circumstances. The defence of lack of training under s 330(7)(B) also remains, as does the defence of 'reasonable excuse' (however vague that term might be).

**21.49** Section 330(9)(A) confirms that legal professional privilege is not lost when professional legal advisers, including solicitors and barristers, discuss matters with the nominated officers in their firms (generally known as the money laundering reporting officer—MRLO).

**21.50** Legal professional privilege remains intact whether or not the nominated officer is himself a professional legal adviser. This provision allows professional legal advisers and relevant professional advisers to take advice from their nominated officers, without formal disclosure being made to the nominated officer. This amendment has the effect of giving some comfort to both the profession and also the client.

Bowman v Fels

The case of *Bowman v Fels* [2005] EWCA Civ 226, [2005] 2 Cr App R 19 raised important **21.51** issues relating to the ambit of POCA and its application to the legal profession. Because of its importance the Bar Council, the Law Society, and the former NCIS were all granted permission to intervene in the appeal.

*Bowman v Fels* focused on the applicability or otherwise of s 328 of POCA in a case where **21.52** information came to the attention of the lawyer for one of the parties in the course of legal proceedings leading him to know or, more likely, suspect that the other party was engaged in money laundering.

The court held that so far as UK domestic law was concerned, it was elementary that when a **21.53** lawyer is advising a client or acting for him in litigation, he may not disclose to a third party any information about his client's affairs without his express or implied consent (see para 78 and *R v Derby Magistrates' Court ex p B* [1996] 1 AC 487 at pp 503–8 and *Three Rivers DC v Bank of England (No 6)* [2004] 3 WLR 1274, where the House of Lords restated emphatically that legal advice privilege was just as important as litigation privilege, and that for good policy reasons the law affords a special privilege to communications between lawyers and their clients, which it denies to all other confidential communications).

The Court concluded that the proper interpretation of s 328 is that it is not intended to **21.54** cover or affect the ordinary conduct of litigation by legal professionals. That included any step taken by them in litigation, from the issue of proceedings and the securing of injunctive relief or a freezing order up to its final disposal by judgment. Legal proceedings were defined as a state-provided mechanism for the resolution of issues according to law.

### Consensual resolution in a litigious context

In *Bowman v Fels*, the Court of Appeal considered the position where parties agreed to dispose **21.55** of the whole or any aspect of legal proceedings on a consensual basis. The consensual resolution of issues is an integral part of the conduct of ordinary civil litigation. There is also within the CPR a need to encourage cooperation and the value of consensual settlement is underlined.

The Court commented that: **21.56**

> any consensual agreement can in abstract dictionary terms be called an arrangement. But we do not consider that it can have been contemplated that taking such a step in the context of civil litigation would amount to 'becoming concerned in an arrangement which...facilitates the acquisition, retention, use or control of criminal property' within the meaning of s 328. Rather it is another ordinary feature of the conduct of civil litigation, facilitating the resolution of a legal dispute and of the parties' legal rights and duties according to law in a manner which is a valuable alternative to the court imposed solution of litigation and judgment.

The Court went on to state that the position could be different if one were concerned with a settlement which did not reflect the legal and practical merits of the parties' respective positions in the proceedings, and was known or suspected to be no more than a pretext for an agreement relating to the acquisition, retention, use, or control of criminal property.

### POCA clauses

The Court in *Bowman v Fels* left open the permissibility or possibility of a POCA clause, **21.57** whereby an arrangement might be entered into, but expressly made subject to it: 'not taking effect until authorised disclosure has been made pursuant to s 328 of POCA and appropriate consent is given or deemed to be given under s 335 of that Act'.

**21.58** The Court commented that a question could arise whether the making of such an arrangement, even though its validity or implementation were to be made subject to the condition, could itself be a prohibited act within ss 328(1) and 338.

**21.59** The Court stated (at para 103) that it remained uneasy about a clause which would disclose to all concerned (including the other party, who might well be the person suspected of money laundering activity) that money laundering was suspected.

**21.60** It commented that, curiously, the prohibition on tipping off under s 333 only applied once a disclosure to the authorities has been made. In *Bowman v Fels*, the Court stated that both s 330(3)(c) and (4) and s 342(3)(c) and (4) preserve a broad freedom to make disclosure not merely to a client when giving legal advice, but to any person in connection with actual or contemplated legal proceedings, so it may be that a POCA clause would create no problem in the context of legal proceedings (see para 104), but clearly caution should be exercised.

**21.61** It is also important to note that whilst litigation in related processes may fall outside of the ambit of the offences, the property itself remains criminal property for the purposes of s 340(3) of POCA. Therefore any future dealings with the property after the terms of any judgment or settlement are carried out will require a re-examination of whether a report to SOCA is required. Solicitors will also need to advise their clients about their own position if ownership of criminal property by them falls outside a court order or other type of settlement covered by the exclusion. The s 329 offence of acquisition, use, and possession may be particularly relevant in these circumstances.

**21.62** It should further be noted that neither common law legal professional privilege nor the s 330(6) exemption apply to communications made with the intention of furthering a criminal purpose.

### Protection for judges

**21.63** In relation to judges who suspect that the subject matter of the dispute may be criminal property, the Court of Appeal has made it clear that their judgments and orders will not constitute an 'arrangement' for the purposes of s 328 (see para 65 of their judgment). While the Court of Appeal does not expressly address the position of either arbitrators or mediators, it can be implied that the same considerations will be applied.

## D. Suspicious Activity Reports: 'SARs'

### Introduction

**21.64** Suspicious Activity Reports (SARs) are one of the government's main weapons in the battle against money laundering and other financial crimes. These reports generate leads that law enforcement agencies use to initiate money laundering investigations. A SAR should be made as soon as the knowledge or suspicion that criminal proceeds exist has arisen, especially if consent may be required, or at the earliest opportunity thereafter.

**21.65** SOCA's preferred method for reporters to submit their suspicion is the SOCA Suspicious Activity Report Form. SOCA prefers these forms to be submitted electronically, but printable hard-copy versions of the forms can be found on the SOCA website or can be obtained directly from SOCA. The standard form consists of six separate sheets ('modules').

SOCA do not usually acknowledge any SAR sent by fax, post, or letter. Electronic submis- **21.66** sions through the SAR Online system will receive an acknowledgment which will include an automatically generated reference number.

### Why is completing a SAR important?

The Money Laundering Regulations 2007 (SI 2007/2157), as amended by the Money **21.67** Laundering (Amendment) Regulations 2011(SI 2011/1781) and 2012 (SI 2012/2299), include requirements that there be due diligence procedures in place in relation to existing clients and customers; and they require the financial, accountancy, legal, and other sectors to take steps to prevent their services being used for money laundering or terrorist financing. The Regulations require firms to apply enhanced customer identification and monitoring measures, and require them to have appropriate anti-money laundering systems in place. One of the 'defences' to the money laundering offences in ss 327 to 329 is the making of an authorised disclosure and the obtaining of appropriate consent.

An authorised disclosure (s 338) is a disclosure which is made: **21.68**

- before a person does the act prohibited by ss 327 to 329 (see Appendix 6),
- while a person is doing the act prohibited by ss 327 to 329, the act having begun at a point when the discloser did not know or suspect that the property is the proceeds of crime and the disclosure being made on the discloser's own initiative as soon as practicable after he first knew or suspected that the property is the proceeds of crime, or
- after the act prohibited by ss 327 to 329, but made on the discloser's own initiative as soon as practicable after the act.

Appropriate consent is the consent of a constable, Customs officer, or SOCA officer to pro- **21.69** ceed with a prohibited act (s 335).

A key element of consent is the specification of time limits within which the authorities must **21.70** respond to an authorised disclosure in circumstances where a consent decision is required. The law specifies that consent decisions must be made within seven working days. The seven-day notice period commences on the day after a disclosure is made and excludes bank holidays and weekends. The purpose of the seven-day notice period is to allow SOCA and its law enforcement partners time to risk assess, analyse, research, and undertake further enquiries relating to the disclosed information in order to determine the best response to the request for consent.

If nothing is heard after that time, then the discloser can go ahead with an otherwise pro- **21.71** hibited act without an offence being committed. If consent is withheld within the seven working days, then the authorities have a further thirty-one calendar days in which to take further action, such as seeking a court order to restrain the assets in question. The thirty-one days include Saturdays, Sundays, and public holidays.

It is an offence to undertake the act during this 'moratorium' period as the participant would **21.72** not have the appropriate consent. The moratorium period enables SOCA to further their investigation into the reported matter using the powers within POCA in relation to the criminal property (eg imposing a restraint order). If nothing is heard after the end of the thirty-one-day period, then the discloser can proceed with the transaction without committing an offence.

### Notification of consent

**21.73** In the first instance, a consent decision will usually be communicated to the reporter by telephone in order to provide the quickest possible response. SOCA will also send a letter by post recording the decision, but there is no requirement to wait for this letter in order to proceed with the prohibited act if consent has been granted verbally.

### The legislative scheme

**21.74** Section 339 of POCA (as amended by s 105 of SOCPA) states:

(1) The Secretary of State may by order prescribe the form and manner in which a disclosure under section 330, 331, 332 or 338 must be made.

   (1A) A person commits an offence if he makes a disclosure under section 330, 331, 332 or 338 otherwise than in the form prescribed under subsection (1) or otherwise than in the manner so prescribed.

   (1B) But a person does not commit an offence under subsection (1A) if he has a reasonable excuse for making the disclosure otherwise than in the form prescribed under subsection (1) or (as the case may be) otherwise than in the manner so prescribed.

(2) The power under subsection (1) to prescribe the form in which a disclosure must be made includes power to provide for the form to include a request to a person making a disclosure that the person provide information specified or described in the form if he has not provided it in making the disclosure.

(3) Where under subsection (2) a request is included in a form prescribed under subsection (1), the form must—

   (a) state that there is no obligation to comply with the request, and

   (b) explain the protection conferred by subsection (4) on a person who complies with the request.

### Completing the form

**21.75** A SAR should be made as soon as the knowledge or suspicion that criminal proceeds exist has arisen, especially if consent may be required, or at the earliest opportunity thereafter. Customer Due Diligence (CDD) is an important aspect of this. Those working within the regulated sector are, pursuant to the Money Laundering Regulations, required to apply due diligence and maintain ongoing monitoring.

**21.76** It is advisable to include as much CDD detail as possible. The type of information likely to be of use to SOCA will be the person's full name, date of birth, passport number, National Insurance number, telephone numbers (home, business, and mobile), company name/registration number, email addresses, associated addresses, and postcodes, if this information is held. Current and previous addresses should also be of assistance if known.

**21.77** It is helpful to also provide an initial summary that sets out the grounds for suspicion and, if appropriate, any known links to criminality. If possible, it is worthwhile detailing chronologically the dates of individual transactions. Where an individual is suspicious because the activity deviates from the normal activity for that customer, business, or sector, it may be necessary to explain what the normal activity is and how this differs, eg an exceptionally large cash payment. Include the value of the transactions involved, the origins/destination of the funds, and, if applicable, the associated crime number. Also, where applicable, give the reference numbers of any previous related SARs.

### Limited Intelligence Value Reports

The Limited Intelligence Value Report (LIVR) is briefer than a full SAR and allows financial **21.78** institutions to adhere to their obligations under POCA when they have reasonable grounds to suspect money laundering, but in circumstances where they may only hold limited information to convey to the law enforcement authority. They are of particular use for minor irregularities where there is nothing to suggest that the conduct is as a result of dishonest behaviour.

SOCA produces full guidance notes that relate to when LIVRs should be used, available on **21.79** their website. If in doubt, use the standard form.

## E. Tipping Off

### The offence of tipping off

If a person was to disclose to the subject of an investigation the fact that law enforcement **21.80** authorities had commenced an enquiry into his affairs, or that a production order had been obtained in relation to his bank accounts, or that a financial institution had disclosed a suspicious transaction, this could seriously prejudice the outcome of the enquiry. Accordingly, the legislation has been framed in such a way that such disclosures can in themselves give rise to criminal charges. POCA has been amended by the Terrorism Act 2000 and Proceeds of Crime Act 2002 (Amendment) Regulations 2007 (SI 2007/3398) to ensure investigations are not curtailed or prejudiced by way of 'tipping off'. These regulations implement, in part, Directive 2005/60/EC of the European Parliament and of the Council of 26 October 2005 on the prevention of the use of the financial system for the purpose of money laundering and terrorist financing ('the Directive'). The regulations give effect to chapter 3 of the Directive. Schedule 2 to the regulations makes amendments to POCA.

Principally, the previous offence of tipping off in s 333 of POCA was repealed by the new **21.81** Regulations. Paragraph 4 inserts a new s 333A into POCA to create an offence of tipping off to cover the regulated sector. New ss 333B to 333D give effect to the exceptions in Art 28 of the above Directive.

In the regulated sector a person commits an offence if (s 333A): **21.82**

(1) ...
    (a) the person discloses any matter within subsection (2);
    (b) the disclosure is likely to prejudice any investigation that might be conducted following the disclosure referred to in that subsection; and
    (c) the information on which the disclosure is based came to the person in the course of a business in the regulated sector.
(2) The matters are that the person or another person has made a disclosure under this Part—
    (a) to a constable,
    (b) to an officer of Revenue and Customs,
    (c) to a nominated officer, or
    (d) to a member of staff of the Serious Organised Crime Agency authorised for the purposes of this Part by the Director General of that Agency,
    of information that came to that person in the course of a business in the regulated sector.
(3) A person commits an offence if—

(a) the person discloses that an investigation into allegations that an offence under this Part has been committed is being contemplated or is being carried out;

(b) the disclosure is likely to prejudice that investigation; and

(c) the information on which the disclosure is based came to the person in the course of a business in the regulated sector.

### Sentence

**21.83** The penalty for an offence under this section is, on summary conviction, a term not exceeding three months, or a fine not exceeding level 5 on the standard scale, or both; and on conviction on indictment, imprisonment for a term not exceeding two years, or a fine, or both.

### 'Defences' available

**21.84** Sections 333B to 333D set out effectively the 'defences' available to a person who may be involved in a tipping-off offence. These sections provide:

333B Disclosures within an undertaking or group etc

(1) An employee, officer or partner of an undertaking does not commit an offence under section 333A if the disclosure is to an employee, officer or partner of the same undertaking.

(2) A person does not commit an offence under section 333A in respect of a disclosure by a credit institution or a financial institution if—

(a) the disclosure is to a credit institution or a financial institution,

(b) the institution to whom the disclosure is made is situated in an EEA State or in a country or territory imposing equivalent money laundering requirements, and

(c) both the institution making the disclosure and the institution to whom it is made belong to the same group.

(3) In subsection (2) 'group' has the same meaning as in Directive 2002/87/EC of the European Parliament and of the Council of 16th December 2002 on the supplementary supervision of credit institutions, insurance undertakings and investment firms in a financial conglomerate.

(4) A professional legal adviser or a relevant professional adviser does not commit an offence under section 333A if—

(a) the disclosure is to a professional legal adviser or a relevant professional adviser,

(b) both the person making the disclosure and the person to whom it is made carry on business in an EEA State or in a country or territory imposing equivalent money laundering requirements, and

(c) those persons perform their professional activities within different undertakings that share common ownership, management or control.

333C Other permitted disclosures between institutions etc

(1) This section applies to a disclosure—

(a) by a credit institution to another credit institution,

(b) by a financial institution to another financial institution,

(c) by a professional legal adviser to another professional legal adviser, or

(d) by a relevant professional adviser of a particular kind to another relevant professional adviser of the same kind.

(2) A person does not commit an offence under section 333A in respect of a disclosure to which this section applies if—

(a) the disclosure relates to—

(i) a client or former client of the institution or adviser making the disclosure and the institution or adviser to whom it is made,

(ii) a transaction involving them both, or

(iii) the provision of a service involving them both;

(b) the disclosure is for the purpose only of preventing an offence under this Part of this Act;

    (c)  the institution or adviser to whom the disclosure is made is situated in an EEA State or in a country or territory imposing equivalent money laundering requirements; and

    (d)  the institution or adviser making the disclosure and the institution or adviser to whom it is made are subject to equivalent duties of professional confidentiality and the protection of personal data (within the meaning of section 1 of the Data Protection Act 1998).

333D Other permitted disclosures etc

(1)  A person does not commit an offence under section 333A if the disclosure is—

    (a)  to the authority that is the supervisory authority for that person by virtue of the Money Laundering Regulations 2007 (SI 2007/2157); or

    (b)  for the purpose of—

        (i)  the detection, investigation or prosecution of a criminal offence (whether in the United Kingdom or elsewhere),

        (ii)  an investigation under this Act, or

        (iii)  the enforcement of any order of a court under this Act.

(2)  A professional legal adviser or a relevant professional adviser does not commit an offence under section 333A if the disclosure—

    (a)  is to the adviser's client, and

    (b)  is made for the purpose of dissuading the client from engaging in conduct amounting to an offence.

(3)  A person does not commit an offence under section 333A(1) if the person does not know or suspect that the disclosure is likely to have the effect mentioned in section 333A(1)(b).

(4)  A person does not commit an offence under section 333A(3) if the person does not know or suspect that the disclosure is likely to have the effect mentioned in section 333A(3)(b).

In the above sections 'relevant professional adviser' means an accountant, auditor, or tax **21.85** adviser who is a member of a professional body which is established for accountants, auditors, or tax advisers (as the case may be) and which makes provision for:

(a)  testing the competence of those seeking admission to membership of such a body as a condition for such admission; and

(b)  imposing and maintaining professional and ethical standards for its members, as well as imposing sanctions for non-compliance with those standards.

As stated elsewhere in this chapter, the language used in POCA is different from that used in **21.86** the CJA; in particular the draftsmen of POCA do not use the word 'defence' in the relevant parts of the statute. Nevertheless, it is clear that an individual will not have committed the offence in question if one of the 'exemptions' or safety nets set out in the Act apply. Arguably it will be for the Crown to show that they do not apply, and therefore the burden will be on the prosecution. Having said that, there is something of an inevitability that the best case for applying the 'exemptions' will come from the defendant.

### Banks and other institutions

The difficulties encountered by virtue of the tipping-off provisions (under the pre-POCA **21.87** legislation) were highlighted in *Bank of Scotland v A* [2001] 1 WLR 751, where the Court of Appeal stated:

> The tipping-off legislation which was the source of the problem with which this appeal deals, gave extensive powers to the police. Properly used they were beneficial. Misused they could create unintended consequences. It is of the greatest importance that the use of those powers is confined to situations where it is appropriate. Institutions such as banks need to be able

to ensure that they are not affected adversely or unnecessarily because of the existence of the police's powers.

**21.88**  The Court of Appeal in *BS v A* [2001] 1 WLR 751 considered a situation where the police informed the bank that money laundering investigations were being conducted into activities closely associated with one of its customers, in consequence of which the bank was put in a dilemma: if it paid out, it might be liable to third parties as a constructive trustee, whereas if it did not, an action could be brought against the bank and it would be unable to defend itself because the police would object to the bank revealing what it had been told. The Court held that the question of what information could be revealed should have been capable of agreement between the bank, the police, and the SFO. Failing such agreement, the appropriate remedy was not to seek an ex parte order freezing the customer's account, but to seek an interim declaration under the CPR.

**21.89**  The difficulties in terms of the tipping off provisions were further considered in *K Ltd v National Westminster Bank plc* [2006] EWCA Civ 1039. The bank found itself in a predicament when its customer asked it to make a payment which the bank suspected would facilitate the use of criminal property and leave it open to the allegation of becoming 'concerned in an arrangement'. The customer, following the bank's refusal, made a claim for an interim injunction requiring the bank to comply with its instructions. It was argued on behalf of the customer that the bank, by refusing to honour its customer's instructions, was acting in breach of the contract whereby the bank had agreed to follow its customer's instructions. The Court found that there could be no doubt that if a banker knows or suspects that money in a customer's account is criminal property and, without making disclosure or without authorised consent (if disclosure is made), he processes a customer's cheque in such a way as to transfer the money in question into the account of another person, then he was facilitating the use or control of that criminal property, and thus committing an offence under s 328 of the 2002 Act. The Court held it would be no defence to a charge under that section that the bank was contractually obliged to obey its customer's instructions (para 9): 'If the law of the land makes it a criminal offence to honour the customer's mandate in these circumstances there can be no breach of contract for the bank to refuse to honour its mandate...'

**21.90**  More recently, in *Jayesh Shah and Shaleetha Mahabeer v HSBC Private Bank (UK) Limited* [2012] EWCA Civ 31 the Court of Appeal confirmed that a bank was not obliged to provide its customer with the details of a disclosure to SOCA. To the contrary, where the provision of that information might amount to a tipping off offence, the bank was obliged not to do so.

# 22

# COSTS, FUNDING ISSUES, AND COMPENSATION

## A. Introduction

Restraint orders are made when the court is satisfied, amongst other things, that there is **22.01** 'reasonable cause to believe' that the defendant has benefited from the criminal activity with which he is charged (s 40(2) of the Proceeds of Crime Act 2002 (POCA)). When the case comes to trial, however, the jury has to be satisfied of the defendant's guilt *beyond reasonable doubt* in order to record the conviction that is the essential prerequisite to a confiscation order being made. Sometimes a defendant who has been subject to a restraint order for a substantial period of time will be acquitted. The restraint order will promptly be discharged (s 42(6)), but he may have incurred costs in defending the proceedings and, together with other parties holding realisable property, have suffered a loss in complying with the terms of the restraint order.

22.02　The purpose of this chapter is to consider the rights of the defendant (and, on occasion, third parties) to seek costs and compensation against the prosecuting authority, and the ability of the prosecuting authority or receiver to obtain costs from the defendant. We have divided it into various parts, including: issues relating to costs; legal fees and legal aid funding; receivership costs; compensation for the acquitted defendant, and the power to award compensation under POCA. There is necessarily some overlap with other chapters to give the reader a complete overview of the costs and compensation regime within asset forfeiture law. The landscape in relation to costs and legal aid has changed substantially since the introduction of the Legal Aid, Sentencing and Punishment of Offenders Act 2012. In particular, the Legal Services Commission was abolished and replaced with the Legal Aid Agency from 1 April 2013.

22.03　The statutory position in relation to costs in criminal proceedings is now complemented by the Practice Direction (Costs in Criminal Proceedings) [2011] 1 Cr App R 13 handed down on 30 July 2010 (the 'Costs Practice Direction'). The Practice Direction and Pt 76 of the Criminal Procedure Rules (CrimPR) as amended from 1 April 2013, provide a useful starting point for any practitioner dealing with costs in criminal proceedings. It is not proposed within this chapter to provide a full overview of the current costs rules in criminal proceedings, but rather to highlight some of the considerations within restraint, receivership, confiscation, and forfeiture proceedings.

### Costs and compensation distinguished

22.04　Orders for costs and orders for compensation are distinct. An order for costs is confined to ordering the payment of legal costs incurred by the defendant in restraint order proceedings, which may extend to related contempt or receivership hearings, but does not extend to any other costs or expenses he may incur as a result of the order. An order for compensation, on the other hand, seeks not to recompense the defendant for legal costs, but to compensate him for any loss he has suffered as a result of complying with the order. Persons other than the defendant who hold realisable property may also seek a compensation order.

## B. The Magistrates' Court and Costs

### The power of the magistrates' court to order costs in civil proceedings

22.05　The magistrates' court commonly hears applications for cash forfeiture and condemnation as described in Chapters 15 and 23 of this book. These are civil proceedings in nature. The power of magistrates to award costs on the hearing of a civil complaint is contained in s 64 of the Magistrates' Courts Act 1980:

(1) On the hearing of a complaint, a magistrates' court shall have the power in its discretion to make such order as to costs—
    (a) on making the order for which the complaint is made, to be paid by the defendant to the complainant;
    (b) on dismissing the complaint, to be paid by the complainant to the defendant, as it thinks just and reasonable . . .

Under s 64(2), the amount of any sum ordered to be paid under s 64(1) shall be specified in **22.06** the order, or order of dismissal, as the case may be. The costs ordered to be paid under this section shall be enforceable as a civil debt (s 64(3)).

The sum ordered should not be in excess of the proper costs incurred, nor should it be a pen- **22.07** alty in the guise of costs (see *R v Highgate Justices ex p Petrou* [1954] 1 All ER 406).

The amount of the costs must be fixed by the court 'as part of the adjudication' (*R v Pwllheli* **22.08** *Justices ex p Soane* [1948] 2 All ER 815) and may include the expenses of the claimant's witnesses, as well as the fee of his solicitor. It follows that the same justices who reached the decision on hearing the complaint must make the award for costs.

An award for costs made by the magistrates' court under s 64 is not enforceable by the **22.09** magistrates' court, but in effect becomes a civil debt enforceable by the successful party on application to the county court.

Under s 52 of the Courts Act 1971, magistrates are entitled to award costs where a complaint **22.10** has not been proceeded with (s 52(3)(b)). Where a complaint is not proceeded with, a magistrates' court may make such order as to costs to be paid by the complainant to the defendant as it thinks is just and reasonable.

The power to award costs is limited to making an order as to the costs of proceedings on the **22.11** complaint in question and does not give the court authority to award costs which may have been incurred in other proceedings. For example, the power to award costs in a forfeiture application would only relate to the costs and hearings which occurred after the lodging of the application for forfeiture. It would not extend to the continued detention hearing that had taken place prior to the application for forfeiture. Each continued detention hearing is a separate application supported by an information in its own right, and costs should be applied for and dealt with at the time of the continued detention hearing (see *R v Magistrates' Court at Dover ex p Customs and Excise Commissioners* (1995) 160 JP 233).

There is no right to appeal to the Crown Court against a costs order by the magistrates (see *R* **22.12** *v Crown Court at Lewis ex p Rogers* [1974] 1 All ER 589); however judicial review is available.

### The issue when seeking to obtain defence costs in civil proceedings

In *The Queen on the application of Perinpanathan v City of Westminster Magistrates' Court and* **22.13** *another* [2010] EWCA Civ 40; [2010] 1 WLR 1508, the test for the award of costs to a successful defendant in cash forfeiture proceedings was considered by the Court of Appeal. The Court of Appeal in dismissing an appeal from the Divisional Court, agreed that the test laid down by Lord Bingham in *Bradford Metropolitan District Council v Booth* (CO/3219/99), The Times, 31 May 2000, should be applied. Lord Bingham stated:

> 23. I would accordingly hold that the proper approach to questions of this kind can for convenience be summarised in three propositions:
>
> 24. (1) Section 64(1) confers a discretion upon a Magistrates' Court to make such order as to costs as it thinks just and reasonable. That provision applies both to the quantum of the costs (if any) to be paid, but also as to the party (if any) which should pay them.
>
> 25. (2) What the court will think just and reasonable will depend on all the relevant facts and circumstances of the case before the court. The court may think it just and reasonable that costs should follow the event, but need not think so in all cases covered by the subsection.

26. (3) Where a complainant has successfully challenged before justices an administrative decision made by a police or regulatory authority acting honestly, reasonably, properly and on grounds that reasonably appeared to be sound, in exercise of its public duty, the court should consider, in addition to any other relevant fact or circumstances, both (i) the financial prejudice to the particular complainant in the particular circumstances if an order for costs is not made in his favour; and (ii) the need to encourage public authorities to make and stand by honest, reasonable and apparently sound administrative decisions made in the public interest without fear of exposure to undue financial prejudice if the decision is successfully challenged.

**22.14** The magistrates' court in *Perinpanathan* had refused to award costs, on the basis that the cash seizure had been properly brought by the police. The Divisional Court in its judgment, [2009] EWHC 762 (Admin), concluded that the police had acted properly, Goldring LJ commenting (at 29):

> ...I accept that there is a difference between administrative decisions such as those referred to in *Bradford* and the present case. The distinction is limited, however. In one case a police officer (at possible risk to someone's livelihood) is saying that the person will not have a licence, for example. In the other, he is saying the person will not have his (or in this case her) money returned. In taking both decisions, it is crucial that the police act honestly, reasonably, properly, and on grounds that reasonably appear to be sound. In both cases there is a need to make and stand by honest, reasonable and apparently sound decisions in the public interest without fear of exposure to undue financial prejudice, in one case if the decision is successfully challenged, in the other if the application fails. There is a real public interest that the police seek an order for forfeiture if they consider that on the evidence it is more probable than not that the money was intended for an unlawful purpose. It would be quite contrary to the public interest if, due to fear of financial consequences, it was decided not to seek its forfeiture, but simply return the money. The public duty requires the police to make an application in such circumstances.

**22.15** The Court of Appeal dismissed an appeal against this decision and Lord Justice Stanley Burnton agreed with the reasoning of Goldring LJ in the Divisional Court. Stanley Burnton LJ stated at para 44 of his judgment:

> In the present case, it is common ground that the police had reasonable grounds to seize and to detain the cash in question. It is accepted that when they commenced the proceedings under section 298 of POCA they had reasonable grounds to believe, and did believe, that this cash was intended for use in unlawful conduct (c.f. section 298(2)). It seems to me that in these circumstances the police, acting responsibly, effectively had no choice but to institute those proceedings. As I have pointed out, they could not detain the cash indefinitely. It would have been irresponsible and a breach of their duty to the public for them to have delivered up the cash to the appellant in those circumstances. The only alternative was to make the application for its forfeiture, as they duly did. They should not have been deterred from making that application in those circumstances by concerns as to their liability for the costs of the appellant. There is nothing in POCA to indicate that the principle in *City of Bradford* should be inapplicable. To the contrary, the restriction of compensation for loss under section 302(4) to cases in which the circumstances are exceptional is consistent with its application.

**22.16** However, notwithstanding the court's refusal to pay costs to the successful party in this instance, the police or HMRC cannot assume that they may proceed with impunity. Goldring LJ made clear at para 33 of his judgment in the Divisional Court:

> ...it should not be thought that those who bring these applications have carte blanche to make applications for forfeiture without any risk of costs being awarded against them. Such applications can result in grave injustice if not made honestly, reasonably, properly and on

grounds that are sound. If applications are made inappropriately, the court should not hesitate to make an order for costs against the applicant.

*Defence costs in criminal proceedings*

**22.17** The position in civil proceedings in the magistrates' court is to be contrasted with criminal proceedings. Attention is drawn to the guidance in the Costs Practice Direction at para 2.1 that the court should make a defendant's costs order from central funds in favour of a successful defendant (one who is acquitted, not proceeded against, or not committed for trial etc) in criminal proceedings in the magistrates' court unless there are positive reasons for not doing so. For example, where the defendant's own conduct has brought suspicion on himself and misled the prosecution into thinking that the case against him was stronger than it was, or the defendant is convicted of at least one offence, the defendant can be left to pay his own costs. See also CrimPR r 76.4(5) where the general rule and exceptions are set out. However, the extent of any defendant's costs order from central funds in magistrates' court criminal proceedings commenced after 1 October 2012 has been restricted to the level payable under legal aid by the coming into force of Sch 7 to the Legal Aid, Sentencing and Punishment of Offenders Act 2012, which has introduced section 16A to the Prosecution of Offences Act 1985.

# C. The Crown Court and Costs

## Restraint and receivership proceedings

**22.18** The power of the Crown Court to award costs in restraint and receivership proceedings is set out within r 61.19 of the CrimPR, which provides:

(2) The court has discretion as to—
    (a) whether costs are payable by one party to another;
    (b) the amount of those costs; and
    (c) when they are to be paid.
(3) If the court decides to make an order about costs—
    (a) the general rule is that the unsuccessful party will be ordered to pay the costs of the successful party; but
    (b) the court may make a different order.
(4) In deciding what order (if any) to make about costs, the court must have regard to all of the circumstances, including—
    (a) the conduct of all the parties; and
    (b) whether a party has succeeded on part of an application, even if he has not been wholly successful.
(5) The orders which the court may make include an order that a party must pay—
    (a) a proportion of another party's costs;
    (b) a stated amount in respect of another party's costs;
    (c) costs from or until a certain date only;
    (d) costs incurred before proceedings have begun;
    (e) costs relating to particular steps taken in the proceedings;
    (f) costs relating only to a distinct part of the proceedings; and
    (g) interest on costs from or until a certain date, including a date before the making of an order.
(6) Where the court would otherwise consider making an order under para (5)(f), it must instead, if practicable, make an order under para (5)(a) or (c).

    (7) Where the court has ordered a party to pay costs, it may order an amount to be paid on account before the costs are assessed.

**22.19**  Rule 61.20(1)–(2) states:

    (1) Where the Crown Court has made an order for costs in restraint proceedings or receivership proceedings it may either—

        (a) make an assessment of the costs itself; or

        (b) order assessment of the costs under rule 76.11.

    (2) In either case, the Crown Court or the assessing authority, as the case may be, must—

        (a) only allow costs which are proportionate to the matters in issue; and

        (b) resolve any doubt which it may have as to whether the costs were reasonably incurred or reasonable and proportionate in favour of the paying party.

**22.20**  Rule 61.21 states, in relation to the time allowed for complying with an order for costs:

    (1) A party to restraint proceedings or receivership proceedings must comply with an order for the payment of costs within 14 days of—

        (a) the date of the order if it states the amount of those costs;

        (b) if the amount of those costs is decided later under rule 76.11, the date of the assessing authority's decision; or

        (c) in either case, such later date as the Crown Court may specify.

**22.21**  Rule 61.20(5) states that, when assessing costs, the court or assessing authority must have particular regard to:

    (a) the conduct of all the parties, including in particular, conduct before, as well as during, the proceedings;

    (b) the amount or value of the property involved;

    (c) the importance of the matter to all the parties;

    (d) the particular complexity of the matter or the difficulty or novelty of the questions raised;

    (e) the skill, effort, specialised knowledge and responsibility involved;

    (f) the time spent on the application; and

    (g) the place where and the circumstances in which work or any part of it was done.

**22.22**  Part 7 of the Costs Practice Direction specifically deals with Crown Court restraint and receivership proceedings. When assessing the costs of restraint and receivership proceedings, further guidance is provided at paras 7.2.5–7.2.8 of the Costs Practice Direction:

    7.2.5 In applying the test of proportionality regard should be had to the objective of dealing with cases justly. Dealing with a case justly includes, so far as practicable, dealing with it in ways which are proportionate to:

        (i) the amount of money involved;

        (ii) the importance of the case;

        (iii) the complexity of the issues; and

        (iv) the financial position of each party.

The relationship between the total of the costs incurred and the financial value of the claim may not be a reliable guide.

    7.2.6 In any proceedings there will be costs which will inevitably be incurred and which are necessary for the successful conduct of the case. Litigators are not required to conduct litigation at rates which are uneconomic, thus in a modest claim the proportion of costs is likely to be higher than in a large claim and may even equal or possibly exceed the amount in dispute.

7.2.7   Where a hearing takes place, the time taken by the court in dealing with a particular issue may not be an accurate guide to the amount of time properly spent by the legal or other representatives in preparing for the trial of that issue.

7.2.8   The Criminal Procedure Rules do not apply to the assessment of costs in proceedings to the extent that section 11 of the Access to Justice Act 1999 (costs in funded cases) applies and statutory instruments made under that Act make different provision (in this regard attention is drawn to the guidance notes issued by the Senior Costs Judge: Costs Orders Against an LSC Funded Client and against the LSC under section 11(1) of the Access to Justice Act 1999).

### Criminal proceedings in the Crown Court

Costs in the Crown Court generally and in criminal proceedings are dealt with in the Costs Practice Direction and CrimPR Pt 76.   **22.23**

### *The acquitted defendant and costs*

In relation to defendants against whom criminal proceedings were brought before 1 October   **22.24** 2012 and who have been acquitted in the Crown Court, paras 2.2.1–2.2.3 of the Costs Practice Direction (mirroring CrimPR r 76.4) provide guidance on defendants' costs orders from central funds in criminal cases:

2.2.1   Where a person is not tried for an offence for which he has been indicted, or in respect of which proceedings against him have been sent for trial or transferred for trial, or has been acquitted on any count in the indictment, the court may make a defendant's costs order in his favour. Such an order should normally be made whether or not an order for costs between the parties is made, unless there are positive reasons for not doing so. For example, where the defendant's own conduct has brought suspicion on himself and has misled the prosecution into thinking that the case against him was stronger than it was, the defendant can be left to pay his own costs. The court when declining to make a costs order should explain, in open court, that the reason for not making an order does not involve any suggestion that the defendant is guilty of any criminal conduct but the order is refused because of the positive reason that should be identified.

2.2.2   Where a person is convicted of some count(s) in the indictment and acquitted on other(s) the court may exercise its discretion to make a defendant's costs order but may order that only part of the costs incurred be paid. The court should make whatever order seems just having regard to the relative importance of the two charges and the conduct of the parties generally. Where the court considers that it would be inappropriate that the defendant should recover all of the costs properly incurred, the amount must be specified in the order.

The Crown Court may make a defendant's costs order in favour of such a successful appellant:

2.2.3   Whether to make such an award is a matter in the discretion of the court in the light of the circumstances of each particular case.

However for criminal proceedings commenced from 1 October 2012 the ability to obtain   **22.25** a defendant's costs order in criminal proceedings in the Crown Court has been restricted. Costs are only payable to defendants following successful appeals against conviction or sentence from the magistrates' court and then only at legal aid rates. Schedule 7 to the Legal Aid, Sentencing and Punishment of Offenders Act 2012 has introduced s 16A to the Prosecution of Offences Act 1985 which has abolished the right to obtain a defendant's costs order from central funds at the Crown Court for those acquitted of indictable offences.

### Assessment of costs

**22.26** Rules 61.20–21 of the CrimPR make specific reference to the assessment of costs under r 76.11. Where the court has made a costs order but not assessed the costs or fixed a sum to be paid, it will be necessary for a claim to be lodged for determination. Assessment of costs is governed by CrimPR r 76.11. Subrules (3)–(4) provide:

> (3) The party in whose favour the court made the costs order ('the applicant') must—
>    (a) apply for an assessment—
>       (i)   in writing, in any form required by the assessing authority
>       (ii)  not more than 3 months after the costs order; and
>    (b) serve the application on
>       (i)   the assessing authority, and
>       (ii)  the party against whom the court made the costs order ('the respondent').
> (4) The applicant must—
>    (a) summarise the work done;
>    (b) specify—
>       (i)   each item of work done, giving the date, time taken and amount claimed,
>       (ii)  any disbursements or expenses, including the fees of any advocate, and
>       (iii) any circumstances of which the applicant wants the assessing authority to take particular account;
>    (c) supply –
>       (i)   receipts or other evidence of the amount claimed, and
>       (ii)  any other information or document for which the assessing authority asks, within such period as the authority may require.

There is currently no set form for the making of a claim, although generally these should follow in broad terms the precedents annexed to the current Practice Direction for civil costs. There is no obligation to import the specific detailed requirements of that Direction—see *John Joseph Morris v The Lord Chancellor* [2000] EWHC 9001 (Costs). This authority also confirms that interest is not recoverable.

**22.27** Rule 76.11(5) sets out the procedure and timetable for the respondent to file any response or challenges (Points of Dispute) thereto in writing and within twenty-one days. As with the application/claim, there is no set form for this document, which generally follows the precedent annexed to the current Practice Direction for civil claims in relation to Points of Dispute.

**22.28** Once in possession of all relevant information required, the assessing authority will carry out a provisional assessment—based upon paper consideration only—which will subsequently be served upon the parties pursuant to r 76.11(6)(c).

**22.29** Rule 76.11(7)(a) provides that:

> Where either party wants the amount allowed re-assessed—
> that party must—
> (i)   apply to the assessing authority in writing and in any form required by that authority,
> (ii)  serve the application on the assessing authority and the other party not more than 21 days after the assessment,
> (iii) explain the objections to the assessment,
> (iv)  supply any additional supporting information or document, and
> (v)   ask for a hearing, if that party wants one.

**22.30** See r 76.11(7)(b)–(c) for the powers on assessment or hearing and para 22.40 below for further appeals thereafter under CrimPR rr 76.12–76.14. An important point to note is, where generally there are no costs recoverable for thareafter assessment proceedings, a party should seriously consider the reasonable prospects of reversing or challenging the provisional assessment and the practical costs of proceeding further.

### Costs against the defendant in confiscation order cases

Orders for the payment of costs should only be made where the defendant has the ability **22.31** to pay them following a confiscation hearing (*R v Ghadami* [1997] Crim LR 606). If a confiscation order is made in what the court finds to be the full value of the defendant's realisable property, no order for costs should be made. In *R v Szrajber* [1994] Crim LR 543, the defendant's benefit from the offences concerned was found to be £524,000, but his realisable property was valued at £407,188 and a confiscation order was accordingly made in this lesser sum. In addition, an order for the payment of costs was made in the sum of £65,428. The Court of Appeal quashed the order for costs on the basis that a confiscation order had been made in the full amount of the defendant's benefit from the offence, and accordingly he had no further assets at his disposal from which the order for costs could be made.

In *R v Smart* [2003] 2 Cr App R (S) 384, the Court determined that where a judge, having **22.32** passed sentence, adjourned the proceedings in contemplation of a confiscation hearing and subsequently said he was reserving the question of costs until the issue of confiscation had been decided, he was exercising his lawful power to postpone part of the sentence, and the fact that he subsequently decided that there could be no confiscation proceedings because of a failure to meet the statutory preconditions for such, did not deprive him of his power to award costs.

In *R v Macatonia* [2009] EWCA Crim 2516, the Court of Appeal confirmed that when **22.33** considering costs against a defendant, an order for costs should never exceed the sum that the prosecutor had actually and reasonably incurred and that the costs incurred should be proportionate to the nature of the hearing. It noted that confiscation proceedings frequently involved more complicated considerations, even where the sums in question were limited.

### Experts' reports and prosecution costs

In *Balshaw v the CPS* [2009] EWCA Crim 470, the defendant argued that the judge at first **22.34** instance had been wrong to order the defendant to pay for the costs of a KPMG forensic report commissioned by the Thames Valley Police for use in confiscation proceedings, on the basis that s 18 of the Prosecutions of Offences Act 1985 only permitted the Crown Court to order costs to be paid by the accused to 'the prosecutor', and the CPS was 'the prosecutor', and not the police.

The Court of Appeal found that there was no principle that the CPS could only recover those **22.35** fees that it had directly incurred. If the court was satisfied that the CPS would compensate the police for the costs of the report, it was proper for the court to make an order requiring the defendant to meet the costs of the report. The position has been clarified by para 3.7 of the Costs Practice Direction, which sets out that:

> 3.7 The principles to be applied in deciding on the amount of costs are those set out by the Court of Appeal in *Neville v Gardner Merchant* [1983] 5 Cr App R (S) 349 (DC). The court when awarding prosecution costs may award costs in respect of time spent in bringing the

offences to light, even if the necessary investigation was carried out, for example, by an environmental health official. Only in very limited circumstances may the Crown Prosecution Service be able to recover particular costs associated with the investigation incurred by the police (as per *Balshaw v Crown Prosecution Service* [2009] EWCA Crim 470). The Divisional Court has held that there is a requirement that any sum ordered to be paid by way of costs should not ordinarily be greatly at variance with any fine imposed. Where substantial research is required in order to counter possible defences, the court may also award costs in respect of that work if it considers it to be justified.

### Interest and costs of assessment

**22.36**  In *Westminster City Council v Wingrove* [1991] 4 All ER 691 the Court determined that there is no basis in statute, regulation, nor order for the payment of interest on costs awarded from central funds in a criminal cause or matter. Sections 17 and 18 of the Judgements Act 1838 do not apply to criminal proceedings. However restraint proceedings (to which receivership orders are ancillary) are 'impossible to conceptualise as criminal proceedings' per the Court of Appeal in *In Re S (Restraint Order—Release of Assets)* [2005] 1 WLR 1333 at para 53, applying *R (McCann) v Crown Court at Manchester* [2003] 1 AC 787.

**22.37**  The cost of drafting and preparing a claim for costs out of central funds (either a bill or schedule) is not itself a recoverable cost (see *Morris v Lord Chancellor* [2000] 1 Costs LR 88 and *R v Mashour* [2004] 3 Costs LR) although these items are often erroneously included and the practitioner (prosecutor) should be aware that neither of these are recoverable (as this could have fairly significant costs consequences, both in terms of what is recoverable and also during negotiations).

## D. Receivership Fees and Costs

**22.38**  It is important to distinguish between a receiver's litigation costs and his remuneration and expenses (fees) incurred in conducting his office. In *Capewell v HMRC* [2007] 1 WLR 386, Lord Walker defined 'remuneration' as the professional fees of the receiver and his own staff, and confined 'expenses' to all other expenditure necessarily or properly incurred by the receiver in the performance of his duties and 'costs' to litigation costs (para 7 of the judgment).

### Receivership fees

**22.39**  In most cases, the receiver will assess his fees on a time-cost basis in accordance with the grade and experience of the fee earner employed and in accordance with the terms agreed with the prosecutor in the letter of agreement. There may be cases in which the defendant considers that the fees charged are excessive. The defendant's interests can be adversely affected by a large bill from a receiver; if he has assets available, they will usually be realised in addition to those required to satisfy the confiscation order. If no such assets are available, the receiver's costs will normally be met out of the assets that have been realised in satisfaction of the confiscation order.

**22.40**  One of the remedies for the aggrieved defendant is to seek an order from the court that the proper remuneration of the receiver be assessed. The assessment will either be conducted by the Crown Court (CrimPR r 60.6(3)) or it may refer this to the taxing authority (CrimPR r 60.6(4)) which then follows the procedure under CrimPR r 76.11. A defendant may appeal the assessment of the assessing authority first to a Costs Judge and then a High Court judge pursuant to CrimPR rr 76.12–76.14. The criteria to be applied by the Crown Court in determining a receiver's remuneration are those under CrimPR r 60.6(3) which are in identical terms to paras 7.3.1 and 7.3.2 of the Costs Practice Direction, which provide that:

7.3.1 The Crown Court (unless it orders otherwise) is required to award such sum as is reasonable and proportionate in all the circumstances. In arriving at the figure for remuneration the court should take into account:
(a) the time properly given by the receiver and his staff to the receivership;
(b) the complexity of the receivership;
(c) any responsibility of an exceptional kind or degree which falls on the receiver in consequence of the receivership;
(d) the effectiveness with which the receiver appears to be carrying out or to have carried out his duties; and
(e) the value and nature of the subject matter of the receivership.

7.3.2 The Crown Court may instead of determining the receiver's remuneration itself refer it to be ascertained by the assessing authority of the Crown Court. In these circumstances rules 76.11 to 76.13 of the Criminal Procedure Rules (which deal with review by the assessing authority, further review by a Costs Judge and appeal to a High Court Judge) have effect.

The defendant should not, however, embark upon this course unless satisfied that he has a rea-  **22.41** sonable prospect of reducing the receiver's charges substantially, because an unsuccessful application is likely to result in a further award of costs against him. The defendant would therefore be well advised to obtain expert evidence (preferably from a costs lawyer) before seeking an order for taxation. In practical terms, the defendant would be well advised, in the first instance, to simply request a detailed breakdown of the work undertaken by the receiver (and/or his/her staff) so that they can form an accurate view as to the reasonableness or otherwise of the work carried out, prior to proceeding further (and potentially incurring any unnecessary cost).

### Receiver's costs in litigation

In most cases, litigation costs will follow the event and the defendant will be required to pay  **22.42** a receiver's costs if he chooses to challenge an application and then loses that challenge. As with all costs decisions, it is a matter of discretion for the court. It is common for the court to order that the litigation costs of the receiver (and, sometimes, the prosecutor) be 'costs in the receivership'—that is to say, met out of the sums realised by the receiver. This empowers the receiver to realise sufficient assets to pay the costs awarded. In *Glatt v Sinclair* [2010] EWHC 3069 (Admin), Kenneth Parker J held that the litigation costs of a receiver of resisting an unsuccessful application for permission to bring an action against that receiver in relation to his conduct as a receiver (ie an allegation that the receiver had been negligent) were also payable out of receivership funds, despite the receivership having been discharged before the application was made. The substantive decision refusing permission, [2010] EWHC 3082 (Admin), and hence also the costs decision cited above, were overturned by the Court of Appeal in *Glatt v Sinclair* [2011] EWCA Civ 1317. However, the principle remains that the receiver can draw any litigation costs awarded to him from the receivership estate or obtain them from a third party where appropriate, see *Sinclair v Dhillon and others* [2012] EWHC 3517 (Admin). This may even include remuneration, expenses, and litigation costs post-discharge—see *Glatt and others v Sinclair* [2013] EWCA Civ 241.

Often a court-appointed receiver will become embroiled in litigation as a third party  **22.43** and sometimes by default. Costs are often said to be 'in the receivership' when either the prosecuting authority or the receiver is successful in litigation, although this expression is rarely, if ever, properly defined. The receiver will often have costs beyond merely instructing solicitors and counsel. Receivers also have to incur costs in preparing witness statements and time in conference, giving instructions etc. Costs have often been awarded 'in the receivership' even when the receiver has been unsuccessful in litigation and this once again gives rise to the question as to who truly should bear those costs. In *Re Nossen's Letter Patent* [1969] 1 WLR 683, Lloyd-Jacob J stated that the established practice of the courts was to disallow any sums claimed in respect of the time spent by the litigant personally in the course of instructing his solicitors, but that, in the case of litigation by a corporation, that practice had not been strictly applied, it being recognised that, if expert assistance is properly required, it may well occur that the corporation's own specialist employees may be the most suitable or convenient experts to employ and that the direct costs incurred, but not a contribution to overheads, should, in principle, be recoverable. He expressed (at p 644) his conclusion this way:

> When it is appropriate that a corporate litigant should recover, on a party and party basis, the sum in respect of expert services of this character performed by its own staff, the amount must be restricted to a reasonable sum for the actual and direct costs of the work undertaken.

**22.44** In *London Scottish Benefit Society v Chorley* (1884) 12 QBD 452; 13 QBD 872 (CA), Sir Gordon Willmer went further and stated that the professional skill can be measured and recognised by law. In his judgment at pp 37–8, he said that costs are 'intended to cover remuneration for the exercise of professional legal skill'. In relation to other skills he said:

> Other professional people, who become involved in litigation and conduct their own case, may recover something in respect of their own professional skill in so far as they qualify as witnesses and are called as such. Nobody else, however, except a solicitor, has ever been held entitled to make any charge, as I understand it, in respect of the exercise of a professional legal skill...

**22.45** In *Sisu Capital Fund Ltd v Tucker and Wallace* [2005] EWHC 2321 (Ch), Warren J accepted that there may be cases where, in the fulfilment of his duties as an office holder, a receiver has to bring or defend litigation:

> The fact that he does so does not mean that it is part of his profession to conduct litigation in the way that it is part of the profession of a solicitor to do so. An office holder is not unique in this respect: trustees of family trusts or of pension funds have fiduciary duties, the fulfilment of which may require them to bring or defend proceedings. That sort of duty on the part of an office holder or other fiduciary does not, in my judgment, afford any basis for a difference in treatment, vis-à-vis payment of costs by an opposing party, from any other litigant. (Paragraph 40 of the judgment.)

Nor in his Lordship's judgment did the fact that an office holder's remuneration was ultimately under the control of the insolvency court make any difference to the result. The real reason he was not able to recover his costs was because he was not a professional seeking to recover costs for time spent in respect of his area of expertise.

**22.46** A similar type of approach was taken by the Crown Court when refusing a former receiver his costs of complying with a witness summons in confiscation proceedings. The former receiver, Nigel Heath Sinclair, applied to His Honour Judge Atherton sitting at Manchester Crown Court in November 2011 for his costs. Mr Sinclair expected that there would be sizeable work involved in retrieving, sorting, and producing the documents ordered which would otherwise be unremunerated. HHJ Atherton accepted that the court had such a jurisdiction to award payment from central funds. The judge relied on s 45(4) of the Senior Courts Act 1981 namely that, 'the Crown Court shall, in relation to the attendance and examination of witnesses, any contempt of court, the enforcement of its orders and all other matters incidental to its jurisdiction, have the like powers, rights, privileges and authority as the High Court'. The judge also relied on the case of *Individual Homes Ltd v Macbream Investments Ltd*, The Times, 14 November 2002 in which the High Court had granted such a category of costs. However, the Costs in Criminal Cases (General) Regulations 1986 make no provision to compensate non-expert witnesses for the costs of complying with a witness summons other than their travel and attendance at court. The judge refused to exercise the discretion to grant the former receiver any payment from central funds based on the facts of the case. He also relied on para 1.2.3 of the Costs Practice Direction, which states: 'Given the present provisions relating to costs, the exercise of the inherent jurisdiction will occur only in the rarest of circumstances.'

It therefore appears that if a receiver has costs that are incurred doing work as an expert as part **22.47** of the litigation (for which, if he was not in office, an expert would have to be employed to carry them out) then those costs are recoverable out of the costs award and the receivership estate. Whether the receiver would be entitled to recover other costs would be determined by his original letter of agreement with the prosecutor and order of appointment.

### Basis of assessment

The basis of assessment for a receiver's remuneration remains unclear as there is no specific **22.48** provision within CrimPR r 60.6 for receivers appointed under POCA nor under CPR r 69.7 (where Pts 43–48 are specifically excluded) for receivers appointed under the CJA or DTA. Under both provisions the receiver will be allowed an amount which is 'reasonable and proportionate in all the circumstances'. There is no mention in the Rules as to where the burden of proof lies. There is currently no authority interpreting the rules, but in practice it may be that the costs are to be assessed upon something of a 'half way house' between the Standard Basis and the Indemnity Basis. In other words, the costs judge will be required to decide whether or not the costs (or any item thereof) are reasonable as opposed to deciding whether or not he has a doubt about the issue. However the requirement for the costs to be *proportionate* is a requirement only for the Standard Basis of assessment and not for the Indemnity Basis: see paras 22.55–22.56 below.

### Payment of receiver's remuneration and expenses from receivership assets

See Chapter 4 on management receivers. **22.49**

### Realisations to be paid to the justices' chief executive

In *Hansford v Southampton Magistrates Court* [2008] 4 All ER 432, the Court made clear **22.50** that, as regards realisations under the CJA, sums realised by a receiver should be paid into the enforcing magistrates' court before deduction of the receiver's own expenses and disbursements, which should be paid to the receiver by the justices' chief executive pursuant to s 81(5) of that Act. Dyson LJ considered that:

> It seems to me that the meaning of section 81(1) is clear. The receiver is obliged to pay the proceeds of realisations to the justices' chief executive as soon as they are in his hands less any authorised payments. Unless he has authority to make those payments at the time the proceeds came into his hands, he may not deduct them from the proceeds. There is nothing

surprising or unfair about such an interpretation. The receiver is obliged to pay the proceeds to the justices' chief executive, but he will receive his remuneration and disbursements pursuant to section 81(5).

**22.51** 'Authorised' was considered to mean authorised by the court prior to the sums being in the hands of the receiver. In practice, this means that the full amount of the receiver's realisations will normally be credited towards payment of the confiscation order prior to payment of the receiver's remuneration and expenses. This procedure is now governed by ss 54–55 of POCA. For further details see Chapter 4 on management receivers and Chapter 11 on enforcement receivers.

## E.  Costs: High Court/Civil Cases

**22.52** The general rule, as in all civil cases, is that costs follow the event, ie the acquitted defendant is entitled to have his costs of the restraint order proceedings paid by the prosecutor, there being no power to direct their payment from central funds (see *Re W (Drug Trafficking) (Restraint Order: Costs)*, The Times, 13 October 1994). The question of costs remains a matter of discretion and where it can be shown that the defendant has behaved in such a way as to bring the proceedings upon himself, it is arguable that he should be left to pay his own costs.

**22.53** If, of course, the defendant makes an unmeritorious application to either the High Court or the Crown Court in restraint proceedings (eg for a variation of the order) he can properly be ordered to bear not only his own costs, but also those of the prosecution, in respect of that particular application—see for example CrimPR 61.19. For costs in High Court civil recovery proceedings under Pt 5 of POCA, see Chapter 13 at para 13.215. Part 44 of the CPR governs costs in civil cases generally.

**Court's discretion and circumstances to be taken into account when exercising its discretion as to costs**

**22.54**  Rule 44.3 of the CPR reads as follows:

(1)  The court has discretion as to—
  (a)  whether costs are payable by one party to another;
  (b)  the amount of those costs; and
  (c)  when they are to be paid.
(2)  If the court decides to make an order about costs—
  (a)  the general rule is that the unsuccessful party will be ordered to pay the costs of the successful party; but
  (b)  the court may make a different order.
(3)  ...
(4)  In deciding what order (if any) to make about costs, the court must have regard to all the circumstances, including—
  (a)  the conduct of all the parties;
  (b)  whether a party has succeeded on part of his case, even if he has not been wholly successful; and
  (c)  any payment into court or admissible offers to settle made by a party which is drawn to the court's attention and which is not an offer to which costs consequences under Part 36 apply.

(5) The conduct of the parties includes—

   (a) conduct before, as well as during, the proceedings, and in particular the extent to which the parties followed the Practice Direction (Pre-Action Conduct) or any relevant pre-action protocol;

   (b) whether it was reasonable for a party to raise, pursue or contest a particular allegation or issue;

   (c) the manner in which a party has pursued or defended his case or a particular allegation or issue;

   (d) whether a claimant who has succeeded in his claim, in whole or in part, exaggerated his claim.

(6) The orders which the court may make under this rule include an order that a party must pay—

   (a) the proportion of another party's costs;

   (b) a stated amount in respect of another party's costs;

   (c) costs from or until a certain date only;

   (d) costs incurred before proceedings have begun;

   (e) costs relating to particular steps taken in the proceedings;

   (f) costs relating only to a distinct part of the proceedings; and

   (g) interest on costs from or until a certain date including a date before judgment.

(7) ...

(8) Where the court has ordered a party to pay costs, it may order an amount to be paid on account before the costs are assessed.

## Basis of assessment

Under r 44.4 of the CPR, where the court is to assess the amounts of costs (whether by **22.55** summary or detailed assessment) it will assess those costs either on the standard basis, or on an indemnity basis, but the court will not in either case allow costs which have been unreasonably incurred or are unreasonable in amount. All costs other than those unreasonably incurred or unreasonable in amount are recoverable under the indemnity basis.

Where the amount of costs is to be assessed on the standard basis, the court will: **22.56**

(a) only allow costs which are proportionate to the matters in issue; and

(b) resolve any doubt that it may have as to whether costs were reasonably incurred or reasonable and proportionate in amount in favour of the paying party.

## Factors to be taken into account in deciding the amount of costs

Rule 44.5 of the CPR states: **22.57**

(1) The court is to have regard to all the circumstances in deciding whether costs were—

   (a) if it is assessing costs on the standard basis—

     (i) proportionately and reasonably incurred; or

     (ii) were proportionate and reasonable in amount, or

   (b) if it is assessing costs on the indemnity basis—

     (i) unreasonably incurred; or

     (ii) unreasonable in amount.

(2) ...

(3) The court must also have regard to—

   (a) the conduct of all the parties including in particular:

     (i) conduct before as well as during the proceedings, and

      (ii) the efforts made, if any, before and during the proceedings in order to try to resolve the dispute;

    (b) the amount or value of any money or property involved;

    (c) the importance of the matter to all the parties;

    (d) the particular complexity of the matter or the difficulty or novelty of the question raised;

    (e) the skill, effort, specialised knowledge and responsibility involved;

    (f) the time spent on the case; and

    (g) the place where and the circumstances in which work or any part of it was done.

### Interim costs orders

**22.58** Most orders will include a provision for costs. Where the court makes an order that does not mention costs, the general rule is that no party is entitled to costs in relation to that order (see r 44.13(1)(a) CPR). This was demonstrated in *Griffiths v Metropolitan Police Commissioner* [2003] EWCA Civ 313 where the Court held not only that an interim order that was silent as to costs prevented either party from any entitlement to recover costs, but also that the trial judge had no jurisdiction to vary that order.

**22.59** The Practice Direction for Pt 44 of the CPR, titled 'General Rules About Costs', sets out the meanings of common interim costs orders (see para 4.2 of the Practice Direction on the court's discretion as to costs: rule 44.2). Commonly encountered costs orders are as follows:

    (1) Costs in any event or simply 'costs': the party in whose favour the order is made is entitled to the costs in respect of the part of the proceedings to which the order relates, whatever other costs orders are made in the proceedings.

    (2) Costs in the case, or costs in the application: the party in whose favour the court makes an order for costs at the end of the proceedings is entitled to his costs of the part of the proceedings to which the order relates.

    (3) Costs reserved: the decision about costs is deferred to a later occasion, but if no later order is made the costs will be 'costs in the case'.

    (4) Claimant's/defendant's costs in the case/application: if the party in whose favour the costs order is made is awarded costs at the end of the proceedings, that party is entitled to his costs of the part of the proceedings to which the order relates. If any other party is awarded costs at the end of the proceedings, the party in whose favour the final costs order is made is not liable to pay the costs of any other party in respect of the part of the proceedings to which the order relates.

    (5) Costs thrown away: where, eg a judgment or order is set aside, the party in whose favour the costs order is made is entitled to the costs that have been incurred as a consequence. This includes the costs of:

        (a) preparing for and attending any hearing at which the judgment order which has been set aside has been made;

        (b) preparing for and attending any hearing to set aside the judgement or order in question;

        (c) preparing for and attending any hearing at which the court orders the proceedings or the part in question to be adjourned;

        (d) any steps taken to enforce a judgment or order which has subsequently been set aside.

    (6) Costs of and caused by: where eg the court makes an order on an application to amend a statement of case, the party in whose favour the costs order is made is entitled to the

costs of preparing for and attending the application and the costs of any consequential amendment to his own statement of case.

(7) Costs here and below: the party in whose favour the costs order is made is entitled not only to his costs in respect of the proceedings in which the court makes the order but also his costs in the proceedings in any lower court. In the case of an appeal from a divisional court the party is not entitled to any costs incurred in any court below the divisional court.

(8) No order as to costs or each party to bear his own costs: each party is to pay his own costs of the part of the proceedings to which the order relates whatever costs order the court makes at the end of the proceedings.

Three further costs orders are: **22.60**

(9) An order that a party or defendant's publicly funded or legally aided costs be subject to assessment; this applies when that party has lost an application and their legal expenses have been publicly funded.

(10) Costs in the receivership: such a costs order implies that the costs of the application will be borne as part of the receivership, ie the receiver will be entitled to claim the costs of the hearing and related legal expenses out of the receivership funds which they manage or control. Where an issue remains over the amount to be paid these costs will be expressed as 'Costs in the receivership, subject to assessment'.

(11) Costs not to be enforced without further leave of the court or 'It is further ordered that the costs of this claim be paid by the claimant/defendant, but the determination of the claimant's/defendant's liability to pay such costs shall be postponed pending further order'. Sometimes referred to as the 'pools coupon' order, it is primarily designed to deal with legally aided claimants who lose an application or matter. The order for costs anticipates that should, at some future point, the claimant/defendant come into funds, then the successful party would be at liberty to get the matter restored and seek their litigation costs.

### Time for commencing detailed assessment

This is an issue of which many practitioners fall foul, as a result of an attempt to commence **22.61** assessment prematurely (upon an interim awards of costs). CPR r 47.1 clearly states that:

> The general rule is that the costs of any proceedings or any part of the proceedings, are *not* to be assessed by the detailed assessment procedure until the conclusion of the proceedings, but the Court may order them to be assessed immediately.

The CPR Part 47 Costs Practice Direction goes on to state at para 1.1: **22.62**

> For the purposes of rule 47.1, proceedings are concluded when the court has finally determined the matters in issue in the claim, whether or not there is an appeal, or made an award of provisional damages under Part 41.

Accordingly, in the absence of agreement, or an order which contains the provisions 'forth- **22.63** with' or 'to be assessed immediately' then any interim orders cannot be pursued/assessed until the conclusion of the proceedings.

## F. Legal Expenses and Legal Funding

### Legal aid funding

Part 7 of POCA deals with criminal proceedings, eg the money laundering offences. **22.64** Representation for defendants in criminal proceedings under POCA is funded in the same way as any other criminal proceedings. Criminal legal aid can be granted by the court or funding provided through the Legal Aid Agency—see the Legal Aid, Sentencing and Punishment of Offenders Act 2012 (LASPO) and regulations thereunder.

**22.65** However, POCA also created a number of types of civil proceedings for which civil legal aid funding may be available. Paragraph 40 of Sch 1 to LASPO brings a range of POCA proceedings in the Crown Court within the scope of civil legal services funding subject to qualifying for representation. For more details see below.

**22.66** The funding for High Court civil recovery proceedings under Pt 5 of POCA, including obtaining legal expenses exclusions from PFOs, is dealt with in Chapter 13.

**22.67** The rates of public funding for advocates and litigators acting in confiscation proceedings under POCA, the CJA or DTA as from 1 April 2013 are set out at paras 14, 26, and 27 of Sch 1 to the Criminal Legal Aid (Remuneration) Regulations 2013.

*Defence costs*

**22.68** The practitioner should note that the Costs in Criminal Cases (General) (Amendment) Regulations 2012 came into force on 1 October 2012 amending the Costs in Criminal Cases (General) Regulations 1986. As noted above, the Legal Aid, Sentencing and Punishment of Offenders Act 2012 has introduced s 16A of the Prosecution of Offences Act 1985 which will restrict the availability of defendants' costs orders from central funds. The main impact of the regulations is that where the recovery of defence costs is continued to be allowed, it will be capped at legal aid rates meaning that privately paying clients who are found not guilty may find themselves substantially out of pocket. As a consequence, the prosecution may find themselves facing significantly reduced claims.

### Funding criteria

**22.69** Where civil legal aid funding is available for proceedings under POCA, applications for legal representation will be subject to the normal criteria for scope, means, and merits. Civil legal aid funding under POCA will only be available for clients who are financially eligible for such funding. Where seized assets have not been taken into account on the basis that they are the subject matter of the dispute, success in the proceedings resulting in the release of assets to the client will be treated as a recovery or preservation. The statutory charge will then apply. Any assets so recovered must therefore be paid to the solicitor and on to the Legal Aid Agency—see LASPO and regulations thereunder.

### Funding and confiscation orders

**22.70** When the court is deciding whether to make a confiscation order, the proceedings will be covered by criminal legal aid funding for the substantive criminal proceedings which led to the court considering confiscation. If for any reason no representation order is in force, application may be made to the court for a representation order to cover the hearing concerning the confiscation order. Such matters come within the definition of 'criminal proceedings' under s 14(b) of LASPO since they concern 'proceedings before a court for dealing with an individual convicted of an offence, including proceedings in respect of a sentence or order'.

**22.71** There are other specific types of proceedings under Pts 2 and 8 of POCA for which civil legal aid funding in the Crown Court is available under Sch 1 to LASPO. These include:

(a) Section 41 restraint order proceedings including orders under section 41(7) which allow the court to make such other order as is appropriate to make the restraint order effective. Civil legal aid funding is available for applications to discharge or vary restraint or ancillary orders under s 42(3) or an order under para 40(1)(a), Sch 1 to LASPO.

(b) When a confiscation order is not satisfied, the Crown Court has power to appoint a receiver in respect of any realisable property. Once a confiscation order is fully satisfied, under s 54(3) an enforcement receiver has power to distribute remaining assets, but can only do so after giving persons who have an interest in the property concerned a reasonable opportunity to make representations. Civil legal aid funding is available to enable any such persons to be represented in hearings in the Crown Court as to the distribution of assets (see para 40(1)(c) of Sch 1 to LASPO).

(c) Any person affected by an action that a receiver takes or proposes to take may apply to the Crown Court under s 62. Civil legal aid funding is available for such applications (see para 40(1)(d) of Sch 1 to LASPO).

(d) Sections 72 and 73 give the Crown Court power to award compensation to persons who have suffered loss as a result of orders made or actions done under Pt 2 of the 2002 Act. Section 72 concerns compensation for serious default. Section 73 concerns compensation where a confiscation order is varied under s 29 (defendant was an absconder) or where a confiscation order is discharged under s 30 (defendant acquitted or not proceeded against). Civil legal aid funding is available to those making applications for compensation under ss 72 or 73 (see para 40(1)(f) of Sch 1 to LASPO).

(e) Sections 351, 362, 369, and 375 give the Crown Court power to discharge or vary Pt 8 investigation orders (production orders, orders to grant entry, disclosure orders, customer information orders, and account monitoring orders). Civil legal aid funding is available for those making such applications (see para 40(1)(g)–(j) of Sch 1 to LASPO).

**Problems with confiscation funding and stays**

In the case of *Crown Prosecution Service v Susan Jane Campbell and others* [2009] EWCA **22.72** Crim 997; [2010] 1 WLR 650 confiscation proceedings were stayed and no order was made. The Legal Services Commission had refused, despite the judge's request, to make an exception to provide funding for an advocate. The judge's request had noted that substantial public funds, in the form of the potential confiscation order, were at risk. On 20 February 2009 the confiscation proceedings came before the Crown Court. Campbell was unrepresented at this hearing, despite there being a representation order in her favour. Her trial counsel had left the independent bar by the time of the confiscation proceedings and her solicitors were unable to find a suitably qualified replacement barrister willing to take the case due to the rate of remuneration under the applicable graduated fee structure—then a fixed daily rate of £178.25 or fixed half daily rate of £99.50 with no funding for preparation of the case unless it involved a very unusual or novel point of law or fact, which this case did not.

The judge at first instance found that any freshly instructed barrister would need to do **22.73** approximately eighty hours of preparation before a final hearing and that the notion that Campbell could have a fair trial without representation was 'pie in the sky'. He then granted her application to stay the proceedings, and made no confiscation order.

The Court of Appeal, refusing an adjournment, was unimpressed by the CPS's submission **22.74** that a review was being conducted into confiscation funding and an adequately funded advocate may be available for Campbell at some future point and the case remained stayed (see paras 8 and 44). The Court pointed out that the problem was not a new one, it having been identified by HHJ Mole QC a year previously (reported on BAILLI as *P* [2008] EW Misc 2 (EWCC)).

**22.75**  Paragraph 14 of Sch 1 to the Criminal Legal Aid (Remuneration) Regulations 2013 has since introduced new legal aid fees for advocacy in confiscation hearings where there are more than fifty pages of evidence. The Regulations came into force on 1 April 2013 and provide that in addition to a daily and half-daily rate, there is to be an increasing fee for papers of 51–250 pages, 251–500 pages, 501–750 pages, and 750–1,000 pages. Above 1,000 pages, an hourly rate is payable.

### Funding for enforcement

**22.76**  In *Taylor v City of Westminster Magistrates' Court* [2009] EWHC 1498, the Divisional Court considered the extent to which a magistrates' court could make a representation order to provide public funding for a court advocate (as opposed to a solicitor alone). The facts were as follows: enforcement proceedings had been instituted against the claimant in 2008, and he had applied for and was granted a representation order by the magistrates' court. It covered a solicitor and was for the purposes of the confiscation enforcement proceedings. Subsequently, the claimant applied to have that order extended to include representation by an advocate. The basis of the application was that the issues for determination before the magistrates' court were such as to require an advocate as well as a solicitor. It was said, for example, that the proceedings before the magistrates' court involved a complex argument about delay by the prosecution in the application for his committal.

**22.77**  The claimant's application was refused, firstly by the Confiscation Order Unit of Her Majesty's Court Service and then subsequently on a renewed oral application before a district judge. The judge, in refusing the request, relied upon reg 12 of the Criminal Defence Service (General) (Number 2) Regulations 2001 (SI 1473/2001).

**22.78**  In Pill LJ's judgment, the District Judge had been correct to refuse the extending of funding:

> 25 . . . regulation 12 does not extend to confiscation enforcement proceedings in the Magistrates' Court, however serious the underlying events . . . The basic principle of interpretation is that a regulation such as this must be construed in context. That means that consideration must be given to this regulation in the context of the 2001 regulations themselves but also against the background legislative scheme, its scope and purpose. Confiscation enforcement proceedings are criminal proceedings for the purposes of the 1999 Act and the 2001 Regulations and fall within the scope of section 12(2)(b) of the 1999 Act. However, the confiscation legislation makes clear that enforcement of a confiscation order is deemed to be equivalent to the enforcement of a fine through the Magistrates' Court. That is far from being proceedings in the case of an indictable offence.

### Funding in civil recovery cases

**22.79**  All proceedings under Chapter 2 of Pt 5 of POCA, High Court Civil Recovery claims, are civil proceedings for which civil legal aid may become available where access to frozen assets is not possible. The proceedings are not currently listed in Sch 1 to LASPO for the purposes of obtaining civil legal aid in general cases under s 9 so that a person would have to satisfy s 10, on exceptional cases, unless the proceedings are historic and are covered by existing funding.

Both a respondent against whom the agency is proceeding or a third party who claims to be an innocent owner of property (eg under s 281 a person who claims to be a victim of theft etc may apply to the court for a declaration that certain property is not recoverable property) may require funding. In most cases legal expenses are released to the respondent from frozen funds or sourced from other parties or assets—this topic is dealt with in detail in Chapter 13 at para 13.215 et seq.

### Funding in cash seizure cases

Chapter 3 of Pt 5 of POCA deals with the recovery of cash in summary proceedings. Civil **22.81** legal aid funding may become available. However, the proceedings are not currently listed in Sch 1 to LASPO for the purposes of obtaining civil legal aid in general cases under s 9 so that a person would have to satisfy s 10, on exceptional cases, unless the proceedings are historic and existing funding is in place. Otherwise, private funds may have to be relied upon.

### Release of restrained funds to cover legal expenses under POCA

Under s 41(3)(a) of POCA, a restraint order may be subject to an exception to allow for rea- **22.83** sonable legal expenses; however, under s 41(4) such an exception must *not* make provision for any legal expenses that relate to an offence (which falls within s 41(5)) and are incurred by either the defendant or a recipient of a tainted gift: see *S v The Commissioners of HM Customs and Excise* [2004] EWCA Crim 2374, [2005] 1 WLR 1338, where the Court said (in para 47) that 'looking at the Act as a whole we are satisfied that Parliament intended to make public funding available to question restraint orders' and that the order should make clear that public funding is available.

A defendant must therefore look to civil legal aid funding, or assets elsewhere. The effect of the **22.84** POCA provisions was confirmed in *Re S* (above) and *Ap and U Ltd v (1) Crown Prosecution Service (2) Revenue & Customs Prosecutions Office* [2007] EWCA Crim 3128; [2008] 1 Cr App R 39, where the Court of Appeal held that Parliament was entitled to take the view that funds which might have criminal origins should not be used to pay lawyers for the benefit of a defendant who was either suspected of, or had been found to be, a criminal; and that Parliament had provided other means for defendants to have legal representation by the provision of state aid. It also held that the measure was not incompatible with any rights under the European Convention.

However, there remain provisions for other unrelated legal costs to be met from restrained **22.85** funds, eg legal charges in relation to conveyancing of property or litigation costs in ongoing proceedings, which are not connected to the criminal matters in question.

In particular, attention is drawn to the potential amendments to s 41 of POCA under s 46 **22.86** of the Crime and Courts Act 2013. These are not yet in force but if they take effect they will allow the release of restrained funds for contributions towards legal aid in contesting criminal and restraint proceedings. In addition, it may also be open to the defendant to contract with his solicitors on a contingent basis, namely that he will be liable to pay the costs only if he is successful in obtaining a discharge of any restraint order. A properly structured conditional fee agreement that did not involve any dissipation or disposal of the restrained assets (and/or breach the terms of the restraint order) may be permissible (albeit there would be an element of risk to the commercial lawyer if they were unsuccessful). This topic is dealt with in some detail in Chapters 2 and 5.

### Drawing legal expenses from living expenses

In *Michael Joseph McInerney v Financial Services Authority* [2009] EWCA Crim 997; [2010] **22.87** 1 WLR 650 the judge made a restraint order against Mr McInerney under s 41 of POCA in connection with alleged money laundering offences. The order restrained all known assets of

McInerney, but allowed him £250 per week towards ordinary living expenses. In November 2008 McInerney applied to the LSC for public funding in order to judicially review the Financial Services Authority (FSA)'s decision to commence a prosecution of the money laundering offences.

**22.88** On 12 February 2009 the LSC offered the requested public funding, subject to the condition that McInerney made a contribution of £117.66 per month from his 'income'. That assessment was made on the basis of his 'income' of £250 per week, that being the sum excluded as living expenses from the terms of the restraint order. McInerney's solicitors argued that the assessment of his income should have been 'nil' due to the restraint order. The LSC rejected this argument. Confirmation was then sought from the FSA that the monthly contribution could be paid to the LSC from the ordinary living allowance. The FSA responded that the payment of the contribution would be a breach of s 41(4) of POCA as it was not possible to make an exception to the order for any legal expenses. McInerney applied to Southwark Crown Court for a variation of the restraint order to make it clear that he was not prohibited from paying the £117.66 contribution. The court refused to make the variation requested. McInerney sought a variation (or a declaration) the effect of which would be to permit him to pay part of the money allowed to him for reasonable living expenses to the LSC as a contribution to the costs incurred in bringing the judicial review application.

**22.89** The Court of Appeal rejected the defendant's request. It agreed with the judge at first instance: payments to the LSC are not ordinary living expenses and thus the defendant would be in contempt of court to pay money to the LSC and the LSC would be in breach of the restraint order to receive it. The court added that s 41(3)(a) makes a distinction between living expenses and legal expenses and if a contribution to the LSC is a legal expense, a payment to the LSC would not be a payment towards ordinary living expenses (para 33). As a result the court held (at para 38): 'In our view the judge was right. A contribution to the LSC to institute judicial review proceedings in connection with the offence in respect of which the restraint order was made is a "legal expense".' For the potential effect of s 46 of the Crime and Courts Act 2013, see para 22.86 above.

### Legal expenses and third parties

**22.90** In *Re S* [2010] EWHC 917 the wife of the defendant had applied to release funds under a CJA restraint order to pay her legal expenses of making an application to discharge the restraint order. The Court considered both *Re D* and *Revenue and Customs Prosecutions Office v Briggs-Price and O'Reilly* (2007) EWCA Civ 568. It considered the application by the defendant's wife to be very different from that in *Briggs-Price*, principally as there was now a 'settled' confiscation order in place—there had to be very strong reasons to permit release of funds to a third party in a post-confiscation situation. The court did not, however, state that a restraint order should never be varied to permit payment towards a third party's legal expenses.

**22.91** As regards civil recovery proceedings, in *Serious Organised Crime Agency v Azam* [2011] EWHC 1551 (Admin) the Court permitted a variation to a PFO obtained by SOCA to fund the legal expenses of the offender's wife.

## G. Compensation

### Compensation for the acquitted defendant under POCA

**22.92** Section 72(1) of POCA sets out the three conditions that need to be satisfied before the Crown Court may make an order for payment of compensation. The amount the Crown

Court may order to be paid is described as an amount 'it believes is just'. Applications must proceed under CrimPR r 58.10.

The first condition is satisfied if a criminal investigation has been started with regard to an **22.93** offence and proceedings are not started for the offence. Under POCA it is possible for a restraint order to be made as soon as the criminal investigation has been started, as distinct to under the CJA and DTA, where it was only possible to obtain a restraint order when proceedings had been started or were about to be. One of the main changes of POCA is that compensation will now be payable not only from when proceedings have been started, but from the beginning of the investigation itself. The first condition is also satisfied if proceedings for an offence are started against the person and they do not result in his conviction for the offence, or he is convicted of the offence but the conviction is quashed or he is pardoned in respect of it (see s 72(3)).

If a criminal investigation has been started with regard to an offence, and proceedings have **22.94** not or are not started for that offence, the second condition is that in the criminal investigation there has been serious default by a person mentioned in s 72(9) of POCA and the investigation would not have continued if the default had not occurred (s 72(9) is in almost identical terms to subs (5) of the corresponding provisions of s 18 of DTA and s 89 of CJA).

If proceedings for an offence are started against a person and they do not result in his convic- **22.95** tion for the offence, or he is convicted of the offence but the conviction is quashed or he is pardoned in respect of it, the second condition (see s 72(4) and (5)) is that in the criminal investigation with regard to the offence or in its prosecution there has been a serious default by a person who is mentioned in subs (9) and the proceedings would not have been started or continued if the default had not occurred.

The third condition is that an application is made under this section by a person who held **22.96** realisable property and has suffered loss in consequence of anything done in relation to it by or in pursuance of an order under Pt 2 of POCA (see s 72(6)).

Section 72 reflects largely the previous legislation under s 18 of the DTA and s 89 of the CJA, **22.97** save that the provisions have been extended to cover the situation where the investigation is started, but proceedings have not been brought. It provides for compensation to be paid to a person whose property has been affected by the enforcement of the confiscation legislation. 'Serious default' is not defined in the Act and therefore each case will need to be determined on its own merits. It is not intended that compensation should be paid on acquittal as a matter of course. The terms of s 72 POCA were considered in passing by the Court of Appeal in *An Informer v Chief Constable* [2012] 3 All ER 601 and by Mr Justice Underhill in the first instance judgment of *Brandon Barnes v Eastenders Cash & Carry Plc & CPS* [2012] EW Misc 6 (CCrimC) (04 April 2012) Case No: U20110135/1/2011.

### Compensation for victims and confiscation orders

POCA contemplates that both a compensation order under s 130 of the Powers of the **22.98** Courts (Criminal Sentencing) Act 2000 and a confiscation order may be made against the same defendant in the same criminal proceedings—see s 13(5) of POCA and para 22.116 below. In *Faithfull v Ipswich Crown Court* [2007] EWHC 2763, the High Court considered whether the Crown Court judge's decision as to whether to order a defendant to pay compensation to a victim could be challenged by judicial review by a third party, such as a potential victim. The Court found that it could not (as there existed alternative civil court remedies), and held that decisions about confiscation and compensation were decisions about sentence, and as such were an integral part of the trial process (*R v Maidstone Crown Court ex p Harrow LBC* [2000] QB 719 distinguished).

22.99    The Act does not contemplate that it shall operate as a means of compensating the Crown where the Crown is the victim, eg by the evasion of duties and taxes, although a confiscation order may in practice have that effect. Following the Supreme Court's decision in *R v Waya* [2012] UKSC 51, the Court of Appeal in *R v Susan Hursthouse* [2013] EWCA Crim 517, *R v Mohid Jawad* [2013] EWCA Crim 644, and *R v Harvey* [2013] EWCA Crim 1104 have emphasised that it would be disproportionate to seek a confiscation order where full compensation has been made to the victim. Compensating the Crown may only be necessary in cases where the Crown has suffered a loss and does not have a civil claim against the defendant. The Court confirmed in *Nugent and Gorman v Commissioners for Revenue and Customs* [2011] UKFTT 329 (TC) that payment in full of a confiscation order did not free a defendant from a tax liability relating to the same conduct. The concept of 'benefit' does not equate with the concept of a 'liability' for tax, and HMRC was able to sue for that liability. However this decision pre-dates *Waya* above.

### Compensation in absconded defendant cases under POCA

22.100    Under s 73(1) of POCA, where a court varies a confiscation order under s 29 of POCA (ie where a defendant has absconded) or discharges a confiscation order under s 30 (where an absconded defendant is later tried for an offence and is acquitted on all counts) and application is made to the Crown Court by a person who held realisable property and has suffered a loss as a result of the making of the order, the court may order the payment of such compensation it believes is just.

22.101    In those circumstance compensation is payable to the applicant by the Lord Chancellor (s 73(3)). It should be noted that this provision is not limited to serious default as in s 72. Applications must proceed under CrimPR r 58.11.

### Civil recovery compensation under POCA

22.102    Under s 283 of POCA, the scheme allows for compensation to be paid under Pt 5 of the Act (Civil recovery of the proceeds etc of unlawful conduct).

22.103    Under s 283(1), where any property to which an Interim Receiving Order (IRO) or Property freezing Order (PFO) has at any time applied and where the court does not in the course of the proceedings decide that the property is recoverable property (or associated property), the person whose property it is may make an application to the court for compensation.

22.104    Section 283(1) does not apply if the court has made a declaration in respect of the property under s 281 (Victims of Theft etc), or makes an order under s 276 (a consent order) (see s 283(2)).

22.105    If the court is satisfied that the applicant has suffered loss as a result of a PFO or IRO it may require the enforcement authority to pay compensation to him. The amount of compensation to be paid under s 283 is the amount the court thinks reasonable having regard to the loss suffered and any other relevant circumstances (see s 283(9)).

22.106    Section 283 deals with cases where there has been a loss to owners of property in circumstances where that property has been made subject to a PFO or IRO, but has not in the end been deemed to be recoverable or associated property for two reasons:

(1) because the court has so determined, or

(2) because the claim or application has been withdrawn.

Under subs (1) the person whose property it is may apply to the court for compensation for **22.107**
any loss relating to that property. In those circumstances the court may order compensation
to be paid by the enforcement authority under subs (5).

The measure of the compensation to be paid is at the court's discretion, having regard to **22.108**
all of the circumstances including any quantifiable losses suffered. If a claimant has himself
contributed to the losses, for example through delays caused by himself, the court is entitled
to take those facts into account.

### Three-month time limit

If the court has decided not to make a recovery order in respect of the property, the appli- **22.109**
cation for compensation must be made within the period of three months beginning, in
relation to a decision of the High Court, with the date of the decision. If any application is
not made for leave to appeal, then the three-month period begins with the date on which
the application is withdrawn or refused or on which any proceedings on appeal are finally
concluded (see s 283(3)).

If the proceedings in respect of the property have been discontinued, the application for **22.110**
compensation must be made within the period of three months beginning with the discontinuance (see s 283(4)).

### Compensation for recovery of cash in summary proceedings

Under s 302 of POCA, when no forfeiture order is made in respect of any cash detained **22.111**
under Chapter 3, the person to whom the cash belongs or from whom it was seized may
make an application to the magistrates' court for compensation. If the seized cash was not
paid into an interest-bearing account at the first opportunity following its initial detention,
the court may make an order for compensation to be paid to the applicant (see s 302(2)).

The amount of compensation to be paid in those circumstances is an amount which the **22.112**
court thinks would have been earned in interest in the period in question if the cash had
been held in an interest-bearing account. It is therefore likely to be of relatively nominal
value (see s 302(3)).

If the court is satisfied that the applicant has suffered any other loss as a result of the detention **22.113**
of the cash and that the circumstances are 'exceptional', the court may order compensation
or additional compensation to be paid to him (see s 302(4)). In those circumstances the
amount of compensation to be paid is the amount the court thinks reasonable, having regard
to the loss suffered and any other relevant circumstances. This subsection was touched on by
the Court of Appeal in *Perinpanathan* cited above at para 22.15.

Where Revenue and Customs officials seize the cash, the compensation is to be paid by the **22.114**
Commissioners of Revenue and Customs (s 302(6)). If the cash was seized by a constable,
the compensation is to be paid by the relevant police force. Section 127 of the MCA sets a
six-month time limit for making an application for compensation under s 302. In *Davis v
Chief Constable of Leicestershire* [2012] EWHC 3388 (Admin) it was held that this time limit
begins to run from the date that the forfeiture proceedings are discontinued.

**22.115**  It should be noted that if a forfeiture order is made in respect of any part of the cash detained under ss 294 and 295 of POCA, the person to whom the cash belongs or from whom it was seized is entitled to claim compensation in relation to any part of the cash that is not ordered to be forfeited (see s 302(8)).

### Compensation and the victims of crime

**22.116**  Section 130 of the (PCC(S)A) provides:

> Compensation orders against convicted persons
>
> (1)  A court by or before which a person is convicted of an offence, instead of or in addition to dealing with him in any other way, may, on application or otherwise, make an order (in this Act referred to as a 'compensation order') requiring him—
>
> > (a)  to pay compensation for any personal injury, loss or damage resulting from that offence or any other offence which is taken into consideration by the court in determining sentence; or
> >
> > (b)  to make payments for funeral expenses or bereavement in respect of a death resulting from any such offence, other than a death due to an accident arising out of the presence of a motor vehicle on a road;
> >
> > but this is subject to the following provisions of this section and to section 131 below.
>
> (2)  …
> (3)  A court shall give reasons, on passing sentence, if it does not make a compensation order in a case where this section empowers it to do so.
> (4)  Compensation under subsection (1) above shall be of such amount as the court considers appropriate, having regard to any evidence and to any representations that are made by or on behalf of the accused or the prosecutor.

**22.117**  Section 131(1) adds:

> The compensation to be paid under a compensation order made by a magistrates' court in respect of any offence of which the court has convicted the offender shall not exceed £5,000.

**22.118**  For the operation of s 130 in practice, see *RCPO v Duffy* [2008] EWHC 848 and the earlier case of *R v Crutchley and Tonks* [1994] 15 Cr App R (S) 627. It has been held that where a defendant has sufficient assets to pay both a confiscation and a compensation order, he can be required to pay both, even where they relate to the same amount (see eg *R v Mitchell and Mitchell* [2001] 2 Cr App R (S) 141). This is specifically contemplated under s 13(5) of POCA. Under s 13(6) of POCA if a defendant has insufficient assets to satisfy both orders in full then the court must direct that so much of the compensation as it specifies be paid from the sums recovered under the confiscation order.

**22.119**  In *R v Dorrian* (2001) 1 Cr App R (S) 135, the appellant submitted that the court had no power to make a compensation order outside the period of twenty-eight days following sentence in the absence of an expressly stated decision to postpone the compensation order as part of the sentence (s 47(2) of the Supreme Court Act 1981). It was conceded that there was a common law power in the court to postpone any part of the sentence, but it was submitted that it must be expressly stated. In *Dorrian* there had been no express statement, but the making of the compensation order was postponed. The Court of Appeal was satisfied that s 72(5)(b) of the CJA did not exclude compensation orders from the consideration of the court making the confiscation order, and that the sentencer had power to make a compensation order or to postpone the making of an order at the time of sentence. It also held that the appellant was correct in his submission that the section dealt with the manner in which funds were allocated if both of the orders were made. The exclusion of compensation orders from s 72A(9) of the CJA provided protection for victims of crime. It meant they could benefit from a compensation order, where a confiscation order was made within the time limit provided. It was not, however, open to the Crown Court to make a compensation order twenty-six months after conviction where no common law power had been exercised to postpone the making of such an order at the date of sentence. No reference was made at the time to the making of a compensation order, or postponing the making of such an order at the time, and accordingly the Crown Court had no power to do so more than two years after conviction. For those reasons the compensation order was not lawful and was quashed.

The position under POCA has been clarified. Under ss 14 and 15 of POCA, when confisca-  **22.120**
tion proceedings are postponed the defendant may be sentenced during the postponement period except that fines, deprivation and forfeiture orders, and any compensation order under s 130 of the PCC(S)A may not be made during this time. Under s 13 of POCA the intention is that all other financial and deprivation and forfeiture orders are considered, and if appropriate, imposed after the confiscation order but at the same hearing so that the confiscation order can be taken into account before they are imposed.

# 23

## CONDEMNATION AND RESTORATION

# A. Introduction

**23.01** In this chapter we give an overview of the law in relation to what some still describe as 'Bootlegging'. Whilst not strictly within the ambit of a book that has as its central focus the proceeds of crime, there is nevertheless a nexus between the two. Cigarette and tobacco smuggling has been successfully deployed by criminal organisations to raise funds for many years, and the extremes to which individuals will go in order to evade the authorities have become increasingly sophisticated.

**23.02** Nowadays the condemnation of goods covers a vast area of legislation. As a result, we have sought to concentrate on those areas that are typical of matters that regularly come before the courts. The objective of condemnation proceedings has been explained in a number of authorities, including *Commissioners of Customs and Excise v Trustee of the property of Sokolow (a bankrupt)* [1954] 2 QB 336, 344 (Hilbery J) where it was said their purpose is to determine the legality of the seizure.

**23.03** The bifurcated jurisdiction adopted by the legislature in relation to the seizure, forfeiture, and condemnation of excise goods and vehicles under ss 49, 139, 141 and Sch 3 to CEMA on the one hand, and on the other, the discretionary power vested in the Commissioners of Revenue and Customs to restore, subject to such conditions (if any) that they think proper, anything forfeited or seized under s 152(b) of CEMA was recognised by Pill LJ in *Gora v Customs and Excise Commissioners* [2003] EWCA Civ 525, at para 57.

**23.04** The present system in relation to forfeiture and restoration has not been without its critics. In *Customs and Excise Commissioners v Weller* [2006] EWHC 237 (Ch), Evans-Lombe J called for a 'statutory rationalisation of the procedure governing the forfeiture of goods by the Commissioners' (para 24). He stated that: 'It seems to me that the present system is confusing to the public and pregnant with the possibility of substantial injustice.'

**23.05** The problem of the two-track system of condemnation and forfeiture, followed by restoration was also subject to scrutiny by the Court of Appeal in *Gascoyne v Customs and Excise Commissioners* [2005] 2 WLR 222, para 5, where Buxton LJ said: 'The procedure has a number of elements which appear to have grown up over the years and which do not always easily fit with each other.' This highlights the practical and very real problems that both appellants, magistrates sitting in their civil jurisdiction, and judges sitting in the First-Tier Tax Tribunals have experienced.

**23.06** Pursuant to s 50 of the Commissioners for Revenue and Customs Act 2005, references to Commissioners of HM Customs and Excise, and HM Customs and Excise in the legislation have been amended to Commissioners of HM Revenue and Customs, and HM Revenue and Customs respectively.

### UK Border Agency

**23.07** The UKBA took over the role of Customs at airports and ports throughout the UK from 5 August 2009. Whilst HMRC has handed over its powers to the UKBA at borders (see s 26 of the Borders, Citizenship and Immigration Act 2009), HMRC inland detection teams continue to operate as before, with much of their work being undertaken in respect of inward and outward diversion fraud cases involving wines, spirits, beers, cigarettes, and other dutiable goods. On 26 March 2013 the Home Secretary announced that the UKBA was to be abolished with its work returning to the Home Office. The Home Secretary told MPs that 'its performance was not good enough'. At the time of going to press further details were unclear. For the purposes of this chapter we have continued with the reference to the UKBA, but with the above caveat.

## B. The Condemnation and Forfeiture of Goods

### The statutory basis

**23.08** The statutory basis for the forfeiture of goods improperly imported derives from s 49 of CEMA. Section 49(1) sets out the circumstances under which goods shall be liable to forfeiture when they have been imported contrary to HMRC restrictions and where the goods in question are chargeable with duty:

(1) Where—
  (a) except as provided by or under the Customs and Excise Acts 1979, any imported goods, being goods chargeable on their importation with customs or excise duty, are, without payment of that duty—
    (i) unshipped in any port,
    (ii) unloaded from any aircraft in the United Kingdom,
    (iii) unloaded from any vehicle in, or otherwise brought across the boundary into, Northern Ireland, or
    (iv) removed from their place of importation or from any approved wharf, examination station or transit shed; or
  (b) any goods are imported, landed or unloaded contrary to any prohibition or restriction for the time being in force with respect thereto under or by virtue of any enactment; or
  (c) any goods, being goods chargeable with any duty or goods the importation of which is for the time being prohibited or restricted by or under any enactment, are found, whether before or after the unloading thereof, to have been concealed in any manner on board any ship or aircraft or, while in Northern Ireland, in any vehicle; or
  (d) any goods are imported concealed in a container holding goods of a different description; or
  (e) any imported goods are found, whether before or after delivery, not to correspond with the entry made thereof; or
  (f) any imported goods are concealed or packed in any manner appearing to be intended to deceive an officer,
  those goods shall, subject to subsection (2) below, be liable to forfeiture.
(2) Where any goods, the importation of which is for the time being prohibited or restricted by or under any enactment, are on their importation either—
  (a) reported as intended for exportation in the same ship, aircraft or vehicle; or
  (b) entered for transit or transhipment; or
  (c) entered to be warehoused for exportation or for use as stores,
  the Commissioners may, if they see fit, permit the goods to be dealt with accordingly.

**23.09** These broad-ranging provisions cover, subject to their own particular legislative provisions, the forfeiture of cigarettes and tobacco (see s 2 of the Tobacco Products Duty Act 1979), alcohol (the Alcoholic Liquor Duties Act 1979, particularly s 5 (spirits), s 36 (beer), s 54 (wine), and s 62 (cider)). They also cover a multitude of other excise goods, including bullion and coins (see *Allgemeine Gold-und Silberscheideanstalt v Customs and Excise Commissioners* [1980] 2 All ER 138 (CA)), pornography, vehicles, as well as goods prohibited from importation by virtue of matters as diverse as trade descriptions and UN sanctions orders.

### Duty payable, unless for own use

**23.10**  UK excise duty is generally payable at the point of importation into the UK—see reg 13 of the Excise Goods (Holding, Movement and Duty Point) Regulations 2010 (SI 2010/593) 'the 2010 Regulations', which provides:

> 13.—(1) Where excise goods already released for consumption in another Member State are held for a commercial purpose in the United Kingdom in order to be delivered or used in the United Kingdom, the excise duty point is the time when those goods are first so held.
>
> (2) Depending on the cases referred to in paragraph (1), the person liable to pay the duty is the person—
>
> (a) making the delivery of the goods;
>
> (b) holding the goods intended for delivery; or
>
> (c) to whom the goods are delivered.
>
> (3) For the purposes of paragraph (1) excise goods are held for a commercial purpose if they are held—
>
> (a) by a person other than a private individual; or
>
> (b) by a private individual ('P'), except in a case where the excise goods are for P's own use and were acquired in, and transported to the United Kingdom from, another Member State by P.
>
> (4) For the purposes of determining whether excise goods referred to in the exception in paragraph (3)(b) are for P's own use regard must be taken of—
>
> (a) P's reasons for having possession or control of those goods;
>
> (b) whether or not P is a revenue trader;
>
> (c) P's conduct, including P's intended use of those goods or any refusal to disclose the intended use of those goods;
>
> (d) the location of those goods;
>
> (e) the mode of transport used to convey those goods;
>
> (f) any document or other information relating to those goods;
>
> (g) the nature of those goods including the nature or condition of any package or container;
>
> (h) the quantity of those goods and, in particular, whether the quantity exceeds any of the following quantities—
>
> - 10 litres of spirits,
> - 20 litres of intermediate products (as defined in article 17(1) of Council Directive 92/83/EEC),
> - 90 litres of wine (including a maximum of 60 litres of sparkling wine),
> - 110 litres of beer,
> - 3200 cigarettes, (after 1.10.11, 800 cigarettes)
> - 400 cigarillos (cigars weighing no more than 3 grammes each),
> - 200 cigars,
> - 3 kilogrammes of any other tobacco products; (after 1.10.11, 1 kg of other tobacco products)
>
> (i) whether P personally financed the purchase of those goods;
>
> (j) any other circumstance that appears to be relevant.
>
> (5) For the purposes of the exception in paragraph (3)(b)—
>
> (a) 'excise goods' does not include any goods chargeable with excise duty by virtue of any provision of the Hydrocarbon Oil Duties Act 1979 or of any order made under section 10 of the Finance Act 1993;
>
> (b) 'own use' includes use as a personal gift but does not include the transfer of the goods to another person for money or money's worth (including any reimbursement of expenses incurred in connection with obtaining them).
>
> (6) Paragraphs (1) and (2) do not apply—
>
> (a) where the excise duty point and the person liable to pay the duty are prescribed by the Excise Goods (Sales on Board Ships and Aircraft) Regulations 1999; or
>
> (b) in the case of chewing tobacco.

For further on the minimum indicative levels, see para 23.29 below.

### Importations for a commercial purpose

Excise duty only becomes payable if the goods are being imported for a commercial purpose **23.11** (ie for onward sale or for money's worth or for profit). Article 32(1) of Council Directive (EC) 2008/118 ('the 2008 Directive') provides:

> Excise duty on excise goods acquired by a private individual for his own use, and transported from one Member State to another by him, shall be charged only in the Member State in which the excise goods are acquired.

As a result, the Regulations confirm that duty and tax must be paid on the goods in the Member State in which they are acquired.

In *Hoverspeed* [2003] 2 WLR 950, the Court of Appeal held that either goods were held for **23.12** personal use within the meaning of the then Directive or they were held for a commercial purpose. This was followed in the Divisional Court case of *Customs and Excise Commissioners v Newbury* [2003] 2 All ER 964; [2003] 1 WLR 2131.

These decisions were applied to the subsequent and similarly worded 2008 Directive and **23.13** 2010 Regulations by the Divisional Court (Laws LJ and Swift J) in *William Stern v UKBA* (unreported 23 January 2013). The Court dismissed a case stated appeal from the magistrates' court and held that a person is required to travel with the goods and be present at the time of importation in order to qualify under reg 13(3)(b) of the 2010 Regulations and Art 32 of the 2008 Directive. On the facts of the case Mr Stern had paid for a large quantity of wine which was going to be distributed for friends and family as gifts and therefore on a non-commercial basis. However, he sent his driver to pick up and transport the wine to the UK and therefore he was not present at the time of importation. As a result, the goods were not 'transported from one Member State to another by him' and therefore the wine was held for a commercial purpose under the definition in Art 32(1) and reg 13(3) and therefore he was liable to pay excise duty upon importation. Laws LJ did, however, make obiter remarks about the potential effects of proportionality and disability discrimination in an appropriate case.

### Civil proceedings

Actions for forfeiture and condemnation are actions *in rem* (against the property as opposed **23.14** to the individual). Nobody stands in jeopardy and the action is by way of complaint heard, in the first instance, usually before a magistrates' court.

Paragraph 8 of Sch 3 to CEMA confirms that the proceedings are civil, and this was further **23.15** confirmed in both *Goldsmith v Customs and Excise Commissioners* The Times, 12 June 2001 and *Mudie v Kent Magistrates' Court* [2003] EWHC (Civ) 237, 2 All ER 631, where the Courts held that condemnation matters do not involve the determination of a criminal charge and that none of the usual consequences of a criminal conviction apply. As a result Art 6 of the ECHR has little application.

This is therefore one of the rare examples of the magistrates' court's civil jurisdiction, and **23.16** because the proceedings are civil, the burden of proof is on the 'balance of probabilities' and not the higher criminal test of 'beyond reasonable doubt'. Civil rules of evidence apply, including the admissibility of hearsay evidence, and there is no necessity for compliance with PACE 1984.

### The legislative scheme

**23.17** The Excise Goods, Beer and Tobacco Products (Amendment) Regulations 2002, SI 2002/2692 came into force on 1 December 2002. They sought to correct any deficiency in the previous Regulations by amending the Excise Goods (Holding, Movement, Warehousing, and REDS) Regulations 1992, SI 2002/3135, to insert a specific provision in relation to 'own use':

> (1A) In the case of excise goods acquired by a person in another member State for his own use and transported by him to the United Kingdom, the excise duty point is the time when those goods are held or used for a commercial purpose by any person.

In other words, excise duty only becomes payable on the goods when they are held for a commercial purpose, or at the point in time when they become held or are used for a commercial purpose. This applies to both the traveller who imported them and/or by any other person who has possession or control of them.

**23.18** SI 2002/2692 also amended the Beer Regulations 1993, SI 1993/1228 and the Tobacco Products Regulations 2001, SI 2001/1712 in identical terms.

**23.19** The effect of these amendments was to reassert that goods being brought into the UK for a traveller's 'own use' were not subject to excise duty. The aim was to ensure that goods purchased on cross-border shopping trips for an individual's own personal use are not subject to the payment of any excise duty (see the Divisional Court's judgment in *R (Hoverspeed) v Customs and Excise Commissioners* [2002] 4 All ER 912 at paras 107–9).

**23.20** In December 2008 EC Directive (EC) 2008/118, which covers general arrangements for products subject to excise duty (and the holding, movement and monitoring of such products), was introduced to replace Council Directive (EEC) No 92/12.

### Gifts

**23.21** The Excise Goods (Holding, Movement and Duty Point) Regulations 2010 (SI 593/2010) provide that 'own use' includes use as a personal gift (reg 13(5)(b)). It is therefore permissible for a traveller to bring in larger than expected consignments of excise goods if he intends to give them away as personal gifts. Much will depend on the credibility of the traveller's story, the likelihood of the assertion, and the evidence the traveller is able to produce to support the claim.

### Transfers for money's worth

**23.22** Regulation 13(5)(b) of the Excise Goods (Holding, Movement and Duty Point) Regulations 2010 states that:

> 'own use'...does not include the transfer of the goods to another person for money or money's worth (including any reimbursement of expenses incurred in connection with obtaining them).

This provision has the effect of catching any importation where the goods concerned are passed on in return for any payment, including any travel expenses. The transaction does not have to be for profit (indeed the legislation is broad enough to cover receiving payment at a loss), and it does not need to be for money, eg payment as a 'thank you' such as a dinner out would make the transfer 'commercial'.

## What factors define 'commercial purpose'?

Regulation 13(4)(a)–(j) of the Excise Goods (Holding, Movement and Duty Point) **23.23**
Regulations 2010 sets out a list of matters that *must* be taken into account by both HMRC/
UKBA and, ultimately, the court in making their determination as to whether the goods in
question were being imported for a commercial purpose. These considerations are:

(a) the person's reasons for having possession or control of the goods;
(b) whether or not the person is a revenue trader (as defined in s 1(1) of CEMA 1979);
(c) the person's conduct, including his intended use of the goods or any refusal to disclose
   his intended use of the goods;
(d) the location of the goods;
(e) the mode of transport used to convey the goods;
(f) any document or other information whatsoever relating to the goods;
(g) the nature of the goods, including the nature and condition of any package or container;
(h) the quantity of the goods, and in particular whether the quantity exceeds the guideline
   quantities (see para 23.29 below);
(i) whether the person personally financed the purchase of the goods in question; and
(j) any other circumstance which appears to be relevant.

Revenue traders, in the context of (b) above, are persons carrying on a trade or business **23.24**
involving the buying, selling, importation, exportation, or dealing in or handling of excise
goods. If the person importing the goods had an obvious outlet through which he could sell
the goods then that would be a matter that the court/Customs may wish to take account of.

Regard should particularly be given to (h), the quantity of the goods. If an individual is **23.25**
importing into the UK 10,000 cigarettes, there is a strong inference that they will not all be
for personal use, although that inference may be rebutted if the individual is a heavy smoker,
rarely travels abroad, or has sufficient means or another legitimate non-commercial reason
for bringing the cigarettes in, eg gifts for family members at Christmas. It should further be
noted that under (j) this list is not intended to be exhaustive.

In *R v Customs and Excise Commissioners ex p Mortimer* [1999] 1 WLR 17 the Court held **23.26**
that Customs officers must take account of the above reasons when considering whether or
not they should seize goods. As a result, in practice, a short interview will take place at the
initial point of interception.

In *Mortimer* Lord Bingham stated at p 22: **23.27**

> . . . fairness demands that the importer has a fair opportunity to satisfy the Customs & Excise,
> despite the quantity of the goods involved, that he is not importing them for a commercial
> purpose. It is plain that the Customs & Excise have no discretion whether or not to give such
> a fair opportunity: it is something they must do.

*Mortimer* was decided under the now defunct Excise Duties (Personal Reliefs) Order 1992.
As a result the mandatory presumption referred to therein no longer applies. Under the
revised regulations, the fact that the goods in question now exceed the Minimum Indicative
Levels (the quantity guidelines) is something which HMRC/UKBA and the court are merely
entitled to have 'regard to'. The assertion, however, that the importer must have a 'fair opportunity' to satisfy HMRC/UKBA of his case remains, it is submitted, good law.

**23.28**   In the Divisional Court's judgment of *R (Hoverspeed) v Customs and Excise Commissioners* [2002] 4 All ER 912, Brooke LJ stated that 'if no satisfactory explanation is forthcoming, then the national official may well conclude that the goods were indeed held for "commercial purposes" '. Refusal to provide an explanation, or a misleading explanation, may therefore both be factors that a court may take into account in deciding the issues it has to determine.

### What are the Minimum Indicative Levels?

**23.29**   The 'Minimum Indicative Level' is now a fairly dated term that relates to the guideline quantities set by the EU.

**23.30**   From October 2011, when travelling within the EU the quantities were:

- 10 litres of spirits;
- 90 litres of wine (including a maximum of 60 litres of sparkling wine);
- 20 litres of 'intermediate products';
- 110 litres of beer;
- 800 cigarettes (prior to 1 October 2011 this was 3,200 cigarettes);
- 400 cigarillos;
- 200 cigars; and
- 1kg of any other tobacco products (prior to 1 October 2011 this was 3kg).

**23.31**   The current minimum indicative levels (as amended on 1 October 2011), are contained in reg 13(4)(h) of the Excise Goods (Holding, Movement and Duty Point) Regulations 2010 and mirror the minimum levels that may be adopted by Member States by implementing in UK legislation Art 32(3)(a) of the EU Council Directive 2008/118/EC.

**23.32**   Whilst they are not defined in Council Directive (EC) 2008/118, 'Intermediate Products' are defined in Art 17(1) of Council Directive (EC) 92/83. They include fortified wine, sherry, and port.

**23.33**   It should be emphasised that these levels are only a guide. As distinct from the purchase of 'duty free' goods from non-EU countries, there are no limits. Genuine shoppers are entitled to bring back greater quantities for their own use. Nor is it unheard of for bootleggers to bring back quantities below the guidelines or matching the guidelines, in an attempt to avoid having their goods seized. In *Harrison v Revenue and Customs Commissioners* (2007), The Times, 8 January 2007, Lightman J held that where quantities less than the prescribed amount were brought into the UK, they could still lawfully be seized where there were ample other circumstances that justified Customs' decision.

**23.34**   It should further be noted:

- if a traveller has over these amounts he should declare the goods in the red channel;
- if the importer is under seventeen the tobacco and alcohol allowances do not apply (ie there are no allowances);
- on transfer flights to other EU countries, it is only necessary to declare what is in hand luggage. Hold baggage contents need only be declared at the final destination;
- from certain EU countries (namely Estonia, Bulgaria, Lithuania, and Romania) other limits currently apply.

**Travelling to the UK from outside the EU**

Similar (albeit more restrictive) levels exist when travelling from a non-EU country (includ- **23.35** ing the Canary Islands and the Channel Islands). Gibraltar is part of the EU, but is outside the EU customs territory, and therefore the 'outside the EU' levels apply. Similarly, although Cyprus is a member of the EU, any importation from an area not deemed under the control of the Government of the Republic of Cyprus is treated as a non-EU import. From 1 January 2010 the 'outside the EU' levels were:

- 200 cigarettes or 100 cigarillos or 50 cigars or 250g of tobacco;
- 4 litres of still table wine;
- 16 litres of beer;
- 1 litre of spirits or strong liqueurs over 22% in volume or 2 litres of fortified wine, sparkling wine or other liqueurs;
- £390 worth of other goods, including perfumes, gifts, and souvenirs.

(See Travellers' Allowances Order 1994 (SI 1994/955) as amended by the Travellers' Allowances (Amendment) Order 2008 (SI 2008/3058) and the Travellers' Allowances (Amendment) Order 2009 (SI 2009/3172).)

## C. Detention, Seizure, and Condemnation

Section 139 of CEMA details the provisions as to detention, seizure, and condemnation of **23.36** goods. Section 139(6) refers to Sch 3 to the Act as having effect for the purpose of forfeiture and condemnation proceedings.

### The forfeiture provisions

Schedule 3 to CEMA sets out the relevant provisions relating to forfeiture, including notice **23.37** of seizure, notice of claim, and condemnation. Paragraph 7 of Sch 3 states that the forfeiture shall have effect as from the date when the liability to forfeiture arose.

### What does 'liable to forfeiture' mean?

Whilst the expression 'liable to forfeiture' is littered throughout the relevant forfeiture Acts **23.38** and statutory provisions, it is not a defined term within the 1979 Act. Accordingly it should be understood by its ordinary and natural meaning. It is submitted that 'liable to forfeiture' denotes something different from 'shall be forfeited' or 'shall automatically be forfeited'. 'Liable' implies some form of discretion by those considering forfeiture, either at the time of seizure or later by a court.

However, that initial elasticity may be somewhat illusory. Paragraph 6 of Sch 3 to CEMA **23.39** states that if the court finds that the thing was at the time of seizure 'liable to forfeiture', the court shall condemn it as forfeit. The draconian nature of these provisions appears to be analogous to strict liability/absolute offences in the criminal sphere, where intention or state of mind becomes irrelevant. This was confirmed in the case of *De Keyser v British Railway Traffic and Electric Co Ltd* [1936] 1 KB 224, where it was held that the justices were bound to condemn prohibited goods and that they possessed no discretion to refuse to do so, eg on the grounds of hardship of an innocent owner.

**23.40**  While Sch 3(6) offers no discretion, it must now be read in the light of recent decisions, particularly *Customs and Excise Commissioners v Newbury* [2003] 2 All ER 964; [2003] 1 WLR 2131, where arguments in terms of proportionality when condemning a vehicle, as well as the goods seized, were successfully raised. The meaning of 'liable to forfeiture' was considered at length by the Court of Appeal in the context of s 139 of CEMA in *Eastenders Cash & Carry Plc and others v The Commissioners of Her Majesty's Revenue & Customs* [2012] EWCA Civ 15, 1 WLR 2067. In considering the wording of s 139 of CEMA, Mummery LJ stated (at para 46):

> … in ordinary English usage, the description of things as 'liable to forfeiture' is, subject to its context, capable of a meaning wider than just the actual satisfaction of a set of specific pre-existing conditions for forfeiture. It would be an accurate use of English to describe a thing as being 'liable to' certain consequences, such as an unwanted sanction or obligation, in specified circumstances, even where those circumstances have not yet been established as fact. 'Liable to' is capable of covering a more general state of affairs of exposure or susceptibility to the possibility or risk of unwanted consequences.

Elias LJ supported this suggestion: 'I accept that the phrase "liable to forfeiture" may, depending on the context, mean no more than "at risk of forfeiture by the court"' (para 82). The Court of Appeal's judgment confirmed that the question of whether goods are 'liable to forfeiture' is an objective question of fact and will involve officers/the court assessing whether there has been a breach of the relevant obligation. HMRC's appeal in this matter has been granted permission, and the appeal is due to take place in November 2013. In *Revenue & Customs Commissioners v First Stop Wholesale Ltd* [2013] EWCA Civ 183 the Court of Appeal held that pending the *Eastenders* appeals to the Supreme Court, the court was bound by the *Eastenders* decisions, finding goods could be liable to forfeiture on grounds which were not advanced or even known at the point of seizure or detention.

### Secondary forfeiture

**23.41**  Section 141(1) of CEMA states where anything has become liable to forfeiture under the Customs & Excise Acts:

> (a) any ship, aircraft, vehicle, animal, container (including any article of passengers' baggage) or other thing which has been used for the carriage, handling or concealment of the thing so liable to forfeiture, either at a time when it was so liable or for the purposes of the commission of the offence for which it later became so liable; and
> (b) any other thing mixed, packed or found with the thing so liable,
>
> shall also be liable to forfeiture.

This section once again highlights the draconian nature of the forfeiture provisions by setting out the consequences for property found and used in connection with goods liable to forfeiture—hence the term 'secondary forfeiture'.

**23.42**  Any vehicle used in the transportation of excise goods where no duty has been paid will itself be liable to forfeiture. Many travellers' motorcars have been forfeited as a result. Similarly, smaller quantities of goods that accompany larger importations of eg tobacco or cigarettes are themselves liable. By way of example: where 60,000 cigarettes are being imported, together with 3 litres of gin and 1 litre of Bacardi, although the 3 litres of gin and the 1 litre of Bacardi may understandably be considered for personal use, because of s 141 and the provision as to any other thing mixed, packed, or found with the thing so liable, the spirits also become liable to forfeiture.

In *Travell v Customs and Excise Commissioners* (1997) 162 JP 181 the Divisional Court held **23.43** that s 141(a) and (b) are to be read disjunctively.

The reference to 'any other thing' should be interpreted to include only things of a like kind. **23.44** By way of example; where 90 kg of hand-rolling tobacco are discovered in the suitcase of an individual, together with his travel alarm clock, the alarm clock is not an excise good, nor sufficiently similar to justify its forfeiture (see *R v Uxbridge Magistrates' ex p Webb* (1998) 162 JP 198 (DC)).

The application of the 'mixed, packed or found' rule must always be a question of fact and **23.45** degree upon which the court must find. This is illustrated by *Travell*, where the Crown Court held that 365 obscene magazines found 'all over the defendant's one bedroom flat' were also liable to forfeiture because they had been 'found with' fifteen imported magazines containing indecent pictures of children. In *Webb* (above) the defendant had imported six obscene videos in a suitcase. The magistrates fast forwarded through two of them and concluded that their content was obscene and that they were liable to forfeiture. They condemned all six videos on the basis that the other four were 'packed with' the two videos that had been viewed.

In *Customs and Excise Commissioners v Jack Bradley (Accrington) Ltd* [1959] 1 QB 219, the **23.46** court held that where kerosene oil had been discovered in the fuel tanks of vehicles, the vehicles themselves would be liable to forfeiture since they had been 'used for the carriage' of the oil.

### More than one person involved

Where excise goods belonging to two people are seized as being liable to forfeiture, the fact **23.47** that one of them makes no claim under Sch 3 cannot trigger the operation of s 141(1)(b) of the Act so as to preclude the other person from arguing that none of the goods were liable to forfeiture. In *Fox v Customs and Excise Commissioners*, The Times, 20 July 2002, Lightman J held:

> As a matter of common sense and as a matter of common justice it must be open to the owner of the seized goods (in this case Mr. Fox) to challenge the facts relied on to establish the liability to forfeiture of the other party's (in this case Mr. Everett) goods. It adds nothing to the point that the other party (in this case Mr. Everett) declined to make a claim or attend the hearing.

Transfers for money's worth and the gift provisions are considered above.

### Proof of other matters

Section 154 of CEMA deals with proof of certain other matters. Section 154(1) states: **23.48**

> An averment in any process in proceedings under the Revenue and Customs Acts—
>    (a) that those proceedings were instituted by the Order of the Commissioners
>    ...
> shall, until the contrary is proved, be sufficient evidence of the matter in question;
> (2) Where in any proceedings relating to Revenue and Customs any question arises as to the place in which any goods have been brought as to whether or not—
>    (a) any duty has been paid or secured in respect of any goods
>    ...
> then,... the burden of proof shall lie upon the other party to the proceedings.

**Stops at Coquelles**

**23.49**  British UKBA officers also operate in Coquelles, France as a result of agreements reached in relation to the Channel Tunnel. As a result, condemnation law also applies to this 'satellite port' pursuant to the Channel Tunnel (Alcoholic Liquor and Tobacco Products) Order 2010, SI 2010/594.

## D.  Condemnation: Practice and Procedure

**Initial seizure**

**23.50**  In the case of *R v Customs and Excise Commissioners ex p Mortimer* [1999] 1 WLR 17, it was determined that:

- fairness required Customs officers to give the importer a full opportunity to satisfy them that the importation was not for a commercial purpose and to alert the traveller to the consequences of his failure to take that opportunity;
- officers were obliged to make plain the purpose of any interview they conducted;
- where their purpose was both to investigate the possible commission of crime and to form a judgement for the purposes of forfeiture, they were required to inform the suspect accordingly (including cautioning him and informing him of his right to remain silent in respect of the criminal investigation);
- officers should explain that under the forfeiture regulations, in the absence of a satisfactory explanation of the traveller's intentions, the goods might be seized.

**23.51**  In *Mortimer*, the Court held that giving the traveller a fair opportunity meant two things:

(1)  that the importer must have a full opportunity to say anything he wanted about his intentions in relation to the goods with a view to showing that his intentions were non-commercial, because he proposed to use them himself or give them to friends or relations as the case may be; and

(2)  that he must be alerted to the possible consequences if he does not take advantage of the opportunity to satisfy Customs that the goods are not being imported for a commercial purpose.

This should mean, in practice, that he is told in general terms of the existence of the Guideline quantities and of the consequence that the goods will be seized if HMRC/UKBA are not satisfied with the explanation they are given. In *Revenue and Customs Commissioners v First Stop Wholesale Ltd* [2013] EWCA Civ 183 the Court held that it was not a pre-condition of lawful seizure that the UKBA explain the reasons for the seizure at the time.

**23.52**  These requirements are usually adhered to when the HMRC/UKBA officer reads to the traveller what is sometimes referred to as the 'Commerciality Statement', which states:

You have excise goods in your possession (control) which appear not to have borne UK duty.

Goods may be held without payment of duty providing they have been acquired and are held for your own use. I suspect that you may be holding goods for a commercial purpose and not for your own use. I intend to ask you some questions to establish whether these goods are held for a commercial purpose.

If no satisfactory explanation is forthcoming or if you do not stay for questioning it may lead me to conclude that the goods are not held for your own use but held for a commercial purpose and your goods (and vehicle) may be seized as liable to forfeiture.

You are not under arrest and are free to leave at any time. Do you understand?

If 'yes', the officer will proceed with a short interview dealing with the relevant issues in reg 13(4) of the Excise Goods (Holding, Movement and Duty Point) Regulations 2010 (SI 2010/593), or explain the Commerciality Statement again. The person intercepted will also be issued with a Notice 1, which sets out the guideline amounts.

It is submitted that best practice dictates that a note of any conversation should be made, **23.53** preferably contemporaneously. The Commerciality Statement should be used and referred to in any statement made by the stopping officer, along with Notice 1, which should be handed to the traveller, preferably before questioning, with the opportunity being given to read it.

The case of *R v Customs and Excise Commissioners ex p Kenneth Stephen Boxall* (15 February **23.54** 1996) (CO 1902/95) although decided before the 1999 amendment, is useful in confirming the procedure for how travellers found with excise goods in their possession should be treated. It repeats that HMRC/UKBA must give the importer the opportunity to tell them why he has the goods in his possession, what he intends to do with them, and produce any document that relates to them. All of this must be done before they make any determination about whether to seize the goods in question as liable to forfeiture (see p 4F of the judgment). It should be emphasised, as it was in *Boxall*, that natural justice obliges HMRC/UKBA to give the person concerned an opportunity to satisfy them that the goods were not imported for a commercial purpose. Not to do so would render the seizing of any excise goods unlawful. Further, in *R (on the application of Blackside Ltd) v Secretary of State for the Home Department* [2013] EWHC 2087 (Admin) the Court held the Border Forces' practice of not sending a notice of seizure when goods were seized and the owner was not present as 'deplorable' and had to stop. (See also *Pash v Revenue and Customs Commissioners* [2013] UKFTT 100 (TC)).

### Possible criminal proceedings

Section 139 of CEMA anticipates the possibility of criminal proceedings. There is the scope **23.55** for charging individuals with an offence of evading duty contrary to s 170(1) and (2) of CEMA or the common law offence of cheating the Revenue. Within the statutory scheme each offence is punishable by up to seven years' imprisonment. If such proceedings are contemplated the codes and regulations set out in PACE 1984 should be followed.

However, it should be noted that for the purposes of a forfeiture hearing, a failure to follow **23.56** PACE is not fatal, as the jurisdiction is civil and therefore falls outside of PACE's remit.

In *Mortimer*, Lord Bingham identified the practical difficulty Revenue and Customs officers **23.57** may find themselves in if they were also investigating the possible commission of a crime. In such circumstances they would be obliged to caution the suspect and that would include the suspect being told that he does not have to say anything. The converse problem is that when dealing with the forfeiture aspect of the seizure, the importer is being actively encouraged to say anything that he wants to about the goods with a view to showing that his intentions are non-commercial. Lord Bingham said there was no entirely simple answer to this practical problem. It would be incumbent on the interviewing officers to make plain the purposes of any interview and, if and when there are two purposes, to explain them both. There must be no watering down of the caution, nor must there be any watering down of the officers' duties in respect of warning the traveller about his failure to not take advantage of the opportunity to satisfy Customs that the goods are not being imported for a commercial purpose.

In *R v Payton* [2006] EWCA Crim 1226, the Court emphasised that nothing must be done **23.58** in civil proceedings that might prejudice the outcome of criminal proceedings. Thus if forfeiture proceedings are initiated it will generally be prudent to adjourn them pending the outcome of the criminal proceedings.

### Notice of claim—the one-month time limit to appeal

**23.59**   Schedule 3 to CEMA states, at para 3, that:

> ...any person claiming that anything seized as liable to forfeiture is not so liable shall within one month of the date of notice of seizure or, where no such notice has been served on him, within one month of the date of the seizure, give notice of his claim in writing to the Commissioners at any office of Revenue and Customs.

**23.60**   Paragraph 4 of the same Schedule states that any notice under para 3 should specify the name and address of the claimant and, in the case of a claimant who is outside the UK, shall specify the name and address of a solicitor in the UK who is authorised to accept service of process and to act on behalf of the claimant. For delay in issuing the Notice of Seizure by the UKBA, see *R (on the Application of Blackside Ltd) v Secretary of State for the Home Department* [2013] EWHC 2087 Admin.

### Six-month time limit on HMRC/UKBA once notice lodged

**23.61**   Paragraph 6 of Sch 3 to CEMA states that where a notice of claim in respect of anything is duly given in accordance with paras 3 and 4 of the same Schedule, the Commissioners shall take proceedings for the condemnation of that thing, and if the court finds that the thing was at the time of seizure liable to forfeiture, the court shall condemn it as forfeited.

**23.62**   Accordingly, s 127 of the MCA states:

> ...a magistrates' court shall not try an information or hear a complaint unless the information was laid, or the complaint made, within 6 months from the time when the offence was committed.

**23.63**   In *Customs and Excise Commissioners v Venn*, The Times, 24 January 2002, the Divisional Court held that CEMA drew a distinction between the detention of goods and the provisions of Sch 3 in respect of forfeiture. Forfeiture depended on there being a seizure of the goods. Where a person gave notice under paras 3 and 4 of Sch 3 claiming that goods seized as liable to forfeiture were not so liable, it was incumbent on the Commissioners to take proceedings for the condemnation of that thing by a court; and where such proceedings were instituted by way of a complaint in a magistrates' court, time ran for the purposes of s 127 of the MCA from the date of service of the notice, not from the date of seizure.

### Preparation for the hearing—service of evidence

**23.64**   There are no rules for service of evidence in the magistrates' court in respect of civil complaints. In the absence of such rules the court is able to regulate its own procedure (*Simms v Moore* [1970] 3 All ER 1). If relevant, all evidence is admissible, unless excluded by some other rule.

**23.65**   Prior to the hearing of any application for forfeiture at the magistrates' court, it is open to HMRC/UKBA to either make voluntary disclosure of the evidence upon which it seeks to rely, or, by correspondence with the defence, to ask for and arrange mutual and simultaneous disclosure.

**23.66**   Voluntary disclosure is useful in cases where, eg, the issues are straightforward, little is challenged, or where the witness in question, giving the statement, is unavailable to attend court. It enables his evidence to be agreed prior to the hearing.

**23.67**   Mutual disclosure can equally be of assistance where the issues are not straightforward and matters are challenged, so as to expedite matters at court and crystallise the arguments. This entails HMRC/UKBA and the other side coming to an agreement whereby Customs will serve their case, ie statements, exhibits, interviews, etc, in return for the appellant revealing his case to HMRC/UKBA, including witness statements he seeks to rely upon. This has the advantage of both parties knowing what the other will say before the case comes to court, and avoids ambushes and costly adjournments.

### Preparation for the hearing—dutiable goods

In *Boxall* (p 6E), the court held that para 6 of Sch 3 made it clear that it is for the court to  **23.68** consider whether the thing seized was at the time liable to forfeiture. Read with s 49(1), para 6 obliges the court to decide whether the goods are dutiable. On this question, the burden of proof lies on HMRC/UKBA and, with the proceedings being civil, the court must be satisfied on the balance of probabilities (in the majority of cases there is little issue over the fact that the goods are dutiable, as they generally relate to excise products like cigarettes and tobacco).

### The hearing—commercial purpose v own use

It will be incumbent upon the court to consider the evidence and determine the issue: namely  **23.69** whether the goods were imported for a commercial purpose, or for personal use.

In so doing they should consider the criteria set out in reg 13(4) of the Excise Goods  **23.70** (Holding, Movement and Duty Point) Regulations 2010 (SI 2010/593). The inclusion of 'any other circumstance that appears to be relevant' covers a multitude of matters, including frequency of travel. For example, an individual who travels abroad frequently does not need to 'stock up' on duty goods such as cigarettes, because he knows he will have the opportunity to purchase more cigarettes on his next trip. Similarly, an individual who makes regular day trips with the sole purpose of bringing back excise goods may have difficulty persuading a court it is not for a commercial purpose, particularly if, for example, he does not smoke heavily, or is purchasing a variety of brands of cigarettes (smokers tend to stick to the same brand), or if he is using a hire car (in the knowledge that it will avoid his own vehicle being seized).

The court may also consider whether the defendant has been stopped before, or had  **23.71** knowledge of the guideline amounts, whether there had been any attempt to hide or conceal the items in question, and whether the traveller's story had changed since the initial stop.

Conversely, if the 'aggravating' matters outlined above do not feature in the defendant's case,  **23.72** or, for example, he has receipts for the purchases, it is a first time stop, and he has verification that the goods are intended for a family party or similar, the court may consider that the importation lacks commerciality.

As has already been observed, the wording of the provisions are mandatory, akin to a strict  **23.73** liability offence, and no discretion is afforded to the court in relation to the goods themselves if the court is satisfied on the balance of probabilities they were imported for a commercial purpose, as per *Fox v Customs and Excise Commissioners* (2002) 166 JP 578 at para 16, where Lightman J held: '...the statutory language is mandatory: where the goods are liable to forfeiture the Court is bound to condemn them'.

However, in relation to secondary forfeiture under s 141, eg a traveller's vehicle, the court  **23.74** is entitled to reach its independent judgment on proportionality, weighing up the evidence and the facts. In *Customs and Excise Commissioners v Newbury* [2003] 2 All ER 964; [2003] 1 WLR 2131, para 35, the court held:

> ... whether forfeiture would be so disproportionate as to be in breach of the particular claimant's rights under Article 1, Protocol 1 to the Convention ... can be resolved by the court. This is not strictly a question of discretion but a matter upon which the court is entitled to reach its own independent judgment.

**23.75** In *Revenue and Customs Commissioners v Berriman and Teeside Combined Court* [2007] 4 All ER 925; [2008] 1 WLR 2171 Customs sought, unsuccessfully, to challenge the finding in *Newbury* by arguing it had erroneously expanded the jurisdiction of the magistrates' court and was leading to unmanageable results (para 32). The court concluded that these arguments had 'much merit', but that *Berriman* was not the case in which to raise them. It found that it was bound by *Newbury*, and that the issues raised would be for a higher court to determine authoritatively (para 36).

**23.76** A useful summary of the statutory procedures to be followed is found in the judgment of Lightman J in *Fox v Commissioners of Customs and Excise* [2003] 1 WLR 1331 at 9–11.

### Court procedure: preliminary matters

**23.77** Paragraph 10(1) and (3) of Sch 3 to CEMA requires the claimant of the goods, ie the defendant, to swear on oath that the thing seized was, or was to the best of his knowledge and belief, his property at the time of the seizure (his solicitor may also take the oath on his behalf for the purposes of this section). Paragraph 10(3) states that if any part of that procedure is not complied with, the court shall (implying must) give judgment for the Commissioners.

**23.78** This means that if the defendant is not prepared to state on oath that the goods seized in fact belonged to him and were his property, then the application for forfeiture on behalf of HMRC/UKBA will succeed. It is advisable that para 10(1) of Sch 3 to CEMA be dealt with at the outset of proceedings, because it may be considered pointless to sit through an entire case if the defendant was not prepared to swear on oath that the goods belonged to him or, alternatively, that he declared that the goods belonged to another for whom he was acting.

**23.79** In giving judgment for HMRC/UKBA in such circumstances, the court will not have considered the facts of the matter. It in effect becomes condemnation by default. A question therefore arises whether or not s 141 would apply, it only having application where there is a finding that the goods are liable to forfeiture. In such circumstances it will be necessary to invite the court to consider the facts and decide whether any of the goods were so liable, in order for the secondary forfeiture provisions of s 141 to bite (see *Fox v Customs and Excise Commissioners* (2002) 166 JP 578).

### Court procedure: condemnation by complaint

**23.80** The procedural rules in relation to the hearing of a complaint and the jurisdiction of the magistrates' court are set out at s 51 et seq of the MCA.

**23.81** Section 52 confirms jurisdiction; s 53 deals with procedure and states that at the hearing of a complaint, the court shall, if the defendant appears, state to him the substance of the complaint; s 54 sets out the adjournment provisions, which may take place 'at any time'; and s 55 confirms that if a defendant does not appear the court may proceed in his absence. Similarly, under s 56 where at the time and place appointed for the hearing or adjourned hearing of a complaint the defendant appears but the complainant does not, the court may dismiss the complaint or, if evidence has been received on a previous occasion, proceed in the absence of the complainant. Section 57 states that where neither party attends, the court may dismiss the complaint; and s 58 deals with the transfer of proceedings.

### Order of speeches

Once ownership of the goods has been established, the procedure to be followed is set out in the Magistrates' Court Rules 1981, r 14, as follows: **23.82**

(i) On the hearing of a complaint, the complainant shall call his evidence and before doing so may address the court.
(ii) At the conclusion of the evidence, for the complainant, the defendant may address the court, whether or not he afterwards calls evidence.
(iii) At the conclusion of the evidence, if any, for the defence, the complainant may call evidence to rebut that evidence.
(iv) At the conclusion of the evidence for the defence and the evidence, if any, in rebuttal, the defendant may address the court if he has not already done so.
(v) Either party may, with the leave of the court, address the court a second time, but where the court grants leave to one party, it shall not refuse leave to the other.
(vi) Where the defendant obtains leave to address the court for a second time, his second address shall be made before the second address, if any, of the complainant.

It follows from the above that HMRC/UKBA only have one opportunity to address the court on the facts without further leave; and that is at the beginning of their case. **23.83**

It should be noted that either party may, with the leave of the court, address the court a second time or, as in any proceedings, either party may address the court on a point of law at any stage. **23.84**

Although the defendant is free to make a submission of no case to answer after the applicant's case, some caution should be exercised, because if it fails and the defendant has been asked to choose between calling evidence and making a submission, he will not be entitled to call evidence thereafter. See *Boyce v Wyatt Engineering*, The Times, 14 June 2001. **23.85**

It should also be noted that HMRC/UKBA have the opportunity to call evidence in rebuttal should they wish to do so. This may occur in forfeiture cases where something has been suggested during the course of the defence case that is either new or was not put to the officer in the case at the first opportunity, and where the officer in the case believes that that aspect of the defence's case needs correcting. **23.86**

### The burden and standard of proof

It is for HMRC/UKBA to satisfy the court, on the balance of probabilities, that the goods were imported for a commercial purpose (*R (Hoverspeed) v Customs and Excise Commissioners* [2002] 4 All ER 912 (DC) para 130/10). **23.87**

It is useful when addressing the court to remind it that it is sitting in its civil jurisdiction and that the burden of proof is that of the 'balance of probabilities' and not that with which it may be more familiar, namely 'beyond reasonable doubt'. **23.88**

### Hearsay in civil cases

The Magistrates' Courts (Hearsay Evidence in Civil Proceedings) Rules 1999, SI 1999/681 set out the rules applying to hearsay in magistrates' courts. **23.89**

**23.90**   These Rules make provision for:

- the procedure to call a witness for cross-examination on hearsay evidence (r 4);
- a notice requirement where a party tenders hearsay evidence but does not call the person who made the statement to give oral evidence, and another party wishes to attack the credibility of the person who made the statement or allege that he has made another statement inconsistent with it (r 5);
- the service of documents required by the Rules (r 6).

**23.91**   However, a failure to comply with the duty to give notice should not affect the admissibility of hearsay evidence (see s 1(1) of the Civil Evidence Act 1995 and s 1(2) which is specifically adopted by r 2(2)). It then becomes a question of weight for the district judge/justices to determine. In assessing the weight, all the relevant circumstances should be considered, including the fact that the individual who made the statement has not been tendered for cross-examination and his evidence has not been tested. The desirability of serving a hearsay notice is obvious as a party may find itself liable for costs if a witness statement tendered at the hearing reveals new evidence that the other side has not had the opportunity of exploring, or fresh evidence that amounts to an ambush.

**23.92**   Section 4(2) of the Civil Evidence Act 1995 gives some guidance that may assist the court when assessing what weight should be given to hearsay evidence. That guidance includes:

(a) whether it would have been reasonable and practicable to have produced the person who made the statements rather than relying on a hearsay report;

(b) whether the person who originally made the statements made them contemporaneously with the matters stated;

(c) whether the evidence is multiple hearsay, in other words whether the hearsay witness is in fact repeating something which itself is hearsay;

(d) whether anyone involved has a motive to conceal or misrepresent matters;

(e) whether the original statement was made for some purpose or produced in collaboration with others;

(f) whether the attempt to rely on hearsay rather than calling the person who made the original statement is designed to prevent a proper valuation of its weight by the court.

**23.93**   In the Crown Court the position is slightly different, although the same principle appears to apply. In *R v Wadmore and Foreman* [2006] EWCA Crim 686, a case that concerned an application for an ASBO, the Court of Appeal held that ASBOs amounted to civil proceedings in a criminal court. The CrimPR do not apply to civil cases. The CPR do not apply in criminal courts. The Magistrates' Courts (Hearsay Evidence in Civil Proceedings) Rules 1999 do not apply to the Crown Court. The Court of Appeal therefore assumed that as the case was civil in nature, hearsay evidence was admissible under s 1 of the Civil Evidence Act 1995. There were no applicable procedural rules and the Court thought that the Magistrates' Court Rules should be applied by analogy.

### Previous convictions

**23.94**   In *R v Halford and Brooks [Senior]*, The Times, 3 October 1991 the Court confirmed that in civil proceedings a different approach to allegations of criminal behaviour may be taken, in that there is no right to silence and evidence of 'bad character' can be admitted (see also *Ali v Best* (1997) 161 JP 399H and *R v Isleworth Crown Court ex p Kevin Marland* (1998) 162 JPR 251).

Previous convictions can be proved by the production of a certificate of conviction, which **23.95** is admissible by virtue of ss 11 and 12 of the Civil Evidence Act 1968 (in force by virtue of the Civil Evidence Act 1968 (Commencement No 1) Order 1968, SI 1968/1734 and not repealed by the Civil Evidence Act 1995).

Where an individual is acquitted in criminal proceedings the evidence of those proceedings **23.96** is admissible (see *Customs and Excise Commissioners v T* (1998) 162 JP 193, citing *Hunter v Chief Constable of West Midlands* [1982] AC 529 (HL)).

### Reasons for stopping the traveller

The only issue before the court is whether the goods were lawfully seized, ie whether **23.97** the goods were held for a commercial purpose or for personal use. The action is against the goods, *in rem*, and not against the individual. Accordingly, the reason why an individual was stopped is not relevant for the purposes of the matter the court has to decide. Similarly, the seizure of the goods cannot be regarded as axiomatically invalid, merely because it occurred as a result of a check that was invalid or unlawful. See *Customs and Excise Commissioners v Atkinson, Dore and Binns* [2003] EWHC 421 (Admin); *Customs and Excise Commissioners v Newbury* [2003] 2 All ER 964; [2003] 1 WLR 2131 (at para 5); and *Hoverspeed v Customs and Excise Commissioners* [2002] EWCA Civ 1804 at paras 44–9, where the Court of Appeal ruled that no link between the legality of the stop and the legality of any subsequent seizure: '. . . can or should in our view be read into the provisions of CEMA' (para 48). In so finding the court held that it did not 'see any unfairness in the seizure of the goods liable to forfeiture, even though their presence happens only to be discovered in the course of an unlawful check. That may be bad luck, but it is not unfair.'

### Power to stop the traveller

The power of HMRC/UKBA to stop and search an individual and his vehicle derives from **23.98** ss 78, 163A, and 164 of CEMA.

### Court should give reasons

The desirability for a court to give at least some brief reasons for its decision and the necessity **23.99** for the parties to prompt the court to do so if the court failed in this regard, was underlined in *R (on the application of Cleary) v Revenue and Customs Commissioners* [2008] EWHC 1987 (Admin). By giving reasons the court will help the parties understand how the decision has been arrived at and it will give the affected party a better steer when evaluating the merits of an appeal. A failure by the court to provide any or any adequate reasons for its decision may also leave the court open to a potential claim for judicial review.

### Sensitive material

Although PII applications do not ordinarily feature in magistrates' courts, exclusion of evi- **23.100** dence on the grounds of public policy applies equally to civil proceedings as it does in criminal. The test is whether the production of a document or other piece of evidence would be 'injurious to the public interest', ie whether the withholding of a document/information is necessary for the proper functioning of a government department. For example, the disclosure of the document may jeopardise an ongoing operation, or the methods deployed, or cooperation received from others in the investigation of an offence.

# E. Condemnation: Costs and Compensation

### Costs

**23.101**  Under s 64(1) of the MCA:

> (1) On the hearing of a complaint, a Magistrates' Court shall have power in its discretion to make such order as to costs—
>
> > (a) on making the order for which the complaint is made, to be paid by the Defendant to the Complainant;
> >
> > (b) on dismissing the complaint, to be paid by the Complainant to the Defendant,
>
> as it thinks just and reasonable...

Pursuant to s 62(2) the amount ordered to be paid shall be specified in the order and s 62(3) confirms that the costs ordered shall be enforceable as a civil debt, in other words, not administered by the magistrates' court.

**23.102**  It is always advisable to apply for costs on the same day and at the same time as the hearing of the forfeiture application. This is because such an order has to be made by the same district judge/magistrates who made the order in relation to the forfeiture application.

**23.103**  Defence solicitors should advise their clients very cautiously about this aspect of the proceedings for three main reasons:

> (1) HMRC/UKBA often seek their full commercial costs in successful forfeiture proceedings. This will include both legal costs (solicitors and counsel) and court costs, and can amount to several thousand pounds. It will sometimes be advisable to take a commercial view on whether to pursue litigation in cases where the value of the goods is not particularly high or where any prospective costs order is likely to make pursuing the claim prohibitive.
>
> (2) Even if the defendant is successful, it will not necessarily follow that he will obtain a costs award if the court finds that HMRC/UKBA have acted honestly, reasonably, and properly, and in the public interest (*Parinpanathan v City of Westminster Magistrates' Court and 2 others* [2010] EWCA Civ 40).
>
> (3) HMRC/UKBA would be entitled to object to such an order if, for example, the defendant had raised matters in the magistrates' court for the first time in dealing with the application for forfeiture which he had not mentioned, either at the time of seizure or subsequently in correspondence.

**23.104**  In exercising its discretion the court can take into account that HMRC/UKBA are exercising their statutory function in condemnation matters. See *R v Uxbridge Justices ex p Metropolitan Police Commissioner* [1981] 1 QB 829; *Bradford City Metropolitan District Council v Booth*, The Times, 31 May 2000; and *R (Chief Constable of Northamptonshire) v Daventry Magistrates' Court* [2001] EWHC 446 (Admin).

**23.105**  Section 144 of CEMA (see para 23.110) provides a partial 'immunity' to HMRC/UKBA in circumstances arising out of the seizure of goods. 'The immunity will apply to any criminal or civil proceedings and will relieve HMRC/UKBA from having to meet any claim for damages or costs or from being subject to any punishment whenever a court is satisfied that there were reasonable grounds for the seizure...' (*Eastenders Cash & Carry PLC and others v Commissioners for HM Revenue & Customs* [2012] EWCA Civ 15, per Elias LJ at paras 83 and 84. As Davis LJ observed (at para 103), s 144 'provides the protection Parliament has thought fit to confer' (but note, this case is currently under appeal to the Supreme Court and is due to be heard in November 2013).

Importantly, costs must not be used as a device to overcompensate the successful party, or punish the unsuccessful party (*R v Highgate Justices ex p Petrou* [1954] 1 All ER 406). **23.106**

The power of the magistrates' court to make a wasted costs order is governed by s 145A of the MCA. For further information on costs, see para 22.05. **23.107**

### Legal aid funding

Legal Aid Agency funding is not generally available for civil proceedings. Section 6(6) of the AJA does not permit the funding of services within Sch 2, and para 2(3) prohibits the funding of advocacy in any proceedings in the magistrates' court. Condemnation proceedings in both the magistrates' court and the Crown Court therefore appear to be excluded. **23.108**

In *R (Mudie) v Kent Magistrates' Court* [2003] 2 All ER 631, the Court of Appeal confirmed that condemnation proceedings could not be extended to criminal proceedings, and therefore CDS funding was not available, although, as Laws LJ observed in *Mudie*, there was nothing to prevent solicitors entering into conditional fee agreements in condemnation proceedings (para 6). **23.109**

### Compensation

Under s 144 of CEMA: **23.110**

(1) Where, in any proceedings for the condemnation of any thing seized as liable to forfeiture under the customs and excise Acts, judgment is given for the claimant, the court may, if it sees fit, certify that there were reasonable grounds for the seizure.

(2) Where any proceedings, whether civil or criminal, are brought against the Commissioners, a law officer of the Crown or any person authorised by or under the Customs and Excise Acts 1979 to seize or detain any thing liable to forfeiture under the customs and excise Acts on account of the seizure or detention of any thing, and judgment is given for the plaintiff or prosecutor, then if either—

(a) a certificate relating to the seizure has been granted under subsection (1) above; or

(b) the court is satisfied that there were reasonable grounds for seizing or detaining that thing under the customs and excise Acts,

the plaintiff or prosecutor shall not be entitled to recover any damages or costs and the defendant shall not be liable to any punishment.

(3) Nothing in subsection (2) above shall affect any right of any person to the return of the thing seized or detained or to compensation in respect of any damage to the thing or in respect of the destruction thereof.

The plaintiff in such a scenario would be the aggrieved traveller or defendant, who had been successful in the magistrates' court, and now sought compensation. However, if the magistrates' court has certified that, notwithstanding its finding against Customs, the original seizure was nevertheless reasonable, then the aggrieved traveller or defendant will not be able to recover costs or damages in any subsequent compensation proceedings (see para 23.105). **23.111**

In the event of not succeeding with a forfeiture application therefore, HMRC/UKBA will always be anxious to ensure that the 's 144 certificate' as to the reasonableness of their original seizure is signed, so to preclude any claim for compensation. This is equally so where the court has condemned (for example) tobacco, but refused to condemn the vehicle that was used to transport it (secondary forfeiture). **23.112**

**Refund for goods destroyed**

**23.113**   Pursuant to paras 16 and 17 of Sch 3 to CEMA, HMRC/UKBA are entitled to destroy any perishable goods, notwithstanding the fact that they may not yet have been condemned.

**23.114**   If this occurs, by para 17, HMRC/UKBA are required to pay a successful appellant an amount equal to the market value of the thing at the time of its seizure. The 'market value' for these purposes was considered by Stanley Burton J in *R (Revenue and Customs Commissioners) v Machell* [2005] EWHC 2593 (Admin). The market value for the purposes of para 17(1)(c) of tobacco goods imported into the UK for the personal use of the importer and seized and destroyed by Customs pursuant to para 16(b) of the Act was to be taken as the retail price at the time of the seizure of such goods in the country of purchase. It was also held that travel costs were not a recoverable amount under para 17. There was no presumption that para 17 conferred a right to compensation in an amount equal to common law damages, and, if anything, there was a presumption that the amount would be less than common law damages. It will be noted that the Court concluded (at para 26 of the judgment) that para 17 of Sch 3 was only directed towards reimbursement for destroyed *perishable* goods. Goods that were destroyed in error that were not perishable (such as alcohol), or by accident, were therefore not covered.

## F.   Condemnation Appeals

**23.115**   HMRC/UKBA and the defendant may appeal from the magistrates' court decision to the Crown Court, or in the alternative invite the court to state a case for the High Court on a matter of law (see para 11 of Sch 3 to CEMA). The Crown Court's jurisdiction and powers of disposal are set out in ss 45 to 48 of the Senior Courts Act 1981.

**Procedure**

**23.116**   On appeal to the Crown Court the hearing is *de novo* (s 79(3) of the Senior Courts Act 1981) and involves a complete rehearing of the original case, including oral evidence. Rule 63.2(2)(b)(iii) of the CrimPR gives a time limit of twenty-one days and the procedure (written notice to the magistrates' court) appears to have been adopted for use in complaint appeals, albeit the appeal is civil.

**23.117**   The procedure adopted at the hearing is generally the same as set out in the Magistrates' Courts Rules above. Pending the rehearing, there is no restriction on either HMRC/UKBA or the defence obtaining more evidence and adducing new evidence at the appeal.

**23.118**   In *R (Customs and Excise Commissioners) v Maidstone Crown Court* [2004] EWHC 1459 (Admin), Customs sought judicial review of two decisions of the Crown Court in relation to granting permission to appeal out of time. The original applications had been made without notice and were made after several months of delay. There was no proper explanation as to why there had been a delay and the judge granted permission without giving any reasons. Newman J held that it was incumbent on a judge in the proper exercise of his discretion to consider the reasons given for any delay and to address the proposed merits of the appeal in the light of said delay. Furthermore, a judge should in the interests of justice give reasons for the grant or refusal of permission and communicate that decision to any affected party. In the event that a Crown Court judge does grant permission to appeal out of time but does so on a misunderstanding of the facts of a particular case, it is open to the aggrieved party to make an application to the Crown Court seeking to set aside the earlier grant of permission. As with the High Court, the Crown Court has an inherent jurisdiction to set aside (*R (on the application of UK Border Agency) v Portsmouth Crown Court* [2011] EWHC 3517 (Admin)).

### Pre-hearing review

It is advisable to have some form of pre-hearing review at the appeal stage. There are a num- **23.119** ber of reasons for this, which include:

- to assist the court with a time estimate; eg if there are four officers being called and two defendants, that is likely to occupy a day, if not two days, of court time;
- to determine which witnesses are required, and ascertain their availability to give evidence;
- to notify any points of law that may prolong matters at the appeal hearing; and
- to deal with other matters that may or may not be relevant to the particular case, eg, whether or not an interpreter is required, etc.

### Pending the hearing of an appeal

It should be noted that Art 12 of Sch 3 to CEMA states that pending the final determination **23.120** by way of appeal of the matter, the goods in question should be left with HMRC/UKBA (see further at para 18.109).

## G. Condemnation in the High Court

Although rare as HMRC nearly always commences proceedings in the magistrates' court, **23.121** condemnation cases may be brought in the High Court. In such cases proceedings are started once a claim form has been issued and follow the CPR. 'How to Start Proceedings' is dealt with in CPR Part 7, whilst the 'General Rules about Costs' are dealt with in CPR Part 44.

## H. Condemnation and the ECHR

The legitimacy of forfeiture proceedings was considered in *Goldsmith v Customs and Excise* **23.122** *Commissioners*, The Times, 12 June 2001. In that case, the Divisional Court considered what application, if any, Art 6(2) of the ECHR had in relation to Sch 3 to CEMA. The Court found that because proceedings for the condemnation of goods liable to forfeiture do not involve the determination of a criminal charge, none of the usual consequences of criminal conviction follow on from such proceedings. Therefore, even if the proceedings were proceedings to which the presumption of innocence in Art 6(2) of the ECHR applied, the burden of proof imposed on the importer of excise goods to rebut Customs' assertion that the importation was for a commercial purpose was proportionate, reasonable, and justified.

This issue had previously been considered in *Salabiaku v France* (1988) 13 EHRR 379, **23.123** where the Court held that there was nothing particularly unfair in imposing a burden of proof on someone where the subject matter was something that he was particularly well placed to prove. See also *The Netherlands v Joustra* C5-05 (ECJ, 23 November 2006).

It will be noted that pursuant to Art 1 of Protocol 1 the right to property is not absolute and **23.124** the state is permitted to secure property in order to control the use of it in accordance with the general interest or securing the payment of taxes and other contributions or penalties. Condemnation proceedings have also been found to be compliant with the ECHR and Art 6 in *Air Canada v UK* (1995) 20 EHRR 150, paras 61–3.

**23.125**  In relation to the condemnation of a vehicle and Art 1, see *Hopping v Customs and Excise Commissioners* (EOO 170) (2001), para 23.210 below.

# I. Red Diesel Cases

**Introduction**

**23.126**  Section 139 and Sch 3 to CEMA are intended to cover a myriad of circumstances where HMRC are entitled to bring proceedings for the condemnation of goods as forfeit.

**23.127**  HMRC/UKBA are allowed, by law, to examine any vehicle, any oil in or on it, and to inspect, test, or sample any oil in the fuel supply. They are also entitled to require vehicle owners or anyone in charge of a vehicle to open a fuel tank or other source of fuel supply, so that the fuel may be located and inspected or tested or sampled. They are also entitled to require anyone in charge of the vehicle to produce any books or documents relating to the vehicle or the oil carried in it. They are entitled to enter and inspect any premises (except private dwelling-houses) and inspect, test, and sample any oil on the premises whether in a vehicle or elsewhere. In short, their powers are wide reaching.

**The legislative provisions**

**23.128**  Red diesel is gas/heavy oil that carries a lower (rebated) rate of duty. It is commonly referred to as 'red diesel' because of the red dye used in its production. The relevant law is found in the Hydrocarbon Oils Duties Act 1979, ss 12(2) and 13(6). Section 12(2) reads:

> No heavy oil on whose delivery for home use rebate has been allowed...shall:
>
> (a)  be used as fuel for a road vehicle; or
> (b)  be taken into a road vehicle as fuel...

Section 12(3) states:

> (a)  Heavy oil shall be deemed to be used as fuel for a road vehicle if, but only if, it is used as fuel for the engine provided for propelling the vehicle or for an engine which draws its fuel from the same supply as that engine; and
> (b)  heavy oil shall be deemed to be taken into a road vehicle as fuel if, but only if, it is taken into it as part of that supply.

**23.129**  Fuel for diesel engine road vehicles (DERV) is heavy oil that carries a higher rate of excise duty than other heavy oils such as aviation kerosene, fuel oil, gas oil, and kerosene. It has now been replaced by the more environmentally friendly ultra low sulphur diesel (ULSD), which is also defined as a heavy oil.

**23.130**  By definition any oil which does not meet the criteria for classification as a light oil is a heavy oil: see s 1(3) and (4) of the Hydrocarbon Oils Duties Act 1979. Section 13(6) states:

> Any heavy oil—
> (a)  taken into a road vehicle as mentioned in s 12(2) above or supplied as mentioned in sub-section 12(2) or (3) above; or
> (b)  taken as fuel into a vehicle at a time when it is not a road vehicle and remaining in the vehicle as part of its fuel supply at a later time when it becomes a road vehicle,
> shall be liable to forfeiture.

Because these matters, like the matters dealt with elsewhere in this chapter, are similar to strict   **23.131**
liability offences (although not criminal), the defendant's state of mind or mitigating circumstances tend to become irrelevant. The action is against the fuel, as opposed to the individual.

In *Customs and Excise Commissioners v Jack Bradley* [1959] 1 QB 219 (one of the few reported   **23.132**
cases on red diesel) Lord Parker held that where oil was being carried and was being consumed it became liable to forfeiture. Lord Parker held (at p 224): 'The offence is the use of oil…one thing at least is clear, that oil is used when it is consumed…' It appears to follow, therefore, that even a vehicle that is shunted stands liable to forfeiture if the fuel is being used, for example, to create pressure, as opposed to propelling the vehicle.

### Excepted vehicles

Excepted vehicles to the provisions of the Hydrocarbon Oils Duties Act are set out in Sch 1   **23.133**
to the Act. Schedule 1 reads:

(1) A vehicle is an excepted vehicle where—
    (a) it is not used on a public road, and
    (b) no licence under the Vehicle Excise and Registration Act 1994 is in force in respect of it.

Public roads are roads repairable at public expense.

Schedule 1 (para 12) states as follows:   **23.134**

(1) A vehicle is an excepted vehicle if it is—
    (a) a road construction vehicle, and
    (b) used or kept solely for the conveyance of built-in road construction machinery (with or without articles or material used for the purposes of the machinery).
(2) In sub-paragraph 1 above 'road construction vehicle' means a vehicle:
    (a) which is constructed or adapted for use for the conveyance of built-in road construction machinery, and
    (b) which is not constructed or adapted for the conveyance of any other load except articles and material used for the purposes of such machinery.
(3) In sub-paragraphs (1) and (2) above 'built-in road construction machinery', in relation to a vehicle, means road construction machinery built-in as part of, or permanently attached to, the vehicle.
(4) In sub-paragraph (3) above 'road construction machinery' means a machine or device suitable for use for the construction or repair of roads and used for no purpose other than the construction or repair of roads.

Provided the vehicle a defendant operates satisfies all of the criteria at subss (1) to (4) above,   **23.135**
it may be classed as a road construction vehicle and is able to use rebated heavy oil (red diesel) as fuel when travelling on a public road.

Depending on circumstances, vehicles excepted under the scheme include tractors, agri-   **23.136**
cultural vehicles, gritters, mobile cranes, digging machines, work trucks, road construction vehicles, and road rollers (a question mark remains over street-lighting vehicles). In terms of penalties, the Misuse of Rebated Oil levy now has the maximum civil penalty of £500. The effect of the legislation is demonstrated by *Charles Michael Rush v Revenue & Customs Commissioners* (2007) (VADT E01027), where the Tribunal held that even an honest mistake, such as erroneously using a fuel can containing red diesel to fuel a vehicle, was not in itself sufficient to establish a defence of reasonable excuse under the Finance Act 1994, s 10 to avoid liability for payment of civil penalties imposed by Customs.

**23.137**  In *Renfrewshire BC v Revenue and Customs Commissioners* (VADT E00963) (2006) the Tribunal held that a tractor was an 'excepted vehicle' when it was being used on a public road, within the meaning of Sch 1, when it was either travelling on its way to a site to perform an agricultural activity or its use on the road had some relationship or connection with such an activity. However, in *Jeff Potts v Revenue & Customs Commissioners* (2007) (VADT E01065) the Tribunal determined that a farmer who, under a contract with a waste disposal company, used his tractor to transport effluent from a brewery and spread it on agricultural land was not using the tractor solely for agricultural purposes within the meaning of the Hydrocarbon Oil Duties Act 1979 Sch 1 para 2.

### Compounding

**23.138**  Often in red diesel cases HMRC will offer to settle the matter upon the payment of a settlement sum. This is known as compounding. The purpose of a compound settlement is to save time and money for Customs and the defendant, and avoid the need for legal proceedings. It is important to note that HMRC are only likely to offer a compound settlement where they have sufficient evidence to proceed to court. It is equally important to note that a compound settlement will not be offered in every case, and much will depend on what is being alleged.

### Procedural requirements

**23.139**  Schedule 5 sets out the procedure that must be followed when a person takes a sample from the motor vehicle for these purposes.

**23.140**  Section 32 of that Schedule states:

> Without prejudice to the admissibility of the evidence of the analyst [who analyses the sample and certifies it as red diesel] such a certificate shall not be admissible as evidence—
>
> (a) unless a copy of it has, not less than 7 days before the hearing, been served by... the Commissioners on all other parties; or
> (b) if any of those other parties, not less than 3 days before the hearing... serves notice on the Commissioners requiring the attendance at the hearing of the person by whom the analysis was made.

The main court procedural requirements for complaints, including appeals, are set out within the condemnation part of this chapter above, and apply equally to red diesel matters.

**23.141**  It is commonplace for somebody who is subject to a seizure to invite HMRC to conduct a review of its decision, as a part of which the person whose property has been seized will have the opportunity to set out his reasons for disagreeing with the decision to seize the property as liable to forfeiture.

### The vehicle and the fuel

**23.142**  Section 141 of CEMA applies, so if the fuel is liable to forfeiture, the vehicle being used to carry it also becomes liable to forfeiture (secondary forfeiture). (See *Customs and Excise Commissioners v Jack Bradley (Accrington) Ltd* [1959] 1 QB 219, where the Court held that where kerosene oil had been discovered in the fuel tank of a vehicle, the vehicle itself would be liable to forfeiture since it had been 'used for the carriage' of the oil.)

**23.143**  Similar arguments in relation to 'bootlegging' matters arise here in terms of proportionality, and whether it would be proportionate to condemn a vehicle with a value of, eg, £20,000, which was carrying a tank load of red diesel (value, eg, £35). See *Customs and Excise*

*Commissioners v Newbury* [2003] 2 All ER 964; [2003] 1 WLR 2131. Much will depend on the circumstances of the seizure, namely: whether it is a first time 'offence'; whether warnings have been previously given; the quantities involved; whether HMRC officials/the court were deliberately misled; or whether there exist other 'aggravating' features. Conversely, if such circumstances do not exist, this may amount to a compelling reason not to order secondary forfeiture.

### The civil burden

If the court finds on the balance of probabilities (these being civil proceedings) that the vehi-  **23.144**
cles were carrying, handling, or concealing oil liable to forfeiture, then it has no discretion and must order forfeiture: see Sch 3(6) to CEMA.

### Criminal offences

While outside the scope of this book, it is worth noting that the criminal law creates  **23.145**
certain offences in relation to the use of oil (other than DERV) to fuel 'road vehicles'. This includes using any oil on which the DERV rate of duty has not been paid. It forbids the use of fully rebated kerosene to propel a vehicle, or fuel an engine (except one only providing heat).

The law goes further in that it makes it an offence to remove any designated chemical marker  **23.146**
or dye from any oil (although how commonplace this is, is questionable). Similarly the law makes it an offence to obstruct any officer from HMRC from obtaining a sample of oil. For completeness, it is also an offence to mix any rebated or duty-free oil with any oil on which no rebate has been allowed. In *R v Owens and Owens* (2006) 150 SJ 1188, it was held that any sample must be taken in the presence of the person concerned.

In the majority of cases, the vehicle in question will be restored to the defendant on payment  **23.147**
of an amount of money known as the 'restoration amount'. This amount will consist of a penalty for any additional offence committed (a penalty of £250 may be imposed for each offence, see s 13(1)(a) and (b) of the Hydrocarbon Oils Duties Act 1979) and an assessment for the duty rebate. If the offence is considered serious the vehicle may be seized and forfeited and may not be restored to the defendant.

## J. Delivery Up

### Introduction

The seizure of goods liable to forfeiture does not mean that the individual from whom they  **23.148**
were seized or the owner of the goods will be unable to regain control of the goods, even if that individual has accepted (or it has been found) that the goods were imported for a commercial purpose. HMRC/UKBA are afforded a discretion to either restore the goods/thing seized or offer 'delivery up'.

### The legislative provisions

The power to offer delivery up is found in para 16 of Sch 3 to CEMA.  **23.149**

This enables HMRC, prior to the condemnation of the goods/thing that has been seized, to  **23.150**
return it upon payment of a sum not exceeding the value of the thing seized (including any duty or tax that was due).

**23.151**  The amount paid for delivery up is in effect a deposit. If the thing is later condemned by the court (or because a valid notice of claim/appeal is not received) the amount paid is forfeited. On the other hand, if the appeal is successful and the court finds in favour of the original owner, HMRC must return the sum. The benefit for the owner is that they have the use of the thing seized while the appeal against seizure is pending.

**23.152**  In terms of most goods/things, HMRC do not usually seek payment of more than the retail value of the thing. The retail value can often be established from valuation guides, eg, for vehicles, *Glass's Guide* (<www.glass.co.uk>).

### Practice

**23.153**  It should be noted that in practice HMRC do not normally offer 'delivery up' if they would not subsequently be prepared to restore the goods (see below). Customs would argue that to do differently would negate the purpose of forfeiture. Nor should the offer of delivery up be construed as an admission by HMRC that they were wrong to seize the thing in the first place. The fact that the goods/thing is delivered up will not avoid the court proceedings or a final determination by the magistrates. HMRC will undoubtedly pursue the court proceedings, not least because they would be liable for repayment of the sum paid (by way of refund) if they were not to.

## K.  Restoration

### The statutory basis

**23.154**  Section 152(b) of CEMA allows for the restoration of goods that have been seized or forfeited:

> The Commissioners may, as they see fit—
>
> ...
>
> (b)  restore, subject to such conditions (if any) as they think proper, any thing forfeited or seized under [those] Acts.

**23.155**  Unlike 'delivery up', restoration will (normally) only take place once a seized thing has been condemned, either following a hearing or because the thing has been deemed forfeit because no valid notice of claim/appeal has been lodged (see para 5 of Sch 3). HMRC/UKBA are entitled to impose such reasonable conditions 'as they think proper' as part of the agreement to restore. Common examples include the payment of a sum; production of an import licence (where one is required to import the thing); or relabelling (where goods were seized under the Trades Description Act because they have false marks of origin). Unlike 'delivery up', a restoration amount is non-refundable.

**23.156**  Restoration is not automatic. HMRC/UKBA may refuse to restore the goods/thing concerned. That refusal is likely to lead in certain cases to complaint. The remedy is by way of an appeal to the First Tier Tax Tribunal ('the Tax Tribunal').

### Appeals against non-restoration

**23.157**  Appeals against decisions not to restore the goods/thing are dealt with by the Tax Tribunal. The Tax Tribunal derives its jurisdiction from s 16(1) of the Finance Act 1994, which gives the Tribunal the power to review the Commissioners'/Director of Border Revenue's decisions in a number of areas.

## Burden and standard of proof

In *Golobiewska v Customs and Excise Commissioners*, The Times, 25 May 2005, the Court of **23.158**
Appeal held that the effect of s 16(6) of the Finance Act 1994 was to impose the burden of proof
on the appellant to establish, on the balance of probabilities, grounds showing that the vehicle
should be restored. Such a burden was to the civil standard. See also *Szukala Trans Pthu Export-
Import v Revenue and Customs Commissioners* (2006) 150 SJ 571 (see para 23.162 below).

However, a distinction must be drawn where one of the factual issues is the question of own **23.159**
use/commercial purpose. In *Bevins and Pyrah v Customs and Excise Commissioners* [2005]
(VADT EO00903) the Tribunal held that Customs had misapplied the law by incorrectly
imposing the burden of proof on the travellers. Both the decision to seize the goods and the
decision not to restore had been made on the basis that the travellers had not made out a
satisfactory case that the goods were for their own use. Following the decision in *Hoverspeed*
(above) such a positive burden could no longer apply. The burden in the first instance was on
Customs to show that the goods were for a commercial use.

## Test of reasonableness

Section 16(4) of the Finance Act 1994 introduces a question of reasonableness for the **23.160**
Tribunal to consider and states:

> In relation to any decision as to an ancillary matter, or any decision on the review of such a
> decision, the powers of an Appeal Tribunal on an appeal under this section shall be confined
> to a power, where the Tribunal are satisfied that the Commissioners... could not reasonably
> have arrived at it...

Appeals against non-restoration are ancillary (see s 14(1)(d) of and Sch 5 para 2(r) to the **23.161**
Finance Act 1994). It is the ancillary decision of HMRC not to restore the thing/goods subject to forfeiture, which is secondary in time (and thus ancillary) to the decision to condemn
the goods as forfeit.

In short, the Tribunal is asking itself whether or not the Commissioners/HMRC acted reason- **23.162**
ably in deciding to refuse to restore the goods/thing concerned. In *Szukala Trans Pthu Export-
Import v Revenue and Customs Commissioners* (2006) 150 SJ 571, the Tribunal held that it
was for the appellant to show that the decision was unreasonable. In order to be reasonable,
a decision must be soundly based factually; and in this regard the Tribunal had a fact-finding
function. Since facts were not a matter of discretion but of evidence, if the decision of the
reviewing officer was found to have been based on facts that were materially incorrect, his
decision would be unreasonable and the Tribunal should direct a fresh review under s 16(4).

In *Ware v Customs and Excise Commissioners* (VADT E00735) the Tribunal recognised a **23.163**
generally accepted test for what is reasonable (at para 18):

- Is this a decision that no reasonable panel of Commissioners could have come to?
- Has some irrelevant matter been taken into account?
- Has some matter which should have been taken into account been ignored?
- Has there been some error of law?

In *Gora* the Court of Appeal held that the issue of whether Customs reasonably arrived at **23.164**
their decision raised questions of *Wednesbury* reasonableness, as identified in *Customs and
Excise Commissioners v J H Corbitt (Numismatists) Ltd* [1980] STC 231.

**23.165** The case of *Associated Provincial Picture Houses Ltd v Wednesbury Corp* [1948] 1 KB 223 is reported extensively and it is not proposed to go into it in any detail within this chapter, the main principles being espoused by Lord Greene MR at p 229 of the judgment, which are also commented upon by Lord Lane at p 663 of his judgment in the case of *Corbitt*. (See also the Court of Appeal decision of *John Dee Ltd v Customs and Excise Commissioners* [1995] STC 941.)

### Proportionality

**23.166** In *Lindsay v Customs and Excise Commissioners* [2002] EWCA Civ 267, the Court of Appeal considered the circumstances in which a failure to offer restoration to a person of his vehicle, which was found to have carried forfeited excise goods, would be unreasonable and disproportionate. Lord Phillips (then Master of the Rolls) held that the aim of the Commissioners' policy was the prevention of the evasion of excise duty that was imposed in accordance with European Community law. He stated that was a legitimate aim under Art 1 of the First Protocol of the Convention (para 55). He went on to note that the trade in smuggled cigarettes was massive and the free movement of persons under Community law greatly facilitated the elicit importation of excise goods, making the smuggler's detection less likely. He also stated that the public were warned that if vehicles were used for smuggling, those vehicles might be forfeited and therefore anybody using their vehicle for smuggling was taking a calculated risk.

**23.167** He added that as a general policy those who used their vehicles for commercial smuggling could not be heard to complain if they then lost their vehicles. In those circumstances, the value of the vehicles did not need to be taken into account (see paras 60–3 of the judgment). However, he also stated that where the importation was not for profit each case had to be considered on its own facts, and introduced a proportionality test. In setting out the factors that should be taken into account, Lord Phillips MR stated at para 64:

> The Commissioners' policy does not, however, draw a distinction between the commercial smuggler and the driver importing goods for social distribution to family or friends in circumstances where there is no attempt to make a profit. Of course, even in such a case the scale of importation, or other circumstances, may be such as to justify forfeiture of the car. But where the importation is not for the purpose of making a profit, I consider that the principle of proportionality requires that each case should be considered on its particular facts, which would include the scale of the importation, whether it is a 'first offence', whether there was an attempt at concealment or dissimulation, the value of the vehicle and the degree of hardship that will be caused by forfeiture.

**23.168** In *Aykut Ates v Customs and Excise Commissioners* (2002) (EOO 188) the Tribunal held that the Commissioners had not acted proportionately when refusing to restore a vehicle used for smuggling to its owner, in circumstances where it was accepted that the owner had lent the car to a friend, and was himself innocent of any smuggling and did not know the use to which the vehicle was being put. The facts suggested that the appellant had been duped into lending his vehicle. Customs had taken the view that in lending his vehicle the appellant had taken a risk that the third party concerned would take the vehicle abroad, and as such there were no exceptional circumstances that justified departing from the policy that vehicles used in smuggling would not be restored to the owner.

### Jurisdiction

**23.169** It should be noted that the above is the limit of the Tribunal's jurisdiction. It is not entitled to, and will not, act as a court of appeal from the magistrates' decision on the question of forfeiture itself. It may, however, hear evidence about the seizure if it is relevant in assisting with the question of whether the ancillary non-restoration decision was correct (see the guidance provided by the Court of Appeal in *Gascoyne* below).

### Personal/commercial use

The Tribunal is not directly concerned with the question of personal use or commercial   **23.170**
importation. That is an issue principally within the confines of the condemnation proceedings/the magistrates' court. (See *Gora v Customs and Excise Commissioners* [2003] EWCA Civ 525 (CA) where Pill LJ recognised that the Tribunal procedure was not intended to enable the appellant to challenge the deemed condemnation of forfeit goods if no claim had been made under Sch 3 to CEMA (see para 58)).

In *Gascoyne v Customs and Excise Commissioners* [2005] 2 WLR 222 (CA), Buxton LJ held   **23.171**
(at para 46 et seq):

> I do not think it can have been intended that the importer before the Tribunal would have a second bite at the cherry of lawfulness, having failed in condemnation proceedings or let them go by default... the reason why the importer cannot have that liberty is not because of the terms of the statute, but because of normal English law rules of *res judicata* or abuse of process.

The reasoning in *Gascoyne* was confirmed by Lindsay J in *Customs and Excise Commissioners v*   **23.172**
*Demack and Eatock* [2005] EWHC 330 (Ch), in which the Court found that Tax Tribunals should not undo findings of fact made by the magistrates in earlier forfeiture proceedings. In *Johnstone v Customs and Excise Commissioners* [2005] EWCA 115 (Admin), the High Court established that if an appellant advances grounds of appeal against non-restoration based on personal use then he has advanced neither a valid ground for restoration nor a valid ground of appeal before the Tax Tribunal. Moses J stated (at para 12 et seq):

> Unfortunately, as I have said, they went on to consider that which has been advanced by Mr. Johnstone, namely that these cigarettes were not for commercial use; they were for personal use. That was not a matter for the Tribunal at all. It is no ground for restoration to say to the Commissioners: these cigarettes were for personal use. This is not a ground upon which restoration can be made.
>
> In the instant case no ground whatever for restoration was advanced. All that was said was that the cigarettes were for personal use. But that issue was solely a matter for the Magistrates' or an appeal to the Crown Court. It was not a matter for the reviewing officer; it was not a matter for the Tribunal; and it is not a matter for the court. If all someone importing cigarettes such as this does is to persist in saying they are for personal use, the correct response is to say: 'You have advanced no ground whatever for restoration in the exercise of powers under section 152(b)'. That, in my judgment, is the view which the Tribunal ought to have taken. But unfortunately, in an excess of kindness, they did look yet again at the issue of whether the grounds were for personal use and decided yet again that they were not. That, as I have said, was not a matter for them.

The judgment of Buxton LJ in *Gascoyne* raised the question of how a Tribunal should pro-   **23.173**
ceed where an appellant has not been afforded a hearing at the condemnation proceedings stage. While most appellants have their 'day in court' at the condemnation hearing, and thus have had the opportunity to make and to argue points on own use/commercial purpose etc (ie a fair hearing pursuant to the ECHR), in cases when no condemnation proceedings have taken place the position will be different. In *Gascoyne* Buxton LJ held (at para 49 et seq):

> The ECHR jurisprudence itself creates a great deal more difficulty in relation to the deeming provisions under paragraph 5 of Schedule 3. One's instincts, if no more, suggest that the extent

to which it was held in *Gora v Customs and Excise Commissioners* [2004] QB 93 CA that those provisions necessarily prevent any further consideration of the legality of the seizure was an excessive limitation…Lord Phillips in *Lindsay* at paragraph 64 of his judgment (states) that the principle of proportionality requires that each case should be considered on its particular facts…As it seems to me, for an importer to be completely shut out in the only Tribunal before which he has in fact appeared from ventilating the matters that are deemed to have been decided against him because of paragraph 5 of Schedule 3 does not adequately enable him to assert his Convention rights. In my view, therefore, in a case where the deeming provisions under paragraph 5 are applied the Tribunal can re-open those issues: so that a Tribunal will always have very well in mind considerations of, or similar to, abuse of process in considering whether such issues should in fact be ventilated before it. The mere fact that the Applicant has not applied to the Commissioners, and therefore there have been no condemnation proceedings, would not in my view be enough. But in my judgment it goes too far to say that the deeming provisions have always, in every case, got to be paramount.

23.174   Lindsay J in *Customs and Excise Commissioners v Demack and Eatock* [2005] EWHC 330 (Ch) suggested (following *Gascoyne*), that in deemed seizure cases the Tribunal could reopen the evidence and make findings of fact on the matter. See also *William McGuiness v Customs and Excise Commissioners* [E00793] and *Customs and Excise Commissioners v Dickinson*, The Times, 3 December 2003, where the Court held it remained open to an importer to raise the issue of personal use for the purposes of seeking to invoke the discretionary procedure of restoration.

23.175   Anecdotally, Tribunals appeared reluctant to see their jurisdiction curtailed in the way that the decision in *Gascoyne* anticipated. Part of the problem was the conflicting messages being sent out in terms of case law. The position was re-examined once again in detail by Evans-Lombe J in the case of *Customs and Excise Commissioners v David Weller* [2006] EWHC 237. In *Weller* the Tribunal proceeded on the basis that it had jurisdiction to consider whether the seized goods were for the appellant's personal use, in a case where there had been no condemnation proceedings and condemnation had not been challenged (para 1).

23.176   His Lordship described the present system as being two track. The first track was to challenge the lawfulness of the forfeiture to the magistrates' court with an appeal to the Crown Court and then to a Divisional Court of the High Court. The second track was to seek the return of the goods forfeited with an appeal to the Tax Tribunal and thereafter to the High Court if unsuccessful (para 10).

23.177   His Lordship proceeded to review both the cases of *Gascoyne* and *Gora*. He noted that Buxton LJ took the view that where there had been deemed forfeiture it was a potential breach of the importer's rights under Art 6 of the ECHR to prevent him from seeking to reopen the issue of whether the original forfeiture was lawful as a reason, or one of the reasons, why his forfeited goods should be returned to him. Buxton LJ had not sought to limit what sort of facts would be relevant to the decision, beyond a recommendation that a Tribunal 'will always have very well in mind considerations of, or similar to, abuse of process'.

23.178   In *Weller*, Evans-Lombe J referred specifically to the case of *Revenue and Customs Commissioners v Smith* (QBD, 17 November 2005). In *Smith*, Lewison J was dealing with a case where an importer was stopped at Dover by Customs officers with 2,000 litres of beer, 250 litres of wine, and 4 litres of spirits in a Toyota Land Cruiser, without having paid duty. He did not give a notice of appeal to the Commissioners under para 3 of Sch 3 to CEMA, but sought to raise the validity of the seizure on appeal with the Tax Tribunal following the Commissioners' refusal to review its decision not to return the forfeited goods to him.

The Tribunal permitted him to raise such an argument. Lewison J, however, set aside the **23.179** Tribunal's ruling. Having referred to Buxton LJ's judgment in *Gascoyne* at para 76, Lewison J stated:

> It is, in my judgment, clear from that passage that in the run-of-the-mill case where there has been a failure to give a paragraph 3 notice invoking the condemnation proceedings, the [provisions] will operate against the applicant in any subsequent appeal to a Tribunal. The Tribunal's function, therefore, is analogous to a sentencing court once a defendant has been convicted. No matter that the defendant still protests his innocence of the charge against him, the function of a sentencing court is to accept mitigation but not to question the original conviction.
>
> Lord Justice Buxton's reference to abuse of power or to considerations analogous to abuse of process are, in my view, references to the well-known principle that it may be an abuse of process to raise in one Tribunal matters that could and should have been raised in another. So the relevant questions will always be, first, could the applicant have raised the question of lawfulness of forfeiture in other proceedings and, if the answer to that question is yes, why did he not do so? In the light of his reasons for not raising the matter in condemnation proceedings, the Tribunal can then answer the question, should he have done so and if the answer to the question is 'yes', then it will be, in most cases, an abuse of process for him to raise the question before the Tribunal.

Evans-Lombe J agreed with this approach. For a time whether an importer was able to raise **23.180** the validity of the forfeiture on a review to a Tribunal depended on two questions:

(1) Did the importer have a realistic opportunity to invoke the condemnation procedure?
(2) If he did, are there nonetheless reasons, disclosed by the facts of the case which should persuade the Commissioners or the Tribunal to permit him to reopen the question of the validity of the original seizure on an application for return of the goods?

Evans-Lombe J stated in *Weller* that the first question would almost always be answered in the **23.181** affirmative, since facts would have to be very unusual to base a conclusion that the importer was prevented, in the thirty days succeeding forfeiture, from giving notice to Customs to initiate condemnation procedure in the magistrates' court (see para 16). It appeared, therefore, that the issue in relation to the Tribunal's jurisdiction had been both clarified and curtailed as a result of the judgments in *Weller* and *Smith*.

However, there then followed a handful of cases where the Tax Tribunal found it appropriate **23.182** to review Customs' decisions notwithstanding a failure to pursue condemnation proceedings: *Peet v Revenue and Customs Commissioners* [2007] LTL 12.7.07 (appellant permitted to reopen lawfulness of seizure on the grounds of human rights); and *Foster v Revenue and Customs Commissioners* [2008] (VADT E01124) (Customs' reasons for seizure had been deemed 'obscure').

Such decisions were unhelpful and once again raised questions as to whether the Tax **23.183** Tribunal's jurisdiction was curtailed to the reasonableness of a review decision or if its power extended to reopening the lawfulness of a seizure, and in turn undertaking a fact-finding exercise as to whether or not the goods were held for a commercial purpose or for own use.

The lack of jurisdiction for an appellant to raise the legality of seizure before the Tax Tribunal **23.184** has now been put beyond doubt by the Court of Appeal in the case of *the Commissioners for HM Revenue & Customs v Lawrence and Joan Jones* [2011] EWCA Civ 824. Per Mummery LJ at para 71 of the judgment:

71. I am in broad agreement with the main submissions of HMRC. For the future guidance of tribunals and their users I will summarise the conclusions that I have reached in this case in the light of the provisions of the 1979 Act, the relevant authorities, the articles of the Convention and the detailed points made by HMRC.

(1) The respondents' goods seized by the customs officers could only be condemned as forfeit pursuant to an order of a court. The FTT and the UTT are statutory appellate bodies that have not been given any such original jurisdiction.

(2) The respondents had the right to invoke the notice of claim procedure to oppose condemnation by the court on the ground that they were importing the goods for their personal use, not for commercial use.

(3) The respondents in fact exercised that right by giving to HMRC a notice of claim to the goods, but, on legal advice, they later decided to withdraw the notice and not to contest condemnation in the court proceedings that would otherwise have been brought by HMRC.

(4) The stipulated statutory effect of the respondents' withdrawal of their notice of claim under paragraph 3 of Schedule 3 was that the goods were deemed by the express language of paragraph 5 to have been condemned and to have been 'duly' condemned as forfeited as illegally imported goods. The tribunal must give effect to the clear deeming provisions in the 1979 Act: it is impossible to read them in any other way than as requiring the goods to be taken as 'duly condemned' if the owner does not challenge the legality of the seizure in the allocated court by invoking and pursuing the appropriate procedure.

(5) The deeming process limited the scope of the issues that the respondents were entitled to ventilate in the FTT on their restoration appeal. The FTT had to take it that the goods had been 'duly' condemned as illegal imports. It was not open to it to conclude that the goods were legal imports illegally seized by HMRC by finding as a fact that they were being imported for own use. The role of the tribunal, as defined in the 1979 Act, does not extend to deciding as a fact that the goods were, as the respondents argued in the tribunal, being imported legally for personal use. That issue could only be decided by the court. The FTT's jurisdiction is limited to hearing an appeal against a discretionary decision by HMRC not to restore the seized goods to the respondents. In brief, the deemed effect of the respondents' failure to contest condemnation of the goods by the court was that the goods were being illegally imported by the respondents for commercial use.

(6) The deeming provisions in paragraph 5 and the restoration procedure are compatible with Article 1 of the First Protocol to the Convention and with Article 6, because the respondents were entitled under the 1979 Act to challenge in court, in accordance with Convention compliant legal procedures, the legality of the seizure of their goods. The notice of claim procedure was initiated but not pursued by the respondents. That was the choice they had made. Their Convention rights were not infringed by the limited nature of the issues that they could raise on a subsequent appeal in the different jurisdiction of the tribunal against a refusal to restore the goods.

(7) I completely agree with the analysis of the domestic law jurisdiction position by Pill LJ in *Gora* and as approved by the Court of Appeal in *Gascoyne*. The key to the understanding of the scheme of deeming is that in the legal world created by legislation the deeming of a fact or of a state of affairs is not contrary to 'reality'; it is a commonly used and legitimate legislative device for spelling out a legal state of affairs consequent on the occurrence of a specified act or omission. Deeming something to be the case carries with it any fact that forms part of the conclusion.

(8) The tentative obiter dicta of Buxton LJ in *Gascoyne* on the possible impact of the Convention on the interpretation and application of the 1979 Act procedures and the potential application of the abuse of process doctrine do not prevent this court from reaching the above conclusions. That case is not binding authority for the proposition that paragraph 5 of Schedule 3 is ineffective as infringing Article 1 of the First Protocol or Article 6 where it is not an abuse to reopen the condemnation issue; nor is it binding

authority for the propositions that paragraph 5 should be construed other than according to its clear terms, or that it should be disapplied judicially, or that the respondents are entitled to argue in the tribunal that the goods ought not to be condemned as forfeited.

(9) It is fortunate that Buxton LJ flagged up potential Convention concerns on Article 1 of the First Protocol and Article 6, which the court in *Gora* did not expressly address, and also considered the doctrine of abuse of process. The Convention concerns expressed in *Gascoyne* are allayed once it has been appreciated, with the benefit of the full argument on the 1979 Act, that there is no question of an owner of goods being deprived of them without having the legal right to have the lawfulness of seizure judicially determined one way or other by an impartial and independent court or tribunal: either through the courts on the issue of the legality of the seizure and/or through the FTT on the application of the principles of judicial review, such as reasonableness and proportionality, to the review decision of HMRC not to restore the goods to the owner.

(10) As for the doctrine of abuse of process, it prevents the owner from litigating a particular issue about the goods otherwise than in the allocated court, but strictly speaking it is unnecessary to have recourse to that common law doctrine in this case, because, according to its own terms, the 1979 Act itself stipulates a deemed state of affairs which the FTT had no power to contradict and the respondents were not entitled to contest. The deeming does not offend against the Convention, because it will only arise if the owner has not taken the available option of challenging the legality of the seizure in the allocated forum.

## L.  Restoration: Practice and Procedure

### Formal departmental reviews

Appeals to the Tribunal are against a formal review decision by HMRC/UKBA. Appeals **23.185** can only be brought by a person who has first requested a formal department review (see the Finance Act 1994, s 16(2)). Persons able to request a review include those affected by the decision, or persons who are liable to pay any duty or penalty in relation to it, together with persons on behalf of whom an application is made (see s 14(2) of the Finance Act 1994).

### Tribunal procedure

The procedure before the Tax Tribunal is governed by the Tribunal Procedure (First-tier **23.186** Tribunal) (Tax Chamber) Rules 2009 ('the Tax Chamber Rules') (SI 2009/273).

### Time limits

Section 14(1) of the Finance Act 1994 requires a request for a review to be made in writ- **23.187** ing within forty-five days from the date of the original decision (s 14(3)). While the Commissioners are not obliged to carry out a review if the request is received outside the forty-five-day limitation period, s 16(1)(b) does afford some scope for out-of-time requests where the Commissioners have agreed to undertake a review after the end of the forty-five day period.

Within forty-five days of receiving the request for a review, HMRC must complete their **23.188** formal review (Finance Act 1994, s 15(2)). Once the forty-five day period expires, the original decision shall be assumed to be upheld and the individual looking to appeal will have an immediate right to pursue that appeal. The forty-five day period afforded to Customs cannot be extended. The appeal itself must be served within thirty days of the date of the document containing the disputed decision (see para 203 of The Transfer of Tribunal Functions and Revenue and Customs Appeals Order 2009 (SI 2009/56), which amends s 16(1) of the Finance Act 1994). It may also be extended by r 5(3)(a), subject to r 20(4), per the Tax Tribunal website:

> You will normally have 30 days to appeal a disputed HMRC decision. If you make use of HMRC's review process you will have 30 days to appeal from the date they tell you the outcome. The time limit runs from both the original decision and any decision following review. The letter you receive from HMRC, both the original decision and any decision following review, will confirm the time you have for appealing.
>
> If you are making your appeal outside the time limit, you must give reasons to the tribunal in writing.

### Lodging the appeal and the statement of case

**23.189**   Rule 20 of the Tax Chamber Rules states an appeal to the Tribunal should be brought by a notice of appeal and the notice of appeal must include:

    (a)   the name and address of the appellant;
    (b)   the name and address of the appellant's representative (if any);
    (c)   an address where documents for the appellant may be sent or delivered;
    (d)   details of the decision appealed against;
    (e)   the result the appellant is seeking; and
    (f)   the grounds for making the appeal.

**23.190**   Rule 20(3) provides:

> The appellant must provide with the notice of appeal a copy of any written record of any decision appealed against, and any statement of reasons for that decision, that the appellant has or can reasonably obtain.

### Respondent's statement of case

**23.191**   In terms of the Commissioners/Director of Border Revenue filing and serving their case in reply, r 25 provides as follows:

> 25.—(1)   A respondent must send or deliver a statement of case to the Tribunal, the appellant and any other respondent so that it is received—
>   (a)   in a Default Paper case, within 42 days after the Tribunal sent the notice of the appeal or a copy of the application notice or notice of reference; or
>   (b)   in a Standard or Complex case, within 60 days after the Tribunal sent the notice of the appeal or a copy of the application notice or notice of reference.
> (2)   A statement of case must—
>   (a)   in an appeal, state the legislative provision under which the decision under appeal was made; and
>   (b)   set out the respondent's position in relation to the case.
> (3)   A statement of case may also contain a request that the case be dealt with at a hearing or without a hearing.
> (4)   If a respondent provides a statement of case to the Tribunal later than the time required by paragraph (1) or by any extension allowed under rule 5(3)(a) (power to extend time), the statement of case must include a request for an extension of time and the reason why the statement of case was not provided in time.

**23.192**   Rules 23 and 28 set out the procedure to be followed depending upon whether the appeal has been designated as a Default Paper, Basic, Standard, or Complex case, including considerations in terms of disclosure. In an attempt to save costs and reduce valuable Tribunal time being taken up unnecessarily, Default Paper cases are dealt with administratively on the papers and will usually be disposed of without a hearing (eg *Ven Hugh Glaisyer v the Director of Border Revenue* (TC/2011/03984)).

While Tribunal procedures tend to be less formal than court procedures, failure to disclose a **23.193** certain document may lead to it being excluded from the hearing (*David Kirk v Customs and Excise Commissioners* (14042)). The risk in non-disclosure is that if the Tribunal is minded to admit any late document, HMRC/UKBA are likely to ask for more time to consider it and that may lead to an adjournment and a possible costs award (see *Customs and Excise Commissioners v Gus Merchandise Corp* [1992] STC 776 at 781–2).

In terms of disclosure generally, legal privilege applies (see *Three Rivers DC (Respondents) v* **23.194** *Governor of the Bank of England* [2004] UKHL 48 at 114–17 and *Alfred Crompton Amusement Machines Ltd v Customs and Excise Commissioners* [1974] AC 405 in relation to internal correspondence between officers and the legal section of Customs).

### Failure to comply with directions

Extensions of time may be sought under r 5(3); however the importance of complying with **23.195** the directions of the Tribunal and the requisite time limits was emphasised by *Customs and Excise Commissioners v Young* [1993] STC 394 where the Commissioners lost the appeal because they had served documents twelve days late.

### Pre-hearing directions

Pre-hearing directions are not uncommon in non-restoration appeals. These may be ordered **23.196** by the Tribunal of its own motion, or following a request of one of the parties (r 6). Often, however, directions are agreed by consent and this can avoid the necessity of a hearing.

Where directions cannot be agreed or where there is a matter of substance which needs to **23.197** be dealt with, a hearing can be arranged that will usually be heard before a Tribunal Judge.

### Preparation for the hearing

In practice, usually each party is responsible for preparing its own bundle for the hearing, **23.198** although the Commissioners/Director of Border Revenue will usually take the lead in this. Rule 15 deals with the procedure in terms of evidence and submissions.

### The hearing

Consideration in terms of whether the hearing should be in private or in public is set out in r **23.199** 32. Usually the hearing will be in public. The correct terms of address for the Tribunal Judge and any lay members are Sir or Madam, as appropriate. It is not usual for counsel to stand when addressing the Tribunal. Gowns are not worn.

During the hearing the judge and any other member of the Tribunal may put questions to **23.200** any witness called to give evidence. While officers are entitled to refer to their notebooks when giving evidence, they should make it clear whether the notes were made contemporaneously or not (*Mori Mohal Indian Restaurant v Customs and Excise Commissioners* (1992) VAT TR 188).

Under r 33, if neither party or if only one party attends, then the Tribunal is entitled to go **23.201** on and hear the matter in any event. Shorthand writers may only be present if permitted by the Tribunal (see *Empire Stores Ltd v Customs and Excise Commissioners* (1992) VAT TR 271).

**Judgment**

23.202  A decision will not necessarily be given immediately and it is usual for there to be a delay while the Tribunal Judge prepares the decision (the rules suggest twenty-eight days or as soon as practicable thereafter, r 35). While there has been complaint in the past about the length of the delay, Moses J held in *R v Customs and Excise Commissioners ex p Dangol* [2000] STC 107 (QBD) that a party could only seek judicial review of a delay in issuing a decision if they could demonstrate that the delay caused an injustice.

23.203  Parties are entitled to have a decision set aside if, eg, there is a procedural irregularity. However, that must be done within twenty-eight days of the release of the decision (r 38). There is no power to set a decision aside outside of that period, the only recourse then being to appeal.

# M. Restoration Appeals

23.204  Rule 39 outlines the procedure to be followed for permission to appeal the Tax Tribunal's decision. Appeals must be filed within fifty-six days (see r 39(2)).

# N. Restoration: Costs and Compensation

**Compensation**

23.205  Traditional thinking has always maintained that the Tax Tribunal does not have any jurisdiction to entertain claims for compensation and such matters are entirely within the remit of the county court. However, this was called into question by *Powell v Revenue and Customs Commissioners* (2005) (EOO 900), where the Tribunal held that a power to pay compensation when restoration was no longer possible was a necessary part of the structure of the legislation, pursuant to s 152(b) of CEMA. The Tribunal found (at paras 102, 109, 112, and 113) that there is a right of appeal to the Tribunal on the question of quantum of compensation and the reasonableness of the payment offered in restoration proceedings where goods have been destroyed. The Tribunal's power would be to return the decision to Customs for review if it found the offer to be unreasonable. It has no power to make its own order in substitution of Customs' decision. It only has the power to keep reviewing the decisions of Customs and if they are unreasonable then returning them for further re-review.

**Costs**

23.206  Costs are dealt with under r 10. Unlike the normal rule in civil proceedings that costs will follow the event, in respect of matters allocated as Default Paper, Basic and Standard cases, there is a general assumption before the Tax Tribunal that each person will pay their own costs when appealing. If, however, any person acts unreasonably during the proceedings, the Tribunal can order them to pay the other person's costs (r 10(1)(b)). There are, however, special rules for costs in 'Complex cases'. A matter is usually allocated as a Complex case where it is lengthy, legally/factually complicated, or high value.

23.207  The Tribunal may decide that costs are not reasonable where the conduct of a party has been improper or where issues have been raised late in the day and without proper notice. Litigants in person are unable to recover their costs in respect of time spent on the case (see *Melina Serpes v Revenue and Customs Commissioners* (VADT 20906) (2008)). The withdrawal of a party from an appeal where costs are applicable will not usually save them from having to pay costs unless, eg, they do so as a result of new evidence of which they were previously unaware (see *JJ McGinty v Customs and Excise Commissioners* (1995) V&DR 193).

## O. The ECHR and Restoration

It is well established that pursuant to s 2(1) of the HRA, a court or tribunal 'must take account' of decisions of the European Commission and Court. Guidance on how matters should be approached is provided by *Hoverspeed Ltd* [2002] EWHC 1630 (Admin) at paras 186–9, and for the court's approach in relation to proportionality see *Lindsay v Customs and Excise Commissioners* [2002] EWCA Civ 267. **23.208**

In *Gora* the Court of Appeal upheld the conclusions of the Tribunal that a decision not to restore seized goods did not involve a criminal charge for the purposes of Art 6 of the Convention (para 48). **23.209**

In *Hopping v Customs and Excise Commissioners* (2001)(EOO 170), the Tribunal held that the policy of 'use it and lose it', namely seizing and refusing to restore to the owner a vehicle used for bootlegging, was proportionate in that a fair balance existed between the legitimate aim pursued and the means employed. The Tribunal commented that seizure and the refusal to restore the vehicle are, on first impression, direct violations of the owner's fundamental right of peaceful enjoyment of his vehicle (Art 1 of Protocol 1 of the ECHR); and that the Commissioners' policy was capable of being arbitrary to the point of being extravagant (para 28), particularly where the financial loss resulting from the refusal to restore an expensive car could many times exceed the loss of revenue sought from the operation. **23.210**

Whilst this decision should be treated with some caution, due to the passage of time, it nevertheless provides a helpful list of criteria which demonstrate that the means employed tend to balance the aim pursued. The Tribunal found: **23.211**

(1)  The policy was a suitable way of preventing smuggling. Take away the vehicle and it can be no longer used for bootlegging.
(2)  To refuse to restore is even-handed. It is the course of action that is blind to the value of the vehicle and to the financial means of the owner. It treats all bootleggers alike.
(3)  The owner who makes a bootlegging trip to France and whose vehicle is taken will know the score before he embarks on his smuggling operations. In a real sense he ventures his vehicle as one of the stakes of his dishonest enterprise. He foregoes his claim to any unqualified fundamental right of peaceful enjoyment of the vehicle before he sets off on his trip.
(4)  So long as the seizure and refusal to restore the vehicle does not cause physical suffering or result in excessive inconvenience to defenceless third parties, its impact will be directed at the owner (see para 28).

Sir Steven Oliver QC added at para 29: **23.212**

Every case will have to be dealt with on its own facts. But in principle we do not see a lack of balance when the factors set out above are brought into the reckoning. Where the owner is the driver he risks losing the vehicle when he sets out to bootleg. He takes the risk and loses when he is caught.

# 24

## TERRORISM AND THE PROCEEDS OF CRIME

## A. Introduction

Terry Davis, the former Secretary General of the Council of Europe, was once quoted as **24.01** saying: 'Terrorists seldom kill for money, but they always need money to kill.' That statement summarises the connection between proceeds of crime law on the one hand and anti-terrorism legislation on the other. This chapter therefore looks at the relationship between terrorist activity and the recovery of the proceeds of crime, and what steps have been taken, both domestically and internationally, to combat terrorism.

### What is terrorism?

There is more than one way of describing what terrorism is, or what a terrorist act may be. **24.02** For many individuals evocative statements such as 'unjustifiable murder', 'lunacy', or 'a hate crime' may well apply. Conversely, for those involved in the commission of such acts, statements such as 'freedom fighting', 'retribution', or 'the necessary product of a system where views have not been listened to' could also apply.

Legislators around the world have attempted to give 'terrorism' more prescriptive definitions. **24.03**

Article 1 of the EU Framework Decision on Combating Terrorism (2002/475/JHA) pro- **24.04** vides that terrorist offences are intentional acts:

> which given their nature and context, may seriously damage a country or an international organisation where committed with the aim of seriously intimidating a population, unduly compelling a Government or international organisation to perform or abstain from performing an act, or seriously destabilising or destroying the fundamental political, constitutional, economic or social structures of a country or an international organisation.

**24.05**   The United Kingdom's Terrorism Act 2000 defines terrorism as follows:

> (1) In this Act 'terrorism' means the use or threat of action where:
>   (a) the action falls within subsection (2),
>   (b) the use or threat is designed to influence the government or to intimidate the public or a section of the public and
>   (c) the use or threat is made for the purpose of advancing a political, religious or ideological cause.
> (2) Action falls within this subsection if it:
>   (a) involves serious violence against a person,
>   (b) involves serious damage to property,
>   (c) endangers a person's life, other than that of the person committing the action,
>   (d) creates a serious risk to the health or safety of the public or a section of the public or
>   (e) is designed seriously to interfere with or seriously to disrupt an electronic system.

**24.06**   In the US by Executive Order 13224 (Blocking and prohibiting transactions with persons who commit, threaten to commit, or support terrorism):

> 'terrorism' means an activity that—
> (i) involves a violent act or an act dangerous to human life, property, or infrastructure; and
> (ii) appears to be intended—
>   (A) to intimidate or coerce a civilian population;
>   (B) to influence the policy of a government by intimidation or coercion; or
>   (C) to affect the conduct of a government by mass destruction, assassination, kidnapping, or hostage-taking.

## B. Terrorism and the International Dimension

**24.07**   Eighteen universal instruments (fourteen instruments and four amendments) against international terrorism have been passed within the framework of the United Nations system relating to specific terrorist activities. Member States through the General Assembly have sought to coordinate their counter-terrorism efforts. The UN's Security Council has also been active in countering terrorism through resolutions and by establishing several subsidiary bodies.

**24.08**   The UN's Security Council resolutions are part of the United Nations Global Counter-Terrorism Strategy, and are aimed at strengthening the effectiveness of the United Nations sanctions regime against terrorist organisations such as Al-Qaida and the Taliban. In particular, certain measures are designed to help Member States combat crimes that might be connected with terrorism (eg drug trafficking, arms trafficking, and money laundering). Security Council decisions taken in this context are binding upon the Member States of the United Nations.

**24.09**   Understandably, efforts to combat terrorist financing are greatly undermined if jurisdictions do not freeze funds or other assets of designated persons quickly and effectively.

### What is a designation?

**24.10**   Designation refers to the identification of an individual or entity that is subject to targeted financial sanctions pursuant to international obligations, particularly UNSCR 1267 (against the Taliban) and successive resolutions such as UNSCR 1373 (post 9/11 attacks).

This includes the legal determination that the relevant sanctions will be applied to the individual or entity and the public communication of that determination.

Resolution 1373 includes a requirement that Member States of the United Nations must:  **24.11**

(a) prevent the financing of terrorist acts, including the freezing of funds and economic resources of persons who commit or attempt to commit terrorist acts or participate in or facilitate such acts: and

(b) prohibit their nationals and those within their territories from making funds, financial services, or economic resources available to such persons.

Resolution 1452 introduces exemptions to prohibitions on making funds, financial assets,  **24.12** or economic resources available to permit payments necessary to meet basic humanitarian needs (such as payments for foodstuffs, rent, or mortgage, medicines and medical treatment, taxes, insurance premiums, public utility charges, and legal fees and expenses) and payments necessary to meet extraordinary expenses.

For discussion on designation, and why Art 6 of the ECHR does not apply to judicial review  **24.13** proceedings brought by individuals listed under UNSCR 1267, see *Secretary of State for the Foreign Office and Commonwealth Affairs* [2011] EWCA Civ 350.

### Why designate and freeze funds?

Freezing terrorist funds and designating groups and individuals is central to combatting ter-  **24.14** rorism and the financing of terrorism. This is because it:

• deters others from dealing with individuals or designated groups and thus prevents the financing of terrorist activity;
• exposes audit trails and allows the authorities time to explore leads;
• encourages both designated persons and other individuals to disassociate themselves from suspected terrorist activity;
• forces terrorists to use more costly and higher risk means of financing their activities, making them more susceptible to detection and disruption.

For further reading, see *FAFT Guidance Document: International Best Practices—*  **24.15** *Freezing of Terrorist Assets; Overview of European and International Legislation on Terrorist Financing: Labayle and Long*; and *Kadi v Council of the European Union* [2008] 3 CMLR 41 and *Kadi II v Commission* (Case T-85/09), where the court confirmed that the terrorist forfeiture scheme was both a permanent sanction and punitive.

## C. The UK Approach

### Terrorism Act 2000

*What is 'Terrorist property'?*

Section 14 of the Terrorism Act 2000 (TA) provides:  **24.16**

> 14 Terrorist property.
> (1) In this Act 'terrorist property' means—
>     (a) money or other property which is likely to be used for the purposes of terrorism (including any resources of a proscribed organisation),

> (b) proceeds of the commission of acts of terrorism, and
> (c) proceeds of acts carried out for the purposes of terrorism.
> (2) In subsection (1)—
>> (a) a reference to proceeds of an act includes a reference to any property which wholly or partly, and directly or indirectly, represents the proceeds of the act (including payments or other rewards in connection with its commission), and
>> (b) the reference to an organisation's resources includes a reference to any money or other property which is applied or made available, or is to be applied or made available, for use by the organisation.

**24.17** The term 'terrorist property' is a catch-all, used to suggest that the offences in the TA apply not only to money, but also to other property and to all forms of terrorism. The definition is particularly relevant to the money laundering offence (s 18) and the power to seize and forfeit cash (see Sch 1 to the Anti-Terrorism, Crime and Security Act 2001, below).

**24.18** Section 14(1) makes it clear that terrorist property can include both property to be used for terrorism and the proceeds of acts of terrorism. Subsection (2)(a) makes explicit that the proceeds of an act of terrorism covers not only the money stolen in, say, a terrorist robbery, but also any money paid in connection with the commission of terrorist acts. Subsection (2)(b) states that any resources of a proscribed organisation are covered: not only the resources they use for eg bomb-making, arms purchases, etc, but also money they have set aside for non-violent purposes such as paying rent.

*Fundraising, use, possession, and funding arrangements*

**24.19** Section 15 of the TA provides as follows:

> (1) A person commits an offence if he—
>> (a) invites another to provide money or other property, and
>> (b) intends that it should be used, or has reasonable cause to suspect that it may be used, for the purposes of terrorism.
> (2) A person commits an offence if he—
>> (a) receives money or other property, and
>> (b) intends that it should be used, or has reasonable cause to suspect that it may be used, for the purposes of terrorism.
> (3) A person commits an offence if he—
>> (a) provides money or other property, and
>> (b) knows or has reasonable cause to suspect that it will or may be used for the purposes of terrorism.
> (4) In this section a reference to the provision of money or other property is a reference to its being given, lent or otherwise made available, whether or not for consideration.

**24.20** By virtue of s 1(5) of the Act the words 'for the purposes of terrorism' can be taken to include 'for the benefit of a proscribed organisation'. As a result, the offences of fund-raising, and using and possessing money, and entering into funding arrangements for a proscribed organisation are caught by these sections.

**24.21** Sections 16 and 17 of the TA provide as follows:

> 16 Use and possession.
> (1) A person commits an offence if he uses money or other property for the purposes of terrorism.
> (2) A person commits an offence if he—
>> (a) possesses money or other property, and

(b) intends that it should be used, or has reasonable cause to suspect that it may be used, for the purposes of terrorism.

17   Funding arrangements.
A person commits an offence if—
(a) he enters into or becomes concerned in an arrangement as a result of which money or other property is made available or is to be made available to another, and
(b) he knows or has reasonable cause to suspect that it will or may be used for the purposes of terrorism.

*Money laundering*

Although s 18 of the TA is entitled 'money laundering' and is most likely to be used for   **24.22** money, it also applies to 'laundering' type arrangements in respect of other property.

18   Money laundering.
(1) A person commits an offence if he enters into or becomes concerned in an arrangement which facilitates the retention or control by or on behalf of another person of terrorist property—
(a) by concealment,
(b) by removal from the jurisdiction,
(c) by transfer to nominees, or
(d) in any other way.
(2) It is a defence for a person charged with an offence under subsection (1) to prove that he did not know and had no reasonable cause to suspect that the arrangement related to terrorist property.

*Penalties*

A person guilty of an offence under any of ss 15 to 18 shall be liable—   **24.23**

(a) on conviction on indictment, to imprisonment for a term not exceeding 14 years, to a fine or to both, or
(b) on summary conviction, to imprisonment for a term not exceeding six months, to a fine not exceeding the statutory maximum or to both.

*Disclosure of information*

Section 19 of the TA requires banks and other businesses to report any suspicion they may   **24.24** have that someone is laundering terrorist money or committing any of the other terrorist property offences in ss 15–18. Section 19(1)(b) ensures the offence is focused on suspicions which arise at work, although, importantly s 19(5) preserves the exemption in respect of legal advisers' privileged material. Section 20 ensures that businesses can disclose information to the police without fear of breaching legal restrictions.

Section 21(1) allows for the activities of informants who may have to be involved with terror-   **24.25** ist property if they are not to be found out and protects others who may innocently become involved.

Sections 21A–21G deal with other types of disclosure and the consequences of failing to   **24.26** disclose. Under s 21A(12) (a failure to disclose in the regulated sector) a person guilty of an offence is liable:

(a) on conviction on indictment, to imprisonment for a term not exceeding five years or to a fine or to both;
(b) on summary conviction, to imprisonment for a term not exceeding six months or to a fine not exceeding the statutory maximum or to both.

**24.27**  Section 21B deals with protected disclosures; s 21C disclosure to SOCA; s 21D tipping off in the regulated sector; s 21E disclosures within an undertaking or group etc; s 21F other permitted disclosures between institutions etc; and s 21G other permitted disclosures etc.

**24.28**  These additional sections were inserted by The Terrorism Act 2000 and Proceeds of Crime Act 2002 (Amendment) Regulations 2007.

*Forfeiture*

**24.29**  Section 23 permits the court 'by or before which a person is convicted of an offence under any of sections 15 to 18' to make a forfeiture order. Section 23(6) allows for forfeiture of the proceeds of a terrorist property-related offence. This could arise in a case where an accountant prepared accounts on behalf of a proscribed organisation—thus facilitating the retention or control of the organisation's money—and was paid for doing so.

**24.30**  Section 23 further provides as follows:

> (2) Where a person is convicted of an offence under section 15(1) or (2) or 16, the court may order the forfeiture of any money or other property which, at the time of the offence, the person had in their possession or under their control and which—
>   (a) had been used for the purposes of terrorism, or
>   (b) they intended should be used, or had reasonable cause to suspect might be used, for those purposes.
> (3) Where a person is convicted of an offence under section 15(3) the court may order the forfeiture of any money or other property which, at the time of the offence, the person had in their possession or under their control and which—
>   (a) had been used for the purposes of terrorism, or
>   (b) which, at that time, they knew or had reasonable cause to suspect would or might be used for those purposes.
> (4) Where a person is convicted of an offence under section 17 or 18 the court may order the forfeiture of any money or other property which, at the time of the offence, the person had in their possession or under their control and which—
>   (a) had been used for the purposes of terrorism, or
>   (b) was, at that time, intended by them to be used for those purposes.
> (5) Where a person is convicted of an offence under section 17 the court may order the forfeiture of the money or other property to which the arrangement in question related, and which—
>   (a) had been used for the purposes of terrorism, or
>   (b) at the time of the offence, the person knew or had reasonable cause to suspect would or might be used for those purposes.
> (6) Where a person is convicted of an offence under section 18 the court may order the forfeiture of the money or other property to which the arrangement in question related.
> (7) Where a person is convicted of an offence under any of sections 15 to 18, the court may order the forfeiture of any money or other property which wholly or partly, and directly or indirectly, is received by any person as a payment or other reward in connection with the commission of the offence.

**24.31**  Section 23A sets out provisions for other terrorism offences and offences with a terrorist connection. The court may order the forfeiture of any money or other property where, at the time of the offence, it was in the possession or control of the person convicted; and

(1)  it had been used for the purposes of terrorism,
(2)  it was intended by that person that it should be used for the purposes of terrorism, or
(3)  the court believes that it will be used for the purposes of terrorism unless forfeited.

Section 23A applies to an offence under:

24.32

(a) any of the following provisions of the TA—
- s 54 (weapons training);
- ss 57, 58, or 58A (possessing things and collecting information for the purposes of terrorism);
- ss 59, 60, or 61 (inciting terrorism outside the United Kingdom);

(b) any of the following provisions of Part 1 of the Terrorism Act 2006 (c. 11)—
- s 2 (dissemination of terrorist publications);
- s 5 (preparation of terrorist acts);
- s 6 (training for terrorism);
- ss 9–11 (offences involving radioactive devices or materials) and ancillary offences (as defined in s 94 of the Counter-Terrorism Act 2008; and Sch 2 to the Counter-Terrorism Act 2008).

Section 23B provides that before making an order under ss 23 or 23A, a court must give an opportunity to be heard to any person, other than the convicted person, who claims to be the owner or otherwise interested in anything which can be forfeited under that section.

24.33

In considering whether to make an order under ss 23 or 23A in respect of any property, a court shall have regard to—

24.34

(a) the value of the property, and
(b) the likely financial and other effects on the convicted person of the making of the order (taken together with any other order that the court contemplates making).

### When an offence is not committed

Sections 21ZA and s 21ZB set out the circumstances where an offence would not be committed, for example, where a prior arrangement or disclosure has been made. Section 21ZA provides a defence to the offences in ss 15 to 18 of the TA, if the person has made a disclosure to an authorised officer before becoming involved in a transaction or an arrangement and the person acts with the consent of the authorised officer. Section 21ZB provides a further defence to the offences in ss 15 to 18 to cover those who become involved in a transaction or an arrangement and then make a disclosure, so long as there is a reasonable excuse for failure to make a disclosure in advance. Section 21ZC provides a defence for those who have a reasonable excuse for failure to make a disclosure.

24.35

> It is a defence for a person charged with an offence under any of sections 15 to 18 to prove that (a) the person intended to make a disclosure of the kind mentioned in section 21ZA or 21ZB, and (b) there is a reasonable excuse for the person's failure to do so.

Sections 21ZA–ZC were inserted by The Terrorism Act 2000 and Proceeds of Crime Act 2002 (Amendment) Regulations 2007 (SI 2007/3398).

24.36

### Terrorist cash

Under Sch 1 to the Anti-Terrorism, Crime and Security Act 2001 an authorised officer may seize any cash if he has reasonable grounds for suspecting that it is terrorist cash (see Pt 2 para 2(1)). The provisions that follow seizure reflect essentially the same provisions that are now set out under s 294 et seq of POCA. Whilst the authorised officer continues to have

24.37

reasonable grounds for his suspicion, cash seized under Sch 1 may be detained initially for a period of forty-eight hours (para 3). That period may be extended by an order made by a magistrate's court, but the order may not authorise the detention of any of the cash beyond the end of the period of three months beginning with the date of the order and, in the case of any further order, beyond the date of the period of two years beginning with the date of the first order (see para 3(2)(a) and (b)). Upon application for continued detention of the cash, a magistrates' court must be satisfied of the following two conditions:

(1) that there are reasonable grounds for suspecting that the cash is intended to be used for the purposes of terrorism and that either (a) its continued detention is justified while its intended use is further investigated or consideration is given to bringing (in the UK or elsewhere) proceedings against any person for an offence with which the cash is connected, or (b) proceedings against any person for an offence with which the cash is connected have been started and have not been concluded;

(2) that there are reasonable grounds for suspecting that the cash consists of resources of an organisation which is a proscribed organisation and that either (a) its continued detention is justified while investigation is made into whether or not it consists of such resources or consideration is given to bringing (in the UK or elsewhere) proceedings against any person for an offence with which the cash is connected, or (b) proceedings against any person for an offence with which the cash is connected have been started and have not been concluded;

(3) that there are reasonable grounds for suspecting that the cash is property earmarked as terrorist property and that either (a) its continued detention is justified while its derivation is further investigated or consideration is given to bringing (in the UK or elsewhere) proceedings against any person for an offence with which the cash is connected, or (b) proceedings against any person for an offence with which the cash is connected have been started and have not been concluded (see paras 5–8 of Sch 1 to the Anti-Terrorism Crime and Security Act 2001).

**24.38** As under POCA, if cash is detained it must be held in an interest-bearing account (para 4). The cash may be released in full or in part if the court is satisfied, on an application by the person from whom it was seized, that the conditions in para 3 for the detention of cash are no longer met (para 5(2)). However, the cash may not be released if an application for its forfeiture has been made under para 6 of Sch 1 or if proceedings have been started against any person for an offence with which the cash is connected (para 5(4)). Under para 6, forfeiture may be applied for and the court may order the forfeiture of the cash or any part of it if it is satisfied that the cash or any part of it is terrorist cash. An appeal against a decision of forfeiture may be made under para 7 of Sch 1 to the Crown Court. An appeal must be made within the period of thirty days beginning with the date on which the order is made and is by way of a rehearing (para 7(3)). Under para 9, a person who claims that any cash detained under the Schedule belongs to him may apply to a magistrates' court for the cash or part of it to be released to him at any time during the course of the proceedings.

**24.39** By para 10(1), if no forfeiture is made in respect of any cash detained under the Schedule, the person to whom the cash belongs or from whom it was seized may make an application to the magistrates' court for compensation. If a forfeiture order is made in respect of only part of the detained cash under Sch 1, compensation may be sought in relation to the other part (para 10(9)). An 'authorised person' for the purposes of this part of the Act includes an officer of Revenue and Customs, a constable or police officer, or an immigration officer (para 19). The Magistrates' Courts (Detention and Forfeiture of Terrorist Cash) (No 2) Rules 2001 (SI 2001 No. 4013) set out the procedure to be followed for an application to a magistrates' court under Sch 1.

### Practice and procedure

For further on practice and procedure in relation to cash forfeiture proceedings in the mag- **24.40** istrates' court, see Chapter 15.

### Judicial review

While there remains obvious scope for judicial review proceedings in cash seizure cases, **24.41** in *M v Bow Street Magistrates' Court*, The Times, 27 July 2005, the Court held that in proceedings under the Anti-Terrorism, Crime and Security Act 2001 it was premature to seek permission to challenge by way of judicial review a district judge's decision on a preliminary ruling when the judge had not yet determined any of the factual issues or received evidence in relation to the substantive matter. The Divisional Court held that it would be impossible to know precisely how the legal issues would arise until the evidence was heard and the facts were found.

### Asset Freezing Unit

The Treasury's Asset Freezing Unit (AFU) became operational from 24 October 2007. **24.42**

The AFU is responsible for: **24.43**

- domestic legislation on financial sanctions;
- the implementation and administration of domestic financial sanctions;
- domestic designations under the Terrorist Asset-Freezing etc. Act 2010 (TAFA);
- providing advice to Treasury Ministers, on the basis of operational advice, on domestic designation decisions;
- the implementation and administration of international financial sanctions in the UK, including those relating to terrorism sanctions in relation to States;
- working with the Foreign and Commonwealth Office on the design of individual financial sanctions regimes and listing decisions at the UN and EU;
- working with international partners to develop the international frameworks for financial sanctions;
- licensing exemptions to financial sanctions where permitted.

The AFU issues Notices and notifications advising of the introduction, amendment, suspen- **24.44** sion, or lifting of financial sanctions regimes with a view to making bodies and individuals likely to be affected by financial sanctions aware of their obligations.

Where there is a legal basis for an asset freeze in the UK, the name of the target will be **24.45** included in the consolidated list of financial sanctions home page of the Treasury website. The AFU also processes applications for licences to release frozen funds or to make funds available to designated/restricted persons and responds to reports and queries from financial institutions, companies, and members of the public concerning financial sanctions.

**Financial Intelligence Unit**

**24.46**   Article 21 of Directive 2005/60/EC of the European Parliament and of the Council of 26 October 2005 on the prevention of the use of the financial system for the purpose of money laundering and terrorist financing requires Member States to establish a Financial Intelligence Unit (FIU). SOCA is currently the UK's FIU. This is further expanded in Recital 29 of the Directive. Recital 29 makes it clear that reports of suspicious activity may be made to persons other than the FIU so long as the information is forwarded promptly and unfiltered to the FIU. Both the TA and POCA allow disclosures to be made to a person other than SOCA and so new s 21C of the TA (inserted by para 5 of Sch 1) and s 339ZA of POCA (inserted by para 7 of Sch 2) give effect to the requirements of Art 21 together with Recital 29. For a summary of the various restrictions imposed by the Terrorism and Investigation Measures Notice, see *CF v Secretary of State for the Home Dept* [2013] EWHC 843 (Admin).

**The Terrorism Act 2000 and Proceeds of Crime Act 2002 (Business in the Regulated Sector) (No 2) Order 2012**

**24.47**   This Order amends the definition of a business in the regulated sector for the purposes of Pt 3 of the TA (terrorist property) and Pt 7 of POCA (money laundering). These Parts contain provisions relating to the reporting of suspicious activity, including requirements and offences specific to such businesses. The amendment includes estate agents selling property outside the UK within the scope of the definition.

**The Terrorist Asset-Freezing etc. Act 2010**

**24.48**   In *Ahmed v HM Treasury* [2010] UKSC 2 the UK Supreme Court ruled on the asset-freezing regime established by the anti-terrorism measures Orders. The Supreme Court found (paras 39 and 192) the Orders to be unlawful because it held that they went much further than was required by the UN Security Council resolutions 1267 (dealing with Taliban assets) and 1373 (introduced after the 9/11 attacks). As one Justice of the Supreme Court put it: 'The draconian nature of the regime imposed under these asset-freezing Orders can hardly be over-stated.'

**24.49**   These anti-terrorism measures Orders were made under s 1 of the UN Act to give effect to obligations created by resolution 1373. Principally, these were the Terrorism (United Nations Measures) Order 2001 (the '2001 Order'), the Terrorism (United Nations Measures) Order 2006 (the '2006 Order') and the Terrorism (United Nations Measures) Order 2009 (the '2009 Order'). These Orders provided for the freezing, without limit of time, of the funds, economic resources, and financial services available to, among others, persons who had been designated. The effect of the Orders was to deprive those persons of all resources. In particular, they provided that the Treasury could give a direction designating any person whom it had 'reasonable grounds for suspecting' was or might be, among other things, a person who committed, attempted to commit, participated in, or facilitated the commission of acts of terrorism.

**24.50**   On 27 January 2010 the Supreme Court decided in the case of *Ahmed* that the 2006 Order was ultra vires, and on 4 February 2010 made an order quashing the 2006 Order. The Supreme Court did not rule upon the lawfulness of the 2001 Order or the 2009 Order, but both Orders were vulnerable to being quashed on the same grounds as the 2006 Order.

**24.51**   Following the quashing of the 2006 Order, the government introduced the Terrorist Asset-Freezing (Temporary Provisions) Act 2010. This provided that the Terrorism Orders were deemed to have been validly made under the UN Act and for directions imposing asset freezes to have continued effect, for the period from Royal Assent (10 February 2010) until 31 December 2010. The Act therefore maintained the terrorist asset-freezing restrictions which had been quashed by the Supreme Court ruling or which were vulnerable to being quashed as a consequence of that ruling.

Under the new rules, the applicant is now required to have a reasonable 'belief' rather than 'suspicion' before imposing final asset-freezing orders. Concerns still remain that no person should have their assets indefinitely frozen on the basis of untested belief alone. However, the new appeal mechanism goes someway to meet that concern. **24.52**

The Terrorist Asset-Freezing (Temporary Provisions) Act 2010 was subsumed into TAFA. The new Act once again gives effect in the UK to SC resolution 1373 and SC resolution 1452 following the *Ahmed* case. **24.53**

The purpose of Pt 2 of the Act is to make amendments to Sch 7 to the Counter-Terrorism Act 2008. Schedule 7 provides the Treasury with powers (by direction) to impose financial restrictions in relation to persons connected with a country (a 'country of concern') in response to money laundering, terrorist financing, or the development or production of nuclear, radiological, biological, or chemical weapons that pose a risk to the national interests of the United Kingdom, or where the Financial Action Task Force has advised that measures should be taken in relation to the country because of the risk of terrorist financing or money laundering activities. **24.54**

Part 2 of the Act also makes amendments to the Sch 7 powers to clarify the persons to whom a direction may be given, to broaden the definition of persons in relation to whom restrictions may be applied, and to introduce a prohibition on circumventing the requirements of a direction. **24.55**

In short, the 2010 Act: **24.56**

- attempts to ensure that no person should have their assets indefinitely frozen on the basis of untested suspicion;
- allows for the Executive to designate individuals as suspected terrorists on the basis of material received (often classified);
- formalises the appeal process;
- works in parallel to the asset-freezing powers in the Anti-Terrorism Crime and Security Act 2001 and the terrorist financing provisions of the TA and POCA.

### Designated persons

The financial restrictions contained in Pt 1 of TAFA apply to 'designated persons'. Section 1 defines 'designated person' as (a) a person designated by the Treasury or (b) a person included in the list provided for by Art 2(3) of the EU Regulation (Council Regulation (EU) No 2580/2001). The EU Regulation was a measure adopted by the EC to implement resolution 1373. It provides that the Council should establish a list of persons to whom asset-freezes apply. The list is made up of persons put forward for inclusion by a 'Competent Authority' in a Member State and on the basis that the Authority has taken relevant steps (eg, to prosecute for a terrorist offence or freeze assets domestically) against that person. The Treasury is a Competent Authority for these purposes. Part 1 of the Terrorist Asset-Freezing etc. Act 2010 gives effect to Resolution 1373 in the UK. **24.57**

*Terrorist activity*

**24.58**  Section 2 of TAFA provides as follows:

> (2) For this purpose involvement in terrorist activity is any one or more of the following—
>> (a) the commission, preparation or instigation of acts of terrorism;
>> (b) conduct that facilitates the commission, preparation or instigation of such acts, or that is intended to do so;
>> (c) conduct that gives support or assistance to persons who are known or believed by the person concerned to be involved in conduct falling within paragraph (a) or (b) of this subsection.
>
> (3) It is immaterial whether the acts of terrorism in question are specific acts of terrorism or acts of terrorism generally.
>
> (4) In this section—
> 'terrorism' has the same meaning as in the Terrorism Act 2000 (see section 1(1) to (4) of that Act).

**24.59**  The Explanatory Notes to the Act summarise the legislative intent, including:

*Confidential information*

**24.60**  Section 10 of TAFA provides that where the Treasury informs only a limited number of persons of an interim designation or a final designation the Treasury may specify that certain information contained in the notification is to be treated as confidential. Such a person (or another person who obtains the information) commits an offence if he or she discloses the information without lawful authority and knowing or having reasonable cause to suspect that it is to be treated as confidential (subss (1), (2), (3), and (6)).

*Making economic resources available to a designated person*

**24.61**  Section 14 of TAFA makes it an offence for a person to make economic resources available (directly or indirectly) to a designated person if the person making the economic resources available knows, or has reasonable cause to suspect, that (a) the economic resources are being made available (directly or indirectly) to a designated person and (b) the designated person would be likely to exchange the economic resources, or use them in exchange, for funds, goods, or services. See also s 15, which also makes it an offence to make economic resources available for the benefit of a designated person.

*Circumventing prohibitions etc*

**24.62**  Under s 18 of TAFA it is an offence for a person intentionally to participate in activities knowing that their object or effect is (whether directly or indirectly) to circumvent, or enable or facilitate the contravention of, the prohibitions in ss 11 to 15 of the Act.

*Appeal to the court in relation to designations*

**24.63**  Section 26 of TAFA provides that a designated person may appeal to the High Court or the Court of Session against a Treasury decision to make or vary, or not to vary or revoke, an interim or final designation, or a Treasury decision to renew a final designation. In determining the appeal the Court may quash the Treasury decision, require the Treasury to revoke the decision, or make such an order as to the validity of the Treasury decision as it thinks appropriate. Subsection (4) provides that where a designated person appeals against a decision relating to a designation this does not suspend the effect of the decision.

*Review of other decisions by the court*

Section 27 of TAFA provides for the review and setting aside of decisions made by the **24.64** Treasury in connection with their functions under Pt 1 of the Act, other than those decisions set out in s 26(1).

*Penalties*

Section 32 of TAFA provides for penalties in relation to breaches of the prohibitions in Part 1 **24.65** of the Act. Subsection (1) provides that a person guilty of any of the offences under ss 11, 12, 13, 14, 15, or 18 is, on conviction on indictment, liable to a maximum of seven years' imprisonment or to a fine or to both or, on summary conviction, to imprisonment for a term not exceeding the 'relevant maximum' (this term is defined in subsection (3)) or to a fine not exceeding the statutory maximum (which is currently set at £5,000) or to both.

# 25

## CIVIL FRAUD BEFORE THE TAX TRIBUNAL

## A. Introduction

In 2005 and 2006 missing trader intra-community (MTIC) fraud was particularly prevalent **25.01** in the UK. The Tax Tribunal continues to deal with many legacy cases that date back to that period. The vast majority of these cases involve trading in mobile telephones and computer components, but the reality is that MTIC fraud can infect any trade in goods that are subject to VAT, especially if the goods are of a high value.

The opportunity for this type of fraud has largely fallen away following the introduction **25.02** of SI 2007/1417 and SI 2007/1418, which introduced a reverse charge system for VAT on goods being dispatched within the EU. But the potential in terms of pre-existing VAT claims assures that these matters are likely to remain in the tribunal system for some time to come. The claims often run into millions of pounds and the stakes for both sides remain high.

The figures speak for themselves. In 2006–07, the scale of attempted MTIC fraud, per the **25.03** UK Treasury, was between £2.25 billion and £3.25 billion. The estimated impact on VAT receipts for 2006–07 was between £1 billion and £2 billion (not all of the attempted frauds having been successful). The significance of these losses to the Exchequer is obvious. The potential profits from this type of scheme are yet another manifestation of the proceeds of unlawful conduct in the UK.

### How the fraud works

In a simple MTIC fraud, the fraud will usually take place in the following way: **25.04**

(1) Trader A, based in an EU Member State (eg France), sells taxable goods to Trader B, in another EU Member State (eg the UK). The supply is zero-rated (ie VAT is charged at zero per cent).

(2) Trader B sells the goods to a UK customer or 'buffer' trader (Buffer 1) and charges VAT on the transaction (Trader B's output VAT). Buffer 1 pays the VAT inclusive price to Trader B (Buffer 1's input VAT). Trader B becomes liable to HMRC for the VAT it has received on the goods. Trader B becomes a 'defaulting trader' by not discharging its VAT liability. Often Trader B 'hijacks' a VAT number (ie uses a VAT number belonging to someone else) or goes 'missing' (hence the name of the fraud).

(3) The goods may then be sold on through a number of UK Buffer companies.

(4) The last UK 'buffer' company (eg Buffer 3) sells the goods to a UK 'broker' ('Trader C') and charges VAT on the transaction. Trader C exports the goods and the transaction is zero rated for VAT. Trader C is placed in a repayment position (received from HMRC) by virtue of the VAT it paid to Buffer 3. Trader C then files a VAT return showing a repayment claim for VAT at the end of its VAT accounting period. Subject to investigations, HMRC would then repay to Trader C the VAT that it has claimed for repayment.

**25.05** The net result of the fraud is that HMRC has to refund an amount that is often more than the original amount that should have been paid by the defaulting/missing trader (Trader B). In short, HMRC loses the VAT that would be due from Trader B and ends up having to pay out a VAT reclaim to Trader C.

**25.06** This illustration, taken from the UK Parliament website, demonstrates how a simple MTIC fraud operates:

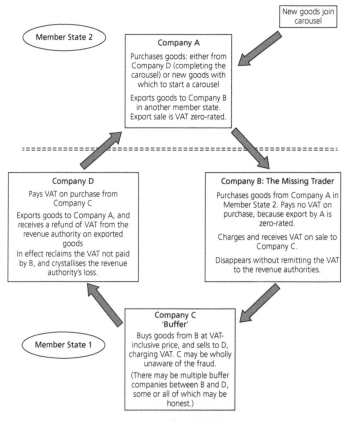

*Note:* Used under the Open Parliament Licence. Adapted from VAT fraud and evasion: what do we know and what can be done? Keen & Smith, National Tax Journal Vol LIX, No 4 December 2006

In a 'carousel fraud' the same goods are traded repeatedly, often by the same companies. **25.07**

The key to understanding the fraud is to bear in mind that imports and exports between EU **25.08** countries are zero-rated for VAT. This gave rise to an entitlement to claim back VAT from HMRC for companies at the end of the supply chain (the exporter). (For the right to set off, see below.)

## Contra trading

'Contra-trading' has been described by HMRC as a mutation of MTIC fraud, which was **25.09** designed by fraudsters to defeat 'extended verification' (ie the process by which HMRC traces chains of transactions to establish if a defaulting trader is present in the chain). The way in which the traders are said to generate such a deception is by orchestrating two chains of transactions: a 'clean chain' and a 'dirty chain' (although, arguably, both chains are 'dirty' because they are part of the same fraud).

(1) The 'dirty chain' possesses the normal characteristics of a simple MTIC fraud, including a defaulting trader (ie 'Trader B' in the example above). Trader C appears as a normal broker in the dirty chain.

(2) In the 'clean chain' Trader C also acts as an acquirer and purchases goods of a similar value to the goods in the 'dirty' chain directly from another EU Member State (Trader X).

(3) Trader C then sells the clean chain goods (plus VAT) to a UK broker (Trader Y) who then exports the goods to outside the UK (zero rated), thus creating a VAT repayment claim for Trader Y.

By offsetting its net output tax as an acquirer in the contra trading chain against its net input **25.10** tax as a broker in the defaulter chain, Trader C ends up disguising its own repayment claim by creating a contra-trading chain with no (apparent) VAT loss. The repayment claim has effectively been shifted, by means of contrived transactions, to Trader Y, who appears not to be participating in a transaction chain that commences with a defaulting trader.

## EU legislation

Articles 167 and 168 of Council Directive 2006/112/EC of 28 November 2006 ('the VAT **25.11** Directive') provide:

167—A right of deduction shall arise at the time the deductible tax becomes charged.

168—In so far as the goods and services are used for the purposes of the taxed transactions of a taxable person, the taxable person shall be entitled, in the Member State in which he carries out these transactions, to deduct the following from the VAT which he is liable to pay:
(a) the VAT due or paid in that Member State in respect of supplies to him of goods or services, carried out or to be carried out by another taxable person.

This VAT Directive recast Council Directive 77/388/EEC of 17 May 1977 ('the Sixth **25.12** Directive') and acted as a codification for the relevant legislation. Article 17 was recast as Article 167.

## Domestic legislation

### *The right to set off*

Sections 24 to 26 of the Value Added Tax Act 1994 (VATA 1994) implemented Art 17(1)–(3) **25.13** of the Sixth Directive. Sections 24 to 26 are mandatory and provide that a taxpayer who has incurred input tax that is properly allowable, is entitled *as of right* to set that input tax off against his output tax liability. The taxpayer is entitled to receive a repayment, in the form of a VAT credit, where the input tax due to him exceeds his liability. The ECJ and the domestic courts are always slow to interfere with this right because it underpins the proper functioning of the VAT system by ensuring fiscal neutrality.

**25.14**  Thus, if a taxable person has incurred input tax that is properly allowable, he is entitled to set it against his output tax liability and, if the input tax credit due to him exceeds the output tax liability, receive a repayment. For the rules concerning the claiming of a deduction of input tax, and the evidence required, see Regulations 13 and 29 of the Value Added Tax Regulations 1995 (SI 1995/2518).

### HMRC's decision to refuse to repay VAT

**25.15**  HMRC introduced Extended Verification to establish whether transactions that formed the basis for claims for VAT repayments were connected to fraud. The validity of such a process was tested in *R (Just Fabulous (UK) Ltd and others) v HMRC* [2007] EWHC 521 (Admin) where the Court held that the length of time that HMRC took to investigate a claim for repayment of VAT must be proportionate and this involved a consideration of both the value of the claim for repayment and the complexity of the investigation. HMRC may often spend a considerable time investigating claims for repayment where the value of the claim is high, before issuing a decision that constitutes a refusal by HMRC to repay VAT to the trader.

**25.16**  Once a decision has been issued by HMRC, a taxpayer has three choices:

(1)  do nothing; or
(2)  ask for a review; or
(3)  appeal to the Tax Tribunal.

### *Right to review*

**25.17**  Pursuant to s 83A(1) of the Value Added Tax Act 1994 (VATA 1994), HMRC must offer a review to a taxpayer who has been given a decision that is capable of appeal to the Tax Tribunal. HMRC must conduct a review where a taxpayer notifies HMRC of his request for a review within thirty days of the date of the decision (s 83C(1)(b) VATA 1994). HMRC may extend the time in which a review must be requested and may also conduct reviews out of time (see ss 83D and 83E VATA 1994 respectively). HMRC must not conduct a review where an appeal has been notified to the Tribunal (s 83C(4)). HMRC have forty-five days in which to conduct the review, but may agree an extension of time with the taxpayer (s 83F(6)). If HMRC uphold the decision upon a review, the taxpayer may then appeal that review decision to the Tax Tribunal within thirty days of the review being concluded (s 83G VATA 1994).

### *Appeals*

**25.18**  If the taxpayer decides to appeal against the decision of HMRC to the Tribunal, rather than request a review by HMRC, he must do so within thirty days of the date of the document that notified him of the decision to which the appeal relates (s 83G(1) VATA 1994).

The Tribunal's jurisdiction to hear an appeal against a decision in an appeal based on an alle- **25.19** gation of knowledge of a connection to MTIC fraud will involve a denial of input tax and thus will fall within VATA 1994 s 83(1)(c):

83 Appeals

[(1)] Subject to [ss 83G and 84], an appeal shall lie to [the tribunal] with respect to any of the following matters—

...

(c) the amount of any input tax which may be credited to a person...

# B. Practice and Procedure

## The procedural rules of the Tax Tribunal

The Tribunal Procedure (First-Tier Tribunal) (Tax Chamber) Rules 2009 (SI 2003/273) **25.20** (as amended) govern all cases litigated in the Tax Tribunal. The Rules have introduced an Overriding Objective (r 2), similar to that found in the CPR. It requires the Tribunal to deal with cases fairly and justly and imposes an obligation upon the parties to cooperate with the Tribunal. The Rules also provide for alternative dispute resolution and arbitration (r 3), although in MTIC cases this is rare. The procedure before the Tribunal is set out in Pt 3 of the Rules and the procedure for starting an appeal is contained in r 20. The Tribunal enjoys broad case management powers, including the ability to strike out a case and make directions in relation to evidence and submissions (see rr 5, 6, 8, and 15).

## Costs

Rule 10 permits the Tribunal to make an order for costs, but its jurisdiction in this respect **25.21** is very limited. This is of particular note in MTIC litigation because the costs incurred by both parties can be significant due to the volume of evidence produced by HMRC. An exception to the limitation placed upon the Tribunal's power to make a costs order is where a case has been categorised as complex, pursuant to r 24, and the taxpayer has not opted out within twenty-eight days of notification of allocation. If costs are likely to be an issue, the parties should raise the matter at a directions hearing or in correspondence at the earliest opportunity.

## The questions for the Tribunal

The questions that the Tribunal must ask itself in an appeal against a decision based upon an **25.22** allegation of knowledge of a connection to MTIC fraud are helpfully set out in the case of *Blue Sphere Global Ltd v HMRC* [2009] EWHC 1150 (Ch) (at [29]):

(1)  Was there a tax loss?
(2)  If so, did this tax loss result from fraudulent evasion?
(3)  If there was a fraudulent evasion of VAT, were the transactions that are the subject of the appeal connected with that evasion?
(4)  If connection is established, did the taxpayer know or should the taxpayer have known, that its purchases were connected with the fraudulent evasion of VAT?

**25.23** The majority of MTIC appeals revolve around what the appellant knew or should have known because this is the issue where the appellant is likely to make a positive case. In some appeals, taxpayers do not concede tax loss, connection, and fraud and thus the hearing can be lengthy. HMRC often produce huge volumes of documentation to prove these issues.

### Burden of proof

**25.24** The burden of proof is upon HMRC. In *Mobilx Limited (In Administration) and others v The Commissioners of Her Majesty's Revenue and Customs* [2010] EWCA Civ 517 Moses LJ stated: 'It is plain that if HMRC wishes to assert that a trader's state of knowledge was such that his purchase is outwith the scope of the right to deduct it must prove that assertion.'

**25.25** In *Livewire v HMRC* [2009] EWHC 15 (Ch), Lewison J referred to HMRC's branding of a taxpayer as a 'contra-trader' as 'HMRC coinage' (para 109) and stated that this is necessarily something that HMRC must prove. Similarly, it must be borne in mind that the terms of art that HMRC freely use in cases such as this are actually allegations that HMRC must prove: a taxpayer is not a defaulter, buffer, or broker until he is proved to be so.

**25.26** In *Red 12 Trading v HMRC* [2009] EWHC 2563 (Ch), Christopher Clarke J said (at para 12):

> … In determining what it was that the taxpayer knew or ought to have known the Tribunal is entitled to look at the *totality of the deals* effected by the taxpayer (and their characteristics), and at what the taxpayer did or omitted to do, and what it could have done, together with the surrounding circumstances in respect of all of them. (Emphasis added.)

**25.27** In *Blue Sphere Global Ltd v Commissioners for Revenue and Customs* (2008) UK VAT 20901 at para 152, the Tribunal found it helpful to adopt the approach taken in the direct tax case of *Hall (Inspector of Taxes) v Lorimer* [1992] STC 599 by Mummery J at 612 and subsequently approved by Nolan LJ [1994] STC 23 at 29:

> The object of the exercise is to paint a picture from the accumulation of detail. The overall effect can only be appreciated by standing back from the detailed picture which has been painted, by viewing it from a distance and by making an informed, considered, qualitative appreciation of the whole. It is a matter of evaluation of the overall effect of the detail, which is not necessarily the same as the sum total of the individual details. Not all details are of equal weight or importance in any given situation. The details may also vary in importance from one situation to another. The process involves painting a picture in each individual case.

**25.28** The Tribunal continued:

> Individual factors may be insufficient in themselves to lead to a conclusion that a trader 'should have known', but the accumulation of a whole series of such factors may prove to be of such weight that, on the evidence before a tribunal, this can be the only conclusion.

**25.29** In *Livewire* (at 102–103), Lewison J stated:

> In my judgment in a case of alleged contra-trading, where the taxable person claiming repayment of input tax is not himself a dishonest co-conspirator, there are two potential frauds:
>
> (i) The dishonest failure to account for VAT by the defaulter or missing trader in the dirty chain; and
> (ii) The dishonest cover-up of that fraud by the contra-trader.
>
> Thus it must be established that the taxable person knew or should have known of a connection between his own transaction and at least one of those frauds. I do not consider that it is necessary that he knew or should have known of a connection between his own transaction

and both of these frauds. If he knows or should have known that the contra-trader is engaging in fraudulent conduct and deals with him, he takes the risk of participating in a fraud, the precise details of which he does not and cannot know.

## Standard of proof

The standard of proof that is applied in all civil proceedings is proof on the balance of prob- **25.30** abilities. In *Secretary of State v Rehman* [2001] UKHL 47, Lord Hoffmann said (at para 55):

> . . . The civil standard of proof always means more likely than not. The only higher degree of probability required by the law is the criminal standard. But, as Lord Nicholls of Birkenhead explained in *In re H (Minors) (Sexual Abuse: Standard of Proof)* [1996] AC 563, 586, some things are inherently more likely than others . . . cogent evidence is generally required to satisfy a civil tribunal that a person has been fraudulent or behaved in some other reprehensible manner. But the question is always whether the tribunal thinks it more probable than not.

## The likely issues

Because of the way that MTIC fraud operates, the basic facts of each case are usually very **25.31** similar. The differences in each case are likely usually to arise in respect of the knowledge/ means of knowledge issue. As explained above, the burden of proving each issue in the appeal is upon HMRC and the way in which HMRC often does this is summarised below.

### Tax loss

There is usually some overlap between tax loss and the fraud issues because HMRC produce **25.32** witness evidence that explains why and how an assessment to VAT has been raised against any given defaulting trader. In large contra-trading cases the volume of evidence that is produced in relation to tax loss can be significant because it may be that many defaulting traders are connected to contra-traders. The volume of evidence in relation to the tax loss issue may also be significant because HMRC can produce evidence, such as purchase orders and sales invoices, to demonstrate the trading that the alleged defaulting trader conducted.

Evidence that an assessment to VAT has not been paid will usually persuade the Tribunal **25.33** that HMRC have suffered a tax loss. Practitioners representing taxpayers can approach this issue by ensuring that the assessments were properly raised and notified to the alleged defaulter in accordance with the relevant law (ss 73–77 VATA 1994). It is often the case that the alleged defaulting trader is also said to have gone missing and that records were not kept by the trader or have not been obtained by HMRC, causing HMRC to raise assessments to VAT using 'best judgment' (s 73(1) VATA 1994). Time limits for the raising of assessments are provided for in s 77 VATA 1994, but this is rarely an issue because s 77(4A) provides for a twenty-year time limit for the raising of an assessment in a case of fraud.

HMRC do not need to assess a tax loss that is equivalent to the tax repayment claim **25.34** of the appellant. That issue was resolved by the Court of Appeal in *Mobilx Limited (In Administration) and others v The Commissioners of Her Majesty's Revenue and Customs* [2010] EWCA Civ 517 and followed by the Upper Tribunal in *S&I Electronics plc v Revenue and Customs Commissioners* [2012] STC 1620.

### Fraud

As Lewison J held in *Livewire*, there are two potential frauds that the appellant could have **25.35** known about: (1) the fraud of a defaulting trader and/or (2) the fraud of a contra-trader (where such an allegation exists in an appeal). The fact that the appellant only needs to have known that his transactions were connected to one of these two frauds does not relieve HMRC of the burden of demonstrating that the two frauds occurred. The tax loss must be shown to be fraudulent and the contra-trader must be demonstrated to be a contra-trader. Only once these frauds, and a connection between the fraudulent transactions and the transactions of the appellant, have been shown can HMRC begin to attempt to prove that knowledge, or the means of knowledge.

### The grey market

**25.36** HMRC often serve expert evidence from a market economist. In short, this expert confirms that a grey market exists, but not to a scale that would support the volume of trading that the appellant has conducted. The expert bases his opinion on an estimate on the size of the grey market for mobile telephones that existed in 2006 and then attempts to opine what market share an appellant would have had. Procedurally, practitioners should be aware of Tribunal Rule 15(1)(c) which provides that the Tribunal may give directions as to 'whether the parties are permitted or required to provide expert evidence, and if so whether the parties must jointly appoint a single expert to provide such evidence'. It is submitted that the wording of this Rule indicates that a party should apply for permission to rely on expert evidence. Technically, practitioners should be aware of the usual duties and responsibilities of experts (see *National Justice Compania Naviera SA v Prudential Assurance Co Ltd (The Ikarian Reefer)* [1993] 2 Lloyd's Rep 68).

### Connection

**25.37** In order to prove connection, HMRC usually produce volumes of commercial documentation that has been uplifted from all of the traders involved in the transaction chains and the freight forwarders that have held and shipped the goods. HMRC will often have summarised their case on connection by producing schedules which they refer to as 'deal sheets'. It is a lengthy task, but it is advisable for practitioners to thoroughly check that each HMRC schedule accurately reflects the evidence served and that the evidence served actually makes out a chain of transactions.

**25.38** The Tribunal has set a fairly low standard for HMRC to reach in order to prove connection (see for example appendix 1 to the decision of the Tribunal in *S&I Electronics plc v Revenue and Customs Commissioners* [2009] UKFTT 108 (TC)). It is submitted that practitioners should have in mind the requirement for cogent evidence of fraud when arguing what documents may or may not constitute 'connection' for the purposes of the *Kittel* test.

### Knowledge and means of knowledge

**25.39** It is quite rare for HMRC to rely on direct evidence of knowledge or means of knowledge of a connection between a taxpayer's transactions and fraud. It is more usual for HMRC to rely on all of the facts of the case to demonstrate that a trader knew or *should have known* of a connection between his transactions and fraud. HMRC usually attempt to identify certain facts from which they invite the Tribunal to infer knowledge or means of knowledge, such as:

- Back-to-back trading. This type of trading involves stock being held by a freight forwarder and then traded by companies in the supply chain. The traders do not take physical possession of the goods. The traders generally sell the same quantity of stock that they bought. HMRC contend that this type of trading is not commercial and is unrealistic and that the taxpayer would know or should have known this. HMRC will pursue this point with vigour where it can be established that the goods were imported, traded, and exported on the same day and that all deals were conducted successfully. The Tribunal has, however, found at first instance that back-to-back trading is not necessarily an indication of fraud or knowledge of the same in itself, and in fact may simply be how trade is conducted in this industry sector. (See *Livewire Telecom Limited v The Commissioners of HM Revenue & Customs*, January 2008, per Judge Avery Jones at para 40(3).)

- No evidence of negotiation. HMRC often contend that because an appellant cannot produce documentary evidence of negotiation, the Tribunal should infer that the deals were pre-arranged and not actually negotiated at all. Appellants often give evidence to the effect that trading was conducted over the phone and notes were kept at the time, but that they had not realised such evidence would be required by HMRC years later in order to make a repayment of VAT. Both cases have found support in the Tribunal and much will turn on the credibility of an appellant when giving evidence.

- No or insufficient insurance. HMRC will often criticise the insurance that traders have in place in respect of the goods that they have traded. This will always be a matter of fact and varies from case to case. Some traders will have purchased their own marine insurance, whilst others may have relied only upon the insurance of their designated freight forwarder.

- No market research and insufficient product knowledge. HMRC will often contend that no evidence of market research has been produced by an appellant and/or that the appellant has not demonstrated any significant product knowledge. Additionally, HMRC may also argue that, where the facts support such a case, there was no rationale for importing products that could not have been readily used within the UK, such as mobile phones with two-pin chargers.

- Lack of or insufficient/inaccurate inspection reports. HMRC may contend that a trader should have inspected the high-value stock that he or she was trading. Equally, HMRC may try to identify a lack of specificity in the documentation (eg the inspection report does not contain enough detail about product condition or the contents of the packaging to be of any use to a trader in assessing whether the correct goods have been delivered to the freight forwarder) or inaccuracies/inconsistencies between the inspection reports and commercial documents.

- High turnover. HMRC will usually measure the increase in turnover that an appellant company has experienced between start-up and the point at which its VAT returns entered into extended verification. In many MTIC cases, the turnover of the appellant quickly rises to very high levels. This argument often finds support in the Tribunal and has done so in the High Court and Court of Appeal. In order to counter this point, appellants often follow the argument that 'turnover is vanity and profit is sanity' and thus measure the gross and net profits achieved over the same period that HMRC measured turnover and then contrast the figures.

- Credit checks. HMRC often contend that a trader should check the creditworthiness of customers. Conversely, traders often contend that they did not trade on credit.

- Due diligence. HMRC will also examine the due diligence records kept by traders for indicators that should have caused the trader to not conduct a deal with a particular party. This issue is discussed in more detail below.

### The FCIB

In most MTIC cases, HMRC will seek to produce evidence obtained from the First Curacao **25.40** International Bank ('FCIB'), established in the Netherlands Antilles. The availability of such evidence is, of course, dependent upon the appellant having maintained an account at the bank. Very many traders did so in 2006, partly because banks in the UK had begun to close the accounts of mobile phones traders.

**25.41** In September 2006 the Investigation Service of the Tax and Customs Administration in the Netherlands took action against FCIB. Arrests and searches were made; and the bank's hard drives and servers were uplifted in the Netherlands. The bank's computers contained FCIB account information and transaction records.

**25.42** In the case of *MSL v HMRC* FTC/35/2010, the taxpayer challenged the admissibility of FCIB evidence in Tax Tribunal proceedings on two key grounds: (1) that the evidence was inadmissible in tax tribunal proceedings without the consent of the Dutch authorities; and (2) that the evidence was unreliable, because it contained errors and was exhibited to the witness statement of a non-expert who gave opinions as to its effect. Mr Justice Arnold, sitting in the Upper Tribunal, dismissed the taxpayer's appeal for the following key reasons: (1) the statutory framework through which the evidence was provided by Dutch Customs to HMRC did not render the evidence inadmissible in Tax Tribunal proceedings and, in any event, the Dutch had given consent for the evidence to be used in such proceedings; and (2) Tribunal Rule 15(2) permits the Tribunal to admit evidence whether or not the evidence would be admissible in a civil trial, including opinion of a non-expert, and the weight to be attached to any such evidence was a matter for the judge.

**25.43** As a result, FCIB evidence continues to be relied on by HMRC, in addition to the other categories of evidence outlined above, to prove fraud, connection, and, where appropriate, knowledge of connection.

### EU authorities

**25.44** MTIC fraud has been considered by the ECJ in several cases over the last seven years. The key decision for the purposes of an appeal against a decision to refuse repayment of input tax based on an allegation of knowledge of a connection to MTIC fraud is *Axel Kittel v Belgian State and Belgian State v Recolta Recycling SPRL* (Joined Cases C-439/04 and C-440/04) [2006] ECR I-6161 ('*Kittel*'). At para 47 the Court held:

> In fact, the right to deduct provided for in Article 17 et seq. of the Sixth Directive is an integral part of the VAT scheme and in principle may not be limited. The right to deduct is exercisable immediately in respect of all the taxes charged on transactions relating to inputs (see, in particular, Case C-62/93 *BP Supergas* [1995] ECR I-1883, paragraph 18, and Joined Cases C-110/98 to C-147/98 *Gabalfrisa and others* [2000] ECR I-1577, paragraph 43).

**25.45** In *Kittel*, at para 45, the ECJ followed its earlier decision in *Optigen Limited v Customs and Excise Commissioners* (Case C-354/03) [2006] ECR I-483 ('*Optigen*') and said:

> The Court observed [in *Optigen*] that the right to deduct input VAT of a taxable person who carries out such transactions likewise cannot be affected by the fact that, in the chain of supply of which those transactions form part, another prior or subsequent transaction is vitiated by VAT fraud, without that taxable person knowing or having any means of knowing (*Optigen*, paragraph 52).

**25.46** The operative part of the judgment in *Kittel* begins at [51], where the ECJ states:

> In the light of the foregoing, it is apparent that traders who take every precaution which could reasonably be required of them to ensure that their transactions are not connected with fraud,

be it the fraudulent evasion of VAT or other fraud, must be able to rely on the legality of those transactions without the risk of losing their right to deduct the input VAT (see, to that effect, Case C-384/04 *Federation of Technological Industries and others* [2006] ECR I-04191, paragraph 33).

The ECJ reiterated at para 55 that the test for the national court to apply in determining whether to refuse the right to deduct is objective: 'It is a matter for the national court to refuse to allow the right to deduct where it is established, on the basis of objective evidence, that that right is being relied on for fraudulent ends (see *Fini H*, paragraph 34).'  **25.47**

Further, the Court held:  **25.48**

> 56  In the same way, a taxable person who knew or should have known that, by his purchase, he was taking part in a transaction connected with fraudulent evasion of VAT must, for the purposes of the Sixth Directive, be regarded as a participant in that fraud, irrespective of whether or not he profited by the resale of the goods.
>
> 57  That is because in such a situation the taxable person aids the perpetrators of the fraud and becomes their accomplice.
>
> 58  In addition, such an interpretation, by making it more difficult to carry out fraudulent transactions, is apt to prevent them.

The ECJ summarised the position at para 61 and expressed the '*Kittel* test':  **25.49**

> By contrast, where it is ascertained, having regard to objective factors, that the supply is to a taxable person who knew or should have known that, by his purchase, he was participating in a transaction connected with fraudulent evasion of VAT, it is for the national court to refuse that taxable person entitlement to the right to deduct.

### Domestic authorities

In *Mobilx Limited (In Administration) and others v The Commissioners of Her Majesty's Revenue and Customs* [2010] EWCA Civ 517 the Court was concerned with two questions (see [4]):  **25.50**

(1) What did the ECJ in *Kittel* mean by 'should have known'?
(2) Is it sufficient that the taxpayer knew or should have known that it was more likely than not that his purchase was connected to fraud or must it be established that he knew or should have known that the transactions in which he was involved *were* connected to fraud?

*Objective test*

Moses LJ recognised that the application of the *Kittel* test required application of objective criteria (para 20):  **25.51**

> The Court's statement of principle [in *Kittel*] depended upon the application of objective criteria which define the scope of VAT. Since the right to deduct is integral to the system of VAT, those objective criteria also define the scope of the right to deduct. It applied those objective criteria to traders who were not themselves fraudulent but knew or should have known their transactions were connected to fraud. By focussing on those objective criteria the court avoided infringing the fundamental principles of fiscal neutrality and legal certainty which lie at the heart of the VAT system.

In terms of the right to deduct where the taxpayer 'should have known' that his transaction was connected to fraud, Moses LJ stated (para 52):  **25.52**

If a taxpayer has the means at his disposal of knowing that by his purchase he is participating in a transaction connected with fraudulent evasion of VAT he loses his right to deduct, not as a penalty for negligence, but because the objective criteria for the scope of that right are not met…A trader who fails to deploy means of knowledge available to him does not satisfy the objective criteria which must be met before his right to deduct arises.

*Knowledge of connection*

**25.53** In answering the question as to what knowledge of connection HMRC must prove in order for a trader to lose his entitlement to deduct, Moses LJ first reiterated the following principle at para 54:

As I have already indicated, the mere existence of that objective and the principle that Community law cannot be relied upon for fraudulent ends (e.g., *Fini H* § 32) does not provide any justification for a general principle that any transaction connected with fraud is vitiated. Such an approach was rejected in *Optigen*.

**25.54** The importance of the recognition that Moses LJ made at para 54 of *Mobilx* is patent: to successfully deny a taxpayer his right to deduct, HMRC must prove tax loss, fraud, connection, and knowledge or means of knowledge of the connection to the fraudulent evasion.

**25.55** At paras 55 and 56, Moses LJ held that the appropriate test for knowledge of a connection to fraud is that the taxpayer knew, *at the time of entering into the transaction*, that the transaction *was* connected to fraud.

*Knowledge of what?*

**25.56** At paras 58 and 59 Moses LJ stated:

The test in *Kittel* is simple and should not be over-refined. It embraces not only those who know of the connection but those who 'should have known'. Thus it includes those who should have known from the circumstances which surround their transactions that they were connected to fraudulent evasion. If a trader should have known that the only reasonable explanation for the transaction in which he was involved was that it was connected with fraud and if it turns out that the transaction was connected with fraudulent evasion of VAT then he should have known of that fact. He may properly be regarded as a participant for the reasons explained in *Kittel*.

The true principle to be derived from *Kittel* does not extend to circumstances in which a taxable person should have known that by his purchase it was more likely than not that his transaction was connected with fraudulent evasion. But a trader may be regarded as a participant where he should have known that the only reasonable explanation for the circumstances in which his purchase took place was that it was a transaction connected with such fraudulent evasion.

*ECHR*

**25.57** When dealing with arguments that were advanced as to whether the application of the *Kittel* test by HMRC amounted to a penalty for the purposes of the ECHR, Moses LJ restated his interpretation of the *Kittel* test at para 64:

On my interpretation of the principle in *Kittel*, there is no question of penalising the traders. If it is established that a trader should have known that by his purchase there was no reasonable explanation for the circumstances in which the transaction was undertaken other than that it was connected with fraud then such a trader was directly and knowingly involved in fraudulent evasion of VAT.

*Due diligence and appropriate questions*

**25.58** In relation to due diligence, Moses LJ stated in *Mobilx* at para 82:

But that is far from saying that the surrounding circumstances cannot establish sufficient knowledge to treat the trader as a participant. As I indicated in relation to the BSG appeal, Tribunals should not unduly focus on the question whether a trader has acted with due diligence. Even if a trader has asked appropriate questions, he is not entitled to ignore the circumstances in which his transactions take place if the *only* reasonable explanation for them is that his transactions have been or will be connected to fraud. The danger in focussing on the question of due diligence is that it may deflect a Tribunal from asking the essential question posed in *Kittel*, namely, whether the trader should have known that by his purchase he was taking part in a transaction connected with fraudulent evasion of VAT. The circumstances may well establish that he was.

Moses LJ quoted from the judgment of Christopher Clarke J in *Red 12* at para 83 and said: **25.59**

The questions posed in BSG (quoted here at § 72) by the Tribunal were important questions which may often need to be asked in relation to the issue of the trader's state of knowledge. I can do no better than repeat the words of Christopher Clarke J in *Red 12 v HMRC* [2009] EWHC 2563:

109 Examining individual transactions on their merits does not, however, require them to be regarded in isolation without regard to their attendant circumstances and context. Nor does it require the tribunal to ignore compelling similarities between one transaction and another or preclude the drawing of inferences, where appropriate, from a pattern of transactions of which the individual transaction in question forms part, as to its true nature e.g. that it is part of a fraudulent scheme. The character of an individual transaction may be discerned from material other than the bare facts of the transaction itself, including circumstantial and 'similar fact' evidence. That is not to alter its character by reference to earlier or later transactions but to discern it.

110 To look only at the purchase in respect of which input tax was sought to be deducted would be wholly artificial. A sale of 1,000 mobile telephones may be entirely regular, or entirely regular so far as the taxpayer is (or ought to be) aware. If so, the fact that there is fraud somewhere else in the chain cannot disentitle the taxpayer to a return of input tax. The same transaction may be viewed differently if it is the fourth in line of a chain of transactions all of which have identical percentage mark ups, made by a trader who has practically no capital as part of a huge and unexplained turnover with no left over stock, and mirrored by over 40 other similar chains in all of which the taxpayer has participated and in each of which there has been a defaulting trader. A tribunal could legitimately think it unlikely that the fact that all 46 of the transactions in issue can be traced to tax losses to HMRC is a result of innocent coincidence. Similarly, three suspicious involvements may pale into insignificance if the trader has been obviously honest in thousands.

111 Further in determining what it was that the taxpayer knew or ought to have known the tribunal is entitled to look at the totality of the deals effected by the taxpayer (and their characteristics), and at what the taxpayer did or omitted to do, and what it could have done, together with the surrounding circumstances in respect of all of them.

## C. Relevant Enquiries and Practical Issues

### Public Notice 726

Public Notice 726 makes clear that its content is not an exhaustive checklist, but provides **25.60** guidance to traders as to what due diligence could be carried out:

- obtaining copies of certificates of incorporation and VAT registration certificates;
- verification of VAT registration;

- obtaining letters of introduction on headed paper;
- obtaining some form of trade reference;
- obtaining credit checks;
- insisting on personal contact with representatives of the prospective supplier and obtaining the prospective supplier's bank details in order to carry out further checks.

**25.61**  In order to verify the transactions, Public Notice 726 encourages traders to keep documentation and additional paperwork including:

- purchase orders;
- proforma invoices;
- delivery notes;
- Convention Merchandises Routiers (CMRs);
- allocation notification;
- inspection records.

**25.62**  Practitioners should be careful to identify the relevant Notice, because the August 2003 version will be of most relevance to 2005/2006 MTIC cases. The August 2003 Notice was cancelled and replaced in March 2008.

**Client enquiries**

**25.63**  Both versions of Public Notice 726 pre-date the decision in *Mobilx* and therefore practitioners may consider it prudent to establish matters such as the following:

- What experience did the directors and operators of the appellant company have in the industry?
- When did trading begin? How and in what form?
- How many employees did the company have? What were the employees responsible for?
- How did the company obtain customers and suppliers?
- What trading process did the company employ and how did the process evolve during the trading history of the company?
- What due diligence process did the company employ and why? How did the process evolve?
- What did the company do with the due diligence it completed and/or obtained?
- What was the minimum due diligence the company would have conducted before trading with a new customer/supplier and/or completing a deal? Did the company manage to meet this standard in respect of every deal?

**25.64**  In respect of each transaction that is the subject of an appeal, it may be useful to enquire as to all of the following (where a supplier is referred to, the question is equally as applicable in respect of the customer of the appellant company):

(a) Why did the company buy from this supplier?
(b) How did the supplier find the company?
(c) How long had the company known the supplier?
(d) How many previous deals had been completed with the supplier?
(e) Who was the point of contact at the supplier?
(f) What due diligence had been completed on the supplier?
(g) Was any additional due diligence (over and above the standards always employed by the company) completed before the deal was completed?

(h) Which employee was responsible for due diligence on the supplier?
(i) Are any of the negotiations with the supplier recorded? Who did the negotiation?
(j) Why was the deal struck with the supplier?
(k) Did anything go wrong during the deal process?
(l) How difficult was the deal to put together relative to other deals?
(m) Why was the transaction reasonable?
(n) How much profit (gross and net) did the company make? How does this compare with other business done by the company?
(o) Were the processes of the company adhered to during the deal process? If they were not adhered to, why were they not adhered to? Why does it not matter to the company? Why did the transaction go ahead?

A failure to give evidence by the individuals who controlled a company allegedly involved in MTIC fraud was viewed dimly *Revenue and Customs v Sunico and others* [2013] EWHC 941 (Ch) and appropriate adverse inferences were drawn. **25.65**

# APPENDICES

# The Proceeds of Crime Act 2002

## Sections 6–18 (as amended)

### PART 2

*Confiscation Orders*

## 6 Making of order

(1) The Crown Court must proceed under this section if the following two conditions are satisfied.
(2) The first condition is that a defendant falls within any of the following paragraphs—
   (a) he is convicted of an offence or offences in proceedings before the Crown Court;
   (b) he is committed to the Crown Court for sentence in respect of an offence or offences under section 3, 4 or 6 of the Sentencing Act;
   (c) he is committed to the Crown Court in respect of an offence or offences under section 70 below (committal with a view to a confiscation order being considered).
(3) The second condition is that—
   (a) the prosecutor asks the court to proceed under this section, or
   (b) the court believes it is appropriate for it to do so.
(4) The court must proceed as follows—
   (a) it must decide whether the defendant has a criminal lifestyle;
   (b) if it decides that he has a criminal lifestyle it must decide whether he has benefited from his general criminal conduct;
   (c) if it decides that he does not have a criminal lifestyle it must decide whether he has benefited from his particular criminal conduct.
(5) If the court decides under subsection (4)(b) or (c) that the defendant has benefited from the conduct referred to it must—
   (a) decide the recoverable amount, and
   (b) make an order (a confiscation order) requiring him to pay that amount.
(6) But the court must treat the duty in subsection (5) as a power if it believes that any victim of the conduct has at any time started or intends to start proceedings against the defendant in respect of loss, injury or damage sustained in connection with the conduct.
(7) The court must decide any question arising under subsection (4) or (5) on a balance of probabilities.
(8) The first condition is not satisfied if the defendant absconds (but section 27 may apply).
(9) References in this Part to the offence (or offences) concerned are to the offence (or offences) mentioned in subsection (2).

## 7 Recoverable amount

(1) The recoverable amount for the purposes of section 6 is an amount equal to the defendant's benefit from the conduct concerned.
(2) But if the defendant shows that the available amount is less than that benefit the recoverable amount is—
   (a) the available amount, or
   (b) a nominal amount, if the available amount is nil.
(3) But if section 6(6) applies the recoverable amount is such amount as—
   (a) the court believes is just, but
   (b) does not exceed the amount found under subsection (1) or (2) (as the case may be).
(4) In calculating the defendant's benefit from the conduct concerned for the purposes of subsection (1), any property in respect of which—

    (a) a recovery order is in force under section 266, or

    (b) a forfeiture order is in force under section 298(2),

    must be ignored.

(5) If the court decides the available amount, it must include in the confiscation order a statement of its findings as to the matters relevant for deciding that amount.

## 8 Defendant's benefit

(1) If the court is proceeding under section 6 this section applies for the purpose of—

    (a) deciding whether the defendant has benefited from conduct, and

    (b) deciding his benefit from the conduct.

(2) The court must—

    (a) take account of conduct occurring up to the time it makes its decision;

    (b) take account of property obtained up to that time.

(3) Subsection (4) applies if—

    (a) the conduct concerned is general criminal conduct,

    (b) a confiscation order mentioned in subsection (5) has at an earlier time been made against the defendant, and

    (c) his benefit for the purposes of that order was benefit from his general criminal conduct.

(4) His benefit found at the time the last confiscation order mentioned in subsection (3)(c) was made against him must be taken for the purposes of this section to be his benefit from his general criminal conduct at that time.

(5) If the conduct concerned is general criminal conduct the court must deduct the aggregate of the following amounts—

    (a) the amount ordered to be paid under each confiscation order previously made against the defendant;

    (b) the amount ordered to be paid under each confiscation order previously made against him under any of the provisions listed in subsection (7).

(6) But subsection (5) does not apply to an amount which has been taken into account for the purposes of a deduction under that subsection on any earlier occasion.

(7) These are the provisions—

    (a) the Drug Trafficking Offences Act 1986 (c. 32);

    (b) Part 1 of the Criminal Justice (Scotland) Act 1987 (c. 41);

    (c) Part 6 of the Criminal Justice Act 1988;

    (d) the Criminal Justice (Confiscation) (Northern Ireland) Order 1990 (S.I. 1990/2588 (N.I. 17));

    (e) Part 1 of the Drug Trafficking Act 1994 (c. 37);

    (f) Part 1 of the Proceeds of Crime (Scotland) Act 1995 (c. 43);

    (g) the Proceeds of Crime (Northern Ireland) Order 1996 (S.I. 1996/1299 (N.I. 9));

    (h) Part 3 or 4 of this Act.

(8) The reference to general criminal conduct in the case of a confiscation order made under any of the provisions listed in subsection (7) is a reference to conduct in respect of which a court is required or entitled to make one or more assumptions for the purpose of assessing a person's benefit from the conduct.

## 9 Available amount

(1) For the purposes of deciding the recoverable amount, the available amount is the aggregate of—

    (a) the total of the values (at the time the confiscation order is made) of all the free property then held by the defendant minus the total amount payable in pursuance of obligations which then have priority, and

    (b) the total of the values (at that time) of all tainted gifts.

(2) An obligation has priority if it is an obligation of the defendant—

    (a) to pay an amount due in respect of a fine or other order of a court which was imposed or made on conviction of an offence and at any time before the time the confiscation order is made, or

(b) to pay a sum which would be included among the preferential debts if the defendant's bankruptcy had commenced on the date of the confiscation order or his winding up had been ordered on that date.

(3) 'Preferential debts' has the meaning given by section 386 of the Insolvency Act 1986 (c. 45).

## 10 Assumptions to be made in case of criminal lifestyle

(1) If the court decides under section 6 that the defendant has a criminal lifestyle it must make the following four assumptions for the purpose of—
    (a) deciding whether he has benefited from his general criminal conduct, and
    (b) deciding his benefit from the conduct.

(2) The first assumption is that any property transferred to the defendant at any time after the relevant day was obtained by him—
    (a) as a result of his general criminal conduct, and
    (b) at the earliest time he appears to have held it.

(3) The second assumption is that any property held by the defendant at any time after the date of conviction was obtained by him—
    (a) as a result of his general criminal conduct, and
    (b) at the earliest time he appears to have held it.

(4) The third assumption is that any expenditure incurred by the defendant at any time after the relevant day was met from property obtained by him as a result of his general criminal conduct.

(5) The fourth assumption is that, for the purpose of valuing any property obtained (or assumed to have been obtained) by the defendant, he obtained it free of any other interests in it.

(6) But the court must not make a required assumption in relation to particular property or expenditure if—
    (a) the assumption is shown to be incorrect, or
    (b) there would be a serious risk of injustice if the assumption were made.

(7) If the court does not make one or more of the required assumptions it must state its reasons.

(8) The relevant day is the first day of the period of six years ending with—
    (a) the day when proceedings for the offence concerned were started against the defendant, or
    (b) if there are two or more offences and proceedings for them were started on different days, the earliest of those days.

(9) But if a confiscation order mentioned in section 8(3)(c) has been made against the defendant at any time during the period mentioned in subsection (8)—
    (a) the relevant day is the day when the defendant's benefit was calculated for the purposes of the last such confiscation order;
    (b) the second assumption does not apply to any property which was held by him on or before the relevant day.

(10) The date of conviction is—
    (a) the date on which the defendant was convicted of the offence concerned, or
    (b) if there are two or more offences and the convictions were on different dates, the date of the latest.

## 11 Time for payment

(1) The amount ordered to be paid under a confiscation order must be paid on the making of the order; but this is subject to the following provisions of this section.

(2) If the defendant shows that he needs time to pay the amount ordered to be paid, the court making the confiscation order may make an order allowing payment to be made in a specified period.

(3) The specified period—
    (a) must start with the day on which the confiscation order is made, and
    (b) must not exceed six months.

(4) If within the specified period the defendant applies to the Crown Court for the period to be extended and the court believes there are exceptional circumstances, it may make an order extending the period.

(5) The extended period—

(a) must start with the day on which the confiscation order is made, and

(b) must not exceed 12 months.

(6) An order under subsection (4)—

   (a) may be made after the end of the specified period, but

   (b) must not be made after the end of the period of 12 months starting with the day on which the confiscation order is made.

(7) The court must not make an order under subsection (2) or (4) unless it gives—

   (a) the prosecutor

   (b) if the Director was appointed as the enforcement authority for the order under section 34, the Director,

an opportunity to make representations.

## 12  Interest on unpaid sums

(1) If the amount required to be paid by a person under a confiscation order is not paid when it is required to be paid, he must pay interest on the amount for the period for which it remains unpaid.

(2) The rate of interest is the same rate as that for the time being specified in section 17 of the Judgments Act 1838 (c. 110) (interest on civil judgment debts).

(3) For the purposes of this section no amount is required to be paid under a confiscation order if—

   (a) an application has been made under section 11(4),

   (b) the application has not been determined by the court, and

   (c) the period of 12 months starting with the day on which the confiscation order was made has not ended.

(4) In applying this Part the amount of the interest must be treated as part of the amount to be paid under the confiscation order.

## 13  Effect of order on court's other powers

(1) If the court makes a confiscation order it must proceed as mentioned in subsections (2) and (4) in respect of the offence or offences concerned.

(2) The court must take account of the confiscation order before—

   (a) it imposes a fine on the defendant, or

   (b) it makes an order falling within subsection (3).

(3) These orders fall within this subsection—

   (a) an order involving payment by the defendant, other than an order under section 130 of the Sentencing Act (compensation orders);

   (b) an order under section 27 of the Misuse of Drugs Act 1971 (c. 38) (forfeiture orders);

   (c) an order under section 143 of the Sentencing Act (deprivation orders);

   (d) an order under section 23 of the Terrorism Act 2000 (c. 11) (forfeiture orders).

(4) Subject to subsection (2), the court must leave the confiscation order out of account in deciding the appropriate sentence for the defendant.

(5) Subsection (6) applies if—

   (a) the Crown Court makes both a confiscation order and an order for the payment of compensation under section 130 of the Sentencing Act against the same person in the same proceedings, and

   (b) the court believes he will not have sufficient means to satisfy both the orders in full.

(6) In such a case the court must direct that so much of the compensation as it specifies is to be paid out of any sums recovered under the confiscation order; and the amount it specifies must be the amount it believes will not be recoverable because of the insufficiency of the person's means.

*Procedural matters*

## 14  Postponement

(1) The court may—

   (a) proceed under section 6 before it sentences the defendant for the offence (or any of the offences) concerned, or

    (b)  postpone proceedings under section 6 for a specified period.

(2)  A period of postponement may be extended.

(3)  A period of postponement (including one as extended) must not end after the permitted period ends.

(4)  But subsection (3) does not apply if there are exceptional circumstances.

(5)  The permitted period is the period of two years starting with the date of conviction.

(6)  But if—

    (a)  the defendant appeals against his conviction for the offence (or any of the offences) concerned, and

    (b)  the period of three months (starting with the day when the appeal is determined or otherwise disposed of) ends after the period found under subsection (5),

  the permitted period is that period of three months.

(7)  A postponement or extension may be made—

    (a)  on application by the defendant;

    (b)  on application by the prosecutor;

    (c)  by the court of its own motion.

(8)  If—

    (a)  proceedings are postponed for a period, and

    (b)  an application to extend the period is made before it ends,

  the application may be granted even after the period ends.

(9)  The date of conviction is—

    (a)  the date on which the defendant was convicted of the offence concerned, or

    (b)  if there are two or more offences and the convictions were on different dates, the date of the latest.

(10)  References to appealing include references to applying under section 111 of the Magistrates' Courts Act 1980 (c. 43) (statement of case).

(11)  A confiscation order must not be quashed only on the ground that there was a defect or omission in the procedure connected with the application for or the granting of a postponement.

(12)  But subsection (11) does not apply if before it made the confiscation order the court—

    (a)  imposed a fine on the defendant;

    (b)  made an order falling within section 13(3);

    (c)  made an order under section 130 of the Sentencing Act (compensation orders).

## 15  Effect of postponement

(1)  If the court postpones proceedings under section 6 it may proceed to sentence the defendant for the offence (or any of the offences) concerned.

(2)  In sentencing the defendant for the offence (or any of the offences) concerned in the postponement period the court must not—

    (a)  impose a fine on him,

    (b)  make an order falling within section 13(3), or

    (c)  make an order for the payment of compensation under section 130 of the Sentencing Act.

(3)  If the court sentences the defendant for the offence (or any of the offences) concerned in the postponement period, after that period ends it may vary the sentence by—

    (a)  imposing a fine on him,

    (b)  making an order falling within section 13(3), or

    (c)  making an order for the payment of compensation under section 130 of the Sentencing Act.

(4)  But the court may proceed under subsection (3) only within the period of 28 days which starts with the last day of the postponement period.

(5)  For the purposes of—

    (a)  section 18(2) of the Criminal Appeal Act 1968 (c. 19) (time limit for notice of appeal or of application for leave to appeal), and

    (b)  paragraph 1 of Schedule 3 to the Criminal Justice Act 1988 (c. 33) (time limit for notice of application for leave to refer a case under section 36 of that Act),

  the sentence must be regarded as imposed or made on the day on which it is varied under subsection (3).

(6) If the court proceeds to sentence the defendant under subsection (1), section 6 has effect as if the defendant's particular criminal conduct included conduct which constitutes offences which the court has taken into consideration in deciding his sentence for the offence or offences concerned.

(7) The postponement period is the period for which proceedings under section 6 are postponed.

## 16 Statement of information

(1) If the court is proceeding under section 6 in a case where section 6(3)(a) applies, the prosecutor must give the court a statement of information within the period the court orders.

(2) If the court is proceeding under section 6 in a case where section 6(3)(b) applies and it orders the prosecutor to give it a statement of information, the prosecutor must give it such a statement within the period the court orders.

(3) If the prosecutor believes the defendant has a criminal lifestyle the statement of information is a statement of matters the prosecutor believes are relevant in connection with deciding these issues—

   (a) whether the defendant has a criminal lifestyle;

   (b) whether he has benefited from his general criminal conduct;

   (c) his benefit from the conduct.

(4) A statement under subsection (3) must include information the prosecutor believes is relevant—

   (a) in connection with the making by the court of a required assumption under section 10;

   (b) for the purpose of enabling the court to decide if the circumstances are such that it must not make such an assumption.

(5) If the prosecutor does not believe the defendant has a criminal lifestyle the statement of information is a statement of matters the prosecutor or the Director believes are relevant in connection with deciding these issues—

   (a) whether the defendant has benefited from his particular criminal conduct;

   (b) his benefit from the conduct.

(6) If the prosecutor gives the court a statement of information—

   (a) he may at any time give the court a further statement of information;

   (b) he must give the court a further statement of information if it orders him to do so, and he must give it within the period the court orders.

(7) If the court makes an order under this section it may at any time vary it by making another one.

## 17 Defendant's response to statement of information

(1) If the prosecutor gives the court a statement of information and a copy is served on the defendant, the court may order the defendant—

   (a) to indicate (within the period it orders) the extent to which he accepts each allegation in the statement, and

   (b) so far as he does not accept such an allegation, to give particulars of any matters he proposes to rely on.

(2) If the defendant accepts to any extent an allegation in a statement of information the court may treat his acceptance as conclusive of the matters to which it relates for the purpose of deciding the issues referred to in section 16(3) or (5) (as the case may be).

(3) If the defendant fails in any respect to comply with an order under subsection (1) he may be treated for the purposes of subsection (2) as accepting every allegation in the statement of information apart from—

   (a) any allegation in respect of which he has complied with the requirement;

   (b) any allegation that he has benefited from his general or particular criminal conduct.

(4) For the purposes of this section an allegation may be accepted or particulars may be given in a manner ordered by the court.

(5) If the court makes an order under this section it may at any time vary it by making another one.

(6) No acceptance under this section that the defendant has benefited from conduct is admissible in evidence in proceedings for an offence.

## 18 Provision of information by defendant

(1) This section applies if—
   (a) the court is proceeding under section 6 in a case where section 6(3)(a) applies, or
   (b) it is proceeding under section 6 in a case where section 6(3)(b) applies or it is considering whether to proceed.

(2) For the purpose of obtaining information to help it in carrying out its functions the court may at any time order the defendant to give it information specified in the order.

(3) An order under this section may require all or a specified part of the information to be given in a specified manner and before a specified date.

(4) If the defendant fails without reasonable excuse to comply with an order under this section the court may draw such inference as it believes is appropriate.

(5) Subsection (4) does not affect any power of the court to deal with the defendant in respect of a failure to comply with an order under this section.

(6) If the prosecutor accepts to any extent an allegation made by the defendant—
   (a) in giving information required by an order under this section, or
   (b) in any other statement given to the court in relation to any matter relevant to deciding the available amount under section 9,
   the court may treat the acceptance as conclusive of the matters to which it relates.

(7) For the purposes of this section an allegation may be accepted in a manner ordered by the court.

(8) If the court makes an order under this section it may at any time vary it by making another one.

(9) No information given under this section which amounts to an admission by the defendant that he has benefited from criminal conduct is admissible in evidence in proceedings for an offence.

# The Proceeds of Crime Act 2002

## Sections 40–42 (as amended)

*Restraint Orders*

### 40 Conditions for exercise of powers

(1) The Crown Court may exercise the powers conferred by section 41 if any of the following conditions is satisfied.

(2) The first condition is that—
  (a) a criminal investigation has been started in England and Wales with regard to an offence, and
  (b) there is reasonable cause to believe that the alleged offender has benefited from his criminal conduct.

(3) The second condition is that—
  (a) proceedings for an offence have been started in England and Wales and not concluded, and
  (b) there is reasonable cause to believe that the defendant has benefited from his criminal conduct.

(4) The third condition is that—
  (a) an application by the prosecutor has been made under section 19, 20, 27 or 28 and not concluded, or the court believes that such an application is to be made, and
  (b) there is reasonable cause to believe that the defendant has benefited from his criminal conduct.

(5) The fourth condition is that—
  (a) an application by the prosecutor has been made under section 21 and not concluded, or the court believes that such an application is to be made, and
  (b) there is reasonable cause to believe that the court will decide under that section that the amount found under the new calculation of the defendant's benefit exceeds the relevant amount (as defined in that section).

(6) The fifth condition is that—
  (a) an application by the prosecutor has been made under section 22 and not concluded, or the court believes that such an application is to be made, and
  (b) there is reasonable cause to believe that the court will decide under that section that the amount found under the new calculation of the available amount exceeds the relevant amount (as defined in that section).

(7) The second condition is not satisfied if the court believes that—
  (a) there has been undue delay in continuing the proceedings, or
  (b) the prosecutor does not intend to proceed.

(8) If an application mentioned in the third, fourth or fifth condition has been made the condition is not satisfied if the court believes that—
  (a) there has been undue delay in continuing the application, or
  (b) the prosecutor does not intend to proceed.

(9) If the first condition is satisfied—
  (a) references in this Part to the defendant are to the alleged offender;
  (b) references in this Part to the prosecutor are to the person the court believes is to have conduct of any proceedings for the offence;
  (c) section 77(9) has effect as if proceedings for the offence had been started against the defendant when the investigation was started.

### 41 Restraint orders

(1) If any condition set out in section 40 is satisfied the Crown Court may make an order (a restraint order) prohibiting any specified person from dealing with any realisable property held by him.

(2) A restraint order may provide that it applies—
  (a) to all realisable property held by the specified person whether or not the property is described in the order;
  (b) to realisable property transferred to the specified person after the order is made.

(3) A restraint order may be made subject to exceptions, and an exception may in particular—
  (a) make provision for reasonable living expenses and reasonable legal expenses;
  (b) make provision for the purpose of enabling any person to carry on any trade, business, profession or occupation;
  (c) be made subject to conditions.

(4) But an exception to a restraint order must not make provision for any legal expenses which—
  (a) relate to an offence which falls within subsection (5), and
  (b) are incurred by the defendant or by a recipient of a tainted gift.

(5) These offences fall within this subsection—
  (a) the offence mentioned in section 40(2) or (3), if the first or second condition (as the case may be) is satisfied;
  (b) the offence (or any of the offences) concerned, if the third, fourth or fifth condition is satisfied.

(6) Subsection (7) applies if—
  (a) a court makes a restraint order, and
  (b) the applicant for the order applies to the court to proceed under subsection (7) (whether as part of the application for the restraint order or at any time afterwards).

(7) The court may make such order as it believes is appropriate for the purpose of ensuring that the restraint order is effective.

(8) A restraint order does not affect property for the time being subject to a charge under any of these provisions—
  (a) section 9 of the Drug Trafficking Offences Act 1986 (c. 32);
  (b) section 78 of the Criminal Justice Act 1988 (c. 33);
  (c) Article 14 of the Criminal Justice (Confiscation) (Northern Ireland) Order 1990 (S.I. 1990/2588 (N.I. 17));
  (d) section 27 of the Drug Trafficking Act 1994 (c. 37);
  (e) Article 32 of the Proceeds of Crime (Northern Ireland) Order 1996 (S.I. 1996/1299 (N.I. 9)).

(9) Dealing with property includes removing it from England and Wales.

## 42 Application, discharge and variation

(1) A restraint order—
  (a) may be made only on an application by an applicant falling within subsection (2);
  (b) may be made on an ex parte application to a judge in chambers.

(2) These applicants fall within this subsection—
  (a) the prosecutor;
  (c) an accredited financial investigator.

(3) An application to discharge or vary a restraint order or an order under section 41(7) may be made to the Crown Court by—
  (a) the person who applied for the order;
  (b) any person affected by the order.

(4) Subsections (5) to (7) apply to an application under subsection (3).

(5) The court—
  (a) may discharge the order;
  (b) may vary the order.

(6) If the condition in section 40 which was satisfied was that proceedings were started or an application was made, the court must discharge the order on the conclusion of the proceedings or of the application (as the case may be).

(7) If the condition in section 40 which was satisfied was that an investigation was started or an application was to be made, the court must discharge the order if within a reasonable time proceedings for the offence are not started or the application is not made (as the case may be).

# The Proceeds of Crime Act 2002

## Sections 48–51 (as amended)

*Management receivers*

### 48  Appointment

(1) Subsection (2) applies if—
  (a) the Crown Court makes a restraint order, and
  (b) the applicant for the restraint order applies to the court to proceed under subsection (2) (whether as part of the application for the restraint order or at any time afterwards).

(2) The Crown Court may by order appoint a receiver in respect of any realisable property to which the restraint order applies.

### 49  Powers

(1) If the court appoints a receiver under section 48 it may act under this section on the application of the person who applied for the restraint order.

(2) The court may by order confer on the receiver the following powers in relation to any realisable property to which the restraint order applies—
  (a) power to take possession of the property;
  (b) power to manage or otherwise deal with the property;
  (c) power to start, carry on or defend any legal proceedings in respect of the property;
  (d) power to realise so much of the property as is necessary to meet the receiver's remuneration and expenses.

(3) The court may by order confer on the receiver power to enter any premises in England and Wales and to do any of the following—
  (a) search for or inspect anything authorised by the court;
  (b) make or obtain a copy, photograph or other record of anything so authorised;
  (c) remove anything which the receiver is required or authorised to take possession of in pursuance of an order of the court.

(4) The court may by order authorise the receiver to do any of the following for the purpose of the exercise of his functions—
  (a) hold property;
  (b) enter into contracts;
  (c) sue and be sued;
  (d) employ agents;
  (e) execute powers of attorney, deeds or other instruments;
  (f) take any other steps the court thinks appropriate.

(5) The court may order any person who has possession of realisable property to which the restraint order applies to give possession of it to the receiver.

(6) The court—
  (a) may order a person holding an interest in realisable property to which the restraint order applies to make to the receiver such payment as the court specifies in respect of a beneficial interest held by the defendant or the recipient of a tainted gift;
  (b) may (on the payment being made) by order transfer, grant or extinguish any interest in the property.

(7) Subsections (2), (5) and (6) do not apply to property for the time being subject to a charge under any of these provisions—
  (a) section 9 of the Drug Trafficking Offences Act 1986 (c. 32);
  (b) section 78 of the Criminal Justice Act 1988 (c. 33);

  (c) Article 14 of the Criminal Justice (Confiscation) (Northern Ireland) Order 1990 (S.I. 1990/2588 (N.I. 17));

  (d) section 27 of the Drug Trafficking Act 1994 (c. 37);

  (e) Article 32 of the Proceeds of Crime (Northern Ireland) Order 1996 (S.I. 1996/1299 (N.I. 9)).

(8) The court must not—

  (a) confer the power mentioned in subsection (2)(b) or (d) in respect of property, or

  (b) exercise the power conferred on it by subsection (6) in respect of property,

  unless it gives persons holding interests in the property a reasonable opportunity to make representations to it.

(8A) Subsection (8), so far as relating to the power mentioned in subsection (2)(b), does not apply to property which—

  (a) is perishable; or

  (b) ought to be disposed of before its value diminishes.

(9) The court may order that a power conferred by an order under this section is subject to such conditions and exceptions as it specifies.

(10) Managing or otherwise dealing with property includes—

  (a) selling the property or any part of it or interest in it;

  (b) carrying on or arranging for another person to carry on any trade or business the assets of which are or are part of the property;

  (c) incurring capital expenditure in respect of the property.

*Enforcement receivers*

## 50 Appointment

(1) This section applies if—

  (a) a confiscation order is made,

  (b) it is not satisfied, and

  (c) it is not subject to appeal.

(2) On the application of the prosecutor the Crown Court may by order appoint a receiver in respect of realisable property.

## 51 Powers

(1) If the court appoints a receiver under section 50 it may act under this section on the application of the prosecutor.

(2) The court may by order confer on the receiver the following powers in relation to the realisable property—

  (a) power to take possession of the property;

  (b) power to manage or otherwise deal with the property;

  (c) power to realise the property, in such manner as the court may specify;

  (d) power to start, carry on or defend any legal proceedings in respect of the property.

(3) The court may by order confer on the receiver power to enter any premises in England and Wales and to do any of the following—

  (a) search for or inspect anything authorised by the court;

  (b) make or obtain a copy, photograph or other record of anything so authorised;

  (c) remove anything which the receiver is required or authorised to take possession of in pursuance of an order of the court.

(4) The court may by order authorise the receiver to do any of the following for the purpose of the exercise of his functions—

  (a) hold property;

  (b) enter into contracts;

  (c) sue and be sued;

  (d) employ agents;

  (e) execute powers of attorney, deeds or other instruments;

  (f) take any other steps the court thinks appropriate.

(5) The court may order any person who has possession of realisable property to give possession of it to the receiver.

(6) The court—

    (a) may order a person holding an interest in realisable property to make to the receiver such payment as the court specifies in respect of a beneficial interest held by the defendant or the recipient of a tainted gift;

    (b) may (on the payment being made) by order transfer, grant or extinguish any interest in the property.

(7) Subsections (2), (5) and (6) do not apply to property for the time being subject to a charge under any of these provisions—

    (a) section 9 of the Drug Trafficking Offences Act 1986 (c. 32);

    (b) section 78 of the Criminal Justice Act 1988 (c. 33);

    (c) Article 14 of the Criminal Justice (Confiscation) (Northern Ireland) Order 1990 (S.I. 1990/2588 (N.I. 17));

    (d) section 27 of the Drug Trafficking Act 1994 (c. 37);

    (e) Article 32 of the Proceeds of Crime (Northern Ireland) Order 1996 (S.I. 1996/1299 (N.I. 9)).

(8) The court must not—

    (a) confer the power mentioned in subsection (2)(b) or (c) in respect of property, or

    (b) exercise the power conferred on it by subsection (6) in respect of property,

    unless it gives persons holding interests in the property a reasonable opportunity to make representations to it.

(8A) Subsection (8), so far as relating to the power mentioned in subsection (2)(b), does not apply to property which—

    (a) is perishable; or

    (b) ought to be disposed of before its value diminishes.

(9) The court may order that a power conferred by an order under this section is subject to such conditions and exceptions as it specifies.

(10) Managing or otherwise dealing with property includes—

    (a) selling the property or any part of it or interest in it;

    (b) carrying on or arranging for another person to carry on any trade or business the assets of which are or are part of the property;

    (c) incurring capital expenditure in respect of the property.

# The Proceeds of Crime Act 2002

## Section 69 (as amended)

*Exercise of powers*

### 69 Powers of court and receiver

(1) This section applies to—
   (a) the powers conferred on a court by sections 41 to 59 and sections 62 to 67;
   (b) the powers of a receiver appointed under section 48 or 50.

(2) The powers—
   (a) must be exercised with a view to the value for the time being of realisable property being made available (by the property's realisation) for satisfying any confiscation order that has been or may be made against the defendant;
   (b) must be exercised, in a case where a confiscation order has not been made, with a view to securing that there is no diminution in the value of realisable property;
   (c) must be exercised without taking account of any obligation of the defendant or a recipient of a tainted gift if the obligation conflicts with the object of satisfying any confiscation order that has been or may be made against the defendant;
   (d) may be exercised in respect of a debt owed by the Crown.

(3) Subsection (2) has effect subject to the following rules—
   (a) the powers must be exercised with a view to allowing a person other than the defendant or a recipient of a tainted gift to retain or recover the value of any interest held by him;
   (b) in the case of realisable property held by a recipient of a tainted gift, the powers must be exercised with a view to realising no more than the value for the time being of the gift;
   (c) in a case where a confiscation order has not been made against the defendant, property must not be sold if the court so orders under subsection (4).

(4) If on an application by the defendant, or by the recipient of a tainted gift, the court decides that property cannot be replaced it may order that it must not be sold.

(5) An order under subsection (4) may be revoked or varied.

# APPENDIX 5

# The Proceeds of Crime Act 2002

## Sections 294–303A (as amended)

### CHAPTER 3

#### *Seizure and detention*

### 294 Seizure of cash

(1) A customs officer, a constable or an accredited financial investigator may seize any cash if he has reasonable grounds for suspecting that it is—
   (a) recoverable property, or
   (b) intended by any person for use in unlawful conduct.
(2) A customs officer, a constable or an accredited financial investigator may also seize cash part of which he has reasonable grounds for suspecting to be—
   (a) recoverable property, or
   (b) intended by any person for use in unlawful conduct,
   if it is not reasonably practicable to seize only that part.
(3) This section does not authorise the seizure of an amount of cash if it or, as the case may be, the part to which his suspicion relates, is less than the minimum amount.
(4) This section does not authorise the seizure by an accredited financial investigator of cash found in Scotland.

### 295 Detention of seized cash

(1) While the customs officer, a constable or an accredited financial investigator continues to have reasonable grounds for his suspicion, cash seized under section 294 may be detained initially for a period of 48 hours.
(1A) The period of 48 hours mentioned in subsection (1) is to be calculated in accordance with subsection (1B).
(1B) In calculating a period of 48 hours in accordance with this subsection, no account shall be taken of—
   (a) any Saturday or Sunday,
   (b) Christmas Day,
   (c) Good Friday,
   (d) any day that is a bank holiday under the Banking and Financial Dealings Act 1971 in the part of the United Kingdom within which the cash is seized, or
   (e) any day prescribed under section 8(2) of the Criminal Procedure (Scotland) Act 1995 as a court holiday in a sheriff court in the sheriff court district within which the cash is seized.
(2) The period for which the cash or any part of it may be detained may be extended by an order made by a magistrates' court or (in Scotland) the sheriff; but the order may not authorise the detention of any of the cash—
   (a) beyond the end of the period of six months[1] beginning with the date of the order,
   (b) in the case of any further order under this section, beyond the end of the period of two years beginning with the date of the first order.
(3) A justice of the peace may also exercise the power of a magistrates' court to make the first order under subsection (2) extending the period.
(4) An application for an order under subsection (2)—

---

[1] Substituted by Policing and Crime Act 2009 c. 26 Pt 5 s 64(1). In force, 25 January 2010.

    (a)  in relation to England and Wales and Northern Ireland, may be made by the Commissioners of Customs and Excise, a constable or an accredited financial investigator,

    (b)  in relation to Scotland, may be made by the Scottish Ministers in connection with their functions under section 298 or by a procurator fiscal,

and the court, sheriff or justice may make the order if satisfied, in relation to any cash to be further detained, that either of the following conditions is met.

(5)  The first condition is that there are reasonable grounds for suspecting that the cash is recoverable property and that either—

    (a)  its continued detention is justified while its derivation is further investigated or consideration is given to bringing (in the United Kingdom or elsewhere) proceedings against any person for an offence with which the cash is connected, or

    (b)  proceedings against any person for an offence with which the cash is connected have been started and have not been concluded.

(6)  The second condition is that there are reasonable grounds for suspecting that the cash is intended to be used in unlawful conduct and that either—

    (a)  its continued detention is justified while its intended use is further investigated or consideration is given to bringing (in the United Kingdom or elsewhere) proceedings against any person for an offence with which the cash is connected, or

    (b)  proceedings against any person for an offence with which the cash is connected have been started and have not been concluded.

(7)  An application for an order under subsection (2) may also be made in respect of any cash seized under section 294(2), and the court, sheriff or justice may make the order if satisfied that—

    (a)  the condition in subsection (5) or (6) is met in respect of part of the cash, and

    (b)  it is not reasonably practicable to detain only that part.

(8)  An order under subsection (2) must provide for notice to be given to persons affected by it.

## 296 Interest

(1)  If cash is detained under section 295 for more than 48 hours (calculated in accordance with s 295(1B)), it is at the first opportunity to be paid into an interest-bearing account and held there; and the interest accruing on it is to be added to it on its forfeiture or release.

(2)  In the case of cash detained under section 295 which was seized under section 294(2), the customs officer, a constable or an accredited financial investigator must, on paying it into the account, release the part of the cash to which the suspicion does not relate.

(3)  Subsection (1) does not apply if the cash or, as the case may be, the part to which the suspicion relates is required as evidence of an offence or evidence in proceedings under this Chapter.

## 297 Release of detained cash

(1)  This section applies while any cash is detained under section 295.

(2)  A magistrates' court or (in Scotland) the sheriff may direct the release of the whole or any part of the cash if the following condition is met.

(3)  The condition is that the court or sheriff is satisfied, on an application by the person from whom the cash was seized, that the conditions in section 295 for the detention of the cash are no longer met in relation to the cash to be released.

(4)  A customs officer, a constable or an accredited financial investigator or (in Scotland) procurator fiscal may, after notifying the magistrates' court, sheriff or justice under whose order cash is being detained, release the whole or any part of it if satisfied that the detention of the cash to be released is no longer justified.

*Forfeiture*

## 298 Forfeiture

(1)  While cash is detained under section 295, an application for the forfeiture of the whole or any part of it may be made—

    (a)  to a magistrates' court by the Commissioners of Customs and Excise, an accredited financial investigator or a constable,

    (b)  (in Scotland) to the sheriff by the Scottish Ministers.

(2) The court or sheriff may order the forfeiture of the cash or any part of it if satisfied that the cash or part—
   (a)  is recoverable property, or
   (b)  is intended by any person for use in unlawful conduct.

(3)  But in the case of recoverable property which belongs to joint tenants, one of whom is an excepted joint owner, the order may not apply to so much of it as the court thinks is attributable to the excepted joint owner's share.

(4)  Where an application for the forfeiture of any cash is made under this section, the cash is to be detained (and may not be released under any power conferred by this Chapter) until any proceedings in pursuance of the application (including any proceedings on appeal) are concluded.

### 299 Appeal against decision under section 298

(1)  Any party to proceedings for an order for the forfeiture of cash under section 298 who is aggrieved by an order under that section or by the decision of the court not to make such an order may appeal—
   (a)  in relation to England and Wales, to the Crown Court;
   (b)  in relation to Scotland, to the Sheriff Principal;
   (c)  in relation to Northern Ireland, to a county court.

(2)  An appeal under subsection (1) must be made before the end of the period of 30 days starting with the day on which the court makes the order or decision.

(3)  The court hearing the appeal may make any order it thinks appropriate.

(4)  If the court upholds an appeal against an order forfeiting the cash, it may order the release of the cash.

### 300 Application of forfeited cash

(1)  Cash forfeited under this Chapter, and any accrued interest on it—
   (a)  if forfeited by a magistrates' court in England and Wales or Northern Ireland, is to be paid into the Consolidated Fund,
   (b)  if forfeited by the sheriff, is to be paid into the Scottish Consolidated Fund.

(2)  But it is not to be paid in—
   (a)  before the end of the period within which an appeal under section 299 may be made, or
   (b)  if a person appeals under that section, before the appeal is determined or otherwise disposed of.

*Supplementary*

### 301 Victims and other owners

(1)  A person who claims that any cash detained under this Chapter, or any part of it, belongs to him may apply to a magistrates' court or (in Scotland) the sheriff for the cash or part to be released to him.

(2)  The application may be made in the course of proceedings under section 295 or 298 or at any other time.

(3)  If it appears to the court or sheriff concerned that—
   (a)  the applicant was deprived of the cash to which the application relates, or of property which it represents, by unlawful conduct,
   (b)  the property he was deprived of was not, immediately before he was deprived of it, recoverable property, and
   (c)  that cash belongs to him,
   the court or sheriff may order the cash to which the application relates to be released to the applicant.

(4)  If—
   (a)  the applicant is not the person from whom the cash to which the application relates was seized,
   (b)  it appears to the court or sheriff that that cash belongs to the applicant,
   (c)  the court or sheriff is satisfied that the conditions in section 295 for the detention of that cash are no longer met or, if an application has been made under section 298, the court or sheriff decides not to make an order under that section in relation to that cash, and

(d) no objection to the making of an order under this subsection has been made by the person from whom that cash was seized,

the court or sheriff may order the cash to which the application relates to be released to the applicant or to the person from whom it was seized.

## 302 Compensation

(1) If no forfeiture order is made in respect of any cash detained under this Chapter, the person to whom the cash belongs or from whom it was seized may make an application to the magistrates' court or (in Scotland) the sheriff for compensation.

(2) If, for any period beginning with the first opportunity to place the cash in an interest-bearing account after the initial detention of the cash for 48 hours (calculated in accordance with s 295(1B)), the cash was not held in an interest-bearing account while detained, the court or sheriff may order an amount of compensation to be paid to the applicant.

(3) The amount of compensation to be paid under subsection (2) is the amount the court or sheriff thinks would have been earned in interest in the period in question if the cash had been held in an interest-bearing account.

(4) If the court or sheriff is satisfied that, taking account of any interest to be paid under section 296 or any amount to be paid under subsection (2), the applicant has suffered loss as a result of the detention of the cash and that the circumstances are exceptional, the court or sheriff may order compensation (or additional compensation) to be paid to him.

(5) The amount of compensation to be paid under subsection (4) is the amount the court or sheriff thinks reasonable, having regard to the loss suffered and any other relevant circumstances.

(6) If the cash was seized by a customs officer, the compensation is to be paid by the Commissioners of Customs and Excise.

(7) If the cash was seized by a constable, the compensation is to be paid as follows—

(a) in the case of a constable of a police force in England and Wales, it is to be paid out of the police fund from which the expenses of the police force are met,

(b) in the case of a constable of a police force in Scotland, it is to be paid by the police authority or joint police board for the police area for which that force is maintained,

(c) in the case of a police officer within the meaning of the Police (Northern Ireland) Act 2000 (c. 32), it is to be paid out of money provided by the Chief Constable.

(7A) If the cash was seized by an accredited financial investigator who was not an officer of Revenue and Customs or a constable, the compensation is to be paid as follows—

(a) in the case of an investigator—

(i) who was a member of the civilian staff of a police force, including the metropolitan police force, (within the meaning of that Part of that Act), or [2]

(ii) who was a member of staff of the City of London police force,

it is to be paid out of the police fund from which the expenses of the police force are met,

(b) in the case of an investigator who was a member of staff of the Police Service of Northern Ireland, it is to be paid out of money provided by the Chief Constable,

(c) in the case of an investigator who was a member of staff of a department of the Government of the United Kingdom, it is to be paid by the Minister of the Crown in charge of the department or by the department,

(d) in the case of an investigator who was a member of staff of a Northern Ireland department, it is to be paid by the department,

(e) in any other case, it is to be paid by the employer of the investigator.

(7B) The Secretary of State may by order amend subsection (7A).

(8) If a forfeiture order is made in respect only of a part of any cash detained under this Chapter, this section has effect in relation to the other part.

---

[2] Substituted by the Police Reform and Social Responsibility Act 2011 c.13 Sch 16(3) para 306. In force, 16 January 2012.

(9) The power in subsection (7B) is exercisable by the Department of Justice (and not by the Secretary of State) so far as it may be used to make provision which could be made by an Act of the Northern Ireland Assembly without the consent of the Secretary of State (see sections 6 to 8 of the Northern Ireland Act 1998)[3].

## 302A  Powers for prosecutors to appear in proceedings

(1) The Director of Public Prosecutions or the Director of Public Prosecutions for Northern Ireland may appear for a constable or an accredited financial investigator in proceedings under this Chapter if the Director—

    (a) is asked by, or on behalf of, a constable or (as the case may be) an accredited financial investigator to do so, and

    (b) considers it appropriate to do so.

(2) The Director of Revenue and Customs Prosecutions may appear for the Commissioners for Her Majesty's Revenue and Customs or an officer of Revenue and Customs in proceedings under this Chapter if the Director—

    (a) is asked by, or on behalf of, the Commissioners for Her Majesty's Revenue and Customs or (as the case may be) an officer of Revenue and Customs to do so, and

    (b) considers it appropriate to do so.

(3) The Directors may charge fees for the provision of services under this section.

(4) The references in subsection (1) to an accredited financial investigator do not include an accredited financial investigator who is an officer of Revenue and Customs but the references in subsection (2) to an officer of Revenue and Customs do include an accredited financial investigator who is an officer of Revenue and Customs.

## 303  "The minimum amount"

(1) In this Chapter, the minimum amount is the amount in sterling specified in an order made by the Secretary of State after consultation with the Scottish Ministers and the Department of Justice[4].

(2) For that purpose the amount of any cash held in a currency other than sterling must be taken to be its sterling equivalent, calculated in accordance with the prevailing rate of exchange.

## 303A  Financial investigators

(1) In this Chapter (apart from this section) any reference in a provision to an accredited financial investigator is a reference to an accredited financial investigator who falls within a description specified in an order made for the purposes of that provision by the Secretary of State under section 453.

(2) Subsection (1) does not apply to the second reference to an accredited financial investigator in section 290(4)(c).

(3) Where an accredited financial investigator of a particular description—

    (a) applies for an order under section 295,

    (b) applies for forfeiture under section 298, or

    (c) brings an appeal under, or relating to, this Chapter,

any subsequent step in the application or appeal, or any further application or appeal relating to the same matter, may be taken, made or brought by a different accredited financial investigator of the same description.

---

[3] Inserted by Northern Ireland Act 1998 (Devolution of Policing and Justice Functions) Order 2010/976 Sch 14 para 62(2). In force 12 April 2010.

[4] Inserted by Northern Ireland Act 1998 (Devolution of Policing and Justice Functions) Order 2010/976 Sch 14 para 63. In force, 12 April 2010.

# The Proceeds of Crime Act 2002

## Sections 327–329

### Money Laundering

#### *Offences*

### 327  Concealing etc

(1) A person commits an offence if he—
  (a)  conceals criminal property;
  (b)  disguises criminal property;
  (c)  converts criminal property;
  (d)  transfers criminal property;
  (e)  removes criminal property from England and Wales or from Scotland or from Northern Ireland.

(2) But a person does not commit such an offence if—
  (a)  he makes an authorised disclosure under section 338 and (if the disclosure is made before he does the act mentioned in subsection (1)) he has the appropriate consent;
  (b)  he intended to make such a disclosure but had a reasonable excuse for not doing so;
  (c)  the act he does is done in carrying out a function he has relating to the enforcement of any provision of this Act or of any other enactment relating to criminal conduct or benefit from criminal conduct.

(3) Concealing or disguising criminal property includes concealing or disguising its nature, source, location, disposition, movement or ownership or any rights with respect to it.

### 328  Arrangements

(1) A person commits an offence if he enters into or becomes concerned in an arrangement which he knows or suspects facilitates (by whatever means) the acquisition, retention, use or control of criminal property by or on behalf of another person.

(2) But a person does not commit such an offence if—

  (a)  he makes an authorised disclosure under section 338 and (if the disclosure is made before he does the act mentioned in subsection (1)) he has the appropriate consent;
  (b)  he intended to make such a disclosure but had a reasonable excuse for not doing so;
  (c)  the act he does is done in carrying out a function he has relating to the enforcement of any provision of this Act or of any other enactment relating to criminal conduct or benefit from criminal conduct.

### 329  Acquisition, use and possession

(1) A person commits an offence if he—
  (a)  acquires criminal property;
  (b)  uses criminal property;
  (c)  has possession of criminal property.

(2) But a person does not commit such an offence if—
  (a)  he makes an authorised disclosure under section 338 and (if the disclosure is made before he does the act mentioned in subsection (1)) he has the appropriate consent;
  (b)  he intended to make such a disclosure but had a reasonable excuse for not doing so;
  (c)  he acquired or used or had possession of the property for adequate consideration;

(d) the act he does is done in carrying out a function he has relating to the enforcement of any provision of this Act or of any other enactment relating to criminal conduct or benefit from criminal conduct.

(3) For the purposes of this section—

(a) a person acquires property for inadequate consideration if the value of the consideration is significantly less than the value of the property;

(b) a person uses or has possession of property for inadequate consideration if the value of the consideration is significantly less than the value of the use or possession;

(c) the provision by a person of goods or services which he knows or suspects may help another to carry out criminal conduct is not consideration.

# The Proceeds of Crime Act 2002

## Section 340

*Interpretation*

### 340 Interpretation

(1) This section applies for the purposes of this Part.

(2) Criminal conduct is conduct which—
  (a) constitutes an offence in any part of the United Kingdom, or
  (b) would constitute an offence in any part of the United Kingdom if it occurred there.

(3) Property is criminal property if—
  (a) it constitutes a person's benefit from criminal conduct or it represents such a benefit (in whole or part and whether directly or indirectly), and
  (b) the alleged offender knows or suspects that it constitutes or represents such a benefit.

(4) It is immaterial—
  (a) who carried out the conduct;
  (b) who benefited from it;
  (c) whether the conduct occurred before or after the passing of this Act.

(5) A person benefits from conduct if he obtains property as a result of or in connection with the conduct.

(6) If a person obtains a pecuniary advantage as a result of or in connection with conduct, he is to be taken to obtain as a result of or in connection with the conduct a sum of money equal to the value of the pecuniary advantage.

(7) References to property or a pecuniary advantage obtained in connection with conduct include references to property or a pecuniary advantage obtained in both that connection and some other.

(8) If a person benefits from conduct his benefit is the property obtained as a result of or in connection with the conduct.

(9) Property is all property wherever situated and includes—
  (a) money;
  (b) all forms of property, real or personal, heritable or moveable;
  (c) things in action and other intangible or incorporeal property.

(10) The following rules apply in relation to property—
  (a) property is obtained by a person if he obtains an interest in it;
  (b) references to an interest, in relation to land in England and Wales or Northern Ireland, are to any legal estate or equitable interest or power;
  (c) references to an interest, in relation to land in Scotland, are to any estate, interest, servitude or other heritable right in or over land, including a heritable security;
  (d) references to an interest, in relation to property other than land, include references to a right (including a right to possession).

(11) Money laundering is an act which—
  (a) constitutes an offence under section 327, 328 or 329,
  (b) constitutes an attempt, conspiracy or incitement to commit an offence specified in paragraph (a),

     (c)  constitutes aiding, abetting, counselling or procuring the commission of an offence specified in paragraph (a), or

     (d)  would constitute an offence specified in paragraph (a), (b) or (c) if done in the United Kingdom.

(12)  For the purposes of a disclosure to a nominated officer—

     (a)  references to a person's employer include any body, association or organisation (including a voluntary organisation) in connection with whose activities the person exercises a function (whether or not for gain or reward), and

     (b)  references to employment must be construed accordingly.

(13)  References to a constable include references to a person authorised for the purposes of this Part by the Director General of the National Criminal Intelligence Service.

# APPENDIX 8

# The Proceeds of Crime Act 2002

## Schedule 6

### POWERS OF INTERIM RECEIVER OR ADMINISTRATOR

*Seizure*

1 Power to seize property to which the order applies.

*Information*

2 (1) Power to obtain information or to require a person to answer any question.

(2) A requirement imposed in the exercise of the power has effect in spite of any restriction on the disclosure of information (however imposed).

(3) An answer given by a person in pursuance of such a requirement may not be used in evidence against him in criminal proceedings.

(4) Sub-paragraph (3) does not apply—

(a) on a prosecution for an offence under section 5 of the Perjury Act 1911, section 44(2) of the Criminal Law (Consolidation) (Scotland) Act 1995 or Article 10 of the Perjury (Northern Ireland) Order 1979 (false statements), or

(b) on a prosecution for some other offence where, in giving evidence, he makes a statement inconsistent with it.

(5) But an answer may not be used by virtue of sub-paragraph (4)(b) against a person unless—

(a) evidence relating to it is adduced, or

(b) a question relating to it is asked,

by him or on his behalf in the proceedings arising out of the prosecution.

*Entry, search, etc.*

3 (1) Power to—

(a) enter any premises in the United Kingdom to which the interim order applies, and

(b) take any of the following steps.

(2) Those steps are—

(a) to carry out a search for or inspection of anything described in the order,

(b) to make or obtain a copy, photograph or other record of anything so described,

(c) to remove anything which he is required to take possession of in pursuance of the order or which may be required as evidence in the proceedings under Chapter 2 of Part 5.

(3) The order may describe anything generally, whether by reference to a class or otherwise.

*Supplementary*

4 (1) An order making any provision under paragraph 2 or 3 must make provision in respect of legal professional privilege (in Scotland, legal privilege within the meaning of Chapter 3 of Part 8).

(2) An order making any provision under paragraph 3 may require any person—

(a) to give the interim receiver or administrator access to any premises which he may enter in pursuance of paragraph 3,

(b) to give the interim receiver or administrator any assistance he may require for taking the steps mentioned in that paragraph.

*Management*

5 (1)  Power to manage any property to which the order applies.

   (2)  Managing property includes—

     (a)  selling or otherwise disposing of assets comprised in the property which are perishable or which ought to be disposed of before their value diminishes,

     (b)  where the property comprises assets of a trade or business, carrying on, or arranging for another to carry on, the trade or business,

     (c)  incurring capital expenditure in respect of the property.

# APPENDIX 9

# Restraint Order

DISOBEDIENCE TO THIS ORDER IS A CONTEMPT OF COURT WHICH IF YOU ARE AN INDIVIDUAL IS PUNISHABLE BY IMPRISONMENT OR IF YOU ARE A BODY CORPORATE IS PUNISHABLE BY SEQUESTRATION OF YOUR ASSETS AND BY IMPRISONMENT OF ANY INDIVIDUAL RESPONSIBLE

IN THE CROWN COURT
SITTING AT SOUTHWARK
Before His Honour Judge Bullingham sitting in Private

No....................................................................

Dated................................................................

### IN THE MATTER OF ALFREDO GERMONT (Defendant)
### AND
### IN THE MATTER OF THE PROCEEDS OF CRIME ACT 2002

---

RESTRAINT ORDER PROHIBITING DISPOSAL OF ASSETS

---

TO: (1) **Mr Alfredo Germont (the Defendant)**
    (2) **Mrs Voiletta Valery (wife of the Defendant)**
    (3) **Traviata Trading Enterprises Limited (a company controlled by the Defendant)**
    (4) **Mr Giorgio Germont (father of the Defendant)**

PENAL NOTICE

If you the Defendant, Mrs Violetta Valery, Traviata Trading Enterprises Limited or Mr Giorgio Germont disobey this Order you may be held to be in contempt of court and may be imprisoned, fined or have your assets seized.

Any other person who knows of this order and does anything which helps or permits the Defendant, Mrs Violetta Valery, Traviata Trading Enterprises Limited or Mr Giorgio Germont to breach the terms of this Order may also be held to be in contempt of court and may be imprisoned, fined or have their assets seized.

**IMPORTANT: NOTICE TO THE DEFENDANT, MRS VIOLETTA VALERY, TRAVIATA TRADING ENTERPRISES LIMITED AND MR GIORGIO GERMONT**

This order prohibits you, the Defendant, from dealing with your assets. It prohibits Mrs Violetta Valery from dealing with the assets identified in paragraph 7 of this Order. It prohibits Traviata Trading Enterprises Limited from dealing with the assets identified in paragraph 8 of this Order. It prohibits Mr Giorgio Germont from dealing with the assets identified in paragraph 9 of this Order.

The Order is subject to the exceptions contained in the Order. You should read it all carefully.

You are advised to consult a solicitor as soon as possible. Under paragraph 2 of schedule 2 of the Access to Justice Act 1999, as amended by paragraph 36 of schedule 11 of Proceeds of Crime Act 2002, you may be entitled to Legal Aid Agency funding in respect of this Order. Your solicitor will be able to provide you with the appropriate forms. These proceedings are not means tested, but are subject to the Interests of Justice test. You should complete form CRM14 and pass it to the magistrates' court where the case was originally dealt with, unless advised otherwise by the court or your solicitor.[1]

---

[1] The reader is referred to s 46 of the Crime and Courts Act 2013 and ss 23 and 24 of the Legal Aid, Sentencing and Punishment of Offenders Act 2012, which set out the relevant provisions for claiming legal aid funding in restraint order matters.

If you are a defendant in criminal proceedings to which this Order is ancillary and you have the benefit of a Representation Order then your solicitor may be able to give you advice and assistance within the scope of that Representation Order.

You have a right to ask this court to vary or discharge this order (see paragraph 20 below). If you wish to do this you must serve the application and the witness statement in support of the application on the Crown Prosecution Service and the Defendant, Mrs Violetta Valery, Traviata Trading Enterprises Limited and Mr Giorgio Germont at least two clear working days before the date fixed by the Crown Court for the hearing of the application.

There is an interpretation section at paragraphs 33 and 34 of this Order.

## The Order

1. This is a Restraint Order made against Mr Alfredo Germont ('the Defendant'), Mrs Violetta Valery, Traviata Trading Enterprises Limited and Mr Giorgio Germont on 1st September 2014 by His Honour Judge Bullingham on the application of the Crown Prosecution Service ('the Prosecutor'). The Judge read the witness statements listed in Schedule A and accepted the undertakings set out in Schedule B at the end of this order.

2. This Order was made without notice to the Defendant, Mrs Violetta Valery, Traviata Trading Enterprises Limited and Mr Giorgio Germont. The Defendant, Mrs Violetta Valery, Traviata Trading Enterprises Limited and Mr Giorgio Germont have a right to apply to the Court to vary or discharge the Order—see paragraph 20 below.

## Optional—Return Date Provision

2A. There will be a further hearing of this matter on 14th September 2014 ('the return date') when the Prosecutor will apply for the continuation of this Order. The Defendant, Mrs Violetta Valery, Traviata Trading Enterprises Limited, Mr Giorgio Germont and any other person affected by this Order are entitled to appear and to object to the continuation of this Order or to ask for it to be varied.

## Disposal of or Dealing with Assets

3. The Defendant must not:—
   (1) remove from England and Wales any of his assets which are in England and Wales whether in his own name or not and whether solely or jointly owned; or
   (2) in any way dispose of, deal with or diminish the value of any of his assets whether they are in or outside England and Wales whether in his own name or not and whether solely or jointly owned.

4. Paragraph 3 applies to all the Defendant's assets whether or not the assets are described in this Order or are transferred to the Defendant after the Order is made, are in his own name and whether they are solely or jointly owned. For the purpose of this Order the Defendant's assets include any asset which he has the power, directly or indirectly, to dispose of or deal with as if it were his own. The Defendant is to be regarded as having such power if a third party holds or controls the asset in accordance with his direct or indirect instructions.

5. This prohibition includes the following assets in particular:—
   (a) the property known as 'Traviata', 123 The Esplanade, Torquay, Devon registered at HM Land Registry under title number DN12345 or the net sale money after payment of any mortgages if it has been sold;
   (b) the property and assets of the Defendant's business known as Traviata Trading Enterprises Limited carried on at 123 The Esplanade, Torquay, Devon or the sale money if any of them have been sold;
   (c) the assets of a company called Traviata Trading Enterprises Limited (company number 12345), registered address 123 The Esplanade, Torquay, Devon;
   (d) the shares held by the Defendant in the company called Traviata Trading Enterprises Limited (company number 12345), registered address 123 The Esplanade, Torquay, Devon;
   (e) any money in the account numbered 12345678 at Anytown Bank PLC, 1 Main Street, Torquay, held in the name of the Defendant;
   (f) any money in the account numbered 98765432 at Anytown Bank PLC, 1 Main Street, Torquay, held in the name of Mrs Violetta Valery;

(g) any money in the account numbered 22334455 at Anytown Bank PLC, 1 Main Street, Torquay, held in the name of Mr Giorgo Germont;

(h) A Rolls Royce motor vehicle registered number AG 123 registered in the name of the Defendant;

(i) A motor vessel named 'Hispaniqla', registered in the joint names of the Defendant and Mrs Violetta Valery;

(j) A racehorse named 'Nabucco', registered in the joint names of the Defendant and Mr Giorgio Germont;

(k) cash totalling £175,000 currently in the possession of the Metropolitan Police Service;

(l) the property known as 'The Heights', Marbella, Spain.

## AND IT IS ORDERED THAT:—

6. The assets of Traviata Trading Enterprises Limited be treated as the personal assets of the Defendant.
7. Mrs Violetta Valery must not:—
   (1) remove from England and Wales or
   (2) in any way dispose of or deal with or diminish the value of the following assets—
       (i) any monies in the account numbered 98765432 at Anytown Bank PLC, 1 Main Street, Torquay, held in the name of Mrs Violetta Valery;
       (ii) a motor vessel named 'Hispaniola', registered in the names of the Defendant and Mrs Violetta Valery.
8. Traviata Trading Enterprises Limited (a company in the Control of the Defendant) must not:—
   (1) remove from England and Wales or
   (2) in any way dispose of or deal with or diminish the value of the following assets—
       (a) The assets of the company called Traviata Trading Enterprises Limited (Company number 12345) registered address 123 The Esplanade, Torquay, Devon;
       (b) Any monies in the account numbered 66778899 at Anytown Bank PLC, 1 Main Street, Torquay, held in the name of Traviata Trading Enterprises Limited.
9. Mr Giorgio Germont must not:—
   (1) remove from England and Wales; or
   (2) in any way dispose of or deal with or diminish the value of the following assets—
       (a) Any monies in the account numbered 22334455 at Anytown Bank PLC, 1 Main Street, Torquay Devon;
       (b) A racehorse called 'Nabucco' registered in the names of the Defendant and Mr Giorgio Germont.

## RENTAL INCOME

10. Any rent received by the Defendant in respect of the properties set out in paragraph 5(a) and (l) above shall be dealt with in the following manner:—
    (a) the tenant shall pay rent to the Defendant in the form of a cheque, standing order or other inter bank transfer;
    (b) the Defendant shall pay the cheque or other payment into bank account number 12345678 at Anytown Bank PLC, 1 Main Street, Torquay in the name of the Defendant ('the account');
    (c) the sums received shall be used by the Defendant each and every month to pay mortgage instalments upon the properties set out in paragraph 5 (a) and (l) above in such amounts as the mortgagees shall require; and
    (d) any surplus held in the account or accounts shall be held restrained in the account subject to this Order.
11. The Defendant shall keep records of rent received and sums paid to the mortgagees, such records to include:—
    (a) the name and address of the tenant from whom each sum is received and the date of receipt;
    (b) the amount paid to the mortgagee and the date of the payment;
    (c) bank statements of the account or accounts into which rents are received and from which mortgage instalments are made;

AND the Defendant shall supply to the Prosecutor each and every calendar month within 14 days after the end of the month a copy of the said records relating to that month.

## DISCLOSURE ORDER

*Provision of Information*

12. The Defendant must serve a witness statement verified by a statement of truth on the Prosecutor within 21 days after this Order has been served on him setting out all his assets and all assets under his control whether in or outside England and Wales and whether in his own name or not and whether solely or jointly owned, giving the value, location and details of all such assets. The witness statement must include:

    (1) the name and address of all persons including financial institutions holding any such assets;

    (2) if the Defendant alleges that any third party or financial institution holds an interest in any such asset then he must identify the nature and extent of that interest, and the name and address of the person who is alleged to hold it;

    (3) details of the Defendant's current salary or other form of income, identifying the amounts paid, by whom they are paid and the account or accounts into which such sums are paid;

    (4) the names and numbers of all accounts held by or under the control of the Defendant, together with the name and address of the place where the account is held and the sums in the account;

    (5) details (including addresses) of any real property in which the Defendant has any interest, including an interest in any of the net sale money if the property were to be sold. These details must include details of any mortgage or charge on the property;

    (6) details of all National Savings Certificates, unit trusts, shares or debentures in any company or corporation, wherever incorporated in the world, owned or controlled by the Defendant or in which he has an interest;

    (7) details of all trusts of which the Defendant is a beneficiary, including the name and address of every trustee;

    (8) particulars of any income or debt due to the Defendant including the name and address of the debtor;

    (9) details of all assets over £1,000 in value received by the Defendant, or anyone on his behalf, since 1st September 2009 identifying the name and address of all persons from whom such property was received;

    (10) details of all assets over £1,000 in value transferred by the Defendant, or anyone on his behalf, to others since 1st September 2009, identifying the name and address of all persons to whom such property was transferred; and

    (11) in the event that any Claim Form, Petition, Statutory Demand, Application Notice, Enforcement Notice, Seizure Notice or other civil court process is pending or is at any time during the currency of this Order served upon him or brought to his attention, the Defendant shall forthwith provide a copy of the process to the Prosecutor.

13. (1) Subject to any further order of the Court any information given in compliance with this Order shall only be used:—

    (a) for the purpose of these proceedings;

    (b) if the Defendant is convicted, for the purposes of any confiscation hearing that may take place; and

    (c) if a confiscation order is made, for the purposes of enforcing that order, including any receivership proceedings.

    (2) Paragraph 13 (1) does not prevent the Prosecutor or counsel instructed by the Prosecutor from considering any information disclosed in compliance with this Order for the purposes of discharging the Prosecutor's disclosure obligations in the criminal proceedings (to which these proceedings are ancillary) whether under the Criminal Procedure and Investigations Act 1996 or the common law.

    (3) There shall be no disclosure of any material disclosed in compliance with this Order to any co-defendant in the criminal proceedings.

    (4) However, nothing in this paragraph shall make inadmissible any disclosure made by the Defendant in any proceedings for perjury relating to that disclosure.

14. The Defendant must serve a witness statement verified by a statement of truth upon the Prosecutor within 21 days after this order has been served on him setting out the following matters:—

    (1) the name and address of every tenant in the properties referred to in paragraph 5 (a) and (l) above; and

(2) the amount of rent paid by each tenant, details of any arrears of such rent and the manner in which the rent is usually paid.

15. (1) Subject to any further order of the court any information given in compliance with this Order shall only be used:—

(a) for the purpose of these proceedings;

(b) if the Defendant is convicted, for the purposes of any confiscation hearing that may take place; and

(c) if a confiscation order is made, for the purposes of enforcing that order, including any receivership proceedings.

(2) Paragraph 15(1) does not prevent the Prosecutor or counsel instructed by the Prosecutor from considering any information disclosed in compliance with this Order for the purposes of discharging the Prosecutor's disclosure obligations in the criminal proceedings (to which these proceedings are ancillary) whether under the Criminal Procedure and Investigations Act 1996 or the common law.

(3) There shall be no disclosure of any material disclosed in compliance with this Order to any co-defendant in the criminal proceedings.

(4) However, nothing in this paragraph shall make inadmissible any disclosure made by the Defendant in any proceedings for perjury relating to that disclosure.

## Repatriation

16. (1) The Defendant must within 21 days after being asked to do so in writing by the Prosecutor bring any moveable asset in respect of which he has an interest, which is outside England and Wales, to a location within England and Wales.

(2) The Defendant must inform the Prosecutor of the location within England and Wales within 7 days of the arrival of the assets.

(3) If the asset is cash or credit in a financial institution it must be paid into an interest bearing account and the account holder, location and account number be notified to the Prosecutor within 7 days.

## Service by an Alternative Method

17. The Prosecutor shall have permission to serve this Order and the witness statement of listed in Schedule A and any further orders or applications or other paperwork relating to this claim by serving the same on Mr Giorgio Germont c/o Messrs Dodson and Fogg, Solicitors, 2 Main Street, Torquay, Devon by pre-paid first class post.

18. The service referred to in paragraph 17 above shall be considered to be good and sufficient service upon the said Mr Giorgio Germont on the second day after posting.

## Exceptions to this Order

19. (1) This Order does not prohibit the Defendant, on the proviso that he is not in prison, from spending up to £250 a week towards his ordinary living expenses, up to the date of the making of any confiscation order. Before starting to withdraw money in respect of his living expenses, the Defendant must contact the Prosecutor to nominate a bank account or source of income from which such monies will be drawn and must obtain the consent of the Prosecutor in writing to the use of that account or income for that purpose.

(2) This Order does not prohibit Mrs Violetta Valery, on the proviso that she is not in prison, from spending up to £250 a week towards her ordinary living expenses, up to the date of the making of any confiscation order. But before spending any money Mrs Violetta Valery must contact the Prosecutor to nominate a bank account or source of income from which such monies will be drawn and must obtain the consent of the Prosecutor in writing to the use of that account or income for that purpose.

(3) This Order does not prohibit the Defendant from spending any money he may receive by way of state benefit from the Department for Work and Pensions and/or Her Majesty's Revenue and Customs.

(4) This Order does not prohibit the Defendant from spending towards his ordinary living expenses any sum earned by him whilst he is in prison.

(5) The Defendant and Mrs Violetta Valery may agree with the Prosecutor that the above spending limit be varied or that this Order be varied in any other respect, but any such agreement must be in writing.

(6) This Order does not prohibit the Defendant from dealing with or disposing of any of his assets in the ordinary and proper course of business, including operating bank account number 667788999 at Anytown Bank PLC, 1 Main Street, Torquay, held in the name of Traviata Trading Enterprises Limited for this purpose. However, to do this, the Defendant must supply to the Prosecutor within 7 days after being asked:—

    (a) the following accounting records of the business:—

        (i) entries from day to day of all sums of money received and expended by the business and the matters in respect of which the receipt and expenditure takes place;

        (ii) a record of the assets and liabilities of the business, including debts owed to and by the business; and

        (iii) if the business involves dealing in goods, statements of stock held by the business.

    (b) bank statements, cheque stubs, paying in books, bank transfer documentation and any correspondence with the bank in relation to the business bank account.

(7) This Order does not prevent:—

    (a) any person from paying any money in satisfaction of the whole or part of any confiscation order which may be made against the Defendant; or

    (b) the levy of distress upon any goods subject to this Order for the purpose of enforcement of any confiscation order which may be made against the Defendant.

## VARIATION OR DISCHARGE OF THIS ORDER

20. Anyone affected by this Order may apply to the court at any time to vary or discharge this Order (or so much of it as affects that person), but they must serve the application and the witness statement in support of the application on the Prosecutor and the Defendant, Mrs Violetta Valery, Traviata Trading Enterprises Limited and Mr Giorgio Germont at least two clear working days before the date fixed by the Crown Court for the hearing of the application.

## EFFECT OF THIS ORDER

21. A person who is an individual who is ordered not to do something must not do it himself or in any other way. He must not do it through others acting on his behalf or on his instructions or with his encouragement.

22. A person who is not an individual which is ordered not to do something must not do it itself or by its directors, officers, partners, employees or agents or in any other way.

## PARTIES OTHER THAN THE DEFENDANT

*Effect of this order*

23. It is a contempt of court for any person notified of this Order knowingly to assist in or permit a breach of this Order. Any person doing so may be imprisoned or fined. He is also at risk of prosecution for a money laundering offence.

*Set off by banks*

24. This Order does not prevent any bank from exercising any right of set off it may have in respect of any facility which it gave to the Defendant before it was notified of this Order.

*Withdrawals by the Defendant*

25. No bank need enquire as to the application or proposed application of any money withdrawn by the Defendant if the withdrawal appears to be permitted by this Order.

*Cash in the custody of Her Majesty's Revenue & Customs or the National Crime Agency*

26. This Order does not apply to any cash while it is seized or detained by Her Majesty's Revenue & Customs or the National Crime Agency under Part 5 of the Proceeds of Crime Act 2002, or while it is detained or forfeited by order of a court under that Part. 'Cash' is to have the meaning given to it by section 289(6) of that Act.

### Existing Charges

27. This Order does not prevent any financial institution or other charge holder from enforcing or taking any other steps to enforce an existing charge it has in respect of a property or properties so secured, providing that the said financial institution gives written notice to the Defendant, the Prosecutor and any other affected third party no later than 21 days before any such application is made. If any evidence is to be relied upon in support of any such application, the substance of it must be communicated to the Prosecutor in advance.

### Persons outside England, Wales, Scotland and Northern Ireland

28. (1) Except as provided in paragraph (2) below, the terms of this Order do not affect or concern anyone outside the jurisdiction of this court, Scotland or Northern Ireland.
    (2) The terms of this Order will affect the following persons in a country or state outside the jurisdiction of this court, Scotland or Northern Ireland:—
    - (a) a person to whom this order is addressed or the officer or agent appointed by power of attorney of such a person;
    - (b) any person who:—
        - (i) is subject to the jurisdiction of this court, Scotland or Northern Ireland;
        - (ii) has been given written notice of this order at his residence or place of business within the jurisdiction of this court, Scotland or Northern Ireland; and
        - (iii) is able to prevent acts or omissions outside the jurisdiction of this court, Scotland or Northern Ireland which constitute or assist in a breach of the terms of this order; and
    - (c) any other person, only to the extent that this order is declared enforceable by or is enforced by a court in that country or state.

### Enforcement in Scotland and Northern Ireland

29. This Order shall have effect in the law of Scotland and Northern Ireland, and may be enforced there, if it is registered under the Proceeds of Crime Act 2002 (Enforcement in Different Parts of the United Kingdom) Order 2002.

### Assets located outside England and Wales

30. Nothing in this Order shall, in respect of assets located outside England and Wales, prevent any third party from complying with:—
    (1) what it reasonably believes to be its obligations, contractual or otherwise, under the laws and obligations of the country or state in which those assets are situated or under the proper law of any contract to which it is a party; and
    (2) any orders of the courts of that country or state, provided that reasonable notice of any application for such an order is given to the Prosecutor;
    unless those assets are situated in Scotland or Northern Ireland, in which case this Order must be obeyed there.

## UNDERTAKINGS

31. The Prosecutor gives to the Court the undertakings set out in Schedule B to this Order.

## DURATION OF THE ORDER

32. This Order will remain in force until it is varied or discharged by a further order of this Court.

## INTERPRETATION

33. Reference to the 'Defendant' means Mr Alfredo Germont. Reference to an asset belonging to the Defendant includes any property in which the Defendant has an interest and any property to which the Defendant has a right.
34. A period of time expressed as a number of days shall be computed as clear days as defined in rule 57.2 of the Criminal Procedure Rules.

## Costs

35. The costs of this Order are reserved.

## Communications with the Court

All communications to the Court about this Order should be sent to the Southwark Crown Court quoting the case number. The office is open between 9am and 5pm Monday to Friday. The telephone number is:

## Address of the Prosecutor for Service and Any Communication in Respect of these Proceedings

All communications to the Prosecutor about this Order should be sent to (insert name, address, telephone and fax numbers of prosecutor).

COURT STAMP

## Schedule A

## Witness Statements

(1)  Witness Statement of [NAME] dated [DATE].

## Schedule B

## Undertakings Given to the Court by the Prosecutor

(1)  The Prosecutor will serve upon the Defendant, Mr Giorgio Germont, Mrs Violetta Valery and Traviata Trading Enterprises Ltd:—
  (a)  a copy of this Order; and
  (b)  a copy of the witness statement containing the evidence relied upon by the Prosecutor, and any other documents provided to the Court on the making of the application.
(2)  Anyone notified of this Order will be given a copy of it by the Prosecutor.
(3)  The Prosecutor will pay the reasonable costs of anyone other than the Defendant, Mrs Violetta Valery, Traviata Trading Enterprises Limited and Mr Giorgio Germont which are incurred as a result of this Order including the costs of finding out whether that person holds any of the Defendant's assets, save that the Prosecutor will not without an order of the Court be obliged to pay any legal or accountancy costs so incurred unless the Prosecutor first gives its consent in writing.

COURT STAMP

# APPENDIX 10

# Management Receivership Order

DISOBEDIENCE OF THIS ORDER IS A CONTEMPT OF COURT WHICH IF YOU ARE AN INDIVIDUAL IS PUNISHABLE BY IMPRISONMENT OR IF YOU ARE A BODY CORPORATE IS PUNISHABLE BY SEQUESTRATION OF YOUR ASSETS AND BY IMPRISONMENT OF ANY INDIVIDUAL RESPONSIBLE

IN THE CROWN COURT
SITTING AT SOUTHWARK
Before His Honour Judge Bullingham sitting in Private

No....................................................................

Dated................................................................

### IN THE MATTER OF ALFREDO GERMONT (Defendant)
### AND
### IN THE MATTER OF THE PROCEEDS OF CRIME ACT 2002

ORDER APPOINTING A MANAGEMENT RECEIVER

**IMPORTANT: NOTICE TO THE DEFENDANT, ALFREDO GERMONT, MR. GIORGIO GERMONT, MISS VIOLETTA VALERY AND TRAVIATA TRADING ENTERPRISES LIMITED AND ANYONE IN POSSESSION OR CONTROL OF THE DEFENDANT'S ASSETS**

1. This Order appoints a Receiver to manage the assets of the Defendant subject to the Restraint Order made by His Honour Judge Bullingham on 1st September 2014.
2. This Order varies the Restraint Order made against the Defendant, Mr Giorgio Germont, Miss Violetta Valery and Traviata Trading Enterprises Limited by His Honour Judge Bullingham on 1st September 2014.
3. If the Defendant or any person in possession or control of his assets disobeys this Order or obstructs the Receiver he or she may be guilty of contempt of court and may be sent to prison or fined or have his or her assets seized.
4. There is an interpretation section at page 4 of this Order.

THE ORDER OF APPOINTMENT

An application was made today by the Crown Prosecution Service to the Crown Court sitting at Southwark for the appointment of a Management Receiver over the assets of the Defendant to enforce the Restraint Order made against him by His Honour Judge Bullingham on 1st September 2014.

The Judge read the witness statement of [insert name] made on the 5th day of November 2014.

As a result of the application THE COURT APPOINTS [insert name and address of receiver] as Management Receiver ['the Receiver'] of the realisable property of the Defendant including those listed in the Schedule to this Order and including the assets and the business and undertakings of Traviata Trading Enterprises Limited.

**AND IT IS ORDERED THAT:—**

1. The assets of Traviata Trading Enterprises Limited be treated as the personal assets of the Defendant.
2. The Receiver shall have the following powers without prejudice to any existing powers vested in her whether by statute or otherwise:—
   a. Power to take possession of, preserve, manage, collect, let charge and sell the assets of the Defendant and Traviata Trading Enterprises Limited.
   b. Power to appoint solicitors, counsel, attorneys, accountants or other agents to advise and/or act on behalf of the Receiver in any part of the world.
   c. Power to discharge all and any costs, charges and expenses of the receivership out of the assets and/or the proceeds of realisation thereof.
   d. Power to bring proceedings in the name of or on behalf of the Defendant and/or Traviata Trading Enterprises Limited, within or without the jurisdiction, against any person having possession of the realisable property of the Defendant and/or Traviata Trading Enterprises Limited for possession thereof or for the payment or delivery up thereof.
   e. Power to execute all such documents in the name of and on behalf of the Defendant and/or Traviata Trading Enterprises Limited as may be necessary to take possession of, preserve, manage, collect, let, charge and/or sell realisable property.
   f. The Defendant, Traviata Trading Enterprises Limited and all other persons in possession of the assets of the Defendant shall take all such reasonable and necessary steps as may be required by the Receiver to enable the receivership to be conducted and the sale of the Defendant's assets to proceed, including but without prejudice to the generality of the foregoing:—
      (i) Providing the Receiver forthwith upon request by the Receiver with such information and documents relating to the management of the said assets as the Receiver so requires.
      (ii) Signing and delivering to the Receiver in accordance with the instructions of the Receiver letters of authority to financial institutions or any other person or body holding any asset of the Defendant authorising the Receiver to receive information or effect the transfer of any asset to the Receiver's control.
      (iii) Executing and delivering within 4 days of being instructed to do so by the Receiver powers of attorney to the Receiver in such form and in such manner as the Receiver directs.
3. No information provided to the Receiver under the powers conferred on the Receiver by this Order shall be used in evidence in the prosecution of an offence alleged to have been committed by the person required to make that disclosure or by any spouse of that person.
4. The costs of the Receivership shall be paid in the Receivership in accordance with the letter of agreement as exhibited to the witness statement of (insert name) made on the 1st day of November 2014.
5. The Receiver shall act in accordance with the letter of agreement as exhibited to the witness statement of (insert name) made on the 1st day of November 2014 and the Receiver shall supply to the Defendant copies of the accounts and reports supplied to the Crown Prosecution Service in accordance with the said letter of agreement.
6. In this Order the realisable property of the Defendant or the Defendant's assets include but is not limited to the assets specified in the Schedule to this Order.

**EFFECT OF THIS ORDER ON PERSONS OUTSIDE ENGLAND, WALES, SCOTLAND AND NORTHERN IRELAND**

7. The terms of this Order do not affect or concern anyone outside England and Wales, Scotland and Northern Ireland until it is declared enforceable or is enforced by a court in the relevant country and then they are to affect him only to the extent they have been declared enforceable or have been enforced, UNLESS such a person is:
   a. a person to whom this Order is addressed or an officer or an agent appointed by power of attorney of such a person; or
   b. a person who is subject to the jurisdiction of this court or Scotland or Northern Ireland and (i) has written notice of this order at his residence or place of business within the jurisdiction of this court or Scotland and (ii) is able lawfully to prevent acts or omissions outside the jurisdiction of this court or Scotland which constitute or assist in a breach of the terms of this Order.

## THE COSTS OF THIS ORDER

8. Costs reserved.

## DURATION OF THIS ORDER

9. This Order shall remain in force until it is varied or discharged by further order of this Court.

## INTERPRETATION OF THIS ORDER

10. In this Order 'the Defendant's assets' or 'assets of the Defendant' means any property in which the Defendant has any interest or to which the Defendant has any right and any property held by any other person to whom the Defendant has made a tainted gift caught by the Proceeds of Crime Act 2002, including but not limited to all property set out in the Schedule hereto.
13. Reference to selling a property includes charging, disposing, transferring, or conveying the legal and/or beneficial interest in the property to the purchaser of it.
14. Reference to the Receiver means [insert name and address of the receiver]
15. Reference to the Defendant means ALFREDO GERMONT.

## VARIATION OR DISCHARGE OF THIS ORDER

16. The Defendant (or anyone notified of this Order) may apply to the court at any time to vary or discharge this Order (or so much of it as affects that person), but anyone wishing to do so must first inform the Receiver and the Crown Prosecution Service giving 2 clear days notice in writing.

**DATED** this the 5th day of November 2014.

All communications to the Receiver about this Order should be sent to [insert name, address and telephone number of the receiver].

All communications to the Court about this Order should be sent to the Chief Clerk at Southwark Crown Court [insert address]. The offices are open between 10am and 4.30pm Monday to Friday. The telephone number is [insert number].

The address for service and telephone number of [insert name of prosecutor] for any communication in respect of these proceedings is:

[insert address and telephone number of the prosecutor].

### SCHEDULE TO THE RECEIVERSHIP ORDER MADE
### ON 5TH NOVEMBER 2014

(a) The Defendant's interest in a company known as Traviata Trading Enterprises Limited;
(b) Anytown Bank PLC account number 12345678 in the name of the Defendant;
(c) Anytown Bank PLC account number 98765432 in the name of the Defendant and Violetta Valery;
(d) Anytown Bank PLC account number 22334455 in the name of Giorgio Germont;
(e) Anytown Bank PLC account number 66778899 in the name of Traviata Trading Enterprises Limited;
(f) The Defendant's interest in all that property and land known as 'The Heights', Marbella, Spain;
(g) The Defendant's interest in a Rolls Royce motor vehicle registered number AG 123 registered in the name of the Defendant;
(h) The Defendant's interest in a motor vessel named 'Hispaniola' registered in the names of the Defendant and Violetta Valery;
(i) A racehorse named 'Nabucco' registered in the names of the Defendant and Giorgio Germont;
(j) A quantity of cash found on the defendant when arrested totalling £175,000 in Sterling bank notes.

# APPENDIX 11

# Enforcement Receivership Order

DISOBEDIENCE TO THIS ORDER IS A CONTEMPT OF COURT WHICH IF YOU ARE AN INDIVIDUAL IS PUNISHABLE BY IMPRISONMENT OR IF YOU ARE A BODY CORPORATE IS PUNISHABLE BY SEQUESTRATION OF YOUR ASSETS AND BY IMPRISONMENT OF ANY INDIVIDUAL RESPONSIBLE

IN THE CROWN COURT
SITTING AT SOUTHWARK
Before His Honour Judge Bullingham sitting in Private

No....................................................................

Dated................................................................

### IN THE MATTER OF ALFREDO GERMONT (Defendant)
### AND
### IN THE MATTER OF THE PROCEEDS OF CRIME ACT 2002

ORDER APPOINTING A RECEIVER OVER THE
ASSETS OF THE DEFENDANT

**IMPORTANT: NOTICE TO THE DEFENDANT AND ANYONE IN POSSESSION OR CONTROL OF HIS ASSETS OR NAMED IN THIS ORDER**

1. This Order appoints a Receiver over the assets of the Defendant to enforce the Confiscation Order made against the Defendant at the Crown Court sitting at Southwark on 7th January 2015. This means that the Receiver must, subject to the terms of this Order, collect the Defendant's assets and sell enough of them to pay the Confiscation Order.
2. If the Defendant or any person in possession or control of his assets disobeys this Order or obstructs the Receiver he or she may be guilty of contempt of court and may be sent to prison or fined or have his or her assets seized.
3. There is an interpretation section at page 5 of this Order.

THE ORDER OF APPOINTMENT

An application was made today by the Crown Prosecution Service to the Crown Court for the appointment of an Enforcement Receiver over the assets of the Defendant to enforce the Confiscation Order made by the Crown Court at Southwark on 7th January 2015 in the sum of £1,000,000.

The Crown Prosecution Service and the Defendant were represented by Counsel. Violetta Valery was represented by Counsel.

The Judge read the witness statements of [insert name of prosecutor] made 1st April 2015, Alfredo Germont made on 10th April 2015 and Violetta Valery made on 12th April 2015.

As a result of the application THE COURT APPOINTS [insert name of Receiver] to act as an Enforcement Receiver to take possession of, or otherwise deal with, all the assets of the Defendant including, but not limited to, those listed in the Schedule to this Order.

**IT IS ORDERED THAT:**

1. The Defendant, Violetta Valery and all other persons having possession of the Defendant's realisable property do forthwith deliver up to the Receiver possession of all such realisable property, together with all deeds, books, documents and papers relating thereto, but without prejudice to the rights of any encumbrancer.

2. The Receiver shall have the following powers without prejudice to any existing powers vested in him whether by statute or otherwise:—
   (a) Power to take possession of, preserve, manage, collect, let, charge and sell the assets of the Defendant;
   (b) Power to apply the net proceeds of the realisation of the Defendant's realisable property towards satisfaction of the Confiscation Order made against the Defendant by the Crown Court sitting at Southwark on 7th January 2015;
   (c) Power to appoint Solicitors, Counsel, Attorneys, Accountants or other Agents to advise and/or act on behalf of the Receiver in any part of the world;
   (d) Power to discharge all and any costs, charges and expenses of the Receivership out of the assets and/or the proceeds of realisation thereof;
   (e) Power to institute, defend or compromise proceedings in connection with the realisation of the Defendant's assets;
   (f) Power to bring proceedings in the name of or on behalf of the Defendant, within or without the jurisdiction, against any person having possession of the realisable property of the Defendant for possession thereof or the payment or delivery up thereof;
   (g) Power to execute all such documents in the name of and on behalf of the Defendant and Violetta Valery as may be necessary to take possession of, preserve, manage, collect, let, charge and/or sell realisable property;
   (h) After satisfaction of the Confiscation Order power to apply out of the realisable property such sum as is required in satisfaction of the legal costs of the Crown Prosecution Service ordered by Paragraph 9 of this Order;
   (i) Power to settle debts and liabilities of the Defendant from the assets of the Defendant; and
   (j) Power to manage the realisable property of the Defendant including the leasing, letting and/or granting of a licence in any real property forming part of the realisable property.
3. The powers of the Receiver shall not be exercisable in relation to any tainted gifts made by the defendant to Violetta Valery until agreement between the parties or further order and that part of the application by the Crown Prosecution Service for the appointment of a receiver in respect of such gifts do stand adjourned generally with the following directions:—
   (a) Any evidence from Violetta Valery to be served by 3rd May 2015;
   (b) Any evidence from the Crown Prosecution Service in reply to be served within 14 days thereafter;
   (c) The application be listed on the first open date thereafter on a date fixed through the list office at the convenience of the parties.
4. The Defendant, Violetta Valery and all other persons in possession of the assets of the Defendant shall take all such reasonable and necessary steps as may be required by the Receiver to enable the receivership to be conducted and the sale of the Defendant's assets to proceed, including but without prejudice to the generality of the foregoing—
   (a) Providing the Receiver forthwith upon request by the Receiver with such information and documentation relating to the said assets as the Receiver requires;
   (b) Signing and delivering to the Receiver in accordance with the instructions of the Receiver, Letters of Authority to financial institutions or any other person or body holding any assets of the Defendant authorising the Receiver to receive information or effect the transfer of any asset to the Receiver's control; and
   (c) Executing and delivering within four days of being instructed to do so by the Receiver power of Attorney to the Receiver in such form and in such manner as the Receiver directs.
5. The costs of the receivership shall be paid in the receivership in accordance with the letter of agreement as exhibited to the witness statement of [insert name of prosecutor].
6. The receiver shall act in accordance with the letter of agreement as exhibited to the witness statement of [insert name of prosecutor] and the Receiver shall supply to the Defendant copies of any accounts and reports supplied to the Crown Prosecution Service in accordance with the said letter of agreement.
7. The Receiver shall be allowed remuneration in accordance with the aforesaid letter of agreement.
8. In this Order the realisable property of the Defendant or the Defendant's assets includes but is not limited to the assets specified in the Schedule to this Order.

## The Costs of this Order

9. The costs of and occasioned by the orders made on 1st September 2014, 5th November 2014 and by this application shall be paid by the Defendant to be subject to detailed assessment by a costs judge if not agreed.

## Effect of this Order on Persons Outside England, Wales, Scotland and Northern Ireland

10. The terms of this Order do not affect or concern anyone outside England, Wales, Scotland and Northern Ireland until it is declared enforceable or is enforced by a court in the relevant country and then they are to affect him only to the extent they have been declared enforceable or have been enforced, UNLESS such person is:
    (a) A person to whom this order is addressed or an officer or an agent appointed by power of attorney of such a person; or
    (b) A person who is subject to the jurisdiction of this court and—
       (i) Has been given written notice of this Order at his residence or place of business within the jurisdiction of this court; and
       (ii) Is able lawfully to prevent acts or omissions outside the jurisdiction of this court which constitute or assist in a breach of the terms of this Order.

## Duration of this Order

11. This Order will remain in force until it is varied or discharged by further order of this Court.

## Interpretation of this Order

12. In this Order 'the Defendant's assets' or 'assets of the Defendant' means any property in which the Defendant has any interest or to which the Defendant has any right and any property held by any person to whom the Defendant has made a tainted gift caught by the Proceeds of Crime Act 2002 including but not limited to all property set out in the Schedule hereto.
13. Reference to selling a property includes charging, disposing transferring or conveying the legal and/ or beneficial interest in the property to the purchaser of it.
14. Reference to the receiver means [insert name and address of the receiver].
15. Reference to the defendant mean Alfredo Germont.

DATED this the 15th day of April 2015.

### Schedule

[List all known realisable assets of the Defendant subject to the order]

# Variation of Restraint Order

DISOBEDIENCE OF THIS ORDER IS A CONTEMPT OF COURT WHICH IF YOU ARE AN INDIVIDUAL IS PUNISHABLE BY IMPRISONMENT OR IF YOU ARE A BODY CORPORATE IS PUNISHABLE BY SEQUESTRATION OF YOUR ASSETS AND BY IMPRISONMENT OF ANY INDIVIDUAL RESPONSIBLE

IN THE CROWN COURT
SITTING AT SOUTHWARK
Before His Honour Judge Bullingham sitting in Private

No.................................................................

Dated...............................................................

## IN THE MATTER OF ALFREDO GERMONT (Defendant)

### AND

## IN THE MATTER OF THE PROCEEDS OF CRIME ACT 2002

ORDER

**UPON HEARING** Counsel for the Defendant and Counsel for the Crown Prosecution Service **AND UPON READING** the witness statement of Alfredo Germont made on the 30th day of November 2014.

IT IS ORDERED THAT

1. The restraint order made by His Honour Judge Bullingham on the 1st day of September 2014 ('the Restraint Order') be varied to the following extent—
   (a) The amount payable to the Defendant by way of general living expenses pursuant to paragraph 19 of the order be increased from £250 per week to £350 per week, to be paid from account number 12345678 held in the name of the Defendant at Anytown Bank PLC; and
   (b) The period for compliance with paragraph 12 of the Order be extended to 1600 hours on 20th December 2014.
2. The Defendant has permission to sell all that property and land known as 'Traviata', 123 The Esplanade, Torquay, Devon ('the property')

PROVIDED THAT

   (i) The Defendant must provide the Crown Prosecution Service with two independent valuations in respect of the property. The Crown Prosecution Service reserves the right to obtain further independent professional property valuations if it wishes to verify those provided by the Defendant;
   (ii) The Defendant must not sell the property for an amount less than its market value as confirmed by the highest valuation obtained under sub-paragraph (i) above;
   (iii) The Defendant shall not pay any fees and charges from the gross sum obtained from the sale of the property (including but not limited to legal fees, agents fees, search fees and charges) without obtaining the prior written consent of the Crown Prosecution Service. The Crown Prosecution Service may withhold its consent for the payment of fees and charges that are unreasonable or are improperly incurred;
   (iv) The Defendant will instruct Messrs. Thorn and Partners, Solicitors, 1a High Street, Torquay, Devon to act for him on the sale of the property and undertakes not to terminate their retainer in

respect thereof save with the written consent of the Crown Prosecution Service or the permission of the court;

(v) The gross proceeds of the sale of the property less:

a. The total amount required to discharge any mortgages and charges that were registered in relation to the property prior to 1st September 2014; and

b. The amount required to pay any fees and/or charges for which the prior consent of the Crown Prosecution Service has been obtained in accordance with sub-paragraph (iii) above

must be paid into an interest bearing account in the name of Messrs. Thorn and Co. The net proceeds will be subject to the terms of the restraint order.

(vi) Within two working days of receiving the net proceeds of sale into their interest bearing account, Messrs. Thorn and Co will inform the Crown Prosecution Service in writing of the date on which the net proceeds of sale were received and the amount of those proceeds. Messrs. Thorn and Co will also provide the Crown Prosecution Service with a completion statement in relation to the said sale.

(vii) Within three working days of the Crown Prosecution Service receiving written confirmation that the net proceeds of sale have been paid into an interest bearing account subject to the terms of the restraint order, the Crown Prosecution Service will apply to HM Land Registry for the removal of the restriction registered against the property.

3. The restraint order will remain in force in relation to the net proceeds of sale pending the conclusion of these proceedings.

4. Paragraph 2 of this Order will cease to have effect if the sale of the property does not take place by 4pm on 31st January, 2015.

5. Costs reserved.

**DATED** this the second day of December, 2014.

# APPENDIX 13

## Certificate of Inadequacy

Claim POCA No. 1234 of 2005

IN THE SOUTHWARK CROWN COURT

Before His Honour Judge Justice Vosper sitting in Private

### IN THE MATTER OF ALFREDO GERMONT (Defendant)

### AND

### IN THE MATTER OF THE PROCEEDS OF CRIME ACT 2002

## Order

**UPON HEARING** Counsel for the Defendant and Counsel for the Crown Prosecution Service
**AND UPON READING** the witness statement of Alfredo Germont made on 1st October 2015.
**IT IS CERTIFIED THAT** the value of the Defendant's realisable property is inadequate for the payment of the amount remaining to be recovered pursuant to the confiscation order ('the order') made against him in the sum of £1,000,000 by the Crown Court sitting at Southwark on 15th January 2014 for the following reasons:—

(a) By order of this Court made on 30th January 2015 it was determined that Violetta Valery had a 50% interest in all that property and land known as 'Traviata', 123 Esplanade, Torquay and in consequence thereof only 50% of the proceeds of sale were available to meet the Order; and

(b) The Crown Court in making the Order determined that the Defendant's Rolls Royce motor vehicle registration number AG 123 was valued at £75,000 whereas upon sale by the Receiver it realised only £35,750.

There be no order for costs.

**DATED** this the 14th day of June 2015.

# APPENDIX 14

## Extract from Practice Direction on POCA: Parts 5 and 8

## SECTION III—APPLICATIONS UNDER PART 8 OF THE ACT IN RESPECT OF CIVIL RECOVERY INVESTIGATIONS AND DETAINED CASH INVESTIGATIONS

### How to apply for an order or warrant

**8.1**

An application for an order or warrant under Part 8 of the Act in connection with a civil recovery investigation or (where applicable) a detained cash investigation must be made—
(1) to a High Court judge;
(2) by filing an application notice.

**8.2**

The application may be made without notice.

### Confidentiality of court documents

**9.1**

CPR rules 5.4, 5.4B and 5.4C do not apply to an application under Part 8 of the Act, and paragraphs 9.2 and 9.3 below have effect in its place.

**9.2**

When an application is issued, the court file will be marked 'Not for disclosure' and, unless a High Court judge grants permission, the court records relating to the application (including the application notice, documents filed in support, and any order or warrant that is made) will not be made available by the court for any person to inspect or copy, either before or after the hearing of the application.

**9.3**

An application for permission under paragraph 9.2 must be made on notice to the appropriate officer in accordance with CPR Part 23.

(CPR rule 23.7(1) requires a copy of the application notice to be served as soon as practicable after it is filed, and in any event at least 3 days before the court is to deal with the application.)

### Application notice and evidence

**10.1**

The application must be supported by written evidence, which must be filed with the application notice.

**10.2**

The evidence must set out all the matters on which the appropriate officer relies in support of the application, including any matters required to be stated by the relevant sections of the Act, and all material facts of which the court should be made aware.

**10.3**

There must also be filed with the application notice a draft of the order sought. This should if possible also be supplied to the court on disk in a form compatible with the word processing software used by the court.

**Hearing of the application**

**11.1**

The application will be heard and determined in private, unless the judge hearing it directs otherwise.

**Variation or discharge of order or warrant**

**12.1**

An application to vary or discharge an order or warrant may be made by—

(1)  the appropriate officer; or
(2)  any person affected by the order or warrant.

**12.2**

An application under paragraph 12.1 to stop an order or warrant from being executed must be made immediately upon it being served.

**12.3**

A person applying to vary or discharge a warrant must first inform the appropriate officer that he is making the application.

**12.4**

The application should be made to the judge who made the order or issued the warrant or, if he is not available, to another High Court judge.

# APPENDIX 15

# Extract From Practice Direction
# on POCA: Parts 5 and 8

## SECTION IV—FURTHER PROVISIONS ABOUT SPECIFIC APPLICATIONS UNDER PART 8 OF THE ACT

### Production order

**13.1**

The application notice must name as a respondent the person believed to be in possession or control of the material in relation to which a production order is sought.

**13.2**

The application notice must specify—

(1) whether the application is for an order under paragraph (a) or (b) of section 345(4) of the Act;
(2) the material, or description of material, in relation to which the order is sought; and
(3) the person who is believed to be in possession or control of the material.

**13.3**

An application under section 347 of the Act for an order to grant entry may be made either—

(1) together with an application for a production order; or
(2) by separate application, after a production order has been made.

**13.4**

An application notice for an order to grant entry must—

(1) specify the premises in relation to which the order is sought; and
(2) be supported by written evidence explaining why the order is needed.

**13.5**

A production order, or an order to grant entry, must contain a statement of the right of any person affected by the order to apply to vary or discharge the order.

### Search and seizure warrant

**14.1**

The application notice should name as the respondent the occupier of the premises to be subject to the warrant, if known.

**14.2**

The evidence in support of the application must state—

(1) the matters relied on by the appropriate officer to show that one of the requirements in section 352(6) of the Act for the issue of a warrant is satisfied;
(2) details of the premises to be subject to the warrant, and of the possible occupier or occupiers of those premises;
(3) the name and position of the member of the staff of the appropriate officer who it is intended will execute the warrant.

**14.3**

There must be filed with the application notice drafts of—

(1) the warrant; and

(2) a written undertaking by the person who is to execute the warrant to comply with paragraph 13.8 of this practice direction.

**14.4**

A search and seizure warrant must—

(1) specify the statutory power under which it is issued and, unless the court orders otherwise, give an indication of the nature of the investigation in respect of which it is issued;

(2) state the address or other identification of the premises to be subject to the warrant;

(3) state the name of the member of the staff of the appropriate officer who is authorised to execute the warrant;

(4) set out the action which the warrant authorises the person executing it to take under the relevant sections of the Act;

(5) give the date on which the warrant is issued;

(6) include a statement that the warrant continues in force until the end of the period of one month beginning with the day on which it is issued;

(7) contain a statement of the right of any person affected by the order to apply to discharge or vary the order.

**14.5**

An example of a search and seizure warrant is annexed to this practice direction. This example may be modified as appropriate in any particular case.

**14.6**

Rule 40.2 applies to a search and seizure warrant.

(CPR rule 40.2 requires every judgment or order to state the name and judicial title of the person making it, to bear the date on which it is given or made, and to be sealed by the court.)

**14.7**

Upon the issue of a warrant the court will provide to the appropriate officer—

(1) the sealed warrant; and

(2) a copy of it for service on the occupier or person in charge of the premises subject to the warrant.

**14.8**

A person attending premises to execute a warrant must, if the premises are occupied produce the warrant on arrival at the premises, and as soon as possible thereafter personally serve a copy of the warrant and an explanatory notice on the occupier or the person appearing to him to be in charge of the premises.

**14.9**

The person executing the warrant must also comply with any order which the court may make for service of any other documents relating to the application.

**Disclosure order**

**15.1**

The application notice should normally name as respondents the persons on whom the appropriate officer intends to serve notices under the disclosure order sought.

**15.2**

A disclosure order must—

(1) give an indication of the nature of the investigation for the purposes of which the order is made;

(2) set out the action which the order authorises the appropriate officer to take in accordance with section 357(4) of the Act;

(3) contain a statement of –

    (a) the offences relating to disclosure orders under section 359 of the Act; and

    (b) the right of any person affected by the order to apply to discharge or vary the order.

**15.3**

Where, pursuant to a disclosure order, the appropriate officer gives to any person a notice under section 357(4) of the Act, he must also at the same time serve on that person a copy of the disclosure order.

### Customer information order

**16.1**

The application notice should normally (unless it is impracticable to do so because they are too numerous) name as respondents the financial institution or institutions to which it is proposed that an order should apply.

**16.2**

A customer information order must –

(1) specify the financial institution, or description of financial institutions, to which it applies;
(2) state the name of the person in relation to whom customer information is to be given, and any other details to identify that person;
(3) contain a statement of—
   (a) the offences relating to disclosure orders under section 366 of the Act; and
   (b) the right of any person affected by the order to apply to discharge or vary the order.

**16.3**

Where, pursuant to a customer information order, the appropriate officer gives to a financial institution a notice to provide customer information, he must also at the same time serve a copy of the order on that institution.

### Account monitoring order

**17.1**

The application notice must name as a respondent the financial institution against which an account monitoring order is sought.

**17.2**

The application notice must—

(1) state the matters required by section 370(2) and (3) of the Act; and
(2) give details of—
   (a) the person whose account or accounts the application relates to;
   (b) each account or description of accounts in relation to which the order is sought, including if known the number of each account and the branch at which it is held;
   (c) the information sought about the account or accounts;
   (d) the period for which the order is sought;
   (e) the manner in which, and the frequency with which, it is proposed that the financial institution should provide account information during that period.

**17.3**

An account monitoring order must contain a statement of the right of any person affected by the order to apply to vary or discharge the order.

# Interim Receiving Order

CO No. 123 of 2014

IN THE HIGH COURT OF JUSTICE
QUEEN'S BENCH DIVISION

Before the Honourable Mr Justice Bellini sitting in Private

### IN THE MATTER OF MR ALFREDO GERMONT (Respondent)

### AND

### IN THE MATTER OF THE PROCEEDS OF CRIME ACT 2002

---

INTERIM RECEIVING ORDER

---

PENAL NOTICE

IF ALFREDO GERMONT FAILS TO COMPLY WITH THE TERMS OF THIS ORDER HE MAY BE HELD IN CONTEMPT OF COURT FOR WHICH HE MAY BE FINED AND BE IMPRISONED OR HAVE HIS ASSETS SEIZED

ANY OTHER PERSON WHO KNOWS OF THIS ORDER AND DOES ANYTHING WHICH HELPS OR PERMITS ALFREDO GERMONT TO BREACH THE TERMS OF THIS ORDER MAY ALSO BE HELD TO BE IN CONTEMPT OF COURT AND MAY BE IMPRISONED, FINED OR HAVE THEIR ASSETS SEIZED.

To: ALFREDO GERMONT

**An application having been made** to the High Court pursuant to section 246 of the Proceeds of Crime Act 2002 by the Director of the National Crime Agency ('the Director').[1]

**And upon reading** the witness statement of **Tony Foot** dated 22 July 2014,

**And upon hearing** Counsel for the Director,

**THE COURT IS SATISFIED** that the relevant requirements for making an interim receiving order are fulfilled.

IMPORTANT NOTICE

TO THE RESPONDENT ALFREDO GERMONT AND TO ANYONE IN POSSESSION OR CONTROL OF THE RESPONDENTS PROPERTY

A.  This Order appoints an Interim Receiver over certain property of the Respondent, limited to the property specified in Schedule 2 of this Order. This Order prohibits the Respondent from dealing with that property.
B.  The Order is subject to the exclusions at the end of this Order.
C.  You should read all of this Order carefully. You are advised to consult a solicitor as soon as possible.

---

[1] The Crime and Courts Act 2013 includes the abolition of the Serious Organised Crime Agency, and the creation of the National Crime Agency (see ss 1–16). Subject to Parliamentary processes the ambition is that it will be fully operational by December 2013.

D. You may be entitled to Legal Aid Agency funding in respect of this Order. You should speak to your solicitor or contact the Legal Aid Agency about funding for proceedings under the Proceeds of Crime Act 2002 involving the National Crime Agency.

E. Subject to the provisions of section 245C of the Proceeds of Crime Act 2002 and the Proceeds of Crime Act 2002 (Legal Expenses in Civil Recovery Proceedings) Regulations 2005, you may be entitled to the release of restrained funds to pay for legal representation in connection with this Order. A request for the release of a sum in respect of reasonable legal expenses must be made in writing to the Director of the National Crime Agency and before any release can be made certain conditions must be fulfilled. You and your legal adviser are referred to Part 3 of the Proceeds of Crime Act 2002 (Legal Expenses in Civil Recovery Proceedings) Regulations 2005 (SI 3382 of 2005).

F. Further to the provisions of section 245C of the Proceeds of Crime Act 2002, you may be entitled to the release of restrained funds to meet your reasonable living expenses or to carry on any trade, business, profession or occupation. A request for the release of property or an asset to meet reasonable living expenses or to carry on any trade, business, profession or occupation can either be made to the Director of the National Crime Agency, in the first instance or to the Court pursuant to section 245B of the Proceeds of Crime Act 2002.

G. You have a right to ask this Court to vary or discharge this Order.

H. If the Respondent or any person in possession or control of the property specified in Schedule 2 to this Order disobeys this Order or obstructs the Receiver he or she may be guilty of contempt of court and may be sent to prison or fined or have their assets seized.

I. There is an interpretation section at page x of this Order.

## AS A RESULT OF THE APPLICATION THE COURT MAKES THE FOLLOWING ORDERS:—

*The Order of Appointment:*

1. THE COURT APPOINTS Ivan I. Dere as Interim Receiver ('the Receiver') of the property listed in Schedule 2 to this Order.

*Order for the detention, custody, preservation and possession of property:*

2. The Respondent must not:
   (i) remove from England and Wales any Schedule 2 property which is in England and Wales whether in their own name or not and whether solely or jointly owned; or
   (ii) in any way dispose of or deal with or diminish the value of any of the Schedule 2 property whether it is in or outside England and Wales whether in the Respondent's own name or not and whether solely or jointly owned.

3. Pursuant to section 250 of the Proceeds of Crime Act 2002, the Respondent shall as soon as reasonably practicable:
   (i) on the demand in writing of the Receiver co-operate in procuring the transfer of the monies specified as item iv of Schedule 2 to this Order to such account as is specified by the Receiver;
   (ii) bring such property as is specified by the Receiver to the offices of the Receiver at Blueberry House, Strawberry Lane, London N1 1AA or to such other place as the Receiver specifies or place it in the custody of the Receiver; and
   (iii) do anything he/she is reasonably required to do by the Receiver for the preservation of the property.

4. Unless otherwise agreed in writing by the Receiver, the Respondent and all other persons having possession of the Schedule 2 property shall forthwith deliver up to the Receiver possession of all such assets, together with all deeds, books, documents and papers relating thereto, but without prejudice to the rights of any encumbrancer and SAVE THAT any person in lawful occupation of any real property is not required, until further order, to give physical possession of the real property to the Receiver.

*Disclosure:*

5. Within 72 hours of personal service of this Order, to the best of his ability, the Respondent must inform the Receiver in writing of all of his assets worldwide exceeding £1000 in value whether in his own name or not and whether solely or jointly owned, giving the value, location and details of all of

his assets. The Respondent must then provide this information in a witness statement verified by a statement of truth within 14 days after being personally served with this Order.

6. Nothing in this Order shall make inadmissible any disclosure made by the Respondent in any proceedings for perjury relating to that disclosure.

7. If the provision of the information required by paragraph 5 is likely to incriminate the Respondent, he may be entitled to refuse to provide it, but he is recommended to take legal advice before refusing to provide the information. Wrongful refusal to provide the information is a contempt of court and may render the Respondent liable to be imprisoned, fined or have his assets seized.

*Powers of the Receiver:*

8. In accordance with Schedule 6 to the Proceeds of Crime Act 2002, the Receiver shall have the following powers without prejudice to any existing powers vested in him whether by statute or otherwise:—

    (i) Power to seize property to which this Order applies;

    (ii) Power to take possession of and manage any property to which this Order applies;

    (iii) Power to enter and search any premises in the United Kingdom in which the Receiver believes or has reasonable grounds to believe that material relevant to his duties under the Act may be located and take the following steps:

        (a) carry out a search for or inspection of anything described in this Order, which shall include, but not be limited to, Suite 1, 2 Commercial Road, Torquay, TQ1 1RR;

        (b) to have Police assistance, if required, when carrying out service of this Order and a search for or inspection of anything described in this Order;

        (c) make or obtain a copy, photograph or other record of anything so described in this Order;

        (d) remove anything which he is entitled to take possession of in pursuance of this Order or which may be required as evidence in proceedings for civil recovery;

        (e) effect and maintain insurance.

    (iv) Power to appoint solicitors, counsel, attorneys, accountants or other agents to advise and/or act on behalf of the Receiver in any part of the world;

    (v) Power to bring proceedings in the name of or on behalf of the Respondent and any other person within or without the jurisdiction, against any person having possession of the property of the Respondent for possession thereof or for the payment or delivery up thereof;

    (vi) Power to execute all such documents in the name of and on behalf of the Respondent and any other person as may be necessary to manage Schedule 2 property;

    (vii) Power to require the Respondent, and all other persons in possession of the property of the Respondent to take all such reasonable and necessary steps as may be required by the Receiver to enable the receivership to be conducted, including but without prejudice to the generality of the foregoing:

        (a) providing the Receiver forthwith upon request by the Receiver with such information and documents including any questions put to them by the Receiver relating to the management of the said property as the Receiver so requires;

        (b) to sign and deliver to the Receiver in accordance with the instructions of the Receiver letters of authority to financial institutions or any other person or body holding any asset of the Respondent authorising the Receiver to receive information or effect the transfer of any such property to the Receiver's control;

        (c) to execute and deliver within 4 days of being instructed to do so by the Receiver power of attorney to the Receiver in such form and in such manner as the Receiver directs.

9. Nothing in this Order shall prevent any person claiming legal professional privilege in relation to the matters set out therein, particularly in relation to communications between the legal adviser and his or her client, or communications made in connection with or in contemplation of legal proceedings and for the purposes of those proceedings. However in such circumstances any person claiming legal professional privilege must still give to the Receiver access to any premises he may enter in pursuance of paragraph 8 and give to the Receiver any assistance he may require pursuant to this Order.

*Duties of the Receiver:*

10. Pursuant to section 247(2)(a) of the Proceeds of Crime Act 2002, the Receiver shall consider such information and documents as are obtained by him in pursuance of this Order to establish whether

or not the Schedule 2 property is recoverable property or associated property, and if the latter, to what extent the property comprises associated property.

11. Pursuant to section 247(2)(b) of the Proceeds of Crime Act 2002, the Receiver shall take all reasonable and necessary steps to establish whether or not any other property is recoverable property (in relation to the same unlawful conduct), and if it is, who holds it.

12. In accordance with section 255(1) of the Proceeds of Crime Act 2002, the Receiver must inform the Director and this Honourable Court as soon as reasonably practicable if he thinks that:

    (i) any property to which the Order applies by virtue of a claim that it is recoverable property is not recoverable property;

    (ii) any property to which this Order applies by virtue of a claim that it is associated property is not associated property;

    (iii) any property to which the Order does not apply is recoverable property (in relation to the same unlawful conduct) or associated property; or

    (iv) any property to which the Order applies is held by a person who is different from the person it is claimed holds it, or if he thinks that there has been a material change in circumstances.

13. In accordance with section 255(2) of the Proceeds of Crime Act 2002, the Receiver shall provide to this Honourable Court a report of his findings and shall serve copies of that report on the Director of the National Crime Agency and on any other person who holds any property to which the Order applies or who may otherwise be affected by the report.

*Orders relating to service:*

14. Permission is given to the National Crime Agency to comply with their undertaking relating to service on the Respondent by serving a copy of the Application Notice, the witness statement of Tony Foot dated 1 July 2014, and this Order on the last known solicitors for the Respondent, namely Messrs Tryitt and Sea, Green House, Blue Road, Torquay TQ1 1LN.

*The Receiver's liability:*

15. If the Receiver deals with any property which is not property to which this Order applies, and at the time he deals with the property he believes on reasonable grounds that he is entitled to do so in pursuance of the Order, the Receiver will not be liable to any person in respect of any loss or damage resulting from his dealing with the property except so far as the loss or damage is caused by his negligence.

16. The Receiver is required to have sufficient security or insurance to cover any liability for their acts or omissions as a Receiver. If the Receiver has appropriate insolvency practitioners' bond or guarantee, then no specific order concerning the security will be necessary from the Court. If, however, the insurance comes in some other form, then provided this form is acceptable, the Court will need to make some direction that the security can be given in this other form.

*The effect of this Order:*

17. A person who is an individual who is ordered not to do something must not do it himself or herself or in any other way. He or she must not do it through others acting on his or her behalf or on his or her instructions or with his or her encouragement.

18. A person which is a corporation and which is ordered not to do something must not do it by its directors, officers, employees or agents or in any other way.

19. Pursuant to Schedule 6(2) to the Proceeds of Crime Act 2002, no answer given by a person to the Receiver in pursuance of paragraph 6 above shall be used in evidence in criminal proceedings against the person, SAVE:

    (i) on a prosecution for an offence under section 5 of the Perjury Act 1911, section 44(2) of the Criminal Law (Consolidation) (Scotland) Act 1995 or Article 10 of the Perjury (Northern Ireland) Order 1979 (false statements); or

    (ii) on a prosecution for some other offence where, in giving evidence, he or she makes a statement inconsistent with it. (But an answer may not be used against a person unless evidence relating to it is adduced, or a question relating to it is asked, by him or her or on his or her behalf in the proceedings arising out of the prosecution).

*Third parties:*

20. It is a contempt of court for any person notified of this Order knowingly to assist in or permit a breach of this Order. Any person doing so may be sent to prison, fined or have his or her assets seized. He or she is also at risk of being prosecuted for a money-laundering offence.

*The effect of this Order on persons outside England, Wales and Scotland:*

21. The terms of this Order do not affect or concern anyone outside England, Wales and Scotland until it is declared enforceable or is enforced by a court in the relevant country and then they are to affect him or her only to the extent they have been declared enforceable or have been enforced, UNLESS such person is:

    (i) a person to whom this Order is addressed or an officer or an agent appointed by power of attorney of such a person; or

    (ii) a person who is subject to the jurisdiction of this court and (i) has been given written notice of this Order at his or her residence or place of business within the jurisdiction of this court and (ii) is able lawfully to prevent acts or omissions outside the jurisdiction of this court which constitute or assist in a breach of the terms of this Order.

*Undertakings:*

22. The Director gives to the Court the undertakings set out in Schedule 1 to this Order.

*Duration of this Order:*

23. This Order will remain in force until it is varied or discharged by further Order of this court.

*Variation or discharge of this Order:*

24. The Respondent (or anyone notified of or affected by this Order) may apply to the Court at any time to vary or discharge this Order (or so much of it as affects that person), but anyone wishing to do so must first inform the National Crime Agency giving at least 2 clear days' notice in writing.

*The costs of the Receivership:*

25. The Receiver may charge for his services and shall prepare and serve accounts in accordance with the letter of nomination as exhibited to the witness statement of Tony Foot dated 1 July 2014.

*The costs of this Order:*

26. The costs of this Order are reserved.

*Communications with the Receiver:*

27. All communications to the Receiver about this Order should be sent to Ivan I. Dere of Blueberry House, Strawberry Lane, London N1 1AA, telephone number 0207 000 1111 quoting the Respondent's name.

*Communications with the National Crime Agency:*

28. All communications to the Director of the National Crime Agency about this Order should be sent to the National Crime Agency, PO Box 8000, London, SE11 5EN, telephone number 0370 496 7622, quoting reference: **GERMONT**.

*Communications with the Court:*

29. All communications to the Court about this Order should be sent to Administrative Crown Office, Royal Courts of Justice, Strand, London, WC2A 2LL quoting the case number. The office is open between 10am and 4:30pm Monday to Friday. The telephone number is 020 7947 6000.

*Interpretation of this Order:*

30. 'Property' is all property wherever situated and includes:
    (i) money;
    (ii) all forms of property, real or personal, heritable or moveable; and
    (iii) things in action and other intangible or incorporeal property.

31. Any reference to a person's property (whether expressed as a reference to the property he or she holds or otherwise) is to be read as follows:
    (i) In relation to land, it is a reference to any interest which he or she holds in the land.
    (ii) In relation to property other than land, it is a reference—
        (a) to the property (if it belongs to him or her), or
        (b) to any other interest which he or she holds in the property.

32. 'The Respondents' recoverable property' or 'recoverable property of the Respondent' means property that has been obtained through unlawful conduct, or property that represents such property.

33. 'Associated property' means property of any of the following descriptions (including property held by the Respondent) which is not itself recoverable property—
    (i) any interest in the recoverable property,
    (ii) any other interest in the property in which the recoverable property subsists,
    (iii) if the recoverable property is a tenancy in common, the tenancy of the other tenant,
    (iv) if (in Scotland) the recoverable property is owned in common, the interest of the other owner,
    (v) if the recoverable property is part of a larger, but not a separate part, the remainder of that property.

34. 'Unlawful conduct' includes conduct occurring in any part of the United Kingdom which is unlawful under the criminal law of that part.

35. The power to 'manage any property' includes:
    (i) selling or otherwise disposing of assets comprised in the property which are perishable or which ought to be disposed of before their value diminishes;
    (ii) where the property comprises assets of a trade or business, carrying on, or arranging for another to carry on, the trade or business;
    (iii) incurring capital expenditure in respect of the property;
    (iv) in respect of any illegitimate business, ceasing the operation of that business.

36. 'Dealing' with property includes (1) disposing of it, (2) removing it from the United Kingdom, (3) relinquishing or cancelling or varying any signing authority over any bank accounts over which he has signing authority or in respect of which he is a signatory on the mandate irrespective of whether there is any money in such accounts, (4) relinquishing or cancelling or varying any power of attorney, directorship, office as trustee or other arrangement pursuant to which he has control of any asset which is not held in his name, or (5) relinquishing, cancelling or varying any arrangements whereby he is empowered to deal with assets which are not in his own name.

37. 'Document' means anything in which information of any description is recorded.

38. Reference to selling or otherwise disposing of assets comprised in the property which are perishable, or which ought to be disposed of before their value diminishes, includes charging, disposing, transferring or conveying the legal and/or beneficial interest in the property to the purchaser of it.

39. 'Act' refers to the Proceeds of Crime Act 2002.

Reference to the Receiver means:

Ivan I. Dere of Blueberry House, Strawberry Lane, London N1 1AA.

Reference to the Respondent means:

MR ALFREDO GERMONT

DATED this 20th day of July 2014.

## Schedule 1

### Undertakings given to the Court by the Director of the National Crime Agency

1. The Director will arrange to serve on the Respondent, ALFREDO GERMONT, a copy of this Order together with a copy of the witness statement containing the evidence relied on by the Applicant when obtaining this Order. Service will take place as soon as practicable after the Order is sealed.

## Schedule 2

(i) The proceeds derived from the sale of the land and property situated at 1 Royal Road, Brixham BX2 1PP registered at HM Land Registry in the name of A Germont with title number TQ11111, and any property acquired from said proceeds.

(ii) The following motor vehicles:
   (a) Mercedes SL500 with number plate ALFREDO 1 registered in the name of Mr Alfredo Germont;
   (b) BMW X5 with number plate ALFY 2 registered in the name of Mr Alfredo Germont;

(iii)  The boat currently being constructed by Boatworks Ltd and located at its premises at Haven Quay, New Road, Brixham BX2 1TT.

(iv)  Monies which have been credited to or have passed through the following accounts:

AND

(v)  Any other such property that the Interim Receiver may believe to be either Recoverable or Associated Property within the meaning of the Act, so long as the Interim Receiver gives notice of this Order to the appropriate person holding or in control of said property.

| Account holder | Institution | Sort Code | Account |
|---|---|---|---|
| Mr Alfredo Germont | Lloyds TSB | 00-00-00 | 12131415 |
| Mr Alfredo Germont | Halifax | 00-10-00 | 654321 |
| Mr A & Mrs T Germont | Lloyds TSB | 00-99-02 | 000011111 |
| Mr A & Mrs T Germont | Co-Op Bank | 00-11-11 | 22223333 |

# Property Freezing Order

IF YOU, ALFREDO GERMONT, OR YOU, VIOLETTA VALERY (OTHERWISE VALERY VIOLETTA), DISOBEY THIS ORDER YOU MAY BE HELD TO BE IN CONTEMPT OF COURT AND MAY BE IMPRISONED, FINED OR HAVE YOUR ASSETS SEIZED.

ANY OTHER PERSON WHO KNOWS OF THIS ORDER AND DOES ANYTHING WHICH HELPS OR PERMITS THE RESPONDENTS TO BREACH THE TERMS OF THIS ORDER MAY ALSO BE HELD TO BE IN CONTEMPT OF COURT AND MAY BE IMPRISONED, FINED OR HAVE THEIR ASSETS SEIZED.

## PROPERTY FREEZING ORDER

(Section 245A of the Proceeds of Crime Act 2002)

POCA no. 107 of 2014

IN THE HIGH COURT OF JUSTICE
QUEEN'S BENCH DIVISION
ADMINISTRATIVE COURT
Before the Honourable Mr Justice Bullingham Sitting in Private
Between

**THE DIRECTOR OF THE NATIONAL CRIME AGENCY (Applicant)**
and
**ALFREDO GERMONT (First Respondent)**
and
**VIOLETTA VALERY**
**(OTHERWISE VALERY VIOLETTA) (Second Respondent)**

TO THE FIRST RESPONDENT

AND TO THE SECOND RESPONDENT

Upon reading the witness statement of Tony Foot dated the 10th day of January 2014,

And Upon Hearing Counsel for the Director of the National Crime Agency ('the Director'),[1]

**THE COURT IS SATISFIED** that the relevant requirements for making a Property Freezing Order are fulfilled.

### This Order

1. This is a Property Freezing Order made against Alfredo Germont 'the First Respondent' and Violetta Valery (otherwise Valery Violetta) 'the Second Respondent' on 11th January 2014 by Mr Justice Bullingham following an application on behalf of the National Crime Agency ('the Agency').
2. This Order prohibits the First Respondent and Second Respondent from dealing with the property and assets set out herein.
3. The Order is subject to the exclusions at the end of this Order.
4. You should read all of this Order carefully. You are advised to consult a solicitor as soon as possible.
5. Subject to the provisions of section 245C of the Proceeds of Crime Act 2002 and the Proceeds of Crime Act 2002 (Legal Expenses in Civil Recovery Proceedings) Regulations 2005, you may be entitled to the release of restrained funds to pay for legal representation in connection with this Order. A request for the release of a sum in respect of reasonable legal expenses must be made in writing to the Director of the National Crime Agency and before any release can be made certain conditions

---

[1] The Crime and Courts Act 2013 includes the abolition of the Serious Organised Crime Agency, and the creation of the National Crime Agency (see ss 1–16). Subject to Parliamentary processes the ambition is that it will be fully operational by December 2013.

must be fulfilled. You and your legal adviser are referred to Part 3 of the Proceeds of Crime Act 2002 (Legal Expenses in Civil Recovery Proceedings) Regulations 2005 (SI 3382 of 2005).

6. Further to the provisions of section 245C of the Proceeds of Crime Act 2002, you may be entitled to the release of restrained funds to meet your reasonable living expenses or to carry on any trade, business, profession or occupation. A request for the release of property or an asset to meet reasonable living expenses or to carry on any trade, business, profession or occupation can either be made to the Director of the National Crime Agency, in the first instance, pursuant to paragraph 12 of this Order, or to the Court pursuant to section 245B of the Proceeds of Crime Act 2002.

7. The First Respondent and Second Respondent and any other person affected by this Order have a right to apply to the Court to vary or discharge it.

*Disposal of or dealing with assets*

8. The First Respondent must not until further order of this Court:–
   (a) remove from England and Wales any of the property or assets set out in paragraph 9 below, whether in his own name or not and whether solely or jointly owned; or
   (b) in any way dispose of or deal with or diminish the value of any of the property or assets set out in paragraph 9 below, whether in his own name or not and whether solely or jointly owned.

9. Paragraph 8 applies to the following property and assets:
   i. The proceeds of the sale of the property situated at 6 Simpson Avenue, Springfield, Torquay TQ1 1AB, previously registered at HM Land Registry in the name of the First Respondent, with title number TQ123456;
   ii. The property situated at 12 Marge Way, Springfield, Torquay TQ2 2AB, and registered at HM Land Registry in the name of the First Respondent, with title number TQ98765;
   iii. Vehicle Registration No. TS02 ACB, a BMW X5 Sport Automatic registered to the First Respondent at Flat 1, 22 Seaview Rise, Paignton TQ6 1PT;
   iv. The following bank accounts
      a. National Westminster Bank account number 12345678 sort code 00-10-00 in the name of the First Respondent;
      b. HSBC account number 98765432 sort code 10-00-10 in the name of the Second Respondent.

10. The Second Respondent must not
    (i) remove from England and Wales; or
    (ii) in any way dispose of or deal with or diminish the value of any of
       i. The proceeds of the sale of the property situated at 6 Simpson Avenue, Springfield, Torquay TQ1 1AB, previously registered at HM Land Registry in the name of the First Respondent, with title number TQ23445;
       ii. The property comprising the land at the back of 12 Marge Way, Springfield, Torquay TQ2 2AB, and registered at HM Land Registry in the name of the First Respondent, with title number TQ98765;
       iii. Vehicle Registration No. TS02 ACB, a BMW X5 Sport Automatic registered to the First Respondent at Flat 1, 22 Seaview Rise, Paignton TQ6 1PT;
       iv. The following bank accounts
          a. National Westminster Bank account number 12345678 sort code 00-10-00 in the name of the First Respondent;
          b. HSBC account number 98765432 sort code 10-00-10 in the name of the Second Respondent.

*Disclosure of information*

11. The First Respondent must:
    (i) inform the Agency in writing within 72 hours of service of this Order on the First Respondent of all his assets whether in or outside England and Wales and whether in his own name or not and whether solely or jointly owned, giving the value, location and details of all such assets;
    (ii) confirm the information in a witness statement which must be verified by a statement of truth and served on the Agency within 21 days after this Order has been served on the First Respondent.

The information in the witness statement must include:
a. the name and address of all persons including financial institutions holding any such assets;
b. details of the First Respondent's current salary or other form of income, identifying the amount paid, by whom it is paid and the account or accounts into which it is paid;

c. the names and numbers of all accounts held by or under the control of the First Respondent, together with the name and address of the place where the account is held and the sums in the account;

d. details (including addresses) of any real property in which the First Respondent has any interest, including an interest in any of the proceeds of sale if the property were to be sold. These details must include details of any mortgage or charge on the property;

e. details of all National Savings Certificates, unit trusts, shares or debentures held by the First Respondent in any company or corporation wherever incorporated in the world, owned or controlled by the First Respondent or in which he has an interest;

f. details of all trusts of which the First Respondent is a beneficiary, including the name and address of every trustee;

g. particulars of any income or debt due to the First Respondent including the name and address of the debtor;

h. details of all assets over £2,000.00 in value received by the First Respondent or anyone on his behalf since 11th January 2004 identifying the name and address of the person from whom such assets were received;

i. details of all assets over £2,000.00 in value transferred by the First Respondent or anyone on his behalf to others since 11th January 2004 identifying the name and address of all persons to whom such property was transferred.

12. The Second Respondent must:

   (i) inform the Agency in writing within 72 hours of service of this Order on the Second Respondent of all her assets whether in or outside England and Wales and whether in her own name or not and whether solely or jointly owned, giving the value, location and details of all such assets;

   (ii) confirm the information in a witness statement which must be verified by a statement of truth and served on the Agency within 21 days after this Order has been served on the Second Respondent.

The information in the witness statement must include:

a. the name and address of all persons including financial institutions holding any such assets;

b. details of the Second Respondent's current salary or other form of income, identifying the amount paid, by whom it is paid and the account or accounts into which it is paid;

c. the names and numbers of all accounts held by or under the control of the Second Respondent, together with the name and address of the place where the account is held and the sums in the account;

d. details (including addresses) of any real property in which the Second Respondent has any interest, including an interest in any of the proceeds of sale if the property were to be sold. These details must include details of any mortgage or charge on the property;

e. details of all National Savings Certificates, unit trusts, shares or debentures held by the Second Respondent in any company or corporation wherever incorporated in the world, owned or controlled by the Second Respondent or in which she has an interest;

f. details of all trusts of which the Second Respondent is a beneficiary, including the name and address of every trustee;

g. particulars of any income or debt due to the Second Respondent including the name and address of the debtor;

h. details of all assets over £2,000.00 in value received by the Second Respondent or anyone on her behalf since 11th January 2004 identifying the name and address of the person from whom such assets were received;

i. details of all assets over £2,000.00 in value transferred by the Second Respondent or anyone on her behalf to others since 11th January 2004 identifying the name and address of all persons to whom such property was transferred.

13. Subject to any further Order of the court any information given in compliance with this Order shall only be used for the purpose of these proceedings and any subsequent civil recovery proceedings.

14. However, nothing in this paragraph shall make inadmissible any disclosure made by the Respondents in any proceedings for perjury relating to that disclosure.

## Costs

15. The costs of this Order are reserved.

## Variation or Discharge of this Order

16. The First Respondent or the Second Respondent may agree with the Agency that this Order be varied in any respect but any such agreement must be in writing.
17. Anyone affected by this Order may apply to the Court at any time to vary or discharge this Order (or so much of it as affects that person), pursuant to section 245B of the Proceeds of Crime Act 2002, but they must first inform the Agency and anyone named on the first page of this Order giving 2 clear days notice. If any evidence is to be relied upon in support of the application it must also be served giving 2 clear days notice.

## Interpretation of this Order

18. A person who is an individual who is ordered not to do something must not do it himself or herself or in any other way. He or she must not do it through others acting on his or her behalf or on his or her instructions or with his or her encouragement.
19. A person that is a corporation and which is ordered not to do something must not do it by its directors, officers, employees or agents or in any other way.

## Parties Other than the Respondents

20. *Effect of this order.* It is a contempt of court for any person notified of this Order knowingly to assist in or permit a breach of the Order. Any person doing so may be sent to prison, fined, or have his assets seized. He is also at risk of prosecution for a money laundering offence.
21. *Set off by banks.* This Order does not prevent any bank from exercising any right of set off it may have in respect of any facility which it gave to the Respondents before it was notified of the Order.
22. *Withdrawals by the Respondent.* No bank need enquire as to the application or proposed application of any money withdrawn by the Respondents if the withdrawal appears to be permitted by this Order.
23. *Persons outside England Wales and Scotland*
    (1) Except as provided by in paragraph (2), the terms of this Order do not affect or concern anyone outside the jurisdiction of this court or Scotland.
    (2) The terms of this Order will affect the following persons in a country or state outside the jurisdiction of this court or Scotland:—
        a. a person to whom this Order is addressed or an officer or an agent appointed by power of attorney of such a person; or
        b. any person who:—
            i. is subject to the jurisdiction of this court,
            ii. has been given written notice of this Order at his residence or place of business within the jurisdiction of this court, and
            iii. is able lawfully to prevent acts or omissions outside the jurisdiction of this court which constitute or assist in a breach of the terms of this Order.
        c. any other person only to the extent that this Order is declared enforceable or is enforced by a court in that country.
24. *Assets located outside England and Wales.* Nothing in this Order shall, in respect of assets located outside England and Wales, prevent any third party from complying with:—
    a. what it reasonably believes to be its obligations, contractual or otherwise, under the laws and obligations of the country or state in which those assets are located or under the proper law of any contract between itself and the Respondents or any of them, or
    b. any Orders of the courts of that country or state, provided that reasonable notice of any application for such an Order is given to the Agency.

## COMMUNICATIONS WITH THE COURT

All communications to the court about this Order should be sent to the Administrative Court Office, Royal Courts of Justice, Strand, London WC2A 2LL quoting the case number. The office is open between 10am and 4pm Monday to Friday. The telephone number is 020 7947 6653.

*Undertaking given by the Agency to the Court*

The Agency will as soon as practicable serve upon the First and Second Respondents:—
a.  A copy of this Order,
b.  The witness statement containing the evidence relied on by the Agency and any other documents provided to the Court on the making of the application.

## ADDRESS AND TELEPHONE NUMBER OF THE AGENCY FOR SERVICE AND ANY COMMUNICATION IN RESPECT OF THESE PROCEEDINGS

The Director

National Crime Agency

PO Box 8000

London

SE11 5EN

Tel: 0370 496 7622

Dated this 11th day of January 2014

# Civil Recovery Order by Consent

## CLAIM NUMBER: CO/0000/2010

IN THE HIGH COURT OF JUSTICE
QUEEN'S BENCH DIVISION
ADMINISTRATIVE COURT
IN THE MATTER OF A RECOVERY ORDER
PURSUANT TO SECTION 266 OF THE PROCEEDS OF CRIME ACT 2002

Between
**THE DIRECTOR OF THE NATIONAL CRIME AGENCY (Claimant)**
and
**ALFREDO GERMONT (First Respondent)**
**VIOLETTA VALERY (Second Respondent)**
**TRAVIATA TRADING ENTERPRISES LTD (Third Respondent)**
**GIORGIO GERMONT (Fourth Respondent)**

### ORDER FOR DISPOSAL BY CONSENT

UPON THE APPLICATION of the Director of the National Crime Agency[1] issued on [insert date]
AND BY THE CONSENT of the Claimant and the Respondents,
AND UPON READING THE FIRST WITNESS STATEMENT of Ivor Edake dated / /2014
AND THE SETTLEMENT AGREEMENT dated / /2014, attached hereto marked Schedule Two

### IT IS ORDERED THAT

1. A Recovery Order is made in respect of the property listed in the first schedule to this Order, marked Schedule One (the 'Scheduled Property').
2. The Scheduled Property shall vest in the Trustee for Civil Recovery (the 'Trustee'), namely Tony Foot of the National Crime Agency, PO Box 8000, London SE11 5EN, forthwith upon the making of this Order.
3. The Trustee shall have the following powers without prejudice to any other powers he may have by virtue of statute or by implication of law:
   a. power to transfer, convey and/or sell the Scheduled Property or any part of it or interest in it;
   b. power to incur expenditure for the purpose of:
      i. acquiring any part of the Scheduled Property, or any interest in it, which is not vested in him; and
      ii. discharging any liabilities, or extinguishing any rights, to which the Scheduled Property is subject;
   c. power to manage the Scheduled Property including:
      i. selling or otherwise disposing of assets comprised in the Scheduled Property which are perishable or which ought to be disposed of before their value diminishes;
      ii. where the Scheduled Property comprises assets of a trade or business, carrying on, or arranging for another to carry on, the trade or business;
      iii. incurring capital expenditure in respect of the Scheduled Property;

---

[1] The Crime and Courts Act 2013 includes the abolition of the Serious Organised Crime Agency, and the creation of the National Crime Agency (see ss 1–16). Subject to Parliamentary processes the ambition is that it will be fully operational by December 2013.

    d. power to start, carry on or defend any legal proceedings in respect of the Scheduled Property;

    e. power to make any compromise or other arrangement in connection with any claim relating to the Scheduled Property;

    f. for the purposes of, or in connection with, the exercise of any of his powers, power by his official name to do any of things mentioned in sub-clause (g) below and power to do any other act which is necessary or expedient;

    g. the things mentioned in sub-clause (f) above are:
   i. holding, entering or seizing the Scheduled Property;
   ii. entering into contracts;
   iii. suing and being sued;
   iv. employing agents; and
   v. executing a power of attorney, deed or other instrument.

4. Upon the Trustee taking possession of the Scheduled Property, the Interim Receiving Order made by this Court on 1 April 2013 shall be discharged and the proceedings brought under case number CO/0000/2009 shall be stayed as against all the Respondents.

5. There be no order for the costs of these proceedings or for the costs of the proceedings relating to the Interim Receiving Order obtained on 1 April 2013 (case number CO/0000/2009).

    Dated this           day of October 2014

    ...................               ...................

    For the Claimant             For the Second Respondent

    ...................               ...................

    For the First Respondent      For the Third Respondent

## SCHEDULE ONE

**Property subject to a Recovery Order pursuant to Section 266 of the Proceeds of Crime Act 2002**

1. The sum of £15,000 held in an account numbered [*insert number*] in the name of the [*insert respondent*] at [*insert location*] branch of [*insert bank*].

2. Zurich Investment Bond 00000 held in the name of the First Respondent.

3. Scottish Provident Investment Bonus Growth policy number 000000 held in the joint names of the First Respondent and the Second Respondent.

4. Funds held by Traviata Trading Enterprises Ltd to the order of the First Respondent with a value at April 2010 of £100,000 plus any interest accrued since that date.

5. AMP Pearl policy held in the name of the First Respondent.

6. Northern Rock policy number 000000 held in the name of the Second Respondent as trustee with a value as at 1st September 2010 of £5000.

7. 5.99% of the current value of the Mercedes 220CE with licence plate numbered TY10 MSW.

8. The real property situate at 11 Simpsons Lane, Springfield, Torquay under Land Registry Number TQ12345678.

# Financial Reporting Order

In the Crown Court

At Southwark

Case No: T2010 0000

Court Code:

---

## FINANCIAL REPORTING ORDER

(Section 76 of the Serious Organised Crime and Police Act 2005)

The Defendant:     ALFREDO GERMONT            Date of birth: 10th August 1955

was convicted on the 1st April 2014 of Conspiracy to Import and Supply Cocaine.

The Court was satisfied that the risk of the Defendant committing another offence listed in section 76(3) of the Serious Organised Crime and Police Act 2005 was sufficiently high to justify the making of a Financial Reporting Order.

On 29th July 2014, the Court ordered that the Defendant be subjected to a Financial Reporting Order, the details of which are specified in the attached Schedule, for a period of 10 years from the date of the making of the order.

Breach of this Order is punishable with imprisonment and/or a fine.

## AN OFFICER OF THE CROWN COURT

**Date:**

## SCHEDULE

**Details of the Financial Reporting Order**

(Any requirement(s) imposed by the Court under section 79 of the Serious Organised Crime and Police Act 2005 must be listed here)

*The Court orders that the Defendant, Alfredo Germont must do the following:*

1. Within one month of 29th July 2014 make a report to the specified person namely, The National Crime Agency[1] Financial Reporting Officer.
2. Thereafter, within 28 days of the end of each succeeding period of 6 months, make further reports to the specified person.
3. This Order shall have effect until 31st July 2024.
4. The report shall be in writing and may be delivered by hand or posted to The Financial Reporting Officer, c/o Deputy Director Proceeds of Crime, PO Box 8000, London SE11 5EN.
5. Each report shall include (if applicable):
    a. Schedule of any current salary or other form of income (save for that which passes through his account held with the Prison Service or any sum earned from prison employment, providing said sum does not exceed £1000 in any six month period), identifying the amount paid, by whom it is paid and the account or accounts into which such sums are paid. The report shall include copies of all payslips for the relevant period.
    b. Schedule of all accounts held by the Defendant, or to which the Defendant is a signatory, including the name in which the account is held, the balance in the account and the name and address of the place where the account is held, together with copies all statements from such accounts for the period in question.
    c. Schedule (including addresses) of any real property in which the Defendant has any interest, including an interest in any of the net sale money if the property were to be sold. These details must include details of any mortgage or charge on the property.
    d. Schedule of any rental income from property, the property to which it relates, the details of who pays the rental income and into which account paid.
    e. Schedule of all beneficial interests the defendant may hold in all business concerns and companies, whether trading or dormant including shares or debentures held in any company or corporation wherever incorporated in the world. If the business is trading to provide annual accounts.
    f. Details of all National Savings Certificates and unit trusts.
    g. Schedule of all assets or property of any value, currently held or received by the Defendant or anyone on his behalf since 01/04/2013, identifying the name and address of the person from whom such asset was received.
    h. Particulars of all trusts of which the Defendant is a trustee, giving the names and addresses of the beneficiaries thereof and particulars of those of which they are beneficiary, giving the names and addresses of the trustees thereof.

---

[1] The Crime and Courts Act 2013 includes the abolition of the Serious Organised Crime Agency, and the creation of the National Crime Agency (see ss 1–16). Subject to Parliamentary processes the ambition is that it will be fully operational by December 2013.

# Proceeds of Crime Litigation
# in Northern Ireland

This appendix provides an overview setting out the principal differences between criminal proceeds law and practice in Northern Ireland as compared with the other jurisdictions within the UK. There have been three generations of proceeds of crime legislation applicable in Northern Ireland. Each of these is still capable of generating litigation under their respective regimes depending on when the underlying criminal offences were committed. The evolution of criminal proceeds legislation in Northern Ireland will be familiar to those who are aware of the way in which the legislation evolved in England and Wales between 1988 and 2006. Since the introduction of the Proceeds of Crime Act 2002 there is now, however, very little difference between the law applying in England and Wales and that applying in Northern Ireland.

## First Generation

The first generation of proceeds of crime legislation consists of:
- The Criminal Justice (Confiscation) (Northern Ireland) Order 1990.
- The Criminal Justice (Confiscation) (1990 Order) (Commencement) Order (Northern Ireland) 1991.
- The Criminal Justice (Confiscation) (Northern Ireland) Order 1993.
- The Criminal Justice (Confiscation) (1993 Order) (Commencement) Order (Northern Ireland) 1994.
- The Criminal Justice (International Co-operation) Act 1990.

The 1990 Order came into operation on 1st July 1991 and established restraint and confiscation legislation in Northern Ireland for the first time. The significant features of this generation of criminal proceeds legislation are:
(i)   The making of a non-drugs trafficking confiscation order is a matter of judicial discretion.
(ii)  Statutory assumptions do not apply in non-drug trafficking confiscation applications.
(iii) Statutory assumptions are discretionary in drug trafficking confiscation applications.
(iv)  Offences of money laundering were introduced for the first time in Northern Ireland under the 1990 Order but applied to the proceeds of drug trafficking only.
(v)   Under the 1993 Order (which came into operation on 1 April 1994) offences of money laundering were extended from drug-trafficking proceeds only to the proceeds of all types of criminal conduct.
(vi)  A restraint order made in England and Wales or Scotland cannot be registered by the High Court in Northern Ireland. The scheme envisaged under the 1990 Order is that a restraint order will be obtained in Northern Ireland on the basis that the 1990 Order treats offences committed in England and Wales or Scotland as if they were committed in Northern Ireland.
(vii) A confiscation order made in England and Wales or Scotland cannot be registered by the High Court in Northern Ireland. The scheme envisaged under the 1990 Order is that a confiscation order will be obtained in Northern Ireland on the basis that the 1990 Order treats offences committed in England and Wales or Scotland as if they were committed in Northern Ireland.

## Second Generation

The second generation of proceeds of crime legislation consisted of:
- The Proceeds of Crime (Northern Ireland) Order 1996.
- The Proceeds of Crime (Northern Ireland) Order 1996 (Amendment) Order 1997.
- The Proceeds of Crime (Countries and Territories designated under the Drug Trafficking Act 1994) Order (Northern Ireland) 1997.

- The Proceeds of Crime (Enforcement of Confiscation Orders made in England and Wales or Scotland) Order (Northern Ireland) 1997.
- The Proceeds of Crime (Countries and Territories designated under the Criminal Justice Act 1988) (1998 Order) (Amendment) (Northern Ireland) Order 1998.
- The Proceeds of Crime (Countries and Territories designated under the Drug Trafficking Act 1994) (1997 Order) (Amendment) (Northern Ireland) Order 1998.
- The Proceeds of Crime (Countries and Territories designated under the Criminal Justice Act 1988) (1998 Order) (Amendment) (Northern Ireland) Order 1999.
- Rules 51-54 of the Crown Court Rules (Northern Ireland) 1979.

The 1996 Order came into operation on 25 August 1996. The significant features of this generation of criminal proceeds legislation are:

(i) The making of a non-drugs trafficking confiscation order is mandatory except where the court is satisfied that a victim has instituted or intends to institute civil proceedings against the defendant in respect of his loss, injury or damage.

(ii) Statutory assumptions are mandatory in a confiscation application for a drugs trafficking offence.

(iii) Statutory assumptions are discretionary in a confiscation application for a non-drugs trafficking offence.

(iv) A restraint order made in England and Wales or Scotland cannot be registered by the High Court in Northern Ireland. The scheme envisaged under the 1996 Order is that a restraint order will be obtained in Northern Ireland on the basis that the 1996 Order treats offences committed in England and Wales or Scotland as if they were committed in Northern Ireland.

(v) A confiscation order made in England and Wales or Scotland cannot be registered by the High Court in Northern Ireland. The scheme envisaged under the 1996 Order is that a confiscation order will be obtained in Northern Ireland on the basis that the 1996 Order treats offences committed in England and Wales or Scotland as if they were committed in Northern Ireland.

# Third Generation

The third generation of proceeds of crime legislation is the most recent evolution of criminal proceeds legislation. From a Northern Ireland perspective the most significant pieces of primary and secondary legislation are:

- The Proceeds of Crime Act 2002.
- The Serious Organised Crime and Police Act 2005.
- The Serious Crime Act 2007.
- The Proceeds of Crime Act 2002 (Commencement No. 5, Transitional Provisions, Savings and Amendment) Order 2003.
- The Proceeds of Crime Act 2002 (Enforcement in different parts of the United Kingdom) Order 2002.
- The Proceeds of Crime Act 2002 (Application of Police and Criminal Evidence Act 1984 and Police and Criminal Evidence (Northern Ireland) Order 1989) Order 2003.
- The Magistrates' Courts (Proceeds of Crime Act 2002) (Confiscation) Rules (Northern Ireland) 2003.
- The Criminal Justice (International Co-operation) Act 1990 (Enforcement of Overseas Forfeiture Orders) (Northern Ireland) Order 2005.
- Order 116 of the Rules of the Court of Judicature (Northern Ireland) 1980—(Terrorism Act 2000 and Confiscation and Forfeiture in Connection with Criminal Proceedings).
- Order 123 of the Rules of the Court of Judicature (Northern Ireland) 1980—(Civil Recovery).
- Rules 74–104 of the Crown Court Rules (Northern Ireland) 1979.

The significant features of the third generation of legislation are similar to those which apply in England and Wales. Worthy of note, however, are the following:

(i) While the 2002 Act had the effect in England and Wales of transferring restraint proceedings from the High Court to the Crown Court, this change was not followed in Northern Ireland. For reasons of practicality, the power to grant restraint orders was retained in the High Court. Where a defendant breaches a restraint order, a contempt application is made to the Queen's Bench judge who granted the original order.

(ii) Similarly, with regard to the appointment of a management receiver, such appointments continue to be made by the High Court.

(iii) There is no role for the magistrates' court in the enforcement of confiscation orders. Confiscation orders are enforced as a Crown Court fine under the Criminal Justice Act (Northern Ireland) 1945. The responsibility of enforcing a confiscation order through an application for the appointment of a receiver falls on the Public Prosecution Service.

(iv) Restraint or receivership orders granted in England and Wales and restraint or administration orders granted in Scotland have effect in Northern Ireland but proceedings for the enforcement of them may only be taken if the order has first been registered in the Northern Ireland High Court.

# Organisational Landscape

### The Role of the Public Prosecution Service

The Public Prosecution Service has the dominant role in confiscation proceedings in Northern Ireland. The principal point of contact is the Assistant Director, High Court, Belfast Chambers with responsibility for High Court proceedings. On rare occasions the Director of the Serious Fraud Office may also institute confiscation proceedings in the jurisdiction.

The Public Prosecution Service prosecutes not only cases investigated by the Police Service of Northern Ireland but also cases investigated by a wide range of government departments. Where those prosecutions give rise to confiscation proceedings (for example in respect of benefit obtained from Customs legislation breaches, social security fraud, or waste management offences) the Public Prosecution Service will handle those proceedings also.

### The Role of the Serious Organised Crime Agency/National Crime Agency

Since the demise of the Assets Recovery Agency, the organisation which plays the dominant role in civil recovery proceedings in Northern Ireland has been SOCA. Civil recovery proceedings are commenced after an investigation initiated by SOCA itself or after a referral by the Police Service of Northern Ireland, HMRC, or by a Northern Ireland Department. SOCA is due in turn to be replaced by the National Crime Agency in December 2013. Although both the Public Prosecution Service and the Serious Fraud Office may also institute civil recovery proceedings, neither organisation has yet done so.

### Cash Forfeiture Proceedings

In practice cash forfeiture proceedings are initiated by three different organisations depending on which has seized the cash. If the cash has been seized following a search carried out by police, then the forfeiture proceedings will be handled by the Crown Solicitor on behalf of the Chief Constable. If cash has been seized by HMRC, then HMRC will handle the forfeiture proceedings. If the cash has been seized by SOCA following a SOCA search, then SOCA (now the National Crime Agency) will handle the proceedings.

# Overview of Money Laundering

| Criminality/ ill-gotten gains | 1. Placement | 2. Layering | 3. Integration |
|---|---|---|---|
| Financially acquisitive crimes | Purpose: to filter the criminal proceeds into the banking/ financial system | Purpose: to disguise the audit trail, so that it is unclear that the money originates from the proceeds of crime | Purpose: to return the ill-gotten gains to the economy, through an apparently legitimate route for personal benefit (or to reinvest into the next criminal venture) |
| From, eg<br>• drugs money<br>• tax or business fraud<br>• theft<br>• corruption<br>• bribery | • deposited in cash into a bank or other financial institution (eg bureau de change)<br>• may involve:<br>  o moving cash to another country by hand<br>  o changing the currency<br>  o changing the denomination (higher value bank notes are more easily transportable/ easier to hide)<br>  o bank or wire transfers | • transfers to different bank accounts<br>• wiring funds to different locations<br>• bank instruction to transfer to a trading company<br>• off-shore company or bank<br>• splitting or merging funds over several transactions<br>• may involve:<br>  o foreign exchange companies<br>  o Internet banking<br>  o cash deposits into several accounts and withdrawals<br>  o creating fictitious contracts, debts and loans<br>  o third-party transactions<br>  o using other people's names | • investments, financial and property<br>• buying assets<br>• other lifestyle purchases<br>• may involve:<br>  o purchase of bearer bonds, shares, or other financial instruments<br>  o land deals, developments, or properties abroad<br>  o yachts, motor cars, race horses<br>  o liquidising assets back into cash<br>  o high-value items, such as jewellery or gold, which can later be sold for cash |

# INDEX